FREQUENTLY USED SYMBOLS (CONTINUED)

Symbol	Meaning
M	Bond's Par Value
MACRS	Modified Accelerated Cost Recovery System
M_e	Market Value of the Stock Trading Ex Rights
MNC	Multinational Company
MPR	Market Price Ratio of Exchange
MRP	Materials Requirement Planning
M_w	Market Value of the Stock With Rights
n	- Number of periods—typically years - Number of Outcomes Considered - Years to Maturity
N	- Number of Rights Needed to Purchase One Share of Stock - Number of Shares of Common Stock Obtainable with one Warrant - Number of Days Payment can be Delayed by Giving up the Cash Discount
N_d	Net Proceeds from the Sale of Debt (Bond)
NE	Number of Shares Needed to Elect a Certain Number of Directors
N_n	Net Proceeds from the Sale of New Common Stock
N_p	Net Proceeds from the Sale of the Preferred Stock
NPV	Net Present Value
O	- Total Number of Shares of Common Stock Outstanding - Order Cost Per Order
OC	Operating Cycle
P	Price (value) of asset
P_o	Value of Common Stock
PAC	Preauthorized Check
$PBDT_t$	Profits Before Depreciation and Taxes in year $_t$
PD	Preferred Stock Dividend
P/E	Price/Earnings Ratio
PMT	Amount of Payment
Pr	Probability
PV	Present Value
PVA_n	Present-Value of an $_n$-Year Annuity
$PVIF_{k,n}$	Present-Value Interest Factor for a Single Amount Discounted at $_k$ Percent for $_n$ Periods
$PVIFA_{k,n}$	Present-Value Interest Factor for an Annuity When Interest is Discounted Annually at $_k$ Percent for $_n$ Periods
Q	- Order Quantity in Units - Sales Quantity in Units
RADR	Risk-Adjusted Discount Rate
R_e	Theoretical Value of a Right When Stock is Trading Ex Rights
RE	Ratio of Exchange
R_F	Risk-Free Rate of Interest
r_l	Risk-Free Cost of the Given Type of Financing, $_l$
ROA	Return on Total Assets
ROE	Return on Equity
RP	Risk Premium
R_w	Theoretical Value of a Right When Stock is Selling With Rights
S	- Sources of Cash
S	- Subscription Price of the Stock - Usage in Units Per Period
SML	Security Market Line
T	Firm's Marginal Tax Rate
t	Time
TN	Total Number of Directors to be Elected
TVW	Theoretical Value of a Warrant
U	Uses of Cash
V	Value of an Asset or Firm
VC	Variable Operating Cost per Unit
WACC	Weighted Average Cost of Capital
w_j	- Proportion of the Portfolio's Total Dollar Value Represented by Asset $_j$ - Proportion of a Specific Source of Financing $_j$ in the Firm's Capital Structure
WMCC	Weighted Marginal Cost of Capital
YTM	Yield to Maturity
α_t	Certainty Equivalent Factor in Year $_t$
σ	Standard Deviation
σ^2	Variance
Σ	Summation Sign

Principles of Managerial Finance

SEVENTH EDITION

Principles of Managerial Finance

Lawrence J. Gitman

San Diego State University

HarperCollins*CollegePublishers*

Acquisitions Editor *Kirsten D. Sandberg*
Developmental Editor *Arlene Bessenoff*
Project Coordination, Text and
Cover Design *York Production Services*
Production Manager *Willie Lane*
Compositor *York Graphic Services, Inc.*
Printer and Binder *R.R. Donnelley & Sons Company*
Cover Printer *The Lehigh Press, Inc.*

Photo/Text Credit: Chapter 13, p. 521: © Davis Freeman, Seattle, WA, 90108 18; Page 71: Excerpt from Eaton Corporation's 1992 Chairman's letter to Stockholders, from Eaton Corporation, 1992 Annual Report, pp. 2 and 3. Reprinted by permission.

Principles of Managerial Finance, Seventh Edition

Library of Congress Cataloging-in-Publication Data

Gitman, Lawrence J.
Principles of managerial finance / Lawrence J. Gitman. — 7th ed.
p. cm.
Includes index.
ISBN 0-06-502347-1
1. Corporations—Finance. 2. Business enterprises—Finance.
I. Title.
HG4011.G5 1993
658. 15—dc20 93-39412
CIP

93 94 95 96 9 8 7 6 5 4 3 2 1

To my wife Robin,
our son, Zachary,
and our daughter, Jessica

Brief contents

part VI Short-term financial decisions 607

part VII Special managerial finance topics 762

Appendixes A-1

Detailed contents

part III Long-term investment decisions 301

part IV Cost of capital, leverage, and capital structure 397

part V Long-term financing decisions 487

part VI Short-term financial decisions 607

List of companies

Page numbers in italics indicate figures; page numbers followed by n indicate notes; page numbers followed by t indicate tables.

To the instructor

Principles of Managerial Finance has consistently met the needs of the introductory finance course at the undergraduate level. It has also worked quite well in the core MBA course and in management development and executive training programs. The seventh edition continues to satisfy these market needs—and more. Incorporating an enhanced learning system, that integrates pedagogy and color with concepts and practical applications, the seventh edition equips instructors to concentrate on the more difficult theories, concepts, and techniques that are needed to make keen financial decisions in an ever-changing and increasingly competitive business environment. The improved pedagogy and generous use of examples also make the text an easily accessible resource for long-distance learning and self-study programs as well as for large lecture-driven courses. From classroom to boardroom the seventh edition of *Principles of Managerial Finance* can help users to get where they want to be.

Major changes in the seventh edition

Improved organization

Although the text is sequential, instructors can assign almost any chapter as a self-contained unit to customize the text to varying course lengths and various teaching strategies. Specific improvements include the following: The chapter on the analysis of financial statements now immediately follows the chapter on financial statements, depreciation, and cash flow so that students can sharpen their analytical skills early in the course. To serve as a motivational device, the material on career opportunities in the field of managerial finance appears in Chapter 1 rather than in an end-of-text appendix. And the chapter on financial planning now opens the part on short-term financial decisions to provide a context for understanding working capital management.

Stronger ties between theory and practice

Practitioner Previews open each chapter with intriguing insights into the financial management of actual companies. These chapter launchers introduce students to industry leaders who explain in their own words the relevance of forthcoming material from a practical point of view. For example, in Chapter 5, William Regan, Senior

Vice President and Corporate Treasurer of USAA, discusses how his firm uses time value of money concepts. Special thanks go to the following contributors:

Charles W. Duddles
Executive Vice President and Chief Financial Officer
Foodmaker, Inc.

Richard Wellek
President and Chief Executive Officer
Varlen Corp.

Adelia Coffman
Senior Vice President and Chief Financial Officer
Qualcomm Incorporated

Richard V.B. Manix
First Vice President
Crédit Agricole

William Regan
Sr. Vice President and Treasurer
USAA

Donald Peters
Vice President, Planning
EG&G Inc.

Martin Fridson
Managing Director
Merrill Lynch Capital Markets

Susan Porth
Chief Financial Officer
Kaiser Foundation Health Plan, Inc.

Oscar Turner
Manager, Strategic Planning
The Quaker Oats Co.

David Lundeen
Director of Corporate Finance
Blockbuster Entertainment Corporation

Kenneth Kwit
President and Chief Executive Officer
Expressions, Inc.

Gerard Halpin III
Assistant Treasurer, Corporate Finance
General Electric Company

Janice LeCocq
Executive Vice President, Finance and Administration
ICOS Corp.

Julian Markby
Managing Director, Media and Communications
Paine Webber Incorporated

Shoon Ledyard
Controller
The Charlotte Hornets

Richard Moorman
Senior Vice President
Bank One Columbus

Karen Leets
Director of Treasury Operations
McDonald's Corp.

Kevin Hall
Controller
Hydro-Scape Products, Inc.

Samuel C. Weaver
Director of Corporate Financial Planning and Analysis
Hershey Foods Corp.

Anthony S. Lucas
Vice President and Controller
The Gillette Company

All-new Concept in Practice examples offer insights into important topics through real company experiences, both large and small, with a range of domestic and global perspectives. Chapter 5, for example, illustrates the concept of future value by highlighting the disadvantages of early withdrawals from retirement accounts.

New Lotus 1-2-3 spreadsheet problems are keyed to the more complex problems in various chapters to familiarize students with a popular commercial spreadsheet program. The *PMF Disk,* once again shrink-wrapped with new copies of the text at no additional cost, now includes the *PMF Lotus Templates.* For quick reference a spreadsheet icon appears next to the applicable problems throughout the end-of-chapter assignment material, with documentation in Appendix B. Appendix C, "Using Computers and Spreadsheets in Managerial Finance," provides insight into the use of computers and spreadsheets in managerial finance.

More contemporary coverage, including key tax provisions of the *Omnibus Budget Reconciliation Act of 1993*

To keep course content current, my colleagues have come to expect and rely upon updated coverage of important current and emerging issues, instruments, and techniques affecting the practice of financial management. Consistent exposure to current practical applications enables students to walk away from the book and onto the job with forward-looking, practical insight, rather than a merely static conceptual grasp of the challenges ahead. In addition to the many current Concept in Practice items, contemporary topics include the following:

- Current thinking on the financial manager's role in total quality management (TQM), agency costs relating to incentive and performance plans, and the associated issue of executive compensation (Chapter 1)
- The changing role of financial intermediaries and the key tax provisions of the recently passed *Omnibus Budget Reconciliation Act of 1993* (Chapter 2)
- An efficient method for calculating the present value of a mixed stream with an embedded annuity (Chapter 5)
- Insights into the stock valuation activities of professional security analysts (Chapter 7)
- Recognition of removal and cleanup costs in the analysis of replacing old assets (Chapter 8)
- The linkage between the optimal capital budget (financing/investment equilibrium) and capital rationing (Chapter 10)
- Practical insight into determination of the optimal capital structure (Chapter 11)
- The latest treatment of voting rights and dividend reinvestment plans (Chapter 13)
- The use of preferred stock, the effects of contingent securities on earnings, and the cause of market premiums on convertibles (Chapter 14)
- Recent findings with regard to the allocation of financial management time to short-term financial management activities (Chapter 16)
- Data on recent yields of popular marketable securities (Chapter 17)
- The problem faced by small businesses in managing their accounts receivable
- NAFTA and the European Open Market (Chapter 20)

Reengineered teaching/learning system

The PMF Teaching/Learning System is really built on proven learning goals (LGs): the LGs, marked by a special icon, are listed at the start of each chapter, tied to first-level heads, reviewed point by point at the chapter's end, and noted in assignment material and supplements such as the Test Bank and Study Guide. Now more than ever, students will know what material they need to learn, where they'll find it in the chapter, and whether they've mastered it by the end of the chapter. In addition, instructors can build lectures and assignments around the LGs.

A key visual aid in the PMF System is the PMF Toolbox, a cluster of icons at the beginning of every major chapter section. Inside the Toolbox, students will find the learning tools and resources—learning goals, software tutorials, problem-solving disk routines, and spreadsheet templates—that are available to them as they attempt to master each learning goal. One example of the Toolbox appears in Chapter 5 next to the heading "Present Value of a Single Amount." Documentation for some of the tools appears in Appendix B, "Instructions for Using the PMF Disk," and in Appendix C, "Using Computers and Spreadsheets in Managerial Finance."

The PMF Example Method is also a key part of PMF System because it infuses practical demonstrations into the learning process. When applicable, this edition reformats the solution of each realistic example to show the use of time lines, tables, and business/financial calculators. Calculator keystrokes of inputs, functions, and outputs are highlighted in discussions and examples of time value techniques in Chapter 5 and the application of those techniques in subsequent chapters. Appendix A contains financial tables.

Chapter cases and end-of-part integrative cases enable students to apply what they've learned by chapter and by part in realistic contexts and to strengthen their practical understanding of techniques presented without the added expense of a separate case book. In Chapter 7, students try their hand at assessing the impact of a proposed risky investment on a firm's bond and stock values. At the end of Part I, students can apply a variety of concepts from Chapters 1 through 4 to assess and make recommendations with regard to the financial strategy of a software company.

International coverage is integrated throughout the text using brief discussions of the international dimensions of chapter topics *and* is treated in a dedicated chapter. For example, Chapter 3 discusses the consolidation of international financial statements. The international material is integrated into the chapter learning goals and the end-of-chapter summaries and problem material.

Important content improvements in the seventh edition

Since users often like to know where new material appears, here are the significant but less sweeping changes that have been made in the seventh edition:

Chapter 1 on the role of finance and the financial manager now includes summary tables on career opportunities in both financial services and managerial finance, discusses the financial manager's role in total quality management (TQM), introduces the concept of stakeholder wealth preservation, and provides timely insights into the agency issue, including descriptions of incentive and performance plans and discussion of the current thinking with regard to executive compensation.

Chapter 2 on the operating environment of the firm now ends rather than begins with business taxation and contains updated coverage of the changing role of financial institutions, the role of the investment banker, and average versus marginal tax rates.

Chapter 3 on financial statements, depreciation, and cash flow now uses the modified accelerated cost recovery system (MACRS) depreciation reference rather than ACRS and includes a streamlined step-by-step presentation of procedures for preparing the statement of cash flows.

Chapter 4 on the analysis of financial statements now concludes its coverage of liquidity ratios with brief insights into the liquidity–profitability tradeoff, includes an evaluation of common-size income statements, introduces the return on total assets (ROA) in place of the ROI, and streamlines discussion of the modified DuPont formula.

Chapter 5 on the time value of money now opens with a brief section on the role of time value in finance, with a conceptual comparison of future and present values using time lines and an explanation of how to use financial tables and business/financial calculators as important computational tools. Keystrokes are shown for all calculator routines.

As a result, discussion of specific financial tables is no longer necessary. A new discussion and demonstration of the procedures for finding the present value of a mixed stream with an embedded annuity has been added.

Chapter 6 on risk and return has been tightened up and now includes an improved discussion of the role of sensitivity analysis in assessing an asset's risk.

Chapter 7 on valuation now contains a clarified discussion of market efficiency with more practical insights, includes an added caveat under coverage of common stock valuation models, and concludes with a look at the valuation activities of professional securities analysts.

Chapter 8 on capital budgeting and cash flow principles now includes a clarified comparison of expansion and replacement decisions, presents a new streamlined and accessible format for finding a project's initial investment, refers to both removal and cleanup costs associated with replacing old assets, better explains the rationale for including changes in the net working capital, and introduces a new format for determining a project's terminal cash flow.

Chapter 9 on capital budgeting techniques now contains an example of the differing reinvestment rate assumptions that are implicit in NPV and IRR and includes a brief discussion of why capital rationing should not exist.

Chapter 10 on the cost of capital includes a demonstration, both by trial and error and with a calculator, of how to determine precisely the before-tax cost of debt; is now consistent in its ongoing example; and ties the process of making financing/investment decisions to capital rationing.

Chapter 11 on leverage and capital structure now includes additional brief discussions of the ability to control leverage and the practical reality of finding a firm's optimal capital structure.

Chapter 12 on long-term debt and investment banking includes streamlined discussion of bonds and bond refunding and an updated description of the role and activities of the investment banker.

Chapter 13 on common stock and dividend policy now contains an example of accounting for outstanding and issued shares and includes enhanced discussions of both voting rights and dividend reinvestment plans.

Chapter 14 on preferred stock, leasing, convertibles, warrants, and options includes a new discussion on the use of preferred stock and provides a new accounting-oriented description of the effects on earnings of contingent securities as well as a brief explanation of why market premiums often exist on convertibles.

Chapter 15 on financial planning has an updated look at the overall planning process, includes added practical insights, and explains more effectively the interpretation of the "plug figure" used in applying the judgmental approach to preparation of the pro forma balance sheet.

Chapter 16 on net working capital and short-term financing stresses even more the importance of short-term financial management and adds practical insights to the discussions of various short-term financing techniques and vehicles.

Chapter 17 on cash and marketable securities now includes a summary table of key features and recent yields on the popular marketable securities.

Chapter 18 on accounts receivable and inventory briefly discusses the rationale for extending credit and now describes the small business problem associated with managing accounts receivable.

Chapter 19 on mergers, LBO's, divestitures, and failure has been refined and updated to include more recent examples and practical wisdom with respect to corporate restructuring and business failure.

Chapter 20 on international managerial finance treats the subject cohesively in a capstone chapter rather than through a series of topics keyed to specific earlier chapters, as in the sixth edition. Coverage includes an introduction to emerging trading blocs—both NAFTA and the European Open Market—along with updated statistics and insights.

Other pedagogical features

Critical-thinking questions, screened in color, follow all first-level heads. These section openers raise key issues so that students grasp the importance of upcoming material.

Concepts in Review questions appear at the end of each section of the chapter (positioned before the next first-level head) and are marked with a special design element. As students progress through the chapter, they can test their understanding of each key theory, concept, and technique before moving on to the next section within the chapter.

End-of-chapter summaries, self-tests, and problem sets are now keyed to learning goals and the *PMF Disk* using icons from the Toolbox. Appendix E contains all Solutions to Self-Test Problems in one convenient location, marked with an easy-to-spot gold tab, and Answers to Selected End-of-Chapter Problems appear in Appendix F. Students get multiple review and self-testing opportunities, and professors get a wide choice of assignable material to reinforce the learning system. These appendixes guide students through the problem-solving process using tables or software and help them to evaluate their progress in preparing detailed problem solutions.

A vibrant, contemporary design, with pedagogical use of four colors in most charts, tables, and graphs, draws reader attention to features of the learning system. Bars of data are highlighted with color in tables and then graphed in the same color so that the more visual learners can immediately see relationships among data.

Marginal material includes running lists of key terms and definitions and, new to this edition, key equations printed in blue when first introduced. Key terms are boldfaced in the index for easy access to the glossary entry, and equations are keyed to routines on the *PMF Disk* in Appendix D, "Key Equations and Disk Routines."

A list of companies discussed in the text appears just before this preface on page xx, in case professors want to assign specific companies for further or ongoing analysis. The endpapers now display frequently used symbols, since many students initially find the notation challenging.

Supplements to the learning system

TEACHING TOOLS FOR INSTRUCTORS

Instructor's Manual *Compiled by Marlene G. Bellamy and Lawrence J. Gitman.* This comprehensive resource really pulls the teaching tools together so that professors can use the text easily and effectively in the classroom. Each chapter provides an overview of key topics, references to the *PMF Disk,* suggested Study Guide assignments, teaching notes to aid in the selection and use of videos as lecture launchers, and detailed answers and solutions to all Concepts in Review questions, end-of-chapter problems, and chapter and part cases, all of which Marlene and I have worked out carefully to ensure accuracy and consistency.

Testing Materials *Created by Hadi Salavitabar, SUNY–New Paltz.* Thoroughly revised to accommodate changes in the text and significantly expanded to increase user flexibility, this test bank contains nearly 2,500 items, including all-new true/false questions, significantly improved multiple-choice items, and rejuvenated problems and essay questions. For quick test selection and construction, each chapter features a handy chart for identifying type of question, skill tested by learning goal, and level of difficulty. Since the test bank is available in both printed and electronic formats—ASCII files, WordPerfect word processing IBM-compatible files, and IBM or Mac TestMaster files—instructors should contact their HarperCollins representative to determine which format best meets their testing needs.

Instructors can also download the TestMaster version of the test bank into *Quiz-Master*, an on-line testing program for IBM and Mac that enables users to conduct timed or untimed exams at computer workstations. Upon completing tests, students can see their scores and view or print a diagnostic report of those topics or objectives requiring more attention. When installed on a local area network, QuizMaster allows instructors to save the scores on disk, print study diagnoses, and monitor progress of students individually or by class section and by all sections of the course.

Presentation Tools *Designed by Thomas J. Liesz, Western State College in Colorado.* Developed from my lecture notes to accompany the sixth edition, the *Lecture Outline Transparency System* includes approximately 20 pages per chapter, all three-hole punched, perforated, and formatted so that an instructor can copy them to acetates or integrate them into his or her own notes. To support the more quantitative and challenging course material, each chapter is comprised of a lecture outline and broad overview of chapter themes; points to introduce transparency acetates; key terms and equations with definitions, plenty of examples and demonstrations, and worked-out table and time-line solutions; a section of teaching tips; and discussion problems, again with worked-out table and time-line solutions where appropriate. The set of approximately 100 *Transparency Acetates* includes key exhibits from the text and from other sources as well as solutions to both end-of-chapter and end-of-part cases. The Instructor's Manual lists all available acetates as a reference for planning classroom presentations. Finally, the *Electronic Lecture Outline Transparency System* combines the best of the printed lecture notes and acetates into a powerful software presentation kit.

Video Lecture Launchers These lecture launchers consist of videos from Fox television combined with a video guide by Cecilia L. Wagner of Seton Hall University. Adopters should ask their local HarperCollins representative about the media supplements to the teaching system, including video segments from Fox Business News, selected on the basis of timeliness, relevance to core topics in finance, and high production quality. Topics covered by the videos include ethics, financial markets, financial statements, the time value of money, risk and return, valuation, capital budgeting, financial planning, valuation, short-term financing, and issues in international managerial finance.

To my colleagues, friends, and family

No textbook can consistently meet market needs without continual feedback from colleagues, students, practitioners, and members of the publishing team. Once again, I invite all my colleagues to relate their classroom experiences using my book and its package to me at San Diego State University or in care of my Acquisitions Editor in Finance, Real Estate, and Insurance, HarperCollins College Publishers, 10 East 53rd Street, New York, NY 10022-5299. Any constructive criticism will undoubtedly help me to enhance the Teaching/Learning System further.

HarperCollins sought the advice of a great many excellent reviewers, all of whom strongly influenced various aspects of this volume. My special thanks go to the following individuals who analyzed all or part of the manuscript of previous editions:

M. Fall Ainina
Gary A. Anderson
Ronald F. Anderson
David A. Arbeit
Allen Atkins
Saul H. Auslander
Peter W. Bacon
Richard E. Ball
Alexander Barges
Scott Besley
Douglas S. Bible
Charles W. Blackwell
Russell L. Block
Calvin M. Boardman
Paul Bolster
Robert J. Bondi
Jeffrey A. Born
Jerry D. Boswell
Denis O. Boudreaux
Kenneth J. Boudreaux
Wayne Boyet
Ron Braswell
William Brunsen
Samuel B. Bulmash
Omer Carey
Patrick A. Casabona
Robert Chatfield
K. C. Chen
Roger G. Clarke
Terrence M. Clauretie
Thomas Cook
Mike Cudd
Donnie L. Daniel
Prabir Datta
Joel J. Dauten
Lee E. Davis
Richard F. DeMong
Peter A. DeVito
James P. D'Mello
R. Gordon Dippel
Vincent R. Driscoll
Betty A. Driver
David R. Durst
Dwayne O. Eberhardt
Ronald L. Ehresman
F. Barney English
Ross A. Flaherty
Rich Fortin
George W. Gallinger
Gerald D. Gay
R. H. Gilmer
Anthony J. Giovino
Philip W. Glasgo
Ron B. Goldfarb
David A. Gordon
J. Charles Granicz
C. Ramon Griffin
Melvin W. Harju
Phil Harrington
George F. Harris
George T. Harris
John D. Harris
Roger G. Hehman
Harvey Heinowitz
Glenn Henderson
Russell H. Hereth
Kathleen T. Hevert
Douglas A. Hibbert
Linda C. Hittle
James Hoban
Hugh A. Hobson
Keith Howe
Kenneth M. Huggins
Jerry G. Hunt
James F. Jackson
Stanley Jacobs
Dale W. Janowsky
Jeannette R. Jesinger
Nalina Jeypalan
Timothy E. Johnson
Ashok K. Kapoor
Daniel J. Kaufman, Jr.
Terrance E. Kingston
Harry R. Kuniansky

William R. Lane
B. E. Lee
Scott Lee
Michael A. Lenarcic
A. Joseph Lerro
Timothy Hoyt McCaughey
Christopher K. Ma
James C. Ma
Dilip B. Madan
Judy Maese
Daniel S. Marrone
William H. Marsh
John F. Marshall
Linda J. Martin
Jay Meiselman
Vincent A. Mercurio
Joseph Messina
Gene P. Morris
Edward A. Moses
Tarun K. Mukherjee
William T. Murphy
Randy Myers
Donald A. Nast
G. Newbould
Dennis T. Officer
Kathleen J. Oldfather
Kathleen F. Oppenheimer
Richard M. Osborne
Jerome S. Osteryoung
Don B. Panton
John Park
Ronda S. Paul
Gerald W. Perritt
Gladys E. Perry
Stanley Piascik
Jerry B. Poe
Gerald A. Pogue
Ronald S. Pretekin
Walter J. Reinhart
Jack H. Reubens
William B. Riley, Jr.
Ron Rizzuto
R. Daniel Sadlier
Hadi Salavitibar
Gary Sanger
William L. Sartoris
Carl J. Schwendiman
Carl Schweser
John W. Settle
Richard A. Shick
A. M. Sibley
Surendra S. Singhvi
Stacy Sirmans
Barry D. Smith
Gerald Smolen
Ira Smolowitz
Jean Snavely
Lester B. Strickler
Elizabeth Strock
John C. Talbott
Gary Tallman
Harry Tamule
Rolf K. Tedefalk
Richard Teweles
Robert D. Tollen
Pieter A. Vandenberg
Kenneth J. Venuto
James A. Verbrugge
Ronald P. Volpe
John M. Wachowicz, Jr.
William H. Weber III
Herbert Weinraub
Jonathan B. Welch
Grant J. Wells
Larry R. White
Peter Wichert
C. Don Wiggins
Howard A. Williams
Richard E. Williams
Glenn A. Wilt, Jr.
Bernard J. Winger
Tony R. Wingler
John C. Woods
Richard H. Yanow
Seung J. Yoon
Charles W. Young
Joe W. Zeman
J. Kenton Zumwalt
Tom Zwirlein

The following individuals provided extremely useful commentary on the seventh edition and its package:

Saul W. Adelman, Miami University of Ohio
Charles Barngrover, University of Cincinnati
Francis E. Canda, University of Akron
Mark Chockalingam, Arizona State University
Maurice P. Corrigan, Teikyo Post University
Thomas W. Donohue, Baldwin-Wallace College
Ted Ellis, College of Notre Dame
Greg Filbeck, Miami University of Ohio
Timothy J. Gallagher, Colorado State University
Jeffrey W. Glazer, San Diego State University, San Marcos
Joel Gold, University of Southern Maine
Reynolds Griffith, Stephen F. Austin State University
R. Stevenson Hawkey, Golden Gate University
Roger P. Hill, University of North Carolina–Wilmington
Jerry G. Hunt, East Carolina University
Mahmood Islam, West Virginia State College
Lawrence Kryzanowsky, Concordia University
Richard E. La Near, Missouri Southern State College
Judy E. Maese, New Mexico State University
Stanley A. Martin, University of Wisconsin
Charles E. Maxwell, Murray State University
Roger R. Palmer, University of St. Thomas

Murray Sabrin, Ramapo College of New Jersey
Kanwal S. Sachdeva, San Diego State University
Jim Scott, Southwest Missouri State University
Joseph V. Stanford, Bridgewater State College
John A Stocker, University of Tampa
Kenneth J. Thygerson, California State University, San Bernadino
Emory A. Trahan, Northeastern University
Nikhil P. Varaiya, San Diego State University
Oscar Varela, University of New Orleans
Robert J. Wright, Wright & Wright CPAs, San Diego
Philip J. Young, Southwest Missouri State University
John T. Zietlow, Indiana State University

My special thanks go to all members of my book team whose vision, creativity, and ongoing support helped me to reengineer all elements of the Teaching/Learning System: to Tom Krueger and Tony Plath for once again preparing the Concept in Practice inserts and for strengthening the *Study Guide*; to Marlene Bellamy for securing the well-received and highly motivating Practitioner Previews and for updating the *Instructor's Manual*; to Bill Megginson of the University of Georgia for enriching the international dimension of managerial finance throughout the book and revising the final chapter, which was originally prepared by Mehdi Salehizadeh of San Diego State University; to Hadi Salavitabar for instituting and cultivating the now-huge and reliable database of test items; to Enrique Roberto Lunski for developing the *PMF Lotus Templates*, to John Hansen, George Flowers, and Bob Bush for upgrading the *PMF Tutor*; to Fred Rexroad for expanding the *PMF Problem-Solver;* to Tom Liesz and his associate Lorna Dotts for creatively cranking through the presentation package; to Cecilia Wagner for screening video segments and preparing the final video teaching guides; and to Tarun Mukherjee of the University of New Orleans for checking the art for the text. I'm pleased by and proud of all their efforts, and I'm confident that my colleagues will appreciate everything they've done to ensure accuracy, consistency, and accessibility throughout the package.

A standing ovation and hearty round of applause also go to the folks back in the home office—Arlene Bessenoff, Susan Bogle, Paula Cousin, Kate Steinbacher, Mike Roche, and Kirsten Sandberg—for the inspiration and perspiration that define team work and ownership. A curtain call is due to Kirsten Sandberg, whose vision, creativity, expertise, and hard work have raised PMF to a new standard of excellence. And to the sales team, to Bob Carlton, Dan Lange, the Road Warriors, and the rest of the formidable force in finance for keeping this business fun!

Finally, and most important, many thanks to my wife, Robin, and to our children, Zachary and Jessica, for patiently providing support, understanding, and good humor throughout the revision process. To them, I will be forever grateful.

Lawrence J. Gitman

To the student

Since you have a good many options for getting your assigned reading materials, I appreciate your choosing this textbook as the best means for learning. You shouldn't be disappointed. To meet your increasingly diverse needs and time constraints (How many courses are you taking this term? How many hours have you worked this week?), my product team has transformed an already strong and accessible learning tool into a powerful and effective learning system by fully integrating learning tools with concepts and practical applications. This means that we have listened carefully to your compliments and complaints about coursework and have tripled our efforts to present the most important concepts and practices of managerial finance in an understanding and—dare I add—lively way. In Practitioner Previews at the beginning of each chapter I introduce you to industry leaders who "tell it like it is" in the world of finance. Concept in Practice inserts offer often humorous insights into the topic at hand through real company experiences. And in the *PMF Toolbox,* a cluster of icons at the beginning of all major chapter sections, you'll find the learning tools and resources—learning goals, software tutorials, problem-solving disk routines, and spreadsheet templates—that are available to you as you attempt to master each learning goal.

Now more than ever, you'll know what material you need to learn, where you'll find it, and whether you've mastered it. After all, managerial finance is an essential component not just in the business curriculum or in professional training programs, but in your daily job activities, *regardless of major.* Finance matters, plain and simple. Beyond the book itself you have access to several resources for success in this course.

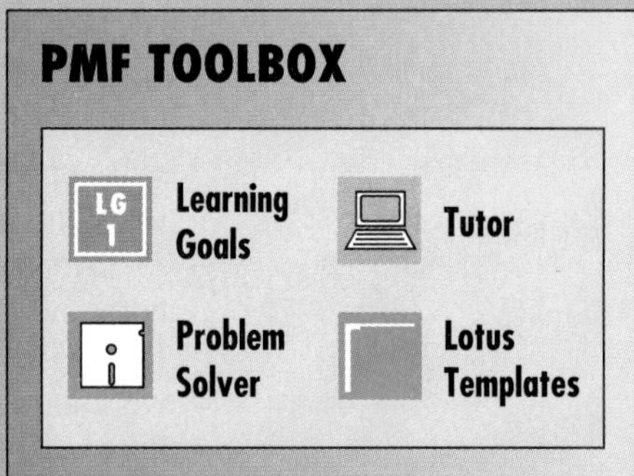

PMF Disk Packaged with new copies of the text at no additional cost, your disk contains three useful tools: the *PMF Tutor,* the *PMF Problem-Solver,* and the *PMF Lotus Templates.* Documentation and practical advice for using the *PMF Disk* appears in Appendix B, "Instructions for Using the *PMF Disk*"; in Appendix C, "Using Computers and Spreadsheets in Managerial Finance"; and in Appendix D, "Key Equations and Disk Routines."

The *PMF Tutor,* by John Hansen, George Flowers, and Robert Bush, all of **Houston Baptist University,** extends

. . . manage-rial finance is an essential component . . . of your daily job activities, *regardless of major.*

self-testing opportunities beyond those on the printed page. The Tutor helps students to identify and solve various types of managerial finance problems. Part of the PMF Toolbox, the Tutor icon, flags all Tutor applications in both text and *Study Guide*. Through user-friendly menus, students can access over fifty-five different problem types, constructed by random number generation for an inexhaustible supply of problems with little chance of repetition. Routines include financial ratios, time value of money, valuation, capital budgeting, and cost of capital. Documentation appears in Appendix B.

The *PMF Problem-Solver,* programmed by Frederick Rexroad of Yellow Springs, Ohio, contains seven short menu-driven programs to accelerate learning by providing an efficient way to perform financial computations. A popular provision of the PMF Toolbox, the Problem-Solver icon points out all related applications throughout the text and *Study Guide.* Referenced to specific text pages for quick review of technique, the routines include financial ratios, time value of money, bond and stock valuation, capital budgeting cash flows, capital budgeting techniques, cost of capital, and cash budgets. Instructions for use also appear in Appendix B.

Lawrence J. Gitman

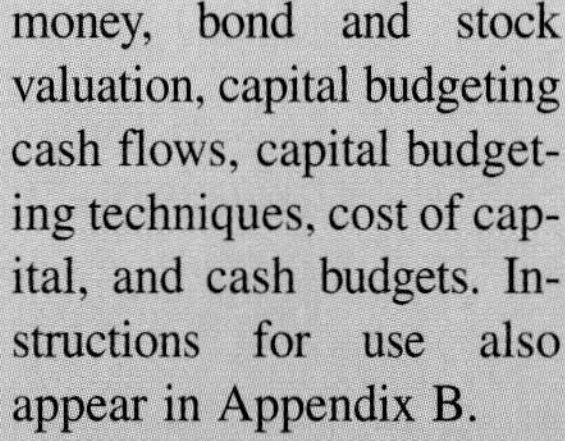

The *PMF Lotus Templates,* developed by Enrique Roberto Lunski, SUNY–New Paltz, provide users with preprogrammed Lotus templates for inputting data and solving problems using perhaps the most popular and widely accepted practical software application. The template files correspond to selected end-of-chapter problems, and the template file names follow the chapter number and the problem number. Documentation also appears in Appendix B.

Given today's rapidly changing technology, who knows what might be available next semester? If you'd prefer electronic versions of texts—on disk or CD-ROM or any other platform—please let my publisher know by writing to the attention of the Acquisitions Editor of Finance, Real Estate, and Insurance, HarperCollins College Publishers, 10 East 53rd Street, New York, NY 10022-5299. We are striving daily to keep apace of your needs and interests, and we wish you all the best in both your academic and professional careers.

Supplements available

Finance Tutor (ISBN 0065013104) *Also by John Hansen, George Flowers, and Robert Bush, all of Houston Baptist University.* If you need help beyond the scope of the *PMF Disk,* then you might obtain a copy of the complete *Finance Tutor.* The Tutor is a combination of a User Manual and a more powerful disk of IBM PC-compatible software designed to help you recognize and solve various basic finance problems. The Tutor contains over 100 types of problems, constructed by random number generation so that you get a fresh problem to work *every time.* Now that's what I call an unlimited return on your investment! The Tutor requires very little start-up or learning time—*it's that easy to use!* It also gives you immediate automated step-by-step feedback so that you can identify and learn from your mistakes in logic or calculations.

Study Guide (ISBN 0065019806) *Created by Thomas M. Krueger, University of Wisconsin–La Crosse, and D. Anthony Plath, University of North Carolina–Charlotte.* This is a fun one! An integral component of the PMF Learning System, this new edition offers a good many tools for studying finance: an introductory section called "And Now a Word from Our Sponsor" on overcoming the fear of finance, getting the most from the guide, and preparing thoroughly for tests and a unique section titled "Want to Win Friends, Fame, and Fortune?" on effective methods for setting up and solving finance problems, with a step-by-step example. Each chapter includes the following features: chapter review enumerated by learning goals; topical chapter outline, also broken down by learning goals for quick review; applications section including definition, objective items, a sample problem with a detailed solution, and then a full set of problems, some of which allow for use of software on the PMF Disk. Answers to definition and multiple-choice items appear in an appendix; however, solutions to problems remain at the end of each chapter. Six pages of the Preface showcasing Chapter 5, "The Time Value of Money," from the study guide follow on pgs. xxxv to xxxvii, so that potential users can preview this superior study tool before making a purchase decision.

Student Lecture Notes (ISBN 0065023293) *Designed by Thomas J. Liesz, Western State College in Colorado.* Derived directly from both printed and electronic versions of the Lecture Outline Transparency System, this handy package of concise notes enables students to follow easily along with classroom presentations. Rather than copying from an instructor's overhead, students can concentrate on understanding what the instructor adds to the overhead or explains in class.

Either your instructor or your bookstore manager should be able to help you obtain and use the above items for learning.

indicates that the topic you are learning in the study guide is also covered in *The PMF Problem-Solver;*

means that the material contained in the study guide is also discussed in the *PMF Tutor; and*

means that this problem can be solved using the *PMF Lotus Templates.*

Naturally, different students will use this study guide in different ways, because different people learn differently. Recognize, however, that reading the study guide without reading the textbook is not a good way to learn financial management. The study guide provides a brief overview of the material contained in the text, and helps you practice using financial concepts and methods. As such, it is intended to *accompany*, rather than *replace*, your r
valuable tool in helping to enhance you

WANT TO WIN
READ

Okay, we confess. We're exaggera
But we can offer you some helpful poin
will help you study more efficiently and
exams, and even result in a higher grad

At the outset, the most important t
other new subject, is hard work. The
finance goes beyond a higher course gra
skills, the ability to solve difficult proble
simply spending time staring at your ope
of time you devote to studying that mat
you get the most out of the hours you d

1. **PLAN.** Develop a strategy
plan throughout the course,
Allocate at least a few hours
of-chapter questions and prob
guide. Don't wait until a few
simply won't work.

The introduction shows how the PMF Toolbox icons are used with study guide materials. The guide also provides effective methods for setting up and solving finance problems. (Shown 55% of actual size.)

order to amortize a loan (i.e., convert it into equal annual payments), the amount of the loan can be divided by the interest factor for the present value of an annuity for the appropriate life and interest rate. An interest or growth rate associated with a stream of cash flows can be determined by dividing the earliest value by the most recent value to obtain what is equivalent to the interest factor for the present value of one dollar. Indexing the table for the appropriate number of years and finding the interest factor closest to that calculated will indicate the approximate rate of growth.

CHAPTER OUTLINE

OUTLINE	NOTES

LG 1 **The financial manager makes decisions based upon the cash flows that are expected to occur at various points in time.**

A. These decisions can be assessed using either future value or present value techniques.

   1. Future value techniques are used to find monetary values measured at the end of a project's life.

   2. Present value techniques are used to find monetary values measured at the beginning of a project's life.

B. A time line illustrates the cash flows associated with a given investment.

   1. The cash flow occurring at time zero and at the end of each year is shown above the line.

   2. Negative values represent cash outflows.

   3. Positive values represent cash inflows.

C. The future value technique uses compounding to find the future value of each cash flow at the end of the investment's life, and then sums these cash flows to find the project's future value.

D. The present value technique uses discounting to find the present value of each cash flow at time zero, and then sums these discounted cash flows to find the investment's present value.

E. Various computational aids simplify the calculations involved with financial mathematics.

Each chapter includes a topical chapter outline, broken down by learning goals for quick review.

EXAMPLE PROBLEM

As a forward-thinking college student, you are planning for your retirement. You plan to work for 25 more years. For the next 10 years, you can save $3,000 per year (with the first deposit being made one year from today). In Year 10, you plan to buy a weekend vacation home in the mountains for $40,000. How much must you save in Years 11 through 25 so that you have exactly $300,000 saved when you retire? Assume you can earn 10 percent, compounded annually, for each of the next 25 years, and ignore any income tax implications associated with your investments.

EXAMPLE SOLUTION

1. *State the problem:*

   To determine the annual pa
   in Year 25, where (a) $3,00
   is withdrawn from savings

2. *Locate the relevant data:*

   A time line captures the rel

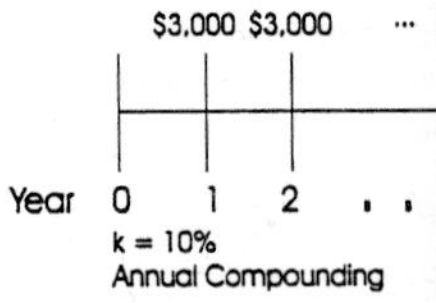

3. *Select the proper tool or eq*

   In this particular problem

   a. The future value of a
   equation we need to

   $FVA_{10\%,\ 10\ years}$

   b. The future value of a
   Year 25 -- at 10 perc

   $FV_{15\ years}$ = PV

LG 6 **Future-value and present-value techniques can be used to solve a variety of problems in personal and managerial financial management.**

A. The annual end-of-year payments necessary to accumulate a given future amount can be determined by dividing the future amount by the appropriate future value interest factor of an ordinary annuity:

$$PMT = \frac{FVA_n}{FVIFA_{k,n}}. \quad (5.30)$$

B. The annual payment necessary to amortize a loan (i.e., convert it to equal annual payments) can be found by dividing the principal balance of the loan by the present value interest factor of an annuity:

$$PMT = \frac{PVA_n}{PVIFA_{k,n}}. \quad (5.32)$$

C. The interest rate or growth rate associated with a stream of cash flows can be found in two steps.

   1. The first step is to divide the earliest value by the most recent value to obtain what is equivalent to an interest factor for the present value of one dollar.

   2. By indexing the present value of one dollar table for the appropriate number of years, the interest rate associated with the interest factor closest to the calculated interest factor is the interest or growth rate for the stream.

   3. When the computed factor falls between two table factors, interpolation may be used to get a more exact answer.

APPLICATIONS

DEFINITION

1. The value of a present sum at a future date found by applying compound interest over a specified period of time is known as ________ ______.

2. Interest earned on a given deposit that becomes part of the principal at the end of a specified period is known as ______________ ______________.

3. A ________ balance is the amount of money on which interest is paid.

The applications section includes definition and objective items (page 5-8), a sample problem with a detailed solution (page 5-12), and a full set of problems.

APPENDIX
ANSWERS TO DEFINITION AND MULTIPLE CHOICE QUESTIONS

CHAPTER 1
The Role of Finance and the Financial Manager

Definition Questions	Learning Goal	Multiple Choice	Learning Goal
1. Finance	1	1. b	1
2. financial services	1	2. b	1
3. financial manager	1	3. c	1
4. unlimited liability	1	4. d	1
5. partnership	1	5. a	1
6. "legal entities"	1	6. a	1
7. stock	1	7. d	1
8. treasurer	1	8. c	1
9. marginal analysis	1	9. b	1
10. accrual method	1	10. a	1
11. risk; return			
12. agents			
13. large private corporations			
14. Ethics training			
15. Owner wealth maximization			

The Op

Definition Ques
1. capital gain
2. S-corporation
3. financial market
4. primary market; secondary ma
5. Bonds; common stock
6. dividends; interest
7. organized security exchange;
8. investment banker
9. real; nominal
10. risk free
11. term structure
12. normal; inverted
13. expectations hypothesis
14. risk-return tradeoff
15. Preferred stock

Answers to definition and multiple-choice items appear in an Appendix.

10.

LG 6

Find the compound annual growth rate associated with the following cash flows:

a. To the nearest 1 percent.
b. Interpolate to the nearest 1/100 of 1 percent.

Year	Cash Flow
1993	$295
1992	275
1991	260
1990	227
1989	209
1988	200

11.

LG 5

Determine the present value of a perpetuity of $1,000 discounted at the firm's opportunity rate of 8 percent.

12.

LG 1 LG 6

Your younger sister will be attending Hibbard College 19 years from today. It will cost $20,000 per year, payable at the beginning of each year, for each of her four years in college, how much will your family need to save for the next 19 years at 6 percent to pay for your sister's education?

SOLUTIONS FOR CHAPTER PROBLEMS

1.

a. In order to find the future sum, the interest factor for the future value of one dollar deposited for three years at 12 percent must be obtained and multiplied by the amount of the deposit (i.e., $3,000). The interest factor for the future value of one dollar at 12 percent for three years is 1.405:

Future sum = (1.405) x ($3,000) = $4,215.

b. In order to evaluate the four alternate compounding periods, the appropriate interest factors to use in indexing the future value of one dollar table must be found:

Solutions to problems appear at the end of each chapter.

A Visual Guide To

Principles of Managerial Finance

Seventh Edition

ISBN: 0-06-501277-1

Lawrence J. Gitman
San Diego State University

Known for its clear explanations together with numerous real-company examples and an extensive array of learning devices, this book has long been a favorite of beginning finance students. Now in its seventh edition, *Principles of Managerial Finance* is more than just a text, it is an accessible learning *system*; a combination of features integrated throughout the text provide a reliable and consistent framework to help students learn the major concepts behind managerial finance. New to this edition is a more logical positioning of the chapter on the analysis of financial statements: *immediately after* the chapter on financial statements. This enables students to use ratio analysis to interpret material which is still fresh in their minds. The author also includes career opportunities in managerial finance in the first chapter. This organizational approach provides a basis for relating the functions of the financial manager and sets the stage for forthcoming, chapter-opening practitioner profiles.

Tool Box

Each section opener includes a **"Tool Box"** that is tied to the **learning goal** for the following material and specifies any software or other resources available to students. This feature is an important aspect of the text's **learning system** which integrates the material into an accessible framework.

Special applications of time value

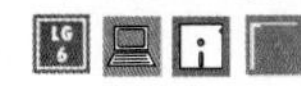

Time-value of money techniques are used in personal financial transactions as well as in managerial finance. In what personal financial transactions would time-value techniques be used? Before reading on, take a few minutes to cite and consider the time-value applications involved in a few such transactions.

FUTURE-VALUE AND PRESENT-VALUE TECHNIQUES HAVE A NUMBER OF IMPORTANT applications. Three will be presented in this section: (1) the calculation of the deposits needed to accumulate a future sum, (2) the calculation of amortization on loans, and (3) the determination of interest or growth rates.

Deposits to Accumulate a Future Sum

Often an individual may wish to determine the annual deposit necessary to accumulate a certain amount of money so many years hence. Suppose a person wishes to purchase a house five years from now and estimates that an initial down payment of $20,000 will be required at that time. She wishes to make equal annual end-of-year deposits in an account paying annual interest of 6 percent, so she must determine what size annuity will result in a lump sum equal to $20,000 at the end of year 5. The solution to this problem is closely related to the process of finding the future value of an annuity.

In an earlier section of this chapter the future value of an n-year annuity, $FVAn$, was found by multiplying the annual deposit, PMT, by the appropriate interest factor (from Table A-2 or using a hand-held business calculator), $FVIFAk,n$. The relationship of the three variables has been defined by Equation 5.15, which is rewritten here as Equation 5.29.

$$FVAn = PMT \times (FVIFAk,n) \qquad (5.29)$$

We can find the annual deposit required to accumulate $FVAn$ dollars, given a specified interest rate, k, and a certain number of years, n, by solving Equation 5.29 for PMT. Isolating PMT on the left side of the equation gives us

$$PMT = FVIFAk,nFVAn \qquad (5.30)$$

Once this is done, we have only to substitute the known values of $FVAn$ and $FVIFAk,n$ into the right side of the equation to find the annual deposit required. An example can be employed to demonstrate this calculation using Table A-2 as well as a hand-held business calculator.

Learning Goals

Learning Goals are enumerated at the beginning of each chapter. They are accompanied by a **"Tool Box"** of resources, and clear, realistic examples of how to use the tools. Throughout the text, these goals are specifically referred to in the assigned material, and summarized point-by-point at the end of the chapter. Students will know what material they need to learn, where they can find it in the chapter, and whether they have mastered it by the end of the chapter.

chapter 5

The time value of money

LEARNING GOALS

After studying this chapter, you should be able to:

LG 1 Discuss the role of time value in finance, particularly the two common views—future value and present value—and the use of financial tables and business/financial calculators to find them.

LG 2 Understand the concept of future value, its calculation for single amounts, and the procedures and effects on interest rates of compounding interest more frequently than annually.

LG 3 Find the future value of the two basic types of annuities—ordinary annuity and annuity due—and compare them.

LG 4 Review the concept of present value, its calculation for a single amount, and the relationship of present to future value.

...e the present value of a mixed ... cash flows, an annuity, a mixed ...th an embedded annuity, and a ...

...the procedures involved in (1) ...ng deposits to accumulate a ...n, (2) loan amortization, and (3) ...terest or growth rates.

As a corporate treasurer for USAA, a large insurance and financial services company, I constantly make decisions based on time value of money concepts. I use time value to raise funds in the money and capital markets for our various business activities and also when evaluating investments that make the best use of corporate financial resources. The time value of money is a building block that is fundamental to areas of finance. It is a factor in many different types of decisions, not only in corporate finance--the basis of the textbook--but also in investments and portfolio analysis in corporations and financial institutions, in government finance, and in personal finance.

The time value of money is, in a way, the language of finance, a common denominator for discussing financial transactions and financial opportunities. It bridges the gap between consumption and investment: money can be converted into tangible goods and consumed now, or you can invest it, deferring consumption, and postpone purchasing goods now because you expect your investment to have even greater value in the future.

The time value of money is, in a way, the language of finance.

The decision either to consume now or to invest now and consume later, involves a tradeoff. For example, your choice to defer working to go to school now is a significant time value tradeoff. There is an opportunity cost—the wages you could earn now. Yet you forego current income because a college education means you can earn considerably more later. How do you equate the money you could earn today with your higher earning potential later? This is really an investment decision, and you use time value of money concepts to decide if you should make that tradeoff.

Time value of money is an essential aspect of most of the concepts presented in later chapters, including risk, or the chance I may lose part or all of my investment, and return, or how much more than initial investment I expect to receive over time; it is also critical for valuation, the integration of risk and return. You will learn in future chapters about other applications of time value: capital budgeting, cost of capital, capital structure, and working capital management. But before you can properly use those tools, you must understand the time value of money and be comfortable with time value techniques. Often the conceptual understanding comes later; it takes time. Time value of money may be one of the most difficult concepts to grasp, but at some point, the tradeoff between time and return becomes evident, and the concepts such as investment tradeoff, risk and return, and compound growth will all begin to fit together.

For example, at USAA I coordinate the investment of corporate financial resources. This means choosing long-term investments that maximize owner wealth. In our case, we do not have stockholders because we are owned by our members, the policyholders. Like other companies (who have investors rather than members), we can return capital to our members as dividends or defer that return and invest it in other financial or tangible assets, such as our subsidiary operations, to earn an even greater return for members in the future. How do we equate the alternative of returning money to members today versus in-

William Regan, Senior Vice President and Treasurer USAA

Practitioner Profiles

Chapter-opening profiles of financial managers from a variety of businesses describe how the chapter material applies to specific real-world situations. These motivational launchers show students the relevance of upcoming material from a practical point of view.

Section Openers

Section openers contain critical analysis questions to prepare students for the section material.

Present value of a single amount

Assume that you wish to purchase the right to receive $50,000 exactly seven years from now by making a single lump-sum payment today. If interest rates suddenly rise, would the amount you should be willing to pay for this opportunity rise or fall? Why? Take a few moments to answer these questions before reading ahead.

present value
The current dollar value of a future amount. The amount of money that would have to be invested today at a given interest rate over a specified period in order to equal the future amount.

IT IS OFTEN USEFUL TO DETERMINE THE "PRESENT VALUE" OF A FUTURE AMOUNT OF money. **Present value** is the current dollar value of a future amount—the amount of money that would have to be invested today at a given interest rate over a specified period to equal the future amount. Present value, like future value, is based on the belief that a dollar today is worth more than a dollar that will be received at some future date. The actual present value of a dollar depends largely on the investment opportunities of the recipient and the point in time at which the dollar is to be received. This section explores the present value of a single amount.

The Concept of Present Value

discounting cash flows
The process of finding present values; the inverse of compounding interest.

The process of finding present values is often referred to as **discounting cash flows**. This process is actually the inverse of compounding interest. It is concerned with answering the question "If I can earn *k* percent on my money, what is the most I would be willing to pay for an opportunity to receive *FVn* dollars n periods from today?" Instead of finding the future value of present dollars invested at a given rate, discounting determines the present value of a future amount, assuming that the decision maker has an opportunity to earn a certain return, *k*, on the money. This annual rate of return is variously referred to as the *discount rate, required return, cost of capital,* or *opportunity cost.*[11] These terms will be used interchangeably in this text. The discounting process can be illustrated by a simple example.

EXAMPLE

Paul Shorter has been given an opportunity to receive $300 one year from now. If he can earn 6 percent on his investments in the normal course of events, what is the most he should pay for this opportunity? To answer this question, we must determine how many dollars would have to be invested at 6 percent today to have $300 one year from now. Letting *PV* equal this unknown amount and using the same notation as in the compounding discussion, the situation can be expressed as follows:

$$PV \times (1 + .06) = \$300 \quad (5.17)$$

Solving Equation 5.17 for *PV* gives us Equation 5.18:

$$PV = \$300\ (1 + .06) = \$283.02 \quad (5.18)$$

Using the notation introduced earlier, the effective interest rate, *keff.*, can be calculated by substituting values for the nominal interest rate, *k*, and the compounding frequency, *m*, into Equation 5.10.

$$keff. = (1 + mk)m - 1 \quad (5.10)$$

Application of this equation can conveniently be demonstrated by using data from the preceding examples.

EXAMPLE

Rich Saver wishes to find the effective interest rate associated with an 8 percent nominal interest rate ($k = .08$) when interest is compounded (1) annually ($m = 1$); (2) semiannually ($m = 2$); and (3) quarterly ($m = 4$). Substituting these values into Equation 5.10, we get

1. *For annual compounding*

$$keff. = (1 + .108)1 - 1 = (1 + .08)1 - 1 = 1 + .08 - 1 = .08 = 8\%$$

2. *For semiannual compounding*

$$keff. = (1 + .282)2 - 1 = (1 + .04)2 - 1 = 1.0816 - 1 = .0816 = 8.16\%$$

3. *For quarterly compounding*

$$keff. = (1 + .084)4 - 1 = (1 + .02)\ 4 - 1 = 1.0824 - 1 = .0824 = 8.24\%$$

Two important points are demonstrated by these values: (1) the nominal and effective interest rates are equivalent for annual compounding, and (2) the effective rate of interest increases with increasing compounding frequency.[8] ■

CONCEPTS IN REVIEW

5-3 How is the *compounding process* related to the payment of interest on savings? What is the general equation for the future value, *FVn*, in period n if *PV* dollars are deposited in an account paying *k* percent annual interest?
5-4 What effect would (a) a *decrease* in the interest rate or (b) an increase in the holding period of a deposit have on its future value? Why?
5-5 What effect does compounding interest more frequently than annually have on (a) the future value generated by a beginning principal and (b) the effective interest rate? Why?
5-6 What is *continuous compounding*? How does the magnitude of the future value of a given deposit at a given rate of interest obtained using continuous compounding compare to the value obtained using annual or any other compounding period?
5-7 Define and differentiate between (a) and *ordinary annuity* and (b) an *annuity due*. Which is the more common form? Which form always has greater future value for otherwise identical annuities and interest rates? Why?
5-8 Explain how one can conveniently determine the future value of an ordinary annuity. How can the future-value interest factors for an ordinary annuity be conveniently modified to find the future-value of an annuity?

Concepts in Review

At the end of each section, **Concepts in Review** reinforce the important concepts covered in the section.

The Gitman Example Method

This feature, which has become a "trademark" of this text, places examples throughout the book to demonstrate the most troublesome concepts for students. This edition formats the solution to realistic examples in four phases: 1. A numerical solution or use of equation; 2. A timeline solution; 3. A table solution; 4. A calculator keystroke solution with calculator buttons highlighted for quick reference. Detailed graphs and figures support the example method.

EXAMPLE

The Braden Company, a small producer of plastic toys, is attempting to determine the most it should pay to purchase a particular annuity. The firm requires a minimum return of 8 percent on all investments, and the annuity consists of cash flows of $700 per year for five years. Table 5.8 shows the long way of finding the present value of the annuity, which is the same as the method used for mixed streams. This procedure yields a present value of $2,795.10, which can be interpreted in the same manner as for the mixed cash-flow stream in the preceding example.

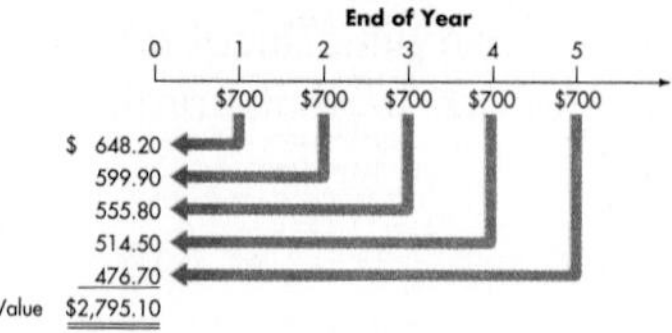

FIGURE 5G
Time line for present value of an annuity ($700 end-of-year cash flows, discounted at 8 percent, over five years)

Time-Line Use Similarly, this situation is depicted graphically on the time-line in shown below. ■

TABLE 5.8

THE LONG METHOD FOR FINDING THE PRESENT VALUE OF AN ANNUITY

Year (n)	Cash flow (1)	$PVIF_{8\%,n}$[a] (2)	Present value [(1) x (2)] (3)
1	$700	.926	$ 648.20
2	700	.857	599.90
3	700	.794	555.80
4	700	.735	514.50
5	700	.681	476.70
		Present value of annuity	$2,795.10

[a] Present-value interest factors at 8 percent are from Table A-3.

THE MATHEMATICS OF THE PRESENT-VALUE-OF-AN ANNUITY CALCULATION

The calculations used in the preceding example can be simplified by recognizing that each of the five multiplications made to get the individual present values involved multiplying the annual amount ($700) by the appropriate present-value interest factor. This method of finding the present value of the annuity can also be written as an equation:

EXAMPLE

If Rich Saver places $100 in a savings account paying 8 percent interest compounded annually, at the end of one year he will have $108 in the account. This $108 represents the initial principal of $100 plus 8 percent ($8) in interest. The future value at the end of the first year is calculated by using Equation 5.1:

$$\text{Future value at end of year 1} = \$100 \times (1 + .08) = \$108 \quad (5.1)$$

If Rich were to leave this money in the account for another year, he would be paid interest at the rate of 8 percent on the new principal of $108. At the end of this second year there would be $116.64 in the account. This amount would represent the principal at the beginning of year 2 ($108) plus 8 percent of the $108 ($8.64) in interest. The future value at the end of the second year is calculated by using Equation 5.2:

$$\text{Future value at end of year 2} = \$108 \times (1 + .08) = \$116.64 \quad (5.2)$$

Substituting the expression between the equal signs in Equation 5.1 for the $108 figure in Equation 5.2 gives us Equation 5.3:

$$\begin{aligned}\text{Future value at end of year 2} &= \$100 \times (1 + .08) \times (1 + .08) \quad (5.3)\\ &= \$100 \times (1+ .08)2\\ &= \$116.64\end{aligned}$$

The Calculation of Future Value

The basic relationship in Equation 5.3 can be generalized to find the future value after any number of periods. Let

FVn = the future value at the end of period n
PV = the initial principal, or present value
k = the annual rate of interest paid
(Note: On business/financial calculators, i is typically used to represent this rate.)
n = the number of periods—typically years—the money is left on deposit

Using this notation, a general equation for the future value at the end of period n can be formulated:

$$FVn = PV \times (1 + k)n \quad (5.4)$$

The usefulness of Equation 5.4 for finding the future value, FVn, in an account paying k percent interest compounded annually for n periods if PV dollars were deposited initially can be illustrated by a simple example.

EXAMPLE

Jane Frugal has placed $800 in a savings account paying 6 percent interest compounded annually. She wishes to determine how much money will be in the account at the end of five years. Substituting PV = $800, k = .06, and n = 5 into Equation 5.4 gives the amount at the end of year 5.

$$FV_5 = \$800 \times (1 + .06)5 = \$800 \times (1.338) = \$1,070.40$$

Concept in Practice

"Concept in Practice," updated for the seventh edition, provides students with insights into real-company experiences in relation to the topic at hand.

CONCEPT IN PRACTICE

Gilligan's Island Reruns Will Never Be the Same

For Silicon Graphics, Inc., a leading supplier of graphic image reproduction technology, 1993 was a very exciting year. The year's accomplishments included: introduction of a new supercomputer that rivaled the fastest computers offered by Cray Research, Inc., a visit by President Bill Clinton and Vice President Al Gore who kicked off their national technology initiative, and a key role for the company's graphic work-station in the production of special effects for Steven Spielberg's recent movie, *Jurassic Park*.

What really excites the firm's managers is a little financial mathematics. Silicon Graphics expects sales growth to rem 30 percent each year over the next several years as the digital media industry explodes. Digital Media, a huge new market combining computers, communication, and consumer electronics, is expected to replace conventional cable TV with such products as Digitized movies, interactive games, and yes, even old reruns from the Gilligan's Island sitcom. With current sales of $1 billion a year and a projected 30 percent annual growth in sales, Silicon Graphics will reach $3.7 billion in sales in just 5 short years.

CONCEPTS IN REVIEW

5-13 How can the size of the equal annual end-of-year deposits necessary to accumulate a certain future sum in a specified future period be determined? How might one use future-value interest factors to aid in this calculation?

5-14 Describe the procedure used to amortize a loan into a series of equal annual payments. What is a loan *amortization schedule*?

5-15 Which present-value interest factors would be used to find (a) the growth rate associated with a stream of cash flows and (b) the interest rate associated with an equal-payment loan? How would each of these be calculated?

Summary

LG **1** Financial managers use time-value of money techniques to explicitly recognize their opportunities to earn positive returns when assessing the value of the expected cash flow streams associated with decision alternatives. While alternatives can be assessed by either compounding to find future-value or discounting to find present-value, financial managers, because they are at time zero when making decisions, rely primarily on present value techniques. Both financial tables, which provide various future- and present-value interest factors, and hand-held business/financial calculators like the BA-35 can be used to streamline the practical application of time value techniques.

LG **2** Future value relies on compound interest to measure the value of future amounts. When interest is compounded, the initial principal or deposit in one period, along with the interest earned on it, becomes the beginning principal of the following period, and so on. Interest can be compounded annually, semiannually, quarterly, monthly, weekly, daily, or even continuously. The more frequently interest is compounded, the larger the future amount that will be accumulated and the higher the effective interest rate. The interest factor formulas and basic equations for the future-value of a single amount are given in Table 5.11.

LG **3** An annuity is a pattern of equal annual cash flows occurring at the end of the period for an ordinary annuity and at the beginning of the period for an annuity due. The future-value of an ordinary annuity can be found using the future-value interest factor for an annuity, which requires an adjustment in the case of an annuity due. The interest factor formulas and basic equations for the future-value of an annuity are given in Table 5.11.

LG **4** Present-value represents the inverse of future value. In finding the present value of a futur[...] amount of money today would b[...] ture amount, considering the fact [...] turn on the current money. The in[...] sic equation for the present valu[...] in Table 5.11.

Graphs

For more visually-oriented students, these graphical features help display information in a clear, concise manner.

FUTURE-VALUE RELATIONSHIP

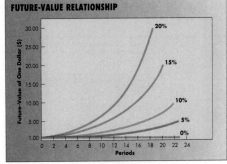

FIGURE 5.5
Interest rates, time periods, and future-value of one dollar.

A Graphic View of Future-Value

It is important to note that we measure future-value at the end of the given period. The relationship between various interest rates, the number of periods interest is earned, and the future-value of one dollar is illustrated in Figure 5.5. It clearly shows two relationships: (1) the higher the interest rate, the higher the future-value, and (2) the longer the period of time, the higher the future-value. Note that for an interest rate of 0 percent, the future-value always equals the present value ($1.00). But for any interest rate greater than zero, the future-value is greater than the present value of $1.00 in Figure 5.5.

Compounding More Frequently than Annually

Interest is often compounded more frequently than once a year. Savings institutions compound interest semiannually, quarterly, monthly, weekly, daily, or even continuously. This section discusses semiannual and quarterly compounding, presents a general equation for compounding more frequently than annually, and briefly describes continuous compounding. It also explains how to use both a table and a hand-held business calculator to simplify calculations.

Marginal Glossary

In addition to an end-of-text glossary a **marginal glossary** defines concepts as soon as they are introduced.

semiannual compounding
Compounding of interest over two periods within the year.

SEMIANNUAL COMPOUNDING

Semiannual compounding of interest involves two compounding periods within the year. Instead of the stated interest rate being paid once a year, one-half of the stated

End-of-Chapter Material

The **end-of-chapter material** includes **chapter summaries** (tied numerically to the **Learning Goals**) that provide a quick review of chapter topics; **self-test problems** designed to strengthen students' understanding of the techniques presented; and a **comprehensive set of problems** that provide professors with a wide range of assignable material.

Problems

5-1 LG 1 Using a Time-Line The financial manager at Starbuck Industries is considering an investment that requires an initial outlay of $25,000 and is expected to result in cash inflows of $3,000 at the end of year 1, $6,000 at the end of years 2 and 3, $10,000 at the end of year 4, $8,000 at the end of year 5, and $7,000 at the end of year 6.

a. Draw and label a time-line depicting the cash flows associated with Starbuck Industries' proposed investment.

b. Use arrows to demonstrate, on the time line in a, how compounding to find future value can be used to measure all cash flows at the end of year 6.

c. Use arrows to demonstrate, on the time-line in b, how discounting to find present-value can be used to measure all cash flows at time zero.

d. Which of the approaches—future-value or present-value is most often relied upon by the financial manager for decision-making purposes?

5-2 LG 2 Future-Value Without tables or the financial routine on your business calculator, use the basic formula for future-value along with the given interest rate, k, and number of periods, n, to calculate the future-value interest factor in each of the following cases. Compare the calculated value to the table value in Appendix Table A-1.

Case	Interest rate, k (%)	Number of periods, n
A	12	2
B	6	3
C	9	2
D	3	4

5-3 LG 2 Future-Value Tables Use the future-value interest factors in Appendix Table A-1 in each of the cases in the following table to estimate, to the nearest year, how long it would take an initial deposit, assuming no withdrawals,

a. To double.

b. To quadruple.

Case	Interest rate (%)
A	12
B	6
C	9
D	3

s Use the future-value interest factors in Appendix Table A-1 in each of the cases in the following table to estimate, to the nearest year, how long it would take an initial deposit, assuming no withdrawals.

5-33 LG 6 Rate of Return—Annuity What is the rate of return on an investment of $10,606 if the company expects to receive $2,000 each year for the next ten years?

5-34 LG 6 Loan Rates of Interest John Fleming has been shopping for a loan to finance the purchase of his new car. He has found three possibilities that seem attractive and wishes to select the one having the lowest interest rate. The information available with respect to each of the three $5,000 loans follows.

Loan	Principal ($)	Annual Payment ($)	Term (years)
A	5,000	1,352.815	
B	5,000	1,543.214	
C	5,000	2,010.453	

5-3 LG 2 Future-Value Tables Use the future-value interest factors in Appendix Table A-1 in each of the cases in the following table to estimate, to the nearest year, how long it would take an initial deposit, assuming no withdrawals,

a. To double.

b. To quadruple.

Chapter 1 Case Funding Jill Moran's Retirement Annuity

Sunrise Industries wishes to accumulate funds to provide a retirement annuity for its Vice President of Research, Jill Moran. By contract, Ms. Moran will retire at the end of exactly 12 years. Upon retirement she is entitled to receive an annual end-of-year payment of $42,000 for exactly 20 years. If she dies before the end of the 20-year period, the annual payments will pass to her heirs. During the 12-year "accumulation period," Sunrise Industries wishes to find the annuity by making equal annual end-of-year deposits into an account earning 9 percent interest. Once the 20-year "distribution period" begins, Sunrise plans to move the accumulated monies into an account earning a guaranteed 12 percent per year. At the end of the distribution period the account balance will equal zero. Note that the first deposit will be made at the end of year 1 and the first distribution will be received at the end of year 13.

Required

a. Draw a time-line depicting all of the cash flows associated with Sunrise's view of the retirement annuity.

b. How large a sum must Sunrise Industries accumulate by the end of year 12 to provide the 20-year, $42,000 annuity?

c. How large must Sunrise's equal annual end-of-year deposits into the account be over the 12-year accumulation period to fully fund Ms. Moran's retirement annuity?

d. How much would Sunrise have to deposit annually during the accumulation period if it could earn 10 percent rather than 9 percent during the accumulation period?

End-of Chapter Case

End-of Chapter Cases tie together the concepts introduced in the text.

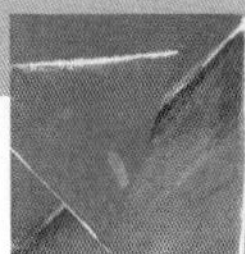

INTEGRATIVE CASE II

Encore International

In the world of trend-setting fashion, instinct and marketing savvy are prerequisites to success. Jordan Ellis had both. His international casual-wear company, Encore, after 10 years in business, rocketed to $300 million in sales during 1994. His fashion line covered the young woman from head to toe with hats, sweaters, dresses, blouses, skirts, pants, sweatshirts, socks, and shoes. In Manhattan there was an Encore shop every five or six blocks, each featuring a different color. There were shops where the entire line was mauve, while others featured the entire line in canary yellow.

Encore had made it. The company's historical growth was so spectacular that no one could have predicted it. However, securities analysts speculated that Encore could not keep up the pace. They warned that competition is fierce in the fashion industry and that the firm might encounter little or no growth in the future. They estimated that stockholders also should except no growth in future dividends.

Contrary to the conservative security analysts, Jordan Ellis, founder of Encore, felt that the company could maintain a constant annual growth rate in dividends per share of 6 percent in the future, or possibly 8 percent for the next two years and 6 percent thereafter. Jordan Ellis based his estimates on an established long-term expansion plan into European and Latin American markets. By venturing into these markets the risk of the firm as measured by beta was expected to immediately increase from 1.10 to 1.25.

In preparing the long-term financial plan, Encore's chief financial officer has assigned a junior financial analyst, Marc Scott, to evaluate the firm's current stock price. He has asked Marc to consider the conservative predictions of the securities analysts and the aggressive predictions of the company founder, Jordan Ellis.

Marc has compiled these 1994 financial data to aid his analysis.

Data Item	1994 value
Earnings per share (EPS)	$6.25
Price per share of common stock equity	$40.00
Book value of common equity	$60,000,000.00
Total common shares outstanding	$2,500,000.00
Common stock dividend per share	$4.00

Integrative Cases

Part-ending **integrative cases** tie together the concepts introduced in each part's chapters. Together with **end-of-chapter cases,** they eliminate the need for a separate casebook.

part I

The goal and environment of managerial finance

CHAPTERS IN THIS PART

chapter 1

The role of finance and the financial manager

LEARNING GOALS

 Define *finance* and describe its major areas—financial services and managerial finance—and the career opportunities within them.

 Review the basic forms of business organization and their respective strengths and weaknesses.

 Describe the managerial finance function and differentiate managerial finance from the closely related disciplines of economics and accounting.

 Identify the key activities of the financial manager within the firm and his or her role in total quality management (TQM).

 Compare the profit maximization and wealth maximization goals and justify the financial manager's focus on owner wealth maximization and the preservation of *stakeholder* wealth.

 Discuss the agency issue as it relates to owner wealth maximization and the role of ethics in the achievement of this goal.

Running a business, whether it is a small business or a large corporation, involves many different functions. Foodmaker, Inc. operates and franchises two types of restaurants: Jack in the Box, the nation's fifth largest fast-food hamburger chain, and Chi-Chi's, the country's largest full-service Mexican chain. Development of new menu items, opening restaurants in new locations, marketing, and customer service are all critical to our company's success. But *finance* is what makes it all happen; it drives everything else. Without capital to meet the company's needs, whether to fund growth or for day-to-day operations, we could not develop and test new products, design marketing campaigns, purchase food, maintain our existing restaurants, or build new restaurants. The role of the financial manager is to ensure that this capital is available in the right amounts, at the right time, and at the lowest cost. If this doesn't happen, a company cannot survive. In fact, the number one cause of business failure in the United States is inadequate capital.

The field of finance is much more complicated and faster paced today. Financial markets are volatile; interest rates can move sharply up or down in a very short time period. These changes affect our financial decisions. Financing projects when interest costs are 14% is different from when they're 7%. Also, there are many more financing strategies to choose from, and new financial products are introduced all the time.

Probably, on a long-term basis, capital expenditure decisions—choosing projects to grow the business—have the biggest impact on the company's overall value. If you make poor capital expenditure decisions, your business won't succeed. For example, we analyze new restaurant proposals over a 20-year time horizon to calculate the return on our original investment and accept the project only if it earns more than a specific rate of return. Otherwise, it won't add to our long-term value. Once we select the projects, we can choose the best way to finance them. If we can raise money at a better cost than our competitors, we may be able to price our products more competitively, thereby improving profitability.

The number one cause of business failure in the United States is inadequate capital.

Our financial decisions, however, can't be made in isolation. Financial people must work hand in hand with marketing and operations people. They must not only "crunch the numbers" but also understand what products cost, how they sell, the tradeoffs between margins and sales volume, and how economic and social trends affect our business. For example, we introduced the teriyaki bowl, a product with good margins that appeals to customers looking for a healthy fast food alternative. But, unlike sandwich items, it doesn't generate sales of high-margin side orders such as French fries. A new product analysis that compares the profitability of the teriyaki bowl to a hamburger without taking side order sales into account could provide misleading information on which to base a decision.

These and other financial decisions are governed by one primary focus: The long-term value of the company. Obviously, you won't get to the long-term if you don't pay attention to short-term financial issues and securities market fluctuations. But maximizing long-term shareholder value, as measured in cash flow terms, is the key to a company's ultimate success and survival. Reported earnings can be misleading because of the various ways to present accounting information. The true strength of the company—what's it really worth to the shareholders—is based on cash flow.

Charles W. Duddles is Foodmaker's Executive Vice President, Chief Administrative Officer, Chief Financial Officer, and also serves on the board of directors. After receiving a bachelor's degree in accounting from Ferris State University in Michigan, he worked for Price Waterhouse, Associates Corp. of North America, and Ralston Purina Co. before joining Foodmaker in 1979 as Controller.

Finance as an area of study

At least one course in managerial finance is required of most business majors. Why do you think exposure to its principles and practices is important, whether you are planning to major in finance or not? Before reading on, spend a few moments answering this question.

THE FIELD OF FINANCE IS BROAD AND DYNAMIC. IT DIRECTLY AFFECTS THE LIVES OF every person and every organization, financial or nonfinancial, private or public, large or small, profit-seeking or not-for-profit. There are many areas for study, and a large number of career opportunities are available in the field of finance.

What is finance?

finance
The art and science of managing money.

Finance can be defined as the art and science of managing money. Virtually all individuals and organizations earn or raise money and spend or invest money. Finance is concerned with the process, institutions, markets, and instruments involved in the transfer of money among and between individuals, businesses, and governments.

Major areas and opportunities in finance

The major areas of finance can be summarized by reviewing the career opportunities in finance. These opportunities can, for convenience, be divided into two broad parts: financial services and managerial finance.

FINANCIAL SERVICES

financial services
The part of finance concerned with design and delivery of advice and financial products to individuals, business, and government.

Financial services is the area of finance concerned with the design and delivery of advice and financial products to individuals, business, and government. It involves a variety of interesting career opportunities within the areas of banking and related institutions, personal financial planning, investments, real estate, and insurance. Table 1.1 describes the career opportunities available in each of these areas.

MANAGERIAL FINANCE

managerial finance
Concerns the duties of the financial manager in the business firm.

financial manager
Actively manages the financial affairs of any type of business, whether financial or nonfinancial, private or public, large or small, profit-seeking or not-for-profit.

Managerial finance is concerned with the duties of the financial manager in the business firm. **Financial managers** actively manage the financial affairs of many types of business—financial and nonfinancial, private and public, large and small, profit-seeking and not-for-profit. They perform such varied tasks as budgeting, financial forecasting, cash management, credit administration, investment analysis, and funds procurement. In recent years the changing economic and regulatory environments have increased the importance and complexity of the financial manager's duties. As a result, many top executives in industry and government have come from the finance area.

Another important recent trend has been the globalization of business activity. U.S. corporations have dramatically increased their sales and investments in other countries, while foreign corporations have increased their sales and direct investments in the United States. These changes have created a need for financial managers who can help a firm to manage cash flows denominated in different currencies and protect against

TABLE 1.1

CAREER OPPORTUNITIES IN FINANCIAL SERVICES

Area	Career opportunities
Banking and related institutions	*Loan officers* evaluate and make recommendations with regard to installment, commercial, real estate, and/or consumer loans. *Retail bank managers* run bank offices and supervise the programs offered by the bank to customers. *Trust officers* administer trust funds for estates, foundations, and business firms. Others offer financial services in personal financial planning, investments, real estate, and insurance.
Personal financial planning	*Financial planners*, working independently or as employees, advise individuals with regard to the management of all aspects—budgeting, taxes, investments, real estate, insurance, and retirement and estate planning—of their personal finances and help them to develop a comprehensive financial plan that meets their objectives.
Investments	*Stockbrokers*, or account executives, assist clients in choosing, buying, and selling securities. *Securities analysts* study stocks and bonds, usually in specific industries, and advise securities firms and their customers, fund managers, and insurance companies with regard to them. *Portfolio managers* build and manage portfolios of securities for firms and individuals. *Investment bankers* provide advice to security issuers and act as middlepersons between issuers and purchasers of newly issued stocks and bonds.
Real estate	*Real estate agents/brokers* list residential and commercial property for sale or lease, find buyers and lessees for listed property, show property, and negotiate the sale or lease of property. *Appraisers* estimate the market values of all types of property. *Real estate lenders* analyze and make recommendations/decisions with regard to loan applications. *Mortgage bankers* find and arrange financing for real estate projects. *Property managers* handle the day-to-day operations of properties to achieve maximum returns for their owners.
Insurance	*Insurance agents/brokers* interview prospects, develop insurance programs to meet their needs, sell them policies, collect premiums, and assist in claims processing and settlement. *Underwriters* appraise and select the risks that their company will insure and set the associated premiums.

the political and foreign exchange risks that naturally arise from international transactions. While this need makes the managerial finance function more demanding and complex, it can also lead to a more rewarding and fulfilling career.

The study of managerial finance

An understanding of the theories, concepts, techniques, and practices presented throughout this text will fully acquaint you with the financial manager's activities and decisions. As you study, you will learn about the career opportunities in managerial finance that are described in Table 1.2. Although the focus of this text is on profit-seeking firms, the principles presented are equally applicable to public and nonprofit organizations. It is important to note that the decision-making principles developed in this text can also be applied to personal financial decisions. I hope that this first exposure to the exciting field of finance will provide the foundation and initiative for further study and possibly even a future career.

TABLE 1.2

CAREER OPPORTUNITIES IN MANAGERIAL FINANCE

Position	Description
Financial analyst	Primarily responsible for preparing and analyzing the firm's financial plans and budgets. Other duties include financial forecasting, performing financial ratio analysis, and working closely with accounting.
Capital budgeting analyst/manager	Responsible for the evaluation and recommendation of proposed asset investments. May be involved in the financial aspects of implementation of approved investments.
Project finance manager	In large firms, arranges financing for approved asset investments. Coordinates consultants, investment bankers, and legal counsel.
Cash manager	Responsible for maintaining and controlling the firm's daily cash balances. Frequently manages the firm's cash collection, short-term investment, transfer, and disbursement activities and coordinates short-term borrowing and banking relationships.
Credit analyst/manager	Administers the firm's credit policy by analyzing or managing the evaluation of credit applications, extending credit, and monitoring and collecting accounts receivable.
Pension fund manager	In large companies, responsible for coordinating the assets and liabilities of the employees' pension fund. Either performs investment management activities or hires and oversees the performance of these activities by a third party.

CONCEPTS IN REVIEW

1-1 What is *finance?* Explain how this field affects the lives of everyone and every organization.

1-2 What is the *financial services* area of finance? Briefly describe each of the following areas of career opportunity:

- **a.** Banking and related institutions
- **b.** Personal financial planning
- **c.** Investments
- **d.** Real estate
- **e.** Insurance

1-3 Describe the field of *managerial finance.* Compare and contrast this field with financial services. List and discuss three career positions in managerial finance.

Basic forms of business organization

Business firms can be organized in any of a number of legal forms. Can you name two popular forms of business organization? Based on what you know about them, which appeals to you as a place you'd prefer to work? Why? See whether your answer changes after you've read the following section.

THE THREE BASIC LEGAL FORMS OF BUSINESS ORGANIZATION ARE THE *SOLE PROPRIETORSHIP,* the *partnership,* and the *corporation.* The sole proprietorship is the most common form of organization. However, the corporation is by far the dominant form with respect to receipts and net profits. Corporations are given primary emphasis in this textbook.

Sole proprietorships

sole proprietorship
A business owned by one person and operated for his or her own profit.

unlimited liability
The condition imposed by a sole proprietorship (or general partnership) allowing the owner's total wealth to be taken to satisfy creditors.

A **sole proprietorship** is a business owned by one person who operates it for his or her own profit. About 75 percent of all business firms are sole proprietorships. The typical sole proprietorship is a small firm, such as a neighborhood grocery, auto-repair shop, or shoe-repair business. Typically, the proprietor, along with a few employees, operates the proprietorship. He or she normally raises capital from personal resources or by borrowing and is responsible for all business decisions. The sole proprietor has **unlimited liability,** which means that his or her total wealth, not merely the amount originally invested, can be taken to satisfy creditors. The majority of sole proprietorships are found in the wholesale, retail, service, and construction industries. The key strengths and weaknesses of sole proprietorships are summarized in Table 1.3.

Partnerships

partnership
A business owned by two or more people and operated for profit.

articles of partnership
The written contract used to formally establish a business partnership.

limited partnership
A partnership in which one or more partners can be designated as having limited liability as long as at least *one* partner has unlimited liability.

A **partnership** consists of two or more owners doing business together for profit. Partnerships, which account for about 10 percent of all businesses, are typically larger than sole proprietorships. Finance, insurance, and real estate firms are the most common types of partnership. Public accounting and stock brokerage partnerships often have large numbers of partners.

Most partnerships are established by a written contract known as the **articles of partnership.** In a *general* (or *regular*) *partnership,* all the partners have unlimited liability. In a **limited partnership,** one or more partners can be designated as having limited liability as long as at least *one* partner has unlimited liability. A *limited partner* is normally prohibited from being active in the management of the firm. Strengths and weaknesses of partnerships are summarized in Table 1.3.

Corporations

corporation
An intangible business entity created by law (often called a "legal entity").

A **corporation** is an artificial being that is created by law. Often called a "legal entity," a corporation has the powers of an individual in that it can sue and be sued, make and be party to contracts, and acquire property in its own name. Although only about 15 percent of all businesses are incorporated, the corporation is the dominant form of business organization. It accounts for nearly 90 percent of business receipts and 80 percent of net profits. Since corporations employ millions of people and have many thousands of shareholders, their activities affect the lives of everyone. Although corporations are involved in all types of business, manufacturing corporations account for the largest portion of corporate business receipts and net profits. The key strengths and weaknesses of large corporations are summarized in Table 1.3. It is important to recognize that there are many small private corporations in addition to the large corporations emphasized throughout this text. For many small corporations there is no access to capital markets, and the requirement that the owner co-sign a loan moderates limited liability.

TABLE 1.3

STRENGTHS AND WEAKNESSES OF THE BASIC LEGAL FORMS OF BUSINESS ORGANIZATION

	Legal form		
	Sole proprietorship	Partnership	Corporation
Strengths	—Owner receives all profits (as well as losses) —Low organizational costs —Income taxed as personal income of proprietor —Secrecy —Ease of dissolution	—Can raise more funds than sole proprietorships —Borrowing power enhanced by more owners —More available brain power and managerial skill —Can retain good employees —Income taxed as personal income of partners	—Owners have *limited liability,* which guarantees that they cannot lose more than they invested —Can achieve large size due to marketability of stock (ownership) —Ownership is readily transferable —Long life of firm–not dissolved by death of owners —Can hire professional managers —Can expand more easily due to access to capital markets —Receives certain tax advantages
Weaknesses	—Owner has *unlimited liability*—total wealth can be taken to satisfy debts —Limited fund-raising power tends to inhibit growth —Proprietor must be jack-of-all-trades —Difficult to give employees long-run career opportunities —Lacks continuity when proprietor dies	—Owners have *unlimited liability* and may have to cover debts of other less financially sound partners —When a partner dies, partnership is dissolved —Difficult to liquidate or transfer partnership —Difficult to achieve large-scale operations	—Taxes generally higher, since corporate income is taxed and dividends paid to owners are again taxed —More expensive to organize than other business forms —Subject to greater government regulation —Employees often lack personal interest in firm —Lacks secrecy, since stockholders must receive financial reports

The major parties in a corporation are the stockholders, the board of directors, and the president. The top portion of Figure 1.1 depicts the relationship among these parties. The **stockholders** are the true owners of the firm by virtue of their equity in preferred and common stock.[1] They vote periodically to elect the members of the board of directors and to amend the firm's corporate charter. The **board of directors** has the ultimate authority in guiding corporate affairs and in making general policy. The directors include key corporate personnel as well as outside individuals who typically are successful businesspeople and executives of other major organizations. Outside directors for major corporations are typically paid an annual fee of $10,000 to $20,000

stockholders
The true owners of the firm by virtue of their equity in the form of preferred and common stock.

board of directors
Group elected by the firm's stockholders and having ultimate authority to guide corporate affairs and make general policy.

[1]Some corporations do not have stockholders but rather have "members" who often have rights similar to those of stockholders—they are entitled to vote and receive dividends. Examples include mutual savings banks, credit unions, mutual insurance companies, and a whole host of charitable organizations.

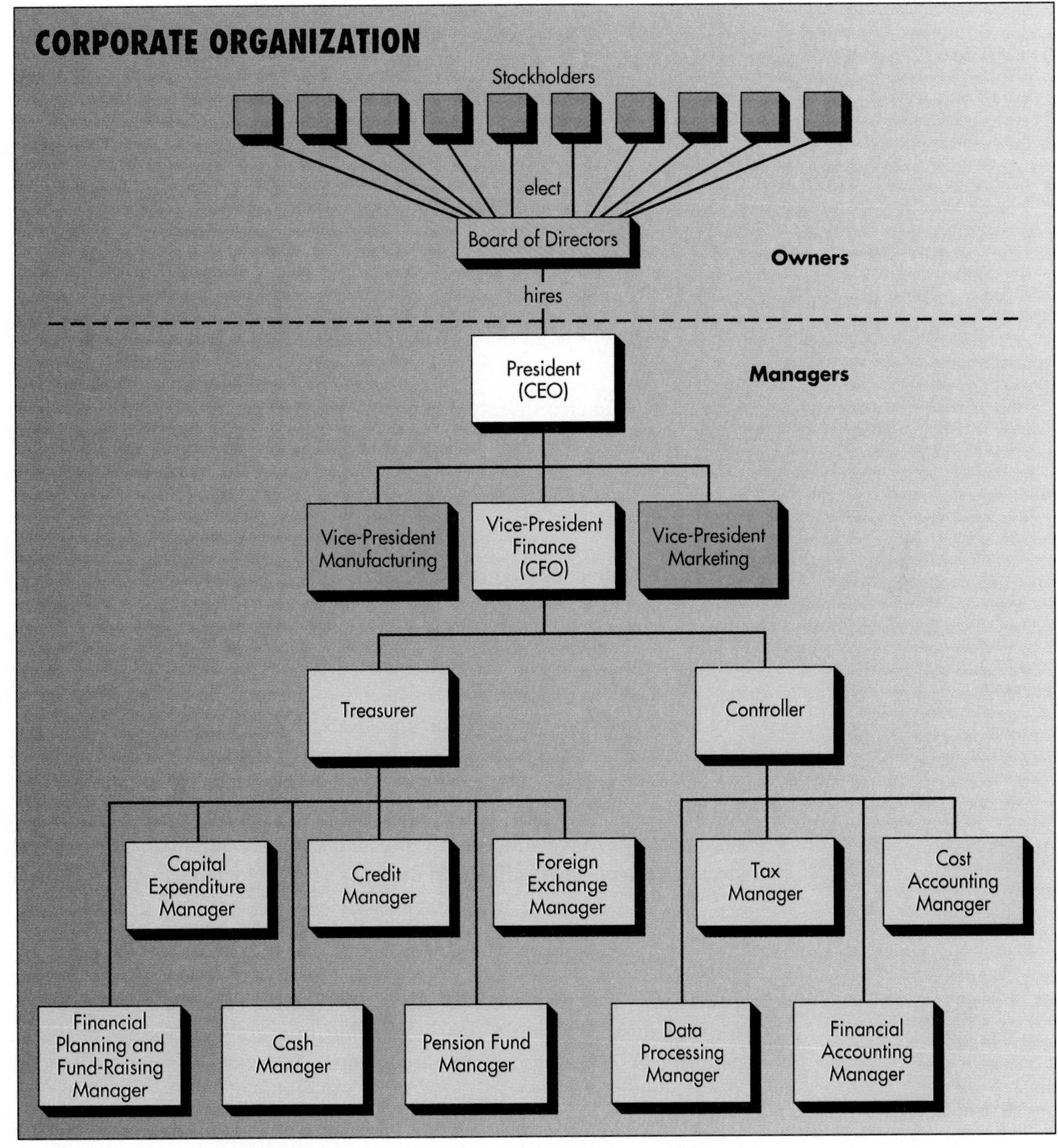

FIGURE 1.1
The general organization of a corporation and the finance function. The finance function is shown in yellow.

or more and, in addition, are frequently granted options to buy a specified number of shares of the firm's stock at a stated—and often attractive—price. The **president or chief executive officer (CEO)** is responsible for managing day-to-day operations and carrying out the policies established by the board. He or she is required to report periodically to the firm's directors. It is important to note the division between owners and managers in a large corporation, as shown by the dashed horizontal line in Figure 1.1. This separation and some of the issues surrounding it will be addressed in the discussion of the agency issue later in this chapter.

president or chief executive officer (CEO)
Corporate official responsible for managing the firm's day-to-day operations and carrying out the policies established by the board of directors.

CONCEPTS IN REVIEW

1-4 What are the three basic forms of business organization? Which form is most common? Which form is dominant in terms of business receipts and net profits? Why?

1-5 Describe the role and basic relationship between the major parties in a corporation—stockholders, board of directors, and president. What typically is the relationship between owners and managers in a large corporation?

The managerial finance function

Managerial finance is closely related to, but quite different from, economics and accounting. Before reading on, spend a few moments considering what might be the differences and similarities between managerial finance and economics and between managerial finance and accounting.

SINCE MOST BUSINESS DECISIONS ARE MEASURED IN FINANCIAL TERMS, THE FINANCIAL manager plays a key role in the operation of the firm. People in all areas of responsibility within the firm—accounting, manufacturing, marketing, human resources, research, and so forth—have to interact with finance staff to get their jobs done. Everyone has to justify personnel requirements, negotiate operating budgets, worry about financial performance appraisals, and sell proposals at least partially on financial merits to get resources from upper management. Of course, financial staff, to make useful forecasts and decisions, must be willing and able to talk to everybody else in the firm. To understand the managerial finance function, we will now look at its organizational role, its relationship to economics and accounting, the key activities of the financial manager, and the financial manager's role in total quality management (TQM).

An organizational view

The size and importance of the managerial finance function depend on the size of the firm. In small firms the finance function is generally performed by the accounting department. As a firm grows, the importance of the finance function typically results in the evolution of a separate department linked directly to the company president or chief executive officer (CEO) through a vice-president of finance, commonly called the chief financial officer (CFO). The lower portion of the organizational chart in Figure 1.1 shows the structure of the finance activity in a typical medium-to-large-size firm. Reporting to the vice-president of finance are the treasurer and the controller. The **treasurer** is commonly responsible for handling financial activities, such as financial planning and fund raising, making capital expenditure decisions, managing cash, managing credit activities, and managing the pension fund. The **controller** typically handles the accounting activities, such as tax management, data processing, and cost and financial accounting. The treasurer's focus tends to be more external, while the controller's focus is more internal. The activities of the treasurer, or financial manager, are the primary concern of this text.

treasurer
The officer responsible for the firm's financial activities, such as financial planning and fund raising, making capital expenditure decisions, managing cash, managing credit activities, and managing the pension fund.

controller
The officer responsible for the firm's accounting activities, such as tax management, data processing, and cost and financial accounting.

If international sales or purchases are important to a firm, it may well employ one or more finance professionals whose job is to monitor and manage the firm's exposure to loss from currency fluctuations. This exposure arises if, for example, a company has booked a sale to a British customer for which delivery and payment will be made, in British pounds, in three months. If the dollar value of the British pound were to decline during the next three months (the pound depreciates), the dollar value of the firm's account receivable would also decline, and the firm would experience a foreign exchange loss, since it would be able to exchange the pounds received for fewer dollars than planned three months earlier. A trained financial manager can "hedge," or protect against, this and similar risks, at reasonable cost, using a variety of financial instruments. These **foreign exchange managers** (or traders) typically report to the firm's treasurer.

foreign exchange manager
The manager responsible for monitoring and managing the firm's exposure to loss from currency fluctuations.

Relationship to economics

The field of finance is closely related to economics. Since every business firm operates within the economy, the financial manager must understand the economic framework and be alert to the consequences of varying levels of economic activity and changes in economic policy. The financial manager must also be able to use economic theories as guidelines for efficient business operation. Examples include supply-and-demand analysis, profit-maximizing strategies, and price theory. The primary economic principle used in managerial finance is **marginal analysis,** the principle that financial decisions should be made and actions taken only when the added benefits exceed the added costs. Nearly all financial decisions ultimately come down to an assessment of their marginal benefits and marginal costs. A basic knowledge of economics is therefore necessary to understand both the environment and the decision-making techniques of managerial finance.

marginal analysis
Economic principle that states that financial decisions should be made and actions taken only when the added benefits exceed the added costs.

EXAMPLE

Jamie Teng is a financial manager for Nord Department Stores—a large chain of upscale department stores operating primarily in the western United States. She is currently trying to decide whether to replace one of the firm's on-line computers with a new, more sophisticated one that would both speed processing time and handle a larger volume of transactions. The new computer would require a cash outlay of $80,000, and the old computer could be sold to net $28,000. The total benefits from the new computer (measured in today's dollars) would be $100,000, and the benefits over a similar time period from the old computer (measured in today's dollars) would be $35,000. Applying marginal analysis to this data, we get:

Benefits with new computer	$100,000	
Less: Benefits with old computer	35,000	
(1) Marginal (added) benefits		$65,000
Cost of new computer	$80,000	
Less: Proceeds from sale of old computer	28,000	
(2) Marginal (added) costs		52,000
Net benefit [(1) − (2)]		$13,000

Since the marginal (added) benefits of $65,000 exceed the marginal (added) costs of $52,000, the purchase of the new computer to replace the old one is recommended. The firm will experience a net gain of $13,000 as a result of this action. ■

Relationship to accounting

The firm's finance and accounting activities are typically within the control of the financial vice-president (CFO), as shown in the lower portion of Figure 1.1. These functions are closely related and generally overlap; indeed, managerial finance and accounting are not often easily distinguishable. In small firms the controller often carries out the finance function, and in large firms many accountants are intimately involved in various finance activities. However, there are two basic differences between finance and accounting; one relates to the emphasis on cash flows and the other to decision making.

EMPHASIS ON CASH FLOWS

accrual method
Recognizes revenue at the point of sale and recognizes expenses when incurred.

cash method
Recognizes revenues and expenses only with respect to actual inflows and outflows of cash.

The accountant's primary function is to develop and provide data for measuring the performance of the firm, assessing its financial position, and paying taxes. Using certain standardized and generally accepted principles, the accountant prepares financial statements that recognize revenue at the point of sale and expenses when incurred. This approach is commonly referred to as the **accrual method.**

The financial manager, on the other hand, places primary emphasis on *cash flows,* the intake and outgo of cash. He or she maintains the firm's solvency by analyzing and planning the cash flows necessary to satisfy its obligations and to acquire assets needed to achieve the firm's goals. The financial manager uses this **cash method** to recognize the revenues and expenses only with respect to actual inflows and outflows of cash.

A simple analogy may help to clarify the basic difference in viewpoint between the accountant and the financial manager. If we consider the human body as a business firm in which each pulsation of the heart represents a transaction, the accountant's primary concern is *recording* each of these pulsations as sales revenues, expenses, and profits. The financial manager is primarily concerned with whether the resulting flow of blood through the arteries reaches the cells and keeps the various organs of the whole body functioning. It is possible for a body to have a strong heart but cease to function due to the development of blockages or clots in its circulatory system. Similarly, a firm may be profitable but still may fail due to an insufficient flow of cash to meet its obligations as they come due.

EXAMPLE

Nassau Corporation, a small yacht dealer, in the calendar year just ended sold one yacht for $100,000; the yacht was purchased during the year at a total cost of $80,000. Although the firm paid in full for the yacht during the year, at year end it has yet to collect the $100,000 from the customer to whom the sale was made. The accounting view and the financial view of the firm's performance during the year are given by the following income and cash flow statements, respectively:

Accounting view	
Income statement Nassau Corporation for the year ended 12/31	
Sales revenue	$100,000
Less: Costs	80,000
Net profit	$ 20,000

Financial view	
Cash flow statement Nassau Corporation for the year ended 12/31	
Cash inflow	$ 0
Less: Cash outflow	80,000
Net cash flow	($80,000)

It can be seen that whereas in an accounting sense the firm is quite profitable, it is a financial failure in terms of actual cash flow. The Nassau Corporation's lack of cash flow resulted from the uncollected account receivable of $100,000. Without adequate cash inflows to meet its obligations the firm will not survive, regardless of its level of profits. ■

The preceding example shows that accrual accounting data do not fully describe the circumstances of a firm. Thus the financial manager must look beyond financial statements to obtain insight into developing or existing problems. The financial manager, by concentrating on cash flow, should be able to avoid insolvency and achieve the firm's financial goals. Of course, while accountants are well aware of the importance of cash flows and financial managers use and understand accrual-based financial statements, the primary emphasis of accountants is on accrual methods, and the primary emphasis of financial managers is on cash methods.

CONCEPT IN PRACTICE

Assessing Cash Flow to Set the Purchase Price of Hauser Communications

Gustave Hauser formed Hauser Communications, a Washington-area cable system, in 1983. In 1992, Southwestern Bell approached Hauser to assess his interest in selling the firm. After initially resisting, Hauser accepted an offer of $650 million in 1993. The offer equated to $2,800 per subscriber, which was 40 percent above the industry average. Absence of a negative reaction in the price of Southwestern Bell's share price suggests that the premium was justified. In this case the cable systems are clustered in high-income areas, which yielded $45 per subscriber monthly compared to $32 on the average. Standard & Poor's reaffirmed the price, saying that anticipated strong cash flows would support interest expense, even if the purchase was funded with debt.

DECISION MAKING

We come now to the second major difference between finance and accounting: decision making. Whereas the accountant devotes the majority of his or her attention to the collection and presentation of financial data, the financial manager evaluates the accountant's statements, develops additional data, and makes decisions based on his or her assessment of the associated returns and risks. The accountant's role is to provide consistently developed and easily interpreted data about the firm's past, present, and future operations. The financial manager uses these data, either in raw form or after certain adjustments and analyses, as an important input to the decision-making process. Of course, this does not mean that accountants never make decisions or that financial managers never gather data; but the primary focuses of accounting and finance are distinctly different.

Key activities of the financial manager

The financial manager's activities can be related to the firm's basic financial statements. His or her primary activities are (1) performing financial analysis and planning, (2) making investment decisions, and (3) making financing decisions. Figure 1.2 relates each of these financial activities to the firm's balance sheet. It is important to note that although investment and financing decisions can be conveniently viewed in terms of the balance sheet, these decisions are made on the basis of their

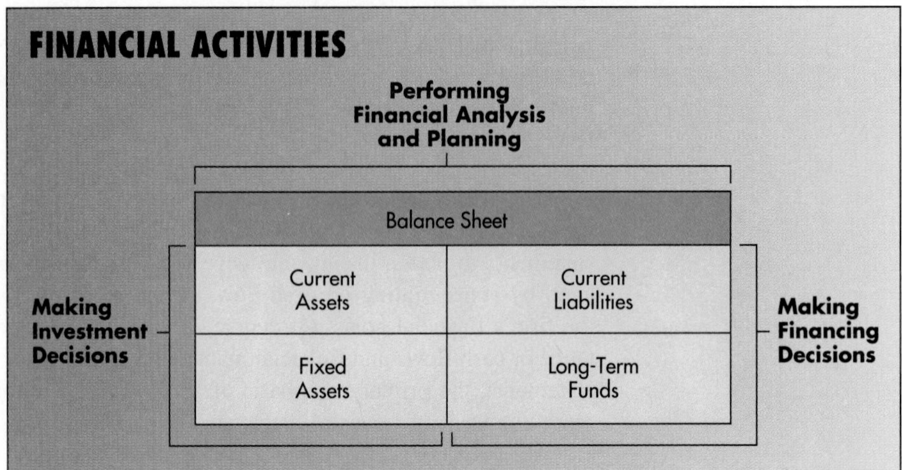

FIGURE 1.2
Key activities of the financial manager

cash flow effects. This emphasis on cash flow will become clearer in Chapter 3 as well as in later chapters.

PERFORMING FINANCIAL ANALYSIS AND PLANNING

Financial analysis and planning is concerned with (1) transforming financial data into a form that can be used to monitor the firm's financial condition, (2) evaluating the need for increased (or reduced) productive capacity, and (3) determining what additional (or reduced) financing is required. These functions encompass the entire balance sheet as well as the firm's income statement and other financial statements. Although this activity relies heavily on accrual-based financial statements, its underlying objective is to assess the firm's cash flows and to develop plans that ensure that adequate cash flow will be available to support achievement of its goals.

MAKING INVESTMENT DECISIONS

The financial manager's investment decisions determine both the mix and the type of assets found on the firm's balance sheet. This activity is concerned with the left-hand side of the balance sheet. *Mix* refers to the number of dollars of current and fixed assets. Once the mix is established, the financial manager must establish and attempt to maintain certain optimal levels of each type of current asset. He or she must also decide which are the best fixed assets to acquire and know when existing fixed assets need to be modified, replaced, or liquidated. These decisions are important in that they affect the firm's success in achieving its goals.

MAKING FINANCING DECISIONS

This activity deals with the right-hand side of the firm's balance sheet and involves two major areas. First, the most appropriate *mix* of short-term and long-term financing must be established. A second and equally important concern is which individual short-term or long-term sources of financing are best at a given point in time. Many of these decisions are dictated by necessity, but some require an in-depth analysis of the available financing alternatives, their costs, and their long-run implications. Again, it is the effect of these decisions on the firms' goal achievement that is of paramount importance.

The financial manager's role in total quality management (TQM)

total quality management (TQM)
The application of quality principles to all aspects of a company's operations.

Total quality management (TQM), the application of quality principles to all aspects of a company's operations, is an important concept for today's financial manager to understand. Quality control was once considered primarily a production responsibility. By contrast, TQM is now a companywide goal affecting *all* departments. TQM principles include continual efforts to improve operations by streamlining processes to achieve greater efficiency and satisfaction of the needs of all customers—both internal and external. (Departments are *internal customers* of each other. For example, the finance department, a user of accounting data, is a customer of the accounting department; the facilities planning group is a customer for the capital budgeting group's project analyses.)

BENEFITS AND COSTS OF TQM

A commitment to TQM directly relates to profitability. In the past, managers considered quality and productivity to be mutually exclusive; one increased only at the expense of the other. More recent experience shows that as quality increases, so does productivity. And improved quality also lowers costs by reducing the time, materials, and service required to correct errors. This obviously should have a positive effect on operating profits. If, by applying TQM, the time to design, develop, and market a new product is shortened, the company will receive sales revenues from this product sooner. The finance department can contribute to the firm's overall quality effort by streamlining its operations so that budgets are available on a timely basis, the level of analysis is appropriate for the size and type of project, and decisions are made more quickly.

The cost of quality includes not only the cost to implement TQM programs that get the job done correctly the first time, but also the cost to correct bad quality when work is *not* performed correctly the first time. The cost of bad quality can be considerable: reprocessing orders, excess demands for service, customer complaints, lost business, and so on.

TQM IN ACTION

Two notable examples of TQM in action at U.S. companies are at Ford Motor Company and Du Pont. Ford, whose motto is "Quality is Job #1," achieved significant cost reductions in labor, overhead, and materials required to produce its cars. It needs one-third fewer labor hours to build its cars than rival General Motors, a savings of about \$800 per car. Du Pont enjoyed an 80 percent market share for its Kalrez plastic until Japanese competition with better customer service began making inroads. The company quickly responded by shortening the production cycle by more than 75 percent, reducing the time to fill orders by more than 50 percent, and increasing on-time deliveries from 70 percent to 100 percent. As a result, sales increased 22 percent.

CONCEPTS IN REVIEW

1-6 How does the finance function evolve within the business firm? What financial activities does the treasurer, or financial manager, perform in the mature firm?

1-7 Describe the close relationship between finance and economics, and explain why the financial manager should possess a basic knowledge of economics. What is the primary economic principle used in managerial finance?

1-8 What are the major differences between accounting and finance with respect to:

a. Emphasis on cash flows?

b. Decision making?

1-9 What are the three key activities of the financial manager? Relate them to the firm's balance sheet.

1-10 What is *total quality management (TQM)?* Discuss the benefits (and costs) of TQM.

Goal of the financial manager

Financial management is a goal-oriented activity. What overriding goal do you think a professional financial manager, typically with a very small ownership interest in the firm, is responsible for pursuing? Why? Before reading on, spend a few moments answering these questions.

As was noted in Figure 1.1, the owners of a corporation are normally distinct from its managers. Actions of the financial manager related to financial analysis and planning, investment decisions, and financing decisions should be taken to achieve the objectives of the firm's owners, its stockholders. In most cases, if the managers are successful in this endeavor, they will also achieve their own financial and professional objectives. In the sections that follow, we first evaluate profit maximization, then describe wealth maximization, consider the preservation of stakeholder wealth, discuss the *agency issue* related to potential conflicts between the goals of stockholders and the actions of management, and finally consider the role of ethics.

Maximize profit?

earnings per share (EPS)
The amount earned during the period on each outstanding share of common stock, calculated by dividing the period's total earnings available for the firm's common stockholders by the number of shares of common stock outstanding.

Some people believe that the owner's objective is always to maximize profits. To achieve the goal of profit maximization, the financial manager takes only those actions that are expected to make a major contribution to the firm's overall profits. Thus for each alternative being considered, the financial manager would choose the one that is expected to result in the highest monetary return. For corporations, profits are commonly measured in terms of **earnings per share (EPS),** which represent the amount earned during the period—typically a quarter (three months) or a year—on each outstanding share of common stock. EPS are calculated by dividing the period's total earnings available for the firm's common stockholders—the firm's owners—by the number of shares of common stock outstanding.

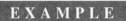

Nick Dukakis, the financial manager of Toros Manufacturing, a major producer of marine engine components, is attempting to choose between two major investments, X and Y. Each is expected to have the following earnings per share effects over its three-year life.

Investment	Earnings per share (EPS) Year 1	Year 2	Year 3	Total for years 1, 2, and 3
X	$1.40	$1.00	$ .40	$2.80
Y	.60	1.00	1.40	3.00

On the basis of the profit-maximization goal, investment Y would be preferred over investment X, since it results in higher earnings per share over the three-year period ($3.00 EPS for Y is greater than $2.80 EPS for X). ■

Profit maximization fails for a number of reasons: It ignores (1) the timing of returns, (2) cash flows available to stockholders, and (3) risk.

TIMING

Because the firm can earn a return on funds it receives, *the receipt of funds sooner rather than later is preferred.* In our example, in spite of the fact that the total earnings from investment X are smaller than those from Y, investment X may be preferred due to the greater EPS it provides in the first year. These earlier returns could be reinvested to provide greater future earnings.

CASH FLOWS

A firm's earnings do *not* represent cash flows available to the stockholders. Owners receive returns either through cash dividends paid them or by selling their shares for a higher price than initially paid. A greater EPS does not necessarily mean that dividend payments will increase, since the payment of dividends results solely from the action of the firm's board of directors. Furthermore, a higher EPS does not necessarily translate into a higher stock price. Firms sometimes experience earnings increases without any correspondingly favorable change in stock price. Only when earnings increases are accompanied by increased current and/or expected cash flows would a higher stock price be expected.

RISK

risk
The chance that actual outcomes may differ from those expected.

risk-averse
Seeking to avoid risk.

Profit maximization disregards not only cash flow but also **risk**—the chance that actual outcomes may differ from those expected. A basic premise in managerial finance is that a tradeoff exists between return (cash flow) and risk. *Return and risk are in fact the key determinants of share price, which represents the wealth of the owners in the firm.* Cash flow and risk affect share price differently: higher cash flow is generally associated with a higher share price, whereas higher risk tends to result in a lower share price since the stockholder must be compensated for the greater risk. In general, stockholders are **risk-averse**—that is, they want to avoid risk. Where risk is involved, stockholders expect to earn higher rates of return on investments of higher risk and lower rates on lower-risk investments.

EXAMPLE

Western Distillers, a manufacturer of bourbon and blended whiskeys, is interested in expanding into one of two new product lines—gin or vodka. Because competition and availability of vodka is significantly affected by political events, it is viewed as a higher-risk line of business than is gin. Today's cost of entering either of these markets is $45 million. The expected annual cash inflows from each product line is expected to average $9 million per year over the next ten years, as shown in column 2 of the following table.

Product line	Risk (1)	Average annual cash inflows (2)	Required rate of return (3)	Present value of cash inflows[a] (4)
Gin	Lower	$9 million	12%	$50.9 million
Vodka	Higher	9 million	15	45.2 million

[a]These values were found by using present-value techniques, which will be fully explained and demonstrated in Chapter 5.

To be compensated for taking risk, the firm must earn a higher rate of return on the higher-risk vodka than on the lower-risk gin line. The firm's required rate of return for each line is shown in column 3 of the preceding table. Applying present-value techniques—quantitative financial techniques that are presented in Chapter 5—we can find the present value (today's value) of the average annual cash inflows over the ten years for each product line as shown in column 4 of the table.

Three important observations can be made:

1. Because the firm's stockholders are *risk-averse,* they must earn a higher rate of return on the higher-risk vodka line than on the lower-risk gin line.
2. Although the vodka line and the gin line have the same expected annual cash inflows, the vodka line's *greater risk causes its cash flows to be worth less* today than the gin line's cash flows ($45.2 million for vodka versus $50.9 million for gin).
3. While both product lines appear attractive, since their benefits (present value of cash inflows) exceed the $45 million cost, the gin alternative would be preferred ($50.9 million for gin and only $45.2 million for vodka).

It should be clear from this example that differences in risk can significantly affect the value of an investment and therefore the wealth of an owner. ■

Maximizing shareholder wealth

The goal of the firm, and therefore of all managers and employees, is to maximize the wealth of the owners for whom it is being operated. The wealth of corporate owners is measured by the share price of the stock, which in turn is based on the timing of returns (cash flows), their magnitude, and their risk. When considering each financial decision alternative or possible action in terms of its impact on the share price of the firm's stock, *financial managers should accept only those actions that are expected to increase share price.* (Figure 1.3 depicts this process.) Since share price represents the owners' wealth in the firm, share-price maximization is consistent with owner-wealth maximization. Note that *return (cash flows) and risk are the key decision variables in the wealth maximization process.* It is also important to recognize that earnings per share (EPS), because they are an important component of the firm's return (cash flows), affect share price.

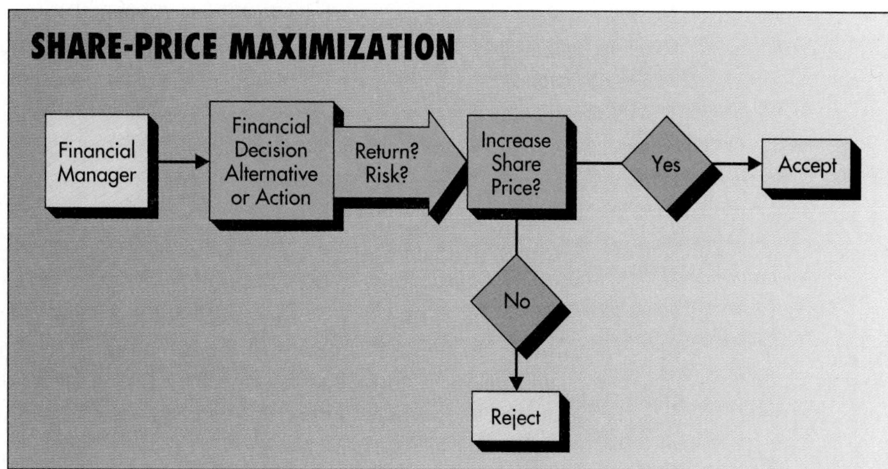

FIGURE 1.3
Financial decisions and share price

Preserving stakeholder wealth

stakeholder
Groups such as employees, customers, suppliers, creditors, and others who have a direct economic link to the firm.

While shareholder wealth maximization is the primary goal, in recent years many firms have broadened their focus to include the interests of *stakeholders* as well as shareholders. **Stakeholders** are groups such as employees, customers, suppliers, creditors, and others who have a direct economic link to the firm. Employees are paid for their labor, customers purchase the firm's products and/or services, suppliers are paid for the materials and services they provide, and creditors provide financing that is to be repaid subject to specified terms. A firm with a stakeholder focus consciously avoids actions that would prove detrimental to stakeholders by damaging their wealth positions through the transfer of stakeholder wealth to the firm. The goal is not to maximize stakeholder well-being but to preserve it.

The stakeholder view, while not altering the shareholder wealth maximization goal, tends to limit the firm's actions to preserve the wealth of stakeholders. Such a view is often considered part of the firm's "social responsibility" and is expected to provide maximum long-run benefit to shareholders by maintaining positive stakeholder relationships. Such relationships should minimize stakeholder turnover, conflicts, and litigation. Clearly, the firm can better achieve its goal of shareholder wealth maximization with the cooperation of—rather than conflict with—its stakeholders.

CONCEPT IN PRACTICE

Pepsico, Greyston, and IBM: The Best Public-Service Corporations

The editors of *Business Week* asked its writers to nominate 1992's most remarkable public-service projects. The three projects selected as the best were sponsored by Pepsico, Greyston Corporation, and IBM. Pepsico distributed water and ice to Hurricane Andrew victims in Florida. Its Pizza Hut unit served hot pizza to victims without kitchens. Greyston, a New York City corporation, hires only the "chronically unemployed," trains them, and pays $7.75 per hour. IBM has made a commitment to provide $35 million in training to inner-city residents. Several sessions will be tailored for learning-disabled people. These projects have the potential to provide a long-run return in addition to the goodwill they generated in 1992. Pizza

Hut may have expanded its customer base, Greyston's employees are more able to make delicious foods, and computer-training graduates will be better able to use IBM systems.

The agency issue

The control of the modern corporation is frequently placed in the hands of professional nonowner managers. (This separation of owners and managers is shown by the dashed horizontal line in Figure 1.1.) We have seen that the goal of the financial manager should be to maximize the wealth of the owners of the firm; thus management can be viewed as *agents* of the owners who have hired them and given them decision-making authority to manage the firm for the owners' benefit. Technically, any manager who owns less than 100 percent of the firm is to some degree an agent of the other owners.

In theory, most financial managers would agree with the goal of owner wealth maximization. In practice, however, managers are also concerned with their personal wealth, job security, lifestyle, and perquisites (benefits such as country club memberships, chauffeured limousines, and impressive offices, all provided at company expense). Such concerns may make managers reluctant or unwilling to take more than moderate risk if they perceive that too much risk might result in a loss of job and damage to personal wealth. The result of such a "satisficing" approach (a compromise between satisfaction and maximization) is a less-than-maximum return and a potential loss of wealth for the owners.

RESOLVING THE AGENCY PROBLEM

agency problem
The likelihood that managers may place personal goals ahead of corporate goals.

From this conflict of owner and personal goals arises what has been called the **agency problem**—the likelihood that managers may place personal goals ahead of corporate goals.[2] Two factors—market forces and *agency costs*—act to prevent or minimize agency problems.

MARKET FORCES During recent years, security market participants, particularly large institutional investors such as mutual funds, life insurance companies, and pension funds, that hold large blocks of a firm's stock, have become more active in management. To ensure management competence and minimize potential agency problems, these shareholders have actively used their votes to oust underperforming management and replace it with more competent management. Note that the formal mechanism through which these shareholders act is by voting their shares in the election of directors, who are empowered to hire and fire operating management. In addition to their legal voting rights, large shareholders are able to communicate with and exert pressure on management to perform or be fired.

hostile takeover
The acquisition of the firm (the *target*) by another firm or group (the *acquirer*) that is *not* supported by management.

Another market force that has in recent years threatened management to perform in the best interest of shareholders is the possibility of a *hostile takeover.* A **hostile takeover** is the acquisition of the firm (the *target*) by another firm or group (the *ac-*

[2]The agency problem and related issues were first addressed by Michael C. Jensen and William H. Meckling, "Theory of the Firm: Managerial Behavior, Agency Costs and Ownership Structure," *Journal of Financial Economics* 3 (October 1976), pp. 305–360. For a comprehensive review of Jensen and Meckling and subsequent research on the agency problem, see Amir Barnea, R. Haugen, and L. Senbet, *Agency Problems and Financial Contracting* (Englewood Cliffs, N.J.: Prentice-Hall, 1985).

quirer) that is *not* supported by management.[3] Hostile takeovers typically occur when the acquirer feels that the target firm is being poorly managed and, as a result, is undervalued in the marketplace. The acquirer believes that by acquiring the target at its current low price and restructuring its management (by firing and replacing them), operations, and financing, it can enhance the firm's value, that is, its share price. Although techniques are available for defending against a hostile takeover, the constant threat of a takeover should motivate management to act in the best interest of the firm's owners.

agency costs
Costs borne by stockholders to prevent or minimize agency problems and to contribute to the maximization of the owners' wealth. They include monitoring and bonding expenditures, opportunity costs, and structuring expenditures.

fidelity bond
A contract under which a bonding company agrees to reimburse a firm for up to a stated amount if a specified manager's dishonest act results in a financial loss to the firm.

incentive plans
Management compensation plans that tend to tie management compensation to share price; most popular incentive plan involves the grant of *stock options.*

stock options
An incentive allowing management to purchase stock at the market price set at the time of the grant.

AGENCY COSTS To respond to potential market forces by preventing or minimizing agency problems and contributing to the maximization of owners' wealth, stockholders incur **agency costs,** of which there are four types.

1. *Monitoring expenditures* prevent satisficing (rather than share-price-maximizing) behavior by management. These outlays pay for audits and control procedures that are used to assess and limit managerial behavior to those actions that tend to be in the best interests of the owners.
2. *Bonding expenditures* protect against the potential consequences of dishonest acts by managers. Typically, the owners pay a third-party bonding company to obtain a **fidelity bond.** This bond is a contract under which the bonding company agrees to reimburse the firm for up to a stated amount if a bonded manager's dishonest act results in financial loss to the firm.
3. *Opportunity costs* result from the difficulties that large organizations typically have in responding to new opportunities. The firm's necessary organizational structure, decision hierarchy, and control mechanisms may cause profitable opportunities to be forgone because of management's inability to seize upon them quickly.
4. *Structuring expenditures* are the most popular, powerful, and expensive agency costs incurred by firms. They result from structuring managerial compensation to correspond with share price maximization. The objective is to give management incentives to act in the best interests of the owners and to compensate managers for such actions. In addition, the resulting compensation packages allow firms to compete for and hire the best managers available. Compensation plans can be divided into two groups—incentive plans and performance plans. **Incentive plans** tend to tie management compensation to share price. The most popular incentive plan is the granting of **stock options** to management. These options allow managers to purchase stock at the market price set at the time of the grant; if the market price rises, they will be rewarded by being able to capture the appreciation of the shares. Therefore a higher future stock price would result in greater management compensation. While in theory these options should motivate, they are often criticized and have declined in popularity during recent years due to the fact that management cannot control general stock market behavior, which can significantly affect share price in spite of positive sales and earnings growth. Even positive management performance can be masked in a generally poor stock market in which share prices in general have declined due to economic and behavioral "market forces" outside of management's control.

[3]Detailed discussion of the important aspects of corporate takeovers—both friendly and hostile—are included in Chapter 19, "Mergers, LBOs, Divestitures, and Failure."

performance plans
Management compensation plans that compensate management on the basis of proven performance measured by EPS, growth in EPS, and other ratios of return. *Performance shares* and/or *cash bonuses* are used as compensation under these plans.

performance shares
Shares of stock given to management for meeting stated performance goals.

cash bonuses
Bonus money paid to management for achieving certain performance goals.

The use of **performance plans** has grown in popularity in recent years due to management's inability to control market forces. These plans compensate management on the basis of its proven performance measured by earnings per share (EPS), growth in EPS, and other ratios of return. **Performance shares**, shares of stock given to management as a result of meeting the stated performance goals, are often used in these plans. Another form of performance-based compensation is **cash bonuses**, cash payments tied to the achievement of certain performance goals. Under performance plans, management understands in advance the formula used to determine the amount of performance shares or cash bonus it can earn during the period. In addition, the minimum benefit (typically $0) and maximum benefit available under the plan are specified.

CONCEPT IN PRACTICE

On Line with Liberty Media

Liberty Media Corporation went on a buying binge in December 1992. The provider of programs to cable networks obtained control of Home Shopping Network and its rival, the QVC Network. Next, Liberty Media combined with Sports Channel to create a network of sports channels serving 41 million households. Wall Street's positive reaction pushed share prices up twelvefold. Among the benefactors was Liberty Media's chairman, John Malone, who received over 10 million shares in Liberty Media stock in lieu of salary. Conservative estimates of Chairman Malone's two-year return exceed $150 million. However, investors have offered few complaints. For instance, William Nygren, research director of a firm with a large stake in Liberty Media, stated, "I sure don't mind being in partnership with the smartest man in cable television, especially if he has his own money on the line."

THE CURRENT VIEW

While academic research[4] as well as intuition support the belief that an effective way to motivate management is to tie compensation to performance, the execution of many compensation plans has been closely scrutinized in recent years. Stockholders—both individuals and institutions—as well as the Securities and Exchange Commission (SEC) have publicly questioned the appropriateness of the multimillion-dollar compensation packages (including salary, bonus, and long-term compensation) that many corporate executives receive. For example, the three highest-paid CEOs in 1992, were (1) Thomas F. Frist, Jr. of Hospital Corp. of America, who earned $127,002,000; (2) Sanford I. Weill of Primerica, who earned $67,635,000; and (3) Charles Lazarus of Toys 'R' Us, who earned $64,231,000. Tenth on the same list was Louis F. Bantle of UST Inc., who earned $24,602,000. During 1992, the compensation of the average CEO of a major U.S. corporation increased about 42 percent over 1991. CEOs of 365 large and medium-sized U.S. industrial companies surveyed by *Business Week* using data from Standard & Poor's Compustat Services Inc., earned an average of $3.8 million in total compen-

[4]See Wilbur G. Lewellen, "Management and Ownership in the Large Firm," *Journal of Finance* 24 (May 1969), pp. 299–322; and Robert T. Masson, "Executive Motivation, Earnings, and Consequent Equity Performance," *Journal of Political Economy* 79 (November–December 1971), pp. 1278–1292. Lewellen concluded that managers appear to make decisions that are largely consistent with share price maximization. Masson found that firms whose executives' compensation was closely tied to the performance of the firm's stock tended to outperform other firms in terms of stock returns.

sation; the average for the 20 largest companies was $33.7 million. While these sizable compensation packages may be justified by significant increases in shareholder wealth, recent studies have failed to find a high correlation between CEO compensation and share price. The publicity surrounding these large compensation packages (without corresponding share price performance) is expected to continue to drive down executive compensation in the future. At the same time, new compensation plans that better link management performance with regard to shareholder wealth to its compensation are expected to be developed and implemented.

Of course, in addition to incurring structuring costs to link management compensation to performance, many firms incur additional agency costs for monitoring, bonding, and streamlining organizational decision making to further ensure congruence of management and owner objectives. Unconstrained, managers may have other goals in addition to share price maximization, but much of the evidence suggests that share price maximization—the focus of this book—is the primary goal of most firms.

The role of ethics

In recent years the legitimacy of actions taken by government officials, businesses, individuals, and even religious leaders have received major media attention. Examples include Senator Robert Packwood's sexual harassment of employees and lobbyists; Big Six public accounting firm Ernst & Young's agreement to pay $400 million to settle federal charges that it inadequately audited four large thrifts that failed at a cost to the government of $6.6 billion; Salomon Brothers' attempts to rig U.S. Treasury bill auctions through the use of fake bids; Volvo's misleading automobile advertisements; Michael Milken's conviction for racketeering, insider trading, and fraud; Charles Keating, Jr.'s self-dealing with depositor funds, resulting in the failure of Lincoln Savings and Loan of California; and televangelist Jim Bakker's personal and financial indiscretions. Clearly, these and other similar actions have raised the question of **ethics**—standards of conduct or moral judgment. Today, society in general and the financial community in particular—primarily because of the notable financial offenders such as Milken and Keating—are developing and enforcing ethical standards. The goal of these standards is to motivate business and market participants to adhere to both the letter and the spirit of laws and regulations concerned with all aspects of business and professional practice.

ethics
Standards of conduct or moral judgment.

OPINIONS

An opinion survey of business leaders, business school deans, and members of Congress showed that 94 percent of the over 1,000 respondents felt that the business community is troubled by ethical problems.[5] In addition, only 32 percent of the respondents felt that this issue had been overblown by the media and political leaders. Most striking was the survey's finding that 63 percent of respondents felt that a business enterprise actually strengthens its competitive position by maintaining high ethical standards. Respondents to the survey believed that the best way to encourage ethical business behavior is for firms to adopt a business code of ethics. They felt that the least effective way is legislation.

[5] *Ethics in American Business* (New York: Touche Ross, 1987).

CONSIDERING ETHICS

Robert A. Cooke, a noted ethicist, suggests that the following questions be used to assess the ethical viability of a proposed action:[6]

1. Is the action . . . arbitrary or capricious? Does it unfairly single out an individual or group?
2. Does the action . . . violate the moral or legal rights of any individual or group?
3. Does the action . . . conform to accepted moral standards?
4. Are there alternative courses of action that are less likely to cause actual or potential harm?

Clearly, considering such questions before taking an action can help to ensure its ethical viability.

Today, more and more firms are directly addressing the issue of ethics by establishing corporate ethics policies and guidelines and by requiring employee compliance with them. Frequently, employees are required to sign a formal pledge to uphold the firm's ethics policies. Such policies typically apply to employee actions in dealing with all corporate constituents—other employees, customers, suppliers, creditors, owners, regulators, and the public at large. Many companies require employees to participate in ethics seminars and training programs that convey and demonstrate corporate ethics policy. Role playing and case exercises are sometimes used to give employees hands-on experience in effectively dealing with potential ethical dilemmas.

CONCEPT IN PRACTICE

Ethics versus Profits: Decision Time at Salomon Brothers

In 1992, Salomon Brothers violated the Federal government's law limiting the number of Treasury securities that may be obtained by a single securities firm. John Meriwether, Salomon's director of bond trading, further violated the law by not reporting the mistake to the government. As punishment the Securities and Exchange Commission fined Meriwether and suspended his trading license for three months. Although Salomon had promised to clean house, its options were to rehire the felon or lose Meriwether to its competition. During 1991 alone, Meriwether's division earned $400 million. Salomon was expected to follow the Salomon credo that "if it makes money, do it" and rehire Meriwether after his suspension was lifted.

ETHICS AND SHARE PRICE

The implementation of a pro-active ethics program is expected to enhance corporate value. An ethics program can produce a number of positive benefits: reduce potential litigation and judgment costs, maintain a positive corporate image, build shareholder confidence, and gain the loyalty, commitment, and respect of all of the firm's constituents. Such actions, by maintaining and enhancing cash flow and reducing perceived risk (as a result of greater investor confidence), are expected to positively affect the firm's share price. *Ethical behavior is therefore viewed as necessary for achievement of the firm's goal of owner wealth maximization.*

[6]"Business Ethics: A Perspective," in *Arthur Andersen Cases on Business Ethics* (Chicago, IL: Arthur Andersen & Co., September 1988), p. 2.

CONCEPTS IN REVIEW

1-11 Briefly describe three basic reasons why profit maximization fails to be consistent with wealth maximization.

1-12 What is *risk?* Why must risk as well as return be considered by the financial manager when evaluating a decision alternative or action?

1-13 What is the goal of the firm and therefore of all managers and employees? Discuss how one measures achievement of this goal.

1-14 Who are a firm's *stakeholders,* and what consideration is often given them in pursuing the firm's goal? Why?

1-15 What is the *agency problem?* How do market forces, both shareholder activism and the threat of hostile takeover, act to prevent or minimize this problem?

1-16 Define *agency costs,* and explain why firms incur them. What are *structuring expenditures,* and how are they used? Describe and differentiate between *incentive* and *performance* compensation plans. What is the current view with regard to the execution of many compensation plans?

1-17 Why has corporate ethics become so important in recent years? Describe the role of corporate ethics policies and guidelines, and discuss the relationship that is believed to exist between ethics and share price.

An overview of the text

THE TEXT'S ORGANIZATION LINKS THE FIRM'S ACTIVITIES TO ITS VALUE, AS DETERMINED in the securities markets. Each major decision area is presented in terms of both return and risk factors and their potential impact on the owner's wealth, as reflected by share value. Coverage of international events and topics is integrated into the chapter discussions.

Keyed to various parts of the text is the *PMF Disk*, a menu-driven computer disk for use with IBM PCs and compatible microcomputers. The disk contains three different sets of routines: the *PMF Tutor,* the *PMF Problem-Solver,* and the *PMF Lotus Templates*. The *PMF Tutor* is a user-friendly program that extends self-testing opportunities in the more quantitative chapters beyond those included in the end-of-chapter materials. It gives immediate feedback with detailed solutions, provides tutorial assistance, and for convenience includes text page references. Text discussions and end-of-chapter problems with which the *PMF Tutor* can be used are marked with a . The *PMF Problem-Solver* can be used as an aid in performing many of the routine financial calculations and procedures presented in the book. For convenience a disk symbol, , is used to identify those text discussions and end-of-chapter problems that can be solved with the *PMF Problem-Solver.* The *PMF Lotus Templates* can be used with Lotus 1-2-3 to input data and solve more complex end-of-chapter problems for selected chapters. These problems are clearly demarked by the spreadsheet symbol, , to enable the student to use this powerful tool to carry out "what if" types of analyses. A detailed discussion of how to use the *PMF Disk*—the *Tutor,* the *Problem-Solver,* and the *Lotus Templates*—is included in Appendix B.

A brief description of each of the text's seven parts is given below. At the end of each chapter is a case that integrates the chapter materials, and at the end of each part is an integrative case that ties together the key topical material covered in the chapters within that part. Both the chapter-end and part-end cases can be used to synthesize and apply related concepts and techniques.

Part I: The goal and environment of managerial finance

Part I sets the stage for subsequent discussion of the managerial finance function. Chapter 1 has discussed finance as an area of study, reviewed the basic forms of business organization, described the managerial finance function, and presented the goal of the financial manager. Chapter 2 describes the operating environment of the firm. Chapter 3 briefly reviews the basic financial statements and discusses the important aspects of depreciation and cash flow. Chapter 4 is concerned with financial statement analysis.

Part II: Basic financial concepts

Part II presents the basic financial concepts underlying the principles and practices of going concerns. The time value of money, the concepts of risk and return, and the valuation process are discussed in Chapters 5, 6, and 7.

Part III: Long-term investment decisions

Part III is concerned with long-term investment decisions (capital budgeting). The primary focus of Chapter 8 is on capital budgeting and cash flow principles. Chapter 9 discusses capital budgeting decision making under both certainty and risk as well some refinements in the capital budgeting process. A knowledge of each of these areas is necessary for a thorough understanding of the management and selection of fixed-asset investments.

Part IV: Cost of capital, leverage, and capital structure

Part IV is devoted to three important topics—the cost of capital, leverage, and capital structure. These closely related topics are directly linked to the firm's value. The cost of capital, discussed in Chapter 10, is an important input in the capital budgeting process. Leverage and capital structure, presented in Chapter 11, affect the firm's cost of capital as well as its share value. These topics show how various suppliers of funds view the firm and enable the financial manager to recognize some important variables that must be considered in obtaining long-term funds.

Part V: Long-term financing decisions

Part V describes the major long-term financing decisions. Chapters 12 through 14 discuss the cost, availability, inherent characteristics, and pros and cons of each of the following: long-term debt and investment banking; common stock and dividend policy; and preferred stock, leasing, convertibles, warrants, and options.

Part VI: Short-term financial decisions

Part VI, Chapters 15 through 18, is devoted to short-term financial (working-capital) management. The first chapter is concerned primarily with short-term financial planning. The focus of the following three chapters is on management of the firm's key current accounts—current assets (cash, marketable securities, accounts receivable, and inventory) and current liabilities (both unsecured and secured sources of short-term financing). The relationship between current assets and current liabilities is discussed along with strategies for their efficient management.

Part VII: Special managerial finance topics

Part VII, Chapters 19 and 20, discusses three other important managerial finance topics: corporate restructuring through mergers, LBOs, and divestitures; the alternatives available to the failed business firm; and the international dimensions of financial decision making.

Summary

LG 1 Define *finance* and describe its major areas—financial services and managerial finance—and the career opportunities within them. Finance, the art and science of managing money, affects the lives of every person and every organization. Major opportunities in financial services are included within the areas of banking and related institutions, personal financial planning, investments, real estate, and insurance. Managerial finance, which is concerned with the duties of the financial manager in the business firm, offers numerous career opportunities such as financial analyst, capital budgeting analyst/manager, project finance manager, cash manager, credit analyst/manager, and pension fund manager. In addition, the recent trend toward globalization of business activity has created new demands and opportunities in managerial finance.

LG 2 Review the basic forms of business organization and their respective strengths and weaknesses. The basic forms of business organization are the sole proprietorship, the partnership, and the corporation. Although there are more sole proprietorships than any other form of business organization, the corporation is dominant in terms of business receipts and profits. Limited liability and the resulting ability to market its ownership are major strengths of the corporation that differentiate it from sole proprietorships and partnerships. The key strengths and weaknesses of each form of business organization are summarized in Table 1.3.

LG 3 Describe the managerial finance function and differentiate managerial finance from the closely related disciplines of economics and accounting. In large firms the managerial finance function might be handled by a separate department headed by the vice-president of finance (CFO), to whom both the treasurer and controller report; in small firms the finance function is generally performed by the accounting department. Managerial finance is closely related to the disciplines of economics and accounting. The financial manager must understand the economic environment and relies heavily on the economic principle of marginal analysis when making decisions. Financial managers use accounting data but differ from accountants, who devote primary attention to accrual methods and to gathering and presenting data, by concentrating on cash flows and decision making.

LG 4 Identify the key activities of the financial manager within the firm and his or her role in total quality management (TQM). The three key activities of the financial manager are (1) performing financial analysis and planning, (2) making investment decisions, and (3) making financing decisions. The financial manager, like all employees, is expected to play an active role in the firm's total quality management (TQM) program. A TQM program involves continual efforts to improve operations by streamlining processes to achieve greater efficiency and satisfaction of the needs of all customers—both internal (departments) and external.

LG 5 Compare the profit maximization and wealth maximization goals and justify the financial manager's focus on owner wealth maximization and the preservation of *stakeholder* wealth. The goal of the financial manager is to maximize the owners' wealth (dependent on stock price) rather than profits, because profit maximization ignores the timing of returns, does not directly consider cash flows, and ignores risk. Because return and risk are the key determinants of share price, both must be assessed by the financial manager when evaluating decision alternatives or actions. The wealth-maximizing actions of financial managers should be consistent with the preservation of the wealth of *stakeholders*, groups such as employees, customers, suppliers, creditors, and others who have a direct economic link to the firm.

LG 6 Discuss the agency issue as it relates to owner wealth maximization and the role of ethics in the achievement of this goal. An agency problem results from the fact that managers as agents for owners may place personal goals ahead of corporate goals. Market forces, both activism on the part of shareholders, particularly large institutional investors, and the threat of hostile takeover, tend to act to prevent or minimize agency problems. In addition, firms incur agency costs in the form of monitoring and bonding expenditures, opportunity costs, and structuring expenditures, which involve both incentive- and performance-based compensation plans to motivate management to act in the best interests of shareholders. Positive ethical practices by the firm and its managers are believed to be necessary for achievement of the firm's goal of owner wealth maximization.

Problem

1-1 LG 2 Liability comparisons Merideth Harper has invested $25,000 in the Southwest Development Company. This firm has recently declared bankruptcy and has $60,000 in unpaid debts. Explain the nature of payments, if any, by Ms. Harper in each of the following situations.

a. The Southwest Development Company is a sole proprietorship owned by Ms. Harper.

b. The Southwest Development Company is a 50–50 partnership of Ms. Harper and Christopher Black.

c. The Southwest Development Company is a corporation.

Chapter 1 Case Assessing the goal of Sports Products, Inc.

Loren Seguara and Dale Johnson both work for Sports Products, Inc., a major producer of boating equipment and accessories. Loren works as a clerical assistant in the Accounting Department, and Dale works as a packager in the Shipping Department. During their lunch break one day, they began talking about the company. Dale complained that he had always worked hard trying not to waste packing materials and efficiently and cost-effectively performing his job. In spite of his efforts and those of his co-workers in the department, the firm's stock price had declined nearly $2 per share over the past nine months. Loren indicated that she shared Dale's frustration, particularly in view of the fact that the firm's profits had been rising. Neither could understand why the firm's stock price was falling as profits rose.

Loren indicated that she had seen documents describing the firm's profit-sharing plan under which all managers were partially compensated on the basis of the firm's profits. She suggested that maybe it was profit that was important to management, since it directly affected their pay. Dale said, "That doesn't make sense, because the stockholders own the firm. Shouldn't management do what's best for stockholders? Something's wrong!" Loren responded, "Well, maybe that explains why the company hasn't concerned itself with the stock price. Look, the only profits stockholders receive are in the form of cash dividends, and this firm has never paid dividends during its 20-year history. We as stockholders therefore don't directly benefit from profits. The only way we benefit is for the stock price to rise." Dale chimed in, "That probably explains why the firm is being sued by state and federal environmental officials for dumping pollutants in the adjacent stream. Why spend money for pollution controls? It increases costs, lowers profits, and therefore lowers management's earnings!"

Loren and Dale realized that the lunch hour had ended and they must quickly return to work. Before leaving, they decided to meet the next day to continue their discussion.

Required

a. What should the management of Sports Products, Inc. pursue as its overriding goal? Why?
b. Does the firm appear to have an *agency problem?* Explain.
c. Evaluate the firm's approach to pollution control. Does it seem to be *ethical?* Why might incurring the expense to control pollution be in the best interests of the firm's owners in spite of its negative impact on profits?
d. On the basis of the information provided, what specific recommendations would you offer the firm?

chapter 2

The operating environment of the firm

LEARNING GOALS

Identify key participants in financial transactions and the basic activities and changing role of financial institutions.

Understand the relationship between financial institutions and markets and the role, operation of, and participants in the money market.

Describe the capital market including the key securities, major exchanges, and the role of the investment banker.

Discuss the fundamentals of interest rates—the real rate of interest and its relationship with the nominal or actual rate of interest (return).

Understand the term structure of interest rates—yield curves and the theories of term structure—and the basic relationship between risk and rates of return.

Describe the fundamentals of business taxation of ordinary income and capital gains, the treatment of tax losses, and S corporations.

A student planning a business career—in fact, *anybody* in business—must understand the entire environment in which businesses operate. This environment is like a fabric woven from many different threads—the federal government, its many regulatory agencies, financial institutions, the money and capital markets—and each thread is an integral part of the business environment.

As a public company that designs, manufactures, and markets engineered industrial products for specialized applications in the transportation and laboratory markets, Varlen deals with many different types of regulations. Today the level of government involvement is greater than ever; it has a larger impact than 10 years ago. Because government regulations and policies change frequently, all managers must stay well informed, to monitor and anticipate change and position the company to respond quickly.

The regulatory environment affects how we operate, evaluate risk, establish and refine product costs, invest corporate resources, and finance our activities. For example, changes in emissions regulations or weight restrictions can dramatically affect our transportation-related business, literally almost overnight, by requiring us to redesign products. Although we don't earn a return on our safety- and environment-related investments and they don't add value, we must make them or face costly penalties. We do business internationally and must consider not only U.S. trade, securities, and customs laws, but also those of any other country where we operate.

Today the level of government involvement is much greater than ever.

Our product demand is directly affected by worldwide economic conditions, because we sell to industries including transportation and petroleum—that are very sensitive to economic changes. Interest rates are influenced by the political and business environments and are a critical factor in the economy's strength. For example, Federal Reserve actions to lower interest rates generally stimulate business activity. Many business decisions, such as timing of capital expenditures and securities offerings, are based upon interest rate levels, and managers must understand the concepts underlying interest rate behavior before they borrow or invest.

Financing a business today is very challenging due to the rapidly changing economic climate. Unless we understand the various financial institutions and capital markets and are nimble enough to adapt to changing market conditions, we can't take advantage of financing opportunities as they arise. The key is to use both the debt and equity markets judiciously. When rates are low we want to lock in favorable long-term interest rates, as we did in spring 1993.

Tax planning is another area where we must track proposed changes and act when—and if—they occur. Dealing with tax changes is very frustrating because we don't know which proposals will become law. Should we put off investing in new equipment or building a new plant to wait for a favorable tax law, or do it now? In addition, changes in tax laws make many perfectly good operating and financial strategies obsolete. They also drive how we structure acquisitions and fund growth plans: whether we use debt or equity, or lease or purchase a piece of equipment.

No matter what the business, a small retail store or a large multinational corporation, managers must understand the operating environment to properly plan and control their business. The ability to track, recognize, and adapt to the changing business climate is a key managerial skill that will be even more critical in the future. A major change in your business environment can significantly affect your whole business—and in some cases put you out of business—if you are not prepared.

Mr. Wellek became President and CEO of Varlen in 1983; from 1968 to 1983 he held senior management positions at Varlen's National Metalwares, Inc., subsidiary. He has a B.S. in Industrial Management from the University of Illinois School of Business Administration and is on its Business Advisory Council.

Financial institutions and markets: An overview

Financial institutions and markets are important elements in a firm's operating environment. Why would a financial manager interact with financial institutions and markets? In what way do you think he or she would do so? Spend a few moments answering these questions before reading on.

FIRMS THAT REQUIRE FUNDS FROM EXTERNAL SOURCES CAN OBTAIN THEM IN THREE ways. One is through a *financial institution* that accepts savings and transfers them to those needing funds. Another is through *financial markets,* organized forums in which the suppliers and demanders of various types of funds can make transactions. A third is through *private placement.* Because of the unstructured nature of private placements, in this section we focus primarily on financial institutions and financial markets. However, private placement of funds is not unusual—especially in the case of debt instruments and preferred stock.

Financial institutions

financial institution
An intermediary that channels the savings of individuals, businesses, and governments into loans or investments.

Financial institutions are intermediaries that channel the savings of individuals, businesses, and governments into loans or investments. Many financial institutions directly or indirectly pay savers interest on deposited funds; others provide services for which they charge depositors (for example, the service charges levied on checking accounts). Some financial institutions accept savings and lend this money to their customers; others invest customers' savings in earning assets such as real estate or stocks and bonds; still others both lend money and invest savings. The government requires financial institutions to operate within established regulatory guidelines.

KEY PARTICIPANTS IN FINANCIAL TRANSACTIONS

The key suppliers and demanders of funds are individuals, businesses, and governments. The savings of individual consumers placed in certain financial institutions provide these institutions with a large portion of their funds. Individuals not only act as suppliers of funds to financial institutions but also demand funds from them in the form of loans. However, the important point here is that individuals as a group are the *net suppliers* for financial institutions; they save more money than they borrow.

Business firms also deposit some of their funds in financial institutions, primarily in checking accounts with various commercial banks. Firms, like individuals, also borrow funds from these institutions. As a group, business firms, unlike individuals, are *net demanders* of funds: They borrow more money than they save.

Governments maintain deposits of temporarily idle funds, certain tax payments, and social security payments in commercial banks. They do not borrow funds directly from financial institutions, although by selling their securities to various institutions, governments indirectly borrow from them. The government, like business firms, is typically a *net demander* of money; it borrows more than it saves. We've all heard about the budget deficits occurring at federal, state, and local levels of government.

MAJOR FINANCIAL INSTITUTIONS

The major financial institutions in the U.S. economy are commercial banks, savings banks, savings and loans, credit unions, life insurance companies, pension funds, and mutual funds. These institutions attract funds from individuals, businesses, and governments, combine them, and perform certain services to make attractive loans available to individuals and businesses. They may also make some of these funds available to fulfill various government demands. A brief description of the major financial institutions is found in Table 2.1.

CHANGING ROLE OF FINANCIAL INSTITUTIONS

Depository Institutions Deregulation and Monetary Control Act of 1980 (DIDMCA)
Signaled the beginning of the "financial services revolution" by eliminating interest-rate ceilings on all accounts and permitting certain institutions to offer new types of accounts and services.

financial supermarket
An institution at which the customer can obtain a full array of the financial services now allowed under DIDMCA.

Passage of the **Depository Institutions Deregulation and Monetary Control Act of 1980 (DIDMCA)** signaled the beginning of the "financial services revolution" that continues to change the nature of financial institutions. By eliminating interest-rate ceilings on all accounts and permitting certain institutions to offer new types of accounts and services, the DIDMCA intensified competition and blurred traditional distinctions among these institutions. The acquisition by Prudential Insurance of Bache & Co. and by American Express of Shearson Lehman Brothers and E. F. Hutton, both brokerage firms, is testimony to this revolution. Until late 1992, what appeared to be evolving was the **financial supermarket,** where a customer could obtain a full array of financial services such as checking, savings, loans, credit cards, securities brokerage, insurance, and retirement and estate planning. Sears, Roebuck and Company's "Sears Financial Network" offered a broad range of financial services and was widely touted as a model financial supermarket. But in late 1992, Sears began to dismantle its supermarket by selling its Dean Witter Financial Services unit, which included both stock brokerage and Discover card operations, most of its Coldwell Banker real estate holdings, and 20 percent of its Allstate insurance unit. At the same time a number of other emerging financial supermarkets, such as American Express, began to dismantle their operations. Apparently, the breakup of the one-stop financial supermarket was the result of an inability to achieve the expected benefits of combining a number of financial service firms. At this time it appears that the financial supermarket may be on its way to extinction.

The role of financial institutions is undergoing further change as a result of the "savings & loan (S&L) crisis" of the late 1980s. Caused by a number of factors including (1) enhanced competition stimulated by DIDMCA, (2) plummeting oil and real estate prices in the "oil patch" (oil-producing areas of the country), (3) defaults on high-risk, high-yield "junk bond" investments, (4) generally poor management, (5) poor regulation by S&L authorities, and (6) the illegal and unethical acts of officers of some major S&Ls, the failures of numerous S&Ls resulted in the Bush administration's thrift bailout plan. This plan—the cost of which is of course being borne by taxpayers—is aimed at resolving the S&L crisis by providing needed financing and more restrictive regulation and enforcement of the nation's S&Ls. It resulted in the creation of two new agencies to bail out the S&L industry. The Office of Thrift Supervision (OTS) regulates the industry. The Resolution Trust Corporation (RTC), a unit of the FDIC, takes over insolvent thrifts, safeguards their deposits, and sells the assets—real estate and loans—of these failed institutions. Through mid-1992 the RTC had taken over more than 700 insolvent institutions, and many more were in danger of insolvency. The cost to taxpayers of the massive S&L bailout has been estimated to be about $500

TABLE 2.1

MAJOR FINANCIAL INSTITUTIONS

Institution	Description
Commercial bank	Accepts both demand (checking) and time (savings) deposits. Also offers negotiable order of withdrawal (NOW) accounts, which are interest-earning savings accounts against which checks can be written. In addition, currently offers money market deposit accounts, which pay interest at rates competitive with those of other short-term investment vehicles. Makes loans directly to borrowers or through the financial markets.
Savings bank	Similar to commercial banks except that it may not hold demand (checking) deposits. Obtains funds from savings, NOW, and money market deposit accounts. Generally lends or invests funds through financial markets, although some residential real estate loans are made to individuals. Located primarily in New York, New Jersey, and the New England states.
Savings and loan	Similar to a savings bank in that it holds savings deposits, NOW accounts, and money market deposit accounts. Also raises capital through the sale of securities in the financial markets. Lends funds primarily to individuals and businesses for real estate mortgage loans. Some funds are channeled into investments in the financial markets.
Credit union	A financial intermediary that deals primarily in transfer of funds between consumers. Membership is generally based on some common bond, such as working for a given employer. Accepts members' savings deposits, NOW account deposits, and money market deposit accounts and lends the majority of these funds to other members, typically to finance automobile or appliance purchases or home improvements.
Life insurance company	The largest type of financial intermediary handling individual savings. Receives premium payments that are placed in loans or investments to accumulate funds to cover future benefit payments. Lends funds to individuals, businesses, and governments or channels them through the financial markets to those who demand them.
Pension fund	Set up so that employees of various corporations or government units can receive income after retirement. Often, employers match the contributions of their employees. Money is sometimes transferred directly to borrowers, but the majority is lent or invested via the financial markets.
Mutual fund	A type of financial intermediary that pools funds of savers and makes them available to business and government demanders. Obtains funds through sale of shares and uses proceeds to acquire bonds and stocks issued by various business and governmental units. Creates a diversified and professionally managed portfolio of securities to achieve a specified investment objective, such as liquidity with a high return. Hundreds of funds, with a variety of investment objectives, exist. Money market mutual funds, which provide competitive returns with very high liquidity, are popular, particularly when short-term interest rates are high.

billion. As a result of government actions, not only should future crises be avoided, but a further blurring of the lines of distinction between banks, S&Ls, and other financial institutions is also expected.

CONCEPT IN PRACTICE

What Does a Bank Look Like?

Most people would probably describe a bank as a large office building with spacious accommodations, fine furniture, and a refined atmosphere. Many people, however, have never seen the inside of a bank or used the services that banks provide. Approximately 15 million U.S. households exist without traditional banking relationships. The people who live in these households are frequently poor, recent immigrants, or others who have avoided or been ignored by traditional commercial banks.

New Valley Corporation wants to change all that. You might not recognize the New Valley name, but you probably know its principal subsidiary—Western Union. While Western Union has handled money transfers for 127 years through its network of 18,000 agents in the United States and abroad, the firm is currently expanding its financial-services product line to include money orders, electronic bill-paying, and other services aimed at low-income consumers. So what does a bank look like? It's not the size of the office that matters, but convenient access for customers and the ability to move money quickly across a wide branch network.

Financial markets

financial markets
Provide a forum in which suppliers of funds and demanders of loans and investments can transact business directly.

Financial markets provide a forum in which suppliers of funds and demanders of loans and investments can transact business directly. Whereas the loans and investments of institutions are made without the direct knowledge of the suppliers of funds (savers), suppliers in the financial markets know where their funds are being lent or invested. The two key financial markets are the *money market* and the *capital market.* Transactions in short-term debt instruments, or marketable securities, take place in the money market. Long-term securities (bonds and stocks) are traded in the capital market.

primary market
Financial market in which securities are initially issued; the only market in which the issuer is directly involved in the transaction.

secondary market
Financial market in which preowned securities (those that are not new issues) are traded.

All securities, whether in the money or capital market, are initially issued in the **primary market.** This is the only market in which the corporate or government issuer is directly involved in the transaction and receives direct benefit from the issue—that is, the company actually receives the proceeds from the sale of securities. Once the securities begin to trade among individual, business, government, or financial institution savers and investors, they become part of the **secondary market.** The primary market is the one in which "new" securities are sold; the secondary market can be viewed as a "used" or "preowned" securities market.

The relationship between institutions and markets

Financial institutions actively participate in the money market and the capital market as both suppliers and demanders of funds. Figure 2.1 depicts the general flow of funds through and between financial institutions and markets; private placement transactions are also shown. The individuals, businesses, and governments that supply and demand funds may be domestic or foreign. In some instances there may be legal constraints on the operations of certain institutions in the financial marketplace. We end this section with a brief description of the money market, including its international

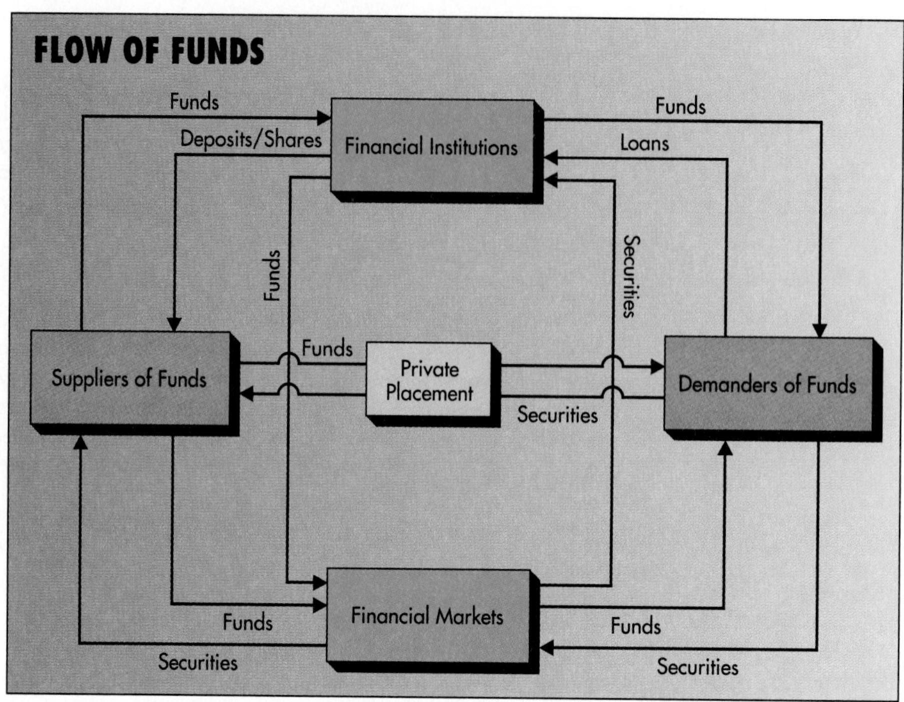

FIGURE 2.1
Flow of funds for financial institutions and markets

equivalent—the *Eurocurrency market.* The next major section of the chapter is devoted to discussion of the capital market because of its key importance to the firm.

The money market

money market
A financial relationship created between suppliers and demanders of *short-term funds.*

marketable securities
Short-term debt instruments, such as U.S. Treasury bills, commercial paper, and negotiable certificates of deposit issued by government, business, and financial institutions, respectively.

The **money market** is created by a financial relationship between suppliers and demanders of *short-term funds,* which have maturities of one year or less. The money market is not an actual organization housed in some central location, although the majority of money market transactions culminate in New York City. Most money market transactions are made in **marketable securities**—short-term debt instruments, such as U.S. Treasury bills, commercial paper, and negotiable certificates of deposit issued by government, business, and financial institutions, respectively. (Marketable securities are described in Chapter 17.)

The money market exists because certain individuals, businesses, governments, and financial institutions have temporarily idle funds that they wish to place in some type of liquid asset or short-term, interest-earning instrument. At the same time, other individuals, businesses, governments, and financial institutions find themselves in need of seasonal or temporary financing. The money market thus brings together these suppliers and demanders of short-term liquid funds.

THE OPERATION OF THE MONEY MARKET

How are suppliers and demanders of short-term funds brought together in the money market? Typically, they are matched through the facilities of large New York banks, through government securities dealers, or through the Federal Reserve banks. The Federal Reserve banks become involved only in loans from one commercial bank to an-

federal funds
Loan transactions between commercial banks in which the Federal Reserve banks become involved.

other; these loans are referred to as transactions in **federal funds.** A number of stock brokerage firms purchase various money market instruments for resale to customers. If a brokerage firm does not have an instrument that a customer has demanded, it will attempt to acquire it. In addition, financial institutions such as banks and mutual funds purchase money market instruments for their portfolios to provide attractive returns on their customers' deposits and share purchases.

Most money market transactions are negotiated by telephone. A firm wishing to purchase a certain marketable security may call its bank, which will then attempt to buy the security by contacting a bank known to "make a market" or to deal in the given security. The bank or the firm may also go directly to a **government security dealer,** an institution that purchases for resale various government securities and other money market instruments. Regardless of whether a business or government is *issuing* a money market instrument (demanding short-term funds) or *purchasing* a money market instrument (supplying short-term funds), one party must go directly to another party or use an intermediary, such as a commercial bank, government security dealer, or brokerage firm, to make a transaction. Individuals wishing to purchase marketable securities generally must go through a dealer firm. The secondary (or resale) market for marketable securities is no different from the primary (or initial issue) market with respect to the basic transactions that are made.

government security dealer
An institution that purchases for resale various government securities and other money market instruments.

PARTICIPANTS IN THE MONEY MARKET

The key participants in the money market are individuals, businesses, governments, and financial institutions. Individuals participate as purchasers and as sellers of money market instruments. Their purchases are somewhat limited due to the large denominations traded—typically $100,000 or more. Certain banks and stock brokerage firms will "break down" marketable securities to make them available in smaller denominations. Individuals sell marketable securities in the money market not as issuers but to liquidate the securities before maturity. Individuals do not issue marketable securities.

Business firms, governments, and financial institutions both buy and sell marketable securities. They may be the primary issuers, or they may sell securities that they have purchased and wish to liquidate before maturity. They therefore may act as primary or secondary sellers of these securities. Of course, each of these parties can issue only certain money market instruments; a business firm, for example, cannot issue a U.S. Treasury bill. Some financial institutions purchase marketable securities specifically for resale, whereas others purchase them as short-term investments. Businesses and governments purchase marketable securities to earn a return on temporarily idle funds.

THE EUROCURRENCY MARKET

Eurocurrency market
International equivalent of the domestic money market.

The international equivalent of the domestic money market is called the **Eurocurrency market.** This is a market for short-term bank deposits denominated in U.S. dollars or other easily convertible currencies. Historically, the Eurocurrency market has been centered in London, but it has evolved into a truly global market with total deposits in excess of $5 trillion.

Eurocurrency deposits arise when a corporation or individual makes a deposit in a bank in a currency other than the local currency of the country where the bank is located. If, for example, a multinational corporation were to deposit U.S. dollars in the London branch of a European or an American bank, this would create a Eurodollar deposit (a dollar deposit at a bank in Europe). Almost all Eurodollar deposits are time deposits, meaning that the bank would promise to repay the deposit, with interest, at a fixed date in the future—say, six months. During the interim the bank is free to lend this dollar deposit to creditworthy corporate or government borrowers, and the bank makes a profit on the "spread" or difference between the interest rate that it pays for the deposit and the rate that it collects on the loan. If the bank cannot find a borrower on its own, it may instead loan the deposit to another international bank. The rate charged on these "interbank loans" is called the **London Interbank Offered Rate (LIBOR),** and this is the base rate that is used to price all Eurocurrency loans.

London Interbank Offered Rate (LIBOR)
The base rate that is used to price all Eurocurrency loans.

The Eurocurrency market has grown rapidly since its creation in the 1950s, primarily because it is an unregulated, wholesale market that capably fills the needs of both borrowers and lenders. Investors with excess cash to lend are able to make large, short-term, and safe deposits at attractive interest rates, while borrowers are able to arrange large loans, quickly and confidentially, also at attractive interest rates. Competition among banks, as well as the wholesale nature of the market, ensures a very small spread between borrowing and lending rates. Finally, since the deposits are not denominated in local currencies, national central banks have never been able to effectively control or regulate the market. Instead, central bankers have promoted Eurocurrency lending by their own nations' banks to capture a larger share of the total market.

CONCEPTS IN REVIEW

2-1 What role do financial institutions play in our economy? Who are the key participants in these transactions? Indicate who are net suppliers and who are net demanders.

2-2 What did the *Depository Institutions Deregulation and Monetary Control Act of 1980 (DIDMCA)* do to begin the "financial services revolution"? Describe the "financial supermarket" and its future. What is the "savings and loan (S&L) crisis," and what effect has it had on financial institutions?

2-3 What are *financial markets,* and what role do they play in our economy? What relationship exists between financial institutions and financial markets?

2-4 What is the *money market?* Where is it housed? How does it differ from the capital market?

2-5 What is the *Eurocurrency market?* What is the *London Interbank Offered Rate (LIBOR)* and how is it used in this market?

The capital market

Securities exchanges are the backbone of the capital, or long-term, market. As the financial manager of a large publicly traded corporation, why would these exchanges be important to you? Take a few moments to think about this question before moving on.

capital market
A financial relationship created by institutions and arrangements that allows suppliers and demanders of *long-term funds* to make transactions.

THE **CAPITAL MARKET** IS A FINANCIAL RELATIONSHIP CREATED BY A NUMBER OF INstitutions and arrangements that allows the suppliers and demanders of *long-term funds*—funds with maturities of more than one year—to make transactions. Included among long-term funds are securities issues of business and government. The backbone of the capital market is formed by the various *securities exchanges* that provide a forum for debt and equity transactions. The smooth functioning of the capital market, which is enhanced through the activities of *investment bankers,* is important to the long-run growth of business.

Key securities

Major securities traded in the capital market include bonds (long-term debt) and both common and preferred stock (equity, or ownership). **Bonds** are long-term debt instruments used by business and government to raise large sums of money, generally from a diverse group of lenders. *Corporate bonds* typically pay interest *semiannually* (every six months) at a stated *coupon interest rate,* have an initial *maturity* of from 10 to 30 years, and have a *par,* or *face, value* of $1,000 that must be repaid at maturity. Bonds are described in detail in Chapter 12.

bond
Long-term debt instrument used by business and government to raise large sums of money, generally from a diverse group of lenders.

EXAMPLE

Cato Industries, a major television picture tube manufacturer, has just issued a 12 percent coupon interest rate, 20-year bond with a $1,000 par value that pays interest semiannually. Investors who buy this bond receive the contractual right to (1) $120 annual interest (12 percent coupon interest rate × $1,000 par value) distributed as $60 at the end of each six months (½ × $120) for 20 years and (2) the $1,000 par value at the end of year 20. ■

Shares of **common stock** are units of ownership interest, or equity, in a corporation. Common stockholders expect to earn a return by receiving **dividends**—periodic distributions of earnings—or by realizing gains through increases in share price. **Preferred stock** is a special form of ownership that has features of both a bond and common stock. Preferred stockholders are promised a fixed periodic dividend that must be paid before payment of any dividends to the owners of common stock. In other words, preferred stock has "preference" over common stock. Common and preferred stock are described in detail in Chapters 13 and 14, respectively.

common stock
Collectively, units of ownership interest, or equity, in a corporation.

dividends
Periodic distributions of earnings to the owners of stock in a firm.

preferred stock
A special form of ownership having a fixed periodic dividend that must be paid before payment of any common stock dividends.

Major securities exchanges

As we noted earlier, **securities exchanges** provide the marketplace in which firms can raise funds through the sale of new securities and purchasers of securities can maintain liquidity by being able to easily resell them when necessary. Many people call securities exchanges "stock markets," but this label is somewhat misleading because bonds, common stock, preferred stock, and a variety of other investment vehicles are all traded on these exchanges. The two key types of securities exchange are the organized exchange and the over-the-counter exchange. In addition, important markets exist outside of the United States.

securities exchanges
Organizations that provide the marketplace in which firms can raise funds through the sale of new securities and purchasers can resell securities.

ORGANIZED SECURITIES EXCHANGES

Organized securities exchanges are tangible organizations that act as *secondary markets* in which outstanding securities are resold. Organized exchanges account for over 72 percent of the *total dollar volume* of domestic shares traded. The dominant organized exchanges are the New York Stock Exchange (NYSE) and the American Stock Exchange (AMEX), both headquartered in New York City. There are also regional ex-

organized securities exchanges
Tangible organizations that act as *secondary markets* in which outstanding securities are resold.

changes, such as the Midwest Stock Exchange (in Chicago) and the Pacific Stock Exchange (in San Francisco).

Most exchanges are modeled after the New York Stock Exchange, which accounts for over 85 percent of the total annual dollar volume of shares traded on organized exchanges. To make transactions on the "floor" of the New York Stock Exchange, an individual or firm must own a "seat" on the exchange. There are a total of 1,366 seats on the NYSE, most of which are owned by brokerage firms. To be listed for trading on an organized stock exchange, a firm must file an application for listing and meet a number of requirements. For example, to be eligible for listing on the NYSE, a firm must have at least 2,000 stockholders owning 100 or more shares, a minimum of 1.1 million shares of publicly held stock, a demonstrated earning power of $2.5 million before taxes at the time of listing and $2 million before taxes for each of the preceding two years, net tangible assets of $18 million, and a total of $18 million in market value of publicly traded shares. Clearly, only large, widely held firms are candidates for listing on the NYSE.

Trading is carried out on the floor of the exchange through an *auction process.* The goal of trading is to fill *buy orders* (orders to purchase securities) at the lowest price and to fill *sell orders* (orders to sell securities) at the highest price, thereby giving both purchasers and sellers the best possible deal. The general procedure for placing and executing an order can be described by a simple example.

EXAMPLE

Kathryn Blake, who has an account with Merrill Lynch, wishes to purchase 200 shares of the Microsoft Corporation at the prevailing market price. Kathryn calls her account executive,[1] Howard Kohn of Merrill Lynch, and places her order. Howard immediately has the order transmitted to the New York headquarters of Merrill Lynch, which immediately forwards the order to the Merrill Lynch clerk on the floor of the exchange. The clerk dispatches the order to one of the firm's seat holders, who goes to the appropriate trading post, executes the order at the best possible price, and returns to the clerk, who then wires the execution price and confirmation of the transaction back to the brokerage office. Howard is given the relevant information and passes it along to Kathryn. Howard then has certain paperwork to do. ■

Once placed, an order to either buy or sell can be executed in minutes, thanks to sophisticated telecommunication devices. Information on the daily trading of securities is reported in various media, including financial publications such as *The Wall Street Journal.*

THE OVER-THE-COUNTER EXCHANGE

over-the-counter (OTC) exchange
Not an organization but an intangible market for the purchase and sale of securities not listed by the organized exchanges.

The **over-the-counter (OTC) exchange** is not an organization but an intangible market for the purchase and sale of securities that are not listed by the organized exchanges. The market price of OTC securities results from a matching of the forces of supply of, and demand for securities by traders known as *dealers.* OTC dealers are linked with the purchasers and sellers of securities through the *National Association of Securities Dealers Automated Quotation (NASDAQ) System,* which is a sophisticated telecom-

[1]The title *account executive* or *financial consultant* is often used to refer to an individual who traditionally has been called a *stockbroker.* These titles are believed to add respectability to the position and change the image of the stockbroker from that of a salesperson to that of a personal financial manager who provides diversified financial services to his or her clients.

munications network that provides current bid and ask prices on thousands of actively traded OTC securities. The *bid price* is the highest price offered by a dealer to purchase a given security, and the *ask price* is the lowest price at which the dealer is willing to sell the security. The dealer in effect adds securities to his or her inventory by purchasing them at the bid price and sells securities from his or her inventory at the ask price, hoping to profit from the *spread* between the bid and ask price. Unlike the auction process on the organized securities exchanges, the prices at which securities are traded in the OTC market result from both competitive bids and negotiation. The OTC, in addition to creating a *secondary (resale) market* for outstanding securities, is a *primary market* in which new public issues are sold. The OTC accounts for nearly 28 percent of the *total dollar volume* of domestic shares traded.

INTERNATIONAL CAPITAL MARKETS

Eurobond market
The oldest and largest international bond market.

Although U.S. capital markets are by far the world's largest, there are important debt and equity markets outside the United States. The oldest and largest international bond market, the **Eurobond market,** is in many ways the long-term equivalent of the Eurocurrency markets discussed earlier. In this market, corporations and governments issue bonds denominated in dollars or other currencies that can be converted into dollars and sell them to investors located outside the United States or the country in whose currency the bonds are denominated. A U.S. corporation might, for example, issue dollar-denominated bonds that would be purchased by investors in Belgium, Germany, Switzerland, or other countries.

bearer bonds
Bonds for which payments are made to the bearer.

Investors find Eurobonds attractive because they provide currency diversification and because, as **bearer bonds** (for which payments are made to the bearer), they provide anonymity to the investor wishing to avoid payment of taxes. Issuing firms and governments appreciate the Eurobond market because it allows them to tap a much larger pool of investors than would generally be available in the local market and because competition keeps their fees attractively low. In recent years, between $150 billion and $250 billion worth of Eurobonds have been issued annually. The currency mix of these bonds fluctuates over time, but in most years at least half of the bonds issued are denominated in U.S. dollars.

foreign bond
Bond issued by a foreign corporation or government that is denominated in the investor's home currency and sold in the investor's home market.

The foreign bond market is another market for long-term debt securities involving international issuers and investors. A **foreign bond** is a bond issued by a foreign corporation or government that is denominated in the investor's home currency and sold in the investor's home market. A bond issued by a U.S. company that is denominated in Swiss francs and sold in Switzerland is an example of a foreign bond. Although the foreign bond market is much smaller than the Eurobond market, many issuers have found this to be an attractive way of tapping debt markets in Switzerland, Germany, the United States, and Japan, as well as other countries.

international equity market
A vibrant equity market that emerged during the past decade to allow corporations to sell large blocks of shares in several different countries simultaneously.

Finally, a vibrant **international equity market** has emerged during the past decade. Many corporations have discovered that they can sell large blocks of shares to investors in several different countries simultaneously. This has not only allowed corporations to diversify their investor base, but has also allowed them to raise far larger amounts of capital than they could have raised in any single national market. International equity sales have also proven to be indispensable to the numerous governments that have executed privatization programs in recent years, since the state-owned companies being sold to private investors are often extremely large. Several recent privatization share issues have raised over $10 billion each and could not have been executed without the active participation of international investors.

CONCEPT IN PRACTICE

Manhattan Isn't the Only Place You Can Trade Stocks

It's easy to forget that stock trading goes on all over the world—not just in New York. Many European stocks, like the stock of the Dutch company Ahold, which trades on the NASDAQ exchange, are available to U.S. investors directly within the U.S. stock market. But some foreign stocks are traded only on their home exchanges. Why might you want to buy one of these stocks? Because you can earn an attractive rate of return on your investment.

The increased value of the dollar in 1993 led many U.S. investors to purchase European stocks—particularly those issued by firms with earnings from U.S. operations or exports to the United States. A strong dollar means that dollar-denominated sales translate into more marks, pounds, or francs. This boosts the profits of foreign firms, raising their stock values. But how can you buy stocks that are traded only in Europe? Any multinational brokerage will accept your business, and many go out of their way to attract U.S. clients. For example, the Dutch brokers Capel and Pierson, Heldring, & Pierson mail out monthly account statements written in English for their U.S. customers.

The role of securities exchanges

efficient market
A market that allocates funds to their most productive uses as a result of competition among wealth-maximizing investors that determines and publicizes prices that are believed to be close to their true value.

In addition to their role in creating continuous liquid markets in which firms can obtain needed financing, the securities exchanges create **efficient markets** that allocate funds to their most productive uses. This is especially true for securities that are actively traded on major exchanges where the competition among wealth-maximizing investors determines and publicizes prices that are believed to be close to their true value. The price of an individual security is determined by what is bought and sold, or the demand for and supply of the security. Figure 2.2 depicts the interaction of the

FIGURE 2.2
Supply of and demand for a security

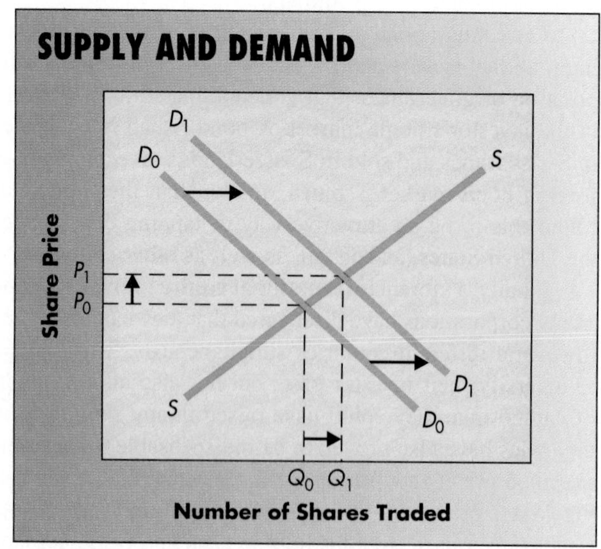

forces of demand (represented by line D_0) and supply (represented by line S) for a given security currently selling at an equilibrium price P_0. At that price, Q_0 shares of the stock are traded.

A capital market brings together buyers and sellers from all geographic areas while affording them some anonymity. This trading forum helps to ensure an efficient market in which the price reflects the true value of the security. Changing evaluations of a firm, of course, cause changes in the demand for and supply of its securities and ultimately result in a new price for the securities. Suppose, for example, that a favorable discovery by the firm shown in Figure 2.2 is announced and investors in the marketplace increase their valuations of the firm's shares. The changing evaluation results in a shift in demand from D_0 to D_1; Q_1 shares will be traded; and a new, higher equilibrium price of P_1 will result. The competitive market created by the major securities exchanges provides a forum in which share price is continuously adjusted to changing demand and supply. Since the prices are readily available, interested parties can use this information to make better purchase and sale decisions.

The role of the investment banker

To raise money in the capital market, firms can use either private placements or public offerings. **Private placement** involves the sale of a new security issue, typically debt or preferred stock, directly to an investor or group of investors, such as an insurance company or pension fund. However, most firms raise money through a **public offering** of securities; this involves the nonexclusive sale of either bonds or stock to the general public. In making a securities offering, whether private or public, most firms hire an investment banker to find buyers for new security issues.

private placement
The sale of a new security issue, typically debt or preferred stock, directly to an investor or group of investors.

public offering
The nonexclusive sale of either bonds or stock to the general public.

The term *investment banker* is somewhat misleading because an investment banker is neither an investor nor a banker; furthermore, he or she neither makes long-term investments nor guards the savings of others. Instead, acting as an intermediary between the issuer and the buyers of new security issues, the **investment banker** purchases securities from corporate and government issuers and resells them to the general public in the *primary market*. In addition to bearing the risk of selling a security issue, investment bankers advise clients. In the United States, for example, during 1992 Goldman Sachs, Morgan Stanley Group, and CS First Boston Group were the top three investment banking firms. (Detailed discussion of the functions, organization, and cost of investment banking is included in Chapter 12.)

investment banker
A financial intermediary that purchases securities from corporate and government issuers and resells them to the general public in the primary market.

CONCEPTS IN REVIEW

2-6 What is the *capital market?* What are *primary* and *secondary* markets? What role do securities exchanges play in the capital market?

2-7 How does the over-the-counter exchange operate? How does it differ from the organized securities exchanges?

2-8 Briefly describe the international capital markets, particularly the *Eurobond market* and the *international equity market.*

2-9 What is an *investment banker?* What role does he or she play in private placements and public offerings?

Interest rates and required returns

Interest rates and required returns represent the costs of using various forms of financing. Indeed, we hear or read about interest rates and their movements almost daily. Can you identify the key factors that make up and affect the level of these rates that are applicable to a given firm? Spend a few minutes trying to answer this question before reading on.

FINANCIAL INSTITUTIONS AND MARKETS CREATE THE MECHANISM THROUGH WHICH FUNDS flow between savers (funds suppliers) and investors (funds demanders). The level of funds flow between suppliers and demanders can significantly affect economic growth. Growth results from the interaction of a variety of economic factors, such as the money supply, trade balances, and economic policies, that affect the cost of money—the interest rate or required return. The level of this rate acts as a regulating device that controls the flow of funds between suppliers and demanders. In general, the lower the interest rate, the greater the funds flow and therefore the greater the economic growth; the higher the interest rate, the lower the funds flow and economic growth. Interest rates and required returns are key variables influencing the actions of the financial manager.

Interest rate fundamentals

interest rate
The compensation paid by the borrower of funds to the lender; from the borrower's point of view, the cost of borrowing funds.

required return
The cost of funds obtained by selling an ownership (or equity) interest; it reflects the funds supplier's level of expected return.

liquidity preferences
General preferences of investors for shorter-term securities.

real rate of interest
The rate that creates an equilibrium between the supply of savings and the demand for investment funds in a perfect world, without inflation, where funds suppliers and demanders have no liquidity preference and all outcomes are certain.

The interest rate or required return represents the cost of money. It is the rent or level of compensation that a demander of funds must pay a supplier. When funds are lent, the cost of borrowing the funds is the **interest rate.** When funds are obtained by selling an ownership (or equity) interest—as in the sale of stock—the cost to the issuer (demander) is commonly called the **required return,** which reflects the funds supplier's level of expected return. In both cases the supplier is compensated for providing either debt or equity funds. Ignoring risk factors, the nominal or actual interest rate (cost of funds) results from the *real rate of interest* adjusted for inflationary expectations and **liquidity preferences**—general preferences of investors for shorter-term securities.

THE REAL RATE OF INTEREST

In a *perfect world* in which there is no inflation and in which funds suppliers and demanders are indifferent to the term of loans or investments because they have no liquidity preference and all outcomes are certain,[2] at a given point in time there would be one cost of money—the **real rate of interest.** The real rate of interest creates an equilibrium between the supply of savings and the demand for investment funds. It is important because it represents the most basic cost of money, which can be adjusted for inflationary expectations and issuer and issue characteristics such as risk to estimate interest rates (returns). The real rate of interest in the United States is assumed

[2]These assumptions are made to describe the most basic interest rate, the *real rate of interest.* Subsequent discussions relax these assumptions to develop the broader concept of the interest rate and required return.

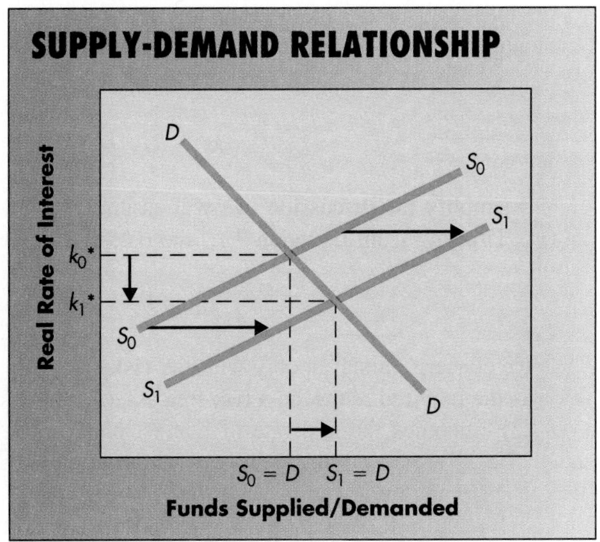

FIGURE 2.3
Supply of savings and demand for investment funds

to be stable and equal to around 2 percent.[3] This supply-demand relationship is shown in Figure 2.3 by the supply function (labeled S_0) and the demand function (labeled D). An equilibrium between the supply of funds and the demand for funds ($S_0 = D$) occurs at a rate of interest k_0*, the real rate of interest.

Clearly, the real rate of interest changes with changing economic conditions, tastes, and preferences. A favorable international trade balance could result in an increased supply of funds, causing the supply function in Figure 2.3 to shift to, say, S_1. This could result in a lower real rate of interest, k_1*, at equilibrium ($S_1 = D$). Likewise, a change in tax laws or other factors could affect the demand for funds, causing the real rate of interest to rise or fall to a new equilibrium level.

NOMINAL OR ACTUAL RATE OF INTEREST (RETURN)

nominal rate of interest
The actual rate of interest charged by the supplier of funds and paid by the demander.

The **nominal rate of interest** is the actual rate of interest charged by the supplier of funds and paid by the demander. It differs from the real rate of interest, k^*, as a result of two factors: (1) inflationary expectations reflected in an inflation premium (IP) and (2) issuer and issue characteristics, such as default risk and contractual provisions, reflected in a risk premium (RP). Using this notation, the nominal rate of interest for security 1, k_1, is given in Equation 2.1:

$$k_1 = \underbrace{k^* + IP}_{\substack{\text{risk-free} \\ \text{rate, } R_F}} + \underbrace{RP_1}_{\substack{\text{risk} \\ \text{premium}}} \tag{2.1}$$

[3]Data in Roger G. Ibbotson and Rex A. Sinquefield, *Stocks, Bonds, Bills and Inflation: Historical Returns* (Chicago: Dow-Jones Irwin, 1989), updated in *SBBI 1992 Yearbook* (Chicago: Ibbotson Associates, 1992), show that over the period 1926–1992, U.S. Treasury bills provided an average annual real rate of return of about .5 percent. Because of certain major economic events that occurred during the 1926–1992 period, many economists believe that the real rate of interest during recent years has been about 2 percent.

As the horizontal braces in the equation indicate, the nominal rate, k_1, can be viewed as having two basic components: a risk-free rate of interest, R_F, plus a risk premium, RP_1:

$$k_1 = R_F + RP_1 \tag{2.2}$$

To simplify the discussion, we will assume that the risk premium, RP_1, is equal to zero. Drawing from Equation 2.1,[4] the risk-free rate can be represented as

$$R_F = k^* + IP \tag{2.3}$$

risk-free rate of interest, R_F
The required return on a risk-free asset, typically a three-month *U.S. Treasury bill.*

U.S. Treasury bills (T-bills)
Short-term IOUs issued by the U.S. Treasury; considered the risk-free asset.

Thus we concern ourselves only with the **risk-free rate of interest, R_F**, which is defined as the required return on a risk-free asset.[5] The risk-free rate (as shown in Equation 2.3) embodies the real rate of interest plus the inflationary expectation. Three-month **U.S. Treasury bills (T-bills),** which are short-term IOUs issued by the U.S. Treasury, are commonly considered the risk-free asset.

The premium for *inflationary expectations* represents the average rate of *inflation* (price-level change) expected over the life of the loan or investment. It is *not* the rate of inflation experienced over the immediate past; rather, it reflects the forecasted rate. Take, for example, the risk-free asset. During the week ended May 29, 1992, three-month T-bills earned a 3.71 percent rate of return. Assuming an approximate 2 percent real rate of interest, funds suppliers were forecasting a 1.71 percent (annual) rate of inflation (3.71% − 2.00%) over the following three months. This expectation was in striking contrast to the expected rate of inflation 11 years earlier in the week ended May 22, 1981. At that time the three-month T-bill rate was 16.60 percent, which meant an expected (annual) inflation rate of 14.60 percent (16.60% − 2.00%). The inflationary expectation premium changes over time in response to many factors, including recent inflation rates, government policies, and international events.

Figure 2.4 illustrates the movement of the rate of inflation and the risk-free rate of interest during the 20-year period 1972–1992. During this period the two rates tended to move in a similar fashion. Between the Arab oil embargo of 1973 and early 1980, inflation and interest rates were quite high, peaking at over 13 percent in 1980–1981. Since 1981 these rates have declined to levels below those existing before the oil embargo. The data clearly illustrate the significant impact of inflation on the nominal rate of interest for the risk-free asset.

Term structure of interest rates

term structure of interest rates
The relationship between the interest rate or rate of return and the time to maturity.

For any class of similar-risk securities the **term structure of interest rates** relates the interest rate or rate of return to the time to maturity. For convenience we will continue to use Treasury securities as a class, but other classes could include securities that have similar overall quality or risk ratings such as Aaa utility bonds, Ba corporate bonds, and so on, as determined by independent agencies like Moody's and Stan-

[4] This equation is commonly called the *Fisher equation,* named for the renowned economist Irving Fisher, who first presented this approximate relationship between nominal interest and the rate of inflation. See Irving Fisher, *The Theory of Interest* (New York: Macmillan, 1930).

[5] In a later part of this discussion the risk premium and its effect on the nominal rate of interest are discussed and illustrated.

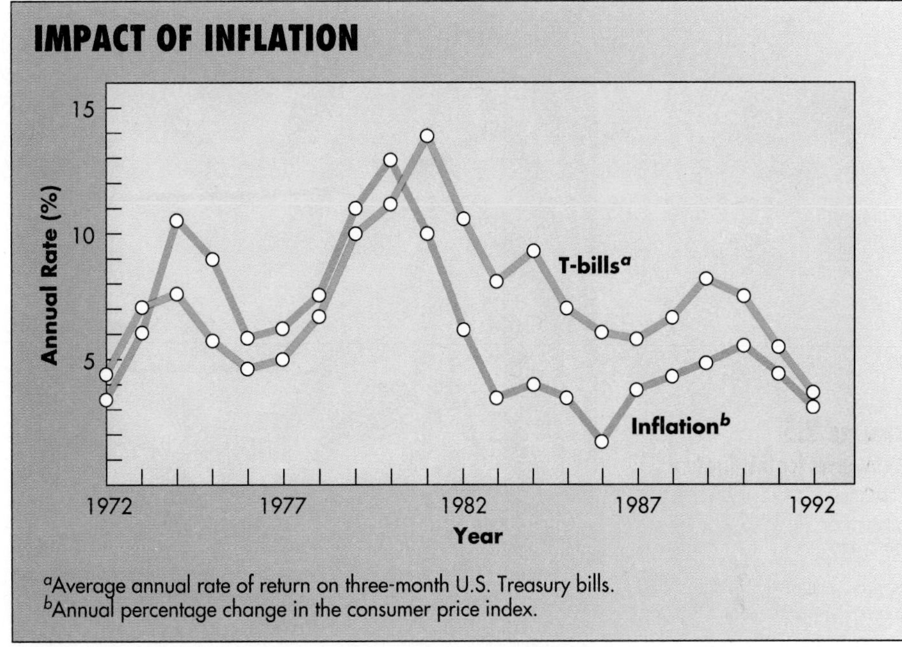

FIGURE 2.4
Relationship between annual rate of inflation and three-month U.S. Treasury bill average yields, 1972–1992

Source: Data from selected *Federal Reserve Bulletins.*

yield to maturity
Annual rate of interest earned on a security purchased on a given day and held to maturity.

yield curve
A graph of the *term structure of interest rates* that depicts the relationship between the *yield to maturity* of a security (*y*-axis) and the time to maturity (*x*-axis); it shows the pattern of interest rates on securities of equal quality and different maturity.

inverted yield curve
A downward-sloping yield curve that indicates generally cheaper long-term borrowing costs than short-term borrowing costs.

normal yield curve
An upward-sloping yield curve that indicates generally cheaper short-term borrowing costs than long-term borrowing costs.

flat yield curve
A yield curve that reflects relatively similar borrowing costs for both short- and longer-term loans.

dard & Poor's. The riskless nature of Treasury securities also provides a laboratory in which to develop the term structure.

YIELD CURVES

At any point in time the relationship between the rate of return or **yield to maturity**—the annual rate of interest earned on a security purchased on a given day and held to maturity—and the remaining time to maturity can be represented by the **yield curve.** In other words, the yield curve shows the pattern of interest rates on securities of equal quality and different maturity; it is a graphic depiction of the term structure of interest rates. Figure 2.5 shows three yield curves for all U.S. Treasury securities—one at May 22, 1981, a second one at September 29, 1989, and a third one at May 29, 1992. It can be seen that both the position and the shape of the yield curves change over time. The May 22, 1981, curve indicates that while short-term interest rates were at that time quite high, the longer-term rates were lower. This curve is described as *downward-sloping,* reflecting generally cheaper long-term borrowing costs than short-term borrowing costs. Historically, the downward-sloping yield curve, which is often called an **inverted yield curve,** has been the exception. More frequently, yield curves similar to that of May 29, 1992, have existed. These *upward-sloping* or **normal yield curves** indicate that short-term borrowing costs are below long-term borrowing costs. Sometimes, a **flat yield curve**, similar to that of September 29, 1989, exists. It reflects relatively similar borrowing costs for both short- and longer-term loans.

CONCEPT IN PRACTICE

Maybe Uncle Sam Needs a New Crystal Ball

Attracted by the lowest long-term interest rates in nearly 20 years, and fearful that rates would rise in the near future, corporations were issuing long-term debt at a

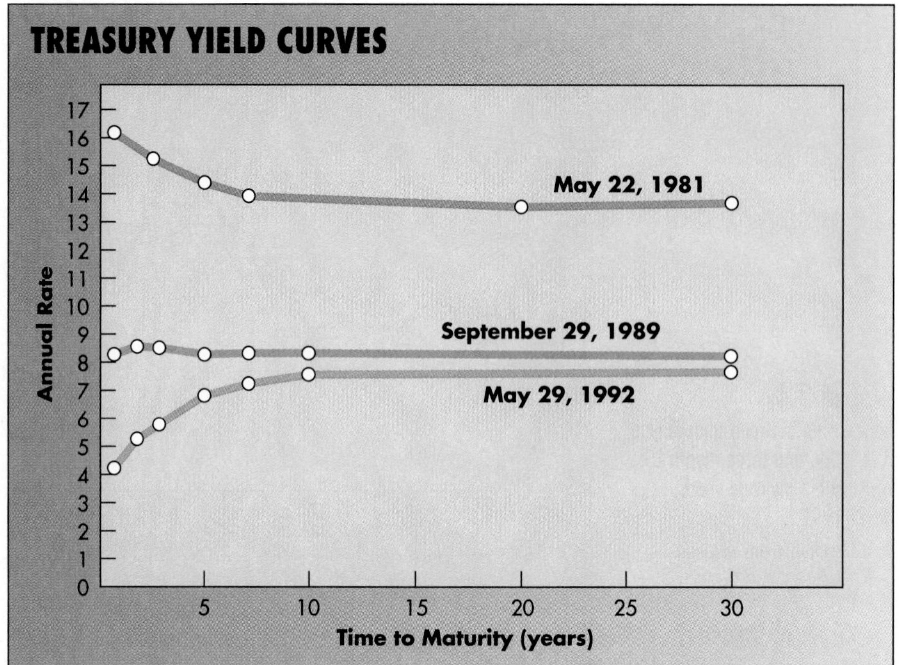

FIGURE 2.5
Yield curves for U.S. Treasury securities: May 22, 1981; September 29, 1989; and May 29, 1992

Source: Data from *Federal Reserve Bulletin*, June 1981, p. A25; December 1989, p. A24; and August 1992, p. A24.

furious pace in 1993 to lock in low interest expenses for the long haul. How should the U.S. Treasury structure its massive borrowings to take advantage of 1993's low interest rates? If you think that the government should follow corporate America's lead and borrow long-term, you score high in common sense but low in your grasp of the logic of public finance. In the spring of 1993, Treasury officials announced plans to reduce the issuance of long-term Treasury bonds and increase sales of short-term Treasury notes. Given the upward slope of the yield curve, the Treasury estimated that increased sales of short-term notes would save taxpayers money. While this logic makes sense in the short run, what about the long run? How much will taxpayers save as the yield curve shifts upward? Unlike Wall Street, perhaps government officials do not believe that interest rates will increase over the next 30 years.

THEORIES OF TERM STRUCTURE

The dominance of the upward-sloping yield curve can be simply explained by the fact that short-term securities are less risky than long-term securities (due to the greater certainty of near-term events than of future events) and therefore have lower returns than long-term securities. Although this explanation is intuitively appealing, it fails to explain why yield curves often take on different shapes such as those shown in Figure 2.5. Three theories are frequently cited to better explain the general shape of the yield curve. They are the expectations hypothesis, liquidity preference theory, and market segmentation theory.

expectations hypothesis
Theory suggesting that the yield curve reflects investor expectations about future interest rates; an increasing inflation expectation results in an upward-sloping yield curve and a decreasing inflation expectation results in a downward-sloping yield curve.

EXPECTATIONS HYPOTHESIS The **expectations hypothesis** suggests that the yield curve reflects investor expectations about future interest rates. The differences in interest-rate expectations result from differing inflationary expectations. Higher future rates of expected inflation will result in higher long-term interest rates; the opposite occurs with lower future rates. This widely accepted explanation of the term structure can be applied to the securities of any issuer. For example, take the case of U.S. Treasury securities. Thus far we have concerned ourselves solely with the risk-free asset, represented by a three-month Treasury bill. In fact, all Treasury securities are *riskless* in terms of (1) the chance that the Treasury will default on the issue by failing to make scheduled interest and principal payments and (2) the ease with which they can be liquidated for cash without experiencing a loss in value. Since it is believed to be easier to forecast inflation over shorter periods of time, the shorter-term three-month Treasury bill is considered the risk-free asset. Of course, differing inflation expectations associated with different maturities will cause nominal interest rates to vary, depending on the maturity of the security. With the addition of a maturity subscript, t, Equation 2.3 can be rewritten as

$$R_{F_t} = k^* + IP_t \tag{2.4}$$

In other words, for U.S. Treasury securities the nominal, or risk-free, rate for a given maturity varies with the inflation expectation over the term of the security.[6]

EXAMPLE

The nominal interest rate, R_{F_t}, for four maturities of U.S. Treasury securities on May 29, 1992, is given in column 1 of the following table. Assuming that the real rate of interest is 2 percent, as noted in column 2, the inflation expectation for each maturity in column 3 is found by solving Equation 2.4 for IP_t. While a 1.71 percent rate of inflation was expected over the three-month period beginning May 29, 1992, a 2.27 percent average rate of inflation was expected over the one-year period, and so on. An analysis of the inflation expectations in column 3 for May 29, 1992, suggests that at that time a general expectation of increasing inflation existed. Simply stated, the May 29, 1992, yield curve for U.S. Treasury securities shown in Figure 2.5 was upward-sloping as a result of the expectation that the rate of inflation would increase in the future.[7]

Maturity, t	Nominal interest rate, R_{F_t} (1)	Real interest rate, k^* (2)	Inflation expectation, IE_t [(1) − (2)] (3)
3 months	3.71%	2.00%	1.71%
1 year	4.27	2.00	2.27
5 years	6.70	2.00	4.70
30 years	7.89	2.00	5.89

Generally, under the expectations hypothesis an increasing inflation expectation results in an upward-sloping yield curve; a decreasing inflation expectation results in a downward-sloping yield curve; and a stable inflation expectation results in a flat yield

[6]Although Treasury securities have no risk of default or illiquidity, they do suffer from "maturity, or interest rate, risk"—the risk that interest rates will change in the future and thereby affect longer maturities more than shorter maturities. Therefore the longer the maturity of a Treasury (or any other) security, the greater its interest rate risk. The impact of interest-rate changes on bond values is discussed in Chapter 7; here we ignore this effect.

[7]It is interesting to note (in Figure 2.5) that the expectations reflected by the September 29, 1989, yield curve were not fully borne out by actual events. By May 1992, interest rates had fallen for all maturities, and the yield curve at that time had shifted downward and become upward-sloping, reflecting an expectation of increasing future interest rates and inflation rates.

curve. Although, as we'll see below, other theories exist, the observed strong relationship between inflation and interest rates (see Figure 2.4) lends significant credence to this widely accepted theory.

liquidity preference theory
Theory suggesting that for any given issuer, long-term interest rates tend to be higher than short-term rates due to the lower liquidity and higher responsiveness to general interest rate movements of longer-term securities; causes the yield curve to be upward-sloping.

LIQUIDITY PREFERENCE THEORY The tendency for yield curves to be upward-sloping can be further explained by **liquidity preference theory.** This intuitively appealing theory indicates that for a given issuer, such as the U.S. Treasury, long-term rates tend to be higher than short-term rates. This belief is based on two behavioral facts:

1. Investors perceive less risk in short-term securities than in longer-term securities and are therefore willing to accept lower yields on them. The reason is the greater liquidity and lower responsiveness to general interest rate movements of shorter-term securities.[8]
2. Borrowers are generally willing to pay a higher rate for long-term than for short-term financing. The reason is that they can lock in funds for a longer period of time and eliminate the potential adverse consequences of having to roll over short-term debt at unknown costs to obtain needed long-term financing.

In a sense, investors (lenders) tend to require a premium for tying up funds for longer periods, while borrowers are generally willing to pay a premium to obtain longer-term financing. These preferences of lenders and borrowers cause the yield curve to tend to be upward-sloping, reflecting a general liquidity preference from the lenders' viewpoint. Simply stated, ignoring other factors such as inflationary expectations, longer maturities tend to have higher interest rates than shorter maturities.

market segmentation theory
Theory suggesting that the market for loans is segmented on the basis of maturity and that the sources of supply and demand for loans within each segment determine its prevailing interest rate; the slope of the yield curve is determined by the general relationship between the prevailing rates in each segment.

MARKET SEGMENTATION THEORY Another often cited theory, **market segmentation theory,** suggests that the market for loans is segmented on the basis of maturity and that the sources of supply of and demand for loans within each segment determine its prevailing interest rate. In other words, the equilibrium between suppliers (lenders) and demanders (borrowers) of short-term loans, such as seasonal business loans, would determine prevailing short-term interest rates, while the equilibrium between suppliers and demanders of long-term loans, such as real estate loans, would determine prevailing long-term interest rates. The slope of the yield curve would therefore be determined by the general relationship between the prevailing rates in each market segment. If supply outstrips the demand for short-term loans, thereby resulting in relatively low short-term rates at a time when long-term rates are high because the demand for long-term loans is far above their supply, an upward-sloping yield curve would result. Simply stated, low rates in the short-term segment and high rates in the long-term segment cause the yield curve to be upward-sloping. The opposite occurs for high short-term rates and low long-term rates.

It is clear that all three theories of term structure have merit. From them we can conclude that at any time the slope of the yield curve is affected by (1) inflationary expectations, (2) liquidity preferences, and (3) the comparative equilibrium of supply and

[8]As is demonstrated in Chapter 7, debt instruments with longer maturities are more sensitive to changing market interest rates. For a given change in market rates, the price or value of longer-term debts will be more significantly changed (up or down) than those with shorter maturities.

demand in the short- and long-term market segments. Upward-sloping yield curves result from higher future inflation expectations, lender preferences for shorter maturity loans, and greater supply of short-term loans than of long-term loans relative to their respective demand. The opposite behaviors would, of course, result in a downward-sloping yield curve. At any point in time it is the interaction of these three forces that will determine the prevailing slope of the yield curve.

Risk premiums: Issuer and issue characteristics

So far we have considered only risk-free U.S. Treasury securities. At this point we reintroduce the risk premium and assess it in view of risky non-Treasury issues. Recall that in Equation 2.1, restated here,

$$k_1 = \underbrace{k^* + IP}_{\substack{\text{risk-free} \\ \text{rate, } R_F}} + \underbrace{RP_1}_{\substack{\text{risk} \\ \text{premium}}}$$

the nominal rate of interest for security 1, k_1, is equal to the risk-free rate, which consists of the real rate of interest (k^*) plus the inflation expectation premium *(IP)* plus the risk premium *(RP_1)*. The *risk premium* varies with specific issuer and issue characteristics; it causes similar-maturity securities[9] to have differing nominal rates of interest.

EXAMPLE

On May 29, 1992, the nominal interest rates on a number of classes of long-term securities were noted as follows.[10]

Security	Nominal interest (%)
U.S. Treasury bonds (average)	7.81
Corporate bonds (by rating):	
Aaa	8.24
Aa	8.61
A	8.80
Baa	9.11
Utility bonds (A-rated)	8.65

Since the Treasury bond would represent the risk-free long-term security, we can calculate the risk premium associated with the other securities listed by subtracting the risk-free rate, 7.81 percent, from each nominal rate (yield).

[9]To provide for the same risk-free rate of interest, $k^* + IP$, it is necessary to assume equal maturities. By doing this the inflationary expectations premium, IP, and therefore R_F, will be held constant, and the issuer and issue characteristics premium, RP, becomes the key factor differentiating the nominal rates of interest on various securities.

[10]These yields were obtained from the *Federal Reserve Bulletin,* August 1992, p. A24.

Security	Risk premium (%)
Corporate bonds (by rating):	
Aaa	8.24 − 7.81 = .43
Aa	8.61 − 7.81 = .80
A	8.80 − 7.81 = .99
Baa	9.11 − 7.81 = 1.30
Utility bonds	8.65 − 7.81 = .84

These risk premiums reflect differing issuer and issue risks. The lower-rated corporate issues—A and Baa—have higher risk premiums than those of the higher-rated corporates—Aaa and Aa—while the utility issue has a risk premium comparable to those of the Aa and A corporates. ■

The risk premium, RP_1, consists of a number of issuer- and issue-related components including default risk, maturity risk, liquidity risk, contractual provisions, and tax risk. Each of these components is briefly defined in Table 2.2. In general, the highest risk premiums and therefore the highest nominal returns are to be found in securities issued by firms with a high risk of default and in long maturities that are traded in thin markets, have unfavorable contractual provisions, and are not tax-exempt.

Risk and return

The fact that a positive relationship exists between risk and the nominal or expected return should be evident. After assessing the risk embodied in a given security, investors tend to purchase those securities that are expected to provide a return commensurate with the perceived risk. The actual return earned on the security will affect their subsequent actions—whether they sell, hold, or buy additional securities. In addition, most investors look to certain types of securities to provide a certain range of risk-return behaviors.

risk-return tradeoff
The expectation that for accepting greater risk, investors must be compensated with greater returns.

A **risk-return tradeoff** exists such that investors must be compensated for accepting greater risk with the expectation of greater returns.[11] Figure 2.6, on page 54, illustrates the typical relationship between risk and return for several popular securities. Clearly, higher returns (costs to the issuer) are expected with greater risk. Financial managers must attempt to keep revenues up and costs down, but they must also consider the risks associated with each investment and financing alternative. Decisions will ultimately rest on an analysis of the impact of risk and return on share price.

CONCEPT IN REVIEW

2-10 What is the *real rate of interest?* Differentiate it from the *nominal rate of interest* for the risk-free asset, a three-month U.S. Treasury bill.

[11]The risk-return tradeoff is discussed in detail in Chapter 6, where certain refinements are introduced to explain why investors are actually rewarded with higher returns for taking only certain types of "nondiversifiable" or inescapable risks.

TABLE 2.2

ISSUER- AND ISSUE-RELATED RISK COMPONENTS

Component	Description
Default risk	The possibility that the issuer of debt will not pay the contractual interest or principal as scheduled. The greater the uncertainty as to the borrower's ability to meet these payments, the greater the risk premium. High bond ratings reflect low default risk, and low bond ratings reflect high default risk.
Maturity risk (also called *interest rate risk*)	The fact that a given change in interest rates will cause the value of the security to change by a greater amount the longer its maturity. If interest rates on otherwise similar-risk securities suddenly rise due to a change in the money supply, the prices of long-term bonds will decline by more than the prices of short-term bonds and vice versa. The longer the time to maturity for a bond, the more significant is the effect of a movement in interest rates on the price of the security.[a]
Liquidity risk	The ease with which securities can be converted into cash without experiencing a loss in value. Generally, securities that are actively traded on major exchanges and over-the-counter are liquid. Less actively traded securities that have a thin market have low liquidity. Since a potential loss in value will result from the need to sell quickly a security with low liquidity, it would have a high liquidity risk.
Contractual provisions	Conditions that are often included in a debt agreement or a stock issue. Certain of these provisions reduce the risk of a security, whereas others may increase risk. For example, ignoring all other risks, a *freely callable bond* (one that can be retired at any time at the issuer's option) would be more risky than a bond that does not have a call feature. The issuer of the freely callable bond will have to offer a higher return to compensate the bondholder for this risk.
Tax risk	The chance that Congress will make unfavorable changes in tax laws. The greater the potential impact of a tax law change on the return of a given security, the greater its tax risk. Undesirable tax-law changes include elimination of tax exempt status,[b] limitation or elimination of tax deductions, and increases in tax rates. By reducing the tax benefits of investments the government can increase its tax revenues at the expense of investors who realize lower after-tax returns and investment values. Generally, long-term securities are subject to greater tax risk than are those that are closer to their maturity dates.

[a]A detailed discussion of the effects of interest rates on the price or value of bonds and other fixed-income securities is presented in Chapter 7.

[b]Many state and local bond issues are tax-exempt for federal income tax purposes; in addition, those issued by the state or locality in which the taxpayer resides are typically exempt from state and local taxes, respectively. Securities that are exempt from federal, state, and local taxes are often called "triple tax-exempts."

2-11 What is the *term structure of interest rates*, and how does it relate to the *yield curve*? For a given class of similar-risk securities, what does each of the following yield curves reflect about interest rates? Which form has been historically dominant?

a. Downward-sloping
b. Upward-sloping
c. Flat

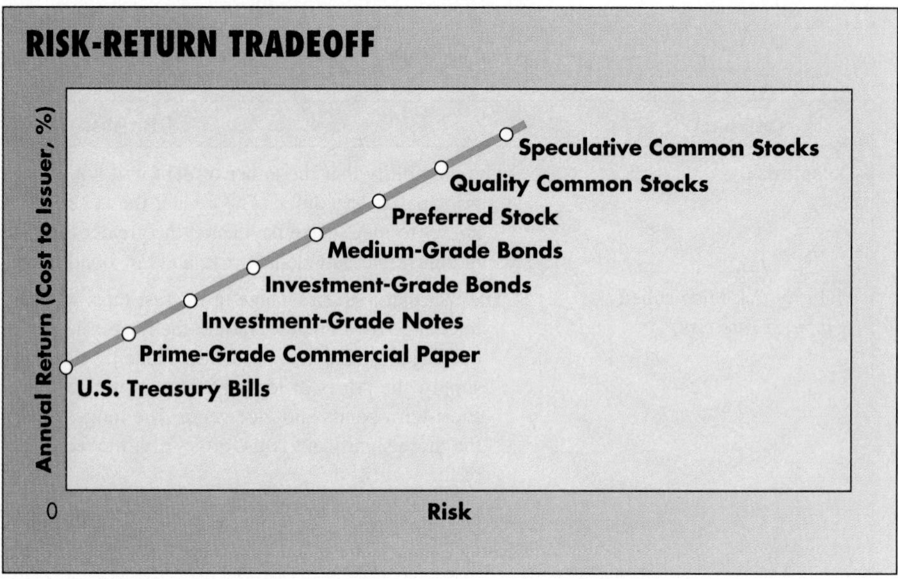

FIGURE 2.6
Risk-return profile for popular securities

2-12 Briefly describe each of the following theories that are frequently cited to explain the general shape of the yield curve.

a. Expectations hypothesis
b. Liquidity preference theory
c. Market segmentation theory

2-13 List and briefly describe the potential component risks that are embodied in the risk premium used to determine the nominal rate of interest on a risky security.

2-14 What is meant by the *risk-return trade-off?* How should this relationship affect the actions of financial managers?

Business taxation

Financial decision making relies heavily on the estimation and analysis of the cash flows associated with alternative courses of action. As a financial manager, why would you need to understand the fundamental aspects of business taxation as an important part of this process? Before reading on, spend a few moments considering this question.

BUSINESSES, LIKE INDIVIDUALS, MUST PAY TAXES ON THEIR INCOME. THE ACTUAL RATES of taxation differ depending on the form of business organization. Income can be subject to either individual or corporate income taxes. The income of sole proprietorships and partnerships is taxed as the income of the individual owners, whereas corporate income is subject to corporate taxes. Regardless of their legal form, all businesses can earn two types of income—ordinary and capital gains. Both types of income are treated similarly for tax purposes under current law. Frequent amendments in the tax code, such as the *Omnibus Budget Reconciliation Act of 1993* that is reflected in the following discussions, make it likely that the 1993 tax rates given below will change before the next edition of this text is published. Because the corporation is financially dominant in our economy, *emphasis here is given to corporate taxation.* A special type of corporate tax-reporting entity is the S corporation, which we will also discuss.

Ordinary income

ordinary income
Income earned through the sale of a firm's goods or services.

The **ordinary income** of a corporation is income earned through the sale of a firm's goods or services. Ordinary income is currently taxed subject to the rates depicted in the corporate tax rate schedule given in Table 2.3.

EXAMPLE

Webster Manufacturing, Inc., a small manufacturer of kitchen knives, has before-tax earnings of \$250,000. The tax on these earnings can be found by using the tax rate schedule given in Table 2.3:

$$\begin{aligned}\text{Total taxes due} &= \$22{,}250 + [.39 \times (\$250{,}000 - \$100{,}000)] \\ &= \$22{,}250 + (.39 \times \$150{,}000) \\ &= \$22{,}250 + \$58{,}500 = \underline{\underline{\$80{,}750}}\end{aligned}$$

The firm's total taxes on its before-tax earnings are therefore \$80,750. If the firm had earned only \$20,000 before taxes, its total tax liability would have been \$3,000 [\$0 + (.15 × \$20,000)]. ■

AVERAGE VERSUS MARGINAL TAX RATES

average tax rate
A firm's taxes divided by its taxable income.

The **average tax rate** paid on the firm's ordinary income can be calculated by dividing its taxes by its taxable income. For firms with taxable income of \$10,000,000 or

TABLE 2.3

CORPORATE TAX RATE SCHEDULE

Range of taxable income	Tax calculation: Base tax	+	(Rate × amount over base bracket)
\$ 0 to \$ 50,000	\$ 0	+	(15% × Amount over \$ 0)
50,000 to 75,000	7,500	+	(25 × Amount over 50,000)
75,000 to 100,000	13,750	+	(34 × Amount over 75,000)
100,000 to 335,000[a]	22,250	+	(39 × Amount over 100,000)
\$335,000 to 10,000,000	113,900	+	(34 × Amount over 335,000)
Over \$10,000,000[b]	3,400,000	+	(35 × Amount over 10,000,000)

[a]Because corporations with taxable income in excess of \$100,000 must increase their tax by the lesser of \$11,750 or 5 percent of the taxable income in excess of \$100,000, they will end up paying a 39 percent tax on taxable income between \$100,000 and \$335,000. The 5 percent surtax that raises the tax rate from 34 percent to 39 percent causes all corporations with taxable income between \$335,000 and \$10,000,000 to have an *average tax rate* of 34 percent, as can be seen in Table 2.4.

[b]This bracket and its associated 35 percent tax rate was created with passage of the *Omnibus Budget Reconciliation Act of 1993,* which was signed into law by President Clinton on August 10, 1993 and was retroactive to its effective date of January 1, 1993.

less, the average tax rate ranges from 15 to 34 percent, reaching 34 percent when taxable income equals or exceeds $335,000. For firms with taxable income in excess of $10,000,000, the average tax rate will range between 34 and 35 percent. The average tax rate paid by Webster Manufacturing, Inc., in our preceding example was 32.3 percent ($80,750 ÷ $250,000). Table 2.4 presents the firm's tax liability and average tax rate for various levels of pretax income; as income increases, the rate approaches and finally reaches 34 percent. It remains at that level up to $10,000,000 of taxable income, beyond which it rises toward but never reaches an average tax rate of 35 percent.

marginal tax rate
The rate at which additional income is taxed.

The **marginal tax rate** represents the rate at which additional income is taxed. In the current corporate tax structure, the marginal tax rate on income up to $50,000 is 15 percent; from $50,000 to $75,000 it is 25 percent; from $75,000 to $100,000 it is 34 percent; for income between $100,000 and $335,000 it is 39 percent; for income between $335,000 and $10,000,000 it is 34 percent; and for income in excess of $10,000,000 it is 35 percent. To simplify calculations in the text, *a fixed 40 percent tax rate is assumed to be applicable to ordinary corporate income.*

EXAMPLE

If Webster Manufacturing's earnings go up to $300,000, the marginal tax rate on the additional $50,000 of income will be 39 percent. The company will therefore have to pay additional taxes of $19,500 (.39 × $50,000). Total taxes on the $300,000, then, will be $100,250 ($80,750 + $19,500). To check this figure using the tax rate schedule in Table 2.3, we would get a total tax liability of $22,250 + [.39 × ($300,000 − $100,000)] = $22,250 + $78,000 = $100,250—the same value that is obtained by applying the marginal tax rate to the added income and adjusting the known tax liability. ■

The *average tax rate* tends to be most useful in evaluating taxes historically, and the *marginal tax rate* is more frequently used in financial decision making. For example, it is often helpful to know the average tax rate at which taxes were paid over a given period. But in making decisions the important concern is the rate at which the earnings from alternative proposals will *actually* be taxed, that is, the marginal tax rate.

TABLE 2.4

PRETAX INCOME, TAX LIABILITIES, AND AVERAGE TAX RATES

Pretax income (1)	Tax liability (2)	Average tax rate [(2) ÷ (1)] (3)
$ 50,000	$ 7,500	15.00%
75,000	13,750	18.33
100,000	22,250	22.25
200,000	61,250	30.63
335,000	113,900	34.00
500,000	170,000	34.00
1,000,000	340,000	34.00
2,500,000	850,000	34.00
10,000,000	3,400,000	34.00
12,000,000	4,100,000	34.17
25,000,000	8,650,000	34.60

With *progressive tax rates*—higher rates for higher levels of taxable income—the average tax rate is always less than or equal to the marginal tax rate. Given our focus on financial decision making, *the tax rates used throughout this text are assumed to represent marginal tax rates.*

INTEREST AND DIVIDEND INCOME

intercorporate dividends
Dividends received on common and preferred stock held in other corporations and representing less than 20 percent ownership in them; they are subject to a 70 percent exclusion for tax purposes.

In the process of determining taxable income, any *interest received* by the corporation is included as ordinary income and is therefore taxed at the firm's applicable tax rates. *Dividends received* on common and preferred stock held in other corporations and representing less than 20 percent ownership in them, on the other hand, are subject to a 70 percent exclusion for tax purposes.[12] Because of the dividend exclusion, only 30 percent of these **intercorporate dividends** are included as ordinary income. The tax law provides this exclusion to avoid *triple taxation*—the first and second corporations are taxed on income before paying the dividend, and the dividend recipient must include the dividend in his or her taxable income. This feature in effect provides some relief by eliminating most of the potential tax liability from the dividend received by the second and any subsequent corporations.

EXAMPLE

Charnes Industries, a large foundry that makes custom castings for the automobile industry, during the year just ended received $100,000 in interest on bonds it held and $100,000 in dividends on common stock it owned in other corporations. The firm is subject to a 40 percent marginal tax rate and is eligible for a 70 percent exclusion on its intercorporate dividend receipts. The after-tax income realized by Charnes from each of these sources of investment income is found as follows:

	Interest income		Dividend income
(1) Before-tax amount	$100,000		$100,000
Less: Applicable exclusion	0	(.70 × $100,000) =	70,000
Taxable amount	$100,000		$ 30,000
(2) Tax (40%)	40,000		12,000
After-tax amount [(1) − (2)]	$ 60,000		$ 88,000

As a result of the 70 percent dividend exclusion, the after-tax amount is greater for the dividend income than for the interest income. Clearly, the dividend exclusion enhances the attractiveness of stock investments relative to bond investments made by one corporation in another corporation. ■

TAX-DEDUCTIBLE EXPENSES

In calculating their taxes, corporations are allowed to deduct operating expenses, such as advertising expense, sales commissions, and bad debts as well as interest expense.

[12]The exclusion is 80 percent if the corporation owns between 20 and 80 percent of the stock in the corporation paying it dividends; 100 percent of the dividends received are excluded if it owns more than 80 percent of the corporation paying it dividends. For convenience, we are assuming here that the ownership interest in the dividend-paying corporation is less than 20 percent.

The tax deductibility of these expenses reduces their after-tax cost, making them less costly than they might at first appear. The following example illustrates the benefit of tax-deductibility.

EXAMPLE

Companies X and Y each expect in the coming year to have earnings before interest and taxes of $200,000. Company X during the year will have to pay $30,000 in interest; Company Y has no debt and therefore will have no interest expense. Calculation of the earnings after taxes for these two firms, which pay a 40 percent tax on ordinary income, are shown below.

	Company X	Company Y
Earnings before interest and taxes	$200,000	$200,000
Less: Interest expense	30,000	0
Earnings before taxes	$170,000	$200,000
Less: Taxes (40%)	68,000	80,000
Earnings after taxes	$102,000	$120,000
Difference in earnings after taxes	$18,000	

The data demonstrate that while Company X had $30,000 more interest expense than Company Y, Company X's earnings after taxes are only $18,000 less than those of Company Y ($102,000 for Company X versus $120,000 for Company Y). This difference is attributable to the fact that Company X's $30,000 interest expense deduction provided a tax savings of $12,000 ($68,000 for Company X versus $80,000 for Company Y). This amount can be calculated directly by multiplying the tax rate by the amount of interest expense (.40 × $30,000 = $12,000). Similarly, the $18,000 *after-tax cost* of the interest expense can be calculated directly by multiplying one minus the tax rate times the amount of interest expense [(1 − .40) × $30,000 = $18,000]. ■

The tax deductibility of certain expenses can be seen to reduce their actual (after-tax) cost to the profitable firm. Note that *interest is a tax-deductible expense, whereas dividends are not.* Because dividends are not tax-deductible, their after-tax cost is equal to the amount of the dividend. Thus a $30,000 cash dividend would have an after-tax cost of $30,000.

CONCEPT IN PRACTICE

Environmental Protection and the IRS

At first glance, you might not see much of a connection between corporate taxes and environmental protection, but there is a direct linkage. In 1993 the Internal Revenue Service issued new rules that required corporate taxpayers to capitalize asbestos-removal expenditures rather than expensing them against taxable income. The IRS reasoned that asbestos removal provides long-term benefits to business by reducing health risks and making certain corporate property more environmentally safe and thus more marketable. Unfortunately, by denying an immediate tax deduction for environmental cleanup costs, the IRS is inadvertently discouraging firms from undertaking projects that protect the environment. Kim Early, Chief Financial Officer at the environmental consulting firm Earth Technology Corp., suggests that allowing corporations to treat asbestos-removal costs as tax-deductible expenses would reduce their federal tax burden and increase cash flow, which would make businesses more willing to finance environmental cleanup projects.

Capital gains[13]

If a firm sells a capital asset such as stock held as an investment for more than its initial purchase price, the difference between the sale price and the purchase price is called a **capital gain.** For corporations, capital gains are added to ordinary corporate income and taxed at the regular corporate rates, with a maximum marginal tax rate of 39 percent.[14] To simplify the computations presented in later chapters of the text, as for ordinary income, *a 40 percent tax rate is assumed to be applicable to corporate capital gains.*

capital gain
The amount by which the price at which an asset was sold exceeds the asset's initial purchase price.

EXAMPLE

The Ross Company, a manufacturer of generic pharmaceuticals, has operating earnings of $500,000 and has just sold for $40,000 a capital asset that was purchased two years ago for $36,000. Since the asset was sold for more than its initial purchase price, there is a capital gain of $4,000 ($40,000 sale price − $36,000 initial purchase price). The corporation's taxable income will total $504,000 ($500,000 ordinary income plus $4,000 capital gain). Since this total is above $335,000, the capital gain will be taxed at the 34 percent rate, resulting in a tax of $1,360 (.34 × $4,000). ■

Tax loss carrybacks and carryforwards

Corporations that are experiencing operating losses may obtain tax relief by using a **tax loss carryback/carryforward.** The tax laws allow corporations to carry tax losses *back up to 3 years* and *forward for as many as 15 years.* The purpose of these laws is to provide a more equitable tax treatment for corporations that are experiencing volatile patterns of income. This feature is especially attractive for firms in cyclic businesses such as durable-goods manufacturing and construction; it effectively allows them to average out their taxes over the good and bad years. The law requires the net amount of losses to first be carried back, applying them to the earliest year allowable, and progressively moving forward until the loss has been fully recovered or the carryforward period has passed. Carrying tax losses back and then forward means using the losses to offset past or future income and recomputing the firm's taxes based on the reduced income. The firm will receive a tax refund on any carrybacks and will have reduced future tax liabilities as a result of the carryforwards.

tax loss carryback/carryforward
A tax benefit that allows corporations experiencing operating losses to carry tax losses *back up to 3 years* and *forward for as many as 15 years.*

EXAMPLE

The Regal Music Company, a growing record producer, had the pretax earnings and associated tax liabilities for the years 1987–1994 given in the table on the next page. The firm paid taxes at a 40 percent rate throughout the period. Column 1 shows these

[13]To simplify the discussion, only capital assets are considered here. The full tax treatment of gains and losses on depreciable assets is presented as part of the discussion of capital-budgeting cash flows in Chapter 8.

[14]The *Omnibus Budget Reconciliation Act of 1993* included a provision that allows the capital gains tax to be halved on gains resulting from investments made after January 1, 1993 in startup firms with a value of less than $50 million that have been held for at least 5 years. This special provision, which is intended to help startup firms, is ignored throughout this text.

amounts before carrybacks and carryforwards have been applied. In 1990 the firm had an operating loss of $500,000 as a result of a major record-industry strike. Column 2 indicates how this operating loss was carried back and then forward. By carrying the loss back three years and then forward, the firm was able to reduce its pretax earnings by $115,000 in 1987; $175,000 in 1988; $85,000 in 1989; $55,000 in 1991; and $70,000 in 1992. The total tax savings was $200,000 ($46,000 in 1987 + $70,000 in 1988 + $34,000 in 1989 + $22,000 in 1991 + $28,000 in 1992).

Year	Item	Before carryback/carryforward (1)	After carryback/carryforward (2)
1987	Pretax earnings	$115,000	$ 0
	Taxes	46,000	0
1988	Pretax earnings	175,000	0
	Taxes	70,000	0
1989	Pretax earnings	85,000	0
	Taxes	34,000	0
1990	Pretax earnings	(500,000)	0
	Taxes	0	0
1991	Pretax earnings	55,000	0
	Taxes	22,000	0
1992	Pretax earnings	80,000	10,000
	Taxes	32,000	4,000
1993	Pretax earnings	100,000	100,000
	Taxes	40,000	40,000
1994	Pretax earnings	110,000	110,000
	Taxes	44,000	44,000

As soon as the company recognized the $500,000 loss in 1990, it was able to file for a tax refund of $150,000 ($46,000 + $70,000 + $34,000) for the years 1987–1989. It then carried the portion of the loss not used to offset past income forward to be applied against positive earnings for the next two years, 1991–1992. If the firm did not have sufficient earnings in the 15-year period 1991–2005 to permit it to write off the 1990 operating loss, it would have had no further tax recourse for recovering it, since such losses can be carried forward only 15 years, and the tax benefit would be lost forever. ■

S corporation
A tax-reporting entity whose earnings are taxed not as a corporation but as the incomes of its stockholders, thus avoiding the usual *double taxation* on corporate earnings.

double taxation
Occurs when the already once-taxed earnings of a corporation are distributed as cash dividends to its stockholders, who are then taxed again on these dividends.

S corporations

Subchapter S of the Internal Revenue Code permits corporations that meet specified requirements and have 35 or fewer stockholders to elect to be taxed like partnerships. That is, income is normally taxed as direct personal income of the shareholders, regardless of whether it is actually distributed to them. The **S corporation** is a tax-reporting entity rather than a tax-paying entity. The key advantage of this form of organization is that the stockholders receive all the organizational benefits of a corporation while escaping the *double taxation* that is normally associated with the distribution of corporate earnings. (**Double taxation** results when the already once-taxed earnings of a corporation are distributed as cash dividends to stockholders, who must pay taxes on these dividends.) S corporations do not receive other tax advantages accorded regular corporations.

CONCEPTS IN REVIEW

2-15 Briefly define ordinary corporate income and capital gains, and describe the tax treatments of each. What is the *average tax rate?* What is the *marginal tax rate?*

2-16 Describe the *intercorporate dividend* exclusion. Why might this feature make corporate stock investments by one corporation in another more attractive than bond investments?

2-17 What benefit results from the tax deductibility of certain corporate expenses? Compare and contrast the tax treatment of corporate interest and dividend payments.

Summary

LG 1 Identify key participants in financial transactions and the basic activities and changing role of financial institutions. Financial institutions, such as banks, savings and loans, and mutual funds, channel the savings of various individuals, businesses, and governments into the hands of demanders of these funds. Both the Depository Institutions Deregulation and Monetary Control Act of 1980 (DIDMCA) and the S&L crisis of the late 1980s have resulted in increased competition and a blurring of the lines of distinction between various institutions. While DIDMCA seemed to usher in the one-stop financial supermarket, in late 1992 Sears and other large financial services companies began to dismantle such operations as a result of their inability to achieve the expected benefits. The role of each of the major financial institutions is briefly described in Table 2.1.

LG 2 Understand the relationship between financial institutions and markets and the role, operation of, and participants in the money market. The financial markets—the money market and the capital market—provide a forum in which suppliers and demanders of loans and investments can transact business directly. Financial institutions actively participate in the financial markets as both suppliers and demanders of funds. In the money market, marketable securities—short-term debt instruments—are traded through large New York banks, government securities dealers, or Federal Reserve banks. Individuals, businesses, governments, and financial institutions participate in the money market, which is created by the financial relationships between these suppliers and demanders of short-term funds. The Eurocurrency market is the international equivalent of the domestic money market.

LG 3 Describe the capital market including the key securities, major exchanges, and the role of the investment banker. In the capital market, long-term debt (bonds) and equity (common and preferred stock) transactions are made. The backbone of the capital market is the securities exchanges. The organized securities exchanges provide secondary markets for securities. The over-the-counter exchange, a telecommunications network linking active participants in this market, in addition to creating a secondary market for securities, is a primary market in which new public issues are sold. Important debt and equity markets—the Eurobond market and the international equity market—exist outside of the United States. The securities exchanges, in addition to creating continuous liquid markets in which firms can obtain needed financing, create efficient markets that determine and publicize security prices and allocate funds to their most productive uses. Investment bankers help firms to make both private placements and public offerings by both bearing the risk of finding buyers and advising clients.

LG 4 Discuss the fundamentals of interest rates—the real rate of interest and its relationship with the nominal or actual rate of interest (return). The flow of funds between savers (suppliers) and investors (demanders) is regulated by the interest rate or required return. In a perfect, inflation-free, certain world there would be one cost of money—the real rate of interest. The nominal or actual interest rate is the sum of the risk-free rate, which is the sum of the real rate of interest and the inflationary expectation premium, and a risk premium reflecting issuer and issue characteristics including default risk, maturity risk, liquidity risk, contractual provisions, and tax risk.

LG 5 Understand the term structure of interest rates—yield curves and the theories of term structure—and the basic relationship between risk and rates of return. For any class of similar-risk securities the term structure of interest rates reflects the relationship between the interest rate, or rate of return, and the time to maturity. Yield curves can be downward-sloping (inverted), upward-sloping (normal), or flat. Three theories—the expectations hypothesis, liquidity preference theory, and market segmentation theory—are frequently cited to explain the general shape of the yield curve. Since investors must be compensated for taking risks, they expect higher returns for greater risk. Each type of security offers a range of potential risk-return tradeoffs.

LG 6 **Describe the fundamentals of business taxation of ordinary income and capital gains, the treatment of tax losses, and S corporations.** While the income of sole proprietorships and partnerships is taxed as the income of the individual owners, corporate income is subject to corporate taxes. Corporate tax rates are applicable to both ordinary income (after deduction of allowable expenses) and capital gains. The average tax rate paid by a corporation ranges from 15 to 35 percent. (For convenience we assume a 40 percent marginal tax rate in this book.) Certain provisions in the tax code such as intercorporate dividend exclusions, tax-deductible expenses, and tax loss carrybacks and carryforwards provide corporate taxpayers with opportunities to reduce their taxes. In addition, S corporations—small corporations meeting special IRS requirements—can elect to be taxed as partnerships.

Self-test problem (Solutions in Appendix E)

ST 2-1 LG 6 **Corporate taxes** Montgomery Enterprises, Inc., had operating earnings of $280,000 for the year just ended. During the year the firm sold stock that it held in another company for $180,000, which was $30,000 above its original purchase price of $150,000, paid one year earlier.

a. What is the amount, if any, of capital gains realized during the year?

b. How much total taxable income did the firm earn during the year?

c. Use the corporate tax rate schedule given in Table 2.3 to calculate the firm's total taxes due.

d. Calculate both the *average tax rate* and the *marginal tax rate* based upon your findings above.

Problems

2-1 LG 4 **Real rate of interest** To estimate the real rate of interest, the economics division of Mountain Banks—a major bank holding company—has gathered the data summarized in the table below. Because there is a high likelihood that new tax legislation will be passed in the near future, current data as well as data reflecting the likely impact of passage of the legislation on the demand for funds are also included in the table. (*Note:* The proposed legislation will not have any impact on the supply schedule of funds. Assume a perfect world in which inflation is expected to be zero, funds suppliers and demanders have no liquidity preference, and all outcomes are certain.)

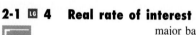

a. Draw the supply curve and the demand curve for funds using the current data. (*Note:* Unlike Figure 2.3, the functions here will not appear as straight lines.)

	Currently		With passage of tax legislation
Amount of funds supplied/demanded ($ billion)	**Interest rate required by funds suppliers (%)**	**Interest rate required by funds demanders (%)**	**Interest rate required by funds demanders (%)**
1	2	7	9
5	3	6	8
10	4	4	7
20	6	3	6
50	7	2	4
100	9	1	3

b. Using your graph, label and note the real rate of interest using current data.

c. Add to the graph drawn in **a** the new demand curve expected in the event the proposed tax legislation becomes effective.

d. What is the new real rate of interest? Compare and analyze this finding in light of your analysis in **b.**

2-2 LG **5** **Yield curve** A firm wishing to evaluate interest rate behavior has gathered yield data on five U.S. Treasury securities, each having a different maturity and all measured at the same point in time. The summarized data follows.

U.S. Treasury security	Time to maturity	Yield (%)
A	1 year	12.6
B	10 years	11.2
C	6 months	13.0
D	20 years	11.0
E	5 years	11.4

a. Draw the yield curve associated with the data given above.

b. Describe the resulting yield curve in **a,** and explain the general expectations embodied in it.

2-3 LG **4,5** **Nominal interest rates and yield curves** A recent study of inflationary expectations has disclosed that the consensus among economic forecasters yields the following average annual rates of inflation expected over the periods noted. (*Note*: Assume that the risk that future interest rate movements will affect longer maturities more than shorter maturities is zero, that is, there is no *maturity risk.*)

Period	Average annual rate of inflation (%)
3 months	5
1 year	6
5 years	8
10 years	8.5
20 years	9

a. If the real rate of interest is currently 2.5 percent, find the nominal interest rate on each of the following U.S. Treasury issues: 20-year bond, 3-month bill, 1-year note, 5-year bond.

b. If the real rate of interest suddenly drops to 2 percent without any change in inflationary expectations, what effect, if any, would this have on your answers in **a**? Explain.

c. Using your findings in **a,** draw a yield curve for U.S. Treasury securities. Describe the general shape and expectations reflected by the curve.

2-4 LG **4,5** **Nominal and real rates and yield curves** A firm wishing to evaluate interest rate behavior has gathered nominal rate of interest and inflationary expectation data on five U.S. Treasury securities, each having a different maturity and each measured at a different point in time during the year just ended. (*Note*: Assume that the risk that future interest rate movements will affect longer maturities more than shorter maturities is zero, that is, there is no *maturity risk.*) These data are summarized in the table next page.

U.S. Treasury security	Point in time	Maturity	Nominal rate of interest (%)	Inflationary expectation (%)
A	Jan. 7	1 year	12.6	9.5
B	Mar. 12	10 years	11.2	8.2
C	May 30	6 months	13.0	10.0
D	Aug. 15	20 years	11.0	8.1
E	Dec. 30	5 years	11.4	8.3

a. Using the data above, find the real rate of interest at each point in time.
b. Describe the behavior of the real rate of interest over the year. What forces might be responsible for such behavior?
c. Draw the yield curve associated with these data, assuming that the nominal rates were measured at the same point in time.
d. Describe the resulting yield curve in **c**, and explain the general expectations embodied in it.

2-5 LG 5 **Term structure of interest rates** The following yield data for a number of highest-quality corporate bonds existed at each of the three points in time noted.

Time to maturity (years)	Yield (%)		
	5 years ago	2 years ago	Today
1	9.1	14.6	9.3
3	9.2	12.8	9.8
5	9.3	12.2	10.9
10	9.5	10.9	12.6
15	9.4	10.7	12.7
20	9.3	10.5	12.9
30	9.4	10.5	13.5

a. On the same set of axes, draw the yield curve at each of the three points of time given.
b. Label each curve in **a** as to its general shape (downward-sloping, upward-sloping, flat).
c. Describe the general inflationary and interest rate expectation existing at each of the three points in time.

2-6 LG 4 **Risk-free rate and risk premiums** The real rate of interest is currently 3 percent; the inflation expectation and risk premiums for a number of securities are given below.

Security	Inflation expectation premium (%)	Risk premium (%)
A	6	3
B	9	2
C	8	2
D	5	4
E	11	1

a. Find the risk-free rate of interest, R_F, that is applicable to each security.
b. Although not noted, what factor must be the cause of the differing risk-free rates found in **a**?
c. Find the nominal rate of interest for each security.

2-7 LG 4 Risk premiums Eleanor Burns is attempting to find the nominal rate of interest for each of two securities—A and B—issued by different firms at the same point in time. She has gathered the following data:

Characteristic	Security A	Security B
Time to maturity	3 years	15 years
Inflation expectation premium	9.0%	7.0%
Risk premium for:		
Default risk	1.0%	2.0%
Maturity risk	0.5%	1.5%
Liquidity risk	1.0%	1.0%
Other risk	0.5%	1.5%

a. If the real rate of interest is currently 2 percent, find the risk-free rate of interest applicable to each security.
b. Find the total risk premium attributable to each security's issuer and issue characteristics.
c. Calculate the nominal rate of interest for each security. Compare and discuss your findings.

2-8 LG 6 Corporate taxes Tantor Supply, Inc., is a small corporation acting as the exclusive distributor of a major line of sporting goods. During 1994 the firm earned $92,500 before taxes.
a. Calculate the firm's tax liability using the corporate tax rate schedule given in Table 2.3.
b. How much is Tantor Supply's 1994 after-tax earnings?
c. What was the firm's average tax rate, based on your findings in **a**?
d. What is the firm's marginal tax rate, based on your findings in **a**?

2-9 LG 6 Average corporate tax rates Using the corporate tax rate schedule given in Table 2.3, perform the following:
a. Calculate the tax liability, after-tax earnings, and average tax rates for the following levels of corporate earnings before taxes: $10,000; $80,000; $300,000; $500,000; $1.5 million; $10 million; $15 million.
b. Plot the average tax rates (measured on the *y*-axis) against the pretax income levels (measured on the *x*-axis). What generalization can be made concerning the relationship between these variables?

2-10 LG 6 Marginal corporate tax rates Using the corporate tax rate schedule given in Table 2.3, perform the following:
a. Find the marginal tax rate for the following levels of corporate earnings before taxes: $15,000; $60,000; $90,000; $200,000; $400,000; $1 million; $20 million.
b. Plot the marginal tax rates (measured on the *y*-axis) against the pretax income levels (measured on the *x*-axis). Explain the relationship between these variables.

2-11 LG 6 Interest versus dividend income During the year just ended, Shering Distributors, Inc., had pretax earnings from operations of $490,000. In addition, during the year it received $20,000 in income from interest on bonds it held in Zig Manufacturing and received $20,000 in income from dividends on its 5 percent common stock holding in Tank Industries, Inc. Shering is in the 40 percent tax bracket and is eligible for a 70 percent dividend exclusion on its Tank Industries stock.

a. Calculate the firm's tax on its operating earnings only.
b. Find the tax and after-tax amount attributable to the interest income from the Zig Manufacturing bonds.

c. Find the tax and after-tax amount attributable to the dividend income from the Tank Industries, Inc., common stock.
d. Compare, contrast, and discuss the after-tax amounts resulting from the interest income and dividend income calculated in **b** and **c.**
e. What is the firm's total tax liability for the year?

2-12 LG 6 **Interest versus dividend expense** The Michaels Corporation expects earnings before interest and taxes to be $40,000 for this period. Assuming an ordinary tax rate of 40 percent, compute the firm's earnings after taxes and earnings available for common stockholders (earnings after taxes and preferred stock dividends, if any) under the following conditions:
a. The firm pays $10,000 in interest.
b. The firm pays $10,000 in preferred stock dividends.

2-13 LG 6 **Capital gains taxes** Perkins Manufacturing is considering the sale of two nondepreciable assets, X and Y. Asset X was purchased for $2,000 and will be sold today for $2,250. Asset Y was purchased for $30,000 and will be sold today for $35,000. The firm is subject to a 40 percent tax rate on capital gains.
a. Calculate the amount of capital gain, if any, realized on each of the assets.
b. Calculate the tax on the sale of each asset.

2-14 LG 6 **Capital gains taxes** The table below contains purchase and sale prices for the nondepreciable capital assets of a major corporation. The firm paid taxes of 40 percent on capital gains.

Asset	Purchase price	Sale price
A	$ 3,000	$ 3,400
B	12,000	12,000
C	62,000	80,000
D	41,000	45,000
E	16,500	18,000

a. Determine the amount of capital gain realized on each of the five assets.
b. Calculate the amount of tax paid on each of the assets.

2-15 LG 6 **Tax loss carryback and carryforward** The Ordway Shipbuilding Company had pretax earnings and associated tax liabilities for the period 1985 to 1994 as indicated below.

Year	Pretax earnings	Tax liability
1985	$600,000	$240,000
1986	450,000	180,000
1987	200,000	80,000
1988	300,000	120,000
1989		
1990	400,000	160,000
1991	300,000	120,000
1992	500,000	200,000
1993	600,000	240,000
1994	300,000	120,000

The firm pays taxes at a 40 percent rate. For each of the following cases, (1) calculate the pretax earnings and taxes after adjustments for any allowable carryback/carryforward for each year, and (2) indicate the *total* change in taxes, if any, resulting from these actions.

a. In 1989, Ordway had an operating loss of $1.8 million.
b. In 1989, Ordway had pretax earnings of $350,000.
c. In 1989, Ordway had an operating loss of $400,000.
d. In 1989, Ordway had pretax earnings of exactly $0.

Chapter 2 Case Determining Sandberg Manufacturing's income and taxes

Marie Clinton, an accountant for Sandberg Manufacturing, has been charged with determining the taxable income and tax liability of the company, which manufactures electronic sensors used primarily in alarm systems, for the year ended December 31, 1994. Shortly after year end, she was able to gather all of the necessary accounting data. She knew that the firm would be taxed at the prevailing corporate rates on both ordinary and capital gains income. The firm had 110,000 shares of common stock outstanding.

Marie found that the firm's 1994 revenues were derived from four sources:

1. Sales revenue:	$2,350,000
2. Interest income:	$ 16,000
3. Dividend income from Sandberg's 15 percent ownership in Southern Switch Corporation:	$ 45,000
4. Capital gains realized on the sales of certain corporate assets:	$ 80,000

Costs and expenditures during the year included:

1. Product costs and operating expenses:	$2,100,000
2. Interest expense:	$ 130,000
3. Total dividends paid:	$ 80,000

Required

a. Find the firm's earnings before taxes for the year ended December 31, 1994.
b. Use your findings in **a** along with the corporate tax rate schedule in Table 2.3 to find the firm's tax liability for calendar year 1994.
c. Find Sandberg's (1) average tax rate and (2) marginal tax rate based on its 1994 income and taxes.
d. Use the marginal tax rate found in **c** to determine the after-tax cost of the firm's 1994 (1) interest expense and (2) dividend payments.
e. Calculate Sandberg's (1) earnings after taxes and (2) earnings per share (EPS) for the year ended December 31, 1994.
f. What were the firm's 1994 retained earnings?

chapter 3

Financial statements, depreciation, and cash flow

LEARNING GOALS

Describe the purpose and basic components of the stockholders' report.

Review the format and key components of the income statement and the balance sheet and interpret these statements.

Identify the purpose and basic content of the statement of retained earnings, the statement of cash flows, and the procedures for consolidating international financial statements.

Understand the effect of depreciation and other noncash charges on the firm's cash flows.

Determine the depreciable value of an asset, its depreciable life, and the amount of depreciation allowed each year for tax purposes using the modified accelerated cost recovery system (MACRS).

Analyze the firm's cash flows and develop and interpret the statement of cash flows.

Understanding financial statements is fundamental to managing a business and knowing how it operates. Financial statements provide an intuitive glimpse of a company, a starting point for further analysis. They are also the basis for business plans and internal budgets.

Most companies have different models and levels of financial statements. The statements of a retail store look quite different from those of a high technology company like QUALCOMM, an international leader in digital wireless communications systems. We have detailed internal statements used by managers to operate their specific business unit, summarized versions of these statements for upper management, audited statements for shareholder reports, and tax statements for the Internal Revenue Service. The company's business structure also affects the financial statements. Classification of businesses for internal reporting may differ from those for external reporting. Managers may break business units down further into product lines.

A company's orientation toward cash flow or profit and loss (P&L) depends on its age and life cycle. Like most young companies, QUALCOMM was very cash oriented at first; now we're more P&L oriented. Once a company goes public, shareholders are more interested in performance, as well as the future possibilities or risks, measured by reported earnings.

At QUALCOMM our general managers must understand cash flow concepts to see trends in cash utilization and generation. From a financial management perspective, I want them to be aware that, although they may be profitable, they should also bring in cash by properly managing inventory and receivables levels. They must look at both the short-term profit perspective and cash generation.

In the beginning, we required tremendous amounts of cash for working capital and research and development (R&D) before we could get our products to market. Our cash flow was mostly negative. In fact, when we sold our first public common stock offering, we had to rework our financial models because they only managed negative numbers! Once we had a successful product, cash flow turned positive and our management focus took a more strategic approach—where do we want to take the business—rather than operating on a day-to-day survival basis.

Our financial statements are quite complex. For example, analysts might question our high R&D expenditures and ask about the results to date. The chairman's letter in the annual report would specifically address this issue. The annual report becomes a marketing tool that informs existing and future shareholders about our accomplishments, successes, future direction, and the status of new technology. It must be easy to follow, with financials that are easy to explain in the chairman's letter and footnotes.

Financial statements provide an intuitive glimpse of a company.

Every company is different, so good managers must be adaptable. The first company I worked for was profitable, with positive cash flow. QUALCOMM struggled for survival until we had a viable product to sell. You need to be intuitive; textbook models and equations will only take you so far. What you learn on the job are basic survival strategies. You must understand management's philosophy and the corporation's strategic objectives to communicate your ideas appropriately. For example, you need to gather the relevant data to develop financial statements that are useful for driving the business. You can create a five-page financial statement, but if management wants it done in two pages in a different presentation style, nobody will look at it.

Dee Coffman, a founder, director and Chief Financial Officer of QUALCOMM, was employed by LINKABIT and M/A-COM LINKABIT from 1970 until 1985 and served as Controller from 1976 until starting QUALCOMM in 1985. She received her B.A. in Business from San Diego State University.

The stockholders' report

A stockholders' report summarizes and documents a publicly held corporation's financial activities over the year. Who receives these reports? What types of information do you think they typically include? Why are they important? Spend a few moments trying to answer these questions before reading ahead.

generally accepted accounting principles (GAAP)
The practice and procedure guidelines used to prepare and maintain financial records and reports; authorized by the *Financial Accounting Standards Board (FASB).*

Financial Accounting Standards Board (FASB)
The accounting profession's rule-setting body, which authorizes *generally accepted accounting principles (GAAP).*

publicly held corporations
Corporations whose stock is traded on either an organized securities exchange or the over-the-counter exchange and/or those with more than $5 million in assets and 500 or more stockholders.

Securities and Exchange Commission (SEC)
The federal regulatory body that governs the sale and listing of securities.

stockholders' report
Annual report required of publicly held corporations that summarizes and documents for stockholders the firm's financial activities during the past year.

letter to stockholders
Typically the first element of the annual stockholders' report and the primary communication from management to the firm's owners.

EVERY CORPORATION HAS MANY AND VARIED USES FOR THE STANDARDIZED RECORDS and reports of its financial activities. Periodically, reports must be prepared for regulators, creditors (lenders), owners, and management. Regulators, such as federal and state securities commissions, enforce the proper and accurate disclosure of corporate financial data. Creditors use financial data to evaluate the firm's ability to meet scheduled debt payments. Owners use corporate financial data in assessing the firm's financial condition and in deciding whether to buy, sell, or hold its stock. Management is concerned with regulatory compliance, satisfying creditors and owners, and monitoring the firm's performance.

The guidelines used to prepare and maintain financial records and reports are known as **generally accepted accounting principles (GAAP).** These accounting practices and procedures are authorized by the accounting profession's rule-setting body, the **Financial Accounting Standards Board (FASB). Publicly held corporations** are those whose stock is traded on either an organized securities exchange or the over-the-counter exchange and/or those with more than $5 million in assets and 500 or more stockholders.[1] These corporations are required by the **Securities and Exchange Commission (SEC)**—the federal regulatory body that governs the sale and listing of securities—and by state securities commissions to provide their stockholders with an annual **stockholders' report.** This report, which summarizes and documents the firm's financial activities during the past year, begins with a letter to the stockholders from the firm's president and/or chairman of the board followed by the key financial statements. In addition, other information about the firm is often included.

The letter to stockholders

The **letter to stockholders** is the primary communication from management to the firm's owners. Typically the first element of the annual stockholders' report, it describes the events that are considered to have had the greatest impact on the firm during the year. In addition, the letter generally discusses management philosophy, strategies, and actions as well as plans for the coming year and their anticipated effects on the firm's financial condition. Figure 3.1 includes the chairman's letter to the stockholders of Eaton Corporation, a major (1992 sales of nearly $3.9 billion) manufacturer of truck components, engine components, automotive and appliance controls, commercial and military controls, industrial controls and power distribution equipment, hy-

[1]Although the Securities and Exchange Commission (SEC) does not have an official definition of "publicly held," these financial parameters mark the cutoff point it uses to require informational reporting, regardless of whether the firm publicly sells its securities. Firms that do not meet these requirements are commonly called "closely held" firms.

TO OUR SHAREHOLDERS

Since the mid-1980s, our strategy has been to fortify and invigorate our primary businesses. In 1992 we sharpened that strategic focus by dedicating Eaton to continuous improvement in the three critical areas of *quality, productivity* and *growth.*

These are prominent concepts in the company's mission and values, which constitute the theme of this annual report.

We are encouraging Eaton's 38,000 employees to contribute their brightest ideas and best efforts to improve quality, increase productivity and maximize growth, and we are empowering them to put their ideas to work. Their progress—and therefore Eaton's—is evident in the improved 1992 earnings from continuous operations. . . .

Productivity and Quality

Last year, we adopted a comprehensive, total cost method of measuring our productivity and set a corporate goal of real productivity improvements of at least 4 percent a year. In 1992, productivity improved 4½ percent; our intent in 1993 is to exceed that figure.

We have embraced total quality management across the corporation as a means of improving productivity, building our businesses and increasing customer satisfaction. Our customers consistently give us high marks. For instance, in 1992 Eaton was ranked highest—by nearly a three-to-one margin—in quality awards received when compared to other major automotive industry suppliers.

We reported last year that 79 percent of our sales came from products that are number 1 or number 2 in the markets they serve. During the prolonged economic downturn, that number remained steady—a testament to the quality of our products and the emphasis on giving our customers total satisfaction.

External Growth

As part of the continuing effort to build our primary businesses, we made three acquisitions in 1992 which are expected to increase Eaton's annual sales by $150 million. . . .

Investments for Internal Growth

To fortify Eaton's excellent market positions, we invested more than $500 million in capital improvements in the last three years. In 1992, these investments totaled $170 million. We expect to invest an additional $500 million over the next two years on equipment and other capital improvements for new product introductions and market expansion.

New and improved products are Eaton's lifeblood. In the past five years, our investments in research, development and engineering have totaled nearly $1.2 billion, including $141 million in R&D expenses and $115 million for manufacturing and product engineering in 1992. We expect to spend up to $1.5 billion in this area during the next five years. . . .

Market Review

Most of our markets have not yet recovered from the recession, but there were two noteworthy exceptions in North America: Heavy truck production jumped to 139,000 units in 1992, more than 30 percent above the 106,000 units a year earlier. Order backlogs indicate strength in this market will continue. The popularity of light trucks, vans and sport utility vehicles—as an alternative to cars—has enabled this market to grow rapidly.

Sales in our automotive and appliance controls business increased 37 percent, much of which is attributed to the acquisitions mentioned earlier. Higher sales in our base markets were partially offset by weakened demand in Europe in the last half of the year.

The strong recovery in the residential market for our power distribution products was offset by continued contractions in the military budget and commercial aircraft industry. In addition, we saw weakened demand in the North American automated materials handling market, as well as significant softening of the semiconductor equipment market. In the fourth quarter, however, sales of specialty controls increased 18 percent, fueled by the highest quarterly shipments of the year in our semiconductor equipment business.

In 1993, we expect improvements in most of our North American markets except for commercial aircraft, military and non-residential construction markets, which account for less than 6 percent of total sales. The economies of western European countries and Japan remain weak, but their recovery usually lags that of the United States. We are committed to offsetting these adverse economic conditions with cost savings that will at least maintain profits from these regions.

Financial Strength

Our balance sheet remains strong. Working capital rose 36 percent from $487 million at the end of 1991 to $663 million at the end of 1992. During that same period, as sales grew by $488 million, or 14 percent, inventories and receivables were essentially flat. At year-end 1992, current assets were double current liabilities. Our financial strength is a formidable asset that positions us to make strategic acquisitions to nourish current businesses and build long-term profitability.

In 1993, we expect a rebounding U.S. economy to give us the sales volumes to produce stronger operating results. We appreciate the continued support of our shareholders, and hope this letter demonstrates that we're pursuing strategies designed to reward long-term holders of Eaton shares.

William E. Butler

William E. Butler
Chairman and Chief Executive Officer
February 26, 1993

FIGURE 3.1
Eaton Corporation's 1992 chairman's letter to stockholders
Source: Eaton Corporation, *1992 Annual Report,* pp. 2 & 3.

draulics and general products, and semi-conductor equipment, from its 1992 stockholders' report. The letter discusses the firm's productivity, quality, growth, markets, and financial strength during its fiscal year ended December 31, 1992 and cites general expectations with regard to 1993.

Financial statements

Following the letter to stockholders will be, at minimum, the four key financial statements required by the Securities and Exchange Commission (SEC). Those statements are (1) the income statement, (2) the balance sheet, (3) the statement of retained earnings, and (4) the statement of cash flows.[2] The annual corporate report must contain these statements for at least the three most recent years of operation (two years for balance sheets). Following the financial statements are *Notes to Financial Statements*—an important source of information on the accounting policies, procedures, calculations, and transactions underlying entries in the financial statements. Historical summaries of key operating statistics and ratios for the past five to ten years are also commonly included with the financial statements. (Financial ratios are discussed in Chapter 4.)

CONCEPT IN PRACTICE

Accounting Changes Can Have Widespread Effects

You might think that the purpose of financial statements is to report objectively the financial condition of corporations, not to influence management decisions about what particular assets and liabilities a firm should hold. But the accounting principles authorized by the FASB often have a significant influence on the asset and liability choices that managers make. Consider FAS 107, a recent modification to GAAP that requires firms to report the market value of financial assets and liabilities in their year-end financial statements. This rule change means that financial institutions must post gains and losses in the market value of financial instruments to capital, which means that their net worth could fluctuate dramatically over time.

To minimize this added volatility, many banks such as Terre Haute First National Bank, North Texas Bancshares, and Grundy National Bank in Iowa plan to shorten the average maturity of their investment portfolios and purchase more securities that offer little interest rate risk. This change in security purchases will have another, unintended impact on the banks—it will reduce the interest income obtained from their security portfolios.

Other features

The stockholders' reports of most widely held corporations also include discussions of the firm's activities, new products, research and development, and the like. Most companies view the annual report not only as a requirement, but also as an important vehicle for influencing owners' perceptions of the company and its future out-

[2]While these statement titles are consistently used throughout this text, it is important to recognize that in practice, companies frequently use different statement titles. For example, General Electric uses "Statement of Earnings" rather than "Income Statement" and "Statement of Financial Position" rather than "Balance Sheet"; Bristol Myers Squibb uses "Statement of Earnings and Retained Earnings" rather than "Income Statement"; and Pfizer uses "Statement of Shareholders' Equity" rather than "Statement of Retained Earnings."

look. Because of the information it contains, the stockholders' report may affect expected risk, return, stock price, and ultimately the viability of the firm.

CONCEPTS IN REVIEW

3-1 What are *generally accepted accounting principles (GAAP)*? Who authorizes GAAP? What role does the *Securities and Exchange Commission (SEC)* play in the financial reporting activities of corporations?

3-2 Describe the basic contents, including the key financial statements, of the stockholders' reports of publicly held corporations.

Basic financial statements

The four basic financial statements are the income statement, the balance sheet, the statement of retained earnings, and the statement of cash flows. Drawing on your background in accounting, before reading on, spend a few moments briefly describing the type and importance of information contained within each of these statements.

OUR CHIEF CONCERN IN THIS SECTION IS TO UNDERSTAND THE FACTUAL INFORMATION presented in the four required corporate financial statements. The financial statements from the 1994 stockholders' report of a hypothetical firm, the Baker Corporation, are presented and briefly discussed below. In addition, the procedures for consolidating international financial statements are briefly described.

Income statement

income statement
Provides a financial summary of the firm's operating results during a specified period.

The **income statement** provides a financial summary of the firm's operating results during a specified period. Most common are income statements covering a one-year period ending at a specified date, ordinarily December 31 of the calendar year. (Many large firms, however, operate on a 12-month financial cycle, or *fiscal year,* that ends at a time other than December 31.) In addition, monthly statements are typically prepared for use by management, and quarterly statements must be made available to the stockholders of publicly held corporations.

Table 3.1 presents Baker Corporation's income statement for the year ended December 31, 1994. The statement begins with *sales revenue*—the total dollar amount of sales during the period—from which the *cost of goods sold* is deducted. The resulting *gross profits* of $700,000 represents the amount remaining to satisfy operating, financial, and tax costs after meeting the costs of producing or purchasing the products sold. Next *operating expenses,* which include sales expense, general and administrative expense, and depreciation expense, are deducted from gross profits.[3] The resulting *operating profits* of $370,000 represent the profit earned from producing and selling products; this amount does not consider financial and tax costs. (Operating profit is often

[3]Depreciation expense can be, and frequently is, included in manufacturing costs—cost of goods sold—to calculate gross profits. Depreciation is shown as an expense in this text to isolate its impact on cash flows.

TABLE 3.1

BAKER CORPORATION INCOME STATEMENT ($000) FOR THE YEAR ENDED DECEMBER 31, 1994

Sales revenue		$1,700
Less: Cost of goods sold		1,000
Gross profits		$ 700
Less: Operating expenses		
Selling expense	$ 80	
General and administrative expense	150	
Depreciation expense	100	
Total operating expense		330
Operating profits		$ 370
Less: Interest expense[a]		70
Net profits before taxes		$ 300
Less: Taxes (rate = 40%)		120
Net profits after taxes		$ 180
Less: Preferred stock dividends		10
Earnings available for common stockholders		$ 170
Earnings per share (EPS)[b]		$ 1.70

[a]Interest expense includes the interest component of the annual financial lease payment as specified by the Financial Accounting Standards Board (FASB).

[b]Calculated by dividing the earnings available for common stockholders by the number of shares of common stock outstanding ($170,000 ÷ 100,000 shares = $1.70 per share).

called *earnings before interest and taxes,* or *EBIT.*) Next, the financial cost—interest expense—is subtracted from operating profits to find *net profits (or earnings) before taxes.* After subtracting $70,000 in 1994 interest, Baker Corporation had $300,000 of net profits before taxes.

After the appropriate tax rates have been applied to before-tax profits, taxes are calculated and deducted to determine *net profits (or earnings) after taxes.* Baker Corporation's net profits after taxes for 1994 were $180,000. Next, any preferred stock dividends must be subtracted from net profits after taxes to arrive at *earnings available for common stockholders.* This is the amount earned by the firm on behalf of the common stockholders during the period. Dividing earnings available for common stockholders by the number of shares of common stock outstanding results in *earnings per share (EPS).* EPS represents the amount earned during the period on each outstanding share of common stock. In 1994 Baker Corporation earned $170,000 for its common stockholders, which represents $1.70 for each outstanding share. (The earnings per share amount rarely equals the amount, if any, of common stock dividends paid to shareholders.)

Balance sheet

balance sheet
Summary statement of the firm's financial position at a given point in time.

The **balance sheet** presents a summary statement of the firm's financial position at a given point in time. The statement balances the firm's *assets* (what it owns) against its financing, which can be either *debt* (what it owes) or *equity* (what was provided by owners). Baker Corporation's balance sheets on December 31 of 1994 and 1993, are

current assets

Short-term assets, expected to be converted into cash within one year or less.

current liabilities

Short-term liabilities, expected to be converted into cash within one year or less.

presented in Table 3.2. They show a variety of asset, liability (debt), and equity accounts. An important distinction is made between short-term and long-term assets and liabilities. The **current assets** and **current liabilities** are *short-term* assets and liabilities. This means that they are expected to be converted into cash within one year or less. All other assets and liabilities, along with stockholders' equity, which is assumed to have an infinite life, are considered *long-term,* or *fixed,* since they are expected to remain on the firm's books for one year or more.

A few points about Baker Corporation's balance sheets need to be highlighted. As is customary, the assets are listed beginning with the most liquid down to the least liq-

TABLE 3.2

BAKER CORPORATION BALANCE SHEETS ($000)

	December 31	
Assets	**1994**	**1993**
Current assets		
Cash	$ 400	$ 300
Marketable securities	600	200
Accounts receivable	400	500
Inventories	600	900
Total current assets	$2,000	$1,900
Gross fixed assets (at cost)		
Land and buildings	$1,200	$1,050
Machinery and equipment	850	800
Furniture and fixtures	300	220
Vehicles	100	80
Other (includes certain leases)	50	50
Total gross fixed assets (at cost)	$2,500	$2,200
Less: Accumulated depreciation	1,300	1,200
Net fixed assets	$1,200	$1,000
Total assets	$3,200	$2,900
Liabilities and stockholders' equity		
Current liabilities		
Accounts payable	$ 700	$ 500
Notes payable	600	700
Accruals	100	200
Total current liabilities	$1,400	$1,400
Long-term debt	$ 600	$ 400
Total liabilities	$2,000	$1,800
Stockholders' equity		
Preferred stock	$ 100	$ 100
Common stock—$1.20 par, 100,000 shares outstanding in 1994 and 1993	120	120
Paid-in capital in excess of par on common stock	380	380
Retained earnings	600	500
Total stockholders' equity	$1,200	$1,100
Total liabilities and stockholders' equity	$3,200	$2,900

uid. Current assets therefore precede fixed assets. *Marketable securities* represent very liquid short-term investments, such as U.S. Treasury bills or certificates of deposit, held by the firm. Because of their highly liquid nature, marketable securities are frequently viewed as a form of cash. *Accounts receivable* represent the total monies owed the firm by its customers on credit sales made to them. Inventories include raw materials, work-in-process (partially finished goods), and finished goods held by the firm. The entry for *gross fixed assets* is the original cost of all fixed (long-term) assets owned by the firm.[4] *Net fixed assets* represent the difference between gross fixed assets and *accumulated depreciation*—the total expense recorded for the depreciation of fixed assets. (The net value of fixed assets is called their *book value.*)

Like assets, the liabilities and equity accounts are listed on the balance sheet from short-term to long-term. Current liabilities include: *accounts payable,* amounts owed for credit purchases by the firm; *notes payable,* outstanding short-term loans, typically from commercial banks; and *accruals,* amounts owed for services for which a bill may not or will not be received. (Examples of accruals include taxes due the government and wages due employees.) *Long-term debt* represents debt for which payment is not due in the current year. *Stockholders' equity* represents the owners' claims on the firm. The *preferred stock* entry shows the historic proceeds from the sale of preferred stock ($100,000 for Baker Corporation). Next, the amount paid in by the original purchasers of common stock is shown by two entries—common stock and paid-in capital in excess of par on common stock. The *common stock* entry is the **par value** of common stock, an arbitrarily assigned per-share value used primarily for accounting purposes. **Paid-in capital in excess of par** represents the amount of proceeds in excess of the par value received from the original sale of common stock. The sum of the common stock and paid-in capital accounts divided by the number of shares outstanding represents the original price per share received by the firm on a single issue of common stock. Baker Corporation therefore received $5.00 per share [($120,000 par + $380,000 paid-in capital in excess of par) ÷ 100,000 shares] from the sale of its common stock. Finally, **retained earnings** represent the cumulative total of all earnings, net of dividends, that have been retained and reinvested in the firm since its inception. It is important to recognize that retained earnings *are not cash* but rather have been utilized to finance the firm's assets.

par value
Per-share value arbitrarily assigned to an issue of common stock primarily for accounting purposes.

paid-in capital in excess of par
The amount of proceeds in excess of the par value received from the original sale of common stock.

retained earnings
The cumulative total of all earnings, net of dividends, that have been retained and reinvested in the firm since its inception.

Baker Corporation's balance sheets in Table 3.2 show that the firm's total assets increased from $2,900,000 in 1993 to $3,200,000 in 1994. The $300,000 increase was due primarily to the $200,000 increase in net fixed assets. The asset increase in turn appears to have been financed primarily by an increase of $200,000 in long-term debt. Better insight into these changes can be derived from the statement of cash flows, which we will discuss shortly.

Statement of retained earnings

statement of retained earnings
Reconciles the net income earned during a given year and any cash dividends paid with the change in retained earnings between the start and end of that year.

The **statement of retained earnings** reconciles the net income earned during a given year, and any cash dividends paid, with the change in retained earnings between the start and end of that year. Table 3.3 presents this statement for Baker Corporation for the year ended December 31, 1994. A review of the statement shows that the com-

[4]For convenience the term *fixed assets* is used throughout this text to refer to what, in a strict accounting sense, is captioned "property, plant, and equipment." This simplification of terminology permits certain financial concepts to be more easily developed.

TABLE 3.3

BAKER CORPORATION STATEMENT OF RETAINED EARNINGS ($000) FOR THE YEAR ENDED DECEMBER 31, 1994

Retained earnings balance (January 1, 1994)		$500
Plus: Net profits after taxes (for 1994)		180
Less: Cash dividends (paid during 1994)		
Preferred stock	($10)	
Common stock	(70)	
Total dividends paid		(80)
Retained earnings balance (December 31, 1994)		$600

pany began the year with $500,000 in retained earnings and had net profits after taxes of $180,000, from which it paid a total of $80,000 in dividends, resulting in year-end retained earnings of $600,000. Thus the net increase for Baker Corporation was $100,000 ($180,000 net profits after taxes minus $80,000 in dividends) during 1994.

Statement of cash flows

statement of cash flows
Provides a summary of the firm's operating, investment, and financing cash flows and reconciles them with changes in its cash and marketable securities during the period of concern.

The **statement of cash flows** provides a summary of the cash flows over the period of concern, typically the year just ended. The statement, which is sometimes called a "source and use statement," provides insight into the firm's operating, investment, and financing cash flows and reconciles them with changes in its cash and marketable securities during the period of concern. Baker Corporation's statement of cash flows for the year ended December 31, 1994, is presented in Table 3.10 on page 91. However, before we look at the preparation of this statement, it is helpful to understand various aspects of depreciation.

CONCEPT IN PRACTICE

Public Accounting Can Be a Nasty Profession

The job of public accountants is to ensure that the corporations that they audit report their financial performance and condition fairly and conservatively to the public. When things go wrong, as they did at Youngstown, Ohio–based Phar-Mor in 1992, the accountants often get the blame. After taking a $350 million charge against earnings for embezzling corporate funds and management fraud, Phar-Mor filed for bankruptcy. The wounded retailer filed suit against its auditor, Coopers & Lybrand, alleging that the accountants were negligent in failing to uncover massive management fraud at the firm. Fighting back, Coopers & Lybrand mounted the first-ever countersuit of a client by an audit firm, claiming that Phar-Mor's senior managers failed to control their employees and deliberately lied to the auditors.

Consolidating international financial statements

So far, this chapter has discussed financial statements involving only one currency, the U.S. dollar. How do we interpret the financial statements of companies that have significant operations in other countries and cash flows denominated in one or more foreign currencies? As it happens, the issue of how to handle consolidation of a company's foreign and domestic financial statements has bedeviled the accounting profession for many years, and the current policy is described in **Financial Accounting Standards Board (FASB) Standard No. 52.** This ruling by the policy-setting body of the accounting profession mandates that U.S.-based companies must translate their foreign-currency-denominated assets and liabilities into dollars (for consolidation with the parent company's financial statements) using a technique called the current rate method.

Financial Accounting Standards Board (FASB) Standard No. 52
Ruling by FASB—the policy-setting body of the U.S. accounting profession—that mandates that U.S.-based companies must translate their foreign-currency-denominated assets and liabilities into dollars using the *current rate (translation) method.*

Under the **current rate (translation) method,** all of a U.S. parent company's foreign currency assets and liabilities are converted into dollar values using the exchange rate prevailing at the fiscal year ending date (the current rate). Income statement items are treated similarly, although they can also be translated by using an average exchange rate for the accounting period in question. Equity accounts, on the other hand, are translated into dollars by using the exchange rate that prevailed when the parent's equity investment was made (the historical rate). Retained earnings are adjusted to reflect each year's operating profits or losses, but this account does not reflect gains or losses resulting from currency movements. Instead, translation gains and losses are accumulated in an equity reserve account on the parent company's books labeled **cumulative translation adjustment.** Translation gains increase this account balance, and translation losses decrease it and can even result in a negative balance. However, the gains and losses are not "realized" (run through the income statement and consolidated to retained earnings) until the parent company sells or shuts down its foreign subsidiary or its assets. While international accounting rules and managerial issues will be discussed in more detail in Chapter 20, an example can be used to briefly describe how translation gains and losses occur.

current rate (translation) method
Technique used by U.S.-based companies to translate their foreign-currency-denominated assets and liabilities into dollars (for consolidation with the parent company's financial statements).

EXAMPLE

Suppose that an American company owns a subsidiary operating in Germany. (The German currency is Deutsche marks, noted DM.) Suppose the subsidiary has total assets worth DM 10,000,000, total liabilities of DM 5,000,000, and DM 5,000,000 in equity. Suppose further that the exchange rate at the beginning of the fiscal year was DM 2.00/US$, which also equals the reciprocal of this, US$.50/DM. Therefore at the beginning of the period the dollar value of the subsidiary's assets, liabilities, and equity is $5,000,000, $2,500,000, and $2,500,000, respectively.

cumulative translation adjustment
Equity reserve account on parent company's books in which translation gains and losses are accumulated.

Now suppose that by the end of the fiscal year the German mark had depreciated to a value of DM 2.50/US$, or US$.40/DM. When the subsidiary's accounts are then translated into dollars, the assets will have declined in value by $1,000,000 to $4,000,000 (DM 10,000,000 × US$.40/DM). The subsidiary's liabilities will also have declined in dollar value, but only by $500,000 to $2,000,000 (DM 5,000,000 × US$.40/DM), and the dollar value of the equity accounts remains unchanged at $2,500,000. Since the parent company experienced a decline in the dollar value of its foreign assets that exceeded the decline in the dollar value of its liabilities, it has experienced a translation loss of $500,000 ($1,000,000 decline in asset value minus $500,000 decline in the value of liabilities). This $500,000 translation loss is recorded as a deficit in the parent company's cumulative translation adjustment account. ■

CONCEPTS IN REVIEW

3-3 What basic information is contained in each of the following financial statements? Briefly describe each.

a. Income statement
b. Balance sheet
c. Statement of retained earnings

3-4 What role does *Financial Accounting Standards Board (FASB) Standard No. 52* play in the consolidation of a company's foreign and domestic financial statements? What is the *current rate (translation) method* and the *cumulative translation adjustment*?

Depreciation

Depreciation is an important accounting concept that is used, in effect, to match the historic costs of fixed assets with the revenues they generate. Why would depreciation be so important to financial managers, who are primarily concerned with cash flows? Take a few moments to consider this question before reading ahead.

depreciation
The systematic charging of a portion of the costs of fixed assets against annual revenues over time.

modified accelerated cost recovery system (MACRS)
System used to determine the depreciation of assets for tax purposes.

noncash charges
Expenses deducted on the income statement but do not involve an actual outlay of cash during the period.

Business firms are permitted to systematically charge a portion of the costs of fixed assets against annual revenues. This allocation of historic cost over time is called **depreciation.** For tax purposes the depreciation of business assets is regulated by the Internal Revenue Code, which experienced major changes under the *Tax Reform Act of 1986.* Because the objectives of financial reporting are sometimes different from those of tax legislation, a firm often will use different depreciation methods for financial reporting than those required for tax purposes. (An observer should therefore not jump to the conclusion that a company is attempting to "cook the books" simply because it keeps two different sets of records.) Tax laws are used to accomplish economic goals such as providing incentives for business investment in certain types of assets, whereas the objectives of financial reporting are of course quite different.

Depreciation for tax purposes is determined by using the **modified accelerated cost recovery system (MACRS),**[5] whereas for financial reporting purposes a variety of depreciation methods are available. Before discussing the methods of depreciating an asset, we must understand the relationship between depreciation and cash flows, the depreciable value of an asset, and the depreciable life of an asset.

Depreciation and cash flows

The financial manager is concerned with cash flows rather than net profits as reported on the income statement. To adjust the income statement to show *cash flow from operations,* all noncash charges must be *added back* to the firm's *net profits after taxes.* **Noncash charges** are expenses that are deducted on the income statement but do not involve an actual outlay of cash during the period. Depreciation, amortization, and depletion allowances are examples. Since depreciation expenses are the most common

[5]This system, which was first established in 1981 with passage of the *Economic Recovery Tax Act,* was initially called the "accelerated cost recovery system (ACRS)." As a result of modifications to this system in the Tax Reform Act of 1986, it is now commonly called the "modified accelerated cost recovery system (MACRS)." Although some people continue to refer to this system as "ACRS," we correctly call it "MACRS" throughout this text.

noncash charges, we shall focus on their treatment; amortization and depletion charges are treated in a similar fashion.

The general rule for adjusting net profits after taxes by adding back all noncash charges is expressed as follows:

$$\text{Cash flow from operations} = \text{net profits after taxes} + \text{noncash charges} \quad (3.1)$$

Applying Equation 3.1 to the 1994 income statement for Baker Corporation presented in Table 3.1 yields a cash flow from operations of $280,000 due to the noncash nature of depreciation:

Net profits after taxes	$180,000
Plus: Depreciation expense	100,000
Cash flow from operations	$280,000

(This value is only approximate, since not all sales are made for cash and not all expenses are paid when they are incurred.)

Depreciation and other noncash charges shield the firm from taxes by lowering taxable income. Some people do not define depreciation as a source of funds; however, it is a source of funds in the sense that it represents a "nonuse" of funds. Table 3.4 shows the Baker Corporation's income statement prepared on a cash basis as an illustration of how depreciation shields income and acts as a nonuse of funds. Ignoring depreciation, except in determining the firm's taxes, results in cash flow from operations of $280,000—the value obtained above. Adjustment of the firm's net profits after taxes by adding back noncash charges such as depreciation will be used on many occasions in this text to estimate cash flow.

Depreciable value of an asset

Under the basic MACRS procedures the depreciable value of an asset (the amount to be depreciated) is its *full* cost including outlays for installation.[6] No adjustment is required for expected salvage value.

EXAMPLE

Baker Corporation acquired a new machine at a cost of $38,000, with installation costs of $2,000. Regardless of its expected salvage value, the depreciable value of the machine is $40,000: ($38,000 cost + $2,000 installation cost). ■

Depreciable life of an asset

depreciable life
Time period over which an asset is depreciated.

The time period over which an asset is depreciated—its **depreciable life**—can significantly affect the pattern of cash flows. The shorter the depreciable life, the more quickly the cash flow created by the depreciation write-off will be received. Given the financial manager's preference for faster receipt of cash flows, a shorter depreciable life is preferred to a longer one. However, the firm must abide by certain Internal Revenue Service (IRS) requirements for determining depreciable life. These MACRS stan-

[6]Land values are *not* depreciable. Therefore to determine the depreciable value of real estate, the value of the land is subtracted from the cost of the real estate. In other words, only buildings and other improvements are depreciable.

TABLE 3.4

BAKER CORPORATION INCOME STATEMENT CALCULATED ON A CASH BASIS ($000) FOR THE YEAR ENDED DECEMBER 31, 1994

Sales revenue		$1,700
Less: Cost of goods sold		1,000
Gross profits		$ 700
Less: Operating expenses		
Selling expense	$ 80	
General and administrative expense	150	
Depreciation expense (noncash charge)	0	
Total operating expense		230
Operating profits		$ 470
Less: Interest expense		70
Net profits before taxes		$ 400
Less: Taxes (from Table 3.1)		120
Cash flow from operations		$ 280

recovery period
The appropriate depreciable life of a particular asset as determined by MACRS.

dards, which apply to both new and used assets, require the taxpayer to use as an asset's depreciable life the appropriate MACRS **recovery period,** except in the case of certain assets depreciated under the *alternative depreciation system.*[7] There are six MACRS recovery periods—3, 5, 7, 10, 15, and 20 years—excluding real estate. As is customary, the property classes (excluding real estate) are referred to, in accordance with their recovery periods, as 3-year, 5-year, 7-year, 10-year, 15-year, and 20-year property. The first four property classes—those routinely used by business—are defined in Table 3.5.

TABLE 3.5

FIRST FOUR PROPERTY CLASSES UNDER MACRS

Property class (recovery period)	Definition
3-year	Research and experiment equipment and certain special tools.
5-year	Computers, typewriters, copiers, duplicating equipment, cars, light-duty trucks, qualified technological equipment, and similar assets.
7-year	Office furniture, fixtures, most manufacturing equipment, railroad track, and single-purpose agricultural and horticultural structures.
10-year	Equipment used in petroleum refining or in the manufacture of tobacco products and certain food products.

[7]For convenience, the depreciation of assets under the *alternative depreciation system* is ignored in this text.

CONCEPT IN PRACTICE

Depreciation Can Be a Complicated Topic

If you think that learning all the various depreciation rules and procedures is tough on students, consider the plight of financial managers at large corporations with several million dollars invested in depreciable assets. Differences in depreciation methods for tax and book accounting records, different recovery periods, and annual revisions in the depreciation section of the federal tax code mean that managers must track the depreciation schedule separately for each asset that the firm owns. Moreover, depreciation expenses influence corporate taxes and cash flow, so managers need the ability to display and compare how various depreciation methods will affect other key financial performance variables.

What's the solution? A special-purpose analytical tool called PRO*FAS, the fixed-asset-management software package offered by Decision Support Technology, Inc. PRO*FAS provides a number of analytical features, including the ability to compare every possible variation in depreciation methods and tax calculations and the ability to share information with general-ledger-accounting software.

Depreciation methods

For *tax purposes,* using MACRS recovery periods, assets in the first four property classes are depreciated by the double-declining balance (200%) method using the half-year convention and switching to straight-line when advantageous. Although tables of depreciation percentages are not provided by law, the *approximate percentages* (i.e., rounded to nearest whole percent) written off each year for the first four property classes are given in Table 3.6. Rather than using the percentages in the table, the firm can either use straight-line depreciation over the asset's recovery period with the half-year convention or use the alternative depreciation system. For purposes of this text we will use the MACRS depreciation percentages given in Table 3.6, since they generally provide for the fastest write-off and therefore the best cash flow effects for the profitable firm.

Because MACRS requires use of the half-year convention, assets are assumed to be acquired in the middle of the year, and therefore only one-half of the first year's depreciation is recovered in the first year. As a result, the final half-year of depreciation is recovered in the year immediately following the asset's stated recovery period. In Table 3.6 the depreciation percentages for an n-year class asset are given for $n + 1$ years. For example, a five-year asset is depreciated over six recovery years. (*Note:* The percentages in Table 3.6 have been rounded to the nearest whole percentage to simplify calculations while retaining realism.)

For *financial reporting purposes* a variety of depreciation methods—straight-line, double-declining balance, and sum-of-the-years'-digits[8]—can be used. Since primary concern in managerial finance centers on cash flows, *only tax depreciation methods will be utilized throughout this textbook.* The application of the tax depreciation percentages given in Table 3.6 can be demonstrated by a simple example.

[8]For a review of these depreciation methods as well as other aspects of financial reporting, see any recently published financial accounting text.

TABLE 3.6

ROUNDED DEPRECIATION PERCENTAGES BY RECOVERY YEAR USING MACRS FOR FIRST FOUR PROPERTY CLASSES

	Percentage by recovery year[a]			
Recovery year	**3-year**	**5-year**	**7-year**	**10-year**
1	33%	20%	14%	10%
2	45	32	25	18
3	15	19	18	14
4	7	12	12	12
5		12	9	9
6		5	9	8
7			9	7
8			4	6
9				6
10				6
11				4
Totals	100%	100%	100%	100%

[a]These percentages have been rounded to the nearest whole percent to simplify calculations while retaining realism. To calculate the *actual* depreciation for tax purposes, be sure to apply the actual unrounded percentages or directly apply double-declining balance (200%) depreciation using the half-year convention.

EXAMPLE

The Baker Corporation acquired, for an installed cost of $40,000, a machine having a recovery period of five years. Using the applicable percentages from Table 3.6, the depreciation in each year is calculated as follows:

Year	Cost (1)	Percentages (from Table 3.6) (2)	Depreciation [(1) × (2)] (3)
1	$40,000	20%	$ 8,000
2	40,000	32	12,800
3	40,000	19	7,600
4	40,000	12	4,800
5	40,000	12	4,800
6	40,000	5	2,000
Totals		100%	$40,000

Column 3 shows that the full cost of the asset is written off over six recovery years. ■

CONCEPTS IN REVIEW

3-5 In what sense does depreciation act as cash inflow? How can a firm's after-tax profits be adjusted to determine cash flow from operations?

3-6 Briefly describe the first four modified accelerated cost recovery system (MACRS) property classes and recovery periods. Explain how the depreciation percentages are determined by using the MACRS recovery periods.

Analyzing the firm's cash flow

The statement of cash flows—one of the firm's four required financial statements—provides a snapshot of the firm's cash flows over a given period of time. As a financial manager, how might this statement prove useful to you? Before reading ahead, spend a few moments responding to this question.

THE *STATEMENT OF CASH FLOWS,* BRIEFLY DESCRIBED EARLIER, SUMMARIZES THE FIRM'S cash flow over a given period of time. Because it can be used to capture historic cash flow, the statement is developed in this section. First, however, we need to discuss cash flow through the firm and the classification of sources and uses.

The firm's cash flows

operating flows
Cash flows directly related to production and sale of the firm's products and services.

investment flows
Cash flows associated with purchase and sale of both fixed assets and business interests.

financing flows
Cash flows that result from debt and equity-financing transactions; includes incurrence and repayment of debt, cash inflow from the sale of stock, and cash outflows to repurchase stock or pay cash dividends.

Figure 3.2 illustrates the firm's cash flows. Note that both cash and marketable securities, which, because of their highly liquid nature, are considered the same as cash, represent a reservoir of liquidity that is increased by cash inflows and decreased by cash outflows. Also note that the firm's cash flows have been divided into (1) operating flows, (2) investment flows, and (3) financing flows. The **operating flows** are cash flows—inflows and outflows—directly related to production and sale of the firm's products and services. These flows capture the income statement and current account transactions (excluding notes payable) occurring during the period. **Investment flows** are cash flows associated with purchase and sale of both fixed assets and business interests. Clearly, purchase transactions would result in cash outflows, whereas sales transactions would generate cash inflows. The **financing flows** result from debt and equity financing transactions. Borrowing and repaying either short-term debt (notes payable) or long-term debt would result in a corresponding cash inflow or outflow. Similarly, the sale of stock would result in a cash inflow, whereas the repurchase of stock or payment of cash dividends would result in a financing outflow. In combination the firm's operating, investment, and financing cash flows during a given period will increase, decrease, or leave unchanged the firm's cash and marketable securities balances.

Classifying sources and uses of cash

The statement of cash flows in effect summarizes the sources and uses of cash during a given period. (Table 3.7 classifies the basic sources and uses of cash.) For example, if a firm's accounts payable increased by $1,000 during the year, this change would be a *source of cash.* If the firm's inventory increased by $2,500, the change would be a *use of cash,* meaning that an additional $2,500 was tied up in inventory.

A few additional points should be made with respect to the classification scheme in Table 3.7:

1. A *decrease* in an asset, such as the firm's cash balance, is a *source of cash flow* because cash that has been tied up in the asset is released and can be used for some other purpose, such as repaying a loan. On the other hand, an *increase* in the firm's cash balance is a *use of cash flow,* since additional cash is being tied up in the firm's cash balance.

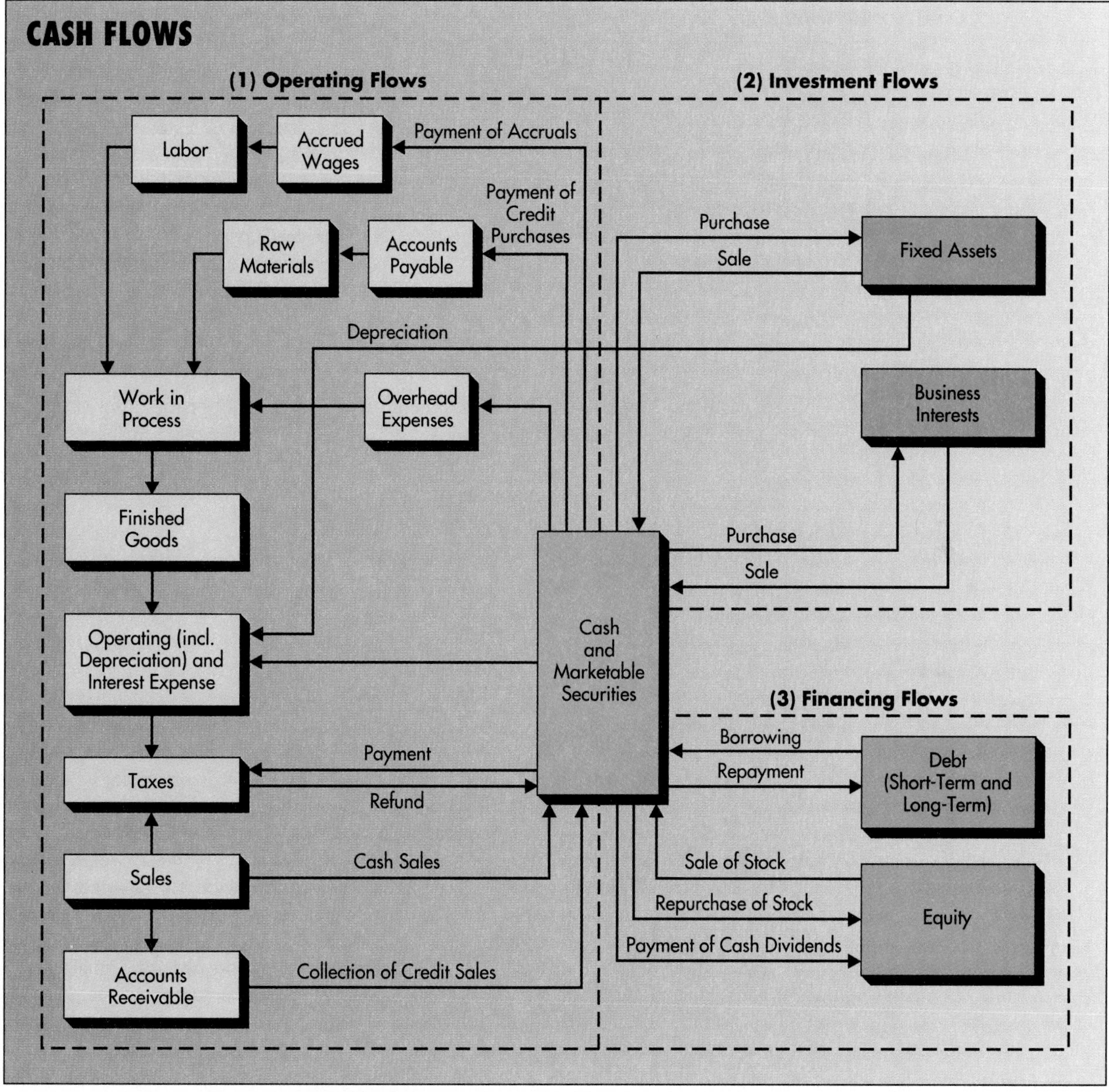

FIGURE 3.2
The firm's cash flows

2. Earlier, Equation 3.1 and the related discussion explained why depreciation and other noncash charges are considered cash inflows, or sources of cash. Adding noncash charges back to the firm's net profits after taxes gives cash flow from operations:

$$\text{Cash flow from operations} = \text{net profits after taxes} + \text{noncash charges}$$

Note that a firm can have a *net loss* (negative net profits after taxes) and still have positive cash flow from operations when noncash charges during the period are

TABLE 3.7

THE SOURCES AND USES OF CASH

Sources	Uses
Decrease in any asset	Increase in any asset
Increase in any liability	Decrease in any liability
Net profits after taxes	Net loss
Depreciation and other noncash charges	Dividends paid
Sale of stock	Repurchase or retirement of stock

greater than the net loss. In the statement of cash flows, net profits after taxes (or net losses) and noncash charges are therefore treated as separate entries.

3. Because depreciation is treated as a separate source of cash, only *gross* rather than *net* changes in fixed assets appear on the statement of cash flows. This treatment avoids the potential double counting of depreciation.
4. Direct entries of changes in retained earnings are not included on the statement of cash flows; instead, entries for items that affect retained earnings appear as net profits or losses after taxes and dividends paid.

CONCEPT IN PRACTICE

Negative Cash Flow Spells the End at Momenta

Cash flow is the lifeblood of any young corporation, but it is particularly important for missionary start-ups, in which a group of managers tries to create a new company and a new industry simultaneously. For example, Momenta Corp. was founded in 1989 to develop, manufacture, and sell pen-based computers, which are notebook-sized PCs that can convert handwritten words and numbers into typed text or data. Momenta set out to create a new market worth an estimated $3.8 billion, yet by August 1991 the firm was bankrupt.

What went wrong? In early 1991, Momenta was spending about $2 million each month, but the firm had no marketable product to generate sales revenue. In 1991 alone, Momenta spent $7 million on advertising and promotion, yet the young firm never produced products that appealed to PC buyers. Fewer than 1,000 Momenta machines were ever sold, and venture capitalists were unwilling to kick in any additional cash until this small trickle of sales turned to a flood of new orders.

Developing the statement of cash flows

The statement of cash flows can be developed in five steps: (1, 2, and 3) prepare a statement of sources and uses of cash, (4) obtain needed income statement data, and (5) properly classify and present relevant data from Steps 1 through 4. With this five-step procedure we can use the financial statements for Baker Corporation presented in Tables 3.1 and 3.2 to demonstrate the preparation of its December 31, 1994, statement of cash flows.

STATEMENT OF SOURCES AND USES OF CASH (STEPS 1, 2, AND 3)

The first three steps in the statement of cash flow preparation process guide the preparation of the statement of sources and uses of cash.

Step 1 Calculate the balance sheet changes in assets, liabilities, and stockholders' equity over the period of concern. (*Note:* Calculate the *gross* fixed asset change for the fixed asset account along with any change in accumulated depreciation.)

Step 2 Using the classification scheme in Table 3.7, classify each change calculated in Step 1 as either a source (S) or a use (U). (*Note:* An increase in accumulated depreciation would be classified as a source, whereas a decrease in accumulated depreciation would be a use. Changes in stockholders' equity accounts are classified in the same way as changes in liabilities—increases are sources, and decreases are uses.)

Step 3 Separately sum all sources and all uses found in Steps 1 and 2. If this statement is prepared correctly, *total sources should equal total uses.*

Application of these first three steps to prepare a statement of sources and uses of cash is demonstrated in the following example.

EXAMPLE

The Baker Corporation's balance sheets in Table 3.2 can be used to develop its statement of sources and uses of cash for the year ended December 31, 1994.

Step 1 The key balance sheet entries from Baker Corporation's balance sheet in Table 3.2 are listed in a stacked format in Table 3.8. Column 1 lists the account name, and columns 2 and 3 give the December 31, 1994 and 1993 values, respectively, for each account. In column 4 the change in the balance sheet account between December 31, 1993, and December 31, 1994, is calculated. Note that for fixed assets, both the gross fixed asset change of +\$300,000 and the accumulated depreciation change of +\$100,000 are calculated.

Step 2 Based on the classification scheme from Table 3.7 and recognizing that changes in stockholders' equity are classified in the same way as changes in liabilities, each change in column 4 of Table 3.8 is listed as either a source in column 5 or a use in column 6.

Step 3 The sources and uses in columns 5 and 6, respectively, of Table 3.8 are totaled at the bottom. Since total sources of \$1,000,000 equal total uses of \$1,000,000, it appears that the statement has been correctly prepared. ■

OBTAINING INCOME STATEMENT DATA (STEP 4)

Step 4 involves obtaining three important inputs to the statement of cash flows from an income statement for the period of concern. These inputs are (1) net profits after taxes, (2) depreciation and any other noncash charges, and (3) cash dividends paid on both preferred and common stock.

TABLE 3.8

BAKER CORPORATION STATEMENT OF SOURCES AND USES OF CASH ($000) FOR THE YEAR ENDED DECEMBER 31, 1994

	Account balance December 31 (from Table 3.2)		Change	Classification	
Account (1)	1994 (2)	1993 (3)	[(2) − (3)] (4)	Source (5)	Use (6)
Assets					
Cash	$ 400	$ 300	+$100		$ 100
Marketable securities	600	200	+ 400		400
Accounts receivable	400	500	− 100	$ 100	
Inventories	600	900	− 300	300	
Gross fixed assets	2,500	2,200	+ 300		300
Accumulated depreciation[a]	1,300	1,200	+ 100	100	
Liabilities					
Accounts payable	700	500	+ 200	200	
Notes payable	600	700	− 100		100
Accruals	100	200	− 100		100
Long-term debt	600	400	+ 200	200	
Stockholders' equity					
Preferred stock	100	100	0		
Common stock at par	120	120	0		
Paid-in capital in excess of par	380	380	0		
Retained earnings	600	500	+ 100	100	
			Totals	$1,000	$1,000

[a]Because accumulated depreciation is treated as a deduction from gross fixed assets, an increase in it is classified as a source; any decrease would be classified as a use.

Step 4 Net profits after taxes and depreciation typically can be taken directly from the income statement; dividends may have to be calculated by using the following equation:

$$\text{Dividends} = \text{net profits after taxes} - \text{change in retained earnings} \quad (3.2)$$

The value of net profits after taxes can be obtained from the income statement, and the change in retained earnings can be found in the statement of sources and uses of cash or can be calculated by using the beginning- and end-of-period balance sheets. The dividend value could be obtained directly from the statement of retained earnings, if available.

EXAMPLE

Baker Corporation's net profits after taxes, depreciation, and dividends can be found in its financial statements.

Step 4 The Baker Corporation's net profits after taxes and depreciation for 1994 can be found on its income statement presented in Table 3.1:

Net profits after taxes ($000)	$180
Depreciation ($000)	$100

Substituting the net profits after taxes value of $180,000 and the increase in retained earnings of $100,000 from Baker Corporation's statement of sources and uses of cash for the year ended December 31, 1994, given in Table 3.8, into Equation 3.2, we find the 1994 cash dividends to be

$$\text{Dividends (\$000)} = \$180 - \$100 = \$80$$

Note that the $80,000 of dividends calculated above could have been drawn directly from Baker's statement of retained earnings, given in Table 3.3. ■

CLASSIFYING AND PRESENTING RELEVANT DATA (STEP 5)

The relevant data from the statement of sources and uses of cash (prepared in Steps 1, 2, and 3) along with the net profit, depreciation, and dividend data obtained (in Step 4) from the income statement can be used to prepare the statement of cash flows.

Step 5 Classify relevant data into one of three categories:

1. Cash flow from operating activities
2. Cash flow from investment activities
3. Cash flow from financing activities

These three categories are consistent with the operating, investment, and financing cash flows depicted in Figure 3.2. Table 3.9 lists the items that would be included in each category on the statement of cash flows. In addition the source of each data item is noted.

Relevant data should be listed in a fashion consistent with the order of the categories and data items given in Table 3.9. All sources as well as net profits after taxes and depreciation would be treated as positive values—cash inflows—while all uses, any losses, and dividends paid would be treated as negative values—cash outflows. The items in each category—operating, investment, and financing—should be totaled, and these three totals should be added to get the "net increase (decrease) in cash and marketable securities" for the period. As a check, this value should reconcile with the actual change in cash and marketable securities for the year, which can be obtained from either the beginning- and end-of-period balance sheets or the statement of sources and uses of cash for the period.

EXAMPLE

The relevant data developed for the Baker Corporation for 1994 can be combined by using the procedure described above to create its statement of cash flows.

Step 5 Classifying and listing the relevant data from earlier steps in a fashion consistent with Table 3.9 results in Baker Corporation's Statement of Cash Flows, presented in Table 3.10. On the basis of this statement, the firm experienced a $500,000 increase in cash and marketable securities during 1994. Looking at Baker Corporation's December 31, 1993 and 1994 balance sheets in Table 3.2 or its statement of sources and uses of cash in Table 3.8, we can see that

TABLE 3.9

CATEGORIES AND SOURCES OF DATA INCLUDED IN THE STATEMENT OF CASH FLOWS

Categories and data items	Data source S/U = Statement of sources and uses of cash I/S = Income statement
Cash Flow from Operating Activities	
Net profits (losses) after taxes	I/S
Depreciation and other noncash charges	I/S
Changes in all current assets other than cash and marketable securities	S/U
Changes in all current liabilities other than notes payable	S/U
Cash Flow from Investment Activities	
Changes in gross fixed assets	S/U
Changes in business interests	S/U
Cash Flow from Financing Activities	
Changes in notes payable	S/U
Changes in long-term debt	S/U
Changes in stockholders' equity other than retained earnings	S/U
Dividends paid	I/S

the firm's cash increased by $100,000 and its marketable securities increased by $400,000 between December 31, 1993, and December 31, 1994. The $500,000 net increase in cash and marketable securities from the statement of cash flows therefore reconciles with the total change of $500,000 in these accounts during 1994. The statement is therefore believed to have been correctly prepared. ■

Interpreting the statement

The statement of cash flows allows the financial manager and other interested parties to analyze the firm's past and possibly future cash flow. The manager should pay special attention to both the major categories of cash flow and the individual items of cash inflow and outflow to assess whether any developments have occurred that are contrary to the company's financial policies. In addition, the statement can be used to evaluate the fulfillment of projected goals. Specific links between cash inflows and outflows cannot be made by using this statement, but it can be used to isolate inefficiencies. For example, increases in accounts receivable and inventories resulting in major cash outflows may signal credit or inventory problems, respectively.

In addition, the financial manager can prepare and analyze a statement of cash flows developed from projected, or pro forma, financial statements. This approach can be used to determine whether planned actions are desirable in view of the resulting cash flows.

TABLE 3.10

BAKER CORPORATION STATEMENT OF CASH FLOWS ($000) FOR THE YEAR ENDED DECEMBER 31, 1994

Cash Flow from Operating Activities		
Net profits after taxes	$ 180	
Depreciation	100	
Decrease in accounts receivable	100	
Decrease in inventories	300	
Increase in accounts payable	200	
Decrease in accruals	(100)[a]	
Cash provided by operating activities		$780
Cash Flow from Investment Activities		
Increase in gross fixed assets	($300)	
Changes in business interests	0	
Cash used for investment activities		(300)
Cash Flow from Financing Activities		
Decrease in notes payable	($100)	
Increase in long-term debts	200	
Changes in stockholders' equity[b]	0	
Dividends paid	(80)	
Cash provided by financing activities		20
Net increase in cash and marketable securities		$500

[a]As is customary, parentheses are used to denote a negative number, which in this case is a cash outflow.

[b]Consistent with this data item in Table 3.9, retained earnings are excluded here, since their change is actually reflected in the combination of the net profits after taxes and dividend entries.

EXAMPLE

Analysis of Baker Corporation's statement of cash flows in Table 3.10 does not seem to indicate the existence of any major problems for the company. Its $780,000 of cash provided by operating activities plus the $20,000 provided by financing activities was used to invest an additional $300,000 in fixed assets and to increase cash and marketable securities by $500,000. The individual items of cash inflow and outflow seem to be distributed in a fashion consistent with prudent financial management. The firm seems to be growing, since (1) less than half of its earnings ($80,000 out of $180,000) was paid to owners as dividends and (2) gross fixed assets increased by three times the amount of historic cost written off through depreciation expense ($300,000 increase in gross fixed assets versus $100,000 in depreciation expense). Major cash inflows were realized by decreasing inventories and increasing accounts payable. The major outflow of cash was to increase cash and marketable securities by $500,000 and thereby improve liquidity. Other inflows and outflows of the Baker Corporation tend to support the fact that the firm was well managed financially during the period. *An understanding of the basic financial principles presented throughout this text is a prerequisite to the effective interpretation of the statement of cash flows.* ■

CONCEPTS IN REVIEW

3-7 Describe the overall cash flow through the firm in terms of (a) operating flows, (b) investment flows, and (c) financing flows.

3-8 List and describe *sources of cash* and *uses of cash*. Discuss why a decrease in cash is a source and an increase in cash is a use.

3-9 Describe the procedure (the first three steps for developing the statement of cash flows) used to develop the statement of sources and uses of cash. How are changes in fixed assets and accumulated depreciation treated on this statement?

3-10 What three inputs to the statement of cash flows are typically obtained (in Step 4) from an income statement for the period of concern? Explain how the income statement and statement of sources and uses of cash can be used to determine dividends for the period of concern. What other methods can be used to obtain the value of dividends?

3-11 Describe the general format of the statement of cash flows, and review the final step (Step 5) involved in preparing the statement. How can the accuracy of the final statement balance, "net increase (decrease) in cash and marketable securities," be conveniently verified?

3-12 How is the statement of cash flows interpreted and used by the financial manager and other interested parties?

Summary

LG **1 Describe the purpose and basic components of the stockholders' report.** The annual stockholders' report, which publicly traded corporations are required to provide to their stockholders, summarizes and documents the firm's financial activities during the past year. It includes, in addition to the letter to stockholders and various subjective and factual information, four key financial statements: (1) the income statement, (2) the balance sheet, (3) the statement of retained earnings, and (4) the statement of cash flows. Notes describing the technical aspects of the financial statements follow them.

LG **2 Review the format and key components of the income statement and the balance sheet and interpret these statements.** The income statement summarizes operating results during the period of concern, subtracting costs, expenses, and taxes from sales revenue to find the period's profits. The balance sheet summarizes the firm's financial position at a given point in time by balancing the firm's assets (what it owns) against its financing, which can be either debt (what it owes) or equity (what was provided by the owners). It makes an important distinction between short-term (current) and long-term assets and liabilities.

LG **3 Identify the purpose and basic content of the statement of retained earnings, the statement of cash flows, and the procedures for consolidating international financial statements.** The statement of retained earnings reconciles the net income earned during a given year and any cash dividends paid with the change in retained earnings between the start and end of that year. The statement of cash flows provides a summary of the cash flows over the period of concern, typically the year just ended. The statement provides insights into the firm's operating, investment, and financing flows and reconciles them with changes in its cash and marketable securities during the period of concern. Financial statements of companies that have operations in other countries where their cash flows are denominated in one or more foreign currency follow Financial Accounting Standards Board (FASB) Standard No. 52, which requires use of the current rate (translation) method to translate foreign-currency-denominated assets and liabilities into dollars.

LG **4 Understand the effect of depreciation and other noncash charges on the firm's cash flows.** Depreciation, or the allocation of historic cost, is the most common type of noncash expenditure made by business. To estimate cash flow from operations, depreciation and any other noncash charges are added back to net profits after taxes. Because they shield the firm from taxes by lowering taxable income without an actual outflow of cash, noncash charges act as a source of funds to the firm.

LG **5 Determine the depreciable value of an asset, its depreciable life, and the amount of depreciation allowed each year for tax purposes using the modified accelerated cost recovery system (MACRS).** The depreciable value of an asset and its depreciable life are determined by using the modified accelerated cost recovery system (MACRS) standards set out in the federal tax code. MACRS groups assets (excluding real estate) into six property classes based on length of recovery period—3, 5, 7, 10, 15, and 20 years—and can be applied over the appropriate period by using a schedule of yearly depreciation percentages for each period.

LG **6 Analyze the firm's cash flows and develop and interpret the statement of cash flows.** The cash flow of a firm over a given period of time can be summarized in the statement of cash flows, which is broken into operating flows, investment flows, and financing flows. The statement can be developed in five steps. The first three steps guide the preparation of a statement of sources and uses of cash; the fourth step involves obtaining needed income statement data; and the fifth and final step is to properly classify and present the relevant data from Steps 1 through 4. The "net increase (decrease) in cash and marketable securities" found in the statement should reconcile with the actual change in cash and marketable securities during the period. Interpretation of the statement of cash flows requires an understanding of basic financial principles and involves evaluation of both the major categories of cash flow and the individual items of cash inflow and outflow.

Self-test problem (Solutions in Appendix E)

ST 3-1 LG 4,5 Depreciation and cash flow A firm expects to have earnings before depreciation and taxes (EBDT) of $160,000 in each of the next six years. It is considering the purchase of an asset costing $140,000, requiring $10,000 in installation costs, and having a recovery period of five years.

a. Calculate the annual depreciation for the asset purchase using the MACRS depreciation percentages in Table 3.6 on page 83.

b. Calculate the annual operating cash flows for each of the six years. Assume that the new asset is the firm's only depreciable asset and that it is subject to a 40 percent ordinary tax rate.

c. Compare and discuss your findings in **a** and **b.**

Problems

3-1 LG 2,3 Reviewing basic financial statements The income statement for the year ended December 31, 1994, the balance sheets for December 31, 1994 and 1993, and the statement of retained earnings for the year ended December 31, 1994, for Technica, Inc., are given on pages 93 and 94. Briefly discuss the form and informational content of each of these statements.

Income statement
Technica, Inc.
for the year ended December 31, 1994

Sales revenue		$600,000
Less: Cost of goods sold		460,000
Gross profits		$140,000
Less: Operating expenses		
General and administrative expense	$30,000	
Depreciation expense	30,000	
Total operating expense		60,000
Operating profits		$ 80,000
Less: Interest expense		10,000
Net profits before taxes		$ 70,000
Less: Taxes		27,100
Earnings available for common stockholders		$ 42,900
Earnings per share (EPS)		$2.15

Balance sheets **Technica, Inc.**		
	December 31,	
Assets	**1994**	**1993**
Cash	$ 15,000	$ 16,000
Marketable securities	7,200	8,000
Accounts receivable	34,100	42,200
Inventories	82,000	50,000
Total current assets	$138,300	$116,200
Land and buildings	$150,000	$150,000
Machinery and equipment	200,000	190,000
Furniture and fixtures	54,000	50,000
Other	11,000	10,000
Total gross fixed assets	$415,000	$400,000
Less: Accumulated depreciation	145,000	115,000
Net fixed assets	$270,000	$285,000
Total assets	$408,300	$401,200
Liabilities and stockholders' equity		
Accounts payable	$ 57,000	$ 49,000
Notes payable	13,000	16,000
Accruals	5,000	6,000
Total current liabilities	$ 75,000	$ 71,000
Long-term debt	$150,000	$160,000
Stockholders' equity		
Common stock equity (shares outstanding: 19,500 in 1994 and 20,000 in 1993)	$110,200	$120,000
Retained earnings	73,100	50,200
Total stockholders' equity	$183,300	$170,200
Total liabilities and stockholders' equity	$408,300	$401,200

Statement of retained earnings **Technica, Inc.** **for the year ended December 31, 1994**	
Retained earnings balance (January 1, 1994)	$50,200
Plus: Net profits after taxes (for 1994)	42,900
Less: Cash dividends (paid during 1994)	(20,000)
Retained earnings balance (December 31, 1994)	$73,100

3-2 LG 2 Financial statement account identification Mark each of the accounts listed in the table on the following page as follows:

a. In column (1), indicate in which statement—income statement (IS) or balance sheet (BS)—the account belongs.

b. In column (2), indicate whether the account is a current asset (CA), current liability (CL), expense (E), fixed asset (FA), long-term debt (LTD), revenue (R), or stockholders' equity (SE).

Account name	(1) Statement	(2) Type of account
Accounts payable	_____	_____
Accounts receivable	_____	_____
Accruals	_____	_____
Accumulated depreciation	_____	_____
Administrative expense	_____	_____
Buildings	_____	_____
Cash	_____	_____
Common stock (at par)	_____	_____
Cost of goods sold	_____	_____
Depreciation	_____	_____
Equipment	_____	_____
General expense	_____	_____
Interest expense	_____	_____
Inventories	_____	_____
Land	_____	_____
Long-term debts	_____	_____
Machinery	_____	_____
Marketable securities	_____	_____
Notes payable	_____	_____
Operating expense	_____	_____
Paid-in capital in excess of par	_____	_____
Preferred stock	_____	_____
Preferred stock dividends	_____	_____
Retained earnings	_____	_____
Sales revenue	_____	_____
Selling expense	_____	_____
Taxes	_____	_____
Vehicles	_____	_____

3-3 LG 2 **Income statement preparation** Use the *appropriate items* from the following list to prepare in good form Perry Corporation's income statement for the year ended December 31, 1994.

Item	Values ($000) at or for year ended December 31, 1994
Accounts receivable	$350
Accumulated depreciation	205
Cost of goods sold	285
Depreciation expense	55
General and administrative expense	60
Interest expense	25
Preferred stock dividends	10
Sales revenue	525
Selling expense	35
Stockholders' equity	265
Taxes	rate = 40%

3-4 LG 2 Income statement preparation Cathy Chen, a self-employed Certified Public Accountant (CPA), on December 31, 1994, completed her first full year in business. During the year she billed $180,000 in business. She had two employees, a bookkeeper and a clerical assistant. In addition to her *monthly* salary of $4,000 she paid annual salaries of $24,000 and $18,000 to the bookkeeper and the clerical assistant, respectively. Employment taxes and benefit costs for health insurance and so on for Ms. Chen and her employees totaled $17,300 for the year. Expenses for office supplies, including postage, totaled $5,200 for the year. In addition, Ms. Chen spent $8,500 during the year on travel and entertainment associated with client visits and new business development. Lease payments for the office space rented (a tax-deductible expense) were $1,350 *per month.* Depreciation expense on the office furniture and fixtures was $7,800 for the year. During the year, Ms. Chen paid interest of $7,500 on the $60,000 borrowed to start the business. She paid an average tax rate of 30 percent during 1994.

a. Prepare an income statement for Cathy Chen, CPA, for the year ended December 31, 1994.
b. How much cash flow from operations did Cathy realize during 1994?
c. Evaluate her 1994 financial performance.

3-5 LG 2 Calculation of EPS and retained earnings Philagem, Inc., ended 1994 with net profit *before* taxes of $218,000. The company is subject to a 40 percent tax rate and must pay $32,000 in preferred stock dividends before distributing any earnings on the 85,000 shares of common stock currently outstanding.

a. Calculate Philagem's 1994 earnings per share (EPS).
b. If the firm paid common stock dividends of $.80 per share, how many dollars would go to retained earnings?

3-6 LG 2 Balance sheet preparation Use the *appropriate items* from the following list to prepare in good form Owen Davis Company's balance sheet at December 31, 1994.

Item	Value ($000) at December 31, 1994
Accounts payable	$ 220
Accounts receivable	450
Accruals	55
Accumulated depreciation	265
Buildings	225
Cash	215
Common stock (at par)	90
Cost of goods sold	2,500
Depreciation expense	45
Equipment	140
Furniture and fixtures	170
General expense	320
Inventories	375
Land	100
Long-term debts	420
Machinery	420
Marketable securities	75
Notes payable	475
Paid-in capital in excess of par	360
Preferred stock	100
Retained earnings	210
Sales revenue	3,600
Vehicles	25

3-7 LG 2 **Initial sale price of common stock** Beck Corporation has one issue of preferred stock and one issue of common stock outstanding. Given Beck's stockholders' equity account below, determine the original price per share at which the firm sold its single issue of common stock.

Stockholders' equity ($000)	
Preferred stock	$ 125
Common stock ($.75 par, 300,000 shares outstanding)	225
Paid-in capital in excess of par on common stock	2,625
Retained earnings	900
Total stockholders' equity	$3,875

3-8 LG 2 **Financial statement preparation** The balance sheet for Rogers Industries for December 31, 1993, follows. Information relevant to Rogers Industries' 1994 operations is given following the balance sheet. Using the data presented:

a. Prepare in good form an income statement for Rogers Industries for the year ended December 31, 1994. Be sure to show earnings per share (EPS).

b. Prepare in good form a balance sheet for Rogers Industries for December 31, 1994.

Balance sheet ($000)
Rogers Industries
December 31, 1993

Assets		Liabilities and stockholders' equity	
Cash	$ 40	Accounts payable	$ 50
Marketable securities	10	Notes payable	80
Accounts receivable	80	Accruals	10
Inventories	100	Total current liabilities	$140
Total current assets	$230	Long-term debt	$270
Gross fixed assets	$890	Preferred stock	$ 40
Less: Accumulated depreciation	240	Common stock ($.75 par, 80,000 shares)	60
Net fixed assets	$650	Paid-in capital in excess of par	260
Total assets	$880	Retained earnings	110
		Total stockholders' equity	$470
		Total liabilities and stockholders' equity	$880

Relevant information Rogers Industries
1. Sales in 1994 were $1,200,000. 2. Cost of goods sold equals 60 percent of sales. 3. Operating expenses equal 15 percent of sales. 4. Interest expense is 10 percent of the total beginning balance of notes payable and long-term debts. 5. The firm pays 40 percent taxes on ordinary income. 6. Preferred stock dividends of $4,000 were paid in 1994. 7. Cash and marketable securities are unchanged. 8. Accounts receivable equal 8 percent of sales. 9. Inventory equals 10 percent of sales. 10. The firm acquired $30,000 of additional fixed assets in 1994. 11. Total depreciation expense in 1994 was $20,000. 12. Accounts payable equal 5 percent of sales. 13. Notes payable, long-term debt, preferred stock, common stock, and paid-in capital in excess of par remain unchanged. 14. Accruals are unchanged. 15. Cash dividends of $119,000 were paid to common stockholders in 1994.

3-9 LG 3 Statement of retained earnings Hayes Enterprises began 1994 with a retained earnings balance of $928,000. During 1994 the firm earned $377,000 after taxes. From this amount, preferred stockholders were paid $47,000 in dividends. At year-end 1994 the firm's retained earnings totaled $1,048,000. The firm had 140,000 shares of common stock outstanding during 1994.

a. Prepare a statement of retained earnings for the year ended December 31, 1994, for Hayes Enterprises. (*Note:* Be sure to calculate and include the amount of common stock dividends paid in 1994.)

b. Calculate the firm's 1994 earnings per share (EPS).

c. How large a per-share cash dividend did the firm pay on common stock during 1994?

3-10 LG 3 Translation of foreign subsidiary's balance sheet Cummings Products, a multinational producer of men's clothing, has a major manufacturing subsidiary operating in Switzerland. (The Swiss currency is francs, noted Sf.) The subsidiary has total assets worth Sf 9,000,000, total liabilities of Sf 6,000,000, and Sf 3,000,000 in equity. The exchange rate at the beginning of 1994 was Sf 1.50/US$, or alternatively, US$.67/Sf. At the end of 1994 the Swiss franc had appreciated to a value of Sf 1.40/US$, or US$.77/Sf.

a. Find the value in US$ of the Swiss subsidiary's assets, liabilities, and equity at the *beginning* of 1994.

b. Find the value in US$ of the Swiss subsidiary's assets and liabilities at the *end* of 1994.

c. Compare your findings in **a** and **b,** and determine the amount, if any, of translation gain or loss experienced by Cummings Products on its Swiss subsidiary during 1994.

d. How would any translation gain or loss found in **c** be treated by Cummings Products?

3-11 LG 4 Cash flow A firm had earnings after taxes of $50,000 in 1994. Depreciation charges were $28,000, and a $2,000 charge for amortization of a bond discount was incurred. What was the firm's cash flow from operations during 1994?

3-12 LG 5 Depreciation On January 1, 1994, Norton Systems acquired two new assets. Asset A was research equipment costing $17,000 and having a three-year recovery period. Asset B was duplicating equipment having an installed cost of $45,000 and a five-year recovery period. Using the MACRS depreciation percentages in Table 3.6 on page 83, prepare a depreciation schedule for each of these assets.

3-13 LG 4,5 Depreciation and cash flow A firm in the third year of depreciating its only asset, originally costing $180,000 and having a five-year MACRS recovery period, has gathered the following data relative to the given year's operations.

Accruals	$ 15,000
Current assets	120,000
Interest expense	15,000
Sales revenue	400,000
Inventory	70,000
Total costs before depreciation, interest, and taxes	290,000
Tax rate on ordinary income	40%

a. Use the *relevant data* above to determine the *cash flow from operations* for the current year.
b. Explain the impact that depreciation, as well as any other noncash charges, has on a firm's cash flows.

3-14 LG 6 Classifying sources and uses Classify each of the following items as a source (S) or a use (U) of funds or as neither (N).

Item	Change ($)	Item	Change ($)
Cash	+100	Accounts receivable	−700
Accounts payable	−1,000	Net profits	+600
Notes payable	+500	Depreciation	+100
Long-term debt	−2,000	Repurchase of stock	+600
Inventory	+200	Cash dividends	+800
Fixed assets	+400	Sale of stock	+1,000

3-15 LG 6 Finding dividends paid Colonial Paint's net profits after taxes in 1994 totaled $186,000. The firm's year-end 1994 and 1993 retained earnings on its balance sheet totaled $812,000 and $736,000, respectively. How many dollars, if any, in dividends did Colonial pay in 1994?

3-16 LG 6 Preparing a statement of cash flows Given the balance sheets and selected data from the income statement of Keith Corporation on the following page:
a. Prepare the firm's statement of cash flows for the year ended December 31, 1994.
b. Reconcile the resulting "net increase (decrease) in cash and marketable securities" with the actual change in cash and marketable securities for the year.
c. Interpret the statement prepared in **a.**

Balance sheets Keith Corporation		
	December 31	
Assets	**1994**	**1993**
Cash	$ 1,500	$ 1,000
Marketable securities	1,800	1,200
Accounts receivable	2,000	1,800
Inventories	2,900	2,800
Total current assets	$ 8,200	$ 6,800
Gross fixed assets	$29,500	$28,100
Less: Accumulated depreciation	14,700	13,100
Net fixed assets	$14,800	$15,000
Total assets	$23,000	$21,800
Liabilities and stockholders' equity		
Accounts payable	$ 1,600	$ 1,500
Notes payable	2,800	2,200
Accruals	200	300
Total current liabilities	$ 4,600	$ 4,000
Long-term debt	$ 5,000	$ 5,000
Common stock	$10,000	$10,000
Retained earnings	3,400	2,800
Total stockholders' equity	$13,400	$12,800
Total liabilities and stockholders' equity	$23,000	$21,800
Income statement data (1994)		
Depreciation expense	$ 1,600	
Net profits after taxes	1,400	

3-17 LG 6 **Preparing a statement of cash flows** Using the 1994 income statement and the 1994 and 1993 balance sheets for Technica, Inc., given in Problem 3-1, do the following:

a. Prepare the firm's statement of cash flows for the year ended December 31, 1994.

b. Reconcile the resulting "net increase (decrease) in cash and marketable securities" with the actual change in cash and marketable securities for the year.

c. Interpret the statement prepared in **a.**

Chapter 3 Case Analyzing Cline Custom Bicycles' cash flows

Darin Cline, formerly an internationally renowned professional bicycle racer, owns and operates Cline Custom Bicycles—a firm that builds and markets custom bicycles to shops throughout the United States. Darin has just received his firm's 1994 income statement, balance sheet, and statement of retained earnings, shown on the following pages along with the firm's 1993 balance sheet. While he is quite pleased to have achieved record earnings of $106,000 in 1994, Darin is concerned about the firm's cash flows. Specifically, he is finding it more and more difficult to pay the firm's bills in a timely manner. To gain insight into the firm's cash flow problems, Darin is planning to have the firm's 1994 statement of cash flows prepared and evaluated.

Income statement ($000)
Cline Custom Bicycles
for the year ended December 31, 1994

Sales revenue		$2,200
Less: Cost of goods sold		1,420
Gross profits		$ 780
Less: Operating expenses		
Selling expense	$300	
General and administrative expense	270	
Depreciation expense	30	
Total operating expense		600
Operating profits		$ 180
Less: Interest expense		29
Net profits before taxes		$ 151
Less: Taxes (30%)		45
Net profits after taxes		$ 106

Balance sheets ($000)
Cline Custom Bicycles

	December 31	
Assets	**1994**	**1993**
Current assets		
Cash	$ 30	$ 50
Marketable securities	10	20
Accounts receivable	320	350
Inventories	460	320
Total current assets	$ 820	$ 740
Gross fixed assets	$ 560	$ 520
Less: Accumulated depreciation	180	150
Net fixed assets	$ 380	$ 370
Total assets	$1,200	$1,110
Liabilities and stockholders' equity		
Current liabilities		
Accounts payable	$ 390	$ 320
Notes payable	110	90
Accruals	20	20
Total current liabilities	$ 520	$ 430
Long-term debt	$ 320	$ 350
Total liabilities	$ 840	$ 780
Stockholders' equity		
Common stock (500,000 shares at $.20 par value)	$ 100	$ 100
Paid-in capital in excess of par	150	150
Retained earnings	110	80
Total stockholders' equity	$ 360	$ 330
Total liabilities and stockholders' equity	$1,200	$1,110

Statement of retained earnings ($000) Cline Custom Bicycles for the year ended December 31, 1994	
Retained earnings balance (January 1, 1994)	$ 80
Plus: Net profits after taxes (for 1994)	106
Less: Cash dividends on common stock (paid during 1994)	(76)
Retained earnings balance (December 31, 1994)	$110

Required

a. Use the financial data presented to prepare Cline Custom Bicycles' statement of cash flows for the year ended December 31, 1994.

b. Evaluate the statement prepared in **a** in light of Cline's current cash flow difficulties.

c. On the basis of your evaluation in **b**, what recommendations might you offer Darin Cline?

chapter 4

The analysis of financial statements

LEARNING GOALS

Understand the parties interested in performing financial ratio analysis and the common types of ratio comparisons.

Describe some of the cautions that should be considered in performing financial ratio analysis.

Use popular ratios to analyze a firm's liquidity and the activity of inventory, accounts receivable, accounts payable, fixed assets, and total assets.

Discuss the relationship between debt and financial leverage and the ratios that can be used to assess the firm's debt position and its ability to meet the payments associated with debt.

Evaluate a firm's profitability relative to its sales, asset investment, owners' equity investment, and share value.

Use the DuPont system and a summary of a large number of ratios to perform a complete financial analysis of all aspects of a firm's financial condition and make appropriate recommendations.

Financial statement analysis provides a starting point for understanding a company. As a bank lender, I used ratios as part of the credit analysis, to help decide whether to make a loan. I am currently working with companies that have serious problems repaying their bank loans. Ratios provide a quick way to monitor a company's condition—although they really only skim the surface. We then focus on selected areas, especially cash flow, as we probe more deeply into the borrower's financial affairs.

Other areas of finance use ratio analysis as well. Security analysts calculate many ratios when preparing an investment recommendation. Credit managers analyze a prospective customer's financial strength, especially liquidity, before granting an accounts receivable line. Corporate financial managers also use ratios to compare the company to its peers and to identify developing trends.

Each industry has different "acceptable" levels for its ratios. They can also vary by geographical region. For example, the current ratio (current assets divided by current liabilities) is generally higher for a retailer (which has substantial receivables and inventory) than for a public utility (which has very little inventory). It is hard to interpret ratios properly without using published industry averages.

Ratio analysis by itself can give a false picture and must be used in conjunction with a more thorough analysis of the company's business.

Ratios act as a "red flag" to signal potential problems. You must ask *why* is this happening and find the cause of the problem. For example, if a company's current ratio is declining, you should first look at changes in the ratio's components to see whether the cause is lower levels of accounts receivable or inventory or higher levels of current liabilities.

It's very dangerous to rely too heavily on ratio analysis, as it has definite limitations. Many ratios are based on historical costs that often reveal little about an asset's revenue-generating ability. In banking we no longer lend primarily on the strength of a company's balance sheet but focus on income and cash flow statements. We are more interested in coverage ratios that show whether a borrower can repay the principal and interest on our loan. Our focus is the *cash* that the company can generate with its assets, not their original cost or the ratio of total liabilities to total assets.

Ratios help you understand relationships between different business areas. For each additional dollar of sales, what is the additional investment in receivables, inventory, and payables? What level of fixed assets supports a certain sales level? You cannot focus on one ratio in isolation but must look at the totality. A company with an excellent debt to equity ratio (low debt) may have stagnant sales growth and not gen-erate sufficient cash to repay the debt. Or perhaps sales are rising, and all the ratios look great. But suddenly the company can't meet its payroll because higher sales require increased investment in receivables and inventory, and cash flow may drop sharply. Another good example is the company on the brink of bankruptcy. Its current ratio is good and it has a high level of net working capital—because it hasn't been collecting receivables or selling inventory. Ratio analysis by itself can give a false picture and *must* be used in conjunction with a more thorough analysis of the company's business.

The ratios in this chapter provide a basic foundation for financial statement analysis. Then the financial analyst, based on a good understanding of the business and industry, can use a series of interrelated ratios or design new ratios that measure what is important for the company's financial management.

Richard Manix received a B.A. in Political Science from Colgate University and an M.B.A. from the Columbia University School of Business. During his 14 years at Bankers Trust, he was a corporate lender to the energy and utility industries as well as a member of the loan workout group. He currently is First Vice President in charge of the U.S. loan workout group for Crédit Agricole, the largest European bank.

The use of financial ratios

Ratio analysis is used to compare a firm's performance and status with that of other firms or to itself over time. As a financial manager, why would you prefer ratios to the use of dollar values of the key variables, such as inventory and fixed assets, when making these comparisons? Spend a few moments answering this question before reading ahead.

IN THE PRECEDING CHAPTER WE STUDIED THE FORMAT, COMPONENTS, AND PRIMARY PURPOSE of each of the firm's four basic financial statements. The information contained in these statements is of major significance to shareholders, creditors, and managers, all of whom regularly need to have relative measures of the company's operating efficiency and condition. *Relative* is the key word here, since the analysis of financial statements is based on the knowledge and use of *ratios* or *relative values.*

ratio analysis
Involves the methods of calculating and interpreting financial ratios to assess the firm's performance and status.

Ratio analysis involves the methods of calculating and interpreting financial ratios to assess the firm's performance and status. The basic inputs to ratio analysis are the firm's income statement and balance sheet for the periods to be examined. However, before proceeding further, we need to describe the various interested parties and the types of ratio comparisons.

Interested parties

Ratio analysis of a firm's financial statements is of interest to shareholders, creditors, and the firm's own management. Both present and prospective shareholders are interested in the firm's current and future level of risk and return. These two dimensions directly affect share price. The firm's creditors are primarily interested in the short-term liquidity of the company and in its ability to make interest and principal payments. A secondary concern of creditors is the firm's profitability; they want assurance that the business is healthy and will continue to be successful. Management, like stockholders, must be concerned with all aspects of the firm's financial situation. Thus it attempts to operate in a manner that will result in financial ratios that will be considered favorable by both owners and creditors. In addition, management uses ratios to monitor the firm's performance from period to period. Any unexpected changes are examined to isolate developing problems.

CONCEPT IN PRACTICE

This Analyst Wins by Picking Losers

Financial statement analysis serves a variety of purposes. Operating managers use it to monitor financial progress, financial analysts use it to identify the best stocks to buy, and the "shorts"—investors who specialize in short-selling common stocks (selling borrowed shares today with the hope of buying them back at a lower price in the future) that they believe are overpriced—use it to find firms that don't deserve the high stock price the market gives them. According to Michael Murphy, the analyst and short-seller who publishes the *Overpriced Stock Service* newsletter, about 15 percent of all publicly traded stocks are overpriced at any given time. Typically, good candidates for short-selling are fundamentally sound companies with problems building up on the balance sheet that have not yet hit the income statement. Another excellent short candidate is the firm whose stock has a chance to lose all its value—that is, a company with very serious financial problems or a firm involved with fraud. In either case, Murphy uses sound financial statement analysis, a little common sense, and some background research to pick the losers that will be winners for his short-selling clients.

Types of ratio comparisons

Ratio analysis does not merely involve the application of a formula to financial data to calculate a given ratio. More important is the *interpretation* of the ratio value. To answer such questions as, Is it too high or too low? Is it good or bad?, a meaningful standard or basis for comparison is needed. Two types of ratio comparisons can be made: cross-sectional and time-series.

CROSS-SECTIONAL ANALYSIS

cross-sectional analysis
The comparison of different firms' financial ratios at the same point in time; involves comparing the firm's ratios to those of an industry leader or to industry averages.

Cross-sectional analysis involves the comparison of different firms' financial ratios at the same point in time. The typical business is interested in how well it has performed in relation to its competitors. (If the competitors are also publicly held corporations, their reported financial statements should be available for analysis.) Often the firm's performance will be compared to that of the industry leader, and the firm may uncover major operating differences, which, if changed, will increase efficiency. Another popular type of comparison is to industry averages. These figures can be found in the *Almanac of Business and Industrial Financial Ratios, Dun & Bradstreet's Key Business Ratios, Business Month, FTC Quarterly Reports, Robert Morris Associates Statement Studies,* and other sources such as industry association publications.[1] A sample from one available source of industry averages is given in Table 4.1.

The comparison of a particular ratio to the standard is made to isolate any *deviations from the norm*. Many people mistakenly believe that in the case of ratios for which higher values are preferred, as long as the firm being analyzed has a value in excess of the industry average, it can be viewed favorably. However, this "bigger is better" viewpoint can be misleading. Quite often, a ratio value that has a large but positive deviation from the norm can indicate problems. These may, upon more careful analysis, be more severe than they would have been had the ratio been below the industry average.[2] It is therefore important for the analyst to investigate *significant deviations to either side* of the industry standard.

The analyst must also recognize that ratio comparisons resulting in large deviations from the norm reflect only the *symptoms* of a problem. Further analysis of the financial statements coupled with discussions with key managers is typically required to isolate the *causes* of the problem. Once this is accomplished, the financial manager

[1]Cross-sectional comparisons of firms operating in several lines of business are difficult to perform. The use of weighted-average industry average ratios based on the firm's product line mix or, if data are available, analysis of the firm on a product-line-by-product-line basis can be performed to evaluate a multiproduct firm.

[2]Similarly, in the case of ratios for which "smaller is better," one must be as concerned with calculated values that deviate significantly *below* the norm, or industry average, as with values that fall above it. Significant deviations, regardless of the side of the norm, require further investigation by the analyst.

TABLE 4.1

INDUSTRY AVERAGE RATIOS (1992) FOR SELECTED LINES OF BUSINESS[a]

Line of business (number of concerns reporting)[b]	Quick ratio (X)	Current ratio (X)	Current liabilities to net worth (%)	Current liabilities to inventory (%)	Total liabilities to net worth (%)	Fixed assets to net worth (%)	Collection period (days)	Sales to inventory (X)	Total assets to sales (%)	Sales to net working capital (X)	Accounts payable to sales (%)	Return on sales (%)	Return on total assets (%)	Return on net worth (%)
Department stores (663)	2.5 **1.2** 0.4	7.5 **3.5** 2.1	13.3 **36.2** 72.8	29.7 **47.6** 78.8	18.0 **57.7** 138.3	7.3 **20.3** 53.2	4.4 **20.6** 50.5	5.9 **4.6** 3.2	35.4 **49.2** 70.8	6.7 **3.8** 2.5	2.8 **4.9** 7.6	3.7 **1.2** (0.8)	6.5 **2.7** (0.8)	14.1 **4.6** (0.7)
Electronic computers (224)	1.9 **1.2** 0.8	3.3 **2.0** 1.3	28.8 **67.2** 187.3	79.1 **146.0** 225.2	39.4 **90.3** 226.7	10.9 **25.3** 47.6	27.7 **49.0** 81.1	19.2 **9.0** 5.6	23.2 **45.9** 76.3	13.0 **7.2** 3.2	3.0 **6.0** 10.6	6.9 **2.7** 0.2	11.1 **4.5** (2.5)	26.6 **11.9** (3.7)
Grocery stores (1424)	1.3 **0.6** 0.3	4.2 **2.1** 1.3	20.3 **51.7** 106.3	37.3 **73.8** 127.3	31.4 **82.5** 190.2	20.3 **52.5** 113.6	1.1 **2.6** 6.2	26.2 **18.2** 12.2	12.5 **18.1** 27.7	35.9 **18.3** 9.7	1.5 **2.5** 3.8	3.2 **1.4** 0.3	15.0 **6.0** 1.2	29.4 **13.8** 3.7
Household audio/video equipment (101)	1.5 **0.9** 0.6	3.9 **2.1** 1.4	33.4 **74.0** 198.0	51.1 **91.1** 153.7	39.9 **119.9** 273.1	14.3 **29.5** 65.2	22.3 **39.5** 56.4	9.7 **5.8** 4.1	30.5 **45.4** 58.9	8.7 **5.2** 3.8	3.4 **6.3** 8.9	8.8 **3.1** 0.6	13.7 **4.8** 0.9	30.1 **12.4** 2.9
Motor vehicles (80)	1.3 **0.7** 0.4	3.2 **1.8** 0.9	33.9 **72.5** 231.5	46.3 **113.8** 179.5	37.2 **89.6** 244.2	12.2 **46.5** 153.8	18.6 **30.3** 48.2	12.6 **6.7** 4.5	23.5 **35.9** 65.0	14.0 **7.9** 4.2	3.8 **6.6** 10.8	6.7 **2.2** (0.2)	13.4 **3.0** (2.0)	39.3 **10.0** (0.1)
Petroleum refining (98)	1.0 **0.8** 0.5	1.9 **1.3** 1.0	38.3 **68.4** 116.4	122.5 **193.7** 374.6	77.2 **147.4** 274.2	82.0 **131.5** 178.5	17.2 **34.8** 44.2	21.1 **14.6** 10.3	38.7 **53.5** 93.4	30.4 **15.8** 9.9	5.6 **9.1** 12.4	4.2 **1.5** 0.3	6.5 **2.3** 0.3	18.0 **6.7** 1.1
Specialized industrial machinery (311)	2.2 **1.0** 0.7	3.6 **1.9** 1.3	125.9 **64.6** 161.6	76.4 **136.4** 239.3	38.2 **95.7** 201.1	14.1 **33.6** 69.2	30.7 **44.2** 57.4	18.4 **8.1** 5.1	32.5 **45.3** 66.5	13.1 **6.0** 3.4	3.0 **5.9** 8.8	8.5 **3.4** 0.8	16.7 **5.7** 0.8	36.7 **11.7** 2.4

[a]These values are given for each ratio for each line of business. The center value is the median, and the values immediately above and below it are the upper and lower quartiles, respectively.

[b]Standard Industrial Classification (SIC) codes for the lines of business shown are, respectively: SIC #5311, SIC #3571, SIC #5411, SIC #3651, SIC #3711, SIC #2911, SIC #3559.

Source: "Industry Norms and Key Business Ratios" Copyright © 1993 Dun & Bradstreet, Inc. Reprinted with permission.

must develop prescriptive actions for eliminating such causes. The fundamental point is that *ratio analysis merely directs the analyst to potential areas of concern; it does not provide conclusive evidence as to the existence of a problem.*

EXAMPLE

In early 1995, Mary Boyle, the chief financial analyst at Caldwell Manufacturing—a manufacturer of heat exchangers—gathered data on the firm's financial performance during 1994, the year just ended. She calculated a variety of ratios and obtained industry averages for use in making comparisons. One ratio in which she was especially interested was inventory turnover, which reflects the speed with which the firm moves its inventory from raw materials through production into finished goods and to the customer as a completed sale. Generally, higher values of this ratio are preferred, since they indicate a quicker turnover of inventory. Caldwell Manufacturing's calculated inventory turnover for 1994 and the industry average inventory turnover were, respectively:

	Inventory turnover, 1994
Caldwell Manufacturing	14.8
Industry average	9.7

Mary's initial reaction to this data was that the firm had managed its inventory significantly better than the average firm in the industry. The turnover was in fact nearly 53 percent faster than the industry average. Upon reflection, however, she felt that there could be a problem, since a very high inventory turnover could also mean very low levels of inventory. In turn, the consequence of low inventory could be excessive stockouts (insufficient inventory). Mary's review of other ratios and discussions with people in the manufacturing and marketing departments did in fact uncover such a problem: The firm's inventories during the year were extremely low as a result of numerous production delays that hindered its ability to meet demand and resulted in lost sales. What had initially appeared to reflect extremely efficient inventory management was actually the symptom of a major problem. ■

TIME-SERIES ANALYSIS

time-series analysis Evaluation of the firm's financial performance over time utilizing financial ratio analysis.

Time-series analysis is applied when a financial analyst evaluates performance over time. Comparison of current to past performance, using ratio analysis, allows the firm to determine whether it is progressing as planned. Developing trends can be seen by using multiyear comparisons, and knowledge of these trends should assist the firm in planning future operations. As in cross-sectional analysis, any significant year-to-year changes can be evaluated to assess whether they are symptomatic of a major problem. The theory behind time-series analysis is that the company must be evaluated in relation to its past performance, developing trends must be isolated, and appropriate action must be taken to direct the firm toward immediate and long-run goals. Time-series analysis is often helpful in checking the reasonableness of a firm's projected (pro forma) financial statements. A comparison of *current* and *past* ratios to those resulting from an analysis of *projected* statements may reveal discrepancies or overoptimism.

COMBINED ANALYSIS

The most informative approach to ratio analysis is one that combines cross-sectional and time-series analyses. A combined view permits assessment of the trend in the behavior of the ratio in relation to the trend for the industry. Figure 4.1 depicts this type of approach using the average collection period ratio of Bartlett Company, a small manufacturer of lawn furniture, over the years 1991–1994. Generally, lower values of this ratio, which reflects the average amount of time it takes the firm to collect bills, are preferred. A look at the figure quickly discloses that (1) Bartlett's effectiveness in collecting its receivables is poor in comparison to the industry and (2) there is a trend toward longer collection periods. Clearly, Bartlett needs to shorten its collection period.

Some words of caution

Before discussing specific ratios, we should consider the following cautions:

1. A single ratio does not generally provide sufficient information from which to judge the overall performance of the firm. Only when a group of ratios is used can

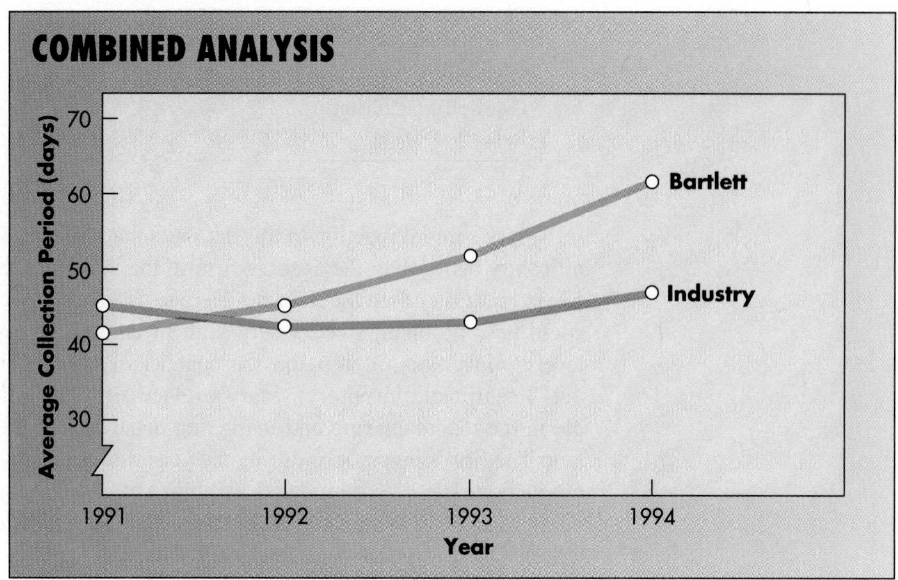

FIGURE 4.1
Combined cross-sectional and time-series view of Bartlett Company's average collection period, 1991–1994

reasonable judgments be made. If an analysis is concerned only with certain specific aspects of a firm's financial position, one or two ratios may be sufficient.

2. The financial statements being compared should be dated at the same point in time during the year. If they are not, the effects of seasonality may produce erroneous conclusions and decisions. For example, comparison of the inventory turnover of a toy manufacturer at the end of June with its end-of-December value can be misleading. The relatively high inventory at the end of June would result in a low inventory turnover, whereas at year-end the low inventory balance would result in a very high inventory turnover. Clearly, the seasonal impact of the December holiday selling season would make the firm's inventory management falsely appear to have greatly improved. Erroneous conclusions such as this can be avoided by comparing results for June of the current year to June of the prior year, December to December, and so forth, to eliminate the effects of seasonality.
3. It is preferable to use audited financial statements for ratio analysis. If the statements have not been audited, there may be no reason to believe that the data contained in them reflect the firm's true financial condition.
4. The financial data being compared should have been developed in the same way. The use of differing accounting treatments—especially relative to inventory and depreciation—can distort the results of ratio analysis, regardless of whether cross-sectional or time-series analysis is used.
5. When the ratios of one firm are compared with those of another or with those of the firm itself over time, results can be distorted due to inflation. Inflation can cause the book values of inventory and depreciable assets to differ greatly from their true (replacement) values. Additionally, inventory costs and depreciation write-offs can differ from their true values, thereby distorting profits. These inflationary effects typically have greater impact the larger the differences in the ages of the assets of the firms being compared. Without adjustment, inflation tends to cause older firms (older assets) to appear more efficient and profitable than newer firms (newer assets). Clearly, care must be taken in comparing ratios of older to newer firms or a firm to itself over a long period of time.

Groups of financial ratios

Financial ratios can for convenience be divided into four basic groups or categories: liquidity ratios, activity ratios, debt ratios, and profitability ratios. Liquidity, activity, and debt ratios primarily measure risk; profitability ratios measure return. In the near-term the important elements are liquidity, activity, and profitability, since these provide the information that is critical to the short-run operation of the firm. (If a firm cannot survive in the short run, we need not be concerned with its longer-term prospects.) Debt ratios are useful primarily when the analyst is sure that the firm will successfully weather the short run.

As a rule, the necessary inputs to an effective financial analysis include, at minimum, the income statement and the balance sheet. The 1994 and 1993 income statements and balance sheets for Bartlett Company are presented in Tables 4.2 and 4.3, respectively, to demonstrate ratio calculations. Note that the ratios presented in the

TABLE 4.2

BARTLETT COMPANY INCOME STATEMENTS ($000)

	For the years ended December 31	
	1994	1993
Sales revenue	$3,074	$2,567
Less: Cost of goods sold	2,088	1,711
Gross profits	$ 986	$ 856
Less: Operating expenses		
Selling expense	$ 100	$ 108
General and administrative expenses	194	187
Lease expense[a]	35	35
Depreciation expense	239	223
Total operating expense	$ 568	$ 553
Operating profits	$ 418	$ 303
Less: Interest expense	93	91
Net profits before taxes	$ 325	$ 212
Less: Taxes (rate = 29%)[b]	94	64
Net profits after taxes	$ 231	$ 148
Less: Preferred stock dividends	10	10
Earnings available for common stockholders	$ 221	$ 138
Earnings per share (EPS)[c]	$ 2.90	$ 1.81

[a]Lease expense is shown here as a separate item rather than being included as interest expense and amortization as specified by the FASB for financial-reporting purposes. The approach used here is consistent with tax-reporting rather than financial-reporting procedures.

[b]The 29 percent tax rate for 1994 results from the fact that the firm has certain special tax write-offs that do not show up directly on its income statement.

[c]Calculated by dividing the earnings available for common stockholders by the number of shares of common stock outstanding—76,262 in 1994 and 76,244 in 1993. Earnings per share in 1994: ($221,000 ÷ 76,262 = $2.90); in 1993: ($138,000 ÷ 76,244 = $1.81).

TABLE 4.3

BARTLETT COMPANY BALANCE SHEETS ($000)

	December 31	
Assets	**1994**	**1993**
Current assets		
Cash	$ 363	$ 288
Marketable securities	68	51
Accounts receivable	503	365
Inventories	289	300
Total current assets	$1,223	$1,004
Gross fixed assets (at cost)[a]		
Land and buildings	$2,072	$1,903
Machinery and equipment	1,866	1,693
Furniture and fixtures	358	316
Vehicles	275	314
Other (includes financial leases)	98	96
Total gross fixed assets (at cost)	$4,669	$4,322
Less: Accumulated depreciation	2,295	2,056
Net fixed assets	$2,374	$2,266
Total assets	$3,597	$3,270
Liabilities and stockholders' equity		
Current liabilities		
Accounts payable	$ 382	$ 270
Notes payable	79	99
Accruals	159	114
Total current liabilities	$ 620	$ 483
Long-term debts (includes financial leases)[b]	$1,023	$ 967
Total liabilities	$1,643	$1,450
Stockholders' equity		
Preferred stock—cumulative 5%, $100 par, 2,000 shares authorized and issued[c]	$ 200	$ 200
Common stock—$2.50 par, 100,000 shares authorized, shares issued and outstanding in 1994: 76,262; in 1993: 76,244	191	190
Paid-in capital in excess of par on common stock	428	418
Retained earnings	1,135	1,012
Total stockholders' equity	$1,954	$1,820
Total liabilities and stockholders' equity	$3,597	$3,270

[a]In 1994 the firm has a six-year financial lease requiring annual beginning-of-year payments of $35,000. Four years of the lease have yet to run.

[b]Annual principal repayments on a portion of the firm's total outstanding debt amount to $71,000.

[c]The annual preferred stock dividend would be $5 per share (5% × $100 par), or a total of $10,000 annually ($5 per share × 2,000 shares).

remainder of this chapter are the "standard" ratios that can be applied to nearly any company. Of course, many companies in different industries use ratios that are particularly focused on aspects peculiar to their industry.

CONCEPTS IN REVIEW

4-1 With regard to financial ratio analyses of a firm, how do the viewpoints held by the firm's present and prospective shareholders, creditors, and management differ? How can these viewpoints be related to the firm's fund-raising ability?

4-2 How can ratio analysis be used for *cross-sectional* and *time-series* comparisons? Which type of comparison would be more common for internal analysis? Why?

4-3 When performing cross-sectional ratio analysis, to what types of deviations from the norm should the analyst devote primary attention? Explain why.

4-4 Why is it preferable to compare financial statements that are dated at the same point in time during the year? What is the problem associated with the analysis of unaudited financial statements?

4-5 Financial ratio analysis is often divided into four areas: *liquidity* ratios, *activity* ratios, *debt* ratios, and *profitability* ratios. Describe and differentiate each of these areas of analysis from the others. Which is of the greatest relative concern to present and prospective creditors?

Analyzing liquidity

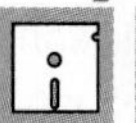

A "liquid firm" is one that can easily meet its short-term obligations as they come due. Given that current assets represent short-term resources and current liabilities represent short-term obligations, how might you go about assessing a firm's liquidity? Before reading on, take a few moments to answer this question.

liquidity
A firm's ability to satisfy its short-term obligations as they come due.

THE LIQUIDITY OF A BUSINESS FIRM IS MEASURED BY ITS ABILITY TO SATISFY ITS SHORT-term obligations *as they come due*. Liquidity refers to the solvency of the firm's *overall* financial position—the ease with which it can pay its bills. The three basic measures of liquidity are (1) net working capital, (2) the current ratio, and (3) the quick (acid-test) ratio.

Net working capital

net working capital
A measure of liquidity calculated by subtracting current liabilities from current assets.

Net working capital, although not actually a ratio, is commonly used to measure a firm's overall liquidity. It is calculated as follows:

$$\text{Net working capital} = \text{current assets} - \text{current liabilities}$$

The net working capital for Bartlett Company in 1994 is

$$\text{Net working capital} = \$1{,}223{,}000 - \$620{,}000 = \$603{,}000$$

This figure is *not* useful for comparing the performance of different firms, but it is quite useful for internal control.[3] Often the contract under which a long-term debt is incurred specifically states a minimum level of net working capital that the firm must maintain. This requirement is intended to force the firm to maintain sufficient operating liquidity and helps to protect the creditor. A time-series comparison of the firm's net working capital is often helpful in evaluating its operations.

Current ratio

current ratio

A measure of liquidity calculated by dividing the firm's current assets by its current liabilities.

The **current ratio,** one of the most commonly cited financial ratios, measures the firm's ability to meet its short-term obligations. It is expressed as follows:

$$\text{Current ratio} = \frac{\text{current assets}}{\text{current liabilities}}$$

The current ratio for Bartlett Company in 1994 is

$$\frac{\$1{,}223{,}000}{\$620{,}000} = 1.97$$

A current ratio of 2.0 is occasionally cited as acceptable, but a value's acceptability depends on the industry in which the firm operates. For example, a current ratio of 1.0 would be considered acceptable for a utility but might be unacceptable for a manufacturing firm. The more predictable a firm's cash flows, the lower the acceptable current ratio. Since Bartlett Company is in a business with a relatively predictable annual cash flow, its current ratio of 1.97 should be quite acceptable.

If the firm's current ratio is divided into 1.0 and the resulting quotient is subtracted from 1.0, the difference multiplied by 100 represents the percentage by which the firm's current assets can shrink without making it impossible for the firm to cover its current liabilities.[4] For example, a current ratio of 2.0 means that the firm can still cover its current liabilities even if its current assets shrink by 50 percent ($[1.0 - (1.0 \div 2.0)] \times 100$).

It is useful to note that whenever a firm's current ratio is 1.0, its net working capital is zero. If a firm has a current ratio of less than 1.0, it will have negative net working capital. Net working capital is useful only in comparing the liquidity of the same firm over time and should not be used to compare the liquidity of different firms; the current ratio should be used instead.

[3]To make cross-sectional as well as better time-series comparisons, *net working capital as a percent of sales* can be calculated. For Bartlett Company in 1994 this ratio would be 19.6 percent ($603,000 ÷ $3,074,000). In general, the larger this value, the greater the firm's liquidity, and the smaller this value, the lesser the firm's liquidity. Because of the relative nature of this measure, it is often used to make liquidity comparisons.

[4]This transformation actually results in the ratio of *net working capital to current assets.* Clearly, current assets can shrink by the amount of net working capital (i.e., their excess over current liabilities) while still retaining adequate current assets to just meet current liabilities.

Quick (acid-test) ratio

quick (acid-test) ratio
A measure of liquidity calculated by dividing the firm's current assets minus inventory by current liabilities.

The **quick (acid-test) ratio** is similar to the current ratio except that it excludes inventory, which is generally the least liquid current asset. The generally low liquidity of inventory results from two primary factors: (1) many types of inventory cannot be easily sold because they are partially completed items, obsolete items, special-purpose items, and the like; and (2) the items are typically sold on credit, which means that they become an account receivable before being converted into cash. The quick ratio is calculated as follows:[5]

$$\text{Quick ratio} = \frac{\text{current assets} - \text{inventory}}{\text{current liabilities}}$$

The quick ratio for Bartlett Company in 1994 is

$$\frac{\$1{,}223{,}000 - \$289{,}000}{\$620{,}000} = \frac{\$934{,}000}{\$620{,}000} = 1.51$$

A quick ratio of 1.0 or greater is occasionally recommended, but as with the current ratio, an acceptable value depends largely on the industry. The quick ratio provides a better measure of overall liquidity only when a firm's inventory cannot easily be converted into cash. If inventory is liquid, the current ratio is a preferred measure of overall liquidity.

Note that for all three liquidity measures—net working capital, current ratio, and quick (acid-test) ratio—the higher their value, the more liquid the firm is typically considered to be. As will be explained in Chapter 16, "Net Working Capital and Short-Term Financing," excessive liquidity reduces a firm's risk of being unable to satisfy its short-term obligations *as they come due* but sacrifices profitability because (1) current assets are less profitable than fixed assets and (2) current liabilities are a less expensive financing source than long-term funds. For now, suffice it to say that there is a cost of increased liquidity—a tradeoff exists between profitability and liquidity (risk).

CONCEPT IN PRACTICE

Over a Barrel at Allied Products Corporation

In the past few years, many financial managers have felt trapped by their bankers. Allied Products Corporation, a $350 million manufacturer of agricultural and heavy industrial equipment made a series of dreadful acquisitions in the 1980s. As a result, the company faced a liquidity squeeze with $230 million in debt soaking up all its free cash flow. After a debt restructuring phase in 1990, Allied faced borrowing costs that rose each time the firm needed an extension on its debt maturity. After

[5]Sometimes the quick ratio is defined as (cash + marketable securities + accounts receivable) ÷ current liabilities. If a firm were to show as current assets items other than cash, marketable securities, accounts receivable, and inventory, its quick ratio might vary, depending on the method of calculation.

several extensions and several increases in its borrowing cost, Allied's liquidity crisis grew deeper, and the firm faced certain bankruptcy. To avert this crisis, Allied offered its bankers one last alternative in 1993: Release the corporate assets securing Allied's debt, allow the firm to sell these assets to one of Allied's profitable subsidiaries, accept $60 million in cash generated from the asset sales, and extend Allied's remaining debt for a two-year period. The bankers agreed to Allied's plan, accepting the firm's proposal to reduce its heavy debt burden and relieve its liquidity crisis.

CONCEPT IN REVIEW

4-6 Why is net working capital useful only in time-series comparisons of overall liquidity whereas the current and quick ratios can be used for both cross-sectional and time-series analysis?

Analyzing activity

Activity ratios can be used to assess the speed with which current accounts—inventory, accounts receivable, and accounts payable—are converted into cash. Why is it important to use these measures to assess the firm's "true" liquidity? Take a few moments to answer this question before reading ahead.

activity ratios
Used to measure the speed with which various accounts are converted into sales or cash.

ACTIVITY RATIOS ARE USED TO MEASURE THE SPEED WITH WHICH VARIOUS ACCOUNTS are converted into sales or cash. Measures of liquidity are generally inadequate because differences in the composition of a firm's current assets and liabilities can significantly affect the firm's "true" liquidity. For example, consider the current portion of the balance sheets for firms A and B in the following table:

Firm A			
Cash	$ 0	Accounts payable	$ 0
Marketable securities	0	Notes payable	10,000
Accounts receivable	0	Accruals	0
Inventories	20,000	Total current liabilities	$10,000
Total current assets	$20,000		
Firm B			
Cash	$ 5,000	Accounts payable	$ 5,000
Marketable securities	5,000	Notes payable	3,000
Accounts receivable	5,000	Accruals	2,000
Inventories	5,000	Total current liabilities	$10,000
Total current assets	$20,000		

Although both firms appear to be equally liquid, since their current ratios are both 2.0 (\$20,000 ÷ \$10,000), a closer look at the differences in the composition of current assets and liabilities suggests that *firm B is more liquid than firm A.* This is true for two reasons: (1) Firm B has more liquid assets in the form of cash and marketable securities than firm A, which has only a single and relatively illiquid asset in the form of inventories, and (2) firm B's current liabilities are in general more flexible than the single current liability—notes payable—of firm A.

It is therefore important to look beyond measures of overall liquidity to assess the activity (liquidity) of specific current accounts. A number of ratios are available for measuring the activity of the most important current accounts, which include inventory, accounts receivable, and accounts payable.[6] The activity (efficiency of utilization) of fixed and total assets can also be assessed.

Inventory turnover

inventory turnover
Measures the activity, or liquidity, of a firm's inventory.

Inventory turnover commonly measures the activity, or liquidity, of a firm's inventory. It is calculated as follows:

$$\text{Inventory turnover} = \frac{\text{cost of goods sold}}{\text{inventory}}$$

Applying this relationship to Bartlett Company in 1994 yields

$$\text{Inventory turnover} = \frac{\$2{,}088{,}000}{\$289{,}000} = 7.2$$

The resulting turnover is meaningful only when it is compared with that of other firms in the same industry or to the firm's past inventory turnover. An inventory turnover of 20.0 would not be unusual for a grocery store, whereas a common inventory turnover for an aircraft manufacturer would be 4.0.

average age of inventory
Average length of time inventory is held by the firm.

Inventory turnover can easily be converted into an **average age of inventory** by dividing it into 360—the number of days in a year.[7] For Bartlett Company the average age of inventory would be 50.0 days (360 ÷ 7.2). This value can also be viewed as the average number of days' sales in inventory.

[6]For convenience the activity ratios involving these current accounts assume that their end-of-period values are good approximations of the average account balance during the period—typically one year. Technically, when the month-end balances of inventory, accounts receivable, or accounts payable vary during the year, the average balance, calculated by summing the 12 month-end account balances and dividing the total by 12, should be used instead of the year-end value. If month-end balances are unavailable, the average can be approximated by dividing the sum of the beginning-of-year and end-of-year balances by 2. These approaches ensure a ratio that on the average better reflects the firm's circumstances. Because the data needed to find averages are generally unavailable to the external analyst, year-end values are frequently used to calculate activity ratios for current accounts.

[7]Unless otherwise specified, a 360-day year consisting of 12 30-day months is assumed throughout this textbook. This assumption allows some simplification of the calculations used to illustrate key concepts.

Average collection period

average collection period
The average amount of time needed to collect accounts receivable.

The **average collection period,** or average age of accounts receivable, is useful in evaluating credit and collection policies.[8] It is arrived at by dividing the average daily sales[9] into the accounts receivable balance:

$$\text{Average collection period} = \frac{\text{accounts receivable}}{\text{average sales per day}} = \frac{\text{accounts receivable}}{\frac{\text{annual sales}}{360}}$$

The average collection period for Bartlett Company in 1994 is

$$\frac{\$503{,}000}{\frac{\$3{,}074{,}000}{360}} = \frac{\$503{,}000}{\$8{,}539} = 58.9 \text{ days}$$

On the average it takes the firm 58.9 days to collect an account receivable.

The average collection period is meaningful only in relation to the firm's credit terms. If, for instance, Bartlett Company extends 30-day credit terms to customers, an average collection period of 58.9 days may indicate a poorly managed credit or collection department or both. Of course, the lengthened collection period could be the result of an intentional relaxation of credit-term enforcement by the firm in response to competitive pressures. If the firm had extended 60-day credit terms, the 58.9-day average collection period would be quite acceptable. Clearly, additional information would be required to draw definitive conclusions about the effectiveness of the firm's credit and collection policies.

Average payment period

average payment period
The average amount of time needed to pay accounts payable.

The **average payment period,** or average age of accounts payable, is calculated in the same manner as the average collection period:

$$\text{Average payment period} = \frac{\text{accounts payable}}{\text{average purchases per day}} = \frac{\text{accounts payable}}{\frac{\text{annual purchases}}{360}}$$

The difficulty in calculating this ratio stems from the need to find annual purchases[10]—a value not available in published financial statements. Ordinarily, purchases are esti-

[8]The average collection period is sometimes called the *days' sales outstanding (DSO)*. A discussion of the evaluation and establishment of credit and collection policies is presented in Chapter 18.

[9]The formula as presented assumes, for simplicity, that all sales are made on a credit basis. If such is not the case, *average credit sales per day* should be substituted for average sales per day.

[10]Technically, annual *credit* purchases—rather than annual purchases—should be used in calculating this ratio. For simplicity this refinement is ignored here.

mated as a given percentage of cost of goods sold. If we assume that Bartlett Company's purchases equaled 70 percent of its cost of goods sold in 1994, its average payment period is

$$\frac{\$382{,}000}{\dfrac{.70 \times \$2{,}088{,}000}{360}} = \frac{\$382{,}000}{\$4{,}060} = 94.1 \text{ days}$$

This figure is meaningful only in relation to the average credit terms extended to the firm. If Bartlett Company's suppliers, on the average, have extended 30-day credit terms, an analyst would give it a low credit rating. If the firm has been generally extended 90-day credit terms, its credit would be acceptable. Prospective lenders and suppliers of trade credit are especially interested in the average payment period, since it provides them with a sense of the bill-paying patterns of the firm.

Fixed asset turnover

fixed asset turnover
Measures the efficiency with which the firm has been using its *fixed,* or earning, assets to generate sales.

The **fixed asset turnover** measures the efficiency with which the firm has been using its *fixed,* or earning, assets to generate sales. It is calculated by dividing the firm's sales by its net fixed assets:

$$\text{Fixed asset turnover} = \frac{\text{sales}}{\text{net fixed assets}}$$

The fixed asset turnover for Bartlett Company in 1994 is

$$\frac{\$3{,}074{,}000}{\$2{,}374{,}000} = 1.29$$

This means that the company turns over its net fixed assets 1.29 times a year. Generally, higher fixed asset turnovers are preferred, since they reflect greater efficiency of fixed-asset utilization.

One caution with respect to use of this ratio and the total asset turnover described next stems from the fact that the calculations use the historical costs of fixed assets. Since some firms have significantly newer or older assets than others, comparing fixed asset turnovers of those firms can be misleading. Because of inflation and the historically based book values of assets, firms with newer assets will tend to have lower turnovers than those with older assets having lower book values.[11] The differences in these turnovers could result from more costly assets rather than from differing operating efficiencies. Therefore the financial manager should be cautious when using these ratios for cross-sectional comparisons.

[11]This problem would not exist if firms were required to use current-cost accounting. Financial Accounting Standards Board (FASB) Standard No. 33, *Financial Reporting and Changing Prices,* issued in 1979 and amended by FASB Standard No. 82, *Financial Reporting and Price Changes: Elimination of Certain Disclosures,* issued in 1984, prescribes procedures for inflation accounting. The standard currently requires only large publicly held corporations to include such reporting as *supplementary information* in their stockholders' reports. For a discussion of these and other FASB statements, see a current edition of an intermediate accounting textbook.

Total asset turnover

total asset turnover
Indicates the efficiency with which the firm uses *all* its assets to generate sales.

The **total asset turnover** indicates the efficiency with which the firm uses *all* its assets to generate sales. Generally, the higher a firm's total asset turnover, the more efficiently its assets have been used. This measure is probably of greatest interest to management, since it indicates whether the firm's operations have been financially efficient. Total asset turnover is calculated as follows:

$$\text{Total asset turnover} = \frac{\text{sales}}{\text{total assets}}$$

The value of Bartlett Company's total asset turnover in 1994 is

$$\frac{\$3{,}074{,}000}{\$3{,}597{,}000} = .85$$

The company therefore turns its assets over .85 times a year.

CONCEPT IN REVIEW

4-7 To assess the reasonableness of the firm's average collection period and average payment period ratios, what additional information is needed in each instance? Explain.

Analyzing debt

A firm's debt position can be assessed by looking at both its degree of indebtedness and its ability to pay its debts. What general relationship would you expect to exist between a firm's degree of indebtedness and its ability to pay its debts? Why? Spend a short time answering these questions before reading ahead.

THE *DEBT POSITION* OF A FIRM INDICATES THE AMOUNT OF OTHER PEOPLE'S MONEY being used in attempting to generate profits. In general, the financial analyst is most concerned with long-term debts, since these commit the firm to paying interest over the long run as well as eventually repaying the principal borrowed. Since creditors' claims must be satisfied before the distribution of earnings to shareholders,[12] present and prospective shareholders pay close attention to degree of indebtedness and ability to repay debts. Lenders are also concerned about the firm's degree of indebtedness and ability to repay debts, since the more indebted the firm, the higher the probability that the firm will be unable to satisfy the claims of all its creditors. Manage-

[12]The law requires that creditors' claims be satisfied before those of the firm's owners. This makes sense, since the creditor is providing a service to the owners and should not be expected to bear the risks of ownership.

ment obviously must be concerned with indebtedness in recognition of the attention paid to it by other parties and in the interest of keeping the firm solvent.

financial leverage
The magnification of risk and return introduced through the use of fixed-cost financing such as debt and preferred stock.

In general, the more debt a firm uses in relation to its total assets, the greater its **financial leverage,** a term used to describe the magnification of risk and return introduced through the use of fixed-cost financing such as debt and preferred stock. In other words, the more fixed-cost debt, or financial leverage, a firm uses, the greater will be its risk and expected return.

Michael Karp and Amy Parsons are in the process of incorporating a new business venture they have formed. After a great deal of analysis they have determined that an initial investment of $50,000—$20,000 in current assets and $30,000 in fixed assets—is necessary. These funds can be obtained in either of two ways. The first is the no-debt plan, under which they would together invest the full $50,000 without borrowing. The other alternative, the debt plan, involves making a combined investment of $25,000 and borrowing the balance of $25,000 at 12 percent annual interest. Regardless of which alternative they choose, Michael and Amy expect sales to average $30,000, costs and operating expenses to average $18,000, and earnings to be taxed at a 40 percent rate. The balance sheets and income statements associated with the no-debt and debt plans are summarized in Table 4.4.

The no-debt plan results in after-tax profits of $7,200, which represent a 14.4 percent rate of return on Michael and Amy's $50,000 investment. The debt plan results in $5,400 of after-tax profits, which represent a 21.6 percent rate of return on their com-

TABLE 4.4

FINANCIAL STATEMENTS ASSOCIATED WITH MICHAEL AND AMY'S ALTERNATIVES

Balance sheets	**No-debt plan**		**Debt plan**	
Current assets	$20,000		$20,000	
Fixed assets	30,000		30,000	
Total assets	$50,000		$50,000	
Debt (12% interest)	$ 0		$25,000	
(1) Equity	50,000		25,000	
Total liabilities and equity	$50,000		$50,000	
Income statements				
Sales	$30,000		$30,000	
Less: Costs and operating expenses	18,000		18,000	
Operating profits	$12,000		$12,000	
Less: Interest expense	0	.12 × $25,000 =	3,000	
Net profit before taxes	$12,000		$ 9,000	
Less: Taxes (rate = 40%)	4,800		3,600	
(2) Net profit after taxes	$ 7,200		$ 5,400	
Return on equity [(2) ÷ (1)]	$\frac{\$\ 7,200}{\$50,000}$	= 14.4%	$\frac{\$\ 5,400}{\$25,000}$	= 21.6%

bined investment of $25,000. It therefore appears that the debt plan provides Michael and Amy with a higher rate of return, but the risk of this plan is also greater, since the annual $3,000 of interest must be paid before receipt of earnings. ■

From the example it should be clear that *with increased debt comes greater risk as well as higher potential return;* therefore the greater the financial leverage, the greater the potential risk and return. A detailed discussion of the impact of debt on the firm's risk, return, and value is included in Chapter 11. Here, emphasis is given to the use of financial debt ratios to externally assess the degree of corporate indebtedness and the ability to meet fixed payments associated with debt.

Measures of debt

degree of indebtedness
Measures amount of debt relative to other significant balance sheet amounts.

ability to service debts
The ability of a firm to make the contractual payments required on a scheduled basis over the life of a debt.

coverage ratios
Ratios that measure the firm's ability to pay certain fixed charges.

There are two general types of debt measures: measures of the degree of indebtedness and measures of the ability to service debts. The **degree of indebtedness** measures the amount of debt relative to other significant balance sheet amounts. Two of the most commonly used measures are the debt ratio and the debt-equity ratio, both of which are discussed next.

The second type of debt measure, the **ability to service debts,** refers to a firm's ability to make the contractual payments required on a scheduled basis over the life of a debt.[13] With debts come scheduled fixed-payment obligations for interest and principal. Lease payments as well as preferred stock dividend payments also represent scheduled obligations. The firm's ability to pay certain fixed charges is measured by using **coverage ratios.** Typically, higher coverage ratios are preferred, but too high a ratio (above industry norms) may indicate underutilization of fixed-payment obligations, which may result in unnecessarily low risk and returns. Alternatively, the lower the firm's coverage ratios, the more risky the firm is considered to be. "Riskiness" here refers to the firm's ability to pay fixed obligations. If a firm is unable to pay these obligations, it will be in default, and its creditors may seek immediate repayment. In most instances this would force a firm into bankruptcy. Two ratios of coverage—the times interest earned ratio and the fixed-payment coverage ratio—are discussed below.[14] Actually, only the first of these ratios is concerned solely with debt; the second one considers other fixed-payment obligations in addition to debt service.

Debt ratio

debt ratio
Measures the proportion of total assets financed by the firm's creditors.

The **debt ratio** measures the proportion of total assets financed by the firm's creditors. The higher this ratio, the greater the amount of other people's money being used in an attempt to generate profits. The ratio is calculated as follows:

---

[13]The term *service* is used throughout this textbook to refer to the payment of interest and repayment of principal associated with a firm's debt obligations. When a firm services its debts, it pays, or fulfills, these obligations.

[14]Coverage ratios use data based on the application of accrual concepts (discussed in Chapter 1) to measure what in a strict sense should be measured with cash flows. This occurs because debts are serviced by using cash flows, not the accounting values shown on the firm's financial statements. But because it is difficult to determine cash flows available for debt service from the firm's financial statements, the calculation of coverage ratios as presented here is quite common due to the ready availability of financial statement data.

$$\text{Debt ratio} = \frac{\text{total liabilities}}{\text{total assets}}$$

The debt ratio for Bartlett Company in 1994 is

$$\frac{\$1{,}643{,}000}{\$3{,}597{,}000} = .457 = 45.7\%$$

This indicates that the company has financed 45.7 percent of its assets with debt. The higher this ratio, the more financial leverage a firm has.

The following ratio differs from the debt ratio by focusing on long-term debts. Short-term debts, or current liabilities, are excluded, since most of them are spontaneous (that is, they are the natural result of doing business) and do not commit the firm to the payment of fixed charges over a long period of time.

Debt-equity ratio

debt-equity ratio
Measures the ratio of long-term debt to stockholders' equity.

The **debt-equity ratio** indicates the relationship between the *long-term* funds provided by creditors and those provided by the firm's owners. It is commonly used to measure the degree of financial leverage of the firm and is calculated as follows:

$$\text{Debt-equity ratio} = \frac{\text{long-term debt}}{\text{stockholders' equity}}$$

The debt-equity ratio for Bartlett Company in 1994 is

$$\frac{\$1{,}023{,}000}{\$1{,}954{,}000} = .524 = 52.4\%$$

The firm's long-term debts therefore are only 52.4 percent as large as stockholders' equity. This figure is meaningful only in light of the firm's line of business. Firms with large amounts of fixed assets, stable cash flows, or both typically have high debt-equity ratios, while less capital-intensive firms, firms with volatile cash flows, or both tend to have lower debt-equity ratios.

Times interest earned ratio

times interest earned ratio
Measures the firm's ability to make contractual interest payments.

The **times interest earned ratio** measures the ability to make contractual interest payments. The higher the value of this ratio, the better able the firm is to fulfill its interest obligations. The times interest earned ratio is calculated as follows:

$$\text{Times interest earned} = \frac{\text{earnings before interest and taxes}}{\text{interest}}$$

Applying this ratio to Bartlett Company yields the following 1994 value:

$$\text{Times interest earned} = \frac{\$418{,}000}{\$93{,}000} = 4.5$$

The value of earnings before interest and taxes is the same as the figure for operating profits shown in the income statement given in Table 4.2. The times interest earned ratio for Bartlett Company seems acceptable. As a rule, a value of at least 3.0—and preferably closer to 5.0—is suggested. If the firm's earnings before interest and taxes were to shrink by 78 percent [(4.5 − 1.0) ÷ 4.5], the firm would still be able to pay the $93,000 in interest it owes. Thus it has a good margin of safety.

CONCEPT IN PRACTICE

Can Adience Avoid Bankruptcy Court?

What happens when a firm can no longer meet its scheduled debt payments? Not only does its credit rating suffer, but the problem usually signals the beginning of a long descent into bankruptcy. In a few cases, however, financial managers and creditors cooperate to avoid a lengthy court battle. In June 1993 Adience, Inc., a Pittsburgh-based supplier of industrial products to the steel industry, failed to meet a scheduled payment on its bonds, and Standard & Poor's Corporation downgraded the firm's debt to a D rating. Lacking the cash flow to make interest payments in a timely manner throughout 1993, Adience offered to exchange $66 million in debt at 15 percent for $45 million in new notes at 11 percent, plus provide creditors with 55 percent of the firm's common equity. If 98 percent of the firm's creditors approve this restructuring package, Adience can arrange an orderly transfer of ownership to its creditors and avoid bankruptcy court. At this writing, 73 percent of the firm's bondholders support the plan. Adience is confident that the rest will approve the plan, because most of these creditors purchased Adience's debt at prices well below its par value in the secondary market, fully anticipating the firm's restructuring proposal.

Fixed-payment coverage ratio

fixed-payment coverage ratio
Measures the firm's ability to meet all fixed-payment obligations.

The **fixed-payment coverage ratio** measures the firm's ability to meet all fixed-payment obligations, such as loan interest and principal, lease payments, and preferred stock dividends. Like the times interest earned ratio, the higher this value, the better. Principal payments on debt, scheduled lease payments, and preferred stock dividends[15] are commonly included in this ratio. The formula for the fixed-payment coverage ratio is as follows:

$$\text{Fixed-payment coverage ratio} = \frac{\text{earnings before interest and taxes} + \text{lease payments}}{\text{interest} + \text{lease payments} + \{(\text{principal payments} + \text{preferred stock dividends}) \times [1/(1 - T)]\}}$$

where T is the corporate tax rate applicable to the firm's income. The term $1/(1 - T)$ is included to adjust the after-tax principal and preferred stock dividend payments back to a before-tax equivalent that is consistent with the before-tax values of all other terms. Applying the formula to Bartlett Company's 1994 data yields

[15]Although preferred stock dividends, which are stated at the time of issue, can be "passed" (not paid) at the option of the firm's directors, it is generally believed that the payment of such dividends is necessary. This text therefore treats the preferred stock dividend as if it were a contractual obligation, not only to be paid as a fixed amount, but also to be paid as scheduled.

Fixed-payment coverage ratio =

$$\frac{\$418{,}000 + \$35{,}000}{\$93{,}000 + \$35{,}000 + \{(\$71{,}000 + \$10{,}000) \times [1/(1 - .29)]\}}$$

$$= \frac{\$453{,}000}{\$242{,}000} = 1.9$$

Since the earnings available are nearly twice as large as its fixed-payment obligations, the firm appears able to safely meet the latter.

Like the times interest earned ratio, the fixed-payment coverage ratio measures risk. The lower the ratio, the greater the risk to both lenders and owners, and the greater the ratio, the lower the risk. This risk results from the fact that if the firm were unable to meet scheduled fixed payments, it could be driven into bankruptcy. An examination of the ratio therefore allows owners, creditors, and managers to assess the firm's ability to handle additional fixed-payment obligations such as debt.

CONCEPT IN REVIEW

4-8 What is *financial leverage*? What ratios can be used to measure the degree of indebtedness? What ratios are used to assess the ability of the firm to meet fixed payments associated with debt?

Analyzing profitability

A firm's profitability can be assessed relative to sales, assets, equity, or share value. Why is it important to view a firm's profitability relative to each of these variables? Before reading on, spend a few moments answering this question.

There are many measures of profitability. Each relates the returns of the firm to its sales, assets, equity, or share value. As a group, these measures allow the analyst to evaluate the firm's earnings with respect to a given level of sales, a certain level of assets, the owners' investment, or share value. Without profits, a firm could not attract outside capital; moreover, present owners and creditors would become concerned about the company's future and attempt to recover their funds. Owners, creditors, and management pay close attention to boosting profits due to the great importance placed on earnings in the marketplace.

Common-size income statements

common-size income statement
An income statement in which each item is expressed as a percentage of sales.

A popular tool for evaluating profitability in relation to sales is the **common-size income statement.**[16] On this statement, each item is expressed as a percentage of sales,

[16]This statement is sometimes called a *percent income statement.* The same treatment is often applied to the firm's balance sheet to make it easier to evaluate changes in the asset and financial structures of the firm. In addition to measuring profitability, these statements can in effect be used as an alternative or supplement to liquidity, activity, and debt-ratio analysis.

TABLE 4.5

BARTLETT COMPANY COMMON-SIZE INCOME STATEMENTS

	For the years ended December 31		Evaluation[a]
	1994	1993	1993–1994
Sales revenue	100.0%	100.0%	same
Less: Cost of goods sold	67.9	66.7	worse
(a) Gross profit margin	32.1%	33.3%	worse
Less: Operating expenses			
Selling expense	3.3%	4.2%	better
General and administrative expenses	6.3	7.3	better
Lease expense	1.1	1.3	better
Depreciation expense	7.8	8.7	better
Total operating expense	18.5%	21.5%	better
(b) Operating profit margin	13.6%	11.8%	better
Less: Interest expense	3.0	3.5	better
Net profits before taxes	10.6%	8.3%	better
Less: Taxes	3.1	2.5	worse
(c) Net profit margin	7.5%	5.8%	better

[a]Subjective assessments based on data provided.

thus enabling the relationship between sales and specific revenues and expenses to be easily evaluated. Common-size income statements are especially useful in comparing the performance for a particular year with that for another year. Three frequently cited ratios of profitability that can be read directly from the common-size income statement are (a) the gross profit margin, (b) the operating profit margin, and (c) the net profit margin. These are discussed below.

Common-size income statements for 1994 and 1993 for Bartlett Company are presented and evaluated in Table 4.5. The evaluation of these statements reveals that the firm's cost of goods sold increased from 66.7 percent of sales in 1993 to 67.9 percent in 1994, resulting in a decrease in the gross profit margin from 33.3 to 32.1 percent. However, thanks to a decrease in operating expenses from 21.5 percent in 1993 to 18.5 percent in 1994, the firm's net profit margin rose from 5.8 percent of sales in 1993 to 7.5 percent in 1994. The decrease in expenses in 1994 more than compensated for the increase in the cost of goods sold. A decrease in the firm's 1994 interest expense (3.0 percent of sales versus 3.5 percent in 1993) added to the increase in 1994 profits.

Gross profit margin

gross profit margin
Measures the percentage of each sales dollar remaining after the firm has paid for its goods.

The **gross profit margin** measures the percentage of each sales dollar remaining after the firm has paid for its goods. The higher the gross profit margin the better and the lower the relative cost of merchandise sold. Of course, the opposite case is also true, as the Bartlett Company example shows. The gross profit margin is calculated as follows:

$$\text{Gross profit margin} = \frac{\text{sales} - \text{cost of goods sold}}{\text{sales}} = \frac{\text{gross profits}}{\text{sales}}$$

The value for Bartlett Company's gross profit margin for 1994 is

$$\frac{\$3{,}074{,}000 - \$2{,}088{,}000}{\$3{,}074{,}000} = \frac{\$986{,}000}{\$3{,}074{,}000} = 32.1\%$$

This value is shown on line (a) of the common-size income statement in Table 4.5.

CONCEPT IN PRACTICE

What Happened to Profitability at The Limited?

How does a retail establishment earn satisfactory profits? The answer varies from store to store and across different market segments, but in general, profitability depends on corporate strategy. At The Limited, the $7 billion women's retail powerhouse, traditionally strong gross margins were built around merchandise that was high in glitz and image but low in quality. This strategy fueled rapid sales growth and increased profits throughout the 1980s, when rapidly changing fashions meant that clothing didn't have to last very long.

In the value-conscious 1990s, however, The Limited's profit-making strategy is in shambles. When customers refused to pay high prices for poor-quality merchandise, the retailer was forced to mark down its apparel to make sales. The firm's gross margin suffered, profits fell by 14 percent in 1993 alone, and the firm's sales dropped 10 percent from 1992 levels at The Limited stores and Lerner. To restore profits and please value-conscious consumers, The Limited is refocusing its corporate strategy to emphasize high-quality merchandise that commands higher retail prices.

Operating profit margin

operating profit margin
Measures the percentage of profit earned on each sales dollar before interest and taxes.

The **operating profit margin** measures what are often called the *pure profits* earned on each sales dollar. Operating profits are pure in the sense that they ignore any financial or government charges (interest or taxes) and measure only the profits earned on operations. A high operating profit margin is preferred. The operating profit margin is calculated as follows:

$$\text{Operating profit margin} = \frac{\text{operating profits}}{\text{sales}}$$

The value for Bartlett Company's operating profit margin for 1994 is

$$\frac{\$418{,}000}{\$3{,}074{,}000} = 13.6\%$$

This value is shown on line (b) of the common-size income statement in Table 4.5.

Net profit margin

net profit margin
Measures the percentage of each sales dollar remaining after all expenses, including taxes, have been deducted.

The **net profit margin** measures the percentage of each sales dollar remaining after all expenses, including taxes, have been deducted. The higher the firm's net profit margin, the better. The net profit margin is a commonly cited measure of the firm's success with respect to earnings on sales. "Good" net profit margins differ considerably across industries. A net profit margin of 1 percent or less would not be unusual for a grocery store, while a net profit margin of 10 percent would be low for a retail jewelry store. The net profit margin is calculated as follows:

$$\text{Net profit margin} = \frac{\text{net profits after taxes}}{\text{sales}}$$

Bartlett Company's net profit margin for 1994 is

$$\frac{\$231{,}000}{\$3{,}074{,}000} = 7.5\%$$

This value is shown on line (c) of the common-size income statement in Table 4.5.

Return on total assets (ROA)

return on total assets (ROA)
Measures the overall effectiveness of management in generating profits with its available assets; also called *return on investment.*

The **return on total assets (ROA),** which is often called the firm's *return on investment,* measures the overall effectiveness of management in generating profits with its available assets. The higher the firm's return on total assets, the better. The return on total assets is calculated as follows:

$$\text{Return on total assets} = \frac{\text{net profits after taxes}}{\text{total assets}}$$

Bartlett Company's return on total assets in 1994 is

$$\frac{\$231{,}000}{\$3{,}597{,}000} = 6.4\%$$

This value, which seems acceptable, could have been derived by using the *DuPont system of analysis,* which will be described in a subsequent section.

Return on equity (ROE)

return on equity (ROE)
Measures the return earned on the owners' (both preferred and common stockholders') investment in the firm.

The **return on equity (ROE)** measures the return earned on the owners' (both preferred and common stockholders') investment in the firm.[17] Generally, the higher this return, the better off are the owners. Return on equity is calculated as follows:

$$\text{Return on equity} = \frac{\text{net profits after taxes}}{\text{stockholders' equity}}$$

[17]This ratio includes preferred stock dividends in the profit figure and preferred stock in the equity value, but because the amount of preferred stock and its impact on a firm are generally quite small or nonexistent, this formula is a reasonably good approximation of the true owners'—that is, the common stockholders'—return.

This ratio for Bartlett Company in 1994 is

$$\frac{\$231{,}000}{\$1{,}954{,}000} = 11.8\%$$

The above value, which seems to be quite good, could also have been derived by using the *DuPont system of analysis,* to be described below.

Earnings per share (EPS)

The firm's *earnings per share (EPS)* are generally of interest to present or prospective stockholders and management. The earnings per share represent the number of dollars earned on behalf of each outstanding share of common stock. They are closely watched by the investing public and are considered an important indicator of corporate success. Earnings per share, as noted in Chapter 1, are calculated as follows:

$$\text{Earnings per share} = \frac{\text{earnings available for common stockholders}}{\text{number of shares of common stock outstanding}}$$

The value of Bartlett Company's earnings per share in 1994 is

$$\frac{\$221{,}000}{76{,}262} = \$2.90$$

The figure represents the dollar amount *earned* on behalf of each share outstanding. It does not represent the amount of earnings actually distributed to shareholders.

Price/Earnings (P/E) ratio

price/earnings (P/E) ratio
Reflects the amount investors are willing to pay for each dollar of the firms earnings; the higher the P/E ratio, the greater the investor confidence in the firm.

Though not a true measure of profitability, the **price/earnings (P/E) ratio** is commonly used to assess the owners' appraisal of share value.[18] The P/E ratio represents the amount investors are willing to pay for each dollar of the firm's earnings. The level of the price/earnings ratio indicates the degree of confidence (or certainty) that investors have in the firm's future performance. The higher the P/E ratio, the greater the investor confidence in the firm's future. The P/E ratio is calculated as follows:

$$\text{Price/earnings (P/E) ratio} = \frac{\text{market price per share of common stock}}{\text{earnings per share}}$$

If Bartlett Company's common stock at the end of 1994 was selling at $32\frac{1}{4}$ (i.e.,

[18]Use of the price/earnings ratio to estimate the value of the firm is part of the discussion of "Other approaches to common stock valuation" in Chapter 7.

$32.25), using the earnings per share (EPS) of $2.90 from the income statement in Table 4.2, the P/E ratio at year-end 1994 is

$$\frac{\$32.25}{\$2.90} = 11.1$$

This figure indicates that investors were paying $11.10 for each $1.00 of earnings.

CONCEPTS IN REVIEW

4-9 What is a *common-size income statement?* Which three ratios of profitability are found on this statement? How is the statement used?

4-10 How can a firm's having a high gross profit margin and a low net profit margin be explained? To what must this situation be attributable?

4-11 Define and differentiate between return on total assets (ROA), return on equity (ROE), and earnings per share (EPS). Which measure is probably of greatest interest to owners? Why?

4-12 What is the *price/earnings (P/E) ratio?* How does its level relate to the degree of confidence (or certainty) of investors in the firm's future performance? Is the P/E ratio a true measure of profitability?

A complete ratio analysis

A complete ratio analysis includes a large number of liquidity, activity, debt, and profitability ratios. Why is it important to periodically perform a complete ratio analysis of a firm's finances? Take a few minutes to answer this question before reading further.

AS INDICATED IN THE CHAPTER, NO SINGLE RATIO IS ADEQUATE FOR ASSESSING ALL aspects of the firm's financial condition. Two popular approaches to a complete ratio analysis are (1) the DuPont system of analysis and (2) the summary analysis of a large number of ratios. Each of these approaches has merit. The DuPont system acts as a *search technique* aimed at finding the key areas responsible for the firm's financial performance. The summary analysis approach tends to view *all aspects* of the firm's financial activities to isolate key areas of responsibility.

DuPont system of analysis

DuPont system of analysis
Used by management as a framework for dissecting the firm's financial statements and assessing its financial condition.

The **DuPont system of analysis** has for many years been used by financial managers as a structure for dissecting the firm's financial statements to assess its financial condition. The DuPont system merges the income statement and balance sheet into two summary measures of profitability: return on total assets (ROA) and return on equity (ROE). Figure 4.2 depicts the basic DuPont system with Bartlett Company's 1994 monetary and ratio values. The upper portion of the chart summarizes the income statement activities; the lower portion summarizes the balance sheet activities.

The DuPont system first brings together the *net profit margin,* which measures the firm's profitability on sales, with its *total asset turnover,* which indicates how efficiently

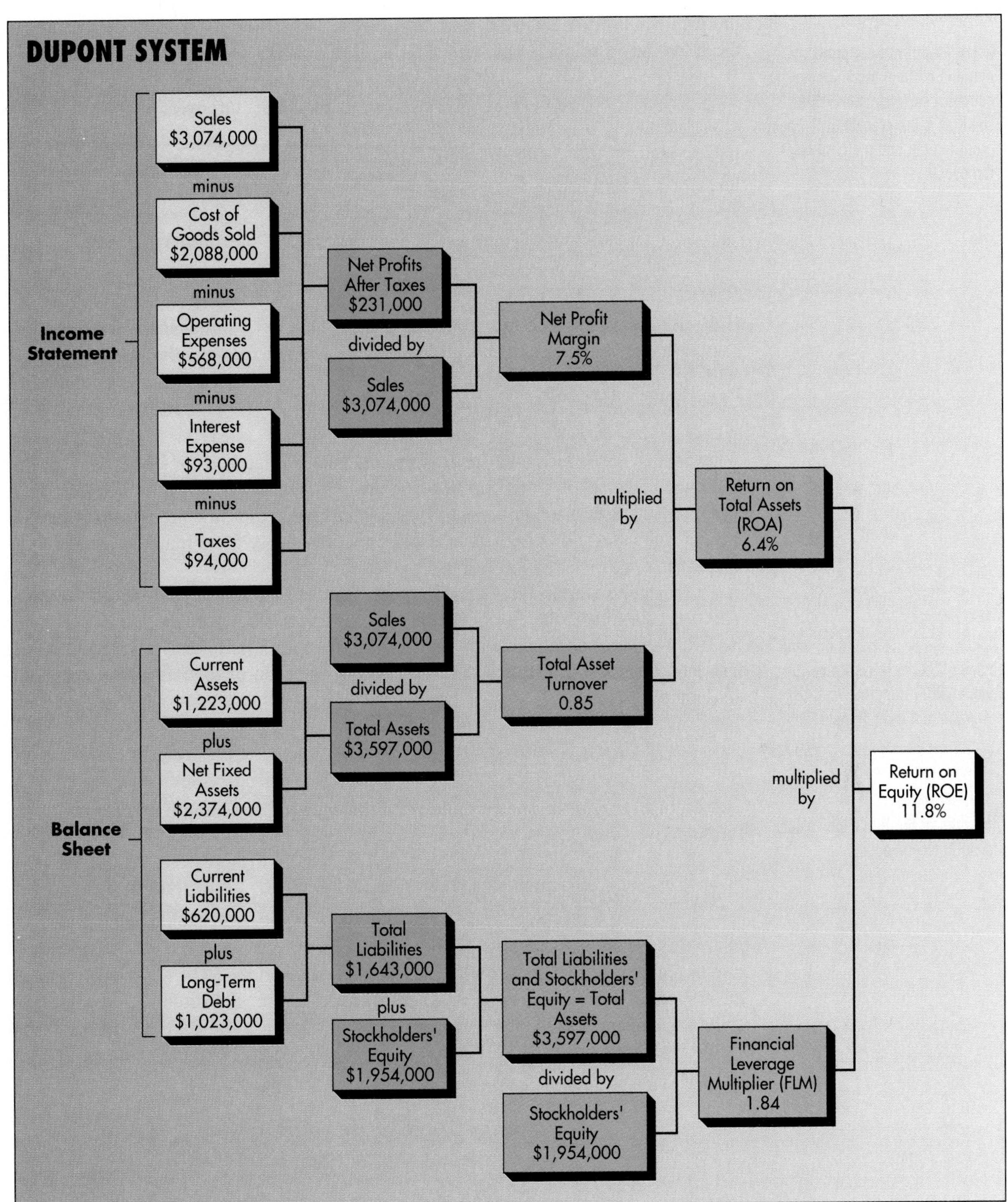

FIGURE 4.2
The DuPont system of analysis with application to Bartlett Company (1994)

DuPont formula
Relates the firm's net profit margin and total asset turnover to its return on total assets (ROA). The ROA is the product of the net profit margin and the total asset turnover.

the firm has used its assets to generate sales. In the **DuPont formula** the product of these two ratios results in the *return on total assets (ROA):*

$$\text{ROA} = \text{net profit margin} \times \text{total asset turnover}$$

Substituting the appropriate formulas into the equation and simplifying results in the formula given earlier,

$$\text{ROA} = \frac{\text{net profits after taxes}}{\text{sales}} \times \frac{\text{sales}}{\text{total assets}} = \frac{\text{net profits after taxes}}{\text{total assets}}$$

If the 1994 values of the net profit margin and total asset turnover for Bartlett Company, calculated earlier, are substituted into the DuPont formula, the result is

$$\text{ROA} = 7.5\% \times 0.85 = 6.4\%$$

As expected, this value is the same as that calculated directly in an earlier section. The DuPont formula allows the firm to break down its return into a profit-on-sales and an efficiency-of-asset-use component. Typically, a firm with a low net profit margin has a high total asset turnover, which results in a reasonably good return on total assets. Often, the opposite situation exists.

modified DuPont formula
Relates the firm's return on total assets (ROA) to its return on equity (ROE) using the *financial leverage multiplier (FLM).*

financial leverage multiplier (FLM)
The ratio of the firm's total assets to stockholders' equity.

The second step in the DuPont system employs the **modified DuPont formula.** This formula relates the firm's return on total assets (ROA) to the return on equity (ROE). The latter is calculated by multiplying the return on total assets (ROA) by the **financial leverage multiplier (FLM),** which is the ratio of total assets to stockholders' equity:[19]

$$\text{ROE} = \text{ROA} \times \text{FLM}$$

Substituting the appropriate formulas into the equation and simplifying results in the formula given earlier,

$$\text{ROE} = \frac{\text{net profits after taxes}}{\text{total assets}} \times \frac{\text{total assets}}{\text{stockholders' equity}} = \frac{\text{net profits after taxes}}{\text{stockholders' equity}}$$

Use of the financial leverage multiplier (FLM) to convert the ROA to the ROE reflects the impact of leverage (use of debt) on owners' return. Substituting the values for Bartlett Company's ROA of 6.4 percent, calculated earlier, and Bartlett's FLM of 1.84 ($3,597,000 total assets ÷ $1,954,000 stockholders' equity) into the modified DuPont formula yields

$$\text{ROE} = 6.4\% \times 1.84 = 11.8\%$$

[19]The financial leverage multiplier is equivalent to $\frac{1}{1 - \text{debt ratio}}$ and represents 1 divided by the percentage of total financing raised with equity. For computational convenience the financial leverage multiplier is utilized here rather than the seemingly more descriptive debt ratio.

The 11.8 percent ROE calculated by using the modified DuPont formula is the same as that calculated directly.

The considerable advantage of the DuPont system is that it allows the firm to break its return on equity into a profit-on-sales component (net profit margin), an efficiency-of-asset-use component (total asset turnover), and a use-of-leverage component (financial leverage multiplier). The total return to the owners can therefore be analyzed in light of these important dimensions. As an illustration, let's look ahead to the ratio values summarized in Table 4.6. Bartlett Company's net profit margin and total asset turnover increased between 1993 and 1994 to levels above the industry average. In combination, improved profit on sales and better asset utilization resulted in an improved return on total assets (ROA). Increased asset return coupled with the increased use of debt reflected in the increased financial leverage multiplier (not shown) caused the owners' return (ROE) to increase. Simply stated, it is clear from the DuPont system of analysis that the improvement in Bartlett Company's 1994 ROE resulted from greater profit on sales, better asset utilization, and the increased use of leverage. Of course, it is important to recognize that the increased return reflected in the ROE may be attributable to the increased risk caused by the higher leverage reflected in the FLM. In other words, the use of more financial leverage increases *both* return and risk.

Summarizing all ratios

The 1994 ratio values calculated earlier and the ratio values calculated for 1992 and 1993 for Bartlett Company, along with the industry average ratios for 1994, are summarized in Table 4.6. The table shows the formula used to calculate each ratio. Using these data, we can discuss the four key aspects of Bartlett's performance—(1) liquidity, (2) activity, (3) debt, and (4) profitability—on a cross-sectional and time-series basis.

LIQUIDITY

The overall liquidity of the firm seems to exhibit a reasonably stable trend, having been maintained at a level that is relatively consistent with the industry average in 1994. The firm's liquidity seems to be good.

ACTIVITY

Bartlett Company's inventory appears to be in good shape. Its inventory management seems to have improved, and in 1994 it performed at a level above that of the industry. The firm may be experiencing some problems with accounts receivable. The average collection period seems to have crept up to a level above that of the industry. Bartlett also appears to be slow in paying its bills; it is paying nearly 30 days later than the industry average. Payment procedures should be examined to make sure that the company's credit standing is not adversely affected. While overall liquidity appears to be good, some attention should be given to the management of accounts receivable and payable. Bartlett's fixed asset turnover and total asset turnover reflect sizable declines in the efficiency of fixed and total asset utilization between 1992 and 1993. Although in 1994 the total asset turnover rose to a level considerably above the industry average, it appears that the pre-1993 level of efficiency has not yet been achieved.

TABLE 4.6

SUMMARY OF BARTLETT COMPANY RATIOS (1992–1994, INCLUDING 1994 INDUSTRY AVERAGES)

		Year				Evaluation[d]		
Ratio	Formula	1992[a]	1993[b]	1994[b]	Industry average 1994[c]	Cross-sectional 1994	Time-series 1992–1994	Overall
Liquidity								
Net working capital	current assets − current liabilities	$583,000	$521,000	$603,000	$427,000	good	good	good
Current ratio	$\frac{\text{current assets}}{\text{current liabilities}}$	2.04	2.08	1.97	2.05	OK	OK	OK
Quick (acid-test) ratio	$\frac{\text{current assets} - \text{inventory}}{\text{current liabilities}}$	1.32	1.46	1.51	1.43	OK	good	good
Activity								
Inventory turnover	$\frac{\text{cost of goods sold}}{\text{inventory}}$	5.1	5.7	7.2	6.6	good	good	good
Average collection period	$\frac{\text{accounts receivable}}{\text{average sales per day}}$	43.9 days	51.2 days	58.9 days	44.3 days	poor	poor	poor
Average payment period	$\frac{\text{accounts payable}}{\text{average purchases per day}}$	75.8 days	81.2 days	94.1 days	66.5 days	poor	poor	poor
Fixed asset turnover	$\frac{\text{sales}}{\text{net fixed assets}}$	1.50	1.13	1.29	1.35	OK	OK	OK
Total asset turnover	$\frac{\text{sales}}{\text{total assets}}$	.94	.79	.85	.75	OK	OK	OK
Debt								
Degree of indebtedness:								
Debt ratio	$\frac{\text{total liabilities}}{\text{total assets}}$	36.8%	44.3%	45.7%	40.0%	OK	OK	OK
Debt-equity ratio	$\frac{\text{long-term debt}}{\text{stockholders' equity}}$	44.2%	53.1%	52.4%	50.0%	OK	OK	OK

Ratio	Formula	Year			Industry average 1994[c]	Evaluation[d]		
		1992[a]	1993[b]	1994[b]		Cross-sectional 1994	Time-series 1992–1994	Overall
Debt (continued)								
Ability to service debts:								
Times interest earned ratio	$\frac{\text{earnings before interest and taxes}}{\text{interest}}$	5.6	3.3	4.5	4.3	good	OK	OK
Fixed-payment coverage ratio	$\frac{\text{earnings before interest and taxes + lease payments}}{\text{int. + lease pay.} + \{(\text{prin. + pref. div.}) \times [1/(1 - T)]\}}$	2.4	1.4	1.9	1.5	good	OK	good
Profitability								
Gross profit margin	$\frac{\text{gross profits}}{\text{sales}}$	31.4%	33.3%	32.1%	30.0%	OK	OK	OK
Operating profit margin	$\frac{\text{operating profits}}{\text{sales}}$	14.6%	11.8%	13.6%	11.0%	good	OK	good
Net profit margin	$\frac{\text{net profits after taxes}}{\text{sales}}$	8.8%	5.8%	7.5%	6.4%	good	OK	good
Return on total assets (ROA)	$\frac{\text{net profits after taxes}}{\text{total assets}}$	8.3%	4.5%	6.4%	4.8%	good	OK	good
Return on equity (ROE)	$\frac{\text{net profits after taxes}}{\text{stockholders' equity}}$	13.1%	8.1%	11.8%	8.0%	good	OK	good
Earnings per share (EPS)	$\frac{\text{earnings available for common stockholders}}{\text{number of shares of common stock outstanding}}$	\$3.26	\$1.81	\$2.90	\$2.26	good	OK	good
Price/earnings (P/E) ratio	$\frac{\text{market price per share of common stock}}{\text{earnings per share}}$	10.5	10.0	11.1	12.5	OK	OK	OK

[a]Calculated from data not included in the chapter.

[b]Calculated by using the financial statements presented in Tables 4.2 and 4.3.

[c]Obtained from sources not included in this chapter.

[d]Subjective assessments based on data provided.

DEBT

Bartlett Company's indebtedness increased over the 1992–1994 period and is currently at a level above the industry average. Although the increase in the debt ratio could be cause for alarm, the firm's ability to meet interest and fixed-payment obligations improved from 1993 to 1994 to a level that outperforms the industry. The firm's increased indebtedness in 1993 apparently caused a deterioration in its ability to pay debt adequately. However, Bartlett has evidently improved its income in 1994 so that it is able to meet its interest and fixed-payment obligations in a fashion consistent with the average firm in the industry. In summary, it appears that although 1993 was an off year, the company's ability to pay debts in 1994 adequately compensates for the increased degree of indebtedness.

PROFITABILITY

Bartlett's profitability relative to sales in 1994 was better than that of the average company in the industry, although it did not match the firm's 1992 performance. While the *gross* profit margin in 1993 and 1994 was better than in 1992, it appears that higher levels of operating and interest expenses in 1993 and 1994 caused the 1994 *net* profit margin to fall below that of 1992. However, Bartlett Company's 1994 net profit margin is quite favorable when compared to the industry average. The firm's return on total assets, return on equity, and earnings per share behaved in a fashion similar to its net profit margin over the 1992–1994 period. Bartlett appears to have experienced either a sizable drop in sales between 1992 and 1993 or a rapid expansion in assets during that period. The owners' return, as evidenced by the exceptionally high 1994 level of return on equity, seems to suggest that the firm is performing quite well. Of course, as was noted in the discussion of the application of the DuPont system of analysis to Bartlett's 1994 results, the firm's increased ROE actually resulted from the increased returns from its improved ROA and the increased risk reflected in its increased degree of indebtedness. This can be seen in its increased debt ratios and financial leverage multiplier (FLM). In addition, although the firm's shares are selling at a price/earnings (P/E) multiple below that of the industry, some improvement occurred between 1993 and 1994. The firm's above-average returns—net profit margin, ROA, ROE, and EPS—may be attributable to its above-average risk as reflected in its below-industry-average P/E ratio.

In summary, it appears that the firm is growing and has recently undergone an expansion in assets, this expansion being financed primarily through the use of debt. The 1993–1994 period seems to reflect a phase of adjustment and recovery from the rapid growth in assets. Bartlett's sales, profits, and other performance factors seem to be growing with the increase in the size of the operation. In short, the firm appears to have done quite well in 1994.

CONCEPTS IN REVIEW

4-13 Three areas of analysis or concern are combined in using the *DuPont system of analysis.* What are these concerns, and how are they combined to explain the firm's return on equity (ROE)? How is risk associated with financial leverage captured using this system?

4-14 Describe how you would approach a complete ratio analysis of the firm on both a cross-sectional and a time-series basis by summarizing a large number of ratios.

Summary

LG **1** **Understand the parties interested in performing financial ratio analysis and the common types of ratio comparisons.** Ratio analysis allows present and prospective stockholders and lenders and the firm's management to evaluate the firm's performance and status. It can be performed on a cross-sectional or a time-series basis. Cross-sectional analysis involves comparisons of different firms' financial ratios at the same point in time. Time-series analysis measures a firm's performance over time.

LG **2** **Describe some of the cautions that should be considered in performing financial ratio analysis.** Cautions in ratio analysis include: (1) a single ratio does not generally provide sufficient information; (2) financial statements being compared should be dated at the same point in time during the year; (3) audited financial statements should be used; (4) data should be checked for consistency of accounting treatment; and (5) inflation and differing asset ages can distort ratio comparisons.

LG **3** **Use popular ratios to analyze a firm's liquidity and the activity of inventory, accounts receivable, accounts payable, fixed assets, and total assets.** The liquidity, or ability of the firm to pay its bills as they come due, can be measured by the firm's net working capital, its current ratio, or its quick (acid-test) ratio. Activity ratios measure the speed with which various accounts are converted into sales or cash. The activity of inventory can be measured by its turnover, that of accounts receivable by the average collection period, and that of accounts payable by the average payment period. Fixed and total asset turnovers can be used to measure the efficiency with which the firm has used its fixed and total assets to generate sales. Formulas for these liquidity and activity ratios are summarized in Table 4.6.

LG **4** **Discuss the relationship between debt and financial leverage and the ratios that can be used to assess the firm's debt position and its ability to meet the payments associated with debt.** The more debt a firm uses, the greater will be its financial leverage, which results in the magnification of both risk and return. Financial debt ratios measure both the degree of indebtedness and the ability to service (pay) debts. Commonly used measures of debt position are the debt ratio and the debt-equity ratio. The ability to pay contractual obligations such as interest, principal, lease payments, and preferred stock dividends can be measured by times-interest-earned and fixed-payment coverage ratios. Formulas for these debt ratios are summarized in Table 4.6.

LG **5** **Evaluate a firm's profitability relative to its sales, asset investment, owners' equity investment, and share value.** Measures of profitability can be made in various ways. The common-size income statement, which shows all items as a percentage of sales, can be used to determine gross profit margin, operating profit margin, and net profit margin. Other measures of profitability include return on total assets, return on equity, earnings per share, and the price/earnings ratio. Formulas for these profitability ratios are summarized in Table 4.6.

LG **6** **Use the DuPont system and a summary of a large number of ratios to perform a complete financial analysis of all aspects of a firm's financial condition and make appropriate recommendations.** The DuPont system of analysis is a search technique aimed at finding the key areas responsible for the firm's financial performance. It allows the firm to break the return on equity into a profit-on-sales component, an efficiency-of-asset-use component, and a use-of-leverage component. The structure of the DuPont system of analysis is summarized in Figure 4.2. By summarizing a large number of ratios, financial analysts can assess all aspects of the firm's activities to isolate key areas of responsibility.

Self-test problems (Solutions in Appendix E)

ST 4-1 LG **3,4,5** **Ratio formulas and interpretations** Without referring to the text, indicate for each of the following ratios the formula for its calculation and the kinds of problems, if any, the firm is likely to have if these ratios are too high relative to the industry average. What if they are too low relative to the industry? Create a table similar to that shown on the next page, and fill in the empty blocks.

Ratio	Too high	Too low
Current ratio =		
Inventory turnover =		
Times interest earned =	X	
Gross profit margin =		
Return on total assets =	X	

ST 4-2 LG 3,4,5 Balance sheet completion using ratios Complete the 1994 balance sheet for O'Keefe Industries using the information that follows it.

Balance sheet O'Keefe Industries December 31, 1994			
Cash	$30,000	Accounts payable	$120,000
Marketable securities	25,000	Notes payable	_____
Accounts receivable	_____	Accruals	20,000
Inventories	_____	Total current liabilities	_____
Total current assets	_____	Long-term debt	_____
Net fixed assets	_____	Stockholders' equity	$600,000
Total assets	_____	Total liabilities and stockholders' equity	_____

The following financial data for 1994 are also available:

(1) Sales totaled $1,800,000.
(2) The gross profit margin was 25 percent.
(3) Inventory turnover was 6.0.
(4) There are 360 days in the year.
(5) The average collection period was 40 days.
(6) The current ratio was 1.60.
(7) The total asset turnover ratio was 1.20.
(8) The debt ratio was 60 percent.

Problems

4-1 LG 3 Liquidity management The Bauman Company's total current assets, net working capital, and inventory for each of the past four years are given below.

Item	1991	1992	1993	1994
Total current assets	$16,950	$21,900	$22,500	$27,000
Net working capital	7,950	9,300	9,900	9,600
Inventory	6,000	6,900	6,900	7,200

a. Calculate the firm's current and quick ratios for each year. Compare the resulting time series of each measure of liquidity (i.e., net working capital, the current ratio, and the quick ratio).
b. Comment on the firm's liquidity over the 1991–1994 period.
c. If you were told that the Bauman Company's inventory turnover for each year in the 1991–1994 period and the industry averages were as follows, would this support or conflict with your evaluation in **b**? Why?

Inventory turnover	1991	1992	1993	1994
Bauman Company	6.3	6.8	7.0	6.4
Industry average	10.6	11.2	10.8	11.0

4-2 LG 3 **Inventory management** Wilkins Manufacturing has sales of $4 million and a gross profit margin of 40 percent. Its *end-of-quarter inventories* are as follows:

Quarter	Inventory
1	$ 400,000
2	800,000
3	1,200,000
4	200,000

a. Find the average quarterly inventory, and use it to calculate the firm's inventory turnover and the average age of inventory.
b. Assuming that the company is in an industry with an average inventory turnover of 2.0, how would you evaluate the activity of Wilkins' inventory?

4-3 LG 3 **Accounts receivable management** An evaluation of the books of Blair Supply, shown in the following table, gives the end-of-year accounts receivable balance, which is believed to consist of amounts originating in the months indicated. The company had annual sales of $2.4 million. The firm extends 30-day credit terms.

Month of origin	Amounts receivable
July	$ 3,875
August	2,000
September	34,025
October	15,100
November	52,000
December	193,000
Year-end accounts receivable	$300,000

a. Use the year-end total to evaluate the firm's collection system.
b. If 70 percent of the firm's sales occur between July and December, would this affect the validity of your conclusion in **a**? Explain.

4-4 LG 4 **Debt analysis** The Springfield Bank is evaluating Creek Enterprises, which has requested a $4,000,000 loan, to assess the firm's financial leverage and financial risk. On the basis of the debt ratios for Creek, along with the industry averages and Creek's recent financial statements (presented on the following pages), evaluate and recommend appropriate action on the loan request.

Income statement Creek Enterprises for the year ended December 31, 1994		
Sales revenue		$30,000,000
Less: Cost of goods sold		21,000,000
Gross profits		$ 9,000,000
Less: Operating expenses		
Selling expense	$3,000,000	
General and administrative expenses	1,800,000	
Lease expense	200,000	
Depreciation expense	1,000,000	
Total operating expense		6,000,000
Operating profits		$ 3,000,000
Less: Interest expense		1,000,000
Net profits before taxes		$ 2,000,000
Less: Taxes (rate = 40%)		800,000
Net profits after taxes		$ 1,200,000

Balance sheet Creek Enterprises December 31, 1994			
Assets		**Liabilities and stockholders' equity**	
Current assets		Current liabilities	
Cash	$ 1,000,000	Accounts payable	$ 8,000,000
Marketable securities	3,000,000	Notes payable	8,000,000
Accounts receivable	12,000,000	Accruals	500,000
Inventories	7,500,000	Total current liabilities	$16,500,000
Total current assets	$23,500,000	Long-term debt (includes financial leases)[b]	$20,000,000
Gross fixed assets (at cost)[a]		Stockholders' equity	
Land and buildings	$11,000,000	Preferred stock (25,000 shares, $4 dividend)	$ 2,500,000
Machinery and equipment	20,500,000	Common stock (1 million shares at $5 par)	5,000,000
Furniture and fixtures	8,000,000	Paid-in capital in excess of par value	4,000,000
Gross fixed assets	$39,500,000	Retained earnings	2,000,000
Less: Accumulated depreciation	13,000,000	Total stockholders' equity	$13,500,000
Net fixed assets	$26,500,000		
Total assets	$50,000,000	Total liabilities and stockholders' equity	$50,000,000

[a]The firm has a four-year financial lease requiring annual beginning-of-year payments of $200,000. Three years of the lease have yet to run.

[b]Required annual principal payments are $800,000.

Industry averages	
Debt ratio	.51
Debt-equity ratio	1.07
Times interest earned ratio	7.30
Fixed-payment coverage ratio	1.85

4-5 LG **5** **Common-size statement analysis** A common-size income statement for Creek Enterprises' 1993 operations is presented below. Using the firm's 1994 income statement presented in Problem 4-4, develop the 1994 common-size income statement and compare it to the 1993 statement. Which areas require further analysis and investigation?

Common-size income statement Creek Enterprises for the year ended December 31, 1993		
Sales revenue ($35,000,000)		100.0%
Less: Cost of goods sold		65.9
Gross profits		34.1%
Less: Operating expenses		
Selling expense	12.7%	
General and administrative expenses	6.3	
Lease expense	0.6	
Depreciation expense	3.6	
Total operating expense		23.2
Operating profits		10.9%
Less: Interest expense		1.5
Net profits before taxes		9.4%
Less: Taxes (rate = 40%)		3.8
Net profits after taxes		5.6%

4-6 LG **6** **Dupont System of analysis** Use the following ratio information for Johnson International and the industry averages for Johnson's line of business to:

a. Construct the DuPont system of analysis for both Johnson and the industry.
b. Evaluate Johnson (and the industry) over the three-year period.
c. In which areas does Johnson require further analysis? Why?

Johnson	1992	1993	1994
Financial leverage multiplier	1.75	1.75	1.85
Net profit margin	.059	.058	.049
Total asset turnover	2.11	2.18	2.34
Industry averages			
Financial leverage multiplier	1.67	1.69	1.64
Net profit margin	.054	.047	.041
Total asset turnover	2.05	2.13	2.15

4-7 LG 6 Cross-sectional ratio analysis Use the following financial statements for Fox Manufacturing Company for the year ended December 31, 1994, along with the industry average ratios also given below, to:

a. Prepare and interpret a ratio analysis of the firm's 1994 operations.

b. Summarize your findings and make recommendations.

Income statement Fox Manufacturing Company for the year ended December 31, 1994		
Sales revenue		$600,000
Less: Cost of goods sold		460,000
Gross profits		$140,000
Less: Operating expenses		
General and administrative expenses	$30,000	
Depreciation expense	30,000	
Total operating expense		60,000
Operating profits		$ 80,000
Less: Interest expense		10,000
Net profits before taxes		$ 70,000
Less: Taxes		27,100
Net profits after taxes (earnings available for common stockholders)		$ 42,900
Earnings per share (EPS)		$2.15

Balance sheet Fox Manufacturing Company December 31, 1994	
Assets	
Cash	$ 15,000
Marketable securities	7,200
Accounts receivable	34,100
Inventories	82,000
Total current assets	$138,300
Net fixed assets	$270,000
Total assets	$408,300
Liabilities and stockholders' equity	
Accounts payable	$ 57,000
Notes payable	13,000
Accruals	5,000
Total current liabilities	$ 75,000
Long-term debt	$150,000
Stockholders' equity	
Common stock equity (20,000 shares outstanding)	$110,200
Retained earnings	73,100
Total stockholders' equity	$183,300
Total liabilities and stockholders' equity	$408,300

Ratio	Industry average, 1994
Net working capital	$125,000
Current ratio	2.35
Quick ratio	.87
Inventory turnover[a]	4.55
Average collection period[a]	35.3 days
Fixed asset turnover	1.97
Total asset turnover	1.09
Debt ratio	.300
Debt-equity ratio	.615
Times interest earned ratio	12.3
Gross profit margin	.202
Operating profit margin	.135
Net profit margin	.091
Return on total assets (ROA)	.099
Return on equity (ROE)	.167
Earnings per share (EPS)	$3.10

[a]Based on a 360-day year and on end-of-year figures.

4-8 LG 6 **Financial statement analysis** The financial statements of Zach Industries for the year ended December 31, 1994, are given below.

Income statement Zach Industries for the year ended December 31, 1994	
Sales revenue	$160,000
Less: Cost of goods sold	106,000
Gross profits	$ 54,000
Less: Operating expenses	
Selling expense	$ 16,000
General and administrative expenses	10,000
Lease expense	1,000
Depreciation expense	10,000
Total operating expense	$ 37,000
Operating profits	$ 17,000
Less: Interest expense	6,100
Net profits before taxes	$ 10,900
Less: Taxes	4,360
Net profits after taxes	$ 6,540

Balance sheet
Zach Industries
December 31, 1994

Assets	
Cash	$ 500
Marketable securities	1,000
Accounts receivable	25,000
Inventories	45,500
Total current assets	$ 72,000
Land	$ 26,000
Buildings and equipment	90,000
Less: Accumulated depreciation	38,000
Net fixed assets	$ 78,000
Total assets	$150,000
Liabilities and stockholders' equity	
Accounts payable	$ 22,000
Notes payable	47,000
Total current liabilities	$ 69,000
Long-term debt	$ 22,950
Common stock	$ 31,500
Retained earnings	$ 26,550
Total liabilities and stockholders' equity	$150,000

a. Use the preceding financial statements to complete the table below. Assume that the industry averages given in the table are applicable for both 1993 and 1994.

b. Analyze Zach Industries' financial condition as it relates to (1) liquidity, (2) activity, (3) debt, and (4) profitability. Summarize the company's overall financial condition.

ZACH INDUSTRIES RATIO ANALYSIS

Ratio	Industry average	Actual 1993	Actual 1994
Current ratio	1.80	1.84	______
Quick ratio	.70	.78	______
Inventory turnover[a]	2.50	2.59	______
Average collection period[a]	37 days	36 days	______
Debt-equity ratio	50%	51%	______
Times interest earned ratio	3.8	4.0	______
Gross profit margin	38%	40%	______
Net profit margin	3.5%	3.6%	______
Return on total assets	4.0%	4.0%	______
Return on equity	9.5%	8.0%	______

[a]Based on a 360-day year and on end-of-year figures.

4-9 LG 6 **Integrative—Complete ratio analysis** Given the following financial statements, historical ratios, and industry averages, calculate the Sterling Company's financial ratios for the most recent year. Analyze its overall financial situation from both a cross-sectional and a time-series viewpoint. Break your analysis into an evaluation of the firm's liquidity, activity, debt, and profitability.

Income statement
Sterling Company
for the year ended December 31, 1994

Sales revenue		$10,000,000
Less: Cost of goods sold		7,500,000
Gross profits		$ 2,500,000
Less: Operating expenses		
Selling expense	$300,000	
General and administrative expenses	650,000	
Lease expense	50,000	
Depreciation expense	200,000	
Total operating expense		1,200,000
Operating profits		$ 1,300,000
Less: Interest expense		200,000
Net profits before taxes		$ 1,100,000
Less: Taxes (rate = 40%)		440,000
Net profits after taxes		$ 660,000
Less: Preferred stock dividends		50,000
Earnings available for common stockholders		$ 610,000
Earnings per share (EPS)		$3.05

Balance sheet
Sterling Company
December 31, 1994

Assets			Liabilities and stockholders' equity	
Current assets			Current liabilities	
Cash		$ 200,000	Accounts payable[b]	$ 900,000
Marketable securities		50,000	Notes payable	200,000
Accounts receivable		800,000	Accruals	100,000
Inventories		950,000	Total current liabilities	$ 1,200,000
Total current assets		$ 2,000,000	Long-term debt (includes financial leases)[c]	$ 3,000,000
Gross fixed assets (at cost)[a]	$12,000,000		Stockholders' equity	
Less: Accumulated depreciation	3,000,000		Preferred stock (25,000 shares, $2 dividend)	$ 1,000,000
Net fixed assets		$ 9,000,000	Common stock (200,000 shares at $3 par)[d]	600,000
Other assets		$ 1,000,000	Paid-in capital in excess of par value	5,200,000
Total assets		$12,000,000	Retained earnings	1,000,000
			Total stockholders' equity	$ 7,800,000
			Total liabilities and stockholders' equity	$12,000,000

[a]The firm has an eight-year financial lease requiring annual beginning-of-year payments of $50,000. Five years of the lease have yet to run.

[b]Annual credit purchases of $6,200,000 were made during the year.

[c]The annual principal payment on the long-term debt is $100,000.

[d]On December 31, 1994, the firm's common stock closed at $27½ (i.e., $27.50).

HISTORICAL AND INDUSTRY-AVERAGE RATIOS FOR STERLING COMPANY

Ratio	Actual 1992	Actual 1993	Industry average, 1994
Net working capital	$760,000	$720,000	$1,600,000
Current ratio	1.40	1.55	1.85
Quick ratio1.00	.92	1.05	
Inventory turnover	9.52	9.21	8.60
Average collection period	45.0 days	36.4 days	35.0 days
Average payment period	58.5 days	60.8 days	45.8 days
Fixed asset turnover	1.08	1.05	1.07
Total asset turnover	.74	.80	.74
Debt ratio .20	.20	.30	
Debt-equity ratio	.25	.27	.39
Times interest earned ratio	8.2	7.3	8.0
Fixed-payment coverage ratio	4.5	4.2	4.2
Gross profit margin	.30	.27	.25
Operating profit margin	.12	.12	.10
Net profit margin	.067	.067	.058
Return on total assets (ROA)	.049	.054	.043
Return on equity (ROE)	.066	.073	.072
Earnings per share (EPS)	$1.75	$2.20	$1.50
Price/earnings (P/E) ratio	12.0	10.5	11.2

Chapter 4 Case Assessing Martin Manufacturing's current financial position

Terri Spiro, an experienced budget analyst at Martin Manufacturing Company, has been charged with assessing the firm's financial performance during 1994 and its financial position at year-end 1994. To complete this assignment, she gathered the firm's 1994 financial statements, which are presented below. In addition, Terri obtained the firm's ratio values for 1992 and 1993, along with the 1994 industry average ratios (also applicable to 1992 and 1993). These are also presented on the facing page.

Income statement ($000) Martin Manufacturing Company for the year ended December 31, 1994		
Sales revenue		$ 5,075,000
Less: Cost of goods sold		3,704,000
Gross profits		$ 1,371,000
Less: Operating expenses		
Selling expense	$650,000	
General and administrative expenses	416,000	
Depreciation expense	152,000	
Total operating expense		1,218,000
Operating profits		$ 153,000
Less: Interest expense		93,000
Net profits before taxes		$ 60,000
Less: Taxes (rate = 40%)		24,000
Net profits after taxes		$ 36,000

Balance sheets
Martin Manufacturing Company

	December 31	
Assets	**1994**	**1993**
Current assets		
Cash	$25,000	$24,100
Accounts receivable	805,556	763,900
Inventories	700,625	763,445
Total current assets	$1,531,181	$1,551,445
Gross fixed assets (at cost)	$2,093,819	$1,691,707
Less: Accumulated depreciation	500,000	348,000
Net fixed assets	$1,593,819	$1,343,707
Total assets	$3,125,000	$2,895,152
Liabilities and stockholders' equity		
Current liabilities		
Accounts payable	$ 230,000	$ 400,500
Notes payable	311,000	370,000
Accruals	75,000	100,902
Total current liabilities	$ 616,000	$ 871,402
Long-term debt	$1,165,250	$ 700,000
Total liabilities	$1,781,250	$1,571,402
Stockholders' equity		
Preferred stock	$ 50,000	$ 50,000
Common stock (at par)	100,000	100,000
Paid-in capital in excess of par value	193,750	193,750
Retained earnings	1,000,000	980,000
Total stockholders' equity	$1,343,750	$1,323,750
Total liabilities and stockholders' equity	$3,125,000	$2,895,152

Historical ratios Martin Manufacturing Company				
Ratio	**Actual 1992**	**Actual 1993**	**Actual 1994**	**Industry average 1994**
Current ratio	1.7	1.8	______	1.5
Quick ratio	1.0	.9	______	1.2
Inventory turnover	5.2	5.0	______	10.2
Average collection period	50 days	55 days	______	46 days
Fixed asset turnover (times)	3.2	3.5	______	4.1
Total asset turnover (times)	1.5	1.5	______	2.0
Debt ratio	45.8%	54.3%	______	24.5%
Times interest earned ratio	2.2	1.9	______	2.5
Gross profit margin	27.5%	28.0%	______	26.0%
Net profit margin	1.1%	1.0%	______	1.2%
Return on total assets (ROA)	1.7%	1.5%	______	2.4%
Return on equity (ROE)	3.1%	3.3%	______	3.2%

Required

a. Calculate the firm's 1994 financial ratios, and then fill in the table above.

b. Analyze the firm's current financial position from both a cross-sectional and a time-series viewpoint. Break your analysis into an evaluation of the firm's liquidity, activity, debt, and profitability.

c. Summarize the firms overall financial position based on your findings in **b**.

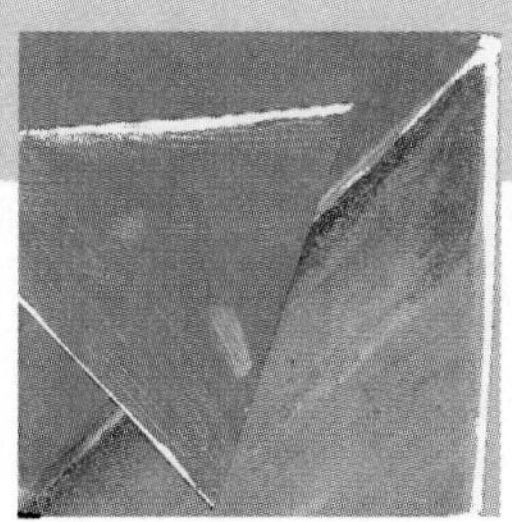

INTEGRATIVE CASE I

TRACK SOFTWARE, INC.

Seven years ago, after 15 years in public accounting, Stanley Booker, CPA, resigned his position as Manager of Cost Systems for Davis, Cohen, and O'Brien Public Accountants and started Track Software, Inc. In the two years preceding his departure from Davis, Cohen, and O'Brien, Stanley had spent nights and weekends developing a sophisticated cost accounting software program that became Track's initial product offering. As the firm grew, Stanley planned to develop and expand the software product offerings—all of which would be related to streamlining the accounting processes of medium- to large-sized manufacturers.

Although Track experienced losses during its first two years of operation—1988 and 1989—its profit has increased steadily from 1990 to the present (1994). The firm's profit history, including dividend payments and contributions to retained earnings, is summarized in Table 1.

TABLE 1

Profit, dividend, and retained earnings, 1988–1994
Track Software, Inc.

Year	Net profits after taxes (1)	Dividends paid (2)	Contribution to retained earnings [(1) − (2)] (3)
1988	($50,000)	$ 0	($50,000)
1989	(20,000)	0	(20,000)
1990	15,000	0	15,000
1991	35,000	0	35,000
1992	40,000	1,000	39,000
1993	43,000	3,000	40,000
1994	48,000	5,000	43,000

Stanley started the firm with a $100,000 investment—his savings of $50,000 as equity and a $50,000 long-term loan from the bank. He had hoped to maintain his initial 100 percent ownership in the corporation, but after experiencing a $50,000 loss during the first year of operation (1988), he sold 60 percent of the stock to a group of investors to obtain needed funds. Since then, no other stock transactions have taken place. Although he owns only 40 percent of the firm, Stanley actively manages all aspects of its activities; the other stockholders are not active in management of the firm.

Stanley has just prepared the firm's 1994 income statement, balance sheet, and statement of retained earnings, shown in Tables 2, 3, and 4, along with the 1993 balance sheet. In addition, he compiled the 1993 ratio values and industry average ratio values, which are applicable to both 1993 and 1994 and summarized in Table 5. He is quite pleased to have achieved record earnings of $48,000 in 1994, but he is concerned about the firm's cash flows. Specifically, he is finding it more and more difficult to pay the firm's bills in a timely manner. To gain insight into these cash flow problems, Stanley is planning to prepare the firm's 1994 statement of cash flows.

Stanley is further frustrated by the firm's inability to afford to hire a software developer to complete development of a cost estimation package that is believed to have "blockbuster" sales potential. Stanley began development of this package two years ago, but the firm's growing complexity has forced him to devote more of his time to administrative duties, thereby halting the development of this product. Stanley's reluctance to fill this position stems from his concern that the added $80,000 per year in salary and benefits for the position would certainly lower the firm's earnings per share (EPS) over the next couple of years. Although the project's success is in no way guaranteed, Stanley believes that if the money were spent to hire the software developer, the firm's sales and earnings would significantly rise once the two- to three-year development, production, and marketing process was completed.

Another of Stanley's concerns is the firm's rising interest expense. Because the firm relies heavily on short-term borrowing to maintain financial flexibility, recent rises in in-

TABLE 2

Income statement ($000) **Track Software, Inc.** **for the year ended December 31, 1994**		
Sales revenue		$1,550
Less: Cost of goods sold		1,030
Gross profits		$ 520
Less: Operating expenses		
Selling expense	$ 150	
General and administrative expense	270	
Depreciation expense	11	
Total operating expense	431	
Operating profits		$ 89
Less: Interest expense		29
Net profits before taxes		$ 60
Less: Taxes (20%)		12
Net profits after taxes		$ 48

TABLE 3

Balance sheets ($000)
Track Software, Inc.

	December 31	
Assets	**1994**	**1993**
Current assets		
Cash	$ 12	$ 31
Marketable securities	66	82
Accounts receivable	152	104
Inventories	191	145
Total current assets	$421	$362
Gross fixed assets	$195	$180
Less: Accumulated depreciation	63	52
Net fixed assets	$132	$128
Total assets	$553	$490
Liabilities and stockholders' equity		
Current liabilities		
Accounts payable	$136	$126
Notes payable	200	190
Accruals	27	25
Total current liabilities	$363	$341
Long-term debts	$ 38	$ 40
Total liabilities	$401	$381
Stockholders' equity		
Common stock (100,000 shares at $.20 par value)	$ 20	$ 20
Paid-in capital in excess of par	30	30
Retained earnings	102	59
Total stockholders' equity	$152	$109
Total liabilities and stockholders' equity	$553	$490

TABLE 4

Statement of retained earnings ($000)
Track Software, Inc.
for the year ended December 31, 1994

Retained earnings balance (January 1, 1994)	$ 59
Plus: Net profits after taxes (for 1994)	48
Less: Cash dividends on common stock (paid during 1994)	(5)
Retained earnings balance (December 31, 1994)	$102

TABLE 5

Ratio	Actual 1993	Industry Average, 1994
Net working capital	$21,000	$96,000
Current ratio	1.06	1.82
Quick ratio	.57	1.10
Inventory turnover	10.40	12.45
Average collection period	29.6 days	20.2 days
Total asset turnover	2.66	3.92
Debt ratio	.78	.55
Times interest earned ratio	3.0	5.6
Gross profit margin	32.1%	42.3%
Operating profit margin	5.5%	12.4%
Net profit margin	3.0%	4.0%
Return on total assets	8.0%	15.6%
Return on equity	36.4%	34.7%

terest rates have resulted in rapid rises in Track's interest expense. In an attempt to get a feel for interest rates, Stanley researched the rates of interest on loans of varying maturities. These are shown in Table 6.

With all of these concerns in mind, Stanley set out to review the various data to develop strategies that would help to ensure a bright future for Track Software, Inc. As part of this process, Stanley believed that a thorough ratio analysis of the firm's 1994 results would provide important additional insights.

TABLE 6

INTEREST RATES FOR VARIOUS LOAN MATURITIES

Loan maturity	Interest rate
3 months	16.0%
6 months	15.5
1 year	14.5
3 years	13.0
5 years	12.4
10 years	11.9
20 years	11.5

Required

a. (1) Upon what financial goal does Stanley seem to be focusing? Is it the correct goal? Why or why not?

(2) Could a potential agency problem exist in this firm? Explain.

b. Calculate the firm's earnings per share (EPS) for each year, recognizing that the number of shares of common stock outstanding has remained unchanged since the firm's inception. Comment on the EPS performance in view of your response in **a**.

c. Use the financial data presented to prepare a statement of cash flows for the year ended December 31, 1994. Evaluate the statement in light of Track's current cash flow difficulties.

d. (1) Use the interest rate data provided to draw the current yield curve facing the firm.

(2) Describe the shape of the yield curve drawn in (1).

(3) In view of the yield curve and other facts given in the case, what financing strategy might be advisable for Track?

e. Analyze the firm's financial condition in 1994 as it relates to (1) liquidity, (2) activity, (3) debt, and (4) profitability using the financial statements provided in Tables 2 and 3 and the ratio data included in Table 5. Be sure to evaluate the firm on both a cross-sectional and a time-series basis.

f. What recommendation would you give to Stanley regarding hiring a new software developer? Relate your recommendation here to your responses in **a**.

part II

Basic financial concepts

CHAPTERS IN THIS PART

chapter 5

The time value of money

LEARNING GOALS

Discuss the role of time value in finance, particularly the two common views—future value and present value—and the use of financial tables and business/financial calculators to find them.

Understand the concept of future value, its calculation for single amounts, and the procedures and effects on interest rates of compounding interest more frequently than annually.

Find the future value of the two basic types of annuities—ordinary annuity and annuity due—and compare them.

Review the concept of present value, its calculation for a single amount, and the relationshiup of present to future value.

Determine the present value of a mixed stream of cash flows, an annuity, a mixed stream with an embedded annuity, and a perpetuity.

Describe the procedures involved in (1) determining deposits to accumulate a future sum, (2) loan amortization, and (3) finding interest or growth rates.

As corporate treasurer for USAA, a large insurance and financial services company, I constantly make decisions based on time value of money concepts. I use time value to raise funds in the money and capital markets for our various business activities and when evaluating investments that make the best use of corporate financial resources. The time value of money is a building block; it's fundamental in so many areas of finance. It plays a role in many different types of decisions, not only in corporate finance but also in investments and portfolio analysis, in government finance, and personal finance.

The time value of money is, in a way, the language of finance, a common denominator for discussing financial transactions and financial opportunities. It bridges the gap between consumption and investment. Money can be converted into tangible goods and consumed now, or you can invest it, deferring consumption. You postpone purchasing goods now because you expect your investment to have even greater value in the future.

The consume versus invest decision involves a tradeoff. For example, your choice to defer working to go to school now is a significant time-value tradeoff.

The time value of money is, in a way, the language of finance . . .

There is an opportunity cost—the wages you could earn now. You forego current income because a college education means you can earn considerably more later. How do you equate the money you could earn today with your higher earning potential later? This is really an investment decision, and you use time value of money concepts to decide if you should make that tradeoff.

Time value of money is an essential aspect of most of the concepts presented in later chapters, including *risk*, the chance I may lose part or all of my investment; *return*, how much more than my initial investment I expect to receive over time; and *valuation*, the integration of risk and return. You will also learn other specific applications of time value: capital budgeting, cost of capital, capital structure, and working capital management. But before you can properly use those tools, you must understand the time value of money and be comfortable with time value techniques. Often the conceptual understanding comes later; it takes time. Time value of money may be one of the most difficult concepts to grasp, but at some point, the tradeoff between time and return becomes evident and the concepts such as investment tradeoff, risk and return, and compound growth will all begin to fit together.

For example, at USAA I coordinate the investment of corporate financial resources, choosing long-term investments that maximize owner wealth. In our case, we do not have stockholders because we are owned by our members, the policyholders. Like companies with investors, we can return capital to members as dividends or defer that return and invest it in other assets to earn an even greater return for them in the future. How do we equate paying dividends today to investing that money and also determine if those investments will pay adequate returns? The answer is time value of money.

Ultimately business professionals think in terms of economic return, of growth, of increased productivity. When comparing alternative decisions, they choose the one providing greater return for the risk involved. The sound business judgment to make such decisions requires the ability to both understand and apply the techniques of financial analysis. To make those decisions in a rational and logical manner, managers have to be very, very comfortable with the time value of money.

William Regan joined USAA in 1986 as Vice President, Corporate Finance, and was promoted to Senior Vice President and Treasurer in 1989. From 1977 to 1985, he held various planning and treasury positions at American Natural Resources. He received a B.S. from the United States Air Force Academy and an M.B.A. and Ph. D. from the University of Wisconsin—Madison and also taught finance at Wayne State University.

The role of time value in finance

The financial manager makes decisions based on the cash flows that are expected to occur at various points in time. Why is it important for the financial manager to somehow quantitatively recognize the differences in the timing of these cash flows? Spend a few minutes answering this question before reading on.

SINCE WE VIEW THE FIRM AS A GOING CONCERN, ITS VALUE AND THE DECISIONS OF THE financial manager must be assesssed in light of both its present and future cash flows—both inflows and outflows. Because firms as well as individuals are always confronted with opportunities to earn positive rates of return on their funds, that is, interest rates are always greater than zero, the timing of cash flows has important economic consequences. Taking a long-term view requires the financial manager to explicitly recognize the time value of money. Before developing the necessary computational procedures, we consider the two common views of time value—future value and present value—and the computational aids that are commonly used to streamline time-value calculations.

Future versus present value

Values and decisions can be assessed by using either future-value or present-value techniques. While these techniques, when correctly applied, will—as demonstrated later in this chapter—result in the same decisions, they view the decision differently. Future-value techniques are used to find *future values*, which are typically measured at the *end* of a project's life, while present-value techniques are used to find *present values*, which are measured at the *start* of a project's life (time zero).

time line
A horizontal line on which time zero is at the leftmost end and future periods are shown as you move from left to right; can be used to depict investment cash flows.

A **time line**, which is a horizontal line on which time zero is at the leftmost end and future periods are shown as you move from left to right, can be used to depict the cash flows associated with a given investment. An illustration of such a line covering five periods (in this case years) is given in Figure 5.1. The cash flow occurring at time zero and at the end of each year is shown above the line, the negative values representing *cash outflows* ($10,000 at time zero) and the positive values representing *cash inflows* ($3,000 inflow at the end of year 1, $5,000 inflow at the end of year 2, and so on). Time lines are frequently used in finance to allow the analyst to fully understand the cash flows associated with a given investment.

FIGURE 5.1
Time line depicting an investment's cash flows

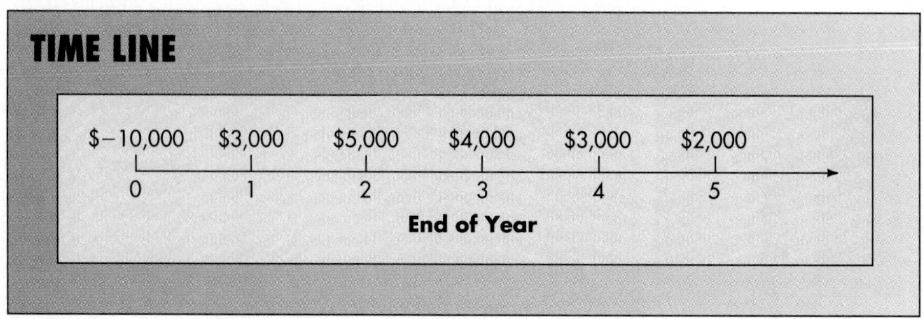

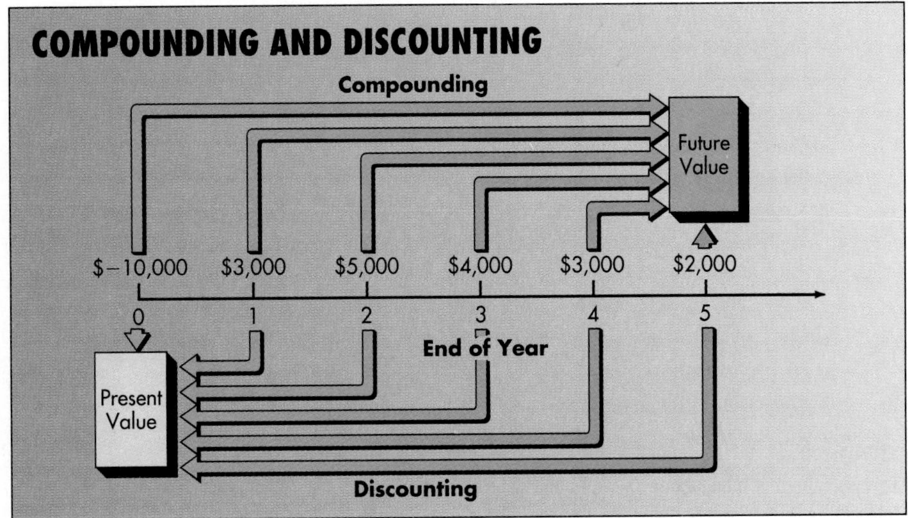

FIGURE 5.2
Time line showing compounding to find future value and discounting to find present value

Because money has a time value (opportunities exist to earn positive rates of return), the cash flows associated with an investment, such as those depicted in Figure 5.1, must be measured at the same point in time. Typically, that point is either the end or the beginning of the investment's life. The future-value technique uses *compounding* to find the future value of each cash flow at the end of the investment's life and then sums them to find the investment's future value. This approach is depicted above the time line in Figure 5.2; it can be seen that the future value of each cash flow is measured at the end of the investment's five-year life. The present-value technique, the other popular approach, uses *discounting* to find the present value of each cash flow at time zero and then sums them to find the investment's present value. Application of this approach is depicted below the time line in Figure 5.2. The meaning and mechanics of both compounding to find future value and discounting to find present value are covered later in this chapter. Although future value and present value, when correctly applied, result in the same decisions, *financial managers, because they make decisions at time zero, tend to rely primarily on present-value techniques.*

Computational aids

Tedious and time-consuming calculations are often involved in finding future and present values. While it is important to understand the concepts and mathematics underlying these calculations, it is also helpful to streamline the practical application of these important time-value techniques. Three computational aids are available—(1) financial tables, (2) hand-held business/financial calculators, and (3) personal computers. Here we focus on the use of financial tables and hand-held business/financial calculators.

FINANCIAL TABLES

Financial tables that include various future- and present-value interest factors can be easily developed from the appropriate formulas and used to simplify time-value calculations. While the degree of decimal precision (rounding to the nearest .01, .001, and

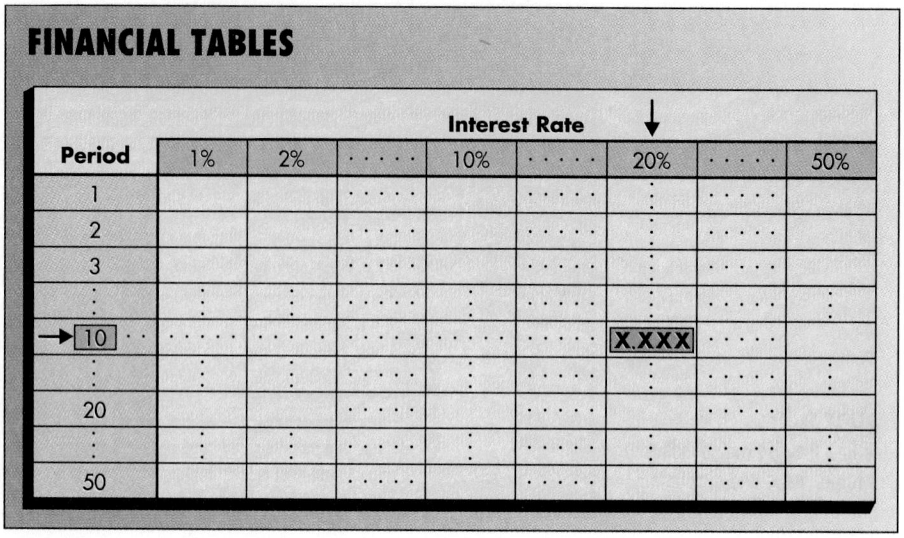

FINANCIAL TABLES

Period	Interest Rate 1%	2%	.....	10%	.....	↓ 20%	.....	50%
1			.....		.....	⋮	.....	
2			.....		.....	⋮	.....	
3			.....		.....	⋮	.....	
⋮	⋮	⋮	.....	⋮	.....	⋮	.....	⋮
→ 10 ..	.....	.....	.....	.....	.....	X.XXX	.....	
⋮	⋮	⋮	.....	⋮	.....	⋮	.....	⋮
20			.....		.....		.....	
⋮	⋮	⋮	.....	⋮	.....	⋮	.....	⋮
50			.....		.....		.....	

FIGURE 5.3
Layout and use of a financial table

so on) varies, the tables are typically indexed by the number of periods (varies by row) and the interest rate (varies by column). Figure 5.3 depicts this general layout of financial tables. If it were the appropriate table and we wished to find the interest factor for 10 years at a 20 percent interest rate, its value would be X.XXX, which is found at the intersection of the 10-year row and the 20% column, as shown. A full set of each of the four basic financial tables is included in Appendix A at the back of the book. The content and role of each of these tables are described later in the chapter, and they are used in the examples presented to demonstrate the application of time-value techniques.

BUSINESS/FINANCIAL CALCULATORS

During the past 10 or so years, the power of the hand-held business/financial calculator has improved dramatically while its cost has become quite low. Today, a powerful hand-held business/financial calculator can be purchased for $15 to $25. Generally, the less expensive calculators are the generic *business calculators*, and the more expensive ones are *financial calculators* that include numerous preprogrammed, often menu-driven financial routines. In addition to describing the use of financial tables included in this text, this and subsequent chapters provide the calculator keystrokes for directly calculating interest factors and making other financial computations. For convenience, we use one of the least expensive ($15 to $20 at a discount store) and most popular business calculators, the Texas Instruments BA-35.

Using the BA-35, we focus primary attention on the keys appearing in its second row of keys, along with two keys in the first row. Figure 5.4 depicts and defines these keys. We typically use only four of the five keys in the second row, with one of the four keys representing the unknown value being calculated. Occasionally, as we'll see in the discussion of finding bond values in Chapter 7, all five of the keys, with one

CALCULATOR KEYS

	CPT	DUE		
N	% i	PMT	PV	FV

CPT – Compute Key Used to Initiate Financial Calculation Once All Values Are Input
DUE – Used to Initiate Calculation for Annuities Due
N – Number of Periods
% i – Interest Rate per Period
PMT – Amount of Payment; Used Only for Annuities
PV – Present Value
FV – Future Value

FIGURE 5.4
Important financial keys on the BA-35 calculator

representing the unknown value, are used. The keystrokes on other business/financial calculators are similar to those of the BA-35. Some of the more sophisticated and expensive calculators are menu-driven so that after you select the appropriate routine, the calculator prompts you to input each value. Regardless, any calculator with the basic future- and present-value functions can be used in lieu of financial tables. The capability and keystrokes of other business/financial calculators are explained in the reference guides that accompany them.

While the use of both financial tables and business/financial calculators is demonstrated throughout this text, you are strongly urged to use a calculator to streamline routine financial calculations *once you understand the basic underlying concepts*. Remember, an ability to solve problems with the aid of a calculator does not necessarily reflect a conceptual understanding of the material—which is the objective of this text. It is therefore important that you make sure you understand concepts before relying on the calculator to streamline required computations. Clearly, with a little practice, both the speed and accuracy of financial computations using a calculator (or personal computer) can be greatly enhanced. Note that because of the calculator's greater precision, slight rounding errors are likely to exist between values calculated by using financial tables and those found with a business/financial calculator.

CONCEPTS IN REVIEW

5-1 Why does the timing of cash flows have important economic consequences? What is a *time line*, and how is it used to depict cash flows?

5-2 What is the difference between *future value* and *present value*? Which approach is preferred by financial managers? Why?

5-3 What computational aids are available for streamlining future- and present-value calculations? How are financial tables laid out and accessed?

Future value of a single amount

Assume that you won $500 in cash and can choose to receive it now or at the end of one year. Ignoring taxes and the utility of the money, what must be true for you to prefer to receive the money sooner rather than later? Before reading on, spend a few minutes answering this question.

IMAGINE THAT AT AGE 25 YOU BEGIN MAKING ANNUAL CASH DEPOSITS OF $2,000 INTO a savings account that pays 5 percent annual interest. At the end of 40 years, at age 65, you would have made deposits totaling $80,000 (40 years × $2,000 per year). Assuming that you have made no withdrawals, what do you think your account balance would be then? $100,000? $150,000? $200,000? No, your $80,000 would have grown to $242,000! Why? Because the time value of money allowed the deposits to earn interest that was compounded over the 40 years. Because opportunities to earn interest on funds are readily available, the time value of money affects everyone—individuals, businesses, and government.

future value
The value of a present amount at a future date found by applying compound interest over a specified period of time.

The **future value** of a present amount is found by applying compound interest over a specified period of time. Savings institutions advertise compound interest returns at a rate of *x* percent or *x* percent interest compounded annually, semiannually, quarterly, monthly, weekly, daily, or even continuously. The principles of future value are quite simple, regardless of the period of time involved.

compounded interest
Interest earned on a given deposit that has become part of the principal at the end of a specified period.

principal
The amount of money on which interest is paid.

The concept of future value

We speak of **compounded interest** when we wish to indicate that the amount earned on a given deposit has become part of the principal at the end of a specified period. The term **principal** refers to the amount of money on which the interest is paid. Annual compounding is the most common type. The concept of future value with annual compounding can be illustrated by a simple example.

If Rich Saver places $100 in a savings account paying 8 percent interest compounded annually, at the end of one year he will have $108 in the account. This $108 represents the initial principal of $100 plus 8 percent ($8) in interest. The future value at the end of the first year is calculated by using Equation 5.1:

$$\text{Future value at end of year 1} = \$100 \times (1 + .08) = \$108 \tag{5.1}$$

If Rich were to leave this money in the account for another year, he would be paid interest at the rate of 8 percent on the new principal of $108. At the end of this second year there would be $116.64 in the account. This amount would represent the principal at the beginning of year 2 ($108) plus 8 percent of the $108 ($8.64) in interest. The future value at the end of the second year is calculated by using Equation 5.2:

$$\begin{aligned}\text{Future value at end of year 2} &= \$108 \times (1 + .08) \\ &= \$116.64\end{aligned} \tag{5.2}$$

Substituting the expression between the equal signs in Equation 5.1 for the \$108 figure in Equation 5.2 gives us Equation 5.3:

$$\begin{aligned}\text{Future value at end of year 2} &= \$100 \times (1 + .08) \times (1 + .08) \\ &= \$100 \times (1 + .08)^2 \\ &= \$116.64 \quad \blacksquare\end{aligned} \tag{5.3}$$

CONCEPT IN PRACTICE

Borrowing a Little Can Cost You a Lot

Employer-sponsored tax-qualified retirement accounts represent a very attractive way to accumulate cash for retirement. At a 7 percent annual rate of interest with annual compounding, a \$50,000 lump-sum retirement account will grow to \$271,372 in just 25 years. Because interest earned on these accounts compounds tax-free, modest monthly contributions made over a long period of time will accumulate into a tidy sum at retirement. But there is one catch—the Internal Revenue Service maintains strict rules and stiff penalties for early withdrawals. What's more, many employee benefits consultants discourage people from removing funds from a retirement account before they retire. According to Alan Nadel, a partner at the accounting firm Arthur Andersen in New York, you should never view a retirement account as a short-term savings plan.

Appearances to the contrary, all the rules and regulations regarding early withdrawal of retirement funds have your best interests at heart. An initial \$20,000 withdrawal from the 7 percent retirement account described above would end up costing \$108,549—plus tax penalties—over a 25-year period. The \$30,000 account (after the initial \$20,000 withdrawal) would grow to only \$162,823 in 25 years' time at 7 percent, compounded annually. To make the power of compound interest work for you, it's important to save as much as you can for as long as you can. Otherwise, you'll find that your retirement nest egg is filled with little more than feathers, not the tidy sum of cash you originally planned to enjoy.

The calculation of future value

The basic relationship in Equation 5.3 can be generalized to find the future value after any number of periods. Let

FV_n = the future value at the end of period n
PV = the initial principal, or present value
k = the annual rate of interest paid (*Note:* On business/financial calculators, i is typically used to represent this rate.)
n = the number of periods—typically years—the money is left on deposit

By using this notation a general equation for the future value at the end of period n can be formulated:

$$FV_n = PV \times (1 + k)^n \tag{5.4}$$

The usefulness of Equation 5.4 for finding the future value, FV_n, in an account paying k percent interest compounded annually for n periods if PV dollars were deposited initially can be illustrated by a simple example.

EXAMPLE

Jane Frugal has placed $800 in a savings account paying 6 percent interest compounded annually. She wishes to determine how much money will be in the account at the end of five years. Substituting $PV = \$800$, $k = .06$, and $n = 5$ into Equation 5.4 gives the amount at the end of year 5:

$$FV_5 = \$800 \times (1 + .06)^5 = \$800 \times (1.338) = \$1{,}070.40$$

Jane will have $1,070.40 in the account at the end of the fifth year.

Time-Line Use This analysis can be depicted diagrammatically on a time line as shown below.

Time line for future value of a single amount ($800 initial principal, earning 6 percent, at the end of five years)

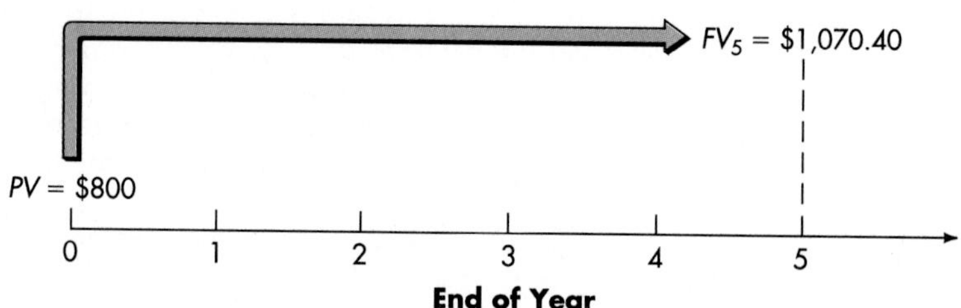

Simplifying future-value calculations

future-value interest factor
The multiplier used to calculate at a specified interest rate the future value of a present amount as of a given time.

Solving the equation in the preceding example is quite time-consuming, since one must raise 1.06 to the fifth power. A future-value interest table or a business/financial calculator can be used to simplify the calculations. A table for the amount generated by the payment of compound interest on an initial principal of $1 is given as Appendix Table A-1 (at the back of the book). The table provides values for $(1 + k)^n$ in Equation 5.4.[1] This portion of Equation 5.4 is called the **future-value interest factor.** This factor is the multiplier used to calculate at a specified interest rate the future value of a present amount as of a given time. The future-value interest factor for an initial principal of $1 compounded at k percent for n periods is referred to as $FVIF_{k,n}$:

$$\text{Future-value interest factor} = FVIF_{k,n} = (1 + k)^n \qquad (5.5)$$

By accessing the table (as shown in Figure 5.3) with respect to the annual interest rate, k, and the appropriate periods,[2] n, the factor relevant to a particular problem can be

[1]This table is commonly referred to as a "compound interest table" or a "table of the future value of one dollar." As long as the reader understands the source of the table values, the various names attached to it should not create confusion, since one can always make a trial calculation of a value for one factor as a check.

[2]Although we commonly deal with years rather than periods, financial tables are frequently presented in terms of periods to provide maximum flexibility.

found. By letting $FVIF_{k,n}$ represent the appropriate factor, we can rewrite Equation 5.4 as follows:

$$FV_n = PV \times (FVIF_{k,n}) \tag{5.6}$$

The expression indicates that to find the future value, FV_n, at the end of period n of an initial deposit, we have merely to multiply the initial deposit, PV, by the appropriate future-value interest factor.[3] An example will illustrate this calculation using both a table and a hand-held business calculator.

EXAMPLE

As was noted in the preceding example, Jane Frugal has placed \$800 in her savings account at 6 percent interest compounded annually. She wishes to find out how much will be in the account at the end of five years.

Table Use The future-value interest factor for an initial principal of \$1 on deposit for five years at 6 percent interest compounded annually, $FVIF_{6\%,5yrs}$, found in Table A-1, is 1.338. Multiplying the initial principal of \$800 by this factor in accordance with Equation 5.6 results in a future value at the end of year 5 of \$1,070.40.

Calculator Use[4] The preprogrammed financial functions in the business calculator[5] can be used to calculate the future value directly. First punch in \$800, and depress **PV**; next punch in 5, and depress **N**; then punch in 6, and depress **%i** (which is equivalent to "*k*" in our notation)[6]; finally, to calculate the future value, depress **CPT** and then **FV**. The future value of \$1,070.58 should appear on the calculator display.

Inputs:	800	5	6		
Functions:	PV	N	%i	CPT	FV
Outputs:					1070.58

[3]Occasionally, the financial manager will want to roughly estimate how long a given sum must earn at a given annual rate to double the amount. The *Rule of 72* is used to make this estimate; dividing the annual rate of interest into 72 results in the approximate period it will take to double one's money at the given rate. For example, to double one's money at a 10 percent annual rate of interest will take about 7.2 years (72 ÷ 10 = 7.2). Looking at Table A-1, we can see that the future-value interest factor for 10 percent and 7 years is slightly below 2 (1.949); this approximation therefore appears to be reasonably accurate.

[4]Many calculators allow the user to set the number of payments per year. Most of these calculators are preset for monthly payments—12 payments per year. Because we work primarily with annual payments—one payment per year—it is important to *make sure that your calculator is set for one payment per year.* Consult the reference guide that accompanies your calculator for instructions for setting this value. Note that the BA-35 is always set for the desired payment frequency of one payment per year.

[5]The BA-35 calculator, like many other multifunction business calculators, has two preprogrammed functions—financial and statistical. It is therefore important always to make sure that the finance function keys have been activated before making financial calculations. On the BA-35 this is done by pressing **2nd** followed by **FIN**. "FIN" will appear in the calculator display to confirm the activation of these functions. Also, to avoid including previous data in current calculations, *always* clear all registers before inputting values and making each computation.

[6]The known values *can be punched into the calculator in any order*; the order specified in this as well as other calculator use demonstrations included in this text results merely from convenience and personal preference.

Note that because the calculator is more accurate than the use of factors from Table A-1, which have been rounded to the nearest .001, a slight difference—in this case \$0.18—will frequently exist between the values found by using these alternative methods. Clearly, the improved accuracy and ease of calculation tend to favor the use of the calculator in making financial calculations such as this. ■

A graphic view of future value

It is important to note that we measure future value at the *end* of the given period. The relationship between various interest rates, the number of periods interest is earned, and the future value of one dollar is illustrated in Figure 5.5. It clearly shows two relationships: (1) the higher the interest rate, the higher the future value, and (2) the longer the period of time, the higher the future value. Note that for an interest rate of 0 percent, the future value always equals the present value (\$1.00). But for any interest rate greater than zero, the future value is greater than the present value of \$1.00 in Figure 5.5.

Compounding more frequently than annually

Interest is often compounded more frequently than once a year. Savings institutions compound interest semiannually, quarterly, monthly, weekly, daily, or even continuously. This section discusses semiannual and quarterly compounding, presents a general equation for compounding more frequently than annually, and briefly describes continuous compounding. It also explains how to use both a table and a hand-held business calculator to simplify calculations.

FIGURE 5.5
Interest rates, time periods, and future value of one dollar

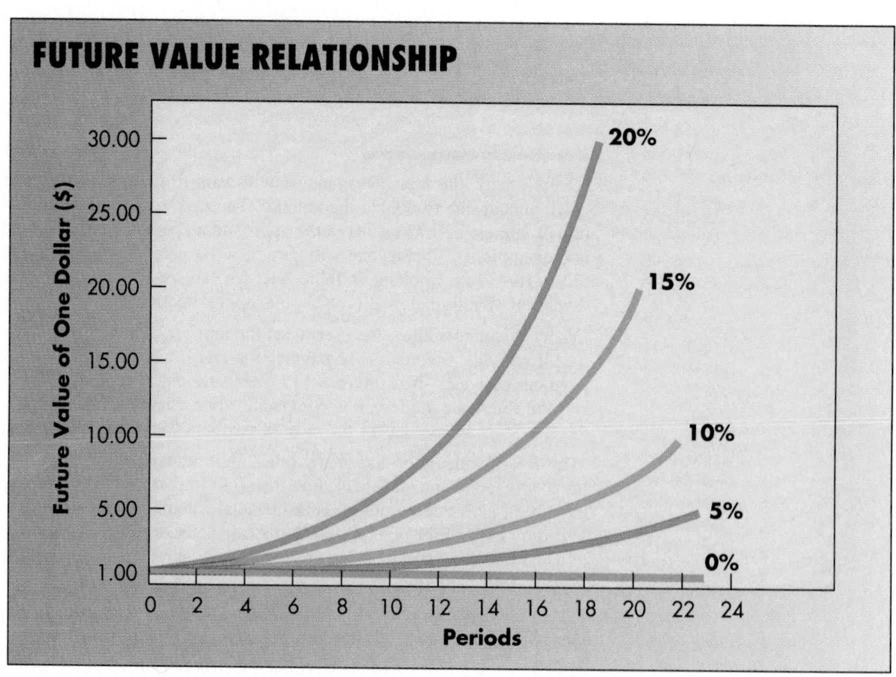

SEMIANNUAL COMPOUNDING

semiannual compounding
Compounding of interest over two periods within the year.

Semiannual compounding of interest involves two compounding periods within the year. Instead of the stated interest rate being paid once a year, one-half of the stated interest rate is paid twice a year.

EXAMPLE

Rich Saver has decided to invest $100 in a savings account paying 8 percent interest *compounded semiannually.* If he leaves his money in the account for two years, he will be paid 4 percent interest compounded over four periods, each of which is six months long. Table 5.1 uses interest factors to show that at the end of one year, when the 8 percent interest is compounded semiannually, Rich will have $108.16; at the end of two years, he will have $116.99. ■

QUARTERLY COMPOUNDING

quarterly compounding
Compounding of interest over four periods within the year.

Quarterly compounding of interest involves four compounding periods within the year. One-fourth of the stated interest rate is paid four times a year.

EXAMPLE

After further investigation of his savings opportunities, Rich Saver has found an institution that will pay him 8 percent interest *compounded quarterly.* If he leaves his money in this account for two years, he will be paid 2 percent interest compounded over eight periods, each of which is three months long. Table 5.2 uses interest factors to present the calculations required to determine the amount Rich will have at the end of two years. As the table shows, at the end of one year, when the 8 percent interest is compounded quarterly, Rich will have $108.24; at the end of two years he will have $117.16. ■

Table 5.3 presents comparative values for Rich Saver's $100 at the end of years 1 and 2 given annual, semiannual, and quarterly compounding at the 8 percent rate. As the table shows, *the more frequently interest is compounded, the greater the amount of money accumulated.* This is true for any interest rate for any period of time.

TABLE 5.1

THE FUTURE VALUE FROM INVESTING $100 AT 8 PERCENT INTEREST COMPOUNDED SEMIANNUALLY OVER TWO YEARS

Period	Beginning principal (1)	Future-value interest factor (2)	Future value at end of period [(1) × (2)] (3)
6 months	$100.00	1.04	$104.00
1 year	104.00	1.04	108.16
18 months	108.16	1.04	112.49
2 years	112.49	1.04	116.99

TABLE 5.2

THE FUTURE VALUE FROM INVESTING $100 AT 8 PERCENT INTEREST COMPOUNDED QUARTERLY OVER TWO YEARS

Period	Beginning principal (1)	Future-value interest factor (2)	Future value at end of period [(1) × (2)] (3)
3 months	$100.00	1.02	$102.00
6 months	102.00	1.02	104.04
9 months	104.04	1.02	106.12
1 year	106.12	1.02	108.24
15 months	108.24	1.02	110.40
18 months	110.40	1.02	112.61
21 months	112.61	1.02	114.86
2 years	114.86	1.02	117.16

TABLE 5.3

THE FUTURE VALUE FROM INVESTING $100 AT 8 PERCENT FOR YEARS 1 AND 2 GIVEN VARIOUS COMPOUNDING PERIODS

End of year	Compounding period		
	Annual	Semiannual	Quarterly
1	$108.00	$108.16	$108.24
2	116.64	116.99	117.16

A GENERAL EQUATION FOR COMPOUNDING MORE FREQUENTLY THAN ANNUALLY

It should be clear from the preceding examples that if m equals the number of times per year interest is compounded, Equation 5.4 (our formula for annual compounding) can be rewritten as

$$FV_n = PV \times \left(1 + \frac{k}{m}\right)^{m \times n} \qquad (5.7)$$

If $m = 1$, Equation 5.7 reduces to Equation 5.4. Thus if interest is compounded annually (once a year), Equation 5.7 will provide the same results as Equation 5.4. The general use of Equation 5.7 can be illustrated with a simple example.

EXAMPLE

The preceding examples calculated the amount that Rich Saver would have at the end of two years if he deposited $100 at 8 percent interest compounded semiannually and quarterly. For semiannual compounding, m would equal 2 in Equation 5.7; for quarterly compounding, m would equal 4. Substituting the appropriate values for semiannual and quarterly compounding into Equation 5.7 would yield

1. *For semiannual compounding:*

$$FV_2 = \$100 \times \left(1 + \frac{.08}{2}\right)^{2\times2} = \$100 \times (1 + .04)^4 = \$116.99$$

2. *For quarterly compounding:*

$$FV_2 = \$100 \times \left(1 + \frac{.08}{4}\right)^{4\times2} = \$100 \times (1 + .02)^8 = \$117.16$$

These results agree with the values for FV_2 in Tables 5.1 and 5.2. If the interest were compounded monthly, weekly, or daily, m would equal 12, 52, or 365, respectively. ■

SIMPLIFYING THE CALCULATIONS

The future-value interest factors for one dollar, given in Table A-1, can be used to find the future value when interest is compounded m times each year. Instead of indexing the table for k percent and n years, as we do when interest is compounded annually, we index it for $(k \div m)$ percent and $(m \times n)$ periods. The usefulness of the table is usually somewhat limited, since it includes only selected rates for a limited number of periods. A business/financial calculator or personal computer is typically required. The following example will demonstrate the use of both a table and a hand-held business calculator.

EXAMPLE

In the earlier examples, Rich Saver wished to find the future value of \$100 invested at 8 percent compounded both semiannually and quarterly for two years. The number of compounding periods, m, was 2 and 4, respectively, in these cases. The interest rate and number of periods used in each case, along with the future-value interest factor, are shown below.

Compounding period	m	Interest rate $(k \div m)$	Periods $(m \times n)$	Future-value interest factor from Table A-1
Semiannual	2	8% ÷ 2 = 4%	2 × 2 = 4	1.170
Quarterly	4	8% ÷ 4 = 2%	4 × 2 = 8	1.172

Table Use The factor for 4 percent and four periods is used for the semiannual compounding, and the factor for 2 percent and eight periods is used for quarterly compounding. Multiplying each of the factors by the initial \$100 deposit results in a value of \$117.00 (1.170 × \$100) for semiannual compounding and a value of \$117.20 (1.172 × \$100) for quarterly compounding.

Calculator Use If the calculator were used for the semiannual compounding calculation, as noted in the preceding table, the number of periods would be 4, and the interest rate would be 4 percent. First punch in $100, and depress **PV**; next punch in 4, and depress **N**; then punch in 4, and depress **%i**; finally, to calculate the future value, depress **CPT** followed by **FV**. The future value of $116.99 should appear on the calculator display.

Inputs:	100	4	4		
Functions:	PV	N	% i	CPT	FV
Outputs:					116.99

For the quarterly compounding case, the number of periods would be 8, and the interest rate would be 2 percent. First punch in $100, and depress **PV**; next punch in 8, and depress **N**; then punch in 2, and depress **%i**; finally, to calculate the future value, depress **CPT** followed by **FV**. The future value of $117.17 should appear on the calculator display.

Inputs:	100	8	2		
Functions:	PV	N	% i	CPT	FV
Outputs:					117.17

Comparing the values found by using the calculator to those based on the use of Table A-1, we can see that the calculator values generally agree with those values given in Table 5.3 but are more precise because the table factors have been rounded. ■

CONTINUOUS COMPOUNDING

continuous compounding
Compounding of interest an infinite number of times per year at intervals of microseconds.

In the extreme case, interest can be (and frequently is) compounded continuously. **Continuous compounding** involves compounding over every microsecond—the smallest time period imaginable. In this case, m in Equation 5.7 would approach infinity, and through the use of calculus the equation would become

$$FV_n \text{ (continuous compounding)} = PV \times (e^{k \times n}) \tag{5.8}$$

where e is the exponential function which has a value of 2.7183.[7] The future-value interest factor for continuous compounding is therefore

$$FVIF_{k,n} \text{ (continuous compounding)} = e^{k \times n} \tag{5.9}$$

[7]Many calculators have the exponential function, typically noted by $\mathbf{e^x}$, built into them. The use of this key is especially helpful in calculating future value when interest is compounded continuously.

EXAMPLE

Continuing with the preceding example, the amount Rich Saver's \$100 deposit (PV = \$100) into an account paying 8 percent annual interest ($k = .08$) would grow to equal at the end of two years ($n = 2$), assuming that interest is compounded continuously, can be found by substituting into Equation 5.8:

$$FV_2 \text{ (continuous compounding)} = \$100 \times e^{.08 \times 2} = \$100 \times 2.7183^{.16}$$
$$= \$100 \times 1.1735 = \$117.35$$

Calculator Use To find this value by using the calculator, first find the value of $e^{.16}$ by punching in .16 and then pressing **2nd** and then **e^x** to get 1.1735. Next multiply this value by \$100 to get the future value of \$117.35. (*Note:* On some calculators, **2nd** may not have to be pressed before pressing **e^x**.)

Inputs:	.16			100
Functions:	2nd	e^x	X	=
Outputs:		1.1735		117.35

The future value with continuous compounding therefore equals \$117.35, which, as expected, is larger than the future value when interest was compounded semiannually (\$116.99) or quarterly (\$117.16). As was noted earlier, \$117.35 is the largest amount that would result from compounding the 8 percent interest more frequently than annually, given an initial deposit of \$100 and a two-year time horizon. ■

NOMINAL AND EFFECTIVE INTEREST RATES

nominal (stated) interest rate
Contractual rate of interest charged by a lender or promised by a borrower.

effective (true) interest rate
The rate of interest actually paid or earned; in personal finance, commonly called the *annual percentage rate (APR).*

annual percentage rate (APR)
In personal finance, the effective interest rate, which must by law be clearly stated to borrowers and depositors.

It is important for both consumers and businesses to be able to make objective comparisons of interest rates. To compare loan costs or investment returns over different compounding periods, we must distinguish between nominal and effective interest rates. The **nominal,** or **stated, interest rate** is the contractual rate charged by a lender or promised by a borrower. The **effective,** or **true, interest rate** is the rate of interest actually paid or earned. In personal finance the effective rate, commonly called the **annual percentage rate (APR),** must by law be clearly stated to borrowers and depositors.

The effective rate differs from the nominal rate in that it reflects the impact of compounding frequency. In terms of interest earnings, it is probably best viewed as the *annual* interest rate that would result in the same future value as that resulting from application of the nominal rate using the stated compounding frequency. Reviewing Table 5.3, we can see that the future value using an 8 percent nominal interest rate increases with increasing compounding frequency. Clearly, the effective rate of interest must also increase with increased compounding frequency.

By using the notation introduced earlier, the effective interest rate, $k_{eff.}$, can be calculated by substituting values for the nominal interest rate, k, and the compounding frequency, m, into Equation 5.10.

$$k_{eff.} = \left(1 + \frac{k}{m}\right)^m - 1 \tag{5.10}$$

Application of this equation can conveniently be demonstrated by using data from the preceding examples.

EXAMPLE

Rich Saver wishes to find the effective interest rate associated with an 8 percent nominal interest rate ($k = .08$) when interest is compounded (1) annually ($m = 1$); (2) semiannually ($m = 2$); and (3) quarterly ($m = 4$). Substituting these values into Equation 5.10, we get

1. *For annual compounding:*

$$k_{eff.} = \left(1 + \frac{.08}{1}\right)^1 - 1 = (1 + .08)^1 - 1 = 1 + .08 - 1 = .08 = 8\%$$

2. *For semiannual compounding:*

$$k_{eff.} = \left(1 + \frac{.08}{2}\right)^2 - 1 = (1 + .04)^2 - 1 = 1.0816 - 1 = .0816 = 8.16\%$$

3. *For quarterly compounding:*

$$k_{eff.} = \left(1 + \frac{.08}{4}\right)^4 - 1 = (1 + .02)^4 - 1 = 1.0824 - 1 = .0824 = 8.24\%$$

Two important points are demonstrated by these values: (1) The nominal and effective interest rates are equivalent for annual compounding, and (2) the effective rate of interest increases with increasing compounding frequency.[8] ■

CONCEPT IN PRACTICE

Effective Rates of Interest Can Be as Individual as You Are

Modern consumer-credit arrangements have become so complicated that it can seem that you need several degrees in finance just to compare your options. For example, look at the two new MasterCards offered by Ford and General Motors. The nominal interest rate on the GM card varies at 10.4 percent plus the prime lending rate, there is no annual fee, and cardholders may claim a credit equal to 5 percent of each charge toward the purchase of a new GM automobile. If you rent a car from Avis, stay at a Marriott Inn, place telephone calls through MCI, or gas up at Mobil, you receive an additional 5 percent credit toward your GM vehicle purchase. The

[8]The *maximum* effective rate for a given nominal rate occurs when interest is compounded *continuously.* The effective rate for this extreme case can be found by using the following equation:

$$k_{eff.} \text{ (continuous compounding)} = e^k - 1 \qquad (5.10a)$$

For the 8 percent nominal rate ($k = .08$), substitution into Equation 5.10a results in an effective rate of

$$e^{.08} - 1 = 1.0833 - 1 = .0833 = 8.33\%$$

in the case of continuous compounding. This is the highest effective rate attainable with an 8 percent nominal rate.

interest rate on Ford's MasterCard varies at 9.4 percent plus the prime lending rate, there is a $20 annual cardholder fee after the first year, and cardholders may claim a 5 percent credit from each charge toward the purchase of a new Ford.

What is the effective rate of interest charged by GM and Ford? The answer depends on (1) how much you charge on a particular credit card, (2) where you make your charge purchases, (3) whether you eventually purchase a new car from the company offering your credit card, (4) the average daily balance you carry on the card, and (5) a bunch of other stuff. Robert McKinley, publisher of a credit card newsletter from RAM Research, feels that rebate cards, like the GM and Ford MasterCards make sense for those who pay off their credit card balances each month. If you don't, your best plan is to ignore all the special options and pick the card with the lowest advertised interest rate. Using McKinley's evaluative yardstick, neither GM nor Ford offers most people the best credit card deal. Keep shopping.

CONCEPTS IN REVIEW

5-4 How is the *compounding process* related to the payment of interest on savings? What is the general equation for the future value, FV_n, in period n if PV dollars are deposited in an account paying k percent annual interest?

5-5 What effect would (a) a *decrease* in the interest rate or (b) an *increase* in the holding period of a deposit have on its future value? Why?

5-6 What effect does compounding interest more frequently than annually have on (a) the future value generated by a beginning principal and (b) the effective interest rate? Why?

5-7 What is *continuous compounding?* How does the magnitude of the future value of a given deposit at a given rate of interest obtained by using continuous compounding compare to the value obtained by using annual or any other compounding period?

Future value of an annuity

Imagine that you have been promised payment of $1,000 annually for the next 10 years. On a strict economic basis, would you have a preference as to whether the payments were made at the beginning or at the end of each year? Why? Spend a few moments thinking about these questions before reading ahead.

annuity
A stream of equal annual cash flows. These cash flows can be *inflows* of returns earned on investments or *outflows* of funds invested to earn future returns.

ordinary annuity
An annuity for which the payments occur at the end of each period.

annuity due
An annuity for which the payments occur at the beginning of each period.

AN ANNUITY IS A STREAM OF EQUAL ANNUAL CASH FLOWS. THESE CASH FLOWS CAN be *inflows* of returns earned on investments or *outflows* of funds invested to earn future returns. Before looking at the mathematics of future value related to annuities, we should distinguish between the two basic types of annuities.

Types of annuities

The two basic types of annuities are the *ordinary annuity* and the *annuity due.* An **ordinary annuity** is an annuity for which the *payments occur at the end of each period,* whereas an **annuity due** is one for which the *payments occur at the beginning of each period.*

TABLE 5.4

COMPARISON OF ORDINARY ANNUITY AND ANNUITY DUE CASH FLOWS ($1,000, FIVE YEARS)

	Annual Cash Flows	
End of Year[a]	Annuity A *(Ordinary)*	Annuity B *(Annuity Due)*
0	$ 0	$1,000
1	1,000	1,000
2	1,000	1,000
3	1,000	1,000
4	1,000	1,000
5	1,000	0
Totals	$5,000	$5,000

[a]The ends of years 0, 1, 2, 3, 4, and 5 are equivalent to the beginnings of years 1, 2, 3, 4, 5, and 6, respectively.

EXAMPLE

Fran Abrams is attempting to choose the better of two annuities. Both are five-year, $1,000 annuities, but annuity A is an ordinary annuity, and annuity B is an annuity due. To better understand the difference between these annuities, she has listed their cash flows in Table 5.4. Note that the amount of each annuity totals $5,000, although the timing of their cash flows differs; the cash flows are received sooner with the annuity due than with the ordinary annuity. ■

In spite of the fact that both annuities in Table 5.4 total $5,000, the annuity due would be of greater value because its cash flows occur earlier and therefore have more time to compound to a higher future value (at a given rate of interest) than those of the ordinary annuity. In general, as will be demonstrated later in this chapter, *the future value of an annuity due is always greater than the future value of an otherwise identical ordinary annuity.* Because ordinary annuities are more frequently used in finance, *unless otherwise specified, the term "annuity" is used throughout this book to refer to ordinary annuities.*

Finding the future value of an ordinary annuity

The calculations required to find the future value of an ordinary annuity on which interest is paid at a specified rate compounded annually can be illustrated by the following example.

EXAMPLE

Fran Abrams wishes to determine how much money she will have at the end of five years if she deposits $1,000 annually at the *end of each* of the next five years into a savings account paying 7 percent annual interest. Her cash flows are represented by annuity A—the ordinary annuity—in Table 5.4. Table 5.5 presents the calculations required to find the future value of this annuity at the end of year 5.

Time-Line Use This situation is depicted diagrammatically on the time line below.

Time line for future value of an ordinary annuity ($1,000 end-of-year deposit, earning 7 percent, at the end of five years)

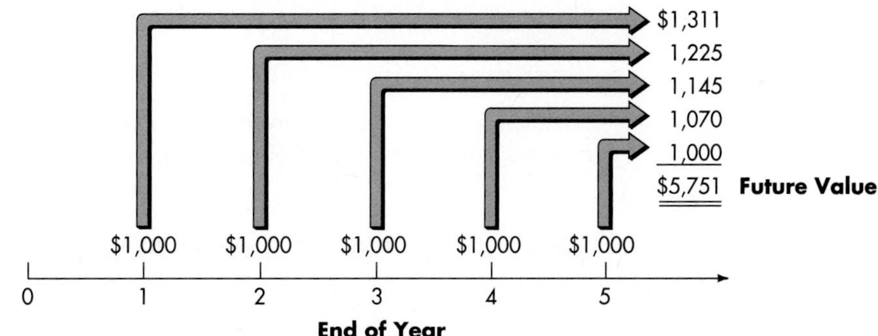

As the table and figure show, at the end of year 5, Fran will have $5,751 in her account. Column 2 of the table indicates that since the deposits are made at the end of the year, the first deposit will earn interest for four years, the second for three years, and so on. The future-value interest factors in column 3 correspond to these interest-earning periods and the 7 percent rate of interest. ■

THE MATHEMATICS OF THE FUTURE-VALUE-OF-AN-ANNUITY CALCULATION

The calculations required in the preceding example can be simplified somewhat, since each of the factors is actually multiplied by the same dollar amount. This is true only in the case of an annuity. The actual calculations required can be expressed as follows:

$$\begin{aligned}\text{Future value of annuity at end of year 5} &= [\$1{,}000 \times (1.311)] \\ &\quad + [\$1{,}000 \times (1.225)] \\ &\quad + [\$1{,}000 \times (1.145)] \\ &\quad + [\$1{,}000 \times (1.070)] \\ &\quad + [\$1{,}000 \times (1.000)] \\ &= \$5{,}751\end{aligned} \tag{5.11}$$

TABLE 5.5

THE FUTURE VALUE OF A $1,000 FIVE-YEAR ORDINARY ANNUITY COMPOUNDED AT 7 PERCENT

End of year	Amount deposited (1)	Number of years compounded (2)	Future-value interest factors from Table A-1 (3)	Future value at end of year [(1) × (3)] (4)
1	$1,000	4	1.311	$1,311
2	1,000	3	1.225	1,225
3	1,000	2	1.145	1,145
4	1,000	1	1.070	1,070
5	1,000	0	1.000	1,000
Future value of ordinary annuity at end of year 5				$5,751

Factoring out the \$1,000, we can rewrite Equation 5.11 as

$$\text{Future value of annuity at end of year 5} = \$1{,}000 \times (1.311 + 1.225 + 1.145 + 1.070 + 1.000) = \$5{,}751 \quad (5.12)$$

Equation 5.12 indicates that to find the future value of the annuity, the annual amount must be multiplied by the sum of the appropriate future-value interest factors.

SIMPLIFYING FUTURE-VALUE-OF-AN-ANNUITY CALCULATIONS

Annuity calculations can be simplified by using a future-value interest table for an annuity or a hand-held business/financial calculator. A table for the future value of a \$1 *ordinary annuity* is given in Appendix Table A-2 (at the back of the book). The factors included in the table are derived by summing the terms in parentheses in equations like Equation 5.12. In the case of Equation 5.12, summing the terms in parentheses results in Equation 5.13:

$$\text{Future value of annuity at end of year 5} = \$1{,}000 \times (5.751) = \$5{,}751 \quad (5.13)$$

future-value interest factor for an annuity
The multiplier used to calculate the future value of an *ordinary annuity* at a specified interest rate over a given period of time.

The formula for the **future-value interest factor for an annuity** when interest is compounded annually at k percent for n periods, $FVIFA_{k,n}$, is

$$FVIFA_{k,n} = \sum_{t=1}^{n} (1 + k)^{t-1} \quad (5.14)$$

This factor is the multiplier used to calculate the future value of an *ordinary annuity* at a specified interest rate over a given period of time. The formula merely states that the future-value interest factor for an n-year ordinary annuity is found by adding the sum of the first $n - 1$ future-value interest factors to 1.000 (i.e., $FVIFA_{k,n} = 1.000 + \sum_{t=1}^{n-1} FVIF_{k,t}$). This relationship can be easily verified by reviewing the terms in Equation 5.12.[9]

Letting FVA_n equal the future value of an n-year annuity, PMT equal the amount to be deposited annually at the end of each year, and $FVIFA_{k,n}$ represent the appropriate *future-value interest factor for a one-dollar annuity compounded at* k *percent for* n *years,* the relationship among these variables can be expressed as follows:

$$FVA_n = PMT \times (FVIFA_{k,n}) \quad (5.15)$$

[9]A mathematical expression that can be applied to calculate the future-value interest factor for an ordinary annuity more efficiently is

$$FVIFA_{k,n} = [(1/k) \times ((1 + k)^n - 1)] \quad (5.14a)$$

The use of this expression is especially attractive in the absence of the appropriate financial tables or a business/financial calculator or personal computer.

An example will illustrate this calculation using both a table and a hand-held business calculator.

EXAMPLE

As was noted in the preceding example, Fran Abrams wishes to find the future value (FVA_n) at the end of five years (n) of an annual *end-of-year deposit* of $1,000 ($PMT$) into an account paying 7 percent annual interest (k) during the next five years.

Table Use The appropriate future-value interest factor for an ordinary five-year annuity at 7 percent, $FVIFA_{7\%,5\text{yrs}}$, found in Table A-2, is 5.751. Multiplying the $1,000 deposit by this factor in accordance with Equation 5.15 results in a future value for the annuity of $5,751.

Calculator Use Using the calculator, first punch in the $1,000, and depress **PMT**; next punch in 5, and depress **N**; then punch in 7, and depress **%i**; to calculate the future value of this ordinary annuity, depress **CPT** followed by **FV**. Ignoring the minus sign,[10] the future value of the ordinary annuity of $5,750.74 should appear on the calculator display. This is basically the same value as that obtained using the factor from Table A-2.

Inputs:	1000	5	7		
Functions:	PMT	N	%i	CPT	FV
Outputs:					5750.74

Finding the future value of an annuity due

The calculations involved in finding the future value of the less common form of an annuity—an annuity due—can be demonstrated by the following example.

EXAMPLE

Fran Abrams, in a fashion similar to her calculations for the ordinary annuity, wishes to find out how much money she will have at the end of five years if she deposits $1,000 annually at the *beginning of each* of the next five years into a savings account paying 7 percent annual interest. Her cash flows in this case are represented by annuity B—the annuity due—in Table 5.4. Table 5.6 demonstrates the calculations required to find the future value of this annuity at the end of year 5. This situation is depicted on the time line shown on the next page.

[10]Note that on many calculators, like the BA-35, the calculated future value of an annuity will be preceded by a minus sign. Technically, this sign is intended to refer to the fact that this future value (*FVA*) is an outflow or withdrawal from the annuity account, since the amount of the annuity (*PMT*) is treated as an inflow or deposit into the annuity account. For our purposes the minus sign is not important and therefore should be ignored.

Time line for future value of an annuity due ($1,000 beginning-of-year deposit, earning 7 percent, at the end of five years)

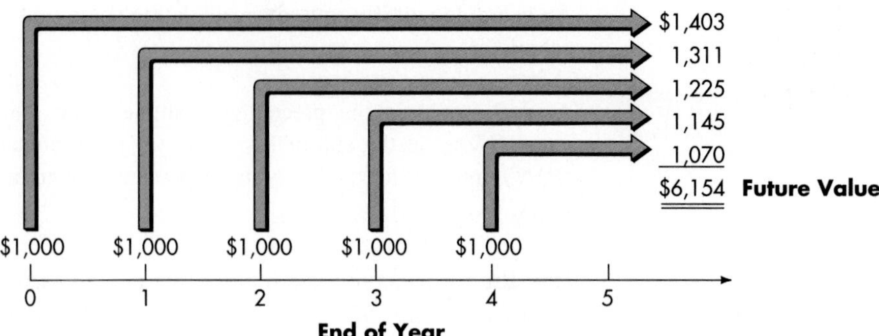

Time-Line Use As the table and figure show, at the end of year 5, Fran will have $6,154 in her account. Column 2 of the table indicates that since the deposits are made at the beginning of each year, the first deposit earns for five years, the second for four years, and so on. The future-value interest factors in column 3 correspond to those interest-earning periods, and the 7 percent rate of interest. ■

SIMPLIFYING FUTURE-VALUE-OF-AN-ANNUITY-DUE CALCULATIONS

Although the future-value interest factors for an annuity in Table A-2 were developed for use with ordinary annuities, a simple conversion can be applied to them to use them with annuities due. Equation 5.16 presents this conversion:

$$FVIFA_{k,n} \text{ (annuity due)} = FVIFA_{k,n} \times (1 + k) \tag{5.16}$$

As can be seen from Equation 5.16, the future-value interest factor for an n-year annuity due at k percent can be found by merely multiplying the future-value interest factor for an ordinary annuity (from Table A-2) at k percent for n years by $(1 + k)$. An example will demonstrate the application of this equation and the use of a hand-held business calculator to find the future value of an annuity due.

TABLE 5.6

THE FUTURE VALUE OF A $1,000 FIVE-YEAR ANNUITY DUE COMPOUNDED AT 7 PERCENT

End of year[a]	Amount deposited (1)	Number of years compounded (2)	Future-value interest factors from Table A-1 (3)	Future value at end of year [(1) × (3)] (4)
0	$1,000	5	1.403	$1,403
1	1,000	4	1.311	1,311
2	1,000	3	1.225	1,225
3	1,000	2	1.145	1,145
4	1,000	1	1.070	1,070
Future value of annuity due at end of year 5				$6,154

[a]The ends of years 0, 1, 2, 3, and 4 are equivalent to the beginnings of years 1, 2, 3, 4, and 5, respectively.

EXAMPLE

As was noted in the preceding example, Fran Abrams wishes to find the future value (FVA_n) at the end of five years (n) of an annual *beginning-of-year deposit* of \$1,000 (PMT) into an account paying 7 percent annual interest (k) during the next five years.

Table Use Substituting $k = 7\%$ and $n = 5$ years into Equation 5.16, with the aid of Table A-2, we get

$$FVIFA_{7\%,5\text{yrs}}\ (\text{annuity due}) = FVIFA_{7\%,5\text{yrs}} \times (1 + .07) = 5.751 \times 1.07 = 6.154$$

Substituting $PMT = \$1,000$ and $FVIFA_{7\%,5\text{yrs}}$ (annuity due) $= 6.154$ into Equation 5.15, we get a future value for the annuity due, FVA_5:

$$FVA_5 = \$1,000 \times 6.154 = \$6,154$$

Calculator Use Using the calculator, first punch in the \$1,000, and depress **PMT**; next punch in 5, and depress **N**; then punch in 7, and depress **%i**; to calculate the future value of this annuity due, depress **DUE** and then **FV**. The future value of the annuity due of \$6,153.29 should appear on the calculator display (ignore the minus sign). Note that this is basically the same value as was obtained earlier in Table 5.6 and above by using Table A-2 in conjunction with Equation 5.16.

Inputs:	1000	5	7		
Functions:	PMT	N	% i	DUE	FV
Outputs:					6153.29

COMPARISON WITH AN ORDINARY ANNUITY

As was noted earlier, the future value of an annuity due is always greater than the future value of an otherwise identical ordinary annuity. This fact is supported by the future values at the end of year 5 of Fran Abrams' two \$1,000 five-year annuities. From Tables 5.5 and 5.6 the *future value* of her ordinary annuity and annuity due, respectively, at the end of year 5 given a 7 percent interest rate were found to be:

Ordinary annuity	\$5,751
Annuity due	\$6,154

Because the annuity due's cash flow occurs at the beginning of the period rather than at the end as is the case for the ordinary annuity, its future value is greater—in the example, Fran would earn about \$400 more with the annuity due.

In spite of their superior earning power, annuities due are much less frequently encountered than are ordinary annuities, and the emphasis throughout the remainder of this text is therefore placed on ordinary annuities. To reiterate, *unless otherwise specified, the term "annuity" refers to ordinary annuities to which the FVIFA factors in Table A-2 directly apply and hand-held business calculators view as standard.*

CONCEPTS IN REVIEW

5-8 Define and differentiate between (a) an *ordinary annuity* and (b) an *annuity due*. Which is the more common form? Which form always has greater future value for otherwise identical annuities and interest rates? Why?

5-9 Explain how one can conveniently determine the future value of an ordinary annuity. How can the future-value interest factors for an ordinary annuity be conveniently modified to find the future value of an annuity due?

Present value of a single amount

Assume that you wish to purchase the right to receive $50,000 exactly seven years from now by making a single lump-sum payment today. If interest rates suddenly rise, would the amount you should be willing to pay for this opportunity rise or fall? Why? Take a few moments to answer these questions before reading ahead.

present value
The current dollar value of a future amount. The amount of money that would have to be invested today at a given interest rate over a specified period to equal the future amount.

IT IS OFTEN USEFUL TO DETERMINE THE "PRESENT VALUE" OF A FUTURE AMOUNT OF money. **Present value** is the current dollar value of a future amount—the amount of money that would have to be invested today at a given interest rate over a specified period to equal the future amount. Present value, like future value, is based on the belief that a dollar today is worth more than a dollar that will be received at some future date. The actual present value of a dollar depends largely on the investment opportunities of the recipient and the point in time at which the dollar is to be received. This section explores the present value of a single amount.

The concept of present value

discounting cash flows
The process of finding present values; the inverse of compounding interest.

The process of finding present values is often referred to as **discounting cash flows.** This process is actually the inverse of compounding interest. It is concerned with answering the question "If I can earn k percent on my money, what is the most I would be willing to pay now for an opportunity to receive FV_n dollars n periods from today?" Instead of finding the future value of present dollars invested at a given rate, discounting determines the present value of a future amount, assuming that the decision maker has an opportunity to earn a certain return, k, on the money. This annual rate of return is variously referred to as the *discount rate, required return, cost of capital,* or *opportunity cost.*[11] These terms will be used interchangeably in this text. The discounting process can be illustrated by a simple example.

EXAMPLE

Paul Shorter has been given an opportunity to receive $300 one year from now. If he can earn 6 percent on his investments in the normal course of events, what is the

[11]The theoretical underpinning of this "required return" is introduced in Chapter 6 and further refined in subsequent chapters.

most he should pay now for this opportunity? To answer this question, we must determine how many dollars would have to be invested at 6 percent today to have $300 one year from now. By letting *PV* equal this unknown amount and using the same notation as in the compounding discussion, the situation can be expressed as follows:

$$PV \times (1 + .06) = \$300 \tag{5.17}$$

Solving Equation 5.17 for *PV* gives us Equation 5.18:

$$PV = \frac{\$300}{(1 + .06)} \tag{5.18}$$

$$= \$283.02$$

which results in a value of $283.02 for *PV*. In other words, the "present value" of $300 received one year from today, given an opportunity cost of 6 percent, is $283.02. Paul should be indifferent to whether he receives $283.02 today or $300.00 one year from now. This is true because the present value of $283.02 is the cash today equivalent of $300 one year from now; investment of $283.02 today at the 6 percent opportunity cost would result in $300 at the end of one year. Clearly, if Paul could receive either amount by paying less than $283.02 today, he should, of course, do so. ■

A mathematical expression for present value

The present value of a future amount can be found mathematically by solving Equation 5.4 for *PV*. In other words, one merely wants to obtain the present value, *PV*, of some future amount, FV_n, to be received n periods from now, assuming an opportunity cost of k. Solving Equation 5.4 for *PV* gives us Equation 5.19, which is the general equation for the present value of a future amount:

$$PV = \frac{FV_n}{(1 + k)^n} = FV_n \times \left[\frac{1}{(1 + k)^n}\right] \tag{5.19}$$

Note the similarity between this general equation for present value and the equation in the preceding example (Equation 5.18). The use of this equation in finding the present value of a future amount can be illustrated by a simple example.

EXAMPLE

Pam Valenti wishes to find the present value of $1,700 that will be received eight years from now. Pam's opportunity cost is 8 percent. Substituting $FV_8 = \$1{,}700$, $n = 8$, and $k = .08$ into Equation 5.19 yields Equation 5.20:

$$PV = \frac{\$1{,}700}{(1 + .08)^8} \tag{5.20}$$

To solve Equation 5.20, the term (1 + .08) must be raised to the eighth power. The value resulting from this time-consuming calculation is 1.851. Dividing this value into $1,700 yields a present value for the $1,700 of $918.42.

Time-Line Use This analysis can be depicted diagrammatically on the time line shown below.

Time line for present value of a single amount ($1,700 future amount, discounted at 8 percent, from the end of eight years)

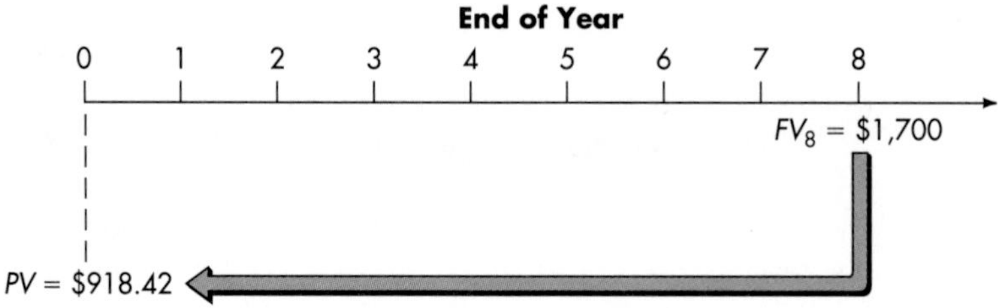

Simplifying present-value calculations

present-value interest factor
The multiplier used to calculate at a specified discount rate the present value of an amount to be received in a future period.

The present-value calculation can be simplified by using a **present-value interest factor.** This factor is the multiplier used to calculate at a specified discount rate the present value of an amount to be received in a future period. The present-value interest factor for the present value of $1 discounted at *k* percent for *n* periods is referred to as $PVIF_{k,n}$:

$$\text{Present-value interest factor} = PVIF_{k,n} = \frac{1}{(1+k)^n} \tag{5.21}$$

Appendix Table A-3 (at the back of the book) presents present-value interest factors for $1. By letting $PVIF_{k,n}$ represent the appropriate interest factor, we can rewrite Equation 5.19 as follows:

$$PV = FV_n \times (PVIF_{k,n}) \tag{5.22}$$

This expression indicates that to find the present value, PV, of an amount to be received in a future period, n, we have merely to multiply the future amount, FV_n, by the appropriate present-value interest factor. An example will illustrate this calculation using both a table and a hand-held business calculator.

EXAMPLE

As was noted in the preceding example, Pam Valenti wishes to find the present value of $1,700 to be received eight years from now, assuming an 8 percent opportunity cost.

Table Use The present-value interest factor for 8 percent and 8 years, $PVIF_{8\%,8\text{yrs}}$, found in Table A-3, is .540. Multiplying the $1,700 future value by this factor in accordance with Equation 5.22 results in a present value of $918.

Calculator Use The present value can alternatively be found by using the business calculator's financial functions. First punch in $1,700, and depress **FV**; next punch in 8, and depress **N**; then punch in 8, and depress **%i**; finally, to calculate the present value, depress **CPT** followed by **PV**. The present value, $918.46, should appear on the calculator display.

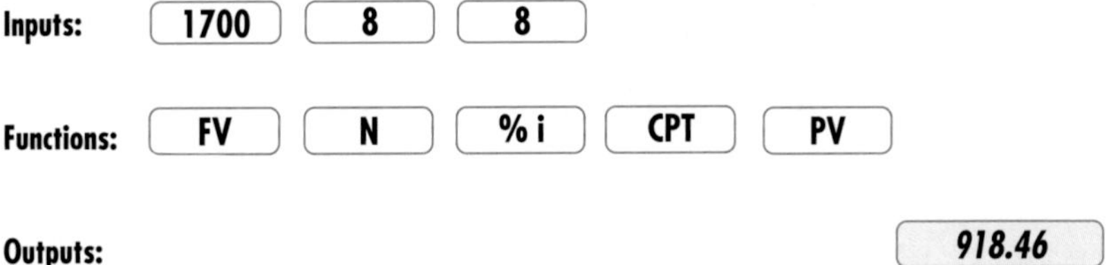

Note that because of rounding in the calculation in Equation 5.20 and of the factors in Table A-3, the value obtained with the calculator—$918.46—is most accurate, although for purposes of this text these differences are deemed insignificant. ■

A graphic view of present value

It is important to note that present-value calculations assume that the future values are measured at the *end* of the given period. The relationship among various discount rates, time periods, and the present value of one dollar is illustrated in Figure 5.6. Everything else being equal, the figure clearly shows two relationships: (1) the higher the discount rate, the lower the present value, and (2) the longer the period of time, the lower the present value. Also note that given a discount rate of 0 percent, the present value always equals the future value ($1.00). But for any discount rate greater than zero, the present value is less than the future value of $1.00 in Figure 5.6.

FIGURE 5.6
Discount rates, time periods, and present value of one dollar

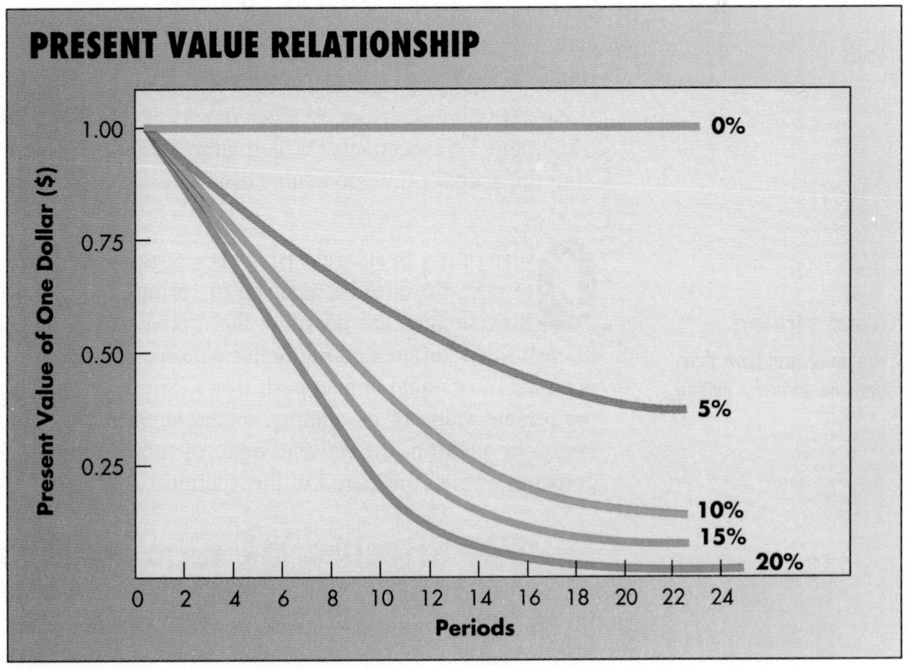

Comparing present value and future value

A few important observations must be made with respect to present values. One is that the expression for the present-value interest factor for k percent and n periods, $1/(1 + k)^n$, is the inverse of the future-value interest factor for k percent and n periods, $(1 + k)^n$. This observation can be confirmed by dividing a present-value interest factor for k percent and n periods, $PVIF_{k,n}$, into 1.0 and comparing the resulting value to the future-value interest factor given in Table A-1 for k percent and n periods, $FVIF_{k,n}$. The two values should be equivalent. Because of the relationship between present-value interest factors and future-value interest factors, we can find the present-value interest factors given a table of future-value interest factors, and vice versa. For example, the future-value interest factor from Table A-1 for 10 percent and five periods is 1.611. Dividing this value into 1.0 yields .621, which is the present-value interest factor given in Table A-3 for 10 percent and five periods.

CONCEPTS IN REVIEW

5-10 What is meant by the phrase "the present value of a future amount"? What is the equation for the present value, PV, of a future amount, FV_n, to be received in period n, assuming that the firm requires a minimum return of k percent? How are present-value and future-value calculations related?

5-11 What effect does *increasing* (a) required return and (b) time periods have on the present value of a future amount? Why?

Present value of cash flow streams

Assume that you can choose between receiving $3,000 either as an ordinary three-year, $1,000 annuity or by receiving $1,500, $1,000, and $500 at the ends of years 1, 2, and 3, respectively. Which alternative would you prefer? Why? Before reading on, spend a few moments answering these questions.

mixed stream
A stream of cash flows that reflects no particular pattern.

QUITE OFTEN IN FINANCE THERE IS A NEED TO FIND THE PRESENT VALUE OF A STREAM of cash flows to be received in various future periods. Two basic types of cash flow streams are possible: the mixed stream and the annuity. A **mixed stream** of cash flows reflects no particular pattern, whereas, as was stated earlier, an *annuity* is a pattern of equal annual cash flows. Since certain shortcuts are possible in finding the present value of an annuity, mixed streams and annuities will be discussed separately. In addition, the present value of mixed streams with embedded annuities and perpetuities are considered in this section.

Present value of a mixed stream

To find the present value of a mixed stream of cash flows, determine the present value of each future amount in the manner described in the preceding section, then add all the individual present values to find the total present value of the stream. An example can be used to illustrate this procedure using Table A-3 or a hand-held business calculator.

EXAMPLE

The Frey Company, a shoe manufacturer, has been offered an opportunity to receive the following mixed stream of cash flows over the next five years:

Year	Cash flow
1	$400
2	800
3	500
4	400
5	300

If the firm must earn 9 percent, at minimum, on its investments, what is the most it should pay for this opportunity?

Table Use To solve this problem, the present value of each cash flow discounted at 9 percent for the appropriate number of years is determined. The sum of all these individual values is then calculated to get the present value of the total stream. The present-value interest factors required are obtained from Table A-3. Table 5.7 presents the calculations needed to find the present value of the cash flow stream, which turns out to be $1,904.60.

Calculator Use A calculator could be used to find the present value of each individual cash flow, using the procedure demonstrated earlier; then the present values could be summed to get the present value of the stream of cash flows. Most more expensive financial calculators have a function that allows you to punch in all cash flows, specify the discount rate, and then directly calculate the present value of the entire cash flow stream. The inexpensive BA-35 business calculator used here does not contain that function. Because calculators provide more precise solutions than those based upon the

TABLE 5.7

THE PRESENT VALUE OF A MIXED STREAM OF CASH FLOWS

Year (n)	Cash flow (1)	$PVIF_{9\%,n}$[a] (2)	Present value [(1) × (2)] (3)
1	$400	.917	$ 366.80
2	800	.842	673.60
3	500	.772	386.00
4	400	.708	283.20
5	300	.650	195.00
	Present value of mixed stream		$1,904.60

[a]Present-value interest factors at 9 percent are from Table A-3.

use of rounded table factors, using a calculator to find the present value of Frey Company's cash flow stream will result in a value that is close to but not precisely equal to the $1,904.60 value calculated above.

Frey should not pay more than $1,904.60 for the opportunity to receive these cash flows, since paying $1,904.60 would provide exactly a 9 percent return.

Time-Line Use This situation is depicted diagrammatically on the time line below.

Time line for present value of a mixed stream (end-of-year cash flows, discounted at 9 percent, over the corresponding number of years)

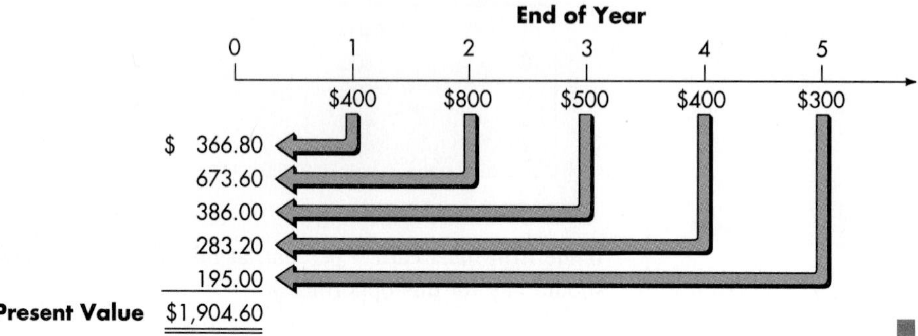

Present value of an annuity

The present value of an annuity can be found in a manner similar to that used for a mixed stream, but a shortcut is possible.

EXAMPLE

The Braden Company, a small producer of plastic toys, is attempting to determine the most it should pay to purchase a particular annuity. The firm requires a minimum return of 8 percent on all investments, and the annuity consists of cash flows of $700 per year for five years. Table 5.8 shows the long way of finding the present value of the

TABLE 5.8

THE LONG METHOD FOR FINDING THE PRESENT VALUE OF AN ANNUITY

Year (*n*)	Cash flow (1)	$PVIF_{8\%,n}$[a] (2)	Present value [(1) × (2)] (3)
1	$700	.926	$ 648.20
2	700	.857	599.90
3	700	.794	555.80
4	700	.735	514.50
5	700	.681	476.70
Present value of annuity			$2,795.10

[a]Present-value interest factors at 8 percent are from Table A-3.

annuity, which is the same as the method used for the mixed stream. This procedure yields a present value of \$2,795.10, which can be interpreted in the same manner as for the mixed cash flow stream in the preceding example.

Time-Line Use Similarly, this situation is depicted graphically on the time line shown below.

Time line for present value of an annuity (\$700 end-of-year cash flows, discounted at 8 percent, over five years)

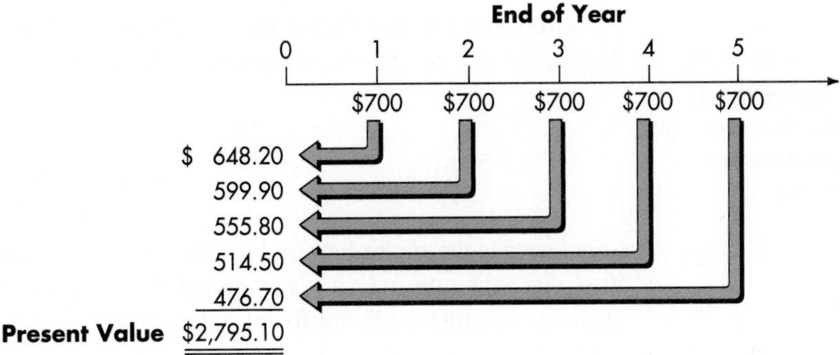

THE MATHEMATICS OF THE PRESENT-VALUE-OF-AN-ANNUITY CALCULATION

The calculations used in the preceding example can be simplified by recognizing that each of the five multiplications made to get the individual present values involved multiplying the annual amount (\$700) by the appropriate present-value interest factor. This method of finding the present value of the annuity can also be written as an equation:

$$\text{Present value of annuity} = [\$700 \times (.926)] + [\$700 \times (.857)] + [\$700 \times (.794)] + [\$700 \times (.735)] + [\$700 \times (.681)] = \$2,795.10 \tag{5.23}$$

Simplifying Equation 5.23 by factoring out the \$700 yields Equation 5.24:

$$\text{Present value of annuity} = \$700 \times (.926 + .857 + .794 + .735 + .681) = \$2,795.10 \tag{5.24}$$

Thus the present value of an annuity can be found by multiplying the annual amount received by the sum of the present-value interest factors for each year of the annuity's life.

SIMPLIFYING PRESENT-VALUE-OF-AN-ANNUITY CALCULATIONS

Annuity calculations can be simplified by using a present-value interest table for an annuity or a business/financial calculator. The values for the present value of a \$1 annuity are given in Appendix Table A-4 (at the back of the book). The factors included in the table are derived by summing the terms in parentheses in equations like Equation 5.24. In the case of Equation 5.24 this results in Equation 5.25:

$$\text{Present value of annuity} = \$700 \times (3.993) = \$2{,}795.10 \tag{5.25}$$

present-value interest factor for an annuity
The multiplier used to calculate the present value of an annuity at a specified discount rate over a given period of time.

The interest factors in Table A-4 actually represent the sum of the first n present-value interest factors in Table A-3 for a given discount rate. The formula for the **present-value interest factor for an annuity** with end-of-year cash flows[12] that are discounted at k percent for n periods, $PVIFA_{k,n}$, is:[13]

$$PVIFA_{k,n} = \sum_{t=1}^{n} \frac{1}{(1+k)^t} \tag{5.26}$$

This factor is the multiplier used to calculate the present value of an annuity at a specified discount rate over a given period of time. The formula merely states that the present-value interest factor for an n-year annuity is found by summing the first n present-value interest factors at the given rate (i.e., $PVIFA_{k,n} = \sum_{t=1}^{n} PVIF_{k,t}$). This relationship can be verified by reviewing the terms in Equation 5.24.[14]

By letting PVA_n equal the present value of an n-year annuity, PMT equal the amount to be received annually at the end of each year, and $PVIFA_{k,n}$ represent the appropriate value for the *present-value interest factor for a one-dollar annuity discounted at* k *percent for* n *years,* the relationship among these variables can be expressed as follows:

$$PVA_n = PMT \times (PVIFA_{k,n}) \tag{5.27}$$

An example will illustrate this calculation using both a table and a hand-held business calculator.

EXAMPLE

The Braden Company, as was noted in the preceding example, wishes to find the present value of a five-year annuity of \$700 assuming an 8 percent opportunity cost.

---

[12]Consistent with the discussions of future value, our concern here is only with *ordinary annuities*—those with cash flows occurring at the *end* of each period.

[13]The formula for the present-value interest factor for an *annuity due* is $\sum_{t=1}^{n} \frac{1}{(1+k)^{t-1}}$, since in this case all cash flows occur at the beginning of each period. The factor therefore merely represents 1.0 plus the sum of the first $n - 1$ present-value interest factors. The present-value interest factor for an annuity due can be found by multiplying the present-value interest factor for an ordinary annuity, $PVIFA_{k,n}$, by $(1 + k)$.

[14]A mathematical expression that can be applied in order to more efficiently calculate the present-value interest factor for an ordinary annuity is

$$PVIFA_{k,n} = \left[(1/k) \times \left(1 - \frac{1}{(1+k)^n}\right)\right]$$

The use of this expression is especially attractive in the absence of the appropriate financial tables or a business/financial calculator or personal computer.

Table Use The present-value interest factor for an annuity at 8 percent for five years, $PVIFA_{8\%,5yrs}$, found in Table A-4, is 3.993. Multiplying the $700 annuity by this factor in accordance with Equation 5.27 results in a present value of $2,795.10.

Calculator Use The present value of an annuity can alternatively be found by using the business calculator's financial functions. First punch in $700, and depress **PMT**; next punch in 5, and depress **N**; then punch in 8, and depress **%i**; finally, to calculate the present value of the annuity, depress **CPT** followed by **PV**. The present value of $2,794.90 should appear on the calculator display.

Inputs:	700	5	8		
Functions:	PMT	N	%i	CPT	PV
Outputs:					2794.90

Note that because of rounding in the calculation in Equation 5.24 and of the factors in Table A-4, the value obtained with the calculator—$2,794.90—is more accurate, although for purposes of this text these differences are deemed insignificant. ■

CONCEPT IN PRACTICE

Taxpayer Bailout of the PBGC?

At first glance, you might think that the Pension Benefit Guarantee Corporation (PBGC), the federal agency that insures private pension plans in corporate America, is on the brink of financial collapse. In 1991 and 1992 the agency's annual deficit, the amount by which newly acquired pension liabilities exceeded newly acquired assets of the corporation, more than doubled, reaching $2.7 billion. Most of this deficit occurred as the PBGC assumed ownership of the failed pension plans belonging to Pan American World Airways and Eastern Airlines.

But don't organize a bake sale to help the PBGC just yet. The federal insurance fund has enjoyed a huge positive cash flow for years, ranging from $200 million in 1987 to over $1 billion in 1991. Then why does the fund show a substantial annual deficit? It's all in the time value of money. Analysts measuring the PBGC's annual deficit assumed that all of the pension money that is currently owed to retirees must be paid immediately in a single lump sum. In truth the PBGC's pension liabilities will be paid monthly for as many as 40 years into the future. As the agency's strong positive cash flow attests, it can easily accommodate these future annuity payments. What's more, the present *discounted* value of all insured pension payments is well below the current market value of all assets supporting these corporate retirement plans. About $1.3 trillion in assets currently back about $900 million in liabilities for the 41 million workers and retirees protected by the PBGC.

Present value of a mixed stream with an embedded annuity

Occasionally, a mixed stream of cash flows will have an annuity embedded within it. Depending upon the number of years in the annuity's life and the life of the mixed stream, the computations can be streamlined by using the following three-step procedure:

Step 1 Find the present value of the annuity at the specified discount rate using the procedure described above. (*Note*: The resulting present value is measured at the beginning of the annuity, which is equivalent to the end of the period immediately preceding the start of the annuity.)

Step 2 Add the present value calculated in Step 1 to any other cash flows occurring in the period immediately preceding the start of that annuity, and eliminate the individual annuity cash flows to determine the revised cash flows.

Step 3 Discount the revised cash flows found in Step 2 back to time zero in the normal fashion at the specified discount rate.

An example can be used to illustrate application of this three-step procedure using both a table and a hand-held business calculator.

EXAMPLE

Powell Products expects an investment to generate the cash flows shown in column 1 of Table 5.9. Given that the firm must earn 9 percent on its investments, what is the present value of the expected cash flow stream?

Table Use The three-step procedure is appllied to Powell's cash flows in Table 5.9, since it has a four-year $7,000 annuity embedded in its cash flows.

Step 1 As noted in column 2 of Table 5.9, the present value of the embedded $7,000 annuity is calculated by multiplying the $7,000 by the present-value-of-an-annuity interest factor at 9 percent for 4 years, $PVIFA_{9\%,4yrs.}$, to find its present value of $22,680 at the end of year 2 (i.e., the beginning of year 3).

Step 2 The end-of-year-2 value of the annuity found in Step 1 is added to the end-of-year-2 cash flow of $6,000, noted in column 3 of Table 5.9, to determine the revised cash flow. This results in total cash flow of $28,680 in year 2 and the elimination of the annuity cash flow for years 3 through 6.

Step 3 Multiplying the revised cash flows in column 3 of Table 5.9 by the appropriate present-value interest factors at 9 percent in column 4 results in the present values shown in column 5 of the table. The present value of this mixed stream of $37,627.56 is found by summing column 5.

Note that by first finding the present value of the embedded $7,000 annuity, the present-value calculation has been simplified.

Calculator Use A similar procedure to that demonstrated above would be applied in using a calculator. The resulting answer would be $37,617.96, which is close to, but more precise than, the value calculated in Table 5.9.[15]

[15]Most financially oriented calculators have a frequency function that allows easy imput of cash flow streams that have annuities embedded in them. The use of this feature, if it is available, is explained in the calculator's reference guide.

TABLE 5.9

THE PRESENT VALUE OF A MIXED STREAM WITH AN EMBEDDED ANNUITY

		Step 1	Step 2	Step 3	
Year(n)	Cash flow (1)	Present value of annuity (2)	Revised cash flow [(1) + (2)] (3)	$PVIF_{9\%,n}$ (4)	Present value [(3) × (4)] (5)
1	$5,000		$ 5,000	.917	$ 4,585.00
2	6,000	22,680	28,680	.842	24,148.56
3	7,000	↑	0	.772	0
4	7,000	$PVIFA_{9\%,4yrs}$	0	.708	0
5	7,000	× 3,240	0	.650	0
6	7,000		0	.596	0
7	8,000		8,000	.547	4,376.00
8	9,000		9,000	.502	4,518.00
			Present value of mixed stream		$37,627.56

Time-Line Use The computational procedure used in this situation is presented diagrammatically on the time line shown below.

Time line for present value of a mixed stream with an embedded annuity (end-of-year cash flows, discounted at 9 percent, over the corresponding number of years)

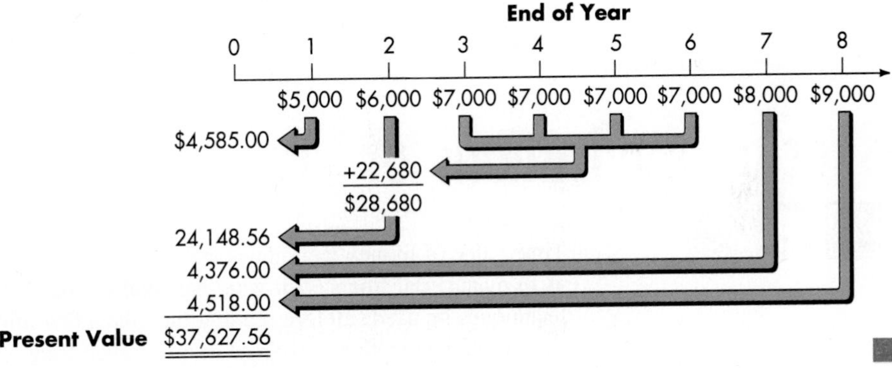

Present value of a perpetuity

perpetuity
An annuity with an infinite life, making continual annual payments.

A **perpetuity** is an annuity with an infinite life—in other words, an annuity that never stops providing its holder with *PMT* dollars at the end of each year. It is sometimes necessary to find the present value of a perpetuity. The present-value interest factor for a perpetuity discounted at the rate *k* is defined by Equation 5.28:

$$PVIFA_{k,\infty} = \frac{1}{k} \tag{5.28}$$

As noted, the appropriate factor, $PVIFA_{k,\infty}$, is found merely by dividing the discount rate, *k* (stated as a decimal), into 1. The validity of this method can be seen by looking at the factors in Table A-4 for 8 percent, 10 percent, 20 percent, and 40 percent.

As the number of periods (typically years) approaches 50, the value of these factors approaches 12.500, 10.000, 5.000, and 2.500, respectively. Dividing .08, .10, .20, and .50 (for k) into 1 gives factors for finding the present value of perpetuities at these rates of 12.500, 10.000, 5.000, and 2.500. An example will help to clarify the application of the factor given in Equation 5.28.

EXAMPLE

A person wishes to determine the present value of a $1,000 perpetuity discounted at 10 percent. The appropriate present-value interest factor can be found by dividing 1 by .10, as noted in Equation 5.28. Substituting the resulting factor, 10, and the amount of the perpetuity, PMT = $1,000, into Equation 5.27 results in a present value of $10,000 for the perpetuity. In other words, the receipt of $1,000 every year for an indefinite period is worth only $10,000 today if a person can earn 10 percent on investments. The reason is that if the person had $10,000 and earned 10 percent interest on it each year, $1,000 a year could be withdrawn indefinitely without affecting the initial $10,000, which would never be drawn upon. ■

CONCEPTS IN REVIEW

5-12 How is the present value of a mixed stream of cash flows calculated? How can the calculations required to find the present value of an annuity be simplified? How can the calculation of the present value of a mixed stream with an embedded annuity be simplified?

5-13 What is a *perpetuity*? How might the present-value interest factor for such a stream of cash flows be determined?

Special applications of time value

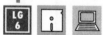

Time value of money techniques are used in personal financial transactions as well as in managerial finance. In what personal financial transactions would time value techniques be used? Before reading on, take a few minutes to cite and consider the time value applications involved in a few such transactions.

FUTURE-VALUE AND PRESENT-VALUE TECHNIQUES HAVE A NUMBER OF IMPORTANT applications. Three will be presented in this section: (1) the calculation of the deposits needed to accumulate a future sum, (2) the calculation of amortization on loans, and (3) the determination of interest or growth rates.

Deposits to accumulate a future sum

Often an individual may wish to determine the annual deposit necessary to accumulate a certain amount of money so many years hence. Suppose a person wishes to purchase a house five years from now and estimates that an initial down payment of $20,000 will be required at that time. She wishes to make equal annual end-of-year deposits in an account paying annual interest of 6 percent, so she must determine what size annuity will result in a lump sum equal to $20,000 at the end of year 5. The solution to this problem is closely related to the process of finding the future value of an annuity.

In an earlier section of this chapter the future value of an n-year annuity, FVA_n, was found by multiplying the annual deposit, PMT, by the appropriate interest factor (from Table A-2 or using a hand-held business calculator), $FVIFA_{k,n}$. The relationship of the three variables has been defined by Equation 5.15, which is rewritten here as Equation 5.29:

$$FVA_n = PMT \times (FVIFA_{k,n}) \tag{5.29}$$

We can find the annual deposit required to accumulate FVA_n dollars, given a specified interest rate, k, and a certain number of years, n, by solving Equation 5.29 for PMT. Isolating PMT on the left side of the equation gives us

$$PMT = \frac{FVA_n}{FVIFA_{k,n}} \tag{5.30}$$

Once this is done, we have only to substitute the known values of FVA_n and $FVIFA_{k,n}$ into the right side of the equation to find the annual deposit required. An example can be employed to demonstrate this calculation using Table A-2 as well as a hand-held business calculator.

EXAMPLE

In the problem just stated, a person wished to determine the equal annual end-of-year deposits required to accumulate $20,000 at the end of five years given an interest rate of 6 percent.

Table Use Table A-2 indicates that the future-value interest factor for an annuity at 6 percent for five years, $FVIFA_{6\%,5yrs}$, is 5.637. Substituting FVA_5 = $20,000 and $FVIFA_{6\%,5yrs}$ = 5.637 into Equation 5.30 yields an annual required deposit, PMT, of $3,547.99 ($20,000 ÷ 5.637). If $3,547.99 is deposited at the end of each year for five years at 6 percent, at the end of the five years there will be $20,000 in the account.

Calculator Use Using the calculator, begin by punching in $20,000 and depressing **FV**; next punch in 5, and depress **N**; then punch in 6, and depress **%i**; finally, to calculate the annual deposit, depress **CPT** followed by **PMT**. The annual deposit amount appearing on the calculator display is $3,547.93 (ignore the minus sign). Note that this value, except for a slight rounding difference, agrees with the value found by using Table A-2 above.

Inputs:	20000	5	6		
Functions:	FV	N	% i	CPT	PMT
Outputs:					3547.93

■

Loan amortization

loan amortization
The determination of the equal annual loan payments necessary to provide a lender with a specified interest return and to repay the loan principal over a specified period.

loan amortization schedule
A schedule of equal payments to repay a loan. It shows the allocation of each loan payment to interest and principal.

The term **loan amortization** refers to the determination of the equal annual loan payments necessary to provide a lender with a specified interest return and repay the loan principal over a specified period. The loan amortization process involves finding the future payments (over the term of the loan) whose present value at the loan interest rate equals the amount of initial principal borrowed. Lenders use a **loan amortization schedule** to determine these payment amounts as well as the allocation of each payment to interest and principal. In the case of home mortgages, these tables are used to find the equal *monthly* payments necessary to amortize, or pay off, the mortgage at a specified interest rate over a 15- to 30-year period.

Amortizing a loan actually involves creating an annuity out of a present amount. For example, an individual may borrow $6,000 at 10 percent and agree to make equal annual end-of-year payments over four years. To determine the size of the payments, the four-year annuity discounted at 10 percent that has a present value of $6,000 must be determined. This process is actually the inverse of finding the present value of an annuity.

Earlier in this chapter the present value, PVA_n, of an n-year annuity of PMT dollars was found by multiplying the annual amount, PMT, by the present-value interest factor for an annuity (from Table A-4 or a hand-held business calculator), $PVIFA_{k,n}$. This relationship, which was originally expressed as Equation 5.27, is rewritten here as Equation 5.31:

$$PVA_n = PMT \times (PVIFA_{k,n}) \tag{5.31}$$

To find the equal annual payment, PMT, required to pay off, or amortize, the loan, PVA_n, over a certain number of years at a specified interest rate, we need to solve Equation 5.31 for PMT. Isolating PMT on the left side of the equation gives us

$$PMT = \frac{PVA_n}{PVIFA_{k,n}} \tag{5.32}$$

Once this is done, we have only to substitute the known values of PVA_n and $PVIFA_{k,n}$ into the right side of the equation to find the annual payment required.

EXAMPLE

In the problem stated above, a person wished to determine the equal annual end-of-year payments necessary to amortize fully a $6,000, 10 percent loan over four years.

Table Use Table A-4 indicates that the present-value interest factor for an annuity corresponding to 10 percent and four years, $PVIFA_{10\%,4yrs}$, is 3.170. Substituting $PVA_4 =$ $6,000 and $PVIFA_{10\%,4yrs} = 3.170$ into Equation 5.32 and solving for PMT yields an annual loan payment of $1,892.74 ($6,000 ÷ 3.170). Thus, to repay the interest and principal on a $6,000, 10 percent, four-year loan, equal annual end-of-year payments of $1,892.74 are necessary.

Calculator Use Using the calculator, begin by punching in $6,000 and depressing **PV**; next punch in 4, and depress **N**; then punch in 10, and depress **%i**; finally, to calculate the annual loan payment, depress **CPT** followed by **PMT**. The annual deposit amount of $1,892.82 appearing on the display, except for a slight rounding difference, agrees with the value found using Table A-4 above.

Inputs:	6000	4	10		
Functions:	PV	N	%i	CPT	PMT
Outputs:					1892.82

The allocation of each loan payment to interest and principal to repay the loan fully can be seen in columns 3 and 4 of the *loan amortization schedule* given in Table 5.10. The portion of each payment representing interest (column 3) declines, and the portion going to principal repayment (column 4) increases over the repayment period. This is typical of amortized loans because with level payments, as the principal is reduced, the interest component declines, leaving a larger portion of each subsequent payment to repay principal.

TABLE 5.10

LOAN AMORTIZATION SCHEDULE ($6,000 PRINCIPAL, 10 PERCENT INTEREST, FOUR-YEAR REPAYMENT PERIOD)

			Payments		
End of year	Loan payment (1)	Beginning-of-year principal (2)	Interest [.10 × (2)] (3)	Principal [(1) − (3)] (4)	End-of-year principal [(2) − (4)] (5)
1	$1,892.74	$6,000.00	$600.00	$1,292.74	$4,707.26
2	1,892.74	4,707.26	470.73	1,422.01	3,285.25
3	1,892.74	3,285.25	328.53	1,564.21	1,721.04
4	1,892.74	1,721.04	172.10	1,720.64	—[a]

[a]Due to rounding, a slight difference ($.40) exists between the beginning-of-year-4 principal (in column 2) and the year-4 principal payment (in column 4).

■

Interest or growth rates

It is often necessary to calculate the compound annual interest or growth rate exhibited by a stream of cash flows. In doing this, either future-value or present-value interest factors can be used. The approach using present-value interest tables is described in this section. The simplest situation is one in which a person wishes to find the rate of interest or growth in a cash flow stream.[16] This can be illustrated by the following example using both present-value tables and a hand-held business calculator.

EXAMPLE

Ray Noble wishes to find the rate of interest or growth of the following stream of cash flows.

[16]Since the calculations required for finding interest rates and growth rates, given certain cash flow streams, are the same, this section refers to the calculations as those required to find interest *or* growth rates.

Year	Cash flow	
1994	$1,520	
		} 4
1993	1,440	
		} 3
1992	1,370	
		} 2
1991	1,300	
		} 1
1990	1,250	

By using the first year (1990) as a base year, it can be seen that interest has been earned (or growth experienced) for four years.

Table Use The first step in finding the interest or growth rate is to divide the amount received in the earliest year by the amount received in the latest year. This gives the present-value interest factor for four years, $PVIF_{k,4yrs}$, which is .822 ($1,250 ÷ $1,520). The interest rate in Table A-3 associated with the factor closest to .822 for four years is the rate of interest or growth rate exhibited by the cash flows. Looking across year 4 of Table A-3 shows that the factor for 5 percent is .823—almost exactly the .822 value. Therefore the rate of interest or growth rate exhibited by the cash flows given is approximately (to the nearest whole percent) 5 percent.[17]

Calculator Use Using the calculator, we treat the earliest value as a present value *(PV)* and the latest value as a future value (FV_n). First punch in the 1990 value of $1,250 and depress **PV**; next punch in the 1994 value of $1,520, and depress **FV**; then punch in the number of years of growth—4—and depress **N**; finally, to get the interest or growth rate, depress **CPT** followed by **%i**. The interest or growth rate appearing on the display is 5.01 percent, which is consistent with, but more precise than, the value found using Table A-3 above. (*Note:* Many calculators require either the *PV* or *FV* value to be input as a negative number to calculate an unknown interest or growth rate.)

[17]In making these and other types of interest or growth-rate estimates using financial tables, *interpolation* can often be used to get a more exact answer. To illustrate, assume that for seven years of data the quotient found by dividing the earliest by latest cash flow value is .575. In the present-value interest table, Table A-3, for *six years* (the number of years of growth) the closest factors to .575 are .596 at 9 percent and .564 at 10 percent. Clearly, the growth rate is between 9 and 10 percent and is closer to the 10 percent value. To interpolate a more precise answer, the following steps are necessary:

1. Find the difference between the 9 and 10 percent present-value interest factors of .596 and .564. The difference is .032 (.596 − .564).
2. Find the *absolute* difference (i.e., ignore a plus or minus sign) between the calculated quotient of .575 and the value of the present-value interest factor for the lower rate (9 percent), which is .596. This difference is .021 (.575 − .596).
3. Divide the value from Step 2 by that found in Step 1 to get the percent of total distance across the range attributable to the calculated value. The result is .6563 (.021 ÷ .032).
4. Multiply the percent found in Step 3 by the interval width over which interpolation is being performed. In this case the interval width is 1 percent (10% − 9%); multiplying we get .6563 percent (.6563 × 1%). Note that when interpolation is being performed over a wider interval, this step becomes more important.
5. Add the value found in Step 4 to the interest rate associated with the lower end of the interval. The result is 9.6563 percent (9% + .6563%). The growth or interest rate is therefore 9.6563 percent.

Of course, an even more accurate result could easily be obtained by using a business/financial calculator or a personal computer. On a hand-held business calculator the more precise rate is found to be 9.6618 percent.

Inputs: 1250 | 1520 | 4

Functions: PV | FV | N | CPT | %i

Outputs: 5.01 ■

Sometimes one wishes to find the interest rate associated with an equal-payment loan. The procedure for doing so can be demonstrated with an example using both financial tables and a hand-held business calculator.

EXAMPLE

Jan Jacobs can borrow $2,000 to be repaid in equal annual end-of-year amounts of $514.14 for the next five years. She would like to calculate the interest rate on this loan.

Table Use Substituting PVA_5 = $2,000 and PMT = $514.14 into Equation 5.31 and rearranging the equation to solve for $PVIFA_{k,5yrs}$, we get:

$$PVIFA_{k,5yrs} = \frac{PVA_5}{PMT} = \frac{\$2{,}000}{\$514.14} = 3.890 \tag{5.33}$$

The interest rate for five years associated with the factor closest to 3.890 in Table A-4 is 9 percent; therefore the interest rate on the loan is approximately (to the nearest whole percent) 9 percent.

Calculator Use Using the calculator, first punch in $514.14, and depress **PMT**; next punch in $2,000, and depress **PV**; then punch in 5, and depress **N**; finally, to get the interest rate, depress **CPT** followed by **%i**. The interest rate appearing on the display is 9 percent, which is consistent with, but more precise than, the approximate value found by using Table A-4 above. (*Note*: Many calculators require either the *PMT* or *PV* value to be input as a negative number to calculate an unknown interest rate on an equal-payment loan.)

Inputs: 514.14 | 2000 | 5

Functions: PMT | PV | N | CPT | %i

Outputs: 9.00 ■

CONCEPT IN PRACTICE

Gilligan's Island Reruns Will Never Be the Same

For Silicon Graphics, Inc., a leading supplier of graphic image-reproduction technology, 1993 was a very exciting year. The year's accomplishments included introduction of a new supercomputer that rivaled the fastest computers offered by Cray Research, Inc., a visit by President Bill Clinton and Vice President Al Gore to kick off their national technology initiative, and a key role for the company's graphic workstations in the production of special effects for Steven Spielberg's movie *Jurassic Park*.

What really excites the firm's managers is a little financial mathematics. Silicon Graphics expects sales growth to run 30 percent each year over the next several years as the digital-media industry explodes. Digital media is a huge new market combining computers, communications, and consumer electronics. It is expected to replace conventional cable TV and provide such products as digitzed movies, interactive games, and even old reruns of *Gilligan's Island.* With current sales of $1 billion a year and a projected 30 percent annual growth in sales, Silicon Graphics will reach $3.7 billion in sales in just five short years.

CONCEPTS IN REVIEW

5-14 How can the size of the equal annual end-of-year deposits that are necessary to accumulate a certain future sum in a specified future period be determined? How might one use future-value interest factors to aid in this calculation?

5-15 Describe the procedure used to amortize a loan into a series of equal annual payments. What is a *loan amortization schedule?*

5-16 Which present-value interest factors would be used to find (a) the growth rate associated with a stream of cash flows and (b) the interest rate associated with an equal-payment loan? How would each of these be calculated?

Summary

LG 1 Discuss the role of time value in finance, particularly the two common views—future value and present value—and the use of financial tables and business/financial calculators to find them. Financial managers use time value of money techniques to explicitly recognize their opportunities to earn positive returns when assessing the value of the expected cash flow streams associated with decision alternatives. While alternatives can be assessed by either compounding to find future value or discounting to find present value, financial managers, because they are at time zero when making decisions, rely primarily on present value techniques. Both financial tables, which provide various future- and present-value interest factors, and hand-held business/financial calculators like the BA-35 can be used to streamline the practical application of time-value techniques.

LG 2 Understand the concept of future value, its calculation for single amounts, and the procedures and effects on interest rates of compounding interest more frequently than annually. Future value relies on compound interest to measure the value of future amounts. When interest is compounded, the initial principal or deposit in one period, along with the interest earned on it, becomes the beginning principal of the following period, and so on. Interest can be compounded annually, semiannually, quarterly, monthly, weekly, daily, or even continuously. The more frequently interest is compounded, the larger the future amount that will be accumulated and the higher the effective interest rate. The interest factor formulas and basic equations for the future value of a single amount are given in Table 5.11.

LG 3 Find the future value of the two basic types of annuities—ordinary annuity and annuity due—and compare them. An annuity is a pattern of equal annual cash flows occurring at the end of the period for an ordinary annuity and at the beginning of the period for an annuity due. The future value of an ordinary annuity can be found by using the future-value interest factor for an annuity, which requires an adjustment in the case of an annuity due. The interest factor formulas and basic equations for the future value of an annuity are given in Table 5.11.

LG 4 Review the concept of present value, its calculation for a single amount, and the relationship of present to future value. Present value represents the inverse of future value. In finding the present value of a future amount, we determine what amount of money today would be equivalent to the given future amount, considering the fact that we can earn a certain return on the current money. The interest-factor formula and basic equation for the present value of a single amount are given in Table 5.11.

LG 5 Determine the present value of a mixed stream of cash flows, an annuity, a mixed stream with an embedded annuity, and a perpetuity. It is frequently necessary to find the present value of a stream of cash flows. For mixed streams, the individual present values must be found and summed. In the case of an annuity the present

TABLE 5.11

SUMMARY OF KEY DEFINITIONS, FORMULAS, AND EQUATIONS FOR TIME VALUE OF MONEY

Variable definitions

FV_n = future value or amount at the end of period n
PV = initial principal, or present value
k = annual rate of interest
n = number of periods—typically years—over which money earns a return
m = number of times per year interest is compounded
t = period number index
e = exponential function = 2.7183
$k_{eff.}$ = effective interest rate
FVA_n = future value of an n-year annuity
PMT = amount deposited or received annually at the end of each year
PVA_n = present value of an n-year annuity

Interest factor formulas

Future value of a single amount

$$FVIF_{k,n} = \left(1 + \frac{k}{m}\right)^{m \times n}$$ [Eq. 5.7]

for annual compounding, $m = 1$

$$FVIF_{k,n} = (1 + k)^n$$ [Eq. 5.5; factors in Table A-1]

for continuous compounding, $m = \infty$

$$FVIF_{k,n} = e^{k \times n}$$ [Eq. 5.9]

to find the effective interest rate

$$k_{eff.} = \left(1 + \frac{k}{m}\right)^m - 1$$ [Eq. 5.10]

Future value of an (ordinary) annuity

$$FVIFA_{k,n} = \sum_{t=1}^{n} (1 + k)^{t-1}$$ [Eq. 5.14; factors in Table A-2]

Future value of an annuity due

$$FVIFA_{k,n} \text{ (annuity due)} = FVIFA_{k,n} \times (1 + k)$$ [Eq. 5.16]

Present value of a single amount

$$PVIF_{k,n} = \frac{1}{(1 + k)^n}$$ [Eq. 5.21; factors in Table A-3]

Present value of an annuity

$$PVIFA_{k,n} = \sum_{t=1}^{n} \frac{1}{(1 + k)^t}$$ [Eq. 5.26; factors in Table A-4]

Present value of a perpetuity

$$PVIFA_{k,\infty} = \frac{1}{k}$$ [Equation 5.28]

Basic equations

Future value (single amount):	$FV_n = PV \times (FVIF_{k,n})$	[Eq. 5.6]
Future value (annuity):	$FVA_n = PMT \times (FVIFA_{k,n})$	[Eq. 5.15]
Present value (single amount):	$PV = FV_n \times (PVIF_{k,n})$	[Eq. 5.22]
Present value (annuity):	$PVA_n = PMT \times (PVIFA_{k,n})$	[Eq. 5.27]

value can be found by using the present-value interest factor for an annuity. For a mixed stream with an embedded annuity the present value of the annuity is found, then used to replace the annuity flows, and the new mixed stream's present value is calculated. The present value of a perpetuity—an infinite-lived annuity—is found by using 1 divided by the discount rate to represent the present-value interest factor.

LG 6 **Describe the procedures involved in (1) determining deposits to accumulate a future sum, (2) loan amortization, and (3) finding interest or growth rates.** The annual deposit to accumulate a given future sum can be found by solving the equation for the future value of an annuity for the annual payment. A loan can be amortized into equal annual payments by solving the equation for the present value of an annuity for the annual payment. Interest or growth rates can be estimated by finding the unknown interest rate in the equation for the present value of either a single amount or an annuity.

Self-test problems (Solutions in Appendix E)

ST 5-1 LG 2 **Future values** Delia Martin has $10,000 that she can deposit in any of three savings accounts for a three-year period. Bank A compounds interest on an annual basis; bank B compounds interest twice each year; and bank C compounds interest each quarter. All three banks have a stated annual interest rate of 4 percent.

a. What amount would Ms. Martin have at the end of the third year, leaving all interest paid on deposit, in each bank?
b. What effective interest rate would she earn in each of the banks?
c. On the basis of your findings in **a** and **b,** which bank should Ms. Martin deal with? Why?
d. If a fourth bank—Bank D, also with a 4 percent stated interest rate—compounds interest continuously, how much would Ms. Martin have at the end of the third year? Does this alternative change your recommendation in **c**? Explain why or why not.

ST 5-2 LG 3 **Future values of annuities** Ramesh Abdul wishes to choose the better of two equally costly cash-flow streams—annuity X and annuity Y. X is an *annuity due* with a cash inflow of $9,000 for each of six years. Y is an *ordinary annuity* with a cash inflow of $10,000 for each of six years. Assume that Ramesh can earn 15 percent on his investments.

a. On a purely subjective basis, which annuity do you think is more attractive? Why?
b. Find the future value at the end of year six, FVA_6, for both annuities—X and Y.
c. Use your finding in **b** to indicate which annuity is more attractive. Why? Compare your finding to your subjective response in **a**.

ST 5-3 LG 5 **Present values** You have a choice of accepting either of two five-year cash flow streams or lump-sum amounts. One cash flow stream is an annuity, and the other is a mixed stream. You may accept alternative A or B—either as a cash flow stream or as a lump sum. Given the cash flow and lump-sum amounts associated with each, and assuming a 9 percent opportunity cost, which alternative (A or B) and in which form (cash flow stream or lump-sum amount) would you prefer?

End of year	Cash flow stream: Alternative A	Cash flow stream: Alternative B
1	$700	$1,100
2	700	900
3	700	700
4	700	500
5	700	300
Lump-sum amount		
At time zero	$2,825	$2,800

ST 5-4 LG 6 Deposits to accumulate a future sum Judi Jordan wishes to accumulate $8,000 by the end of five years by making equal annual end-of-year deposits over the next five years. If Judi can earn 7 percent on her investments, how much must she deposit at the *end of each year* to meet this goal?

Problems

5-1 LG 1 Using a time line The finanical manager at Starbuck Industries is considering an investment that requires an initial outlay of $25,000 and is expected to result in cash inflows of $3,000 at the end of year 1, $6,000 at the end of years 2 and 3, $10,000 at the end of year 4, $8,000 at the end of year 5, and $7,000 at the end of year 6.

a. Draw and label a time line depicting the cash flows associated with Starbuck Industries' proposed investment.

b. Use arrows to demonstrate, on the time line in **a**, how compounding to find future value can be used to measure all cash flows at the end of year 6.

c. Use arrows to demonstrate, on the time line in **b**, how discounting to find present value can be used to measure all cash flows at time zero.

d. Which of the approaches—future value or present value—is most often relied upon by the financial manager for decision-making purposes? Why?

5-2 LG 2 Future-value calculation *Without tables or the financial routine on your business calculator,* use the basic formula for future value along with the given interest rate, k, and number of periods, n, to calculate the future-value interest factor in each of the following cases. Compare the calculated value to the table value in Appendix Table A-1.

Case	Interest rate, k (%)	Number of periods, n
A	12	2
B	6	3
C	9	2
D	3	4

5-3 LG 2 Future-value tables Use the future-value interest factors in Appendix Table A-1 in each of the cases in the following table to estimate, to the nearest year, how long it would take an initial deposit, assuming no withdrawals,

a. To double.
b. To quadruple.

Case	Interest rate (%)
A	7
B	40
C	20
D	10

5-4 LG 2 Future values For each of the following cases, calculate the future value of the single cash flow deposited today that will be available at the end of the deposit period if the interest is compounded annually at the rate specified over the given period.

Case	Single cash flow ($)	Interest rate (%)	Deposit period (years)
A	200	5	20
B	4,500	8	7
C	10,000	9	10
D	25,000	10	12
E	37,000	11	5
F	40,000	12	9

5-5 LG 2 Single-payment loan repayment A person borrows $200 to be repaid in eight years with 14 percent annually compounded interest. The loan may be repaid at the end of any earlier year with no prepayment penalty.

a. What amount would be due if the loan is repaid at the end of year 1?
b. What is the repayment at the end of year 4?
c. What amount is due at the end of the eighth year?

5-6 LG 2 Changing compounding frequency Using annual, semiannual, and quarterly compounding periods, for each of the following (1) calculate the future value if $5,000 is initially deposited, and (2) determine the effective interest rate

a. At 12 percent annual interest for 5 years.
b. At 16 percent annual interest for 6 years.
c. At 20 percent annual interest for 10 years.

5-7 LG 2 Compounding frequency, future value, and effective interest rates For each of the following cases:

Case	Amount of initial deposit ($)	Nominal interest rate, k (%)	Compounding frequency, m (times/year)	Deposit period (years)
A	2,500	6	2	5
B	50,000	12	6	3
C	1,000	5	1	10
D	20,000	16	4	6

a. Calculate the future value at the end of the specified deposit period.
b. Determine the effective interest rate, $k_{eff.}$.
c. Compare the nominal interest rate, k, to the effective interest rate, $k_{eff.}$. What relationship exists between compounding frequency and the nominal and effective interest rates?

5-8 LG 2 Continuous compounding For each of the following cases, find the future value at the end of the deposit period, assuming that interest is compounded continuously at the given nominal interest rate.

Case	Amount of initial deposit ($)	Nominal interest rate, k (%)	Deposit period (years)
A	1,000	9	2
B	600	10	10
C	4,000	8	7
D	2,500	12	4

5-9 LG 2 Comparing compounding periods René Levin wishes to determine the future value at the end of two years of a $15,000 deposit made today into an account paying a nominal annual rate of interest of 12 percent.

a. Find the future value of René's deposit assuming that interest is compounded
(1) annually,
(2) quarterly,
(3) monthly,
(4) continuously.

b. Compare your findings in **a**, and use them to demonstrate the relationship between compounding frequency and future value.

c. What is the maximum future value obtainable given the $15,000 deposit, two-year time period, and 12 percent nominal interest rate? Use your findings in **a** to explain.

5-10 LG 3 Future value of an annuity For each of the following cases:

Case	Amount of annuity ($)	Interest rate (%)	Deposit period (years)
A	2,500	8	10
B	500	12	6
C	30,000	20	5
D	11,500	9	8
E	6,000	14	30

a. Calculate the future value of the annuity assuming that it is an
(1) ordinary annuity,
(2) annuity due.

b. Compare your findings in **a**(1) and **a**(2). All else being identical, which type of annuity—ordinary or annuity due—is preferable? Explain why.

5-11 LG 3 Ordinary annuity versus annuity due Marian Kirk wishes to select the better of two 10-year annuities—C and D—described below.

Annuity C An ordinary annuity of $2,500 per year for 10 years.

Annuity D An annuity due of $2,200 per year for 10 years.

a. Find the future value of both annuities at the end of year 10 assuming that Marian can earn
(1) 10 percent annual interest,
(2) 20 percent annual interest.

b. Use your findings in **a** to indicate which annuity has the greater future value at the end of year 10 for both the (1) 10 percent and (2) 20 percent interest rates.

c. Briefly compare, contrast, and explain any differences between your findings using the 10 percent and 20 percent interest rates in **b.**

5-12 LG 2,3 Annuities and compounding Janet Boyle intends to deposit $300 per year in a credit union for the next 10 years, and the credit union pays an annual interest rate of 8 percent. Determine the future value that Janet will have at the end of 10 years given that end-of-period deposits are made and no interest is withdrawn if

a. $300 is deposited annually, and the credit union pays interest annually.

b. $150 is deposited semiannually, and the credit union pays interest semiannually.

c. $75 is deposited quarterly, and the credit union pays interest quarterly.

5-13 LG 3 Future value of a mixed stream For each of the following mixed streams of cash flows, determine the future value at the end of the final year if deposits are made at the *beginning of each year* into an account paying annual interest of 12 percent, assuming that no withdrawals are made during the period.

Year	Cash flow stream		
	A	B	C
1	$ 900	$30,000	$1,200
2	1,000	25,000	1,200
3	1,200	20,000	1,000
4		10,000	1,900
5		5,000	

5-14 LG 4 **Present-value calculation** *Without tables or the finanical routine on your business calculator,* use the basic formula for present value along with the given opportunity cost, k, and number of periods, n, to calculate the present-value interest factor in each of the following cases. Compare the calculated value to the table value.

Case	Opportunity cost, k (%)	Number of periods, n
A	2	4
B	10	2
C	5	3
D	13	2

5-15 LG 4 **Present values** For each of the following cases, calculate the present value of the cash flow, discounting at the rate given and assuming that the cash flow will be received at the end of the period noted.

Case	Single cash flow ($)	Discount rate (%)	End of period (years)
A	7,000	12	4
B	28,000	8	20
C	10,000	14	12
D	150,000	11	6
E	45,000	20	8

5-16 LG 4 **Present value** Jim Nance has been offered a future payment of $500 three years from today. If his opportunity cost is 7 percent compounded annually, what value would he place on this opportunity?

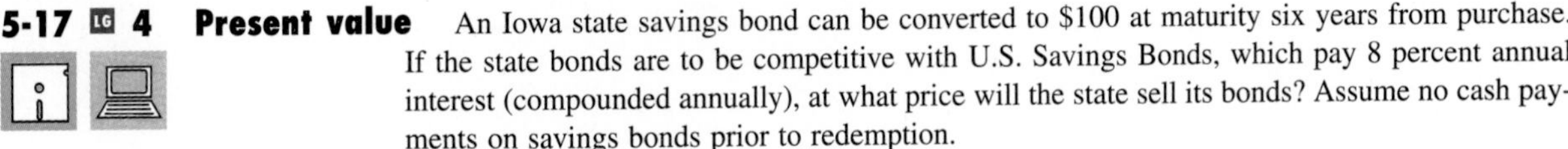

5-17 LG 4 **Present value** An Iowa state savings bond can be converted to $100 at maturity six years from purchase. If the state bonds are to be competitive with U.S. Savings Bonds, which pay 8 percent annual interest (compounded annually), at what price will the state sell its bonds? Assume no cash payments on savings bonds prior to redemption.

5-18 LG 5 **Present value—Mixed streams** Given the following mixed streams of cash flows:

	Cash flow stream	
Year	A	B
1	$ 50,000	$ 10,000
2	40,000	20,000
3	30,000	30,000
4	20,000	40,000
5	10,000	50,000
Totals	$150,000	$150,000

a. Find the present value of each stream using a 15 percent discount rate.

b. Compare the calculated present values and discuss them in light of the fact that the undiscounted total cash flows amount to $150,000 in each case.

5-19 LG 5 **Present value—Mixed streams** Find the present value of the following streams of cash flows. Assume that the firm's opportunity cost is 12 percent.

A		B		C	
Year	Cash flow	Year	Cash flow	Year	Cash flow
1	−$2,000	1	$10,000	1–5	$10,000/yr.
2	3,000	2–5	5,000/yr.	6–10	8,000/yr.
3	4,000	6	7,000		
4	6,000				
5	8,000				

5-20 LG 4,5 **Relationship between future value and present value** Using *only* the following information:

Year (*n*)	Cash flow ($)	Future-value interest factor at 5 percent ($FVIF_{5\%,n}$)
1	800	1.050
2	900	1.102
3	1,000	1.158
4	1,500	1.216
5	2,000	1.276

a. Determine the *present value* of the mixed stream of cash flows using a 5 percent discount rate.
b. How much would you be willing to pay for an opportunity to buy this stream, assuming that you can at best earn 5 percent on your investments?
c. What effect, if any, would a 7 percent rather than a 5 percent opportunity cost have on your analysis? (Explain verbally.)

5-21 LG 5 **Present value of an annuity** For each of the following cases, calculate the present value of the annuity, assuming that the annuity cash flows occur at the end of each year.

Case	Amount of annuity ($)	Interest rate (%)	Period (years)
A	12,000	7	3
B	55,000	12	15
C	700	20	9
D	140,000	5	7
E	22,500	10	5

5-22 LG 5 **Present value of a mixed stream with an embedded annuity** In each of the following cases the mixed cash flow stream has an annuity embedded within it. Use the three-step procedure presented in the text to streamline the calculation of the present value of each of these streams, assuming a 12 percent discount rate in each case.

A		B		C	
Year	Cash flow	Year	Cash flow	Year	Cash flow
1	$12,000	1	$15,000	1–5	$ 1,000/yr.
2	10,000	2–10	20,000/yr.	6	6,000
3	8,000	11–30	25,000/yr.	7	7,000
4	8,000			8	8,000
5	8,000			9–15	10,000/yr.
6	8,000				
7	8,000				
8	5,000				

5-23 LG 5 **Present value of an annuity versus a lump sum** Assume that you just won the state lottery. Your prize can be taken either in the form of $40,000 at the end of each of the next 25 years (i.e., $1,000,000 over 25 years) or as a lump sum of $500,000 paid immediately.
a. If you expect to be able to earn 5 percent annually on your investments over the next 25 years, ignoring taxes and other considerations, which alternative should you take? Why?

b. Would your decision in **a** be altered if you could earn 7 percent, rather than 5 percent, on your investments over the next 25 years? Why?

c. On a strict economic basis, at approximately what earnings rate would you be indifferent between the two plans?

5-24 LG 5 **Cash flow investment decision** Tom Alexander has an opportunity to purchase any of the following investments. The purchase price, the amount of the single cash inflow, and its year of receipt are given below for each investment. Which purchase recommendations would you make, assuming that Tom can earn 10 percent on his investments?

Investment	Price ($)	Single cash inflow ($)	Year of receipt
A	18,000	30,000	5
B	600	3,000	20
C	3,500	10,000	10
D	1,000	15,000	40

5-25 LG 5 **Perpetuities** Given the following data, determine for each of the following perpetuities:

Perpetuity	Annual amount ($)	Discount rate (%)
A	20,000	8
B	100,000	10
C	3,000	6
D	60,000	5

a. The appropriate present-value interest factor.

b. The present value.

5-26 LG 6 **Deposits to accumulate future sums** For each of the following cases, determine the amount of the equal annual end-of-year deposit that would be required to accumulate the given sum at the end of the specified period, assuming the stated annual interest rate.

Case	Sum to be accumulated ($)	Accumulation period (years)	Interest rate (%)
A	5,000	3	12
B	100,000	20	7
C	30,000	8	10
D	15,000	12	8

5-27 LG 6 Accumulating a growing future sum A retirement home at Deer Trail Estates now costs $85,000. Inflation is expected to cause this price to increase at 6 percent per year over the 20 years before C. L. Donovan retires. How large an equal annual end-of-year deposit must be made each year into an account paying an annual interest rate of 10 percent for Donovan to have the cash to purchase a home at retirement?

5-28 LG 5,6 Deposits to create a perpetuity You have decided to endow your favorite university with a scholarship in honor of your successful completion of managerial finance. It is expected that it will cost $6,000 per year to attend the university into perpetuity. You expect to give the university the endowment in 10 years and will accumulate it by making annual (end-of-year) deposits into an account. The rate of interest is expected to be 10 percent for all future time periods.

a. How large must the endowment be?

b. How much must you deposit at the end of each of the next 10 years to accumulate the required amount?

5-29 LG 6 Loan amortization Determine the equal annual end-of-year payment required each year over the life of the following loans to repay them fully during the stated term of the loan.

Loan	Principal ($)	Interest rate (%)	Term of loan (years)
A	12,000	8	3
B	60,000	12	10
C	75,000	10	30
D	4,000	15	5

5-30 LG 6 Loan amortization schedule Joan Messineo borrowed $15,000 at a 14 percent annual rate of interest to be repaid over three years. The loan is amortized into three equal annual end-of-year payments.

a. Calculate the annual end-of-year loan payment.

b. Prepare a loan amortization schedule showing the interest and principal breakdown of each of the three loan payments.

c. Explain why the interest portion of each payment declines with the passage of time.

5-31 LG 6 Growth rates You are given the following series of cash flows:

	Cash flows		
Year	A	B	C
1	$500	$1,500	$2,500
2	560	1,550	2,600
3	640	1,610	2,650
4	720	1,680	2,650
5	800	1,760	2,800
6		1,850	2,850
7		1,950	2,900
8		2,060	
9		2,170	
10		2,280	

a. Calculate the compound growth rate associated with each cash flow stream.
b. If year 1 values represent initial deposits in a savings account paying annual interest, what is the rate of interest earned on each account?
c. Compare and discuss the growth rates and interest rates found in **a** and **b,** respectively.

5-32 LG 6 **Rate of return** Rishi Singh has $1,500 to invest. His investment counselor suggests an investment that pays no stated interest but will return $2,000 at the end of three years.
a. What annual rate of return will Mr. Singh earn with this investment?
b. Mr. Singh is considering another investment, of equal risk, which earns a return of 8 percent. Which investment should he take, and why?

5-33 LG 6 **Rate of return—Annuity** What is the rate of return on an investment of $10,606 if the company expects to receive $2,000 each year for the next ten years?

5-34 LG 6 **Loan rates of interest** John Fleming has been shopping for a loan to finance the purchase of his new car. He has found three possibilities that seem attractive and wishes to select the one having the lowest interest rate. The information available with respect to each of the three $5,000 loans follows.

Loan	Principal ($)	Annual payment ($)	Term (years)
A	5,000	1,352.81	5
B	5,000	1,543.21	4
C	5,000	2,010.45	3

a. Determine the interest rate that would be associated with each of the loans.
b. Which loan should Mr. Fleming take?

Chapter 5 Case Finding Jill Moran's retirement annuity

Sunrise Industries wishes to accumulate funds to provide a retirement annuity for its Vice-President of Research, Jill Moran. By contract, Ms. Moran will retire at the end of exactly 12 years. Upon retirement she is entitled to receive an annual end-of-year payment of $42,000 for exactly 20 years. If she dies before the end of the 20-year period, the annual payments will pass to her heirs. During the 12-year "accumulation period," Sunrise Industries wishes to fund the annuity by makaing equal annual end-of-year deposits into an account earning 9 percent interest. Once the 20-year "distribution period" begins, Sunrise plans to move the accumulated monies into an account earning a gurarанteed 12 percent per year. At the end of the distribution period the account balance will equal zero. Note that the first deposit will be made at the end of year 1 and the first distribution will occur at the end of year 13.

Required

a. Draw a time line depicting all of the cash flows associated with Sunrise's view of the retirement annuity.

b. How large a sum must Sunrise Industries accumulate by the end of year 12 to provide the 20-year, $42,000 annuity?

c. How large must Sunrise's equal annual end-of-year deposits into the account be over the 12-year accumulation period to fully fund Ms. Moran's retirement annuity?

d. How much would Sunrise have to deposit annually during the accumulation period if it could earn 10 percent rather than 9 percent during the accumulation period?

e. How much would Sunrise have to deposit annually during the accumulation period if Ms. Moran's retirement annuity was a perpetuity and all other terms were the same as initially described?

chapter 6

Risk and return

LEARNING GOALS

Understand the meaning and fundamentals of risk, return, and risk preferences.

Describe the basic risk concepts related to the measurement of risk for a single asset and the relationship between risk and time.

Discuss the measurement of return and standard deviation for a portfolio and the various types of correlation that can exist between series of numbers.

Understand diversification in terms of correlation, its relationship to the risk and return of a portfolio, and the impact of international assets on a portfolio.

Review the two components of a security's risk and the derivation and role of beta in measuring the relevant risk of both an individual security and a portfolio.

Explain the capital asset pricing model (CAPM), its relationship to the security market line (SML), and shifts in the SML caused by changes in inflationary expectations and risk aversion.

The concepts of risk and return presented in this chapter are of great importance to business managers worldwide. The idea that return should increase as risk increases is fundamental to modern economics and management. Indeed, the ideas you are about to study are of great interest in both theory and practice. Nobel prizes were awarded for them; they have led to the creation of new investment forms, and they provide an analytical framework practiced by investors throughout the world.

Corporate managers should understand the relevance of risk and return to their daily actions. Rational people are always taking risks. What level of risk is associated with each of our decisions? Are two alternatives of equal or different risk? What is the compensation for choosing the more risky alternative? Such questions demand that managers define, identify, analyze, and measure risk and decide what return is required to make a risky venture worthwhile.

EG&G is a technology-based diverse corporation that provides scientific and technical products and services for government and industrial customers. I am responsible for the strategic planning ideas and processes used worldwide. Our business plans provide *information* to make decisions but are not used to make decisions mechanically. Risk is inherent in these plans. The sources and characteristics of risk vary widely from one business to another. Only occasionally do we attempt to quantify the risk; more often, we consider it subjectively and intuitively based on our experience with similar businesses and situations. Higher risk projects must have higher returns.

For a technology-based corporation like EG&G, the biggest source of risk today is the tremendous uncertainty and change in the U.S. and world economies. For the past 45 years, the technological competition between the U.S. and the former Soviet Union drove us to fund and develop technology to compete as a major world power. Now, federal spending for technology is much less predictable. Since roughly 65 percent of our revenue comes from contracts with the U.S. government, our risk clearly increases but is not easily quantified. For example, statistical techniques are of limited help in characterizing the uncertainty of political change in Eastern Europe.

We face financial risks as well. We compete globally and have manufacturing and service facilities worldwide. Changing perceptions of financial risks and returns drive international currency and interest rate markets. Costs and competitive position can be dramatically affected by changes in exchange rates that are extremely difficult to forecast. Within the U.S. economy the prospective paths of interest rates and federal spending are very uncertain, a consequence of expectations about future government and Federal Reserve actions.

As you read this chapter, then, ponder the questions "What is risk?", "What are its sources?", and "How will I measure it?" Businesses that sell high volume products may find quantitative methods very useful. In other markets with specialized products, services, and customers, dealing with risk is more difficult, and performance is dramatically affected by the decisions of a few market participants. These are our markets, and quantitative techniques typically help us to think about the opportunity analytically but aren't techniques for decision making.

Donald Peters received his B.S. in Physics from the University of Rochester, M.B.A. from the University of Pittsburgh, and Ph.D. from the Sloan School of Management, Massachusetts Institute of Technology. Since 1968 he has held management positions at EG&G in management sciences, operations, information services, and planning and is currently Vice President and director of Planning.

For a technology-based corporation like EG&G, the biggest source of risk today is the tremendous uncertainty and change in the U.S. and world economies

Risk and return fundamentals

Risk in the most basic sense is defined as the chance of a financial loss. From a strict financial point of view, are only those assets that exhibit a chance of loss considered risky? Before reading on, spend a few moments answering this question.

portfolio
A collection, or group, of assets.

TO ACHIEVE THE GOAL OF SHARE-PRICE MAXIMIZATION, THE FINANCIAL MANAGER MUST learn to assess the two key determinants of share price: risk and return.[1] Each financial decision presents certain risk and return characteristics, and all major financial decisions must be viewed in terms of expected risk, expected return, and their combined impact on share price. Risk can be viewed as it relates either to a single asset held in isolation or to a **portfolio**—a collection, or group, of assets. Although portfolio risk is probably more important to the financial manager, the general concept of risk is more readily developed in terms of a single asset. Before considering risk in each of these forms, it is important to understand the fundamentals of risk, return, and risk preferences.

Risk defined

risk
The chance of financial loss, or more formally, the variability of returns associated with a given asset.

In the most basic sense, **risk** can be defined as the chance of financial loss. Assets having greater chances of loss are viewed as more risky than those with lesser chances of loss. More formally, the term *risk* is used interchangeably with *uncertainty* to refer to the *variability of returns associated with a given asset.* For instance, a government bond that guarantees its holder $100 interest after 30 days has no risk, since there is no variability associated with the return. An equivalent investment in a firm's common stock that may earn over the same period anywhere from $0 to $200 is very risky due to the high variability of return. The more certain the return from an asset, the less variability and therefore the less risk.

CONCEPT IN PRACTICE

Loan Pricing Corporation's Measure of Risk

If a loan is too risky, lenders simply don't extend financing. A question that remains is that of the perceived riskiness of loans that are extended. To answer this question, Loan Pricing Corporation tabulated the risk ratings that 85 banks gave to more than 7,000 loans. The loan ratings were sorted by industry, and averages were calculated for each industry. Manufacturing businesses, especially textile and furniture products, were considered the most risky. Service businesses, especially legal and educational businesses, were considered the least risky. Given the difference in the fixed-asset requirements of these industries, such results are not surprising. The risks of loss are greater in businesses with heavy, large, and potentially unique machinery.

[1]Two important points should be recognized here: (1) While for convenience the publicly traded corporation is being discussed, the risk and return concepts presented apply equally well to all firms; and (2) concern centers only on the wealth of common stockholders, since they are the "residual owners" whose returns are in no way specified in advance.

Return defined

return

The total gain or loss experienced on behalf of the owner of an investment over a given period of time; calculated by dividing the asset's change in value plus any cash distributions during the period by its beginning-of-period investment value.

The **return** on an investment is measured as the total gain or loss experienced on behalf of its owner over a given period of time. It is commonly stated as the change in value plus any cash distribution, expressed as a percentage of the beginning-of-period investment value. The expression for calculating the rate of return earned on any asset over period t, k_t, is commonly defined as

$$\frac{k_t P_t - P_{t-1} + C_t}{P_{t-1}} \qquad (6.1)$$

where

k_t = actual, expected, or required rate of return[2] during period t
P_t = price (value) of asset at time t
P_{t-1} = price (value) of asset at time $t - 1$
C_t = cash (flow) received from the asset investment in the time period $t - 1$ to t

The return, k_t, reflects the combined effect of changes in value, $P_t - P_{t-1}$, and cash flow, C_t, realized over the period t.

Equation 6.1 is used to determine the rate of return over a time period as short as one day or as long as 10 years or more. However, in most cases, t is equal to one year, and k therefore represents an annual rate of return. The beginning-of-period value, P_{t-1}, and the end-of-period value, P_t, are not necessarily *realized values*. They are often *unrealized,* which means that although the asset was *not* actually purchased at time $t - 1$ and sold at time t, the values P_{t-1} and P_t could have been realized had they been.

EXAMPLE

Robin's Gameroom, a high-traffic video arcade, wishes to determine the actual rate of return on two of its video machines, Conqueror and Demolition. Conqueror was purchased exactly one year ago for $20,000 and currently has a market value of $21,500. During the year it generated $800 of after-tax cash receipts. Demolition was purchased four years ago, and its value at the beginning and end of the year just completed declined from $12,000 to $11,800. During the year it generated $1,700 of after-tax cash receipts. By substituting into Equation 6.1, the annual rate of return, k, for each video machine is calculated.

Conqueror (C)

$$k_C = \frac{\$21{,}500 - \$20{,}000 + \$800}{\$20{,}000} = \frac{\$2{,}300}{\$20{,}000} = \underline{\underline{11.5\%}}$$

Demolition (D)

$$k_D = \frac{\$11{,}800 - \$12{,}000 + \$1{,}700}{\$12{,}000} = \frac{\$1{,}500}{\$12{,}000} = \underline{\underline{12.5\%}}$$

[2]The terms *expected return* and *required return* are used interchangeably throughout this text, since in an efficient market (discussed later) they would be expected to be equal. The actual return is an *ex post* value, whereas expected and required returns are *ex ante* values. Therefore the actual return may be greater than, equal to, or less than the expected/required return.

Although the value of Demolition declined during the year, its relatively high cash flow caused it to earn a higher rate of return than that earned by Conqueror during the same period. Clearly, it is the combined impact of changes in value and cash flow measured by the rate of return that is important. ■

Risk preferences

Because of differing managerial (firm) preferences, it is important to specify a generally acceptable level of risk.[3] The three basic risk preference behaviors—risk-averse, risk-indifferent, and risk-seeking—are depicted graphically in Figure 6.1. Note that as risk goes from x_1 to x_2, for the **risk-indifferent** manager the required return does not change. In essence, no change in return would be required for the increase in risk. In the case of the **risk-averse** manager, the required return increases for an increase in risk. Because they shy away from risk, these managers require higher expected returns to compensate them for taking greater risk. For the **risk-seeking** manager the required return decreases for an increase in risk. Theoretically, because they enjoy risk, these managers are willing to give up some return to take more risk. *Most managers are risk-averse, since for a given increase in risk they require an increase in return.* Although in theory the risk disposition of each manager could be measured, in practice managers tend to accept only those risks with which they feel comfortable. And they generally tend to be conservative rather than aggressive when accepting risk. Accordingly, *a risk-averse financial manager requiring higher returns for greater risk is assumed throughout this text.*

risk-indifferent
The attitude toward risk in which no change in return would be required for an increase in risk.

risk-averse
The attitude toward risk in which an increased return would be required for an increase in risk.

risk-seeking
The attitude toward risk in which a decreased return would be accepted for an increase in risk.

CONCEPTS IN REVIEW

6-1 Define *risk* as it relates to financial decision making. Why is it important for a decision maker to have some sense of the risk or uncertainty associated with an investment in an asset? Do any assets have perfectly certain returns?

6-2 Describe the basic calculation involved in finding the return on an investment. Differentiate between realized and unrealized returns.

6-3 Compare and contrast the following risk-preference behaviors, and indicate which is most commonly exhibited by the financial manager.

a. Risk-averse
b. Risk-indifferent
c. Risk-seeking

Basic risk concepts: A single asset

From a strict financial viewpoint, risk refers to the variability of returns associated with a given asset. If you had historic data on the returns earned on a given asset, how would you go about assessing and measuring its risk? Take a few moments to answer this question before reading ahead.

[3]The risk preferences of the managers should in theory be consistent with the risk preferences of the firm. Although the *agency problem* suggests that in practice managers may not behave in a manner consistent with the firm's risk preferences, it is assumed here that they do. Therefore the manager's risk preferences and those of the firm are assumed to be identical.

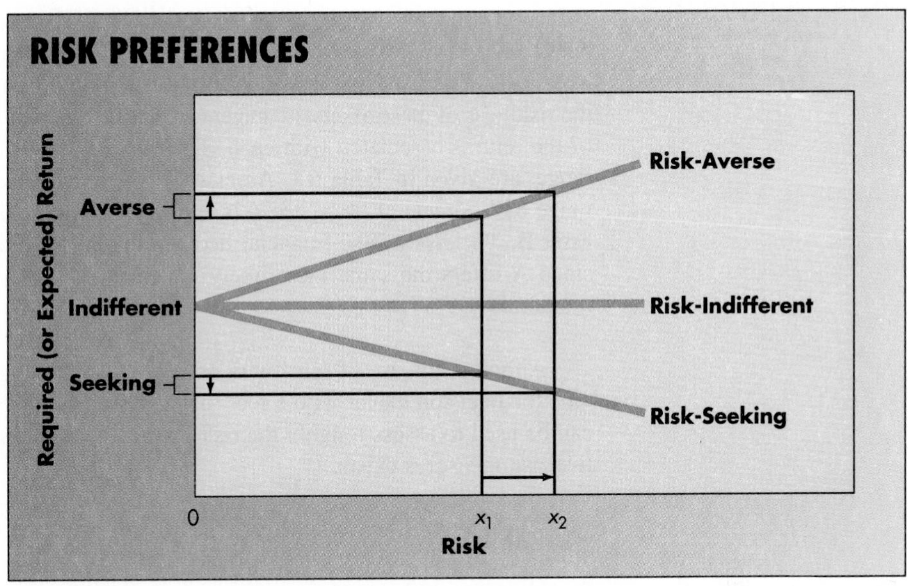

FIGURE 6.1
Risk preference behaviors

THE CONCEPT OF RISK IS MOST READILY DEVELOPED BY FIRST CONSIDERING A SINGLE asset held in isolation. Such an approach creates a situation in which the potential interactions of asset returns can be ignored. The relationship between risk and time is important in understanding the role of risk in financial decision making.

Risk of a single asset

Although the risk of a single asset is measured in much the same way as the risk of an entire portfolio of assets, it is important to differentiate between these two entities, since certain benefits accrue to holders of portfolios. It is also useful to assess risk from both a behavioral and a quantitative point of view. Sensitivity analysis can be used to get a feel for risk, while probabilities, probability distributions, the standard deviation, and the coefficient of variation can be used to more quantitatively assess risk.

sensitivity analysis
A behavioral approach for assessing risk that uses a number of possible return estimates to obtain a sense of the variability among outcomes.

range
A measure of an asset's risk, which is found by subtracting the pessimistic (worst) outcome from the optimistic (best) outcome.

SENSITIVITY ANALYSIS

Sensitivity analysis is a behavioral approach that uses a number of possible return estimates to obtain a sense of the variability among outcomes.[4] One common method involves the estimation of the pessimistic (worst), the most likely (expected), and the optimistic (best) returns associated with a given asset. In this case the asset's risk can be measured by the **range,** which is found by subtracting the pessimistic (worst) outcome from the optimistic (best) outcome. The greater the range for a given asset, the more variability, or risk, it is said to have.

[4]The term "sensitivity analysis" is intentionally used in a general rather than technically correct fashion here to simplify this discussion. A more technical and precise definition and discussion of this technique and "scenario analysis" is presented in Chapter 9.

EXAMPLE

Norman Company, a custom golf equipment manufacturer, is attempting to choose the better of two alternative investments, A and B, each requiring an initial outlay of $10,000 and each having a *most likely* annual rate of return of 15 percent. To evaluate the riskiness of these assets, management has made *pessimistic* and *optimistic* estimates of the returns associated with each. The three estimates for each asset, along with its range, are given in Table 6.1. Asset A appears to be less risky than asset B, since its range of 4 percent (17% − 13%) is less than the range of 16 percent (23% − 7%) for asset B. The risk-averse financial decision maker would prefer asset A over asset B, since A offers the same most likely return as B (15%) but with lower risk (smaller range). ■

Although the use of sensitivity analysis and the range is rather crude, it does provide the decision maker with a feel for the behavior of returns. This behavioral insight can be used to assess roughly the risk involved. Of course, a variety of more quantitative risk measures exists.

PROBABILITIES

probability
The *chance* that a given outcome will occur.

Probabilities can be used to more precisely assess an asset's risk. The **probability** of a given outcome is its *chance* of occurring. If an outcome has an 80 percent probability of occurrence, the given outcome would be expected to occur 8 out of 10 times. If an outcome has a probability of 100 percent, it is certain to occur. Outcomes having a probability of zero will never occur.

EXAMPLE

An evaluation of Norman Company's past estimates indicates that the probabilities of the pessimistic, most likely, and optimistic outcomes' occurring are 25 percent, 50 percent, and 25 percent, respectively. The sum of these probabilities must equal 100 percent; that is, they must be based on all the alternatives considered. ■

PROBABILITY DISTRIBUTIONS

probability distribution
A model that relates probabilities to the associated outcomes.

bar chart
The simplest type of probability distribution; shows only a limited number of outcomes and associated probabilities for a given event.

A **probability distribution** is a model that relates probabilities to the associated outcomes. The simplest type of probability distribution is the **bar chart,** which shows only a limited number of outcome-probability coordinates. The bar charts for Norman Company's assets A and B are shown in Figure 6.2. Although both assets have the same most likely return, the range of return is much more dispersed for asset B than

TABLE 6.1

ASSETS A AND B

	Asset A	Asset B
Initial investment	$10,000	$10,000
Annual rate of return		
Pessimistic	13%	7%
Most likely	15	15
Optimistic	17	23
Range	4%	16%

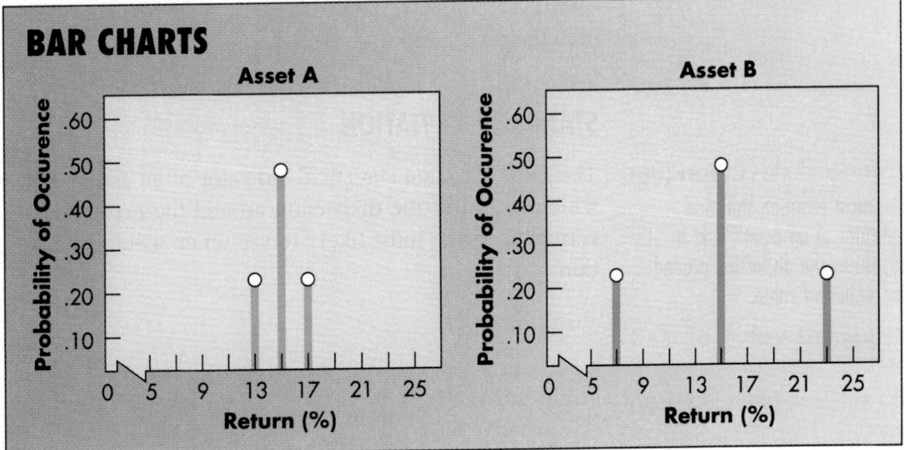

FIGURE 6.2
Bar charts for asset A's and asset B's returns

continuous probability distribution
A probability distribution showing all the possible outcomes and associated probabilities for a given event.

for asset A—16 percent versus 4 percent. If we knew all the possible outcomes and associated probabilities, we could develop a **continuous probability distribution.** This type of distribution can be thought of as a bar chart for a very large number of outcomes.[5] Figure 6.3 presents continuous probability distributions for assets A and B.[6] Note in Figure 6.3 that although assets A and B have the same most likely

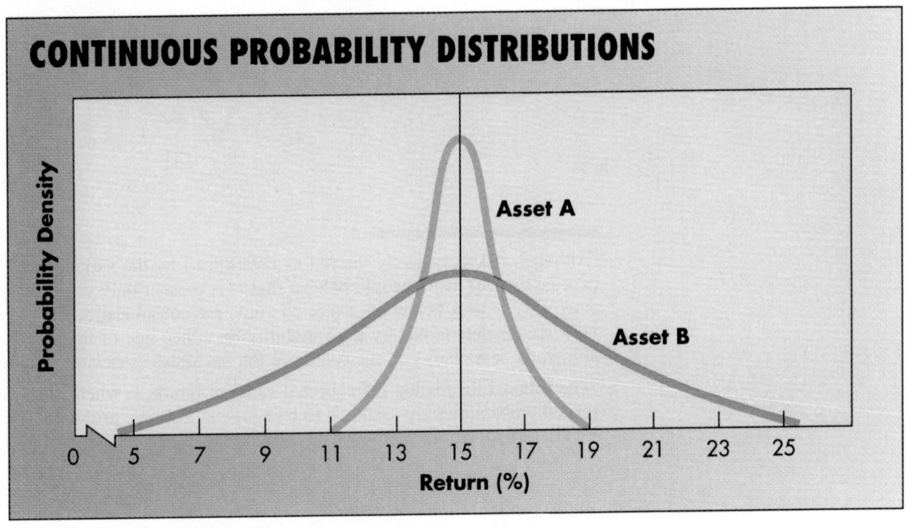

FIGURE 6.3
Continuous probability distributions for asset A's and asset B's returns

---

[5]To develop a continuous probability distribution, one must have data on a large number of historical occurrences. Then, by developing a frequency distribution indicating how many times each outcome has occurred over the given time horizon, one can convert these data into a probability distribution. Probability distributions for risky events can also be developed by using *simulation*—a process discussed briefly in Chapter 9.

[6]The continuous distribution's probabilities change due to the large number of additional outcomes considered. The area under each of the curves is equal to 1, which means that 100 percent of the outcomes, or all the possible outcomes, are considered. Often "probability density functions," such as those in Figure 6.3, are converted into *cumulative probability distributions,* which show the probability of obtaining *at least* a given value.

return (15 percent), the distribution of returns for asset B has much greater *dispersion* than the distribution for asset A. Clearly, asset B is more risky than asset A.

STANDARD DEVIATION

standard deviation (σ_k)
The most common statistical indicator of an asset's risk; it measures the dispersion around the *expected* value.

expected value of a return ($\bar{k}$)
The most likely return on a given asset.

The most common statistical indicator of an asset's risk is the **standard deviation σ_k**, which measures the dispersion around the *expected* value.[7] The **expected value of a return, $\bar{k}$**, is the most likely return on an asset. This can be calculated by using Equation 6.2:[8]

$$\bar{k} = \sum_{i=1}^{n} k_i \times Pr_i \tag{6.2}$$

where

k_i = return for the ith outcome
Pr_i = probability of occurrence of the ith outcome
n = number of outcomes considered

EXAMPLE

The calculations of the expected values for Norman Company's assets A and B are presented in Table 6.2. Column 1 gives the Pr_i's and column 2 gives the k_i's, n equaling 3 in each case. The expected value for each asset's return is 15 percent. ■

The expression for the *standard deviation of returns,* σ_k, is given in Equation 6.3:[9]

$$\sigma_k = \sqrt{\sum_{i=1}^{n} (k_i - \bar{k})^2 \times Pr_i} \tag{6.3}$$

[7]Although risk is typically viewed as determined by the variability, or dispersion, of outcomes around an expected value, many people believe that it is present only when outcomes are below the expected value, since only returns below the expected value are considered bad. Nevertheless, the common approach is to view risk as determined by the variability on either side of the expected value, since the greater this variability, the less confident one can be of the outcomes associated with an asset investment.

[8]The formula for finding the expected value of return, $\bar{k}$, when all of the outcomes, k_i, are known and their related probabilities are assumed to be equal, is a simple arithmetic average.

$$\bar{k} = \frac{\sum_{i=1}^{n} k_i}{n} \tag{6.2a}$$

where n is the number of observations. Because, in analyzing asset investments, returns and related probabilities are often available, the formula given in Equation 6.2 is emphasized in this chapter.

[9]The formula that is commonly used to find the standard deviation of returns, σ_k, in a situation in which *all* of the outcomes are known and their related probabilities are assumed equal, is

$$\sigma_k = \sqrt{\frac{\sum_{i=1}^{n} (k_i - \bar{k})^2}{n-1}} \tag{6.3a}$$

where n is the number of observations. Because, in analyzing asset investments, returns and related probabilities are often available, the formula given in Equation 6.3 is emphasized in this chapter.

TABLE 6.2

EXPECTED VALUES OF RETURNS FOR ASSETS A AND B

Possible outcomes	Probability (1)	Returns (%) (2)	Weighted value (%) [(1) × (2)] (3)
		Asset A	
Pessimistic	.25	13	3.25
Most likely	.50	15	7.50
Optimistic	.25	17	4.25
Total	1.00	Expected return	15.00
		Asset B	
Pessimistic	.25	7	1.75
Most likely	.50	15	7.50
Optimistic	.25	23	5.75
Total	1.00	Expected return	15.00

In general, the higher the standard deviation, the greater the risk.

EXAMPLE

Table 6.3 presents the calculation of standard deviations for Norman Company's assets A and B, based on the data presented earlier. The standard deviation for asset A is 1.41 percent, and the standard deviation for asset B is 5.66 percent. The higher risk of asset B is clearly reflected in its higher standard deviation. ■

normal probability distribution

A symmetrical probability distribution whose shape resembles a bell-shaped curve.

A **normal probability distribution,** depicted in Figure 6.4, is one that always resembles a "bell-shaped" curve. It is symmetrical: From the peak of the graph, the curve's extensions are mirror images of each other. The symmetry of the curve means that half the curve's area lies to the left of the peak and half to the right. Therefore, half the probability is associated with the values to the left of the peak and half with values to the right. As is noted on the figure, for normal probability distributions, 68 percent of the possible outcomes will lie between ±1 standard deviation from the expected value, 95 percent of all outcomes will lie between ±2 standard deviations from the expected value, and 99 percent of all outcomes will lie between ±3 standard deviations from the expected value.[10]

EXAMPLE

If we assume that the probability distribution of returns for the Norman Company is normal, 68 percent of the possible outcomes would be expected to have a return ranging between 13.59 and 16.41 percent for asset A and between 9.34 and 20.66 percent

[10]Tables of values indicating the probabilities associated with various deviations from the expected value of a normal distribution can be found in any basic statistics text. These values can be used to establish confidence limits and make inferences about possible outcomes. Such applications are not discussed in this text but may be found in most basic statistics and upper-level managerial finance texts.

TABLE 6.3

THE CALCULATION OF THE STANDARD DEVIATION OF THE RETURNS FOR ASSETS A AND B[a]

Asset A

i	k_i	$\bar{k}$	$k_i - \bar{k}$	$(k_i - \bar{k})^2$	Pr_i	$(k_i - \bar{k})^2 \times Pr_i$
1	13%	15%	−2%	4%	.25	1%
2	15	15	0	0	.50	0
3	17	15	2	4	.25	1

$$\sum_{i=1}^{3} (k_i - \bar{k})^2 \times Pr_i = 2\%$$

$$\sigma_{K_A} = \sqrt{\sum_{i=1}^{3} (k_i = \bar{k})^2 \times Pr_i} = \sqrt{2\%} = \underline{\underline{1.41\%}}$$

Asset B

i	k_i	$\bar{k}$	$k_i - \bar{k}$	$(k_i - \bar{k})^2$	Pr_i	$(k_i - \bar{k})^2 \times Pr_i$
1	7%	15%	−8%	64%	.25	16%
2	15	15	0	0	.50	0
3	23	15	8	64	.25	16

$$\sum_{i=1}^{3} (k_i - \bar{k})^2 \times Pr_i = 32\%$$

$$\sigma_{k_B} = \sqrt{\sum_{i=1}^{3} (k_i = \bar{k})^2 \times Pr_i} = \sqrt{32\%} = \underline{\underline{5.66\%}}$$

[a] Calculations in this table are made in percentage form rather than decimal form, e.g., 13% rather than .13. As a result, some of the intermediate computations may appear to be inconsistent with those that would result from using decimal form. Regardless, the resulting standard deviations are correct and identical to those that would result from using decimal rather than percentage form.

for asset B; 95 percent of the possible return outcomes would range between 12.18 and 17.82 percent for asset A and between 3.68 and 26.32 percent for asset B; and 99 percent of the possible return outcomes would range between 10.77 and 19.23 percent for asset A and between −1.98 and 31.98 percent for asset B. The greater risk of asset B is clearly reflected by its much wider range of possible returns for each level of confidence (68 percent, 95 percent, etc.). ■

COEFFICIENT OF VARIATION

coefficient of variation (CV)
A measure of relative dispersion used in comparing the risk of assets with differing expected returns.

The **coefficient of variation, *CV*,** is a measure of relative dispersion that is useful in comparing the risk of assets with differing expected returns. Equation 6.4 gives the expression for the coefficient of variation:

$$CV = \frac{\sigma_k}{\bar{k}} \tag{6.4}$$

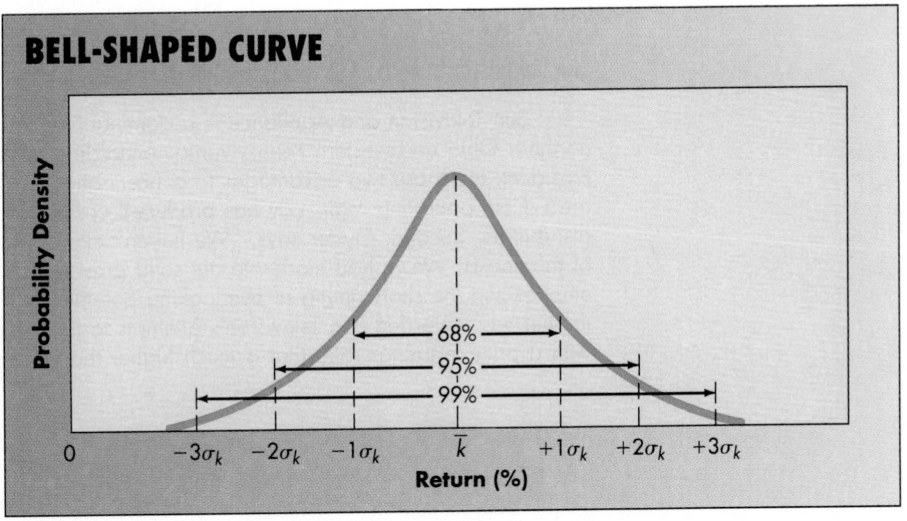

FIGURE 6.4
Normal probability distribution, with ranges

The higher the coefficient of variation, the greater the risk.

EXAMPLE

When the standard deviation values (from Table 6.3) and the expected returns (from Table 6.2) for assets A and B are substituted into Equation 6.4, the coefficients of variation for A and B are .094 (1.41% ÷ 15%) and .377 (5.66% ÷ 15%) respectively. Asset B has the higher coefficient of variation and is therefore more risky than asset A. Since both assets have the same expected return, the coefficient of variation has not provided any more information than the standard deviation. ■

The real utility of the coefficient of variation is in comparing assets that have *different* expected returns. A simple example will illustrate this point.

EXAMPLE

A firm is attempting to select the less risky of two alternative assets—X and Y. The expected return, standard deviation, and coefficient of variation for each of these assets' returns follow.

Statistics	Asset X	Asset Y
(1) Expected return	12%	20%
(2) Standard deviation	9%[a]	10%
(3) Coefficient of variation [(2) ÷ (1)]	.75	.50[a]

[a]Preferred asset using the given risk measure.

If the firm were to compare the assets solely on the basis of their standard deviations, it would prefer asset X, since asset X has a lower standard deviation than asset Y (9 percent versus 10 percent). However, comparing the coefficients of variation of the assets shows that management would be making a serious error in choosing asset X over asset Y, since the relative dispersion, or risk, of the assets as reflected in the coefficient of variation is lower for Y than for X (.50 versus .75). Clearly, the use of the coefficient of variation to compare asset risk is effective because it also considers the relative size, or expected return, of the assets. ■

CONCEPT IN PRACTICE

Sun Television's Focus Cuts Potential Returns and Risks

Sun Television and Appliance is a dominant electronics and appliance retailer in northern Ohio and western Pennsylvania. According to Robert Oyster, Sun Television's President, there are two advantages to concentrating its 31 superstores in a limited area. First, operating regionally has produced cost efficiencies in advertising and distribution. Second, Oyster says, "We haven't experienced the boom-and-bust cycles of the coasts. We've had moderate but solid growth." Kidder Peabody critically emphasized the shortcoming of overlooking potential markets. Nonetheless, the stock market has rewarded Sun Television's attempts to limit risk, even if it limits earnings, with a price/earnings ratio that is much higher than average.

Risk and time

Risk can be viewed not only with respect to the current time period but also as an *increasing function of time.* Figure 6.5 depicts probability distributions of returns for a one-year, 10-year, 15-year, and 20-year forecast, assuming that each year's expectd returns are equal. A band representing $\pm$ 1 standard deviation, σ, from the expected return, $\bar{k}$, is indicated in the figure. It can be seen that the *variability of the returns, and therefore the risk, increases with the passage of time.* Generally, the longer-lived an asset investment, the greater its risk due to increasing variability of returns resulting from increased forecasting errors for distant years.[11]

FIGURE 6.5
Risk as a function of time

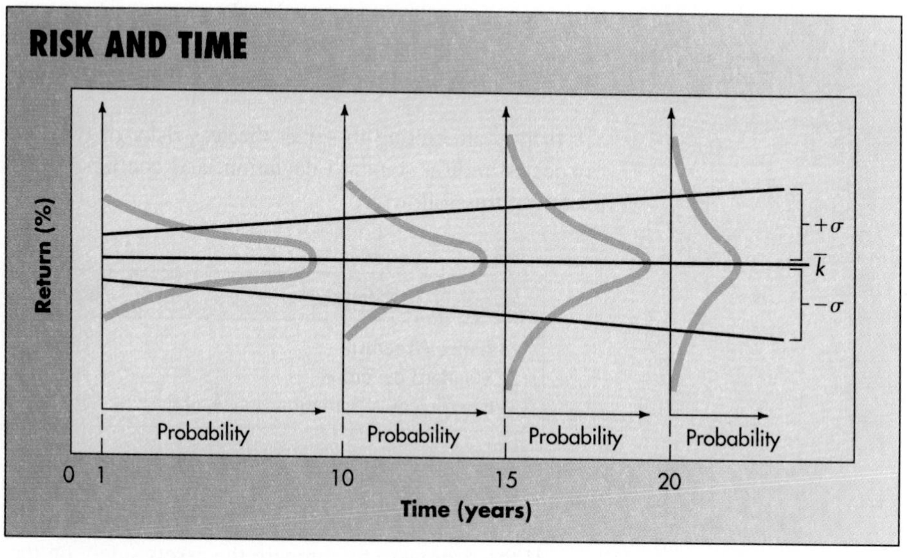

[11]These forecasting errors are normal, since in most situations, uncontrollable factors, such as strikes, wars, and inflation, are difficult, if not impossible, to predict but can have a very real effect on future returns.

CONCEPTS IN REVIEW

6-4 How can *sensitivity analysis* be used to assess asset risk? What is one of the most common methods of sensitivity analysis? Define and describe the role of the *range* as an aid in sensitivity analysis.

6-5 How does a plot of the *probability distribution* of outcomes allow the decision maker to evaluate asset risk? What is the difference between a *bar chart* and *a continuous probability distribution?*

6-6 What does the *standard deviation* of a distribution of asset returns indicate? What relationship exists between the size of the standard deviation and the degree of asset risk?

6-7 What is the *coefficient of variation?* How is it calculated? When is the coefficient of variation preferred over the standard deviation for comparing asset risk?

Risk of a portfolio

A portfolio is a collection, or group, of assets. From a strict risk-return point of view, what general benefit results from holding a portfolio of assets rather than a single asset? Why? Spend a few moments answering these questions before reading ahead.

efficient portfolio
A portfolio that maximizes return for a given level of risk or minimizes risk for a given level of return.

THE RISK OF ANY SINGLE PROPOSED ASSET INVESTMENT SHOULD NOT BE VIEWED INDEPENDENT of other assets. New investments must be considered in light of their impact on the risk and return of the *portfolio* of assets.[12] The financial manager's goal for the firm is to create an **efficient portfolio,** one that maximizes return for a given level of risk or minimizes risk for a given level of return. The statistical concept of *correlation* underlies the process of diversification that is used to develop an efficient portfolio of assets. Before discussing these and other aspects of portfolio risk, we will look at the procedures for calculating portfolio return and standard deviation.

Portfolio return and standard deviation

The *return* on a portfolio is calculated as a weighted average of the returns on the individual assets from which it is formed. Letting w_j equal the proportion of the portfolio's total dollar value represented by asset j and k_j equal the return on asset j, we can use Equation 6.5 to find the portfolio return, k_p:

$$k_p = (w_1 \times k_1) + (w_2 \times k_2) + \cdots + (w_n \times k_n) = \sum_{j=1}^{n} w_j \times k_j \qquad (6.5)$$

[12]The portfolio of a firm, which would consist of its total assets, is not differentiated from the portfolio of an owner, which would likely contain a variety of different investment vehicles (i.e., assets). The differing characteristics of these two types of portfolios should become clear upon completion of Chapter 9.

Of course, $\sum_{j=1}^{n} w_j = 1$, which means that 100 percent of the portfolio's assets must be included in this computation.

The *standard deviation* of a portfolio's returns is found by applying the formula used earlier to find the standard deviation of a single asset. Specifically, Equation 6.3 would be used when the probabilities of the returns are known, and Equation 6.3a (from footnote 9) would be applied when the outcomes are known and their related probabilities of occurrence are assumed to be equal.

EXAMPLE

Assume that we wish to determine the expected value and standard deviation of returns for portfolio XY, created by combining equal portions (50 percent) of assets X and Y. The expected returns of assets X and Y for each of the next five years (1995–1999) are given in columns 1 and 2, respectively, in part A of Table 6.4. In columns 3 and 4 the weights of 50 percent for both assets X and Y along with their respective returns from columns 1 and 2 are substituted into Equation 6.5 to get an expected portfolio return of 12 percent for each year, 1995 to 1999. Furthermore, as shown in part B of Table 6.4, the expected value (calculated by using Equation 6.2a found in

TABLE 6.4

EXPECTED RETURN, EXPECTED VALUE, AND STANDARD DEVIATION OF RETURNS FOR PORTFOLIO XY

A. Expected portfolio returns

	Expected return			
	Asset X	Asset Y	Portfolio return calculation[a]	Expected portfolio return, k_p
Year	(1)	(2)	(3)	(4)
1995	8%	16%	(.50 × 8%) + (.50 × 16%) =	12%
1996	10	14	(.50 × 10) + (.50 × 14) =	12
1997	12	12	(.50 × 12) + (.50 × 12) =	12
1998	14	10	(.50 × 14) + (.50 × 10) =	12
1999	16	8	(.50 × 16) + (.50 × 8) =	12

B. Expected value of portfolio returns, 1995–1999[b]

$$\bar{k}_p = \frac{12\% + 12\% + 12\% + 12\% + 12\%}{5} = \frac{60\%}{5} = 12\%$$

C. Standard deviation of expected portfolio returns[c]

$$\sigma_{k_p} = \sqrt{\frac{(12\% - 12\%)^2 + (12\% - 12\%)^2 + (12\% - 12\%)^2 + (12\% - 12\%)^2 + (12\% - 12\%)^2}{5 - 1}}$$

$$= \sqrt{\frac{0\% + 0\% + 0\% + 0\% + 0\%}{4}} = \sqrt{\frac{0\%}{4}} = \underline{\underline{0\%}}$$

[a]Using Equation 6.5.

[b]Using Equation 6.2a found in footnote 8.

[c]Using Equation 6.3a found in footnote 9.

footnote 8) of these portfolio returns over the five-year period is also 12 percent. Substituting into the formula given earlier (Equation 6.3a found in footnote 9), portfolio XY's standard deviation of 0 percent is calculated in part C of Table 6.4. This value should not be surprising since the expected return each year is the same—12 percent—and therefore no variability is exhibited in the expected returns from year to year shown in column 4 of part A of the table. ■

Correlation

correlation
A statistical measure of the relationship, if any, between series of numbers representing data of any kind.

positively correlated
Descriptive of two series that move in the same direction.

negatively correlated
Descriptive of two series that move in opposite directions.

correlation coefficient
A measure of the degree of correlation between two series.

perfectly positively correlated
Describes two positively correlated series that have a *correlation coefficient* of +1.

perfectly negatively correlated
Describes two negatively correlated series that have a *correlation coefficient* of −1.

Correlation is a statistical measure of the relationship, if any, between series of numbers representing data of any kind, from returns to test scores. If two series move in the same direction, they are **positively correlated;** if the series move in opposite directions, they are **negatively correlated.**[13] The degree of correlation is measured by the **correlation coefficient,** which ranges from +1 for **perfectly positively correlated** series to −1 for **perfectly negatively correlated** series. These two extremes are depicted for series M and N in Figure 6.6. The perfectly positively correlated series move exactly together, while the perfectly negatively correlated series move in exactly opposite directions.

Diversification

To reduce overall risk, it is best to combine or add to the portfolio assets that have a negative (or a low positive) correlation. By combining negatively correlated assets the overall variability of returns, or risk, σ_k, can be reduced. Figure 6.7 shows that a portfolio containing the negatively correlated assets F and G, both having the same

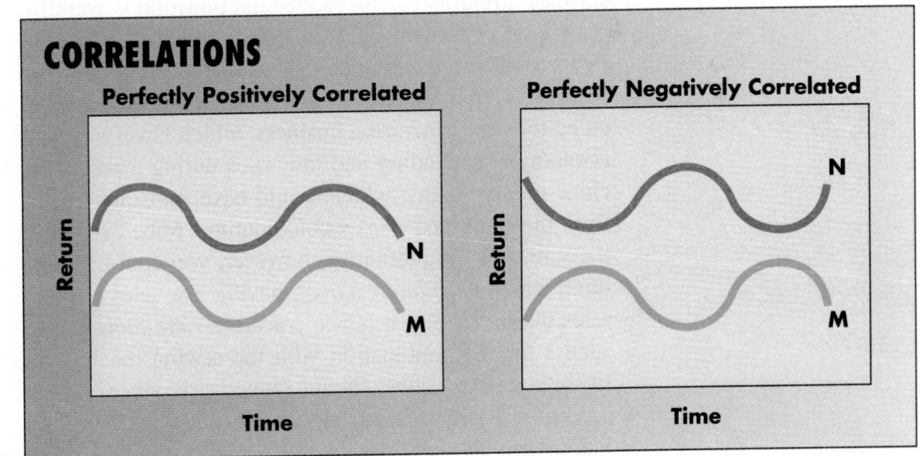

FIGURE 6.6
The correlation between series M and N

[13]The general *long-term trend* of two series could be the same (both increasing or both decreasing) or different (one increasing, the other decreasing), while the correlation of their *short-term (point-to-point) movements* could in both situations be either positive or negative. In other words, the pattern of movement around the trends could be correlated independent of the actual relationship between the trends. Further clarification of this seemingly inconsistent behavior can be found in most basic statistics texts.

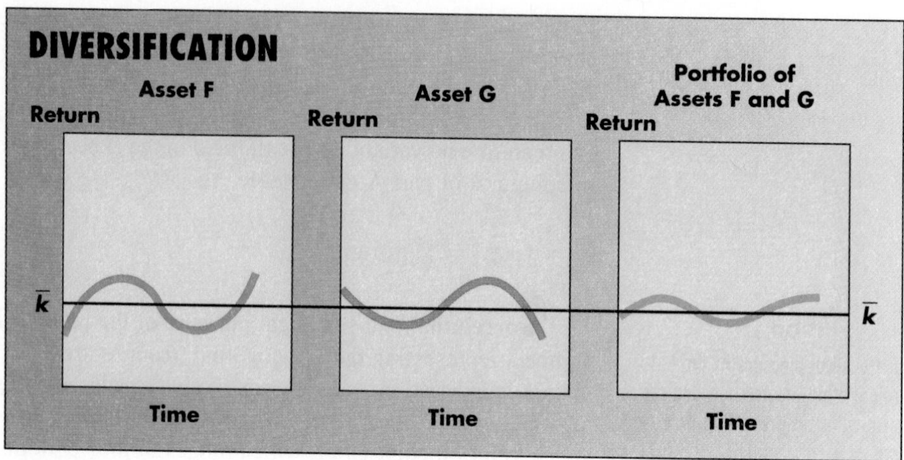

FIGURE 6.7
Combining negatively correlated assets to diversify risk

expected return, $\bar{k}$, also has the return $\bar{k}$ but has less risk (variability) than either of the individual assets. Even if assets are not negatively correlated, the lower the positive correlation between them, the lower the resulting risk. Some assets are **uncorrelated**, that is, they are completely unrelated in the sense that there is no interaction between their returns. Combining uncorrelated assets can reduce risk—not as effectively as combining negatively correlated assets but more effectively than combining positively correlated assets. The correlation coefficient for uncorrelated assets is close to zero and acts as the midpoint between perfect positive and perfect negative correlation.

uncorrelated
Describes two series that lack any relationship or interaction and therefore have a *correlation coefficient* close to zero.

The creation of a portfolio by combining two assets having perfectly positively correlated returns *cannot* reduce the portfolio's overall risk below the risk of the least risky asset. Alternatively, a portfolio combining two assets with less than perfectly positive correlation *can* reduce total risk to a level below that of either of the components, which in certain situations may be zero. For example, assume that you are in the machine-tool manufacturing business, which is very *cyclical,* having high sales when the economy is expanding and low sales during a recession. If you acquired another machine-tool company, which would have sales positively correlated with those of your firm, the combined sales would continue to be cyclical. As a result, risk would remain the same. As an alternative, however, you could acquire a sewing-machine manufacturer, which is *countercyclical,* having low sales during economic expansion and high sales during recession (since consumers are more likely to make their own clothes at such a time). Combination with the sewing machine manufacturer, which has negatively correlated sales, should reduce risk, since the low machine-tool sales during a recession would be balanced out by high sewing-machine sales, and vice versa. A numeric example will provide a better understanding of the role of correlation in the diversification process.

EXAMPLE

Table 6.5 presents the anticipated returns from three different assets—X, Y, and Z—over the next five years, along with their expected values and standard deviations. Each of the assets has an expected value of return of 12 percent and a standard deviation of 3.16 percent. The assets therefore have equal return and equal risk, although their return patterns are not necessarily identical. A comparison of the return patterns of assets X and Y shows that they are perfectly negatively correlated, since they move in exactly opposite directions over time. A comparison of assets X and Z shows that they

TABLE 6.5

RETURNS, EXPECTED VALUES, AND STANDARD DEVIATIONS FOR ASSETS X, Y, AND Z AND PORTFOLIOS XY AND XZ

	Assets			Portfolios	
Year	X	Y	Z	XY[a] (50%X + 50%Y)	XZ[b] (50%X + 50%Z)
1995	8%	16%	8%	12%	8%
1996	10	14	10	12	10
1997	12	12	12	12	12
1998	14	10	14	12	14
1999	16	8	16	12	16
Statistics:[c]					
Expected value	12%	12%	12%	12%	12%
Standard deviation[d]	3.16%	3.16%	3.16%	0%	3.16%

[a]Portfolio XY, which consists of 50 percent of asset X and 50 percent of asset Y, illustrates *perfect negative correlation,* since these two return streams behave in completely opposite fashion over the five-year period. The return values shown here were calculated in part A of Table 6.4.

[b]Portfolio XZ, which consists of 50 percent of asset X and 50 percent of asset Z, illustrates *perfect positive correlation,* since these two return streams behave identically over the five-year period. These return values were calculated by using the same method demonstrated for portfolio XY in part A of Table 6.4.

[c]Since the probabilities associated with the returns are not given, the general equations, Equation 6.2a in footnote 8 and Equation 6.3a in footnote 9, were used to calculate expected values and standard deviations, respectively. Calculation of the expected value and standard deviation for portfolio XY is demonstrated in parts B and C, respectively, of Table 6.4.

[d]The portfolio standard deviations can be directly calculated from the standard deviations of the component assets using the following formula:

$$\sigma_{k_p} = \sqrt{w_1{}^2\sigma_1{}^2 + w_2{}^2\sigma_2{}^2 + 2w_1w_2r_{1,2}r_{1,2}\sigma_1\sigma_2}$$

where w_1 and w_2 are the proportions of the component assets 1 and 2, σ_1 and σ_2 are the standard deviations of the component assets 1 and 2, and $r_{1,2}$ is the correlation coefficient between the returns of component assets 1 and 2.

are perfectly positively correlated, since they move in precisely the same direction. (Note that the returns for X and Z are identical.)[14]

Portfolio XY By combining equal portions of assets X and Y—the perfectly negatively correlated assets—portfolio XY (shown in Table 6.5) is created.[15] Calculation of portfolio XY's annual expected returns, their expected value, and the standard deviation of expected portfolio returns is demonstrated in Table 6.4 as part of the preceding example. The risk in the portfolio created by this combination, as reflected by its standard deviation, is reduced to 0 percent, while the expected return value remains at 12 percent. Since both assets have the same expected return values, are combined in equal parts, and are perfectly negatively correlated, the combination results in the complete

[14]It is *not* necessary for return streams to be identical for them to be perfectly positively correlated. Identical return streams are used in this example to permit the concepts to be illustrated in the simplest, most straightforward fashion. Any return streams that move (i.e., vary) exactly together—regardless of the relative magnitude of the returns—are perfectly positively correlated.

[15]Although the assets are not divisible in actuality, for illustrative purposes it has been assumed that each of the assets—X, Y, and Z—can be divided up and combined with other assets to create portfolios. This assumption is made only to permit the concepts again to be illustrated in the simplest, most straightforward fashion.

elimination of risk. Whenever assets are perfectly negatively correlated, an optimum combination (similar to the 50–50 mix in the case of assets X and Y) exists for which the resulting standard deviation will equal 0.

Portfolio XZ By combining equal portions of assets X and Z—the perfectly positively correlated assets—portfolio XZ (shown in Table 6.5) is created. The risk in this portfolio, as reflected by its standard deviation, which remains at 3.16 percent, is unaffected by this combination, and the expected return value remains at 12 percent. Whenever perfectly positively correlated assets such as X and Z are combined, the standard deviation of the resulting portfolio cannot be reduced below that of the least risky asset; the maximum portfolio standard deviation will be that of the riskiest asset. Since assets X and Z have the same standard deviation (3.16 percent), the minimum and maximum standard deviations are both 3.16 percent, which is the only value that could be taken on by a combination of these assets. This result can be attributed to the unlikely situation that X and Z are identical assets. ■

Correlation, diversification, risk, and return

In general, the lower (less positive and more negative) the correlation between asset returns, the greater the potential diversification of risk. (This should be clear from the behaviors illustrated in Table 6.5.) For each pair of assets there is a combination that will result in the lowest risk (standard deviation) possible. The amount of potential risk reduction at this combination depends on the degree of correlation. This concept is a bit difficult to grasp, since many potential combinations (assuming divisibility) could be made, given the expected return for each of two assets, the standard deviation for each asset, and the correlation coefficient. Note that only one combination of the infinite number of possibilities will minimize risk.

Three possible correlations—perfect positive, uncorrelated, and perfect negative—can be used to illustrate the effect of correlation on the diversification of risk and return. Table 6.6 summarizes the impact of correlation on the range of return and risk for various two-asset portfolio combinations. It should be clear from the table that as we move from perfect positive correlation to uncorrelated assets to perfect negative correlation, the ability to reduce risk is improved. Note that in no case will creating portfolios of assets result in greater risk than that of the riskiest asset included in the portfolio. An example may clarify this concept further.

EXAMPLE

A firm has carefully calculated the expected return, $\bar{k}$, and risk, σ, for each of two assets—R and S—as summarized below:

Asset	Expected return, $\bar{k}$	Risk (standard deviation), σ
R	6%	3%
S	8%	8%

From these data it can be seen that asset R is clearly a lower-risk, lower-return asset than asset S.

TABLE 6.6

CORRELATION, RETURN, AND RISK FOR VARIOUS TWO-ASSET PORTFOLIO COMBINATIONS

Correlation coefficient	Range of return	Range of risk
+1 (perfect positive)	Between returns of two assets held in isolation	Between risk of two assets held in isolation
0 (uncorrelated)	Between returns of two assets held in isolation	Between risk of most risky asset and an amount less than risk of least risky asset but greater than 0
−1 (perfect negative)	Between returns of two assets held in isolation	Between risk of most risky asset and 0

To evaluate possible combinations (assuming divisibility of the two assets), the firm considered three possible correlations—perfect positive, uncorrelated, and perfect negative. The results of the analysis are shown in Figure 6.8. The ranges of return and risk exhibited are consistent with those noted in Table 6.6. In all cases the return will range between the 6 percent return of R and the 8 percent return of S. The risk, on the other hand, ranges between the individual risks of R and S (from 3 percent to 8 percent) in the case of perfect positive correlation, from below 3 percent (the risk of R) to 8 percent (the risk of S) and greater than 0 percent in the uncorrelated case, and between 0 percent and 8 percent (the risk of S) in the perfectly negatively correlated case.

Note that *only in the case of perfect negative correlation can the risk be reduced to 0.* It can also be seen in Figure 6.8 that as the correlation becomes less positive and more negative (moving from the top of the figure down), the ability to reduce risk im-

FIGURE 6.8
Range of portfolio return (k_p) and risk (σ_{k_p}) for combinations of assets R and S for various correlation coefficients

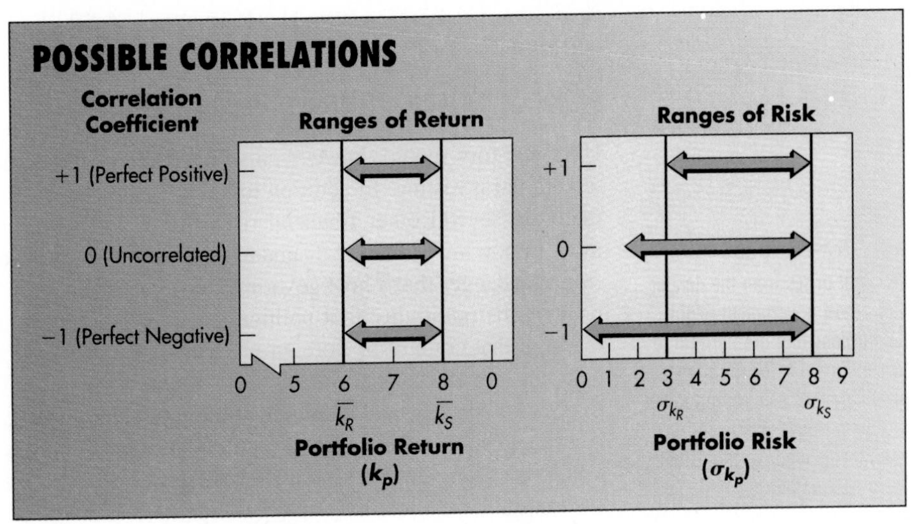

proves. Keep in mind that the amount of risk reduction achieved also depends on the proportions in which the assets are combined. While determination of the risk-minimizing combination is beyond the scope of this discussion, it is an important issue in developing portfolios of assets. ■

International diversification

The ultimate example of portfolio diversification involves including foreign assets in a portfolio of domestic assets. This strategy enhances risk reduction in two ways. First, by including assets with payoffs denominated in foreign currencies, the correlations of the returns of the portfolio's assets are reduced when all investment returns are translated into dollars. Second, by including assets from countries that are less sensitive to the business cycle of the United States than are domestic financial assets, the portfolio's responsiveness to market movements is reduced.

RETURNS FROM INTERNATIONAL DIVERSIFICATION

Over long investment horizons, international diversification strategies tend to yield returns that are superior to those yielded by purely domestic strategies. Over any single short or intermediate period, however, international diversification can yield subpar returns—particularly during periods when the dollar is appreciating in value relative to other currencies. When the U.S. currency gains in value, the dollar value of a foreign-currency-denominated portfolio of assets declines, and even if this portfolio yields a satisfactory return in local currency, the return to U.S. investors will be reduced when translated into dollars. Furthermore, if the dollar is appreciating because the U.S. economy is performing relatively better than other economies, then foreign-currency-denominated protfolios will tend to have lower nominal (local currency) returns than will U.S. domestic portfolios. Subpar local currency portfolio returns, coupled with an appreciating dollar, can yield truly dismal dollar returns to U.S. investors. Of course, if the U.S. economy is performing relatively poorly and the dollar is depreciating against most foreign currencies, then the dollar returns to U.S. investors on a portfolio of foreign assets can be very attractive indeed. The logic of international portfolio diversification assumes that these fluctuations in currency values and relative performance will average out over long periods and that an internationally diversified portfolio will tend to yield a comparable return at a lower level of risk than will similar purely domestic portfolios.

RISKS OF INTERNATIONAL DIVERSIFICATION

U.S. investors should, however, also be aware of the potential dangers involved in international investing. In addition to the risk induced by potential currency fluctuations there are several other financial risks that are unique to international investing. The most important of these fall under the heading of **political risk.** Political risk arises from the danger that a host government might take actions harmful to foreign investors or from the possibility that political turmoil in a country might endanger investments made in that country by foreign nationals. Political risks are particularly acute in developing counties, where unstable or ideologically motivated governments often attempt to block return of profits by multinational companies and other foreign investors or even seize (nationalize) their assets in the host country.

political risk
Risk that arises from the danger that a host government might take actions that are harmful to foreign investors or from the possibility that political turmoil in a country might endanger investments made in that country by foreign nationals.

Even where governments do not resort to deliberate exchange controls or seizure, international investors may suffer if a general shortage of hard currency prevents payment of dividends or interest to foreigners. When governments are forced to allocate scarce foreign exchange, they rarely give top priority to the interests of foreign investors. Instead, hard currency reserves are typically used to pay for necessary imports such as food and industrial materials and to pay interest on the government's own debts. Since most of the debt of developing countries is held by banks rather than individuals, portfolio investors are often harmed very badly when a country experiences political or economic problems.

CONCEPTS IN REVIEW

6-8 Why must assets be evaluated in a portfolio context? What is an *efficient portfolio*? How can the return and standard deviation of a portfolio be determined?

6-9 Why is the *correlation* between asset returns important? How does diversification of risk in the asset selection process allow the investor to combine risky assets so that the risk of the portfolio is less than the risk of the individual assets in it?

6-10 How does international diversification enhance risk reduction? Why, particularly during periods when the dollar is appreciating, can international diversification result in subpar returns? What are *political risks,* and how do they affect international diversification?

Risk and return: The capital asset pricing model (CAPM)

Research has shown that investors are rewarded for taking only those risks that cannot be eliminated through diversification. Why is it important for the financial manager to be concerned with those "nondiversifiable" risks and their relationship to the required level of return? Before reading ahead, spend a few moments considering this question.

THE MOST IMPORTANT ASPECT OF RISK IS THE *OVERALL RISK* OF THE FIRM AS VIEWED BY investors in the marketplace. Overall risk significantly affects investment opportunities—and even more important, the owners' wealth. The basic theory that links together risk and return for all assets is commonly called the **capital asset pricing model (CAPM).**[16] Here we will use CAPM to understand the basic risk-return tradeoffs that are involved in all types of financial decisions.[17]

capital asset pricing model (CAPM)
The basic theory that links together risk and return for all assets.

[16]The initial development of this theory is generally attributed to William F. Sharpe, "Capital Asset Prices: A Theory of Market Equilibrium Under Conditions of Risk," *Journal of Finance* 19 (September 1964), pp. 425–442, and John Lintner, "The Valuation of Risk Assets and the Selection of Risky Investments in Stock Portfolios and Capital Budgets," *Review of Economics and Statistics* 47 (February 1965), pp 13–37. A number of authors subsequently advanced, refined, and tested this now widely accepted theory.

[17]While CAPM has been widely accepted, a broader theory, *arbitrage pricing theory (APT),* first described by Stephen A. Ross, "The Arbitrage Theory of Capital Asset Pricing," *Journal of Economic Theory* (December 1976), pp. 341–360, has in recent years received a great deal of attention in the financial literature. The theory suggests that the risk premium on securities may be better explained by a number of factors underlying and in place of the market return used in CAPM. The CAPM in effect can be viewed as being derived from APT. While testing of APT theory confirms the importance of the market return, it has thus far failed to clearly identify other risk factors. As a result of this failure as well as APT's lack of practical acceptance and usage, we concentrate our attention here on CAPM.

Types of risk

To understand the basic types of risk, consider what happens when we begin with a single security (asset) in a portfolio. Then we expand the portfolio by randomly selecting additional securities from, say, the population of all actively traded securities. Using the standard deviation of return, σ_k, to measure the total portfolio risk, Figure 6.9 depicts the behavior of the total portfolio risk (y-axis) as more securities are added (x-axis). With the addition of securities, the total portfolio risk declines, due to the effects of diversification (as explained in the previous section), and tends to approach a limit. Research has shown that most of the benefits of diversification, in terms of risk reduction, can be gained by forming portfolios containing 15 to 20 randomly selected securities.[18]

total risk
The combination of a security's nondiversifiable and diversifiable risk.

diversifiable risk
The portion of an asset's risk that is attributable to firm-specific, random causes; can be eliminated through diversification.

nondiversifiable risk
The relevant portion of an asset's risk attributable to market factors that affect all firms; cannot be eliminated through diversification.

The **total risk** of a security can be viewed as consisting of two parts:

$$\text{Total security risk} = \text{nondiversifiable risk} + \text{diversifiable risk} \tag{6.6}$$

Diversifiable risk, which is sometimes called *unsystematic risk,* represents the portion of an asset's risk that is associated with random causes that can be eliminated through diversification. It is attributable to firm-specific events, such as strikes, lawsuits, regulatory actions, and loss of a key account. **Nondiversifiable risk,** which is also called *systematic risk,* is attributable to market factors that affect all firms, and it cannot be eliminated through diversification. Factors such as war, inflation, international incidents, and political events account for nondiversifiable risk.

FIGURE 6.9
Portfolio risk and diversification

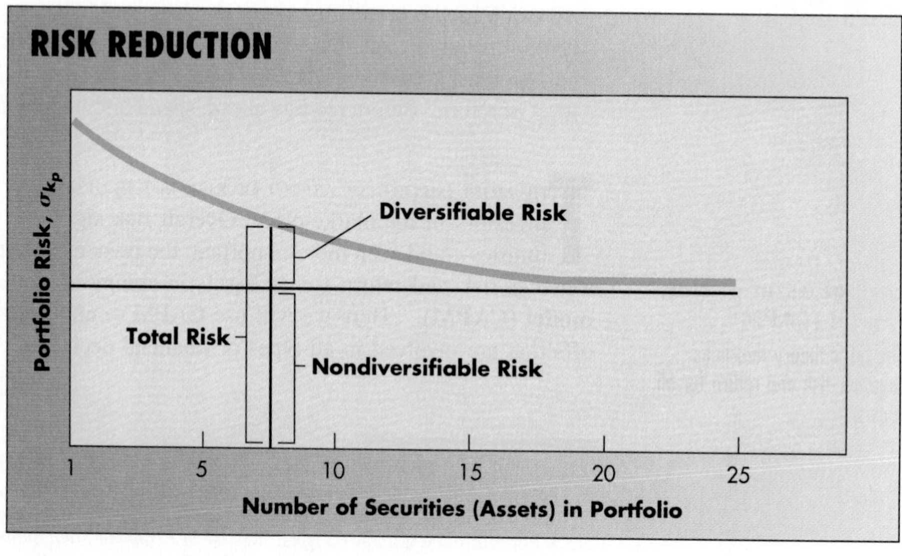

[18]See, for example, W. H. Wagner and S. C. Lau, "The Effect of Diversification on Risk," *Financial Analysts Journal* 26 (November–December 1971), pp. 48–53; and Jack Evans and Stephen H. Archer, "Diversification and the Reduction of Dispersion: An Empirical Analysis," *Journal of Finance* 23 (December 1968), pp. 761–767.

Because, as illustrated in Figure 6.9, any investor can create a portfolio of assets that will eliminate all, or virtually all, diversifiable risk, *the only relevant risk is nondiversifiable risk.* Any investor (or firm) must therefore be concerned solely with nondiversifiable risk, which reflects the contribution of an asset to the risk of the portfolio. The measurement of nondiversifiable risk is thus of primary importance in selecting those assets possessing the most desired risk-return characteristics.

CONCEPT IN PRACTICE

Southwestern Bell Is No Longer Solely Southwestern or Bell

In 1993, Southwestern Bell, which operates telephone systems in an area that includes Arkansas, Kansas, Missouri, Oklahoma, and Texas, became the first regional Bell Telephone company to own U.S. cable television properties. Southwestern Bell entered the cable market in the Washington, D.C., area because phone companies are barred by federal law from owning cable systems within their own service territories. Such rules do not apply to ownership in other nations. For instance, Southwestern Bell provides cable and telephone service to 1.2 million homes in Great Britain. The move to cable also allows Southwestern Bell to diversify away from the regulations it encounters in the telephone industry.

The model: CAPM

The capital asset pricing model (CAPM) links together nondiversifiable risk and return for all assets. We will discuss the model in five parts. The first part defines, derives, and describes the beta coefficient, which is a measure of nondiversifiable risk, for both individual assets and portfolios. The second part presents an equation of the model itself, and the third part graphically describes the relationship between risk and return. In the fourth part the effects of changes in inflationary expectations and risk aversion on the relationship between risk and return are discussed. The final part presents some general comments on CAPM.

BETA COEFFICIENT

beta coefficient (b)
A measure of nondiversifiable risk. An *index* of the degree of movement of an asset's return in response to a change in the *market return.*

market return
The return on the market portfolio of all traded securities.

The **beta coefficient, b,** is used to measure nondiversifiable risk. It is an *index* of the degree of movement of an asset's return in response to a change in the *market return.* The beta coefficient for an asset can be found by examining the asset's historical returns relative to the returns for the market. The **market return** is the return on the market portfolio of all traded securities. The return on a portfolio of the stocks in *Standard & Poor's 500 Stock Composite Index* or some similar stock index is commonly used to measure the market return. Although betas for actively traded securities can be obtained from a variety of sources, it is important to understand their derivation, interpretation, and application to portfolios.

DERIVING BETA FROM RETURN DATA The relationship between an asset's return and the market return and its use in deriving beta can be demonstrated graphically. Figure 6.10 plots the relationship between the returns of two assets—R and S—and the market return. Note that the horizontal (x) axis measures the market returns and the vertical (y) axis measures the individual asset's (R or S) returns. The first step in deriving beta involves plotting the coordinates for the market return and asset returns at various points in time. Such annual market return–asset return coordinates are shown in Figure 6.10 for asset S only for the years 1987 through 1994 (with the year

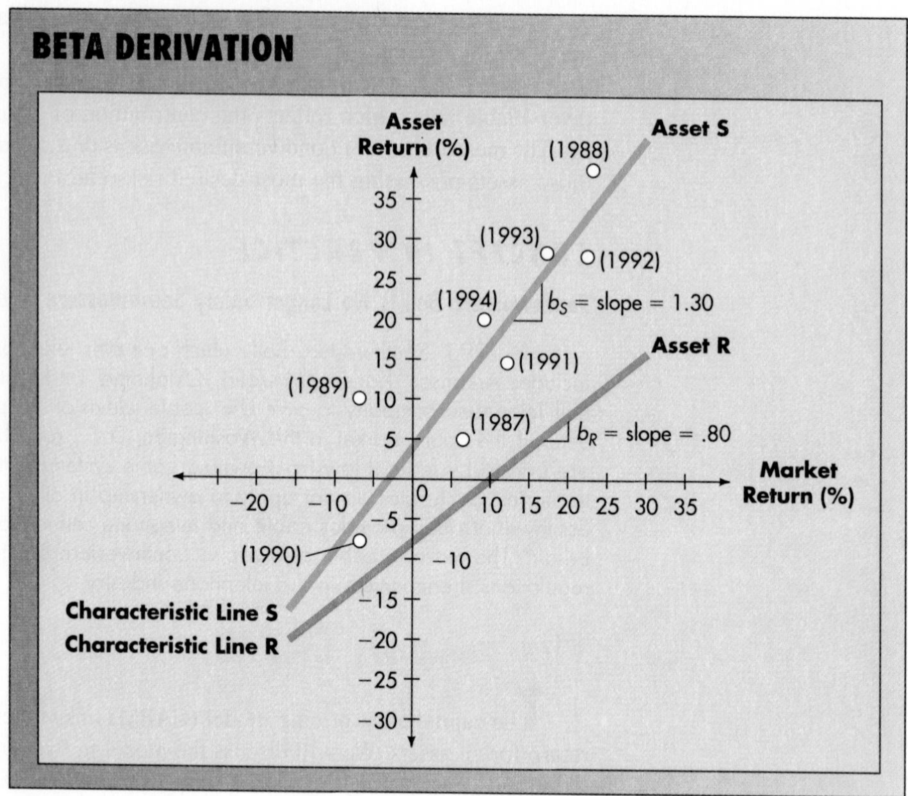

FIGURE 6.10
Graphic derivation of beta for assets R and S

noted in parentheses). For example, in 1994, asset S's return was 20 percent when the market return was 10 percent. By use of statistical techniques the "characteristic line" that best explains the relationship between the asset return and the market return coordinates is fit to the data points.[19] The slope of this line is beta. The beta for asset R

[19]The empirical measurement of beta is approached by using least-squares regression analysis to find the regression coefficient (b_j) in the equation for the "characteristic line":

$$k_j = a_j + b_j k_m + e_j$$

where

k_j = the return on asset j
a_j = the intercept
b_j = the beta coefficient, which equals $\frac{Cov\ (k_j, k_m)}{\sigma_m{}^2}$

where

$Cov\ (k_j, k_m)$ = covariance of the return on asset j, k_j, and the market portfolio, k_m
$\sigma_m{}^2$ = variance of the return on the market portfolio
k_m = the required rate of return on the market portfolio of securities
e_j = random error term, which reflects the diversifiable or unsystematic risk of asset j

Because of the somewhat rigorous calculations involved in finding betas, the interested reader is referred to an advanced managerial finance or investments text for a more detailed discussion of this topic.

is about .80, and that for asset S is about 1.30. Clearly, asset S's higher beta (steeper characteristic line slope) indicates that its return is more responsive to changing market returns and therefore it is more risky than asset R.[20]

OBTAINING AND INTERPRETING BETAS Beta coefficients can be obtained for actively traded stocks from published sources, such as *Value Line Investment Survey,* or through brokerage firms. Betas for some selected stocks are given in Table 6.7. The beta coefficient for the market is considered to be equal to 1.0; all other betas are viewed in relation to this value. Asset betas may take on values that are either positive or negative, but positive betas are the norm. The majority of beta coefficients fall between .5 and 2.0. Table 6.8 provides some selected beta values and their associated interpretations.

PORTFOLIO BETAS The beta of a portfolio can be easily estimated by using the betas of the individual assets it includes. Letting w_j represent the proportion of the portfolio's total dollar value represented by asset j and b_j equal the beta of asset j, we can use Equation 6.7 to find the portfolio beta, b_p:

$$b_p = (w_1 \times b_1) + (w_2 \times b_2) + \cdots + (w_n \times b_n) = \sum_{j=1}^{n} w_j \times b_j \tag{6.7}$$

Of course, $\sum_{j=1}^{n} w_j = 1$, which means that 100 percent of the portfolio's assets must be included in this computation.

Portfolio betas are interpreted in exactly the same fashion as individual asset betas. They indicate the degree of responsiveness of the portfolio's return to changes in the market return. For example, when the market return increases by 10 percent, a port-

TABLE 6.7

Stock	Beta	Stock	Beta
Anheuser-Busch	1.05	IBM	.95
Apple Computer	1.15	Merrill Lynch & Company	1.65
Boston Edison	.70	Occidental Petroleum	.80
CBS, Inc.	.95	Procter & Gamble	1.10
Caesar's World	1.30	Seagram Company	1.05
Cascade Natural Gas	.55	Sony Corporation	.75
Delta Air Lines	1.10	Tandy Corporation	1.25
Exxon Corporation	.75	Union Electric	.65
General Motors	1.10	Universal Foods	.85
Hilton Hotels	1.30	Xerox Corporation	1.15

Source: Value Line Investment Survey (New York: Value Line Publishing, Inc., May 28, 1993).

[20]The values of beta also depend on the time interval used for return calculations and the number of returns used in the regression analysis. In other words, betas calculated by using monthly returns would not necessarily be comparable to those calculated by using a similar number of daily returns.

TABLE 6.8

SELECTED BETA COEFFICIENTS AND THEIR INTERPRETATIONS

Beta	Comment	Interpretation[a]
2.0	Move in same direction as market	Twice as responsive, or risky, as the market
1.0		Same response or risk as the market (i.e., average risk)
.5		Only half as responsive, or risky, as the market
0		Unaffected by market movement
−.5	Move in opposite direction to market	Only half as responsive, or risky, as the market
−1.0		Same response or risk as the market (i.e., average risk)
−2.0		Twice as responsive, or risky, as the market

[a]A stock that is twice as responsive as the market is expected to experience a 2 percent change in its return for each 1 percent change in the return of the market portfolio, whereas the return of a stock that is half as responsive as the market is expected to change by 1/2 of 1 percent for each 1 percent change in the return of the market portfolio.

folio with a beta of .75 will experience a 7.5 percent increase in its return (.75 × 10%), whereas a portfolio with a beta of 1.25 will experience a 12.5 percent increase in its return (1.25 × 10%). Low-beta portfolios are less responsive and therefore less risky than high-beta portfolios. Clearly, a portfolio containing mostly low-beta assets will have a low beta, and one containing mostly high-beta assets will have a high beta.

EXAMPLE

The Austin Fund, a large investment company, wishes to asses the risk of two portfolios—V and W. Both portfolios contain five assets, with the proportions and betas shown in Table 6.9. The betas for portfolios V and W, b_V and b_W, can be calculated by substituting the appropriate data from the table into Equation 6.7 as follows:

$$\begin{aligned} b_V &= (.10 \times 1.65) + (.30 \times 1.00) + (.20 \times 1.30) \\ &\quad + (.20 \times 1.10) + (.20 \times 1.25) \\ &= .165 + .300 + .260 + .220 + .250 = 1.195 \approx \underline{\underline{1.20}} \end{aligned}$$

$$\begin{aligned} b_W &= (.10 \times .80) + (.10 \times 1.00) + (.20 \times .65) \\ &\quad + (.10 \times .75) + (.50 \times 1.05) \\ &= .080 + .100 + .130 + .075 + .525 = \underline{\underline{.91}} \end{aligned}$$

Portfolio V's beta is 1.20, and portfolio W's is .91. These values make sense, since portfolio V contains relatively high-beta assets and portfolio W contains relatively low-beta assets. Clearly, portfolio V's returns are more responsive to changes in market returns and are therefore more risky than portfolio W's. ■

THE EQUATION

Using the beta coefficient, b, to measure nondiversifiable risk, the *capital asset pricing model (CAPM)* is given in Equation 6.8:

$$k_j = R_F + [b_j \times (k_m - R_F)] \tag{6.8}$$

TABLE 6.9

AUSTIN FUND'S PORTFOLIOS V AND W

	Portfolio V		Portfolio W	
Asset	**Proportion**	**Beta**	**Proportion**	**Beta**
1	.10	1.65	.10	.80
2	.30	1.00	.10	1.00
3	.20	1.30	.20	.65
4	.20	1.10	.10	.75
5	.20	1.25	.50	1.05
Totals	1.00		1.00	

where

k_j = required return on asset j
R_F = risk-free rate of return, commonly measured by the return on a U.S. Treasury bill
b_j = beta coefficient or index of nondiversifiable risk for asset j
k_m = market return; the return on the market portfolio of assets

The required return on an asset, k_j, is an increasing function of beta, b_j, which measures nondiversifiable risk. In other words, *the higher the risk, the higher the required return, and the lower the risk, the lower the required return.* The model can be broken into two parts: (1) the *risk-free rate,* R_F and (2) the *risk premium,* $b_j \times (k_m - R_F)$. The $(k_m - R_F)$ portion of the risk premium is called the *market risk premium,* since it represents the premium the investor must receive for taking the average amount of risk associated with holding the market portfolio of assets. Let us look at an example.

EXAMPLE

Benjamin Corporation, a growing computer-software developer, wishes to determine the required return on an asset—asset Z—that has a beta, b_z, of 1.5. The risk-free rate of return is found to be 7 percent; the return on the market portfolio of assets is 11 percent. Substituting $b_z = 1.5$, $R_F = 7$ percent, and $k_m = 11$ percent into the capital asset pricing model given in Equation 6.8 yields a required return:

$$k_z = 7\% + [1.5 \times (11\% - 7\%)] = 7\% + 6\% = \underline{\underline{13\%}}$$

The market risk premium of 4 percent (11% − 7%), when adjusted for the asset's index of risk (beta) of 1.5, results in a risk premium of 6 percent (1.5 × 4%), which, when added to the 7 percent risk-free rate, results in a 13 percent required return. Other things being equal, the higher the beta, the greater the required return, and the lower the beta, the less the required return. ■

security market line (SML)
The depiction of the *capital asset pricing model (CAPM)* as a graph that reflects the required return for each level of nondiversifiable risk (beta).

THE GRAPH: THE SECURITY MARKET LINE (SML)

When the capital asset pricing model (Equation 6.8) is depicted graphically, it is called the **security market line (SML).** The SML will, in fact, be a straight line. It reflects for each level of nondiversifiable risk (beta) the required return in the marketplace. In the graph, risk as measured by beta, b, is plotted on the x-axis, and required returns, k, are plotted on the y-axis. The risk-return tradeoff is clearly represented by the SML. Let us look at an illustration.

EXAMPLE

In the preceding example for the Benjamin Corporation the risk-free rate, R_F, was 7 percent, and the market return, k_m, was 11 percent. Since the betas associated with R_F and k_m, b_{R_F} and b_m, are by definition 0[21] and 1, respectively, the SML can be plotted by using these two sets of coordinates (i.e., $b_{R_F} = 0$, $R_F = 7\%$; and $b_m = 1$, $k_m = 11\%$). Figure 6.11 presents the security market line that results from plotting the coordinates given. As traditionally shown, the security market line in Figure 6.11 presents the required return associated with all positive betas. The market risk premium of 4 percent (k_m of 11% − R_F of 7%) has been highlighted. For a beta for asset Z, b_z, of 1.5, its corresponding required return, k_z, is 13 percent. Also shown in the figure is asset Z's risk premium of 6 percent (k_z of 13% − R_F of 7%). It should be clear that for assets with betas greater than 1, the risk premium is greater than that for the market; for assets with betas less than 1, the risk premium is less than that for the market. ■

FIGURE 6.11
The security market line (SML) with Benjamin Corporation's asset Z data shown

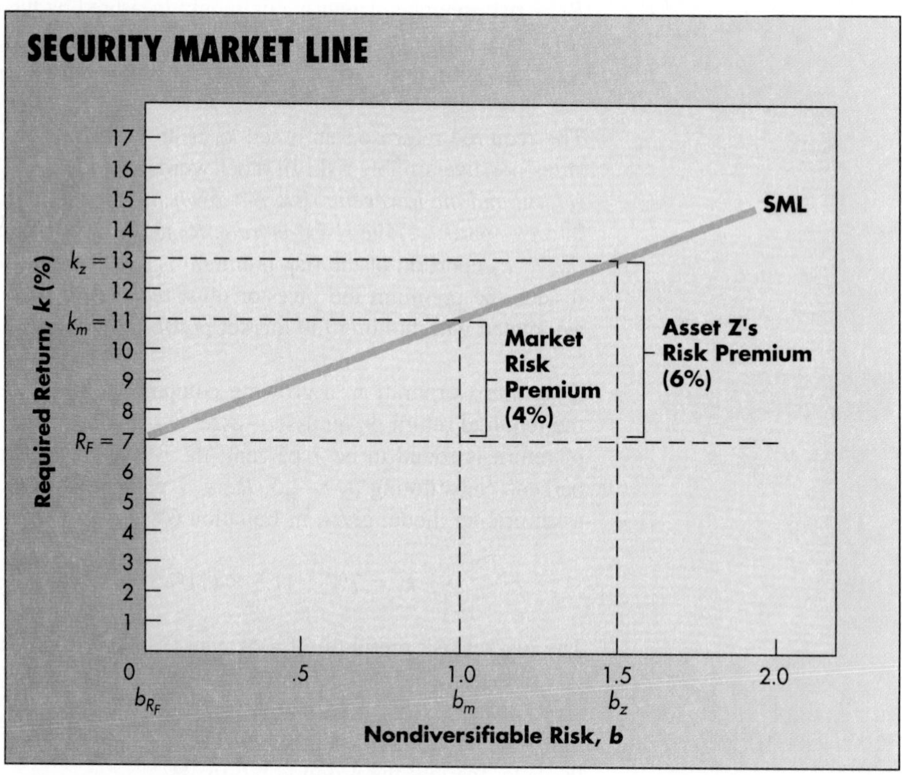

[21]Since R_F is the rate of return on a risk-free asset, the beta associated with the risk-free asset, b_{R_F}, would equal 0. The 0 beta on the risk-free asset reflects not only its absence of risk but also that the asset's return is unaffected by movements in the market return.

SHIFTS IN THE SECURITY MARKET LINE

The security market line is not stable over time. While the firm's risk as measured by beta may not change,[22] shifts in the security market line can result in a change in required return. The position and slope of the SML is affected by two major forces—inflationary expectations and risk aversion—which are separately analyzed below.

CHANGES IN INFLATIONARY EXPECTATIONS Changes in inflationary expectations, as noted in Chapter 2, affect the risk-free rate of return, R_F. Equation 2.3 is rewritten below as Equation 6.9:

$$R_F = k^* + IP \qquad (6.9)$$

This equation shows that assuming a constant real rate of interest, k^*, increases or decreases in inflationary expectations reflected in an inflation premium, IP, will result in corresponding changes in the risk-free rate. Therefore a change in inflationary expectations resulting from events such as international trade embargoes or major changes in Federal Reserve policy will result in a shift in the SML. Because the risk-free rate is a basic component of all rates of return (see Equation 2.2 in Chapter 2), any change in R_F will be reflected in *all* required rates of return. Changes in inflationary expectations therefore result in parallel shifts in the SML in direct response to the magnitude and direction of the change. This effect can best be illustrated by an example.

EXAMPLE

In the preceding example the risk-free rate, R_F, was 7 percent; the market return, k_m, was 11 percent; and the beta for asset Z, b_Z, was 1.5. By using CAPM, the required return for asset Z, k_Z, was found to be 13 percent. Assuming that the risk-free rate includes a 2 percent real rate of interest, k^*, and a 5 percent inflation premium, IP, then Equation 6.9 confirms that

$$R_F = 2\% + 5\% = 7\%$$

In addition, we assume that recent economic events have resulted in an *increase of 3 percent in inflationary expectations, raising the inflation premium* from 5 percent (IP) to 8 percent (IP_1). As a result, all returns would likewise rise by 3 percent. In this case the new returns (noted by the subscript 1) are

$$R_{F_1} = 10\% \text{ (rises from 7\% to 10\%)}$$
$$k_{m_1} = 14\% \text{ (rises from 11\% to 14\%)}$$

Substituting these values, along with asset Z's beta (b_Z) of 1.5, into the CAPM (Equation 6.8), we find that asset Z's new required return (k_{Z_1}) can be calculated:

$$k_{Z_1} = 10\% + [1.5 \times (14\% - 10\%)] = 10\% + 6\% = \underline{\underline{16\%}}$$

[22]A firm's beta can change over time as a result of changes in the firm's asset mix, in its financing mix, or in external factors not within management's control, such as earthquakes, toxic spills, etc. The impacts of changes in beta on value are discussed in Chapter 7.

Comparing k_{Z_1} of 16 percent to k_Z of 13 percent, we see that the change in asset Z's required return of 3 percent exactly equals the change in the inflation premium. The same 3 percent increase would result for all assets.

Figure 6.12 graphically depicts the situation described above. It shows that the 3 percent increase in inflationary expectations results in a parallel shift upward by a vertical distance of 3 percent in the SML. Clearly, the required returns on all assets rise by 3 percent. Note that the rise in the inflation premium from 5 percent to 8 percent (IP to IP_1) causes the risk-free rate to rise from 7 percent to 10 percent (R_F to R_{F_1}) and the market return to increase from 11 percent to 14 percent (k_m to k_{m_1}). The security market line therefore shifts upward by 3 percent (SML to SML$_1$), causing the required return on all risky assets such as asset Z to rise by 3 percent; as noted, asset Z's required return rises from 13 percent to 16 percent (k_Z to k_{Z_1}). It should now be clear that *a given change in inflationary expectations will be fully reflected in a corresponding change in the returns of all assets as reflected graphically in a parallel shift of the SML.* ■

CHANGES IN RISK AVERSION The slope of the security market line reflects the general risk preferences of investors in the marketplace. As discussed earlier and noted graphically in Figure 6.1, most investors are risk-averse—they require increased returns for increased risk. This positive relationship between risk and return is graphically represented by the SML, which depicts the relationship between nondiversifiable risk as measured by beta, *b* (*x*-axis), and the required return, *k* (*y*-axis). The slope of the SML reflects the degree of risk aversion; the steeper its slope, the greater the degree of risk aversion, since a higher level of return would be required for each level

FIGURE 6.12
Impact of increased inflationary expectations on the SML

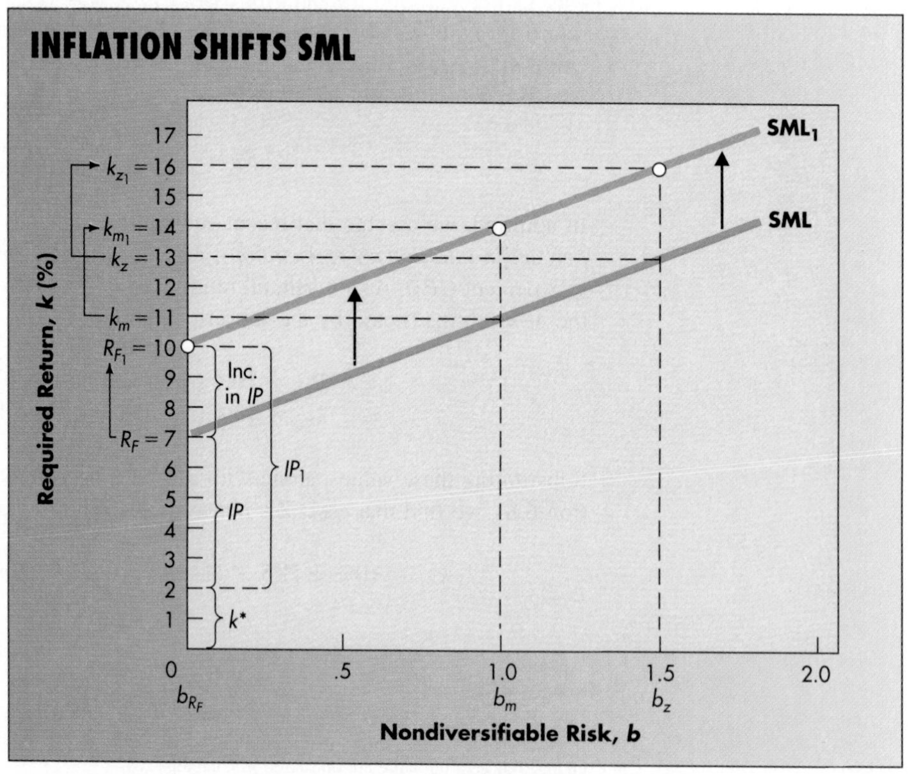

of risk as measured by beta. In other words, *risk premiums increase with increasing risk avoidance.*

Changes in risk aversion, and therefore shifts in the SML, result from changing tastes and preferences of investors, which generally result from various economic, political, and social events. Examples of events that *increase* risk aversion include a stock market crash, assassination of a key political leader, the outbreak of war, and so forth. In general, widely accepted expectations of hard times ahead tend to cause investors to become more risk-averse, requiring higher returns as compensation for accepting a given level of risk. The impact of increased risk aversion on the SML can best be demonstrated by example.

EXAMPLE

In the preceding examples the SML in Figure 6.11 reflected a risk-free rate (R_F) of 7 percent, a market return (k_m) of 11 percent, a market risk premium ($k_m - R_F$) of 4 percent, and a required return on asset Z (k_Z) with a beta (b_Z) of 1.5 of 13 percent. Assume that as a result of recent economic events investors have become more risk-averse, causing a new higher market return (k_{m_1}) of 14 percent. Graphically, this change would cause the SML to shift upward as noted in Figure 6.13, causing a new market risk premium ($k_{m_1} - R_F$) of 7 percent. As a result, the required return on all risky assets will increase. In the case of asset Z with a beta of 1.5, its new required return (k_{Z_1}) can be calculated by using CAPM (Equation 6.8):

FIGURE 6.13
Impact of increased risk aversion on the SML

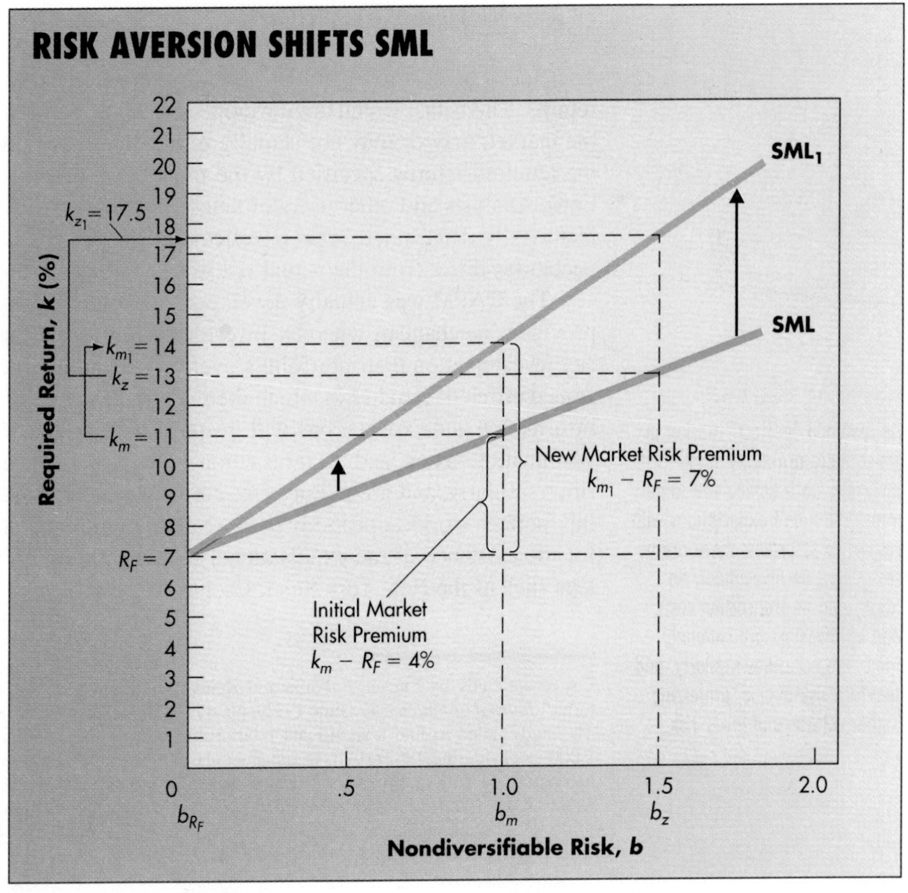

$$k_{Z_1} = 7\% + [1.5 \times (14\% - 7\%) = 7\% + 10.5\% = \underline{\underline{17.5\%}}$$

This value can be seen on the new security market line (SML_1) in Figure 6.13. Note that although asset Z's risk as measured by beta does not change, its required return has increased due to the increased risk aversion reflected in the market risk premium, which rose from 4 percent to 7 percent. It should now be clear that *greater risk aversion results in higher required returns for each level of risk, whereas a reduction in risk aversion would cause the required return for each level of risk to decline.* ■

CONCEPT IN PRACTICE

Sensitivity of Boeing's Systematic Risk to Economic Conditions

Boeing's measure of risk, beta, in 1993 stood at 1.1, which was 10 percent greater than the market portfolio's beta of 1.0. To compensate its shareholders for the firm's greater nondiversifiable risk, the airplane manufacturer's return needed to be 10 percent greater than the market risk premium. Boeing's financial managers also estimate betas in up-markets, when stock prices in general increase, and down-markets, when stock prices in general decline. For Boeing the beta in up-markets was .6, while the beta in down-markets was 2.8. As might be expected, given Boeing's large investment in fixed assets, the required rate of return used in the selection of projects is much higher at Boeing if the economy is forecast to decline.

SOME COMMENTS ON CAPM

The capital asset pricing model generally relies on historical data to estimate required returns. The betas, which are developed by using data for the given asset as well as for the market, may or may not actually reflect the *future* variability of returns. Therefore the required returns specified by the model can be viewed only as rough approximations. Analysts and other users of betas commonly make subjective adjustments to the historically determined betas to reflect their expectations of the future when such expectations differ from the actual risk-return behaviors of the past.

The CAPM was actually developed to explain the behavior of security prices and provide a mechanism whereby investors could assess the impact of a proposed security investment on their portfolio's overall risk and return. It is actually based on an assumed **efficient market** in which there are many small investors, each having the same information and expectations with respect to securities; there are no restrictions on investment, no taxes, and no transaction costs; and all investors are rational, view securities similarly, and are risk-averse, preferring higher returns and lower risk. Although this perfect world appears to be unrealistic, empirical studies have provided support for the existence of the expectational relationship described by CAPM in active markets such as the New York Stock Exchange.[23] In the case of real corporate assets, such

efficient market
An assumed "perfect" market in which there are many small investors, each having the same information and expectations with respect to securities; there are no restrictions on investment, no taxes, and no transaction costs; and all investors are rational, they view securities similarly, and they are risk-averse, preferring higher returns and lower risk.

[23] A recent study by Eugene F. Fama and Kenneth R. French, "The Cross-Section of Expected Stock Returns," *Journal of Finance* 47 (June 1992), pp. 427–465, raised serious questions about the validity of CAPM. The study failed to find a significant relationship between the historic betas and historic returns on over 2,000 stocks during 1963–1990. In other words, they found that the magnitude of a stock's historical beta had no relationship to the level of its historical return. While Fama and French's study continues to receive attention, CAPM has not been abandoned because its rejection as a *historical* model fails to reject its validity as an *expectational* model. Therefore in spite of this challenge, CAPM continues to be viewed as a logical and useful framework for linking *expected* risk and return.

as plant and equipment, research thus far has failed to prove the general applicability of CAPM because of indivisibility, relatively large size, limited number of transactions, and absence of an efficient market for such assets.

In spite of the fact that the risk-return tradeoff described by CAPM is not generally applicable to all assets, it provides a useful conceptual framework for evaluating and linking risk and return. An awareness of this tradeoff and an attempt to somehow capture and consider risk as well as return in financial decision making should aid the financial manager in achieving the goal of owner wealth maximization.

CONCEPTS IN REVIEW

6-11 What is the relationship of total risk, nondiversifiable risk, and diversifiable risk? Why would someone argue that nondiversifiable risk is the only relevant risk?

6-12 What risk is measured by *beta?* Define beta. How are asset betas derived, and where can they be obtained? How can you find the beta of a portfolio?

6-13 What is the equation for the *capital asset pricing model (CAPM)*? Explain the meaning of each variable. Assuming a risk-free rate of 8 percent and a market return of 12 percent, draw the *security market line (SML).*

6-14 What impact would the following changes have on the security market line and therefore on the required return for a given level of risk?

a. An increase in inflationary expectations.

b. Investors become less risk-averse.

6-15 Why do financial managers have difficulty applying CAPM in decision making? Generally, what benefit does CAPM provide them?

Summary

LG **1** **Understand the meaning and fundamentals of risk, return, and risk preferences.** Risk is the chance of loss or, more formally, refers to the variability of returns. Return is the change in value plus any cash distributions expressed as a percentage of the initial value. The variable definitions and equation for the rate of return are given in Table 6.10. The three basic risk-preference behaviors are risk-indifference, risk-aversion, and risk-seeking. Most financial decision makers are risk-averse because they require higher expected returns as compensation for taking greater risk.

LG **2** **Describe the basic risk concepts related to the measurement of risk for a single asset and the relationship between risk and time.** The risk of a single asset is measured in much the same way as the risk of a portfolio, or collection, of assets. Sensitivity analysis is a behavioral approach that can be used to get a feel for risk. More quantitative risk measures include probabilities, probability distributions, the standard deviation, and the coefficient of variation. The key variable definitions and equations for the expected value of a return, standard deviation of returns, and the coefficient of variation are summarized in Table 6.10. Risk is an increasing function of time because the variability of returns tends to increase with the passage of time.

LG **3** **Discuss the measurement of return and standard deviation for a portfolio and the various types of correlation that can exist between series of numbers.** The return of a portfolio is calculated as the weighted average of returns on the individual assets from which it is formed. The variable definitions and equation for portfolio return are given in Table 6.10. The portfolio standard deviation is found by using the formula for the standard deviation of a single asset. Correlation, the statistical relationship between series of numbers, can be positive (the series move in the same direction), negative (the series move in opposite directions), or uncorrelated (the series exhibit no discernable relationship). At the extremes the series can be perfectly positively correlated (have a correlation coefficient of $+1$) or perfectly negatively correlated (have a correlation coefficient of -1).

TABLE 6.10

SUMMARY OF KEY DEFINITIONS AND FORMULAS FOR RISK AND RETURN

Variable definitions

k_t = actual, expected, or required rate of return during period t
P_t = price (value) of asset at time t
P_{t-1} = price (value) of asset at time $t-1$
C_t = cash received from the asset investment in the time period $t-1$ to t
$\bar{k}$ = expected value of a return
k_i = return for the ith outcome
Pr_i = probability of occurrence of the ith outcome
n = number of outcomes considered
σ_k = standard deviation of returns
CV = coefficient of variation
k_p = portfolio return
w_j = proportion of total portfolio dollar value represented by asset j
k_j = required return on asset j
b_p = portfolio beta
b_j = beta coefficient or index of nondiversifiable risk for asset j
R_F = risk-free rate of return
k_m = market return; the return on the market portfolio of assets

Risk and return formulas

Rate of return during period t

$$k_t = \frac{P_t - P_{t-1} + C_t}{P_{t-1}} \quad \text{[Eq. 6.1]}$$

Expected value of a return:
for probabilistic data

$$\bar{k} = \sum_{i=1}^{n} k_i \times Pr_i \quad \text{[Eq. 6.2]}$$

general formula

$$\bar{k} = \frac{\sum_{i=1}^{n} k_i}{n} \quad \text{[Eq. 6.2a]}$$

Standard deviation of returns:
for probabilistic data

$$\sigma_k = \sqrt{\sum_{i=1}^{n} (k_i - \bar{k})^2 \times Pr_i} \quad \text{[Eq. 6.3]}$$

general formula

$$\sigma_k = \sqrt{\frac{\sum_{i=1}^{n} (k_i - \bar{k})^2}{n-1}} \quad \text{[Eq. 6.3a]}$$

Coefficient of variation

$$CV = \frac{\sigma_k}{\bar{k}} \quad \text{[Eq. 6.4]}$$

Portfolio return

$$k_p = \sum_{j=1}^{n} w_j \times k_j \quad \text{[Eq. 6.5]}$$

Total security risk = nondiversifiable risk + diversifiable risk [Eq. 6.6]

Portfolio beta

$$b_p = \sum_{j=1}^{n} w_j \times b_j \quad \text{[Eq. 6.7]}$$

Capital asset pricing model (CAPM)

$$k_j = R_F + [b_j \times (k_m - R_F)] \quad \text{[Eq. 6.8]}$$

LG 4 Understand diversification in terms of correlation, its relationship to the risk and return of a portfolio, and the impact of international assets on a portfolio. Diversification involves combining assets with low (less positive and more negative) correlation to reduce the risk of the portfolio. While the return on a two-asset portfolio will lie between the returns of the two assets held in isolation, the range of risk depends on the correlation between the two assets. If they are perfectly positively correlated, the portfolio's risk will be between the individual asset's risks. If uncorrelated, the portfolio's risk will be between the risk of the most risky asset and an amount less than the risk of the least risky asset but greater than zero. If negatively correlated, the portfolio's risk will be between the risk of the most risky asset and zero. International diversification, which involves including foreign assets in a portfolio of domestic assets, can be used to further reduce a portfolio's risk.

LG 5 Review the two components of a security's risk and the derivation and role of beta in measuring the relevant risk of both an individual security and a portfolio. The total risk of a security consists of nondiversifiable and diversifiable risk. Only nondiversifiable risk is relevant, since diversifiable risk can be easily eliminated through diversification. Nondiversifiable risk can be measured by the beta coefficient, which reflects the relationship between an asset's return and the market return. Beta is derived by using statistical techniques to find the slope of the "characteristic line" that best explains the historic relationship between the asset's return and the market return. The beta of a portfolio is a weighted average of the betas of the individual assets that it includes.

LG 6 Explain the capital asset pricing model (CAPM), its relationship to the security market line (SML), and shifts in the SML caused by changes in inflationary expectations and risk aversion. The capital asset pricing model (CAPM) uses beta to relate an asset's risk relative to the market to the asset's required return. The variable definitions and equation for CAPM are given in Table 6.10. The graphic depiction of CAPM is the security market line (SML), which shifts over time in response to changing inflationary expectations and/or changes in investor risk aversion. Changes in inflationary expectations result in parallel shifts in the SML in direct response to the magnitude and direction of change. Increasing risk aversion results in a steepening in the slope of the SML, while decreasing risk aversion reduces the slope of the SML.

Self-test problems (Solutions in Appendix E)

ST 6-1 LG 3,4 Portfolio analysis You have been asked for your advice in selecting a portfolio of assets and have been supplied with the following data:

	Expected return (%)		
Year	**Asset A**	**Asset B**	**Asset C**
1995	12	16	12
1996	14	14	14
1997	16	12	16

No probabilities have been supplied. You have been told that you can create two portfolios—one consisting of assets A and B and the other consisting of assets A and C—by investing equal proportions (i.e., 50 percent) in each of the two component assets.

a. What is the expected return for each asset over the three-year period?
b. What is the standard deviation for each asset's return?
c. What is the expected return for each of the two portfolios?
d. How would you characterize the correlations of returns of the two assets making up each of the two portfolios identified in **c**?
e. What is the standard deviation for each portfolio?
f. Which portfolio do you recommend? Why?

ST 6-2 LG 5,6 Beta and CAPM Currently under consideration is a project with a beta, b, of 1.50. At this time the risk-free rate of return, R_F, is 7 percent, and the return on the market portfolio of assets, k_m, is 10 percent. The project is actually *expected* to earn an annual rate of return of 11 percent.

a. If the return on the market portfolio were to increase by 10 percent, what would be expected to happen to the project's *required return?* What if the market return were to decline by 10 percent?

b. Use the capital asset pricing model (CAPM) to find the *required return* on this investment.

c. On the basis of your calculation in **b**, would you recommend this investment? Why or why not?

d. Assume that as a result of investors becoming less risk-averse, the market return drops by 1 percent to 9 percent. What impact would this change have on your responses in **b** and **c**?

Problems

6-1 LG 1 Rate of return Douglas Keel, a financial analyst for Orange Industries, wishes to estimate the rate of return for two similar-risk investments—X and Y. Keel's research indicates that the immediate past returns will act as reasonable estimates of future return. A year earlier, investment X had a market value of $20,000 and investment Y, of $55,000. During the year, investment X generated cash flow of $1,500, and investment Y generated cash flow of $6,800. The current market values of investments X and Y are $21,000 and $55,000, respectively.

a. Calculate the expected rate of return on investments X and Y using the most recent year's data.

b. Assuming that the two investments are equally risky, which one should Keel recommend? Why?

6-2 LG 1 Return calculations For each of the following investments, calculate the rate of return earned over the unspecified time period.

Investment	Beginning-of-period value ($)	End-of-period value ($)	Cash flow during period ($)
A	800	1,100	−100
B	120,000	118,000	15,000
C	45,000	48,000	7,000
D	600	500	80
E	12,500	12,400	1,500

6-3 LG 1 Risk preferences Sharon Smith, the financial manager for Barnett Corporation, wishes to evaluate three prospective investments—X, Y, and Z. Currently, the firm earns 12 percent on its investments, which have a risk index of 6 percent. The three investments under consideration are profiled below in terms of expected return and expected risk.

Investment	Expected return (%)	Expected risk index (%)
X	14	7
Y	12	8
Z	10	9

a. If Sharon Smith were *risk-indifferent,* which investments would she select? Explain why.

b. If Sharon Smith were *risk-averse,* which investments would she select? Explain why.

c. If Sharon Smith were a *risk seeker,* which investments would she select? Explain why.
d. Given the traditional risk-preference behavior exhibited by financial managers, which investment would be preferred? Why?

6-4 LG 2 Risk analysis Solar Designs is considering an investment in an expanded product line. Two possible types of expansion are being considered. After investigating the possible outcomes, the company made the following estimates:

	Expansion A	Expansion B
Initial investment	$12,000	$12,000
Annual rate of return		
Pessimistic	16%	10%
Most likely	20	20
Optimistic	24	30

a. Determine the range of the rates of return for each of the two projects.
b. Which project is less risky? Why?
c. If you were making the investment decision, which one would you choose? Why? What does this imply about your feelings toward risk?
d. Assume that the most likely outcome of expansion B is 21 percent per year and all other facts remain the same. Does this change your answer to part **c**? Why?

6-5 LG 2 Risk and probability Micro-Pub, Inc., is considering the purchase of one of two microfilm cameras—R or S. Both should provide benefits over a ten-year period, and each requires an initial investment of $4,000. Management has constructed the following table of estimates of probabilities and rates of return for pessimistic, most likely, and optimistic results:

	Camera R		Camera S	
	Amount	Probability	Amount	Probability
Initial investment	$4,000	1.00	$4,000	1.00
Annual rate of return				
Pessimistic	20%	.25	15%	.20
Most likely	25	.50	25	.55
Optimistic	30	.25	35	.25

a. Determine the range for the rate of return for each of the two cameras.
b. Determine the expected rate of return for each camera.
c. Which camera is more risky? Why?

6-6 LG 2 Bar charts and risk Swan's Sportswear is considering bringing out a line of designer jeans. Currently, it is negotiating with two different well-known designers. Because of the highly competitive nature of the industry, the two designs have been given code names. After market research, the firm has established the following expectations about the annual rates of return:

		Annual rate of return	
Market acceptance	Probability	Line J	Line K
Very poor	.05	.0075	.010
Poor	.15	.0125	.025
Average	.60	.0850	.080
Good	.15	.1475	.135
Excellent	.05	.1625	.150

Use the table to:

a. Construct a bar chart for each line's annual rate of return.
b. Calculate the expected value of return for each line.
c. Evaluate the relative riskiness for each jean line's rate of return using the bar charts.

6-7 LG 2 Coefficient of variation Metal Manufacturing has isolated four alternatives for meeting its need for increased production capacity. The data gathered relative to each of these alternatives is summarized in the following table.

Alternative	Expected return (%)	Standard deviation of return (%)
A	20	7.0
B	22	9.5
C	19	6.0
D	16	5.5

a. Calculate the coefficient of variation for each alternative.
b. If the firm wishes to minimize risk, which alternative would you recommend? Why?

6-8 LG 2 Assessing return and risk Swift Manufacturing must choose between two asset purchases. The annual rate of return and the related probabilities given in the following table summarize the firm's analysis to this point.

Project 257		Project 432	
Rate of return	Probability	Rate of return	Probability
−10%	.01	10%	.05
10	.04	15	.10
20	.05	20	.10
30	.10	25	.15
40	.15	30	.20
45	.30	35	.15
50	.15	40	.10
60	.10	45	.10
70	.05	50	.05
80	.04		
100	.01		

a. For each project, compute:
(1) The range of possible rates of return.
(2) The expected value of return.
(3) The standard deviation of the returns.
(4) The coefficient of variation.
b. Construct a bar chart of each distribution of rates of return.
c. Which project would you consider the less risky? Why?

6-9 LG 2 Integrative—Expected return, standard deviation, and coefficient of variation Three assets—F, G, and H—are currently being considered by Perth Industries. The following probability distributions of expected returns for these assets have been developed.

	Asset F		Asset G		Asset H	
i	Pr_i	Return, k_i	Pr_i	Return, k_i	Pr_i	Return, k_i
1	.10	40%	.40	35%	.10	40%
2	.20	10	.30	10	.20	20
3	.40	0	.30	−20	.40	10
4	.20	−5			.20	0
5	.10	−10			.10	−20

a. Calculate the expected value of return, $\bar{k}$, for each of the three assets. Which provides the largest expected return?

b. Calculate the standard deviation, σ_k, for each of the three assets' returns. Which appears to have the greatest risk?

c. Calculate the coefficient of variation, CV, for each of the three assets. Which appears to have the largest *relative* risk?

6-10 LG 2 Normal probability distribution Assuming that the rates of return associated with a given asset investment are normally distributed and that the expected return, $\bar{k}$, is 18.9 percent and the coefficient of variation, CV, is .75, answer the following questions.

a. Find the standard deviation of returns, σ_k.

b. Calculate the range of expected return outcomes associated with the following probabilities of occurrence.

(1) 68 percent
(2) 95 percent
(3) 99 percent

c. Draw the probability distribution associated with your findings in **a** and **b**.

6-11 LG 3 Portfolio return and standard deviation Jamie Wong is considering building a portfolio containing two assets, L and M. Asset L will represent 40 percent of the dollar value of the portfolio, and asset M will account for the other 60 percent. The expected returns over the next six years, 1995–2000, for each of these assets, is summarized in the following table.

	Expected return (%)	
Year	Asset L	Asset M
1995	14	20
1996	14	18
1997	16	16
1998	17	14
1999	17	12
2000	19	10

a. Calculate the expected portfolio return, k_p, for *each* of the six years.

b. Calculate the expected value of portfolio returns, $\bar{k}_p$, over the six-year period.

c. Calculate the standard deviation of expected portfolio returns, σ_{k_p}, over the six-year period.

d. How would you characterize the correlation of returns of the two assets L and M?

e. Discuss any benefits of diversification achieved through creation of the portfolio.

6-12 LG 3 Portfolio analysis You have been given the following return data on three assets—F, G, and H—over the period 1995–1998.

Year	Expected return (%) Asset F	Asset G	Asset H
1995	16	17	14
1996	17	16	15
1997	18	15	16
1998	19	14	17

Using these assets, you have isolated three investment alternatives:

Alternative	Investment
1	100% of asset F
2	50% of asset F and 50% of asset G
3	50% of asset F and 50% of asset H

a. Calculate the expected return over the four-year period for each of the three alternatives.

b. Calculate the standard deviation of returns over the four-year period for each of the three alternatives.

c. Use your findings in **a** and **b** to calculate the coefficient of variation for each of the three alternatives.

d. On the basis of your findings above, which of the three investment alternatives would you recommend? Why?

6-13 LG 4 Correlation, risk, and return Matt Peters wishes to evaluate the risk and return behaviors associated with various combinations of assets V and W under three assumed degrees of correlation—perfect positive, uncorrelated, and perfect negative. The following expected return and risk values were calculated for each of the assets.

Asset	Expected return, $\bar{k}$ (%)	Risk (standard deviation), σ_k (%)
V	8	5
W	13	10

a. If the returns of assets V and W are *perfectly positively correlated* (correlation coefficient = +1), describe the *range* of (1) expected return and (2) risk associated with all possible portfolio combinations.

b. If the returns of assets V and W are *uncorrelated* (correlation coefficient = 0), describe the *approximate range* of (1) expected return and (2) risk associated with all possible portfolio combinations.

c. If the returns of assets V and W are *perfectly negatively correlated* (correlation coefficient = −1), describe the *range* of (1) expected return and (2) risk associated with all possible portfolio combinations.

6-14 LG 5 Total, nondiversifiable, and diversifiable risk David Talbot randomly selected securities from all those listed on the New York Stock Exchange for his portfolio. He began with one security and added securities one by one until a total of 20 securities were held in the portfolio. After each security was added, David calculated the portfolio standard deviation, σ_{k_p}. The calculated values are given below:

Number of securities	Portfolio risk, σ_{k_p} (%)	Number of securities	Portfolio risk, σ_{k_p} (%)
1	14.50	11	7.00
2	13.30	12	6.80
3	12.20	13	6.70
4	11.20	14	6.65
5	10.30	15	6.60
6	9.50	16	6.56
7	8.80	17	6.52
8	8.20	18	6.50
9	7.70	19	6.48
10	7.30	20	6.47

a. On a set number of securities in portfolio (x-axis)–portfolio risk (y-axis) axes, plot the portfolio risk data given in the preceding table.

b. Divide the total portfolio risk in the graph into its *nondiversifiable* and *diversifiable* risk components and label each of these on the graph.

c. Describe which of the two risk components is the *relevant risk,* and explain why it is relevant. How much of this risk exists in David Talbot's portfolio?

6-15 LG 5 Graphic derivation of beta A firm wishes to graphically estimate the betas for two assets—A and B. It has gathered the following return data for the market portfolio and both assets over the last ten years, 1985–1994.

	Actual return (%)		
Year	Market portfolio	Asset A	Asset B
1985	6	11	16
1986	2	8	11
1987	−13	−4	−10
1988	−4	3	3
1989	−8	0	−3
1990	16	19	30
1991	10	14	22
1992	15	18	29
1993	8	12	19
1994	13	17	26

a. On a set of market return (x-axis)–asset return (y-axis) axes, use the data given to draw the characteristic line for asset A and for asset B (on the same set of axes).

b. Use the characteristic lines from **a** to estimate the betas for assets A and B.

c. Use the betas found in **b** to comment on the relative risks of assets A and B.

6-16 LG 5 **Interpreting beta** A firm wishes to assess the impact of changes in the market return on an asset that has a beta of 1.20.

a. If the market return increased by 15 percent, what impact would this change be expected to have on the asset's return?

b. If the market return decreased by 8 percent, what impact would this change be expected to have on the asset's return?

c. If the market return did not change, what impact, if any, would be expected on the asset's return?

d. Would this asset be considered more or less risky than the market? Explain.

6-17 LG 5 **Betas** Answer the questions below for the following assets A–D.

Asset	Beta
A	.50
B	1.60
C	−.20
D	.90

a. What impact would a *10 percent increase* in the market return be expected to have on each asset's return?

b. What impact would a *10 percent decrease* in the market return be expected to have on each asset's return?

c. If you were certain that the market return would *increase* in the near future, which asset would you prefer? Why?

d. If you were certain that the market return would *decrease* in the near future, which asset would you prefer? Why?

6-18 LG 5 **Betas and risk rankings** Stock A has a beta of .80, stock B has a beta of 1.40, and stock C has a beta of −.30.

a. Rank these stocks from the most risky to the least risky.

b. If the return on the market portfolio increases by 12 percent, what change in the return for each of the stocks would you expect?

c. If the return on the market portfolio declines by 5 percent, what change in the return for each of the stocks would you expect?

d. If you felt that the stock market was just ready to experience a significant decline, which stock would you likely add to your portfolio? Why?

e. If you anticipated a major stock market rally, which stock would you add to your portfolio? Why?

6-19 LG 5 **Portfolio betas** Rose Berry is attempting to evaluate two possible portfolios—both consisting of the same five assets but held in different proportions. She is particularly interested in using beta to compare the risk of the portfolios and in this regard has gathered the following data.

		Portfolio weights (%)	
Asset	Asset beta	Portfolio A	Portfolio B
1	1.30	10	30
2	.70	30	10
3	1.25	10	20
4	1.10	10	20
5	.90	40	20
	Total	100	100

a. Calculate the betas for portfolios A and B.
b. Compare the risk of each portfolio to the market as well as to each other. Which portfolio is more risky?

6-20 LG 6 Capital asset pricing model—CAPM For each of the following cases, use the capital asset pricing model to find the required return.

Case	Risk-free rate, R_F (%)	Market return, k_m (%)	Beta, b
A	5	8	1.30
B	8	13	.90
C	9	12	−.20
D	10	15	1.00
E	6	10	.60

6-21 LG 6 Manipulating CAPM Use the basic equation for the capital asset pricing model (CAPM) to work each of the following:

a. Find the *required return* for an asset with a beta of .90 when the risk-free rate and market return are 8 percent and 12 percent, respectively.
b. Find the *risk-free rate* for a firm with a required return of 15 percent and a beta of 1.25 when the market return is 14 percent.
c. Find the *market return* for an asset with a required return of 16 percent and a beta of 1.10 when the risk-free rate is 9 percent.
d. Find the *beta* for an asset with a required return of 15 percent when the risk-free rate and market return are 10 percent and 12.5 percent, respectively.

6-22 LG 6 Security market line, SML Assume that the risk-free rate, R_F, is currently 9 percent and that the market return, k_m, is currently 13 percent.

a. Draw the security market line (SML) on a set of nondiversifiable risk (x-axis)–required return (y-axis) axes.
b. Calculate and label on the axes in **a** the *market risk premium.*
c. Given the data above, calculate the required return on asset A having a beta of .80 and asset B having a beta of 1.30.
d. Draw in the betas and required returns from **c** for assets A and B on the axes in **a**. Label the *risk premium* associated with each of these assets, and discuss them.

6-23 LG 6 Shifts in the security market line Assume that the risk-free rate, R_F, is currently 8 percent, the market return, k_m, is 12 percent, and asset A has a beta, b_A, of 1.10.

a. Draw the security market line (SML) on a set of nondiversifiable risk (x-axis)–required return (y-axis) axes.
b. Use the CAPM to calculate the required return, k_A, on asset A, and depict asset A's beta and required return on the SML drawn in **a**.
c. Assume that as a result of recent economic events, inflationary expectations have declined by 2 percent, lowering R_F and k_m to 6 and 10 percent, respectively. Draw the new SML on the axes in **a**, and calculate and show the new required return for asset A.
d. Assume that as a result of recent events, investors have become more risk-averse, causing the market return to rise by 1 percent to 13 percent. Ignoring the shift in part **c**, draw the new SML on the same set of axes as used above, and calculate and show the new required return for asset A.
e. From the changes above, what conclusions can be drawn about the impact of (1) decreased inflationary expectations and (2) increased risk aversion on the required returns of risky assets?

6-24 LG 1,2,5,6 **Integrative—Risk, return, and CAPM** Wolff Enterprises must consider several investment projects, A through E, using the capital asset pricing model (CAPM) and its graphic representation, the security market line (SML). Use the table below to answer the questions that follow it.

Item	Rate of return (%)	Beta (*b*) value
Risk-free asset	9	0
Market portfolio	14	1.00
Project A	—	1.50
Project B	—	.75
Project C	—	2.00
Project D	—	0
Project E	—	−.50

a. Calculate the required return and risk premium for each project, given its level of nondiversifiable risk.

b. Use your findings in **a** to draw the security market line (required return relative to nondiversifiable risk).

c. Discuss the relative nondiversifiable risk of projects A through E.

d. Assume that recent economic events have caused investors to become less risk-averse, causing the market return to decline by 2 percent to 12 percent. Calculate the new required returns for assets A through E, and draw the new security market line on the same set of axes as used in **b**.

e. Compare your findings in **a** and **b** with those in **d**. What conclusion can you draw about the impact of a decline in investor risk aversion on the required returns of risky assets?

Chapter 6 Case Analyzing risk and return on Chargers Products' investments

Junior Seau, a financial analyst for Chargers Products, a manufacturer of stadium benches, must evaluate the risk and return of two assets—X and Y. The firm is considering adding these assets to its diversified asset portfolio. To assess the return and risk of each asset, Junior gathered data on the annual cash flow and beginning- and end-of-year values of each asset over the immediately preceding ten years, 1985–1994. These data are summarized in the following table. Junior's investigation suggests that both of the assets will, on average, tend to perform in the future just as they have during the past 10 years. He therefore believes that the expected annual return can be estimated by finding the average annual return for each asset over the past 10 years.

Junior believes that each asset's risk can be assessed in two ways: in isolation and as part of the firm's diversified portfolio of assets. The risk of the assets in isolation can be found by using the standard deviation and coefficient of variation of returns over the past ten years. The capital asset pricing model (CAPM) can be used to assess the asset's risk as part of the firm's portfolio of assets. Applying some sophisticated quantitative techniques, Junior estimated betas for assets X and Y of 1.60 and 1.10, respectively. In addition, he found that the risk-free rate is currently 7 percent and the market return is 10 percent.

RETURN DATA FOR ASSETS X AND Y, 1985–1994

	Asset X			Asset Y		
		Value			Value	
Year	Cash flow	Beginning	Ending	Cash flow	Beginning	Ending
1985	$1,000	$20,000	$22,000	$1,500	$20,000	$20,000
1986	1,500	22,000	21,000	1,600	20,000	20,000
1987	1,400	21,000	24,000	1,700	20,000	21,000
1988	1,700	24,000	22,000	1,800	21,000	21,000
1989	1,900	22,000	23,000	1,900	21,000	22,000
1990	1,600	23,000	26,000	2,000	22,000	23,000
1991	1,700	26,000	25,000	2,100	23,000	23,000
1992	2,000	25,000	24,000	2,200	23,000	24,000
1993	2,100	24,000	27,000	2,300	24,000	25,000
1994	2,200	27,000	30,000	2,400	25,000	25,000

Required

a. Calculate the annual rate of return for each asset in *each* of the 10 preceding years, and use those values to find the average annual return for each asset over the 10-year period.

b. Use the returns calculated in **a** to find (1) the standard deviation and (2) the coefficient of variation of the returns for each asset over the 10-year period 1985–1994.

c. Use your findings in **a** and **b** to evaluate and discuss the return and risk associated with each asset. Which asset appears to be preferable? Explain.

d. Use the CAPM to find the required return for each asset. Compare this value with the average annual returns calculated in **a**.

e. Compare and contrast your findings in **c** and **d**. What recommendations would you give Junior with regard to investing in either of the two assets? Explain to Junior why he is better off using beta rather than the standard deviation and coefficient of variation to assess the risk of each asset.

f. Rework **d** and **e** under each of the following circumstances:

(1) A rise of 1 percent in inflationary expectations causes the risk-free rate to rise to 8 percent and the market return to rise to 11 percent.

(2) As a result of favorable political events, investors suddenly become less risk-averse, causing the market return to drop by 1 percent to 9 percent.

chapter 7

Valuation

LEARNING GOALS

Describe the key inputs—cash flows (returns), timing, and required return (risk)—and basic model used in the valuation process.

Apply the basic valuation model to bonds and evaluate the relationships between both required return and time to maturity and bond values.

Explain yield to maturity (YTM), its calculation, and the procedure used to value bonds that pay interest semiannually.

Understand the concept of market efficiency and basic common-stock valuation under each of three cases: zero growth, constant growth, and variable growth.

Discuss three other approaches—book value, liquidation value, and price/earnings (P/E) multiples—that are used to estimate common stock values.

Review the relationship between the impact of financial decisions on both expected return and risk and their combined effect on the firm's value.

At Merrill Lynch, one of Wall Street's largest stock brokerage and investment banking firms, valuation is a fundamental concept used in many different areas. As investment bankers, clients may ask us to perform valuation studies on privately held companies to establish a sale price, set the price per share prior to the company's first public stock offering, or value publicly traded companies as part of our investment advisory services.

Financial managers—in fact, *all* managers—should understand the underlying importance of valuation. I have seen an increasing appreciation by corporate managers of their *stewardship* role. They recognize that their decisions ultimately affect shareholder wealth. To maximize shareholder wealth, you must understand what creates it. First, you must use valuation models like those in this chapter to measure the current market value of the company. You must also understand the dynamics of market valuation, because value changes frequently. Follow a company's bond and stock prices for a month or two, and you'll see how much they can fluctuate.

While most decisions affect shareholder value, financial decisions are especially critical in creating value. If I am a corporate treasurer with $25 million to invest, should I purchase more inventory to capture additional sales or new manufacturing equipment to improve operating efficency? Choosing among the options means knowing which best maximizes the firm's value.

A major concern for any company is the cost to raise short- or long-term debt or issue common stock. Financial, operational, or marketing decisions may affect the market perception of the company's prospects and therefore influence its borrowing costs. For public companies, bond quality is determined by the rating given by an independent rating agency; the higher the rating, the lower the cost of bonds.

To maximize shareholder wealth, you must understand what *creates* it.

Merrill Lynch must continually consider the impact of its operating and financing decisions on borrowing costs and bond ratings. The two are closely intertwined; as a financial services company, we borrow funds for many reasons, including the financing of our large inventory of stocks and bonds, as well as making loans to customers with margin brokerage accounts. Interest costs are therefore a very major factor in our profitability: a small rate differential can substantially affect our bottom line.

In this chapter you will learn about different valuation models that may seem very straightforward, but using them is really more of an art than a science. The key to using *any* model is developing good inputs. Effective valuation depends on cash flow estimates, and this can be the most difficult part—it's a moving target. There are so many variables, and every input is a function of several others. With some industries—for example, chemicals, paper, and building products industries—the availability of good information makes it easier to forecast cash flows. The uncertainty is in the economic outlook. At the other extreme, biotechnology companies are difficult to value because many don't have products or revenues yet. We overcome these difficulties by using probabilities and applying scenario analysis to a range of potential outcomes. You can't focus on a single forecast; obviously, the probability of achieving it is pretty low.

It's really a matter of experience, and our analysts must know the companies and industries well, then make judgments—and it's an imperfect process. Whether you become an analyst at an investment banking firm, working with many different companies, or choose the managerial finance career path and focus on one company, you should understand the models and how to use them, but you also need excellent analytical skills and good business judgment so you can analyze the assumptions.

Martin S. Fridson, Managing Director, High Yield Research and Product Development, received a B.A. from Harvard University and M.B.A from Harvard Business School. Before joining Merrill Lynch in 1989, he was a Principal at Morgan Stanley & Co., Inc. (1984–1989) and a Vice President at Salomon Brothers Inc. (1981–1984).

Valuation fundamentals

The value of any asset is the present value of all its future cash flows. How are the important inputs to valuation—risk and return—embodied in this basic definition of value? Spend a few moments answering this question before reading ahead.

valuation
The process that links risk and return to determine the worth of an asset.

As was noted in Chapter 6, all major financial decisions must be viewed in terms of expected risk, expected return, and their combined impact on share price. **Valuation** is the process that links risk and return to determine the worth of an asset. It is a relatively simple process that can be applied to expected streams of benefits from bonds, stocks, income properties, oil wells, and so on to determine their worth at a given point in time. To do this, the manager uses the time-value-of-money techniques presented in Chapter 5 and the concepts of risk and return developed in Chapter 6.

Key inputs

The key inputs to the valuation process include cash flows (returns), timing, and the required return (risk). Each is described briefly below.

CASH FLOWS (RETURNS)

The value of any asset depends on the cash flow(s) it is expected to provide over the ownership period. To have value, an asset does not have to provide an annual cash flow; it can provide an intermittent cash flow or even a single cash flow over the period.

EXAMPLE

Celia Sargent, the financial analyst for Groton Corporation, a diversified holding company, wishes to estimate the value of three of its assets—common stock in Michaels Enterprises, an interest in an oil well, and an original painting by a well-known artist. Her cash flow estimates for each were:

Stock in Michaels Enterprises Expect to receive cash dividends of $300 per year indefinitely.

Oil well Expect to receive cash flow of $2,000 at the end of one year, $4,000 at the end of two years, and $10,000 at the end of four years, when the well is to be sold.

Original painting Expect to be able to sell the painting in five years for $85,000.

Having developed these cash flow estimates, Celia has taken the first step toward placing a value on each of these assets. ■

TIMING

In addition to making cash flow estimates, we must know the timing of the cash flows.[1] It is customary to specify the timing along with the amounts of cash flow. For exam-

[1]Although cash flows can occur at any time during a year, for computational convenience as well as custom, we will assume that they occur at the *end* of the year unless otherwise noted.

ple, the cash flows of $2,000, $4,000, and $10,000 for the oil well in the example were expected to occur at the end of years 1, 2, and 4, respectively. In combination the cash flow and its timing fully define the return expected from the asset.

REQUIRED RETURN (RISK)

Risk, as was noted in Chapter 6, describes the chance that an expected outcome will not be realized. The level of risk associated with a given cash flow can significantly affect its value. In general, the greater the risk of (or the less certain) a cash flow, the lower its value. In terms of present value (see Chapter 5), greater risk can be incorporated into an analysis by using a higher required return or discount rate. Recall that in the capital asset pricing model (CAPM) presented in Chapter 6 (see Equation 6.8), the greater the risk as measured by beta, b, the higher the required return, k. In the valuation process, too, the required return is used to incorporate risk into the analysis—the higher the risk, the greater the required return (discount rate), and the lower the risk, the less the required return.

EXAMPLE

Let's return to Celia Sargent's task of placing a value on Groton Corporation's original painting, which is expected to provide a single cash flow of $85,000 from its sale at the end of five years, and consider two scenarios.

Scenario 1—Certainty A major art gallery has contracted to buy the painting for $85,000 at the end of five years. Because this is considered a certain situation, Celia views this asset as "money in the bank" and would use the prevailing risk-free rate, R_F, of 9 percent as the required return (discount rate) when calculating the value of the painting.

Scenario 2—High Risk The value of original paintings by this artist has fluctuated widely over the past 10 years, and although Celia expects to be able to get $85,000 for the painting, she realizes that its sale price in five years could range between $30,000 and $140,000. Due to the high uncertainty surrounding the painting's value, Celia believes that a 15 percent required return (discount rate) is appropriate. ■

The preceding example and the associated estimates of the appropriate required return illustrate the role this rate plays in capturing risk. The often subjective nature of such estimates is also clear.[2]

The basic valuation model

Simply stated, the value of any asset is *the present value of all future cash flows it is expected to provide over the relevant time period.* The time period can be as short as one year or as long as infinity. The value of an asset is therefore determined by discounting the expected cash flows back to their present value, using the required return commensurate with the asset's risk as the appropriate discount rate. Utilizing the

[2]Straightforward techniques for estimating required returns do not exist. Actual practice tends to rely on subjective estimates based on the conceptual risk-return framework of the capital asset pricing model. Subsequent discussions describe some of these "practical" approaches.

present-value techniques presented in Chapter 5, we can express the value of any asset at time zero, V_0, as

$$V_0 = \frac{CF_1}{(1+k)^1} + \frac{CF_2}{(1+k)^2} + \cdots + \frac{CF_n}{(1+k)^n} \tag{7.1}$$

where

V_0 = value of the asset at time zero
CF_t = cash flow expected at the end of year t
k = appropriate required return (discount rate)
n = relevant time period

Using present-value interest factor notation, $PVIF_{k,n}$ from Chapter 5, Equation 7.1 can be rewritten as

$$V_0 = [CF_1 \times (PVIF_{k,1})] + [CF_2 \times (PVIF_{k,2})] + \cdots + [CF_n \times (PVIF_{k,n})] \tag{7.2}$$

Substituting the expected cash flows, CF_t, over the relevant time period, n, and the appropriate required return, k, into Equation 7.2, we can determine the value of any asset.

EXAMPLE

Celia Sargent, using appropriate required returns and Equation 7.2, calculated the value of each asset (using present-value interest factors from Table A-3) as shown in Table 7.1. The Michaels Enterprises stock has a value of \$2,500, the oil well's value is \$9,262, and the original painting has a value of \$42,245. Had she instead used a calculator, the values of the oil well and original painting would have been \$9,266.98 and \$42,260.03, respectively. Note that regardless of the pattern of the expected cash flow from an asset, the basic valuation equation can be used to determine its value. ■

CONCEPTS IN REVIEW

7-1 Define *valuation,* and explain why it is important for the financial manager to understand the valuation process.

7-2 Briefly describe the three key inputs—cash flows, timing, and the required return—to the valuation process. Does the valuation process apply only to assets providing an annual cash flow? Explain.

7-3 Define and specify the general equation for the value of any asset, V_0, in terms of its expected cash flow, CF_t, in each year t, and the appropriate required return (discount rate), k.

Bond valuation

Bonds provide their holders with fixed, contractual cash flows at prespecified points in time. Given the highly predictable nature of their cash flows, why do the market values of bonds often differ from their stated maturity values and frequently change over time? Before reading on, take a few moments to answer this question.

TABLE 7.1

VALUATION OF GROTON CORPORATION'S ASSETS BY CELIA SARGENT

Asset	Cash flow, *CF*	Appropriate required return (%)	Valuation
Michaels Enterprises stock[a]	\$300/year indefinitely	12	$V_0 = \$300 \times (PVIFA_{12\%,\infty})$ $= \frac{\$300}{.12} = \underline{\underline{\$2{,}500}}$
Oil well[b]	Year (t) / CF_t: 1 — \$2,000; 2 — 4,000; 3 — 0; 4 — 10,000	20	$V_0 = [\$2{,}000 \times (PVIF_{20\%,1})]$ $+ [\$4{,}000 \times (PVIF_{20\%,2})]$ $+ [\$0 \times (PVIF_{20\%,3})]$ $+ [\$10{,}000 \times (PVIF_{20\%,4})]$ $= [\$2{,}000 \times (.833)]$ $+ [\$4{,}000 \times (.694)]$ $+ [\$0 \times (.579)]$ $+ [\$10{,}000 \times (.482)]$ $= \$1{,}666 + \$2{,}776$ $+ \$0 + \$4{,}820$ $= \underline{\underline{\$9{,}262}}$
Original painting[c]	\$85,000 at end of year 5	15	$V_0 = \$85{,}000 \times (PVIF_{15\%,5})$ $= \$85{,}000 \times (.497)$ $= \underline{\underline{\$42{,}245}}$

[a]This is a perpetuity (infinite-lived annuity), and therefore Equation 5.28 is applied.

[b]This is a mixed stream of cash flows and therefore requires a number of *PVIF*s as noted.

[c]This is a lump-sum cash flow and therefore requires a single *PVIF*.

THE BASIC VALUATION EQUATION CAN BE CUSTOMIZED FOR USE IN VALUING SPECIFIED securities—bonds, preferred stock, and common stock. Bonds and preferred stock are similar, since they have stated contractual interest and dividend cash flows. The dividends on common stock, on the other hand, are not known in advance. Bond valuation is described in this section, and common stock valuation is discussed in the following section.[3]

Bond fundamentals

Bonds, which are discussed in detail in Chapter 12, are long-term debt instruments used by business and government to raise large sums of money, typically from

[3]Because the procedures are identical, the valuation of preferred stock is demonstrated as a special case in the discussion of using the *zero growth model* to value common stock.

a diverse group of lenders. As was noted in Chapter 2, most corporate bonds pay interest *semiannually* (every six months) at a stated *coupon interest rate,* have an initial *maturity* of 10 to 30 years, and have a *par,* or *face, value* of $1,000 that must be repaid at maturity.[4] An example will illustrate the point.

EXAMPLE

The Mills Company, a large defense contractor, on January 1, 1995, issued a 10 percent coupon interest rate, 10-year bond with a $1,000 par value that pays interest semiannually. Investors who buy this bond receive the contractual right to (1) $100 annual interest (10 percent coupon interest rate × $1,000 par value) distributed as $50 (½ × $100) at the end of each six months and (2) the $1,000 par value at the end of the tenth year. ■

Using data presented for Mills Company's new issue, we look now at basic bond valuation and other issues.

Basic bond valuation

The value of a bond is the present value of the contractual payments its issuer is obligated to make from the current time until it matures. The appropriate discount rate would be the required return, k_d, which depends on prevailing interest rates and risk. The basic equation for the value, B_0, of a bond that pays *annual* interest of I dollars,[5] that has n years to maturity, that has an M dollar par value, and for which the required return is k_d is given by Equation 7.3:

$$B_0 = I \times \left[\sum_{t=1}^{n} \frac{1}{(1+k_d)^t}\right] + M \times \left[\frac{1}{(1+k_d)^n}\right] \tag{7.3}$$

$$= I \times (PVIFA_{k_d,n}) + M \times (PVIF_{k_d,n}) \tag{7.3a}$$

Equation 7.3a along with the appropriate financial tables (A-3 and A-4) or a hand-held business/financial calculator can be used to calculate bond value.

EXAMPLE

Using the Mills Company data for the January 1, 1995, new issue and *assuming that interest is paid annually* and that the required return is equal to the bond's coupon interest rate, I = $100, k_d = 10 percent, M = $1,000, and n = 10 years.

Table Use Substituting the values noted above into Equation 7.3a yields:

$$B_0 = \$100 \times (PVIFA_{10\%,10\text{yrs}}) + \$1{,}000 \times (PVIF_{10\%,10\text{yrs}})$$
$$= \$100 \times (6.145) + \$1{,}000 \times (.386)$$
$$= \$614.50 + \$386.00 = \underline{\underline{\$1{,}000.50}}$$

The bond therefore has a value of approximately $1,000.[6]

[4]Bonds often have features that allow them to be retired by the issuer prior to maturity; these *call* and *conversion* features are presented in Chapters 12 and 14. For the purpose of the current discussion, these features are ignored.

[5]The payment of annual rather than semiannual bond interest is assumed throughout the following discussion. This assumption simplifies the calculations involved while maintaining the conceptual accuracy of the valuation procedures presented.

[6]Note that a slight rounding error ($.50) results here due to the use of the table factors, which are rounded to the nearest thousandth.

Calculator Use Using the calculator, first punch in 10, and depress **N**; then punch in the required return, k_d, of 10, and depress **%i**; next punch in the annual interest, *I*, of \$100, and depress **PMT**; then punch in the maturity value, *M*, of \$1,000, and depress **FV**; and to calculate the bond value, depress **CPT** followed by **PV**. The bond value of exactly \$1,000 should appear on the calculator display.

Inputs:	10	10	100	1000		
Functions:	N	%i	PMT	FV	CPT	PV
Outputs:						*1000*

Note that *the bond value calculated in the example above is equal to its par value; this will always be the case when the required return is equal to the coupon interest rate.*[7]

Time-Line Use The computations involved in finding the bond value are depicted graphically on the time line shown below.

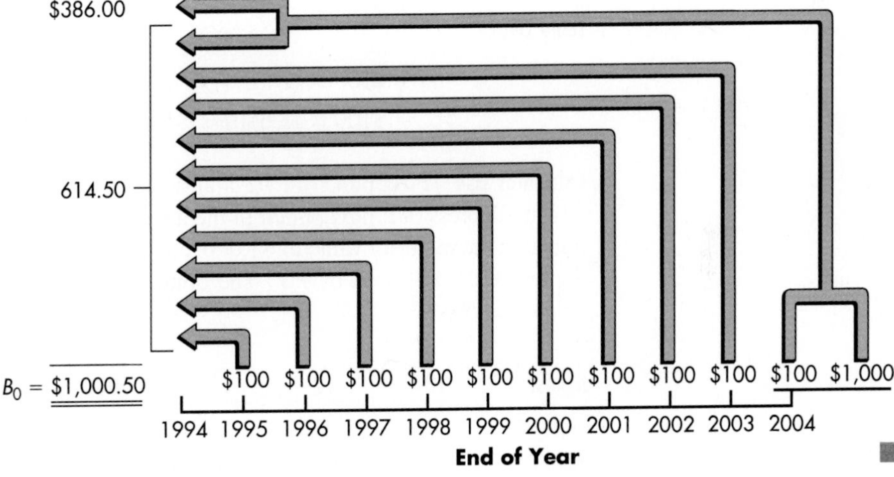

Graphic depiction of bond valuation (Mills Company's 10 percent coupon interest rate, 10-year maturity, \$1,000 par, January 1, 1995, issue paying annual interest; required return = 10 percent)

Bond value behavior

The value of a bond in the marketplace is rarely constant over its life. A variety of forces in the economy as well as the mere passage of time tend to affect value. Since

[7]Note that because bonds pay interest in arrears, the prices at which they are quoted and traded reflect their value *plus* any accrued interest. For example, a \$1,000 par value, 10 percent coupon bond paying interest semiannually and having a calculated value of \$900 would pay interest of \$50 at the end of each six-month period. If it is now three months since the beginning of the interest period, three-sixths of the \$50 interest, or \$25 (i.e., 3/6 × \$50), would be accrued. The bond would therefore be quoted at \$925—its \$900 value plus the \$25 in accrued interest. For convenience, *throughout this book, bond values will always be assumed to be calculated at the beginning of the interest period,* thereby avoiding the need to consider accrued interest.

these external forces are really in no way controlled by bond issuers or investors, it is useful to understand the impact that required return and time to maturity have on bond value.

REQUIRED RETURNS AND BOND VALUES

discount
The amount by which a bond sells at a value that is less than its par, or face, value.

premium
The amount by which a bond sells at a value that is greater than its par, or face, value.

Whenever the required return on a bond differs from the bond's coupon interest rate, the bond's value will differ from its par, or face, value. The required return on the bond is likely to differ from the coupon interest rate because either (1) economic conditions have changed, causing a shift in the basic cost of long-term funds, or (2) the firm's risk has changed. Increases in the basic cost of long-term funds or in risk will raise the required return, and decreases in the basic cost or risk will lower the required return.

Regardless of the exact cause, the important point is that when the required return is greater than the coupon interest rate, the bond value, B_0, will be less than its par value, M. In this case the bond is said to sell at a **discount**, which will equal $M - B_0$. On the other hand, when the required rate of return falls below the coupon interest rate, the bond value will be greater than par. In this situation the bond is said to sell at a **premium**, which will equal $B_0 - M$. An example will illustrate this point using Equation 7.3a along with either financial tables or a hand-held business/financial calculator.

EXAMPLE

In the preceding example we saw that when the required return equaled the coupon interest rate, the bond's value equaled its $1,000 par value. If for the same bond the required return were to rise to 12 percent, its value would be found as follows:

Table Use

$$B_0 = \$100 \times (PVIFA_{12\%,10\text{yrs}}) + \$1{,}000 \times (PVIF_{12\%,10\text{yrs}})$$
$$= \$100 \times (5.650) + \$1{,}000 \times (.322) = \underline{\underline{\$887.00}}$$

Calculator Use First punch in 10, and depress **N**; then punch in the required return of 12, and depress **%i**; next punch in the annual interest of $100, and depress **PMT**; then punch in the maturity value of $1,000, and depress **FV**; and to calculate the bond value, depress **CPT** followed by **PV**. The bond value of $887.00 should appear on the calculator display.

Inputs:	10	12	100	1000		
Functions:	N	%i	PMT	FV	CPT	PV
Outputs:						887.00

The bond would therefore sell at a *discount* of $113.00 ($1,000 par value − $887.00 value).

If, on the other hand, the required return fell to, say, 8 percent, the bond's value would be found as follows:

Table Use

$$B_0 = \$100 \times (PVIFA_{8\%,10\text{yrs}}) + \$1{,}000 \times (PVIF_{8\%,10\text{yrs}})$$
$$= \$100 \times (6.710) + \$1{,}000 \times (.463) = \underline{\underline{\$1{,}134.00}}$$

Calculator Use First punch in 10, and depress **N**; then punch in the required return of 8, and depress **%i**; next punch in the annual interest of $100, and depress **PMT**; then punch in the maturity value of $1,000, and depress **FV**; and to calculate the bond value, depress **CPT** followed by **PV**. The bond value of $1,134.20 should appear on the calculator display. Note that this value is more precise than the $1,134 value calculated above by using the rounded financial table factors.

Inputs:	10	8	100	1000		
Functions:	N	%i	PMT	FV	CPT	PV
Outputs:						*1134.20*

The bond would therefore sell for a premium of about $134 ($1,134.00 value − $1,000 par value). The results of this and earlier calculations for the Mills Company's bond values are summarized in Table 7.2 and graphically depicted in Figure 7.1 on page 268. ■

CONCEPT IN PRACTICE

Generating a High Return for Tucson Electric Power's Bondholders

At the outset of 1992, operating conditions were bleak at Tucson Electric Power. Due to heavy operating losses and a negative cash flow, the utility issued a moratorium on certain debt payments in January 1991 and asked its creditors for time to iron out its difficulties. To make a restructuring plan workable, virtually all parties having any relationship with the utility had to make concessions. Fortunately, by November, existing common shareholders had agreed to give up all but 16 percent of ownership. SCECorp agreed to pay $40 million for damages and court costs to settle Tucson Electric's claim that SCECorp had interfered with Tucson Electric's efforts to merge with San Diego Gas and Electric. Despite the reorganization and the court case, Tucson Electric continued to pay interest on its publicly held bonds, because they would immediately become due in bankruptcy.

TABLE 7.2

BOND VALUES FOR VARIOUS REQUIRED RETURNS (10 PERCENT COUPON INTEREST RATE, 10-YEAR MATURITY, $1,000 PAR, INTEREST PAID ANNUALLY) FOR MILLS COMPANY'S BOND

Required return, k_d (%)	Bond value, B_0	Status
12	$ 887.00	Discount
10	1,000.00	Par value
8	1,134.00	Premium

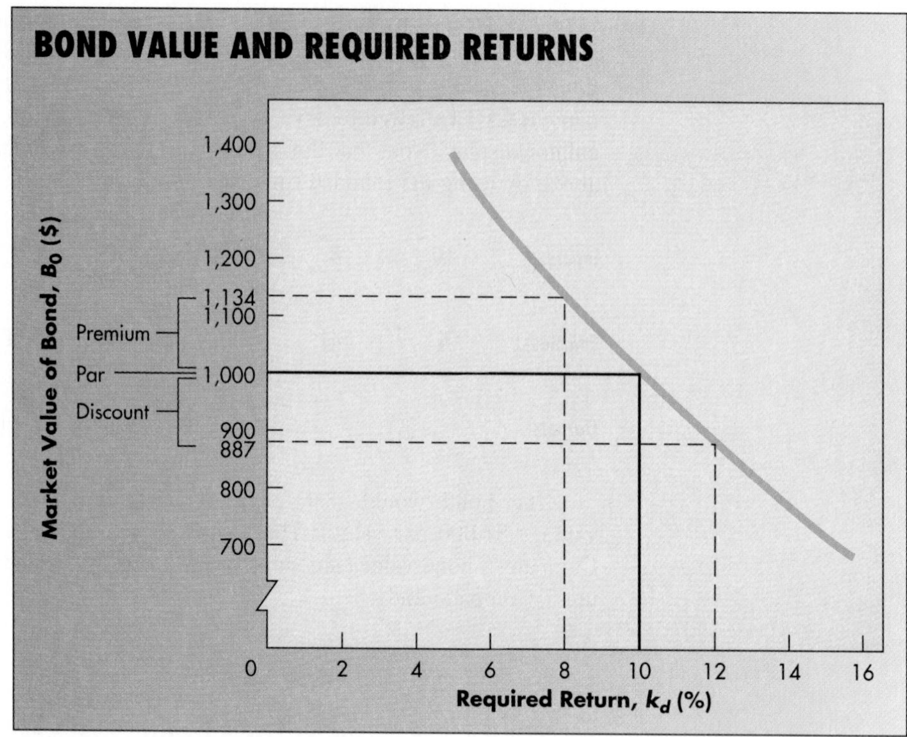

FIGURE 7.1
Bond value and required return (Mills Company's 10 percent coupon interest rate, 10-year maturity, $1,000 par, January 1, 1995, issue paying annual interest)

Another change pushing bond prices higher was the decline in expected inflation rates. The required rate of return on Treasury bonds maturing in 2001 declined from 7.00 percent to 6.52 percent. In total, bondholders earned a 23 percent return on the firm's 8⅛ percent-coupon-interest-rate bond maturing in 2001, consisting of a 15 percent price increase and an 8 percent interest payment.

TIME TO MATURITY AND BOND VALUES

Whenever the required return is different from the coupon interest rate, the amount of time to maturity affects bond value, even if the required return remains constant until maturity. Two important relationships exist among time to maturity, required return, and bond value. They are concerned with constant required returns and changing required returns.

CONSTANT REQUIRED RETURNS When the required return is different from the coupon interest rate and is assumed to be *constant until maturity,* the value of the bond will approach its par value as the passage of time moves the bond's value closer to maturity. Of course, when the required return equals the coupon interest rate, the bond's value will remain at par until it matures.

EXAMPLE

Figure 7.2 depicts the behavior of the bond values calculated earlier and presented in Table 7.2 for Mills Company's 10 percent coupon interest rate bond paying annual interest and having 10 years to maturity. Each of the three required returns—12 percent, 10 percent, and 8 percent—is assumed to remain constant over the 10 years to the

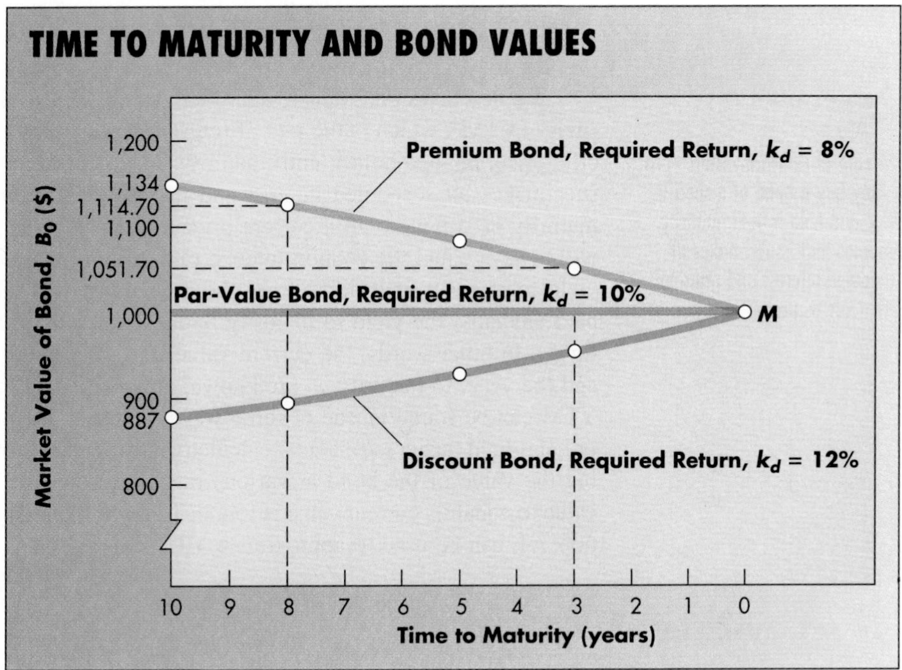

FIGURE 7.2
Relationship between time to maturity, required return, and bond value (Mills Company's 10 percent coupon interest rate, 10-year maturity, $1,000 par issue paying annual interest)

bond's maturity. The bond's value in each case approaches and ultimately equals the bond's $1,000 par value at its maturity. At the 12 percent required return, the bond's discount declines with the passage of time as the bond's value increases from $887 to $1,000. When the 10 percent required return equals the bond's coupon interest rate, its value remains unchanged at $1,000 over its maturity. Finally, at the 8 percent required return, the bond's premium will decline as its value drops from $1,134 to $1,000 at maturity. With the required return assumed to be constant to maturity, the bond's value approaches its $1,000 par or maturity value as the time to maturity declines. ■

CHANGING REQUIRED RETURNS The shorter the amount of time until a bond's maturity, the less responsive is its market value to a given change in the required return. In other words, short maturities have less "interest rate risk" than do long maturities when all other features—coupon interest rate, par value, and interest payment frequency—are the same.

EXAMPLE

The effect of changing required returns on bonds of differing maturity can be illustrated by using Mills Company's bond and Figure 7.2. If, as denoted by the dashed line at eight years to maturity, the required return declines from 10 to 8 percent, the bond's value rises from $1,000 to $1,114.70—an 11.47 percent increase. If the same change in required return had occurred with only three years to maturity, as denoted by the dashed line, the bond's value would have risen to just $1,051.70—only a 5.17 percent increase. Similar types of responses can be seen in terms of the change in bond value associated with increases in required returns. The shorter the time to maturity, the smaller the impact on bond value caused by a given change in the required return. ■

Yield to maturity (YTM)

yield to maturity (YTM)
The rate of return investors earn if they buy a bond at a specific price and hold it until maturity. Assumes that issuer makes all scheduled interest and principal payments as promised.

When investors evaluate and trade bonds, they commonly consider **yield to maturity (YTM),** which is the rate of return investors earn if they buy the bond at a specific price, B_0, and hold it until maturity. The measure assumes, of course, that the issuer makes all scheduled interest and principal payments as promised. The yield to maturity on a bond with a current price equal to its par, or face, value (i.e., $B_0 = M$) will always equal the coupon interest rate. When the bond value differs from par, the yield to maturity will differ from the coupon interest rate. Assuming that interest is paid annually, the yield to maturity on a bond can be found by solving Equation 7.3 for k_d. In other words, the current value, B_0, the annual interest, I, the par value, M, and the years to maturity, n, are known, and the yield to maturity must be found. The YTM can be found in one of three ways—by trial and error, approximation formula, or hand-held business/financial calculator. The *trial-and-error approach* involves finding the value of the bond at various rates until the rate causing the calculated bond value to equal its current value is found. The *approximate yield formula*, given in Equation 7.4, can be used to approximate YTM:

$$\text{Approximate yield} = \frac{I + \dfrac{M - B_0}{n}}{\dfrac{M + B_0}{2}} \tag{7.4}$$

The *hand-held business/financial calculator* provides accurate YTM values with minimum effort. Application of each of these methods for finding YTM is demonstrated in the following example.

EXAMPLE

The Mills Company bond, which currently sells for $1,080, has a 10 percent coupon interest rate and $1,000 par value, pays interest annually, and has 10 years to maturity. Since $B_0 = \$1{,}080$, $I = \$100$ $(.10 \times \$1{,}000)$, $M = \$1{,}000$, and $n = 10$ years, substituting into Equation 7.3a, we get

$$\$1{,}080 = \$100 \times (PVIFA_{kd,10\text{yrs}}) + \$1{,}000 \times (PVIF_{kd,10\text{yrs}})$$

Our objective is to solve the equation for k_d—the YTM.

Trial and Error Since we know that a required return, k_d, of 10 percent (which equals the bond's 10 percent coupon interest rate) would result in a value of $1,000, the discount rate that would result in $1,080 must be less than 10 percent. (Remember that the lower the discount rate, the higher the present value, and the higher the discount rate, the lower the present value.) Trying 9 percent, we get

$$\begin{aligned}
&\$100 \times (PVIFA_{9\%,10\text{yrs}}) + \$1{,}000 \times (PVIF_{9\%,10\text{yrs}}) \\
&\qquad = \$100 \times (6.418) + \$1{,}000 \times (.422) \\
&\qquad = \$641.80 + \$422.00 = \$1{,}063.80
\end{aligned}$$

Since the 9 percent rate is not quite low enough to bring the value up to $1,080, we next try 8 percent and get

$$\$100 \times (PVIFA_{8\%,10\text{yrs}}) + \$1{,}000 \times (PVIF_{8\%,10\text{yrs}})$$
$$= \$100 \times (6.710) + \$1{,}000 \times (.463)$$
$$= \$671.00 + \$463.00 = \$1{,}134.00$$

Since the resulting value of $1,134 at the 8 percent rate is higher than $1,080 and the $1,063.80 value at the 9 percent rate is lower than $1,080, the bond's yield to maturity must be between 8 and 9 percent. Since the $1,063.80 is closer to $1,080, to the nearest whole percent the YTM is 9 percent. By using *interpolation* (as described in footnote 17 in Chapter 5), the more precise YTM value is 8.77 percent.[8]

Approximation Formula Substituting the relevant data into the approximate yield formula given in Equation 7.4, we get

$$\text{Approximate yield} = \frac{\$100 + \dfrac{\$1{,}000 - \$1{,}080}{10}}{\dfrac{\$1{,}000 + \$1{,}080}{2}}$$

$$= \frac{\$100 + (-\$8)}{\$1{,}040} = \frac{\$92}{\$1{,}040} = .0885 = \underline{\underline{8.85\%}}$$

The approximate YTM is therefore 8.85 percent, which does not differ greatly from the 8.77 percent YTM calculated above by using the trial-and-error approach.

Calculator Use Using the calculator, first punch in 10, and depress **N**; then punch in the annual interest of $100, and depress **PMT**; next punch in the current bond value, B_0, of $1,080, and depress **PV**; then punch in the bond's maturity value, M, of $1,000, and depress **FV**; and to calculate the YTM of this bond, depress **CPT** followed by **%i**. The YTM of 8.766 should appear on the calculator display. Note that this number is the precise value of YTM, which agrees with the interpolated value found above by using the trial-and-error approach.

[8]To interpolate in this case, the following steps are involved:

1. Find the difference between the bond values at 8 and 9 percent. The difference is $70.20 ($1,134.00 − $1,063.80).
2. Find the *absolute* difference between the desired value of $1,080 and the value associated with the lower discount rate. The difference is $54 ($1,134 − $1,080).
3. Divide the value from Step 2 by the value found in Step 1 to get the percent of the distance across the discount rate range between 8 and 9 percent. The result is .77 ($54.00 ÷ $70.20).
4. Multiply the percent found in Step 3 by the interval width of 1 percent (9% − 8%) over which interpolation is being performed. The result is .77 percent (.77 × 1%).
5. Add the value found in Step 4 to the interest rate associated with the lower end of the interval. The result is 8.77 percent (8% + .77%). The yield to maturity is therefore 8.77 percent.

Inputs:	10	100	1080	1000		
Functions:	N	PMT	PV	FV	CPT	%i
Outputs:						8.766

Semiannual interest and bond values

The procedure used to value bonds paying interest semiannually is similar to that illustrated in Chapter 5 for compounding interest more frequently than annually—except that here we need to find present instead of future value. It involves

1. Converting annual interest, I, to semiannual interest by dividing it by 2.
2. Converting the number of years to maturity, n, to the number of six-month periods to maturity by multiplying n by 2.
3. Converting the required stated (rather than effective)[9] return for similar-risk bonds that also pay semiannual interest from an annual rate, k_d, to a semiannual rate by dividing it by 2.

Substituting the three changes noted above into Equation 7.3 yields

$$B_0 = \frac{I}{2} \times \left[\sum_{t=1}^{2n} \frac{1}{\left(1 + \frac{k_d}{2}\right)^t} \right] + M \times \left[\frac{1}{\left(1 + \frac{k_d}{2}\right)^{2n}} \right] \qquad (7.5)^{10}$$

$$= \frac{I}{2} \times \left(PVIFA_{\frac{k_d}{2},2n}\right) + M \times \left(PVIF_{\frac{k_d}{2},2n}\right) \qquad (7.5a)$$

An example can be used to illustrate the application of this equation using either financial tables or a hand-held business/financial calculator.

[9]As was noted in Chapter 5, the effective annual rate of interest, $k_{eff.}$, for stated interest rate k, when interest is paid semiannually (m=2), can be found by using Equation 5.10:

$$k_{eff.} = \left(1 + \frac{k}{2}\right)^2 - 1$$

For example, a bond with a 12 percent required stated return, k_d, that pays semiannual interest would have an effective annual rate of return of

$$k_{eff.} = \left(1 + \frac{.12}{2}\right)^2 - 1 = (1.06)^2 - 1 = 1.1236 - 1 = .1236 = \underline{\underline{12.36\%}}$$

Because most bonds pay semiannual interest at semiannual rates equal to 50 percent of the stated annual rate, their effective annual rates of return are generally higher than their stated rates.

[10]Although it may appear inappropriate to use the semiannual discounting procedure on the maturity value, M, this technique is necessary to find the correct bond value. One way to confirm the accuracy of this approach is to calculate the bond value in the case that the required stated return and coupon interest rate are equal; for B_0 to equal M, as would be expected in such a case, the maturity value must be discounted on a semiannual basis.

EXAMPLE

Assuming that the Mills Company bond pays interest semiannually and that the required stated return, k_d, is 12 percent for similar-risk bonds that also pay semiannual interest, substituting into Equation 7.5a yields

$$B_0 = \frac{\$100}{2} \times \left(PVIFA_{\frac{12\%}{2},2 \times 10\text{yrs}}\right) + \$1{,}000 \times \left(PVIF_{\frac{12\%}{2},2 \times 10\text{yrs}}\right)$$

Table Use

$$B_0 = \$50 \times (PVIFA_{6\%,20 \text{ periods}}) + \$1{,}000 \times (PVIF_{6\%,20 \text{ periods}})$$
$$= \$50 \times (11.470) + \$1{,}000 \times (.312) = \underline{\underline{\$885.50}}$$

Calculator Use When using a calculator to find bond value in the case in which interest is paid semiannually, we must double the number of periods and divide both the required stated return and the annual interest by 2. For the Mills Company bond, we would use 20 periods (2 × 10 years), a required return of 6 percent (12 percent ÷ 2), and an interest payment of $50 ($100 ÷ 2). First punch in the number of semiannual periods, 20, and depress **N**; punch in the semiannual required return of 6, and depress **%i**; next punch in the semiannual interest of $50, and depress **PMT**; then punch in the maturity value of $1,000, and depress **FV**; and to calculate the bond value, depress **CPT** followed by **PV**. The bond value of $885.30 should appear on the calculator display. Note that this value is more precise than the $885.50 value calculated by using the rounded financial table factors.

Inputs:	20	6	50	1000		
Functions:	N	%i	PMT	FV	CPT	PV
Outputs:						*885.30*

Comparing the $885.30 result above with the $887.00 value found earlier by using annual compounding (see Table 7.2), we can see that the bond's value is lower when semiannual interest is used. This will always occur when the bond sells at a discount. For bonds selling at a premium, the opposite will occur. (Value with semiannual interest is greater than with annual interest.)

CONCEPTS IN REVIEW

7-4 Describe the basic procedure used to value a bond that pays *annual* interest. What procedure is used to value bonds paying interest *semiannually*?

7-5 In terms of the required return and the coupon interest rate, what relationship between them will cause a bond to sell (a) at a discount? (b) at a premium? (c) at its par value? Explain.

7-6 If the required return on a bond differs from its coupon interest rate and is assumed to be constant until maturity, describe the behavior of the bond value as the passage of time moves the bond toward its maturity.

7-7 If you were a risk-averse investor, to protect against the potential impact of rising interest rates on bond value, would you prefer bonds with short or long periods until maturity? Explain why.

7-8 What is meant by the *yield to maturity (YTM)* on a bond? Briefly describe both the trial-and-error approach and the approximate approach for calculating YTM.

Common stock valuation

Common stockholders require the firm, at minimum, to earn a return consistent with its risk. What effect would the general expectation among investors that the firm will not earn its *required* return have on its share price and *expected* return? Spend a few moments answering this question before reading on.

COMMON STOCKHOLDERS EXPECT TO BE REWARDED THROUGH THE RECEIPT OF PERIODIC cash dividends and an increasing—or at least nondeclining—share value. Like current owners, prospective owners and security analysts frequently estimate the firm's value. They choose to purchase the stock when they believe that it is *undervalued* (i.e., that its true value is greater than its market price) and to sell it when they feel that it is *overvalued* (i.e., that its market price is greater than its true value). Before describing specific stock valuation techniques, we will look at the concept of an efficient market, which tends to dispel the belief that the prices of actively traded stocks can differ from their true values.

Market efficiency[11]

Economically rational buyers and sellers use their assessment of an asset's risk and return to determine its value. To a buyer the asset's value represents the maximum price that he or she would pay to acquire it, while a seller views the asset's value as a minimum sale price. In competitive markets with many active participants, such as the New York Stock Exchange, the interactions of many buyers (demanders of shares) and sellers (suppliers of shares) result in an equilibrium price or *market value* for each security. This price reflects the collective actions of buyers and sellers based on all available information. As new information becomes available, buyers and sellers are assumed to immediately digest such information and through their purchase and sale activities to quickly create a new market equilibrium price.

required return, k
A specified return required each period by investors for a given level of risk.

expected return, $\hat{k}$
The return that is expected to be earned each period on a given asset over an infinite time horizon.

This process of market adjustment to new information can be viewed in terms of rates of return. From the discussions in Chapter 6 we know that for a given level of risk, investors require a specified periodic return—the **required return, k**—which can be estimated by using beta and CAPM (see Equation 6.8). At each point in time, investors estimate the **expected return, $\hat{k}$**—the return that is expected to be earned on a

[11] A great deal of theoretical and empirical research has been performed in the area of market efficiency. For purposes of this discussion, generally accepted beliefs about market efficiency are described rather than the technical aspects of the various forms of market efficiency and their theoretical implications. For a good discussion of the theory and evidence relative to market efficiency, see Thomas E. Copeland and J. Fred Weston, *Financial Theory and Corporate Policy,* 3rd ed. (Reading, MA: Addison-Wesley Publishing Co., 1988), Chapters 10 and 11.

given asset each period over an infinite time horizon. The expected return can be estimated by using a simplified form of Equation 6.1, given below in Equation 7.6:

$$\hat{k} = \frac{\text{Expected benefit during each period}}{\text{Current price of asset}} \tag{7.6}$$

Whenever investors find that the expected return is not equal to the required return ($\hat{k} \neq k$), a market price adjustment will occur. If the expected return is less than the required return ($\hat{k} < k$), investors will sell the asset, since it is not expected to earn a return commensurate with its risk. Such action would drive the price down, which, assuming no change in expected benefits, will cause the expected return to rise to the level of the required return. This relationship can be seen in Equation 7.6, where a decrease in asset price will result in an increase in the expected return. If the expected return were above the required return ($\hat{k} > k$), investors would buy the asset, driving its price up and its expected return down to the point that it equals the required return. This market adjustment process can be demonstrated with an example.

EXAMPLE

The common stock of Alton Industries (AI) is currently selling for \$50 per share, and market participants expect it to generate benefits of \$6.50 per share during each coming period. In addition the risk-free rate, R_F, is currently 7 percent; the market return, k_m, is 12 percent; and the stock's beta, b_{AI}, is 1.20. When these values are substituted into Equation 7.6, the firm's current expected return, $\hat{k}_0$, is

$$\hat{k}_0 = \frac{\$6.50}{\$50.00} = \underline{\underline{13\%}}$$

When the appropriate values are substituted into the CAPM (Equation 6.8), the current required return, k_0, is

$$\hat{k}_0 = 7\% + [1.20 \times (12\% - 7\%)] = 7\% + 6\% = \underline{\underline{13\%}}$$

Since $\hat{k}_0 = k_0$, the market is currently in equilibrium, and the stock is fairly priced at \$50 per share.

Assume that a just-issued press release indicates that a major product liability suit has been filed against Alton Industries. As a result, investors immediately adjust their risk assessment upward, raising the firm's beta from 1.20 to 1.40. The new required return, k_1, becomes

$$k_1 = 7\% + [1.40 \times (12\% - 7\%)] = 7\% + 7\% = \underline{\underline{14\%}}$$

Because the expected return of 13 percent is now below the required return of 14 percent, many investors would sell the stock—driving its price down to about \$46.43—the price that would result in a 14 percent expected return, $\hat{k}_1$.

$$\hat{k}_1 = \frac{\$6.50}{\$46.43} = \underline{\underline{14\%}}$$

The new price of \$46.43 brings the market back into equilibrium, since the expected return, $\hat{k}_1$, of 14 percent now equals the required return, k_1, of 14 percent. ■

CONCEPT IN PRACTICE

Forecasting Interest Rates with Utility Stock Prices at Federated Investors

Federated Investors uses changes in the Dow Jones Utility Average to predict changes in interest rates. According to the Pittsburgh-based investment analyst, many money managers use stock issued by electric utilities and natural-gas companies as substitutes for bonds. When investors anticipate that interest rates will fall, they supposedly bid up stock prices. The theory is that low bond yields will make these stocks more competitive investments. To get the best returns, investors must move their wealth to utility stocks before the stock prices rise, which precedes the decline in bond interest rates. The reduction in the anticipated rate of inflation reduces k, the required return, and increases price. According to Federated Investors, the yields on utilities accurately anticipated drops in long-term Treasury rates over the 1989–1993 period.

efficient market hypothesis

Theory describing the behavior of an assumed "perfect" market in which securities are typically in equilibrium, security prices fully reflect all public information available and react swiftly to new information, and, since stocks are fairly priced, investors need not waste time looking for mispriced securities.

As was noted in Chapter 6, active markets such as the New York Stock Exchange are efficient—they are made up of many rational investors who react quickly and objectively to new information. The **efficient market hypothesis,** which is the basic theory describing the behavior of such a "perfect" market, specifically states:

1. Securities are typically in equilibrium, meaning that they are fairly priced and their expected returns equal their required returns.
2. At any point in time, security prices fully reflect all public information[12] available about the firm and its securities, and these prices react swiftly to new information.
3. Since stocks are fully and fairly priced, it follows that investors should not waste their time trying to find and capitalize on mispriced (undervalued or overvalued) securities.

Not all market participants are believers in the efficient market hypothesis. Some feel that it is worthwhile to search for undervalued or overvalued securities and to trade them to profit from market inefficiencies that cause expected returns to differ from required returns. Others argue that it is mere luck that would allow market participants to correctly anticipate new information and as a result earn excess returns, that is, actual returns > required returns. They believe that it is unlikely that market participants can over the *long run* earn excess returns. *Throughout this text we ignore the disbelievers and continue to assume market efficiency.* This means that *the terms "expected return" and "required return" are used interchangeably,* since they should be equal in an efficient market. This also means that stock prices accurately reflect true value based on risk and return. In other words, we will operate under the assumption that the market price at any point in time is the best estimate of value. Next we look closely at the mechanics of stock valuation.

[12]Those market participants who have nonpublic—*inside*—information may have an unfair advantage that permits them to earn an excess return. Since the mid-1980s with the disclosure of the insider-trading activities of Ivan Boesky, Michael Milken, and others, major national attention has been focused on the "problem" of insider trading and its resolution. Clearly, those who trade securities based on inside information have an unfair and illegal advantage. Empirical research has confirmed that those with inside information do indeed have an opportunity to earn an excess return. Here we ignore this possibility, given its illegality and the fact that current actions by the securities industry and the government will (it is hoped) eliminate the possibility of insider trading. We, in effect, assume that all relevant information is public, and therefore the market is efficient.

The basic stock valuation equation

Like bonds, the value of a share of common stock is equal to the present value of all future benefits it is expected to provide. Simply stated, *the value of a share of common stock is equal to the present value of all future dividends it is expected to provide over an infinite time horizon.*[13] Although by selling stock at a price above that originally paid, a stockholder can earn capital gains in addition to dividends, what is really sold is the right to all future dividends. Stocks that are not expected to pay dividends in the foreseeable future have a value attributable to a distant dividend that is expected to result from the sale of the company or liquidation of its assets. Therefore from a valuation viewpoint, only dividends are relevant. Redefining terms, the basic valuation model in Equation 7.1 can be specified for common stock as given in Equation 7.7:

$$P_0 = \frac{D_1}{(1+k_s)^1} + \frac{D_2}{(1+k_s)^2} + \cdots + \frac{D_\infty}{(1+k_s)^\infty} \tag{7.7}$$

where

P_0 = value of common stock
D_t = per-share dividend expected at the end of year t
k_s = required return on common stock

The equation can be simplified somewhat by redefining each year's dividend, D_t, in terms of anticipated growth. We will consider three cases here—zero growth, constant growth, and variable growth.

ZERO GROWTH

zero growth model
An approach to dividend valuation that assumes a constant, nongrowing dividend stream.

The simplest approach to dividend valuation, the **zero growth model,** assumes a constant, nongrowing dividend stream. In terms of the notation already introduced,

$$D_1 = D_2 = \cdots = D_\infty$$

Letting D_1 represent the amount of the annual dividend, Equation 7.7 under zero growth would reduce to

$$P_0 = D_1 \times \sum_{t=1}^{\infty} \frac{1}{(1+k_s)^t} = D_1 \times (PVIFA_{k_s,\infty}) = \frac{D_1}{k_s} \tag{7.8}$$

The equation shows that with zero growth the value of a share of stock would equal the present value of a perpetuity of D_1 dollars discounted at a rate k_s. Let us look at an example.

[13]The need to consider an infinite time horizon is not critical, since a sufficiently long period, say, 50 years, will result in about the same present value as an infinite period for moderate-sized required returns. For example, at 15 percent a dollar to be received 50 years from now, $PVIF_{15\%,50\text{yrs}}$, is worth only about \$.001 today.

EXAMPLE

The dividend of the Denham Company, an established textile producer, is expected to remain constant at \$3 per share indefinitely. If the required return on its stock is 15 percent, the stock's value is \$20 (\$3 ÷ .15). ■

Since preferred stock typically provides its holders with a fixed annual dividend over its assumed infinite life, Equation 7.8 can be used to find the *value of preferred stock.* The value of preferred stock can be estimated by substituting the stated preferred dividend and the required return on the preferred stock for D_1 and k_s, respectively, in Equation 7.8. For example, a preferred stock paying a \$5 stated annual dividend and having a required return of 13 percent would have a value of \$38.46 (\$5 + .13). Detailed discussion of preferred stock is included in Chapter 14.

CONSTANT GROWTH

constant growth model

A widely cited dividend valuation approach that assumes that dividends will grow at a constant rate that is less than the required return.

The most widely cited dividend valuation approach, the **constant growth model,** assumes that dividends will grow at a constant rate, g, that is less than the required return, k_s ($g < k_s$).[14] Letting D_0 represent the most recent dividend, Equation 7.7 can be rewritten as follows:

$$P_0 = \frac{D_0 \times (1+g)^1}{(1+k_s)^1} + \frac{D_0 \times (1+g)^2}{(1+k_s)^2} + \cdots + \frac{D_0 \times (1+g)^\infty}{(1+k_s)^\infty} \tag{7.9}$$

If we simplify Equation 7.9, it can be rewritten as follows:[15]

$$P_0 = \frac{D_1}{k_s - g} \tag{7.10}$$

---

[14]One of the assumptions of the constant growth model as presented is that earnings and dividends grow at the same rate. This assumption is true only in cases in which a firm pays out a fixed percentage of its earnings each year (has a fixed payout ratio). In the case of a declining industry, a negative growth rate ($g < 0$) might exist. In such a case the constant growth model, as well as the variable growth model presented in the next section, remains fully applicable to the valuation process.

[15]For the interested reader the calculations necessary to derive Equation 7.10 from Equation 7.9 follow. The first step is to multiply each side of Equation 7.9 by $(1 + k_s)/(1 + g)$ and subtract Equation 7.9 from the resulting expression. This yields

$$\frac{P_0 \times (1 + k_s)}{1+g} - P_0 = D_0 - \frac{D_0 \times (1+g)^\infty}{(1+k_s)^\infty} \tag{1}$$

Since k_s is assumed to be greater than g, the second term on the right side of Equation 1 should be zero. Thus

$$P_0 \times \left(\frac{1+k_s}{1+g} - 1\right) = D_0 \tag{2}$$

Equation 2 is simplified as follows:

$$P_0 \times \left(\frac{(1+k_s) - (1+g)}{1+g}\right) = D_0 \tag{3}$$

$$P_0 \times (k_s - g) = D_0 \times (1+g) \tag{4}$$

$$P_0 = \frac{D_1}{k_s - g} \tag{5}$$

Equation 5 equals Equation 7.10 above.

Gordon model
A common name for the *constant growth model* that is widely cited in dividend valuation.

The constant growth model in Equation 7.10 is commonly called the **Gordon model.** An example will show how it works.

EXAMPLE

The Lamar Company, a small cosmetics company, from 1989 through 1994 paid the per-share dividends shown below.

Year	Dividend per share ($)
1994	1.40
1993	1.29
1992	1.20
1991	1.12
1990	1.05
1989	1.00

Using Appendix Table A-3 for the present-value interest factor, *PVIF,* or a hand-held business calculator in conjunction with the technique described for finding growth rates in Chapter 5, the annual growth rate of dividends, which is assumed to equal the expected constant rate of dividend growth, g, is found to equal 7 percent.[16] The company estimates that its dividend in 1995, D_1, will equal $1.50. The required return, k_s, is assumed to be 15 percent. When these values are substituted into Equation 7.10, the value of the stock is

$$P_0 = \frac{\$1.50}{.15 - .07} = \frac{\$1.50}{.08} = \underline{\underline{\$18.75 \text{ per share}}}$$

Assuming that the values of D_1, k_s, and g are accurately estimated, Lamar Company's stock value is $18.75. ■

[16]The technique involves solving the following equation for g:

$$D_{1994} = D_{1989} \times (1 + g)^5$$

$$\frac{D_{1989}}{D_{1994}} = \frac{1}{(1 + g)^5} = PVIF_{g,5}$$

Two basic steps can be followed using the present-value table. First, dividing the earliest dividend (D_{1989} = $1.00) by the most recent dividend (D_{1994} = $1.40), a factor for the present value of one dollar, *PVIF,* of .714 ($1.00 ÷ $1.40) results. Although six dividends are shown, *they reflect only five years of growth.* Looking across the table at the present-value interest factors, *PVIF,* for five years, the factor closest to .714 occurs at 7 percent (.713). Therefore the growth rate of the dividends, rounded to the nearest whole percentage, is 7 percent.

Alternatively, using a hand-held business/financial calculator, begin by punching in the 1989 value of $1.00, and depress **PV**; next punch in the 1994 value of $1.40, and depress **FV**; then punch in the number of years of growth—5—and depress **N**; finally, to get the growth rate, depress **CPT** followed by **%i**. The growth rate of 6.96 percent, which we round to 7 percent, appears on the display.

Inputs: 1.00 | 1.40 | 5

Functions: PV | FV | N | CPT | %i

Outputs: 6.96

VARIABLE GROWTH

variable growth model
A dividend valuation approach that allows for a change in the dividend growth rate.

The zero and constant growth common-stock models presented in Equations 7.8 and 7.10, respectively, do not allow for any shift in expected growth rates. Because future growth rates might shift up or down due to changing expectations, it is useful to consider a **variable growth model** that allows for a change in the dividend growth rate.[17] Letting g_1 equal the initial growth rate and g_2 equal the subsequent growth rate and assuming a single shift in growth rates (from g_1 to g_2) occurs at the end of year N, we can use the following four-step procedure to determine the value of a share of stock.

Step 1 Find the value of the cash dividends at the end of *each year,* D_t, during the initial growth period—years 1 through N. This step may require adjusting the most recent dividend, D_0, using the initial growth rate, g_1, to calculate the dividend amount for each year. Therefore for the first N years:

$$D_t = D_0 \times (1 + g_1)^t = D_0 \times FVIF_{g_1,t}$$

Step 2 Find the present value of the dividends expected during the initial growth period. Using the notation presented earlier, this value can be given as

$$\sum_{t=1}^{N} \frac{D_0 \times (1 + g_1)^t}{(1 + k_s)^t} = \sum_{t=1}^{N} \frac{D_t}{(1 + k_s)^t} = \sum_{t=1}^{N} (D_t \times PVIF_{k_s,t})$$

Step 3 Find the value of the stock at the end of the initial growth period, $P_N = \frac{D_{N+1}}{k_s - g_2}$, which is the present value of all dividends expected from year $N + 1$ to infinity—assuming a constant dividend growth rate, g_2. This value is found by applying the constant growth model (presented as Equation 7.10 in the preceding section) to the dividends expected from year $N + 1$ to infinity. The present value of P_N would represent the value today of all dividends that are expected to be received from year $N+1$ to infinity. This value can be represented by

$$\frac{1}{(1 + k_s)^N} \times \frac{D_{N+1}}{k_s - g_2} = PVIF_{k_s}, N \times P_N$$

Step 4 Add the present-value components found in Steps 2 and 3 to find the value of the stock, P_0, given in Equation 7.11:

$$P_0 = \underbrace{\sum_{t=1}^{N} \frac{D_0 \times (1 + g_1)^t}{(1 + k_s)^t}}_{\substack{\text{Present value}\\ \text{of dividends}\\ \text{during initial}\\ \text{growth period}}} + \underbrace{\left(\frac{1}{(1 + k_s)^N} \times \frac{D_{N+1}}{k_s - g_2}\right)}_{\substack{\text{Present value of}\\ \text{price of stock at}\\ \text{end of initial}\\ \text{growth period}}} \qquad (7.11)$$

[17]Although more than one change in the growth rate can be incorporated in the model, to simplify the discussion, we will consider only a single growth-rate change. The number of variable growth valuation models is technically unlimited, but concern over all likely shifts in growth is unlikely to yield much more accuracy than a simpler model.

The application of these steps to a variable growth situation with only one growth rate change is illustrated in the following example.

EXAMPLE

The most recent (1994) annual dividend payment of Warren Industries, a rapidly growing boat manufacturer, was \$1.50 per share. The firm's financial manager expects that these dividends will increase at a 10 percent annual rate, g_1, over the next three years (1995, 1996, and 1997) due to the introduction of a hot new boat. At the end of the three years (end of 1997) the firm's mature product line is expected to result in a slowing of the dividend growth rate to 5 percent per year forever (noted as g_2). The firm's required return, k_s, is 15 percent. To estimate the current (end-of-1994) value of Warren's common stock, $P_0 = P_{1994}$, the four-step procedure presented above must be applied to these data.

Step 1 The value of the cash dividends in each of the next three years is calculated in columns 1, 2, and 3 of Table 7.3. The 1995, 1996, and 1997 dividends are \$1.65, \$1.82, and \$2.00, respectively.

Step 2 The present value of the three dividends expected during the 1995–1997 initial growth period is calculated in columns 3, 4, and 5 of Table 7.3. The sum of the present values of the three dividends is \$4.14—the total of the column 5 values.

Step 3 The value of the stock at the end of the initial growth period (N = 1997) can be found by first calculating $D_{N+1} = D_{1998}$:

$$D_{1998} = D_{1997} \times (1 + .05) = \$2.00 \times (1.05) = \$2.10$$

By using D_{1998} = \$2.10, k_s = .15, and g_2 = .05, the value of the stock at the end of 1997 can be calculated:

$$P_{1997} = \frac{D_{1998}}{k_s - g_2} = \frac{\$2.10}{.15 - .05} = \frac{\$2.10}{.10} = \$21.00$$

TABLE 7.3

CALCULATION OF PRESENT VALUE OF WARREN INDUSTRIES' DIVIDENDS (1995–1997)

t	End of year	$D_0 = D_{1994}$ (1)	$PVIF_{10\%,t}$ (2)	D_t [(1) × (2)] (3)	$PVIF_{15\%,t}$ (4)	Present value of dividends [(3) × (4)] (5)
1	1995	\$1.50	1.100	\$1.65	.870	\$1.44
2	1996	1.50	1.210	1.82	.756	1.38
3	1997	1.50	1.331	2.00	.658	1.32

$$\text{Sum of present value of dividends} = \sum_{t=1}^{3} \frac{D_0 \times (1 + g_1)^t}{(1 + k_s)^t} = \$4.14$$

Finally, in this step, the share value of \$21 at the end of 1997 must be converted into a present (end-of-1994) value. Using the 15 percent required return, we get

$$PVIF_{k_s,N} \times P_N = PVIF_{15\%,3} \times P_{1997} = .658 \times \$21.00 = \$13.82$$

Step 4 Adding the present value of the initial dividend stream (found in Step 2) to the present value of the stock at the end of the initial growth period (found in Step 3) as specified in Equation 7.11, we get the current (end-of-1994) value of Warren Industries' stock:

$$P_{1994} = \$4.14 + \$13.82 = \$17.96$$

The stock is currently worth \$17.96 per share.

Time-Line Use The calculation of this value is summarized diagramatically below.

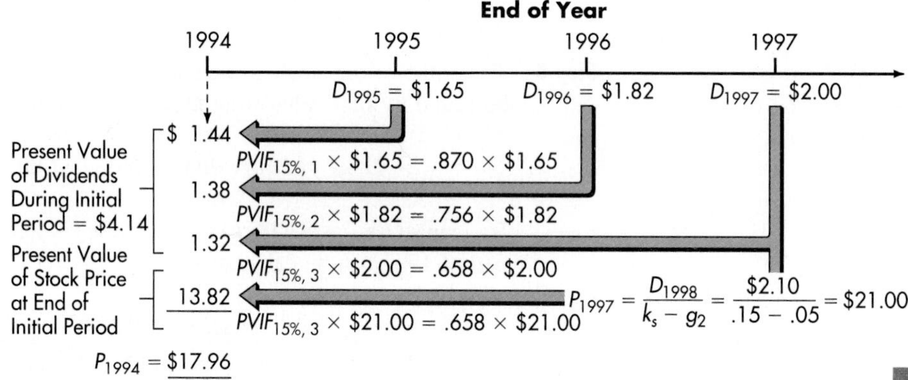

Finding Warren Industries' current (end-of-1994) value with variable growth

It is important to recognize that the zero, constant, and variable growth valuation models presented above provide useful frameworks for estimating stock value. Clearly, the estimates produced cannot possibly be very precise, given that the forecasts of future growth and discount rates are themselves necessarily approximate. Looked at another way, a great deal of rounding error can be introduced into the stock price estimate as a result of rounding growth and discount rate estimates to the nearest whole percent. In applying valuation models, it is therefore advisable to carefully estimate these rates and conservatively round them, probably to the nearest tenth of a percent.

Other approaches to common stock valuation

Many other approaches to common stock valuation exist, but only one is widely accepted. The more popular approaches include the use of book value, liquidation value, and some type of a price/earnings multiple.

book value per share
The amount per share of common stock to be received if all of the firm's assets are sold for their book value and if the proceeds remaining after payment of all liabilities (including preferred stock) are divided among the common stockholders.

BOOK VALUE

Book value per share is simply the amount per share of common stock to be received if all of the firm's assets are sold for their exact book (accounting) value and if the proceeds remaining after all liabilities (including preferred stock) are paid among the common stockholders. This method lacks sophistication and can be criticized on the basis of its reliance on historical balance sheet data. It ignores the firm's expected earnings potential and generally lacks any true relationship to the firm's value in the marketplace. Let us look at an example.

EXAMPLE

The Lamar Company currently (December 31, 1994) has total assets of $6 million, total liabilities including preferred stock of $4.5 million, and 100,000 shares of common stock outstanding. Its book value per share would therefore be

$$\frac{\$6{,}000{,}000 - \$4{,}500{,}000}{100{,}000 \text{ shares}} = \underline{\underline{\$15 \text{ per share}}}$$

Since this value assumes that assets are sold for their book value, it may not represent the minimum share value. As a matter of fact, although most stocks sell above book value, it is not unusual to find stocks selling below book value. ■

liquidation value per share
The *actual* amount per share of common stock to be received if all of the firm's assets are sold, liabilities (including preferred stock) are paid, and any remaining money is divided among the common stockholders.

LIQUIDATION VALUE

Liquidation value per share is the *actual* amount per share of common stock to be received if all of the firm's assets are sold, liabilities (including preferred stock) are paid, and any remaining money is divided among the common stockholders.[18] This measure is more realistic than book value, but it still fails to consider the earning power of the firm's assets. An example will illustrate.

EXAMPLE

The Lamar Company found upon investigation that it would obtain only $5.25 million if it sold its assets today. The firm's liquidation value per share would therefore be

$$\frac{\$5{,}250{,}000 - \$4{,}500{,}000}{100{,}000 \text{ shares}} = \underline{\underline{\$7.50 \text{ per share}}}$$

Ignoring any expenses of liquidation, this amount would be the firm's minimum value. ■

price/earnings multiple approach
A technique to estimate the firm's share value; calculated by multiplying the firm's expected earnings per share (EPS) by the average price/earnings (P/E) ratio for the industry.

PRICE/EARNINGS (P/E) MULTIPLES

The *price/earnings (P/E) ratio*, introduced in Chapter 4, reflects the amount investors are willing to pay for each dollar of earnings. The average P/E ratio in a particular industry can be used as the guide to a firm's value if it is assumed that investors value the earnings of a given firm in the same manner as they do the "average" firm in that industry. The **price/earnings multiple approach** to value is a popular technique whereby the firm's expected earnings per share (EPS) are multiplied by the average price/earnings (P/E) ratio for the industry to estimate the firm's share value. The aver-

[18]In the event of liquidation, creditors' claims must be satisfied first, then those of the preferred stockholders. Anything left goes to common stockholders. A more detailed discussion of liquidation procedures is presented in Chapter 19.

age P/E ratio for the industry can be obtained from a source such as *Standard & Poor's Industrial Ratios.*

The use of P/E multiples is especially helpful in valuing firms that are not publicly traded, whereas the use of the market price may be preferable in the case of a publicly traded firm.[19] In any case the price/earnings multiple approach is considered superior to the use of book or liquidation values, since it considers *expected* earnings.[20] An example will demonstrate the use of price/earnings multiples.

EXAMPLE

The Lamar Company is expected to earn $2.60 per share next year (1995). This expectation is based on an analysis of the firm's historical earnings trend and expected economic and industry conditions. The average price/earnings ratio for firms in the same industry is 7. Multiplying Lamar's expected earnings per share (EPS) of $2.60 by this ratio gives us a value for the firm's shares of $18.20, assuming that investors will continue to measure the value of the average firm at 7 times its earnings. ■

It is important to recognize that professional securities analysts typically use a variety of models and techniques to value stocks. For example, an analyst might use the constant growth model, liquidation value, and price/earnings (P/E) multiples to estimate the true worth of a given stock. If the analyst feels comfortable with his or her estimates, the stock value would be viewed as being not greater than the largest estimate. Of course, should the firm's estimated liquidation value per share exceed its "going concern" value per share estimated by using one of the valuation models (zero, constant, or variable growth) or the P/E multiple approach, it would be viewed as being worth more dead than alive. In such an event the firm would lack sufficient earning power to justify its existence and should probably be liquidated. From an investor's perspective the stock in this situation would be an attractive investment only if it could be purchased at a price below its liquidation value, which in an *efficient market* would never occur.

CONCEPT IN PRACTICE

Multiple Measures Indicate That Wedco Technology Is Underpriced

In early 1993, prices of shares issued by Wedco Technology, which custom-grinds plastic for chemical firms, rose from $8 to $10. Nonetheless, many brokers believed that Wedco's shares were still undervalued. Without a dividend payment to rely on for valuation purposes, financial analysts at Thomas James Associates used price/earnings, price/cash-flow, and price/book-value ratios to set a projected value of $20 per share. Furthermore, Thomas James' analysts asked clients to consider 1994 earnings projections in predicting future prices. Specifically, Wedco's earnings were projected to rise by 40 percent while the price/earnings ratio was held constant. The result was a forecast price increase of $4.40 per share of Wedco Technology.

---

[19]Generally, when the P/E ratio is used to value private or closely held corporations, a premium is added to adjust for the issue of control. This adjustment is necessary, since the P/E ratio implicitly reflects minority interests of noncontrolling investors in publicly traded companies—a condition that does not exist in the private or closely held corporation.

[20]The price/earnings multiple approach to valuation does have a theoretical explanation. If we view 1 divided by the price/earnings ratio, or the earnings/price ratio, as the rate at which investors discount the firm's earnings and if we assume that the projected earnings per share will be earned indefinitely (i.e., no growth in earnings per share), the price/earnings multiple approach can be looked on as a method of finding the present value of a perpetuity of projected earnings per share at a rate equal to the earnings/price ratio. This method is in effect a form of the zero growth model presented in Equation 7.8 on page 277.

CONCEPTS IN REVIEW

7-9 In an *efficient market,* describe the events that occur in response to new information that causes the expected return to exceed the required return. What happens to the market value?

7-10 What does the *efficient market hypothesis* say about (a) securities prices, (b) their reaction to new information, and (c) investor opportunities to profit? Is this hypothesis reasonable?

7-11 Describe, compare, and contrast each of the following common stock valuation models.

a. Zero growth
b. Constant growth
c. Variable growth

7-12 Explain each of the three other approaches to common stock valuation—(a) book value, (b) liquidation value, and (c) price/earnings (P/E) multiples. Which of these is considered the best?

Decision making and common stock value

The value of a share of stock at a given point in time is determined by its expected return and risk. What impact would a sudden decrease in expected return or an increase in risk have on stock value? Why? Before reading ahead, spend a few moments answering these questions.

Valuation equations measure the stock value at a point in time based on expected return (D_1, g) and risk (k_s) data. The decisions of the financial manager, through their effect on these variables, can cause the value of the firm, P_0, to change. Figure 7.3 depicts the relationship among financial decisions, return, risk, and stock value.

FIGURE 7.3
Financial decisions, return, risk, and stock value

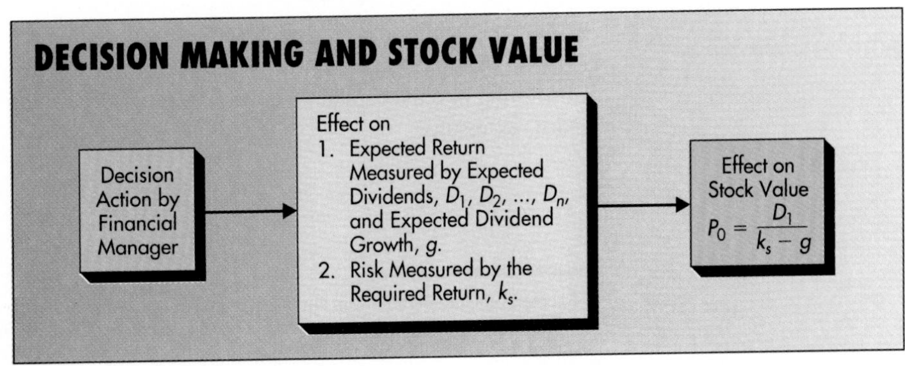

Changes in expected return

Assuming that economic conditions remain stable, any management action that would cause current and prospective stockholders to raise their dividend expectations should increase the firm's value. In Equation 7.10[21] we can see that P_0 will increase for any increase in D_1 or g. Any action of the financial manager that will increase the level of expected returns without changing risk (the required return) should be undertaken, since it will positively affect owners' wealth. An example will illustrate.

EXAMPLE

Imagine that Lamar Company, which was found to have a share value of \$18.75 in an earlier example using the constant growth model, on the following day announced a major technological breakthrough that would revolutionize its industry. Current and prospective stockholders are not expected to adjust their required return of 15 percent, but they do expect that future dividends will be increased. Specifically, they feel that although the dividend next year, D_1, will remain at \$1.50, the expected rate of growth will increase from 7 to 9 percent. If we substitute $D_1 = \$1.50$, $k_s = .15$, and $g = .09$ into Equation 7.10, the resulting value equals \$25 [i.e., $\$1.50 \div (.15 - .09)$]. The increased value therefore resulted from the higher expected future dividends reflected in the increase in the growth rate, g. ■

Changes in risk

Although k_s is defined as the required return, it is, as was pointed out in Chapter 6, directly related to the nondiversifiable risk, which can be measured by beta. The *capital asset pricing model (CAPM)* given in Equation 6.8 is restated as Equation 7.12:

$$k_s = R_F + [b \times (k_m - R_F)] \tag{7.12}$$

Reviewing the model, with the risk-free rate, R_F, and the required return on the market, k_m, held constant, the required return, k_s, depends directly on beta. In other words, any action taken by the financial manager that increases risk will also increase the required return. In Equation 7.10 it can be seen that with all else constant, an increase in the required return, k_s, will reduce share value, P_0, and a decrease in the required return will increase share value. Thus any action of the financial manager that increases risk contributes toward a reduction in value, and any action that decreases risk contributes toward an increase in value. An example will illustrate.

EXAMPLE

Assume that the Lamar Company's 15 percent required return resulted from a risk-free rate, R_F, of 9 percent, a market return, k_m, of 13 percent, and a beta, b, of 1.50. By substituting into the capital asset pricing model, Equation 7.12, the 15 percent required return, k_s, results:

$$k_s = 9\% + [1.50 \times (13\% - 9\%)] = \underline{\underline{15\%}}$$

[21]To convey the interrelationship among financial decisions, return, risk, and stock value, the constant growth dividend-valuation model is used. Other models—zero growth or variable growth—could be used, but the simplicity of exposition using the constant growth model justifies its use here.

By using this return, the value of the firm, P_0, was calculated to be $18.75 in the earli- er example.

Now imagine that the financial manager makes a decision that, without changing expected dividends, increases the firm's beta to 1.75. Assuming that R_F and k_m remain at 9 and 13 percent, respectively, the required return will increase to 16 percent (i.e., 9% + [1.75 × (13% − 9%)]) to compensate stockholders for the increased risk. By substituting D_1 = $1.50, k_s = .16, and g = .07 into the valuation equation, Equation 7.10, results in a share value of $16.67 [i.e., $1.50 ÷ (.16 − .07)]. As expected, the owners, by raising the required return (without any corresponding increase in expected return), cause the firm's stock value to decline. Clearly, the financial manager's action was not in the owners' best interest. ■

CONCEPT IN PRACTICE

Government Influence on the Required Rate of Return Helps to Keep USAir Flying High

Among the factors contributing to USAir's multimillion-dollar loss in 1992 was a long-term debt of almost 2.4 billion dollars. Fortunately for USAir and other big borrowers, the U.S. Treasury and Federal Reserve were attempting to reduce long-term interest rates in 1993. The Clinton Administration directed the Treasury Department to reduce its issuance of longer-term debt in favor of securities with shorter maturities. Reduced Treasury demand for long-term funds was expected to cut long-term interest rates. Meanwhile, the Federal Reserve increased its willingness to buy the remaining long-term Treasury issues, thereby increasing the supply of money available to purchase long-term corporate bonds. Bondholders would also benefit from rising bond values created by a decline in the required rate of return.

Combined effect

A financial decision rarely affects return and risk independently; most decisions affect both factors. In terms of the measures presented, with an increase in risk (beta, b) one would expect an increase in return (D_1 or g, or both), assuming that R_F and k_m remain unchanged. Depending on the relative magnitude of the changes in these variables, the net effect on value can be assessed.

EXAMPLE

If we assume that the two changes illustrated for Lamar Company in the preceding examples occur simultaneously as a result of an action of the financial decision maker, key variable values would be D_1 = $1.50, k_s = .16, and g = .09. By substituting into the valuation model, a share price of $21.43 [i.e., $1.50 ÷ (.16 − .09)] is obtained. The net result of the decision, which increased return (g from 7 to 9 percent) as well as risk (b from 1.50 to 1.75 and therefore k_s from 15 to 16 percent), is positive, since the share price increased from $18.75 to $21.43. Assuming that the key variables are accurately measured, the decision appears to be in the best interest of the firm's owners, since it increases their wealth. ■

CONCEPTS IN REVIEW

7-13 Explain the linkages among financial decisions, return, risk, and stock value. How do the *capital asset pricing model (CAPM)* and the *Gordon model* fit into this basic framework? Explain.

7-14 Assuming that all other variables remain unchanged, what impact would *each* of the following have on stock price? Explain your answer.

a. The firm's beta increases.
b. The firm's required return decreases.
c. The dividend expected next year decreases.
d. The rate of growth in dividends is expected to increase.

Summary

LG 1 Describe the key inputs—cash flows (returns), timing, and required return (risk)—and basic model used in the valuation process. Key inputs to the valuation process include cash flows (returns), timing, and the required return (risk). The value, or worth, of any asset is equal to the present value of all future cash flows it is expected to provide over the relevant time period. The key variable definitions and the basic valuation formula for any asset are summarized in Table 7.4.

LG 2 Apply the basic valuation model to bonds and evaluate the relationships between both required return and time to maturity and bond values. The value of a bond is the present value of interest payments plus the present value of its par, or face, value. The key variable definitions and the basic valuation formula for a bond are summarized in Table 7.4. The discount rate used to determine bond value is the required return, which may differ from the bond's stated coupon interest rate. A bond can sell at a discount, at par, or at a premium, depending upon whether the required return is respectively greater than, equal to, or less than its coupon interest rate. The amount of time to maturity affects bond values even if required return remains constant. When required return is constant, the value of a bond will approach its par value as the passage of time moves the bond closer to maturity. The shorter the amount of time until a bond's maturity, the less responsive is its market value to a given change in the required return.

LG 3 Explain yield to maturity (YTM), its calculation, and the procedure used to value bonds that pay interest semiannually. Yield to maturity (YTM) is the rate of return investors earn if they buy a bond at a specific price and hold it until maturity, assuming that the issuer makes all scheduled interest and principal payments as promised. YTM can be calculated by trial and error, approximation formula, or hand-held business/financial calculator. Bonds that pay interest semiannually are valued by using the same procedure that is used to value bonds paying annual interest except that the interest payments are one-half of the annual interest payments, the number of periods is twice the number of years to maturity, and the required return used is one-half of the stated annual required return on similar-risk bonds.

LG 4 Understand the concept of market efficiency and basic common-stock valuation under each of three cases: zero growth, constant growth, and variable growth. Market efficiency, which is assumed throughout the text, suggests that there are many rational investors whose quick reactions to new information cause the market value of common stock to adjust upward or downward depending upon whether the expected return is above or below, respectively, the required return for the period. The efficient market hypothesis suggests that securities are fairly priced, they reflect fully all publicly available information, and investors should therefore not waste time trying to find and capitalize on mispriced securities. The value of a share of common stock is the present value of all future dividends that it is expected to provide over an infinite time horizon. Three cases of dividend growth—zero growth, constant growth, and variable growth—can be considered in common stock valuation. The key variable definitions and the basic valuation formulas for each of these cases are summarized in Table 7.4. The most widely cited model is the constant growth model.

LG 5 Discuss three other approaches—book value, liquidation value, and price/earnings (P/E) multiples—that are used to estimate common stock values. Book value per share is merely the amount per share of common stock that would be received if the firm sold all of its assets for their exact book (accounting) value, paid off its liabilities (including preferred stock), and divided the remaining funds among the common stockholders. Liquidation value per share is the amount received by each shareholder, assuming that assets are sold at their market value, liabilities (including preferred stock) are paid, and the remaining funds are distributed among the common stockholders. The price/earnings (P/E) multiples approach estimates stock value by multiplying the firm's expected earnings per share (EPS) by the average price/earnings (P/E) ratio for the industry. Of these three approaches, P/E multiples are the most popular in practice because, unlike book and liquidation value, they view the firm as a going concern whose value lies in its earning power rather than its asset values.

LG 6 Review the relationship between the impact of financial decisions on both expected return and risk and their combined effect on the firm's value. In a stable economy, any action of the financial manager that increases the level of expected return without changing risk should increase share value, and any action that reduces the level of expected return without changing risk should reduce share value. Similarly, any action that increases risk (required return) will reduce share value, and any action that reduces risk will increase share value. In the constant growth model, returns are measured by next year's dividend (D_1) and its growth rate (g), and risk is measured by the required return (k_s). Because most financial decisions affect both return and risk, an assessment of their combined effect on value must be part of the financial decision-making process.

TABLE 7.4

SUMMARY OF KEY VALUATION DEFINITIONS AND FORMULAS

Variable definitions

V_0 = value of the asset at time zero
CF_t = cash flow expected at the end of year t
k = appropriate required return (discount rate)
n = relevant time period, or number of years to maturity
B_0 = bond value
I = annual interest on a bond
k_d = required return on a bond
M = par, or face, value of a bond
P_0 = value of common stock
D_t = per-share dividend expected at the end of year t
k_s = required return on common stock
g = constant rate of growth in dividends
D_0 = most recent per-share dividend
N = last year of initial growth period (in variable growth model)
g_1 = initial dividend growth rate (in variable growth model)
g_2 = subsequent dividend growth rate (in variable growth model)

Valuation formulas

Value of any asset

$$V_0 = \frac{CF_1}{(1+k)^1} + \frac{CF_2}{(1+k)^2} + \cdots + \frac{CF_n}{(1+k)^n} \quad \text{[Eq. 7.1]}$$

$$= [CF_1 \times (PVIF_{k,1})] + [CF_2 \times (PVIF_{k,2})] + \cdots + [CF_n \times (PVIF_{k,n})] \quad \text{[Eq. 7.2]}$$

Bond value

$$B_0 = I \times \left[\sum_{t=1}^{n} \frac{1}{(1+k_d)^t}\right] + M \times \left[\frac{1}{(1+k_d)^n}\right] \quad \text{[Eq. 7.3]}$$

$$= I \times (PVIFA_{k_d,n}) + M \times (PVIF_{k_d,n}) \quad \text{[Eq. 7.3a]}$$

Common-stock value

Zero growth: $P_0 = \frac{D_1}{k_s}$ (also used to value preferred stock) [Eq. 7.8]

Constant growth: $P_0 = \frac{D_1}{k_s - g}$ [Eq. 7.10]

Variable growth: $P_0 = \sum_{t=1}^{N} \frac{D_0 \times (1+g_1)^t}{(1+k_s)^t} + \left(\frac{1}{(1+k_s)^N} \times \frac{D_{N+1}}{k_s - g_2}\right)$ [Eq. 7.11]

Self-test problems (Solutions in Appendix E)

ST 7-1 LG 2 Bond valuation Lahey Industries has a $1,000 par value bond with an 8 percent coupon interest rate outstanding. The bond has 12 years remaining to its maturity date.

a. If interest is paid *annually,* what is the value of the bond when the required return is (1) 7 percent, (2) 8 percent, and (3) 10 percent?

b. Indicate for each case in **a** whether the bond is selling at a discount, at a premium, or at its par value.

c. Using the 10 percent required return, find the bond's value when interest is paid *semiannually.*

ST 7-2 LG 3 Yield to maturity Elliot Enterprises' bonds currently sell for $1,150, have an 11 percent coupon interest rate and a $1,000 par value, pay interest *annually,* and have 18 years to maturity.

a. Calculate the bonds' yield to maturity (YTM) to the nearest whole percent.

b. Estimate the bonds' YTM using the *approximate yield formula.*

c. Compare and discuss your findings in **a** and **b**.

d. Compare the YTM calculated in **a** to the bonds' coupon interest rate, and use a comparison of the bonds' current price and their par value to explain this difference.

ST 7-3 LG 4 Common stock valuation Perry Motors' common stock currently pays an annual dividend of $1.80 per share. The required return on the common stock is 12 percent. Estimate the value of the common stock under each of the following dividend-growth-rate assumptions.

a. Dividends are expected to grow at an annual rate of 0 percent to infinity.

b. Dividends are expected to grow at a constant annual rate of 5 percent to infinity.

c. Dividends are expected to grow at an annual rate of 5 percent for each of the next three years followed by a constant annual growth rate of 4 percent from year 4 to infinity.

Problems

7-1 LG 1 Valuation fundamentals Imagine that you are trying to evaluate the economics of purchasing an automobile. Assume that you expect the car to provide annual after-tax cash benefits of $1,200 and that you can sell the car for after-tax proceeds of $5,000 at the end of the planned five-year ownership period. All funds for purchasing the car will be drawn from your savings, which are currently earning 6 percent after taxes.

a. Identify the cash flows, their timing, and the required return applicable to valuing the car.

b. What is the maximum price you would be willing to pay to acquire the car? Explain why.

7-2 LG 1 Valuation of assets Using the information provided in the table at the top of page 291, find the value of each of the assets given.

7-3 LG 1 Asset valuation and risk Laura Drake wishes to estimate the value of an asset that is expected to provide cash inflows of $3,000 per year at the end of years 1 through 4 and $15,000 at the end of year 5. Her research indicates that she must earn 10 percent on low-risk assets, 15 percent on average-risk assets, and 22 percent on high-risk assets.

a. What is the most Laura should pay for the asset if it is classified as (1) low risk? (2) average risk? (3) high risk?

b. If Laura is unable to assess the risk of the asset and wants to be certain she makes a good deal, on the basis of your findings in **a**, what is the most she should pay? Why?

c. All else being the same, what effect does increasing risk have on the value of an asset? Explain in light of your findings in **a**.

Asset	Cash flow: End of year	Cash flow: Amount ($)	Appropriate required return (%)
A	1	5,000	18
	2	5,000	
	3	5,000	
B	1 through ∞	300	15
C	1	0	16
	2	0	
	3	0	
	4	0	
	5	35,000	
D	1 through 5	1,500	12
	6	8,500	
E	1	2,000	14
	2	3,000	
	3	5,000	
	4	7,000	
	5	4,000	
	6	1,000	

7-4 LG 2 Basic bond valuation Complex Systems has an issue of $1,000-par-value bonds with a 12 percent coupon interest rate outstanding. The issue pays interest annually and has 16 years remaining to its maturity date.

a. If bonds of similar risk are currently earning a 10 percent rate of return, how much will the Complex Systems bond sell for today?

b. Describe the *two* possible reasons that similar-risk bonds are currently earning a return below the coupon interest rate on the Complex Systems bond.

c. If the required return were at 12 percent instead of 10 percent, what would the current value of Complex Systems' bond be? Contrast this finding with your findings in **a** and discuss.

7-5 LG 2 Bond valuation—Annual interest Calculate the value of each of the following bonds, all of which pay interest *annually*.

Bond	Par value ($)	Coupon interest rate (%)	Years to maturity	Required return (%)
A	1,000	14	20	12
B	1,000	8	16	8
C	100	10	8	13
D	500	16	13	18
E	1,000	12	10	10

7-6 LG 2 Bond value and changing required returns Midland Utilities has outstanding a bond issue that will mature to its $1,000 par value in 12 years. The bond has a coupon interest rate of 11 percent and pays interest *annually.*

a. Find the value of the bond if the required return is (1) 11 percent, (2) 15 percent, (3) 8 percent.

b. Plot your findings in **a** on a set of required return (*x*-axis)–market value of bond (*y*-axis) axes.

c. Use your findings in **a** and **b** to discuss the relationship between the coupon interest rate on a bond and the required return and the market value of the bond relative to its par value.

d. What two reasons cause the required return to differ from the coupon interest rate?

7-7 LG 2 **Bond value and time—Constant required returns** Pecos Manufacturing has just issued a 15-year, 12 percent coupon interest rate, $1,000-par bond that pays interest *annually.* The required return is currently 14 percent, and the company is certain it will remain at 14 percent until the bond matures in 15 years.

a. Assuming that the required return does remain at 14 percent until maturity, find the value of the bond with (1) 15 years, (2) 12 years, (3) 9 years, (4) 6 years, (5) 3 years, and (6) 1 year to maturity.

b. Plot your findings on a set of time to maturity (*x*-axis)–market value of bond (*y*-axis) axes constructed similarly to Figure 7.2.

c. All else remaining the same, when the required return differs from the coupon interest rate and is assumed to be constant to maturity, what happens to the bond value as time moves toward maturity? Explain in light of the graph in **b**.

7-8 LG 2 **Bond value and time—Changing required returns** Lynn Parsons is considering investing in either of two outstanding bonds. The bonds both have $1,000 par values and 11 percent coupon interest rates and pay *annual* interest. Bond A has exactly five years to maturity, while bond B has 15 years remaining until it matures.

a. Calculate the value of bond A if the required return is (1) 8 percent, (2) 11 percent, and (3) 14 percent.

b. Calculate the value of bond B if the required return is (1) 8 percent, (2) 11 percent, and (3) 14 percent.

c. From your findings in **a** and **b,** complete the following table, and discuss the relationship between time to maturity and changing required returns.

Required return (%)	Value of bond A	Value of bond B
8	?	?
11	?	?
14	?	?

d. If Lynn wanted to minimize "interest rate risk," which bond should she purchase? Why?

7-9 LG 3 **Yield to maturity—Trial-and-error and approximate approaches** The Salem Company bond currently sells for $955, has a 12 percent coupon interest rate and $1,000 par value, pays interest *annually,* and has 15 years to maturity.

a. Calculate the yield to maturity (YTM) on this bond using the trial-and-error present-value-based approach.

b. Use the *approximate yield formula* to estimate the YTM on this bond.

c. Compare the yields calculated in **a** and **b**, and discuss the relative utility of the approximation formula. Which approach would you recommend?

d. Explain the relationship that exists between the coupon interest rate and yield to maturity and the par value and market value of a bond.

7-10 LG 3 Yield to maturity Each of the following bonds pays interest *annually.*

Bond	Par value ($)	Coupon interest rate (%)	Years to maturity	Current value ($)
A	1,000	9	8	820
B	1,000	12	16	1,000
C	500	12	12	560
D	1,000	15	10	1,120
E	1,000	5	3	900

a. Use the approximate yield *formula* to find the yield to maturity (YTM) for each bond.
b. Calculate the YTM for each bond using the trial-and-error present-value-based approach.
c. Compare and contrast your findings in **a** and **b** for each bond. Comment on the accuracy of your estimates from **a**.
d. What relationship exists between the coupon interest rate and yield to maturity and the par value and market value of a bond? Explain.

7-11 LG 3 Bond valuation—Semiannual interest Find the value of a bond maturing in six years, with a $1,000 par value and a coupon interest rate of 10 percent (5 percent paid semiannually) if the required stated return on similar-risk bonds is 14 percent annual interest (7 percent paid semiannually).

7-12 LG 3 Bond valuation—Semiannual interest Calculate the value of each of the following bonds, all of which pay interest *semiannually.*

Bond	Par value ($)	Coupon interest rate (%)	Years to maturity	Required stated return (%)
A	1,000	10	12	8
B	1,000	12	20	12
C	500	12	5	14
D	1,000	14	10	10
E	100	6	4	14

7-13 LG 3 Bond valuation—Quarterly interest Calculate the value of a $5,000-par-value bond paying quarterly interest at an annual coupon interest rate of 10 percent and having 10 years until maturity if the required stated return on similar-risk bonds is currently a 12 percent annual rate paid *quarterly.*

7-14 LG 4 Common stock valuation—Zero growth Scotto Manufacturing is a mature firm in the machine-tool-component industry. The firm's most recent common-stock dividend was $2.40 per share. Due to its maturity as well as stable sales and earnings, the firm's management feels that dividends will remain at the current level for the foreseeable future.
a. If the required return is 12 percent, what is the value of Scotto's common stock?
b. If the firm's risk as perceived by market participants suddenly increases, causing the required return to rise to 20 percent, what will be the common stock value?
c. On the basis of your findings in **a** and **b,** what impact does risk have on value? Explain.

7-15 LG 4 Preferred stock valuation Jones Design wishes to estimate the value of its outstanding preferred stock. The preferred issue has an $80 par value and pays an annual dividend of $6.40 per share. Similar-risk preferred stocks are currently earning a 9.3 percent annual rate of return.

a. What is the market value of the outstanding preferred stock?

b. If an investor purchases the preferred stock at the value calculated in **a**, how much would she gain or lose per share if she sells the stock when the required return on similar-risk preferreds has risen to 10.5 percent? Explain.

7-16 LG 4 **Common stock value—Constant growth** Use the constant growth valuation model (Gordon model) to find the value of each of the following firms.

Firm	Dividend expected next year ($)	Dividend growth rate (%)	Required return (%)
A	1.20	8	13
B	4.00	5	15
C	.65	10	14
D	6.00	8	9
E	2.25	8	20

7-17 LG 4 **Common stock value—Constant growth** Elk County Telephone has paid the following dividends over the past six years:

Year	Dividend per share ($)
1994	2.87
1993	2.76
1992	2.60
1991	2.46
1990	2.37
1989	2.25

The firm's dividend per share next year is expected to be $3.02.

a. If you can earn 13 percent on similar-risk investments, what is the most you would pay per share for this firm?

b. If you can earn only 10 percent on similar-risk investments, what is the most you would be willing to pay per share?

c. Compare and contrast your findings in **a** and **b**, and discuss the impact of changing risk on share value.

7-18 LG 4 **Common stock value—Variable growth** Newman Manufacturing is considering a cash purchase of the stock of Grips Tool. During the year just completed, Grips earned $4.25 per share and paid cash dividends of $2.55 per share. Grips' earnings and dividends are expected to grow at 25 percent per year for the next three years, after which they are expected to grow at 10 percent per year to infinity. What is the maximum price per share Newman should pay for Grips if it has a required return of 15 percent on investments with risk characteristics similar to those of Grips?

7-19 LG 4 **Common stock value—Variable growth** Lawrence Industries' most recent annual dividend was $1.80 per share ($D_0$ = $1.80), and the firm's required return is 11 percent. Find the market value of Lawrence's shares when:

a. Dividends are expected to grow at 8 percent annually for three years followed by a 5 percent constant annual growth rate from year 4 to infinity.

b. Dividends are expected to grow at 8 percent annually for three years followed by zero percent annual growth in years 4 to infinity.

c. Dividends are expected to grow at 8 percent annually for three years followed by a 10 percent constant annual growth rate in years 4 to infinity.

7-20 LG 4 Common stock value—All growth models You are evaluating the potential purchase of a small business that is currently generating $42,500 of after-tax cash flow (D_0 = $42,500). On the basis of a review of similar-risk investment opportunities, you must earn an 18 percent rate of return on the proposed purchase. Since you are relatively uncertain as to future cash flows, you have decided to estimate the firm's value using several possible cash-flow growth-rate assumptions.

a. What is the firm's value if cash flows are expected to grow at an annual rate of 0 percent to infinity?

b. What is the firm's value if cash flows are expected to grow at a constant annual rate of 7 percent to infinity?

c. What is the firm's value if cash flows are expected to grow at an annual rate of 12 percent for the first two years followed by a constant annual rate of 7 percent from year 3 to infinity?

7-21 LG 5 Book and liquidation value The balance sheet for Gallinas Industries follows.

Balance sheet
Gallinas Industries
December 31

Assets		Liabilities and stockholders' equity	
Cash	$ 40,000	Accounts payable	$100,000
Marketable securities	60,000	Notes payable	30,000
Accounts receivable	120,000	Accrued wages	30,000
Inventories	160,000	Total current liabilities	$160,000
Total current assets	$380,000	Long-term debt	$180,000
Land and buildings (net)	$150,000	Preferred stock	$ 80,000
Machinery and equipment	250,000	Common stock (10,000 shares)	360,000
Total fixed assets (net)	$400,000	Total liabilities and	
Total assets	$780,000	stockholders' equity	$780,000

Additional information with respect to the firm is available:

(1) Preferred stock can be liquidated for its book value.
(2) Accounts receivable and inventories can be liquidated at 90 percent of book value.
(3) The firm has 10,000 shares of common stock outstanding.
(4) All interest and dividends are currently paid up.
(5) Land and buildings can be liquidated for 130 percent of their book value.
(6) Machinery and equipment can be liquidated at 70 percent of book value.
(7) Cash and marketable securities can be liquidated at book value.

Given this information, answer the following:

a. What is Gallinas Industries' book value per share?
b. What is the liquidation value per share?
c. Compare, contrast, and discuss the values found in **a** and **b**.

7-22 LG 5 Valuation with price/earnings multiples For each of the following firms, use the data given to estimate their common stock value employing price/earnings (P/E) multiples.

Firm	Expected EPS ($)	Price/earnings multiple
A	3.00	6.2
B	4.50	10.0
C	1.80	12.6
D	2.40	8.9
E	5.10	15.0

7-23 LG **6** **Management action and stock value** REH Corporation's most recent dividend was $3 per share, its expected annual rate of dividend growth is 5 percent, and the required return is now 15 percent. A variety of proposals are being considered by management to redirect the firm's activities. For each of the proposed actions below, determine the resulting impact on share price and indicate the best alternative.

a. Do nothing, which will leave the key financial variables unchanged.
b. Invest in a new machine that will increase the dividend growth rate to 6 percent and lower the required return to 14 percent.
c. Eliminate an unprofitable product line, which will increase the dividend growth rate to 7 percent and raise the required return to 17 percent.
d. Merge with another firm, which will reduce the growth rate to 4 percent and raise the required return to 16 percent.
e. Acquire a subsidiary operation from another manufacturer. The acquisition should increase the dividend growth rate to 8 percent and increase the required return to 17 percent.

7-24 LG **4,6** **Integrative—Valuation and CAPM formulas** Given the following information for the stock of Foster Company, calculate its beta.

Current price per share of common	$50.00
Expected dividend per share next year	$ 3.00
Constant annual dividend growth rate	9%
Risk-free rate of return	7%
Required return on market portfolio	10%

7-25 LG **4,6** **Integrative—Risk and valuation** Giant Enterprises has a beta of 1.20, the risk-free rate of return is currently 10 percent, and the required return on the market portfolio is 14 percent. The company, which plans to pay a dividend of $2.60 per share in the coming year, anticipates that its future dividends will increase at an annual rate consistent with that experienced over the 1988–1994 period, when the following dividends were paid:

Year	Dividend per share ($)	Year	Dividend per share ($)
1994	2.45	1990	1.82
1993	2.28	1989	1.80
1992	2.10	1988	1.73
1991	1.95		

a. Use the capital asset pricing model (CAPM) to determine the required return on Giant Enterprises' stock.
b. Using the constant growth dividend valuation model and your finding in **a,** estimate the value of Giant Enterprises' stock.
c. Explain what effect, if any, a decrease in beta would have on the value of Giant's stock.

7-26 LG **4,6** **Integrative—Valuation and CAPM** Hamlin Steel Company wishes to determine the value of Craft Foundry, a firm that it is considering acquiring for cash. Hamlin wishes to use the capital asset pricing model (CAPM) to determine the applicable discount rate to use as an input to the constant growth valuation model. Craft's stock is not publicly traded. After studying the betas of firms similar to Craft that are publicly traded, Hamlin believes that an appropriate beta for Craft's stock would be 1.25. The risk-free rate is currently 9 percent, and the market return is 13 percent. Craft's historical dividend per share for each of the past six years is given below:

Year	Dividend per share ($)
1994	3.44
1993	3.28
1992	3.15
1991	2.90
1990	2.75
1989	2.45

a. Given that Craft is expected to pay a dividend of $3.68 next year, determine the maximum cash price Hamlin should pay for each share of Craft.

b. Discuss the use of the CAPM for estimating the value of common stock, and describe the effect on the resulting value of Craft of:
(1) A decrease in the dividend growth rate of 2 percent from that exhibited over the 1989–1994 period.
(2) A decrease in the beta to 1.

Chapter 7 Case Assessing the impact of Suarez Manufacturing's proposed risky investment on its bond and stock values

Early in 1995, Inez Marcus, the chief financial officer for Suarez Manufacturing, was given the task of assessing the impact of a proposed risky investment on the firm's bond and stock values. To perform the necessary analysis, Inez gathered the following relevant data on the firm's bonds and stock.

Bonds The firm has one bond issue currently outstanding. It has a $1,000 par value, a 9 percent coupon interest rate, and 18 years remaining to maturity. Interest on the bond is paid annually, and the bond's required return is currently 8 percent. After a great deal of research and consultation, Inez concluded that the proposed investment would not violate any of the bond's numerous provisions. Because the proposed investment will increase the overall risk of the firm, she expects that if it is undertaken, the required return on these bonds will increase to 10 percent.

Stock During the immediate past five years (1990–1994) the annual dividends paid on the firm's common stock were as follows:

Year	Dividend per share ($)
1994	1.90
1993	1.70
1992	1.55
1991	1.40
1990	1.30

The firm expects that without the proposed investment the dividend in 1995 will be $2.09 per share and the annual rate of growth (rounded to the nearest whole percent) will continue in the future. Currently, the required return on the common stock is 14 percent. Inez's research indicates that if the proposed investment is undertaken, the 1995 dividend will rise to $2.15 per share and the annual rate of dividend growth will increase to 13 percent. She feels that in the *best case* the dividend would continue to grow at this rate each year into the future, and in the *worst case* the 13 percent annual rate of growth in dividends would continue only through 1997, and then at the beginning of 1998 the rate of growth would return to the rate that was experienced between 1990 and 1994. As a result of the increased risk associated with the proposed risky investment, the required return on the common stock is expected to increase by 2 percent to an annual rate of 16 percent, regardless of which dividend-growth outcome occurs.

Armed with the above data, Inez must now assess the impact of the proposed risky investment on the market value of Suarez's bonds and stock. To simplify her calculations, she plans to round the historic growth rate in common-stock dividends to the nearest whole percent.

Required

a. Find the *current* value of each of Suarez Manufacturing's bonds.

b. Find the *current* value per share of Suarez Manufacturing's common stock.

c. Find the value of Suarez's bonds in the event that it *undertakes the proposed risky investment*. Compare this value to that found in **a**. What effect would the proposed investment have on the firm's bondholders? Explain.

d. Find the value of Suarez's common stock in the event that it *undertakes the proposed risky investment* and assuming that the dividend growth rate stays at 13 percent forever. Compare this value to that found in **b**. What effect would the proposed investment have on the firm's stockholders? Explain.

e. On the basis of your findings in **c** and **d**, who wins and who loses as a result of undertaking the proposed risky investment? Should the firm do it? Why?

f. Rework parts **d** and **e** assuming that at the beginning of 1998 the annual dividend growth rate returns to the rate experienced between 1990 and 1994.

INTEGRATIVE CASE II
ENCORE INTERNATIONAL

In the world of trend-setting fashion, instinct and marketing savvy are prerequisites to success. Jordan Ellis had both. His international casual-wear company, Encore, after 10 years in business rocketed to $300 million in sales during 1994. His fashion line covered the young woman from head to toe with hats, sweaters, dresses, blouses, skirts, pants, sweatshirts, socks, and shoes. In Manhattan there was an Encore shop every five or six blocks, each featuring a different color. There were shops where the entire line was mauve, while others featured the entire line in canary yellow.

Encore had made it. The company's historical growth was so spectacular that no one could have predicted it. However, securities analysts speculated that Encore could not keep up the pace. They warned that competition is fierce in the fashion industry and that the firm might encounter little or no growth in the future. They estimated that stockholders also should expect no growth in future dividends.

Contrary to the conservative security analysts, Jordan Ellis, founder of Encore, felt that the company could maintain a constant annual growth rate in dividends per share of 6 percent in the future, or possibly 8 percent for the next two years and 6 percent thereafter. Jordan Ellis based his estimates on an established long-term expansion plan into European and Latin American markets. By venturing into these markets the risk of the firm as measured by beta was expected to immediately increase from 1.10 to 1.25.

In preparing the long-term financial plan, Encore's chief financial officer has assigned a junior financial analyst, Marc Scott, to evaluate the firm's current stock price. He has asked Marc to consider the conservative predictions of the securities analysts and the aggressive predictions of the company founder, Jordan Ellis.

Marc has compiled these 1994 financial data to aid his analysis.

Data item	1994 value
Earnings per share (EPS)	$6.25
Price per share of common stock	$40.00
Book value of common stock equity	$60,000,000
Total common shares outstanding	2,500,000
Common stock dividend per share	$4.00

Required

a. What is the firm's current book value per share?

b. What is the firm's current P/E ratio?

c. (1) What are the required return and risk premium for Encore stock using the capital asset pricing model, assuming a beta of 1.10? (*Hint:* Use the security market line—with data points noted—given in the figure below to find the market return.)
(2) What are the required return and risk premium for Encore stock using the capital asset pricing model, assuming a beta of 1.25?
(3) What is the effect on the required return if the beta rises as expected?

d. If the securities analysts are correct and there is no growth in future dividends, what is the value per share of the Encore stock? (*Note:* Beta = 1.25.)

e. (1) If Jordan Ellis' predictions are correct, what is the value per share of Encore stock if the firm maintains a constant annual 6 percent growth rate in future dividends? (*Note:* Beta = 1.25.)
(2) If Jordan Ellis' predictions are correct, what is the value per share of Encore stock if the firm maintains a constant annual 8 percent growth rate in dividends per share over the next two years and 6 percent thereafter? (*Note:* Beta = 1.25.)

f. Compare the current (1994) price of the stock and the stock values found in **b**, **d**, and **e**. Discuss why these values may differ. Which valuation method do you believe most clearly represents the true value of the Encore stock?

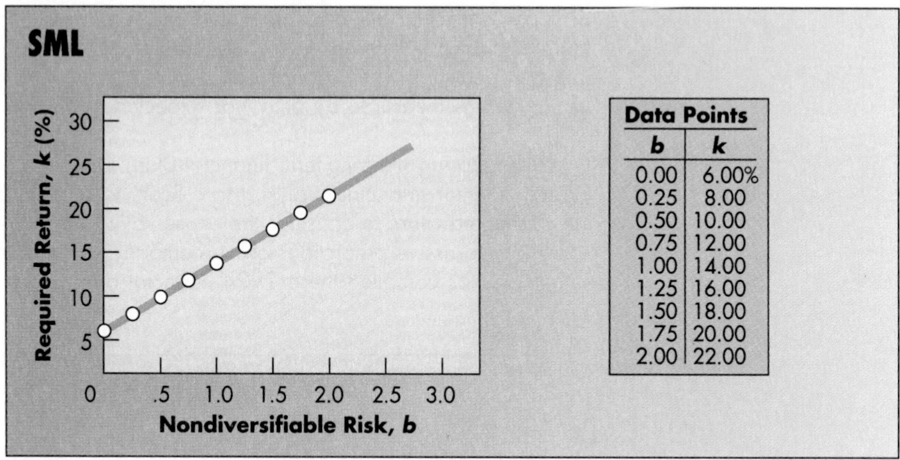

Security market line for Encore International

part III

Long-term investment decisions

CHAPTERS IN THIS PART

chapter 8

Capital budgeting and cash flow principles

LEARNING GOALS

 Understand the key capital expenditure motives and the steps in the capital budgeting process, beginning with proposal generation and ending with follow-up.

 Describe the basic terminology used to describe projects, funds availability, decision approaches, and cash flow patterns.

 Discuss the major components of relevant cash flows, differences in the development of expansion- versus replacement-decision cash flows, and international capital budgeting and long-term investments.

 Calculate the initial investment associated with a proposed capital expenditure, given relevant cost, depreciation, tax, and net working capital data.

 Determine the operating cash inflows that are relevant to a capital budgeting proposal using the income statement format.

 Find the terminal cash flow associated with a capital budgeting proposal, given relevant sale price, depreciation, tax, and net working capital data.

Kaiser Foundation Health Plan, Inc. is the country's largest health maintenance organization (HMO). The Health Plan, together with Kaiser Foundation Hospitals, has about 6.6 million members who pay monthly membership dues for medical and hospital services. Both Kaiser Foundation Health Plan and Kaiser Foundation Hospitals are non-profit organizations, and this affects financial management in several ways. First, we have fewer financing sources. We don't issue common stock; we either earn money on operations or borrow. We own our medical facilities and equipment (whereas some HMOs contract with local physicians and hospitals) and our current capital budget is about $1 billion a year. So we need to maintain access to the debt market. Second, we have no shareholders and can focus on the longer-term view and achieving stakeholder (member, employer, employee, and community) satisfaction, rather than short-term profitability. Third, we don't worry about the tax implications of financial strategies, because we don't pay income taxes. Finally, it is much harder to monitor performance; there are many factors as important as the bottom line—such as whether we're growing, offering good care at reasonable rates, and providing community service benefits. It's always a struggle to figure out how well we're doing as an organization.

Making sound capital investment decisions is important for any company, whether for-profit or non-profit, and Kaiser is no exception. Our large annual capital budget requires a well-developed capital budgeting process. Also, health care facilities and equipment purchases have a long approval and construction phases. We must plan our financing and spread the facilities cost to the members. Many of our projects are large and complex—for example, a $200 million medical center with hospital plus doctor's offices. We analyze these projects very carefully before committing our resources.

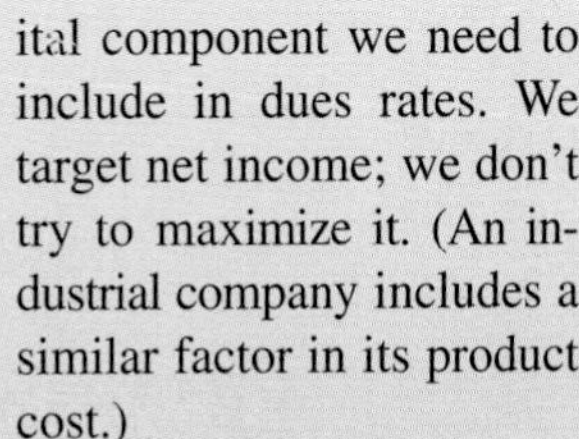

Our large annual capital budget requires a well-developed capital budgeting process.

Our long-range capital planning process covers a 10 to 15 year period, probably longer than many organizations'. Each of our 12 regions develops its own capital forecast, translating membership forecasts into required services for existing and new members and equipment and facilities needs. Finally, we review and consolidate them and make our centralized financing plans.

Next, we prepare a forecast of internally generated funds that, when supplemented with debt, will cover the all planned capital expenditures. Then each region estimates its net income and cash flow for the next year, and we calculate the capital component we need to include in dues rates. We target net income; we don't try to maximize it. (An industrial company includes a similar factor in its product cost.)

The hardest part of developing capital budgeting cash flows is the timing of cash payments on facilities projects. While we can reasonably forecast the project's total cost and overall timeframe, we can't predict when the cash payments will be made to the contractors; inevitably there are delays. Forecasting our working capital is also somewhat difficult because it varies so much. Timing land purchases is also hard due to lengthy negotiations, soil tests, and maybe zoning.

Recently we began integrating our capital and strategic plans, to link capital and operating decisions more closely. In the past we did not always understand the operational implications of a capital investment. We're also trying to better define the non-quantifiable benefits of our capital projects that can't be measured in dollars or rate of return, such as better quality of care and greater membership satisfaction.

Susan Porth joined Kaiser Foundation Health Plan and Kaiser Foundation Hospitals in 1978 as Treasurer and became Senior Vice President–Finance in 1988. She held various finance positions, in the Treasury Department during her seven years at Crown Zellerbach, a major paper manufacturer. Ms Porth received an A.B. in Economics from Smith College and an M.B.A. from Harvard Business School.

The capital budgeting decision process

The capital budgeting process involves generating long-term investment proposals; reviewing, analyzing, and selecting them; and implementing and following up on those selected. Why do financial managers give these long-term investment decisions so much attention? Before reading on, spend a few moments answering this question in light of the firm's goal.

BECAUSE LONG-TERM INVESTMENTS REPRESENT SIZABLE OUTLAYS OF FUNDS THAT COMmit a firm to some course of action, procedures are needed to analyze and select them properly. Attention must be given to measuring relevant cash flows and applying appropriate decision techniques. As time passes, fixed assets may become obsolete or may require an overhaul; at these points, too, financial decisions may be required. **Capital budgeting** is the process of evaluating and selecting long-term investments that are consistent with the firm's goal of owner wealth maximization. Firms typically make a variety of long-term investments, but the most common such investment for the manufacturing firm is in *fixed assets,* which include property (land), plant, and equipment. These assets are quite often referred to as *earning assets* because they generally provide the basis for the firm's earning power and value. Note that for ease of presentation and study, both this and the following chapter are devoted to coverage of capital budgeting.

capital budgeting
The process of evaluating and selecting long-term investments that are consistent with the firm's goal of owner wealth maximization.

Capital budgeting (investment) and financing decisions are treated *separately,* although it should become clear in the following chapter that the use of the cost of capital as a discount rate links these two decisions. Typically, once a proposed investment has been determined to be acceptable, the financial manager then chooses the best financing method. Therefore we concentrate here on fixed asset acquisition without regard to the specific method of financing used. Chapters 10 through 14 address the key issues related to long-term financing of fixed assets. This section of the chapter discusses capital expenditure motives, the steps in the capital budgeting process, and basic capital budgeting terminology.

Capital expenditure motives

A **capital expenditure** is an outlay of funds by the firm that is expected to produce benefits over a period of time *greater than* one year. A **current expenditure** is an outlay resulting in benefits received *within* one year. Fixed-asset outlays are capital expenditures, but not all capital expenditures are classified as fixed assets. A $60,000 outlay for a new machine with a usable life of 15 years is a capital expenditure that would appear as a fixed asset on the firm's balance sheet. A $60,000 outlay for advertising that produces benefits over a long period is also a capital expenditure. However, an outlay for advertising would rarely be shown as a fixed asset.[1]

capital expenditure
An outlay of funds by the firm that is expected to produce benefits over a period of time *greater than* one year.

current expenditure
An outlay of funds by the firm resulting in benefits received *within* one year.

[1]Some firms do, in effect, capitalize advertising outlays if there is reason to believe that the benefit of the outlay will be received at some future date. The capitalized advertising may appear as a deferred charge such as "deferred advertising expense," which is then amortized over the future. Expenses of this type are often deferred for reporting purposes to increase reported earnings, while for tax purposes the entire amount will be expensed to reduce the tax liability.

Capital expenditures are made for many reasons, but although the motives differ, the evaluation techniques are the same. The basic motives for capital expenditures are to expand, replace, or renew fixed assets or to obtain some other less tangible benefit over a long period. Table 8.1 provides brief descriptions of the key motives for making capital expenditures.

Steps in the process

capital budgeting process
Consists of five distinct but interrelated steps: proposal generation, review and analysis, decision making, implementation, and follow-up.

The **capital budgeting process** can be viewed as consisting of five distinct but interrelated steps. It begins with *proposal generation.* This is followed by *review and analysis, decision making, implementation,* and *follow-up.* A brief description of each of these steps is given in Table 8.2. Each step in the process is important; major time and effort, however, are devoted to review and analysis and decision making. These are the steps that are given the most attention in this and the following chapter.

Basic terminology

Before beginning to develop the concepts, tools, and techniques related to the review and analysis and decision-making steps in the capital budgeting process, it is useful to understand some of the basic terminology of these areas. In addition, we present a number of key assumptions that are used to simplify the discussion in the remainder of this chapter as well as in Chapter 9.

TABLE 8.1

KEY MOTIVES FOR MAKING CAPITAL EXPENDITURES

Motive	Description
Expansion	The most common motive for a capital expenditure is to expand the level of operations—usually through acquisition of fixed assets. A growing firm often finds it necessary to acquire new fixed assets rapidly; sometimes this includes the purchase of additional physical facilities, such as additional property and plant.
Replacement	As a firm's growth slows and it reaches maturity, most of its capital expenditures will be for the replacement or renewal of obsolete or worn-out assets. Each time a machine requires a major repair, the outlay for the repair should be evaluated in terms of the outlay to replace the machine and the benefits of replacement.
Renewal	Often an alternative to replacement. Renewal may involve rebuilding, overhauling, or retrofitting an existing machine or facility. For example, an existing drill press could be renewed by replacing its motor and adding a numeric control system, or a physical facility could be renewed by rewiring, adding air conditioning, and so on. Firms wishing to improve efficiency may find that both replacing and renewing existing machinery are suitable solutions.
Other purposes	Some capital expenditures do not result in the acquisition or transformation of tangible fixed assets shown on the firm's balance sheet. Instead, they involve a long-term commitment of funds by the firm in expectation of a future return. These expenditures include outlays for advertising, research and development, management consulting, and new products. Other capital expenditure proposals—such as the installment of pollution-control and safety devices mandated by the government—are difficult to evaluate because they provide intangible returns rather than clearly measurable cash flows.

TABLE 8.2

STEPS IN THE CAPITAL BUDGETING PROCESS

Steps (listed in order)	Description
Proposal generation	Proposals for capital expenditures are made by people at all levels within a business organization. To stimulate a flow of ideas that could result in potential cost savings, many firms offer cash rewards to employees whose proposals are ultimately adopted. Capital expenditure proposals typically travel from the originator to a reviewer at a higher level in the organization. Clearly, proposals requiring large outlays will be much more carefully scrutinized than less costly ones.
Review and analysis	Capital expenditure proposals are formally reviewed (1) to assess their appropriateness in light of the firm's overall objectives and plans and, more important, (2) to evaluate their economic validity. The proposed costs and benefits are estimated and then converted into a series of relevant cash flows to which various capital budgeting techniques are applied to measure the investment merit of the potential outlay. In addition, various aspects of the *risk* associated with the proposal are either incorporated into the economic analysis or rated and recorded along with the economic measures. Once the economic analysis is completed, a summary report, often with a recommendation, is submitted to the decision maker(s).
Decision making	The actual dollar outlay and the importance of a capital expenditure determine the organizational level at which the expenditure decision is made. Firms typically delegate capital-expenditure authority on the basis of certain dollar limits. Generally, the board of directors reserves the right to make final decisions on capital expenditures requiring outlays beyond a certain amount, while the authority for making smaller expenditures is given to other organizational levels. Inexpensive capital expenditures such as the purchase of a hammer for $15 are treated as operating outlays not requiring formal analysis.[a] Generally, firms operating under critical time constraints with respect to production often find it necessary to provide exceptions to a strict dollar-outlay scheme. In such cases the plant manager is often given the power to make decisions necessary to keep the production line moving, even though the outlays entailed are larger than he or she would normally be allowed to authorize.
Implementation	Once a proposal has been approved and funding has been made available,[b] the implementation phase begins. For minor outlays, implementation is relatively routine; the expenditure is made, and payment is rendered. For major expenditures, greater control is required to ensure that what has been proposed and approved is acquired at the budgeted costs. Often the expenditures for a single proposal may occur in phases, each outlay requiring the signed approval of company officers.
Follow-up	Involves monitoring the results during the operating phase of a project. The comparisons of actual outcomes in terms of costs and benefits with those expected and those of previous projects are vital. When actual outcomes deviate from projected outcomes, action may be required to cut costs, improve benefits, or possibly terminate the project.

[a]There is a certain dollar limit beyond which outlays are *capitalized* (i.e., treated as a fixed asset) and *depreciated* rather than *expensed.* This dollar limit depends largely on what the U.S. Internal Revenue Service will permit. In accounting, the issue of whether to expense or capitalize an outlay is resolved by using the *principle of materiality,* which suggests that any outlays deemed material (i.e., large) relative to the firm's scale of operations should be capitalized, whereas others should be expensed in the current period.

[b]Capital expenditures are often approved as part of the annual budgeting process, although funding will not be made available until the budget is implemented—frequently as long as six months after approval.

INDEPENDENT VERSUS MUTUALLY EXCLUSIVE PROJECTS

independent projects
Projects whose cash flows are unrelated or independent of one another; the acceptance of one *does not eliminate* the others from further consideration.

mutually exclusive projects
Projects that compete with one another, so that the acceptance of one *eliminates* the others from further consideration.

The two most common project types are (1) independent projects and (2) mutually exclusive projects. **Independent projects** are projects whose cash flows are unrelated or independent of one another; the acceptance of one *does not eliminate* the others from further consideration. If a firm has unlimited funds to invest, all the independent projects that meet its minimum investment criteria can be implemented. For example, a firm with unlimited funds may be faced with three acceptable independent projects—(1) installing air conditioning in the plant, (2) acquiring a small supplier, and (3) purchasing a new computer system. Clearly, the acceptance of any one of these projects does not eliminate the others from further consideration; all three could be undertaken. **Mutually exclusive projects** are projects that have the same function and therefore compete with one another. The acceptance of one of a group of mutually exclusive projects *eliminates* all other projects in the group from further consideration. For example, a firm in need of increased production capacity could obtain it by (1) expanding its plant, (2) acquiring another company, or (3) contracting with another company for production. Clearly, the acceptance of one of these alternatives eliminates the need for either of the others.

UNLIMITED FUNDS VERSUS CAPITAL RATIONING

unlimited funds
The financial situation in which a firm is able to accept all independent projects that provide an acceptable return.

capital rationing
The financial situation in which a firm has only a fixed number of dollars for allocation among competing capital expenditures.

The availability of funds for capital expenditures affects the firm's decision environment. If a firm has **unlimited funds** for investment, making capital budgeting decisions is quite simple. All independent projects that will provide returns greater than some predetermined level can be accepted. Typically, firms are not in such a situation; they instead operate under **capital rationing.** This means that they have only a fixed number of dollars available for capital expenditures and that numerous projects will compete for these limited dollars. The firm must therefore ration its funds by allocating them to projects that will maximize share value. Procedures for dealing with capital rationing are presented in Chapter 9. The discussions that follow assume unlimited funds.

CONCEPT IN PRACTICE

A Grand Slam Is Tough to Follow

One grand slam does not a grand-slammer make. Consider the enigmatic visionary Steve Jobs, who, as part of the personal computer revolution of the 1980s, started Apple Computer Company. After leaving Apple in 1985, Jobs founded NeXT, Inc. and boasted that NeXT would "kill" the now-giant workstation manufacturer, Sun Microsystems.

How is the superstar of the microcomputer industry doing these days? NeXT has yet to earn a profit and has nearly exhausted its $125 million of venture capital provided by Ross Perot, Canon, Inc., and others. In 1993, NeXT stopped making computers, its president and chief financial officer resigned, and several large PC manufacturers formed a software alliance excluding NeXT. And so NeXT has focused on developing software for Intel. On the competitive field of business, hitting a home run every time at bat is tough—but an all-star entrepreneur will never stop swinging for the fences.

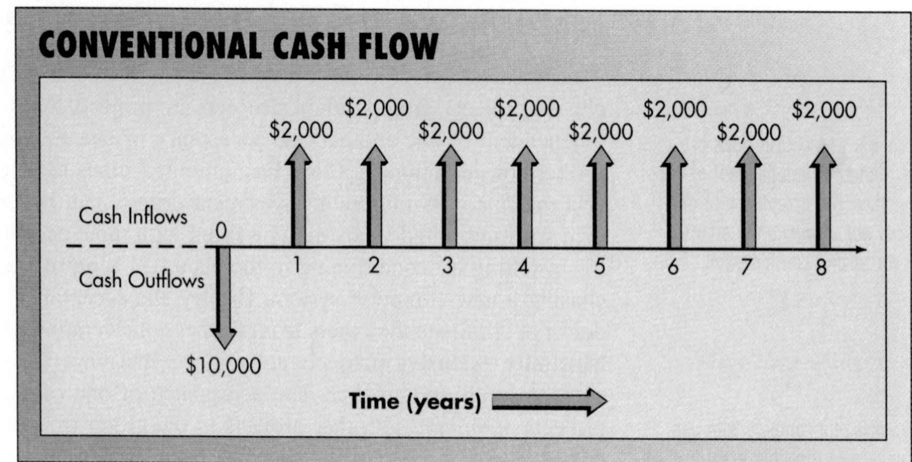

FIGURE 8.1
Time line for a conventional cash flow pattern

ACCEPT-REJECT VERSUS RANKING APPROACHES

accept-reject approach
The evaluation of capital expenditure proposals to determine whether they meet the firm's minimum acceptance criterion.

ranking approach
The ranking of capital expenditure projects on the basis of some predetermined measure such as the rate of return.

Two basic approaches to capital budgeting decisions are available. The **accept-reject approach** involves evaluating capital expenditure proposals to determine whether they meet the firm's minimum acceptance criterion. This approach can be used when the firm has unlimited funds, as a preliminary step in evaluating mutually exclusive projects, or in a situation in which capital must be rationed. In these cases, only acceptable projects should be considered. The second method, the **ranking approach,** involves ranking projects on the basis of some predetermined measure such as the rate of return. The project with the highest return is ranked first, and the project with the lowest return is ranked last. Only acceptable projects should be ranked. Ranking is useful in selecting the "best" of a group of mutually exclusive projects and in evaluating projects with a view to capital rationing.

CONVENTIONAL VERSUS NONCONVENTIONAL CASH FLOW PATTERNS

conventional cash flow pattern
An initial outflow followed by a series of inflows.

nonconventional cash flow pattern
A pattern in which an initial outflow is *not* followed by a series of inflows.

Cash flow patterns associated with capital investment projects can be classified as *conventional* or *nonconventional.* A **conventional cash flow pattern** consists of an initial outflow followed by a series of inflows. This pattern is associated with many types of capital expenditures. For example, a firm may spend $10,000 today and as a result expect to receive cash inflows of $2,000 each year for the next eight years. This conventional pattern is diagrammed on the time line in Figure 8.1.[2] A **nonconventional cash flow pattern** is any pattern in which an initial outflow is *not* followed by a series of inflows. For example, the purchase of a machine may require an initial cash outflow of $20,000 and may generate cash inflows of $5,000 each year for four years. In the fifth year after purchase, an outflow of $8,000 may be required to overhaul the

[2]Arrows rather than plus or minus signs are frequently used on time lines to distinguish between cash inflows and cash outflows. Upward-pointing arrows represent cash inflows (positive cash flows), and downward-pointing arrows represent cash outflows (negative cash flows).

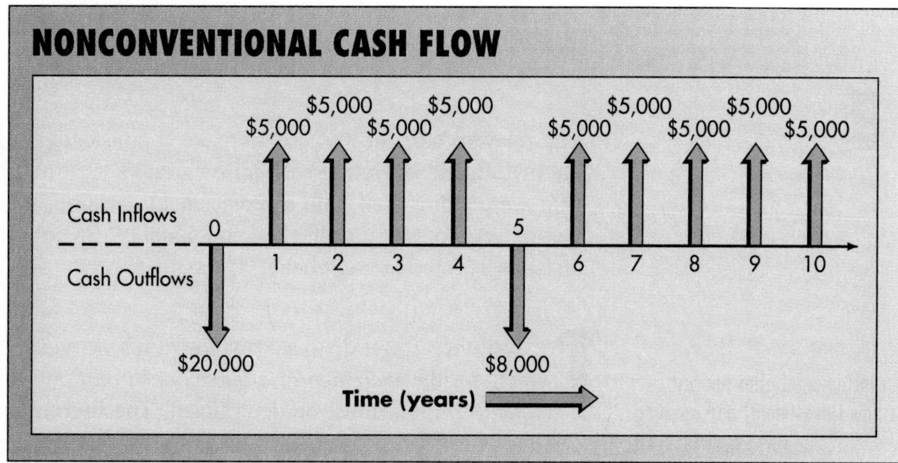

FIGURE 8.2
Time line for a nonconventional cash flow pattern

machine, after which it generates inflows of $5,000 each year for five years. This nonconventional pattern is illustrated on the time line in Figure 8.2.

Difficulties often arise in evaluating projects involving a nonconventional pattern of cash flows. The discussions in the remainder of this chapter and in the following chapter are therefore limited to the evaluation of conventional patterns.

ANNUITY VERSUS MIXED STREAM CASH FLOWS

annuity
A stream of equal annual cash flows.

mixed stream
A series of cash flows exhibiting any pattern other than that of an annuity.

As was pointed out in Chapter 5, an **annuity** is a stream of equal annual cash flows. A series of cash flows exhibiting any pattern other than that of an annuity is a **mixed stream** of cash flows. The cash inflows of $2,000 per year (for eight years) in Figure 8.1 are inflows from an annuity, whereas the unequal pattern of inflows in Figure 8.3 (page 311) represents a mixed stream. As was pointed out in Chapter 5, the techniques required to evaluate cash flows are much simpler to use when the pattern of flows is an annuity.

CONCEPTS IN REVIEW

8-1 What is *capital budgeting*? How do capital expenditures relate to the capital budgeting process? Do all capital expenditures involve fixed assets? Explain.

8-2 What are the basic motives described in the chapter for making capital expenditures? Discuss, compare, and contrast them.

8-3 Briefly describe each of the steps—proposal generation, review and analysis, decision making, implementation, and follow-up—involved in the capital budgeting process.

8-4 Define and differentiate between each of the following sets of capital budgeting terms.

- **a.** Independent versus mutually exclusive projects.
- **b.** Unlimited funds versus capital rationing.
- **c.** Accept-reject versus ranking approaches.
- **d.** Conventional versus nonconventional cash flow patterns.
- **e.** Annuity versus mixed stream cash flows.

The relevant cash flows

The relevant cash flows used to make capital budgeting decisions include the initial investment, operating cash inflows, and a terminal cash flow. In general, if your firm were confronted with a replacement decision, how would you go about estimating each of those cash flow components? Spend a few minutes answering this question before reading ahead.

relevant cash flows
The incremental after-tax cash outflow (investment) and resulting subsequent inflows associated with a proposed capital expenditure.

incremental cash flows
The *additional* cash flows—outflows or inflows—that are expected to result from a proposed capital expenditure.

TO EVALUATE CAPITAL EXPENDITURE ALTERNATIVES, THE **RELEVANT CASH FLOWS,** which are the *incremental after-tax cash outflow (investment) and resulting subsequent inflows,* must be determined. The **incremental cash flows** represent the *additional* cash flows—outflows or inflows—that are expected to result from a proposed capital expenditure. As was noted in Chapter 3, cash flows, rather than accounting figures, are used because it is these flows that directly affect the firm's ability to pay bills and purchase assets. Furthermore, accounting figures and cash flows are not necessarily the same, due to the presence of certain noncash expenditures on the firm's income statement. The remainder of this chapter is devoted to the procedures for measuring the relevant cash flows associated with proposed capital expenditures.

Major cash flow components

initial investment
The relevant cash outflow for a proposed project at time zero.

operating cash inflows
The incremental after-tax cash inflows resulting from use of a project during its life.

terminal cash flow
The after-tax nonoperating cash flow occurring in the final year of a project, usually attributable to liquidation of the project.

The cash flows of any project having the *conventional pattern* can include three basic components: (1) an initial investment, (2) operating cash inflows, and (3) terminal cash flow. All projects—whether for expansion, replacement, renewal, or some other purpose—have the first two components. Some, however, lack the final component, terminal cash flow.

Figure 8.3 depicts on a time line the cash flows for a project. Each of the cash flow components is labeled. The **initial investment,** which is the relevant cash outflow at time zero, is $50,000 for the proposed project. The **operating cash inflows,** which are the incremental after-tax cash inflows resulting from use of the project during its life, gradually increase from $4,000 in the first year to $10,000 in the tenth and final year of the project. The **terminal cash flow,** which is the after-tax nonoperating cash flow occurring in the final year of the project, usually attributable to liquidation of the project, is $25,000 received at the end of the project's 10-year life. Note that the terminal cash flow does *not* include the $10,000 operating cash inflow for year 10.

CONCEPT IN PRACTICE

Happily, Intel's Cash Flow Estimates Were Quite Off

When scheming up new capital projects with which to storm the market, how do companies estimate resulting future cash inflows? By accurately predicting demand for the new product. This is no easy task. As Intel Corp. designed its new Pentium processor, a replacement for the 80486-class microcomputer chip in many PCs, Intel realized that Pentium would be more popular than originally expected. So the firm delayed the chip's release by two months to build inventory. Still, impatient computer manufacturers said that there were too few Pentium chips available. When Intel announced its plan to ship over 10,000 more chips to customers by the end of the fourth quarter of 1993, one large PC-maker griped that it needed all 10,000 chips!

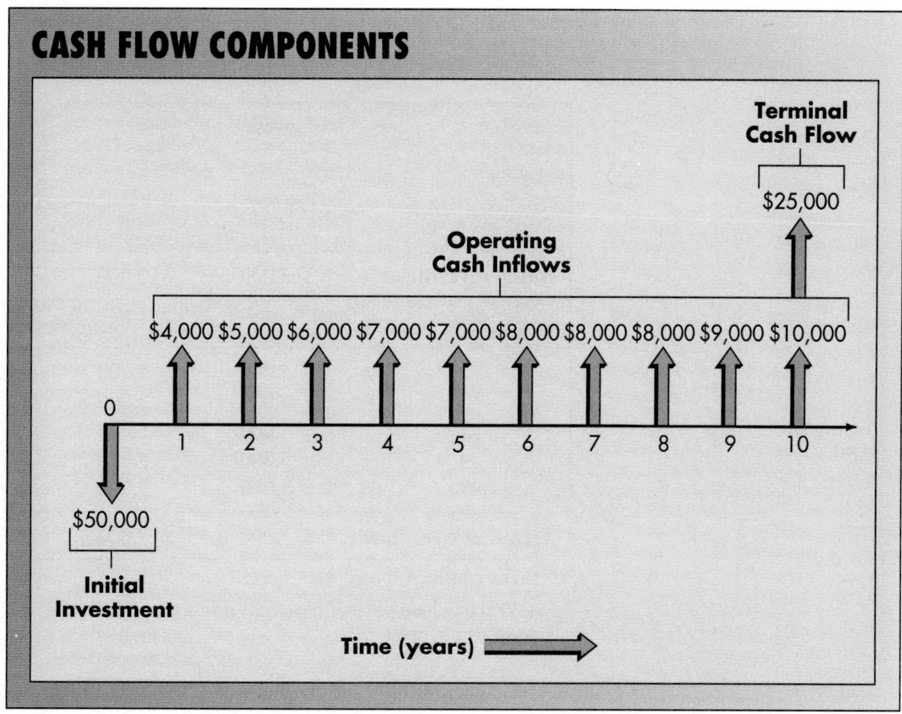

FIGURE 8.3
Time line for major cash flow components

While happily revising its capital budgeting forecast to reflect greater revenue from Pentium sales, Intel is also figuring out how to make enough new chips to keep its customers happy.

Expansion versus replacement cash flows

The development of relevant cash flows is most straightforward in the case of *expansion decisions.* In this case the initial investment, operating cash inflows, and terminal cash flow are merely the after-tax cash outflow and inflows associated with the proposed outlay. The development of relevant cash flows for *replacement decisions* is more complicated; the firm must find the *incremental* cash outflows and inflows that will result from the proposed replacement. The initial investment in this case would be found by subtracting from the initial investment needed to acquire the new asset any after-tax cash inflows expected from liquidation today of the old asset being replaced. The operating cash inflows would be found by taking the difference between the operating cash inflows from the new asset and from the replaced asset. The terminal cash flow would be found by taking the difference between the after-tax cash flows expected upon termination of the new and the old assets.

EXAMPLE

Column 1 of Table 8.3 shows the initial investment, operating cash inflows, and terminal cash flow for an *expansion decision* involving the acquisition of new asset A. As a result of a $13,000 purchase price, the firm would expect operating cash inflows of $5,000 in each of the next five years and a terminal cash flow of $7,000 at the end of year 5.

TABLE 8.3

EXPANSION AND REPLACEMENT CASH FLOWS

	Expansion	Replacement		
	New Asset A (1)	New Asset A (2)	Old Asset A (3)	Relevant cash flows [(2) − (3)] (4)
Initial investment	$13,000[a]	$10,000[b]	. . .	$10,000
Year		Operating cash inflows		
1	$ 5,000	$ 5,000	$3,000	$ 2,000
2	5,000	5,000	2,500	2,500
3	5,000	5,000	2,000	3,000
4	5,000	5,000	1,500	3,500
5	5,000	5,000	1,000	4,000
Terminal cash flow	$ 7,000	$ 7,000	$2,000	$ 5,000

[a]Purchase price.

[b]$13,000 purchase price of new asset A less the $3,000 expected after-tax cash inflow from liquidating old asset A.

If new asset A is being considered as a *replacement* for old asset A, the relevant cash flows would be found by subtracting the expected cash flows attributed to old asset A from the expected cash flows for new asset A. The expected after-tax cash flows for new and old Asset A are shown in columns 2 and 3, respectively, of Table 8.3. Because old asset A can be liquidated for $3,000, the initial investment in new asset A is $10,000, as shown in column 2. Replacement of old asset A would eliminate both its expected operating cash inflows in years 1 through 5 of $3,000, $2,500, $2,000, $1,500, and $1,000 and its terminal cash flow of $2,000 in year 5—all shown in column 3 of Table 8.3. Therefore the relevant cash flows resulting from the *replacement decision* would be the difference in expected cash flows between new asset A (column 2) and old asset A (column 3), as shown in column 4 of Table 8.3. ■

Actually, all capital budgeting decisions can be viewed as replacement decisions. Expansion decisions are merely replacement decisions in which all cash flows from the old asset are zero. In light of this fact, the following discussions emphasize the more general replacement decisions.

International capital budgeting and long-term investments

Although the same basic capital budgeting principles are used for domestic and international projects, several additional factors must be addressed in evaluating foreign investment opportunities. International capital budgeting differs from the domestic version because (1) cash inflows and outflows occur in a foreign currency (the dollar value of these cash flows can change radically if exchange rates fluctuate), and (2) foreign investments potentially face significant political risk, including the risk that the company's assets may be seized. Both of these risks can be minimized through careful corporate planning.

Companies face both long- and short-term currency risks relating to both the invested capital and the cash flows resulting from it. Long-term currency risk can be minimized by at least partly financing the foreign investment in the local capital markets rather than with a dollar-denominated capital contribution from the parent company. This step ensures that the project's revenues, operating costs, and financing costs will be in the local currency, rather than having the financing costs in dollars. Likewise, the dollar value of short-term, local currency cash flows can be protected by using special securities and strategies such as futures, forwards, and options market instruments.

Political risks can be minimized by using both financial and operating strategies. For example, by structuring the investment as a joint venture and by selecting a competent and well-connected local partner, the U.S. company can minimize the risk that its operations will be seized or harassed. Furthermore, companies can protect themselves from having their investment returns blocked by local governments by structuring the financing of such investments as debt rather than as equity. Debt-service payments are legally enforceable claims, whereas equity returns (such as dividends) are not. Even if local courts do not support the claims of the U.S. company, the company can threaten to pursue its case in U.S. courts.

foreign direct investment
The transfer of capital, managerial, and technical assets to a foreign country.

In spite of the above difficulties, **foreign direct investment,** which involves the transfer of capital, managerial, and technical assets to a foreign country, by U.S., European, and Japanese multinational companies has surged in recent years. For example, the market value of foreign assets owned by U.S.-based companies now exceeds $800 billion, although because many of these investments have been in place for over 20 years, the book value of these assets is less than $400 billion. Likewise, foreign direct investment in the United States now exceeds $500 billion in both market and book value, with British companies holding the largest stake, followed by Japanese, Canadian, Dutch, and German companies. Furthermore, foreign direct investment by U.S. companies now exceeds $50 billion per year and seems to be accelerating, particularly in East Asia and Latin America.

CONCEPTS IN REVIEW

8-5 Why is it important to evaluate capital budgeting projects on the basis of *incremental after-tax cash flows?* How can expansion decisions be treated as replacement decisions? Explain.

8-6 How does international capital budgeting differ from the domestic version? How can currency risk—both long- and short-term—and political risk be minimized when making *foreign direct investment?*

Finding the initial investment

The initial investment is the relevant cash outflow required at time zero to implement a proposed long-term investment. What cash flow components would be included in determining the initial investment associated with a proposed replacement decision? Take a few minutes to answer this question before reading ahead.

As was previously stated, the term *initial investment* as used here refers to the relevant cash outflow to be considered in evaluating a prospective capital expenditure. It is calculated by subtracting all cash inflows occurring at time zero from all cash outflows occurring at time zero (the time the expenditure is made). Since our discussion of capital budgeting is concerned only with investments exhibiting conventional cash flows, the initial investment must occur at time zero.

The basic variables that must be considered in determining the initial investment associated with a capital expenditure are the installed cost of the new asset, the after-tax proceeds (if any) from the sale of an old asset, and the change (if any) in net working capital. The basic format for determining the initial investment is given in Table 8.4. Note that if there are no installation costs and the firm is not replacing an existing asset, the purchase price of the asset adjusted for any change in net working capital is equal to the initial investment.

Installed cost of new asset

cost of new asset
The net outflow required to acquire a new asset.

installation costs
Any added costs that are necessary to place an asset into operation.

installed cost of new asset
The cost of the asset plus its installation costs; equals the asset's depreciable value.

As shown in Table 8.4, the installed cost of the new asset is found by adding the cost of the new asset to its installation costs. The **cost of new asset** is the net outflow its acquisition requires. Usually, we are concerned with the acquisition of a fixed asset for which a definite purchase price is paid. **Installation costs** are any added costs that are necessary to place an asset into operation. They are considered part of the firm's capital expenditure. Each capital expenditure decision should be checked to make sure installation costs have not been overlooked. The Internal Revenue Service (IRS) requires the firm to add installation costs to the purchase price of an asset to determine its depreciable value, which is depreciated over a period of years. The **installed cost of new asset**, calculated by adding the cost of the asset to its installation costs, equals its depreciable value.

After-tax proceeds from sale of old asset

after-tax proceeds from sale of old asset
Found by subtracting applicable taxes from the *proceeds from the sale of an old asset.*

Table 8.4 shows that the **after-tax proceeds from sale of old asset** decrease the firm's initial investment in the new asset. These proceeds are found by subtracting ap-

TABLE 8.4

THE BASIC FORMAT FOR DETERMINING INITIAL INVESTMENT

Installed cost of new asset =
Cost of new asset
+Installation costs
−After-tax proceeds from sale of old asset =
Proceeds from sale of old asset
∓Tax on sale of old asset
±Change in net working capital
Initial investment

proceeds from sale of old asset
The cash inflows, net of any removal or cleanup costs, resulting from the sale of an existing asset.

tax on sale of old asset
Tax that depends upon the relationship between the old asset's sale price, initial purchase price, and *book value.*

book value
The strict accounting value of an asset, calculated by subtracting its accumulated depreciation from installed cost.

plicable taxes from (or adding any tax refunds to) the old asset's sale proceeds. The **proceeds from sale of old asset** are the net cash inflows it provides. This amount is net of any costs incurred in the process of removing the asset. Included in these *removal costs* are *cleanup costs*, particularly those related to removal and proper disposal of chemical and nuclear wastes. These costs may not be trivial.

The proceeds from the sale of an old asset are normally subject to some type of tax.[3] This **tax on sale of old asset** depends upon the relationship between its sale price, initial purchase price, and book value. The actual tax treatment is not controlled by the firm but rather is dictated by government tax laws, procedures, and forms, all of which are periodically revised. An understanding of (1) book value and (2) basic tax rules is necessary to determine the tax on sale of an asset.

BOOK VALUE

The **book value** of an asset is its strict accounting value. It can be calculated using the following equation:

$$\text{Book value} = \text{installed cost of asset} - \text{accumulated depreciation} \qquad (8.1)$$

EXAMPLE

Hudson Industries, a small electronics company, acquired a machine tool with an installed cost of $100,000 two years ago. The asset was being depreciated under MACRS (see Chapter 3) using a five-year recovery period.[4] Table 3.6 (page 83) shows that under MACRS for a five-year recovery period, 20 percent and 32 percent of the installed cost would be depreciated in years 1 and 2, respectively. In other words, 52 percent (20% + 32%) of the $100,000 cost, or $52,000 (.52 × $100,000), would represent the accumulated depreciation at the end of year 2. Substituting into Equation 8.1, we get

$$\text{Book value} = \$100{,}000 - \$52{,}000 = \$48{,}000$$

The book value of Hudson's asset at the end of year 2 is therefore $48,000. ■

BASIC TAX RULES

Four potential tax situations can occur in selling an asset. These situations differ, depending upon the relationship between the asset's sale price, its initial purchase price, and its book value. The three key forms of taxable income and their associated tax treatments are defined and summarized in Table 8.5. The assumed tax rates used throughout this text are noted in the final column of the same table. The four possible tax situations resulting in one or more forms of taxable income are the following: (1) the asset is sold for more than its initial purchase price; (2) the asset is sold for more than its book value but less than its initial purchase price; (3) the asset is sold for its book value; and (4) the asset is sold for less than its book value. An example will illustrate.

[3]A brief discussion of the tax treatment of ordinary and capital gains income was presented in Chapter 2.

[4]Under the *Tax Reform Act of 1986* most manufacturing machinery and equipment has a seven-year recovery period as noted in Chapter 3 (Table 3.5). Using this recovery period results in eight years of depreciation, which unnecessarily complicates examples and problems. To simplify, *machinery and equipment are treated as five-year assets throughout this and the following chapters.*

TABLE 8.5

TAX TREATMENT ON SALES OF ASSETS

Form of taxable income	Definition	Tax treatment	Assumed tax rate
Capital gain	Portion of the sale price that is in excess of the initial purchase price.	Regardless of how long the asset has been held, the total capital gain is taxed as ordinary income.	40%
Recaptured depreciation	Portion of the sale price that is in excess of book value and represents a recovery of previously taken depreciation.	All recaptured depreciation is taxed as ordinary income.	40%
Loss on sale of asset	Amount by which sale price is *less than* book value.	If asset is depreciable and used in business, loss is deducted from ordinary income.	40% of loss is a tax savings
		If asset is *not* depreciable or is *not* used in business, loss is deductible only against capital gains.	40% of loss is a tax savings

EXAMPLE

The old asset purchased two years ago for $100,000 by Hudson Industries has a current book value of $48,000. What will happen if the firm now decides to sell the asset and replace it? The tax consequences associated with sale of the asset depend upon the sale price. Let us consider each of the four possible situations.

The sale of the asset for more than its initial purchase price If Hudson sells the old asset for $110,000, it realizes a capital gain of $10,000 (the amount by which the sale price exceeds the initial purchase price of $100,000), which is taxed as ordinary income.[5] The firm also experiences ordinary income in the form of **recaptured depreciation,** which is the portion of the sale price that is above book value and below the initial purchase price. In this case there is recaptured depreciation of $52,000 ($100,000 − $48,000). The taxes on the total gain of $62,000 are calculated as follows:

recaptured depreciation
The portion of the sale price that is above book value and below the initial purchase price.

[5]Although the *Tax Reform Act of 1986* requires corporate capital gains to be treated as ordinary income, the structure for corporate capital gains is retained under the law to facilitate a rate differential in the likely event of future tax revisions. Therefore this distinction is made throughout the text discussions.

	Amount (1)	Rate (2)	Tax [(1) × (2)] (3)
Capital gain	$10,000	.40	$ 4,000
Recaptured depreciation	52,000	.40	20,800
Totals	$62,000		$24,800

These taxes should be used in calculating the initial investment in the new asset, using the format in Table 8.4. In effect, the taxes raise the amount of the firm's initial investment in the new asset by reducing the proceeds from the sale of the old asset.

The sale of the asset for more than its book value but less than its initial purchase price If Hudson sells the old asset for $70,000, which is less than its original purchase price but more than its book value, there is no capital gain. However, the firm still experiences a gain in the form of recaptured depreciation of $22,000 ($70,000 − $48,000), which is taxed as ordinary income. Since the firm is assumed to be in the 40 percent tax bracket, the taxes on the $22,000 gain are $8,800. This amount in taxes should be used in calculating the initial investment in the new asset.

The sale of the asset for its book value If the asset is sold for $48,000, which is its book value, the firm breaks even. Since *no tax results from selling an asset for its book value,* there is no effect on the initial investment in the new asset.

The sale of the asset for less than its book value If Hudson sells the asset for $30,000, an amount less than its book value, it experiences a loss of $18,000 ($48,000 − $30,000). If this is a depreciable asset used in the business, the loss may be used to offset ordinary operating income. If the asset is *not* depreciable or *not* used in the business, the loss can be used only to offset capital gains. In both cases the loss will save the firm $7,200 ($18,000 × .40) in taxes. In either case, if current operating earnings or capital gains are not sufficient to offset the loss, the firm may be able to apply these losses to prior years' taxes or future years' taxes.[6] ■

Change in net working capital[7]

Net working capital, as was noted in Chapter 4, is the amount by which a firm's current assets exceed its current liabilities. This topic is treated in depth in Part VI, especially in Chapter 16, but at this point it is important to note that changes in net working capital often accompany capital expenditure decisions, regardless of their motive. If a firm acquires new machinery to expand its level of operations, accompanying such expansion will be increased levels of cash, accounts receivable, inventories, accounts payable, and accruals. These increases result from the need for more cash to support expanded operations, more accounts receivable and inventories to support increased sales, and more accounts payable and accruals to support increased purchases made to

[6]As was noted in Chapter 2, the tax law provides detailed procedures for using *tax loss carrybacks and carryforwards.* Application of such procedures to capital budgeting is beyond the scope of this text, and they are therefore ignored in subsequent discussions.

[7]Occasionally, this factor is intentionally ignored to enhance the attractiveness of a proposed investment and thereby improve its likelihood of acceptance. Similar intentional omissions and/or overly optimistic estimates are sometimes made to enhance project acceptance. The presence of formal review and analysis procedures should help the firm to ensure that capital budgeting cash flow estimates are realistic and unbiased and that the "best" projects—those making the maximum contribution to owner wealth—are accepted.

TABLE 8.6

CALCULATION OF CHANGE IN NET WORKING CAPITAL FOR DANSON COMPANY

Current account	Change in balance	
Cash	+ $ 4,000	
Accounts receivable	+ 10,000	
Inventories	+ 8,000	
(1) Current assets		+ $22,000
Accounts payable	+ $ 7,000	
Accruals	+ 2,000	
(2) Current liabilities		+ 9,000
Change in net working capital [(1) − (2)]		+ $13,000

meet expanded product demand. As was noted in Chapter 3, increases in cash, accounts receivable, and inventories are *uses of cash* (cash outflows or investments), while increases in accounts payable and accruals are *sources of cash* (cash inflows or financing). As long as the expanded operations continue, the increased investment in current assets (cash, accounts receivable, and inventories) and increased current liability financing (accounts payable and accruals) would be expected to continue.

change in net working capital
The difference between a change in current assets and a change in current liabilities.

The difference between the change in current assets and the change in current liabilities would be the **change in net working capital.** Generally, current assets increase by more than current liabilities, resulting in an increased investment in net working capital, which would be treated as an initial outflow associated with the project.[8] If the change in net working capital were negative, it would be shown as an initial inflow associated with the project. The change in net working capital—regardless of whether an increase or a decrease—*is not taxable* because it merely involves a net build-up or reduction of current accounts.

EXAMPLE

Danson Company, a metal products manufacturer, is contemplating expanding its operations to meet the growing demand for its products. In addition to Danson's acquiring a variety of new capital equipment, financial analysts expect that the changes in current accounts summarized in Table 8.6 will occur and be maintained over the life of the expansion. Current assets are expected to increase by $22,000, and current liabilities are expected to increase by $9,000, resulting in a $13,000 increase in net working capital. In this case the increase would represent an increased net working capital investment and be treated as a cash outflow in calculating the initial investment. ■

Calculating the initial investment

It should be clear that a variety of tax and other considerations enter into the initial investment calculation. The following example illustrates how the basic variables

[8]When net working capital changes apply to the calculation of the initial investment associated with a proposed capital expenditure, they are for convenience assumed to be instantaneous and thereby occurring at time zero. In practice, the change in net working capital will frequently occur over a period of months as the capital expenditure is implemented.

described in the preceding discussions are used to calculate the initial investment according to the format in Table 8.4.[9]

EXAMPLE

Powell Corporation, a large diversified manufacturer of aircraft components, is trying to determine the initial investment required to replace an old machine with a new, much more sophisticated model. The proposed (new) machine's purchase price is $380,000, and an additional $20,000 will be required to install it. It will be depreciated under MACRS using a five-year recovery period. The present (old) machine was purchased three years ago at a cost of $240,000 and was being depreciated under MACRS using a five-year recovery period. The firm has found a buyer willing to pay $280,000 for the present machine and remove it at the buyer's own expense. The firm expects that a $35,000 increase in current assets and an $18,000 increase in current liabilities will accompany the replacement; these changes will result in a $17,000 ($35,000 − $18,000) *increase* in net working capital. Both ordinary income and capital gains are taxed at a rate of 40 percent.

The only component of the initial investment calculation that is difficult to obtain is taxes. Since the firm is planning to sell the present machine for $40,000 more than its initial purchase price, it will realize a *capital gain of $40,000.* The book value of the present machine can be found by using the depreciation percentages from Table 3.6 (page 83) of 20 percent, 32 percent, and 19 percent for years 1, 2 and 3, respectively. The resulting book value is $69,600 ($240,000 − [(.20 + .32 + .19) × $240,000]). An *ordinary gain of $170,400* ($240,000 − $69,600) in recaptured depreciation is also realized on the sale. The total taxes on the gain are $84,160 [($40,000 + $170,400) × .40]. Substituting these taxes along with the purchase price and installation cost of the proposed machine, the proceeds from the sale of the present machine, and the change in net working capital, into the format in Table 8.4 results in an initial investment of $221,160. This represents the net cash outflow required at time zero:

Installed cost of proposed machine		
Cost of proposed machine	$380,000	
+ Installation costs	20,000	
Total installed cost—proposed (depreciable value)		$400,000
− After-tax proceeds from sale of present machine		
Proceeds from sale of present machine	$280,000	
− Tax on sale of present machine	84,160	
Total after-tax proceeds—present		195,840
+ Change in net working capital		17,000
Initial investment		$221,160

CONCEPTS IN REVIEW

8-7 Describe each of the following inputs to the initial investment, and use the basic format presented in this chapter to explain how the initial investment is calculated by using them.

[9]Throughout our discussions of capital budgeting, all assets evaluated as candidates for replacement are assumed to be depreciable assets that are directly used in the business, so any losses on the sale of these assets can be applied against ordinary operating income. The decisions are also structured to ensure that the usable life remaining on the old asset is just equal to the life of the new asset; this assumption permits the avoidance of the problem of unequal lives, which is discussed in Chapter 9.

a. Cost of new asset.
b. Installation costs.
c. Proceeds from sale of old asset.
d. Tax on sale of old asset.
e. Change in net working capital.

8-8 What is the *book value* of an asset, and how is it calculated? Describe the three key forms of taxable income and their associated tax treatments.

8-9 What four tax situations may result from the sale of an asset that is being replaced? Describe the tax treatment in each situation.

8-10 Referring to the basic format for calculating initial investment presented in this chapter, explain how a firm would determine the *depreciable value* of the new asset.

Finding the operating cash inflows

Operating cash inflows are the relevant cash inflows resulting from the use of a proposed long-term investment during its life. Given estimates of the revenues, expenses, and depreciation associated with both the old and new asset, how would you go about estimating the operating cash inflows for a replacement decision? Before reading on, take a few moments to answer this question.

THE BENEFITS EXPECTED FROM A CAPITAL EXPENDITURE ARE MEASURED BY ITS *OPERating cash inflows,* which are *incremental after-tax cash inflows.* In this section we use the income statement format to develop clear definitions of the terms *after-tax, cash inflows,* and *incremental.*

Interpreting the term *after-tax*

Benefits that are expected to result from proposed capital expenditures must be measured on an after-tax basis, since the firm will not have the use of any benefits until it has satisfied the government's tax claims. These claims depend on the firm's taxable income, so the deduction of taxes *prior to* making comparisons between proposed investments is necessary for consistency. Consistency is required in evaluating capital expenditure alternatives, since the intention is to compare like benefits.

Interpreting the term *cash inflows*

All benefits that are expected from a proposed project must be measured on a cash flow basis. Cash inflows represent dollars that can be spent, not merely "accounting profits," which are not necessarily available for paying the firm's bills. A simple technique for converting after-tax net profits into operating cash inflows was illustrated in Chapter 3. The basic calculation requires adding any *noncash charges* deducted as expenses on the firm's income statement back to net profits after taxes. Probably the most common noncash charge found on income statements is depreciation. It is the only noncash charge that will be considered in this section. The following example shows

TABLE 8.7

POWELL CORPORATION'S REVENUE AND EXPENSES (EXCLUDING DEPRECIATION) FOR PROPOSED AND PRESENT MACHINES

Year	Revenue (1)	Expenses (excl. depr.) (2)
With proposed machine		
1	$2,520,000	$2,300,000
2	2,520,000	2,300,000
3	2,520,000	2,300,000
4	2,520,000	2,300,000
5	2,520,000	2,300,000
With present machine		
1	$2,200,000	$1,990,000
2	2,300,000	2,110,000
3	2,400,000	2,230,000
4	2,400,000	2,250,000
5	2,250,000	2,120,000

how after-tax operating cash inflows can be calculated for a present and a proposed project.

EXAMPLE

Powell Corporation's estimates of its revenue and expenses (excluding depreciation), with and without the proposed capital expenditure described in the preceding example, are given in Table 8.7. Note that both the expected usable life of the proposed machine and the remaining usable life of the present machine is five years. The amount to be depreciated with the proposed machine is calculated by summing the purchase price of $380,000 and the installation costs of $20,000. Since the machine is to be depreciated under MACRS using a five-year recovery period, 20, 32, 19, 12, 12, and 5 percent would be recovered in years 1 through 6, respectively (see Chapter 3 and Table 3.6 on page 83 for more detail).[10] The resulting depreciation on this machine for each of the six years, as well as the remaining three years of depreciation on the old machine, are calculated in Table 8.8.[11]

[10]As was noted in Chapter 3, it takes $n + 1$ years to depreciate an n-year class asset under the provisions of the *Tax Reform Act of 1986*. Therefore MACRS percentages are given for each of six years for use in depreciating an asset with a five-year recovery period.

[11]It is important to recognize that although both machines will provide five years of use, the proposed new machine will be depreciated over the six-year period, whereas the present machine—as noted in the preceding example—has been depreciated over three years and therefore has only its final three years (years 4, 5, and 6) of depreciation (i.e., 12, 12, and 5 percent, respectively, under MACRS) remaining.

TABLE 8.8

DEPRECIATION EXPENSE FOR PROPOSED AND PRESENT MACHINES FOR POWELL CORPORATION

Year	Cost (1)	Applicable MACRS depreciation percentages (from Table 3.6) (2)	Depreciation [(1) × (2)] (3)
With proposed machine			
1	$400,000	20%	$ 80,000
2	400,000	32	128,000
3	400,000	19	76,000
4	400,000	12	48,000
5	400,000	12	48,000
6	400,000	5	20,000
Totals		100%	$400,000
With present machine			
1	$240,000	12% (year-4 depreciation)	$ 28,800
2	240,000	12 (year-5 depreciation)	28,800
3	240,000	5 (year-6 depreciation)	12,000
4	Since the present machine is at the end of the third year of its cost recovery at the time the analysis is performed, it has only the final three years of depreciation (years 4, 5, and 6) yet applicable.		0
5			0
6			0
		Total	$69,600[a]

[a]The total $69,600 represents the book value of the present machine at the end of the third year, which was calculated in the preceding example.

The operating cash inflows in each year can be calculated by using the following income statement format:

Revenue
− Expenses (excluding depreciation)
Profits before depreciation and taxes
− Depreciation
Net profits before taxes
− Taxes
Net profits after taxes
+ Depreciation
Operating cash inflows

When the data from Tables 8.7 and 8.8 are substituted into this format and assuming a 40 percent tax rate, Table 8.9 demonstrates the calculation of operating cash inflows for each year for both the proposed and the present machine. Since the proposed machine will be depreciated over six years, the analysis must be performed over the six-year period to fully capture the tax effect of depreciation in year 6 for the new asset. The resulting operating cash inflows are shown in column 8 of the table. The year-6 cash inflow for the proposed machine of $8,000 results solely from the tax benefit of the year-6 depreciation deduction. ■

TABLE 8.9

CALCULATION OF OPERATING CASH INFLOWS FOR POWELL CORPORATION'S PROPOSED AND PRESENT MACHINES

Year	Revenue[a] (1)	Expenses (excl. depr.)[b] (2)	Profits before depreciation and taxes [(1) − (2)] (3)	Depreciation[c] (4)	Net profits before taxes [(3) − (4)] (5)	Taxes [.40 × (5)] (6)	Net profits after taxes [(5) − (6)] (7)	Operating cash inflows [(4) + (7)] (8)
With proposed machine								
1	$2,520,000	$2,300,000	$220,000	$ 80,000	$140,000	$56,000	$ 84,000	$164,000
2	2,520,000	2,300,000	220,000	128,000	92,000	36,800	55,200	183,200
3	2,520,000	2,300,000	220,000	76,000	144,000	57,600	86,400	162,400
4	2,520,000	2,300,000	220,000	48,000	172,000	68,800	103,200	151,200
5	2,520,000	2,300,000	220,000	48,000	172,000	68,800	103,200	151,200
6	0	0	0	20,000	− 20,000	− 8,000	− 12,000	8,000
With present machine								
1	$2,200,000	$1,990,000	$210,000	$ 28,800	$181,200	$72,480	$108,720	$137,520
2	2,300,000	2,110,000	190,000	28,800	161,200	64,480	96,720	125,520
3	2,400,000	2,230,000	170,000	12,000	158,000	63,200	94,800	106,800
4	2,400,000	2,250,000	150,000	0	150,000	60,000	90,000	90,000
5	2,250,000	2,120,000	130,000	0	130,000	52,000	78,000	78,000
6	0	0	0	0	0	0	0	0

[a]From column 1 of Table 8.7.

[b]From column 2 of Table 8.7.

[c]From column 3 of Table 8.8.

Interpreting the term *incremental*

The final step in estimating the operating cash inflows to be used in evaluating a proposed project is to calculate the *incremental (relevant)* cash inflows. Incremental operating cash inflows are needed, since our concern is *only* with how much more or less operating cash will flow into the firm as a result of the proposed project.

EXAMPLE

Table 8.10 demonstrates the calculation of Powell Corporation's incremental (relevant) operating cash inflows for each year. The estimates of operating cash inflows developed in Table 8.9 are given in columns 1 and 2. The column 2 values represent the amount of operating cash inflows that Powell Corporation will receive if it does not replace the present machine. If the proposed machine replaces the present machine, the firm's operating cash inflows for each year will be those shown in column 1. Subtracting the operating cash inflows with the present machine from the operating cash inflows with the proposed machine in each year results in the incremental operating cash inflows for each year, shown in column 3 of Table 8.10. These cash flows in effect represent the amounts by which each respective year's cash inflows will increase as a result of replacing the present machine with the proposed machine. For example,

TABLE 8.10

INCREMENTAL (RELEVANT) OPERATING CASH INFLOWS FOR POWELL CORPORATION

	Operating cash inflows		
Year	Proposed machine[a] (1)	Present machine[a] (2)	Incremental (relevant) [(1) − (2)] (3)
1	$164,000	$137,520	$26,480
2	183,200	125,520	57,680
3	162,400	106,800	55,600
4	151,200	90,000	61,200
5	151,200	78,000	73,200
6	8,000	0	8,000

[a]From column 8 of Table 8.9.

in year 1, Powell Corporation's cash inflows would increase by $26,480 if the proposed project were undertaken. Clearly, these are the relevant inflows to be considered in evaluating the benefits of making a capital expenditure for the proposed machine.[12] ■

CONCEPT IN PRACTICE

Making "Rent-A-Doc" More Than a Temporary Success

Firms frequently fail to realize the operating cash inflows forecasted for a project because they lose sight of their original business objectives. On Assignment, Inc., did just that. Initially, the agency provided scientists to firms needing skilled staff for short-

---

[12]The following equation can be used to more directly calculate the incremental cash inflow in year t, ICI_t.

$$ICI_t = [\Delta PBDT_t \times (1 - T)] + [\Delta D_t \times T]$$

where:

$\Delta PBDT_t$ = the change in profits before depreciation and taxes [revenues − expenses (excl. depr.)] in year t
ΔD_t = the change in depreciation expense in year t
T = the firm's marginal tax rate

Applying this formula to the Powell Corporation data given in Tables 8.7 and 8.8 for year 3, we get variable values of

$$\Delta PBDT_3 = (\$2{,}520{,}000 - \$2{,}300{,}000) - (\$2{,}400{,}000 - \$2{,}230{,}000)$$
$$= \$220{,}000 - \$170{,}000 = \$50{,}000$$
$$\Delta D_3 = \$76{,}000 - \$12{,}000 = \$64{,}000$$
$$T = .40$$

Substituting into the equation, we get

$$ICI_3 = [\$50{,}000 \times (1 - .40)] + [\$64{,}000 \times .40]$$
$$= \$30{,}000 + \$25{,}600 = \underline{\underline{\$55{,}600}}$$

The $55,600 of incremental cash inflow for year 3 is the same value as that calculated for year 3 in column 3 of Table 8.10.

term, temporary assignments. Since the "Rent-A-Doc" concept worked well, the firm expanded into areas such as consulting and executive recruiting. This lack of focus caused costs to soar. In 1989, On Assignment lost $1.5 million on sales of just $7 million.

Then the firm's managers reviewed their original goals. They closed the consulting and recruiting offices and focused again on the temporary service. As corporations began downsizing in the early 1990s, On Assignment found new customers that were eager to hire temporaries to replace laid-off employees. By 1993 the agency expected earnings of $2.5 million on sales of $38.1 million, with a work force of over 1,000 scientists. By revisiting its business plan, On Assignment got on track.

CONCEPTS IN REVIEW

8-11 How is the *Modified Accelerated Cost Recovery System (MACRS)* used to depreciate an asset? How does depreciation enter into the operating cash inflow calculation?

8-12 Given the revenues, expenses (excluding depreciation), and depreciation associated with a present asset and a proposed replacement for it, how would the incremental (relevant) operating cash inflows associated with the decision be calculated?

Finding the terminal cash flow

The terminal cash flow is the relevant cash flow attributable to liquidation of a long-term investment at the end of its life. If you were making the terminal cash flow calculation for a replacement decision, what items would you include? Spend a few moments answering this question before reading on.

THE CASH FLOW RESULTING FROM TERMINATION AND LIQUIDATION OF A PROJECT AT THE end of its economic life is its *terminal cash flow*. It represents the after-tax cash flow, exclusive of operating cash inflows, occurring in the final year of the project. When they apply, it is important to recognize these flows because they could significantly affect the capital expenditure decision. Consideration of these flows also provides closure to the analysis, allowing the firm to return to its initial position in terms of the expenditures being considered. Terminal cash flow, which is most often positive, can be calculated for replacement projects by using the basic format presented in Table 8.11.

Proceeds from sale of assets

The proceeds from sale of the new and old asset, often called "salvage value," represent the amount *net of any removal or cleanup costs* expected upon termination of the project. For replacement projects, proceeds from both the new asset and the old asset must be considered as noted. For expansion, renewal, and other types of capital expenditures, the proceeds from the old asset would be zero. Of course, it is not unusual for the values of assets to be zero at termination of a project.

TABLE 8.11

THE BASIC FORMAT FOR DETERMINING TERMINAL CASH FLOW

After-tax proceeds from sale of new asset =
  Proceeds from sale of new asset
  ∓Tax on sale of new asset
−After-tax proceeds from sale of old asset =
  Proceeds from sale of old asset
  ∓Tax on sale of old asset
±Change in net working capital

Terminal cash flow

Taxes on sale of assets

Like the tax calculation on sale of old assets (demonstrated earlier as part of finding the initial investment), taxes must be considered on the terminal sale of both the new and the old asset for replacement projects and on only the new asset in other cases. The tax calculations apply whenever an asset is sold for a value different from its book value. If the net proceeds from the sale are expected to exceed book value, a tax payment shown as an *outflow* (deduction from sale proceeds) would occur. When the net proceeds from the sale are below book value, a tax rebate shown as a cash *inflow* (addition to sale proceeds) would result. Of course, for assets sold to net exactly their book value, no taxes would be due.

Change in net working capital

The change in net working capital reflects the reversion to its original status of any net working capital investment reflected as part of the initial investment. Most often this will show up as a cash inflow attributed to the reduction in net working capital; with termination of the project the need for the increased net working capital investment is assumed to end.[13] Since the net working capital investment is in no way consumed, the amount recovered at termination will equal the amount shown in the calculation of the initial investment.[14] Tax considerations are not involved because the change in net working capital results from an internal reduction or build-up of current accounts. Of course, occasionally net working capital will not be changed by the proposed investment and therefore will not enter into the analysis.

It should be clear that the terminal cash flow calculation, when applicable, involves the same procedures as those used to find the initial investment. The following example demonstrates how the terminal cash flow is calculated for a replacement decision.

[13]As was noted earlier, the change in net working capital is, for convenience, assumed to occur instantaneously—in this case, upon termination of the project. In actuality it may take a number of months for the original increase in net working capital to be worked down to zero.

[14]In practice the full net working capital investment may not be recovered. This occurs because some accounts receivable may not be collectible and some inventory will likely be obsolete, and therefore their book values cannot be realized.

EXAMPLE

Continuing with the Powell Corporation example, assume that the firm expects to be able to liquidate the new machine at the end of its five-year usable life to net $50,000 after paying removal and cleanup costs. The old machine can be liquidated at the end of the five years to net $0 because it will then be completely obsolete. The firm expects to recover its $17,000 net working capital investment upon termination of the project. As was noted earlier, both ordinary income and capital gains are taxed at a rate of 40 percent.

From the analysis of the operating cash inflows presented earlier, it can be seen that while the present (old) machine will be fully depreciated and therefore have a book value of zero at the end of the five years, the proposed (new) machine will have a book value of $20,000 (equal to the year-6 depreciation) at the end of five years. Since the sale price of $50,000 for the proposed machine is below its initial installed cost of $400,000 but greater than its book value of $20,000, taxes will have to be paid only on the recaptured depreciation of $30,000 ($50,000 sale proceeds − $20,000 book value). Applying the ordinary tax rate of 40 percent to the $30,000 results in a tax of $12,000 (.40 × $30,000) on the sale of the proposed machine. Its after-tax sale proceeds would therefore equal $38,000 ($50,000 sale proceeds − $12,000 taxes). Since the present machine would net $0 at termination and its book value would be $0, no tax would be due on sale of the present machine. Its after-tax sale proceeds would therefore equal $0 ($0 sale proceeds − $0 taxes). Substituting the appropriate values into the format in Table 8.11 results in the terminal cash inflow value of $55,000 derived below. This represents the after-tax cash flow, exclusive of operating cash inflows, occurring upon termination of the project at the end of year 5.

After-tax proceeds from sale of proposed machine		
Proceeds from sale of proposed machine	$50,000	
− Tax on sale of proposed machine	12,000	
Total after-tax proceeds—proposed		$38,000
− After-tax proceeds from sale of present machine		
Proceeds from sale of present machine	$ 0	
∓ Tax on sale of present machine	0	
Total after-tax proceeds—present		0
+ Change in net working capital		17,000
Terminal cash flow		$55,000

CONCEPT IN REVIEW

8-13 What is the *terminal cash flow*? Use the basic format presented to explain how the value of this cash flow is calculated for replacement projects.

Summarizing the relevant cash flows

A project's cash flows are estimated over its usable life, at the end of which the project is assumed to be liquidated. Given this treatment, where is the benefit of the unused depreciation reflected in the project's relevant cash flows? Before reading further, take a few moments to answer this question.

THE THREE CASH FLOW COMPONENTS—THE INITIAL INVESTMENT, OPERATING CASH inflows, and terminal cash flow—together represent a project's *relevant cash flows.* These cash flows can be viewed as the incremental after-tax cash flows attributable to the proposed project. They represent, in a cash flow sense, how much better or worse off the firm will be if it chooses to implement the proposal.

EXAMPLE

The relevant cash flows for Powell Corporation's proposed replacement expenditure can now be presented.

Time-Line Use They are shown graphically on the time line shown below. Note that because the new asset is assumed to be sold at the end of its five-year usable life, the year-6 incremental operating cash inflow calculated in Table 8.10 has no relevance; the terminal cash flow effectively replaces this value in the analysis. As the figure shows, the relevant cash flows follow a conventional pattern (an initial outflow followed by a series of inflows). Techniques for analyzing this type of pattern to determine whether to undertake a proposed capital investment are discussed in Chapter 9.

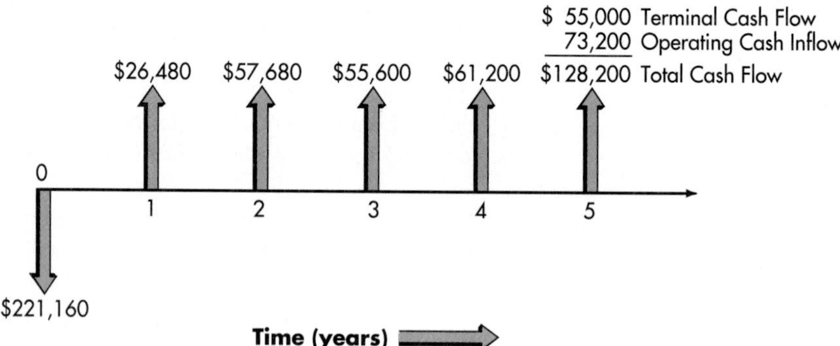

Powell Corporation's relevant cash flows with the proposed machine

CONCEPT IN PRACTICE

Good Projects Pump Up Expectations at Urethane Technologies

Capital budgeting isn't just for corporate financial managers. It's also for outside investors and analysts who want to ride a good investment. Urethane Technologies' stock price rose from $6 in December 1992 to $13.50 in May 1993, even though the young firm had not generated a penny's worth of earnings for its common shareholders. What pumped up the stock price? Urethane Technologies developed a specially formulated liquid chemical compound for making polyurethane-based products such as nonpneumatic (airless) bicycle tires. These tires ride as comfortably as pneumatic ones but last longer because they are inflated by foam, not air. The market's estimation of net cash flows from the airless-tire project inflated the firm's stock price. If all goes according to plan, these cash flows should reach Urethane Technologies' shareholders by the end of 1993, when the firm expects to report its first operating profit.

CONCEPT IN REVIEW

8-14 Diagram and describe the three elements representing the *relevant cash flows* for a conventional capital budgeting project.

Summary

LG 1 **Understand the key capital expenditure motives and the steps in the capital budgeting process, beginning with proposal generation and ending with follow-up.** Capital budgeting is the process used to evaluate and select capital expenditures consistent with the goal of owner wealth maximization. Capital expenditures are long-term investments made to expand, replace, or renew fixed assets or to obtain some other less tangible benefit. The capital budgeting process contains five distinct but interrelated steps: proposal generation, review and analysis, decision making, implementation, and follow-up.

LG 2 **Describe the basic terminology used to describe projects, funds availability, decision approaches, and cash flow patterns.** Capital expenditure proposals may be independent or mutually exclusive. Typically, firms have only limited funds for capital investments and must ration them among carefully selected projects. To make investment decisions when proposals are mutually exclusive or when capital must be rationed, projects must be ranked; otherwise, accept-reject decisions must be made. Conventional cash flow patterns consist of an initial outflow followed by a series of inflows; any other pattern is nonconventional. These patterns can be either annuities or mixed streams.

LG 3 **Discuss the major components of relevant cash flows, differences in the development of expansion- versus replacement-decision cash flows, and international capital budgeting and long-term investments.** The relevant cash flows necessary for making capital budgeting decisions are the initial investment, the operating cash inflows, and the terminal cash flow associated with a given proposal. For replacement decisions these flows are found by determining the difference between the cash flows associated with the new asset and the old asset. Expansion decisions are viewed as replacement decisions in which all cash flows from the old asset are zero. International capital budgeting differs from the domestic version because cash flows occur in a foreign currency and foreign investments potentially face significant political risk. A number of techniques are available for minimizing both currency and political risks when making foreign direct investment.

LG 4 **Calculate the initial investment associated with a proposed capital expenditure, given relevant cost, depreciation, tax, and net working capital data.** The initial investment is the initial outflow required, taking into account the installed cost of the new asset, the after-tax proceeds from the sale of the old asset, and any change in net working capital. Finding the after-tax proceeds from sale of the old asset, which reduces the initial investment, involves cost, depreciation, and tax data. The book value of an asset is its strict accounting value, which is used to determine what, if any, taxes are owed as a result of selling an asset. Any of three forms of taxable income—capital gain, recaptured depreciation, or a loss—can result from sale of an asset. The form of taxable income that applies depends upon whether it is sold for: (1) more than its initial purchase price, (2) more than book value but less than initially paid, (3) book value, or (4) less than book value. The change in net working capital is found by subtracting the increases in current liabilities (cash inflows or financing) from increases in current assets (cash outflows or investments) that are expected to accompany a given capital expenditure.

LG 5 **Determine the operating cash inflows that are relevant to a capital budgeting proposal using the income statement format.** The operating cash inflows are the incremental after-tax operating cash inflows that are expected to result from implementing a proposal. The income statement format, which involves adding depreciation back to net profits after taxes, gives the operating cash inflows associated with the present and proposed projects. The relevant (incremental) cash inflows, which are used to evaluate the proposed project, are found by subtracting the operating cash inflows associated with the present project from those of the proposed project.

LG 6 **Find the terminal cash flow associated with a capital budgeting proposal, given relevant sale price, depreciation, tax, and net working capital data.** The terminal cash flow represents the after-tax cash flow, exclusive of operating cash inflows, that is expected to result from liquidation of the project at the end of its life. It is found by calculating and then finding the difference between the after-tax proceeds from sale of the new and the old asset at project termination and then adjusting this difference for any change in net working capital. Sale price and depreciation data are used to find the taxes and therefore the after-tax sale proceeds on the new and old asset. The change in net working capital typically represents the recovery of the net working capital investment included in the initial investment.

Self-test problems (Solutions in Appendix E)

ST 8-1 LG 4 **Book value, taxes, and initial investment** Irvin Enterprises is considering the purchase of a new piece of equipment to replace the current equipment. The new equipment will cost $75,000 and will require $5,000 in installation costs. It will be depreciated under MACRS using a five-year recovery period. The old piece of equipment was purchased for an installed cost of $50,000 four

years ago; it was being depreciated under MACRS using a five-year recovery period. The old equipment can be sold today for $55,000 net of any removal or cleanup costs. As a result of the proposed replacement the firm's investment in net working capital is expected to increase by $15,000. The firm pays taxes at a rate of 40 percent on both ordinary income and capital gains. (Table 3.6 on page 83 contains the applicable MACRS depreciation percentages.)

a. Calculate the book value of the old piece of equipment.
b. Determine the taxes, if any, attributable to the sale of the old equipment.
c. Find the initial investment associated with the proposed equipment replacement.

ST 8-2 LG 4,5,6 Determining relevant cash flows A machine currently in use was originally purchased two years ago for $40,000. The machine is being depreciated under MACRS using a five-year recovery period; it has three years of usable life remaining. The current machine can be sold today to net $42,000 after removal and cleanup costs. A new machine, using a three-year MACRS recovery period, can be purchased at a price of $140,000. It will require $10,000 to install and has a three-year usable life. If the new machine is acquired, the investment in accounts receivable is expected to rise by $10,000, the inventory investment will increase by $25,000, and accounts payable will increase by $15,000. *Profits before depreciation and taxes* are expected to be $70,000 for each of the next three years with the old machine and $120,000 in the first year and $130,000 in the second and third years with the new machine. At the end of three years the market value of the old machine would equal zero, but the new machine could be sold to net $35,000 before taxes. Both ordinary corporate income and capital gains are subject to a 40 percent tax. (Table 3.6 on page 83 contains the applicable MACRS depreciation percentages.)

a. Determine the initial investment associated with the proposed replacement decision.
b. Calculate the incremental operating cash inflows for years 1 to 4 associated with the proposed replacement. (*Note:* Only depreciation cash flows must be considered in year 4.)
c. Calculate the terminal cash flow associated with the proposed replacement decision. (*Note:* This is at the end of year 3.)
d. Diagram the relevant cash flows found in **a, b,** and **c** associated with the proposed replacement decision assuming that it is terminated at the end of year 3.

Problems

8-1 LG 1 Classification of expenditures Given the following list of outlays, indicate whether each would normally be considered a capital or a current expenditure. Explain your answers.

a. An initial lease payment of $5,000 for electronic point-of-sale cash register systems.
b. An outlay of $20,000 to purchase patent rights from an inventor.
c. An outlay of $80,000 for a major research and development program.
d. An $80,000 investment in a portfolio of marketable securities.
e. A $300 outlay for an office machine.
f. An outlay of $2,000 for a new machine tool.
g. An outlay of $240,000 for a new building.
h. An outlay of $1,000 for a marketing research report.

8-2 LG 2 Basic terminology A firm is considering the following three separate situations.

Situation A Build either a small office building or a convenience store on a parcel of land located in a high-traffic area. Adequate funding is available, and both projects are known to be acceptable. The office building will require an initial investment of $620,000 and is expected to provide operating cash inflows of $40,000 per year for 20 years. The convenience store is expected to cost $500,000 and provide a growing stream of operating cash inflows over its 20-year life. The initial operating cash inflow is $20,000 and will increase by 5 percent each year.

Situation B Replace a machine with a new one requiring a $60,000 initial investment and providing operating cash inflows of $10,000 per year for the first five years. At the end of year 5 a machine overhaul costing $20,000 is required. After it is completed, expected operating cash inflows are $10,000 in year 6; $7,000 in year 7; $4,000 in year 8; and $1,000 in year 9, at the end of which the machine will be scrapped.

Situation C Invest in any or all of the four machines whose relevant cash flows are given in the following table. The firm has $500,000 budgeted to fund these machines, all of which are known to be acceptable. Initial investment for each machine is $250,000.

	Operating cash inflows			
Year	**Machine 1**	**Machine 2**	**Machine 3**	**Machine 4**
1	$ 50,000	$70,000	$65,000	$90,000
2	70,000	70,000	65,000	80,000
3	90,000	70,000	80,000	70,000
4	−30,000	70,000	80,000	60,000
5	100,000	70,000	−20,000	50,000

For each situation or project, indicate

a. Whether the *situation* is independent or mutually exclusive.
b. Whether the availability of funds is unlimited or capital rationing exists.
c. Whether accept-reject or ranking decisions are required.
d. Whether each *project's* cash flows are conventional or nonconventional.
e. Whether each *project's* cash flow pattern is an annuity or a mixed stream.

8-3 LG 3 Expansion versus replacement cash flows Edison Systems has estimated the cash flows over the five-year lives for two projects, A and B. These cash flows are summarized below:

	Project A	**Project B**
Initial investment	$40,000	$12,000[a]
Year	**Operating cash inflows**	
1	$10,000	$ 6,000
2	12,000	6,000
3	14,000	6,000
4	16,000	6,000
5	10,000	6,000

[a]After-tax cash inflows expected from liquidation.

a. If project A were actually a *replacement* for project B and the $12,000 initial investment shown for B was the after-tax cash inflows expected from liquidating it, what would be the relevant cash flows for this replacement decision?
b. How can an *expansion decision* such as project A be viewed as a special form of a replacement decision? Explain.

8-4 LG 4 Relevant cash flow pattern fundamentals For each of the following projects, determine the *relevant cash flows,* classify the cash flow pattern, and diagram the pattern.

a. A project requiring an initial investment of $120,000 that generates annual operating cash inflows of $25,000 for the next 18 years. In each of the 18 years, maintenance of the project will require a $5,000 cash outflow.

b. A new machine having an installed cost of $85,000. Sale of the old machine will yield $30,000 after taxes. Operating cash inflows generated by the replacement will exceed the operating cash inflows of the old machine by $20,000 in each year of a six-year period. At the end of year 6, liquidation of the new machine will yield $20,000 after taxes, which is $10,000 greater than the after-tax proceeds expected from the old machine had it been retained and liquidated at the end of year 6.

c. An asset requiring an initial investment of $2 million that will yield annual operating cash inflows of $300,000 for each of the next 10 years. Operating cash outlays will be $20,000 for each year except year 6, when an overhaul requiring an additional cash outlay of $500,000 will be required. The asset's liquidation value at the end of year 10 is expected to be $0.

8-5 LG 4 **Book value** Find the book value for each of the assets below, assuming that MACRS depreciation is being used. (*Note:* See Table 3.6 on page 83 for the applicable depreciation percentages.)

Asset	Installed cost	Recovery period	Elapsed time since purchase
A	$ 950,000	5 years	3 years
B	40,000	3 years	1 year
C	96,000	5 years	4 years
D	350,000	5 years	1 year
E	1,500,000	7 years	5 years

8-6 LG 4 **Book value and taxes on sale of assets** Troy Industries purchased a new machine three years ago for $80,000. It is being depreciated under MACRS with a five-year recovery period using the percentages given in Table 3.6 on page 83. Assume 40 percent ordinary and capital gains tax rates.

a. What is the book value of the machine?

b. Calculate the firm's tax liability if it sells the machine for the following amounts: $100,000; $56,000; $23,200; $15,000.

8-7 LG 4 **Tax calculations** For each of the following cases, describe the various taxable components of the funds received through sale of the asset, and determine the total taxes resulting from the transaction. Assume 40 percent ordinary and capital gains tax rates. The asset was purchased for $200,000 two years ago and is being depreciated under MACRS using a five-year recovery period. (See Table 3.6 on page 83 for the applicable depreciation percentages.)

a. The asset is sold for $220,000.

b. The asset is sold for $150,000.

c. The asset is sold for $96,000.

d. The asset is sold for $80,000.

8-8 LG 4 **Change in net working capital calculation** Samuels Manufacturing is considering the purchase of a new machine to replace one they feel is obsolete. The firm has total current assets of $920,000 and total current liabilities of $640,000. As a result of the proposed replacement, the following *changes* are anticipated in the levels of the current asset and current liability accounts noted.

Account	Change
Accruals	+ $ 40,000
Marketable securities	0
Inventories	− 10,000
Accounts payable	+ 90,000
Notes payable	0
Accounts receivable	+ 150,000
Cash	+ 15,000

a. Using the information given, calculate the change, if any, in net working capital that is expected to result from the proposed replacement action.
b. Explain why a change in these current accounts would be relevant in determining the initial investment for the proposed capital expenditure.
c. Would the change in net working capital enter into any of the other cash flow components comprising the relevant cash flows? Explain.

8-9 LG 4 **Initial investment—Basic calculation** Cushing Corporation is considering the purchase of a new grading machine to replace the existing one. The existing machine was purchased three years ago at an installed cost of $20,000; it was being depreciated under MACRS using a five-year recovery period. (See Table 3.6 on page 83 for the applicable depreciation percentages.) The existing machine is expected to have a usable life of at least five more years. The new machine would cost $35,000 and require $5,000 in installation costs; it would be depreciated by using a five-year recovery period under MACRS. The existing machine can currently be sold for $25,000 without incurring any removal or cleanup costs. The firm pays 40 percent taxes on both ordinary income and capital gains. Calculate the *initial investment* associated with the proposed purchase of a new grading machine.

8-10 LG 4 **Initial investment at various sale prices** Edwards Manufacturing Company is considering replacement of one machine with another. The old machine was purchased three years ago for an installed cost of $10,000. The firm is depreciating the machine under MACRS using a five-year recovery period. (See Table 3.6 on page 83 for the applicable depreciation percentages.) The new machine costs $24,000 and requires $2,000 in installation costs. Assume that the firm is subject to a 40 percent tax rate on both ordinary income and capital gains. In each of the following cases, calculate the initial investment for the replacement.

a. Edwards Manufacturing Company (EMC) sells the old machine for $11,000.
b. EMC sells the old machine for $7,000.
c. EMC sells the old machine for $2,900.
d. EMC sells the old machine for $1,500.

8-11 LG 4 **Depreciation** A firm is evaluating the acquisition of an asset that costs $64,000 and requires $4,000 in installation costs. If the firm depreciates the asset under MACRS using a five-year recovery period (see Table 3.6 on page 83 for the applicable depreciation percentages), determine the depreciation charge for each year.

8-12 LG 5 **Incremental operating cash inflows** A firm is considering renewing its equipment to meet increased demand for its product. The cost of equipment modifications will be $1.9 million plus $100,000 in installation costs. The firm will depreciate the equipment modifications under MACRS using a five-year recovery period. (See Table 3.6 on page 83 for the applicable depreciation percentages.) Additional sales revenue from the renewal should amount to $1.2 million per year, and additional operating expenses and other costs (excluding depreciation) will amount to 40 percent of the additional sales. The firm has an ordinary tax rate of 40 percent. (*Note:* Answer the following questions for each of the next *six* years.)

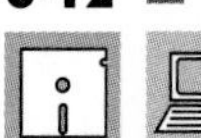

a. What incremental earnings before depreciation and taxes will result from the renewal?
b. What incremental earnings after taxes will result from the renewal?
c. What incremental operating cash inflows will result from the renewal?

8-13 LG 5 **Incremental operating cash inflows—Expense reduction** Miller Corporation is considering replacement of a machine. The replacement will reduce operating expenses (i.e., increase revenues) by $16,000 per year for each of the five years the new machine is expected to last. Although the old machine has zero book value, it can be used for five more years. The depreciable value of the new machine is $48,000. The firm will depreciate the machine under MACRS using a five-year recovery period (see Table 3.6 on page 83 for the applicable depreciation percentages) and is subject to a 40 percent tax rate on ordinary income. Estimate the incremental operating cash inflows generated by the replacement. (*Note:* Be sure to consider the depreciation in year 6.)

8-14 LG 5 **Incremental operating cash inflows** Strong Tool Company has been considering purchasing a new lathe to replace a fully depreciated lathe that will last five more years. The new lathe is expected to have a five-year life and depreciation charges of $2,000 in year 1; $3,200 in year 2; $1,900

in year 3; $1,200 in both year 4 and year 5; and $500 in year 6. The firm estimates the revenues and expenses (excluding depreciation) for the new and the old lathes as shown in the following table. The firm is subject to a 40 percent tax rate on ordinary income.

	New lathe		Old lathe	
Year	**Revenue**	**Expenses (excl. depr.)**	**Revenue**	**Expenses (excl. depr.)**
1	$40,000	$30,000	$35,000	$25,000
2	41,000	30,000	35,000	25,000
3	42,000	30,000	35,000	25,000
4	43,000	30,000	35,000	25,000
5	44,000	30,000	35,000	25,000

a. Calculate the operating cash inflows associated with each lathe. (*Note:* Be sure to consider the depreciation in year 6.)

b. Calculate the incremental (relevant) operating cash inflows resulting from the proposed lathe replacement.

c. Diagram the incremental operating cash inflows calculated in **b.**

8-15 LG 6 **Terminal cash flows—Various lives and sale prices** Looner Industries is currently analyzing the purchase of a new machine costing $160,000 and requiring $20,000 in installation costs. Purchase of this machine is expected to result in an increase in net working capital of $30,000 to support the expanded level of operations. The firm plans to depreciate the asset under MACRS using a five-year recovery period and expects to sell the machine to net $10,000 before taxes at the end of its usable life. The firm is subject to a 40 percent tax rate on both ordinary and capital gains income.

a. Calculate the terminal cash flow for a usable life of (1) three years, (2) five years, and (3) seven years.

b. Discuss the effect of usable life on terminal cash flows using your findings in **a.**

c. Assuming a five-year usable life, calculate the terminal cash flow if the machine were sold to net (1) $9,000 or (2) $170,000 (before taxes) at the end of the five years.

d. Discuss the effect of sale price on terminal cash flows using your findings in **c.**

8-16 LG 6 **Terminal cash flow—Replacement decision** Russell Industries is considering replacing a fully depreciated machine having a remaining useful life of 10 years with a newer, more sophisticated machine. The new machine will cost $200,000 and will require $30,000 in installation costs. It will be depreciated under MACRS using a five-year recovery period. A $25,000 increase in net working capital will be required to support the new machine. The firm plans to evaluate the potential replacement over a four-year period. They estimate that the old machine could be sold at the end of four years to net $15,000 before taxes; the new machine at the end of four years will be worth $75,000 before taxes. Calculate the terminal cash flow that is relevant to the proposed purchase of the new machine. The firm is subject to a 40 percent tax rate on both ordinary and capital gains income.

8-17 LG 4,5,6 **Relevant cash flows for a marketing campaign** Marcus Tube, a manufacturer of high-quality aluminum tubing has maintained stable sales and profits over the past 10 years. While the market for aluminum tubing has been expanding by 3 percent per year, Marcus has been unsuccessful in sharing this growth. To increase its sales, the firm is considering an aggressive marketing campaign that centers on regularly running ads in all relevant trade journals and exhibiting products at all major regional and national trade shows. The campaign is expected to require an *annual* tax-deductible expenditure of $150,000 over the next five years. Sales revenue, as noted in the income statement for 1994 shown, totaled $20,000,000. If the proposed marketing

campaign is not initiated, sales are expected to remain at this level in each of the next five years, 1995–1999. With the marketing campaign, sales are expected to rise to the levels shown in the following table for each of the next five years; cost of goods sold is expected to remain at 80 percent of sales; general and administrative expense (exclusive of any marketing campaign outlays) is expected to remain at 10 percent of sales; and annual depreciation expense is expected to remain at $500,000. Assuming a 40 percent tax rate, find the relevant cash flows over the next five years associated with the proposed marketing campaign.

Income statement Marcus Tube for the year ended December 31, 1994		
Sales revenue		$20,000,000
Less: Cost of good sold (80%)		16,000,000
Gross profits		$ 4,000,000
Less: Operating expenses		
General and administrative expense (10%)	$2,000,000	
Depreciation expense	500,000	
Total operating expense		2,500,000
Net profits before taxes		$ 1,500,000
Less: Taxes (rate = 40%)		600,000
Net profits after taxes		$ 900,000

Sales forecast Marcus Tube	
Year	**Sales revenue**
1995	$20,500,000
1996	21,000,000
1997	21,500,000
1998	22,500,000
1999	23,500,000

8-18 LG 4,5 **Relevant cash flows—No terminal value** Central Laundry and Cleaners is considering replacing an existing piece of machinery with a more sophisticated machine. The old machine was purchased three years ago at a cost of $50,000, and this amount was being depreciated under MACRS using a five-year recovery period. The machine has five years of usable life remaining. The new machine being considered will cost $76,000 and requires $4,000 in installation costs. The new machine would be depreciated under MACRS using a five-year recovery period. The old machine can currently be sold for $55,000 without incurring any removal or cleanup costs. The firm pays 40 percent taxes on both ordinary income and capital gains. The revenues and expenses (excluding depreciation) associated with the new and the old machine for the next five years are given in the table on page 336. (Table 3.6 on page 83 contains the applicable MACRS depreciation percentages.)

a. Calculate the initial investment associated with replacement of the old machine by the new one.

b. Determine the incremental operating cash inflows associated with the proposed replacement. (*Note:* Be sure to consider the depreciation in year 6.)

	New machine		Old machine	
Year	Revenue	Expenses (excl. depr.)	Revenue	Expenses (excl. depr.)
1	$750,000	$720,000	$674,000	$660,000
2	750,000	720,000	676,000	660,000
3	750,000	720,000	680,000	660,000
4	750,000	720,000	678,000	660,000
5	750,000	720,000	674,000	660,000

c. Diagram the relevant cash flows found in **a** and **b** that are associated with the proposed replacement decision.

8-19 LG 4,5,6 **Integrative—Determining relevant cash flows** The Lombard Company is contemplating the purchase of a new high-speed widget grinder to replace the existing grinder. The existing grinder was purchased two years ago at an installed cost of $60,000; it was being depreciated under MACRS using a five-year recovery period. The existing grinder is expected to have a usable life of five more years. The new grinder would cost $105,000 and would require $5,000 in installation costs; it has a five-year usable life and would be depreciated under MACRS using a five-year recovery period. The existing grinder can currently be sold for $70,000 without incurring any removal or cleanup costs. To support the increased business resulting from purchase of the new grinder, accounts receivable would increase by $40,000, inventories by $30,000, and accounts payable by $58,000. At the end of five years the existing grinder is expected to have a market value of zero; the new grinder would be sold to net $29,000 after removal and cleanup costs and before taxes. The firm pays 40 percent taxes on both ordinary income and capital gains. The estimated *profits before depreciation and taxes* over the five years for both the new and existing grinder are shown in the following table. (Table 3.6 on page 83 contains the applicable MACRS depreciation percentages.)

	Profits before depreciation and taxes	
Year	New grinder	Existing grinder
1	$43,000	$26,000
2	43,000	24,000
3	43,000	22,000
4	43,000	20,000
5	43,000	18,000

a. Calculate the initial investment associated with the replacement of the existing grinder by the new one.

b. Determine the incremental operating cash inflows associated with the proposed grinder replacement. (*Note:* Be sure to consider the depreciation in year 6.)

c. Determine the terminal cash flow expected from the proposed grinder replacement.

d. Diagram the relevant cash flows associated with the proposed grinder replacement decision.

8-20 LG 4,5,6 **Integrative—Determining relevant cash flows** Atlantic Drydock is considering replacement of an existing hoist with one of two newer, more efficient pieces of equipment. The existing hoist is three years old, cost $32,000, and is being depreciated under MACRS using a five-year recovery period. Although the existing hoist has only three years (years 4, 5, and 6) of depreci-

ation remaining under MACRS, it has a remaining usable life of five years. Hoist A, one of the two possible replacement hoists, costs $40,000 to purchase and $8,000 to install. It has a five-year usable life and will be depreciated under MACRS using a five-year recovery period. The other hoist, B, costs $54,000 to purchase and $6,000 to install. It also has a five-year usable life, and it will be depreciated under MACRS using a five-year recovery period.

Increased investments in net working capital will accompany the decision to acquire hoist A or hoist B. Purchase of hoist A would result in a $4,000 increase in net working capital; hoist B would result in a $6,000 increase in net working capital. The projected *profits before depreciation and taxes* with each alternative hoist and the existing hoist are given in the following table.

	Profits before depreciation and taxes		
Year	With hoist A	With hoist B	With existing hoist
1	$21,000	$22,000	$14,000
2	21,000	24,000	14,000
3	21,000	26,000	14,000
4	21,000	26,000	14,000
5	21,000	26,000	14,000

The existing hoist can currently be sold for $18,000 and will not incur any removal or cleanup costs. At the end of five years the existing hoist can be sold to net $1,000 before taxes. Hoists A and B can be sold to net $12,000 and $20,000 before taxes, respectively, at the end of the five-year period. The firm is subject to a 40 percent tax rate on both ordinary income and capital gains. (Table 3.6 on page 83 contains the applicable MACRS depreciation percentages.)

a. Calculate the initial investment associated with each alternative.

b. Calculate the incremental operating cash inflows associated with each alternative. (*Note:* Be sure to consider the depreciation in year 6.)

c. Calculate the terminal cash flow associated with each alternative. (*Note:* This is at the end of year 5.)

d. Diagram the relevant cash flows associated with each alternative.

Chapter 8 Case Developing relevant cash flows for Clark Upholstery Company's machine renewal or replacement decision

Bo Humphries, chief financial officer of Clark Upholstery Company, expects the firm's *net profits after taxes* for the next five years to be as shown in the following table.

Year	Net profits after taxes
1	$100,000
2	150,000
3	200,000
4	250,000
5	320,000

Bo is beginning to develop the relevant cash flows needed to analyze whether to renew or replace Clark's *only* depreciable asset, a machine that originally cost $30,000, has a current book value of zero, and can now be sold for $20,000. (*Note:* Because the firm's only depreciable asset is fully depreciated—its book value is zero—its expected net profits after taxes equal its operating cash inflows.) He estimates that at the end of five years the existing machine can be sold to net $2,000 before taxes. Bo planned to use the information given below to develop the relevant cash flows for each of the alternatives.

Alternative 1 Renew the existing machine at a total depreciable cost of $90,000. The renewed machine would have a five-year usable life and would be depreciated under MACRS using a five-year recovery period. Renewing the machine would result in the following projected revenues and expenses (excluding depreciation):

Year	Revenue	Expenses (excluding depreciation)
1	$1,000,000	$801,500
2	1,175,000	884,200
3	1,300,000	918,100
4	1,425,000	943,100
5	1,550,000	968,100

The renewed machine would result in an increased investment of $15,000 in net working capital. At the end of five years the machine could be sold to net $8,000 before taxes.

Alternative 2 Replace the existing machine with a new machine costing $100,000 and requiring installation costs of $10,000. The new machine would have a five-year usable life and be depreciated under MACRS using a five-year recovery period. The firm's projected revenues and expenses (excluding depreciation), if it acquires the machine, are as follows:

Year	Revenue	Expenses (excluding depreciation)
1	$1,000,000	$764,500
2	1,175,000	839,800
3	1,300,000	914,900
4	1,425,000	989,900
5	1,550,000	998,900

The new machine would result in an increased investment of $22,000 in net working capital. At the end of five years the new machine could be sold to net $25,000 before taxes.

The firm is subject to a 40 percent tax on both ordinary income and capital gains. As noted, the company uses MACRS depreciation. (See Table 3.6 on page 83 for the applicable depreciation percentages.)

Required

a. Calculate the initial investment associated with each of Clark Upholstery's alternatives.

b. Calculate the incremental operating cash inflows associated with each of Clark's alternatives. (*Note:* Be sure to consider the depreciation in year 6.)

c. Calculate the terminal cash flow associated with each of Clark's alternatives. (*Note:* This is at the end of year 5.)

d. Use your findings in **a, b,** and **c** to diagram the relevant cash flows associated with each of Clark Upholstery's alternatives.

e. Based solely upon your comparison of their relevant cash flows, which alternative appears to be better? Why?

chapter 9

Capital budgeting techniques: Certainty, risk, and some refinements

LEARNING GOALS

 Calculate, interpret, and evaluate one of the most commonly used unsophisticated capital budgeting techniques—the payback period.

 Apply the sophisticated capital budgeting techniques—net present value (NPV) and internal rate of return (IRR)—to relevant cash flows to choose acceptable as well as preferred capital expenditures.

 Use net present value profiles to compare net present value and internal rate of return techniques in light of conflicting rankings from both theoretical and practical viewpoints.

 Recognize the basic behavioral approaches—breakeven cash flow, sensitivity and scenario analysis, and simulation—for dealing with project risk and the unique risks and other issues facing multinational companies (MNCs).

 Understand the calculation, differing approaches, and practical aspects of the two basic risk-adjustment techniques—certainty equivalents (CEs) and risk-adjusted discount rates (RADRs).

 Describe two capital budgeting refinements—comparing projects with unequal lives and capital rationing—that frequently require special forms of analysis.

Capital budgeting is a process for analyzing and selecting appropriate long-term investment projects. At times this pursuit represents art more than science; in many cases, factors determining a capital investment project's ultimate success (general economic conditions, competition, interest rates, government regulations, etc.) are beyond a company 's direct control. Also, the time horizon for many capital projects extends far into the future (10 years or more), so projecting the timing and benefit of these investment activities can be a highly uncertain process.

The Quaker Oats Company spends several hundred million dollars a year or more on capital investment projects. Given the amount of money involved, capital budgeting represents an important organizational activity for us. When we evaluate any capital project, we try to determine the source, timing, amount, and potential variability of its cash flows—a process that is sometimes more easily said than done.

Like most companies, Quaker's objective is to maximize its return on capital investments. Our capital-budgeting decision depends on many quantitative and qualitative factors including project length, involvement of existing or cutting-edge technology, and the project's size and scope. Techniques used to evaluate the financial viability of capital projects include payback, internal rate of return (IRR), and net present value (NPV). At Quaker we prefer the NPV (discounted cash flow) methodology because this approach provides the most appropriate decision-making criteria.

It is easy to get a false sense of confidence by looking strictly at the numbers.

For example, assume that you are considering whether to invest $1 million in a project (A) with an IRR of 20% and an NPV of $200,000 or to invest $10,000 in an alternative project (B) with an IRR of 100% and an NPV of $10,000. The IRR rule would lead us to choose project B (higher return). However, life experience (reality) tells us that project A (more money) is the preferable alternative. All else being equal, it is better to achieve significant wealth than significant returns. NPV correctly leads us to this conclusion and, accordingly, creates behavior that we believe is more in line with true shareholder objectives.

Typically, several factors are critical to a project's success. Through sensitivity analysis we try to understand the nature and degree of risk associated with these factors. By preparing a base case set of realistic assumptions, we can assess the impact of changing key variables on the financial results. This important planning consideration allows us to monitor the critical success factors from the outset of the project and quickly adjust our strategy in the future, if necessary.

In general, the risk characteristics throughout our various businesses are similar, so we apply a consistent discount rate across divisions for capital budgeting. However, if a new project's business characteristics (production process, mode of distribution, customer base, technology, or geographic market) differ significantly from those of our basic business, we might use a higher, risk-adjusted discount rate to evaluate that investment.

Finally, it is easy to get a false sense of confidence by looking strictly at the numbers. Financial analysis alone cannot replace common sense or business judgment. Consequently, before starting any financial analysis, we ask such basic questions as: "What is the purpose of this investment?"; "Is it consistent with the business strategic objective?"; and "What would happen if we did not invest?". The answers to these questions often determine whether a project is accepted or not.

Oscar Turner received a B.A. in Economics from UCLA, an M.A. in Accounting from DePaul University (Chicago), and an M.B.A. from Columbia Business School. He joined Quaker Oats in 1990 as Planning Controller for New Ventures and became Manager, Strategic Planning, U.S. Grocery Products in 1991. From 1985 to 1990 he was a corporate lender for Continental Bank.

Capital budgeting techniques

Capital budgeting techniques are used by firms to select projects that will enhance owner wealth. How would you go about applying present value techniques to a project's relevant cash flows in a fashion consistent with owner wealth maximization? Before reading on, spend a few moments answering this question.

THE RELEVANT CASH FLOWS DEVELOPED IN CHAPTER 8 MUST BE ANALYZED TO ASSESS whether a project is acceptable or to rank projects. A number of techniques are available for performing such analyses. The preferred approaches integrate time value procedures (Chapter 5), risk and return considerations (Chapter 6), and valuation concepts (Chapter 7) to select capital expenditures that are consistent with the firm's goal of maximizing owners' wealth. This and the following section focus on the use of these techniques to evaluate capital expenditure proposals for decision-making purposes.

We shall use the same basic problem to illustrate the application of all the techniques described in this chapter. The problem concerns the Bennett Company, a medium-sized metal fabricator that is currently contemplating two projects—project A, requiring an initial investment of $42,000, and project B, requiring an initial investment of $45,000. The projected incremental (relevant) operating cash inflows for the two projects are presented in Table 9.1.[1] The projects exhibit conventional cash flow patterns, which are assumed throughout the text. In addition, we continue to assume that all projects' cash flows have the same level of risk, that projects being compared

TABLE 9.1

CAPITAL EXPENDITURE DATA FOR BENNETT COMPANY

	Project A	Project B
Initial investment	$42,000	$45,000
Year	**Operating cash inflows**	
1	$14,000	$28,000
2	14,000	12,000
3	14,000	10,000
4	14,000	10,000
5	14,000	10,000
Average	$14,000	$14,000

[1]For simplification these five-year-lived projects with five years of cash inflows are used throughout this chapter. Projects with usable lives equal to the number of years of cash inflows are also included in the end-of-chapter problems. It is important to recall from Chapter 8 that under the *Tax Reform Act of 1986*, MACRS depreciation results in $n + 1$ years of depreciation for an n-year class asset. This means that projects will commonly have at least one year of cash flow beyond their recovery period. In actual practice, usable lives of projects (and the associated cash inflows) may differ significantly from their depreciable lives. Generally, under MACRS, usable lives are longer than depreciable lives.

have equal usable lives, and that the firm has unlimited funds. Since very few decisions are actually made under such conditions, these simplifying assumptions are relaxed in later sections of the chapter. Here we begin with a look at the three most popular capital budgeting techniques—payback period, net present value, and internal rate of return.[2]

Payback period

payback period
The exact amount of time required for a firm to recover its initial investment in a project as calculated from *cash inflows.*

Payback periods are a commonly used criterion for evaluating proposed investments. The **payback period** is the exact amount of time required for the firm to recover its initial investment in a project as calculated from *cash inflows.* In the case of an *annuity* the payback period can be found by dividing the initial investment by the annual cash inflow; for a *mixed stream* the yearly cash inflows must be accumulated until the initial investment is recovered. Although popular, the payback period is generally viewed as an *unsophisticated capital budgeting technique,* since it does *not* explicitly consider the time value of money by discounting cash flows to find present value.

THE DECISION CRITERION

The decision criterion when payback is used to make accept-reject decisions is as follows: *If the payback period is less than the maximum acceptable payback period, accept the project; if the payback period is greater than the maximum acceptable payback period, reject the project.*

EXAMPLE

The data for Bennett Company's projects A and B presented in Table 9.1 can be used to demonstrate the calculation of the payback period. For project A, which is an annuity, the payback period is 3.0 years ($42,000 initial investment ÷ $14,000 annual cash inflow). Since project B generates a mixed stream of cash inflows, the calculation of the payback period is not quite as clear-cut. In year 1 the firm will recover $28,000 of its $45,000 initial investment. At the end of year 2, $40,000 ($28,000 from year 1 + $12,000 from year 2) will be recovered. At the end of year 3, $50,000 ($40,000 from years 1 and 2 + $10,000 from year 3) will be recovered. Since the amount received by the end of year 3 is greater than the initial investment of $45,000, the payback period is somewhere between two and three years. Only $5,000 ($45,000 − $40,000) must be recovered during year 3. Actually, $10,000 is recovered, but only 50 percent of this cash inflow ($5,000 ÷ $10,000) is needed to complete the payback of the initial $45,000. The payback period for project B is therefore 2.5 years (2 years + 50 percent of year 3).

If Bennett's maximum acceptable payback period is 2.75 years, project A would be rejected, and project B would be accepted. If the maximum payback were 2.25 years,

[2]Two other closely related techniques that are sometimes used to evaluate capital budgeting projects are the *average (or accounting) rate of return (ARR)* and the *profitability index (PI).* The ARR is an unsophisticated technique that is calculated by dividing a project's average profits after taxes by its average investment. Because it fails to consider cash flows and the time value of money, it is ignored here. The PI, sometimes called the *benefit-cost ratio,* is calculated by dividing the present value of cash inflows by the initial investment. This technique, which does consider the time value of money, is sometimes used as a starting point in the selection of projects under capital rationing; the more popular NPV and IRR methods are discussed here.

both projects would be rejected. If the projects were being ranked, project B would be preferred over project A, since it has a shorter payback period (2.5 years versus 3.0 years). ■

CONCEPT IN PRACTICE

Brewing a Quick Payback from New-Employee Training at Starbucks Coffee

Howard Schultz has transformed Seattle's Starbucks Coffee Company from a local coffee grinder to a profitable 90-million-dollar national retailer. His strategy is based on the belief that more than every dollar you invest in your employees shows up on the bottom line. Employee training is one area that Schultz has found to be a gold mine. Starbucks normally spends 25 hours of classroom training time on every new employee before he or she works behind the counter. Trainees attend classes with such appropriate titles as Coffee Knowledge 101.

Schultz estimates that he spends $1,000 to train each new worker. However, his documents show that overhead cost as a percentage of sales declines from 12.3 percent to 8 percent following training. Given Starbucks weekly per-employee average sales of $350, the weekly savings from training is $15.05 [(.123 − .080) × $350] per employee. Division of the training cost, $1,000, by the savings per week results in a payback period of 66.5 weeks. Fifteen weeks into the second year following training, Starbucks Coffee is in the black with respect to new-employee-training costs.

PROS AND CONS OF PAYBACK PERIODS

The payback period's popularity, particularly among small firms, results from its ease of calculation and simple intuitive appeal. It is appealing in light of the fact that it considers cash flows rather than accounting profits; it also gives *some* implicit consideration to the timing of cash flows and therefore to the time value of money. Because it can be viewed as a measure of *risk exposure,* many firms use the payback period as a decision criterion or as a supplement to sophisticated decision techniques. The longer the firm must wait to recover its invested funds, the greater the possibility of a calamity. Therefore the shorter the payback period, the lower the firm's exposure to such risk.

The major weakness of payback is that the appropriate payback period cannot be specified in light of the wealth maximization goal because it is not based upon discounting cash flows to determine whether they add to the firm's value. Instead, the appropriate payback period is merely a subjectively determined maximum acceptable period of time over which a project's cash flows must break even (i.e., just equal the initial investment). A second weakness is that this approach fails to take *fully* into account the time factor in the value of money; by measuring how quickly the firm recovers its initial investment, it only implicitly considers the timing of cash flows.[3] A third weakness is the failure to recognize cash flows that occur *after* the payback period. This weakness can be illustrated by an example.

EXAMPLE

Data for two investment opportunities—X and Y—are given in Table 9.2. The payback period for project X is two years; for project Y it is three years. Strict adherence to the payback approach suggests that project X is preferable to project Y. However, if we

---

[3]To consider differences in timing *explicitly* in applying the payback method, the *present-value payback period* is sometimes used. It is found by first calculating the present value of the cash inflows at the appropriate discount rate and then finding the payback period by using the present value of the cash inflows.

TABLE 9.2

CALCULATION OF THE PAYBACK PERIOD FOR TWO ALTERNATIVE INVESTMENT PROJECTS

	Project X	Project Y
Initial investment	$10,000	$10,000
Year	**Cash inflows**	
1	$ 5,000	$ 3,000
2	5,000	4,000
3	1,000	3,000
4	100	4,000
5	100	3,000
Payback period	2 years	3 years

look beyond the payback period, we see that project X returns only an additional $1,200 ($1,000 in year 3, $100 in year 4, and $100 in year 5), whereas project Y returns an additional $7,000 ($4,000 in year 4 and $3,000 in year 5). On the basis of this information, it appears that project Y is preferable to X. The payback approach ignores the cash inflows in years 3, 4, and 5 for project X and in years 4 and 5 for project Y.[4] ■

Net present value (NPV)

Because *net present value* gives explicit consideration to the time value of money, it is considered a *sophisticated capital budgeting technique.* All such techniques in one way or another discount the firm's cash flows at a specified rate. This rate—often called the *discount rate, opportunity cost,* or *cost of capital* (the topic of Chapter 10)—refers to the minimum return that must be earned on a project to leave the firm's market value unchanged.

net present value (NPV)
A sophisticated capital budgeting technique; found by subtracting a project's initial investment from the present value of its cash inflows discounted at a rate equal to the firm's cost of capital.

The **net present value (NPV),** as noted in Equation 9.1, is found by subtracting the initial investment *(II)* from the present value of the cash inflows (CF_t) discounted at a rate equal to the firm's cost of capital *(k).*

$$\text{NPV} = \text{present value of cash inflows} - \text{initial investment}$$

$$\text{NPV} = \sum_{t=1}^{n} \frac{\text{CF}_t}{(1+k)^t} - II \quad (9.1)$$

Using NPV, both inflows and outflows are measured in terms of present dollars. Since we are dealing with conventional investments, the initial investment is automatically

[4]To get around this weakness, some analysts add a desired dollar return to the initial investment and then calculate the payback period for the increased amount. For example, if the analyst wished to pay back the initial investment plus 20 percent for projects X and Y in Table 9.2, the amount to be recovered would be $12,000 [$10,000 + (.20 × $10,000)]. For project X the payback period would be infinite because the $12,000 would never be recovered; for project Y the payback period would be 3.50 years [3 years + ($2,000 + $4,000) years]. Clearly, project Y would be preferred.

stated in terms of today's dollars. If it were not, the present value of a project would be found by subtracting the present value of outflows from the present value of inflows.

THE DECISION CRITERION

The decision criterion when NPV is used to make accept-reject decisions is as follows: *If NPV is greater than $0, accept the project; if NPV is less than $0, reject the project.* If NPV is greater than zero, the firm will earn a return greater than its cost of capital. Such action should enhance the market value of the firm and therefore the wealth of its owners.

EXAMPLE

The net present value (NPV) approach can be illustrated by using the Bennett Company data presented in Table 9.1. If the firm has a 10 percent cost of capital, the net present values for projects A (an annuity) and B (a mixed stream) can be calculated as in Table 9.3. These calculations are based on the application of the techniques presented in Chapter 5 using the appropriate present-value table factors.[5] The results show that the net present values of projects A and B are $11,074 and $10,914 respectively. Both projects are acceptable, since the net present value of each is greater than zero. If the projects were being ranked, however, project A would be considered superior to B, since it has a higher net present value ($11,074 versus $10,914) than that of B. ■

Internal rate of return (IRR)

internal rate of return (IRR)
The discount rate that equates the present value of cash inflows with the initial investment associated with a project, thereby causing NPV = $0.

The internal rate of return (IRR), although considerably more difficult to calculate by hand than NPV, is probably the most used *sophisticated capital budgeting technique* for evaluating investment alternatives. The **internal rate of return (IRR)** is defined as the discount rate that equates the present value of cash inflows with the initial investment associated with a project. The IRR, in other words, is the discount rate that equates the NPV of an investment opportunity with zero (since the present value of cash inflows equals the initial investment). Mathematically, the IRR is found by solving Equation 9.1 for the value of k that causes NPV to equal zero.

$$\$0 = \sum_{t=1}^{n} \frac{CF_t}{(1 + \text{IRR})^t} - II$$

$$\sum_{t=1}^{n} \frac{CF_t}{(1 + \text{IRR})^t} = II \qquad (9.2)$$

As will be demonstrated shortly, the actual calculation by hand of the IRR from Equation 9.2 is no easy chore.

[5]Alternatively, a hand-held business/financial calculator such as the Texas Instruments BA-35 could have been used to streamline these calculations as described in Chapter 5. Most of the more sophisticated (and more expensive) financial calculators are preprogrammed to find NPVs. With these calculators you merely punch in all cash flows along with the cost of capital or discount rate and depress **NPV** to find the net present value. When such a calculator is used, the resulting values for projects A and B are $11,071 and $10,924, respectively.

TABLE 9.3

THE CALCULATION OF NPVs FOR BENNETT COMPANY'S CAPITAL EXPENDITURE ALTERNATIVES

Project A	
Annual cash inflow	$14,000
× Present-value annuity interest factor, *PVIFA*[a]	3,791
Present value of cash inflows	$53,074
− Initial investment	42,000
Net present value (NPV)	$11,074

Project B

Year	Cash inflows (1)	Present-value interest factor, *PVIF*[b] (2)	Present value [(1) × (2)] (3)
1	$28,000	.909	$25,452
2	12,000	.826	9,912
3	10,000	.751	7,510
4	10,000	.683	6,830
5	10,000	.621	6,210
		Present value of cash inflows	$55,914
		− Initial investment	45,000
		Net present value (NPV)	$10,914

[a]From Table A-4, for 5 years and 10 percent.

[b]From Table A-3, for given year and 10 percent.

THE DECISION CRITERION

The decision criterion, when the IRR is used in making accept-reject decisions, is as follows: *If the IRR is greater than the cost of capital, accept the project; if the IRR is less than the cost of capital, reject the project.* This criterion guarantees that the firm earns at least its required return. Such an outcome should enhance the market value of the firm and therefore the wealth of its owners.

CALCULATING THE IRR

The IRR can be found either by using trial-and-error techniques or with the aid of a sophisticated financial calculator or a computer.[6] Here we demonstrate the trial-and-

[6]The Texas Instruments BA-35 calculator—the inexpensive hand-held business/financial calculator used throughout this text—can be employed to find the IRR of an annuity, but it lacks a function for use in finding the IRR of a mixed stream of cash flows. Most of the more sophisticated (and more expensive) financial calculators are preprogrammed to find IRRs. With these calculators you merely punch in all cash flows and depress **IRR** to find the internal rate of return. Computer software, like the *PMF Disk*, described in Appendix B, is also available for use in calculating IRRs.

error approach. Calculating the IRR for an annuity is considerably easier than calculating it for a mixed stream of operating cash inflows.[7] The steps involved in calculating the IRR in each case are given in Table 9.4. The application of these steps can be illustrated by the following example.

EXAMPLE

The two-step procedure given in Table 9.4 for finding the IRR of an *annuity* can be demonstrated by using Bennett Company's project A cash flows given in Table 9.1.

Step 1 Dividing the initial investment of \$42,000 by the annual cash inflow of \$14,000 results in a payback period of 3.000 years (\$42,000 ÷ \$14,000 = 3.000).

Step 2 According to Table A-4, the *PVIFA* factors closest to 3.000 for five years are 3.058 (for 19 percent) and 2.991 (for 20 percent). The value closest to 3.000 is 2.991; therefore the IRR for project A, to the nearest 1 percent, is *20 percent.* The actual value, which is between 19 and 20 percent, could be found by using a calculator[8] or computer or by interpolation[9]; it is 19.86 percent. (*Note:* For our purposes, values rounded to the nearest 1 percent will suffice.) Project A with an IRR of 20 percent is quite acceptable, since this IRR is above the firm's 10 percent cost of capital (20 percent IRR > 10 percent cost of capital).

The application of the seven-step procedure given in Table 9.4 for finding the internal rate of return of a *mixed stream* of cash inflows can be illustrated by using Bennett Company's project B cash flows given in Table 9.1.

Step 1 Summing the cash inflows for years 1 through 5 results in total cash inflows of \$70,000, which, when divided by the number of years in the project's life, results in an average annual cash inflow of \$14,000 [(\$28,000 + \$12,000 + \$10,000 + \$10,000 + \$10,000) ÷ 5].

---

[7]The ease of calculating the IRR for an annuity as well as the steps in the process results from an ability to simplify Equation 9.2. Since for annuities, $CF_1 = CF_2 = \ldots = CF_n$, the CF_t term can be factored from Equation 9.2. Doing this, we get

$$CF_t \sum_{t=1}^{n} \frac{1}{(1+\text{IRR})^t} = II$$

Dividing both sides of the equation by CF_t, we get

$$\sum_{t=1}^{n} \frac{1}{(1+\text{IRR})^t} = \frac{II}{CF_t}$$

Since the left side of the equation is equal to $PVIFA_{\text{IRR},n}$ and the right side equals the payback period—the initial investment divided by the annual cash inflow—it is not difficult to estimate the IRR for annuities.

[8]The procedure for using a hand-held business/financial calculator to find the unknown interest rate on an equal-payment loan described in Chapter 5 can be used to find the IRR for an annuity. When applying this procedure, we treat the life of the annuity the same as the term of the loan, the initial investment the same as the loan principal, and the annual cash inflows the same as the annual loan payments. The resulting solution is the IRR for the annuity rather than the interest rate on the loan.

[9]*Interpolation* is a mathematical technique used to find intermediate or fractional values when only integer data are provided. Since interest factors for whole percentages are included in the financial tables in Appendix A, interpolation is required to calculate more precisely the internal rate of return. See footnote 17 in Chapter 5 for a demonstration of the use of interpolation to obtain better estimates of rates of return.

TABLE 9.4

STEPS FOR CALCULATING THE INTERNAL RATES OF RETURN (IRRs) OF ANNUITIES AND MIXED STREAMS

FOR AN ANNUITY

Step 1: Calculate the payback period for the project.[a]

Step 2: Use Table A-4 (the present-value interest factors for a $1 annuity, *PVIFA*) to find, for the life of the project, the factor closest to the payback value. The discount rate associated with that factor is the internal rate of return (IRR) to the nearest 1 percent.

FOR A MIXED STREAM[b]

Step 1: Calculate the average annual cash inflow.

Step 2: Divide the average annual cash inflow into the initial investment to get an "average payback period" (or present-value interest factor for a $1 annuity, *PVIFA*). The average payback is needed to estimate the IRR for the average annual cash inflow.

Step 3: Use Table A-4 *(PVIFA)* and the average payback period in the same manner as described in Step 2 for finding the IRR of an annuity. The result will be a *very rough* approximation of the IRR based on the assumption that the mixed stream of cash inflows is an annuity.

Step 4:[c] Adjust subjectively the IRR obtained in Step 3 by comparing the pattern of average annual cash inflows (calculated in Step 1) to the actual mixed stream of cash inflows. If the actual cash flow stream seems to have higher inflows in the earlier years than the average stream, adjust the IRR up. If the actual cash inflows in the earlier years are below the average, adjust the IRR down. The amount of adjustment up or down typically ranges from 1 to 3 percentage points, depending upon how much the actual cash inflow stream's pattern deviates from the average annual cash inflows. For small deviations an adjustment of around 1 percentage point may be best, whereas for large deviations, adjustments of around 3 percentage points are generally appropriate. If the average cash inflows seem fairly close to the actual pattern, make no adjustment in the IRR.

Step 5: Using the IRR from Step 4, calculate the net present value of the mixed-stream project. Be sure to use Table A-3 (the present-value interest factors for $1, *PVIF*), treating the estimated IRR as the discount rate.

Step 6: If the resulting NPV is greater than zero, subjectively raise the discount rate; if the resulting NPV is less than zero, subjectively lower the discount rate. The greater the deviation of the resulting NPV from zero, the larger the subjective adjustment. Typically, adjustments of 1 to 3 percentage points are used for relatively small deviations, whereas larger adjustments are required for relatively large deviations.

Step 7: Calculate the NPV using the new discount rate. Repeat Step 6. Stop as soon as two *consecutive* discount rates that cause the NPV to be positive and negative, respectively, have been found.[d] Whichever of these rates causes the NPV to be closer to zero is the IRR to the nearest 1 percent.

[a]The payback period calculated actually represents the interest factor for the present value of an annuity *(PVIFA)* for the given life discounted at an unknown rate, which, once determined, represents the IRR for the project.

[b]Note that subjective estimates are suggested in Steps 4 and 6. After working a number of these problems, a "feel" for the appropriate subjective adjustment, or "educated guess," may result.

[c]The purpose of this step is to provide a more accurate first estimate of the IRR. This step can be skipped.

[d]A shortcut method is to find a discount rate that results in a positive NPV and another that results in a negative NPV. Using only these two values, one can interpolate between the two discount rates to find the IRR. This approach, which may be nearly as accurate as that described above, can guarantee an answer after only two NPV calculations. Of course, because interpolation involves a straight-line approximation to an exponential function, the wider the interpolation interval, the less accurate the estimate.

Step 2 Dividing the initial outlay of $45,000 by the average annual cash inflow of $14,000 (calculated in Step 1) results in an "average payback period" (or present value of an annuity factor, *PVIFA*) of 3.214 years.

Step 3 In Table A-4 the factor closest to 3.214 for five years is 3.199, the factor for a discount rate of 17 percent. The starting estimate of the IRR is therefore 17 percent.

Step 4 Since the actual early-year cash inflows are greater than the average annual cash inflows of $14,000, a *subjective* increase of 2 percent is made in the discount rate. This makes the estimated IRR 19 percent.

Step 5 Using the present-value interest factors *(PVIF)* for 19 percent and the correct year from Table A-3, the net present value of the mixed stream is calculated as follows:

Year *(t)*	Cash inflows (1)	$PVIF_{19\%,t}$ (2)	Present value at 19% [(1) × (2)] (3)
1	$28,000	.840	$23,520
2	12,000	.706	8,472
3	10,000	.593	5,930
4	10,000	.499	4,990
5	10,000	.419	4,190
	Present value of cash inflows		$47,102
	− Initial investment		45,000
	Net present value (NPV)		$ 2,102

Steps 6 and 7 Since the net present value of $2,102, calculated in Step 5, is greater than zero, the discount rate should be subjectively increased. Since the NPV deviates by only about 5 percent from the $45,000 initial investment, let's try a 2 percentage point increase to 21 percent.

Year *(t)*	Cash inflows (1)	$PVIF_{21\%,t}$ (2)	Present value at 21% [(1) × (2)] (3)
1	$28,000	.826	$23,128
2	12,000	.683	8,196
3	10,000	.564	5,640
4	10,000	.467	4,670
5	10,000	.386	3,860
	Present value of cash inflows		$45,494
	− Initial investment		45,000
	Net present value (NPV)		$ 494

These calculations indicate that the NPV of $494 for an IRR of 21 percent is reasonably close to, but still greater than, zero. Thus a higher discount rate should be tried. Since we are so close, let's try a 1 percentage point increase to 22 percent. As the following calculations show, the net present value using a discount rate of 22 percent is −$256.

Year (t)	Cash inflows (1)	$PVIF_{22\%,t}$ (2)	Present value at 22% [(1) × (2)] (3)
1	$28,000	.820	$22,960
2	12,000	.672	8,064
3	10,000	.551	5,510
4	10,000	.451	4,510
5	10,000	.370	3,700
	Present value of cash inflows		$44,744
	− Initial investment		45,000
	Net present value (NPV)		−$ 256

Since 21 and 22 percent are consecutive discount rates that give positive and negative net present values, the trial-and-error process can be terminated. The IRR that we are seeking is the discount rate for which the NPV is closest to zero. For this project, 22 percent causes the NPV to be closer to zero than 21 percent, so 22 percent is the IRR that we shall use. If we had used a financial calculator, a computer, or interpolation, the exact IRR would be 21.65 percent; as indicated earlier, for our purposes the IRR rounded to the nearest 1 percent will suffice. Therefore the IRR of project B is approximately *22 percent.*

Project B is acceptable, since its IRR of approximately 22 percent is greater than the Bennett Company's 10 percent cost of capital. This is the same conclusion as was reached by using the NPV criterion. It is interesting to note that the IRR suggests that project B is preferable to project A, which has an IRR of approximately 20 percent. This conflicts with the rankings of the projects obtained by using NPV. Such conflicts are not unusual; *there is no guarantee that these two techniques (NPV and IRR) will rank projects in the same order. However, both methods should reach the same conclusion about the acceptability or nonacceptability of projects.* ■

CONCEPT IN PRACTICE

Canada's Energy Boondoggle Has a Negative NPV

In 1993 the Canadian government voted to further subsidize the Hibernia Project, which will drill for oil in the iceberg-filled waters 200 miles off the Newfoundland coast. Production, storage, and housing facilities will have to be anchored in 240 feet of water near the spot where the Titanic sunk. Mobil, Chevron, Murphy Oil, and Petro-Canada expect to spend $4.1 billion on construction. Total anticipated capital and operating expenditures will push the cost of Hibernia oil to about $25 per barrel. That is five times the current cost to recover a barrel of oil. In addition to paying $226 million for an 8.5 percent share of ownership, the Canadian government has extended a $2.1 billion grant to the other owners as compensation for participating in the project. Mobil admitted that "it wasn't economical to proceed without government money." Clearly, without the government subsidy, nongovernment participants would have experienced negative NPVs, thereby reducing both the value of the firm and its owners' wealth.

CONCEPTS IN REVIEW

9-1 What is the *payback period*? How is it calculated? What weaknesses are commonly associated with the use of the payback period to evaluate a proposed investment?

9-2 What is the formula for finding the *net present value (NPV)* of a project with conventional cash flows? What is the acceptance criterion for NPV?

9-3 What is the *internal rate of return (IRR)* on an investment? How is it determined? What is its acceptance criterion?

9-4 Do the net present value (NPV) and internal rate of return (IRR) always agree with respect to accept-reject decisions? With respect to ranking decisions? Explain.

Comparing NPV and IRR techniques

The NPV and IRR often rank projects differently due to their differing assumptions regarding reinvestment of the cash inflows they generate. Which assumption do you think is better—the NPV's assumption of reinvestment at the cost of capital or the IRR's assumption of reinvestment at the IRR? Take a few moments to think about this question before reading ahead.

FOR CONVENTIONAL PROJECTS, NET PRESENT VALUE (NPV) AND INTERNAL RATE OF RETURN *(IRR) will always generate the same accept-reject decision, but differences in their underlying assumptions can cause them to rank projects differently.* To understand the differences and preferences surrounding these techniques, we need to look at net present value profiles, conflicting rankings, and the question of which approach is better.

Net present value profiles

net present value profiles
Graphs that depict the net present value of a project for various discount rates.

Projects can be compared graphically by constructing **net present value profiles** that depict the net present value for various discount rates. These profiles are useful in evaluating and comparing projects, especially when conflicting rankings exist. Their development and interpretation are best demonstrated via an example.

EXAMPLE

To prepare net present value profiles for Bennett Company's two projects, A and B, the first step is to develop a number of discount-rate–net-present-value coordinates. Three coordinates can easily be obtained for each project; they are at discount rates of 0 percent, 10 percent (the cost of capital, k), and the IRR. The net present value at a

TABLE 9.5

DISCOUNT-RATE–NPV COORDINATES FOR PROJECTS A AND B

	Net present value	
Discount rate	Project A	Project B
0%	$28,000	$25,000
10	11,074	10,914
20	0	—
22	—	0

0 percent discount rate is found by merely adding all the cash inflows and subtracting the initial investment. Using the data in Table 9.1, for project A we get

$$(\$14,000 + \$14,000 + \$14,000 + \$14,000 + \$14,000) - \$42,000 = \$28,000$$

and for project B we get

$$(\$28,000 + \$12,000 + \$10,000 + \$10,000 + \$10,000) - \$45,000 = \$25,000$$

The net present values for projects A and B at the 10 percent cost of capital were found to be $11,074 and $10,914, respectively (in Table 9.3). Since the IRR is the discount rate for which net present value equals zero, the IRRs of 20 percent for project A and 22 percent for project B result in $0 NPVs. The three sets of coordinates for each of the projects are summarized in Table 9.5.

Plotting the data in Table 9.5 on a set of discount-rate–NPV axes results in the net present value profiles for projects A and B plotted in Figure 9.1. An analysis of Figure 9.1 indicates that for any discount rate less than approximately 10.7 percent, the NPV for project A is greater than the NPV for project B. Beyond this point, the NPV for project B is greater than that for project A. Since the net present value profiles for projects A and B cross at a positive NPV, the IRRs for the projects cause conflicting rankings whenever they are compared to NPVs calculated at discount rates below 10.7 percent. ■

Conflicting rankings

The possibility of *conflicting rankings* of projects by NPV and IRR should be clear from the Bennett Company example. Ranking is an important consideration when projects are mutually exclusive or when capital rationing is necessary. When projects are mutually exclusive, ranking enables the firm to determine the best project from a financial viewpoint. When capital rationing is necessary, ranking projects may not determine the group of projects to accept, but it will provide a logical starting point.

conflicting rankings
Conflicts in the ranking of a given project by NPV and IRR that result from *differences in the magnitude and timing of cash flows.*

Conflicting rankings using NPV and IRR result from *differences in the magnitude and timing of cash flows.* Although these two factors can be used to explain conflicting rankings, the underlying cause results from the implicit assumption concern-

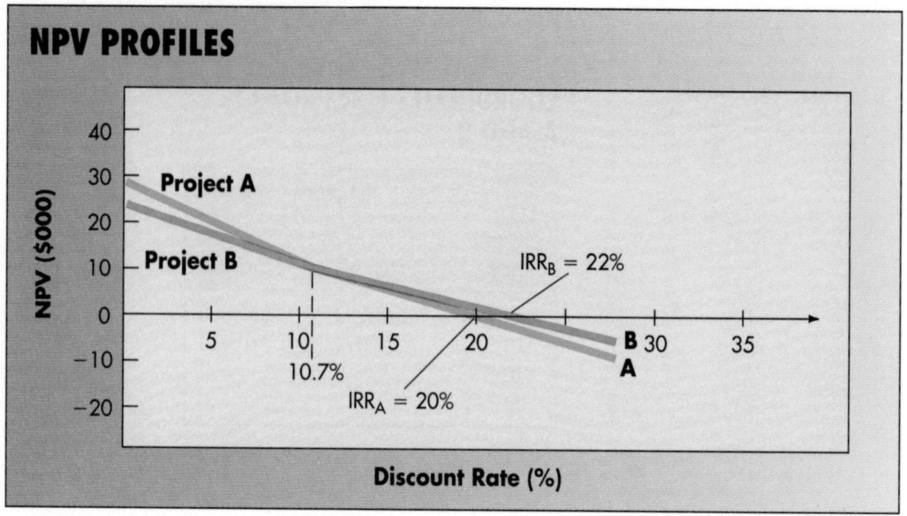

FIGURE 9.1
Net present value profiles for Bennett Company's projects A and B

intermediate cash inflows
Cash inflows received before the termination of a project.

ing the reinvestment of **intermediate cash inflows**—cash inflows received before the termination of a project. NPV assumes that intermediate cash inflows are reinvested at the cost of capital, whereas IRR assumes that intermediate cash inflows can be invested at a rate equal to the project's IRR.[10] These differing assumptions can be demonstrated with an example.

EXAMPLE

A project requiring a $170,000 initial investment is expected to provide operating cash inflows of $52,000, $78,000, and $100,000 at the end of each of the next three years. The NPV of the project (at the firm's 10 percent cost of capital) is $16,867, and its IRR is 15 percent. Clearly, the project is acceptable (NPV = $16,867 > $0 and IRR = 15 percent > 10 percent cost of capital). Table 9.6 demonstrates calculation of the project's future value at the end of its three-year life, assuming both a 10 percent (its cost of capital) and a 15 percent (its IRR) rate of return. A future value of $248,720 results from reinvestment at the 10 percent cost of capital (total in column 5), and a future value of $258,496 results from reinvestment at the 15 percent IRR (total in column 7).

If the future value in each case in Table 9.6 is viewed as the return received three years from today from the $170,000 initial investment, the cash flows are those given in Table 9.7. The NPVs and IRRs in each case are shown below the cash flows in Table 9.7. It can be seen that when the 10 percent reinvestment rate is used, the NPV remains at $16,867, while a different NPV ($24,213) results from reinvestment at the 15 percent IRR. From this it should be clear that NPV assumes reinvestment at the cost of

[10]To eliminate the reinvestment rate assumption of the IRR, some practitioners calculate the *modified internal rate of return (MIRR).* The MIRR is found by converting each operating cash inflow to its future value measured at the end of the project's life and then summing the future values of all inflows to get the project's *terminal value.* Each future value is found by using the cost of capital, thereby eliminating the reinvestment rate criticism of the traditional IRR. The MIRR represents the discount rate that causes the terminal value to just equal the initial investment. Because it uses the cost of capital as the reinvestment rate, the MIRR is generally viewed as a better measure of a project's true profitability than the IRR. Although this technique is frequently used in commercial real estate valuation and is a preprogrammed function on some sophisticated financial calculators, its failure to resolve the issue of conflicting rankings and its theoretical inferiority to NPV have resulted in the MIRR's receiving only limited attention and acceptance in the financial literature. For a thorough analysis of the arguments surrounding IRR and MIRR, see Anthony D. Plath and William F. Kennedy, "Teaching Return-Based Measures of Project Evaluation," *Financial Practice and Education*, forthcoming, Fall 1993.

TABLE 9.6

REINVESTMENT RATE COMPARISONS FOR A PROJECT

			Reinvestment rate			
			10%		15%	
Year (1)	Cash inflows (2)	Number of years earning interest (t) [3 − (1)] (3)	$FVIF_{10\%,t}$ (4)	Future value [(2) × (4)] (5)	$FVIF_{15\%,t}$ (6)	Future value [(2) × (6)] (7)
1	$ 52,000	2	1.210	$ 62,920	1.323	$ 68,796
2	78,000	1	1.100	85,800	1.150	89,700
3	100,000	0	1.000	100,000	1.000	100,000
		Future value end of year 3		$248,720		$258,496
NPV @ 10% = $16,867						
IRR = 15%						

capital (10 percent in this example). Note that with reinvestment at 10 percent, the IRR would be 13.5 percent rather than the 15 percent value that results with the 15 percent reinvestment rate. It should be clear that the IRR assumes an ability to reinvest intermediate cash inflows at the IRR; if reinvestment does not occur at this rate, the IRR will differ from 15 percent. Reinvestment at a rate below the IRR would (as demonstrated in Table 9.7) result in an IRR below that calculated, and reinvestment at a rate above the IRR would result in an IRR above that calculated. ■

In general, projects with similar-sized investments and lower early-year cash inflows (lower cash inflows in the early years) tend to be preferred at lower discount rates.[11] Projects having higher early-year cash inflows (higher cash inflows in the early

TABLE 9.7

PROJECT CASH FLOWS AFTER REINVESTMENT

		Reinvestment rate	
		10%	15%
Initial investment		$170,000	
Year		Operating cash inflows	
1		$ 0	$ 0
2		0	0
3		248,720	258,496
	NPV @ 10%	$ 16,867	$ 24,213
	IRR	13.5%	15.0%

[11]Because differences in the relative sizes of initial investments can also affect conflicts in rankings, the initial investments are assumed to be similar. This permits isolation of the effect of differences in the magnitude and timing of cash inflows on project rankings.

years) tend to be preferred at higher discount rates. These behaviors can be explained by the fact that at high discount rates, later-year cash inflows tend to be severely penalized in present-value terms. Of course, annuities (projects with level cash inflows) cannot be characterized in this fashion; they can best be evaluated in comparison to other cash inflow streams. Table 9.8 summarizes the preferences associated with extreme discount rates and dissimilar cash inflow patterns.

EXAMPLE

In an earlier example, the Bennett Company's projects A and B were found to have conflicting rankings at the firm's 10 percent cost of capital. This finding is depicted in Figure 9.1. If we review each project's cash inflow pattern as presented in Table 9.1, we see that although the projects require similar initial investments, they have dissimilar cash inflow patterns—project A has level cash inflows, and project B has higher early-year cash inflows. Table 9.8 indicates that project B would be preferred over project A at higher discount rates. Figure 9.1 shows that this is in fact the case. At a discount rate in excess of 10.7 percent, project B's NPV is above that of project A. Clearly, the magnitude and timing of the projects' cash inflows do affect their rankings. ■

Although the classification of cash inflow patterns in Table 9.8 is useful in explaining conflicting rankings, differences in the magnitude and timing of cash inflows do not guarantee conflicts in ranking. In general, the greater the difference between the magnitude and timing of cash inflows, the greater the likelihood of conflicting rankings. Conflicts based on NPV and IRR can be reconciled computationally; to do so, one creates and analyzes an incremental project reflecting the difference in cash flows between the two mutually exclusive projects. Because a detailed description of this procedure is beyond the scope of an introductory text, suffice it to say that IRR techniques can be used to generate consistently the same project rankings as would be obtained by using NPV.

Which approach is better?

The better approach for evaluating capital expenditures is difficult to determine because the theoretical and practical strengths of the approaches differ. It is therefore wise to view both NPV and IRR techniques in light of each of the following dimensions.

TABLE 9.8

PREFERENCES ASSOCIATED WITH EXTREME DISCOUNT RATES AND DISSIMILAR CASH INFLOW PATTERNS

	Cash inflow pattern	
Discount rate	Lower early-year cash inflows	Higher early-year cash inflows
Low	Preferred	Not preferred
High	Not preferred	Preferred

THEORETICAL VIEW

On a purely theoretical basis, NPV is the better approach to capital budgeting. Its theoretical superiority is attributed to a number of factors. Most important is the fact that the use of NPV implicitly assumes that any intermediate cash inflows generated by an investment are reinvested at the firm's cost of capital. The use of IRR assumes reinvestment at the often high rate specified by the IRR. Since the cost of capital tends to be a reasonable estimate of the rate at which the firm could actually reinvest intermediate cash inflows, the use of NPV with its more conservative and realistic reinvestment rate is in theory preferable. In addition, certain mathematical properties may cause a project with nonconventional cash flows to have zero or more than one IRR; this problem does not occur with the NPV approach.

PRACTICAL VIEW

Evidence suggests[12] that in spite of the theoretical superiority of NPV, *financial managers prefer to use IRR.* The preference for IRR is attributable to the general disposition of businesspeople toward *rates of return* rather than actual *dollar returns.* Because interest rates, profitability, and so on are most often expressed as annual rates of return, the use of IRR makes sense to financial decision makers. They tend to find NPV more difficult to use because it does not really measure benefits *relative to the amount invested.* Because a variety of methods and techniques are available for avoiding the pitfalls of the IRR, its widespread use should not be viewed as reflecting a lack of sophistication on the part of financial decision makers.

CONCEPTS IN REVIEW

9-5 What is a *net present value profile*? How can it be used to compare projects when conflicting rankings exist? What causes conflicts in the ranking of projects using net present value (NPV) and internal rate of return (IRR)?

9-6 Explain how, on a purely theoretical basis, the assumption concerning the reinvestment of intermediate cash inflows tends to favor the use of net present value (NPV) over internal rate of return (IRR). In practice, which technique is preferred? Why?

Approaches for dealing with risk

LG 4

The risk of a conventional capital budgeting project is reflected in the variability of its cash inflows. As a financial manager, how might you use sensitivity analysis to get a feel for the risk of a given project? Before reading ahead, take a few moments to think about this question.

UP TO THIS POINT, THE DISCUSSION OF CAPITAL BUDGETING TECHNIQUES HAS BEEN based on the assumption that all projects' cash flows have the same level of risk as the firm. Project cash inflows were equally risky. In actuality, there are very

[12]For example, see Lawrence J. Gitman and Charles E. Maxwell, "A Longitudinal Comparison of Capital Budgeting Techniques Used by Major U.S. Firms: 1986 versus 1976," *Journal of Applied Business Research* (Fall 1987), pp. 41–50, for a discussion of evidence with respect to capital budgeting decision-making practices in major U.S. firms.

few capital budgeting projects for which cash inflows have the same risk as the firm. Using the basic risk concepts presented in Chapter 6, here we present a few behavioral approaches for dealing with risk in capital budgeting: risk and cash inflows, sensitivity and scenario analysis, and simulation. In addition, some international risk considerations are discussed.

Risk and cash inflows

In the discussion of capital budgeting, *risk* refers to the chance that a project will prove unacceptable (i.e., NPV < \$0 or IRR < cost of capital, k) or, more formally, to the degree of variability of cash flows. Projects with a small chance of being acceptable and a broad range of expected cash flows are more risky than projects having a high chance of being acceptable and a narrow range of expected cash flows.

In the conventional capital budgeting projects assumed here, risk therefore stems almost entirely from *cash inflows,* since the initial investment is generally known with relative certainty. These inflows, of course, derive from a number of risky variables related to revenues, expenditures, and taxes. Examples would include the level of sales, cost of raw materials, labor rates, utility costs, and tax rates. We will concentrate on the risk in the cash inflows, but remember that this risk actually results from the interaction of these underlying variables. Therefore, to assess the risk of a proposed capital expenditure, the analyst needs to evaluate the probability that the cash inflows will be large enough to provide for project acceptance. This behavioral approach is best demonstrated by a simple example.

EXAMPLE

Treadwell Tire Company, a tire retailer with a 10 percent cost of capital, is considering investing in either of two mutually exclusive projects, A and B, each requiring a \$10,000 initial investment *(II)* and expected to provide equal annual cash inflows *(CF)* over their 15-year lives. For either project to be acceptable according to the net present value technique, its NPV must be greater than zero. If we let CF equal the annual cash inflow and II equal the initial investment, the following condition must be met for projects with annuity cash inflows, such as A and B, to be acceptable:

$$\text{NPV} = [CF \times (PVIFA_{k,n})] - II > \$0 \qquad (9.3)$$

breakeven cash inflow
The minimum level of cash inflow necessary for a project to be acceptable, that is, NPV > \$0.

By substituting $k = 10\%$, $n = 15$ years, and $II = \$10,000$, the **breakeven cash inflow**—the minimum level of cash inflow necessary for Treadwell's projects to be acceptable—can be found:

$$[CF \times (PVIFA_{10\%,15\text{yrs}})] - \$10,000 > \$0$$
$$CF \times (7.606) > \$10,000$$
$$CF > \frac{\$10,000}{7.606} = \underline{\underline{\$1,315}}$$

In other words, for the projects to be acceptable, they must have annual cash inflows of at least \$1,315.

Given this breakeven level of cash inflows, the risk of each project could be assessed by determining—using various statistical techniques that are beyond the scope of this text[13]—the probability that the firm's cash inflows will equal or exceed this breakeven level. Assume that such a statistical analysis results in the following:

Probability of $CF_A > \$1,315$	100%
Probability of $CF_B > \$1,315$	65%

Since project A is certain (100 percent probability) to have a positive net present value, while there is only a 65 percent chance that project B will have a positive NPV, project A is less risky than project B. Of course, the potential level of returns associated with each project must be evaluated in view of the firm's risk preference before the preferred project is selected. ■

The example clearly identifies risk as it relates to the chance that a project is acceptable, but it does not address the issue of cash flow variability. Even though project B has a greater chance of loss than project A, it might result in higher potential NPVs. Recall from Chapters 6 and 7 that it is the combination of risk and return that determines value. Similarly, the worth of a capital expenditure and its impact on the firm's value must be viewed in light of both risk and return. The analyst must therefore consider the *variability* of cash inflows and NPVs to assess project risk and return fully.

Sensitivity and scenario analysis

sensitivity analysis
A behavioral approach that uses a number of possible values for a given variable to assess its impact on a firm's return.

Two approaches for dealing with project risk to capture the variability of cash inflows and NPVs are sensitivity analysis and scenario analysis. **Sensitivity analysis,** as was noted in Chapter 6, is a behavioral approach that uses a number of possible values for a given variable, such as cash inflows, to assess its impact on the firm's return, measured here by NPV. This technique is often useful in getting a feel for the variability of return in response to changes in a key variable. In capital budgeting, one of the most common sensitivity approaches is to estimate the NPVs associated with pessimistic (worst), most likely (expected), and optimistic (best) cash inflow estimates. By subtracting the pessimistic-outcome NPV from the optimistic-outcome NPV, the *range* can be determined.

EXAMPLE

Continuing with Treadwell Tire, assume that the financial manager made pessimistic, most likely, and optimistic estimates of the cash inflows for each project. The cash inflow estimates and resulting NPVs in each case are summarized in Table 9.9. Comparing the ranges of cash inflows ($1,000 for project A and $4,000 for B) and, more important, the ranges of NPVs ($7,606 for project A and $30,424 for B) makes it clear that project A is less risky than project B. Given that both projects have the same most likely NPV of $5,212, the assumed risk-averse decision maker will take project A because it has less risk and no possibility of loss. ■

scenario analysis
A behavioral approach that evaluates the impact on return of simultaneous changes in a number of variables.

Scenario analysis, which is a behavioral approach similar to sensitivity analysis but broader in scope, is used to evaluate the impact of various circumstances on the

[13]Normal distributions are commonly used to develop the concept of the probability of success—that is, of a project having a positive NPV. The reader who is interested in learning more about this technique should see any second- or MBA-level managerial finance text.

TABLE 9.9

SENSITIVITY ANALYSIS OF TREADWELL'S PROJECTS A AND B

	Project A	Project B
Initial investment	$10,000	$10,000
	Annual cash inflows	
Outcome		
Pessimistic	$ 1,500	$0
Most likely	2,000	2,000
Optimistic	2,500	4,000
Range	$ 1,000	$ 4,000
	Net present values[a]	
Outcome		
Pessimistic	$ 1,409	−$10,000
Most likely	5,212	5,212
Optimistic	9,015	20,424
Range	$ 7,606	$30,424

[a]These values were calculated by using the corresponding annual cash inflows. A 10 percent cost of capital and a 15-year life for the annual cash inflows were used.

firm's return. Rather than isolating the effect of a change in a single variable, scenario analysis is used to evaluate the impact on return of simultaneous changes in a number of variables, such as cash inflows, cash outflows, and the cost of capital, resulting from differing assumptions relative to economic and competitive conditions. For example, the firm could evaluate the impact of both high inflation (scenario 1) and low inflation (scenario 2) on a project's NPV. Each scenario will affect the firm's cash inflows, cash outflows, and cost of capital, thereby resulting in different levels of NPV. The decision maker can use these NPV estimates to roughly assess the risk involved with respect to the level of inflation. The widespread availability of computer-based spreadsheet programs (such as *Lotus 1–2–3*) has greatly enhanced the ease and popularity of use of scenario as well as sensitivity analysis.

CONCEPT IN PRACTICE

Reducing Basic's Quality so that Philip Morris' Marlboro Man Can Ride Again

William Campbell, CEO of Philip Morris, is constantly evaluating the impact of operating and marketing changes on the profitability of products ranging from Kraft's Macaroni and Cheese to Toblerone Nougats. In the tobacco division, Campbell's analysis considers tradeoffs between the premium Marlboro cigarette and discount Basic cigarette. Anticigarette publicity, increased prices for Marlboro, and improved Basic cigarette quality resulted in approximately 366 million fewer Marlboro packs being sold in the United States in 1992 than in 1991. Although much of the decline was offset by surging sales of Basic, the profit on a single pack of Marlboro exceeds that of Basic by almost 50 cents. To stem the loss, Campbell plans to reduce the quality of the Basic brand and use the savings to fund Marlboro Adventure Team promotions. The net effect is expected to increase 1993 profits by 16 million dollars.

Simulation

simulation
A statistically based behavioral approach used in capital budgeting to get a feel for risk by applying predetermined probability distributions and random numbers to estimate risky outcomes.

Simulation is a statistically based behavioral approach used in capital budgeting to get a feel for risk by applying predetermined probability distributions and random numbers to estimate risky outcomes. By tying the various cash flow components together in a mathematical model and repeating the process numerous times, the financial manager can develop a probability distribution of project returns. Figure 9.2 presents a flowchart of the simulation of the net present value of a project. The process of generating random numbers and using the probability distributions for cash inflows and outflows allows values for each of these variables to be determined. Substituting these values into the mathematical model results in an NPV. By repeating this process perhaps a thousand times, a probability distribution of net present values is created.

Although only gross cash inflows and outflows are simulated in Figure 9.2, more sophisticated simulations using individual inflow and outflow components, such as sales volume, sale price, raw material cost, labor cost, maintenance expense, and so on, are quite common. From the distribution of returns, regardless of how they are measured (NPV, IRR, and so on), the decision maker can determine not only the expected value of the return but also the probability of achieving or surpassing a given return. The use

FIGURE 9.2
Flowchart of a net present value simulation

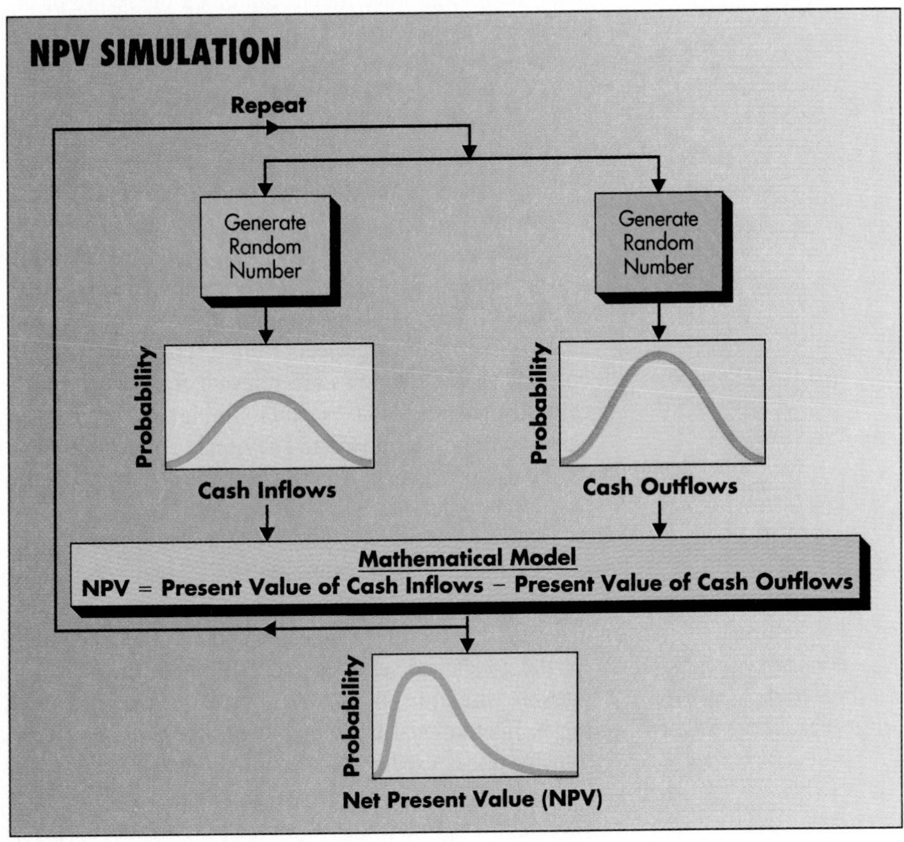

of computers has made the simulation approach quite feasible. The output of simulation provides an excellent basis for decision making, since it allows the decision maker to view a continuum of risk-return tradeoffs rather than a single-point estimate.

International risk considerations

Although the basic techniques of capital budgeting are the same for purely domestic firms as for multinational companies (MNCs), firms that operate in several countries face risks that are unique to the international arena. Two types of risk are particularly important and have been discussed briefly in earlier chapters: exchange rate risk and political risk—including, in the extreme, the risk that assets in foreign countries will be seized by the host government.

exchange rate risk
The danger that an unexpected change in the exchange rate between the dollar and the currency in which a project's cash flows are demoninated can reduce the market value of that project's cash flow.

Exchange rate risk refers to the danger that an unexpected change in the exchange rate between the dollar and the currency in which a project's cash flows are denominated can reduce the market value of that project's cash flow. While a project's initial investment can, as usual, be predicted with some certainty in either local currency or dollar value, the dollar value of future cash inflows can be dramatically altered if the local currency depreciates against the dollar. In the short term, specific cash flows can be hedged by using financial instruments such as currency futures and options. Long-term exchange rate risk can best be minimized by financing the project in whole or in part in local currency.

Political risk is much harder to protect against once a foreign project is accepted, since the foreign government can block the return of profits, seize the firm's assets, or otherwise interfere with a project's operation. This inability to manage risk after the fact makes it even more important that managers account for political risks before making an investment. They can do this either by adjusting a project's expected cash inflows to account for the probability of political interference or by using risk-adjusted discount rates (discussed later in this chapter) in the capital budgeting formulas. In general, it is much better to subjectively adjust individual project cash flows for political risk than to use a blanket adjustment for all projects.

In addition to unique risks that MNCs must face, there are several other special issues that are relevant only for international capital budgeting. These include tax law differences, the importance of *transfer pricing* in evaluating projects, and the need to analyze international projects from a strategic as well as a financial perspective. Since only after-tax cash flows are relevant for capital budgeting, financial managers must carefully account for taxes paid to foreign governments on profits (or even on revenues) earned within their borders. They must also address the impact of these tax payments on the parent company's U.S. tax liability, because full or partial credit is generally allowed for foreign tax payments.

transfer prices
Prices that subsidiaries charge each other for the goods and services traded between them.

Much of the international trade involving MNCs is, in reality, simply the shipment of goods and services from one of a parent company's wholly owned subsidiaries to another subsidiary located abroad. The parent company therefore has great discretion in setting the **transfer prices**, which are the prices that subsidiaries charge each other for the goods and services traded between them, because they are not traded in open markets with arms-length prices. The importance and widespread use of transfer pricing in international trade makes capital budgeting in MNCs very difficult unless the transfer prices used accurately reflect actual costs and incremental cash flows.

Finally, MNCs often must approach international capital projects from a strategic point of view, rather than from a strictly financial perspective. For example, an MNC may feel compelled to invest in a country to ensure continued access, even if the project itself may not have a positive net present value. This motivation was important for Japanese automakers who set up assembly plants in the United States even when the strong dollar of the early 1980s made export from Japan more economically rational. For much the same reason, U.S. investment in Europe surged during the years before the market integration of the European Community in 1992. MNCs often will invest in production facilities in the home country of major rivals to deny these competitors a profitable, uncontested home market. Finally, MNCs may feel compelled to invest in certain industries or countries to achieve a broad corporate objective such as completing a product line or diversifying raw material sources, even when the project's cash flows may not be sufficiently profitable.

CONCEPTS IN REVIEW

9-7 Define *risk* in terms of the cash inflows from a project. How can determination of the *breakeven cash inflow* be used to gauge project risk? Explain.

9-8 Briefly describe, compare, and explain how each of the following behavioral approaches can be used to deal with project risk:

- **a.** Sensitivity analysis
- **b.** Scenario analysis
- **c.** Simulation

9-9 Briefly define and explain how each of the following items that are unique to multinational companies (MNCs) affect their capital budgeting decisions.

- **a.** Exchange rate risk
- **b.** Political risk
- **c.** Tax law differences
- **d.** Transfer pricing
- **e.** Strategic rather than financial viewpoint

Risk-adjustment techniques

Differences in project risk should be somehow incorporated into the capital budgeting techniques that are used to evaluate projects. How might you go about adjusting for risk when applying the net present value technique to projects? Spend a short time answering this question before reading ahead.

THE APPROACHES FOR DEALING WITH RISK THAT HAVE BEEN PRESENTED SO FAR ALLOW the financial manager to get a "feel" for project risk. Unfortunately, they do not really provide a straightforward basis for evaluating risky projects. We will now illustrate the two major risk-adjustment techniques using the net present value (NPV) decision method.[14] The NPV decision rule of accepting only those projects with NPVs > \$0 will continue to hold. The basic equation for NPV was presented in Equation 9.1. Close examination of that equation should make it clear that since the initial

[14]The IRR could just as well have been used, but since NPV is theoretically preferable, it is used instead.

investment *(II),* which occurs at time zero, is known with certainty, a project's risk is embodied in the present value of cash inflows:

$$\sum_{t=1}^{n} \frac{CF_t}{(1+k)^t} \tag{9.4}$$

Two opportunities to adjust the present value of cash inflows for risk exist: (1) the cash inflows, CF_t, can be adjusted, or (2) the discount rate, k, can be adjusted. Here we describe and compare two techniques—the cash inflow adjustment process, using *certainty equivalents,* and the discount rate adjustment process, using *risk-adjusted discount rates.* In addition, we consider the portfolio effects of project analysis as well as the practical aspects of certainty equivalents and risk-adjusted discount rates.

Certainty equivalents (CEs)

certainty equivalents (CEs)
Risk-adjustment factors that represent the percent of estimated cash inflow that investors would be satisfied to receive *for certain* rather than the cash inflows that are *possible* for each year.

One of the most direct and theoretically preferred approaches for risk adjustment is the use of **certainty equivalents (CEs),** which represent the percent of estimated cash inflow that investors would be satisfied to receive *for certain* rather than the cash inflows that are *possible* for each year. Equation 9.5 presents the basic expression for NPV when certainty equivalents are used for risk adjustment:

$$\text{NPV} = \sum_{t=1}^{n} \frac{\alpha_t \times CF_t}{(1+R_F)^t} - II \tag{9.5}$$

where

α_t = certainty equivalent factor in year t ($0 \leq \alpha_t \leq 1$)
CF_t = relevant cash inflow in year t
R_F = risk-free rate of return

risk-free rate, R_F
The rate of return that one would earn on a virtually riskless investment such as a U.S. Treasury bill.

The equation shows that the project is adjusted for risk by first converting the expected cash inflows to certain amounts, $\alpha_t \times CF_t$, and then discounting the cash inflows at the risk-free rate, R_F.[15] The **risk-free rate, R_F,** is the rate of return that one would earn on a virtually riskless investment such as a U.S. Treasury bill. It is used to discount the certain cash inflows and is not to be confused with a risk-adjusted discount rate. (If a risk-adjusted rate were used, the risk would in effect be counted twice.) Although the process described here of converting risky cash inflows to certain cash inflows is somewhat subjective, the technique is theoretically sound.

EXAMPLE

Bennett Company wishes to consider risk in the analysis of two projects, A and B. The basic data for these projects were initially presented in Table 9.1, and the analysis of the projects using net present value and assuming that the projects had equivalent risks was presented in Table 9.3. By ignoring risk differences and using net present value, it was shown earlier that at the firm's 10 percent cost of capital, project A was preferred over project B, since its NPV of $11,074 was greater than B's NPV of $10,914. Assume, however, that on further analysis the firm found that project A was actually

[15] Alternatively, the internal rate of return could be calculated for the risk-adjusted cash inflows and then compared to the risk-free rate to make the accept-reject decision.

TABLE 9.10

ANALYSIS OF BENNETT COMPANY'S PROJECTS A AND B USING CERTAINTY EQUIVALENTS

Project A					
Year (*t*)	**Cash inflows (1)**	**Certainty equivalent factors[a] (2)**	**Certain cash inflows [(1) × (2)] (3)**	**$PVIF_{6\%,t}$ (4)**	**Present value [(3) × (4)] (5)**
1	$14,000	.90	$12,600	.943	$11,882
2	14,000	.90	12,600	.890	11,214
3	14,000	.80	11,200	.840	9,408
4	14,000	.70	9,800	.792	7,762
5	14,000	.60	8,400	.747	6,275
			Present value of cash inflows		$46,541
			− Initial investment		42,000
			Net present value (NPV)		$ 4,541

Project B					
Year (*t*)	**Cash inflows (6)**	**Certainty equivalent factors[a] (7)**	**Certain cash inflows [(6) × (7)] (8)**	**$PVIF_{6\%,t}$ (9)**	**Present value [(8) × (9)] (10)**
1	$28,000	1.00	$28,000	.943	$26,404
2	12,000	.90	10,800	.890	9,612
3	10,000	.90	9,000	.840	7,560
4	10,000	.80	8,000	.792	6,336
5	10,000	.70	7,000	.747	5,229
			Present value of cash inflows		$55,141
			− Initial investment		45,000
			Net present value (NPV)		$10,141

Note: The basic cash flows for these projects were presented in Table 9.1, and the analysis of the projects using NPV and assuming equal risk was presented in Table 9.3.

[a]These values were estimated by management; they reflect the risk that managers perceive in the cash inflows.

more risky than project B. To consider the differing risks, the firm estimated the certainty equivalent factors for each project's cash inflows for each year. Columns 2 and 7 of Table 9.10 show the estimated values for projects A and B, respectively. Multiplying the risky cash inflows (given in columns 1 and 6) by the corresponding certainty equivalent factors (CEs) (columns 2 and 7, respectively) gives the certain cash inflows for projects A and B shown in columns 3 and 8, respectively.

Upon investigation, Bennett's management estimated the prevailing risk-free rate of return, R_F, to be 6 percent. Using the 6 percent risk-free rate to discount the certain cash inflows for each of the projects results in the net present values of $4,541 for project A and $10,141 for project B, as calculated in Table 9.10. (The calculated values using a hand-held business/financial calculator are \$4,544 and \$10,151 for projects A and B, respectively.) Note that as a result of the risk adjustment, project B is now preferred. The usefulness of the certainty equivalent approach for risk adjustment should be quite clear; the only difficulty lies in the need to make subjective estimates of the certainty equivalent factors. ■

Risk-adjusted discount rates (RADRs)

A more practical approach for risk adjustment involves the use of risk-adjusted discount rates (RADRs). Instead of adjusting the cash inflows for risk, as was done in the certainty equivalent approach, this approach adjusts the discount rate.[16] Equation 9.6 presents the basic expression for NPV when risk-adjusted discount rates are used:

$$\text{NPV} = \sum_{t=1}^{n} \frac{CF_t}{(1 + \text{RADR})^t} - II \qquad (9.6)$$

risk-adjusted discount rate (RADR)
The rate of return that must be earned on a given project to compensate the firm's owners adequately, thereby resulting in the maintenance or improvement of share price.

The **risk-adjusted discount rate (RADR)** is the rate of return that must be earned on a given project to compensate the firm's owners adequately, thereby resulting in the maintenance or improvement of share price. The higher the risk of a project, the higher the RADR and therefore the lower the net present value for a given stream of cash inflows. Because the logic underlying the use of RADRs is closely linked to the capital asset pricing model developed in Chapter 6, we will review some of its basic constructs here before demonstrating the development and use of RADRs. It is, of course, important to recognize that because real corporate assets, unlike securities, are not traded in an efficient market, *the CAPM cannot be directly applied in making real asset decisions.*

RADR AND CAPM

In Chapter 6 the *capital asset pricing model (CAPM)* was used to link the *relevant* risk and return for all assets traded in *efficient markets.* In the development of the CAPM, the *total risk* of an asset was defined as

$$\text{Total risk} = \text{nondiversifiable risk} + \text{diversifiable risk} \qquad (9.7)$$

For assets traded in an efficient market, the *diversifiable risk,* which results from uncontrollable or random events, can be eliminated through diversification. The relevant risk is therefore the *nondiversifiable risk*—the risk for which owners of these assets are rewarded. Nondiversifiable risk for securities is commonly measured by using *beta,* which is an index of the degree of movement of an asset's return in response to a change in the market return.

By using beta, b_j, to measure the relevant risk of any asset j, the CAPM is

$$k_j = R_F + [b_j \times (k_m - R_F)] \qquad (9.8)$$

[16]The risk-adjusted discount rate approach can be applied in using the internal rate of return as well as net present value. If the IRR is used, the risk-adjusted discount rate becomes the cutoff rate that must be exceeded by the IRR for the project to be accepted. In using NPV, the projected cash inflows are merely discounted at the risk-adjusted discount rate.

where

k_j = required return on asset j
R_F = risk-free rate of return
b_j = beta coefficient for asset j
k_m = return on the market portfolio of assets

In Chapter 6 we demonstrated that the required return on any asset, j, could be determined by substituting values of R_F, b_j, and k_m into the CAPM—Equation 9.8. Any security that is expected to earn in excess of its required return would be acceptable, and those that are expected to earn an inferior return would be rejected.

If we assume for a moment that real corporate assets such as computers, machine tools, and special-purpose machinery are traded in efficient markets, the CAPM could be redefined as noted in Equation 9.9:

$$k_{\text{project } j} = R_F + [b_{\text{project } j} \times (k_m - R_F)] \quad (9.9)$$

The security market line (SML), which is a graphic depiction of the CAPM, is shown for Equation 9.9 in Figure 9.3. As noted, any project having an IRR falling above the SML would be acceptable, since its IRR would exceed the required return, k_{project}; any project with an IRR below k_{project} would be rejected. In terms of NPV, any project falling above the SML would have a positive NPV, and any project falling below the SML would have a negative NPV.[17]

FIGURE 9.3
CAPM and SML in capital budgeting decision making

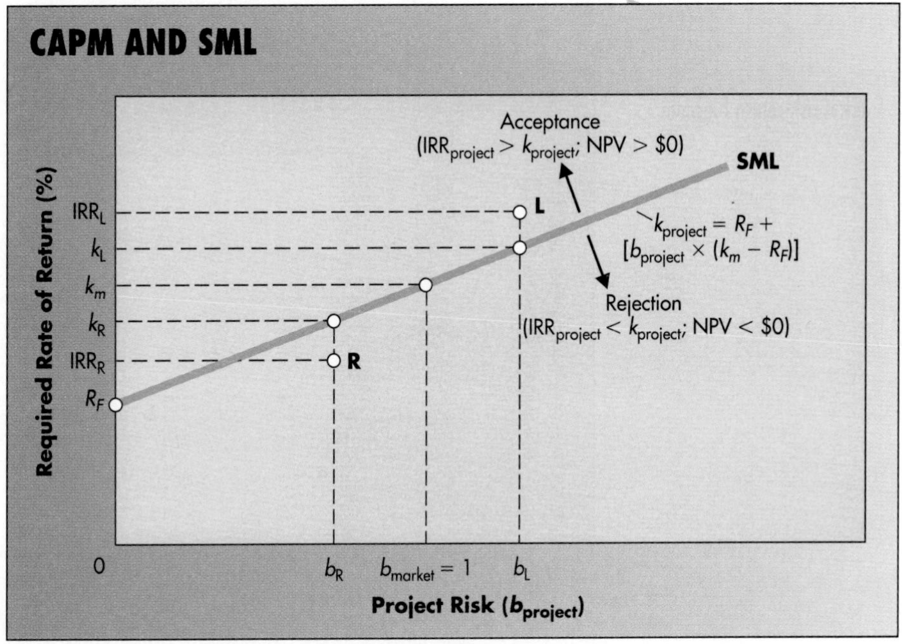

[17]As was noted earlier, whenever the IRR is above the cost of capital or required return (IRR > k), the NPV is positive, and whenever the IRR is below the cost of capital or required return (IRR < k), the NPV is negative. Since by definition the IRR is the discount rate that causes NPV to equal zero and the IRR and NPV always agree on accept-reject decisions, the relationship noted in Figure 9.3 logically follows.

EXAMPLE

Two projects, L and R, are shown in Figure 9.3. Project L has a beta, b_L, and generates an internal rate of return, IRR_L. The required return for a project with risk b_L is k_L. Since project L generates a return greater than that required ($IRR_L > k_L$), project L would be acceptable. Project L would have a positive NPV when its cash inflows are discounted at its required return, k_L. Project R, on the other hand, generates an IRR below that required for its risk, b_R ($IRR_R < k_R$). This project would have a negative NPV when its cash inflows are discounted at its required return, k_R. Project R should be rejected. ■

APPLYING RADRs

Because the CAPM is based upon an assumed efficient market, which as noted in Chapter 6 does *not* exist for real corporate assets such as plant and equipment, it is not directly applicable in making real corporate asset investment decisions. Attention is therefore typically devoted to assessing the *total risk* of a project as measured by its standard deviation or coefficient of variation. Relating these measures (described in Chapter 6) to the required level of return would then result in a risk-adjusted rate of return (RADR), which can be used in Equation 9.6 to find the NPV. To adjust the discount rate, it is necessary to develop a function that expresses the return for each level of project risk required to at least maintain the firm's value.

market risk-return function
A graph of the discount rates associated with each level of project risk.

By using the coefficient of variation *(CV)*[18] as a measure of project risk, the firm can develop some type of **market risk-return function**—a graph of the discount rates associated with each level of project risk. An example of such a function is given in Figure 9.4, which relates the risk-adjusted discount rate, RADR, to the project risk as measured by the coefficient of variation, *CV.* In a fashion similar to CAPM, the rela-

FIGURE 9.4
A market risk-return function

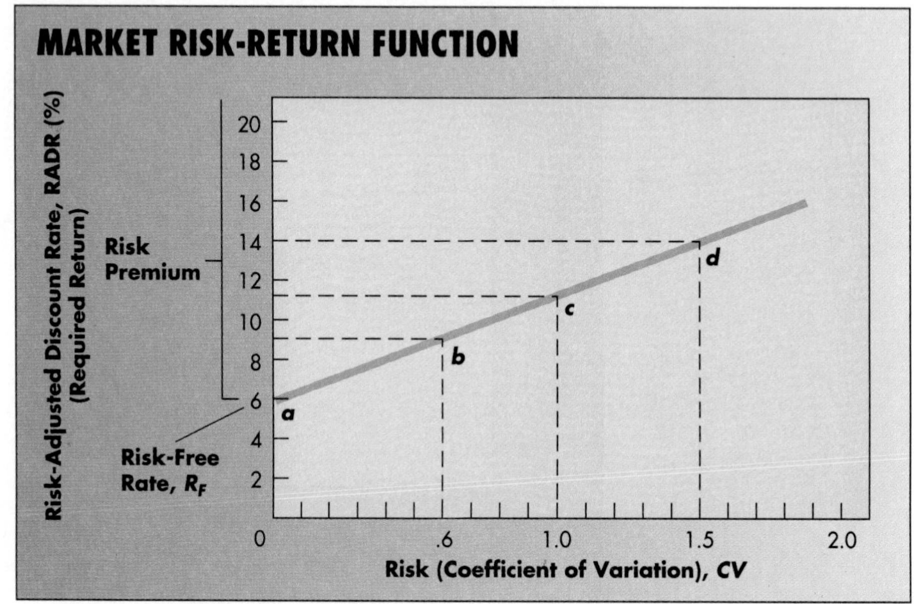

[18]The coefficient of variation is used here because it provides a relative basis for comparing risk. Although it is a project-specific measure that embodies both nondiversifiable and diversifiable risk, it is assumed to represent a reasonable measure of the relative risk of real-asset projects.

tionship is assumed to be linear. The risk-return function in Figure 9.4 indicates that project cash inflows associated with a riskless event ($CV = 0$) should be discounted at a 6 percent rate. This rate of return therefore represents the risk-free rate, R_F (point *a* in the figure). For all levels of risk greater than certainty ($CV > 0$), the associated required rate of return is indicated. Points *b*, *c*, and *d* indicate that rates of return of approximately 9, 11, and 14 percent will be required on projects with coefficients of variation of 0.6, 1.0, and 1.5, respectively.

Figure 9.4 is a *market risk-return function,* which means that investors will discount cash inflows with the given levels of risk at the corresponding rates. Therefore in order not to damage its market value, the firm must use the correct discount rate for evaluating a project. If a firm discounts a risky project's cash inflows at too low a rate and accepts the project, the firm's market price may drop as investors recognize that the firm itself has become more risky.[19] The amount by which the required discount rate for a project exceeds the risk-free rate is called the **risk premium.** It of course increases with increasing project risk. A simple example will clarify the use of the risk-adjusted discount rate, RADR, in evaluating capital budgeting projects.

risk premium
The amount by which the required discount rate for a project exceeds the risk-free rate.

EXAMPLE

Bennett Company wishes to use the risk-adjusted discount rate approach to determine, according to NPV, whether to implement project A or project B. In addition to the data presented earlier, Bennett's management has estimated the coefficient of variation for project A to be 1.5 and that for project B to be 1.0. According to Figure 9.4, the RADR for project A is approximately 14 percent; for project B it is approximately 11 percent. Due to the riskier nature of project A, its risk premium is 8 percent (14% − 6%); for project B the risk premium is 5 percent (11% − 6%). The net present value of each project, using its RADR, is calculated in Table 9.11. (The calculated values using a hand-held business/financial calculator are $6,063 and $9,798 for projects A and B, respectively.) The results clearly show that project B is preferable, since its risk-adjusted net present value (NPV) of $9,802 is greater than the $6,062 risk-adjusted NPV for project A. This is the same conclusion that resulted from using certainty equivalents in the preceding example. As was noted earlier (see Table 9.3), when the discount rates are not adjusted for risk, project A would be preferred to project B. The usefulness of risk-adjusted discount rates should now be clear; the real difficulty of this approach lies in estimating the market risk-return function. ■

Portfolio effects

As was noted in Chapter 6, since investors are not rewarded for taking diversifiable risk, they should hold a diversified portfolio of securities. Since a business firm can be viewed as a portfolio of assets, is it similarly important that the firm maintain a diversified portfolio of assets?

By holding a diversified portfolio the firm could reduce the variability of its cash flows. By combining two projects with negatively correlated cash inflows, the combined cash inflow variability—and therefore the risk—could be reduced. But are firms rewarded for diversifying risk in this fashion? If they are, the value of the firm could be enhanced through diversification into other lines of business. Surprisingly, the value

[19]It is also true that if the firm discounts a project's cash inflows at too high a rate, resulting in the rejection of an acceptable project, the firm's market price may drop because investors believe that it is being overly conservative and sell their stock, putting downward pressure on the firm's market value.

TABLE 9.11

ANALYSIS OF BENNETT COMPANY'S PROJECTS A AND B USING RISK-ADJUSTED DISCOUNT RATES

Project A

Annual cash inflow	$14,000
× $PVIFA_{14\%,5yrs}$	3.433
Present value of cash inflows	$48,062
− Initial investment	42,000
Net present value (NPV)	$ 6,062

Project B

Year (t)	Cash inflows (1)	$PVIF_{11\%,t}$ (2)	Present value [(1) × (2)] (3)
1	$28,000	.901	$25,228
2	12,000	.812	9,744
3	10,000	.731	7,310
4	10,000	.659	6,590
5	10,000	.593	5,930
	Present value of cash inflows		$54,802
	− Initial investment		45,000
	Net present value (NPV)		$ 9,802

Note: By using Figure 9.4 and the coefficients of variation of 1.5 and 1.0 for projects A and B, respectively, a discount rate of 14 percent is used for project A and a discount rate of 11 percent is used for project B.

of the stock of firms whose shares are traded publicly in an efficient marketplace is generally *not* affected by diversification. In other words, diversification is not normally rewarded and therefore is generally not necessary.

The lack of reward for diversification results from the fact that investors themselves can diversify by holding securities in a variety of firms; they do not need to have the firm do it for them. And investors can diversify more readily due to the ease of making transactions and at a lower cost because of the greater availability of information and trading mechanisms. Of course, if as a result of acquiring a new line of business the firm's cash flows tend to respond more to changing economic conditions (i.e., greater nondiversifiable risk), greater returns would be expected. If, for the additional risk, the firm earned a return in excess of that required (IRR $> k$), the value of the firm could be enhanced. Also, other benefits such as increased cash, greater borrowing capacity, guaranteed availability of raw materials, and so forth could result from, and therefore justify, diversification in spite of any immediate cash flow impact.

In spite of the fact that a strict theoretical view supports the use of a technique that relies on the CAPM framework, the presence of market imperfections causes the market for real corporate assets to be inefficient. The relative inefficiency of this market coupled with difficulties associated with measurement of nondiversifiable project risk and the market risk-return function tend to favor the use of *total risk* to evaluate capital budgeting projects. Therefore the use of total risk as an approximation for the relevant risk tends to have widespread practical appeal.

CE versus RADR in practice

Certainty equivalents (CEs) are the *theoretically preferred* approach for project risk adjustment because they separately adjust for risk and time; they first eliminate risk from the cash flows and then discount the certain cash flows at a risk-free rate. Risk-adjusted discount rates (RADRs), on the other hand, have a major theoretical problem: They combine the risk and time adjustments in a single discount-rate adjustment. Because of the basic mathematics of compounding and discounting, the RADR approach therefore implicitly assumes that risk is an increasing function of time. Rather than demonstrate this implicit assumption, suffice it to say that *CEs are theoretically superior to RADRs.*

However, because of the complexity of developing CEs, *RADRs are most often used in practice.* (*Note:* The RADR is very much the same kind of stated discount rate that has been assumed throughout this book.) Their popularity stems from two major facts: (1) They are consistent with the general disposition of financial decision makers toward rates of return,[20] and (2) they are easily estimated and applied. The first reason is clearly a matter of personal preference, but the second is based on the computational convenience and well-developed procedures involved in the use of RADRs. In practice, risk is often subjectively categorized rather than related to a continuum of RADRs associated with each level of risk, as is illustrated by the market risk-return function in Figure 9.4. Firms often establish a number of *risk classes,* with an RADR assigned to each. Each project is then subjectively placed in the appropriate risk class, and the corresponding RADR is used to evaluate it. This is sometimes done on a division-by-division basis, each division having its own set of risk classes and associated RADRs similar to those in Table 9.12. The use of *divisional costs of capital* and associated risk classes allows the large multidivisional firm to incorporate differing levels of divisional risk into the capital budgeting process while still recognizing differences in the levels of individual project risk. An example will help to illustrate the general use of risk classes and RADRs.

EXAMPLE

Assume that the management of Bennett Company decided to use a more subjective but practical RADR approach to analyze projects. Each project would be placed in one of four risk classes according to its perceived risk. The classes were ranged from I for the lowest-risk projects to IV for the highest-risk projects. Associated with each class was an RADR that was appropriate to the level of risk of projects in the class. A brief description of each class, along with the associated RADR, is given in Table 9.12. It shows that lower-risk projects tend to involve routine replacement or renewal activities, whereas higher-risk projects involve expansion, often into new or unfamiliar activities.

[20]Recall that while NPV was the theoretically preferred evaluation technique, IRR was more popular in actual business practice due to the general preference of businesspeople for rates of return rather than pure dollar returns. The preference for RADRs over CEs is therefore consistent with the preference for IRR over NPV.

TABLE 9.12

BENNETT COMPANY'S RISK CLASSES AND RADRs

Risk class	Description	Risk-adjusted discount rate, RADR
I	*Below-average risk:* Projects with low risk. Typically involve routine replacement without renewal of existing activities.	8%
II	*Average risk:* Projects similar to those currently implemented. Typically involve replacement or renewal of existing activities.	10%
III	*Above-average risk:* Projects with higher than normal, but not excessive, risk. Typically involve expansion of existing or similar activities.	14%
IV	*Highest risk:* Projects with very high risk. Typically involve expansion into new or unfamiliar activities.	20%

The financial manager of Bennett has assigned project A to Class III and project B to Class II. The cash flows for project A would therefore be evaluated by using a 14 percent RADR, and project B's would be evaluated by using a 10 percent RADR.[21] The net present value of project A at 14 percent was calculated in Table 9.11 to be $6,062, and the NPV for project B at a 10 percent RADR was found to be $10,914 in Table 9.3. Clearly, with RADRs based on the use of risk classes, project B is preferred over project A. As was noted earlier, this result is contrary to the findings in Table 9.3, in which no attention was given to the differing risk of projects A and B. ■

CONCEPTS IN REVIEW

9-10 Explain the concept of *certainty equivalents (CEs)*. How are they used in the risk-adjustment process?

9-11 Describe the logic as well as the basic procedures involved in using *risk-adjusted discount rates (RADRs)*. How does this approach relate to the *capital asset pricing model (CAPM)*? Explain.

9-12 Explain why a firm whose stock is actively traded in the securities markets need not concern itself with diversification. In spite of this, how is the risk of capital budgeting projects frequently measured? Why?

9-13 Compare and contrast certainty equivalents (CEs) and risk-adjusted discount rates (RADRs) from both a theoretical and a practical point of view. In practice, how are risk classes often used to apply RADRs? Explain.

[21]Note that the 10 percent RADR for project B using the risk classes in Table 9.12 differs from the 11 percent RADR found earlier for project B by using the market risk-return function. This difference is attributable to the less precise nature of the use of risk classes.

Capital budgeting refinements

Most firms operate under capital rationing, which means that they have more acceptable projects than they can fund with the available capital budget. When selecting acceptable projects under capital rationing, what specific objective should the firm pursue to enhance owner wealth? Before reading further, spend a few moments answering this question.

Refinements must often be made in the analysis of capital budgeting projects to accommodate special circumstances. These adjustments permit the relaxation of certain simplifying assumptions presented earlier. Two areas in which special forms of analysis are frequently needed are (1) comparison of mutually exclusive projects having unequal lives and (2) capital rationing caused by a binding budget constraint.

Comparing projects with unequal lives

The financial manager must often select the best of a group of unequal-lived projects. If the projects are independent, the length of the project lives is not critical. But when unequal-lived projects are mutually exclusive, the impact of differing lives must be considered because the projects do not provide service over comparable time periods. This is especially important when continuing service is needed from the project under consideration. The discussions that follow assume that the unequal-lived mutually exclusive projects being compared *are ongoing.* If such were not the case, the project with the highest net present value (NPV) would be selected.

THE PROBLEM

A simple example will demonstrate the basic problem of noncomparability caused by the need to select the best of a group of mutually exclusive projects with differing usable lives.

EXAMPLE

The AT Company, a regional cable-television company, is in the process of evaluating two projects, X and Y. The relevant cash flows for each project are given in the table. The applicable cost of capital for use in evaluating these equally risky projects is 10 percent.

	Project X	Project Y
Initial investment	$70,000	$85,000
Year	**Cash inflows**	
1	$28,000	$35,000
2	33,000	30,000
3	38,000	25,000
4	—	20,000
5	—	15,000
6	—	10,000

The net present value (NPV) of each project at the 10 percent cost of capital is found to be

$$\begin{aligned}\text{NPV}_X &= [\$28{,}000 \times (.909)] + [\$33{,}000 \times (.826)] + [\$38{,}000 \text{ times } (.751)] - \$70{,}000\\ &= (\$25{,}452 + \$27{,}258 + \$28{,}538) - \$70{,}000\\ &= \$81{,}248 - \$70{,}000 = \underline{\underline{\$11{,}248}}\end{aligned}$$

$$\begin{aligned}\text{NPV}_Y &= [\$35{,}000 \times (.909)] + [\$30{,}000 \times (.826)] + [\$25{,}000 \times (.751)]\\ &\quad + [\$20{,}000 \times (.683)] + [\$15{,}000 \times (.621)]\\ &\quad + [\$10{,}000 \times (.564)] - \$85{,}000\\ &= (\$31{,}815 + \$24{,}780 + \$18{,}775 + \$13{,}660 + \$9{,}315 + \$5{,}640) - \$85{,}000\\ &= \$103{,}985 - \$85{,}000 = \underline{\underline{\$18{,}985}}\end{aligned}$$

The NPV for project X is \$11,248; that for project Y is \$18,985. Ignoring the differences in project lives, we can see that both projects are acceptable (NPVs greater than zero) and that project Y is preferred over project X. In other words, if the projects are independent and, due to limited funds, only one could be accepted, project Y, with the larger NPV, would be preferred. On the other hand, if the projects are mutually exclusive, their differing lives must be considered; project X provides three years of service, and project Y provides six years of service. ■

The analysis in this example is incomplete if the projects are mutually exclusive (which will be our assumption throughout the remaining discussions). To compare these unequal-lived, mutually exclusive projects correctly, the differing lives must be considered in the analysis; an incorrect decision could result from use of NPV to select the better project. Although a number of approaches are available for dealing with unequal lives, here we present only the most efficient technique—the annualized net present value (ANPV) approach.

ANNUALIZED NET PRESENT VALUE (ANPV) APPROACH

annualized net present value (ANPV) approach
An approach to evaluating unequal-lived projects that converts the net present value of unequal-lived, mutually exclusive projects into an equivalent (in NPV terms) annual amount.

The **annualized net present value (ANPV) approach** converts the net present value of unequal-lived projects into an equivalent (in NPV terms) annual amount that can be used to select the best project.[22] This net-present-value-based approach can be applied to unequal-lived, mutually exclusive projects by using the following steps.

Step 1 Calculate the net present value of each project j, NPV_j, over its life, n_j, using the appropriate cost of capital, k.

Step 2 Divide the net present value of each project having a positive NPV by the present-value interest factor for an annuity at the given cost of capital and the project's life to get the annualized net present value for each project j, ANPV_j:

[22] The theory underlying this as well as other approaches for comparing projects with unequal lives assumes that each project can be replaced in the future for the same initial investment and that each will provide the same expected future cash inflows. While changing technology and inflation will affect the initial investment and expected cash inflows, the lack of specific attention to them does not detract from the usefulness of this technique.

$$\text{ANPV}_j = \frac{\text{NPV}_j}{PVIFA_{k,n_j}} \tag{9.10}$$

Step 3 The project having the highest ANPV would be the best, followed by the project with the next highest ANPV, and so on.

Application of these steps can be illustrated by using data from the preceding example.

EXAMPLE

Using the AT Company data presented earlier for projects X and Y, the three-step ANPV approach can be applied as follows:

Step 1 The net present values of projects X and Y discounted at 10 percent—calculated in the preceding example for a single purchase of each asset—are

$$\text{NPV}_X = \$11{,}248$$
$$\text{NPV}_Y = \$18{,}985$$

As was noted earlier, on the basis of these NPVs, which ignore the differing lives, project Y is preferred over project X.

Step 2 By applying Equation 9.10 to the NPVs, the annualized net present value for each project can be calculated:

$$\text{ANPV}_X = \frac{\$11{,}248}{PVIFA_{10\%,3\text{yrs}}} = \frac{\$11{,}248}{2.487} = \underline{\underline{\$4{,}523}}$$

$$\text{ANPV}_Y = \frac{\$18{,}985}{PVIFA_{10\%,6\text{yrs}}} = \frac{\$18{,}985}{4.355} = \underline{\underline{\$4{,}359}}$$

Step 3 Reviewing the ANPVs calculated in Step 2, we can see that project X would be preferred over project Y. Given that projects X and Y are mutually exclusive, project X would be the recommended project because it provides the higher annualized net present value. ■

Capital rationing

Firms commonly operate under *capital rationing*—they have more acceptable independent projects than they can fund. *In theory*, capital rationing should not exist. Firms should, as will be discussed in Chapter 10, accept all projects that have positive NPVs (or IRRs > the cost of capital). However, *in practice* most firms operate under capital rationing. Generally, firms attempt to isolate and select the best acceptable projects subject to a capital expenditure budget set by management. Research has found that management internally imposes capital expenditure constraints to avoid what it deems to be "excessive" levels of new financing, particularly debt. In spite of the fact that failing to fund all acceptable independent projects is theoretically inconsistent with the goal of owner wealth maximization, here we discuss capital rationing procedures because they are widely used in practice.

The objective of *capital rationing* is to select the group of projects that provides the *highest overall net present value* and does not require more dollars than are budgeted. As a prerequisite to capital rationing, the best of any mutually exclusive projects must be chosen and placed in the group of independent projects. Two basic approaches to project selection under capital rationing are discussed here.

CONCEPT IN PRACTICE

Capital Rationing at Apple Computer Is Not What the Doctor Ordered

The average holding period for stock has shortened from seven years in 1960 to two years today. Among the chief executive officers who hate to disappoint fidgety shareholders is Apple Computer's John Sculley. Believing that investors in high-tech firms are quick to sell shares at the slightest hint of trouble, he has viewed research and development as a necessary evil. By comparison, Andrew Grove, CEO of Intel, plans to invest almost half of 1992's revenues in research and development and capital outlays in 1993. In Grove's opinion you need to have the best product possible and capacity to meet demand, or your research and development dollar is wasted. Shareholders appear to have preferred Intel's aggressive approach to capital budgeting. While Apple's stock price rose 2 percent in the six months ending in January 1993, happy investors bid Intel's stock price up from $47 to $100 during that same period.

internal rate of return approach
An approach to capital rationing that involves the graphic plotting of project IRRs in descending order against the total dollar investment.

investment opportunities schedule (IOS)
The graph that plots project IRRs in descending order against total dollar investment.

INTERNAL RATE OF RETURN APPROACH

The **internal rate of return approach** involves graphically plotting IRRs in descending order against the total dollar investment. This graph, which is discussed in some detail in Chapter 10, is called the **investment opportunities schedule (IOS).** By drawing the cost of capital line and then imposing a budget constraint, the financial manager can determine the group of acceptable projects. The problem with this technique is that it does not guarantee the maximum dollar return to the firm. It merely provides a satisfactory solution to capital rationing problems.

EXAMPLE

The Tate Company, a fast-growing plastics company, is confronted with six projects competing for its fixed budget of $250,000. The initial investment and IRR for each project are as follows:

Project	Initial investment	IRR
A	$ 80,000	12%
B	70,000	20
C	100,000	16
D	40,000	8
E	60,000	15
F	110,000	11

The firm has a cost of capital of 10 percent. Figure 9.5 presents the investment opportunities schedule (IOS) resulting from ranking the six projects in descending order based on IRRs. According to the schedule, only projects B, C, and E should be accepted. Together they will absorb $230,000 of the $250,000 budget. Project D is not worthy of consideration, since its IRR is less than the firm's 10 percent cost of capital. The drawback of this approach, however, is that there is no guarantee that the acceptance of projects B, C, and E will maximize *total dollar returns* and therefore owners' wealth. ■

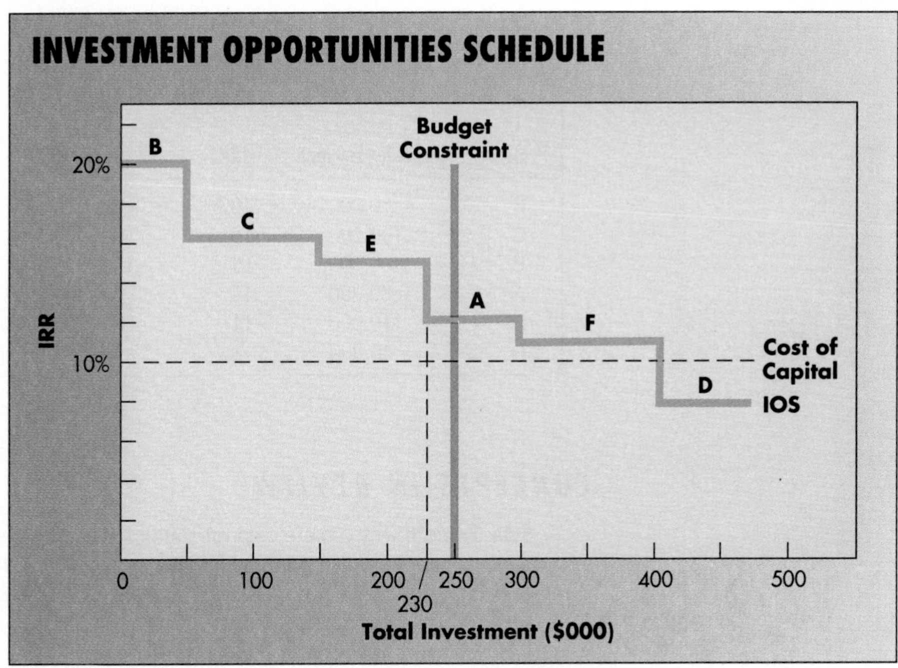

FIGURE 9.5
Investment opportunities schedule (IOS) for Tate Company projects

NET PRESENT VALUE APPROACH

net present value approach
An approach to capital rationing that is based on the use of present values to determine the group of projects that will maximize owners' wealth.

The **net present value approach** is based on the use of present values to determine the group of projects that will maximize owners' wealth. It is implemented by ranking projects on the basis of IRRs and then evaluating the present value of the benefits from each potential project to *determine the combination of projects with the highest overall present value.* This is the same as maximizing net present value, since whether the entire budget is used or not, it is viewed as the total initial investment. The portion of the firm's budget that is not used does not increase the firm's value. At best, the unused money can be invested in marketable securities or returned to the owners in the form of cash dividends. In either case the wealth of the owners is not likely to be enhanced.

EXAMPLE

The group of projects described in the preceding example is ranked in Table 9.13 on the basis of IRRs. The present value of the cash inflows associated with the projects is also included in the table. Projects B, C, and E, which together require $230,000, yield a present value of $336,000. However, if projects B, C, and A were implemented, the total budget of $250,000 would be used, and the present value of the cash inflows would be $357,000. This is greater than the return expected from selecting the projects on the basis of the highest IRRs. Implementing B, C, and A is preferable, since they maximize the present value for the given budget. *The firm's objective is to use its budget to generate the highest present value of inflows.* Assuming that any unused portion of the budget does not gain or lose money, the total NPV for projects B, C, and E would be $106,000 ($336,000 − $230,000), whereas for projects B, C, and A the total NPV would be $107,000 ($357,000 − $250,000). Selection of projects B, C, and A will therefore maximize NPV. ■

TABLE 9.13

RANKINGS FOR TATE COMPANY PROJECTS

Project	Initial investment	IRR	Present value of inflows at 10%	
B	$ 70,000	20%	$112,000	
C	100,000	16	145,000	
E	60,000	15	79,000	
A	80,000	12	100,000	
F	110,000	11	126,500	Cutoff point
D	40,000	8	36,000	(IRR < 10%)

CONCEPTS IN REVIEW

9-14 Explain why a mere comparison of the NPVs of unequal-lived ongoing mutually exclusive projects is inappropriate. Describe the *annualized net present value (ANPV)* approach for comparing unequal-lived mutually exclusive projects.

9-15 What is *capital rationing*? In theory, should capital rationing exist? Why does it frequently occur in practice?

9-16 Compare and contrast the *internal rate of return approach* and *net present value approach* to capital rationing. Which is better? Why?

Summary

LG 1 Calculate, interpret, and evaluate one of the most commonly used unsophisticated capital budgeting techniques—the payback period. The payback period is an unsophisticated capital budgeting technique that measures the amount of time required for the firm to recover its initial investment from cash inflows. The formula and decision criteria for the payback period are summarized in Table 9.14. Shorter payback periods are preferred. In addition to its ease of calculation and simple intuitive appeal, the payback period's appeal lies in its consideration of cash flows, the implicit consideration given to timing, and its ability to measure risk exposure. Its weaknesses include its lack of linkage to the wealth maximization goal, failure to explicitly consider time value, and the fact that it ignores cash flows after the payback period.

LG 2 Apply the sophisticated capital budgeting techniques—net present value (NPV) and internal rate of return (IRR)—to relevant cash flows to choose acceptable as well as preferred capital expenditures. Sophisticated capital budgeting techniques use the cost of capital to consider the time factor in the value of money. Two such techniques are the net present value (NPV) and internal rate of return (IRR). The key formulas and decision criteria for them are summarized in Table 9.14. Both NPV and IRR provide the same accept-reject decisions for a given project but often conflict in ranking projects.

LG 3 Use net present value profiles to compare net present value and internal rate of return techniques in light of conflicting rankings from both theoretical and practical viewpoints. Net present value profiles are useful in comparing projects, especially when conflicting rankings exist between NPV and IRR. On a purely theoretical basis, NPV is preferred over IRR, since NPV assumes reinvestment of intermediate cash inflows at the cost of capital and does not exhibit the mathematical problems that often occur in calculating IRRs for nonconventional cash flows. In practice, the IRR is more commonly used by major firms because it is consistent with the general preference of businesspeople toward rates of return.

LG 4 Recognize the basic behavioral approaches—breakeven cash flow, sensitivity and scenario analysis, and simulation—for dealing with project risk and the unique risks and other issues facing multinational companies (MNCs). Risk in capital budgeting is concerned with either the chance that a project will prove unacceptable or, more formally, the degree of variability of cash flows. Finding the breakeven cash inflow and assessing the probability that it will be realized make up one behavioral approach that is used to assess the chance of success. Sensitivity analysis and scenario analysis are also behavioral approaches for dealing with project risk to capture the variability of cash inflows and NPVs. Simulation is a

TABLE 9.14

SUMMARY OF KEY FORMULAS/DEFINITIONS AND DECISION CRITERIA FOR CAPITAL-BUDGETING TECHNIQUES

Technique	Formula/Definition	Decision criteria
Payback period[a]	*For annuity:* $\frac{\text{initial investment}}{\text{annual cash inflow}}$ *For mixed stream:* Calculate cumulative cash inflows on year-to-year basis until the initial investment is recovered.	*Accept* if < maximum acceptable payback period; *reject* if > maximum acceptable payback period.
Net present value (NPV)[b]	Present value of cash inflows − initial investment	*Accept* if > $0; *reject* if < $0.
Internal rate of return (IRR)[b]	The discount rate that equates the present value of cash inflows with the initial investment, thereby causing NPV = $0.	*Accept* if > the cost of capital; *reject* if < the cost of capital.

[a]Unsophisticated technique, since it does not give explicit consideration to the time value of money.

[b]Sophisticated technique, since it gives explicit consideration to the time value of money.

statistically based approach that results in a probability distribution of expected returns. It usually requires a computer and allows the decision maker to understand the risk-return tradeoffs that are involved in a proposed investment. Although the basic capital budgeting techniques are the same for purely domestic and multinational companies (MNCs), firms that operate in several countries must also deal with both exchange rate and political risks, tax law differences, transfer pricing, and strategic rather than strict financial issues.

LG **5 Understand the calculation, differing approaches, and practical aspects of the two basic risk-adjustment techniques—certainty equivalents (CEs) and risk-adjusted discount rates (RADRs).** Certainty equivalents (CEs) are used to adjust the risky cash inflows to certain amounts, which are discounted at a risk-free rate in order to find the NPV. The risk-adjusted discount rate (RADR) technique involves a market-based adjustment of the discount rate that is used to calculate NPV. The RADR is closely linked to the CAPM, but because real corporate assets, unlike securities, are generally not traded in an efficient market, the CAPM cannot be applied directly to capital budgeting. CEs are the theoretically superior risk-adjustment technique, but RADRs are more commonly used in practice because decision makers prefer rates of return and find them easier to estimate and apply.

LG **6 Describe two capital budgeting refinements—comparing projects with unequal lives and capital rationing—that frequently require special forms of analysis.** The annualized net present value (ANPV) approach is the most efficient method of comparing ongoing mutually exclusive projects having unequal usable lives. It converts the NPVs of unequal-lived projects into an equivalent annual amount—its ANPV—by dividing each project's NPV by the present-value interest factor for an annuity at the given cost of capital and project life. The project with the highest ANPV is best, and so on. Although in theory capital rationing should not exist, in practice it commonly occurs. The two basic approaches for choosing projects under capital rationing are the internal rate of return approach and the net present value approach. Of the two, the net present value approach better achieves the objective of using the budget to generate the highest present value of inflows.

Self-test problems (Solutions in Appendix E)

ST 9-1 LG **1,2,3** **All techniques with NPV profile—Mutually exclusive projects** Fitch Industries is in the process of choosing the better of two equal-risk, mutually exclusive capital expenditure projects—M and N. The relevant cash flows for each project are given below. The firm's cost of capital is 14 percent.

	Project M	Project N
Initial investment (*II*)	$28,500	$27,000
Year (t)	**Cash inflows (CF_t)**	
1	$10,000	$11,000
2	10,000	10,000
3	10,000	9,000
4	10,000	8,000

a. Calculate each project's payback period.
b. Calculate the net present value (NPV) for each project.
c. Calculate the internal rate of return (IRR) for each project.
d. Summarize the preferences dictated by each measure, and indicate which project you would recommend. Explain why.
e. Draw the net present value profiles for each project on the same set of axes, and explain the circumstances under which a conflict in rankings might exist.

ST 9-2 LG 5 **Certainty equivalents and risk-adjusted discount rates** The market risk-return data and certainty equivalent factors applicable to the CBA Company's mutually exclusive projects A and B are given below.

Market risk-return data	
Coefficient of variation	**Market discount rate**
0.0 (risk-free rate, R_F)	7.0%
0.2	8.0
0.4	9.0
0.6	10.0
0.8	11.0
1.0	12.0
1.2	13.0
1.4	14.0
1.6	15.0
1.8	16.0
2.0	17.0

Certainty equivalent factors (α_t)		
Year (t)	**Project A**	**Project B**
0	1.00	1.00
1	.95	.90
2	.90	.85
3	.90	.70

The firm is considering two mutually exclusive projects, A and B. Project data are given at the top of the following page.

	Project A	Project B
Initial investment *(II)*	$15,000	$20,000
Project life	3 years	3 years
Annual cash inflow *(CF)*	$ 7,000	$10,000
Coefficient of variation	0.4	1.8

a. Ignoring any differences in risk and assuming that the firm's cost of capital is 10 percent, calculate the net present value (NPV) of each project.
b. Use NPV to evaluate the projects using *certainty equivalents* to account for risk.
c. Use NPV to evaluate the projects using *risk-adjusted discount rates* to account for risk.
d. Compare, contrast, and explain your findings in **a, b,** and **c**.

Problems

9-1 LG 1 **Payback period** Jordan Enterprises is considering a capital expenditure that requires an initial investment of $42,000 and returns after-tax cash inflows of $7,000 per year for 10 years. The firm has a maximum acceptable payback period of eight years.

a. Determine the payback period for this project.
b. Should the company accept the project? Why or why not?

9-2 LG 1 **Payback comparisons** Nova Products has a five-year maximum acceptable payback period. The firm is considering the purchase of a new machine and must choose between two alternative ones. The first machine requires an initial investment of $14,000 and generates annual after-tax cash inflows of $3,000 for each of the next seven years. The second machine requires an initial investment of $21,000 and provides an annual cash inflow after taxes of $4,000 for 20 years.

a. Determine the payback period for each machine.
b. Comment on the acceptability of the machines, assuming that they are independent projects.
c. Which machine should the firm accept? Why?
d. Do the machines in this problem illustrate any of the criticisms of using payback? Discuss.

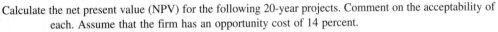

9-3 LG 2 **NPV** Calculate the net present value (NPV) for the following 20-year projects. Comment on the acceptability of each. Assume that the firm has an opportunity cost of 14 percent.

a. Initial investment is $10,000; cash inflows are $2,000 per year.
b. Initial investment is $25,000; cash inflows are $3,000 per year.
c. Initial investment is $30,000; cash inflows are $5,000 per year.

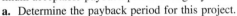

9-4 LG 2 **NPV for varying required returns** Dane Cosmetics is evaluating a new fragrance-mixing machine. The asset requires an initial investment of $24,000 and will generate after-tax cash inflows of $5,000 per year for eight years. For each of the required rates of return listed, (1) calculate the net present value (NPV), (2) indicate whether to accept or reject the machine, and (3) explain your decision.

a. The cost of capital is 10 percent.
b. The cost of capital is 12 percent.
c. The cost of capital is 14 percent.

9-5 LG 2 Net present value—Independent projects Using a 14 percent cost of capital, calculate the net present value for each of the independent projects given in the following table and indicate whether or not each is acceptable.

	Project A	Project B	Project C	Project D	Project E
Initial investment (*II*)	$26,000	$500,000	$170,000	$950,000	$80,000
Year (t)			**Cash inflows (CF_t)**		
1	$4,000	$100,000	$20,000	$230,000	$ 0
2	4,000	120,000	19,000	230,000	0
3	4,000	140,000	18,000	230,000	0
4	4,000	160,000	17,000	230,000	20,000
5	4,000	180,000	16,000	230,000	30,000
6	4,000	200,000	15,000	230,000	0
7	4,000		14,000	230,000	50,000
8	4,000		13,000	230,000	60,000
9	4,000		12,000		70,000
10	4,000		11,000		

9-6 LG 2 NPV and maximum return A firm can purchase a fixed asset for a $13,000 initial investment. If the asset generates an annual after-tax cash inflow of $4,000 for four years:

a. Determine the net present value (NPV) of the asset, assuming that the firm has a 10 percent cost of capital. Is the project acceptable?

b. Determine the maximum required rate of return (closest whole-percentage rate) that the firm can have and still accept the asset. Discuss this finding in light of your response in **a**.

9-7 LG 2 NPV—Mutually exclusive projects Hook Industries is considering the replacement of one of its old drill presses. Three alternative replacement presses are under consideration. The relevant cash flows associated with each are given in the following table. The firm's cost of capital is 15 percent.

	Press A	Press B	Press C
Initial investment (*II*)	$85,000	$60,000	$130,000
Year (t)		**Cash inflows (CF_t)**	
1	$18,000	$12,000	$ 50,000
2	18,000	14,000	30,000
3	18,000	16,000	20,000
4	18,000	18,000	20,000
5	18,000	20,000	20,000
6	18,000	25,000	30,000
7	18,000	—	40,000
8	18,000	—	50,000

a. Calculate the net present value (NPV) of each press.

b. Using NPV, evaluate the acceptability of each press.

c. Rank the presses from best to worst using NPV.

9-8 LG 1,2 Payback and NPV Neil Corporation has three projects under consideration. The cash flows for each of them are given in the following table. The firm has a 16 percent cost of capital.

	Project A	Project B	Project C
Initial investment (*II*)	$40,000	$40,000	$40,000
Year (*t*)	Cash inflows (CF_t)		
1	$13,000	$ 7,000	$19,000
2	13,000	10,000	16,000
3	13,000	13,000	13,000
4	13,000	16,000	10,000
5	13,000	19,000	7,000

a. Calculate each project's payback period. Which project is preferred according to this method?
b. Calculate each project's net present value (NPV). Which project is preferred according to this method?
c. Comment on your findings in **a** and **b,** and recommend the best project. Explain your recommendation.

9-9 LG 2 Internal rate of return For each of the following projects, calculate the internal rate of return (IRR), and indicate for each project the maximum cost of capital that the firm could have and find the IRR acceptable.

	Project A	Project B	Project C	Project D
Initial investment (*II*)	$90,000	$490,000	$20,000	$240,000
Year (*t*)	Cash inflows (CF_t)			
1	$20,000	$150,000	$ 7,500	$120,000
2	25,000	150,000	7,500	100,000
3	30,000	150,000	7,500	80,000
4	35,000	150,000	7,500	60,000
5	40,000	—	7,500	—

9-10 LG 2 IRR—Mutually exclusive projects Bell Manufacturing is attempting to choose the better of two mutually exclusive projects for expanding the firm's warehouse capacity. The relevant cash flows for the projects are given. The firm's cost of capital is 15 percent.

	Project X	Project Y
Initial investment (*II*)	$500,000	$325,000
Year (*t*)	Cash inflows (CF_t)	
1	$100,000	$140,000
2	120,000	120,000
3	150,000	95,000
4	190,000	70,000
5	250,000	50,000

a. Calculate the IRR to the nearest whole percent for each of the projects.
b. Assess the acceptability of each project based on the IRRs found in **a**.
c. Which project is preferred on the basis of the IRRs found in **a**?

9-11 LG 2 **IRR, investment life, and cash inflows** Oak Enterprises accepts projects earning more than the firm's 15 percent cost of capital. Oak is currently considering a 10-year project that provides annual cash inflows of $10,000 and requires an initial investment of $61,450. (*Note:* All amounts are after taxes.)

a. Determine the IRR of this project. Is it acceptable?
b. Assuming that the cash inflows continue to be $10,000 per year, how many *additional years* would the flows have to continue to make the project acceptable (i.e., have an IRR of 15 percent)?
c. With the given life, initial investment, and cost of capital, what is the minimum annual cash inflow that the firm should accept?

9-12 LG 2 **NPV and IRR** Benson Designs has prepared the following estimates for a long-term project it is considering. The initial investment will be $18,250, and the project is expected to yield after-tax cash inflows of $4,000 per year for seven years. The firm has a 10 percent cost of capital.

a. Determine the net present value (NPV) for the project.
b. Determine the internal rate of return (IRR) for the project.
c. Would you recommend that the firm accept or reject the project? Explain your answer.

9-13 LG 1,2 **Payback, NPV, and IRR** Rieger International is attempting to evaluate the feasibility of investing $95,000 in a piece of equipment having a five-year life. The firm has estimated the *cash inflows* associated with the proposal as follows:

Year (t)	Cash inflows (CF_t)
1	$20,000
2	25,000
3	30,000
4	35,000
5	40,000

The firm has a 12 percent cost of capital.

a. Calculate the payback period for the proposed investment.
b. Calculate the net present value (NPV) for the proposed investment.
c. Calculate the internal rate of return (IRR), rounded to the nearest whole percent, for the proposed investment.
d. Evaluate the acceptability of the proposed investment using NPV and IRR. What recommendation would you make relative to implementation of the project? Why?

9-14 LG 2,3 **NPV, IRR, and NPV profiles** Thomas Company is considering two mutually exclusive projects. The firm, which has a 12 percent cost of capital, has estimated its cash flows as shown in the table at the top of page 385.

a. Calculate the NPV of each project, and assess its acceptability.
b. Calculate the IRR for each project, and assess its acceptability.
c. Draw the NPV profile for each project on the same set of axes.
d. Evaluate and discuss the rankings of the two projects based on your findings in **a, b,** and **c**.
e. Explain your findings in **d** in light of the pattern of cash inflows associated with each project.

	Project A	Project B
Initial investment (*II*)	$130,000	$85,000
Year (*t*)	**Cash inflows (CF_t)**	
1	$ 25,000	$40,000
2	35,000	35,000
3	45,000	30,000
4	50,000	10,000
5	55,000	5,000

9-15 LG **1,2,3** **All techniques—Mutually exclusive investment decision** Pound Industries is attempting to select the best of three mutually exclusive projects. The initial investment and after-tax cash inflows associated with each project are given in the following table.

Cash flows	Project A	Project B	Project C
Initial investment (*II*)	$60,000	$100,000	$110,000
Cash inflows (*CF*), years 1–5	$20,000	$ 31,500	$ 32,500

a. Calculate the payback period for each project.
b. Calculate the net present value (NPV) of each project, assuming that the firm has a cost of capital equal to 13 percent.
c. Calculate the internal rate of return (IRR) for each project.
d. Draw the net present value profile for each project on the same set of axes, and discuss any conflict in ranking that may exist between NPV and IRR.
e. Summarize the preferences, and indicate which project you would recommend. Explain why.

9-16 LG **1,2,3** **All techniques with NPV profile—Mutually exclusive projects** The following two projects of equal risk are being considered for the purchase of new equipment. The firm's cost of capital is 13 percent. The cash flows for each project are given in the following table.

	Project A	Project B
Initial investment (*II*)	$80,000	$50,000
Year (*t*)	**Cash inflows (CF_t)**	
1	$15,000	$15,000
2	20,000	15,000
3	25,000	15,000
4	30,000	15,000
5	35,000	15,000

a. Calculate each project's payback period.
b. Calculate the net present value (NPV) for each project.
c. Calculate the internal rate of return (IRR) for each project.

d. Draw a net present value profile for each project on the same set of axes, and discuss any conflict in ranking that may exist between NPV and IRR.

e. Summarize the preferences dictated by each measure, and indicate which project you would recommend. Explain why.

9-17 LG 1,2 **Integrative—Complete investment decision** Wells Printing is considering the purchase of a new printing press. The total installed cost of the press would be \$2.2 million. This outlay would be partially offset by the sale of an existing press. The old press has zero book value, cost \$1 million 10 year ago, and can be sold currently for \$1.2 million before taxes. As a result of the new press, sales in each of the next five years are expected to increase by \$1.6 million, but product costs (excluding depreciation) will represent 50 percent of sales. The new press will not affect the firm's net working capital requirements. The new press will be depreciated under MACRS using a five-year recovery period (see Table 3.6 on page 83). The firm is subject to a 40 percent tax rate on both ordinary income and capital gains. Wells Printing's cost of capital is 11 percent. (*Note:* Assume that both the old and new press will have terminal values of \$0 at the end of year 6.)

a. Determine the initial investment required by the new press.

b. Determine the operating cash inflows attributable to the new press. (*Note:* Be sure to consider the depreciation in year 6.)

c. Determine the payback period.

d. Determine the net present value (NPV) and the internal rate of return (IRR) related to the proposed new press.

e. Make a recommendation to accept or reject the new press, and justify your answer.

9-18 LG 2 **Integrative—Investment decision** Holliday Manufacturing is considering the replacement of an existing machine. The new machine costs \$1.2 million and requires installation costs of \$150,000. The existing machine can be sold currently for \$185,000 before taxes. It is two years old, cost \$800,000 new, and has a \$384,000 book value and a remaining useful life of five years. It was being depreciated under MACRS using a five-year recovery period (see Table 3.6 on page 83) and therefore has the final four years of depreciation remaining. If held until the end of five years, the machine's market value would be zero. Over its five-year life, the new machine should reduce operating costs by \$350,000 per year. The new machine will be depreciated under MACRS using a five-year recovery period (see Table 3.6 on page 83). The new machine can be sold for \$200,000 net of removal and clean up costs at the end of five years. An increased investment in net working capital of \$25,000 will be needed to support operations if the new machine is acquired. Assume that the firm has adequate operating income against which to deduct any loss experienced on the sale of the existing machine. The firm has a 9 percent cost of capital and is subject to a 40 percent tax rate on both ordinary income and capital gains.

a. Develop the relevant cash flows needed to analyze the proposed replacement.

b. Determine the net present value (NPV) of the proposal.

c. Determine the internal rate of return (IRR) on the proposal.

d. Make a recommendation to accept or reject the replacement proposal, and justify your answer.

e. What is the highest cost of capital the firm could have and still accept the proposal? Explain.

9-19 LG 2,4 **Breakeven cash inflows and risk** Pueblo Enterprises is considering investment in either of two mutually exclusive projects, X and Y. Project X requires an initial investment of \$30,000; project Y requires \$40,000. Each project's cash inflows are five-year annuities; project X's inflows are \$10,000 per year; project Y's are \$15,000. The firm has unlimited funds and, in the absence of risk differences, accepts the project with the highest NPV. The cost of capital is 15 percent.

a. Find the NPV for each project. Are the projects acceptable?

b. Find the *breakeven cash inflow* for each project.

c. The firm has estimated the probabilities of achieving various ranges of cash inflow for the two projects, as noted in the table at the top of page 387. What is the probability that each project will achieve the breakeven cash inflow found in **b**?

Range of cash inflow	Probability of achieving cash inflow in given range	
	Project X	Project Y
\$0 to \$5,000	0%	5%
\$5,000 to \$7,500	10	10
\$7,500 to \$10,000	60	15
\$10,000 to \$12,500	25	25
\$12,500 to \$15,000	5	20
\$15,000 to \$20,000	0	15
Above \$20,000	0	10

d. Which project is more risky? Which project has the potentially higher NPV? Discuss the risk-return tradeoffs of the two projects.

e. If the firm wished to minimize losses (i.e., NPV < \$0), which project would you recommend? Which would you recommend if the goal, instead, was achieving the higher NPV?

9-20 LG 4 Basic sensitivity analysis Murdock Paints is in the process of evaluating two mutually exclusive additions to their processing capacity. The firm's financial analysts have developed pessimistic, most likely, and optimistic estimates of the annual cash inflows associated with each project. These estimates are given in the following table.

	Project A	Project B
Initial investment (*II*)	\$8,000	\$8,000
Outcome	**Annual cash inflows (*CF*)**	
Pessimistic	\$ 200	\$ 900
Most likely	1,000	1,000
Optimistic	1,800	1,100

a. Determine the range of annual cash inflows for each of the two projects.

b. Assume that the firm's cost of capital is 10 percent and that both projects have 20-year lives. Construct a table similar to that above for the NPVs for each project. Include the *range* of NPVs for each project.

c. Do **a** and **b** provide consistent views of the two projects? Explain.

d. Which project would you recommend? Why?

9-21 LG 4 Sensitivity analysis James Secretarial Services is considering the purchase of one of two new personal computers, P and Q. Both are expected to provide benefits over a 10-year period, and each has a required investment of $3,000. The firm uses a 10 percent cost of capital. Management has constructed the following table of estimates of probabilities and annual cash inflows for pessimistic, most likely, and optimistic results.

	Computer P	Computer Q
Initial investment (*II*)	$3,000	$3,000
Outcome	**Annual cash inflows (*CF*)**	
Pessimistic	$ 500	$ 400
Most likely	750	750
Optimistic	1,000	1,200

a. Determine the range of annual cash inflows for each of the two computers.
b. Construct a table similar to that above for the NPVs associated with each outcome for both computers.
c. Find the range of NPVs, and subjectively compare the risk of each computer.

9-22 LG 4 Simulation Ogden Corporation has compiled the following information on a capital expenditure proposal:
(1) The projected cash *inflows* are normally distributed with a mean of $36,000 and a standard deviation of $9,000.
(2) The projected cash *outflows* are normally distributed with a mean of $30,000 and a standard deviation of $6,000.
(3) The firm has an 11 percent cost of capital.
(4) The probability distributions of cash inflows and cash outflows are not expected to change over the project's 10-year life.
a. Describe how the preceding data could be used to develop a simulation model for finding the net present value of the project.
b. Discuss the advantages of using a simulation to evaluate the proposed project.

9-23 LG 5 Certainty equivalents—Accept-reject decision Allison Industries has constructed a table, shown below, that gives expected cash inflows and certainty equivalent factors for these cash inflows. These measures are for a new machine that lasts five years and requires an initial investment of $95,000. The firm has a 15 percent cost of capital, and the risk-free rate is 10 percent.

Year (t)	Cash inflows (CF_t)	Certainty equivalent factors (α_t)
1	$35,000	1.0
2	35,000	.8
3	35,000	.6
4	35,000	.6
5	35,000	.2

a. What is the net present value (unadjusted for risk)?
b. What is the certainty equivalent net present value?
c. Should the firm accept the project? Explain.
d. Management has some doubts about the estimate of the certainty equivalent factor for year 5. There is some evidence that it may not be any lower than that for year 4. What impact might this have on the decision you recommended in **c**? Explain.

9-24 LG 5 **Certainty equivalents—Mutually exclusive decision** Kent Manufacturing is considering investing in either of two mutually exclusive projects, C and D. The firm has a 14 percent cost of capital, and the risk-free rate is currently 9 percent. The initial investment, expected cash inflows, and certainty equivalent factors associated with each of the projects are presented in the following table.

	Project C		Project D	
Initial investment (*II*)	$40,000		$56,000	
Year (t)	**Cash inflows (CF_t)**	**Certainty equivalent factors (α_t)**	**Cash inflows (CF_t)**	**Certainty equivalent factors (α_t)**
1	$20,000	.90	$20,000	.95
2	16,000	.80	25,000	.90
3	12,000	.60	15,000	.85
4	10,000	.50	20,000	.80
5	10,000	.40	10,000	.80

a. Find the net present value (unadjusted for risk) for each project. Which is preferred according to this measure?

b. Find the certainty equivalent net present value for each project. Which is preferred according to this risk-adjustment technique?

c. Compare and discuss your findings in **a** and **b**. Which, if either, of the projects would you recommend that the firm accept? Explain.

9-25 LG 5 **Risk-adjusted discount rates—Basic** Country Wallpapers is considering investment in one of three mutually exclusive projects, E, F, and G. The firm's cost of capital is 15 percent, and the risk-free rate, R_F, is 10 percent. The firm has gathered the following basic cash flow and risk index data for each project.

	Project (j)		
	E	**F**	**G**
Initial investment (*II*)	$15,000	$11,000	$19,000
Year (t)	**Cash inflows (CF_t)**		
1	$ 6,000	$ 6,000	$ 4,000
2	6,000	4,000	6,000
3	6,000	5,000	8,000
4	6,000	2,000	12,000
Risk index (RI_j)	1.80	1.00	0.60

a. Find the net present value (NPV) of each project using the firm's cost of capital. Which project is preferred in this situation?

b. The firm uses the following equation to determine the risk-adjusted discount rate, RADR_j, for each project j:

$$\text{RADR}_j = R_F + [RI_j \times (k - R_F)]$$

where

R_F = risk-free rate of return
RI_j = risk index for project j
k = cost of capital

Substitute each project's risk index into this equation to determine its RADR.

c. Use the RADR for each project to determine its risk-adjusted NPV. Which project is preferable in this situation?

d. Compare and discuss your findings in **a** and **c**. Which project would you recommend that the firm accept?

9-26 LG 5 Integrative—Certainty equivalents and risk-adjusted discount rates After a careful evaluation of investment alternatives and opportunities, Masters School Supplies has determined the best estimate of the market risk-return function as shown in the following table.

Risk index	Appropriate discount rate
0.0	7.0% (risk-free rate, R_F)
0.2	8.0
0.4	9.0
0.6	10.0
0.8	11.0
1.0	12.0
1.2	13.0
1.4	14.0
1.6	15.0
1.8	16.0
2.0	17.0

The firm is faced with two mutually exclusive projects, A and B. The following are the data the firm has been able to gather about the projects:

	Project A	Project B
Initial investment *(II)*	$20,000	$30,000
Project life	5 years	5 years
Annual cash inflow *(CF)*	$ 7,000	$10,000
Risk index	0.2	1.4
	Certainty equivalent factors (α_t)	
Year *(t)*	**Project A**	**Project B**
0	1.00	1.00
1	0.95	0.90
2	0.90	0.80
3	0.90	0.70
4	0.85	0.70
Greater than 4	0.80	0.60

All the firm's cash inflows have already been adjusted for taxes.

a. Evaluate the projects using *certainty equivalents.*

b. Evaluate the projects using *risk-adjusted discount rates.*

c. Discuss your findings in **a** and **b**, and explain why the two approaches are alternative techniques for considering risk in capital budgeting.

9-27 LG 5 **Risk classes and RADR** Moses Manufacturing is attempting to select the best of three mutually exclusive projects, X, Y, and Z. Though all the projects have five-year lives, they possess differing degrees of risk. Project X is in Class V, the highest-risk class; project Y is in Class II, the below-average-risk class; and project Z is in Class III, the average-risk class. The basic cash flow data for each project and the risk classes and risk-adjusted discount rates (RADRs) used by the firm are given in the following tables.

	Project X	Project Y	Project Z
Initial investment	$180,000	$235,000	$310,000
Year		**Cash inflows**	
1	$80,000	$50,000	$90,000
2	70,000	60,000	90,000
3	60,000	70,000	90,000
4	60,000	80,000	90,000
5	60,000	90,000	90,000

RISK CLASSES AND RADRS

Risk Class	Description	Risk-adjusted discount rate (RADR)
I	Lowest risk	10%
II	Below-average risk	13
III	Average risk	15
IV	Above-average risk	19
V	Highest risk	22

a. Find the risk-adjusted NPV for each project.

b. Which, if any, project would you recommend that the firm undertake?

9-28 LG 6 **Unequal lives—ANPV approach** Evans Industries wishes to select the best of three possible machines, each expected to fulfill the firm's ongoing need for additional aluminum-extrusion capacity. The three machines—A, B, and C—are equally risky. The firm plans to use a 12 percent cost of capital to evaluate each of them. The initial investment and annual cash inflows over the life of each machine are given in the following table.

	Machine A	Machine B	Machine C
Initial investment (*II*)	$92,000	$65,000	$100,500
Year (*t*)	**Cash inflows (CF_t)**		
1	$12,000	$10,000	$30,000
2	12,000	20,000	30,000
3	12,000	30,000	30,000
4	12,000	40,000	30,000
5	12,000	—	30,000
6	12,000	—	—

a. Calculate the NPV for each machine over its life. Rank the machines in descending order based on NPV.

b. Use the *annualized net present value (ANPV)* approach to evaluate and rank the machines in descending order based on the ANPV.

c. Compare and contrast your findings in **a** and **b**. Which machine would you recommend that the firm acquire? Why?

9-29 LG 6 **Unequal lives—ANPV approach** Portland Products is considering the purchase of one of three mutually exclusive projects for increasing production efficiency. The firm plans to use a 14 percent cost of capital to evaluate these equal-risk projects. The initial investment and annual cash inflows over the life of each project are summarized as follows:

	Project X	Project Y	Project Z
Initial investment (*II*)	$78,000	$52,000	$66,000
Year (*t*)	**Cash inflows (CF_t)**		
1	$17,000	$28,000	$15,000
2	25,000	38,000	15,000
3	33,000	—	15,000
4	41,000	—	15,000
5	—	—	15,000
6	—	—	15,000
7	—	—	15,000
8	—	—	15,000

a. Calculate the NPV for each project over its life. Rank the projects in descending order based on NPV.

b. Use the *annualized net present value (ANPV)* approach to evaluate and rank the projects in descending order based on the ANPV.

c. Compare and contrast your findings in **a** and **b**. Which project would you recommend that the firm purchase? Why?

9-30 LG 6 **Capital rationing—IRR and NPV approaches** Valley Corporation is attempting to select the best of a group of independent projects competing for the firm's fixed capital budget of $4.5 million. The firm recognizes that any unused portion of this budget will earn less than its 15 percent cost of capital, thereby resulting in a present value of inflows that is less than the initial investment. The firm has summarized the key data to be used in selecting the best group of projects in the following table.

Project	Initial investment	IRR	Present value of inflows at 15%
A	$5,000,000	17%	$5,400,000
B	800,000	18	1,100,000
C	2,000,000	19	2,300,000
D	1,500,000	16	1,600,000
E	800,000	22	900,000
F	2,500,000	23	3,000,000
G	1,200,000	20	1,300,000

a. Use the *internal rate of return (IRR) approach* to select the best group of projects.
b. Use the *net present value (NPV) approach* to select the best group of projects.
c. Compare, contrast, and discuss your findings in **a** and **b**.
d. Which projects should the firm implement? Why?

9-31 LG 6 **Capital rationing—NPV approach** A firm with a 13 percent cost of capital must select the optimal group of projects from those in the table, given its capital budget of $1 million.

Project	Initial investment	NPV at 13% cost of capital
A	$300,000	$ 84,000
B	200,000	10,000
C	100,000	25,000
D	900,000	90,000
E	500,000	70,000
F	100,000	50,000
G	800,000	160,000

a. Calculate the *present value of cash inflows* associated with each project.
b. Select the optimal group of projects, keeping in mind that unused funds are costly.

Chapter 9 Case Making Norwich Tool's lathe investment decision

Norwich Tool, a large machine shop, is considering replacing one of its lathes with either of two new lathes—lathe A or lathe B. Lathe A is a highly automated, computer-controlled lathe; lathe B is a less expensive lathe that uses standard technology. To analyze these alternatives, Mario Jackson, a financial analyst, prepared estimates of the initial investment and incremental (relevant) cash inflows associated with each lathe. These are summarized in the following table.

	Lathe A	Lathe B
Initial Investment	$660,000	$360,000
Year	**Cash inflows**	
1	$128,000	$ 88,000
2	182,000	120,000
3	166,000	96,000
4	168,000	86,000
5	450,000	207,000

Note that Mario planned to analyze both lathes over a five-year period. At the end of that time the lathes would be sold, thus accounting for the large fifth-year cash inflows.

One of Mario's major dilemmas centered on the risk of the two lathes. He felt that although the two lathes had similar risk, lathe A had a much higher risk of breakdown and repair due to its sophisticated and not fully proven solid-state electronic technology. Because he was unable to effectively quantify this possibility, Mario decided to apply the firm's 13 percent cost of capital when analyzing the lathes. Norwich Tool required all projects to have a maximum payback period of 4.0 years.

Required

a. Use the payback period to assess the acceptability and relative ranking of each lathe.

b. Assuming equal risk, use the following sophisticated capital budgeting techniques to assess the acceptability and relative ranking of each lathe.
(1) Net present value (NPV).
(2) Internal rate of return (IRR).

c. Summarize the preferences indicated by the techniques used in **a** and **b**, and indicate which lathe you would recommend, if either, if the firm has (1) unlimited funds or (2) capital rationing.

d. Repeat part **b** assuming that Mario has decided that, due to its greater risk, lathe A's cash inflows should be evaluated by using a 15 percent cost of capital.

e. What effect, if any, does recognition of lathe A's greater risk in **d** have on your recommendation in **c**?

INTEGRATIVE CASE III
LASTING IMPRESSIONS COMPANY

Lasting Impressions (LI) Company is a medium-sized commercial printer of promotional advertising brochures, booklets, and other direct-mail pieces. The firm's major clients are New York- and Chicago-based ad agencies. The typical job is characterized by high quality and production runs of over 50,000 units. LI has not been able to compete effectively with larger printers because of its existing older, inefficient presses. The firm is currently having problems cost effectively meeting run length requirements as well as meeting quality standards.

The general manager has proposed the purchase of one of two large six-color presses designed for long, high-quality runs. The purchase of a new press would enable LI to reduce its cost of labor and therefore the price to the client, putting the firm in a more competitive position. The key financial characteristics of the old press and the two proposed presses are summarized below.

Old press Originally purchased three years ago at an installed cost of $400,000, it is being depreciated under MACRS using a five-year recovery period. The old press has a remaining economic life of five years. It can be sold today to net $420,000 before taxes; if it is retained, it can be sold to net $150,000 before taxes at the end of five years.

Press A This highly automated press can be purchased for $830,000 and will require $40,000 in installation costs. It will be depreciated under MACRS using a five-year recovery period. At the end of the five years, the machine could be sold to net $400,000 before taxes. If this machine is acquired, it is anticipated that the following current account changes would result.

Cash	+ $ 25,400
Accounts receivable	+ 120,000
Inventories	− 20,000
Accounts payable	+ 35,000

Press B This press is not as sophisticated as press A. It costs $640,000 and requires $20,000 in installation costs. It will be depreciated under MACRS using a five-year recovery period. At the end of five years it can be sold to net $330,000 before taxes. Acquisition of this press will have no effect on the firm's net working capital investment.

The firm estimates that its profits before depreciation and taxes with the old press and with press A or press B for each of the five years would be as shown in Table 1. The firm is subject to a 40 percent tax rate on both ordinary income and capital gains. The firm's cost of capital, k, applicable to the proposed replacement is 14 percent.

TABLE 1

PROFITS BEFORE DEPRECIATION AND TAXES FOR LASTING IMPRESSIONS COMPANY'S PRESSES

Year	Old press	Press A	Press B
1	$120,000	$250,000	$210,000
2	120,000	270,000	210,000
3	120,000	300,000	210,000
4	120,000	330,000	210,000
5	120,000	370,000	210,000

Required

a. For each of the two proposed replacement presses, determine:
(1) Initial investment.
(2) Operating cash inflows. (*Note:* Be sure to consider the depreciation in year 6.)
(3) Terminal cash flow. (*Note:* This is at the end of year 5.)

b. Using the data developed in **a**, find and diagram the relevant cash flow stream associated with each of the two proposed replacement presses assuming that each is terminated at the end of five years.

c. Using the data developed in **b**, apply each of the following decision techniques:
(1) Payback period. (*Note:* For year 5, use only the operating cash inflows—exclude terminal cash flow—when making this calculation.)
(2) Net present value (NPV).
(3) Internal rate of return (IRR).

d. Draw net present value profiles for the two replacement presses on the same set of axes, and discuss conflicting rankings of the two presses, if any, resulting from use of NPV and IRR decision techniques.

e. Recommend which, if either, of the presses the firm should acquire if the firm has (1) unlimited funds and (2) capital rationing.

f. What is the impact on your recommendation of the fact that the operating cash inflows associated with press A are characterized as very risky in contrast to the low-risk operating cash inflows of press B?

part IV

Cost of capital, leverage, and capital structure

CHAPTERS IN THIS PART

chapter 10

The cost of capital

LEARNING GOALS

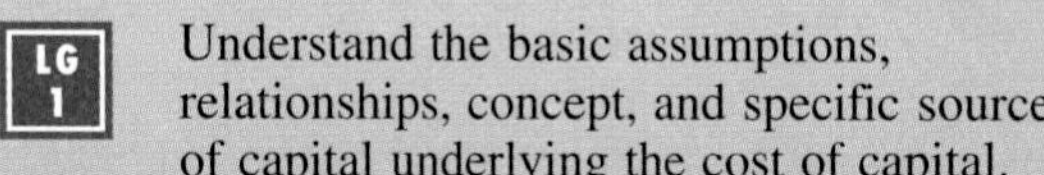

LG 1 Understand the basic assumptions, relationships, concept, and specific sources of capital underlying the cost of capital.

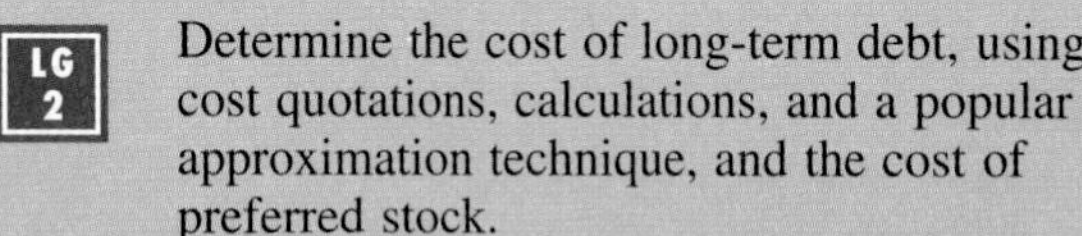

LG 2 Determine the cost of long-term debt, using cost quotations, calculations, and a popular approximation technique, and the cost of preferred stock.

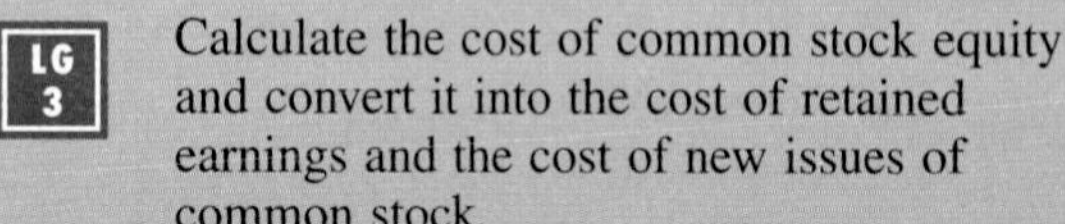

LG 3 Calculate the cost of common stock equity and convert it into the cost of retained earnings and the cost of new issues of common stock.

LG 4 Find the weighted average cost of capital (WACC) and discuss the alternative weighting schemes.

LG 5 Describe the rationale for and procedures used to determine breaking points and the weighted marginal cost of capital (WMCC).

LG 6 Explain how the weighted marginal cost of capital (WMCC) can be used with the investment opportunities schedule (IOS) to make the firm's financing/investment decisions.

Like other corporate resources, capital is limited, and there is a cost involved in choosing among investment projects. Capital—whether debt or equity—is not free; it is a cost of doing business. To an extent, capital is found and purchased just like a videotape. We "buy" capital from lenders and equity investors and invest this capital in projects, such as regional video and music store chains, that not only cover the cost of capital but also provide a return above this cost. If we can't increase profitability and earn a good return on shareholder equity, then we shouldn't do the project.

The way a company views cost of capital depends on its business, financial condition, and stage in its life cycle. A mature company with good access to capital markets may calculate its cost of capital by using a weighted average based on either its current capital structure or a target, optimal capital structure. Then it develops financing strategies to stay within those guidelines.

In our case the cost of capital depends more on *when* and *where* we get the funds required to finance our growth than on *whether* we will issue debt or equity to get to a target capital structure. Blockbuster Entertainment is a young, rapidly growing company. From 1988 to 1992 we grew from 589 to 3,127 video stores; and revenues increased from $137 million to $1.2 billion; earnings per share (EPS) rose from $0.15 to $0.76 during the same period. We financed much of this growth with equity-related securities.

We base our optimal debt and equity levels on achieving a high return on equity, which is critical in providing access to equity markets. If we can raise debt at, say, 6 percent and leverage that capital into 25 to 30 percent returns by investing it in our core business, we've earned a respectable return for our shareholders. Using debt improves return on equity, but only up to a point. If you add too much debt, lenders worry whether you'll have adequate cash flow to repay them, and then borrowing costs rise significantly.

Trends in securities markets obviously influence the type of securities that we sell at a particular time. We monitor the capital markets and evaluate different financing strategies to reduce our cost of capital and take advantage of more investment opportunities. As a public company, we are very earnings conscious, and we track price/earnings ratios for comparable companies. If they traded in the 18 to 20 times earnings range and we traded at 10 times earnings, we would consider our equity underpriced and seek other ways to raise money. For example, in early 1993 we considered our stock to be underpriced relative to our earnings base. The interest rate environment was very favorable, so we issued $150 million in long-term debt rather than sell equity.

To an extent, capital is found and purchased just like a videotape.

The cost of capital relates to many other areas of finance. If our cost of capital is very high, it limits our investment opportunities. To minimize cost of capital, we try to keep our growth rate and profitability high. That's within our control, and a track record of growth and increasing profits provides greater access to capital markets. The more profitable we are, the more we are recognized and respected by the investor community. It also makes our securities attractive to a broad range of investors, which increases demand, so the price tends to rise, lowering our overall cost of capital. If we can demonstrate the success of our strategic decisions to a broad pool of investors, the price of our securities will reflect our true future growth expectations.

David Lundeen joined Blockbuster Entertainment in 1990 as Director of Corporate Finance. He is also an executive of its two technology investment and development subsidiaries. He was formerly in the Corporate Finance Group of Drexel Burnham Lambert and with Booz-Allen and Hamilton. He received his B.S. in Industrial Engineering from the University of Michigan and an M.B.A. from the University of Chicago.

An overview of the cost of capital

The cost of capital is the rate of return that a firm must earn on investments to leave share price unchanged. Why is use of a weighted average of the current costs of the firm's financing mix preferred over use of the cost of the specific source of funds used to finance a given investment? Before reading on, spend a few moments answering this question.

THE COST OF CAPITAL IS AN EXTREMELY IMPORTANT FINANCIAL CONCEPT. IT ACTS AS A major link between the firm's long-term investment decisions (discussed in Part III) and the wealth of the owners as determined by investors in the marketplace. It is in effect the "magic number" that is used to decide whether a proposed corporate investment will increase or decrease the firm's stock price. Clearly, only those investments that are expected to increase stock price [NPV (at cost of capital) > \$0, or IRR > cost of capital] would be recommended. Due to its key role in financial decision making, the importance of the cost of capital cannot be overemphasized.

cost of capital
The rate of return that a firm must earn on its project investments to maintain its market value and attract needed funds.

The **cost of capital** can be defined as the rate of return that a firm must earn on its project investments to maintain the market value of its stock. It can also be thought of as the rate of return required by the market suppliers of capital to attract their funds to the firm. If risk is held constant, the implementation of projects with a rate of return above the cost of capital will increase the value of the firm, and the implementation of projects with a rate of return below the cost of capital will decrease the value of the firm.

Basic assumptions

The cost of capital is a dynamic concept affected by a variety of economic and firm factors. To isolate the basic structure of the cost of capital, we make some key assumptions relative to risk and taxes:

business risk
The risk to the firm of being unable to cover operating costs.

financial risk
The risk to the firm of being unable to cover required financial obligations (interest, lease payments, preferred stock dividends).

1. **Business risk**—the risk to the firm of being unable to cover operating costs—*is assumed to be unchanged.* This assumption means that the acceptance of a given project by the firm leaves its ability to meet operating costs unchanged.
2. **Financial risk**—the risk to the firm of being unable to cover required financial obligations (interest, lease payments, preferred stock dividends)—*is assumed to be unchanged.* This assumption means that the projects are financed in such a way that the firm's ability to meet required financing costs is unchanged.
3. After-tax costs are considered relevant. In other words, *the cost of capital is measured on an after-tax basis.* Note that this assumption is consistent with the framework used to make capital budgeting decisions.

Risk and financing costs

Regardless of the type of financing employed, the following equation can be used to explain the general relationship between risk and financing costs:

$$k_l = r_l + bp + fp \qquad (10.1)$$

where

k_l = the specific (or nominal) cost of the various types of long-term financing, l
r_l = the risk-free cost of the given type of financing, l
bp = the business risk premium
fp = the financial risk premium

Equation 10.1 is merely another form of the nominal interest equation—Equation 2.2 presented in Chapter 2—where r_l equals R_F and $bp + fp$ equals RP_1, the factor for issuer and issue characteristics. It indicates that the cost of each type of capital depends on the risk-free cost of that type of funds, the business risk of the firm, and the financial risk of the firm.[1] We can evaluate the equation in either of two ways:

1. *Time-series comparisons* are made by comparing the firm's cost of each type of financing *over time.* Here the differentiating factor is the risk-free cost of the given type of financing.
2. *Comparisons between firms* are made at a point in time by comparing the cost of each type of capital to a given firm with its cost *to another firm.* In this case the risk-free cost of the given type of funds would remain constant,[2] while the cost differences would be attributable to the differing business and financial risk of each firm.

An example may help to clarify these two comparisons.

EXAMPLE

The Hobson Company, a midwestern meat packer, had a cost of long-term debt two years ago of 8 percent. This 8 percent was found to represent a 4 percent risk-free cost of long-term debt, a 2 percent business risk premium, and a 2 percent financial risk premium. Currently, the risk-free cost of long-term debt is 6 percent. How much would you expect the company's cost of long-term debt to be today, assuming that its business and financial risk have remained unchanged? The previous business risk premium of 2 percent and financial risk premium of 2 percent will still prevail, since neither has changed. Adding the 4 percent total risk premium (the 2 percent business risk premium plus the 2 percent financial risk premium) to the 6 percent risk-free cost of long-term debt results in a cost of long-term debt to Hobson Company of 10 percent. In this *time-series comparison,* in which business and financial risk are assumed to be constant, the cost of the long-term funds changes only in response to changes in the risk-free cost of the given type of funds.

Another company, Raj Company, which has a 2 percent business risk premium and a 4 percent financial risk premium, can be used to demonstrate *comparisons* between firms. Although Raj and Hobson are both in the meat packing business (and thus have the same business risk premium of 2 percent), the cost of long-term debt to Raj Com-

[1] Although the relationship between r_l bp, and fp is presented as linear in Equation 10.1, this is only for simplicity; the actual relationship is likely to be much more complex mathematically. The only definite conclusion that can be drawn is that the cost of a specific type of financing for a firm is somehow functionally related to the risk-free cost of that type of financing adjusted for the firm's business and financial risks [i.e., that $k_l = f(r_l, bp, fp)$].

[2] The risk-free cost of each type of financing, r_l, may differ considerably. In other words, at a given point in time, the risk-free cost of long-term debt may be 6 percent while the risk-free cost of common stock may be 9 percent. The risk-free cost is expected to be different for each type of financing, l. The risk-free cost of different *maturities* of the same type of debt may differ, since, as was discussed in Chapter 2, long-term issues are generally viewed as more risky than short-term issues.

pany is currently 12 percent (the 6 percent risk-free cost plus a 2 percent business risk premium plus a 4 percent financial risk premium). This is greater than the 10 percent cost of long-term debt for Hobson. The difference is attributable to the greater financial risk associated with Raj. ■

The basic concept

target capital structure
The desired optimal mix of debt and equity financing that most firms attempt to achieve and maintain.

The cost of capital is estimated at a given point in time. It reflects the expected average future cost of funds over the long run, based on the best information available. This view is consistent with the use of the cost of capital to make long-term financial investment decisions. Although firms typically raise money in lumps, the cost of capital should reflect the interrelatedness of financing activities. For example, if a firm raises funds with debt (borrowing) today, it is likely that some form of equity, such as common stock, will have to be used next time. Most firms maintain a deliberate, optimal mix of debt and equity financing. This mix is commonly called a **target capital structure**—a topic that will be discussed in greater detail in Chapter 11. It is sufficient here to say that although firms raise money in lumps, they tend toward some desired *mix of financing* to maximize owner wealth.

To capture the interrelatedness of financing assuming the presence of a target capital structure, we need to look at the *overall cost of capital* rather than the cost of the specific source of funds used to finance a given expenditure. The importance of such a view can be illustrated by a simple example.

EXAMPLE

A firm is *currently* faced with an investment opportunity. Assume the following:

Best project available

Cost = $100,000
Life = 20 years
IRR = 7 percent

Cost of least-cost financing source available

Debt = 6 percent

Since it can earn 7 percent on the investment of funds costing only 6 percent, the firm undertakes the opportunity. Imagine that *one week later* a new investment opportunity is available:

Best project available

Cost = $100,000
Life = 20 years
IRR = 12 percent

Cost of least-cost financing source available

Equity = 14 percent

In this instance the firm rejects the opportunity, since the 14 percent financing cost is greater than the 12 percent return expected.

The firm's actions were not in the best interests of its owners. It accepted a project yielding a 7 percent return and rejected one with a 12 percent return. Clearly, there is a better way. Due to the interrelatedness of financing decisions, the firm must use a combined cost, which over the long run would provide for better decisions. By weighting the cost of each source of financing by its target proportion in the firm's capital structure, a *weighted average cost* that reflects the interrelationship of financing decisions can be obtained. Assuming that a 50–50 mix of debt and equity is desired, the weighted average cost above would be 10 percent [(.50 × 6% debt) + (.50 × 14% equity)]. With this cost, the first opportunity would have been rejected (7% IRR < 10% weighted average cost), and the second one would have been accepted (12% IRR > 10% weighted average cost). Such an outcome would clearly be more desirable. ■

CONCEPT IN PRACTICE

Patient Suppliers of Capital are Paid Off

Investors can be deadly if they withdraw their financial interests at the first sign of trouble. Or they can be life-giving if they wait for returns on their investment. Cummins Engine Company, the world's largest manufacturer of diesel engines, relied on the financial support of Ford Motor Company, Tenneco, Inc., and Kubota, Inc., which collectively provided $250 million in new equity capital for a 15 percent annual return, but in six years.

Cummins needed the time. In 1980 the firm began retooling its production process, pouring $200 million yearly into technical projects. Then came an unexpected sales slump, a mistimed pricing strategy, two unsolicited takeover attempts, a Japanese assault on its markets, an economic recession, and a major product failure. Cummins lost $223 million in four years, yet its investment partners held fast. The payoff for this patience? $67.1 million in operating profits in 1993! Without its patient partners, Cummins might never have gotten the capital—or the time—it needed to prepare itself for the 1990s.

The cost of specific sources of capital

This chapter focuses on finding the costs of specific sources of capital and combining them to determine and apply the weighted average cost of capital. Our concern is only with the long-term sources of funds available to a business firm, since these sources supply the permanent financing. Long-term financing supports the firm's fixed-asset investments,[3] which, we assume, are selected by using appropriate techniques.

There are four basic sources of long-term funds for the business firm: long-term debt, preferred stock, common stock, and retained earnings. The right-hand side of a balance sheet can be used to illustrate these sources.

Balance sheet		
Assets	Current liabilities	
	Long-term debt	Sources of long-term funds
	Stockholders' equity Preferred stock Common stock equity Common stock Retained earnings	

[3]The role of both long-term and short-term financing in supporting both fixed and current asset investments is addressed in Chapter 16. Suffice it to say that long-term funds are at minimum used to finance fixed assets.

Although not all firms will use each of these methods of financing, each firm is expected to have funds from some of these sources in its capital structure. The *specific cost* of each source of financing is the *after-tax* cost of obtaining the financing *today,* not the historically based cost reflected by the existing financing on the firm's books. Techniques for determining the specific cost of each source of long-term funds are presented on the following pages. Although these techniques tend to develop precisely calculated values of specific as well as weighted average costs, the resulting values are at best *rough approximations* because of the numerous assumptions and forecasts that underlie them. While we round calculated costs to the nearest 0.1 percent throughout this chapter, it is not unusual for practicing financial managers to use costs rounded to the nearest 1 percent because these values are merely estimates.

CONCEPTS IN REVIEW

10-1 What is the *cost of capital?* What role does it play in making long-term investment decisions? Why is use of a weighted average cost rather than the specific cost recommended?

10-2 Why are business and financial risk assumed to be unchanged when evaluating the cost of capital? Discuss the implications of these assumptions on the acceptance and financing of new projects.

10-3 Why is the cost of capital most appropriately measured on an after-tax basis? What effect, if any, does this have on specific cost components?

10-4 You have just been told, "Since we are going to finance this project with debt, its required rate of return must exceed the cost of debt." Do you agree or disagree? Explain.

The cost of long-term debt

The cost of long-term debt is typically viewed as the after-tax cost to maturity of a bond issue. From the issuer's viewpoint, what are the items of cash inflow and outflow associated with the issuance and scheduled repayment of a bond? Take a few moments to respond to this question before reading further.

cost of long-term debt, k_i
The after-tax cost today of raising long-term funds through borrowing.

THE **COST OF LONG-TERM DEBT,** k_i**,** IS THE AFTER-TAX COST TODAY OF RAISING LONG-term funds through borrowing. For convenience we typically assume that the funds are raised through issuance and sale of bonds. In addition, consistent with Chapter 7, we assume that the bonds pay *annual*—rather than *semiannual*—interest.

Net proceeds

net proceeds
Funds actually received from the sale of a security.

flotation costs
The total costs of issuing and selling a security.

Most corporate long-term debts are incurred through the sale of bonds. The **net proceeds** from the sale of a bond, or any security, are the funds that are actually received from the sale. **Flotation costs**—the total costs of issuing and selling a security—reduce the net proceeds from the sale of a bond, whether sold at a premium, at a discount, or at its par (face) value.

EXAMPLE

Duchess Corporation, a major hardware manufacturer, is contemplating selling $10 million worth of 20-year, 9 percent coupon (stated *annual* interest rate) bonds, each with a par value of $1,000. Since similar-risk bonds earn returns greater than 9 percent, the firm must sell the bonds for $980 to compensate for the lower coupon interest rate. The flotation costs paid to the investment banker are 2 percent of the par value of the bond (2% × $1,000), or $20.[4] The net proceeds to the firm from the sale of each bond are therefore $960 ($980 − $20). ■

Before-tax cost of debt

The before-tax cost of debt, k_d, for a bond can be obtained in any of three ways—quotation, calculation, or approximation.

USING COST QUOTATIONS

When the net proceeds from sale of a bond equal its par value, the before-tax cost would just equal the coupon interest rate. For example, a 10 percent coupon interest rate bond that nets proceeds equal to the bond's $1,000 par value would have a before-tax cost, k_d, of 10 percent. A second quotation that is sometimes used is the *yield to maturity (YTM)* (see Chapter 7) on a similar-risk bond.[5] For example, if a similar-risk bond has a YTM of 9.7 percent, this value can be used as the before-tax cost of debt, k_d.

CALCULATING THE COST

This approach finds the before-tax cost of debt by calculating the *internal rate of return (IRR)* on the bond cash flows. From the issuer's point of view, this value can be referred to as the *cost to maturity* of the cash flows associated with the debt. The cost to maturity can be calculated by using either the trial-and-error techniques for finding IRR demonstrated in Chapter 9 or a hand-held business/financial calculator. It represents the annual before-tax percentage cost of the debt to the firm.

EXAMPLE

In the preceding example the net proceeds of a $1,000, 9 percent coupon interest rate, 20-year bond were found to be $960. Although the cash flows from the bond issue do not have a conventional pattern, the calculation of the annual cost is quite simple. Actually, the cash flow pattern is exactly the opposite of a conventional pattern in that it consists of an initial inflow (the net proceeds) followed by a series of annual outlays (the interest payments). In the final year, when the debt is retired, an outlay representing the repayment of the principal also occurs. The cash flows associated with the Duchess Corporation's bond issue are as follows:

[4]As was noted in Chapter 2, firms often hire investment bankers to find buyers for new security issues, regardless of whether they are privately placed or sold through a public offering. The flotation cost includes compensation to the investment banker for marketing the issue. Detailed discussion of the functions, organization, and cost of investment banking is included in Chapter 12.

[5]Generally, the yield to maturity of bonds with a similar "rating" is used. Bond ratings, which are published by independent agencies, are discussed in Chapter 12.

End of year(s)	Cash flow
0	$ 960
1–20	−$ 90
20	−$1,000

The initial $960 inflow is followed by annual interest outflows of $90 (9% coupon interest rate × $1,000 par value) over the 20-year life of the bond. In year 20 an outflow of $1,000, representing the repayment of the principal, occurs. The before-tax cost of debt can be determined by finding the IRR—the discount rate that equates the present value of the outflows with the initial inflow.

Trial-and-Error Since we know from the discussions in Chapter 7 that discounting a bond's future cash flows at its coupon interest rate will result in its $1,000 par value, the discount rate necessary to cause Duchess Corporation's bond value to equal $960 must be greater than its 9 percent coupon interest rate. (Remember that the higher the discount rate, the lower the present value, and the lower the discount rate, the higher the present value.) Applying a 10 percent discount rate to the bond's future cash flows, we get

$$\begin{aligned}\$90 \times (PVIFA_{10\%,\,20\text{yrs.}}) &+ \$1{,}000 \times (PVIF_{10\%,\,20\text{yrs.}})\\ &= \$90 \times (8.514) + \$1{,}000 \times (.149)\\ &= \$766.26 + \$149.00 = \$915.26\end{aligned}$$

Since the bond's value of $1,000 at its 9 percent coupon interest rate is higher than $960 and the $915.26 value at the 10 percent discount rate is lower than $960, the bond's before-tax cost must be between 9 and 10 percent. Since the $1,000 value is closer to $960, the before-tax cost of the bond rounded to the nearest whole percent would be 9 percent. By using interpolation (as described in footnote 17 in Chapter 5) the more precise value for the bond's before-tax cost is *9.47 percent.*[6]

Calculator Use Using the calculator, first punch in 20, and depress **N**; then punch in the annual interest of $90, and depress **PMT**. Next punch in the value of the bond's initial net proceeds of $960, and depress **PV**; then punch in the bond's maturity value of $1,000, and depress **FV**. To calculate the bond's before-tax cost, depress **CPT** followed by ***%i***. The before-tax cost (cost to maturity) of *9.452* should appear on the calculator display. Note that this number is the precise value of the bond's cost to maturity, which is closely approximated by the interpolated value found above by using the trial-and-error approach.

---

[6]To interpolate in this case, the following steps are involved:

1. Find the differences between the bond values at 9 and 10 percent. The difference is $84.74 ($1,000 − $915.26).
2. Find the *absolute* difference between the desired value of $960 and the value associated with the lower discount rate. The difference is $40.00 ($1,000 − $960).
3. Divide the value from Step 2 by the value found in Step 1 to get the percent of the distance acorss the discount rate range between 9 and 10 percent. The result is .47 ($40.00 ÷ $84.74).
4. Multiply the percent found in Step 3 by the interval width of 1 percent (10% − 9%) over which interpolation is being performed. The result is .47 percent (.47 × 1%).
5. Add the value found in Step 4 to the interest rate associated with the lower end of the interval. The result is 9.47 percent (9% + .47%). The before-tax cost of the debt is therefore 9.47 percent.

Inputs:	20	90	960	1000		
Functions:	N	PMT	PV	FV	CPT	%i
Outputs:						9.452

■

CONCEPT IN PRACTICE

Cost of Debt Drives Up the Number of Debt Offerings

Financial managers resort to public offerings of debt securities only when raising large amounts of cash, because fixed investment banking fees for small public bond issues force the cost of debt to a prohibitive level. Yet in 1993, relatively small public offerings of debt were all the rage, with issues ranging from $1 million to $50 million. What made these managers change their minds?

Cooker Restaurant Corporation of Columbus, Ohio, sold $20 million of convertible debt; Trans Leasing International, Inc., a lessor of medical and scientific equipment, offered $13 million in subordinated debentures; and Fortune Petroleum Corp. of Agoura Hills, California, sold $1.7 million in convertible debentures. Typically, large insurance companies buy such issues in the private placement market. But with market interest rates at their lowest in 20 years, the cost of debt decreased to offset the banking fees. Furthermore, public offerings often took less time than private placements did. Fortune Petroleum arranged its public sale in four months, compared to nearly a year for private placement. Not bad for a company needing new financing fast to replace its maturing debt!

APPROXIMATING THE COST

The before-tax cost of debt, k_d, for a bond with a \$1,000 par value can be approximated by using the following equation:

$$k_d = \frac{I + \dfrac{\$1{,}000 - N_d}{n}}{\dfrac{N_d + \$1{,}000}{2}} \tag{10.2}$$

where

I = annual interest in dollars
N_d = net proceeds from the sale of debt (bond)
n = number of years to the bond's maturity

EXAMPLE

Substituting the appropriate values from the Duchess Corporation example into the approximation formula given in Equation 10.2, we get

$$k_d = \frac{\$90 + \dfrac{\$1{,}000 - \$960}{20}}{\dfrac{\$960 + \$1{,}000}{2}} = \frac{\$90 + \$2}{\$980}$$

$$= \frac{\$92}{\$980} = \underline{\underline{9.4\%}}$$

The approximate before-tax cost of debt, k_d, is therefore 9.4 percent, which does not differ greatly from the 9.45 percent value calculated precisely in the preceding example. ■

After-tax cost of debt

As was indicated earlier, the *specific cost* of financing must be stated on an after-tax basis. Since (as discussed in Chapter 2) interest on debt is tax-deductible, it reduces the firm's taxable income by the amount of deductible interest. The interest deduction therefore reduces taxes by an amount equal to the product of the deductible interest and the firm's tax rate, T. In light of this, the after-tax cost of debt, k_i, can be found by multiplying the before-tax cost, k_d, by 1 minus the tax rate as stated in the following equation:

$$k_i = k_d \times (1 - T) \tag{10.3}$$

EXAMPLE

We can use the 9.4 percent before-tax debt cost approximation for Duchess Corporation, which has a 40 percent tax rate, to demonstrate the after-tax debt cost calculation. Applying Equation 10.3 results in an after-tax cost of debt of 5.6 percent [9.4% × (1 − .40)]. Typically, the explicit cost of long-term debt is less than the explicit cost of any of the alternative forms of long-term financing, primarily because of the tax-deductibility of interest. ■

CONCEPTS IN REVIEW

10-5 What is meant by the *net proceeds* from the sale of a bond? In which circumstances is a bond expected to sell at a discount or at a premium?

10-6 Describe the trial-and-error approach used to calculate the before-tax cost of debt. How does this calculation relate to a bond's *cost to maturity* and IRR? How can this value be found more efficiently and accurately?

10-7 What sort of general approximation can be used to find the before-tax cost of debt? How is the before-tax cost of debt converted into the after-tax cost?

The cost of preferred stock

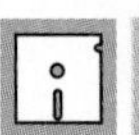

The cost of preferred stock is today's cost of using it to raise funds. Given its assumed infinite life, how would you find the cost of using preferred stock as a source of long-term financing? Before reading further, spend a short time answering this question.

PREFERRED STOCK REPRESENTS A SPECIAL TYPE OF OWNERSHIP INTEREST IN THE FIRM. Preferred stockholders must receive their *stated* dividends before any earnings can be distributed to common stockholders. Since preferred stock is a form of ownership, the proceeds from the sale of preferred stock are expected to be held for an infinite period of time. A complete discussion of the various characteristics of preferred stock is presented in Chapter 14. However, the one aspect of preferred stock that requires clarification at this point is dividends.

Preferred stock dividends

Most preferred stock dividends are stated as a *dollar amount*—"x dollars per year." When dividends are stated this way, the stock is often referred to as "x-dollar preferred stock." Thus a $4 preferred stock is expected to pay preferred stockholders $4 in dividends each year on each share of preferred stock owned. Sometimes preferred stock dividends are stated as an *annual percentage rate.* This rate represents the percentage of the stock's par, or face, value that equals the annual dividend. For instance, an 8 percent preferred stock with a $50 par value would be expected to pay an annual dividend of $4 a share (.08 × $50 par = $4). Before the cost of preferred stock is calculated, any dividends stated as percentages should be converted to annual dollar dividends.

Calculating the cost of preferred stock

cost of preferred stock, k_p
The annual preferred stock dividend, D_p, divided by the net proceeds from the sale of the preferred stock, N_p.

The **cost of preferred stock, k_p,** is found by dividing the annual preferred stock dividend, D_p, by the net proceeds from the sale of the preferred stock, N_p. The net proceeds represent the amount of money to be received net of any flotation costs required to issue and sell the stock. Equation 10.4 gives the cost of preferred stock, k_p, in terms of the annual dollar dividend, D_p, and the net proceeds from the sale of the stock, N_p:

$$k_p = \frac{D_p}{N_p} \tag{10.4}$$

Since preferred stock dividends are paid out of the firm's *after-tax* cash flows, a tax adjustment is not required.

EXAMPLE

Duchess Corporation is contemplating issuance of a 10 percent (annual dividend) preferred stock that is expected to sell for its $87 per share par value. The cost of issuing and selling the stock is expected to be $5 per share. The firm would like to determine the cost of the stock. The first step in finding this cost is to calculate the dollar amount of the annual preferred dividend, since the annual dividend is stated as a percentage of the stock's $87 par value. The annual dollar dividend is $8.70 (.10 × $87). The net proceeds from the proposed sale of stock can be found by subtracting the flotation costs from the sale price. This gives a value of $82 per share. Substituting the annual dividend, D_p, of $8.70 and the net proceeds, N_p, of $82 into Equation 10.4 gives the cost of preferred stock, 10.6 percent ($8.70 ÷ $82). ■

Comparing the 10.6 percent cost of preferred stock to the 5.6 percent cost of long-term debt shows that the preferred stock is more expensive. This difference results primarily because the cost of long-term debt—interest—is tax deductible.

CONCEPT IN REVIEW

10-8 How would you calculate the cost of preferred stock? Why do we concern ourselves with the net proceeds from the sale of the stock instead of its sale price?

The cost of common stock

The cost of common stock is the level of return that the firm must earn on it to maintain its share price. How could you use the constant growth valuation (Gordon) model or CAPM to find the cost of a firm's common stock equity? Take a few moments to answer this question before reading on.

THE *COST OF COMMON STOCK* IS THE RETURN REQUIRED ON THE STOCK BY INVESTORS in the marketplace. There are two forms of common stock financing: (1) retained earnings and (2) new issues of common stock. As a first step in finding each of these costs, we must estimate the cost of common stock equity.

Finding the cost of common stock equity

cost of common stock equity, k_s
The rate at which investors discount the expected dividends of the firm to determine its share value.

The **cost of common stock equity, k_s,** is the rate at which investors discount the expected dividends of the firm to determine its share value. Two techniques for measuring the cost of common stock equity capital are available. One uses the constant growth valuation model; the other relies on the capital asset pricing model (CAPM).

USING THE CONSTANT GROWTH VALUATION (GORDON) MODEL

constant growth valuation (Gordon) model
Assumes that the value of a share of stock equals the present value of all future dividends (assumed to grow at a constant rate) that it is expected to provide over an infinite time horizon.

The **constant growth valuation model**—the **Gordon model**—was presented in Chapter 7. It is based on the widely accepted premise that the value of a share of stock is equal to the present value of all future dividends it is expected to provide over an infinite time horizon. The key expression derived in Chapter 7 and presented as Equation 7.10 is restated in Equation 10.5:

$$P_0 = \frac{D_1}{k_s - g} \tag{10.5}$$

where

P_0 = value of common stock
D_1 = per-share dividend expected at the end of year 1
k_s = required return on common stock
g = constant rate of growth in dividends

Solving Equation 10.5 for k_s results in the following expression for the cost of *common stock equity:*

$$k_s = \frac{D_1}{P_0} + g \tag{10.6}$$

Equation 10.6 indicates that the cost of common stock equity can be found by dividing the dividend expected at the end of year 1 by the current price of the stock and adding the expected growth rate. Since common stock dividends are paid from *after-tax* income, no tax adjustment is required.

EXAMPLE

Duchess Corporation wishes to determine its cost of common stock equity capital, k_s. The market price, P_0, of its common stock is $50 per share. The firm expects to pay a dividend, D_1, of $4 at the end of the coming year, 1995. The dividends paid on the outstanding stock over the past six years (1989–1994) were as follows:

Year	Dividend
1994	$3.80
1993	3.62
1992	3.47
1991	3.33
1990	3.12
1989	2.97

Using the table for the present-value interest factors, *PVIF* (Table A-3) or a business/financial calculator in conjunction with the technique described for finding growth rates in Chapter 5, we can calculate the annual growth rate of dividends, g. It turns out to be approximately 5 percent (more precisely, it is 5.05 percent). Substituting $D_1 = \$4$, $P_0 = \$50$, and $g = 5$ percent into Equation 10.6 results in the cost of common stock equity:

$$k_s = \frac{\$4}{\$50} + 5.0\% = 8.0\% + 5.0\% = \underline{\underline{13.0\%}}$$

The 13.0 percent cost of common stock equity capital represents the return required by *existing* shareholders on their investment to leave the market price of the firm's outstanding shares unchanged. ■

CONCEPT IN PRACTICE

Cost of Equity Capital Feeds Rapid Growth at Lone Star Steakhouse

If you think everyone in our cholesterol-conscious society lives by chicken and fish alone, think again. Lone Star Steakhouse & Saloon, Inc., serves big, juicy steaks in medium-sized towns far from the grilled-chicken-breast crowd of big cities. Lone Star's recipe for success is mighty tasty, with earnings quadrupling to $15.6 million in 1993 on sales of $109 million and share value reaching $25 by mid-1993. Its lofty price/earnings ratio stands at 104, meaning that its current cost of equity capital is lower than the Texas plains.

By 1994, Lone Star wants to add 36 new locations to its current 29. How will it fund this whopping 124 percent expansion? Believing that the firm's share price cannot sustain its sizzling growth rate, short sellers (investors using a technique that allows them to profit from a decline in share price) are building strong positions in the stock and could make equity capital more expensive for Lone Star. Better to expand now than to wait for short sellers to send its stock price plummeting and its cost of equity capital rising.

capital asset pricing model (CAPM)
Describes the relationship between the required return, or cost of common stock equity capital, k_s, and the nondiversifiable risk of the firm as measured by the beta coefficient, b.

USING THE CAPITAL ASSET PRICING MODEL (CAPM)

The **capital asset pricing model (CAPM)** was developed and discussed in Chapter 6. It describes the relationship between the required return, or cost of common stock equity capital, k_s, and the nondiversifiable risk of the firm as measured by the beta coefficient, b. The basic CAPM is given in Equation 10.7:

$$k_s = R_F + [b \times (k_m - R_F)] \tag{10.7}$$

where

R_F = risk-free rate of return

k_m = market return; the return on the market portfolio of assets

Using CAPM, the cost of common stock equity is the return required by investors as compensation for the firm's nondiversifiable risk, which is measured by beta, b.

EXAMPLE

Duchess Corporation, which calculated its cost of common stock equity capital, k_s, using the constant growth valuation model in the preceding example, also wishes to calculate this cost by using the capital asset pricing model. From information provided by the firm's investment advisers and its own analyses, it is found that the risk-free rate, R_F, equals 7 percent; the firm's beta, b, equals 1.5; and the market return, k_m, equals 11 percent. Substituting these values into Equation 10.7, the company estimates the cost of common stock equity capital, k_s, as follows:

$$k_s = 7.0\% + [1.5 \times (11.0\% - 7.0\%)] = 7.0\% + 6.0\% = 13.0\%$$

The 13.0 percent cost of common stock equity capital, which is the same as that found by using the constant growth valuation model, represents the required return of investors in Duchess Corporation common stock. ■

COMPARING THE CONSTANT GROWTH AND CAPM TECHNIQUES

Use of CAPM differs from the constant growth valuation model in that it directly considers the firm's risk as reflected by beta to determine the *required* return or cost of common stock equity capital. The constant growth model does not look at risk; it uses the market price, P_0, as a reflection of the *expected* risk-return preference of investors in the marketplace. While theoretical equivalency exists between the constant growth valuation model and CAPM techniques for finding k_s, in a practical sense it is difficult to demonstrate due to measurement problems associated with growth, beta, the risk-free rate (what maturity of government security to use), and the market return. The use of the constant growth valuation model is often preferred because the data required are more readily available.

Another difference lies in the fact that when the constant growth valuation model is used to find the cost of common stock equity capital, it can easily be adjusted for flotation costs to find the cost of new common stock; the CAPM does not provide a simple adjustment mechanism. The difficulty in adjusting the cost of common stock equity capital calculated by using CAPM for these costs stems from the fact that in its common form the model does not include the market price, P_0, a variable that is needed to make such an adjustment. Although CAPM has a stronger theoretical foundation, the computational appeal of the traditional constant growth valuation model justifies its use throughout this text to measure common stock costs.

The cost of retained earnings

cost of retained earnings, k_r
The same as the cost of an equivalent fully subscribed issue of additional common stock, which is measured by the cost of common stock equity, k_s.

If earnings were not retained, dividends would be charged to retained earnings and paid out of cash to the common stockholders. Thus the **cost of retained earnings, k_r,** to the firm is the same as the cost of an *equivalent fully subscribed issue of additional common stock.* This means that retained earnings increase the stockholders' equity in the same way as a new issue of common stock. Stockholders find the firm's retention of earnings acceptable only if they expect that it will earn at least their required return on the reinvested funds.

Viewing retained earnings as a fully subscribed issue of additional common stock, we can set the firm's cost of retained earnings, k_r, equal to the cost of common stock equity as given by Equations 10.6 and 10.7.[7]

$$k_r = k_s \tag{10.8}$$

It is not necessary to adjust the cost of retained earnings for flotation costs, since by retaining earnings the firm raises equity capital without incurring these costs.

EXAMPLE

The cost of retained earnings for Duchess Corporation was actually calculated in the preceding examples, since it is equal to the cost of common stock equity. Thus k_r equals 13.0 percent. As we will show in the next section, the cost of retained earnings is always lower than the cost of a new issue of common stock, due to the absence of flotation costs when financing projects with retained earnings. ■

The cost of new issues of common stock

cost of a new issue of common stock, k_n
Determined by calculating the cost of common stock after considering both the amount of underpricing and the associated flotation costs.

underpriced
Stock sold at a price below its current market price, P_0.

Our purpose in finding the firm's overall cost of capital is to determine the after-tax cost of *new* funds required for financing projects. Attention must therefore be given to the **cost of a new issue of common stock, k_n.** As we will explain later, this cost is important only when sufficient retained earnings are unavailable. The cost of a new issue of common stock is determined by calculating the cost of common stock after considering both the amount of underpricing and the associated flotation costs. Normally, to sell a new issue, it will have to be **underpriced**—sold at a price below the current market price, P_0. In addition, flotation costs paid for issuing and selling the new issue will reduce proceeds.

The cost of new issues can be calculated by determining the net proceeds after underpricing and flotation costs, using the constant growth valuation model expression for the cost of existing common stock, k_s, as a starting point. If we let N_n represent the

[7]Technically, if a stockholder received dividends and wished to invest them in additional shares of the firm's stock, he or she would have to first pay personal taxes on the dividends and then pay brokerage fees before acquiring additional shares. Using *pt* as the average stockholder's personal tax rate and *bf* as the average brokerage fees stated as a percentage, the cost of retained earnings, k_r, can be specified as: $k_r = k_s \times (1 - pt) \times (1 - bf)$. Due to the difficulty in estimating *pt* and *bf*, only the simpler definition of k_r given in Equation 10.8 is used here.

net proceeds from the sale of new common stock after allowing for underpricing and flotation costs, the cost of the new issue, k_n, can be expressed as follows:[8]

$$k_n = \frac{D_1}{N_n} + g \tag{10.9}$$

Since the net proceeds from sale of new common stock, N_n, will be less than the current market price, P_0, the cost of new issues, k_n, will always be greater than the cost of existing issues, k_s, which, as was noted above, is equal to the cost of retained earnings, k_r. The cost of new common stock is normally greater than any other long-term financing cost. Since common stock dividends are paid from after-tax cash flows, no tax adjustment is required.

EXAMPLE

In the example using the constant growth valuation model, an expected dividend, D_1, of \$4; a current market price, P_0, of \$50; and an expected growth rate of dividends, g, of 5 percent were used to calculate Duchess Corporation's cost of common stock equity capital, k_s, which was found to be 13.0 percent. To determine its cost of *new* common stock, k_n, Duchess Corporation, with the aid of its advisers, has estimated that, on the average, new shares can be sold for \$47. The \$3 per share underpricing is necessary because of the competitive nature of the market. A second cost associated with a new issue is an underwriting fee of \$2.50 per share that would be paid to cover the costs of issuing and selling the new issue. The total underpricing and flotation costs per share are therefore expected to be \$5.50.

Subtracting the \$5.50 per share underpricing and flotation cost from the current \$50 share price, P_0, results in expected net proceeds, N_n, of \$44.50 per share (\$50.00 − \$5.50). Substituting $D_1 = \$4$, $N_n = \$44.50$, and $g = 5$ percent into Equation 10.9 results in a cost of new common stock, k_n, as follows:

$$k_n = \frac{\$4.00}{\$44.50} + 5.0\% = 9.0\% + 5.0\% = \underline{\underline{14.0\%}}$$

Duchess Corporation's cost of new common stock, k_n, is therefore 14.0 percent. This is the value to be used in the subsequent calculation of the firm's overall cost of capital. ■

CONCEPTS IN REVIEW

10-9 What premise about share value underlies the constant growth valuation (Gordon) model that is used to measure the cost of common stock equity, k_s? What does each component of the equation represent?

[8]An alternative, but computationally less straightforward, form of this equation is

$$k_n = \frac{D_1}{P_0 \times (1 - f)} + g \tag{10.9a}$$

where f represents the *percentage* reduction in current market price expected as a result of underpricing and flotation costs. Simply stated, N_n in Equation 10.9 is equivalent to $P_0 \times (1 - f)$ in Equation 10.9a. For convenience, Equation 10.9 is used to define the cost of a new issue of common stock, k_n.

10-10 If retained earnings are viewed as a fully subscribed issue of additional common stock, why is the cost of financing a project with retained earnings technically less than the cost of using a new issue of common stock?

The weighted average cost of capital (WACC)

The weighted average cost of capital (WACC) reflects, on the average, the firm's cost of long-term financing. Given the costs of the specific sources of financing, how would you obtain the appropriate weights for use in calculating a firm's WACC? Before reading ahead, spend a few moments considering this question.

NOW THAT METHODS FOR CALCULATING THE COST OF SPECIFIC SOURCES OF FINANCING have been reviewed, we can present techniques for determining the overall cost of capital. As was noted earlier, the **weighted average cost of capital (WACC),** k_a, reflects the expected average future cost of funds over the long run. It is found by weighting the cost of each specific type of capital by its proportion in the firm's capital structure. Let us look at the computational procedures and weighting schemes that are involved.

weighted average cost of capital (WACC), k_a
Reflects the expected average future cost of funds over the long run; determined by weighting the cost of each specific type of capital by its proportion in the firm's capital structure.

Calculating the weighted average cost of capital (WACC)

Once the costs of the specific sources of financing have been determined, the weighted average cost of capital (WACC) can be calculated. This calculation is performed by multiplying the specific cost of each form of financing by its proportion in the firm's capital structure and summing the weighted values. As an equation, the weighted average cost of capital, k_a, can be specified as follows:

$$k_a = (w_i \times k_i) + (w_p \times k_p) + (w_s \times k_{r \text{ or } n}) \tag{10.10}$$

where

w_i = proportion of long-term debt in capital structure
w_p = proportion of preferred stock in capital structure
w_s = proportion of common stock equity in capital structure
$w_i + w_p + w_s = 1.0$

Three important points should be noted in Equation 10.10:

1. For computational convenience it is best to convert the weights to decimal form and leave the specific costs in percentage terms.
2. *The sum of weights must equal 1.0.* Simply stated, all capital structure components must be accounted for.

3. The firm's common stock equity weight, w_s, is multiplied by either the cost of retained earnings, k_r, or the cost of new common stock, k_n. The specific cost used in the common stock equity term depends on whether the firm's common stock equity financing will be obtained using retained earnings, k_r, or new common stock, k_n.

EXAMPLE

Earlier in the chapter, we found the costs of the various types of capital for Duchess Corporation to be as follows:

Cost of debt, k_i = 5.6 percent
Cost of preferred stock, k_p = 10.6 percent
Cost of retained earnings, k_r = 13.0 percent
Cost of new common stock, k_n = 14.0 percent

The company uses the following weights in calculating its weighted average cost of capital:

Source of capital	Weight
Long-term debt	40%
Preferred stock	10
Common stock equity	50
Total	100%

Because the firm expects to have a sizable amount of retained earnings available ($300,000), it plans to use its cost of retained earnings, k_r, as the cost of common stock equity. Using this value along with the other data presented, Duchess Corporation's weighted average cost of capital is calculated in Table 10.1. (*Note:* For computational convenience the financing proportion weights are listed in decimal form in column 1 and the specific costs are shown in percentage terms in column 2.) The resulting weighted average cost of capital for Duchess is 9.8 percent. In view of this cost of cap-

TABLE 10.1

CALCULATION OF THE WEIGHTED AVERAGE COST OF CAPITAL FOR DUCHESS CORPORATION

Source of capital	Weight (1)	Cost (2)	Weighted cost [(1) × (2)] (3)
Long-term debt	.40	5.6%	2.2%
Preferred stock	.10	10.6	1.1
Common stock equity	.50	13.0	6.5
Totals	1.00		9.8%

Weighted average cost of capital = 9.8%

ital and assuming an unchanged risk level, the firm should accept all projects that earn a return greater than or equal to 9.8 percent. ■

CONCEPT IN PRACTICE

Can Stock Dividends Reduce the Weighted Average Cost of Capital?

Financial managers strive to reduce the weighted average cost of capital at the firms they manage because a lower cost of capital signals that the firm can support a larger capital budget and undertake more corporate projects. Are there easy ways to cut corporate capital costs? Firms like Del Electronics Corp., Vishay Intertechnology, Inc., and Citizens Utilities Company think so. They introduce a regular stock dividend payment to boost share price and to decrease the cost of equity capital. But stock dividends should have no impact on stock price. When a firm pays a 5 percent stock dividend, current equity holders get a 5 percent increase in number of shares owned, but each shareholder's claim against the firm's earnings falls by 5 percent. Market price of the stock should not change. Why does this simple technique work? Some managers believe that investors prefer stock dividends to compound wealth tax-free and pay capital gains taxes only when selling shares. Other managers feel that stock dividends signal increases in expected corporate profits.

Weighting schemes

Weights can be calculated as *book value* or *market value* and as *historic* or *target.*

book value weights
Weights that use accounting values to measure the proportion of each type of capital in the firm's financial structure; used in calculating the weighted average cost of capital.

market value weights
Weights that use market values to measure the proportion of each type of capital in the firm's financial structure; used in calculating the weighted average cost of capital.

historic weights
Either book or market value weights based on *actual* capital structure proportions; used in calculating the weighted average cost of capital.

target weights
Either book or market value weights based on *desired* capital structure proportions; used in calculating the weighted average cost of capital.

BOOK VALUE VERSUS MARKET VALUE

Book value weights use accounting values to measure the proportion of each type of capital in the firm's financial structure. **Market value weights** measure the proportion of each type of capital at its market value. Market value weights are appealing, since the market values of securities closely approximate the actual dollars to be received from their sale. Moreover, since the costs of the various types of capital are calculated by using prevailing market prices, it seems reasonable to use market value weights. In addition, the long-term investment cash flows to which the cost of capital is applied are estimated in terms of current as well as future market values. *Market value weights are clearly preferred over book value weights.*

HISTORIC VERSUS TARGET

Historic weights can be either book or market value weights based on *actual* capital structure proportions. For example, past as well as current book value proportions would constitute a form of historic weighting. Likewise, past or current market value proportions would represent a historic weighting scheme. Such a weighting scheme would therefore be based on real—rather than desired—proportions. **Target weights,** which can also be based on either book or market values, reflect the firm's *desired* capital structure proportions. Firms using target weights establish such proportions on the basis of the "optimal" capital structure they wish to achieve. When one considers the somewhat approximate nature of the calculations, the choice of weights may not be critical. However, from a strictly theoretical point of view the *preferred weighting scheme is target market value proportions,* and these are assumed throughout this chapter.

CONCEPT IN REVIEW

10-11 What is the *weighted average cost of capital (WACC),* and how is it calculated? Describe the logic underlying the use of *target capital structure weights,* and compare and contrast this approach with the use of historic weights.

The marginal cost and investment decisions

The weighted marginal cost of capital (WMCC) is the firm's weighted average cost of capital (WACC) associated with its next dollar of new financing. Why is the WMCC an increasing function of the level of total new financing raised at a given point in time? Take a few moments to consider this question before reading on.

The firm's weighted average cost of capital is a key input to the investment decision-making process. As was demonstrated earlier in the chapter, the firm should make only those investments for which the expected return is greater than the weighted average cost of capital. Of course, at any given time the firm's financing costs and investment returns will be affected by the volume of financing/investment undertaken. The concepts of a *weighted marginal cost of capital* and an *investment opportunities schedule* provide the mechanisms whereby financing and investment decisions can be made simultaneously at any point in time.

The weighted marginal cost of capital (WMCC)

The weighted average cost of capital may vary at any time depending on the volume of financing the firm plans to raise. *As the volume of financing increases, the costs of the various types of financing will increase, raising the firm's weighted average cost of capital.* The **weighted marginal cost of capital (WMCC)** is simply the firm's weighted average cost of capital (WACC) associated with its next dollar of total new financing. The financial manager is interested in this marginal cost because it is relevant to current decisions.

weighted marginal cost of capital (WMCC)
The firm's weighted average cost of capital (WACC) associated with its next dollar of total new financing.

Because the costs of the financing components—debt, preferred stock, and common stock—rise as larger amounts are raised, the WMCC is an increasing function of the level of total new financing. Increases in the component financing costs result from the fact that at a given point in time, the larger the amount of new financing, the greater the risk to the fund supplier. Risk rises in response to the increased uncertainty as to the outcomes of the investments financed with these funds. In other words, fund suppliers require greater returns in the form of interest, dividends, or growth as compensation for the increased risk introduced as larger volumes of *new* financing are incurred.

Another factor causing the weighted average cost of capital to increase relates to the use of common stock equity financing. The portion of new financing provided by common stock equity will be taken from available retained earnings until exhausted and then obtained through new common stock financing. Since retained earnings are a less expensive form of common stock equity financing than the sale of new common stock, it should be clear that once retained earnings have been exhausted, the weighted average cost of capital will rise with the addition of more expensive new common stock.

FINDING BREAKING POINTS

breaking point
The level of *total* new financing at which the cost of one of the financing components rises, thereby causing an upward shift in the *weighted marginal cost of capital (WMCC).*

To calculate the WMCC, the **breaking points,** which reflect the level of *total* new financing at which the cost of one of the financing components rises, must be calculated. The following general equation can be used to find breaking points:

$$BP_j = \frac{AF_j}{w_j} \tag{10.11}$$

where

BP_j = breaking point for financing source j
AF_j = amount of funds available from financing source j at a given cost
w_j = capital structure weight (historic or target, stated in decimal form) for financing source j

EXAMPLE

When Duchess Corporation exhausts its \$300,000 of available retained earnings (k_r = 13.0%), it must use the more expensive new common stock financing (k_n = 14.0%) to meet its common stock equity needs. In addition, the firm expects that it can borrow only \$400,000 of debt at the 5.6 percent cost; additional debt will have an after-tax cost (k_i) of 8.4 percent. Two breaking points therefore exist—(1) when the \$300,000 of retained earnings costing 13.0 percent is exhausted and (2) when the \$400,000 of long-term debt costing 5.6 percent is exhausted. The breaking points can be found by substituting these values and the corresponding capital structure weights given earlier into Equation 10.11. We get

$$BP_{\text{common equity}} = \frac{\$300{,}000}{.50} = \$600{,}000$$

$$BP_{\text{long-term debt}} = \frac{\$400{,}000}{.40} = \$1{,}000{,}000 \ \blacksquare$$

CALCULATING THE WMCC

weighted marginal cost of capital (WMCC) schedule
Graph that relates the firm's weighted average cost of capital (WACC) to the level of total new financing.

Once the breaking points have been determined, the weighted average cost of capital over the range of total new financing between breaking points must be calculated. First, the weighted average cost of capital for a level of total new financing between zero and the first breaking point is found. Next, the weighted average cost of capital for a level of total new financing between the first and second breaking points is found, and so on. By definition, for each of the ranges of total new financing between breaking points, certain component capital costs will increase, causing the weighted average cost of capital to increase to a higher level than that over the preceding range. Together these data can be used to prepare the **weighted marginal cost of capital (WMCC) schedule,** which is a graph that relates the firm's weighted average cost of capital (WACC) to the level of total new financing.

TABLE 10.2

WEIGHTED AVERAGE COST OF CAPITAL FOR RANGES OF TOTAL NEW FINANCING FOR DUCHESS CORPORATION

Range of total new financing	Source of capital (1)	Weight (2)	Cost (3)	Weighted cost [(2) × (3)] (4)
$0 to $600,000	Debt	.40	5.6%	2.2%
	Preferred	.10	10.6	1.1
	Common	.50	13.0	6.5
	Weighted average cost of capital			9.8%
$600,000 to $1,000,000	Debt	.40	5.6%	2.2%
	Preferred	.10	10.6	1.1
	Common	.50	14.0	7.0
	Weighted average cost of capital			10.3%
$1,000,000 and above	Debt	.40	8.4%	3.4%
	Preferred	.10	10.6	1.1
	Common	.50	14.0	7.0
	Weighted average cost of capital			11.5%

EXAMPLE

Table 10.2 summarizes the calculation of the weighted average cost of capital for Duchess Corporation over the three total new financing ranges created by the two breaking points—$600,000 and $1,000,000. Comparing the costs in column 3 of the table for each of the three ranges, we can see that the costs in the first range ($0 to $600,000) are those calculated in earlier examples and used in Table 10.1. In the second range ($600,000 to $1,000,000) the increase in the common stock equity cost to 14.0 percent is reflected. In the final range the increase in the long-term debt cost to 8.4 percent is introduced.

The weighted average costs of capital (WACC) for the three ranges created by the two breaking points are summarized in the table shown in Figure 10.1. These data describe the weighted marginal cost of capital (WMCC), which can be seen to increase with increasing levels of total new financing. Figure 10.1 presents the WMCC schedule. Again, it is clear that the WMCC is an increasing function of the amount of total new financing raised. ■

The investment opportunities schedule (IOS)

investment opportunities schedule (IOS)
A ranking of investment possibilities from best (highest returns) to worst (lowest returns).

At any given time a firm has certain investment opportunities available to it. These opportunities differ with respect to the size of investment anticipated, risk, and return. (Because the calculated weighted average cost of capital does not apply to risk-changing investments, we continue to assume that all opportunities have equal risk similar to the firm's risk.) The firm's **investment opportunities schedule (IOS)** is a ranking of investment possibilities from best (highest returns) to worst (lowest returns). As the cumulative amount of money invested in a firm's capital projects increases, its return (IRR) on the projects will decrease; generally, the first project selected will have

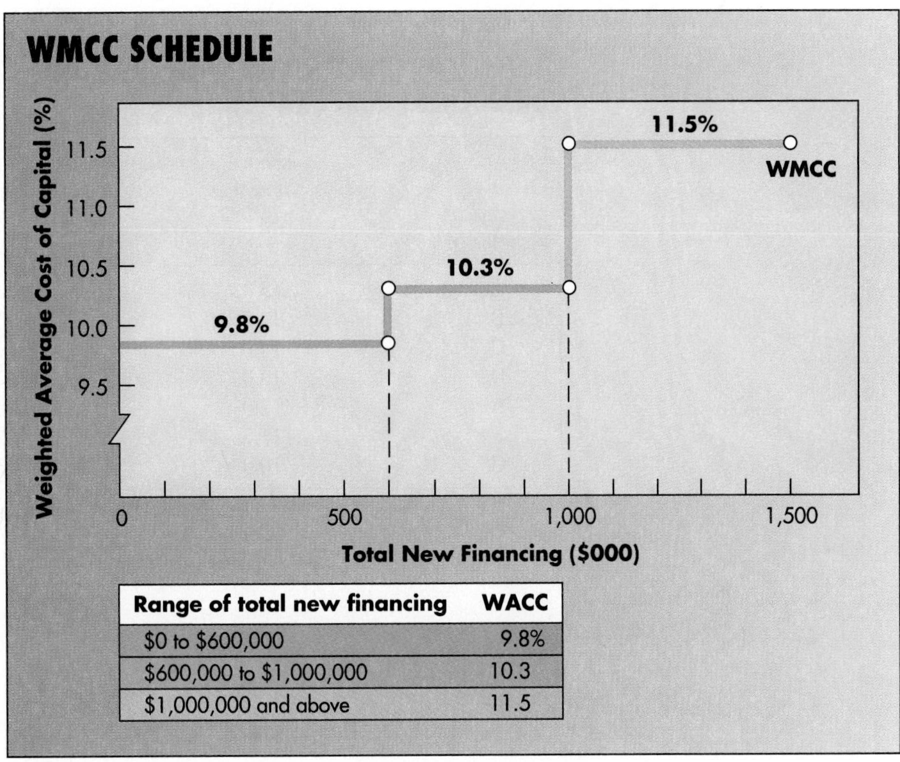

Range of total new financing	WACC
$0 to $600,000	9.8%
$600,000 to $1,000,000	10.3
$1,000,000 and above	11.5

FIGURE 10.1
Weighted marginal cost of capital (WMCC) schedule for Duchess Corporation

the highest return, the next project the second highest, and so on. In other words, the return on investments will *decrease* as the firm accepts additional projects.

EXAMPLE

Duchess Corporation's current investment opportunities schedule (IOS) lists the best (highest return) to the worst (lowest return) investment possibilities in column 1 of Table 10.3. In column 2 of the table the initial investment required by each project is shown, and in column 3 the cumulative total invested funds required to finance all projects better than and including the corresponding investment opportunity is given. Plotting the project returns against the cumulative investment (column 1 against column 3 in Table 10.3) on a set of total new financing or investment–weighted average cost of capital and IRR axes results in the firm's investment opportunities schedule (IOS). A graph of the IOS for Duchess Corporation is given in Figure 10.2. ■

Making financing/investment decisions

As long as a project's internal rate of return[9] is greater than the weighted marginal cost of new financing, the firm should accept the project. While the return will decrease with the acceptance of more projects, the weighted marginal cost of capital

[9]Although net present value could be used to make these decisions, the internal rate of return is used here because of the ease of comparison it offers.

TABLE 10.3

INVESTMENT OPPORTUNITIES SCHEDULE (IOS) FOR DUCHESS CORPORATION

Investment opportunity	Internal rate of return (IRR) (1)	Initial investment (2)	Cumulative investment[a] (3)
A	15.0%	$100,000	$ 100,000
B	14.5	200,000	300,000
C	14.0	400,000	700,000
D	13.0	100,000	800,000
E	12.0	300,000	1,100,000
F	11.0	200,000	1,300,000
G	10.0	100,000	1,400,000

[a]The cumulative investment represents the total amount invested in projects with higher returns plus the investment required for the given investment opportunity.

FIGURE 10.2
Using the IOS and WMCC to select projects

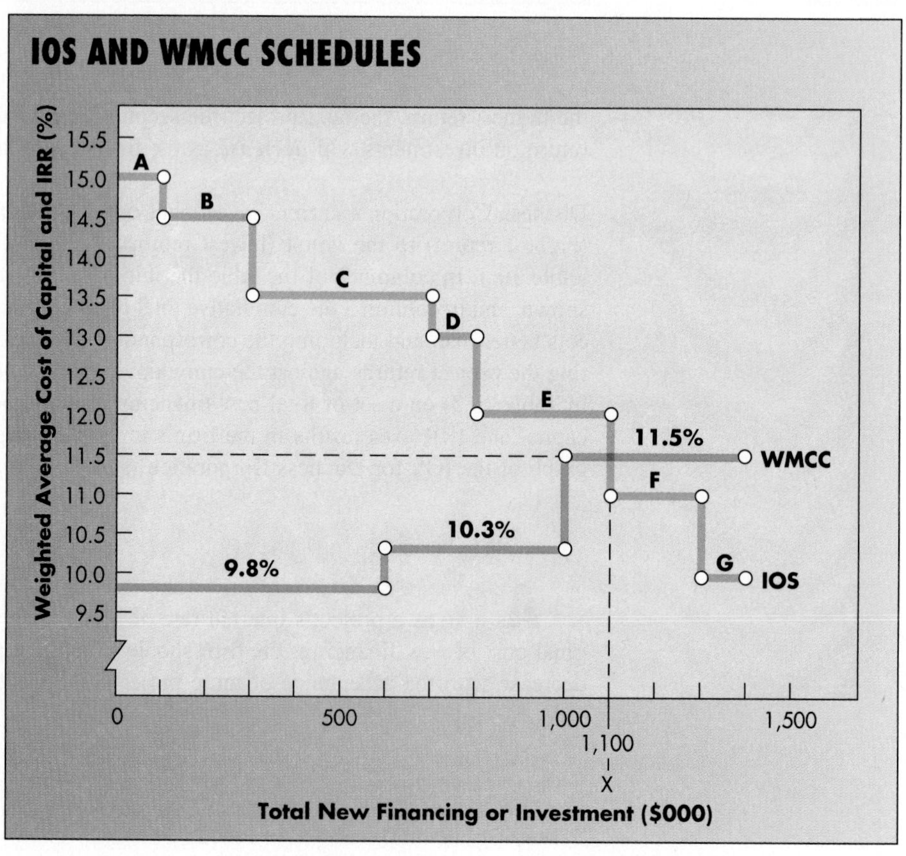

will increase because greater amounts of financing will be required. The firm would therefore *accept projects up to the point at which the marginal return on its investment equals its weighted marginal cost of capital.* Beyond that point, its investment return will be less than its capital cost.[10] This approach is consistent with the maximization of net present value (NPV), since for conventional projects (1) the NPV is positive as long as the IRR exceeds the weighted average cost of capital, k_a, and (2) the larger the difference between the IRR and k_a, the larger the resulting NPV. Therefore the acceptance of projects beginning with those having the greatest positive difference between IRR and k_a down to the point at which IRR just equals k_a should result in the maximum total NPV for all independent projects accepted. Such an outcome is completely consistent with the firm's goal of owner wealth maximization. Returning to the Duchess Corporation example, we can demonstrate the application of this procedure.

EXAMPLE

Figure 10.2 shows the Duchess Corporation's WMCC schedule and IOS on the same set of axes. By using these two functions in combination the firm's optimal capital budget ("X" in the figure) is determined. By raising \$1.1 million of new financing and investing these funds in projects A, B, C, D, and E, the firm should maximize the wealth of its owners, since these projects result in the maximum total net present value. Note that the 12.0 percent return on the last dollar invested (in project E) *exceeds* its 11.5 percent weighted average cost, and investment in project F is not feasible because its 11.0 percent return is *less than* the 11.5 percent cost of funds available for investment. The importance of the WMCC and the IOS for investment decision making should now be quite clear. ■

It is important to note that at the point at which the IRR equals the weighted average cost of capital, k_a—the optimal capital budget of \$1,100,000 at point X in Figure 10.2—the firm's size as well as its shareholder value will be optimized. In a sense the size of the firm is determined by the market—the availability of and returns on investment opportunities, and the availability and cost of financing. Of course, as was noted in Chapter 9, most firms operate under *capital rationing* because management imposes an internal capital expenditure (and therefore financing) budget constraint that is below the optimum capital budget (where IRR $= k_a$). Suffice it to say that due to capital rationing, a gap frequently exists between the theoretically optimal capital budget and the firm's actual level of financing/investment.

CONCEPTS IN REVIEW

10-12 What is the *weighted marginal cost of capital (WMCC)*? What does the *WMCC schedule* represent? Why does this schedule increase?

10-13 What is the *investment opportunities schedule (IOS)*? Is it typically depicted as an increasing or decreasing function of the level of investment at a given point in time? Why?

10-14 Use a graph to show how the weighted marginal cost of capital (WMCC) schedule and the investment opportunities schedule (IOS) can be used to find the level of financing/investment that maximizes owners' wealth. Why, on a practical basis, do many firms finance/invest at a level below this optimum?

[10] So as not to confuse the discussion presented here, the fact that the use of the IRR for selecting projects may not provide optimum decisions is ignored. The problems associated with the IRR and its use in capital rationing were discussed in greater detail in Chapter 9.

Summary

LG 1 **Understand the basic assumptions, relationships, concept, and specific sources of capital underlying the cost of capital.** The cost of capital is the rate of return that a firm must earn on its investments to maintain its market value and attract needed funds. The specific costs of the basic sources of capital (long-term debt, preferred stock, retained earnings, and common stock) can be calculated individually. Only the cost of debt must be adjusted for taxes. The cost of each is affected by business and financial risks, which are assumed to be unchanged, and by the risk-free cost of the given type of financing. To capture the interrelatedness of financing, an overall or weighted average cost of capital should be used.

LG 2 **Determine the cost of long-term debt, using cost quotations, calculations, and a popular approximation technique, and the cost of preferred stock.** The cost of long-term debt is the after-tax cost today of raising long-term funds through borrowing. Cost quotations, calculation using either trial-and-error techniques or a hand-held business/financial calculator, or an approximation can be used to find the before-tax cost of debt, which must then be tax-adjusted. The cost of preferred stock is the stated annual dividend expressed as a percentage of the net proceeds from the sale of preferred shares. The key variable definitions and formulas for the before- and after-tax cost of debt and the cost of preferred stock are given in Table 10.4.

LG 3 **Calculate the cost of common stock equity and convert it into the cost of retained earnings and the cost of new issues of common stock.** The cost of common stock equity can be calculated by using the constant growth valuation model or the capital asset pricing model (CAPM). The cost of retained earnings is equal to the cost of common stock equity. An adjustment in the cost of common stock equity to reflect underpricing and flotation cost is required to find the cost of new issues of common stock. The key variable definitions and formulas for the cost of common stock equity, the cost of retained earnings, and the cost of new issues of common stock are given in Table 10.4.

LG 4 **Find the weighted average cost of capital (WACC) and discuss the alternative weighting schemes.** The firm's weighted average cost of capital (WACC) reflects the expected average future cost of funds over the long run. It can be determined by combining the costs of specific types of capital after weighting each cost using historical book or market value weights or target book or market value weights. The theoretically preferred approach uses target weights based on market values. The key variable definitions and formula for WACC are given in Table 10.4.

LG 5 **Describe the rationale for and procedures used to determine breaking points and the weighted marginal cost of capital (WMCC).** A firm's weighted marginal cost of capital (WMCC) reflects the fact that as the volume of financing increases, the costs of the various types of financing will increase, raising the firm's weighted average cost of capital (WACC). Breaking points, which are found by dividing the amount of funds available from a given financing source by its capital structure weight, represent the level of total new financing at which the cost of one of the financing components rises, thereby causing an upward shift in the WMCC. The WMCC is the firm's WACC associated with its next dollar of total financing. The WMCC schedule relates the WACC to each level of total new financing.

LG 6 **Explain how the weighted marginal cost of capital (WMCC) can be used with the investment opportunities schedule (IOS) to make the firm's financing/investment decisions.** The investment opportunities schedule (IOS) presents a ranking of currently available investments from those with the highest returns to those with the lowest returns. It is used in combination with the WMCC to find the level of financing/investment that maximizes owners' wealth. With this approach, the firm would accept projects up to the point at which the marginal return on its investment equals its weighted marginal cost of capital.

Self-test problem (Solution in Appendix E)

ST 10-1 LG 2,3,4,5,6 **Specific costs, WACC, WMCC, and IOS** Humble Manufacturing is interested in measuring its overall cost of capital. Current investigation has gathered the following data. The firm is in the 40 percent tax bracket.

Debt The firm can raise an unlimited amount of debt by selling $1,000 par value, 10 percent coupon interest rate, 10-year bonds on which *annual interest* payments will be made. To sell the issue, an average discount of $30 per bond would have to be given. The firm must also pay flotation costs of $20 per bond.

Preferred stock The firm can sell 11 percent (annual dividend) preferred stock at its $100-per-share par value. The cost of issuing and selling the preferred stock is expected to be $4 per share. An unlimited amount of preferred stock can be sold under these terms.

TABLE 10.4

SUMMARY OF KEY DEFINITIONS AND FORMULAS FOR COST OF CAPITAL

Variable definitions

k_d = before-tax cost of debt
I = annual interest in dollars
N_d = net proceeds from the sale of debt (bond)
n = number of years to the bond's maturity
k_i = after-tax cost of debt
T = firm's tax rate
k_p = cost of preferred stock
D_p = annual preferred stock dividend (in dollars)
N_p = net proceeds from the sale of preferred stock
k_s = required return on common stock
D_1 = per-share dividend expected at the end of year 1
P_0 = value of common stock
g = constant rate of growth in dividends
R_F = risk-free rate of return
b = beta coefficient or measure of nondiversifiable risk
k_m = required return on the market portfolio
k_r = cost of retained earnings
k_n = cost of a new issue of common stock
N_n = net proceeds from sale of new common stock
k_a = weighted average cost of capital
w_i = proportion of long-term debt in capital structure
w_p = proportion of preferred stock in capital structure
w_s = proportion of common stock equity in capital structure
BP_j = breaking point for financing source j
AF_j = amount of funds available from financing source j at a given cost
w_j = capital structure proportion (historic or target, stated in decimal form) for financing source j

Cost of capital formulas

Before-tax cost of debt

$$k_d = \frac{I + \dfrac{\$1{,}000 - N_d}{n}}{\dfrac{N_d + \$1{,}000}{2}} \qquad \text{[Eq. 10.2]}$$

After-tax cost of debt $k_i = k_d \times (1 - T)$ [Eq. 10.3]

Cost of preferred stock

$$k_p = \frac{D_p}{N_p} \qquad \text{[Eq. 10.4]}$$

Cost of common stock equity

Using constant growth valuation model: $k_s = \dfrac{D_1}{P_0} + g$ [Eq. 10.6]

Using CAPM: $k_s = R_F + [b \times (k_m - R_F)]$ [Eq. 10.7]

Cost of retained earnings $k_r = k_s$ [Eq. 10.8]

Cost of new issues of common stock

$$k_n = \frac{D_1}{N_n} + g \qquad \text{[Eq. 10.9]}$$

Weighted average cost of capital (WACC)

$$k_a = (w_i \times k_i) + (w_p \times k_p) + (w_s \times k_{r \text{ or } n}) \qquad \text{[Eq. 10.10]}$$

Breaking point $BP_j = \dfrac{AF_j}{w_j}$ [Eq. 10.11]

Common stock The firm's common stock is currently selling for $80 per share. The firm expects to pay cash dividends of $6 per share next year. The firm's dividends have been growing at an annual rate of 6 percent, and this rate is expected to continue in the future. The stock will have to be underpriced by $4 per share, and flotation costs are expected to amount to $4 per share. The firm can sell an unlimited amount of new common stock under these terms.

Retained earnings The firm expects to have $225,000 of retained earnings available in the coming year. Once these retained earnings are exhausted, the firm will use new common stock as the form of common stock equity financing.

a. Calculate the specific cost of each source of financing. (Round to the nearest 0.1 percent.)

b. The firm uses the following weights based on target capital structure proportions to calculate its weighted average cost of capital. (Round to the nearest 0.1 percent.)

Source of capital	Weight
Long-term debt	40%
Preferred stock	15
Common stock equity	45
Total	100%

(1) Calculate the single breaking point associated with the firm's financial situation. (*Hint:* This point results from the exhaustion of the firm's retained earnings.)

(2) Calculate the weighted average cost of capital associated with total financing below the breaking point calculated in (1).

(3) Calculate the weighted average cost of capital associated with total financing above the breaking point calculated in (1).

c. Using the results of **b** along with the following information on the available investment opportunities, draw the firm's weighted marginal cost of capital (WMCC) schedule and investment opportunities schedule (IOS) on the same set of total new financing or investment (x-axis)–weighted average cost of capital and IRR (y-axis) axes.

Investment opportunity	Internal rate of return (IRR)	Initial investment
A	11.2%	$100,000
B	9.7	500,000
C	12.9	150,000
D	16.5	200,000
E	11.8	450,000
F	10.1	600,000
G	10.5	300,000

d. Which, if any, of the available investments would you recommend that the firm accept? Explain your answer. How much total new financing will be required?

Problems

10-1 LG 1 Cost of debt—Risk premiums Mulberry Printing's cost of long-term debt last year was 10 percent. This rate was attributable to a 7 percent risk-free cost of long-term debt, a 2 percent business risk premium, and a 1 percent financial risk premium. The firm currently wishes to obtain a long-term loan.

a. If the firm's business and financial risk are unchanged from the previous period and the risk-free cost of long-term debt is now 8 percent, at what rate would you expect the firm to obtain a long-term loan?

b. If, as a result of borrowing, the firm's financial risk will increase enough to raise the financial risk premium to 3 percent, how much would you expect the firm's borrowing cost to be?

c. One of the firm's competitors has a 1 percent business risk premium and a 2 percent financial risk premium. What is that firm's cost of long-term debt likely to be?

10-2 LG 1 Concept of cost of capital Wren Manufacturing is in the process of analyzing its investment decision-making procedures. The two projects evaluated by the firm during the past month were projects 263 and 264. The basic variables surrounding each project analysis using the IRR decision technique and the resulting decision actions are summarized in the following table.

Basic variables	Project 263	Project 264
Cost	$64,000	$58,000
Life	15 years	15 years
IRR	8%	15%
Least-cost financing		
Source	Debt	Equity
Cost (after-tax)	7%	16%
Decision		
Action	Accept	Reject
Reason	8% IRR > 7% cost	15% IRR < 16% cost

a. Evaluate the firm's decision-making procedures, and explain why the acceptance of project 263 and rejection of project 264 may not be in the owners' best interest.

b. If the firm maintains a capital structure containing 40 percent debt and 60 percent equity, find its weighted average cost using the data in the table.

c. Had the firm used the weighted average cost calculated in **b**, what actions would have been taken relative to projects 263 and 264?

d. Compare and contrast the firm's actions with your findings in **c**. Which decision method seems more appropriate? Explain why.

10-3 LG 2 Cost of debt using both methods Currently, Warren Industries can sell 15-year, $1,000 par-value bonds paying annual interest at a 12 percent coupon rate. As a result of current interest rates, the bonds can be sold for $1,010 each; flotation costs of $30 per bond will be incurred in this process. The firm is in the 40 percent tax bracket.

a. Find the net proceeds from sale of the bond, N_d.

b. Show the cash flows from the firm's point of view over the maturity of the bond.

c. Use the *IRR approach* with interpolation (see footnote 6) to calculate the before-tax and after-tax cost of debt.

d. Use the *approximation formula* to estimate the before-tax and after-tax cost of debt.

e. Compare and contrast the cost of debt calculated in **c** and **d**. Which approach do you prefer? Why?

10-4 LG 2 Cost of debt using the approximation formula For each of the following $1,000 bonds, assuming annual interest payment and a 40 percent tax rate, calculate the *after-tax* cost to maturity using the *approximation formula.*

Bond	Life	Underwriting fee	Discount (−) or premium (+)	Coupon interest rate
A	20 years	$25	$−20	9%
B	16	40	+10	10
C	15	30	−15	12
D	25	15	Par	9
E	22	20	−60	11

10-5 LG 2 Cost of preferred stock Taylor Systems has just issued preferred stock. The stock has a 12 percent annual dividend and a $100 par value and was sold at $97.50 per share. In addition, flotation costs of $2.50 per share must be paid.

a. Calculate the cost of the preferred stock.

b. If the firm had sold the preferred stock with a 10 percent annual dividend and netted $90.00 after flotation costs, what would its cost have been?

10-6 LG 2 Cost of preferred stock Determine the cost for each of the following preferred stocks.

Preferred stock	Par value	Sale price	Flotation cost	Annual dividend
A	$100	$101	$9.00	11%
B	40	38	$3.50	8%
C	35	37	$4.00	$5.00
D	30	26	5% of par	$3.00
E	20	20	$2.50	9%

10-7 LG 3 Cost of common stock equity—CAPM J&M Corporation common stock has a beta, *b*, of 1.2. The risk-free rate is 6 percent, and the market return is 11 percent.

a. Determine the risk premium on J&M common stock.

b. Determine the required return that J&M common stock should provide.

c. Determine J&M's cost of common stock equity using the CAPM.

10-8 LG 3 Cost of common stock equity Ross Textiles wishes to measure its cost of common stock equity. The firm's stock is currently selling for $57.50. The firm expects to pay a $3.40 dividend at the end of the year (1995). The dividends for the past five years were as shown below.

Year	Dividend
1994	$3.10
1993	2.92
1992	2.60
1991	2.30
1990	2.12

After underpricing and flotation costs, the firm expects to net $52 per share on a new issue.

a. Determine the growth rate of dividends.
b. Determine the net proceeds, N_n, that the firm actually receives.
c. Using the constant growth valuation model, determine the cost of retained earnings, k_r.
d. Using the constant growth valuation model, determine the cost of new common stock, k_n.

10-9 LG 3 Retained earnings versus new common stock Using the data for each firm in the following table, calculate the cost of retained earnings and the cost of new common stock using the constant growth valuation model.

Firm	Current market price per share	Dividend growth rate	Projected dividend per share next year	Underpricing per share	Flotation cost per share
A	$50.00	8%	$2.25	$2.00	$1.00
B	20.00	4	1.00	.50	1.50
C	42.50	6	2.00	1.00	2.00
D	19.00	2	2.10	1.30	1.70

10-10 LG 4 WACC—Book weights Ridge Tool has on its books the following amounts and specific (after-tax) costs for each source of capital:

Source of capital	Book value	Specific cost
Long-term debt	$700,000	5.3%
Preferred stock	50,000	12.0
Common stock equity	650,000	16.0

a. Calculate the firm's weighted average cost of capital using book value weights.
b. Explain how the firm can use this cost in the investment decision-making process.

10-11 LG 4 WACC—Book weights and market weights The Webster Company has compiled the following information.

Source of capital	Book value	Market value	After-tax cost
Long-term debt	$4,000,000	$3,840,000	6.0%
Preferred stock	40,000	60,000	13.0
Common stock equity	1,060,000	3,000,000	17.0
Totals	$5,100,000	$6,900,000	

a. Calculate the weighted average cost of capital using book value weights.
b. Calculate the weighted average cost of capital using market value weights.
c. Compare the answers obtained in **a** and **b**. Explain the differences.

10-12 LG 4 **WACC and target weights** After careful analysis, Dexter Brothers has determined that its optimal capital structure is composed of the following sources and target market value weights:

Source of capital	Target market value weight
Long-term debt	30%
Preferred stock	15
Common stock equity	55
Total	100%

The cost of debt is estimated to be 7.2 percent; the cost of preferred stock is estimated to be 13.5 percent; the cost of retained earnings is estimated to be 16.0 percent; and the cost of new common stock is estimated to be 18.0 percent. All of these are after-tax rates. Currently, the company's debt represents 25 percent, the preferred stock represents 10 percent, and the common stock equity represents 65 percent of total capital based on the market values of the three components. The company expects to have a significant amount of retained earnings available and does not expect to sell any new common stock.

a. Calculate the weighted average cost of capital based on historic market value weights.

b. Calculate the weighted average cost of capital based on target market value weights.

10-13 LG 2,3,4,5 **Calculation of specific costs, WACC, and WMCC** Dillon Labs has asked its financial manager to measure the cost of each specific type of capital as well as the weighted average cost of capital. The weighted average cost is to be measured by using the following weights: 40 percent long-term debt, 10 percent preferred stock, and 50 percent common stock equity (retained earnings, new common stock, or both). The firm's tax rate is 40 percent.

Debt The firm can sell for $980 a 10-year, $1,000-par-value bond paying annual interest at a 10 percent coupon rate. A flotation cost of 3 percent of the par value would be required in addition to the discount of $20 per bond.

Preferred stock Eight percent (annual dividend) preferred stock having a par value of $100 can be sold for $65. An additional fee of $2 per share must be paid to the underwriters.

Common stock The firm's common stock is currently selling for $50 per share. The dividend expected to be paid at the end of the coming year (1995) is $4. Its dividend payments, which have been approximately 60 percent of earnings per share in each of the past five years, were as follows:

Year	Dividend
1994	$3.75
1993	3.50
1992	3.30
1991	3.15
1990	2.85

It is expected that, to sell, new common stock must be underpriced $5 per share and the firm must also pay $3 per share in flotation costs. Dividend payments are expected to continue at 60 percent of earnings.

a. Calculate the specific cost of each source of financing. (Assume that $k_r = k_s$.)
b. If earnings available to common shareholders are expected to be $7 million, what is the breaking point associated with the exhaustion of retained earnings?
c. Determine the weighted average cost of capital between zero and the breaking point given in **b.**
d. Determine the weighted average cost of capital just beyond the breaking point calculated in **b.**

10-14 LG 2,3,4,5 **Calculation of specific costs, WACC, and WMCC** Lang Enterprises is interested in measuring its overall cost of capital. Current investigation has gathered the following data. The firm is in the 40 percent tax bracket.

Debt The firm can raise an unlimited amount of debt by selling $1,000, 8 percent coupon interest rate, 20-year bonds on which annual interest payments will be made. To sell the issue, an average discount of $30 per bond would have to be given. The firm also must pay flotation costs of $30 per bond.

Preferred stock The firm can sell 8 percent preferred stock at its $95-per-share par value. The cost of issuing and selling the preferred stock is expected to be $5 per share. An unlimited amount of preferred stock can be sold under these terms.

Common stock The firm's common stock is currently selling for $90 per share. The firm expects to pay cash dividends of $7 per share next year. The firm's dividends have been growing at an annual rate of 6 percent, and this is expected to continue into the future. The stock will have to be underpriced by $7 per share, and flotation costs are expected to amount to $5 per share. The firm can sell an unlimited amount of new common stock under these terms.

Retained earnings When measuring this cost, the firm does not concern itself with the tax bracket or brokerage fees of owners. It expects to have available $100,000 of retained earnings in the coming year; once these retained earnings are exhausted, the firm will use new common stock as the form of common stock equity financing.

a. Calculate the specific cost of each source of financing. (Round answers to the nearest 0.1 percent.)
b. The firm's capital structure weights used in calculating its weighted average cost of capital are given. (Round answer to the nearest 0.1 percent.)

Source of capital	Weight
Long-term debt	30%
Preferred stock	20
Common stock equity	50
Total	100%

(1) Calculate the single breaking point associated with the firm's financial situation. (*Hint:* This point results from exhaustion of the firm's retained earnings.)
(2) Calculate the weighted average cost of capital associated with total financing below the breaking point calculated in (1).
(3) Calculate the weighted average cost of capital associated with total financing above the breaking point calculated in (1).

10-15 LG **4,5,6** **Integrative—WACC, WMCC, and IOS** Cartwell Products has compiled the data given in the following table relative to the current costs of its three basic sources of external capital—long-term debt, preferred stock, and common stock equity—for various ranges of new financing.

Source of capital	Range of new financing	After-tax cost
Long-term debt	$0 to $320,000 $320,000 and above	6.% 8
Preferred stock	$0 and above	17
Common stock equity	$0 to $200,000 $200,000 and above	20 24

The company's capital structure weights used in calculating its weighted average cost of capital are as follows:

Source of capital	Weight
Long-term debt	40%
Preferred stock	20
Common stock equity	40
Total	100%

a. Determine the breaking points and ranges of *total* new financing associated with each source of capital.

b. Using the data developed in **a**, determine the breaking points (levels of *total* new financing) at which the firm's weighted average cost of capital will change.

c. Calculate the weighted average cost of capital for each range of total new financing found in **b**. (*Hint:* There are three ranges.)

d. Using the results of **c** along with the following information on the available investment opportunities, draw the firm's weighted marginal cost of capital (WMCC) schedule and investment opportunities schedule (IOS) on the same set of total new financing or investment (*x*-axis)–weighted average cost of capital and IRR (*y*-axis) axes.

Investment opportunity	Internal rate of return (IRR)	Initial investment
A	19%	$200,000
B	15	300,000
C	22	100,000
D	14	600,000
E	23	200,000
F	13	100,000
G	21	300,000
H	17	100,000
I	16	400,000

e. Which, if any, of the available investments would you recommend that the firm accept? Explain your answer.

Chapter 10 Case Making Star Products' financing/investment decision

Star Products Company is a growing manufacturer of automobile accessories whose stock is actively traded on the over-the-counter exchange. During 1994 the Dallas-based company experienced sharp increases in both sales and earnings. Because of this recent growth, Melissa Jen, the company's treasurer, wants to make sure that available funds are being used to their fullest. Management has set a policy to maintain the current capital structure proportions of 30 percent long-term debt, 10 percent preferred stock, and 60 percent common stock equity for at least the next three years. The firm is in the 40 percent tax bracket.

Star's division and product managers have presented several competing investment opportunities to Ms. Jen. However, since funds are limited, choices must be made of which projects to accept. The investment opportunities schedule (IOS) is given below.

INVESTMENT OPPORTUNITIES SCHEDULE (IOS) FOR STAR PRODUCTS COMPANY

Investment opportunity	Rate of return	Initial investment
A	15%	$400,000
B	22	200,000
C	25	700,000
D	23	400,000
E	17	500,000
F	19	600,000
G	14	500,000

To estimate the firm's weighted average cost of capital (WACC), Ms. Jen contacted a leading investment banking firm, which provided the financing cost data given below.

Financing cost data
Star Products Company

Long-term debt: The firm can raise $450,000 of additional debt by selling fifteen-year, $1,000, 9 percent coupon interest rate bonds that pay annual interest. It expects to net $960 per bond after flotation costs. Any debt in excess of $450,000 will have a before-tax cost, k_d, of 13 percent.

Preferred stock: Preferred stock, regardless of the amount sold, can be issued with a $70 par value, 14 percent annual dividend rate, and will net $65 per share after flotation costs.

Common stock equity: The firm expects dividends and earnings per share to be $.96 and $3.20, respectively, in 1995 and to continue to grow at a constant rate of 11 percent per year. The firm's stock currently sells for $12 per share. Star expects to have $1,500,000 of retained earnings available in the coming year. Once the retained earnings have been exhausted, the firm can raise additional funds by selling new common stock, netting $9 per share after flotation costs.

Required

a. Calculate the cost of each source of financing, as specified below:
  (1) Long-term debt, first \$450,000
  (2) Long-term debt, greater than \$450,000
  (3) Preferred stock, all amounts
  (4) Common stock equity, first \$1,500,000
  (5) Common stock equity, greater than \$1,500,000

b. Find the breaking points associated with each source of capital, and use them to specify each of the ranges of total new financing over which the firm's weighted average cost of capital (WACC) remains constant.

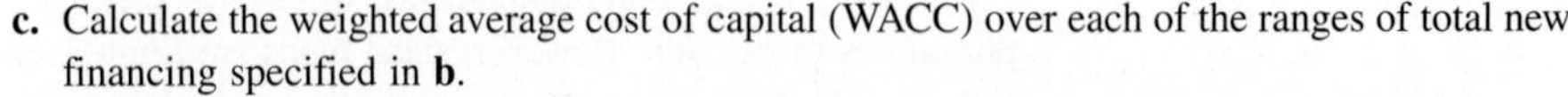

c. Calculate the weighted average cost of capital (WACC) over each of the ranges of total new financing specified in **b**.

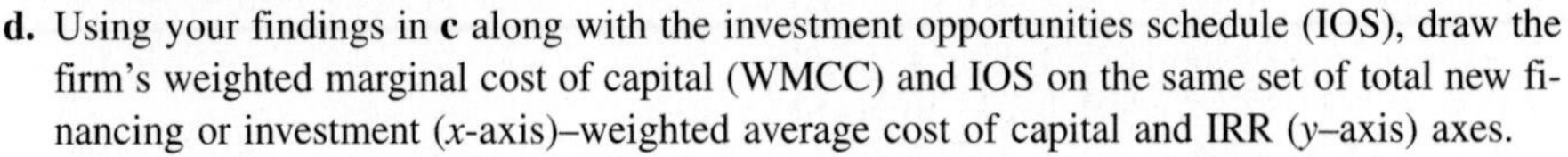

d. Using your findings in **c** along with the investment opportunities schedule (IOS), draw the firm's weighted marginal cost of capital (WMCC) and IOS on the same set of total new financing or investment (*x*-axis)–weighted average cost of capital and IRR (*y*–axis) axes.

e. Which, if any, of the available investments would you recommend that the firm accept? Explain your answer.

chapter 11

Leverage and capital structure

LEARNING GOALS

 Discuss the role of breakeven analysis, algebraic and graphic determination of the operating breakeven point, and the effect of changing costs on it.

 Understand the concepts, measurement, and behavior of operating, financial, and total leverage and the relationship between them.

 Describe the basic types of capital, external assessment of capital structure, capital structure of non-U.S. firms, and capital structure theory in terms of tax benefits, probability of bankruptcy, agency costs imposed by lenders, and asymmetric information.

 Explain the optimal capital structure using a graphic view of the firm's debt, equity, and weighted average cost of capital functions, along with a modified form of the zero growth valuation model.

 Discuss the graphic presentation, risk considerations, and basic shortcomings of using the EBIT–EPS approach to comparing alternative capital structures.

 Review the procedures for linking the return and risk associated with alternative capital structures to market value to select the best capital structure and other important capital structure considerations.

In 1991 I led a group of investors in purchasing EXPRESSIONS, Inc. using a leveraged buyout (LBO), a technique in which an acquisition is financed mostly with debt. This 15-year-old company is both a manufacturer and a retailer of customized upholstered furniture, producing about 70 percent of the products that it sells through a national network of franchised and company-owned retail stores. In both businesses, total leverage—using fixed operating and financial costs to increase returns—significantly affects our bottom line. Our retail operations demonstrate clearly the importance of operating leverage, while our acquisition strategy demonstrates financial leverage and its effect on capital structure.

When we acquired EXPRESSIONS, after-tax earnings were about $1 million a year. Although after-tax earnings dropped to about $500,000 in year one, we believe that the company improved. Operating and financial leverage produced a significantly higher level of earnings before interest, taxes, depreciation, and amortization (EBITDA)—about $2.5 million versus an average of $1.8 million in the prior two years. EBITDA, which tells more about our true operational earning power—cash flow generation—was more important to investors than after-tax earnings.

Our retail business demonstrates the effect of operating leverage on EXPRES-

SIONS. When planning for new stores, we assume that a store must at least break even in year one. Our typical store has approximately $150,000 to $180,000 in fixed expenses, items such as rent, insurance, and utilities that don't vary with volume but must be paid whether sales are $500 or $5 million. Most other expenses such as advertising, sales commissions, and local delivery are variable and average 23% of sales. To break even, a proposed new store with $150,000 in fixed expenses needs sales of about $575,000. When sales are above or below break-even, our high fixed costs result in a much greater than proportional increase or decrease in operating profits. If sales increase 50 percent, from $575,000 (where operating profit is slightly over $5,000) to $862,500, operating profit increases by nearly 1,500%!

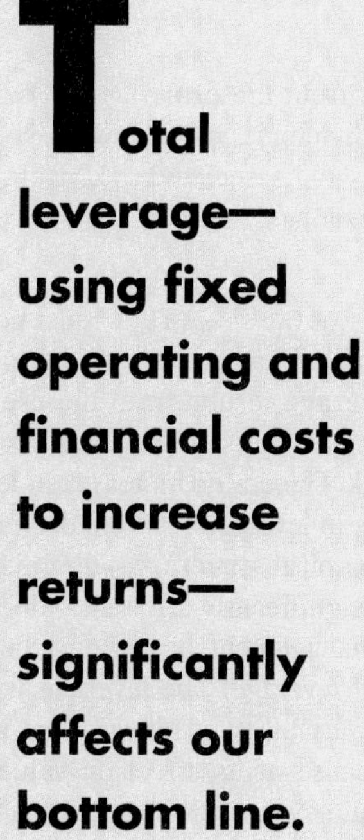
Total leverage—using fixed operating and financial costs to increase returns—significantly affects our bottom line.

Financial leverage definitely shaped our acquisition financing strategy. When we bought the company, its debt/equity ratio was low, just over 40%. We set our target capital structure—the mix of long-term debt and equity—on the basis of the debt level supported by historic and projected EBITDA. At closing, the debt/equity ratio was about 90%, extremely high by industry standards but not unusual for an LBO.

There is no absolute number that defines whether financial leverage is too high. The key is *the relationship of EBITDA to fixed financial costs and future capital investment requirements.* Comparing our leverage to industry standards gives an inaccurate picture of our financial condition, since our operational and cash flow characteristics are quite different; our retail sales return is well above the industry norm, and franchisees finance most capital expenditures. After the acquisition our total long-term debt was about $6 million, and our interest charge was about $800,000. On the basis of historical EBITDA of about $1.8 million, we had interest coverage of over two times, which rose to over three times in our first year of ownership. By increasing the debt in our capital structure, we increased the earnings available to equity owners at a much higher rate than the corresponding increases in EBITDA.

After receiving a B.A. in Economics from Cornell University and a J.D. from Columbia Law School, Kenneth Kwit practiced corporate law for about 12 years and then served as Vice President and General Counsel of Norton Simon, Inc., where he was responsible for over $1 billion of acquisitions. Before becoming part-owner and CEO of EXPRESSIONS in 1992, he was CEO of two high-growth consumer products companies, including the largest publicly held winery in the United States.

Leverage

Leverage results from the firm's use of fixed operating and financial (interest and preferred stock dividend) costs. How do you suppose the level of fixed costs affects the firm's returns and associated risk? Before reading on, spend a few moments answering this question.

leverage
Results from the use of fixed-cost assets or funds to magnify returns to the firm's owners.

capital structure
The mix of long-term debt and equity maintained by the firm.

LEVERAGE AND CAPITAL STRUCTURE ARE CLOSELY RELATED CONCEPTS THAT ARE LINKED to cost of capital (Chapter 10) and therefore capital budgeting decisions (Chapters 8 and 9). **Leverage** results from the use of fixed-cost assets or funds to magnify returns to the firm's owners. Changes in leverage result in changes in level of return and associated risk. Generally, increases in leverage result in increased return and risk, whereas decreases in leverage result in decreased return and risk. The amount of leverage in the firm's **capital structure**—the mix of long-term debt and equity maintained by the firm—can significantly affect its value by affecting return and risk. Unlike some causes of risk, management has almost complete control over the risk introduced through the use of leverage. The levels of fixed-cost assets or funds that management selects affect the variability of returns, that is, risk, which is therefore controllable by management. Because of its effect on value, the financial manager must understand how to measure and evaluate leverage, particularly when attempting to create the best capital structure.

The three basic types of leverage can best be defined with reference to the firm's income statement. In the general income statement format in Table 11.1, the portions related to the firm's operating leverage, financial leverage, and total leverage are clearly labeled. *Operating leverage* is concerned with the relationship between the firm's sales revenue and its earnings before interest and taxes, or EBIT (EBIT is a descriptive label for *operating profits*). *Financial leverage* is concerned with the relationship between the firm's earnings before interest and taxes (EBIT) and its common stock earnings per share (EPS). *Total leverage* is concerned with the relationship between the firm's sales revenue and earnings per share (EPS). It is important to recognize that the

TABLE 11.1

GENERAL INCOME STATEMENT FORMAT AND TYPES OF LEVERAGE

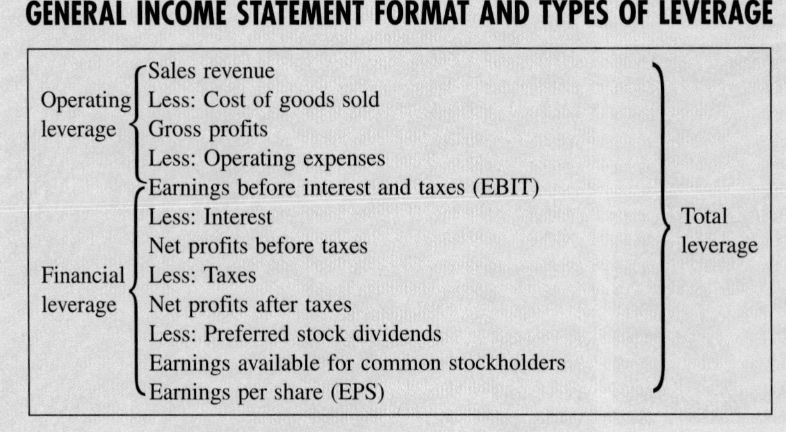

Operating leverage	Sales revenue	Total leverage
	Less: Cost of goods sold	
	Gross profits	
	Less: Operating expenses	
	Earnings before interest and taxes (EBIT)	
Financial leverage	Less: Interest	
	Net profits before taxes	
	Less: Taxes	
	Net profits after taxes	
	Less: Preferred stock dividends	
	Earnings available for common stockholders	
	Earnings per share (EPS)	

demonstrations of these three forms of leverage that follow are conceptual in nature and that the measures presented are *not* routinely used by financial managers for decision-making purposes. But first, before we examine the three leverage concepts separately in detail, we will use breakeven analysis to demonstrate the effects of fixed costs on the firm's operations.

Breakeven analysis

breakeven analysis (cost-volume-profit analysis)
Used (1) to determine the level of operations necessary to cover all operating costs and (2) to evaluate the profitability associated with various levels of sales.

operating breakeven point
The level of sales necessary to cover all operating costs; the point at which EBIT = $0.

Breakeven analysis, which is sometimes called **cost-volume-profit analysis,** is used by the firm (1) to determine the level of operations necessary to cover all operating costs and (2) to evaluate the profitability associated with various levels of sales. The firm's **operating breakeven point** is the level of sales necessary to cover all operating costs. At the operating breakeven point, earnings before interest and taxes, or EBIT, equals zero.[1] The first step in finding the operating breakeven point is to divide the cost of goods sold and operating expenses into fixed and variable operating costs. (*Fixed costs* are a function of time, not sales volume, and are typically contractual; rent, for example, is a fixed cost. *Variable costs* vary directly with sales and are a function of volume, not time; shipping costs, for example, are a variable cost.)[2] The top portion of Table 11.1 can then be recast as shown in the left-hand side of Table 11.2. By using this framework the firm's operating breakeven point can be developed and evaluated.

THE ALGEBRAIC APPROACH

Using the following variables, we can represent the operating portion of the firm's income statement as shown in the right-hand portion of Table 11.2.

$$\begin{aligned} P &= \text{sale price per unit} \\ Q &= \text{sales quantity in units} \\ FC &= \text{fixed operating cost per period} \\ VC &= \text{variable operating cost per unit} \end{aligned}$$

TABLE 11.2

OPERATING LEVERAGE, COSTS, AND BREAKEVEN ANALYSIS

	Item	Algebraic representation
Operating leverage	Sales revenue	$(P \times Q)$
	Less: Fixed operating costs	$-\ FC$
	Less: Variable operating costs	$-(VC \times Q)$
	Earnings before interest and taxes	EBIT

[1]Quite often, the breakeven point is calculated so that it represents the point at which *all operating and financial costs* are covered. Our concern in this chapter is not with this overall breakeven point.

[2]Some costs, commonly called *semifixed* or *semivariable*, are partly fixed and partly variable. One example would be sales commissions that are fixed for a certain volume of sales and then increase to higher levels for higher volumes. For convenience and clarity we assume that all costs can be classified as either fixed or variable.

Rewriting the algebraic calculations in Table 11.2 as a formula for earnings before interest and taxes yields Equation 11.1:

$$\text{EBIT} = (P \times Q) - FC - (VC \times Q) \tag{11.1}$$

Simplifying Equation 11.1 yields

$$\text{EBIT} = Q \times (P - VC) - FC \tag{11.2}$$

As was noted above, the operating breakeven point is the level of sales at which all fixed and variable operating costs are covered—that is, the level at which EBIT equals zero. Setting EBIT equal to zero and solving Equation 11.2 for Q yields

$$Q = \frac{FC}{P - VC} \tag{11.3}$$

Q is the firm's operating breakeven point. Let us look at an example.

EXAMPLE

Assume that Cheryl's Posters, a small poster retailer, has fixed operating costs of \$2,500, its sale price per unit (poster) is \$10, and its variable operating cost per unit is \$5. Applying Equation 11.3 to these data yields

$$Q = \frac{\$2{,}500}{\$10 - \$5} = \frac{\$2{,}500}{\$5} = 500 \text{ units}$$

At sales of 500 units the firm's EBIT should just equal zero. ■

In the example the firm will have positive EBIT for sales greater than 500 units and negative EBIT, or a loss, for sales less than 500 units. We can confirm this by substituting values above and below 500 units, along with the other values given, into Equation 11.1.

THE GRAPHIC APPROACH

Figure 11.1 presents in graph form the breakeven analysis of the data in the example above. The firm's operating breakeven point is the point at which its *total operating cost,* or the sum of its fixed and variable operating costs, equals sales revenue. At this point, EBIT equals zero. The figure shows that a loss occurs when the firm's sales are *below* the operating breakeven point. In other words, for sales less than 500 units, total operating costs exceed sales revenue, and EBIT is less than zero. For sales levels *above* the breakeven point of 500 units, sales revenue exceeds total operating costs, and EBIT is greater than zero.

CONCEPT IN PRACTICE

How Can Zenith Labs Make Any Money?

Over the next five years, brand-name pharmaceuticals—like SmithKline Beecham PLC's ulcer treatment, *Tagamet,* and Bristol-Myers Squibb Company's antihypertensive

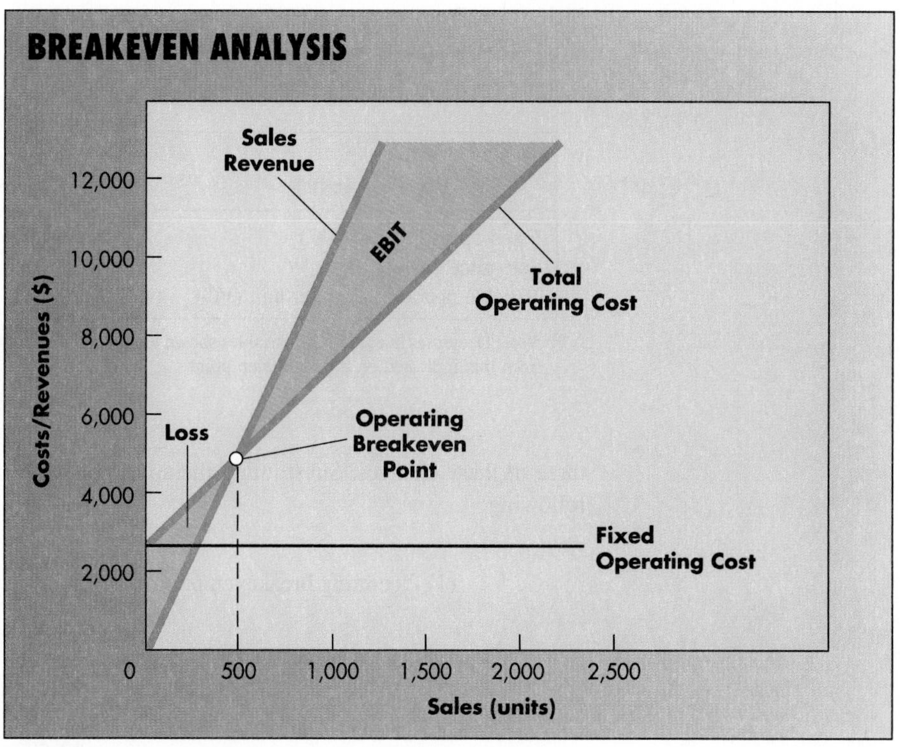

FIGURE 11.1
Graphic operating breakeven analysis

drug, *Capoten*—worth nearly $20 billion in annual sales are expected to go off-patent. These brand-name drugs will be competing against their generic equivalents, which sell for about one-half the brand-name price to capture around one-third of total market share for a particular drug. Given the significantly lower selling price and unit volume of new generic compounds, you might expect generic drug manufacturers like Zenith Laboratories, Inc., to face dismal earnings prospects.

Not so! By selling two-thirds fewer units at one-half the unit price of name brands, generics manufacturers will still be awash in cash because they incur zero research and development costs. So small sales volumes, trim profit margins, and lower fixed costs can provide healthy profits for these firms.

CHANGING COSTS AND THE OPERATING BREAKEVEN POINT

A firm's operating breakeven point is sensitive to a number of variables: fixed operating costs (FC), the sale price per unit (P), and the variable operating cost per unit (VC). The effects of increases or decreases in each of these variables can be readily assessed by referring to Equation 11.3. The sensitivity of the breakeven sales volume (Q) to an *increase* in each of these variables is summarized in Table 11.3. As might be expected, the table indicates that an increase in cost (FC or VC) tends to increase the operating breakeven point, whereas an increase in the sale price per unit (P) will decrease the operating breakeven point.

EXAMPLE

Assume that Cheryl's Posters wishes to evaluate the impact of (1) increasing fixed operating costs to $3,000, (2) increasing the sale price per unit to $12.50, (3) increasing the variable operating cost per unit to $7.50, and (4) simultaneously implementing all

TABLE 11.3

SENSITIVITY OF OPERATING BREAKEVEN POINT TO INCREASES IN KEY BREAKEVEN VARIABLES

Increase in variable	Effect on operating breakeven point
Fixed operating cost (FC)	Increase
Sale price per unit (P)	Decrease
Variable operating cost per unit (VC)	Increase

Note: Decreases in each of the variables shown would have the opposite effect from that indicated on the breakeven point.

three of these changes. Substituting the appropriate data into Equation 11.3 yields the following:

$$\text{(1) Operating breakeven point} = \frac{\$3{,}000}{\$10 - \$5} = 600 \text{ units}$$

$$\text{(2) Operating breakeven point} = \frac{\$2{,}500}{\$12.50 - \$5} = 333\tfrac{1}{3} \text{ units}$$

$$\text{(3) Operating breakeven point} = \frac{\$2{,}500}{\$10 - \$7.50} = 1{,}000 \text{ units}$$

$$\text{(4) Operating breakeven point} = \frac{\$3{,}000}{\$12.50 - \$7.50} = 600 \text{ units}$$

Comparing the resulting operating breakeven points to the initial value of 500 units, we can see that, as noted in Table 11.3, the cost increases (actions 1 and 3) raise the breakeven point (600 units and 1,000 units, respectively), whereas the revenue increase (action 2) lowers the breakeven point to 333⅓ units. The combined effect of increasing all three variables (action 4) results in an increased breakeven point of 600 units. ■

Operating leverage

operating leverage
The potential use of *fixed operating costs* to magnify the effects of changes in sales on the firm's earnings before interest and taxes (EBIT).

Operating leverage results from the existence of *fixed operating costs* in the firm's income stream. Using the structure presented in Table 11.2, we can define **operating leverage** as the potential use of *fixed operating costs* to magnify the effects of changes in sales on the firm's earnings before interest and taxes (EBIT). The following example illustrates how operating leverage works.

EXAMPLE

Using the data presented earlier for Cheryl's Posters (sale price, P = \$10 per unit; variable operating cost, VC = \$5 per unit; fixed operating cost, FC = \$2,500), Figure 11.2 presents the operating breakeven chart originally shown in Figure 11.1. The additional notations on the chart indicate that as the firm's sales increase from 1,000 to 1,500 units (Q_1 to Q_2), its EBIT increases from \$2,500 to \$5,000 (EBIT_1 to EBIT_2). In other

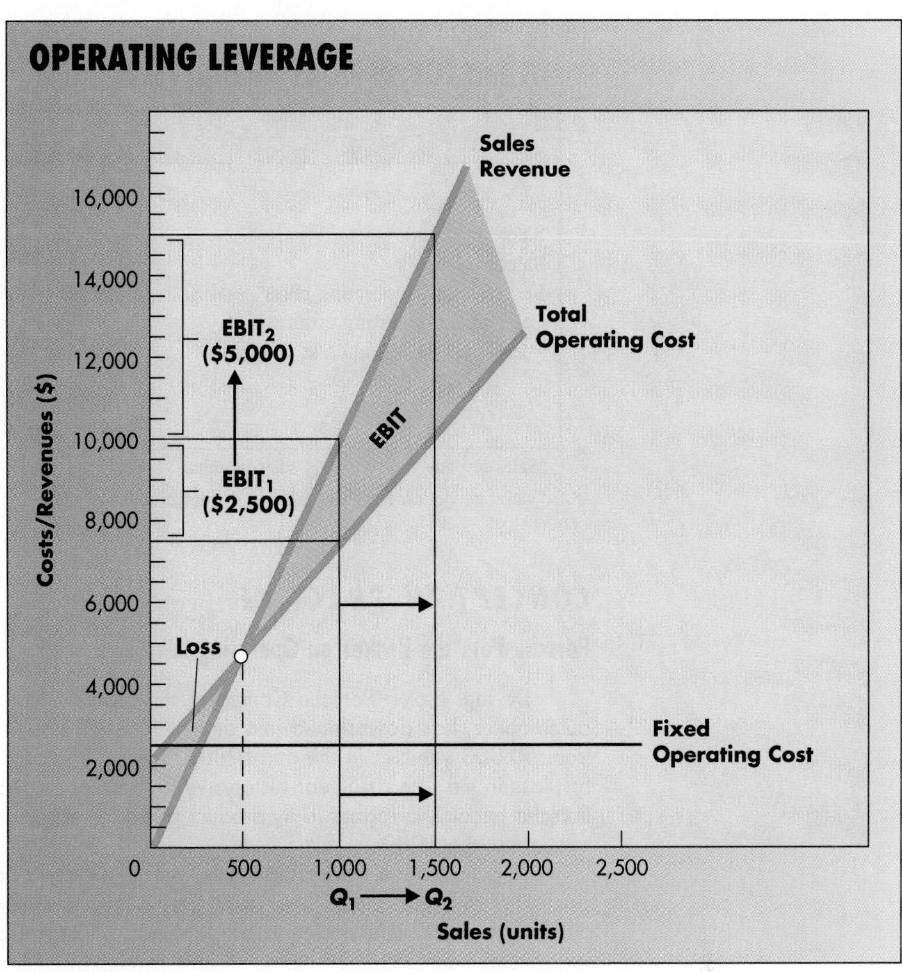

FIGURE 11.2
Breakeven analysis and operating leverage

words, a 50 percent increase in sales (1,000 to 1,500 units) results in a 100 percent increase in EBIT. Table 11.4 includes the data for Figure 11.2 as well as relevant data for a 500-unit sales level. We can illustrate two cases using the 1,000-unit sales level as a reference point.

Case 1 A 50 percent *increase* in sales (from 1,000 to 1,500 units) results in a 100 percent *increase* in earnings before interest and taxes (from \$2,500 to \$5,000).

Case 2 A 50 percent *decrease* in sales (from 1,000 to 500 units) results in a 100 percent *decrease* in earnings before interest and taxes (from \$2,500 to \$0). ■

From the above example we see that operating leverage works in both directions. When a firm has fixed operating costs, operating leverage is present. An increase in sales results in a more-than-proportional increase in earnings before interest and taxes; a decrease in sales results in a more-than-proportional decrease in earnings before interest and taxes.

TABLE 11.4

THE EBIT FOR VARIOUS SALES LEVELS

		Case 2	Case 1
		−50%	+50%
Sales (in units)	500	1,000	1,500
Sales revenue[a]	$5,000	$10,000	$15,000
Less: Variable operating costs[b]	2,500	5,000	7,500
Less: Fixed operating costs	2,500	2,500	2,500
Earnings before interest and taxes (EBIT)	$ 0	$ 2,500	$ 5,000
		−100%	+100%

[a]Sales revenue = $10/unit × sales in units.

[b]Variable operating costs = $5/unit × sales in units.

CONCEPT IN PRACTICE

Porsche Puts the Brakes on Operating Leverage

Dr. Ing. h.c. F. Porsche Company, the German manufacturer of Porsche automobiles, has downshifted into difficult times. Worldwide annual sales have skidded from 50,000 vehicles in the mid-1980s to an estimated 15,000 cars in 1993 for the first loss in the firm's 45-year history. What happened to the King of the Road? Porsche became arrogant in its product pricing, and operating expenses soared throughout the 1980s.

To get back on track, Porsche is cutting its fixed operating expenses to reduce its operating leverage and its breakeven point. The company has dropped off the highly visible, expensive auto racing circuit, trimmed personnel by 25 percent, formed teams for development and engineering of new production models, and reassigned production work from outside manufacturers to in-house staff. Without such swift, severe moves to reduce costs, Porsche might not survive as an independent manufacturer of fine automobiles.

MEASURING THE DEGREE OF OPERATING LEVERAGE (DOL)

degree of operating leverage (DOL)
The numerical measure of the firm's operating leverage.

The **degree of operating leverage (DOL)** is the numerical measure of the firm's operating leverage. It can be derived by using the following equation:[3]

$$\text{DOL} = \frac{\text{percentage change in EBIT}}{\text{percentage change in sales}} \tag{11.4}$$

Whenever the percentage change in EBIT resulting from a given percentage change in sales is greater than the percentage change in sales, operating leverage exists. This means that as long as DOL is greater than 1, there is operating leverage.

[3]The degree of operating leverage also depends on the base level of sales used as a point of reference. The closer the base sales level used is to the operating breakeven point, the greater the operating leverage. *Comparison of the degree of operating leverage of two firms is valid only when the base level of sales used for each firm is the same.*

EXAMPLE

Applying Equation 11.4 to cases 1 and 2 in Table 11.4 yields the following results:[4]

$$\text{Case 1: } \frac{+\ 100\%}{+\ 50\%} = 2.0$$

$$\text{Case 2: } \frac{-\ 100\%}{-\ 50\%} = 2.0$$

Since the result is greater than 1, operating leverage exists. For a given base level of sales, the higher the value resulting from applying Equation 11.4, the greater the degree of operating leverage. ■

A more direct formula for calculating the degree of operating leverage at a base sales level, Q, is shown in Equation 11.5, using the symbols given earlier.[5]

$$\text{DOL at base sales level } Q = \frac{Q \times (P - VC)}{Q \times (P - VC) - FC} \qquad (11.5)$$

EXAMPLE

Substituting $Q = 1{,}000$, $P = \$10$, $VC = \$5$, and $FC = \$2{,}500$ into Equation 11.5 yields the following result:

$$\text{DOL at 1,000 units} = \frac{1{,}000 \times (\$10 - \$5)}{1{,}000 \times (\$10 - \$5) - \$2{,}500} = \frac{\$5{,}000}{\$2{,}500} = 2.0$$

The use of the formula results in the same value for DOL (2.0) as that found by using Table 11.4 and Equation 11.4.[6] ■

FIXED COSTS AND OPERATING LEVERAGE

Changes in fixed operating costs affect operating leverage significantly. Firms can sometimes incur fixed operating costs rather than variable operating costs and at other times may be able to substitute one type of cost for the other. For example, a firm could make fixed-dollar lease payments rather than payments equal to a specified percentage of sales, or it could compensate sales representatives with a fixed salary and bonus rather than on a pure percent-of-sales commission basis. The effects of changes in fixed operating costs on operating leverage can best be illustrated by continuing our example.

---

[4]Because the concept of leverage is *linear,* positive and negative changes of equal magnitude will always result in equal degrees of leverage when the same base sales level is used as a point of reference. This relationship holds for all types of leverage discussed in this chapter.

[5]Technically, the formula for DOL given in Equation 11.5 should include absolute value signs because it is possible to get a negative DOL when the EBIT for the base sales level is negative. Since we assume that the EBIT for the base level of sales is positive, the absolute value signs are not included.

[6]When total sales in dollars—instead of unit sales—are available, the following equation in which TR = dollar level of base sales and TVC = total variable operating costs in dollars can be used:

$$\text{DOL at base dollar sales } TR = \frac{TR - TVC}{TR - TVC - FC}$$

This formula is especially useful for finding the DOL for multiproduct firms. It should be clear that since in the case of a single-product firm, $TR = P \times Q$ and $TVC = VC \times Q$, substitution of these values into Equation 11.5 results in the equation given here.

EXAMPLE

Assume that Cheryl's Posters is able to exchange a portion of its variable operating costs (by eliminating sales commissions) for fixed operating costs (by increasing sales salaries). This exchange results in a reduction in the variable operating cost per unit from \$5 to \$4.50 and an increase in the fixed operating costs from \$2,500 to \$3,000. Table 11.5 presents an analysis similar to that given in Table 11.4 using these new costs. Although the EBIT of \$2,500 at the 1,000-unit sales level is the same as before the shift in operating cost structure, Table 11.5 shows that by shifting to greater fixed operating costs, the firm has increased its operating leverage.

With the substitution of the appropriate values into Equation 11.5, the degree of operating leverage at the 1,000-unit base level of sales becomes

$$\text{DOL at 1,000 units} = \frac{1{,}000 \times (\$10 - \$4.50)}{1{,}000 \times (\$10 - \$4.50) - \$3{,}000} = \frac{\$5{,}500}{\$2{,}500} = 2.2$$

By comparing this value to the DOL of 2.0 before the shift to more fixed costs, it is clear that the higher the firm's fixed operating costs relative to variable operating costs, the greater the degree of operating leverage. ■

Financial leverage

financial leverage
The potential use of *fixed financial costs* to magnify the effects of changes in earning before interest and taxes (EBIT) on the firm's earnings per share (EPS).

Financial leverage results from the presence of *fixed financial costs* in the firm's income stream. Using the framework in Table 11.1, we can define **financial leverage** as the potential use of *fixed financial costs* to magnify the effects of changes in earnings before interest and taxes (EBIT) on the firm's earnings per share (EPS). The two fixed financial costs that may be found on the firm's income statement are (1) interest on debt and (2) preferred stock dividends. These charges must be paid regardless of the amount of EBIT available to pay them.[7] The following example illustrates how financial leverage works.

TABLE 11.5

OPERATING LEVERAGE AND INCREASED FIXED COSTS

	Case 2		Case 1
	−50%		+50%
Sales (in units)	500	1,000	1,500
Sales revenue[a]	\$5,000	\$10,000	\$15,000
Less: Variable operating costs[b]	2,250	4,500	6,750
Less: Fixed operating costs	3,000	3,000	2,500
Earnings before interest and taxes (EBIT)	−\$250	\$ 2,500	\$ 5,250
	−110%		+110%

[a]Sales revenue was calculated as indicated in Table 11.4.
[b]Variable operating costs = \$4.50/unit × sales in units.

[7]As was noted in Chapter 4, although preferred stock dividends can be "passed" (not paid) at the option of the firm's directors, it is generally believed that the payment of such dividends is necessary. *This text therefore treats the preferred stock dividend as if it were a contractual obligation, not only to be paid as a fixed amount, but also to be paid as scheduled.* Although failure to pay preferred dividends cannot force the firm into bankruptcy, it increases the common stockholders' risk because they cannot be paid dividends until the claims of preferred stockholders are satisfied.

EXAMPLE

Chen Foods, a small Oriental food company, expects earnings before interest and taxes of $10,000 in the current year. It has a $20,000 bond with a 10 percent (annual) coupon rate of interest and an issue of 600 shares of $4 (annual dividend per share) preferred stock outstanding. It also has 1,000 shares of common stock outstanding. The annual interest on the bond issue is $2,000 (.10 × $20,000). The annual dividends on the preferred stock are $2,400 ($4.00/share × 600 shares). Table 11.6 presents the earnings per share corresponding to levels of earnings before interest and taxes of $6,000, $10,000, and $14,000, assuming that the firm is in the 40 percent tax bracket. Two situations are illustrated in the table.

Case 1 A 40 percent *increase* in EBIT (from $10,000 to $14,000) results in a 100 percent *increase* in earnings per share (from $2.40 to $4.80).

Case 2 A 40 percent *decrease* in EBIT (from $10,000 to $6,000) results in a 100 percent *decrease* in earnings per share (from $2.40 to $0). ■

The effect of financial leverage is such that an increase in the firm's EBIT results in a more-than-proportional increase in the firm's earnings per share, whereas a decrease in the firm's EBIT results in a more-than-proportional decrease in EPS.

MEASURING THE DEGREE OF FINANCIAL LEVERAGE (DFL)

degree of financial leverage (DFL)
The numerical measure of the firm's financial leverage.

The **degree of financial leverage (DFL)** is the numerical measure of the firm's financial leverage. It can be computed in a fashion similar to that used to measure the degree of operating leverage. The following equation presents one approach for obtaining the DFL.[8]

TABLE 11.6

THE EPS FOR VARIOUS EBIT LEVELS

		Case 2		Case 1	
		−40%		+40%	
EBIT	$6,000		$10,000		$14,000
Less: Interest (I)	2,000		2,000		2,000
Net profits before taxes	$4,000		$ 8,000		$12,000
Less: Taxes (T = .40)	1,600		3,200		4,800
Net profits after taxes	$2,400		$ 4,800		$ 7,200
Less: Preferred stock dividends (PD)	2,400		2,400		2,400
Earnings available for common (EAC)	$ 0		$ 2,400		$ 4,800
Earnings per share (EPS)	$\frac{\$0}{1,000} = \$0$		$\frac{\$2,400}{1,000} = \$2.40$		$\frac{\$4,800}{1,000} = \$4.80$
		−100%		+100%	

[8]This approach is valid only when the base level of EBIT used to calculate and compare these values is the same. In other words, *the base level of EBIT must be held constant to compare the financial leverage associated with different levels of fixed financial costs.*

$$\text{DFL} = \frac{\text{percentage change in EPS}}{\text{percentage change in EBIT}} \tag{11.6}$$

Whenever the percentage change in EPS resulting from a given percentage change in EBIT is greater than the percentage change in EBIT, financial leverage exists. This means that whenever DFL is greater than 1, there is financial leverage.

EXAMPLE

Applying Equation 11.6 to cases 1 and 2 in Table 11.6 yields

$$\text{Case 1:} \quad \frac{+\,100\%}{+\,40\%} = 2.5$$

$$\text{Case 2:} \quad \frac{-100\%}{-\,40\%} = 2.5$$

In both cases the quotient is greater than 1, and financial leverage exists. The higher this value, the greater the degree of financial leverage. ■

A more direct formula for calculating the degree of financial leverage at a base level of EBIT is given by Equation 11.7, using the notation from Table 11.6.[9] Note that in the denominator the term $\frac{1}{1-T}$ converts the after-tax preferred stock dividend to a before-tax amount for consistency with the other terms in the equation.

$$\text{DFL at base level EBIT} = \frac{\text{EBIT}}{\text{EBIT} - I - \left(PD \times \frac{1}{1-T}\right)} \tag{11.7}$$

EXAMPLE

Substituting EBIT = \$10,000, I = \$2,000, PD = \$2,400, and the tax rate (T = .40) into Equation 11.7 yields the following result:

$$\text{DFL at \$10,000 EBIT} = \frac{\$10{,}000}{\$10{,}000 - \$2{,}000 - \left(\$2{,}400 \times \frac{1}{1-.40}\right)}$$

$$= \frac{\$10{,}000}{\$4{,}000} = 2.5$$

Notice that the formula given in Equation 11.7 provides a more direct method for calculating the degree of financial leverage than the approach illustrated by using Table 11.6 and Equation 11.6. ■

Total leverage: The combined effect

The combined effect of operating and financial leverage on the firm's risk can be assessed by using a framework similar to that used to develop the individual concepts of leverage. This combined effect, or **total leverage,** can be defined as the potential use of *fixed costs, both operating and financial,* to magnify the effect of changes in sales on the firm's earnings per share (EPS). Total leverage can therefore be viewed as the total impact of the fixed costs in the firm's operating and financial structure.

total leverage
The potential use of *fixed costs, both operating and financial,* to magnify the effect of changes in sales on the firm's earnings per share (EPS).

[9] By using the formula for DFL in Equation 11.7, it is possible to get a negative value for the DFL if the EPS for the base level of EBIT is negative. Rather than show absolute value signs in the equation, it is instead assumed that the base-level EPS is positive.

EXAMPLE

Cables Inc., a computer cable manufacturer, expects sales of 20,000 units at $5 per unit in the coming year and must meet the following: variable operating costs of $2 per unit, fixed operating costs of $10,000, interest of $20,000, and preferred stock dividends of $12,000. The firm is in the 40 percent tax bracket and has 5,000 shares of common stock outstanding. Table 11.7, on page 450, presents the levels of earnings per share (EPS) associated with the expected sales of 20,000 units and with sales of 30,000 units.

The table illustrates that as a result of a 50 percent increase in sales (from 20,000 to 30,000 units), the firm would experience a 300 percent increase in earnings per share (from $1.20 to $4.80). Although not shown in the table, a 50 percent decrease in sales would, conversely, result in a 300 percent decrease in earnings per share. The linear nature of the leverage relationship accounts for the fact that sales changes of equal magnitude in opposite directions result in earnings-per-share changes of equal magnitude in the corresponding direction. At this point it should be clear that whenever a firm has fixed costs—operating or financial—in its structure, total leverage will exist. ■

MEASURING THE DEGREE OF TOTAL LEVERAGE (DTL)

degree of total leverage (DTL)
The numerical measure of the firm's total leverage.

The **degree of total leverage (DTL)** is the numerical measure of the firm's total leverage. It can be obtained in a fashion similar to that used to measure operating and financial leverage. The following equation presents one approach for measuring DTL.[10]

$$\text{DTL} = \frac{\text{percentage change in EPS}}{\text{percentage change in sales}} \tag{11.8}$$

Whenever the percentage change in EPS resulting from a given percentage change in sales is greater than the percentage change in sales, total leverage exists. This means that as long as the DTL is greater than 1, there is total leverage.

EXAMPLE

Applying Equation 11.8 to the data in Table 11.7 yields

$$\text{DTL} = \frac{+300\%}{+\ 50\%} = 6.0$$

Since this result is greater than 1, total leverage exists. The higher the value, the greater the degree of total leverage. ■

A more direct formula for calculating the degree of total leverage at a given base level of sales, Q, is given by Equation 11.9,[11] which uses the same notation presented earlier:

$$\text{DTL at base sales level } Q = \frac{Q \times (P - VC)}{Q \times (P - VC) - FC - I - \left(PD \times \dfrac{1}{1-T}\right)} \tag{11.9}$$

[10]This approach is valid only when the base level of sales used to calculate and compare these values is the same. In other words, *the base level of sales must be held constant to compare the total leverage associated with different levels of fixed costs.*

[11]By using the formula for DTL in Equation 11.9, it is possible to get a negative value for the DTL if the EPS for the base level of sales is negative. For our purposes, rather than show absolute value signs in the equation, we instead assume that the base-level EPS is positive.

TABLE 11.7

THE TOTAL LEVERAGE EFFECT

	+50%	
Sales (in units)	20,000	30,000
Sales revenue[a]	$100,000	$150,000
Less: Variable operating costs[b]	40,000	60,000
Less: Fixed operating costs	10,000	10,000
Earnings before interest and taxes (EBIT)	$ 50,000	$ 80,000
	+60%	
Less: Interest	20,000	20,000
Net profits before taxes	$ 30,000	$ 60,000
Less: Taxes (T = .40)	12,000	24,000
Net profits after taxes	$ 18,000	$ 36,000
Less: Preferred stock dividends	12,000	12,000
Earnings available for common	$ 6,000	$ 24,000
Earnings per share (EPS)	$\frac{\$6{,}000}{5{,}000} = \$1.20$	$\frac{\$24{,}000}{5{,}000} = \$4.80$
	+300%	

$$\text{DOL} = \frac{+60\%}{+50\%} = 1.2$$

$$\text{DFL} = \frac{+300\%}{+60\%} = 5.0$$

$$\text{DTL} = \frac{+300\%}{+50\%} = 6.0$$

[a] Sales revenue = \$5/unit × sales in units.

[b] Variable operating costs = \$2/unit × sales in units.

EXAMPLE

Substituting Q = 20,000, P = \$5, VC = \$2, FC = \$10,000, I = \$20,000, PD = \$12,000, and the tax rate (T = .40) into Equation 11.9 yields the following result:

DTL at 20,000 units

$$= \frac{20{,}000 \times (\$5 - \$2)}{20{,}000 \times (\$5 - \$2) - \$10{,}000 - \$20{,}000 - \left(\$12{,}000 \times \frac{1}{1 - .40}\right)}$$

$$= \frac{\$60{,}000}{\$10{,}000} = 6.0$$

Clearly, the formula used in Equation 11.9 provides a more direct method for calculating the degree of total leverage than the approach illustrated using Table 11.7 and Equation 11.8. ■

THE RELATIONSHIP OF OPERATING, FINANCIAL, AND TOTAL LEVERAGE

Total leverage reflects the combined impact of operating and financial leverage on the firm. High operating leverage and high financial leverage will cause total leverage to be high. The opposite will also be true. The relationship between operating leverage and financial leverage is *multiplicative* rather than *additive.* The relationship between the degree of total leverage (DTL) and the degrees of operating leverage (DOL) and financial leverage (DFL) is given by Equation 11.10.

$$\text{DTL} = \text{DOL} \times \text{DFL} \tag{11.10}$$

EXAMPLE

Substituting the values calculated for DOL and DFL, shown on the right-hand side of Table 11.7, into Equation 11.10 yields

$$DTL = 1.2 \times 5.0 = 6.0$$

The resulting degree of total leverage (6.0) is the same value as was calculated directly in the preceding examples. ■

CONCEPTS IN REVIEW

11-1 What is meant by the term *leverage*? How do operating leverage, financial leverage, and total leverage relate to the income statement?

11-2 What is the *operating breakeven point*? How do changes in fixed operating costs, the sale price per unit, and the variable operating cost per unit affect it?

11-3 What is meant by *operating leverage*? What causes it? How is the *degree of operating leverage (DOL)* measured?

11-4 What is meant by *financial leverage*? What causes it? How is the *degree of financial leverage (DFL)* measured?

11-5 What is the general relationship among operating leverage, financial leverage, and the total leverage of the firm? Do these types of leverage complement each other? Why or why not?

The firm's capital structure

The firm's optimal capital structure results from balancing the benefits and costs of debt financing to minimize its weighted average cost of capital. Assuming that a firm's after-tax operating earnings available to its debt and equity holders are constant, how does minimizing the weighted average cost of capital relate to its goal of owner wealth maximization? Spend a few moments answering this question before reading ahead.

CAPITAL STRUCTURE IS ONE OF THE MOST COMPLEX AREAS OF FINANCIAL DECISION MAKing due to its interrelationship with other financial decision variables.[12] To achieve the firm's goal of owner wealth maximization, the financial manager must be able to assess the firm's capital structure and understand its relationship to risk, return, and value. This section links together the concepts presented in Chapters 5, 6, 7, and 10 and the discussion of leverage in this chapter.

Types of capital

capital
The long-term funds of the firm; all items on the right-hand side of the firm's balance sheet, excluding current liabilities.

The term **capital** denotes the long-term funds of the firm. All of the items on the right-hand side of the firm's balance sheet, excluding current liabilities, are sources of capital. The following simplified balance sheet illustrates the basic breakdown of total capital into its two components—*debt capital* and *equity capital.*

[12]Of course, while capital structure is financially important, it, like many business decisions, is generally not as important as the firm's products or services. In a practical sense a firm can probably more readily increase its value by improving quality and reducing costs rather than fine-tuning its capital structure.

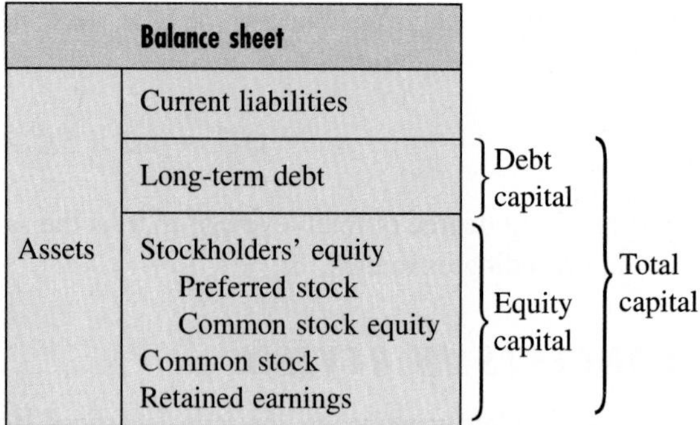

debt capital
All long-term borrowing incurred by the firm.

Debt capital includes all long-term borrowing incurred by the firm. The various types and characteristics of long-term debt are discussed in detail in Chapter 12. In Chapter 10 the cost of debt was found to be less than the cost of other forms of financing. The relative inexpensiveness of debt capital is due to the fact that the lenders take the least risk of any long-term contributors of capital. Their risk is less than that of others because (1) they have a higher priority of claim against any earnings or assets available for payment, (2) they have a far stronger legal pressure against the company to make payment than do preferred or common stockholders, and (3) the tax-deductibility of interest payments lowers the debt cost to the firm substantially.

equity capital
The long-term funds provided by the firm's owners, the stockholders.

Equity capital consists of the long-term funds provided by the firm's owners, the stockholders. Unlike borrowed funds that must be repaid at a specified future date, equity capital is expected to remain in the firm for an indefinite period of time. The two basic sources of equity capital are (1) preferred stock and (2) common stock equity, which includes common stock and retained earnings. As was demonstrated in Chapter 10, common stock is typically the most expensive form of equity, followed by retained earnings and preferred stock, respectively. The characteristics of common stock and retained earnings are discussed in Chapter 13; preferred stock is discussed further in Chapter 14.

Our concern here is the relationship between debt and equity capital. Key differences between these two types of capital, relative to voice in management, claims on income and assets, maturity, and tax treatment, are summarized in Table 11.8. It should be clear that due to its secondary position relative to debt, suppliers of equity capital take greater risk and therefore must be compensated with higher expected returns than suppliers of debt capital.

TABLE 11.8

KEY DIFFERENCES BETWEEN DEBT AND EQUITY CAPITAL

	Type of capital	
Characteristic	**Debt**	**Equity**
Voice in management[a]	No	Yes
Claims on income and assets	Senior to equity	Subordinate to debt
Maturity	Stated	None
Tax treatment	Interest deduction	No deduction

[a]In default, debtholders and preferred stockholders *may* receive a voice in management; otherwise, only common stockholders have voting rights.

External assessment of capital structure

Earlier it was shown that *financial leverage* results from the use of fixed-payment financing, such as debt and preferred stock, to magnify return and risk. Debt ratios, which measure, directly and indirectly, the firm's degree of financial leverage were presented in Chapter 4. The direct measures of the degree of indebtedness are the *debt ratio* and the *debt-equity ratio:* The higher these ratios, the greater the firm's financial leverage. The measures of the firm's ability to meet fixed payments associated with debt include the *times interest earned ratio* and the *fixed-payment coverage ratio.* These ratios provide indirect information on leverage. The smaller these ratios, the less able the firm is to meet payments as they come due. In general, low debt-payment ratios are associated with high degrees of financial leverage. The more risk a firm is willing to take, the greater will be its financial leverage. In theory, the firm should maintain financial leverage consistent with a capital structure that maximizes owners' wealth.

An acceptable degree of financial leverage for one industry or line of business can be highly risky in another due to differing operating characteristics between industries or lines of business. Table 11.9 presents the debt and times interest earned ratios for selected industries and lines of business. Significant industry differences can be seen in these data. For example, the debt ratio for electronic computer manufacturers is 58.3 percent, whereas for auto retailers it is 79.0 percent. Of course, differences in debt positions are also likely to exist *within* an industry or line of business.

Capital structure of non-U.S. firms

Modern capital structure theory (discussed in the next section) has developed largely within the framework of the U.S. financial system, and most empirical studies of these theories have employed data from U.S. companies. In recent years, however, both corporate executives and academic researchers have focused much greater attention on financing patterns shown by European, Japanese, Canadian, and other non-U.S. companies. They have found striking similarities and important differences between U.S. and international companies.

In general, non-U.S. companies have much higher leverage ratios than do their U.S. counterparts, whether these ratios are computed by using book values or market values of debt and equity securities. There are several reasons for this, most of which are related to the fact that capital markets are much more developed in the United States than elsewhere and have played a much greater role in corporate financing than has been the case in other countries. In most European countries and especially in Japan and other Pacific Rim nations, large commercial banks are much more actively involved in the financing of corporate activity than has been true in the United States. Furthermore, in many of these countries, banks are allowed to make large equity investments in nonfinancial corporations—a practice that is prohibited for U.S.banks. Finally, share ownership tends to be much more tightly controlled among founding family, institutional, and even public investors in Europe and Asia than is the case for most large U.S. corporations, many of which have up to one million individual shareholders. This tight ownership structure of non-U.S. firms helps to resolve many agency problems that affect large U.S. companies, thus allowing the non-U.S. firms to tolerate a higher level of indebtedness.

On the other hand, there are important similarities between U.S. corporations and those of other countries. First, the same industry patterns of capital structure tend to

TABLE 11.9

DEBT RATIOS FOR SELECTED INDUSTRIES AND LINES OF BUSINESS (FISCAL YEARS ENDED 4/1/91 THROUGH 3/31/92)

Industry or line of business	Debt ratio	Times interest earned ratio
Manufacturing industries		
Books: publishing and printing	63.1%	2.6
Dairy products	62.3	2.4
Electronic computers	58.3	2.0
Fertilizers	56.8	2.5
Iron and steel foundries	61.3	2.2
Jewelry and precious metals	56.5	2.3
Machine tools and metalworking equipment	57.3	1.9
Wines, distilled liquors, liqueurs	56.5	2.4
Women's dresses	62.0	3.3
Wholesaling industries		
Furniture	65.9	2.1
General groceries	67.3	2.3
Hardware and paints	59.2	2.2
Men's and boys' clothing	63.7	2.6
Petroleum products	65.7	2.0
Retailing industries		
Autos, new and used	79.0	1.4
Department stores	56.3	1.6
Radios, TV, consumer electronics	65.8	2.2
Restaurants	71.0	2.4
Shoes	65.7	2.2
Service industries		
Accounting, auditing, bookkeeping	52.7	5.4
Advertising agencies	75.0	3.0
Auto repair—general	63.5	2.3
Insurance agents and brokers	78.9	2.4
Physicians	67.2	2.4
Travel agencies	71.7	2.5

Source: RMA Annual Statement Studies, 1992 (fiscal years ended 4/1/91 through 3/31/92) (Philadelphia: Robert Morris Associates, 1992) Copyright © 1992 by Robert Morris Associates.

Note: Robert Morris Associates recommends that these ratios be regarded only as general guidelines and not as absolute industry norms. No claim is made as to the representativeness of their figures.

be revealed around the world. In almost all countries, pharmaceutical and other high-growth industrial firms tend to have lower debt ratios than do steel companies, airlines, and electric utility companies. Second, the capital structures of the largest U.S.-based multinational companies, which have access to many different capital markets and financing techniques around the world, typically resemble the capital structures of multinational companies from other countries more than they resemble those of smaller national companies. Finally, there is a worldwide trend away from reliance on banks for corporate financing and toward greater reliance on security issuance, so over time the differences in the capital structures of U.S. and non-U.S. firms will probably lessen.

Capital structure theory

Theoretical and empirical research suggests that there is an optimal capital structure range for a firm. However, the understanding of capital structure at this point does not provide financial managers with a specified methodology for use in determining a firm's optimal capital structure. But financial theory does provide help in understanding how the chosen financing mix affects the firm's value.

In 1958, Franco Modigliani and Merton H. Miller[13] (commonly referred to as "M and M") demonstrated algebraically that assuming perfect markets,[14] the capital structure that a firm chooses does not affect its value. Many researchers, including M and M, have examined the effects of less restrictive assumptions on the relationship between capital structure and the firm's value. The result is a theoretical *optimal* capital structure based on balancing the benefits and costs of debt financing. The major benefit of debt financing is the tax shield provided by the government, which allows interest payments to be deducted in calculating taxable income. The cost of debt financing results from (1) the increased probability of bankruptcy caused by debt obligations, (2) the *agency costs* of the lender's monitoring and controlling the firm's actions, and (3) the costs associated with managers having more information about the firm's prospects than do investors.

TAX BENEFITS

Allowing firms to deduct interest payments on debt when calculating taxable income reduces the amount of the firm's earnings paid in taxes, thereby making more earnings available for investors (bondholders and stockholders). The deductibility of interest means the cost of debt, k_i, to the firm is subsidized by the government. Letting k_d equal the before-tax cost of debt and T equal the tax rate, from Chapter 10 (Equation 10.3) we have $k_i = k_d \times (1 - T)$.

PROBABILITY OF BANKRUPTCY

The probability, or chance, that a firm will become bankrupt due to an inability to meet its obligations as they come due depends largely on its level of both business risk and financial risk.

BUSINESS RISK In Chapter 10 we defined *business risk* as the risk to the firm of being unable to cover its operating costs. In general, the greater the firm's operating leverage—the use of fixed operating costs—the higher its business risk. Although operating leverage is an important factor affecting business risk, two other factors—revenue stability and cost stability—also affect it. *Revenue stability* refers to the relative variability of the firm's sales revenues. Firms with reasonably stable levels of demand and with products that have stable prices have stable revenues that result in low levels of business risk. Firms with highly volatile product demand and prices have unstable revenues that result in high levels of business risk. *Cost stability* refers to the

[13]Franco Modigliani and Merton H. Miller, "The Cost of Capital, Corporation Finance, and the Theory of Investment," *American Economic Review,* June 1958, pp. 261–297.

[14]Perfect market assumptions include (1) no taxes, (2) no brokerage or flotation costs for securities, (3) symmetrical information—investors and managers have the same information about the firm's investment prospects, and (4) investors can borrow at the same rate as corporations.

relative predictability of input prices such as those for labor and materials. The more predictable and stable these input prices are, the lower the business risk, and the less predictable and stable they are, the higher the business risk.

Business risk varies among firms, regardless of their lines of business, and is not affected by capital structure decisions. The level of business risk must be taken as given. The higher a firm's business risk, the more cautious the firm must be in establishing its capital structure. Firms with high business risk therefore tend toward less highly leveraged capital structures, and firms with low business risk tend toward more highly leveraged capital structures. Here, as in Chapter 10, we will hold business risk constant throughout the discussions that follow. Let us look at an example.

EXAMPLE

Cooke Company, a soft drink manufacturer, in preparing to make a capital structure decision has obtained estimates of sales and the associated levels of EBIT. The firm's forecasting group feels that there is a 25 percent chance that sales will total $400,000, a 50 percent chance that sales will total $600,000, and a 25 percent chance that sales will total $800,000. Fixed operating costs total $200,000, and variable operating costs equal 50 percent of sales. These data are summarized and the resulting earnings before interest and taxes (EBIT) calculated in Table 11.10.

The table shows that there is a 25 percent chance that the EBIT will be zero, a 50 percent chance that it will be $100,000, and a 25 percent chance that it will be $200,000. The financial manager must accept as given these levels of EBIT and their associated probabilities when developing the firm's capital structure. These EBIT data effectively reflect a certain level of business risk that captures the firm's operating leverage, sales revenue variability, and cost variability. ■

FINANCIAL RISK The firm's capital structure directly affects its *financial risk,* which is the risk to the firm of being unable to cover required financial obligations. The penalty for not meeting financial obligations is bankruptcy. The more fixed-cost financing—debt (including financial leases) and preferred stock—a firm has in its capital structure, the greater its financial leverage and risk. Financial risk depends on the capital structure decision made by the management, and that decision is affected by the business risk the firm faces. The total risk of a firm (business and financial risk combined) determines its probability of bankruptcy. Financial risk, its relationship to business risk, and their combined impact can be demonstrated by continuing with the Cooke Company example.

TABLE 11.10

SALES AND ASSOCIATED EBIT CALCULATIONS FOR COOKE COMPANY ($000)

Probability of sales	0.25	0.50	0.25
Sales revenue	$400	$600	$800
Less: Fixed operating costs	200	200	200
Less: Variable operating costs (50% of sales)	200	300	400
Earnings before interest and taxes (EBIT)	$ 0	$100	$200

EXAMPLE

Cooke Company's current capital structure is as shown:

Current capital structure	
Long-term debt	$ 0
Common stock equity (25,000 shares at $20)	500,000
Total capital	$500,000

Let us assume that the firm is considering seven alternative capital structures. If we measure these structures using the debt ratio, they are associated with ratios of 0, 10, 20, 30, 40, 50, and 60 percent. If (1) the firm has no current liabilities, (2) its capital structure currently contains all equity as shown, and (3) the total amount of capital remains constant[15] at $500,000, the mix of debt and equity associated with the debt ratios just stated would be as noted in Table 11.11. Also shown in the table is the number of shares of common stock remaining outstanding under each alternative.

Associated with each of the debt levels in column 3 of Table 11.11 would be an interest rate that is expected to increase with increases in financial leverage, as reflected in the debt ratio. The level of debt, the associated interest rate (assumed to apply to *all* debt), and the dollar amount of annual interest associated with each of the alternative capital structures are summarized in Table 11.12. Since both the level of debt and the interest rate increase with increasing financial leverage (debt ratios), the annual interest increases as well.

TABLE 11.11

CAPITAL STRUCTURES ASSOCIATED WITH ALTERNATIVE DEBT RATIOS FOR COOKE COMPANY

	Capital structure ($000)			Shares of common stock outstanding (000)
Debt ratio (%) (1)	Total assets[a] (2)	Debt [(1) × (2)] (3)	Equity [(2) − (3)] (4)	[(4) ÷ $20][b] (5)
0%	$500	$ 0	$500	25.00
10	500	50	450	22.50
20	500	100	400	20.00
30	500	150	350	17.50
40	500	200	300	15.00
50	500	250	250	12.50
60	500	300	200	10.00

[a]Because the firm, for convenience, is assumed to have no current liabilities, its total assets equal its total capital of $500,000.

[b]The $20 value represents the book value per share of common stock equity noted earlier.

[15]This assumption is needed to permit the assessment of alternative capital structures without having to consider the returns associated with the investment of additional funds raised. Attention here is given only to the *mix* of capital rather than to its investment.

TABLE 11.12

LEVEL OF DEBT, INTEREST RATE, AND DOLLAR AMOUNT OF ANNUAL INTEREST ASSOCIATED WITH COOKE COMPANY'S ALTERNATIVE CAPITAL STRUCTURES

Capital structure debt ratio (%)	Debt ($000) (1)	Interest rate on *all* debt (%) (2)	Interest ($000) [(1) × (2)] (3)
0%	$ 0	0.0%	$ 0.00
10	50	9.0	4.50
20	100	9.5	9.50
30	150	10.0	15.00
40	200	11.0	22.00
50	250	13.5	33.75
60	300	16.5	49.50

Table 11.13 uses the levels of earnings before interest and taxes (EBIT) and associated probabilities developed in Table 11.10, the number of shares of common stock found in column 5 of Table 11.11, and the interest values calculated in column 3 of Table 11.12 to calculate the earnings per share (EPS) for debt ratios of 0, 30, and 60 percent. A 40 percent tax rate is assumed. Also shown are the resulting expected EPS, the standard deviation of EPS, and the coefficient of variation of EPS associated with each debt ratio.[16]

The resulting statistics from the calculations in Table 11.13, along with the same statistics for the other debt ratios (10, 20, 40, and 50 percent—calculations not shown), are summarized for the seven alternative capital structures in Table 11.14 on page 460. Because the coefficient of variation measures the risk relative to the expected EPS, it is the preferred risk measure for use in comparing capital structures. As the firm's financial leverage increases, so does its coefficient of variation of EPS. As expected, an increasing level of risk is associated with increased levels of financial leverage.

The relative risk of two of the capital structures evaluated in Table 11.13 (debt ratios = 0% and 60%) can be illustrated by showing the probability distribution of EPS associated with each of them. Figure 11.3 on page 460 shows these two distributions. While the expected level of EPS increases with increasing financial leverage, so does risk, as reflected in the relative dispersion of each of the distributions. Clearly, the uncertainty of the expected EPS, as well as the chance of experiencing negative EPS, is greater when higher degrees of leverage are employed.

The nature of the risk-return tradeoff associated with the seven capital structures under consideration can clearly be observed by plotting the expected EPS and coefficient of variation relative to the debt ratio. Plotting the data obtained from Table 11.14 results in Figure 11.4 on page 461. An analysis of the figure shows that as debt is substituted for equity (as the debt ratio increases), the level of earnings per share rises and

[16]For explanatory convenience the coefficient of variation of EPS, which measures total (nondiversifiable and diversifiable) risk, is used throughout this chapter as a proxy for beta, which measures the relevant nondiversifiable risk.

TABLE 11.13

CALCULATION OF EPS FOR SELECTED DEBT RATIOS ($000) FOR COOKE COMPANY

	Debt ratio = 0%		
Probability of EBIT	**0.25**	**0.50**	**0.25**
EBIT (Table 11.10)	$ 0.00	$100.00	$200.00
Less: Interest (Table 11.12)	0.00	0.00	0.00
Net profits before taxes	$ 0.00	$100.00	$200.00
Less: Taxes ($T = .40$)	0.00	40.00	80.00
Net profits after taxes	$ 0.00	$ 60.00	$120.00
EPS (25.0 shares, Table 11.11)	$ 0.00	$ 2.40	$ 4.80
Expected EPS[a]		$ 2.40	
Standard deviation of EPS[a]		$ 1.70	
Coefficient of variation of EPS[a]		0.71	
	Debt ratio = 30%		
Probability of EBIT	**0.25**	**0.50**	**0.25**
EBIT (Table 11.10)	$ 0.00	$100.00	$200.00
Less: Interest (Table 11.12)	15.00	15.00	15.00
Net profits before taxes	($15.00)	$ 85.00	$185.00
Less: Taxes ($T = .40$)	(6.00)[b]	34.00	74.00
Net profits after taxes	($ 9.00)	$ 51.00	$111.00
EPS (17.50 shares, Table 11.11)	($ 0.51)	$ 2.91	$ 6.34
Expected EPS[a]		$ 2.91	
Standard deviation of EPS[a]		$ 2.42	
Coefficient of variation of EPS[a]		0.83	
	Debt ratio = 60%		
Probability of EBIT	**0.25**	**0.50**	**0.25**
EBIT (Table 11.10)	$ 0.00	$100.00	$200.00
Less: Interest (Table 11.12)	49.50	49.50	49.50
Net profits before taxes	($49.50)	$ 50.50	$150.50
Less: Taxes ($T = .40$)	(19.80)[b]	20.20	60.20
Net profits after taxes	($29.70)	$ 30.30	$90.30
EPS (10.00 shares, Table 11.11)	($ 2.97)	$ 3.03	$ 9.03
Expected EPS[a]		$ 3.03	
Standard deviation of EPS[a]		$ 4.24	
Coefficient of variation of EPS[a]		1.40	

[a]The procedures used to calculate the expected value, standard deviation, and coefficient of variation were presented in Equations 6.2, 6.3, and 6.4, respectively, in Chapter 6.

[b]It is assumed that the firm receives the tax benefit from its loss in the current period as a result of applying the tax loss carryback procedures specified in the tax law (see Chapter 2).

TABLE 11.14

EXPECTED EPS, STANDARD DEVIATION, AND COEFFICIENT OF VARIATION FOR ALTERNATIVE CAPITAL STRUCTURES FOR COOKE COMPANY

Capital structure debt ratio (%)	Expected EPS ($) (1)	Standard deviation of EPS ($) (2)	Coefficient of variation of EPS [(2) ÷ (1)] (3)
0%	$2.40	$1.70	0.71
10	2.55	1.88	0.74
20	2.72	2.13	0.78
30	2.91	2.42	0.83
40	3.12	2.83	0.91
50	3.18	3.39	1.07
60	3.03	4.24	1.40

then begins to fall (graph *a*). The graph demonstrates that the peak earnings per share occur at a debt ratio of 50 percent. The decline in earnings per share beyond that ratio results from the fact that the significant increases in interest are not fully offset by the reduction in the number of shares of common stock outstanding.

If we look at the risk behavior as measured by the coefficient of variation, we can see that risk increases with increasing leverage (graph *b*). As noted, a portion of the risk can be attributed to business risk, while that portion changing in response to increasing financial leverage would be attributed to financial risk. Clearly, a risk-return tradeoff exists relative to the use of financial leverage. How to combine these risk-

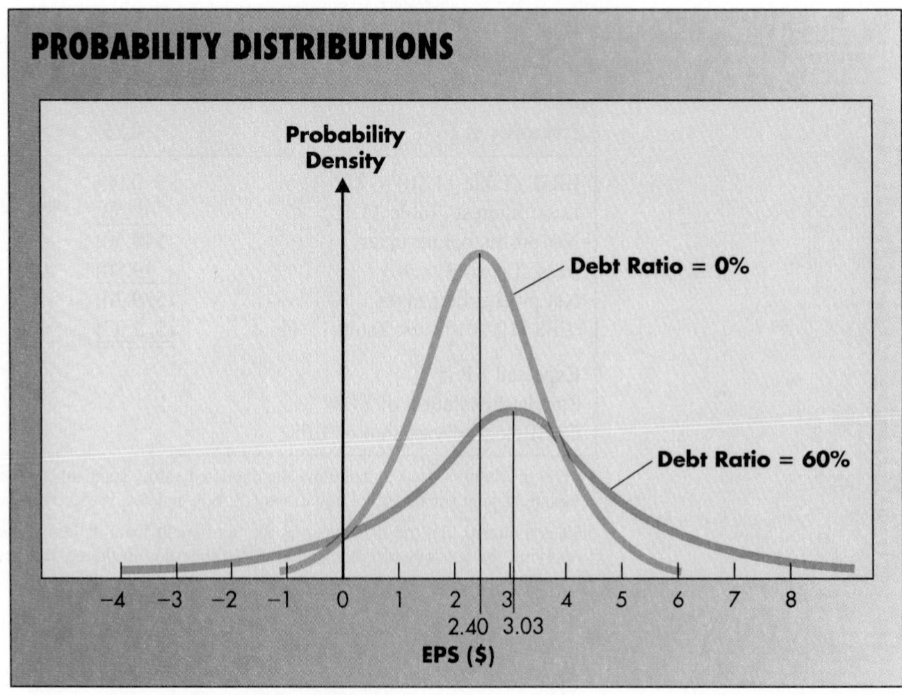

FIGURE 11.3
Probability distributions of EPS for debt ratios of 0 and 60 percent for Cooke Company

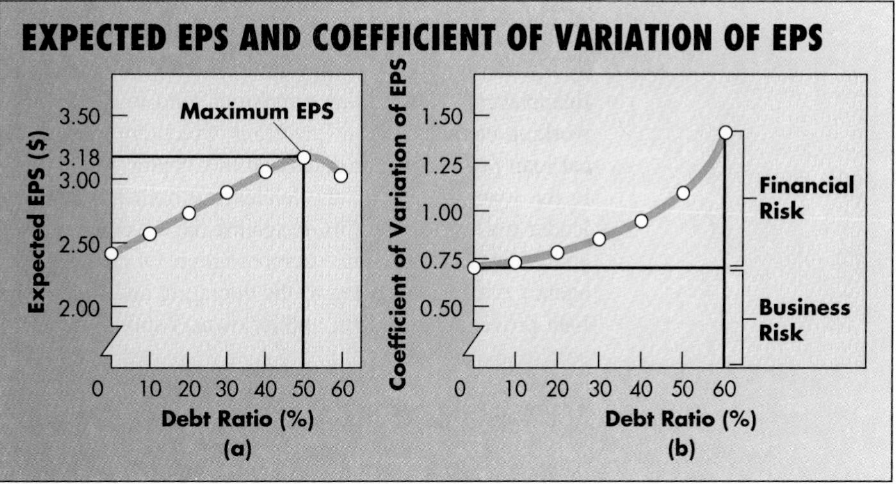

FIGURE 11.4
Expected EPS and coefficient of variation of EPS for alternative capital structures for Cooke Company

return factors into a valuation framework will be addressed later in the chapter. The key point to recognize here is that as a firm introduces more leverage into its capital structure, it will experience increases in both the expected level of return and the associated risk. ■

AGENCY COSTS IMPOSED BY LENDERS

As was noted in Chapter 1, the managers of firms typically act as *agents* of the owners. The owners hire the managers and give them the authority to manage the firm for the owners' benefit. The *agency problem* created by this relationship extends not only to the relationship between owners and managers, but also to the relationship between owners and lenders. This latter problem is due to the fact that lenders provide funds to the firm on the basis of their expectations for the firm's current and future capital expenditures and capital structure. These factors determine the firm's business and financial risk.

When a lender provides funds to a firm, the interest rate charged is based on the lender's assessment of the firm's risk. The lender-borrower relationship, therefore, depends on the lender's expectations for the firm's subsequent behavior. If unconstrained, this arrangement creates incentives for the firm to increase its risk without increasing current borrowing costs. The borrowing rates are, in effect, locked in when the loans are negotiated. After obtaining a loan at a certain rate from a bank or through the sale of bonds, the firm could increase its risk by investing in risky projects or by incurring additional debt. Such action could weaken the lender's position in terms of its claim on the cash flow of the firm. From another point of view, if these risky investment strategies paid off, the stockholders would benefit, since their payment obligations to the lender remain unchanged; the excess cash flows generated by a positive outcome from the riskier action would enhance the value of the firm to its owners. In other words, if the risky investments pay off, the owners receive all the benefits, but if the risky investments do not pay off, the lenders share in the costs.

Clearly, an incentive exists for the managers acting on behalf of the stockholders to "take advantage" of lenders. To avoid this type of situation, lenders impose certain monitoring and controlling techniques on borrowers, who, as a result, incur *agency costs.* The most obvious strategy is to deny subsequent loan requests or to increase the cost of future loans to the firm. Because this strategy is an after-the-fact approach, other controls must be included in the loan agreement. Lenders typically protect themselves by including provisions that limit the firm's ability to significantly alter its business or financial risk. These loan provisions tend to center on issues such as the level of net working capital, asset acquisitions, executive salaries, and dividend payments. (Typical loan provisions are discussed in Chapter 12.) By including appropriate provisions in the loan agreement, the lender can both monitor and control the firm's risk. The lender thus can protect itself against the adverse consequences of this agency problem and assure itself adequate compensation for risk. Of course, in exchange for incurring agency costs by agreeing to the operating and financial constraints placed on it by the loan provisions, the firm and its owners should benefit by obtaining funds at a lower cost.

ASYMMETRIC INFORMATION

pecking order
A hierarchy of financing beginning with retained earnings followed by debt financing and finally external equity financing.

asymmetric information
The situation in which managers of a firm have more information about operations and future prospects than do investors.

A relatively recent survey of financial executives examined capital structure decisions.[17] The managers were asked which of two major criteria determined their financing decisions: (1) maintaining a *target capital structure* or (2) following a hierarchy of financing, called a **pecking order,** which begins with retained earnings followed by debt financing and finally external equity financing. Thirty percent answered target capital structure, and 70 percent chose the pecking order. At first glance, on the basis of financial theory, this choice appears to be inconsistent with wealth-maximizing goals. However, in an earlier address to the American Finance Association entitled "The Capital Structure Puzzle," Stewart Myers explained how "asymmetric information" could account for the pecking order financing preferences of financial managers.[18] **Asymmetric information** results when managers of a firm have more information about operations and future prospects than do investors. Assuming that managers make decisions with the goal of maximizing the wealth of existing stockholders, then asymmetric information can affect the capital structure decisions that managers make.

signal
A financing action by management that is believed to reflect its view with respect to the firm's stock value; generally, debt financing is viewed as a *positive signal* that management believes that the stock is "undervalued," and a stock issue is viewed as a *negative signal* that management believes that the stock is "overvalued."

Suppose, for example, that management has found a valuable investment that will require additional financing. Management believes that the prospects for the firm's future are very good and that the market does not fully appreciate the firm's value. The firm's current stock price is low given management's knowledge of the firm's prospects. It would be more advantageous to current stockholders if management raised the required funds using debt rather than issuing new stock. Such an action by management is frequently viewed as a **signal** that reflects its view with respect to the firm's stock value. In this case the use of debt financing is a *positive signal* suggesting that management believes that the stock is "undervalued" and therefore a bargain. If, instead, new stock was issued, when the firm's positive future outlook became known to the market, the increased value would be shared with new stockholders rather than fully captured by existing owners.

If, however, the outlook for the firm is poor, management may believe that the firm's stock is overvalued; then it would be in the best interest of existing stockholders for the firm to issue new stock. Therefore investors often interpret the announcement of a stock issue as a *negative signal*—bad news concerning the firm's prospects—

[17]J. Michael Pinegar and Lisa Wilbricht, "What Managers Think of Capital Structure Theory: A Survey," *Financial Management,* Winter 1989, pp. 82–91.

[18]Stewart C. Myers, "The Capital Structure Puzzle," *Journal of Finance,* July 1984, pp. 575–592.

and the stock price declines. This decrease in stock value along with high underwriting costs for stock issues (compared to debt issues) make new stock financing very expensive. Since asymmetric information conditions exist from time to time, firms should maintain some reserve borrowing capacity (low debt levels). This reserve allows the firm to take advantage of good investment opportunities without selling stock at a low value.

The optimal capital structure

To provide some insight into what is meant by an optimal capital structure, we will examine some basic financial relationships. It is generally believed that *the value of the firm is maximized when the cost of capital is minimized.* By using a modification of the simple zero growth valuation model (see Equation 7.8 in Chapter 7), the value of the firm, V, can be defined by Equation 11.11, where EBIT equals earnings before interest and taxes, T is the tax rate, EBIT $\times$ $(1 - T)$ represents the after-tax operating earnings available to the debt and equity holders, and k_a is the weighted average cost of capital:

$$V = \frac{\text{EBIT} \times (1 - T)}{k_a} \tag{11.11}$$

Clearly, if we assume that EBIT is constant, the value of the firm, V, is maximized by minimizing the weighted average cost of capital, k_a.

COST FUNCTIONS

Figure 11.5(a) plots three cost functions—the after-tax cost of debt, k_i; the cost of equity, k_s; and the weighted average cost of capital, k_a—as a function of financial leverage measured by the debt ratio (debt-to-total assets). The *cost of debt,* k_i, remains low due to the tax subsidy (interest is tax-deductible) but slowly increases with increasing leverage to compensate lenders for increasing risk. The *cost of equity,* k_s, is above the cost of debt and increases with increasing financial leverage but generally more rapidly than the cost of debt. The increase in the cost of equity occurs because, to compensate

FIGURE 11.5
Capital costs and the optimal capital structure

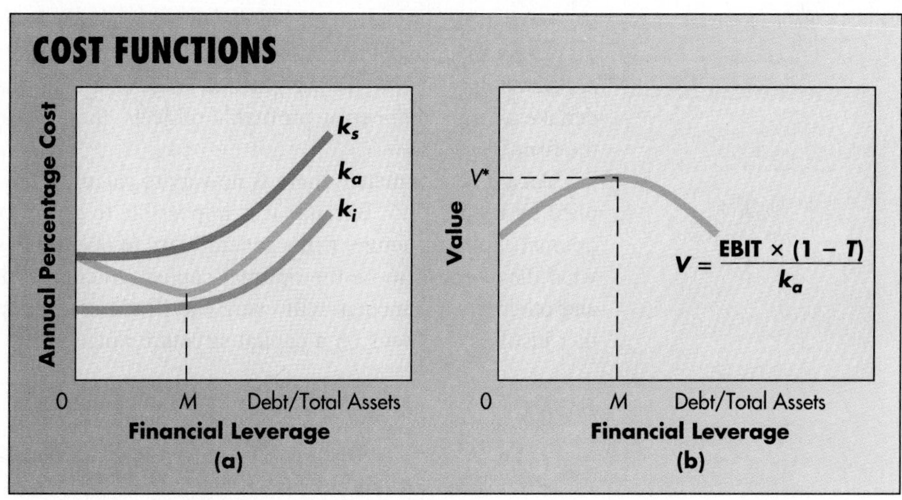

for the higher degree of financial risk, the stockholders require a higher return as leverage increases.

The *weighted average cost of capital,* k_a, results from a weighted average of the firm's debt and equity capital costs. At a debt ratio of zero, the firm is 100 percent equity-financed. As debt is substituted for equity and as the debt ratio increases, the weighted average cost of capital declines because the debt cost is less than the equity cost ($k_i < k_s$). As the debt ratio continues to increase, the increased debt and equity costs eventually cause the weighted average cost of capital to rise (after point M in Figure 11.5(a)). This behavior results in a U-shaped, or saucer-shaped, weighted average cost of capital function, k_a.

CONCEPT IN PRACTICE

Reilley's Acquisition Relies on the Right Capital Structure

William F. Reilley wants his old company back. Reilley, current CEO of K-III Communications and former president of Macmillan, Inc., lost a bitter takover brawl for Macmillan to British media baron Robert Maxwell in 1990. When Maxwell Communications, Inc. went under after Maxwell's mysterious drowning in 1991, Reilley saw a chance to get his former employer for about $700 million.

So what's stopping him? In order to maintain a viable capital structure at K-III after the Macmillan acquisition, Reilley must fund at least 25 percent of the $700 million purchase price with new equity. Borrowing the remaining $525 million, 66 percent of K-III's financing will be debt, compared to the firm's current 52 percent debt ratio. While Reilley has the financial backing of the leverage-buyout firm Kohlberg, Kravis Roberts & Company (KKR), many analysts believe that KKR may be hesitant to buy $175 million in new equity from K-III, because the Macmillan acquisition will extend K-III's debt ratio to a risky 66 percent of total assets.

A GRAPHIC VIEW OF THE OPTIMAL STRUCTURE

optimal capital structure
The capital structure at which the weighted average cost of capital is minimized, thereby maximizing the firm's value.

Since the maximization of value, V, is achieved when the overall cost of capital, k_a, is at a minimum (see Equation 11.11), the **optimal capital structure** is therefore that at which the weighted average cost of capital, k_a, is minimized. In Figure 11.5(a) the point M represents the minimum weighted average cost of capital—the point of optimal financial leverage and hence of optimal capital structure for the firm; as shown in Figure 11.5(b), at that point, M, the value of the firm is maximized at V^*. Generally, the lower the firm's weighted average cost of capital, the greater the difference between the return on a project and this cost, and therefore the greater the owners' return. Simply stated, minimizing the weighted average cost of capital allows management to undertake a larger number of profitable projects, thereby further increasing the value of the firm.

As a practical matter, there is no way to calculate the optimal capital structure implied by Figure 11.5. Because it is impossible to either know or remain at the precise optimal capital structure, firms generally try to operate in a range that places them near what they believe to be the optimal capital structure. The fact that retained earnings and other new financings will cause the firm's actual capital structure to change further justifies the focus on a capital structure range rather than a single optimum.

CONCEPTS IN REVIEW

11-6 What is a firm's *capital structure*? How do *debt* and *equity* capital differ? What ratios can be used to assess the degree of financial leverage in the firm's capital structure?

11-7 Discuss the differences, and the reasons for them, in the capital structures of U.S. and non-U.S. corporations. In what ways are the capital structures of U.S. and non-U.S. corporations similar?

11-8 What is the major benefit of debt financing? How does it affect the firm's cost of debt?

11-9 Define *business risk,* and discuss the three factors that affect it. What influence does business risk have on the firm's capital structure decisions? Define *financial risk,* and explain its relationship to the firm's capital structure.

11-10 Briefly describe the agency problem that exists between owners and lenders. Explain how the firm must incur *agency costs* for the lender to resolve this problem.

11-11 What is *asymmetric information,* and how does it affect the financial manager's capital structure decisions? Explain how and why the firm's financing actions are often viewed as signals by investors.

11-12 Describe the generally accepted theory concerning the behavior of the cost of debt, the cost of equity, and the weighted average cost of capital as the firm's financial leverage increases from zero. Where is the *optimal capital structure* under this theory, and what is its relationship to the firm's value at that point?

The EBIT–EPS approach to capital structure

The EBIT–EPS approach to capital structure focuses on selection of the capital structure that maximizes earning per share (EPS) over the expected range of earnings before interest and taxes (EBIT). What do you think is the major shortcoming of this approach? Take a few moments to answer this question before reading further.

EBIT–EPS approach
An approach for selecting the capital structure that maximizes earnings per share (EPS) over the expected range of earnings before interest and taxes (EBIT).

THE **EBIT–EPS APPROACH** TO CAPITAL STRUCTURE INVOLVES SELECTING THE CAPITAL structure that maximizes earnings per share (EPS) over the expected range of earnings before interest and taxes (EBIT). Here the main emphasis is on the effects of various capital structures on *owners' returns.* Since one of the key variables affecting the market value of the firm's shares is its earnings, EPS can be conveniently used to analyze alternative capital structures.

Presenting a financing plan graphically

To analyze the effects of a firm's capital structure on the owners' returns, we consider the relationship between earnings before interest and taxes (EBIT) and earnings per share (EPS). A constant level of EBIT—constant business risk—is assumed to isolate the impact on returns of the financing costs associated with alternative capital structures (financing plans). EPS is used to measure the owners' returns, which are expected to be closely related to share price.[19]

[19]The relationship that is expected to exist between earnings per share and owners' wealth is not one of cause and effect. As was indicated in Chapter 1, the maximization of profits does not necessarily assure the firm that owners' wealth is also being maximized. Nevertheless, it is expected that the movement of earnings per share will have some effect on owners' wealth, since EPS data constitute one of the few pieces of information investors receive, and they often bid the firm's share price up or down in response to the level of these earnings.

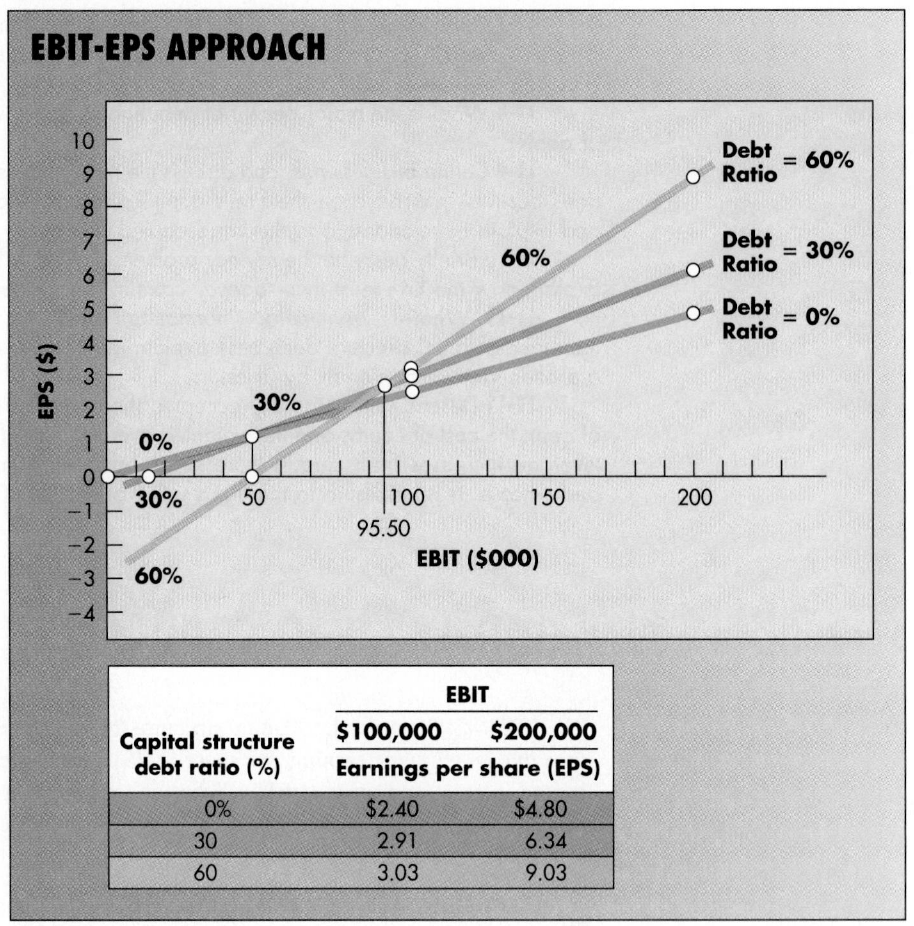

Capital structure debt ratio (%)	EBIT $100,000	EBIT $200,000
	Earnings per share (EPS)	
0%	$2.40	$4.80
30	2.91	6.34
60	3.03	9.03

FIGURE 11.6
A comparison of selected capital structures for Cooke Company *(data from Table 11.13)*

THE DATA REQUIRED

To graph a financing plan, at least two EBIT–EPS coordinates are required. The approach for obtaining coordinates can be illustrated by the following simple example.

EXAMPLE

Cooke Company data developed earlier can be used to illustrate the EBIT–EPS approach. The EBIT–EPS coordinates can be found by assuming two EBIT values and calculating the EPS associated with them.[20] Such calculations for three capital structures—debt ratios of 0, 30, and 60 percent—for Cooke Company were presented in Table 11.13. Using the EBIT values of $100,000 and $200,000, the associated EPS values calculated there are summarized in the table within Figure 11.6. ■

[20]A convenient method for finding one EBIT–EPS coordinate is to calculate the *financial breakeven point,* the level of EBIT for which the firm's EPS just equals zero. It is the level of EBIT needed just to cover all fixed financial costs—annual interest (I) and preferred stock dividends (PD). The equation for the financial breakeven point is

$$\text{Financial breakeven point} = I + \frac{PD}{1 - T}$$

where T is the tax rate. It can be seen that when $PD = \$0$, the financial breakeven point is equal to I, the annual interest payment.

PLOTTING THE DATA

financial breakeven point
The level of EBIT necessary just to cover all fixed financial costs; the level of EBIT for which EPS = $0.

The data summarized for Cooke Company can be plotted on a set of EBIT–EPS axes, as shown in Figure 11.6. The figure shows the level of EPS expected for each level of EBIT. For levels of EBIT below the x-axis intercept–known as the **financial breakeven point,** where EBIT just covers all fixed financial costs (EPS = $0)—it can be seen that a loss (negative EPS) results.

Comparing alternative capital structures

The graphic display of financing plans in a fashion similar to Figure 11.6 can be used to compare alternative capital structures. The following example illustrates this procedure.

EXAMPLE

Cooke Company's capital structure alternatives were plotted on the EBIT–EPS axes in Figure 11.6. An analysis of this figure discloses that over certain ranges of EBIT, each capital structure reflects superiority over the others in terms of maximizing EPS. The zero-leverage capital structure (debt ratio = 0 percent) would be superior to either of the other capital structures for levels of EBIT between $0 and $50,000; between $50,000 and $95,500 of EBIT, the capital structure associated with a debt ratio of 30 percent would be preferred; and at a level of EBIT in excess of $95,500, the capital structure associated with a debt ratio of 60 percent would provide the highest earnings per share.[21] ■

Considering risk in EBIT–EPS analysis

When interpreting EBIT–EPS analysis, it is important to consider the risk of each capital structure alternative. Graphically, the risk of each capital structure can be viewed in light of the *financial breakeven point* (EBIT-axis intercept) and the *degree of financial leverage* reflected in the slope of the capital structure line. The higher the financial breakeven point and the steeper the slope of the capital structure line, the

[21]An algebraic technique can be used to find the *indifference points* between the capital structure alternatives. This technique involves expressing each capital structure as an equation stated in terms of earnings per share, setting the equations for two capital structures equal to each other, and solving for the level of EBIT that causes the equations to be equal. By using the notation from footnote 20 and letting n equal the number of shares of common stock outstanding, the general equation for the earnings per share from a financing plan is

$$\text{EPS} = \frac{(1 - T) \times (\text{EBIT} - I) - \text{PD}}{n}$$

Comparing Cooke Company's 0 percent and 30 percent capital structures, we get

$$\frac{(1 - .40) \times (\text{EBIT} - \$0) - \$0}{25.00} = \frac{(1 - .40) \times (\text{EBIT} - \$15.00) - \$0}{17.50}$$

$$\frac{.60 \times \text{EBIT}}{25.00} = \frac{.60 \times \text{EBIT} - \$9.00}{17.50}$$

$$10.50 \times \text{EBIT} = 15.00 \times \text{EBIT} - \$225.00$$

$$\$225.00 = 4.50 \times \text{EBIT}$$

$$\text{EBIT} = \$50$$

The calculated value of the indifference point between the 0 percent and 30 percent capital structures is therefore $50,000, as can be seen in Figure 11.6.

greater the financial risk.[22] Further assessment of risk can be performed by using ratios. With increased financial leverage, as measured by using the debt ratio, we would expect a corresponding decline in the firm's ability to make scheduled interest payments, as measured by using the times interest earned ratio.

EXAMPLE

Reviewing the three capital structures plotted for Cooke Company in Figure 11.6, we can see that as the debt ratio increases, so does the financial risk of each alternative. Both the financial breakeven point and the slope of the capital structure lines increase with increasing debt ratios. If we use the \$100,000 EBIT value, the times interest earned ratio (EBIT ÷ interest) for the zero-leverage capital structure is infinity (\$100,000 ÷ 0); for the 30 percent debt case it is 6.67 (\$100,000 ÷ \$15,000); and for the 60 percent debt case it is 2.02 (\$100,000 ÷ \$49,500). Since lower times interest earned ratios reflect higher risk, these ratios support the earlier conclusion that the risk of the capital structures increases with increasing financial leverage. The capital structure for a debt ratio of 60 percent is more risky than that for a debt ratio of 30 percent, which in turn is more risky than the capital structure for a debt ratio of 0 percent. ■

Basic shortcoming of EBIT–EPS analysis

The most important point to recognize in using EBIT–EPS analysis is that this technique tends to concentrate on *maximization of earnings rather than maximization of owners' wealth.* Although there may be a positive relationship between these two objectives, the use of an EPS-maximizing approach ignores risk. If investors did not require risk premiums (additional returns) as the firm increased the proportion of debt in its capital structure, a strategy involving maximizing earnings per share would also maximize owner's wealth. Because risk premiums increase with increases in financial leverage, the maximization of EPS *does not* ensure owners' wealth maximization. To select the best capital structure, both return (EPS) and risk (via the required return, k_s) must be integrated into a valuation framework in a fashion consistent with the capital structure theory presented earlier.

CONCEPT IN REVIEW

11-13 Explain the EBIT–EPS approach to capital structure. Include in your answer a graph indicating the financial breakeven point; label the axes.

Choosing the optimal capital structure

The optimal capital structure is the one that balances return and risk factors in a fashion that maximizes market value (owner wealth). Is there reason to believe that this wealth-maximizing capital structure is generally the same one that maximizes earnings per share (EPS)? Before reading further, devote a few minutes to answering this question.

[22]The degree of financial leverage (DFL) is reflected in the slope of the EBIT–EPS function. The steeper the slope, the greater the degree of financial leverage, since the change in EPS (y-axis) resulting from a given change in EBIT (x-axis) will increase with increasing slope and will decrease with decreasing slope.

CREATING A WEALTH MAXIMIZATION FRAMEWORK FOR USE IN MAKING CAPITAL STRUCture decisions is not easy. Although the two key factors—return and risk—can be used separately to make capital structure decisions, integration of them into a market value context should provide the best results. This section describes the procedures for linking the return and risk associated with alternative capital structures to market value to select the best capital structure.

Linkage

To determine its value under alternative capital structures, the firm must find the level of return that must be earned to compensate investors and owners for the risk being incurred. That is, the risk associated with each structure must be linked to the required rate of return. Such a framework is consistent with the overall valuation framework developed in Chapter 7 and applied to capital budgeting decisions in Chapter 9.

The required return associated with a given level of financial risk can be estimated in a number of ways. Theoretically, the preferred approach would be to first estimate the beta associated with each alternative capital structure and then use the CAPM framework presented in Chapter 6 (see Equation 6.8) to calculate the required return, k_s. Another approach would involve linking the financial risk associated with each capital structure alternative directly to the required return. Such an approach is similar to the market risk-return function presented in Chapter 9 (see Figure 9.4). It would require estimation of the required return associated with each level of financial risk, as measured by a statistic such as the coefficient of variation of EPS. Regardless of the approach used, one would expect that the required return would be greater the greater the financial risk involved. An example will illustrate.

EXAMPLE

Cooke Company, using the coefficients of variation of EPS associated with each of the seven alternative capital structures (see column 3 of Table 11.14) as a risk measure, estimated the associated required returns, k_s. These are shown in Table 11.15. As expected, the estimated required return, k_s, increases with increasing risk, as measured by the coefficient of variation of EPS. ■

TABLE 11.15

REQUIRED RETURNS FOR COOKE COMPANY'S ALTERNATIVE CAPITAL STRUCTURES

Capital structure debt ratio (%)	Coefficient of variation of EPS (from column 3 of Table 11.14) (1)	Estimated required return, k_s (%) (2)
0%	0.71	11.5%
10	0.74	11.7
20	0.78	12.1
30	0.83	12.5
40	0.91	14.0
50	1.07	16.5
60	1.40	19.0

Estimating value

The value of the firm associated with alternative capital structures can be estimated by using one of the standard valuation models. If, for simplicity, we assume that all earnings are paid out as dividends, a zero growth valuation model such as that developed in Chapter 7 can be used. The model, originally stated in Equation 7.8, is restated here with EPS substituted for dividends, since in each year the dividends would equal EPS.

$$P_0 = \frac{\text{EPS}}{k_s} \tag{11.12}$$

By substituting the estimated level of EPS and the associated required return, k_s, into Equation 11.12, we can estimate the per-share value of the firm, P_0.

EXAMPLE

Returning again to Cooke Company, we can now estimate the value of its stock under each of the alternative capital structures. Substituting the expected EPS (from column 1 of Table 11.14) and the required returns, k_s (from column 2 of Table 11.15), into Equation 11.12 for each of the alternative capital structures results in the share values given in column 3 of Table 11.16. Plotting the resulting share values against the associated debt ratios as shown in Figure 11.7 clearly illustrates that the maximum share value occurs at the capital structure associated with a debt ratio of 30 percent. ■

Maximizing value versus maximizing EPS

Throughout this text, for a variety of reasons, the goal of the financial manager has been specified as maximizing owners' wealth, not profit. Although there is some relationship between the level of expected profit and value, there is no reason to be-

TABLE 11.16

CALCULATION OF SHARE VALUE ESTIMATES ASSOCIATED WITH ALTERNATIVE CAPITAL STRUCTURES FOR COOKE COMPANY

Capital structure debt ratio (%)	Expected EPS ($) (from column 1 of Table 11.14) (1)	Estimated required return, k_s (from column 2 of Table 11.15) (2)	Estimated share value ($) [(1) ÷ (2)] (3)
0%	$2.40	.115	$20.87
10	2.55	.117	21.79
20	2.72	.121	22.48
30	2.91	.125	23.28
40	3.12	.140	22.29
50	3.18	.165	19.27
60	3.03	.190	15.95

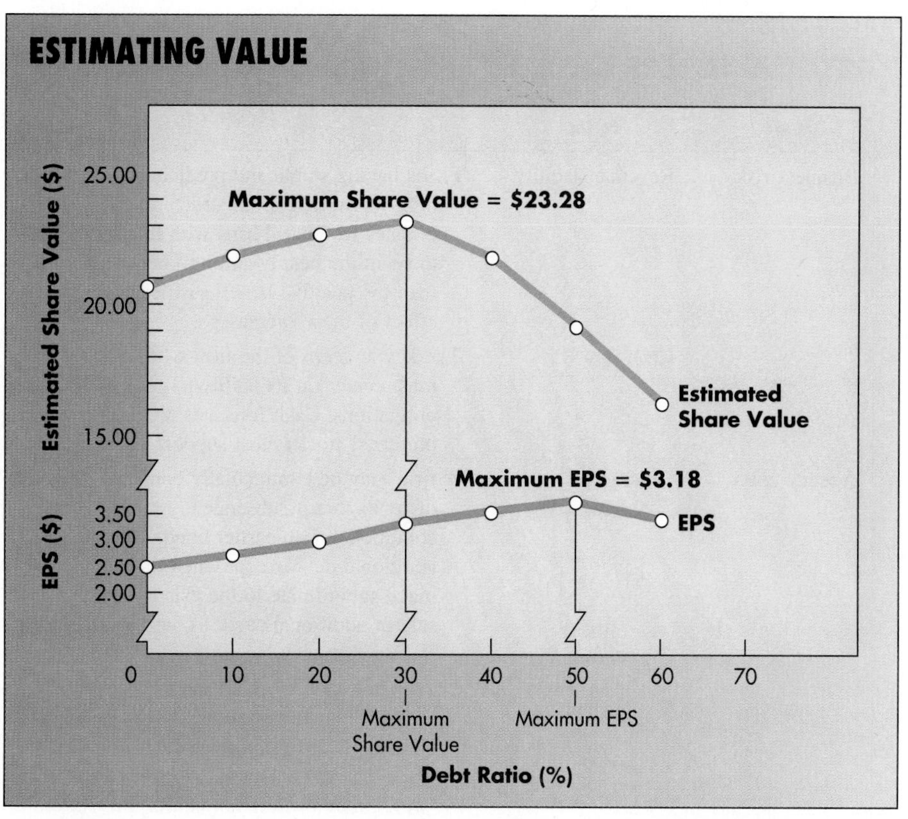

FIGURE 11.7
Estimated share value and EPS for alternative capital structures for Cooke Company

lieve that profit-maximizing strategies necessarily result in wealth maximization. It is therefore the wealth of the owners as reflected in the estimated share value that should act as the criterion for selecting the best capital structure. A final look at Cooke Company will help to highlight this point.

EXAMPLE

Further analysis of Figure 11.7 clearly shows that although the firm's profits (EPS) are maximized at a debt ratio of 50 percent, share price is maximized at a 30 percent debt ratio. In this case the preferred capital structure would be the 30 percent debt ratio. The failure of the EPS-maximization approach to provide a similar conclusion stems from its lack of consideration of risk. Solely on the basis of the quantitative analysis presented, Cooke Company should employ the capital structure that results in a 30 percent debt ratio. ■

Some other important considerations

Because, as was noted earlier, there is really no practical way to calculate the optimal capital structure, any quantitative analysis of capital structure must be tempered with other important considerations. A nearly endless list of additional factors relative to capital structure decisions could be created; some of the more important of these factors, categorized relative to the broad area of concern, are summarized in Table 11.17.

TABLE 11.17

IMPORTANT FACTORS TO CONSIDER IN MAKING CAPITAL STRUCTURE DECISIONS

Concern	Factor	Description
Business risk	Revenue stability	Firms having stable and predictable revenues can more safely undertake highly levered capital structures than can firms with volatile patterns of sales revenue. Firms with increasing revenues (growing sales) tend to be in the best position to benefit from added debt because they can reap the positive benefits of leverage, which tends to magnify the effect of these increases.
	Cash flow	The key concern of the firm when it is considering a new capital structure must center on its ability to generate the necessary cash flows to meet obligations. Cash forecasts reflecting an ability to service debts (and preferred stock) must support any capital structure shift.
Agency costs	Contractual obligations	A firm may be contractually constrained with respect to the type or form of funds that it subsequently raises. For example, a contract describing conditions of an earlier bond issue might prohibit the firm from selling additional debt except when the claims of holders of such debt are made subordinate to the existing debt. Contractual constraints on the sale of additional stock as well as the ability to distribute dividends on stock might also exist.
	Management preferences	Occasionally, a firm will impose an internal constraint on the use of debt to limit the firm's risk exposure to a level deemed acceptable to its management. In other words, due to risk aversion, the firm's management constrains the firm's capital structure at a certain level, which may or may not be the true optimum.
	Control	A management that is concerned about control may prefer to issue debt rather than (voting) common stock to raise funds. Of course, if market conditions are favorable, a firm that wanted to sell equity could issue *nonvoting shares* or make a *preemptive offering* (see Chapter 13), allowing each shareholder to maintain proportionate ownership. Generally, only in closely held firms or firms threatened by takeover does control become a major concern in the capital structure decision process.
Asymmetric information	External risk assessment	The firm's ability to raise funds quickly and at favorable rates will clearly depend on the external risk assessments of lenders and bond raters. The financial manager must therefore consider the potential impact of capital structure decisions not only on share value but also on published financial statements from which lenders and raters tend to assess the firm's risk.
	Timing	At certain points in time, when the general level of interest rates is low, the use of debt financing might be more attractive; when interest rates are high, the sale of stock may become more appealing. Sometimes the sources of both debt and equity capital dry up and become unavailable under what would be viewed as reasonable terms. General economic conditions—especially those of the capital market—can thus significantly affect capital structure decisions.

CONCEPT IN PRACTICE

Financial Capital Creates the Ties That Bind

When you consider optimal capital structure, you probably recall the relationship among operating leverage, debt, and financial leverage. While optimal capital structure indeed involves operating and financial risk, *political* risk can also factor into a firm's optimal capital structure. The Hongkong & Shanghai Banking Corp., Hong Kong's $258 billion banking giant, understands this factor well. In 1997, control of the British colony of Hong Kong will revert to mainland China under Communist rule. The capitalists are restless.

What can they do? As the leading provider of bank credit in China's Shanghai province, the Hong Kong bank is helping firms in mainland China to integrate Hong Kong debt within their capital structures. The bank is also selling minority stakes in its common equity to the Bank of China and other government institutions. The bank is carefully using financial capital—including debt and equity securities—to create ties between Hong Kong and China that jointly serve the interests of investors and businesses in both places.

CONCEPTS IN REVIEW

11-14 Do *maximizing value* and *maximizing EPS* lead to the same conclusion about the optimal capital structure? If the conclusions are different, what is the cause?

11-15 How might a firm go about determining its optimal capital structure? In addition to quantitative considerations, what other important factors should a firm consider when it is making capital structure decisions?

Summary

LG **1** **Discuss the role of breakeven analysis, algebraic and graphic determination of the operating breakeven point, and the effect of changing costs on it.** Breakeven analysis is used to measure the level of sales necessary to cover total operating costs. The operating breakeven point may be calculated algebraically, by dividing fixed operating costs by the difference between the sale price per unit and variable operating cost per unit, or determined graphically. The operating breakeven point increases with increased fixed and variable operating costs and decreases with an increase in sale price and vice versa.

LG **2** **Understand the concepts, measurement, and behavior of operating, financial, and total leverage and the relationship between them.** Operating leverage is the potential use of fixed operating costs by the firm to magnify the effects of changes in sales on earnings before interest and taxes (EBIT). The higher the fixed operating costs, the greater the operating leverage. Financial leverage is the potential use of fixed financial costs by the firm to magnify the effects of changes in earnings before interest and taxes (EBIT) on earnings per share (EPS). The higher the fixed financial costs—typically interest on debt and preferred stock dividends—the greater the financial leverage. The total leverage of the firm is the potential use of fixed costs—both operating and financial—to magnify the effects of changes in sales on earnings per share (EPS). Total leverage reflects the combined effect of operating and financial leverage.

LG **3** **Describe the basic types of capital, external assessment of capital structure, and capital structure theory in terms of tax benefits, probability of bankruptcy, agency costs imposed by lenders, and asymmetric information.** The two basic types of capital—debt and equity—making up a firm's capital structure differ with respect to voice in management, claims on income and assets, maturity, and tax treatment. Capital structure can be externally assessed by using financial ratios—debt ratio, debt-equity ratio, times interest earned ratio, and fixed payment coverage ratio. Non-U.S. companies tend to have much higher leverage ratios than do their U.S. counterparts, primarily because the United States' capital markets are much better developed. Similarities between U.S. corporations and those of other countries include industry patterns of capital structures, large multinational company capital structures, and the trend toward greater reliance on securities issuance and less reliance on banks for financing.

Research suggests that there is an optimal capital structure that balances the firms benefits and cost of debt financing. The major benefit of debt financing is the tax-deductible interest, and the costs of debt financing include the probability of bankruptcy, caused by business and financial risk; agency costs imposed by lenders in their loan agreements to protect themselves against potential agency problems; and asymmetric information, which causes firms to typically raise funds in a pecking order of retained earnings first, then debt, and finally external equity financing, to send positive signals to the market and thereby enhance the wealth of existing shareholders.

LG 4 Explain the optimal capital structure using a graphic view of the firm's debt, equity, and weighted average cost of capital functions, along with a modified form of the zero growth valuation model. The zero growth valuation model can be used to define the firm's value as its after-tax EBIT divided by its weighted average cost of capital. Assuming that EBIT is constant, the value of the firm is maximized by minimizing its weighted average cost of capital (WACC). The optimal capital structure is therefore the one that minimizes the WACC. Graphically, although both debt and equity costs rise with increasing financial leverage, the lower cost of debt causes the WACC to decline and then rise with increasing financial leverage. As a result, the firm's WACC exhibits a U-shape having a minimum value, which defines the optimum capital structure—the one that maximizes the owners' wealth.

LG 5 Discuss the graphic presentation, risk considerations, and basic shortcomings of using the EBIT–EPS approach to comparing alternative capital structures. The EBIT–EPS approach can be used to evaluate various capital structures in light of the returns they provide the firm's owners and their degree of financial risk. Under the EBIT–EPS approach, the preferred capital structure would be the one that is expected to provide maximum EPS over the firm's expected range of EBIT. Graphically, this approach reflects risk in terms of the financial breakeven point and the slope of the capital structure-line. The major shortcoming of EBIT–EPS analysis is that by ignoring risk, it concentrates on maximization of earnings rather than maximization of owners' wealth.

LG 6 Review the procedures for linking the return and risk associated with alternative capital structures to market value to select the best capital structure, and other important capital structure considerations. The best capital structure can be selected from various alternatives by using a valuation model to link return and risk factors. The preferred capital structure would be the one that results in the highest estimated share value—not the highest profits (EPS). Of course, other important nonquantitative factors, such as revenue stability, cash flow, contractual obligations, management preferences, control, external-risk assessment, and timing, must also be considered in making capital structure decisions.

Self-test problems (Solutions in Appendix E)

ST 11-1 LG 1,2 Breakeven point and all forms of leverage TOR most recently sold 100,000 units at $7.50 each; its variable operating costs are $3.00 per unit, and its fixed operating costs are $250,000. Annual interest charges total $80,000, and the firm has 8,000 shares of $5 (annual dividend) preferred stock outstanding. It currently has 20,000 shares of common stock outstanding. Assume that the firm has a 40 percent tax rate.

a. At what level of sales (in units) would the firm break even on operations (i.e., EBIT = $0)?

b. Calculate the firm's earnings per share (EPS) in tabular form at (1) the current level of sales and (2) a 120,000-unit sales level.

c. Using the current *$750,000 level of sales as a base,* calculate the firm's degree of operating leverage (DOL).

d. Using the EBIT *associated with the $750,000 level of sales as a base,* calculate the firm's degree of financial leverage (DFL).

e. Use the degree of total leverage (DTL) concept to determine the effect (in percentage terms) of a 50 percent increase in TOR's sales *from the $750,000 base level* on its earnings per share.

ST 11-2 LG 5 EBIT–EPS analysis Newlin Electronics is considering additional financing of $10,000. It currently has $50,000 of 12 percent (annual interest) bonds and 10,000 shares of common stock outstanding. The firm can obtain the financing through a 12 percent (annual interest) bond issue or the sale of 1,000 shares of common stock. The firm has a 40 percent tax rate.

a. Calculate two EBIT–EPS coordinates for each plan by selecting any two EBIT values and finding their associated EPS.

b. Plot the two financing plans on a set of EBIT–EPS axes.

c. On the basis of your graph in **b**, at what level of EBIT does the bond plan become superior to the stock plan?

ST 11-3 LG 3,6 Optimal capital structure The Hawaiian Macadamia Nut Company has collected the following data with respect to its capital structure, expected earnings per share, and required return.

Capital structure debt ratio (%)	Expected earnings per share ($)	Required return, k_s (%)
0%	$3.12	13%
10	3.90	15
20	4.80	16
30	5.44	17
40	5.51	19
50	5.00	20
60	4.40	22

a. Compute the estimated share value using the simplified method described in this chapter (see Equation 11.12).
b. Determine the optimal capital structure based on (1) maximization of expected earnings per share and (2) maximization of share value.
c. Which capital structure do you recommend? Why?

Problems

11-1 LG 1 Breakeven point—Algebraic Kate Rowland wishes to estimate the number of flower arrangements she must sell at $24.95 to break even. She has estimated fixed operating costs of $12,350 per year and variable operating costs of $15.45 per arrangement. How many flower arrangements must Kate sell to break even on operating costs?

11-2 LG 1 Breakeven comparisons—Algebraic Given the following price and cost data for each of the three firms F, G, and H, answer the questions below.

Firm	F	G	H
Sale price per unit	$18.00	$21.00	$30.00
Variable operating cost per unit	6.75	13.50	12.00
Fixed operating cost	45,000	30,000	90,000

a. What is the operating breakeven point in units for each firm?
b. How would you rank these firms in terms of their risk?

11-3 LG 1 Breakeven point—Algebraic and graphic Fine Leather Enterprises sells its single product for $129.00 per unit. The firm's fixed operating costs are $473,000 annually, and its variable operating costs are $86.00 per unit.
a. Find the firm's operating breakeven point in units.

b. Label the *x*-axis "Sales (units)" and the *y*-axis "Costs/Revenues ($)," and then graph the firm's sales revenue, total operating cost, and fixed operating cost functions on these axes. In addition, label the operating breakeven point and the areas of loss and profit (EBIT).

11-4 LG 1 **Breakeven analysis** Barry Carter is considering opening a record store. He wants to estimate the number of CDs he must sell to break even. The CDs will be sold for $13.98 each, variable operating costs are $10.48 per CD, and annual fixed operating costs are $73,500.

a. Find the operating breakeven point in CDs.
b. Calculate the total operating costs at the breakeven volume found in **a**.
c. If Barry estimates that at a minimum he can sell 2,000 CDs *per month,* should he go into the record business?
d. How much EBIT would Barry realize if he sells the minimum 2,000 CDs per month noted in **c**?

11-5 LG 1 **Breakeven point—Changing costs/revenues** JWG Company publishes *Creative Crosswords.* Last year the book of puzzles sold for $10 with variable operating cost per book of $8 and fixed operating costs of $40,000. How many books must be sold this year to achieve the breakeven point for the stated operating costs, given the following different circumstances?

a. All figures remain the same as last year.
b. Fixed operating costs increase to $44,000; all other figures remain the same as last year.
c. The selling price increases to $10.50; all costs remain the same as last year.
d. Variable operating cost per book increases to $8.50; all other figures remain the same.
e. What conclusions about the operating breakeven point can be drawn from your answers?

11-6 LG 1 **EBIT sensitivity** Stewart Industries sells its finished product for $9 per unit. Its fixed operating costs are $20,000, and the variable operating cost per unit is $5.

a. Calculate the firm's earnings before interest and taxes (EBIT) for sales of 10,000 units.
b. Calculate the firm's EBIT for sales of 8,000 and 12,000 units, respectively.
c. Calculate the percentage changes in sales (from the 10,000-unit base level) and associated percentage changes in EBIT for the shifts in sales indicated in **b**.
d. On the basis of your findings in **c**, comment on the sensitivity of changes in EBIT in response to changes in sales.

11-7 LG 2 **Degree of operating leverage** Grey Products has fixed operating costs of $380,000, variable operating costs per unit of $16, and a selling price of $63.50 per unit.

a. Calculate the operating breakeven point in units.
b. Calculate the firm's EBIT at 9,000, 10,000, and 11,000 units, respectively.
c. Using 10,000 units as a base, what are the percentage changes in units sold and EBIT as sales move from the base to the other sales levels used in **b**?
d. Use the percentages computed in **c** to determine the degree of operating leverage (DOL).
e. Use the degree of operating leverage formula to determine the DOL at 10,000 units.

11-8 LG 2 **Degree of operating leverage—Graphic** Levin Corporation has fixed operating costs of $72,000, variable operating costs of $6.75 per unit, and a selling price of $9.75 per unit.

a. Calculate the operating breakeven point in units.
b. Compute the degree of operating leverage (DOL) for the following unit sales levels: 25,000, 30,000, 40,000. Use the formula given in the chapter.
c. Graph the DOL figures that you computed in **b** (on the *y*-axis) against sales levels (on the *x*-axis).
d. Compute the degree of operating leverage at 24,000 units; add this point to your graph.
e. What principle is illustrated by your graph and figures?

11-9 LG 2 **EPS calculations** Southland Industries has $60,000 of 16 percent (annual interest) bonds outstanding, 1,500 shares of preferred stock paying an annual dividend of $5 per share, and 4,000 shares of common stock outstanding. Assuming that the firm has a 40 percent tax rate, compute earnings per share (EPS) for the following levels of EBIT:

a. $24,600
b. $30,600
c. $35,000

11-10 LG 2 Degree of financial leverage Northwestern Savings and Loan has a current capital structure consisting of $250,000 of 16 percent (annual interest) debt and 2,000 shares of common stock. The firm pays taxes at the rate of 40 percent.

a. Using EBIT values of $80,000 and $120,000, determine the associated earnings per share (EPS).
b. Using $80,000 of EBIT as a base, calculate the degree of financial leverage (DFL).
c. Rework parts **a** and **b** assuming that the firm has $100,000 of 16 percent (annual interest) debt and 3,000 shares of common stock.

11-11 LG 2 DFL and graphic display of financing plans Wells and Associates has EBIT of $67,500. Interest costs are $22,500, and the firm has 15,000 shares of common stock outstanding. Assume a 40 percent tax rate.

a. Use the degree of financial leverage (DFL) formula to calculate the DFL for the firm.
b. Using a set of EBIT–EPS axes, plot Wells and Associates' financing plan.
c. Assuming that the firm also has 1,000 shares of preferred stock paying a $6.00 annual dividend per share, what is the DFL?
d. Plot the financing plan including the 1,000 shares of $6.00 preferred stock on the axes used in **b**.
e. Briefly discuss the graph of the two financing plans.

11-12 LG 2 Integrative—Multiple leverage measures Play-More Toys produces inflatable beach balls, selling 400,000 balls a year. Each ball produced has a variable operating cost of $.84 and sells for $1.00. Fixed operating costs are $28,000. The firm has annual interest charges of $6,000, preferred dividends of $2,000, and a 40 percent tax rate.

a. Calculate the operating breakeven point in units.
b. Use the degree of operating leverage (DOL) formula to calculate DOL.
c. Use the degree of financial leverage (DFL) formula to calculate DFL.
d. Use the degree of total leverage (DTL) formula to calculate DTL. Compare this to the product of DOL and DFL calculated in **b** and **c**.

11-13 LG 2 Integrative—Leverage and risk Firm R has sales of 100,000 units at $2.00 per unit, variable operating costs of $1.70 per unit, and fixed operating costs of $6,000. Interest is $10,000 per year. Firm W has sales of 100,000 units at $2.50 per unit, variable operating costs of $1.00 per unit, and fixed operating costs of $62,500. Interest is $17,500 per year. Assume that both firms are in the 40 percent tax bracket.

a. Compute the degree of operating, financial, and total leverage for firm R.
b. Compute the degree of operating, financial, and total leverage for firm W.
c. Compare the relative risks of the two firms.
d. Discuss the principles of leverage illustrated in your answers.

11-14 LG 3 Various capital structures Charter Enterprises currently has $1 million in total assets and is totally equity-financed. It is contemplating a change in capital structure. Compute the amount of debt and equity that would be outstanding if the firm were to shift to one of the following debt ratios: 10, 20, 30, 40, 50, 60, and 90 percent. (The amount of total assets would not change.) Is there a limit to the debt ratio's value?

11-15 LG 3 Debt and financial risk Tower Interiors has made the following forecast of sales. Also given is the probability of each level of sales.

Sales	Probability
$200,000	.20
300,000	.60
400,000	.20

The firm has fixed operating costs of $75,000 and variable operating costs equal to 70 percent of the sales level. The company pays $12,000 in interest per period. The tax rate is 40 percent.

a. Compute the earnings before interest and taxes (EBIT) for each level of sales.

b. Compute the earnings per share (EPS) for each level of sales, the expected EPS, the standard deviation of the EPS, and the coefficient of variation of EPS, assuming that there are 10,000 shares of common stock outstanding.

c. Tower has the opportunity to reduce leverage to zero and pay no interest. This will require that the number of shares outstanding be increased to 15,000. Repeat **b** under this assumption.

d. Compare your findings in **b** and **c**, and comment on the effect of the reduction of debt to zero on the firm's financial risk.

11-16 LG 4 EPS and optimal debt ratio Williams Glassware has estimated, at various debt ratios, the expected earnings per share and the standard deviation of the earnings per share as follows:

Debt ratio (%)	Earnings per share (EPS)	Standard deviation of EPS
0%	$2.30	$1.15
20	3.00	1.80
40	3.50	2.80
60	3.95	3.95
80	3.80	5.53

a. Estimate the optimal debt ratio based on the relationship between earnings per share and the debt ratio. You will probably find it helpful to graph the relationship.

b. Graph the relationship between the coefficient of variation and the debt ratio. Label the areas associated with business risk and financial risk.

11-17 LG 5 EBIT–EPS and structure Data-Check is considering two capital structures. The key information follows. Assume a 40 percent tax rate.

Source of capital	Structure A	Structure B
Long-term debt	$100,000 at 16% coupon rate	$200,000 at 17% coupon rate
Common stock	4,000 shares	2,000 shares

a. Calculate two EBIT–EPS coordinates for each of the structures by selecting any two EBIT values and finding their associated EPS.

b. Plot the two capital structures on a set of EBIT–EPS axes.

c. Indicate over what EBIT range, if any, each structure is preferred.

d. Discuss the leverage and risk aspects of each structure.

e. If the firm is fairly certain that its EBIT will exceed $75,000, which structure would you recommend? Why?

11-18 LG 5 EBIT–EPS and preferred stock Litho-Print is considering two possible capital structures, A and B, shown below. Assume a 40 percent tax rate.

Source of capital	Structure A	Structure B
Long-term debt	$75,000 at 16% coupon rate	$50,000 at 15% coupon rate
Preferred stock	$10,000 with an 18% annual dividend	$15,000 with an 18% annual dividend
Common stock	8,000 shares	10,000 shares

a. Calculate two EBIT–EPS coordinates for each of the structures by selecting any two EBIT values and finding their associated EPS.
b. Graph the two capital structures on the same set of EBIT–EPS axes.
c. Discuss the leverage and risk associated with each of the structures.
d. Over what range of EBIT would each structure be preferred?
e. Which structure would you recommend if the firm expects its EBIT to be $35,000? Explain.

11-19 LG 4,5,6 Integrative—Optimal capital structure Nelson Corporation has made the following forecast of sales, with the associated probability of occurrence noted.

Sales	Probability
$200,000	.20
300,000	.60
400,000	.20

The company has fixed operating costs of $100,000 per year, and variable operating costs represent 40 percent of sales. The existing capital structure consists of 25,000 shares of common stock that have a $10 per share book value. No other capital items are outstanding. The marketplace has assigned the following discount rates to risky earnings per share.

Coefficient of variation of EPS	Estimated required return, k_s (%)
.43	15%
.47	16
.51	17
.56	18
.60	22
.64	24

The company is contemplating *shifting its capital structure* by substituting debt in the capital structure for common stock. The three different debt ratios under consideration are given in the table at the top of page 480, along with an estimate of the corresponding required interest rate on *all* debt.

Debt ratio (%)	Interest rate on *all* debt
20%	10%
40	12
60	14

The tax rate is 40 percent. The market value of the equity for a levered firm can be found by using the simplified method (see Equation 11.12).

a. Calculate the expected earnings per share (EPS), the standard deviation of EPS, and the coefficient of variation of EPS for the three proposed capital structures.

b. Determine the optimal capital structure, assuming (1) maximization of earnings per share and (2) maximization of share value.

c. Construct a graph (similar to Figure 11.7) showing the relationships in **b**. (*Note:* You will probably have to sketch the lines, since you have only three data points.)

11-20 LG 4,5,6 **Integrative—Optimal capital structure** Country Textiles, which has fixed operating costs of $300,000 and variable operating costs equal to 40 percent of sales, has made the following three sales estimates, with their probabilities noted.

Sales	Probability
$ 600,000	.30
900,000	.40
1,200,000	.30

The firm wishes to analyze five possible capital structures—0, 15, 30, 45, and 60 percent debt ratios. The firm's total assets of $1 million are assumed to be constant. Its common stock has a book value of $25 per share, and the firm is in the 40 percent tax bracket. The following additional data have been gathered for use in analyzing the five capital structures under consideration.

Capital structure debt ratio (%)	Before-tax cost of debt, k_d (%)	Required return, k_s (%)
0%	0.0%	10.0%
15	8.0	10.5
30	10.0	11.6
45	13.0	14.0
60	17.0	20.0

a. Calculate the level of EBIT associated with each of the three levels of sales.

b. Calculate the amount of debt, the amount of equity, and the number of shares of common stock outstanding for each of the capital structures being considered.

c. Calculate the annual interest on the debt under each of the capital structures being considered. (*Note:* The before-tax cost of debt, k_d, is the interest rate applicable to *all* debt associated with the corresponding debt ratio.)

d. Calculate the EPS associated with each of the three levels of EBIT calculated in **a** for each of the five capital structures being considered.

e. Calculate the (1) expected EPS, (2) standard deviation of EPS, and (3) coefficient of variation of EPS for each of the capital structures, using your findings in d.

f. Plot the expected EPS and coefficient of variation of EPS against the capital structures (x-axis) on separate sets of axes, and comment on the return and risk relative to capital structure.

g. Using the EBIT–EPS data developed in **d**, plot the 0, 30, and 60 percent capital structures on the same set of EBIT–EPS axes, and discuss the ranges over which each is preferred. What is the major problem with the use of this approach?

h. Using the valuation model given in Equation 11.12 and your findings in **e**, estimate the share value for each of the capital structures being considered.

i. Compare and contrast your findings in **f** and **h**. Which structure is preferred if the goal is to maximize EPS? Which structure is preferred if the goal is to maximize value? Which capital structure do you recommend? Explain.

Chapter 11 Case Evaluating Tampa Manufacturing's capital structure

Tampa Manufacturing, an established producer of printing equipment, expects its sales to remain flat for the next three to five years due to both a weak economic outlook and an expectation of little new printing technology development over that period. On the basis of this scenario the firms management has been instructed by its board to institute programs that will allow it to operate more efficiently, earn higher profits, and, most important, maximize share value. In this regard, the firm's chief financial officer (CFO), Jon Lawson, has been charged with evaluating the firm's capital structure. Lawson believes that the current capital structure, which contains 10 percent debt and 90 percent equity, may lack adequate financial leverage. To evaluate the firm's capital structure, Lawson has gathered the data summarized below on the current capital structure (10% debt ratio) and two alternative capital structures—A (30% debt ratio) and B (50% debt ratio)—that he would like to consider.

	Capital structure[a]		
Source of capital	**Current (10% debt)**	**A (30% debt)**	**B (50% debt)**
Long-term debt	$1,000,000	$3,000,000	$5,000,000
Coupon interest rate[b]	9%	10%	12%
Common stock	100,000 shares	70,000 shares	40,000 shares
Required return on equity, k_s[c]	12%	13%	18%

[a]These structures are based on maintaining the firm's current level of $10,000,000 of total financing.

[b]Interest rate applicable to *all* debt.

[c]Market-based returns for the given level of risk.

Lawson expects the firm's earnings before interest and taxes (EBIT) to remain at its current level of $1,200,000. The firm has a 40 percent tax rate.

Required

a. Use the current level of EBIT to calculate the times interest earned ratio for each capital structure. Evaluate the current and two alternative capital structures using the times interest earned and debt ratios.

b. Prepare a single EBIT–EPS graph showing the current and two alternative capital structures.

c. On the basis of the graph in **b**, which capital structure will maximize Tampa's earnings per share (EPS) at its expected level of EBIT of $1,200,000? Why might this *not* be the best capital structure?

d. Using the zero growth valuation model given in Equation 11.12, find the market value of Tampa's equity under each of the three capital structures at the $1,200,000 level of expected EBIT.

e. On the basis of your findings in **c** and **d**, which capital structure would you recommend? Why?

INTEGRATIVE CASE IV
O'GRADY APPAREL COMPANY

O'Grady Apparel Company was founded nearly 140 years ago when an Irish merchant named Garrett O'Grady landed in Los Angeles with an inventory of heavy canvas, which he hoped to sell for tents and wagon covers to miners headed for the California goldfields. Instead, he turned to the sale of harder-weaing clothing.

Today, the O'Grady Apparel Company is a small manufacturer of fabrics and clothing whose stock is traded on the over-the-counter exchange. In 1994 the Los Angeles–based company experienced sharp increases in both domestic and European markets resulting in record earnings. Sales rose from \$15.9 million in 1993 to \$18.3 million in 1994 with earnings per share of \$3.28 and \$3.84, respectively.

The European sales represented 29 percent of total sales in 1994, up from 24 percent the year before and only 3 percent in 1989, one year after foreign operations were launched. Although foreign sales represent nearly one-third of total sales, the growth in the domestic market is expected to affect the company most markedly. In 1995, management expects sales to surpass \$21 million, while earnings per share are expected to rise to \$4.40. (Selected income statement items are presented in Table 1.)

Because of the recent growth, Margaret Jennings, the corporate treasurer, is concerned that available funds are not being used to their fullest. The projected \$1,300,000 of internally generated 1995 funds are expected to be insufficient to meet the company's expansion needs. Management has set a policy to maintain the current capital structure proportions of 25 percent long-term debt, 10 percent preferred stock, and 65 percent common stock equity for at least the next three years. In addition, it plans to pay out about 40 percent of its earnings as dividends. Total capital expenditures are yet to be determined.

Ms. Jennings has been presented with several competing investment opportunities by division and product managers. However, since funds are limited, choices of which projects to accept must be made. The investment opportunities schedule (IOS) is shown in Table 2. To analyze the affect of the increased financing requirements on the weighted average cost of capital (WACC), Ms. Jennings contacted a leading investment banking firm which provided the financing cost data given in Table 3. The firm is in the 40 percent tax bracket.

TABLE 1

SELECTED INCOME STATEMENT ITEMS

	1992	1993	1994	Projected 1995
Net sales	$13,860,000	$15,940,000	$18,330,000	$21,080,000
Net profits after taxes	1,520,000	1,750,000	2,020,000	2,323,000
Earnings per share (EPS)	2.88	3.28	3.84	4.40
Dividends per share	1.15	1.31	1.54	1.76

TABLE 2

INVESTMENT OPPORTUNITIES SCHEDULE (IOS)

Investment opportunity	Internal rate of return (IRR)	Initial investment
A	21%	$400,000
B	19	200,000
C	24	700,000
D	27	500,000
E	18	300,000
F	22	600,000
G	17	500,000

TABLE 3

FINANCING COST DATA

Long-term debt: The firm can raise $700,000 of additional debt by selling ten-year, $1,000, 12 percent annual interest rate bonds to net $970 after flotation costs. Any debt in excess of $700,000 will have a before-tax cost, k_d, of 18 percent.

Preferred stock: Preferred stock, regardless of the amount sold, can be issued with a $60 par value, 17 percent annual dividend rate, and will net $57 per share after flotation costs.

Common stock equity: The firm expects its dividends and earnings to continue to grow at a constant rate of 15 percent per year. The firm's stock is currently selling for $20 per share. The firm expects to have $1,300,000 of available retained earnings. Once the retained earnings have been exhausted, the firm can raise additional funds by selling new common stock, netting $16 per share after flotation costs.

Required

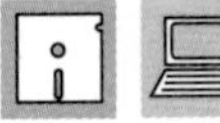

a. Over the relevant ranges noted in the following table, calculate the after-tax cost of each source of financing needed to complete the table.

Source of capital	Range of new financing	After-tax cost (%)
Long-term debt	\$0–\$700,000	____
	\$700,000 and above	____
Preferred stock	\$0 and above	____
Common stock equity	\$0–\$1,300,000	____
	\$1,300,000 and above	____

b. (1) Determine the breaking points associated with each source of capital.

(2) Using the breaking points developed in (1) determine each of the ranges of *total* new financing over which the firm's weighted average cost of capital (WACC) remains constant.

(3) Calculate the weighted average cost of capital for each range of total new financing.

c. (1) Using your findings in **b**(3) with the investment opportunities schedule (IOS), draw the firm's weighted marginal cost of capital (WMCC) schedule and IOS on the same set of total new financing or investment (*x*-axis)–weighted average cost of capital and IRR (*y*-axis) axes.

(2) Which, if any, of the available investments would you recommend that the firm accept? Explain your answer.

d. (1) Assuming that the specific financing costs do not change, what effect would a shift to a more highly levered capital structure consisting of 50 percent long-term debt, 10 percent preferred stock, and 40 percent common stock have on your findings above? (*Note:* Rework **b** and **c** above using these capital structure weights.)

(2) Which capital structure—the original one or this one—seems better? Why?

part V

Long-term financing decisions

CHAPTERS IN THIS PART

chapter 12

Long-term debt and investment banking

LEARNING GOALS

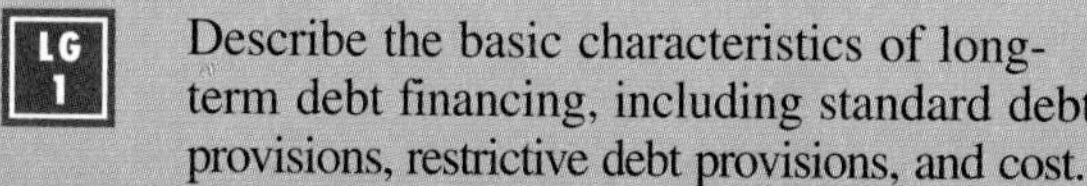

LG 1 Describe the basic characteristics of long-term debt financing, including standard debt provisions, restrictive debt provisions, and cost.

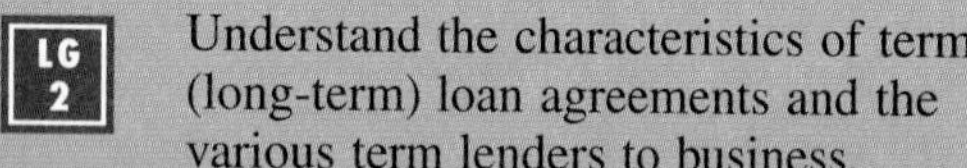

LG 2 Understand the characteristics of term (long-term) loan agreements and the various term lenders to business.

LG 3 Discuss the legal aspects of corporate bonds, general features of a bond issue, bond ratings, popular types of bonds, and international long-term debt financing.

LG 4 Review the logic and computational procedures involved in bond-refunding options, particularly exercising a call to refund a bond with new bonds issued at a lower interest rate.

LG 5 Define the investment bankers' role and the two major functions that they perform in helping firms to raise long-term financing—both debt and equity.

LG 6 Discuss the investment banking process—from selecting an investment banker through stabilizing the price, the cost of investment banking services, and the private placement as an alternative to a public offering.

General Electric Company is actually two companies: an industrial company (General Electric, GE) and a financial company (General Electric Capital Services, GECS). We have two treasury organizations because there is a fundamental difference in the approach to financing these two entities. An industrial company emphasizes cash flow financing: How will we repay the debt, how much do we need, and for what maturity? A finance company focuses on managing the spread between the interest rates on the funds that it borrows and the interest rates on the funds that it lends.

I am responsible for financing on the industrial side, which includes diverse business units—aircraft engines, appliances, broadcasting (NBC), industrial manufacturing, and power systems. Basically, GE finances its U.S. operations at the parent level. For example, if one of our businesses needs money, we use the GE name and credit rating—AAA, the highest. The strength of the consolidated entity helps us get the lowest total financing cost.

Financial managers should understand the impact of debt on the entire company. A company's debt level changes its risk characteristics; more debt means greater financial risk. Management must decide how much debt a company can support, when to finance with debt or equity, and how much of each is appropriate.

Bond ratings are another critical component in determining the company's debt level. As a rule, GE's financial decisions are consistent with maintaining our AAA rating, which is extremely valuable. A company's credit rating affects both borrowing cost and access to debt markets. For example, I worked for a large publishing company when it was a takeover target. At one point we couldn't borrow at all because of rumors. This obviously put the company at a disadvantage.

Financial managers should understand the impact of debt on the entire company.

Managing debt involves choosing maturities. We try to match debt maturities to cash flow from projects being financed. Even in mid-1993, when long-term rates were very low, we generally didn't finance for over seven years. Our time horizon has shortened in recent years. Twenty years ago, GE, like most companies, issued 25- or 30-year bonds whenever short-term financing reached a certain level. Today, it's rare for us to go beyond 10 years. Our philosophy is different from that of other companies in that regard. Most of our debt is issued with five- to seven-year maturities, and we refinance as necessary. We think that this strategy is more efficient and cost-effective over time than 30-year debt. It's certainly not an exact science, and we monitor the market carefully to make these decisions. Another company may prefer to lock in rates for a longer time frame.

Another important change is the growing importance of short-term debt—commercial paper (corporate IOUs), for example—in our overall debt picture. Today the commercial paper markets are larger and more liquid, and a certain amount of commercial paper is a permanent part of our balance sheet. We include short-term debt with long-term debt and equity as part of GE's capital structure.

GE uses investment bankers for two primary reasons: to underwrite securities and as a sounding board to get the pulse of the market. Investment bankers may also bring GE structured deals targeting a particular investor demand. Smaller or less experienced firms may rely more on investment bankers for advance preparation and analysis. Whatever the relationship, investment bankers are the link between the company (borrower) and the investor (lender) and play a key role in implementing a company's desired capital structure.

A graduate of Holy Cross College in Worcester, Massachusetts, Gerry Halpin received his M.B.A. degree from The Darden School at the University of Virginia. Before joining GE as Assistant Treasurer in 1988, he worked for the accounting firm of Arthur Andersen and was in the Treasury Departments of PepsiCo and Macmillan Publishing.

Characteristics of long-term debt financing

Because a borrowing firm, once it has received the loan proceeds, may be able to increase its risk without being required to pay the lender an increased return (interest), a potential agency problem exists between owners and lenders. If you were a lender, how would you go about protecting yourself against this agency problem? Before reading on, spend a few moments answering this question.

long-term financing
Financing with an initial maturity of more than one year.

LONG-TERM DEBT IS AN IMPORTANT FORM OF **LONG-TERM FINANCING**—FINANCING WITH an initial maturity of more than one year. It can be obtained with a *term loan,* which is negotiated from a financial institution, or through the sale of *bonds,* which are marketable debt sold to a number of institutional and individual lenders. The process of selling bonds, as well as stock, is generally accomplished by using an *investment banker*—an institution that can assist in private placements and take a lead role in public offerings. Long-term debt provides financial leverage and is a desirable component of capital structure (see Chapter 11), since it tends to lower the weighted average cost of capital[1] (see Chapter 10).

The long-term debts of a business typically have maturities of between 5 and 20 years.[2] When a long-term debt has one year or less to maturity, accountants will show the balance of the long-term debt as a current liability because at that point it becomes a short-term obligation. Similar treatment is given to portions of long-term debts that are payable in the coming year. These entries are normally labeled "current portion of long-term debt." Here we discuss long-term debt provisions and costs. In subsequent sections we'll turn our attention to term loans, corporate bonds, and investment banking.

Standard debt provisions

standard debt provisions
Provisions in long-term debt agreements specifying certain criteria of satisfactory record keeping and reporting, tax payment, and general business maintenance on the part of the borrowing firm; normally, they do not place a burden on the financially sound business.

A number of **standard debt provisions** are included in long-term debt agreements. These provisions specify certain criteria of satisfactory record keeping and reporting, tax payment, and general business maintenance on the part of the borrowing firm. Standard debt provisions do not normally place a burden on the financially sound business. Commonly included standard provisions are listed below.

1. The borrower is required to maintain satisfactory accounting records in accordance with generally accepted accounting principles (GAAP).
2. The borrower is required to periodically *supply audited financial statements*, which are used by the lender to monitor the firm and enforce the debt agreement.

---

[1]Long-term debt tends to lower the WACC primarily because of the tax-deductibility of interest, which causes the explicit cost of long-term debt to be quite low. Of course, as was noted in Chapter 11, the introduction of large quantities of debt into the firm's capital structure can result in high levels of financial risk, which cause the weighted average cost of capital to rise.

[2]Some texts classify debts with maturities between one and seven years as *intermediate-term debt.* This text uses a strict short-term–long-term classification. Debts with maturities of one year or less are considered short-term, and debts with maturities greater than one year are considered long-term. This classification is consistent with the firm's balance sheet classification of current liabilities and long-term debts.

3. The borrower is required to *pay taxes and other liabilities when due.*
4. The borrower is required to *maintain all facilities in good working order,* thereby behaving as a "going concern."

Restrictive debt provisions

restrictive covenants
Contractual clauses in long-term debt agreements that place certain operating and financial constraints on the borrower.

Long-term debt agreements, whether resulting from a term loan or a bond issue, normally include certain **restrictive covenants,** contractual clauses that place certain operating and financial constraints on the borrower. Since the lender is committing funds for a long period, it of course seeks to protect itself. Restrictive covenants, coupled with standard debt provisions, allow the lender to monitor and control the borrower's activities to protect itself against the *agency problem* created by the relationship between owners and lenders (described in Chapter 11). Without these provisions the borrower could "take advantage" of the lender by acting to increase the firm's risk, perhaps by investing all of the firm's capital in the state lottery, while not being required to pay the lender an increased return (interest).

Restrictive covenants remain in force for the life of the debt agreement. The most common restrictive covenants are listed below.

1. The borrower is required to maintain a minimum level of net working capital. Net working capital below the minimum is considered indicative of inadequate liquidity, a common precursor to loan default and ultimate failure.
2. Borrowers are *prohibited from selling accounts receivable* to generate cash, since doing so could cause a long-run cash shortage if proceeds are used to meet current obligations.
3. Long-term lenders commonly impose *fixed-asset restrictions* on the firm. These constrain the firm with respect to the liquidation, acquisition, and encumbrance of fixed assets, since any of these actions could damage the firm's ability to repay its debt.
4. Many debt agreements *constrain subsequent borrowing* by prohibiting additional long-term debt or by requiring that additional borrowing be "*subordinated*" to the original loan. **Subordination** means that all subsequent or less important creditors agree to wait until all claims of the *senior debt* are satisfied before having their claims satisfied.

subordination
In a long-term debt agreement, the stipulation that all subsequent or less important creditors agree to wait until all claims of the *senior debt* are satisfied before having their claims satisfied.

5. Borrowers may be *prohibited from entering into certain types of leases* to limit additional fixed-payment obligations.
6. Occasionally, the lender *prohibits combinations* by requiring the borrower to agree not to consolidate, merge, or combine in any way with another firm, since such an action could significantly change the borrower's business and financial risk.
7. To prevent liquidation of assets through large salary payments, the lender may *prohibit or limit salary increases for specified employees.*
8. The lender may include *management restrictions* requiring the borrower to maintain certain "key employees" without whom the future of the firm would be uncertain.
9. Occasionally, the lender includes a covenant *limiting the borrower's security investment* alternatives. This restriction protects the lender by controlling the risk and marketability of the borrower's security investments.
10. Occasionally, a covenant specifically requires the borrower to *spend the borrowed funds on a proven financial need.*
11. A relatively common provision *limits the firm's annual cash dividend payments* to a maximum of 50 to 70 percent of its net earnings or a specified dollar amount.

In the process of negotiating the terms of long-term debt, borrower and lender must ultimately agree to acceptable restrictive covenants. A good financial manager will know in advance the relative impact of proposed restrictions and will "hold the line" on those that may have a severely negative or damaging effect. The violation of any standard or restrictive provision by the borrower gives the lender the right to demand immediate repayment of the debt. Generally, the lender will evaluate any violation to determine whether it is serious enough to jeopardize the loan. On the basis of such an evaluation the lender may demand immediate repayment of the loan, waive the violation and continue the loan, or waive the violation but alter the terms of the initial debt agreement.

Cost of long-term debt

The cost of long-term debt is generally greater than that of short-term borrowing. In addition to standard and restrictive provisions, the long-term debt agreement specifies the interest rate, the timing of payments, and the dollar amount of payments. The major factors affecting the cost, or interest rate, of long-term debt are loan maturity, loan size, and, more important, borrower risk and the basic cost of money.

CONCEPT IN PRACTICE

A Sale at Sears That You Won't Want to Miss

What can a firm do when its cost of long-term debt, plus associated restrictive covenants, become too much of a burden? If it has the cash, it can simply pay off its creditors. If it doesn't, then it can do what Sears Roebuck & Company is doing: selling subsidiaries. By the end of 1993, managers at Sears must raise $3 billion in cash to retire $4 billion in debt. To achieve this goal, Sears has already sold its mortgage banking group to PNC Bank in Pittsburgh for $328 million and offered a 20 percent equity stake in its retail brokerage unit, Dean Witter, for $775 million. It plans to sell 20 percent of common stock in its Allstate Insurance to the public for $2 billion. Now if Sears could only sell socks . . . .

LOAN MATURITY

Generally, long-term loans have higher interest rates than short-term loans. As was noted in Chapter 2, there is a tendency for yield curves to be upward sloping (long-term interest rates higher than short-term rates) as a result of several factors: (1) the general expectation of higher future rates of inflation; (2) lender preferences for shorter-term, more liquid loans; and (3) greater demand for long-term rather than short-term loans relative to the supply of such loans. In a more practical sense, the longer the term of a loan, the less accuracy there is in predicting future interest rates and therefore the greater the lender's risk of forgoing an opportunity to loan money at a higher rate. In addition, the longer the term, the greater the repayment risk associated with the loan. To compensate for all of these factors, the lender typically charges a higher interest rate on long-term loans.

LOAN SIZE

The size of the loan affects the interest cost of borrowing in an inverse manner. Loan administration costs per dollar borrowed are likely to decrease with increasing loan size. On the other hand, the risk to the lender increases, since larger loans result in less diversification. The size of the loan sought by each borrower must therefore be evaluated to determine the net administrative cost-risk tradeoff.

BORROWER RISK

As was noted in Chapter 11, the higher the firm's operating leverage, the greater its business risk. Also, the higher the borrower's debt ratio or debt-equity ratio (or the lower its times interest earned ratio or fixed-payment coverage ratio), the greater its financial risk. The lender's main concern is with the borrower's ability to fully repay the loan as prescribed in the debt agreement. The overall assessment of the borrower's business and financial risk, along with information on past payment patterns, is used by the lender in setting the interest rate on any loan.

BASIC COST OF MONEY

The cost of money is the basis for determining the actual interest rate charged. Generally, the rate on U.S. Treasury securities with *equivalent maturities* is used as the basic (lowest-risk) cost of money. To determine the actual interest rate to be charged, the lender will add premiums for loan size and borrower risk to this basic cost of money for the given maturity. Alternatively, some lenders determine a prospective borrower's risk class[3] and find the rates charged on similar-maturity loans to firms that are believed to be in the same risk class. Instead of having to determine a risk premium, the lender can use the risk premium prevailing in the marketplace for similar loans.

CONCEPTS IN REVIEW

12-1 What are the two key methods of raising long-term debt financing? What motives does the lender have for including certain *restrictive covenants* in a debt agreement? How do these covenants differ from so-called *standard debt provisions?*

12-2 What sort of negotiation process is required in settling on a set of restrictive loan covenants? What are the consequences of violation of a standard or restrictive provision by the borrower?

12-3 What is the general relationship between the cost of short-term and long-term debt? Why? In addition to loan maturity, what other major factors affect the cost, or interest rate, of long-term debt?

Term loans

A term loan is a loan with an initial maturity of more than one year. What specific financial institutions do you think make term loans to businesses? Take some time to answer this question before reading further.

[3]A *risk class* reflects the firm's overall risk profile. One must envision a continuum of risk, break it into discrete classes, and place the firm in an appropriate class. Looking at other firms that are perceived to be in the same risk class will help the lender to make certain decisions about the appropriate rate of interest. For publicly traded firms, betas (see Chapter 6) are often used to classify firms into homogeneous risk classes. If the firm's debt is rated by an independent bond-rating agency, the ratings will effectively determine the risk class and associated interest rate.

term (long-term) loan
A loan made by a financial institution to a business and having an initial maturity of more than one year.

A TERM (LONG-TERM) LOAN IS A LOAN MADE BY A FINANCIAL INSTITUTION TO A BUSINESS and having an initial maturity of more than one year. These loans generally have maturities of 5 to 12 years; shorter maturities are available, but minimum 5-year maturities are common. Term loans are often made to finance *permanent* working capital needs, to pay for machinery and equipment, or to liquidate other loans.

Characteristics of term loan agreements

term loan agreement
A formal contract, ranging from a few to a few hundred pages, specifying the conditions under which a financial institution has made a long-term loan.

The actual **term loan agreement** is a formal contract ranging from a few to a few hundred pages. The following items are commonly specified in the document: the amount and maturity of the loan, payment dates, interest rate, standard provisions, restrictive provisions, collateral (if any), purpose of the loan, action to be taken in the event the agreement is violated, and stock-purchase warrants. Of these, only payment dates, collateral requirements, and stock-purchase warrants require further discussion.

PAYMENT DATES

balloon payment
At the maturity of a loan, a large lump-sum payment representing the entire loan principal if the periodic payments represent only interest.

Term loan agreements generally specify monthly, quarterly, semiannual, or annual loan payments. Generally, these equal payments fully repay the interest and principal over the life of the loan. Occasionally, a term loan agreement will require periodic payments over the life of the loan followed by a large lump-sum payment at maturity. This so-called **balloon payment** represents the entire loan principal if the periodic payments represent only interest.

COLLATERAL REQUIREMENTS

secured loan
A loan that has specific assets pledged as collateral.

collateral
The items used by a borrower to back up a loan; any assets against which a lender has a legal claim if the borrower defaults on some provision of the loan.

unsecured loan
A loan that has no assets pledged as collateral.

Term lending arrangements may be unsecured or secured. **Secured loans** have specific assets pledged as collateral.[4] The **collateral** commonly takes the form of an asset such as machinery and equipment, plant, inventory, pledges of accounts receivable, and pledges of securities. **Unsecured loans** are obtained without pledging specific assets as collateral. Whether collateral is required depends on the lender's evaluation of the borrower's financial condition. Any collateral required and its disposition under various circumstances are specifically described in the term loan agreement. In addition, the lender will file necessary legal documents to (1) establish clearly its right to seize and liquidate loan collateral in the event the borrower defaults and (2) serve notice to subsequent lenders of a prior claim on the asset(s).

STOCK-PURCHASE WARRANTS

stock-purchase warrants
Instruments that give their holder the right to purchase a certain number of shares of the firm's common stock at a specified price over a certain period of time.

A trend in term lending is for the corporate borrower to give the lender certain financial perquisites in addition to the payment of interest and repayment of principal. **Stock-purchase warrants** are instruments that give their holder the right to purchase a certain number of shares of the firm's common stock at a specified price over a certain

[4]The terms *security* and *collateral* are used interchangeably to refer to the items used by a borrower to back up a loan. Loan security or collateral may be any assets against which a lender, as a result of making a loan, has a legal claim that is exercisable if the borrower defaults on some provision of the loan. If the borrower defaults, the lender can sell the security or collateral to satisfy the claim against the borrower. Some of the more technical aspects of loan defaults are presented in Chapter 19.

period of time. These are used to entice institutional lenders to make long-term loans, possibly under more-than-normally-favorable terms. Stock-purchase warrants are discussed in greater detail in Chapter 14.

Term lenders

The primary lenders making term loans to business are commercial banks, insurance companies, pension funds, regional development companies, the federal government's Small Business Administration, small business investment companies, commercial finance companies, and equipment manufacturers' financing subsidiaries. Although the characteristics and provisions of term lending agreements made by these lenders are similar, a number of basic differences exist. Table 12.1 summarizes the key characteristics and types of loans made.

CONCEPTS IN REVIEW

12-4 What types of payment dates are generally required in a term (long-term) loan agreement? What is a *balloon payment?*

12-5 What role do commercial banks, insurance companies, pension funds, regional development companies, the Small Business Administration, small business investment companies, commercial finance companies, and equipment manufacturers play in lending long-term funds to businesses?

Corporate bonds

When interest rates decline, a firm may wish to consider issuing new bonds at the lower rate and using the funds obtained to retire its outstanding higher-rate bonds. How does such a decision lend itself to the application of the capital budgeting techniques presented in earlier chapters? Spend a few moments answering this question before reading ahead.

corporate bond
A certificate indicating that a corporation has borrowed a certain amount of money from an institution or an individual and promises to repay it in the future under clearly defined terms.

A **CORPORATE BOND** IS A CERTIFICATE INDICATING THAT A CORPORATION HAS BORROWED a certain amount of money from an institution or an individual and promises to repay it in the future under clearly defined terms. Most bonds are issued with maturities of 10 to 30 years and with a par, or face, value of $1,000. The coupon interest rate on a bond represents the percentage of the bond's par value that will be paid annually, typically in two equal semiannual payments. The bondholders, who are the lenders, are promised the semiannual interest payments and, at maturity, repayment of the principal amount (par value).

Legal aspects of corporate bonds

Since a corporate bond issue may be for hundreds of millions of dollars obtained by selling portions of the debt to numerous unrelated people, certain legal arrangements are required to protect purchasers. Bondholders are protected legally primarily through the indenture and the trustee.

TABLE 12.1

CHARACTERISTICS AND TYPES OF TERM LOANS MADE BY MAJOR TERM LENDERS

Lender	Characteristics	Types of loans
Commercial bank	Makes some term loans to businesses.	Generally less than 12-year maturity except for real estate. Often participates in large loans made by a group of banks, since banks are legally limited[a] in the amount they can loan a single borrower. Loans typically secured by collateral.
Insurance company	Life insurers are most active lenders.	Maturities of 10 to 20 years. Generally to larger firms and in larger amounts than commercial bank loans. Both unsecured and secured loans.
Pension fund	Invests a small portion of its funds in term loans to businesses.	Generally mortgage loans to large firms. Similar to insurance company loans.
Regional development company	An association generally attached to local or regional governments. Attempts to promote business development in a given area by offering attractive financing deals. Obtains funds from various governmental bodies and through sale of tax-exempt bonds.	Term loans are made at competitive rates.
Small Business Administration (SBA)	An agency of the federal government that makes loans to "eligible" small and minority-owned businesses.	Joins with private lender and lends or guarantees repayment of all or part of the loan. Most loans are made for less than $750,000 at or below commercial bank interest rates. The average loan amount is around $300,000.
Small business investment company (SBIC)	Licensed by the government. Makes both debt and equity investments in small firms.	Makes loans to small firms with high growth potential. Term loans with 5- to 20-year maturities and interest rates above those on bank loans. Generally receives, in addition, an equity interest in the borrowing firm.
Commercial finance company (CFC)	Involved in financing equipment purchases. Often a subsidiary of the manufacturer of equipment.	Makes secured loans for purchase of equipment. Typically installment loans with less-than-10-year maturities at higher-than-bank interest rates.
Equipment manufacturers' financing subsidiary	A type of "captive finance company" owned by the equipment manufacturer.	Makes long-term installment loans on equipment sales. Similar to commercial finance companies.

[a]Commercial banks are legally prohibited from loaning amounts in excess of 15 percent (plus an additional 10 percent for loans secured by readily marketable collateral) of the bank's unimpaired capital and surplus to any one borrower. This restriction is intended to protect depositors by forcing the commercial bank to spread its risk across a number of borrowers.

BOND INDENTURE

bond indenture
A complex and lengthy legal document stating the conditions under which a bond has been issued.

A **bond indenture** is a complex and lengthy legal document stating the conditions under which a bond has been issued. It specifies both the rights of the bondholders and the duties of the issuing corporation. In addition to specifying the interest and principal payments and dates and containing various standard and restrictive provisions, it frequently contains sinking-fund requirements and provisions with respect to a security interest (if the bond is secured).

SINKING-FUND REQUIREMENTS The standard and restrictive provisions for long-term debt and for bond issues have already been described in an earlier section of this chapter. However, an additional restrictive provision often included in a bond indenture is a **sinking-fund requirement.** Its objective is to provide for the systematic retirement of bonds prior to their maturity. To carry out this requirement, the corporation makes semiannual or annual payments to a *trustee,* who uses these funds to retire bonds by purchasing them in the marketplace. This process is simplified by inclusion of a *call feature,* which permits the issuer to repurchase bonds at a stated price prior to maturity. The trustee will "call" bonds only when sufficient bonds cannot be purchased in the marketplace or when the market price of the bond is above the stated (call) price.[5]

sinking-fund requirement
A restrictive provision that is often included in a bond indenture providing for the systematic retirement of bonds prior to their maturity.

SECURITY INTEREST The bond indenture is similar to a loan agreement in that any collateral pledged against the bond is specifically identified in the document. Usually, the title to the collateral is attached to the indenture, and the disposition of the collateral in various circumstances is specifically described. The protection of bond collateral is crucial to increase the safety and thereby enhance the marketability of a bond issue.

TRUSTEE

trustee
A paid individual, corporation, or commercial bank trust department that acts as the third party to a bond indenture to ensure that the issuer does not default on its contractual responsibilities to the bondholders.

A **trustee** is a third party to a bond indenture. The trustee can be an individual, a corporation, or, most often, a commercial bank trust department. The trustee, whose services are paid for, acts as a "watchdog" on behalf of the bondholders, making sure that the issuer does not default on its contractual responsibilities. The trustee is empowered to take specified actions on behalf of the bondholders if the terms of the indenture are violated.

CONCEPT IN PRACTICE

Bondholders Aren't Passive Investors at Marriott Corporation

Bondholders may lack corporate voting rights but not voices in running a business. Ask Stephen Bollenbach, CEO of the Marriott Corporation. He proposed dividing the $9.1 billion company into two firms: Marriott International, a fast-growth service business operating Marriott's hotels and providing food and facilities management for health care and educational institutions; and Host Marriott

[5]The market price of a callable bond will not generally exceed its call price, except in the case of a *convertible bond*—a bond that can be converted into a specified number of shares of common stock at the bondholders' option. Because, as we will explain in Chapter 14, the market price of a convertible bond often reflects the value of its underlying stock, it is not unusual for it to trade at prices above its call price.

Corporation, a slow-growth, capital-intensive unit overseeing the firm's real estate. Marriott International would enjoy projected income of $136 million on sales of $7.8 billion. Host Marriott would assume the company's $2.1 billion in debt.

Marriott's stockholders support the plan. Bondholders argue that, should Host Marriott enter default, such restructuring would cut them from Marriott International's cash flows but would protect current shareholders from possible bankruptcy. Since a majority of bondholders must approve the plan, Bollenbach is drafting Plan B to divide Marriott's total debt more equitably between the two new units.

General features of a bond issue

Three common features of a bond issue are (1) a conversion feature, (2) a call feature, and (3) stock-purchase warrants. These features provide both the issuer and the purchaser with certain opportunities for replacing, retiring, and (or) supplementing the bond with some type of equity issue.

CONVERSION FEATURE

conversion feature
A feature of so-called *convertible bonds* that allows bondholders to change each bond into a specified number of shares of common stock.

The **conversion feature** of certain so-called *convertible bonds* allows bondholders to change each bond into a specified number of shares of common stock. Bondholders will convert their bonds only when the market price of the stock is greater than the conversion price, hence providing a profit for the bondholder. Chapter 14 discusses convertible bonds in detail.

CALL FEATURE

call feature
A feature that is included in almost all corporate bond issues that gives the issuer the opportunity to repurchase bonds prior to maturity at a stated price.

call price
The stated price at which a bond may be repurchased, by use of a *call feature,* prior to maturity.

call premium
The amount by which a bond's call price exceeds its par value.

The **call feature** is included in almost all corporate bond issues. It gives the issuer the opportunity to repurchase bonds prior to maturity. The **call price** is the stated price at which bonds may be repurchased prior to maturity. Sometimes the call privilege is exercisable only during a certain period. As a rule, the call price exceeds the par value of a bond by an amount equal to one year's interest. For example, a $1,000 bond with a 10 percent coupon interest rate would be callable for around $1,100 [$1,000 + (10% × $1,000)]. The amount by which the call price exceeds the bond's par value is commonly referred to as the **call premium.** This premium compensates bondholders for having the bond called away from them, and it is the cost to the issuer of calling the bonds. A higher call premium is required by investors when interest rates are high because there is an increased likelihood that rates will decline, the issuer will exercise the call, and the bondholders will experience large opportunity losses.

The call feature is generally advantageous to the issuer, since it enables the issuer to retire outstanding debt prior to maturity. Thus when interest rates fall, an issuer can call an outstanding bond and reissue a new bond at a lower interest rate. When interest rates rise, the call privilege will not be exercised, except possibly to meet sinking-fund requirements. Of course, to sell a callable bond, the issuer must pay a higher interest rate than on noncallable bonds of equal risk to compensate bondholders for the risk of having the bonds called away from them.

STOCK-PURCHASE WARRANTS

Like term loans, warrants are occasionally attached to bonds as "sweeteners" to make them more attractive to prospective buyers. As was noted earlier, a stock-purchase warrant gives its holder the right to purchase a certain number of shares of common stock at a specified price over a certain period of time. An in-depth discussion of stock-purchase warrants is included in Chapter 14.

debentures
See Table 12.3.

subordinated debentures
See Table 12.3.

income bonds
See Table 12.3.

mortgage bonds
See Table 12.3.

collateral trust bonds
See Table 12.3.

equipment trust certificates
See Table 12.3.

zero (or low) coupon bonds
See Table 12.4.

junk bonds
See Table 12.4.

floating rate bonds
See Table 12.4.

extendable notes
See Table 12.4.

putable bonds
See Table 12.4.

Bond ratings

The riskiness of publicly traded bond issues is assessed by independent agencies such as Moody's and Standard & Poor's. Moody's has nine major ratings; Standard & Poor's has ten. These agencies derive the ratings by using financial ratio and cash flow analyses. Table 12.2 summarizes these ratings. There is normally an inverse relationship between the quality or rating of a bond and the rate of return that it must provide bondholders. High-quality (high-rated) bonds provide lower returns than lower-quality (low-rated) bonds. This reflects the lender's risk-return tradeoff. When considering bond financing, the financial manager must therefore be concerned with the expected ratings of the firm's bond issue, since these ratings can significantly affect salability and cost.

Popular types of bonds

Bonds can be classified in a variety of ways. Here we break them into traditional bonds—the basic types that have been around for years—and contemporary bonds—newer, more innovative types of bonds that have been developed and/or become popular in recent years. The traditional types of bonds are summarized in terms of their key characteristics and priority of lenders' claim in Table 12.3. Note that the first three types—**debentures, subordinated debentures,** and **income bonds**—are unsecured, whereas the last three—**mortgage bonds, collateral trust bonds,** and **equipment trust certificates**—are secured.

Table 12.4 describes the key characteristics of five contemporary types of bonds—**zero** (or **low**) **coupon bonds, junk bonds, floating rate bonds, extendable notes,** and **putable bonds.** These bonds can be either unsecured or secured. These contemporary bonds have been introduced in recent years in response to changing capital market conditions and investor preferences. Zero (or low) coupon bonds are designed to provide

TABLE 12.2

MOODY'S AND STANDARD & POOR'S BOND RATINGS[a]

Moody's	Interpretation	Standard & Poor's	Interpretation
Aaa	Prime quality	AAA	Bank investment quality
Aa	High grade	AA	
A	Upper medium grade	A	
Baa	Medium grade	BBB	
Ba	Lower medium grade or speculative	BB	Speculative
		B	
B	Speculative		
Caa	From very speculative	CCC	
Ca	to near or in default	CC	
C	Lowest grade	C	Income bond
		D	In default

[a]Some ratings may be modified to show relative standing within a major rating category; for example, Moody's uses numerical modifiers (1, 2, 3), whereas Standard & Poor's uses plus (+) and minus (−) signs.

Source: Moody's Investors Services, Inc., and Standard & Poor's Corporation.

TABLE 12.3

SUMMARY OF CHARACTERISTICS AND PRIORITY OF CLAIM OF TRADITIONAL TYPES OF BONDS

Bond type	Characteristics	Priority of lenders' claim
Debentures	Unsecured bonds that only creditworthy firms can issue. Convertible bonds are normally debentures.	Claims are the same as those of any general creditor. May have other unsecured bonds subordinated to them.
Subordinated debentures	Claims are not satisfied until those of the creditors holding certain (senior) debts have been fully satisfied.	Claim is that of a general creditor but not as good as a senior debt claim.
Income bonds	Payment of interest is required only when earnings are available from which to make such payment. Commonly issued in reorganization of a failed or failing firm.	Claim is that of a general creditor. Not in default when interest payments are missed, since they are contingent only on earnings being available.
Mortgage bonds	Secured by real estate or buildings. Can be *open-end* (other bonds issued against collateral), *limited open-end* (a specified amount of additional bonds can be issued against collateral), or *closed-end;* may contain an *after-acquired clause* (property subsequently acquired becomes part of mortgage collateral).	Claim is on proceeds from sale of mortgaged assets; if not fully satisfied, the lender becomes a general creditor. The *first-mortgage* claim must be fully satisfied before distribution of proceeds to *second-mortgage* holders, and so on. A number of mortgages can be issued against the same collateral.
Collateral trust bonds	Secured by stock and (or) bonds that are owned by the issuer. Collateral value is generally 25 to 35 percent greater than bond value.	Claim is on proceeds from stock and (or) bond collateral; if not fully satisfied, the holder becomes a general creditor.
Equipment trust certificates	Used to finance "rolling stock"—airplanes, trucks, boats, railroad cars. A mechanism whereby a trustee buys such an asset with funds raised through the sale of trust certificates and then leases it to the firm, which, after making the final scheduled lease payment, receives title to the asset. A type of leasing.	Claim is on proceeds from the sale of the asset; if proceeds do not satisfy outstanding debt, trust certificate holders become general creditors.

tax benefits to both issuer and purchaser; junk bonds were recently widely used to finance mergers and takeovers; both floating rate bonds and extendable notes give purchasers inflation protection; and putable bonds give the bondholder an option to sell the bond at par. These contemporary bonds allow the firm to more easily raise funds at a reasonable cost by better meeting the needs of investors. Changing capital market conditions, investor preferences, and corporate financing needs will likely result in development of further innovations in bond financing.

International long-term debt financing

Companies and governments borrow internationally by tapping one of three principal financial markets: the Eurobond, foreign bond, and Eurocurrency loan markets.

TABLE 12.4

CHARACTERISTICS OF CONTEMPORARY TYPES OF BONDS

Bond type	Characteristics[a]
Zero (or low) coupon bonds	Issued with no (zero) or a very low coupon (stated interest) rate and sold at a large discount from par. A significant portion (or all) of the investor's return therefore comes from gain in value (i.e., par value minus purchase price). Generally callable at par value. Because the issuer can annually deduct the current year's interest accrual without having to actually pay the interest until the bond matures (or is called), its cash flow each year is increased by the amount of the tax shield provided by the interest deduction.
Junk bonds	Debt rated Ba or lower by Moody's or BB or lower by Standard & Poor's. During the 1980s, commonly used by rapidly growing firms to obtain growth capital, most often as a way to finance mergers and takeovers of other firms. High-risk bonds with high yields—typically yielding 3 percent more than the best-quality corporate debt. As a result of a number of major defaults during the early 1990s, the popularity of these bonds has been somewhat reduced.
Floating rate bonds	Stated interest rate is adjusted periodically within stated limits in response to changes in specified money or capital market rates. Popular when future inflation and interest rates are uncertain. Tend to sell at close to par as a result of the automatic adjustment to changing market conditions. Some issues provide for annual redemption at par at the option of the bondholder.
Extendable notes	Short maturities, typically one to five years, which can be redeemed or renewed for a similar period at the option of their holders. Similar to a floating rate bond. An issue might be a series of three-year renewable notes over a period of 15 years; every three years the notes could be extended for another three years, at a new rate that is competitive with market interest rates prevailing at the time of renewal.
Putable bonds	Bonds that can be redeemed at par (typically $1,000) at the option of their holder either at specific dates such as three to five years after the date of issue and every 1 to 5 years thereafter or when and if the firm takes specified actions such as being acquired, acquiring another company, or issuing a large amount of additional debt. In return for the right to "put the bond" at specified times or actions by the firm, the bond's yield is lower than that of a nonputable bond.

[a]The claims of lenders against holders of each of these types of bonds vary depending on their other features. Each of these bonds can be unsecured or secured.

Each of these provides established, creditworthy borrowers the opportunity to obtain large amounts of long-term debt financing quickly and efficiently, in their choice of currency, and with very flexible repayment terms. Each of these markets is briefly described below.

EUROBONDS

Eurobond

A bond issued by an international borrower and sold to investors in countries with currencies other than the currency in which the bond is denominated.

A **Eurobond** is a bond issued by an international borrower and sold to investors in countries with currencies other than the currency in which the bond is denominated. A dollar-denominated bond issued by a U.S. corporation and sold to Belgian investors is an example of a Eurobond. The Eurobond market first developed in the early 1960s, when several European and U.S. borrowers discovered that many European investors wanted to hold dollar-denominated, bearer bonds that would both shelter investment income from taxation (since coupon interest payments were made to the "bearer" of the bond and names were not reported to tax authorities) and provide protection against exchange rate risk. From its founding until the mid-1980s, "blue chip" U.S. corporations were the largest single class of Eurobond issuers, and many of these companies were able to borrow in this market at interest rates below those the federal government paid on Treasury bonds it issued. As the market matured, issuers were able to choose the currency in which they borrowed, and European corporate and public-sector borrowers rose to prominence. By 1986, total Eurobond new issues had reached $187.7 billion dollars, two-thirds of which were dollar-denominated.

Several regulatory changes in U.S. financial markets during the mid-1980s caused U.S. corporations to switch their debt issues from the Eurobond market to the domestic bond market. The most important change was the adoption of the *shelf registration* procedure (discussed later in this chapter) by the SEC in 1984. After a sharp decline in volume in 1987 the Eurobond market reached almost $220 billion in total new issues in 1989 as new borrowers, particularly Japanese corporations issuing convertible "Euroyen" bonds, surged to prominence. In more recent years the Eurobond market has become much more balanced in terms of the mix of borrowers, total issue volume, and currency of denomination. Today, most Eurobond issues are in fact executed as one part of a complicated financial engineering transaction known as a "currency swap," wherein companies headquartered in different countries issue bonds in their home country currencies and then exchange principal and interest payments with each other.

FOREIGN BONDS

foreign bond
A bond issued in a host country's financial market, in the host country's currency, by a foreign borrower.

Whereas a Eurobond is issued by an international borrower in a single currency (initially dollars) in a variety of countries, a **foreign bond** is a bond issued in a host country's financial market, in the host country's currency, by a foreign borrower. A Deutsche mark–denominated bond issued in Germany by a U.S. company is an example of a foreign bond. In most years, at least $40 billion worth of foreign bonds are issued. The three largest foreign bond markets are Japan, Switzerland, and the United States.

EUROCURRENCY LOAN MARKET

Eurocurrency loan market
A large number of international banks that make long-term, floating rate, hard-currency (typically U.S. dollar–denominated) loans in the form of lines of credit to international corporate and government borrowers.

The **Eurocurrency loan market** consists of a large number of international banks that stand ready to make long-term, floating rate, hard-currency (typically U.S. dollar–denominated) loans to international corporate and government borrowers. These bank loans are usually structured as lines of credit on which borrowers can draw. Most large (over $500 million) loans are syndicated, meaning that pieces of each loan are sold to dozens of banks, thereby providing a measure of diversification to the lenders. Individual syndicated loans have ranged as large as $14 billion, and loans of $1 billion are quite common. Furthermore, in total size the Eurocurrency market, at over $500 billion in new credits per year in peak periods, dwarfs all other international financial markets. Finally, while the Eurocurrency market is best known for its role in the Third World "debt crisis" of the early 1980s, it has become an overwhelmingly important corporate financing market during the last decade.

Bond-refunding options

A firm that wishes to retire or refund a bond prior to maturity has two options. Both require some foresight on the part of the issuer.

SERIAL ISSUES

serial bonds
An issue of bonds for which a certain proportion matures each year.

The borrower can issue **serial bonds,** a certain proportion of which matures each year. When serial bonds are issued, a schedule showing the interest rate associated with each maturity is given. An example would be a $30 million, 20-year bond issue for which $1.5 million of the bonds ($30 million ÷ 20 years) mature each year. The interest rates associated with shorter maturities would, of course, differ from the rates associated with longer maturities. Although serial bonds cannot necessarily be retired at the option of the issuer, they do permit the issuer to systematically retire the debt.

REFUNDING BONDS BY EXERCISING A CALL

If interest rates drop following the issuance of a bond, the issuer may wish to refund (refinance) the debt with new bonds at the lower interest rate. If a call feature has been included in the issue, the issuer can easily retire it. In an accounting sense, bond refunding will increase earnings per share and reduce risk by lowering interest expense. Of course, the desirability of refunding a bond through exercise of a call is not necessarily obvious; its long-term consequences require the use of present-value techniques. This **bond-refunding decision** is another application of the capital budgeting techniques described in Chapters 8 and 9. Here the firm must find the net present value (NPV) of the bond refunding cash flows. The *initial investment* is the incremental after-tax cash outflows associated with calling the old bonds and issuing new bonds, and the *annual cash flow savings* are the after-tax cash savings that are expected to result from the reduced debt payments on the new lower-interest bond. These cash flows are the same each year. The resulting cash flow pattern surrounding this decision is *conventional*—an outflow followed by a series of inflows. The bond-refunding decision can be made by using the following three-step procedure.

bond-refunding decision
The decision facing firms, when bond interest rates drop, whether to refund (refinance) existing bonds with new bonds at the lower interest rate.

Step 1 *Find the initial investment* by estimating the incremental after-tax cash outflow required at time zero to call the old bond and issue a new bond in its place. Any overlapping interest resulting from the need to pay interest on both the old and new bond is treated as part of the initial investment.

Step 2 *Find the annual cash flow savings,* which is the difference between the annual after-tax debt payments with the old and new bond. This cash flow stream will be an annuity with a life equal to the maturity of the new bond.[6]

Step 3 Use the after-tax cost of debt (as the discount rate) to *find the net present value (NPV)* by subtracting the initial investment from the present value of annual cash flow savings. The *after-tax cost of debt* is used because the decision involves very low risk.[7] *If the resulting NPV is greater than zero, the proposed refunding is recommended;* otherwise, it should be rejected.

Application of these bond-refunding decision procedures can be illustrated with a simple example. However, a few tax-related points should be clarified first.

CALL PREMIUMS The amount by which the call price exceeds the par value of the bond is the *call premium.* It is paid by the issuer to the bondholder to buy back outstanding bonds prior to maturity. The call premium is treated as a tax-deductible expense in the year of the call.

[6]To simplify this procedure, the maturity of the new bond is set equal to the number of years to maturity remaining on the old bond. A procedure using annualized net present value (ANPV) techniques as presented in Chapter 9 would be required in comparing bonds having unequal maturities remaining.

[7]Because the refunding decision involves the choice of retaining an existing debt or substituting a new, lower-cost debt, it is viewed as a low-risk decision that will not significantly affect the firm's financial risk. The low-risk nature of the decision warrants the use of a very low rate, such as the firm's after-tax cost of debt.

BOND DISCOUNTS AND PREMIUMS When bonds are sold at a discount or at a premium, the firm is required to amortize (write off) the discount or premium in equal portions over the life of the bond. The amortized discount is treated as a tax-deductible expenditure, whereas the amortized premium is treated as taxable income. If a bond is retired prior to maturity, any unamortized portion of a discount or premium is deducted from or added to pretax income at that time.

FLOTATION OR ISSUANCE COSTS Any costs incurred in the process of issuing a bond must be amortized over the life of the bond. The annual write-off is therefore a tax-deductible expenditure. If a bond is retired prior to maturity, any unamortized portion of this cost is deducted from pretax income at that time.

EXAMPLE

Halda Industries, a manufacturer of copper pipe, is contemplating calling $30 million of 30-year, $1,000 bonds (30,000 bonds) issued five years ago with a coupon interest rate of 14 percent. The bonds have a call price of $1,140 and initially netted proceeds of $29.1 million due to a discount of $30 per bond. The initial flotation cost was $360,000. The company intends to sell $30 million of 12 percent coupon interest rate, 25-year bonds to raise funds for retiring the old bonds. The firm intends to sell the new bonds at their par value of $1,000. The flotation costs on the new issue are estimated to be $440,000. The firm is currently in the 40 percent tax bracket and estimates its after-tax cost of debt to be 8 percent.[8] Because the new bonds must first be sold and their proceeds then used to retire the old bonds, the firm expects a two-month period of overlapping interest, during which interest must be paid on both the old and the new bonds.

Step 1 *Find the Initial Investment* A number of calculations are required to find the initial investment.

a. *Call premium* The call premium per bond is $140 ($1,140 call price − $1,000 par value). Because the total call premium is deductible in the year of the call, its after-tax cost is

Before tax ($140 × 30,000 bonds)	$4,200,000
Less: Taxes (.40 × $4,200,000)	1,680,000
After-tax cost of call premium	$2,520,000

b. *Flotation cost of new bond* This cost was given as $440,000.

c. *Overlapping interest*[9] Treated as part of the initial investment, the after-tax cost of the overlapping interest on the old bond is

Before tax (.14 × 2/12 × $30,000,000)	$700,000
Less: Taxes (.40 × $700,000)	280,000
After-tax cost of overlapping interest	$420,000

[8]Ignoring any flotation costs, the firm's after-tax cost of debt would be 7.2 percent [12 percent debt cost × (1 − .40 tax rate)]. To reflect the flotation costs associated with selling new debt, the use of an after-tax debt cost of 8 percent was believed to be the applicable discount rate. A more detailed discussion of techniques for calculating a firm's after-tax cost of debt can be found in Chapter 10.

[9]Technically, the after-tax amount of overlapping interest could be reduced by the after-tax interest earnings from investment of the average proceeds available from sale of the new bonds during the interest overlap period. For clarity any interest earned on the proceeds from sale of the new bond during the overlap period are ignored in this chapter.

d. *Unamortized discount on old bond* The $900,000 discount ($30,000,000 par value − $29,100,000 net proceeds from sale) on the old bond was being amortized over 30 years. Because only five of the 30 years' amortization of the discount has been applied, the remaining 25 years of unamortized discount can be deducted as a lump sum, thereby reducing taxes by $300,000 (25/30 × $900,000 × .40).

e. *Unamortized flotation cost of old bond* The $360,000 initial flotation cost on the old bond was being amortized over 30 years. Because only five of the 30 years' amortization of this cost has been applied, the remaining 25 years of unamortized flotation cost can be deducted as a lump sum, thereby reducing taxes by $120,000 (25/30 × $360,000 × .40).

Summarizing these calculations in Table 12.5, we find the initial investment to be $2,960,000. This means that Halda Industries must pay out $2,960,000 now to implement the proposed bond refunding.

Step 2 *Find the Annual Cash Flow Savings* To find the annual cash flow savings, a number of calculations are required.

a. *Interest cost of old bond* The after-tax annual interest cost of the old bond is

Before tax (.14 × $30,000,000)	$4,200,000
Less: Taxes (.40 × $4,200,000)	1,680,000
After-tax interest cost	$2,520,000

b. *Amortization of discount on old bond* The $900,000 discount ($30,000,000 par value − $29,100,000 net proceeds from sale) on the old bond was being amortized over 30 years, resulting in an annual write-off of $30,000 ($900,000 ÷ 30). Because it is a tax-deductible noncash charge, the amortization of this discount results in an annual tax savings of $12,000 (.40 × $30,000).

TABLE 12.5

FINDING THE INITIAL INVESTMENT FOR HALDA INDUSTRIES' BOND-REFUNDING DECISION

a. Call premium		
Before tax [($1,140 − $1,000) × 30,000 bonds]	$4,200,000	
Less: Taxes (.40 × $4,200,000)	1,680,000	
After-tax cost of call premium		$2,520,000
b. Flotation cost of new bond		440,000
c. Overlapping interest		
Before tax (.14 × 2/12 × $30,000,000)	$700,000	
Less: Taxes (.40 × $700,000)	280,000	
After-tax cost of overlapping interest		420,000
d. Tax savings from unamortized discount on old bond [25/30 × ($30,000,000 − $29,100,000) × .40]		(300,000)
e. Tax savings from unamortized flotation cost of old bond (25/30 × $360,000 × .40)		(120,000)
Initial investment		$2,960,000

c. *Amortization of flotation cost on old bond* The $360,000 flotation cost on the old bond was being amortized over 30 years, resulting in an annual write-off of $12,000 ($360,000 ÷ 30). Because it is a tax-deductible non-cash charge, the amortization of the flotation cost results in an annual tax savings of $4,800 (.40 × $12,000).

d. *Interest cost of new bond* The after-tax annual interest cost of the new bond is

Before tax (.12 × $30,000,000)	$3,600,000
Less: Taxes (.40 × $3,600,000)	1,440,000
After-tax interest cost	$2,160,000

e. *Amortization of flotation cost on new bond* The $440,000 flotation cost on the new bond will be amortized over 25 years, resulting in an annual write-off of $17,600 ($440,000 ÷ 25). Because it is a tax-deductible non-cash charge, the amortization of the flotation cost results in an annual tax savings of $7,040 (.40 × $17,600).

These calculations are summarized in Table 12.6. It can be seen that totaling the first three values (**a**, **b**, and **c**), that the annual after-tax debt payment for the old bond is $2,503,200. When the values for the new bond (**d** and **e**) are totaled, the annual after-tax debt payment for the new bond is $2,152,960.

Subtracting the new bond's annual debt payment from that of the old bond, we find the annual cash flow savings to be $350,240 ($2,503,200 − $2,152,960). This means that implementation of the proposed bond refunding will result in an annual cash flow savings of $350,240.

TABLE 12.6

FINDING THE ANNUAL CASH FLOW SAVINGS FOR HALDA INDUSTRIES' BOND-REFUNDING DECISION

Old bond			
a. Interest cost			
Before tax (.14 × $30,000,000)	$4,200,000		
Less: Taxes (.40 × $4,200,000)	1,680,000		
After-tax interest cost		$2,520,000	
b. Tax savings from amortization of discount [($900,000[a] ÷ 30) × .40]		(12,000)	
c. Tax savings from amortization of flotation cost [($360,000 ÷ 30) × .40]		(4,800)	
(1) Annual after-tax debt payment			$2,503,200
New bond			
d. Interest cost			
Before tax (.12 × $30,000,000)	$3,600,000		
Less: Taxes (.40 × $3,600,000)	1,440,000		
After-tax interest cost		$2,160,000	
e. Tax savings from amortization of flotation cost [($440,000 ÷ 25) × .40]		(7,040)	
(2) Annual after-tax debt payment			2,152,960
Annual cash flow savings [(1) − (2)]			$ 350,240

[a] $30,000,000 par value − $29,100,000 net proceeds from sale

TABLE 12.7

FINDING THE NET PRESENT VALUE OF HALDA INDUSTRIES' BOND-REFUNDING DECISION

Present value of annual cash flow savings (from Table 12.6)	
$\$350,240 \times PVIFA_{8\%,25\text{yrs}}$	
$350,240 × 10.675 =	$3,738,812
Less: Initial investment (from Table 12.5)	2,960,000
Net present value (NPV) of refunding[a]	$ 778,812

Decision: The proposed refunding is *recommended* because the NPV of refunding of $778,812 is greater than $0.

[a]By using a hand-held business/financial calculator, the present value of the cash flow savings would be $3,738,734, which would have resulted in a NPV of refunding of $778,734.

Step 3 *Find the Net Present Value (NPV)* The net present value (NPV) of the proposed bond refunding is calculated in Table 12.7. It can be seen that the present value of the annual cash flow savings of $350,240 at the 8 percent after-tax cost of debt over the 25 years is $3,738,812. Subtracting the initial investment of $2,960,000 from the present value of annual cash flow savings results in a net present value (NPV) of $778,812. Because a positive NPV results, *the proposed bond refunding is recommended.* ■

CONCEPTS IN REVIEW

12-6 What types of maturities, denominations, and interest payments are associated with a typical corporate bond? Describe the role of the *bond indenture* and the *trustee.*

12-7 What does it mean if a bond has a *conversion feature?* A *call feature? Stock-purchase warrants?* How are bonds rated, and why?

12-8 Describe the basic characteristics of each of the following popular types of bonds.

a. Debentures
b. Subordinated debentures
c. Income bonds
d. Zero (or low) coupon bonds
e. Junk bonds
f. Floating rate bonds
g. Extendable notes
h. Putable bonds

12-9 Describe, compare, and contrast the basic features of the following secured bonds.

a. Mortgage bond
b. Collateral trust bond
c. Equipment trust certificate

12-10 Describe and compare the basic characteristics of the following sources of international long-term debt financing:

a. Eurobonds
b. Foreign bonds
c. Eurocurrency loans

12-11 What two options may be available to a firm that wants to retire or refund an outstanding bond issue prior to maturity? Must these options be provided for in advance of issuance? Why might the issuer wish to retire or refund a bond prior to its maturity?

12-12 Why does the *bond-refunding decision* lend itself to the application of capital budgeting techniques? Describe the three-step procedure that is used to make these decisions.

Investment banking

Investment bankers act as financial intermediaries that purchase securities from corporate and government issuers and resell them to the general public. What functions in addition to selling do you think investment bankers perform? Before reading ahead, take a few moments to answer this question.

INVESTMENT BANKING PLAYS AN IMPORTANT ROLE IN HELPING FIRMS TO RAISE LONG-TERM financing—both debt and equity—in the capital markets. It is the investment banker's job to find buyers for new security issues. As was noted briefly in Chapter 2, investment bankers are neither investors nor bankers; they neither make long-term investments nor guard the savings of others. Instead, acting as an intermediary between the issuer and the buyers of new security issues, the **investment banker** purchases securities from corporate and government issuers and resells them to the general public. In the United States, for example, during 1992 the top three investment banking firms were Goldman Sachs, Morgan Stanley Group, and CS First Boston Group. Many investment banking firms operate in other areas as well; for example, Merrill Lynch is a major investment banker in addition to being one of the nation's leading securities brokerage firms.

investment banker
A financial intermediary that purchases securities from corporate and government issuers and resells them to the general public.

Functions of the investment banker

The investment banker's primary function is underwriting security issues. A secondary function is advising clients.

UNDERWRITING

underwriting
The process in which an investment banker buys a security issue from the issuing firm at a lower price than that for which he or she plans to sell it, thereby guaranteeing the issuer a specified amount from the issue and assuming the risk of price changes between the time of purchase and the time of sale.

When **underwriting** a security issue, an investment banker guarantees the issuer that it will receive a specified amount from the issue. The banker buys the securities at a lower price than that for which he or she plans to sell them, thereby expecting to make a profit. The investment banker therefore bears the risk of price changes and a market collapse between the time of purchase and the time of sale of securities. There is always the possibility that the banker will be "stuck" with a large amount of the securities. In some instances he or she may be able to sell the securities only at a price lower than the initial purchase price.

EXAMPLE

Gigantica Corporation, a regional investment banking firm, has agreed to underwrite a new \$50 million common stock issue for Leader Electronics, an established manufacturer of consumer electronics. It has agreed to purchase the stock for \$48 million. Since

Gigantica must pay Leader $48 million for the stock, it must attempt to sell the stock for net proceeds of at least $48 million. Actually, it will attempt to sell the stock for at least $50 million, thereby obtaining a $2 million commission. If it is unable to raise $50 million, the investment banking firm will not realize the full $2 million commission and will possibly lose part of the $48 million that it initially paid for the stock. In some cases a security issue can be sold in a few days; in other situations, months are required to negotiate a sale. The investment banker therefore bears the risk of unfavorable price changes before the issue is sold as well as the risk of being unable to sell the issue at all. ■

Many security issues are not underwritten but rather are *privately placed* or sold on a *best efforts basis.* These functions are also handled by investment bankers.

private placement
The direct sale of a new security issue to one or more purchasers.

PRIVATE PLACEMENT **Private placement** occurs when an investment banker arranges for the direct sale of a new security issue to an individual, several individuals, a firm, or a group of firms. The investment banker is then paid a commission for acting as an intermediary in the transaction.

best efforts basis
A public offering in which the investment banker uses his or her resources to sell the security issue without taking on the risk of underwriting and is compensated on the basis of the number of securities sold.

BEST EFFORTS BASIS In the case of some public offerings, the investment banker may not actually underwrite the issue; rather, the banker may use his or her resources to sell the securities on a **best efforts basis.** In this case, the banker does not take on the risk associated with underwriting, and compensation is based on the number of securities sold.

ADVISING

The investment banker performs an advisory function by analyzing the firm's financial needs and recommending appropriate means of financing. Since an investment banker has a feel for the pulse of the capital markets, he or she can also provide useful advice on mergers, acquisitions, and refinancing decisions.

Organization of investment banking activity

The investment banker's functions of underwriting security issues and advising clients come into play as a result of a logical sequence of events. The process begins when a firm that is in need of additional financing selects an investment banking firm, which then confers with the issuer, syndicates the underwriting, forms a selling group, fulfills legal requirements for a sale, sets a price, distributes the issue, and stabilizes the price.

SELECTING AN INVESTMENT BANKER

competitive bidding
A method of choosing an investment banker in which the banker or group of bankers that bids the highest price for a security issue is awarded the issue.

negotiated offering
A security issue for which the investment banker is merely hired rather than awarded the issue through competitive bidding.

A firm that needs additional financing through the capital markets initiates the fund-raising process by selecting an investment banker to underwrite the new issue and provide advice. The investment banker may be selected through **competitive bidding** or may be chosen by the issuing firm. In the case of competitive bidding, the investment banker or group of bankers that bids the highest price for the issue is awarded it. If the investment banker is merely hired by the issuing firm, the security issue is called a **negotiated offering.**

CONFERRING WITH THE ISSUER

Once selected, the investment banker helps the firm determine how much capital should be raised and in what form—debt or equity. The banker analyzes the firm's financial position and proposed disposition of the funds to be raised to make sure that the firm is financially sound and that the proposed expenditures are justifiable. After an examination of certain legal aspects of the firm and its proposed offering, a tentative underwriting agreement is drawn up.

SYNDICATING THE UNDERWRITING

underwriting syndicate

A group of investment banking firms, each of which will underwrite a portion of a large security issue, thus lessening the risk of loss to any single firm.

Due to the size of many new security issues, it is often necessary for the originating investment banker to form an **underwriting syndicate,** which is a group of investment banking firms. The use of an underwriting syndicate lessens the risk of loss to any single firm. Each underwriter in the syndicate must sell its portion of the issue. This is likely to result in a wider distribution of the new securities.

FORMING A SELLING GROUP

selling group

A group of brokerage firms, each of which agrees to sell a portion of a security issue and expects to make a profit on the *spread* between the price at which they buy and sell the securities.

The originating underwriter with the assistance of syndicate members puts together a **selling group,** which is responsible for distributing the new issue to the investing public. The selling group is normally made up of a large number of brokerage firms, each of which accepts the responsibility for selling a certain portion of the issue. Members of the selling group, like underwriters, expect to make a profit on the *spread* between the price at which they buy and sell the securities. Figure 12.1 depicts the selling process for a new security issue.

FULFILLING LEGAL REQUIREMENTS

Through the Securities and Exchange Commission (SEC), the federal government regulates the initial and subsequent trading of securities. Initial regulation tends to center on the public sale of new issues; subsequent regulation is concerned with the sale of securities in *secondary markets*—both organized and over-the-counter.

REGISTRATION REQUIREMENTS Before a new security can be issued, the issuer must obtain the approval of the SEC. According to the Securities Act of 1933, which was passed to ensure the full disclosure of information with respect to new security issues and prevent a stock market collapse similar to the one that occurred in 1929–1932, the issuer is required to file a registration statement with the SEC. The firm cannot sell the security until the SEC approves the registration statement. This procedure usually requires 20 days.

prospectus

A portion of a security registration statement filed with the SEC that details the firm's operating and financial position; it must be made available to all potential buyers.

red herring

On a prospectus, a statement, printed in red ink, indicating the tentative nature of a security offer while it is being reviewed by the SEC.

One portion of the registration statement is called the **prospectus**; it details the firms operating and financial position. This prospectus may be issued to potential buyers during the waiting period between filing the registration statement and its approval as long as a **red herring**—a statement indicating the tentative nature of the offer—is printed in red ink on the prospectus. Once the registration statement has been approved, the new security can be offered for sale if the prospectus is made available to all interested parties. If the registration statement is found to be fraudulent, the SEC not only will reject the issue but also can sue the directors and others responsible for the misrepresentation. *Approval of the registration statement by the SEC does not mean that the security is a good investment; it indicates only that the facts presented in the statement accurately reflect the firm's operating and financial position.*

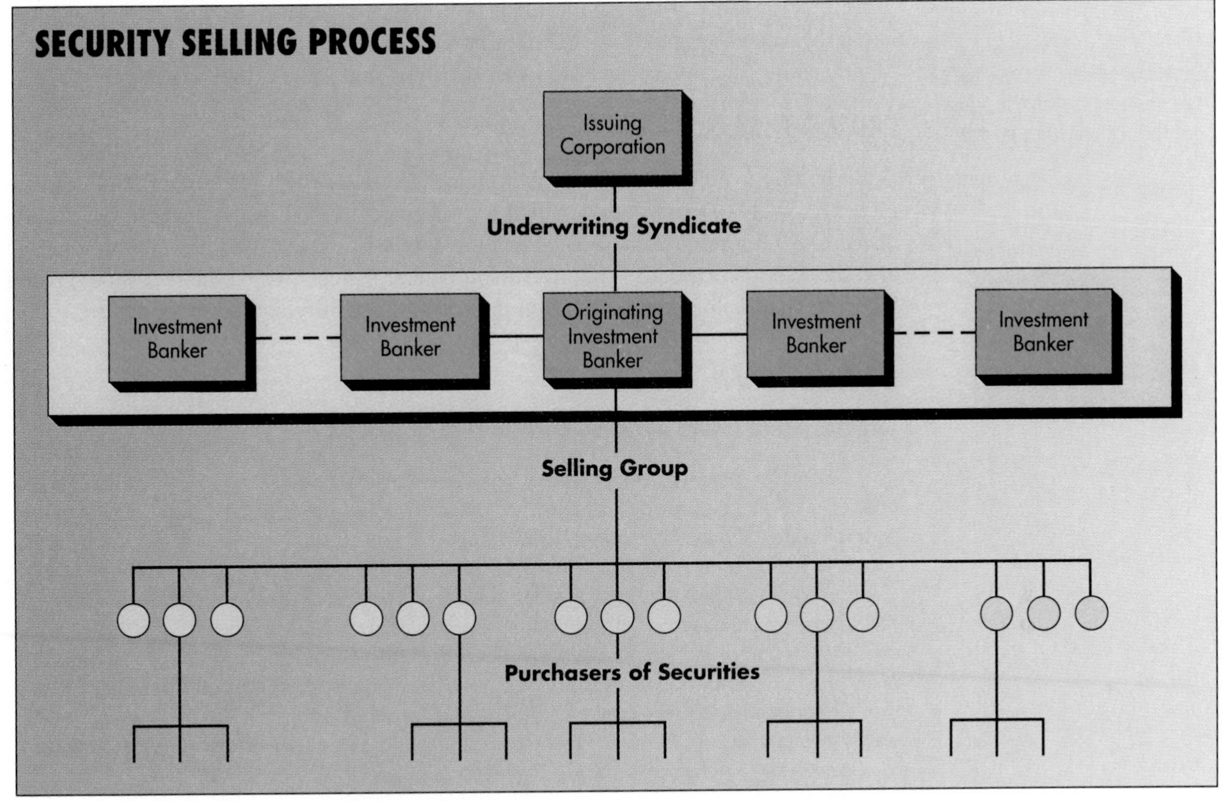

FIGURE 12.1
The selling process for a new security issue

As an alternative to filing a lengthy registration statement and awaiting SEC approval, firms with more than $150 million in outstanding common stock can use a procedure known as **shelf registration.** This procedure allows a firm to file a "master registration statement"—a single document summarizing planned financing—covering a two-year period. At any time during the two years, the firm, after filing a "short statement," can sell securities that have already been approved under the master statement. By using this procedure the approved securities are effectively warehoused and kept "on the shelf" until the need exists or market conditions are appropriate for selling the securities. The use of shelf registration is especially popular with large firms that frequently need access to the capital markets to raise debt or equity funds. Although some firms using shelf registration can reduce their reliance on investment bankers, the investment banker continues to be the key link between the firm and the capital markets.

shelf registration
An SEC procedure that allows firms with more than $150 million in outstanding common stock to file a "master registration statement" covering a two-year period and then, during that period, to sell securities that have already been approved under the master statement.

TRADING REQUIREMENTS Another important piece of legislation regulating the securities markets is the Securities Exchange Act of 1934, which is aimed at controlling the secondary trading of securities by providing for the regulation of securities exchanges, listed securities, and the general activities of the securities markets. The act provides for the disclosure of information on and accurate representation of securities traded. This piece of legislation and the Securities Act of 1933 are the key laws protecting participants in the capital markets. Many states also have laws aimed at regulating the sale of securities within their borders. These **blue sky laws** protect investors by preventing the sale of securities that provide "nothing but blue sky."

blue sky laws
State laws aimed at regulating the sale of securities within the state and thereby protecting investors.

PRICING THE ISSUE

Underwriting syndicates generally wait until the end of the registration period to price securities so that they will have a feel for the current mood of the market. The pricing decision is important because it affects the ease with which the issue can be sold and also the issuer's proceeds. The investment banker's "feel" for the market should result in a price that achieves the optimum mix of marketability and financial return.

CONCEPT IN PRACTICE

Targeted Stock Issues Redefine Basic Arithmetic at USX

Can two plus two equal three? Yes, with targeted equity issues! These issues offer investors a claim against part, not all, of a firm's residual cash flow. For example, USX Corporation offers USX equity in three forms: in the firm's oil and gas subsidiary, Marathon Group; in its U.S. Steel Group; and in its natural gas unit, Delhi Group. Each of these stocks trades on the New York Stock Exchange, and each pays dividends from its own cash flow, compensates its own senior officers, and files separate financial statements with the SEC. Yet USX Corporation remains one legal entity: Its bondholders have claims against assets and earnings of all three units. The firm's financial managers contend that issuing targeted equity rather than a single equity security allows USX to raise more money at lower cost. It also enables investors to choose only one of USX's three businesses.

DISTRIBUTING THE ISSUE

Before the actual offering of a new security for sale, the issue is publicized. This can be done only after the registration statement has been approved by the SEC. Publicity is obtained by advertising and personal contacts through the brokerage firms handling the issue. When the security is formally placed on the market, orders are accepted from the selling groups and from outsiders. If the issue is sold out, it is considered **oversubscribed;** if all shares are not sold immediately, it is said to be **undersubscribed.**

oversubscribed issue
A security issue that is sold out.

undersubscribed issue
A security issue whose shares are not immediately sold.

STABILIZING THE PRICE

Once an issue has been offered for sale, the underwriting syndicate attempts to stabilize its price so that the entire issue can be sold at or near the initial offering price. By placing orders to buy the security, the underwriting syndicate can keep the demand for the issue, and therefore its price, at the desired level. This activity, sometimes referred to as **market stabilization,** is legal as long as the intent is disclosed in the registration statement filed with the SEC. Market stabilization is in the best interests of both the issuer and the underwriting syndicate in that it reduces the syndicate's risk, thereby justifying payment of a higher price to the issuer by the syndicate.

market stabilization
The process in which an underwriting syndicate places orders to buy the security that it is attempting to sell to keep the demand for the issue, and therefore its price, at the desired level.

Cost of investment banking services

The investment banker is compensated by purchasing the security issue at a discount from the proposed sale price. On an individual per-bond or per-share basis, the difference between the price paid for a security by the investment banker and the sale price is referred to as the **spread.** The size of the spread depends on the cost of in-

spread
The difference between the price paid for a security by the investment banker and the sale price.

vestigations, printing, and registration; the discount to the underwriting syndicate; and the discount given to the selling group. The issuer's overall flotation cost has two basic components—administrative cost and underwriting cost. Generally, the larger the issue, the lower the overall cost in percentage terms. It is also generally true that the overall flotation cost for common stock is highest, followed by preferred stock and bonds in that order. The overall flotation cost ranges from as little as 1 percent of the total proceeds on a large bond issue to as much as 20 percent or more on a small common stock issue. The type of security issued affects the cost because it affects the ease with which large blocks can be placed with one purchaser. A firm that is contemplating a security issue must therefore weigh the cost of public sale against the cost and feasibility of private placement.

Private placement

As an alternative to a public offering, a firm can sometimes negotiate private (or direct) placement of a security issue. Interestingly, the trend in recent years is toward increasing use of private placements and diminished use of public offerings. Ordinarily, private placements are used primarily for bonds or preferred stock. Recently, a number of large firms have created in-house services for private placement of their short- and long-term debt. Common stock is sometimes directly placed when the firm believes that the existing shareholders might purchase the issue through an arrangement known as a *rights offering,* which is described in detail in Chapter 13.

Private placement usually reduces administrative and issuance costs and provides the issuer with a great deal of flexibility, since the firm need not file registration statements and is not required to obtain the approval of the Securities and Exchange Commission. In addition, private placement is often advantageous because the issuer has more flexibility in tailoring covenants and later renegotiating them, should the need arise, than it does with a public offering. On the other hand, private placement poses a disadvantage to the buyer who at some future date may wish to sell the securities on the open market, because prior to public sale, registration and approval by the Securities and Exchange Commission are required. In the case of private placements an investment banker is frequently employed to assist in finding a buyer and to provide pricing advice.

Direct placement of common stock is sometimes achieved through stock options or stock-purchase plans. **Stock options** are generally extended to management and permit the purchase of a certain number of shares of the firm's common stock at a specified price over a stated period of time. These options are intended to minimize *agency problems* by stimulating managerial actions consistent with the goal of owner wealth maximization. **Stock-purchase plans** are a fringe benefit offered to a firm's employees. They allow the employees to purchase the firm's stock at a discount or on a matching basis with a part of the cost absorbed by the firm. Both plans provide equity capital and at the same time increase employee motivation and interest in the company.

stock options
Options, generally extended to management, that permit purchase of the firm's common stock at a specified price over a stated period of time.

stock-purchase plans
An employee fringe benefit that allows the purchase of a firm's stock at a discount or on a matching basis with a part of the cost absorbed by the firm.

CONCEPT IN PRACTICE

Communications Skills Pay Off in Private Placements

In 1990, Symbus Technology, Inc., a Massachusetts-based firm specializing in neural network software, won a $1 million contract from Electronic Data Systems Corporation based on specifications for a new software product, not on the functional software itself. Great news, right? Seemingly yes, but Symbus would not realize this future sales revenue until it met EDS's production and performance requirements. To be able to pay its software developers, Symbus had to convince venture capitalists to fund software development despite the firm's negative net worth. So its investment bankers, Janney Montgomery Scott, Inc., sponsored a private syndicated equity offering to wealthy sponsors and got a $100,000 bridge loan convertible to common stock if the offering succeeded. Symbus's financial managers prepared and peddled their offering prospectus to Janney's accountants, attorneys, and managers and then pitched the stock to private investors. In late 1992, after a full year of presentations and correspondence, Symbus had raised $3.1 million.

CONCEPTS IN REVIEW

12-13 Describe the role and functions performed by the *investment banker.* Explain the sequence of events involved in the investment banking activity.

12-14 How is the investment banker compensated for its services? How are underwriting costs affected by the size and type of an issue?

12-15 What role, if any, does an investment banker play in private placements? How are *stock options* and *stock-purchase plans* used to directly place common stock?

Summary

LG 1 Describe the basic characteristics of long-term debt financing, including standard debt provisions, restrictive debt provisions, and cost. Standard and restrictive provisions are included in long-term debt agreements to protect the lender. Standard debt provisions do not ordinarily place a burden on a financially sound business. Restrictive covenants tend to place certain operating and financial constraints on the borrower. The cost (interest rate) of long-term debt is normally higher than the cost of short-term borrowing. Major factors affecting the cost of long-term debt are loan maturity, loan size, and, more important, borrower risk and the basic cost of money.

LG 2 Understand the characteristics of term (long-term) loan agreements and the various term lenders to business. The conditions of a term (long-term) loan are specified in the term loan agreement. Term loans generally require periodic installment payments; some require balloon payments at maturity. Term loans may be either unsecured or secured. Some term lenders receive stock-purchase warrants. Term loans can be obtained from a number of types of major lenders ranging from commercial banks and insurance companies to the federal government's Small Business Administration to the financing subsidiaries of equipment manufacturers. Table 12.1 provides a complete listing of term lenders along with the characteristics and types of loans they make.

LG 3 Discuss the legal aspects of corporate bonds, general features of a bond issue, bond ratings, popular types of bonds, and international long-term debt financing. Corporate bonds are certificates indicating that a corporation has borrowed a certain amount that it promises to repay in the future under clearly defined terms. Most bonds are issued with maturities of 10 to 30 years and a par value of $1,000. All conditions of the bond issue are detailed in the indenture, which is enforced by the trustee. A bond issue may include a conversion feature, a call feature, or stock-purchase warrants. Bond ratings by independent agencies indicate the risk of a bond issue. A variety of traditional and contemporary types of bonds, some unsecured and others secured, are available; Tables 12.3 and 12.4 list them and summarize their characteristics. The Eurobond, foreign bond, and Eurocurrency loan markets allow established creditworthy companies and governments to quickly and efficiently borrow large amounts of debt internationally in their choice of currency and with very flexible repayment terms.

LG 4 Review the logic and computational procedures involved in bond-refunding options, particularly exercising a call to refund a bond with new bonds issued at a lower interest rate. Firms sometimes retire or refund (refinance) bonds prior to their maturity. When serial bonds are issued, retirement is on a planned basis. Bonds are refunded (refinanced) when there is a drop in interest rates sufficient to result in a positive net present value (NPV) from calling the old bonds and replacing them with new lower-interest-rate bonds. The NPV is found by first finding the initial investment, which is the estimated incremental after-tax cash outflow required at time zero to call the old bond and issue the new bond in its place. Next, the annual cash flow savings is found by determining the difference between the annual after-tax debt payments with the old and new bond. Finally, the after-tax cost of debt is used to find NPV by subtracting the initial investment from the present value of annual cash flow savings.

LG 5 Define the investment bankers' role and the two major functions that they perform in helping firms to raise long-term financing—both debt and equity. Investment bankers act as financial intermediaries between the issuers and buyers of new securities. They purchase securities from corporate and government issuers and resell them to the general public. The investment banker's primary function is underwriting, which involves buying a security issue from the issuing firm at a lower price than he or she plans to sell it for, thereby guaranteeing the issuer a specified amount from the issue and assuming the risk of price changes between the points of purchase and sale. Investment bankers also assist in private placements and can be hired to sell new issues on a best efforts basis. A secondary, but important, function performed by investment bankers involves providing advice to issuers on appropriate financing, mergers, acquisitions, and refinancing decisions.

LG 6 Discuss the investment banking process—from selecting an investment banker through stabilizing the price, the cost of investment banking services, and the private placement as an alternative to a public offering. Once selected, the investment banker confers with the issuer to determine the amount and form of capital to raise, may syndicate the underwriting to lessen the risk to any single investment banking firm, forms a selling group to distribute the new issue to the investing public, fulfills the legal requirements of the Securities and Exchange Commission with regard to the initial as well as subsequent sale of the securities, prices and distributes the issue, and stabilizes the price so that the entire issue can be sold at or near the initial offering price. The cost of investment banking services ranges from as little as 1 percent of the total proceeds on a large bond issue to as much as 20 percent or more on a small common stock issue. An alternative to public offerings is private (direct) placement of securities—primarily bonds and preferred stocks. In private placements an investment banker is usually employed to assist in finding a buyer and to provide pricing advice. Stock options and stock purchase plans are sometimes used to directly place common stock.

Self-test problem (Solution in Appendix E)

ST 12-1 LG 4 Bond-refunding decision Torbert Manufacturing is considering refunding $20 million of outstanding bonds (20,000 bonds at $1,000 par value) as a result of recent declines in long-term interest rates. The plan would involve issuing $20 million of new bonds at the lower interest rate and using the proceeds to call and retire the $20 million in outstanding bonds. The details of both bond issues are outlined below. The firm is in the 40 percent tax bracket.

Old bonds Torbert's old bonds were initially issued 10 years ago with a 30-year maturity and a 13 percent coupon rate of interest. The bonds were initially sold at a $12 discount from their $1,000 par value, flotation costs were $150,000, and their call price is $1,130.

New bonds The new bonds are expected to sell at their $1,000 par value, have an 11 percent coupon interest rate, have a 20-year maturity, and require $400,000 in flotation costs. The firm will have a three-month period of overlapping interest while it retires the old bonds.

a. Calculate the initial investment required to call the old bonds and issue the new bonds.
b. Calculate the annual cash flow savings, if any, that are expected from the proposed bond-refunding decision.
c. If the firm uses its 7 percent after-tax cost of debt to evaluate low-risk decisions, find the net present value (NPV) of the bond-refunding decision. Would you recommend the proposed refunding? Explain your answer.

Problems

12-1 LG 4 Bond discounts or premiums The initial proceeds per bond, the size of the issue, the initial maturity of the bond, and the years remaining to maturity are given in the table at the top of page 516 for a number of bonds. In each case the firm is in the 40 percent tax bracket, and the bond has a $1,000 par value.

Bond	Proceeds per bond	Size of issue	Initial maturity of bond	Years remaining to maturity
A	$ 980	20,000 bonds	25 years	20
B	1,020	14,000 bonds	20 years	12
C	1,000	10,500 bonds	10 years	8
D	950	9,000 bonds	30 years	21
E	1,030	3,000 bonds	30 years	15

a. Indicate whether each bond was sold at a discount, at a premium, or at its par value.
b. Determine the total discount or premium for each issue.
c. Determine the annual amount of discount or premium amortized for each bond.
d. Calculate the unamortized discount or premium for each bond.
e. Determine the after-tax cash flow associated with the retirement now of each of these bonds, using the values developed in d.

12-2 LG 4 Cost of a call For each of the callable bond issues in the table, calculate the after-tax cost of calling the issue. Each bond has a $1,000 par value; the various issue sizes and call prices are summarized in the following table. The firm is in the 40 percent tax bracket.

Bond	Size of issue	Call price
A	8,000 bonds	$1,080
B	10,000 bonds	1,060
C	6,000 bonds	1,010
D	3,000 bonds	1,050
E	9,000 bonds	1,040
F	13,000 bonds	1,090

12-3 LG 4 Amortization of flotation cost The flotation cost, the initial maturity, and the number of years remaining to maturity are given for a number of bonds. The firm is in the 40 percent tax bracket.

Bond	Flotation cost	Initial maturity of bond	Years remaining to maturity
A	$500,000	30 years	24
B	200,000	20 years	5
C	40,000	25 years	10
D	100,000	10 years	2
E	80,000	15 years	9

a. Calculate the annual amortization of the flotation cost for each bond.
b. Determine the tax savings, if any, that would be expected to result from the unamortized flotation cost if the bond were called today.

12-4 LG 4 Interest overlap cost and tax shield The principal, coupon interest rate, and interest overlap period are given for a number of bonds in the table at the top of page 517.

Bond	Principal	Coupon interest rate	Interest overlap period
A	$ 2,000,000	12.0%	2 months
B	60,000,000	14.0	4 months
C	40,000,000	10.0	3 months
D	10,000,000	11.0	4 months
E	25,000,000	9.5	1 month

a. Calculate the dollar amount of interest that must be paid for each bond during the interest overlap period.

b. Calculate the after-tax cost of overlapping interest for each bond if the firm is in the 40 percent tax bracket.

12-5 LG 4 **Bond-refunding decision—No interest overlap** The North Company is contemplating offering a new $30 million bond issue to replace an outstanding $30 million bond issue. The firm wishes to do this to take advantage of the decline in interest rates that has occurred since the initial bond issuance. The old and new bonds are described below. The firm is in the 40 percent tax bracket.

Old bonds The outstanding bonds have a $1,000 par value and a 14 percent coupon interest rate. They were issued five years ago with a 25-year maturity. They were initially sold for their par value of $1,000, and the firm incurred $250,000 in flotation costs. They are callable at $1,140.

New bonds The new bonds would have a $1,000 par value and a 12 percent coupon interest rate. They would have a 20-year maturity and could be sold at their par value. The flotation cost of the new bonds would be $400,000. The firm does not expect to have any overlapping interest.

a. Calculate the tax savings that are expected from the unamortized portion of the old bonds' flotation cost.

b. Calculate the annual tax savings from the flotation cost of the new bonds, assuming the 20-year amortization.

c. Calculate the after-tax cost of the call premium that is required to retire the old bonds.

d. Determine the initial investment that is required to call the old bonds and issue the new bonds.

e. Calculate the annual cash flow savings, if any, that are expected from the proposed bond-refunding decision.

f. If the firm has a 7 percent after-tax cost of debt, find the net present value (NPV) of the bond-refunding decision. Would you recommend the proposed refunding? Why or why not?

12-6 LG 4 **Bond-refunding decision—With interest overlap** Rubens Paper Company is considering offering a new $10 million bond issue to replace an outstanding $10 million bond issue. The firm wishes to do this to take advantage of the decline in interest rates that has occurred since the original issue. The two bond issues are described below; the firm is in the 40 percent tax bracket.

Old bonds The outstanding bonds have a $1,000 par value and a 17 percent coupon interest rate. They were issued five years ago with a 20-year maturity. They were initially sold at a $20 per-bond discount, and a $120,000 flotation cost was incurred. They are callable at $1,170.

New bonds The new bonds would have a 15-year maturity, a par value of $1,000, and a 14 percent coupon interest rate. It is expected that these bonds can be sold at par for a flotation cost of $200,000. The firm expects a two-month period of overlapping interest while it retires the old bonds.

a. Calculate the initial investment that is required to call the old bonds and issue the new bonds.

b. Calculate the annual cash flow savings, if any, that are expected from the proposed bond-refunding decision.

c. If the firm uses its after-tax cost of debt of 8 percent to evaluate low-risk decisions, find the net present value (NPV) of the bond-refunding decision. Would you recommend the proposed refunding? Explain your answer.

12-7 LG 4 **Bond-refunding decision—With interest overlap and sensitivity analysis** L-D Hauling is considering using the proceeds from a new $14 million bond issue to call and retire its outstanding $14 million bond issue. The details of both bond issues are outlined below. The firm is in the 40 percent tax bracket.

Old bonds The firm's old issue has a coupon interest rate of 14 percent, was issued six years ago, and had a 30-year maturity. The bonds sold at a $15 discount from their $1,000 par value, flotation costs were $120,000, and their call price is $1,140.

New bonds The new bonds are expected to sell at par ($1,000), have a 24-year maturity, and have flotation costs of $360,000. The firm will have a one-month period of overlapping interest while it retires the old bonds.

a. What is the initial investment that is required to call the old bonds and issue the new bonds?
b. What are the annual cash flow savings, if any, from the proposed bond-refunding decision if (1) the new bonds have a 12.5 percent coupon interest rate and (2) the new bonds have a 13 percent coupon interest rate?
c. Construct a table showing the net present value (NPV) of refunding under the two circumstances given in **b** when (1) the firm has an after-tax cost of debt of 6 percent and (2) the firm has an after-tax cost of debt of 8 percent.
d. Discuss the set(s) of circumstances (described in **c**) when the refunding would be favorable and when it would not.
e. If the four circumstances summarized in **d** were equally probable (each had .25 probability), would you recommend the refunding? Why or why not?

12-8 LG 6 **Underwriting spread** Hildreth Recycling is interested in selling common stock to raise capital for plant expansion. The firm has consulted the First Atlanta Company, a large underwriting firm, which believes that the stock can be sold for $80 per share. The underwriter, on investigation, has found that its administrative costs will be 2 percent of the sale price and its selling costs will be 1.5 percent of the sale price. If the underwriter requires a profit equal to 1 percent of the sale price, how much will the *spread* have to be *in dollars* to cover the underwriter's costs and profit?

12-9 LG 6 **Bond underwriting analysis** RM International wishes to sell $100 million of bonds whose net proceeds will be used in the acquisition of Little Books. The company has estimated that the net proceeds after paying the underwriting costs should provide an amount sufficient to make the acquisition. The underwriter believes that the 100,000 bonds can be sold to the public at their $1,000 par value. The underwriter estimates that its administrative costs will be $3.5 million. It also must sell the bonds at a .75 percent discount from their par value to members of the selling group. The underwriting commission (in addition to recovery of its administrative costs) is 1 percent of the par value of the offering.

a. Calculate the per-bond spread required by the underwriter to cover its costs.
b. How much will RM International net from the issue?
c. How much will the selling group receive? How much will the underwriter receive?
d. Assuming that this is a public offering, describe the nature of the underwriter's risk.

Chapter 12 Case Making California Food's bond-refunding decision

Margaret Stone, chief financial officer of California Foods, believes that long-term interest rates are currently lower than they'll be in the next five years. With this belief she has begun investigating whether it might be the right time to offer a new bond issue to replace an outstanding $25 million bond issue. After consulting a number of investment bankers, Margaret chose an established firm that offered to underwrite the issue at the lowest flotation costs. Under the proposed terms of the underwriting agreement, California Foods (CF) would reimburse the investment banker for $100,000 in administrative costs plus the .3 percent of par discount given to members of the selling group. In addition, CF would pay an underwriting commission equal to .5 percent of the par value of the offering. To analyze the appropriateness of the bond refunding, Margaret gathered the data presented below for the old and the new bonds. California Foods has a 6 percent after-tax cost of debt and is in the 40 percent tax bracket.

Old bonds The old bonds were initially issued 10 years ago with a 30-year maturity and a 12 1/4 percent coupon interest rate. The $1,000-par-value bonds were initially sold for $970, flotation costs were $240,000, and their call price is $1,125.

New bonds The bonds are expected to sell at their $1,000 par value, have a 10 3/4 percent coupon interest rate, have a 20-year maturity, and require the flotation costs noted above. The firm expects a three-month period of overlapping interest while it retires the old bonds.

Required

a. Calculate the dollar amount of flotation costs associated with the proposed 10 3/4 percent bond issue.

b. Use the data provided along with the flotation costs calculated in **a** to evaluate and make a recommendation relative to the proposed bond refunding.

c. What, if any, impact would the fact that the least-expensive flotation costs are $500,000 rather than the amount calculated in **a** have on your findings in **b**? Would your recommendation change?

chapter 13

Common stock and dividend policy

LEARNING GOALS

LG 1 Differentiate between debt and equity capital in terms of ownership rights, claims on income and assets, maturity, and tax treatment.

LG 2 Discuss common stock fundamentals, including ownership; par value; authorized, outstanding, and issued shares; voting rights; dividends; the distribution of earnings and assets; *and international common stock.*

LG 3 Describe stock rights, the sale of common stock, and the advantages and disadvantages of common stock financing.

LG 4 Understand cash dividend payment procedures, dividend reinvestment plans, dividend policy theories and arguments with regard to its relevance, and the key factors that affect dividend policy.

LG 5 Review and evaluate the three basic types of dividend policies—constant-payout-ratio, regular, and low-regular-and-extra.

LG 6 Contrast the basic features, objectives, and procedures for paying other forms of dividends, including stock dividends, stock splits, and stock repurchases.

It's critical for financial managers—especially in biotechnology companies—to understand the importance of common stock. Equity is the cornerstone of biotechnology companies' capital structure because of the very high risk and substantial cash required for product development. It generally takes about $200 million and 7 to 10 years to get a product from research to market. ICOS, a development-stage biotechnology company that began operations on September 1, 1990, has no products in the market yet and therefore can't fund growth from product revenues. Common stock is the only form of financing that provides our stockholders with rewards (in the form of high returns from capital gains) that are commensurate with the risk.

For most companies, debt is the least expensive form of capital, and equity is the most expensive. But for us, common stock is the cheapest way to raise money. It's very difficult for young biotech firms to sell debt without offering a cash equivalent as security. This reduces our liquidity, so we can't lower our cost of capital by using debt in our financing mix. That's pretty frustrating when interest rates are low.

Unlike other industries, we must raise cash in advance, without earnings or dividends to attract investors. Our founders had started major biotech companies before and believed that ICOS would have a competitive advantage if it could prerecruit and fund for two years a critical mass of leading scientists and their associates. On the basis of the founders' reputations and the company's strategic plan, ICOS raised $33 million through a private placement of common stock, setting the stage for rapid research and development progress. It was a departure from traditional biotech financing: self-financing by the founders followed by an equity investment from venture capital firms, which provide funds in exchange for common stock and a management role.

A year later, we faced a major financial decision: whether to sell equity to the general public (an initial public offering, IPO). Going public is a major step for any company. There are many reporting requirements, and the shareholder base typically expands from a handful to thousands. In our case, 450 private shareholders increased to over 25,000 after we went public. We hadn't planned to go public so soon, but market conditions, our growth, and progress in product development were positive factors to attract investors. Ideally, managers in all areas need to be aware of the impact of their decisions on the company's capital raising activities so that a company can respond quickly when market conditions are good. Fortunately we were ready.

Equity is the cornerstone of biotechnology companies' capital structure because of the very high risk and substantial cash required for product development.

Pricing an equity offering is always difficult. When we did our IPO, the market was just starting to move down, but we were able to sell our stock within the filing range. When we did our second equity offering, biotech stocks were again under pressure. (Timing is everything!) We filed on February 24, 1992, at $12 per share and priced it at $9 in a sinking market on April 7. We were criticized for accepting a lower price, but the fundamental issue was getting cash to secure the company's future. In retrospect, $9 was pretty good; the market and our stock soon fell even lower.

To be successful in the biotechnology industry, management must constantly survey the options in the current capital markets, exploring every opportunity to build a strong cash position. This provides a reserve to survive both the inevitable disappointments in these high risk product development efforts and down cycles on Wall Street.

Janice LeCocq joined ICOS in 1990 as Executive Vice President, Finance and Administration, Chief Financial Officer, and Director. Her prior experience includes nine years as a securities analyst and investment banker with Montgomery Securities. She received an A.B. in Human Biology and a Ph.D. in Medical Anthropology from Stanford University.

The nature of equity capital

Sources of long-term financing are often compared with respect to ownership rights, claims on the firm's income and assets, maturity, and tax treatment. What do you think the key differences are in each of these areas between debt and equity capital? Before reading on, spend a few moments answering this question.

A FIRM NEEDS TO MAINTAIN AN EQUITY BASE THAT IS LARGE ENOUGH TO ALLOW IT TO take advantage of low-cost debt and build an optimal capital structure (see Chapter 11). Equity capital can be raised *internally* through retained earnings, which are significantly affected by dividend policy, or *externally* by selling common or preferred stock. Although preferred stock, which is discussed in Chapter 14, is a less costly form of financing than common stock or retained earnings, it is not frequently used. Here we discuss the key features of equity capital, followed by discussions of common stock, stock rights, and dividends.

The key differences between debt and equity capital were summarized in Chapter 11 (see specifically Table 11.8). These differences relate to ownership rights, claims on the firm's income and assets, maturity, and tax treatment.

Ownership rights

Unlike creditors (lenders), holders of equity capital (common and preferred stockholders) are owners of the firm. Holders of equity capital often have voting rights that permit them to select the firm's directors and to vote on special issues. In contrast, debtholders may receive voting privileges only when the firm has violated the conditions of a *term loan agreement* or *bond indenture.*

Claims on income and assets

Holders of equity capital receive claims on both income and assets that are secondary to the claims of creditors.

CLAIMS ON INCOME

The claims of equity holders on income cannot be paid until the claims of all creditors have been satisfied. These claims include both interest and scheduled principal payments. Once these claims have been satisfied, the firm's board of directors can decide whether to distribute dividends to the owners. Of course, as will be explained later in this chapter, a firm's ability to pay dividends may be limited by legal, contractual, or internal constraints.

CLAIMS ON ASSETS

The claims of equity holders on the firm's assets are secondary to the claims of creditors. When the firm becomes bankrupt, assets are sold, and the proceeds are distributed in this order: to employees and customers, to the government, to secured creditors, to unsecured creditors, and finally to equity holders.[1] Because equity holders are the last to receive any distribution of assets during bankruptcy proceedings, they expect greater returns from dividends and/or stock price appreciation.

As was noted in Chapter 10, the costs of the various forms of equity financing are generally higher than debt costs. This is partially explained by the fact that the suppliers of equity capital take more risk as a result of their claims on income and assets being subordinate to those of debtholders. Despite its being more costly, equity capital is necessary for the firm to grow and mature. All firms must initially be financed with some common stock equity.

Maturity

Unlike debt, equity capital is a permanent form of financing. It does not "mature," and therefore repayment of the initial amount paid in is not required. Since equity does not mature and will be liquidated only during bankruptcy proceedings, the owners must recognize that although a ready market may exist for the firm's shares, the price that can be realized may fluctuate. This potential fluctuation of the market price of equity makes the overall returns to a firm's owners even more risky.

Tax treatment

As was noted in Chapter 2, interest payments to debtholders are treated as tax-deductible expenses on the firm's income statement, whereas dividend payments to common and preferred stockholders are not tax-deductible. The tax-deductibility of interest, as was pointed out in Chapter 10, primarily accounts for the fact that the explicit cost of debt is generally less than the explicit cost of equity.

CONCEPT IN REVIEW

13-1 How do debt and equity capital differ? What are the key differences between them with respect to ownership rights, claims on income and assets, maturity, and tax treatment?

Common stock fundamentals

During recent years many firms have issued two or more classes of common stock—some shares having voting rights and other shares are nonvoting. Why do you think some firms have chosen to issue nonvoting common stock? Spend a short time answering this question before reading on.

THE TRUE OWNERS OF BUSINESS FIRMS ARE THE COMMON STOCKHOLDERS, WHO INVEST their money with the expectation of receiving future returns. A common stockholder is sometimes referred to as a *residual owner,* since in essence he or she re-

[1]The procedures followed when a firm becomes bankrupt are described in Chapter 19.

ceives what is left—the residual—after all other claims on the firm's income and assets have been satisfied. As a result of this generally uncertain position, the common stockholder expects to be compensated with adequate dividends and, ultimately, capital gains. Here we discuss the fundamental aspects of common stock: ownership; par value; authorized, outstanding, and issued shares; voting rights; dividends; the distribution of earnings and assets; and international common stock.

privately owned stock
All common stock of a firm owned by a single individual.

closely owned stock
All common stock of a firm owned by a small group of investors such as a family.

publicly owned stock
Common stock of a firm owned by a broad group of unrelated individual and (or) institutional investors.

Ownership

The common stock of a firm can be **privately owned** by a single individual, **closely owned** by a small group of investors, such as a family, or **publicly owned** by a broad group of unrelated individual and (or) institutional investors. Typically, small corporations are privately or closely owned, and if their shares are traded, this occurs privately or on the over-the-counter exchange (see Chapter 2). Large corporations, which are emphasized in the following discussions, are publicly owned, and their shares are generally actively traded on the organized or over-the-counter exchanges, which were briefly described in Chapter 2.

par value
A relatively useless value that is arbitrarily placed on stock in the firm's corporate charter.

no par value
Used to describe stock that is issued without a par value, in which case the stock may be assigned a value or placed on the firm's books at the price at which it is sold.

Par value

Common stock may be sold with or without a par value. A **par value** is a relatively useless value that is arbitrarily placed on the stock in the firm's corporate charter. It is generally quite low, somewhere in the range of $1. Firms often issue stock with **no par value,** in which case they may assign it a value or place it on the books at the price at which it is sold. A low par value may be advantageous in states where certain corporate taxes are based on the par value of stock; if a stock has no par value, the tax may be based on an arbitrarily determined per-share figure. The accounting entries resulting from the sale of common stock can be illustrated by a simple example.

EXAMPLE

Bubble Soda Company, a soft drink manufacturer, has issued 1,000,000 shares of $2 par-value common stock, receiving proceeds of $50 per share. This results in the following entries on the firm's books:

Common stock (1,000,000 shares at $2 par)	$ 2,000,000
Paid-in capital in excess of par	48,000,000
Common stock equity	$50,000,000

Sometimes the entry labeled "paid-in capital in excess of par" is labeled "capital surplus." This value is important because firms are usually prohibited by state law from distributing any paid-in capital as dividends. ■

Authorized, outstanding, and issued shares

authorized shares
The number of shares of common stock that a firm's corporate charter allows without further stockholder approval.

A firm's corporate charter defines the number of **authorized shares** that it can issue. The firm cannot sell more shares than the charter authorizes without obtaining approval from its owners through a shareholder vote. Because it is often difficult to amend the charter to authorize the issuance of additional shares, firms generally at-

outstanding shares
The number of shares of common stock sold to the public.

tempt to authorize more shares than they initially plan to issue. Authorized shares become **outstanding shares** when they are sold to the public. If the firm repurchases any of its outstanding shares, these shares are recorded as **treasury stock** and shown as a deduction from stockholders' equity on the firm's balance sheet. **Issued shares** are the number of shares of common stock that have been put into circulation; they represent the sum of outstanding shares and treasury stock.

EXAMPLE

treasury stock
The number of shares of outstanding stock that have been repurchased and held by the firm; shown on the firm's balance sheet as a deduction from stockholders' equity.

issued shares
The number of shares of common stock that have been put into circulation; they represent the sum of outstanding shares and treasury stock.

Golden Enterprises, a producer of medical pumps, has the following stockholders' equity account on December 31, of the year just ended.

Stockholders' equity	
Common stock—$0.80 par value:	
Authorized 35,000,000 shares; issued 15,000,000 shares	$ 12,000,000
Paid-in capital in excess of par	63,000,000
Retained earnings	31,000,000
	$106,000,000
Less: Cost of treasury stock (1,000,000 shares)	4,000,000
Total stockholders' equity	$102,000,000

If Golden decides to sell additional common stock, how many shares can it sell without gaining approval from its shareholders? Note that the firm has 35 million authorized shares, 15 million issued shares, and 1 million shares of treasury stock. Thus 14 million shares are outstanding (15 million issued shares − 1 million shares of treasury stock), and Golden can issue 21 million additional shares (35 million authorized shares − 14 million outstanding shares) without seeking shareholder approval to amend its corporate charter. This total includes the treasury shares currently held by Golden, which the firm can always reissue to the public without obtaining shareholder approval for their sale. ■

Voting rights

hostile takeover
A maneuver in which an outside group, without management support, tries to gain voting control of a firm by buying its shares in the marketplace.

nonvoting common stock
Common stock that carries no voting rights; issued when the firm wishes to raise capital through the sale of common stock but does not want to relinquish its voting control.

supervoting shares
Stock that carries with it more votes per share than a share of regular common stock.

Generally, each share of common stock entitles the holder to one vote in the election of directors and in other special elections. Votes are generally assignable and must be cast at the annual stockholders' meeting. In recent years many firms have issued two or more classes of common stock—unequal voting rights being their key difference. The issuance of different classes of stock has been frequently used as a defense against a **hostile takeover** in which an outside group, without management support, tries to gain voting control of the firm by buying its shares in the marketplace. At other times a class of **nonvoting common stock** is issued when the firm wishes to raise capital through the sale of common stock but does not want to relinquish its voting control. This and other approaches to issuing classes of stock with unequal voting rights result in some **supervoting shares,** which, by giving their holders more votes per share, allow them to better control the firm's future. An interesting variation on this theme was put in place by J.M. Smucker Co. The firm initially had only one class of stock, which, once it was held for four years, provided 10 votes per share. Since the Smucker family owned 30 percent of the stock, this procedure, when it was initiated a number of years ago, effectively ruled out a hostile takeover of the company.

When different classes of common stock are issued on the basis of unequal voting rights, class A common is typically—but not universally—designated as nonvoting, and class B common would have voting rights. Generally, higher classes of shares are given preference with respect to the distribution of earnings (dividends) and assets (in liquidation) over the lower-class shares, which in exchange receive more voting rights. In other words, because class A shares are not given voting rights, they are generally given preference over class B shares in terms of the distribution of dividends and assets. Treasury stock, which resides within the corporation, generally *does not* have voting rights, *does not* earn dividends, and *does not* have a claim on assets in liquidation. Three aspects of voting require special attention—proxies, majority voting, and cumulative voting.

PROXIES

proxy statement
A statement giving the votes of a stockholder or stockholders to another party.

proxy battle
The attempt by a nonmanagement group to gain control of the management of a firm through the solicitation of a sufficient number of proxy votes.

Since most small stockholders do not attend the annual meeting to vote, they may sign a **proxy statement** giving their votes to another party. The solicitation of proxies from shareholders is closely controlled by the Securities and Exchange Commission, since there is a possibility that proxies will be solicited on the basis of false or misleading information. The existing management generally receives the stockholders' proxies, since it is able to solicit them at company expense. Occasionally, when the ownership of the firm is widely disseminated, outsiders may attempt to gain control by waging a **proxy battle.** This requires soliciting a sufficient number of votes to unseat the existing management. To win a corporate election, votes from a majority of the shares voted are required. Proxy battles generally occur when the existing management is performing poorly; however, the odds of a nonmanagement group winning a proxy battle are generally slim.

MAJORITY VOTING

majority voting system
The system whereby, in the election of the board of directors, each stockholder is entitled to one vote for each share of stock owned and he or she can vote all shares for each director.

In the **majority voting system,** each stockholder is entitled to one vote for each share of stock owned. The stockholders vote for each position on the board of directors separately, and each stockholder is permitted to vote all of his or her shares for *each* director he or she favors. The directors who receive the majority of the votes are elected. It is impossible for minority interests to select a director, since each shareholder can vote his or her shares for as many of the candidates as he or she wishes. As long as management controls a majority of the votes, it can elect all the directors. An example will clarify this point.

EXAMPLE

Merritt Company, a producer of high-quality paper, is in the process of electing three directors. There are 1,000 shares of stock outstanding, of which management controls 60 percent. The management-backed candidates are A, B, and C; the minority candidates are D, E, and F. By voting its 600 shares (60 percent of 1,000) for *each* of its candidates, management can elect A, B, and C; the minority shareholders, with only 400 votes for each of their candidates, cannot elect any directors. Management's candidates will receive 600 votes each, and other candidates will receive 400 votes each. ■

CUMULATIVE VOTING

cumulative voting system
The system under which each share of common stock is allotted a number of votes equal to the total number of corporate directors to be elected and votes can be given to *any* director(s).

Nearly half of all the states, including California, Illinois, and Michigan, require corporations chartered by them to use a **cumulative voting system** in the election of directors; other states permit cumulative voting as long as it is provided for in the corporation's charter. This system gives a number of votes equal to the total number of directors to be elected to each share of common stock. The votes can be given to *any* director(s) the stockholder desires. The advantage of this system is that it provides the minority shareholders with an opportunity to elect at least some directors.

EXAMPLE

Dearing Company, a competitor of Merritt Company, is also in the process of electing three directors. In this case, however, each share of common stock entitles the holder to three votes, which may be voted in any manner desired. Again, there are 1,000 shares outstanding, and management controls 600. It therefore has a total of 1,800 votes (3×600), while the minority shareholders have 1,200 votes (3×400). In this situation the majority shareholders can elect only two directors, and the minority shareholders can elect at least one director. The majority shareholders can split their votes evenly among the three candidates (give them 600 votes each); but if the minority shareholders give all their votes to one of their candidates, he or she will win. ■

A commonly cited formula for determining the number of shares necessary to elect a certain number of directors, *NE*, under cumulative voting is given by Equation 13.1:

$$NE = \frac{O \times D}{TN + 1} + 1 \qquad (13.1)$$

where

NE = number of shares needed to elect a certain number of directors
O = total number of shares of common stock outstanding
D = number of directors desired
TN = total number of directors to be elected

EXAMPLE

Substituting the values in the preceding example for O (1,000) and TN (3) into Equation 13.1 and letting $D = 1$, 2, and 3 yields values of NE equal to 251, 501, and 751, respectively. Since the minority stockholders control only 400 shares, they can elect only one director. ■

The advantage of cumulative voting from the viewpoint of minority shareholders should be clear from the example. However, even with cumulative voting, certain election procedures such as staggered terms for directors can be used to prevent minority representation on a board. Also, the majority shareholders may control a large enough number of shares, or the total number of directors to be elected may be small enough to prevent minority representation.

Dividends

The payment of corporate dividends is at the discretion of the board of directors. Most corporations pay dividends quarterly. Dividends may be paid in cash, stock, or merchandise. Cash dividends are the most common; merchandise dividends are the least common. The common stockholder is not promised a dividend, but he or she comes to expect certain payments based on the historical dividend pattern of the firm. Before dividends are paid to common stockholders, the claims of the government, all creditors, and preferred stockholders must be satisfied. Because of the importance of the dividend decision to the growth and valuation of the firm, discussion of dividends is included in detail later in this chapter.

Distribution of earnings and assets

As was mentioned in previous sections, holders of common stock have no guarantee of receiving any periodic distribution of earnings in the form of dividends, nor are they guaranteed anything in the event of liquidation. However, one thing they are assured of is that they cannot lose any more than they have invested in the firm. Moreover, the common stockholder can receive unlimited returns through dividends and through the appreciation in the value of his or her holdings. In other words, although nothing is guaranteed, the *possible* rewards for providing risk capital can be considerable, even great.

International common stock

While the international market for common stock is not—and probably never will be—as large as the international market for debt securities, cross-border trading and issuance of common stock have increased dramatically during the past 15 years. Much of this increase can be accounted for simply as a growing desire on the part of institutional and individual investors to obtain internationally diversified investment portfolios. For example, the total value of international stock trading now exceeds $1.6 *trillion*, and since foreign stocks still account for a small fraction of U.S. and foreign institutional holdings, this total will surely grow rapidly in the years ahead.

INTERNATIONAL STOCK ISSUES

Besides investors, corporations have also discovered the benefits of issuing stock outside of their home markets. For example, several top U.S. multinational companies have chosen to list their stock in half a dozen or more stock markets, the London, Frankfurt, and Tokyo markets being the most popular. Issuing stock internationally not only broadens the investor base, it can also help a company to integrate itself into the local business scene, since a local stock listing both increases local business press coverage and serves as effective corporate advertising. Having locally traded stock can also facilitate corporate acquisitions because shares can then be used as an acceptable method of payment.

American Depositary Receipts (ADRs)
Claims issued by U.S. banks representing ownership of shares of a foreign company's stock held on deposit by the U.S. bank in the foreign market and issued in dollars to U.S. investors.

sponsored ADR
An ADR for which the issuing (foreign) company absorbs the legal and financial costs of creating and trading the security.

unsponsored ADR
An ADR for which the issuing firm is not involved with the issue and may even oppose it; usually results from U.S. investor demand.

AMERICAN DEPOSITARY RECEIPTS

Foreign corporations have also discovered the benefits of trading their stock in the United States. The disclosure and reporting requirements mandated by the U.S. Securities and Exchange Commission have historically discouraged all but the largest foreign firms from directly listing their shares on the New York or American Stock Exchanges. For example, in mid-1993, Daimler Benz announced that it would become the first large German company to seek such a listing. Instead, most foreign companies tap the U.S. market through **American Depositary Receipts (ADRs)**. These are claims issued by U.S. banks representing ownership of shares of a foreign company's stock held on deposit by the U.S. bank in the foreign market. Since ADRs are issued, in dollars, by a U.S. bank to U.S. investors, they are subject to U.S. securities laws yet still give investors the opportunity to diversify their portfolios internationally.

ADRs can be either sponsored or unsponsored. A **sponsored ADR** is one for which the issuing (foreign) company absorbs the legal and financial costs of creating and trading the security, while an **unsponsored ADR** is one in which the issuing firm is not involved with the issue at all—and may even oppose it. Unsponsored ADRs typically result from U.S. investor demand for shares of particular foreign companies. The shares of over 800 foreign companies are traded in the United States in the form of sponsored and unsponsored ADRs.

RECENT TRENDS

There have been two very important recent trends in international equity issues. The first is the increasing frequency with which European companies are making multinational equity issues within the European Community in preparation for the open market and unified currency expected to develop during the 1990s. These multinational equity issues have coincided with a surge in cross-border mergers and acquisitions undertaken for the same purpose. The second, and more fundamental, trend affecting global equity trading is the increasing frequency and size of share issues involving *privatization* of formerly state-owned enterprises. Over $200 billion of privatizing share issues were executed during the last 15 years, and over 25 of these were worth at least $1 billion. As privatization continues to spread through Western and Eastern Europe, the Commonwealth of Independent States, and, ultimately, the People's Republic of China, these equity issues will play a major role in international equity trading.

CONCEPTS IN REVIEW

13-2 Why is the common stockholder considered the true owner of a firm? What risks do common stockholders take that other suppliers of long-term capital do not?

13-3 What are *proxies?* How are they used? How do majority and cumulative voting systems differ? Which of these voting systems would be preferred by the minority shareholders? Why?

13-4 Discuss the following with regard to international equity issues:

a. The reasons for the increase in cross-border common stock trading and issuance

b. The advantages, to both U.S.-based and foreign corporations, of issuing stock outside of their home markets

c. The use of *American Depositary Receipts (ADRs)* and the difference between *sponsored* and *unsponsored* ADRs.

d. Recent market and political events that affect international equity issues

Stock rights and other considerations

Stock rights give their holders the privilege to purchase additional shares of stock in direct proportion to their number of owned shares. Why do the corporate charters of smaller corporations, whose shares are closely owned or publicly owned and not actively traded, often specify the use of rights offerings? Take a few minutes to answer this question before reading on.

IN ADDITION TO COMMON STOCK FUNDAMENTALS, STOCK RIGHTS, SELLING COMMON stock, and the advantages and disadvantages of common stock are important considerations.

Stock rights

stock rights
Provide stockholders with the privilege to purchase additional shares of stock in direct proportion to their number of owned shares.

Stock rights provide stockholders with the privilege to purchase additional shares of stock in direct proportion to their number of owned shares. Today, rights are primarily used by smaller corporations whose shares are either *closely owned* or *publicly owned* and not actively traded. In these situations, rights are an important common stock financing tool without which shareholders would run the risk of losing their proportionate control of the corporation. Rights are rarely used by large publicly owned corporations whose shares are widely held and actively traded because maintenance of proportionate control is not a major concern of their shareholders.

PREEMPTIVE RIGHTS

preemptive rights
Allow common stockholders to maintain their *proportionate* ownership in the corporation when new issues are made.

dilution of ownership
Occurs when a new stock issue results in each present stockholder having a claim on a *smaller* part of the firm's earnings than previously.

Preemptive rights allow common stockholders to maintain their *proportionate* ownership in the corporation when new issues are made. While most states permit shareholders to be extended this privilege in the corporate charter, only two states require corporations chartered by them to provide these rights to common stockholders. Preemptive rights allow existing shareholders to maintain their voting control and protect against the dilution of their ownership and earnings. **Dilution of ownership** usually results in the dilution of earnings, since each present shareholder will have a claim on a *smaller* part of the firm's earnings than previously. Of course, if total earnings simultaneously increase, the long-run effect may be an overall increase in earnings per share.

From the firm's viewpoint, the use of rights offerings to raise new equity capital may be easier and less costly and generate more interest than a public offering of stock. An example may help to clarify the use of rights.

EXAMPLE

The Patrick Company, a large national advertising firm, currently has 100,000 shares of common stock outstanding and is contemplating issuing an additional 10,000 shares through a rights offering. Each existing shareholder will receive one right per share, and each right will entitle the shareholder to purchase one-tenth of a share of new common stock (10,000 ÷ 100,000), so 10 rights will be required to purchase one share of the stock. The holder of 1,000 shares (1 percent) of the outstanding common stock will receive 1,000 rights, each permitting the purchase of one-tenth of a share of new common stock, for a total of 100 shares of new common stock. If the shareholder exercises the rights, he or she will end up with a total of 1,100 shares of common stock, or 1 percent of the total number of shares then outstanding (110,000). Thus the shareholder maintains the same proportion of ownership as he or she had before the rights offering. ■

MECHANICS OF RIGHTS OFFERINGS

date of record (rights)
The last date on which the recipient of a right must be the legal owner indicated in the company's stock ledger.

ex rights
Period beginning four *business days* prior to the date of record during which a stock will be sold without announced rights being attached to it.

holders of record
Owners of the firm's shares on the *date of record.*

subscription price
The price at which stock rights are exercisable for a specified period of time; is set below the prevailing market price.

When a company makes a rights offering, the board of directors must set a **date of record,** which is the last date on which the recipient of a right must be the legal owner indicated in the company's stock ledger. Because of the time needed to make bookkeeping entries when a stock is traded, stocks usually begin selling **ex rights**—without the rights being attached to the stock—four *business days* prior to the date of record.

The issuing firm sends rights to **holders of record**—owners of the firm's shares on the date of record, who may exercise their rights, sell them, or let them expire. Rights are transferable, and many are traded actively enough to be listed on the various securities exchanges. They are exercisable for a specified period of time, generally not more than a few months, at a price, called the **subscription price,** that is set somewhat below the prevailing market price. Since fractions of shares are not always issued, it is sometimes necessary to purchase additional rights or sell any extra rights. The value of a right depends largely on the number of rights needed to purchase a share of stock and the amount by which the right's subscription price is below the current market price. If the rights have a very low value and an individual owns only a small number of shares, the rights may be allowed to expire.

MANAGEMENT DECISIONS

A firm's management must make two basic decisions when preparing for a rights offering. The first is the price at which the rights holders can purchase a new share of common stock. The subscription price must be set *below* the current market price, but how far below depends on management's evaluation of the sensitivity of the market demand to a price change, the degree of dilution of ownership and earnings expected, and the size of the offering. Management will consider the rights offering successful if approximately 90 percent of the rights are exercised.

Once management has determined the subscription price, it must determine the number of rights required to purchase a share of stock. Since the amount of funds to be raised is known in advance, the subscription price can be divided into this value to get the total number of shares that must be sold. Dividing the total number of shares outstanding by the total number of shares to be sold will give management the number of rights required to purchase a share of stock.

EXAMPLE

Ingram Company, a closely owned hand tool manufacturer, intends to raise $1 million through a rights offering. The firm currently has 160,000 shares outstanding, which have been most recently trading for $53 to $58 per share. The company has consulted an investment banking firm, which has recommended setting the subscription price for the rights at $50 per share. It believes that at this price the offering will be fully subscribed. The firm must therefore sell an additional 20,000 shares ($1,000,000 ÷ $50 per share). This means that eight rights (160,000 ÷ 20,000) will be needed to purchase a new share at $50. Each right will entitle its holder to purchase one-eighth of a share of common stock. ■

VALUE OF A RIGHT

Theoretically, the value of a right should be the same if the stock is selling *with rights* or *ex rights*. In either case the market value of a right may differ from its theoretical value.

WITH RIGHTS Once a rights offering has been declared, shares will trade with rights for only a few days. Equation 13.2 is used to find the theoretical value of a right when the stock is trading with rights, R_w:

$$R_w = \frac{M_w - S}{N + 1} \tag{13.2}$$

where

R_w = theoretical value of a right when stock is selling with rights
M_w = market value of the stock with rights
S = subscription price of the stock
N = number of rights needed to purchase one share of stock

EXAMPLE

Ingram Company's stock is currently selling with rights at a price of \$54.50 per share, the subscription price is \$50 per share, and eight rights are required to purchase a new share of stock. According to Equation 13.2, the value of a right is \$.50 [(\$54.50 − \$50.00) ÷ (8 + 1)]. A right should therefore be worth \$.50 in the marketplace. ■

EX RIGHTS When a share of stock is traded ex rights, meaning that the value of the right is no longer included in the stock's market price, the share price of the stock is expected to drop by the value of a right. Equation 13.3 is used to find the market value of the stock trading ex rights, M_e. The same notation is used as in Equation 13.2:

$$M_e = M_w - R_w \tag{13.3}$$

The theoretical value of a right when the stock is trading ex rights, R_e, is given by Equation 13.4:

$$R_e = \frac{M_e - S}{N} \tag{13.4}$$

The use of these equations can be illustrated by returning to the Ingram Company example.

EXAMPLE

According to Equation 13.3, the market price of the Ingram Company stock selling ex rights is \$54 (\$54.50 − \$.50). Substituting this value into Equation 13.4 gives the value of a right when the stock is selling ex rights, which is \$.50 [(\$54.00 − \$50.00) ÷ 8]. The theoretical value of the right when the stock is selling with rights or ex rights is therefore the same. ■

MARKET BEHAVIOR OF RIGHTS

As was indicated earlier, stock rights are negotiable instruments, often traded on securities exchanges. The market price of a right will generally differ from its theoretical value. The extent to which it will differ will depend on how the firm's stock price is expected to behave during the period when the right is exercisable. By buying rights instead of the stock itself, investors can achieve much higher returns on their money when stock prices rise.

CONCEPT IN PRACTICE

Reno Air Has More to Offer High-Rollers

Reno Air is a small, full-service airline that uses Reno, Nevada, as its hub. The bulk of Reno Air's passengers are skiers and people who trek to the Reno–Lake Tahoe area for its gambling casinos. While investing in a start-up airline is a gamble, Reno Air offers a special twist by issuing units in the over-the-counter market. Each unit represents two shares of common stock and a right to buy another share at a fixed price. Until shareholders exercise their right, they can experience capital gains on three shares for the price of only two.

UNDERSUBSCRIBED AND OVERSUBSCRIBED OFFERINGS

standby arrangement
A formal guarantee that any shares that are not subscribed or sold publicly will be purchased by the investment banker.

Rights offerings may be made through an *investment banker* or directly by the issuing company. Most rights offerings are made through investment bankers, who agree to issue and sell the rights. In most cases the investment banker agrees to a **standby arrangement**, which is a formal guarantee that any shares not subscribed or sold publicly will be purchased by the investment banker. This guarantee assures the firm that the entire issue will be sold; it will not be *undersubscribed.* The investment banker, of course, charges a higher fee for making this guarantee.

oversubscription privilege
Provides for distribution of shares for which rights were not exercised to interested shareholders on a pro rata basis at the stated subscription price.

Most rights offerings include an **oversubscription privilege,** which provides for the distribution of shares for which the rights were not exercised to interested shareholders on a pro rata basis at the stated subscription price. This privilege is a method of restricting ownership to the same group, although ownership proportions may change slightly. Shares that cannot be sold through the oversubscription privilege may be offered to the public. If an investment banker is used, the disposition of unsubscribed shares may be left up to the banker.

Selling common stock

Aside from the sale of new common stock through a rights offering, the firm may be able to sell new shares of common stock directly through some type of stock option or stock-purchase plan. (Both of these instruments were introduced and defined in Chapter 12.) *Stock options* are generally extended to management and permit it to purchase a certain number of shares of the firm's common stock at a specified price over a certain period of time. *Stock-purchase plans* are fringe benefits that are occasionally offered to employees that allow them to purchase the firm's stock at a discount or on a matching basis, with the firm absorbing part of the cost.

New issues of common stock, like bonds, can also be sold publicly through an *investment banker.* Of course, these sales are closely regulated by the *Securities and Exchange Commission (SEC)* as well as by state securities commissions. Public sale is commonly used in situations in which rights offerings are not required or are unsuccessful. As was noted in Chapter 12, the *public offering* of common stock through an investment banker is generally more expensive than any type of *private placement,* but the investment banker provides useful advice as well as a convenient forum for selling new common stock. For large public stock offerings, the total cost—administrative cost plus underwriting cost—ranges between 5 and 10 percent of the amount of funds raised. The total cost can rise as high as 20 percent or more on a small common stock issue. (A detailed discussion of the role of the investment banker was presented in Chapter 12.)

Advantages and disadvantages of common stock

A number of key advantages and disadvantages of common stock are often cited.

ADVANTAGES

The basic advantages of common stock stem from the fact that it is a source of financing that places a *minimum of constraints* on the firm. Since dividends do *not* have to be paid on common stock and their nonpayment does not jeopardize the receipt of payment by other security holders, common stock financing is quite attractive. The fact that common stock has *no maturity,* thereby eliminating a future repayment obligation, also enhances its desirability as a form of financing. Another advantage of common stock over other forms of long-term financing is its *ability to increase the firm's borrowing power.* The more common stock a firm sells, the larger its equity base and therefore the more easily and cheaply long-term debt financing can be obtained.

DISADVANTAGES

The disadvantages of common stock financing include the *potential dilution of earnings*. Clearly, when additional shares are issued, more shares have a claim on the firm's earnings. This often results in a short-run decline in earnings per share (EPS), which in turn can and often does negatively affect the stock's market price. A related disadvantage is the *potential dilution of control*. Particularly for smaller corporations the issuance is additional common shares could shift ownership proportions, and therefore voting control, from one party to another. Another disadvantage, as was noted in Chapter 11, is the *negative signal* that common stock financing sends to the marketplace. Market participants perceive the sale of common stock by the firm to reflect management's belief that the stock is "overvalued"; as a result, the stock price declines. A final disadvantage of common stock financing is its *high cost*. In Chapter 10, common stock equity was shown to be, normally, the most expensive form of long-term financing. The reason is that dividends are not tax-deductible and common stock is a riskier security than either debt or preferred stock.

CONCEPT IN PRACTICE

Chrysler's Stock Issue Receives Credit

The price of Chrysler's common stock rose by over 100 percent in 1992. To benefit from its high-octane performance, Chrysler issued 40 million new shares in 1993. Half of the $1.4 billion sales proceeds was used to reduce Chrysler's unfunded pension liability, while the remaining half was used to reduce debt and finance new acquisitions. Moody's and Standard & Poor's, the two primary credit-rating agencies, immediately upgraded Chrysler's credit rating. Recognition that the improved credit rating would reduce interest expenses limited shareholder aversion. Chrysler's share price declined by only 3 percent, despite a 14 percent dilution of ownership.

CONCEPTS IN REVIEW

13-5 What are *stock rights?* Compare the theoretical value of rights when a stock is selling *with rights* with its *ex rights* value.

13-6 How are *stock options* and *stock-purchase plans* used to sell new common stock directly? How is new common stock sold publicly?

13-7 What are the key advantages and disadvantages of using common stock financing as a source of new capital funds?

Dividend fundamentals

Some people believe that because dividends are irrelevant, they should be treated as a residual—the amount remaining after all acceptable investment opportunities have been undertaken. What arguments would you make in support of the relevance of dividends to the achievement of the firm's goal of owner-wealth maximization? Spend a few moments answering this question before reading further.

retained earnings
Earnings that are not distributed as dividends; a form of *internal* financing.

EXPECTED CASH DIVIDENDS ARE THE KEY RETURN VARIABLE FROM WHICH OWNERS AND investors determine share price (see Chapter 7). They represent a source of cash flow to stockholders and provide them with information about the firm's current and future performance. Because **retained earnings**—earnings that are not distributed as dividends—are a form of *internal* financing, the dividend decision can significantly affect the firm's *external* financing requirements. In other words, if the firm needs financing, the larger the cash dividend paid, the greater the amount of financing that must be raised externally through borrowing or through the sale of common or preferred stock. (Remember that although dividends are charged to retained earnings, they are actually paid out of cash.) To provide an understanding of the fundamentals of dividend policy, we discuss the procedures for paying cash dividends, dividend reinvestment plans, dividend policy theories, and the key factors affecting dividend policy.

Cash dividend payment procedures

The payment of cash dividends to corporate stockholders is decided by the firm's board of directors. The directors normally hold a quarterly or semiannual dividend meeting at which they evaluate the past period's financial performance and future outlook to determine whether and in what amount dividends should be paid. Insight into recent dividends paid, if any, can typically be found in their annual stockholders' reports. The payment date of the cash dividend, if one is declared, must also be established.

AMOUNT OF DIVIDENDS

Whether dividends should be paid and, if they are, how large they should be are important decisions that depend largely on the firm's dividend policy. Most firms pay some cash dividends each period. The amount is generally fixed, although significant increases or decreases in earnings may justify changing it. Most firms have a set policy with respect to the amount of the periodic dividend, but the firm's directors can change this amount at the dividend meeting.

RELEVANT DATES

date of record (dividends)
The date, set by the firm's directors, on which every person whose name is recorded as a stockholder will at a specified future time receive a declared dividend.

If the directors of the firm declare a dividend, they will also indicate the record and payment dates associated with the dividend. Typically, the directors issue a statement indicating their dividend decision, the record date, and the payment date. This statement is generally quoted in *The Wall Street Journal, Barron's,* and other financial news media.

ex dividend
Period beginning four *business days* prior to the date of record during which a stock will be sold without the right to receive the current dividend.

RECORD DATE Every person whose name is recorded as a stockholder on the **date of record,** which is set by the directors, will at a specified future time receive a declared dividend. These stockholders are often referred to as *holders of record.* Due to the time needed to make bookkeeping entries when a stock is traded, the stock will begin selling **ex dividend** four *business days* prior to the date of record. A simple way to determine the first day on which the stock sells ex dividend is to subtract four days from the date of record; if a weekend intervenes, subtract six days. Purchasers of a stock selling ex dividend do not receive the current dividend. Ignoring general market fluctuations, the stock's price would be expected to drop by the amount of the declared dividend on the ex dividend date.

payment date
The actual date on which the firm will mail the dividend payment to the holders of record.

PAYMENT DATE The payment date is also set by the directors. It is generally set a few weeks after the record date. The **payment date** is the actual date on which the firm will mail the dividend payment to the holders of record. An example will clarify the various dates and accounting entries.

EXAMPLE

At the quarterly dividend meeting of the Rudolf Company, a distributor of office products, held June 10, the directors declared an $.80 per share cash dividend for holders of record on Monday, July 1. The firm had 100,000 shares of common stock outstanding. The payment date for the dividend was August 1. Before the dividend was declared, the key accounts of the firm were as follows:

Cash	$200,000	Dividends payable	$ 0
		Retained earnings	1,000,000

When the directors announced the dividend, $80,000 of the retained earnings ($.80 per share × 100,000 shares) was transferred to the dividends payable account. The key accounts thus became

Cash	$200,000	Dividends payable	$ 80,000
		Retained earnings	920,000

The Rudolf Company's stock began selling ex dividend four *business days* prior to the date of record, which was June 25. This date was found by subtracting six days (since a weekend intervened) from the July 1 date of record. Purchasers of Rudolf's stock on June 24 or earlier received the rights to the dividends; those who purchased the stock on or after June 25 did not. Assuming a stable market, Rudolf's stock price would be expected to drop by approximately $.80 per share when it began selling ex dividend on June 25. When the August 1 payment date arrived, the firm mailed dividend checks to the holders of record as of July 1. This produced the following balances in the key accounts of the firm:

Cash	$120,000	Dividends payable	$ 0
		Retained earnings	920,000

The net effect of declaration and payment of the dividend was to reduce the firm's total assets (and stockholders' equity) by $80,000. ■

Dividend reinvestment plans

dividend reinvestment plans (DRPs)
Plans that enable stockholders to use dividends received on the firms stock to acquire additional full or fractional shares at little or no transaction (brokerage) cost.

Today about 900 firms offer **dividend reinvestment plans (DRPs),** which enable stockholders to use dividends received on the firm's stock to acquire additional shares—even fractional shares—at little or no transaction (brokerage) cost. (A small number of these companies, such as Exxon, Texaco, and W.R. Grace, allow investors to make their initial purchases of the firm's stock directly from the company without going through a broker.) Under current tax law, cash dividends from all plans (or the value of the stocks received through a DRP) are taxed as ordinary income. In addition, when the acquired shares are sold, if the proceeds are in excess of the original purchase price, the capital gain will also be taxed as ordinary income.

Dividend reinvestment plans can be handled by a company in either of two ways. Both allow the stockholder to elect to have dividends reinvested in the firm's shares. In one approach, a third-party trustee is paid a fee to buy the firm's outstanding shares in the open market on behalf of the shareholders who wish to reinvest their dividends. This type of plan benefits participating shareholders by allowing them to use their dividends to purchase shares generally at a lower transaction cost than they would otherwise pay. The second approach involves buying *newly issued shares* directly from the firm without paying any transaction costs. This approach allows the firm to raise new capital while permitting owners to reinvest their dividends, frequently at about 5 percent below the current market price. Clearly, the existence of a DRP may enhance the appeal of a firm's shares.

Dividend policy theories

Numerous theories and empirical findings concerning dividend policy have been reported in the financial literature over the past 35 or so years. Although this research has provided some interesting arguments and insights about dividend policy, capital budgeting and capital structure decisions are generally considered far more important than dividend decisions. In other words, good investment and financing decisions should not be sacrificed for a dividend policy of questionable importance. A number of key questions have yet to be resolved: Does dividend policy matter? What effect does dividend policy have on share price? Is there a model that can be used to evaluate alternative dividend policies in view of share value? Here we begin by describing the residual theory of dividends, which is used as a backdrop for discussion of the key arguments in support of dividend irrelevance and then those in support of dividend relevance.

THE RESIDUAL THEORY OF DIVIDENDS

residual theory of dividends
A theory that the dividend paid by a firm should be the amount left over after all acceptable investment opportunities have been undertaken.

One school of thought—the **residual theory of dividends**—suggests that the dividend paid by a firm should be viewed as a *residual*—the amount left over after all acceptable investment opportunities have been undertaken. Using this approach, the firm would treat the dividend decision in three steps as follows:

1. Determine its optimum level of capital expenditures, which would be the level generated by the point of intersection of the investment opportunities schedule (IOS) and weighted marginal cost of capital (WMCC) function (see Chapter 10).
2. Using the optimal capital structure proportions (see Chapter 11), estimate the total amount of equity financing needed to support the expenditures generated in Step 1.
3. Because the cost of retained earnings, k_r, is less than the cost of new common stock, k_n (see Chapter 10), use retained earnings to meet the equity requirement determined in Step 2. If retained earnings are inadequate to meet this need, sell new common stock. If the available retained earnings are in excess of this need, distribute the surplus amount as dividends.

According to this approach, as long as the firm's equity need is in excess of the amount of retained earnings, no cash dividend would be paid. If an excess of retained earnings exists, the residual amount would then be distributed as a cash dividend. The argument supporting this approach is that it is sound management to be certain that the company has the money it needs to compete effectively and therefore increase share price. This view of dividends tends to suggest that the required return of investors, k_s, is *not* influenced by the firm's dividend policy—a premise that in turn suggests that dividend policy is irrelevant. Let us look at an example.

EXAMPLE

Overbrook Industries, a manufacturer of canoes and other small watercraft, has available from the current period's operations $1.8 million that can be retained or paid out in dividends. The firm's optimal capital structure is at a debt ratio of 30 percent, which represents 30 percent debt and 70 percent equity. Figure 13.1 depicts the firm's weighted marginal cost of capital (WMCC) function along with three investment opportunities schedules, IOS_1, IOS_2, and IOS_3. For each IOS the level of total new financing or investment determined by the point of intersection of the IOS and the WMCC has been noted. For IOS_1 it is \$1.5 million, for IOS_2 it is \$2.4 million, and for IOS_3 it is \$3.2 million. Although only one IOS will actually exist, it is useful to look at the dividend decisions generated by applying the residual theory in each of the three cases. Table 13.1 summarizes this analysis.

Table 13.1 shows that if IOS_1 exists, the firm will pay out \$750,000 in dividends, since only \$1,050,000 of the \$1,800,000 of available earnings is needed. A 41.7 percent payout ratio results. For IOS_2, dividends of \$120,000 (a payout ratio of 6.7 percent) result. Should IOS_3 exist, the firm would pay no dividends (a zero payout ratio), since its retained earnings of \$1,800,000 would be less than the \$2,240,000 of equity needed. In this case the firm would have to obtain additional new common stock financing to meet the new requirements generated by the intersection of the IOS_3 and WMCC. Depending on which IOS exists, the firm's dividend would in effect be the residual, if any, remaining after financing all acceptable investments. ■

dividend irrelevance theory
A theory put forth by Miller and Modigliani that, in a perfect world, the value of a firm is unaffected by the distribution of dividends and is determined solely by the earning power and risk of its assets.

DIVIDEND IRRELEVANCE ARGUMENTS

The residual theory of dividends suggests that dividends are irrelevant—that they represent an earnings residual rather than an active decision variable that affects the firm's value. This view is consistent with the **dividend irrelevance theory** put forth by Merton H. Miller and Franco Modigliani[2] (as noted in Chapter 11, commonly called

FIGURE 13.1
WMCC and IOSs for Overbrook Industries

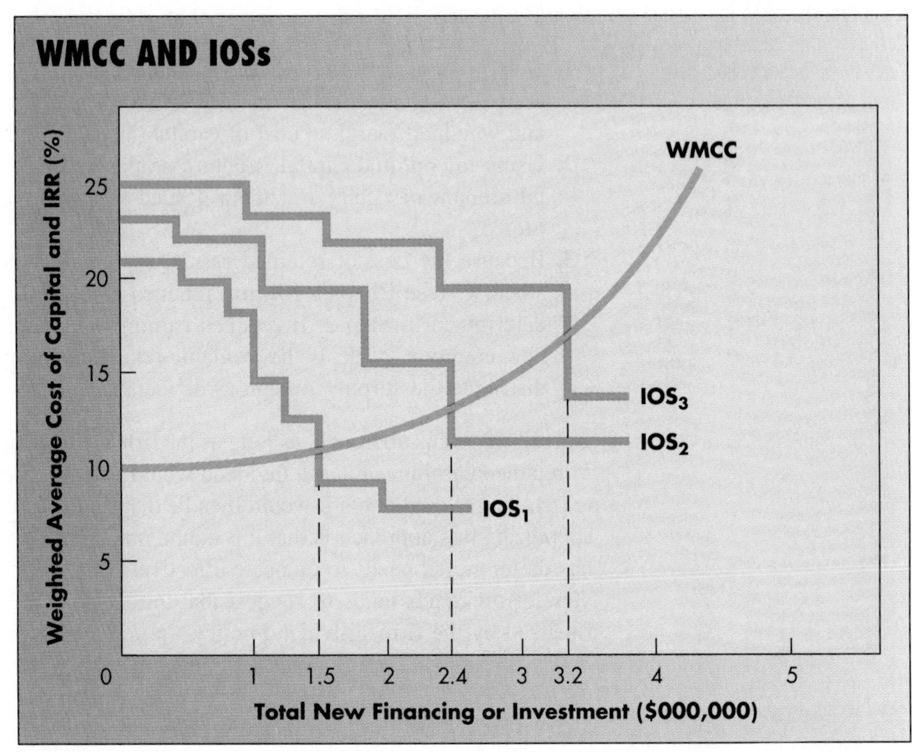

[2]Merton H. Miller and Franco Modigliani, "Dividend Policy, Growth and the Valuation of Shares," *Journal of Business* 34 (October 1961), pp. 411–433.

TABLE 13.1

APPLYING THE RESIDUAL THEORY OF DIVIDENDS TO OVERBROOK INDUSTRIES FOR EACH OF THREE IOSs (SHOWN IN FIGURE 13.1)

	Investment opportunities schedules		
Item	IOS_1	IOS_2	IOS_3
(1) New financing or investment (Fig. 13.1)	$1,500,000	$2,400,000	$3,200,000
(2) Retained earnings available (given)	$1,800,000	$1,800,000	$1,800,000
(3) Equity needed [70% × (1)]	1,050,000	1,680,000	2,240,000
(4) Dividends [(2) − (3)]	$ 750,000	$ 120,000	$ 0[a]
(5) Dividend payout ratio [(4) ÷ (2)]	41.7%	6.7%	0%

[a]In this case, additional new common stock in the amount of $440,000 ($2,240,000 needed − $1,800,000 available) would have to be sold; no dividends would be paid.

"M and M"). M and M's theory shows that in a perfect world (certainty, no taxes, no transactions costs, and no other market imperfections) the value of the firm is unaffected by the distribution of dividends. They argue that the firm's value is determined solely by the earning power and risk of its assets (investments) and that the manner in which it splits its earnings stream between dividends and internally retained (and reinvested) funds does not affect this value.

In response to studies showing that large dividend changes affect share price in the same direction—increases in dividends result in increased share price, and decreases in dividends result in decreased share price—M and M argue that these effects are attributable not to the dividend itself but rather to the **informational content** of dividends with respect to future earnings. In other words, it is not the preference of shareholders for current dividends rather than future capital gains (expected to result from the retention of earnings) that is responsible for this behavior. Instead, a change, up or down, in dividends is viewed as a *signal* (see Chapter 11) that management expects future earnings to change in the same direction. An increase in dividends would be viewed as a *positive signal* that would cause investors to bid up the share price, and a decrease in dividends would be a *negative signal* that would cause a decrease in share price.

informational content
The information provided by the dividends of a firm with respect to future earnings, which causes owners to bid up (or down) the price of the firm's stock.

M and M further argue that a **clientele effect** exists: A firm will attract shareholders whose preferences with respect to the payment and stability of dividends correspond to the payment pattern and stability of the firm itself. In other words, investors desiring stable and predictable dividends as a source of income would hold the stock of firms that pay about the same dividend amount each period; investors who prefer to earn capital gains would be more attracted to growing firms that reinvest a large portion of their earnings, which results in a fairly unstable pattern of dividends. Since the shareholders get what they expect, M and M argue that the value of their firm's stock is unaffected by dividend policy.

clientele effect
The theory that a firm will attract shareholders whose preferences with respect to the payment and stability of dividends correspond to the payment pattern and stability of the firm itself.

In summary, it can be seen that M and M and other dividend irrelevance proponents argue that—all else being equal—an investor's required return, k_s, and therefore the value of the firm, are unaffected by dividend policy because (1) the firm's value is determined solely by the earning power and risk of its assets; (2) if dividends do affect value, they do so solely because of their informational content, which signals management's earnings expectations; and (3) a clientele effect exists that causes a firm's shareholders to receive the dividends that they expect. These views of M and M with respect to dividend irrelevance are consistent with the residual theory, which focuses on making the best investment decisions to maximize share value. The proponents of dividend irrelevance conclude that since dividends are irrelevant to a firm's value, the firm does not need to have a dividend policy. Although many research studies have been performed to validate or refute the dividend irrelevance theory, none have been successful in providing irrefutable evidence.

DIVIDEND RELEVANCE ARGUMENTS

dividend relevance theory

The theory, attributed to Gordon and Lintner, that stockholders prefer current dividends and that there is a direct relationship between a firm's dividend policy and its market value.

bird-in-the-hand argument

The belief, in support of dividend relevance theory, that current dividend payments ("a bird in the hand") reduce investor uncertainty and ultimately result in a higher value for the firm's stock.

The key argument in support of **dividend relevance theory** is attributed to Myron J. Gordon and John Lintner,[3] who suggest that stockholders prefer current dividends and that there is, in fact, a direct relationship between the dividend policy of the firm and its market value. Fundamental to this proposition is their **bird-in-the-hand argument,** which suggests that investors are generally risk averse and attach less risk to current than to future dividends or capital gains. Simply stated, "a bird in the hand is worth two in the bush." Current dividend payments are therefore believed to reduce investor uncertainty, causing investors to discount the firm's earnings at a lower rate, k_s, thereby—all else being equal—placing a higher value on the firm's stock. Conversely, if dividends are reduced or not paid, investor uncertainty will increase, raising the required return, k_s, and lowering the stock's value.

Although many other arguments and counterarguments relating to the question of dividend relevance have been put forward, the *numerous empirical studies of this issue fail to provide conclusive evidence in support of the intuitively appealing dividend relevance argument.* In addition, researchers have yet to develop a model that can be used to evaluate alternative policies in view of share value. In practice, however, the actions of financial managers and stockholders alike tend to support the belief that dividend policy affects stock value.[4] Since our concern centers on the day-to-day behavior of business firms, the remainder of this chapter is consistent with the belief that dividends *are relevant*—that each firm must develop a dividend policy that fulfills the goals of owners and maximizes their wealth as reflected in the firm's share price.

CONCEPT IN PRACTICE

Merrill Lynch Views Excessive Dividends Negatively

Good dividends can often lure investors. Higher demand increases price and the price/earnings (P/E) ratio. Merrill Lynch believes that investors who pay premium P/Es for stocks want strong growth in earnings and share price, even though they originally chose the stock for its attractive dividend payouts. Drug companies were considered to be particularly unattractive investments because their dividend payouts were

[3]Myron J. Gordon, "Optimal Investment and Financing Policy," *Journal of Finance* 18 (May 1963), pp. 264–272, and John Lintner, "Dividends, Earnings, Leverage, Stock Prices, and the Supply of Capital to Corporations," *Review of Economics and Statistics* 44 (August 1962), pp. 243–269.

[4]A common exception is small firms, since they frequently treat dividends as a residual remaining after all acceptable investments have been initiated. This course of action occurs because small firms usually do not have ready access to capital markets. The use of retained earnings therefore acts as a key source of financing for growth, which is generally an important goal of a small firm.

significantly above that of the market. According to Charles Clough, Merrill Lynch's chief investment strategist, high dividends were a sign that the drug firms were generating more cash than they could reinvest. Compounding the problem was President Clinton's assertion that drug companies were profiteering.

Factors affecting dividend policy

Before discussing the basic types of dividend policies, we should consider the factors involved in formulating dividend policy. These include legal constraints, contractual constraints, internal constraints, the firm's growth prospects, owner considerations, and market considerations.

LEGAL CONSTRAINTS

Most states prohibit corporations from paying out as cash dividends any portion of the firm's "legal capital," which is measured by the par value of common stock. Other states define legal capital to include not only the par value of the common stock but also any paid-in capital in excess of par. These "capital impairment restrictions" are generally established to provide a sufficient equity base to protect creditors' claims. An example will clarify the differing definitions of capital.

EXAMPLE

The stockholders' equity account of Miller Flour Company, a large grain processor, is presented below.

MILLER FLOUR COMPANY'S STOCKHOLDERS' EQUITY

Common stock at par	$100,000
Paid-in capital in excess of par	200,000
Retained earnings	140,000
Total stockholders' equity	$440,000

In states where the firm's legal capital is defined as the par value of its common stock, the firm could pay out $340,000 ($200,000 + $140,000) in cash dividends without impairing its capital. In states where the firm's legal capital includes all paid-in capital, the firm could pay out only $140,000 in cash dividends. ■

An earnings requirement limiting the amount of dividends to the sum of the firm's present and past earnings is sometimes imposed. In other words, the firm cannot pay more in cash dividends than the sum of its most recent and past retained earnings. However, *the firm is not prohibited from paying more in dividends than its current earnings.*[5]

EXAMPLE

Assume that the Miller Flour Company, presented in the preceding example, in the year just ended has $30,000 in earnings available for common stock dividends. An analy-

[5]A firm that has an operating loss in the current period could still pay cash dividends as long as sufficient retained earnings against which to charge the dividend were available and, of course, as long as it had the cash with which to make the payments.

sis of the stockholders' equity account above indicates that the firm has past retained earnings of $140,000. Thus it could legally pay dividends of up to $170,000. ■

If a firm has overdue liabilities or is legally insolvent or bankrupt (if the fair market value of its assets is less than its liabilities), most states prohibit its payment of cash dividends. In addition, the Internal Revenue Service prohibits firms from accumulating earnings to reduce the owners' taxes. A firm's owners must pay income taxes on dividends when received, but the owners are not taxed on capital gains in market value until the stock is sold. A firm may retain a large portion of earnings to delay the payment of taxes by its owners. If the IRS can determine that a firm has accumulated an excess of earnings to allow owners to delay paying ordinary income taxes, it may levy an **excess earnings accumulation tax** on any retained earnings above $250,000—the amount that is currently exempt from this tax for all firms except personal service corporations.

excess earnings accumulation tax
The tax levied by the IRS on retained earnings above $250,000, when it has determined that the firm has accumulated an excess of earnings to allow owners to delay paying ordinary income taxes.

CONTRACTUAL CONSTRAINTS

Often the firm's ability to pay cash dividends is constrained by certain restrictive provisions in a loan agreement. Generally, these constraints prohibit the payment of cash dividends until a certain level of earnings has been achieved or limit the dividends paid to a certain dollar amount or percentage of earnings. Constraints on dividend payments help to protect creditors from losses due to insolvency on the part of the firm. The violation of a contractual constraint is generally grounds for a demand of immediate payment by the funds supplier affected.

INTERNAL CONSTRAINTS

The firm's ability to pay cash dividends is generally constrained by the amount of excess cash available rather than the level of retained earnings against which to charge them. Although it is possible for a firm to borrow funds to pay dividends, lenders are generally reluctant to make such loans, since they produce no tangible or operating benefits that will help the firm repay the loan. Although a firm may have high earnings, its ability to pay dividends may be constrained by a low level of liquid assets (cash and marketable securities).

EXAMPLE

The Miller Flour Company's stockholders' equity account presented earlier indicates that if the firm's legal capital is defined as all paid-in capital, the firm can pay $140,000 in dividends. If the firm has total liquid assets of $50,000 ($20,000 in cash plus marketable securities worth $30,000) and $35,000 of this is needed for operations, the maximum dividend the firm can pay is $15,000 ($50,000 − $35,000). ■

GROWTH PROSPECTS

The firm's financial requirements are directly related to the degree of asset expansion that is anticipated. If the firm is in a growth stage, it may need all the funds it can get to finance capital expenditures. A growing firm also requires funds to maintain and improve its assets. High-growth firms typically find themselves constantly in need of funds. Their financial requirements may be characterized as large and immediate. Firms exhibiting little or no growth may nevertheless periodically need funds to replace or renew assets.

A firm must evaluate its financial position from the standpoint of profitability and risk to develop insight into its ability to raise capital externally. It must determine not only its ability to raise funds but also the cost and speed with which financing can be obtained. Generally, a large, mature firm has adequate access to new capital, whereas the funds that are available to a rapidly growing firm may not be sufficient to support its numerous acceptable projects. A growth firm is likely to have to depend heavily on internal financing through retained earnings to take advantage of profitable projects; it is likely to pay out only a very small percentage of its earnings as dividends. A more stable firm that needs long-term funds only for planned outlays is in a better position to pay out a large proportion of its earnings, especially if it has ready sources of financing.

OWNER CONSIDERATIONS[6]

In establishing a dividend policy the primary concern of the firm should be to maximize owners' wealth. Although it is impossible to establish a policy that will maximize each owner's wealth, the firm must establish a policy that has a favorable effect on the wealth of the *majority* of owners.

One consideration is the *tax status of a firm's owners.* If a firm has a large percentage of wealthy stockholders who are in a high tax bracket, it may decide to pay out a *lower* percentage of its earnings to allow the owners to delay the payment of taxes until they sell the stock.[7] Of course, when the stock is sold, if the proceeds are in excess of the original purchase price, the capital gain will be taxed as ordinary income. Lower-income shareholders, however, who need dividend income, will prefer a *higher* payout of earnings.

A second consideration is the *owners' investment opportunities.* A firm should not retain funds for investment in projects yielding lower returns than the owners could obtain from external investments of equal risk. The firm should evaluate the returns that are expected on its own investment opportunities and, using present-value techniques, determine whether greater returns are obtainable from external investments such as government securities or other corporate stocks. If it appears that the owners would have better opportunities externally, the firm should pay out a higher percentage of its earnings. If the firm's investment opportunities are at least as good as similar-risk external investments, a lower payout is justifiable.

A final consideration is the *potential dilution of ownership.* If a firm pays out a higher percentage of earnings, new equity capital will have to be raised with common stock, which may result in the dilution of both control and earnings for the existing owners. By paying out a low percentage of its earnings, the firm can minimize such possibility of dilution.

MARKET CONSIDERATIONS

Since the wealth of the firm's owners is reflected in the market price of the firm's shares, an awareness of the market's probable response to certain types of policies is helpful in formulating a suitable dividend policy. Stockholders are believed to value a *fixed or*

[6]Theoretically, in an *efficient market* owner considerations are automatically handled by the pricing mechanism. The logic is as follows. A firm that pays a dividend that is smaller than required by a large number of owners will experience a decline in price because the dissatisfied shareholders will sell their shares. The resulting drop in share price will (as was explained in Chapter 7) raise the expected return to investors, which will cause the firm's WMCC to rise. As a result—all else being equal—the firm's optimal capital budget will become smaller and the demand for retained earnings will fall. This decrease should allow the firm to satisfy shareholders by paying the larger dividends that they demand. In spite of this logic it is helpful to understand some of the important considerations underlying owner behavior.

[7]The consideration of the owners' tax status in making dividend policy decisions is illegal, although it is difficult for the IRS to enforce this law. Rather, the IRS will look for high retained earnings and high liquidity. Firms in this situation are penalized through the *excess earnings accumulation tax.* It is quite difficult, if not impossible, to determine the extent to which the tax status of a firm's owners affects dividend policy decisions.

increasing level of dividends as opposed to a fluctuating pattern of dividends. This belief is supported by the research of John Lintner, who found that corporate managers are averse to changing the dollar amount of dividends in response to changes in earnings, particularly when earnings decline.[8] In addition, stockholders are believed to value a policy of *continuous dividend payment.* Since regularly paying a fixed or increasing dividend eliminates uncertainty about the frequency and magnitude of dividends, the earnings of the firm are likely to be discounted at a lower rate. This should result in an increase in the market value of the stock and therefore increased owners' wealth.

A final market consideration is the *informational content* of dividends. Shareholders often view the firm's dividend payment as a *signal* relative to its future success. A stable and continuous dividend is a *positive signal* that conveys to the owners that the firm is in good health and that there is no reason for concern. If the firm skips a dividend payment in a given period due to a loss or to very low earnings, shareholders are likely to react unfavorably to this *negative signal.* The nonpayment of the dividend creates uncertainty about the future, and this uncertainty is likely to result in lower stock value. Owners and investors generally construe a dividend payment during a period of losses as an indication that the loss is merely temporary.

CONCEPTS IN REVIEW

13-8 How do the date of record and the holders of record relate to the payment of cash dividends? What does the term *ex dividend* mean? Who sets the dividend payment date?

13-9 What is a *dividend reinvestment plan?* What benefit is available to plan participants? Describe the two ways in which companies can handle such plans.

13-10 Describe the *residual theory of dividends.* Would following this approach lead to a stable dividend? Is this approach consistent with dividend relevance? Explain.

13-11 Describe, compare, and contrast the basic arguments relative to the irrelevance or relevance of dividend policy given by:

a. Merton H. Miller and Franco Modigliani (M and M)
b. Myron J. Gordon and John Lintner

13-12 Briefly describe each of the following factors affecting dividend policy:

a. Legal constraints
b. Contractual constraints
c. Internal constraints
d. Growth prospects
e. Owner considerations
f. Market considerations

Types of dividend policies

LG 5

Owners tend to respond most favorably to generally positive information that signals to them that the firm is okay and minimizes their uncertainty. In light of this behavioral fact, what general characteristics would you include in your firm's dividend policy? Take a short time to answer this question before reading on.

dividend policy
The firm's plan of action to be followed whenever a decision concerning dividends must be made.

THE FIRM'S **DIVIDEND POLICY** REPRESENTS A PLAN OF ACTION TO BE FOLLOWED WHENever the dividend decision must be made. The dividend policy must be formulated with two basic objectives in mind: maximizing the wealth of the firm's owners and

[8]John Lintner, "Distribution of Income of Corporations among Dividends, Retained Earnings, and Taxes," *American Economic Review* 46 (May 1956), pp. 97–113.

providing for sufficient financing. These two objectives are interrelated. They must be fulfilled in light of a number of factors—legal, contractual, internal, growth, owner-related, and market-related—that limit the policy alternatives. Three of the more commonly used dividend policies are described below. A particular firm's cash dividend policy may incorporate elements of each.

dividend payout ratio
Indicates the percentage of each dollar earned that is distributed to the owners in the form of cash; calculated by dividing the firm's cash dividend per share by its earnings per share.

constant-payout-ratio dividend policy
A dividend policy based on the payment of a certain percentage of earnings to owners in each dividend period.

Constant-payout-ratio dividend policy

One type of dividend policy that firms occasionally adopt is the use of a constant payout ratio. The **dividend payout ratio,** calculated by dividing the firm's cash dividend per share by its earnings per share, indicates the percentage of each dollar earned that is distributed to the owners in the form of cash. With a **constant-payout-ratio dividend policy** the firm establishes that a certain percentage of earnings will be paid to owners in each dividend period. The problem with this policy is that if the firm's earnings drop or if a loss occurs in a given period, the dividends may be low or even nonexistent. Since dividends are often considered an indicator of the firm's future condition and status, the firm's stock price may thus be adversely affected by this type of action. An example will clarify the problems stemming from a constant-payout-ratio policy.

EXAMPLE

Peachtree Industries, a miner of potassium, has a policy of paying out 40 percent of earnings in cash dividends. In periods when a loss occurs, the firm's policy is to pay no cash dividends. Peachtree's earnings per share, dividends per share, and average price per share for the past six years were as follows:

Year	Earnings/share	Dividends/share	Average price/share
1994	$ − 0.50	$0.00	$42.00
1993	3.00	1.20	52.00
1992	1.75	0.70	48.00
1991	− 1.50	0.00	38.00
1990	2.00	0.80	46.00
1989	4.50	1.80	50.00

Dividends increased in 1991–1992 and in 1992–1993 and decreased in 1989–1990, 1990–1991, and 1993–1994. The data show that in years of decreasing dividends, the firm's stock price dropped; when dividends increased, the price of the stock increased. Peachtree's sporadic dividend payments appear to make its owners uncertain about the returns they can expect from their investment in the firm and therefore tend to generally depress the stock's price. Although a constant-payout-ratio dividend policy is used by some firms, it is *not* recommended. ■

Regular dividend policy

regular dividend policy
A dividend policy based on the payment of a fixed-dollar dividend in each period.

Another type of dividend policy, the **regular dividend policy,** is based on the payment of a fixed-dollar dividend in each period. The regular dividend policy provides the owners with generally positive information, indicating that the firm is okay and thereby minimizing their uncertainty. Often, firms using this policy will increase the regular dividend once a *proven* increase in earnings has occurred. Under this policy, dividends are almost never decreased.

EXAMPLE

The dividend policy of Woodward Laboratories, a producer of a popular artificial sweetener, is to pay annual dividends of $1.00 per share until per-share earnings have exceeded $4.00 for three consecutive years, at which time the annual dividend is raised to $1.50 per share and a new earnings plateau is established. The firm does not anticipate decreasing its dividend unless its liquidity is in jeopardy. Woodward's earnings per share, dividends per share, and average price per share for the past 12 years were as follows:

Year	Earnings/share	Dividends/share	Average price/share
1994	$4.50	$1.50	$47.50
1993	3.90	1.50	46.50
1992	4.60	1.50	45.00
1991	4.20	1.00	43.00
1990	5.00	1.00	42.00
1989	2.00	1.00	38.50
1988	6.00	1.00	38.00
1987	3.00	1.00	36.00
1986	0.75	1.00	33.00
1985	0.50	1.00	33.00
1984	2.70	1.00	33.50
1983	2.85	1.00	35.00

It can be seen that regardless of the level of earnings, Woodward Labs paid dividends of $1.00 per share through 1991. In 1992 the dividend was raised to $1.50 per share, since earnings in excess of $4.00 per share had been achieved for three years. In 1992 the firm would also have had to establish a new earnings plateau for further dividend increases. Woodward Laboratories' average price per share exhibited a stable, increasing behavior in spite of a somewhat volatile pattern of earnings. ■

target dividend-payout ratio
A policy under which the firm attempts to pay out a certain percentage of earnings as a stated dollar dividend, which it adjusts toward a target payout as proven earnings increases occur.

Often, a regular dividend policy is built around a **target dividend-payout ratio.** Under this policy the firm attempts to pay out a certain percentage of earnings, but rather than let dividends fluctuate, it pays a stated dollar dividend and adjusts it toward the target payout as proven earnings increases occur. For instance, Woodward Laboratories appears to have a target payout ratio of around 35 percent. The payout was about 35 percent ($1.00 ÷ $2.85) when the dividend policy was set in 1983, and when the dividend was raised to $1.50 in 1992, the payout ratio was about 33 percent ($1.50 ÷ $4.60).

CONCEPT IN PRACTICE

Salving the Wounds Arising from IBM's Dividends Cut

In January 1993, John Akers, IBM's Chairman and CEO, informed shareholders that the firm was cutting the dividends paid on common stock. Specifically, the once sacred $1.21 quarterly dividend was being reduced to $.54. Akers sent a letter to every shareholder asserting that the dividend cut was in the shareholders' best long-run interest. Akers gave three reasons in support of cutting IBM's dividend.

1. IBM's recent earnings performance was dismal.
2. Retained earnings had to be increased to update plant and equipment.
3. The 7-plus percent dividend yield that arose from IBM's stock price decline from $100 to $50 greatly exceeded the normal dividend yield.

To stop the bleeding, Akers' letter closed with a report that a selection team had been chosen to find a replacement for him as Chairman and CEO of IBM. A few months later Louis V. Gerstner, Jr. was hired to replace Akers.

Low-regular-and-extra dividend policy

low-regular-and-extra dividend policy
A dividend policy based on paying a low regular dividend, supplemented by an additional dividend when earnings warrant it.

extra dividend
An additional dividend optionally paid by the firm if earnings are higher than normal in a given period.

Some firms establish a **low-regular-and-extra dividend policy,** paying a low regular dividend, supplemented by an additional dividend when earnings warrant it. If earnings are higher than normal in a given period, the firm may pay this additional dividend, which will be designated an **extra dividend.** By designating the amount by which the dividend exceeds the regular payment as an extra dividend, the firm avoids giving shareholders false hopes. The use of the "extra" designation is especially common among companies that experience cyclical shifts in earnings.

By establishing a low regular dividend that is paid each period, the firm gives investors the stable income that is necessary to build confidence in the firm, and the extra dividend permits them to share in the earnings if the firm experiences an especially good period. Firms using this policy must raise the level of the regular dividend once proven increases in earnings have been achieved. The extra dividend should not be a regular event, or it becomes meaningless. The use of a target dividend-payout ratio in establishing the regular dividend level is advisable.

CONCEPT IN REVIEW

13-13 What are (1) a constant-payout-ratio dividend policy, (2) a regular dividend policy, and (3) a low-regular-and-extra dividend policy? What are the effects of these policies?

Other forms of dividends

Stock dividends and stock repurchases can be viewed as alternatives to the payment of cash dividends to owners. How would the firm's repurchase and retirement of outstanding common stock have effects similar to those resulting from its payment of cash dividends? Before reading further, devote a few minutes to answering this question.

A NUMBER OF OTHER FORMS OF DIVIDENDS ARE AVAILABLE TO THE FIRM. IN THIS SECtion we will discuss two other methods of paying dividends—stock dividends and stock repurchases—as well as a closely related topic, stock splits.

Stock dividends

stock dividend
The payment to existing owners of a dividend in the form of stock.

A **stock dividend** is the payment to existing owners of a dividend in the form of stock. Often, firms pay stock dividends as a replacement for or a supplement to cash dividends. Although stock dividends do not have a real value, stockholders may perceive them to represent something they did not have before and therefore to have value.

ACCOUNTING ASPECTS

small (ordinary) stock dividend
A stock dividend that represents less than 20 to 25 percent of the common stock outstanding at the time the dividend is declared.

In an accounting sense, the payment of a stock dividend is a shifting of funds between capital accounts rather than a use of funds. When a firm declares a stock dividend, the procedures with respect to announcement and distribution are the same as those described earlier for a cash dividend. The accounting entries associated with the payment of stock dividends vary depending upon whether or not it is a **small (ordinary) stock dividend,** which is generally viewed as a stock dividend representing less than 20 to 25 percent of the common stock outstanding at the time the dividend is declared. Because small stock dividends are most common, the accounting entries associated with them are illustrated in the following example.

EXAMPLE

The current stockholders' equity on the balance sheet of Garrison Corporation, a distributor of prefabricated cabinets, is as follows:

Preferred stock	$ 300,000
Common stock (100,000 shares at $4 par)	400,000
Paid-in capital in excess of par	600,000
Retained earnings	700,000
Total stockholders' equity	$2,000,000

If Garrison declares a 10 percent stock dividend and the market price of its stock is $15 per share, $150,000 of retained earnings (10% × 100,000 shares × $15 per share) will be capitalized.[9] The $150,000 will be distributed between common stock and paid-in capital in excess of par accounts based on the par value of the common stock. The resulting account balances are as follows:

Preferred stock	$ 300,000
Common stock (110,000 shares at $4 par)	440,000
Paid-in capital in excess of par	710,000
Retained earnings	550,000
Total stockholders' equity	$2,000,000

Since 10,000 new shares (10% of 100,000) have been issued and the prevailing market price is $15 per share, $150,000 ($15 per share × 10,000 shares) has been shifted from retained earnings to the common stock and paid-in capital accounts. A total of $40,000 ($4 par × 10,000 shares) has been added to common stock, and the re-

[9]The accounting treatment of *large stock dividends* can as an alternative involve capitalizing only an amount equal to the *par value* of the stock issued as a dividend. For a more detailed discussion of the accounting treatment of stock dividends, see Donald E. Kieso and Jerry Weygandt, *Intermediate Accounting,* 7th edition (New York: John Wiley & Sons, 1992), pp. 801–803.

maining \$110,000 [(\$15 − \$4) × 10,000 shares] has been added to the paid-in capital in excess of par. The firm's total stockholders' equity has not changed; funds have only been *redistributed* among stockholders' equity accounts. ■

THE SHAREHOLDER'S VIEWPOINT

The shareholder receiving a stock dividend receives nothing of value. After the dividend is paid, the per-share value of the shareholder's stock will decrease in proportion to the dividend in such a way that the market value of his or her total holdings in the firm will remain unchanged. The shareholder's proportion of ownership in the firm will also remain the same, and *as long as the firm's earnings remain unchanged*, so will his or her share of total earnings. (Clearly, if the firm's earnings and cash dividends increase at the time the stock dividend is issued, an increase in share value is likely to result.) A continuation of the preceding example will clarify this point.

EXAMPLE

Ms. X owned 10,000 shares of Garrison Corporation's stock. The company's most recent earnings were \$220,000, and earnings are not expected to change in the near future. Before the stock dividend, Ms. X owned 10 percent (10,000 shares ÷ 100,000 shares) of the firm's stock, which was selling for \$15 per share. Earnings per share were \$2.20 (\$220,000 ÷ 100,000 shares). Since Ms. X owned 10,000 shares, her earnings were \$22,000 (\$2.20 per share × 10,000 shares). After receiving the 10 percent stock dividend, Ms. X has 11,000 shares, which again is 10 percent (11,000 shares ÷ 110,000 shares) of the ownership. The market price of the stock can be expected to drop to \$13.64 per share [\$15 × (1.00 ÷ 1.10)], which means that the market value of Ms. X's holdings will be \$150,000 (11,000 shares × \$13.64 per share). This is the same as the initial value of her holdings (10,000 shares × \$15 per share). The future earnings per share will drop to \$2 (\$220,000 ÷ 110,000 shares), since the same \$220,000 in earnings must now be divided among 110,000 shares. Since Ms. X still owns 10 percent of the stock, her share of total earnings is still \$22,000 (\$2 per share × 11,000 shares). In summary, if the firm's earnings remain constant and total cash dividends do not increase, a stock dividend will result in a lower per-share market value for the firm's stock. ■

THE COMPANY'S VIEWPOINT

Stock dividends are more costly to issue than cash dividends, but the advantages generally outweigh these costs. Firms find the stock dividend to be a means of giving owners something without having to use cash. Generally, when a firm is growing rapidly and needs to preserve cash to finance this growth, a stock dividend is used. As long as the stockholders recognize that the firm is reinvesting the cash flow generated from earnings in a manner that should tend to maximize future earnings, the market value of the firm should at least remain unchanged. If the stock dividend is paid so that cash can be retained to satisfy past-due bills, a decline in market value may result.

Stock splits

stock split
A method that is commonly used to lower the market price of a firm's stock by increasing the number of shares belonging to each shareholder.

Although not a type of dividend, *stock splits* have an effect on a firm's share price similar to that of stock dividends. A **stock split** is a method that is commonly used to lower the market price of a firm's stock by increasing the number of shares belonging to each shareholder. Quite often, a firm believes that its stock is priced too high and that lowering the market price will enhance trading activity. Stock splits are often made prior to new issues of a stock to enhance the marketability of the stock and stimulate market activity.

A stock split has no effect on the firm's capital structure. It commonly increases the number of shares outstanding and reduces the stock's per-share par value. In other words, when a stock is split, a specified number of new shares are exchanged for a given number of outstanding shares. In a 2-for-1 split, two new shares are exchanged for each old share; in a 3-for-2 split, three new shares are exchanged for each two old shares, and so on.

EXAMPLE

Delphi Company, a forest products concern, had 200,000 shares of $2 par-value common stock and no preferred stock outstanding. Since the stock is selling at a high market price, the firm has declared a 2-for-1 stock split. The total before- and after-split stockholders' equity is given below.

Before split	
Common stock (200,000 shares at $2 par)	$ 400,000
Paid-in capital in excess of par	4,000,000
Retained earnings	2,000,000
Total stockholders' equity	$6,400,000
After 2-for-1 split	
Common stock (400,000 shares at $1 par)	$ 400,000
Paid-in capital in excess of par	4,000,000
Retained earnings	2,000,000
Total stockholders' equity	$6,400,000

The insignificant effect of the stock split on the firm's books is obvious. ■

reverse stock split
A method that is used to raise the market price of a firm's stock by exchanging a certain number of outstanding shares for one new share of stock.

Stock can be split in any way desired. Sometimes a **reverse stock split** is made: A certain number of outstanding shares are exchanged for one new share. For example, in a 1-for-2 split, one new share is exchanged for two old shares; in a 2-for-3 split, two new shares are exchanged for three old shares, and so on. Reverse stock splits are initiated when a stock is selling at too low a price to appear respectable.[10]

It is not unusual for a stock split to cause a slight increase in the market value of the stock. This is attributable to the informational content of stock splits and the fact that *total* dividends paid commonly increase slightly after a split.[11]

[10] If a firm's stock is selling at a low price—possibly less than a few dollars—many investors are hesitant to purchase it because they believe it is "cheap." These somewhat unsophisticated investors correlate cheapness and quality, and they feel that a low-priced stock is a low-quality investment. A reverse stock split raises the stock price and increases per-share earnings.

[11] Eugene F. Fama, Lawrence Fisher, Michael C. Jensen, and Richard Roll, "The Adjustment of Stock Prices to New Information," *International Economic Review* 10 (February 1969), pp. 1–21, found that the stock price increases before the split announcement, and the increase in stock price is maintained if dividends per share are increased but is lost if dividends per share are *not* increased following the split.

Stock repurchases

stock repurchase
The repurchasing by the firm of outstanding shares of its common stock in the marketplace; desired effects of stock repurchases are that they enhance shareholder value and/or help to discourage unfriendly takeovers.

Over the past 5 to 10 years, firms have increased their repurchasing of outstanding common stock in the marketplace. While the practical motives for **stock repurchases** include obtaining shares to be used in acquisitions, having shares available for employee stock option plans, or retiring shares, the recent increase in frequency and importance of stock repurchases is attributable to the fact that they either enhance shareholder value or help to discourage an unfriendly takeover. Enhancement of shareholder value through stock repurchase is achieved by (1) reducing the number of shares outstanding and thereby raising earnings per share (EPS), (2) sending a *positive signal* to investors in the marketplace that management believes that the stock is undervalued, and (3) providing a temporary floor for the stock price, which may have been declining. The use of repurchases to discourage unfriendly takeovers is predicated on the belief that by reducing the number of publicly traded shares, it is less likely that a corporate raider can gain control of the firm. Here we focus on the repurchase of shares for retirement, since this motive for repurchase is similar to the payment of cash dividends.

ACCOUNTING ENTRIES

The accounting entries that result when common stock is repurchased are a reduction in cash and the establishment of a contra capital account called "treasury stock," which is shown as a deduction from stockholders' equity. The label *treasury stock* is used to indicate the presence of repurchased shares on the balance sheet. The repurchase of stock can be viewed as a cash dividend, since it involves the distribution of cash to the firm's owners, who are the sellers of the shares.

VIEWED AS A CASH DIVIDEND

When common stock is repurchased for retirement, the underlying motive is to distribute excess cash to the owners. As a result of any repurchase, the owners receive cash for their shares. Generally, as long as earnings remain constant, the repurchase of shares reduces the number of outstanding shares, raising the earnings per share and therefore the market price per share. In addition, certain owner tax benefits may result from stock repurchases. The repurchase of common stock results in a type of reverse dilution, since the earnings per share and the market price of stock are increased by reducing the number of shares outstanding. The net effect of the repurchase is similar to the payment of a cash dividend. A simple example will clarify this point.

EXAMPLE

The Benton Company, a national sportswear chain, has released the following financial data:

Earnings available for common stockholders	$1,000,000
Number of shares of common outstanding	400,000
Earnings per share ($1,000,000 ÷ 400,000)	$2.50
Market price per share	$50
Price/earnings (P/E) ratio ($50 ÷ $2.50)	20

The firm is contemplating using $800,000 of its earnings either to pay cash dividends or to repurchase shares. If the firm pays cash dividends, the amount of the dividend would be $2 per share ($800,000 ÷ 400,000 shares). If the firm pays $52 per share to repurchase stock, it could repurchase approximately 15,385 shares ($800,000 ÷ $52 per share). As a result of this repurchase, 384,615 shares (400,000 shares − 15,385 shares) of common stock would remain outstanding. Earnings per share (EPS) would rise to \$2.60 (\$1,000,000 ÷ 384,615). If the stock still sold at 20 times earnings (P/E = 20), applying the price/earnings (P/E) multiple approach presented in Chapter 7, its market price would rise to \$52 per share (\$2.60 × 20). In both cases the stockholders would receive \$2 per share—a \$2 cash dividend in the dividend case or a \$2 increase in share price (\$50 per share to \$52 per share) in the repurchase case. ■

The advantages of stock repurchases are an increase in per-share earnings and certain owner tax benefits. The tax advantage stems from the fact that if the cash dividend is paid, the owners will have to pay ordinary income taxes on it, whereas the \$2 increase in the market value of the stock due to the repurchase will not be taxed until the owner sells the stock. Of course, when the stock is sold, if the proceeds are in excess of the original purchase price, the capital gain will be taxed as ordinary income. The IRS allegedly watches firms that regularly repurchase stock and levies a penalty if it believes that the repurchases have been made to delay the payment of taxes by the stockholders. Enforcement in this area appears to be relatively lax.

THE REPURCHASE PROCESS

When a company intends to repurchase a block of outstanding shares, it should make shareholders aware of its intentions. Specifically, it should advise them of the purpose of the repurchase (acquisitions, stock options, retirement, and so forth) and the disposition (if any) planned for the repurchased shares (traded for shares of another firm, distribution to executives, held in the treasury, and so forth).

Three basic methods of repurchase are commonly used. One is to purchase shares on the *open market.* This places upward pressure on the price of shares if the number of shares being repurchased is reasonably large in comparison with the total number outstanding. The second method is through tender offers.[12] A **tender offer** is a formal offer to purchase a given number of shares of a firm's stock at a specified price. The price at which a tender offer is made is set above the current market price to attract sellers. If the number of shares desired cannot be repurchased through the tender offer, open-market purchases can be used to obtain the additional shares. Tender offers are preferred when large numbers of shares are repurchased, since the company's intentions are clearly stated and each stockholder has an opportunity to sell his or her shares at the tendered price. The third method that is sometimes used to repurchase shares involves arranging to purchase on a *negotiated basis* a large block of shares from one or more major stockholders. Again, in this case the firm would have to state its intentions and make certain that the purchase price is fair and equitable in view of the interests and opportunities of the remaining shareholders.

tender offer
A formal offer to purchase a given number of shares of a firms stock at a specified price.

CONCEPTS IN REVIEW

13-14 What is a *stock dividend?* Why do firms issue stock dividends? Comment on the following statement: "I have a stock that promises to pay a 20 percent stock dividend every year, and therefore it guarantees that I will break even in five years."

[12]Tender offers are discussed in greater detail in Chapter 19. The motive for these offers may be to acquire control of another firm rather than to tender the firm's own shares.

13-15 What is a *stock split?* Compare and contrast it to a stock dividend.

13-16 What is the logic behind *repurchasing shares* of common stock to distribute excess cash to the firm's owners? How might this raise the per-share earnings and market price of outstanding shares?

Summary

LG 1 **Differentiate between debt and equity capital in terms of ownership rights, claims on income and assets, maturity, and tax treatment.** Holders of equity capital (common and preferred stock) are owners of the firm. Holders of common stock have voting rights that permit them to select the firm's directors and vote on special issues. They have claims on income and assets that are secondary to the claims of creditors, have no maturity date, and do not receive tax benefits similar to those given to debtholders.

LG 2 **Discuss common stock fundamentals, including ownership; par value; authorized, outstanding, and issued shares; voting rights; dividends; the distribution of earnings and assets; and international common stock.** The common stock of a firm can be privately owned, closely owned, or publicly owned. It can be sold with or without a par value. Not all shares authorized in the corporate charter will be outstanding. If a firm has treasury stock, it will have issued more shares than are outstanding. Some firms issue two or more classes of common stock, unequal voting rights being their key difference. Proxies can be used to transfer voting rights from one party to another. Either majority voting or cumulative voting may be used by the firm to elect its directors. Common stockholders are guaranteed neither the periodic distribution of earnings in the form of dividends nor the receipt of funds in the event of liquidation. International trading of common stock dramatically increased during the past 15 years as corporations discovered the benefits of using stock outside of their home markets and foreign corporations discovered the benefits of trading their stock in the U.S. either through listing on U.S. exchanges or through the issuance of sponsored or unsponsored American Depositary Receipts (ADRs). This trend is expected to continue.

LG 3 **Describe stock rights, the sale of common stock, and the advantages and disadvantages of common stock financing.** Holders of common stock—especially in smaller corporations—may receive stock rights that give them an opportunity to purchase new common stock at a reduced price on a pro rata basis. A certain number of rights are required to purchase the new shares at the reduced price, which causes each right to have a monetary value. Rights may be exercised, sold, purchased, or allowed to expire. In addition to rights offerings, new common stock can be sold directly through stock options or a stock-purchase plan or publicly through an investment banker. Basic advantages of common stock include the minimum of constraints it places on the firm, its lack of a maturity date, and its ability to increase the firm's borrowing power. Disadvantages include the potential dilution of earnings and control, the negative signal it sends to the marketplace, and its high cost.

LG 4 **Understand cash dividend payment procedures, dividend reinvestment plans, dividend policy theories and arguments with regard to its relevance, and the key factors that affect dividend policy.** The cash dividend decision is normally a quarterly decision made by the corporate board of directors, which establishes the record date and payment date. Generally, the larger the dividend charged to retained earnings and paid in cash, the greater the amount of financing that must be raised externally. Some firms offer dividend reinvestment plans that allow stockholders to acquire shares in lieu of cash dividends, often at an attractive price. The residual theory suggests that dividends should be viewed as the residual earnings left after all acceptable investment opportunities have been undertaken. Dividend irrelevance, which supports the residual theory, is argued by Miller and Modigliani using a perfect world wherein information content and clientele effects exist. Gordon and Lintner argue dividend relevance based upon the uncertainty-reducing effect of dividends, supported by their bird-in-the-hand argument. Although intuitively appealing, empirical studies fail to provide clear support of dividend relevance in the context of its effect on the firm's share price. Certain legal, contractual, and internal constraints as well as growth prospects, owner considerations, and certain market considerations affect a firm's dividend policy, which should maximize the wealth of its owners while providing for sufficient financing.

LG 5 **Review and evaluate the three basic types of dividend policies—constant-payout-ratio, regular, and low-regular-and-extra.** With a constant-payout-ratio dividend policy the firm pays a fixed percentage of earnings out to the owners each period. The problem with this policy is that dividends move up and down with earnings, and no dividend is paid when the firm has a loss. Under a regular dividend policy the firm pays a fixed-dollar dividend each period; it increases the amount of dividends only after a proven increase in earnings has occurred. The low-regular-and-extra dividend policy is similar to the regular dividend policy, except that it pays an "extra dividend" in periods when the firm's earnings are higher than normal. The regular and the low-regular-and-extra dividend policies are generally preferred over the constant-payout-ratio dividend policy because of the uncertainty-reducing effect of their stable patterns of dividends.

LG 6 **Contrast the basic features, objectives, and procedures for paying other forms of dividends, including stock dividends, stock splits, and stock repurchases.** Occasionally, firms may pay stock dividends as a replacement or supplement to cash dividends. The payment of stock dividends involves a shifting of funds between capital accounts rather than a use of funds. Stock splits are sometimes used to enhance trading activity in a firm's shares by lowering or raising the market price of a firm's stock by increasing or decreasing, respectively, the number of shares belonging to each shareholder. A stock split has no effect on the firm's capital structure. Stock repurchases can be made in lieu of cash dividend payments to retire outstanding shares and delay the payment of taxes. Whereas stock dividends and stock repurchases can be viewed as dividend alternatives, stock splits are used to deliberately adjust the market price of shares. Only stock repurchases involve the actual outflow of cash—both stock dividends and stock splits involve accounting adjustments in the capital accounts.

Self-test problems (Solutions in Appendix E)

ST 13-1 LG 3 **Sale of common equity using rights** Bulah Gas wishes to raise $1 million in common equity financing using a rights offering. The company has 500,000 shares of common stock outstanding that have recently traded for $25 to $28 per share. The firm believes that if the subscription price is set at $25, the shares will be fully subscribed.

a. Determine the number of new shares the firm must sell to raise the desired amount of capital.
b. How many shares will each right entitle a holder of one share to purchase?
c. If Candy Lopez, who holds 5,000 shares of Bulah Gas, exercises her rights, how many additional shares can she purchase?
d. What is the theoretical value of a right if the current market price is $27 *with rights* and the subscription price is $25? Answer for both stock selling *with rights* and stock selling *ex rights.*
e. Approximately how much could Candy get for her rights immediately after the stock goes *ex rights?*

ST 13-2 LG 6 **Stock repurchase** The Off-Shore Steel Company has earnings available for common stockholders of $2 million and 500,000 shares of common stock outstanding at $60 per share. The firm is currently contemplating the payment of $2 per share in cash dividends.

a. Calculate the firm's current earnings per share (EPS) and price/earnings (P/E) ratio.
b. If the firm can repurchase stock at $62 per share, how many shares can be purchased in lieu of making the proposed cash dividend payment?
c. How much will the EPS be after the proposed repurchase? Why?
d. If the stock will sell at the old P/E ratio, what will the market price be after repurchase?
e. Compare and contrast the earnings per share before and after the proposed repurchase.
f. Compare and contrast the stockholders' position under the dividend and repurchase alternatives.

Problems

13-1 LG 2 **Accounting for common stock** What accounting entries on the firm's balance sheet would result from the following cases?

a. A firm sells 10,000 shares of $1-par common stock at $13 per share.
b. A firm sells 20,000 shares of $2-par common stock and receives $100,000.
c. A firm sells 200,000 shares of no-par common stock for $8 million.
d. A firm sells 14,000 shares of common stock for the par value of $5 per share.

13-2 LG 2 **Authorized and available shares** Aspin Corporation's charter authorizes issuance of 2,000,000 shares of common stock. Currently, 1,400,000 shares are outstanding, and 100,000 shares are being held as treasury stock. The firm wishes to raise $48,000,000 for a plant expansion. Discussions with its investment bankers indicate that the sale of new common stock will net the firm $60 per share.

a. What is the maximum number of new shares of common stock the firm can sell without receiving further authorization from shareholders?

b. On the basis of the data given above and your finding in **a**, will the firm be able to raise the needed funds without receiving further authorization?

c. What must the firm do to obtain authorization to issue more than the number of shares found in **a**?

13-3 LG 2 **Majority versus cumulative voting** Mountain Products is electing five new directors to its board. The company has 1,000 shares of common stock outstanding. The management, which controls 54 percent of the common shares outstanding, backs candidates A through E; the minority shareholders are backing candidates F through J.

a. If the firm uses a *majority voting system,* how many directors will each group elect?

b. If the firm uses a *cumulative voting system,* how many directors will each group elect?

c. Discuss the differences between these two approaches and the resulting election outcomes.

13-4 LG 2 **Majority versus cumulative voting** Determine the number of directors that can be elected by the *minority shareholders* using (1) majority voting and (2) cumulative voting in each of the following cases.

Case	Number of shares outstanding	Percentage of shares held by minority	Number of directors to be elected
A	140,000	20%	3
B	100,000	40	7
C	175,000	30	4
D	880,000	40	5
E	1,000,000	18	9

13-5 LG 3 **Number of rights** Indicate (1) how many shares of stock one right is worth and (2) the number of shares a given stockholder, X, can purchase in each of the following cases:

Case	Number of shares outstanding	Number of new shares to be issued	Number of shares held by stockholder X
A	900,000	30,000	600
B	1,400,000	35,000	200
C	800,000	40,000	2,000
D	60,000	12,000	1,200
E	180,000	36,000	1,000

13-6 LG 3 Theoretical value of rights Determine the theoretical value of the right when the stock is selling (1) *with rights* and (2) *ex rights* in each of the following cases:

Case	Market value of stock *with rights*	Subscription price of stock	Number of rights needed to purchase one share of stock
A	$20.00	$17.50	4
B	56.00	50.00	3
C	41.00	30.00	6
D	50.00	40.00	5
E	92.00	82.00	8

13-7 LG 3 Value of a right Your sister-in-law is a stockholder in a corporation that recently declared a rights offering. In need of cash, she has offered to sell you her rights for 30 cents each. The key data relative to the stock and associated rights are as follows:

Current stock price *with rights*	$37.25/share
Subscription price of stock rights	$36.00/share
Number of rights needed to purchase one share of common stock	4

a. Determine the theoretical value of the rights when the stock is trading *with rights.*
b. Determine the theoretical value of the rights when the stock is trading *ex rights.*
c. Discuss your findings in **a** and **b**. Would it be desirable to accept your sister-in-law's offer?

13-8 LG 3 Sale of common equity—Using rights Ziegler Manufacturing is interested in raising $600,000 of new equity capital through a rights offering. The firm currently has 300,000 shares of common stock outstanding. It expects to set the subscription price at $25 and anticipates that the stock will sell for $29 *with rights.*

a. Calculate the number of new shares the firm must sell to raise the desired amount of funds.
b. How many rights will be needed to purchase one share of stock at the subscription price?
c. Willie Jones holds 48,000 shares of Ziegler common stock. If he exercises his rights, how many additional shares can he purchase?
d. Determine the theoretical value of a right when the stock is selling (1) *with rights* and (2) *ex rights.*
e. Approximately how much could Mr. Jones get for his rights immediately after the stock goes *ex rights?*
f. If the date of record for Ziegler Manufacturing was Monday, March 15, on what dates would the stock sell (1) *with rights* and (2) *ex rights?*

13-9 LG 4 Dividend payment procedures Wood Shoes, at the quarterly dividend meeting, declared a cash dividend of $1.10 per share for holders of record on Monday, July 10. The firm has 300,000 shares of common stock outstanding and has set a payment date of July 31. Before the dividend declaration, the firm's key accounts were as follows:

Cash	$500,000	Dividends payable	$ 0
		Retained earnings	2,500,000

a. Show the entries after the meeting adjourned.
b. When is the ex dividend date?
c. After the July 31 payment date, what values would the key accounts have?
d. What effect, if any, will the dividend have on the firm's total assets?
e. Ignoring general market fluctuations, what effect, if any, will the dividend have on the firm's stock price on the ex dividend date?

13-10 LG 4 **Residual dividend policy** As president of Young's of California, a large clothing chain, you have just received a letter from a major stockholder. The stockholder asks about the company's dividend policy. In fact, the stockholder has asked you to estimate the amount of the dividend that you are likely to pay next year. You have not yet collected all the information about the expected dividend payment, but you do know the following:

(1) The company will follow a residual dividend policy.

(2) The total capital budget for next year is likely to be one of three amounts, depending on the results of capital budgeting studies that are currently under way. The capital expenditure amounts are $2 million, $3 million, and $4 million.

(3) The forecasted level of potential retained earnings next year is $2 million.

(4) The target or optimal capital structure is a debt ratio of 40 percent.

You have decided to respond by sending the stockholder the best information available to you.

a. Describe a residual dividend policy.

b. Compute the amount of the dividend (or the amount of new equity needed) and the dividend-payout ratio for each of the three capital expenditure amounts.

c. Compare, contrast, and discuss the amount of dividends (calculated in **b**) associated with each of the three capital expenditure amounts.

13-11 LG 4 **Dividend constraints** The Howe Company's stockholders' equity account is as follows:

Common stock (400,000 shares at $4 par)	$1,600,000
Paid-in capital in excess of par	1,000,000
Retained earnings	1,900,000
Total stockholders' equity	$4,500,000

The earnings available for common stockholders from this period's operations are $100,000, which have been included as part of the $1.9 million retained earnings.

a. What is the maximum dividend per share that the firm can pay? (Assume that legal capital includes *all* paid-in capital.)

b. If the firm has $160,000 in cash, what is the largest per-share dividend it can pay without borrowing?

c. Indicate the accounts and changes, if any, that will result if the firm pays the dividends indicated in **a** and **b**.

d. Indicate the effects of an $80,000 cash dividend on stockholders' equity.

13-12 LG 4 **Dividend constraints** A firm has $800,000 in paid-in capital, retained earnings of $40,000 (including the current year's earnings), and 25,000 shares of common stock outstanding. In the current year it has $29,000 of earnings available for the common stockholders.

a. What is the most the firm can pay in cash dividends to each common stockholder? (Assume that legal capital includes *all* paid-in capital.)

b. What effect would a cash dividend of $.80 per share have on the firm's balance sheet entries?

c. If the firm cannot raise any new funds from external sources, what do you consider the key constraint with respect to the magnitude of the firm's dividend payments? Why?

13-13 LG 5 **Alternative dividend policies** A firm has had the earnings per share over the last 10 years shown in the table at the top of page 558.

a. If the firm's dividend policy was based on a constant payout ratio of 40 percent for all years with positive earnings and a zero payout otherwise, determine the annual dividend for each year.

b. If the firm had a dividend payout of $1.00 per share, increasing by $.10 per share whenever the dividend payout fell below 50 percent for two consecutive years, what annual dividend did the firm pay each year?

c. If the firm's policy was to pay $.50 per share each period except when earnings per share exceed $3.00, when an extra dividend equal to 80 percent of earnings beyond $3.00 would be paid, what annual dividend did the firm pay each year?

Year	Earnings per share
1994	$4.00
1993	3.80
1992	3.20
1991	2.80
1990	3.20
1989	2.40
1988	1.20
1987	1.80
1986	−0.50
1985	0.25

d. Discuss the pros and cons of each dividend policy described in **a** through **c.**

13-14 LG 5 **Alternative dividend policies** Given the following earnings per share over the period 1987—1994, determine the annual dividend per share under each of the policies set forth in **a** through **d**.

Year	Earnings per share
1994	$1.40
1993	1.56
1992	1.20
1991	−0.85
1990	1.05
1989	0.60
1988	1.00
1987	0.44

a. Pay out 50 percent of earnings in all years with positive earnings.

b. Pay $.50 per share and increase to $.60 per share whenever earnings per share rise above $.90 per share for two consecutive years.

c. Pay $.50 per share except when earnings exceed $1.00 per share, when there would be an extra dividend equal to 60 percent of earnings above $1.00 per share.

d. Combine policies in **b** and **c**. When the dividend is raised (in **b**), raise the excess dividend base (in **c**) from $1.00 to $1.10 per share.

e. Compare and contrast each of the dividend policies described in **a** through **d**.

13-15 LG 6 **Stock dividend—Firm** Columbia Paper has the stockholders' equity account, given here. The firm's common stock has a current market price of $30 per share.

Preferred stock	$100,000
Common stock (10,000 shares at $2 par)	20,000
Paid-in capital in excess of par	280,000
Retained earnings	100,000
Total stockholders' equity	$500,000

a. Show the effects on Columbia Paper of a 5 percent stock dividend.

b. Show the effects of (1) a 10 percent and (2) a 20 percent stock dividend.

c. In light of your answers to **a** and **b**, discuss the effects of stock dividends on stockholders' equity.

13-16 LG 6 **Cash versus stock dividend** Milwaukee Tool has a stockholders' equity account as given. The firm's common stock currently sells for $4 per share.

Preferred stock	$ 100,000
Common stock (400,000 shares at $1 par)	400,000
Paid-in capital in excess of par	200,000
Retained earnings	320,000
Total stockholders' equity	$1,020,000

a. Show the effects on the firm of a $.01, $.05, $.10, and $.20 per-share *cash* dividend.
b. Show the effects on the firm of a 1 percent, 5 percent, 10 percent, and 20 percent *stock* dividend.
c. Compare the effects in **a** and **b**. What are the significant differences in the two methods of paying dividends?

13-17 LG 6 **Stock dividend—Investor** Sarah Warren currently holds 400 shares of Nutri-Foods. The firm has 40,000 shares outstanding. The firm most recently had earnings available for common stockholders of $80,000, and its stock has been selling for $22 per share. The firm intends to retain its earnings and pay a 10 percent stock dividend.
a. How much does the firm currently earn per share?
b. What proportion of the firm does Sarah Warren currently own?
c. What proportion of the firm will Ms. Warren own after the stock dividend? Explain your answer.
d. At what market price would you expect the stock to sell after the stock dividend?
e. Discuss what effect, if any, the payment of stock dividends will have on Ms. Warren's share of the ownership and earnings of Nutri-Foods.

13-18 LG 6 **Stock dividend—Investor** Security Data Company has outstanding 50,000 shares of common stock currently selling at $40 per share. The firm most recently had earnings available for common stockholders of $120,000, but it has decided to retain these funds and is considering either a 5 percent or a 10 percent stock dividend in lieu of a cash dividend.
a. Determine the firm's current earnings per share.
b. If Sam Waller currently owns 500 shares of the firm's stock, determine his proportion of ownership currently and under each of the proposed dividend plans. Explain your findings.
c. Calculate and explain the market price per share under each of the stock dividend plans.
d. For each of the proposed stock dividends, calculate the earnings per share after payment of the stock dividend.
e. What would the value of Sam Waller's holdings be under each of the plans? Explain.
f. As Mr. Waller, would you have any preference with respect to the proposed stock dividends? Why or why not?

13-19 LG 6 **Stock split—Firm** Growth Industries' current stockholders' equity account is as follows:

Preferred stock	$ 400,000
Common stock (600,000 shares at $3 par)	1,800,000
Paid-in capital in excess of par	200,000
Retained earnings	800,000
Total stockholders' equity	$3,200,000

a. Indicate the change, if any, expected if the firm declares a 2-for-1 stock split.
b. Indicate the change, if any, expected if the firm declares a 1-for-1½ *reverse* stock split.
c. Indicate the change, if any, expected if the firm declares a 3-for-1 stock split.
d. Indicate the change, if any, expected if the firm declares a 6-for-1 stock split.
e. Indicate the change, if any, expected if the firm declares a 1-for-4 *reverse* stock split.

13-20 LG 6 **Stock split—Firm** Mammoth Corporation is considering a 3-for-2 stock split. It currently has the stockholders' equity position shown below. The current stock price is $120 per share. The most recent period's earnings available for common stock is included in retained earnings.

Preferred stock	$ 1,000,000
Common stock (100,000 shares at $3 par)	300,000
Paid-in capital in excess of par	1,700,000
Retained earnings	10,000,000
Total stockholders' equity	$13,000,000

a. What effects on Mammoth would result from the stock split?
b. What change in stock price would you expect to result from the stock split?
c. What is the maximum cash dividend *per share* that the firm could pay on common stock before and after the stock split? (Assume that legal capital includes *all* paid-in capital.)
d. Contrast your answers to **a** through **c** with the circumstances surrounding a 50 percent stock dividend.
e. Explain the differences between stock splits and stock dividends.

13-21 LG 6 **Stock repurchase** The following financial data on the Boyd Recording Company are available:

Earnings available for common stockholders	$800,000
Number of shares of common stock outstanding	400,000
Earnings per share ($800,000 ÷ 400,000)	$2
Market price per share	$20
Price/earnings (P/E) ratio ($20 ÷ $2)	10

The firm is currently contemplating using $400,000 of its earnings to pay cash dividends of $1 per share or repurchasing stock at $21 per share.
a. Approximately how many shares of stock can the firm repurchase at the $21-per-share price using the funds that would have gone to pay the cash dividend?
b. Calculate earnings per share (EPS) after the repurchase. Explain your calculations.
c. If the stock still sells at 10 times earnings, how much will the market price be after the repurchase?
d. Compare and contrast the pre- and post-repurchase earnings per share.
e. Compare and contrast the stockholders' position under the dividend and repurchase alternatives. What are the tax implications under each alternative?

Chapter 13 Case Examining the impact of a rights offering on Meg International's dividends

Meg International, a global food products concern, employs a constant-payout-ratio dividend policy. Its dividends have consistently equaled 30 percent of its earnings available for common stockholders. The firm is a bit unusual in that it pays a single year-end dividend rather than the more traditional quarterly dividends. During the past ten years the firm's earnings were stable to slightly increasing. Expecting this trend to continue, in late 1994 the firm forecasted 1995 earnings after taxes of $4,600,000. Because the firm has no preferred stock outstanding, this amount will be available to its 1 million common stockholders. Recently, the firms Board decided to shift the firm's capital structure to a less highly levered position by selling $5,000,000 of common stock and using the proceeds to retire that amount of bonds. The sale would be made through a rights offering, which was required by the firm's corporate charter. The Board charged the firm's chief financial officer, Haim Lev, with examining this proposed strategy. It instructed him not to cut the *per-share* dividend below what it would have been without the rights offering. In this regard the Board indicated its willingness to pay stock dividends should its cash position be inadequate to permit full payment of cash dividends.

In preparation for examining the Board's proposal and making a recommendation to the board, Haim gathered the needed data. He estimated that at the end of 1995 the firm would have total cash and marketable securities of $1,500,000, but it must maintain minimum balances of $62,500 in cash and $200,000 in marketable securities. The firm's shares were recently trading for $42 to $45 per share, and Haim believed that if the subscription price were set at $40 per share, the rights offering would be fully subscribed. The new shares, like existing shares, would have a par value of $2. Should the firm find it necessary, due to its cash and marketable security constraints, to supplement its cash dividend with a stock dividend, the market price of the stock is assumed to be $42 at the end of 1995. Meg International's stockholders' equity account on January 1, 1995, is as follows:

Common stock (1,000,000 shares at $2 par)	$ 2,000,000
Paid-in capital in excess of par	13,000,000
Retained earnings	3,200,000
Total stockholders' equity	$18,200,000

Given this information, Haim began to examine the impact of the proposed rights offering on Meg International's dividends.

Required

a. Calculate Meg International's expected earnings per share (EPS) and dividends per share for 1995 *without* the sale of additional shares.

b. How many new shares must Meg International sell to raise the $5,000,000? How many shares will each right entitle a holder of one share of stock to purchase?

c. What would the theoretical value of a right be if the current market price is $42 *with rights* and the subscription price is $40? Answer for both when the stock is selling *with rights* and *ex rights*.

d. After the rights offering is fully subscribed, how many shares will be outstanding? Show the stockholders' equity account after the rights offering is complete.

e. How much cash does the firm need to pay the per-share dividend calculated in **a** on all shares outstanding, found in **d**, after the rights offering? How much cash will be available for paying cash dividends? What would the amount of this dividend be on a per-share basis? How many dollars, if any, in stock dividends will the firm need to pay to maintain the planned per-share dividend calculated in **a**?

f. *To the nearest whole percent*, what percent stock dividend does the firm need to issue to supplement its cash dividend consistent with its stated dividend goal? How many shares must be issued? Revise the stockholders' equity account in **d** to reflect payment of the stock dividend. What would be the share price after payment of the stock dividend?

g. How much in cash and stock dividends will the firm pay? Comment on the firm's use of a constant-payout-ratio dividend policy.

chapter 14

Preferred stock, leasing, convertibles, warrants, and options

LEARNING GOALS

Understand the basic rights of preferred stockholders, the features of preferred stock, special types of preferred stock, and the advantages and disadvantages of preferred stock financing.

Review the basic types of leases, leasing arrangements, the lease contract, the lease-versus-purchase decision, the effects of leasing on future financing, and the advantages and disadvantages of leasing.

Describe the basic types of convertible securities and their general features—including the conversion ratio, conversion period, conversion (or stock) value, and effects on earnings—and the use of convertible financing to raise long-term funds.

Demonstrate the procedures for determining the straight bond value, conversion (or stock) value, and market value of a convertible bond.

Explain the basic characteristics of stock-purchase warrants, the implied price of an attached warrant, and the values of warrants—theoretical, market, and market premium.

Define options, and discuss the basics of calls and puts, options markets, options trading, the role of call and put options in fund raising, and using options to protect against foreign currency exposures.

Successful financing of companies now and in the future requires a thorough understanding of all parts of the capital structure. Knowledge of preferred stock, leasing, convertibles, warrants, and options is critical for a well-rounded financial executive, whether he or she is going to be in commercial banking, investment banking, or a corporation's finance department.

Convertible securities are popular today because they offer an attractive current yield. Investors may benefit from the issuer's upside potential because convertible debt or preferred stock gives the holder the right to change the security into a stated number of shares of common stock, typically any time during the security's life. When stock prices are high, convertibles allow issuers to effectively sell stock at a higher price and are less dilutive than issuing common stock. During the 1980s the media industry raised a significant amount of capital for acquisitions and internal growth by issuing convertible debt.

Although the coupon on convertible debt is lower than that on nonconvertible debt, convertibles are more expensive overall because they convert into equity—the most expensive form of capital. However, convertibles have several attractive elements for issuers. First, they are inexpensive if the issuer's stock price doesn't rise and conversion does not occur because the issuer has locked in below-market-rate debt. Second, convertibles have minimum business covenants compared to traditional debt securities. Third, more senior debt lenders treat convertibles as quasi-equity because they offer minimal rights to the holder in the event of financial difficulty. This is particularly important for non-investment-grade issuers (bond ratings below Baa3/BBB−), the majority of convertible issuers today.

During the 1980s the media industry raised a significant amount of capital . . . by issuing convertible debt.

A classic example of why a company should use convertible debt is the recent $72 million acquisition by Thomas Nelson of The Word, a subsidiary of Capital Cities/ABC. We served as financial advisor to Thomas Nelson and raised $55 million of the acquisition cost in the form of convertible debt. Before the acquisition, Thomas Nelson was substantially debt-free. The merger made tremendous economic sense because each publishing company sold to primarily the same buyers. On a pro forma basis the acquisition looked risky because Thomas Nelson doubled in size. Convertible debt reduced the transaction's risk because it had a lower interest rate than other forms of financing and none of the usual business performance covenants associated with bank or public high-yield debt. The investors expect to gain from the eventual increase in stock price resulting from Thomas Nelson's management expertise and economies of scale.

Basically, a "convert" is a debt security combined with options to purchase the issuer's stock at a specified price in the future. If a convert is correctly priced, the amount of interest paid on it should equal the interest paid on the principal amount of a similar nonconvertible security less the value of the option on the stock. A buyer or seller can capitalize on pricing inefficiencies by separating the debt and options portions of the security by selling mirror options to reduce the invested capital. The goal is an above-market-yielding debt instrument that could be either sold or kept. This cutting edge technique represents just one type of derivative financing. It is important for bankers and financial managers to understand the convertible and options markets to achieve the best results for their clients or firms.

Julian Markby received an M.B.A. from the Columbia University School of Business and was with Bank of Boston's Media Group from 1980 to 1987, serving ultimately as Vice President and Team Leader. After three years as First Vice President for Investment Banking at Drexel Burnham Lambert, in 1990 he joined PaineWebber Incorporated as a Managing Director and head of its Media and Communications Group.

Preferred stock

Preferred stock is like debt in that it has a stated dividend that is given priority over common stock dividends and like equity in that it is a form of ownership with no maturity date. Why do you think a firm would use preferred stock rather than debt or common stock to obtain needed long-term funds? Before reading on, spend a few moments answering this question.

par-value preferred stock
Preferred stock with a stated face value that is used with the specified dividend percentage to determine the annual dollar dividend.

no-par preferred stock
Preferred stock that has a specified annual dollar dividend but no stated face value.

PREFERRED STOCK GIVES ITS HOLDERS CERTAIN PRIVILEGES THAT MAKE THEM SENIOR to common stockholders. Because of this, firms generally do not issue large quantities of preferred stock. Preferred stockholders are promised a fixed periodic return, which is stated either as a percentage or as a dollar amount. In other words, a 5 percent preferred stock or a $5 preferred stock can be issued. The way the dividend is stated depends on whether the preferred stock has a par value. **Par-value preferred stock** has a stated face value. The annual dividend is specified as a percentage on par-value preferred stock and in dollars on **no-par preferred stock,** which does not have a stated face value. Thus a 5 percent preferred stock with a $100 par value is expected to pay $5 (5% of $100) in dividends per year, and a $5 preferred stock with no par value is also expected to pay its $5 stated dividend each year.

Preferred stock is most often issued by public utilities, by acquiring firms in merger transactions, or by firms that are experiencing losses and need additional financing. Public utilities issue preferred stock to increase their financial leverage while increasing equity and avoiding the higher risk associated with debt financing. Preferred stock is used in connection with mergers to give the acquired firm's shareholders a fixed-income security that, when exchanged for their stock, results in certain tax advantages. In addition, preferred stock is frequently used by firms that are experiencing losses to raise needed funds. These firms can more easily sell preferred stock than common stock because it gives the preferred stockholder a claim that is senior to that of the common stockholders and therefore is less risky than common stock. Frequently, special features, such as conversion or warrants (described later in this chapter) are included to enhance the attractiveness of the preferred stock and lower its cost to the issuer.

Basic rights of preferred stockholders

The basic rights of preferred stockholders with respect to the distribution of earnings, the distribution of assets, and voting are somewhat more favorable than the rights of common stockholders. Because preferred stock is a form of ownership and has no maturity date, its claims on income and assets are secondary to those of the firm's creditors.

DISTRIBUTION OF EARNINGS

Preferred stockholders are given preference over common stockholders with respect to the distribution of earnings. If the stated preferred stock dividend is *passed* (not paid) by the board of directors, the payment of dividends to common stockholders is prohibited. It is this preference in dividend distribution that makes common stockholders the true risk takers with respect to receipt of periodic returns.

DISTRIBUTION OF ASSETS

Preferred stockholders are usually given preference over common stockholders in the liquidation of assets as a result of a firm's bankruptcy, although they must wait until all creditors have been satisfied. The amount of the claim of preferred stockholders in liquidation is normally equal to the par, or stated, value of the preferred stock. The preferred stockholder's preference over the common stockholder places the common stockholder in the more risky position with respect to recovery of investment.

VOTING RIGHTS

Preferred stock is often considered a *quasi-debt* since, much like interest on debt, it yields a fixed periodic (dividend) payment. Of course, as ownership, preferred stock is unlike debt in that it has no maturity date. Because their claim on the firm's income is fixed and takes precedence over the claim of common stockholders, preferred stockholders are therefore not exposed to the same degree of risk as common stockholders. They are consequently *not* normally given the right to vote.

Features of preferred stock

A number of features are generally included as part of a preferred stock issue. These features, along with a statement of the stock's par value, the amount of dividend payments, the dividend payment dates, and any restrictive covenants, are specified in an agreement that is similar to a *term loan agreement* or *bond indenture* (see Chapter 12).

RESTRICTIVE COVENANTS

The restrictive covenants that are commonly found in a preferred stock issue are aimed at ensuring the continued existence of the firm and, most important, regular payment of the stated dividend. These covenants include provisions related to passing dividends, the sale of senior securities, mergers, sales of assets, net working capital requirements, and the payment of common stock dividends or common stock repurchases. The violation of preferred stock covenants usually permits preferred stockholders either to obtain representation on the firm's board of directors or to force the retirement of their stock at or above its par, or stated, value.

CUMULATION

cumulative preferred stock
Preferred stock for which all passed (unpaid) dividends in arrears must be paid along with the current dividend before payment of dividends to common stockholders.

noncumulative preferred stock
Preferred stock for which passed (unpaid) dividends do not accumulate.

Most preferred stock is **cumulative** with respect to any dividends passed. That is, all dividends in arrears must be paid along with the current dividend before payment of dividends to common stockholders. If preferred stock is **noncumulative,** passed (unpaid) dividends do not accumulate. In this case, only the current dividend must be paid before paying dividends to common stockholders. Since the common stockholders, who are the firm's true owners, can receive dividends only after the dividend claims of preferred stockholders have been satisfied, it is in the firm's best interest to pay preferred dividends when they are due.[1] The following example will help to clarify the distinction between cumulative and noncumulative preferred stock.

[1]Most preferred stock is cumulative, since it is difficult to sell noncumulative stock. Common stockholders obviously prefer issuance of noncumulative preferred, since it does not place them in quite as risky a position. But it is often in the best interest of the firm to sell *cumulative* preferred stock due to its lower cost.

EXAMPLE

Zimmer Corporation, a manufacturer of specialty automobiles, currently has outstanding an issue of $6 preferred stock on which quarterly dividends of $1.50 are to be paid. Because of a cash shortage, the last two quarterly dividends were passed. The directors of the company have been receiving a large number of complaints from common stockholders, who have of course not received any dividends in the past two quarters either. If the preferred stock is cumulative, the company will have to pay its preferred stockholders $4.50 per share ($3.00 of dividends in arrears plus the current $1.50 dividend) before paying dividends to its common stockholders. If the preferred stock is noncumulative, however, the firm must pay only the current $1.50 dividend to its preferred stockholders before paying dividends to its common stockholders. ■

PARTICIPATION

nonparticipating preferred stock
Preferred stock whose stockholders receive only the specified dividend payments.

participating preferred stock
Preferred stock that provides for dividend payments based on certain formulas allowing preferred stockholders to participate with common stockholders in the receipt of dividends beyond a specified amount.

Most issues of preferred stock are **nonparticipating,** which means that preferred stockholders receive only the specified dividend payments. Occasionally, **participating preferred stock** is issued. This type provides for dividend payments based on certain formulas allowing preferred stockholders to participate with common stockholders in the receipt of dividends beyond a specified amount. This feature is included only when the firm considers it absolutely necessary in order to obtain badly needed funds.

CALL FEATURE

Preferred stock is generally *callable,* which means that the issuer can retire outstanding stock within a certain period of time at a specified price. The call option generally cannot be exercised until a period of years has elapsed since the issuance of the stock. The call price is normally set above the initial issuance price, but it may decrease according to a predetermined schedule as time passes. Making preferred stock callable provides the issuer with a method of bringing the fixed-payment commitment of the preferred issue to an end.

CONVERSION FEATURE

conversion feature
A feature that allows preferred stockholders to change each share into a stated number of shares of common stock.

Preferred stock quite often contains a **conversion feature** that allows preferred stockholders to change each share into a stated number of shares of common stock. Sometimes the conversion ratio, or number of shares of common stock, changes according to a prespecified formula. A detailed discussion of conversion is presented later in this chapter.

Special types of preferred stock

adjustable-rate (or floating-rate) preferred stock (ARPS)
Preferred stock whose dividend rate is tied to interest rates on specific government securities.

Most preferred stock has a fixed dividend, but some firms issue **adjustable-rate (or floating-rate) preferred stock (ARPS).** Such stocks have a dividend rate that is tied to interest rates on specific government securities. Rate adjustments are commonly made quarterly, and typically the rate must be maintained within certain preset limits. The appeal of ARPS is the protection that it offers investors against sharp rises in interest rates, since the dividend rate on ARPS will rise with interest rates. From the firm's perspective, adjustable-rate preferreds have appeal, since they can be sold at an initially lower dividend rate and the scheduled dividend rate will fall if interest rates decline.

payment-in-kind (PIK) preferred stock
Preferred stock that pays dividends in additional shares of preferred stock rather than cash.

A relatively recent innovation in preferred stock financing, **payment-in-kind (PIK) preferred stock,** usually doesn't pay cash dividends but rather pays in additional shares of preferred stock, which pay dividends in even more preferred stock. Typical dividend rates on PIK preferred stock range from 15 to 18 percent. After a stated time period, generally five or six years, PIK preferreds are supposed to begin paying cash dividends or provide holders with a chance to swap for another, more traditional security. These preferreds are essentially the equivalent of *junk bonds* (see Chapter 12) and, like them, are issued to finance corporate takeovers. A good deal of uncertainty surrounds PIK preferreds, since if the issuer runs into trouble, holders may end up with nothing—little chance of receiving cash dividends and little possibility of legal recourse against the issuer. Because they are primarily used to finance takeovers, PIK preferreds are not viewed as a major corporate financing tool.

CONCEPT IN PRACTICE

Convertible Preferred Stock Saves Triad

In 1989, Drexel Burnham Lambert, Inc. failed to take over Triad Systems Corporation, a California-based technology firm specializing in inventory management software. To defend itself, Triad paid shareholders a huge cash dividend financed by $80 million in new debt, carrying a 14 percent annual coupon interest rate and redeemable in 1992. If Triad could not fund redemption by July 1992, its bondholders could extend the maturity and continue to earn the 14 percent annual coupon interest rate.

In early 1992, Triad began arranging new debt financing and issuing new equity to realign its capital structure. With net worth plummeting to negative $35 million, the firm found no customers for common stock and arranged private placement of $20 million in perpetual preferred stock, featuring a floating 4 percent dividend for three years and convertible into common stock. With an option of forced conversion after 1995 if the firm's common share price reached 150 percent of the original conversion price, this type of equity enabled Triad to get new debt financing and complete its recapitalization by July 1992.

Advantages and disadvantages of preferred stock

It is difficult to generalize about the advantages and disadvantages of preferred stock because of the variety of features that may be incorporated in a preferred stock issue. The attractiveness of preferred stock is also affected by current interest rates and the firm's existing capital structure. Nevertheless, some key advantages and disadvantages are often cited.

ADVANTAGES

One commonly cited advantage of preferred stock is its *ability to increase financial leverage.* Since preferred stock obligates the firm to pay only fixed dividends to its holders, its presence helps to increase the firm's financial leverage. (The effects of preferred stock on a firm's financial leverage were discussed in Chapter 11.) Increased financial leverage will magnify the effects of increased earnings on common stockholders' returns.

A second advantage is the *flexibility* provided by preferred stock. Although preferred stock provides added financial leverage in much the same way as bonds, it differs from bonds in that the issuer can pass a dividend payment without suffering the consequences that result when an interest payment is missed on a bond. Preferred stock allows the issuer to keep its levered position without running as great a risk of being forced out of business in a lean year as it might if it missed interest payments on actual debt.

A third advantage of preferred stock has been its *use in corporate restructuring—mergers, leveraged buyouts (LBOs), and divestitures.* Often preferred stock is exchanged for the common stock of an acquired firm, with the preferred dividend set at a level equivalent to the historic dividend of the acquired firm. This exchange allows the acquiring firm to state at the time of the acquisition that only a fixed dividend will be paid. All other earnings can be reinvested to perpetuate the growth of the new enterprise. In addition, the owners of the acquired firm will be assured of a continuing stream of dividends equivalent to that which may have been provided before the restructuring.

DISADVANTAGES

Three major disadvantages are often cited for preferred stock. One is the *seniority of the preferred stockholder's claim.* Since holders of preferred stock are given preference over common stockholders with respect to the distribution of earnings and assets, the presence of preferred stock in a sense jeopardizes common stockholders' returns. If a firm has preferred stockholders to pay, and if the firm's after-tax earnings are quite variable, its ability to pay at least token dividends to common stockholders may be seriously impaired.

A second disadvantage of preferred stock is cost. The *cost of preferred stock financing is generally higher than that of debt financing.* The reason is that, unlike the payment of interest to bondholders, the payment of dividends to preferred stockholders is not guaranteed. Since preferred shareholders are willing to accept the added risk of purchasing preferred stock rather than long-term debt, they must be compensated with a higher return. Another factor causing the cost of preferred stock to be greater than that of long-term debt is the fact that interest on debt is tax-deductible, whereas preferred stock dividends must be paid from after-tax earnings.

A third disadvantage of preferred stock is that it is *generally difficult to sell.* Most investors find preferred stock unattractive relative to bonds (due to the issuer's ability to pass dividends) and to common stock (due to its limited return). As a consequence, most preferred stock includes special features, such as conversion or warrants, to enhance its marketability.

CONCEPTS IN REVIEW

14-1 What is *preferred stock?* What claims do preferred stockholders have with respect to the distribution of earnings (dividends) and assets? What types of firms and circumstances are typically involved in the issuance of preferred stock?

14-2 What are *cumulative* and *noncumulative* preferred stock? Which form is more common? Why?

14-3 What is a *call feature* in a preferred stock issue? What is an *adjustable-rate (or floating-rate) preferred stock (ARPS)?* What is *payment-in-kind (PIK) preferred* stock?

14-4 What are the key advantages and disadvantages of using preferred stock financing as a source of new long-term funds?

Leasing

Financial (or capital) leases are noncancelable long-term arrangements under which a firm can obtain the use of certain assets in exchange for agreeing to make scheduled lease payments over the term of the lease. Why would financial managers frequently compare the economics of a financial lease to the alternative of borrowing to purchase a needed asset? Take a few moments to answer this question before reading further.

leasing
The process by which a firm can obtain the use of certain fixed assets for which it must make a series of contractual, periodic, tax-deductible payments.

lessee
The receiver of the services of the assets under a lease contract.

lessor
The owner of assets that are being leased.

LEASING, LIKE LONG-TERM DEBT, ALLOWS THE FIRM TO OBTAIN THE USE OF CERTAIN fixed assets for which it must make a series of contractual, periodic, tax-deductible payments. The **lessee** is the receiver of the services of the assets under the lease contract; the **lessor** is the owner of the assets. Leasing can take a number of forms. Here we discuss the basic types of leases, leasing arrangements, the lease contract, the lease-versus-purchase decision, the effects of leasing on future financing, and the advantages and disadvantages of leasing.

Basic types of leases

The two basic types of leases that are available to a business are *operating* and *financial* leases, the latter of which are often called *capital leases* by accountants. Each is briefly described below.

OPERATING LEASES

operating lease
A *cancelable* contractual arrangement whereby the lessee agrees to make periodic payments to the lessor, often for five or fewer years, for an asset's services; generally, the total payments over the term of the lease are *less* than the lessor's initial cost of the leased asset.

An **operating lease** is normally a contractual arrangement whereby the lessee agrees to make periodic payments to the lessor, often for five or fewer years, to obtain an asset's services. Such leases are generally *cancelable* at the option of the lessee, who may be required to pay a predetermined penalty for cancellation. Assets that are leased under operating leases have a usable life that is *longer* than the term of the lease. Usually, however, they would become less efficient and technologically obsolete if leased for a longer period of years. Computer systems are prime examples of assets whose relative efficiency is expected to diminish with new technological developments. The operating lease is therefore a common arrangement for obtaining such systems, as well as for other relatively short-lived assets such as automobiles.

If an operating lease is held to maturity, the lessee at that time returns the leased asset to the lessor, who may lease it again or sell the asset. Normally, the asset still has a positive market value at the termination of the lease. In some instances the lease contract will give the lessee the opportunity to purchase the leased asset. Generally, the total payments made by the lessee to the lessor are *less* than the lessor's initial cost of the leased asset.

financial (or capital) lease
A *longer-term* lease than an operating lease that is *noncancelable* and obligates the lessee to make payments for the use of an asset over a predefined period of time; the total payments over the term of the lease are *greater* than the lessor's initial cost of the leased asset.

FINANCIAL (OR CAPITAL) LEASES

A **financial (or capital) lease** is a *longer-term* lease than an operating lease. Financial leases are *noncancelable* and therefore obligate the lessee to make payments for the use of an asset over a predefined period of time. Even if the lessee does not require the service of the leased asset, it is contractually obligated to make payments over the life of the lease contract. Financial leases are commonly used for leasing land, buildings, and large pieces of equipment. The noncancelable feature of the financial lease makes it quite similar to certain types of long-term debt. The lease payment becomes a fixed, tax-deductible expenditure that must be paid at predefined dates over a definite period. Like debt, failure to make the contractual lease payments can result in bankruptcy for the lessee.

Another distinguishing characteristic of the financial lease is that the total payments over the lease period are *greater* than the lessor's initial cost of the leased asset. In other words, the lessor must receive more than the asset's purchase price to earn its required return on the investment. Technically, under Financial Accounting Standards Board (FASB) Standard No. 13, "Accounting for Leases," a financial (or capital) lease is defined as one having *any* of the following elements:

1. The lease transfers ownership of the property to the lessee by the end of the lease term.
2. The lease contains an option to purchase the property at a "bargain price." Such an option must be exercisable at a "fair market value."
3. The lease term is equal to 75 percent or more of the estimated economic life of the property (exceptions exist for property leased toward the end of its usable economic life).
4. At the beginning of the lease, the present value of the lease payments is equal to 90 percent or more of the fair market value of the leased property.

The emphasis in this chapter is on financial leases because they result in inescapable long-term financial commitments by the firm.

direct lease
A lease under which a lessor owns or acquires the assets that are leased to a given lessee.

sale-leaseback arrangement
A lease under which the lessee sells an asset for cash to a prospective lessor and then leases back the same asset, making fixed periodic payments for its use.

leveraged lease
A lease under which the lessor acts as an equity participant, supplying only about 20 percent of the cost of the asset, while a lender supplies the balance.

maintenance clauses
Provisions within an operating lease requiring the lessor to maintain the assets and to make insurance and tax payments.

renewal options
Provisions especially common in operating leases that grant the lessee the option to re-lease assets at their expiration.

Leasing arrangements

Lessors use three primary techniques for obtaining assets to be leased. The method depends largely on the desires of the prospective lessee. A **direct lease** results when a lessor owns or acquires the assets that are leased to a given lessee. In other words, the lessee did not previously own the assets that it is leasing. A second technique that is commonly used by lessors to acquire leased assets is to purchase assets already owned by the lessee and lease them back. A **sale-leaseback arrangement** is normally initiated by a firm that needs funds for operations. By selling an existing asset to a lessor and then *leasing it back,* the lessee receives cash for the asset immediately while at the same time obligating itself to make fixed periodic payments for use of the leased asset. Leasing arrangements that include one or more third-party lenders are leveraged leases. Unlike direct and sale-leaseback arrangements, under a **leveraged lease** the lessor acts as an equity participant, supplying only about 20 percent of the cost of the asset, and a lender supplies the balance. In recent years, leveraged leases have become especially popular in structuring leases of very expensive assets.

A lease agreement normally specifies whether the lessee is responsible for maintenance of the leased assets. Operating leases normally include **maintenance clauses** requiring the lessor to maintain the assets and to make insurance and tax payments. Financial leases almost always require the lessee to pay maintenance and other costs. The lessee is usually given the option to renew a lease at its expiration. **Renewal options,** which grant lessees the right to re-lease assets at expiration, are especially common in operating leases, since their term is generally shorter than the usable life of the

purchase options
Provisions frequently included in both operating and financial leases that allow the lessee to purchase the leased asset at maturity, typically for a prespecified price.

leased assets. **Purchase options** allowing the lessee to purchase the leased asset at maturity, typically for a prespecified price, are frequently included in both operating and financial leases.

The lessor can be one of a number of parties. In operating lease arrangements the lessor is quite likely to be the manufacturer's leasing subsidiary or an independent leasing company. Financial leases are frequently handled by independent leasing companies or by the leasing subsidiaries of large financial institutions such as commercial banks and life insurance companies. Life insurance companies are especially active in real estate leasing. Pension funds, like commercial banks, have also been increasing their leasing activities.

The lease contract

The key items in the lease contract normally include a description of the leased assets, the term, or duration, of the lease, provisions for its cancelation, lease payment amounts and dates, maintenance and associated cost provisions, renewal features, purchase options, and other provisions specified in the lease negotiation process. Although some provisions are optional, the leased assets, the terms of the agreement, the lease payment, and the payment interval must all be clearly specified in every lease agreement. Furthermore, the consequences of the lessee missing a payment or the violation of any other lease provisions by either the lessee or lessor must be clearly stated in the contract.

CONCEPT IN PRACTICE

Commercial Tenant Services Specializes in Lease Pricing Errors

Commercial real estate lease contracts can be complex beasts: lease payments can fluctuate during the term of a lease because of changes in inflation rates, utility usage at a site, and space requirements of the lessee or as a result of a change in building management or ownership, when lessees can renegotiate contract provisions. Commercial Tenant Services (CTS), Inc. of New York specializes in auditing commercial property leases. Working solely on a contingency basis, the firm checks lease contracts on behalf of lessees to ensure that tenants have not overpaid their leases and lessors have not overcharged their tenants. In one recent lease audit, CTS discovered $30,000 in overbillings to Johnson, Smith and Kinsley/Accord, a New York executive recruiting firm, during the seven-year term of the lease!

The lease-versus-purchase decision

lease-versus-purchase (or lease-versus-buy) decision
The decision facing firms needing to acquire new fixed assets: whether to lease the assets or to purchase them, using borrowed funds or available liquid resources.

The **lease-versus-purchase (or lease-versus-buy) decision** is one that commonly confronts firms that are contemplating the acquisition of new fixed assets. The alternatives available are (1) lease the assets, (2) borrow funds to purchase the assets, or (3) purchase the assets using available liquid resources. Alternatives 2 and 3, although they differ, are analyzed in a similar fashion. Even if the firm has the liquid resources with which to purchase the assets, the use of these funds is viewed as equivalent to borrowing. Therefore, here we need to compare only the leasing and purchasing alternatives.

The lease-versus-purchase decision is made by using basic present-value techniques. The following steps are involved in the analysis:

Step 1 Find the *after-tax cash outflows for each year under the lease alternative.* This step generally involves a fairly simple tax adjustment of the annual lease payments. In addition, the cost of exercising a purchase option in the final year of the lease term must frequently be included.[2]

Step 2 Find the *after-tax cash outflows for each year under the purchase alternative.* This step involves adjusting the sum of the scheduled loan payment and maintenance cost outlay for the tax shields resulting from the tax deductions attributable to maintenance, depreciation, and interest.

Step 3 Calculate the *present value of the cash outflows* associated with the lease (from Step 1) and purchase (from Step 2) alternatives using the *after-tax cost of debt* as the discount rate. Although some controversy surrounds the appropriate discount rate, the after-tax cost of debt is used to evaluate the lease-versus-purchase decision because the decision itself involves the choice between two financing alternatives having very low risk. If we were evaluating whether a given machine should be acquired, the appropriate risk-adjusted rate or cost of capital would be used, but in this type of analysis we are attempting only to determine the better *financing* technique—leasing or borrowing.

Step 4 Choose the alternative with the *lower present value* of cash outflows from Step 3. This will be the *least cost* financing alternative.

The application of each of these steps is demonstrated in the following example.

EXAMPLE

Roberts Company, a small machine shop, is contemplating acquiring a new machine tool costing $24,000. Arrangements can be made to lease or purchase the machine. The firm is in the 40 percent tax bracket.

Lease The firm would obtain a five-year lease requiring annual end-of-year lease payments of $6,000.[3] All maintenance costs would be paid by the lessor, while insurance and other costs would be borne by the lessee. The lessee will exercise its option to purchase the equipment for $4,000 at termination of the lease.

Purchase The firm would finance the purchase of the machine with a 9 percent, five-year loan requiring end-of-year installment payments of $6,170.[4] The machine would be depreciated under MACRS using a five-year recovery period. The firm will pay $1,500 per year for a service contract that covers all maintenance costs; insurance and

[2]Including the cost of exercising a purchase option in the lease alternative cash flows ensures that under both the lease and purchase alternatives the firm owns the asset at the end of the relevant time horizon. The alternative would be to include the cash flows from sale of the asset in the purchase alternative cash flows at the end of the lease term. These approaches guarantee avoidance of unequal lives, which were discussed in Chapter 9. In addition, they make any subsequent cash flows irrelevant because they would either be identical or nonexistent, respectively, under each alternative.

[3]Lease payments are generally made at the beginning of the year. To simplify the following discussions, end-of-year lease payments have been assumed.

[4]The annual loan payment on the 9 percent, five-year loan of $24,000 is calculated by using the loan amortization technique described in Chapter 5. Dividing the present-value interest factor for an annuity, *PVIFA*, from Table A-4 at 9 percent for five years (3.890) into the loan principal of $24,000 results in the annual loan payment of $6,170. (*Note:* By using a hand-held business/financial calculator the annual loan payment would be $6,170.22.) For a more detailed discussion of loan amortization, see Chapter 5.

TABLE 14.1

DETERMINING THE INTEREST AND PRINCIPAL COMPONENTS OF THE ROBERTS COMPANY LOAN PAYMENTS

			Payments		
End of year	**Loan payments (1)**	**Beginning-of-year principal (2)**	Interest [.09 × (2)] **(3)**	Principal [(1) − (3)] **(4)**	**End-of-year principal [(2) − (4)] (5)**
1	$6,170	$24,000	$2,160	$4,010	$19,990
2	6,170	19,990	1,799	4,371	15,619
3	6,170	15,619	1,406	4,764	10,855
4	6,170	10,855	977	5,193	5,662
5	6,170	5,662	510	5,660	—[a]

[a]The values in this table have been rounded to the nearest dollar, which results in a slight difference ($2) between the beginning-of-year-5 principal (in column 2) and the year-5 principal payment (in column 4).

other costs will be borne by the firm. The firm plans to keep the equipment and use it beyond its five-year recovery period.

Using these data, we can apply the steps presented earlier.

Step 1 The after-tax cash outflow from the lease payments can be found by multiplying the before-tax payment of $6,000 by 1 minus the tax rate, T, of 40 percent.

$$\text{After-tax cash outflow from lease} = \$6{,}000 \times (1 - T) = \$6{,}000 \times (1 - .40) = \$3{,}600$$

Therefore the lease alternative will result in annual cash outflows over the five-year lease of $3,600. In the final year the $4,000 cost of the purchase option would be added to the $3,600 lease outflow to get a total cash outflow in year 5 of $7,600 ($3,600 + $4,000).

Step 2 The after-tax cash outflow from the purchase alternative is a bit more difficult to find. First, the interest component of each annual loan payment must be determined, since the Internal Revenue Service allows the deduction of interest only—not principal—from income for tax purposes.[5] Table 14.1 presents the calculations required to split the loan payments into their interest and principal components. Columns 3 and 4 show the annual interest and principal paid in each of the five years.

[5]When the rate of interest on the loan used to finance the purchase just equals the cost of debt, the present value of the after-tax loan payments (annual principal payments − interest tax shields) discounted at the after-tax cost of debt would just equal the initial loan principal. In such a case it is unnecessary to amortize the loan to determine the payment amount and the amounts of interest when finding after-tax cash outflows. The loan payments and interest payments (columns 1 and 4 in Table 14.2) could be ignored, and in their place the initial loan principal ($24,000) would be shown as an outflow occurring at time zero. To allow for a loan interest rate that is different from the firm's cost of debt and for easier understanding, here we isolate the loan payments and interest rather than use this computationally more efficient approach.

TABLE 14.2

AFTER-TAX CASH OUTFLOWS ASSOCIATED WITH PURCHASING FOR ROBERTS COMPANY

End of year	Loan payments (1)	Maintenance costs (2)	Depreciation (3)	Interest[a] (4)	Total deductions [(2) + (3) + (4)] (5)	Tax shields [(.40 × (5)] (6)	After-tax cash outflows [(1) + (2) − (6)] (7)
1	$6,170	$1,500	$4,800	$2,160	$ 8,460	$3,384	$4,286
2	6,170	1,500	7,680	1,799	10,979	4,392	3,278
3	6,170	1,500	4,560	1,406	7,466	2,986	4,684
4	6,170	1,500	2,880	977	5,357	2,143	5,527
5	6,170	1,500	2,880	510	4,890	1,956	5,714

[a]From Table 14.1, column 3.

The annual loan payment is shown in column 1, and the annual maintenance cost, which is a tax-deductible expense, is shown in column 2 of Table 14.2. Next, we find the annual depreciation write-off resulting from the $24,000 machine. Using the applicable MACRS five-year recovery period depreciation percentages—20 percent in year 1, 32 percent in year 2, 19 percent in year 3, and 12 percent in years 4 and 5—given in Table 3.6 on page 83 results in the annual depreciation for years 1 through 5 given in column 3 of Table 14.2.[6]

Table 14.2 presents the calculations required to determine the cash outflows[7] associated with borrowing to purchase the new machine. Column 7 of the table presents the after-tax cash outflows associated with the purchase alternative. A few points should be clarified with respect to the calculations in Table 14.2. The major cash outflows are the total loan payment for each year given in column 1 and the annual maintenance cost in column 2. The sum of these two outflows is reduced by the tax savings from writing off the maintenance, depreciation, and interest expenses associated with the new machine and its financing, respectively. The resulting cash outflows are the after-tax cash outflows associated with the purchase alternative.

Step 3 The present values of the cash outflows associated with the lease (from Step 1) and purchase (from Step 2) alternatives are calculated in Table 14.3 using the firm's 6 percent after-tax cost of debt.[8] Applying the appropriate present-

[6]The year 6 depreciation is ignored, since we are considering the cash flows solely over a five-year time horizon. Similarly, depreciation on the leased asset when purchased at the end of the lease for $4,000 is ignored. The tax benefits resulting from this depreciation would make the lease alternative even more attractive. Clearly, the analysis would become both more precise and more complex if we chose to look beyond the five-year time horizon.

[7]Although other cash outflows such as insurance and operating expenses may be relevant here, they would be the same under the lease and purchase alternatives and therefore would cancel out in the final analysis.

[8]If we ignore any flotation costs, the firm's after-tax cost of debt would be 5.4 percent [9% debt cost × (1 − .40 tax rate)]. To reflect both the flotation costs associated with selling new debt and the need to sell the debt at a discount, an after-tax debt cost of 6 percent was used as the applicable discount rate. A more detailed discussion of techniques for calculating the after-tax cost of debt can be found in Chapter 10.

TABLE 14.3

A COMPARISON OF THE CASH OUTFLOWS ASSOCIATED WITH LEASING VERSUS PURCHASING FOR ROBERTS COMPANY

	Leasing			Purchasing		
End of year	After-tax cash outflows (1)	Present-value factors[a] (2)	Present value of outflows [(1) × (2)] (3)	After-tax cash outflows[b] (4)	Present-value factors[a] (5)	Present value of outflows [(4) × (5)] (6)
1	$3,600	.943	$3,395	$4,286	.943	$4,042
2	3,600	.890	3,204	3,278	.890	2,917
3	3,600	.840	3,024	4,684	.840	3,935
4	3,600	.792	2,851	5,527	.792	4,377
5	7,600[c]	.747	5,677	5,714	.747	4,268
	PV of cash outflows		$18,151	PV of cash outflows		$19,539

[a]From Table A-3, *PVIF,* for 6 percent and the corresponding year.

[b]From column 7 of Table 14.2.

[c]After-tax lease payment outflow of $3,600 plus the $4,000 cost of exercising the purchase option.

value interest factors given in columns 2 and 5 to the after-tax cash outflows in columns 1 and 4 results in the present values of lease and purchase cash outflows given in columns 3 and 6, respectively. The sum of the present values of the cash outflows for the leasing alternative is given in column 3 of Table 14.3, and the sum for the purchasing alternative is given in column 6 of Table 14.3.

Step 4 Since the present value of cash outflows for leasing ($18,151) is lower than that for purchasing ($19,539), *the leasing alternative is preferred.* Leasing results in an incremental savings of $1,388 ($19,539 − $18,151) and is therefore the less costly alternative.[9] ■

The techniques described here for comparing lease and purchase alternatives may be applied in different ways. The approach illustrated by using the Roberts Company data is one of the most straightforward. It is important to recognize that the lower cost of one alternative over the other results from factors such as the differing tax brackets of the lessor and lessee, different tax treatments of leases versus purchases, and differing risks and borrowing costs for lessor and lessee. Therefore, when making a lease-versus-purchase decision, the firm will find that inexpensive borrowing opportunities, high required lessor returns, and a low risk of obsolescence increase the attractiveness of purchasing. Subjective factors must also be included in the decision-making process. Like most financial decisions, the lease-versus-purchase decision requires a certain degree of judgment or intuition.

[9]By using a hand-held business/financial calculator the present value of the cash outflows for the lease would be $18,154, and that for the purchase would be $19,541, resulting in an incremental savings of $1,387.

Effects of leasing on future financing

Since leasing is considered a type of financing, it affects the firm's future financing. Lease payments are shown as a tax-deductible expense on the firm's income statement. Anyone analyzing the firm's income statement would probably recognize that an asset is being leased, although the actual details of the amount and term of the lease would be unclear. The following sections discuss the lease disclosure requirements established by the Financial Accounting Standards Board (FASB) and the effect of leases on financial ratios.

LEASE DISCLOSURE REQUIREMENTS

capitalized lease
A financial (capital) lease that has the present value of all its payments included as an asset and corresponding liability on the firm's balance sheet, as required by Financial Accounting Standards Board (FASB) Standard No. 13.

The Financial Accounting Standards Board (FASB), in Standard No. 13, "Accounting for Leases," requires explicit disclosure of *financial (capital) lease* obligations on the firm's balance sheet. Such a lease must be shown as a **capitalized lease,** meaning that the present value of all its payments is included as an asset and corresponding liability on the firm's balance sheet. An *operating lease*, on the other hand, need not be capitalized, but its basic features must be disclosed in a footnote to the financial statements. Standard No. 13, of course, establishes detailed guidelines to be used in capitalizing leases to reflect them as an asset and corresponding liability on the balance sheet. Subsequent standards have further refined lease capitalization and disclosure procedures. Let us look at an example.

EXAMPLE

Lawrence Company, a manufacturer of water purifiers, is leasing an asset under a 10-year lease requiring annual end-of-year payments of \$15,000. The lease can be capitalized merely by calculating the present value of the lease payments over the life of the lease. However, the rate at which the payments should be discounted is difficult to determine.[10] If 10 percent were used, the present, or capitalized, value of the lease would be \$92,175 (\$15,000 × 6.145). (The value calculated by using a hand-held business/financial calculator is \$92,169.) This value would be shown as an asset and corresponding liability on the firm's balance sheet, which should result in an accurate reflection of the firm's true financial position. ■

LEASES AND FINANCIAL RATIOS

Since the consequences of missing a financial lease payment are the same as those of missing an interest or principal payment on debt, a financial analyst must view the lease as a long-term financial commitment of the lessee. With FASB No. 13, the inclusion of financial (capital) leases as an asset and corresponding liability (i.e., long-term debt) provides for a balance sheet that more accurately reflects the firm's financial status. It thereby permits various types of financial ratio analyses to be performed directly on the statement by any interested party.

[10]The Financial Accounting Standards Board in Standard No. 13 established certain guidelines for the appropriate discount rate to use in capitalizing leases. Most commonly, the rate that the lessee would have incurred to borrow the funds to buy the asset with a secured loan under terms similar to the lease repayment schedule would be used. This simply represents the *before-tax cost of a secured debt.*

Advantages and disadvantages of leasing

Leasing has a number of commonly cited advantages and disadvantages that should be considered in making a lease-versus-purchase decision. Although not all these advantages and disadvantages hold in every case, it is not unusual for a number of them to apply in a given situation.

ADVANTAGES

The commonly cited advantages of leasing are listed below.

1. Leasing allows the lessee, in effect, to *depreciate land,* which is prohibited if the land were purchased. Since the lessee who leases land is permitted to deduct the *total lease payment* as an expense for tax purposes, the effect is the same as if the firm had purchased the land and then depreciated it.
2. Since it results in the receipt of service from an asset possibly without increasing the assets or liabilities on the firm's balance sheet, leasing may result in misleading *financial ratios.* With the passage of FASB No. 13 this advantage no longer applies to financial leases, although in the case of operating leases it remains a potential advantage.
3. The use of sale-leaseback arrangements may permit the firm to *increase its liquidity* by converting an *existing* asset into cash, which can then be used as working capital. A firm short of working capital or in a liquidity bind can sell an owned asset to a lessor and lease the asset back for a specified number of years.
4. Leasing provides *100 percent financing.* Most loan agreements for the purchase of fixed assets require the borrower to pay a portion of the purchase price as a down payment. As a result the borrower is able to borrow only 90 to 95 percent of the purchase price of the asset.
5. When a *firm becomes bankrupt* or is reorganized, the maximum claim of lessors against the corporation is three years of lease payments, and the lessor of course gets the asset back. If debt is used to purchase an asset, the creditors have a claim that is equal to the total outstanding loan balance.
6. In a lease arrangement the firm may *avoid the cost of obsolescence* if the lessor fails to accurately anticipate the obsolescence of assets and sets the lease payment too low. This is especially true in the case of operating leases, which generally have relatively short lives.
7. A lessee *avoids many of the restrictive covenants* that are normally included as part of a long-term loan. Requirements with respect to minimum net working capital, subsequent borrowing, changes in management, and so on are *not* normally found in a lease agreement.
8. In the case of low-cost assets that are infrequently acquired, leasing—especially operating leases—may provide the firm with needed *financing flexibility.* That is, the firm does not have to arrange other financing for these assets and can somewhat conveniently obtain them through a lease.

DISADVANTAGES

The commonly cited disadvantages of leasing are the following:

1. A lease does not have a stated interest cost. Thus in many leases, the *return to the lessor is quite high,* so the firm might be better off borrowing to purchase the asset.

2. At the end of the term of the lease agreement the *salvage value* of an asset, if any, is realized by the lessor. If the lessee had purchased the asset, it could have claimed its salvage value. Of course, an expected salvage value when recognized by the lessor results in lower lease payments.
3. Under a lease, the lessee is generally *prohibited from making improvements* on the leased property or asset without the approval of the lessor. If the property were owned outright, this difficulty would not arise. Of course, lessors generally encourage leasehold improvements that are expected to enhance the asset's salvage value.
4. If a lessee leases an *asset that subsequently becomes obsolete,* it still must make lease payments over the remaining term of the lease. This is true even if the asset is unusable.

CONCEPTS IN REVIEW

14-5 What is *leasing?* Define, compare, and contrast *operating leases* and *financial (or capital) leases*. How does the Financial Accounting Standards Board (FASB) Standard No. 13 define a financial (or capital) lease? Describe three methods used by lessors to acquire assets to be leased.

14-6 Describe the four basic steps involved in the *lease-versus-purchase decision* process. Why must present-value techniques be used in this process?

14-7 What type of lease must be treated as a *capitalized lease* on the balance sheet? How does the financial manager capitalize a lease?

14-8 List and discuss the commonly cited advantages and disadvantages that should be considered in making a lease-versus-purchase decision.

Convertible securities

A convertible security allows its holder to change the bond (or preferred stock) into a stated number of shares of common stock. Why would a firm use convertible bonds rather than straight (nonconvertible) bonds or common stock to raise needed long-term funds? Spend a short time answering this question before reading further.

conversion feature
An option that is included as part of a bond or a preferred stock issue that allows its holder to change the security into a stated number of shares of common stock.

A **CONVERSION FEATURE** IS AN OPTION THAT IS INCLUDED AS PART OF A BOND OR A preferred stock issue that allows its holder to change the security into a stated number of shares of common stock. The conversion feature typically enhances the marketability of an issue.

Types of convertible securities

Corporate bonds and preferred stocks may be convertible into common stock. The most common type of convertible security is the bond. Convertibles normally have an accompanying *call feature.* This feature permits the issuer to retire or encourage conversion of outstanding convertibles when appropriate.

CONVERTIBLE BONDS

convertible bond
A bond that can be changed into a specified number of shares of common stock.

straight bond
A bond that is nonconvertible, having no conversion feature.

A **convertible bond** is a bond that can be changed into a specified number of shares of common stock. It is almost always a *debenture*—an unsecured bond—with a call feature. Because the conversion feature provides the purchaser of a convertible bond with the possibility of becoming a stockholder on favorable terms, convertible bonds are generally a less expensive form of financing than similar-risk nonconvertible or **straight bonds.** The conversion feature adds a degree of speculation to a bond issue, although the issue still maintains its value as a bond.

CONVERTIBLE PREFERRED STOCK

convertible preferred stock
Preferred stock that can be changed into a specified number of shares of common stock.

straight preferred stock
Preferred stock that is nonconvertible, having no conversion feature.

Convertible preferred stock is preferred stock that can be changed into a specified number of shares of common stock. It can normally be sold with a lower stated dividend than a similar-risk nonconvertible or **straight preferred stock.** The reason is that the convertible preferred holder is assured of the fixed dividend payment associated with a preferred stock and also may receive the appreciation resulting from increases in the market price of the underlying common stock. Although convertible preferred stock behaves in a fashion similar to convertible bonds, the following discussions will concentrate on the more popular convertible bonds.

General features of convertibles

The general features of convertible securities include the conversion ratio, the conversion period, the conversion (or stock) value, and the effect on earnings.

CONVERSION RATIO

conversion ratio
The ratio at which a convertible security can be exchanged for common stock.

conversion price
The per-share price that is effectively paid for common stock as the result of conversion of a convertible security.

The **conversion ratio** is the ratio at which a convertible security can be exchanged for common stock. The conversion ratio can be stated in two ways.

1. Sometimes the conversion ratio is stated by indicating that the security is convertible into a given number of shares of common stock. In this situation the conversion ratio is *given*. To find the **conversion price,** which is the per-share price that is effectively paid for common stock as the result of conversion, the par value (not the market value) of the convertible security must be divided by the conversion ratio.

EXAMPLE

Western Wear Company, a manufacturer of denim products, has outstanding a bond with a $1,000 par value and convertible into 25 shares of common stock. The bond's conversion ratio is 25. The conversion price for the bond is $40 per share ($1,000 ÷ 25). ■

2. Sometimes, instead of the conversion ratio, the conversion price is given. The conversion ratio can be obtained by dividing the par value of the convertible by the conversion price.

EXAMPLE

The Mosher Company, a franchisor of seafood restaurants, has outstanding a convertible 20-year bond with a par value of $1,000. The bond is convertible at $50 per share into common stock. The conversion ratio is 20 ($1,000 ÷ $50). ■

The issuer of a convertible security normally establishes a conversion ratio or conversion price that sets the conversion price per share at the time of issuance above the current market price of the firm's stock. If the prospective purchasers do not expect conversion ever to be feasible, they will purchase a straight security or some other convertible issue. A predictable chance of conversion must be provided for to enhance the marketability of a convertible security.

CONVERSION PERIOD

Convertible securities are almost always convertible anytime during the life of the security. Occasionally, conversion is permitted only for a limited number of years, say, for 5 or 10 years after issuance of the convertible.

conversion (or stock) value
The value of a convertible security measured in terms of the market price of the common stock into which it can be converted.

CONVERSION (OR STOCK) VALUE

The **conversion (or stock) value** is the value of the convertible measured in terms of the market price of the common stock into which it can be converted. The conversion value can be found simply by multiplying the conversion ratio by the current market price of the firm's common stock.

EXAMPLE

McNamara Industries, a petroleum processor, has outstanding a $1,000 bond that is convertible into common stock at $62.50 a share. The conversion ratio is therefore 16 ($1,000 ÷ $62.50). Since the current market price of the common stock is $65 per share, the conversion value is $1,040 (16 × $65). Since the conversion value is above the bond value of $1,000, conversion is a viable option for the owner of the convertible security. ■

contingent securities
Convertibles, warrants, and stock options. Their presence affects the reporting of a firm's earnings per share (EPS).

primary EPS
Earnings per share (EPS) calculated under the assumption that all contingent securities *that derive the major portion of their value from their conversion privileges or common stock characteristics* are converted and exercised, and are therefore common stock.

common stock equivalents (CSEs)
All contingent securities that derive a major portion of their value from their conversion privileges or common stock characteristics.

fully diluted EPS
Earnings per share (EPS) calculated under the assumption that *all* contingent securities are converted and exercised and are therefore common stock.

EFFECT ON EARNINGS

The presence of **contingent securities**, which include convertibles as well as warrants (described later in this chapter) and stock options (described in Chapters 1, 12, and 13), affects the reporting of the firm's earnings per share (EPS). Firms with contingent securities that if converted or exercised would increase by more than 3 percent the number of shares outstanding are required to report earnings in two other ways—on a *primary* basis and on a *fully diluted* basis. **Primary EPS** treats as common stock all contingent securities *that derive the major portion of their value from their conversion privileges or common stock characteristics.* These securities are technically called **common stock equivalents (CSEs)**. Primary EPS is calculated by dividing earnings available for common stockholders (adjusted for interest and preferred stock dividends that would *not* be paid given assumed conversion) by the sum of the number of shares outstanding and the CSE. **Fully diluted EPS** treats as common stock *all* contingent securities. It is calculated by dividing earnings available for common stockholders (adjusted for interest and preferred stock dividends that would *not* be paid given assumed conversion of *all* outstanding contingent securities) by the number of shares of common stock that would be outstanding if *all* contingent securities are converted and exercised. Rather than demonstrate these accounting calculations,[11] suffice it to say that

[11]For excellent discussions and demonstrations of the various methods of reporting EPS, see Leopold A. Bernstein, *Financial Statement Analysis: Theory, Application, and Interpretation*, 5th edition (Homewood, IL: Irwin, 1993), Chapter 12.

firms with outstanding convertibles, warrants, and/or stock options must report primary and fully diluted EPS on their income statements.

Financing with convertibles

Using convertible securities to raise long-term funds can help the firm to achieve its cost of capital and capital structure goals (see Chapters 10 and 11, respectively). There are a number of more specific motives and considerations involved in evaluating convertible financing.

MOTIVES FOR CONVERTIBLE FINANCING

Convertibles can be used for a variety of reasons. One popular motive is their use as a form of *deferred common stock financing.* When a convertible security is issued, both issuer and purchaser expect the security to be converted into common stock at some point in the future. Since the security is first sold with a conversion price above the current market price of the firm's stock, conversion is initially not attractive. The issuer of a convertible could alternatively sell common stock, but only at or below its current market price. By selling the convertible the issuer in effect makes a *deferred sale* of common stock. As the market price of the firm's common stock rises to a higher level, conversion may occur. By deferring the issuance of new common stock until the market price of the stock has increased, fewer shares will have to be issued, thereby decreasing the dilution of both ownership and earnings.

Another motive for convertible financing is its *use as a "sweetener" for financing.* Since the purchaser of the convertible is given the opportunity to become a common stockholder and share in the firm's future success, *convertibles can normally be sold with lower interest rates than nonconvertibles.* Therefore, from the firm's viewpoint, including a conversion feature reduces the effective interest cost of debt. The purchaser of the issue sacrifices a portion of his or her interest return for the potential opportunity to become a common stockholder in the future. Another important motive for issuing convertibles is that, generally speaking, *convertible securities can be issued with far fewer restrictive covenants than nonconvertibles.* This results due to the fact that because many investors view convertibles as common stock (i.e., equity), the covenant issue is not important to them.

A final motive for using convertibles is to *raise cheap funds temporarily.* By using convertible bonds the firm can temporarily raise debt, which is typically less expensive than common stock (see Chapter 10), to finance projects. Once such projects are on line, the firm may wish to shift its capital structure to a less highly levered position. A conversion feature gives the issuer the opportunity, through actions of convertible holders, to shift its capital structure at a future point in time.

CONCEPT IN PRACTICE

Kodak Develops a Picture-Perfect Risk-Return Tradeoff

Every investor dreams of high potential returns on common stock without risk of falling prices. Eastman Kodak Company is making dreams come true with convertible bonds or notes with multiple redemption options, for which redemption prices rise over the term of the note to guarantee investors a 5 percent annual return on their investment. Each note is convertible into 5.622 shares of Kodak's common stock. When Kodak's equity sold for $50 a share in 1993, the conversion value of the note was \$281 (\$50 × 5.622 = \$281), and the market price was \$310, for a conversion premium of about 10 percent. Why would you pay such a premium to buy Kodak's stock? Because even if Kodak's stock price declines, you suffer no loss on your investment as long as you hold the notes until October 15, 1994. At that time you can exercise your first redemption option and have Kodak repurchase each note at a predetermined price.

OTHER CONSIDERATIONS

When the price of the firm's common stock rises above the conversion price, the market price of the convertible security will normally rise to a level close to its conversion value. When this happens, many convertible holders will not convert, since they already have the market price benefit obtainable from conversion and can still receive fixed periodic interest payments. Because of this behavior, virtually all convertible securities have a *call feature* that enables the issuer to encourage or *"force" conversion.* The call price of the security generally exceeds the security's par value by an amount equal to one year's stated interest on the security. Although the issuer must pay a premium for calling a security, the call privilege is generally not exercised until the conversion value of the security is 10 to 15 percent *above the call price.* This type of premium above the call price helps to assure the issuer that when the call is made, the holders of the convertible will convert it instead of accepting the call price.

Unfortunately, there are instances when the market price of a security does not reach a level sufficient to stimulate the conversion of associated convertibles. A convertible security that cannot be forced into conversion using the call feature is called an **overhanging issue.** An overhanging issue can be quite detrimental to a firm. If the firm were to call the issue, the bondholders would accept the call price rather than convert the bonds and effectively pay an excessive price for the stock. In this case the firm not only would have to pay the call premium but would require additional financing to pay off the bonds at their par value. If the firm raised these funds through the sale of equity, a large number of shares would have to be issued due to their low market price. This, in turn, could result in the dilution of existing ownership. Another source of financing the call would be the use of debt or preferred stock, but this use would leave the firm's capital structure no less levered than before the call.

overhanging issue
A convertible security that cannot be forced into conversion by using the call feature.

Determining the value of a convertible bond

The key characteristic of convertible securities that greatly enhances their marketability is their ability to minimize the possibility of a loss while providing a possibility of capital gains. Here we discuss the three values of a convertible bond: (1) the straight bond value, (2) the conversion (or stock) value, and (3) the market value.

STRAIGHT BOND VALUE

The **straight bond value** of a convertible bond is the price at which it would sell in the market without the conversion feature. This value is found by determining the value of a nonconvertible bond with similar payments issued by a firm having the same risk. The straight bond value is typically the *floor,* or minimum, price at which the convertible bond would be traded. The straight bond value equals the present value of the bond's interest and principal payments discounted at the interest rate the firm would have to pay on a nonconvertible bond.

straight bond value
The price at which a convertible bond would sell in the market without the conversion feature.

EXAMPLE

Duncan Company, a southeastern discount store chain, has just sold a $1,000, 20-year convertible bond with a 12 percent coupon interest rate. The bond interest will be paid at the end of each year, and the principal will be repaid at maturity.[12] A straight bond could have been sold with a 14 percent coupon interest rate, but the conversion feature compensates for the lower rate on the convertible. The straight bond value of the convertible is calculated as shown below.

Year(s)	Payments (1)	Present-value interest factor at 14 percent (2)	Present value [(1) × (2)] (3)
1–20	$ 120[a]	6.623[b]	$794.76
20	1,000	.073[c]	73.00
		Straight bond value	$867.76

[a]$1,000 at 12% = $120 interest per year.

[b]Present-value interest factor for an annuity, *PVIFA*, discounted at 14% for 20 years, from Table A-4.

[c]Present-value interest factor for $1, *PVIF*, discounted at 14% for year 20, from Table A-3.

This value, $867.76, is the minimum price at which the convertible bond is expected to sell. (The value calculated by using a hand-held business/financial calculator is $867.54.) Generally, only in certain instances in which the stock's market price is below the conversion price will the bond be expected to sell at this level. ■

CONVERSION (OR STOCK) VALUE

The *conversion (or stock) value* of a convertible security was defined earlier as the value of the convertible measured in terms of the market price of the common stock into which the security can be converted. When the market price of the common stock exceeds the conversion price, the conversion (or stock) value exceeds the par value. An example will clarify the point.

EXAMPLE

Duncan Company's convertible bond described earlier is convertible at $50 per share. This means that each bond can be converted into 20 shares, since each bond has a $1,000 par value. The conversion values of the bond when the stock is selling at $30, $40, $50, $60, $70, and $80 per share are shown in the following table.

Market price of stock	Conversion value
$30	$ 600
40	800
50 (conversion price)	1,000 (par value)
60	1,200
70	1,400
80	1,600

[12]Consistent with Chapter 7, we continue to assume the payment of annual rather than semiannual bond interest. This assumption simplifies the calculations involved while maintaining the conceptual accuracy of the procedures presented.

When the market price of the common stock exceeds the $50 conversion price, the conversion value exceeds the $1,000 par value. Since the straight bond value (calculated in the preceding example) is $867.76, the bond will, in a stable environment, never sell for less than this amount, regardless of how low its conversion value is. If the market price per share were $30, the bond would still sell for $867.76—not $600—because its value as a bond would dominate. ■

MARKET VALUE

market premium
The amount by which the market value exceeds the straight or conversion value of a convertible security.

The market value of a convertible is likely to be greater than its straight value or its conversion value. The amount by which the market value exceeds its straight or conversion value is often called the **market premium.** The general relationship of the straight bond value, conversion value, market value, and market premium for Duncan Company's convertible bond is shown in Figure 14.1. The straight bond value acts as a floor for the security's value up to the point X, where the stock price is high enough to cause the conversion value to exceed the straight bond value. The market value of the convertible often exceeds both its straight and conversion values, thus resulting in a market premium. The premium is attributed to the fact that the convertible gives investors a chance to experience attractive capital gains from increases in the stock price while at the same time taking less risk. The reduced risk is attributable to the fact that the floor (straight bond value) provides protection against losses resulting from a decline in the stock price caused by falling profits or other factors. The market premium tends to be greatest when the straight bond value and conversion (or stock) value are nearly equal. This probably results from the fact that investors perceive the benefits of these two sources of value to be greatest at this point.

FIGURE 14.1
The values and market premium for Duncan Company's convertible bond

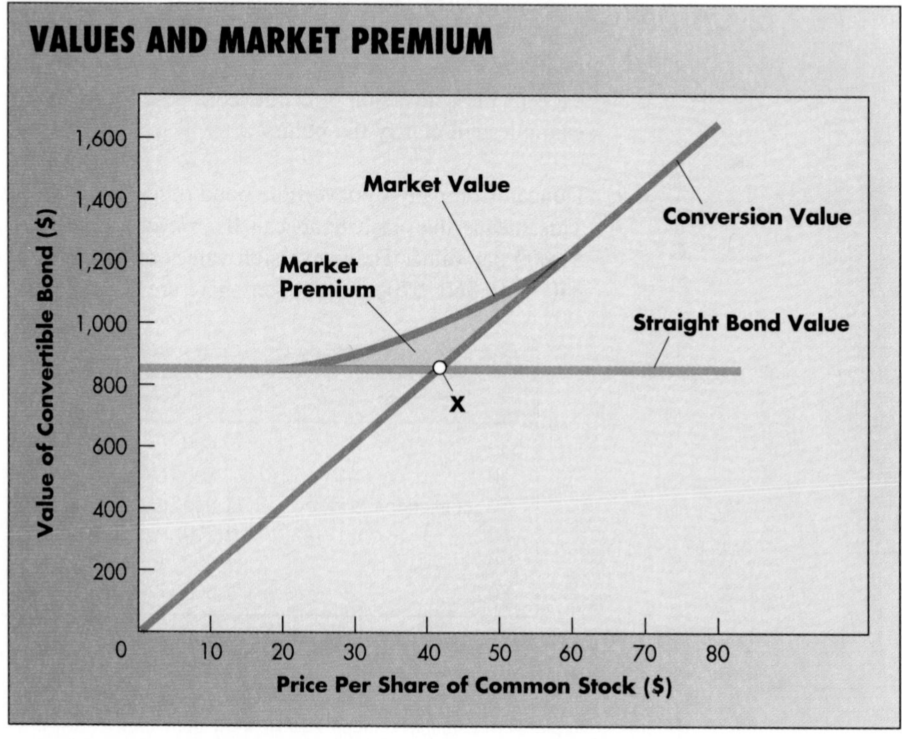

CONCEPTS IN REVIEW

14-9 What is the *conversion feature?* What is a *conversion ratio?* How do convertibles and other *contingent securities* affect EPS? Briefly describe the motives for convertible financing.

14-10 When the market price of the stock rises above the conversion price, why may a convertible security *not* be converted? How can the *call feature* be used to force conversion in this situation? What is an *overhanging issue?*

14-11 Define the *straight bond value, conversion value, market value,* and *market premium* associated with a convertible bond, and describe the general relationships among them.

Stock-purchase warrants

Stock-purchase warrants, which give their holder the right to purchase a certain number of shares of common stock at a specified price over a certain period of time, are often attached as an enhancement to a debt issue. How, if at all, do you think the impact of the exercise of warrants on the firm's capital structure differs from the impact resulting from conversion of a convertible bond? Before reading further, devote a few moments to answering this question.

stock-purchase warrant
An instrument that gives its holder the right to purchase a certain number of shares of common stock at a specified price over a certain period of time.

STOCK-PURCHASE WARRANTS ARE QUITE SIMILAR TO STOCK RIGHTS, WHICH WERE DEscribed in detail in Chapter 13. A **stock-purchase warrant** gives the holder the right to purchase a certain number of shares of common stock at a specified price over a certain period of time. (Of course, holders of warrants earn no income from them until the warrant is exercised or sold.) Warrants also bear some similarity to convertibles in that they provide for the injection of additional equity capital into the firm at some future date.

Basic characteristics

Some of the basic characteristics of stock-purchase warrants are discussed here.

WARRANTS AS "SWEETENERS"

Warrants are often attached to debt issues as "sweeteners," or added benefits. When a firm makes a large bond issue, the attachment of stock-purchase warrants may add to the marketability of the issue while lowering the required interest rate. As sweeteners, warrants are similar to conversion features. Often, when a new firm is raising its initial capital, suppliers of debt will require warrants to permit them to share in whatever success the firm achieves. In addition, established companies sometimes offer warrants with debt to compensate for risk and thereby lower the interest rate and/or provide for fewer *restrictive covenants.*

CONCEPT IN PRACTICE

Covered Warrants Incite the Wrath of Hong Kong

Members of the Hong Kong Stock Exchange have been lobbying the exchange to restrict independent financial institutions, particularly investment and merchant bankers like Salomon Brothers and Barclays de Zoete Wedd, from issuing covered warrants, which represent debt backed by a call option on the underlying firm's common equity. Even though Hong Kong exchange regulations make sure that issuers of these synthetic securities are well capitalized, listed firms are worried. They argue that their share prices could fall if the security's issuer fails to acquire enough stock to meet warrantholder demand when the warrants are exercised, and they fear that movements in price of covered warrants could adversely affect the price of underlying common stock, perhaps to the extent that the listed firms lose control of their equity prices.

EXERCISE PRICES

exercise (or option) price
The price at which holders of warrants can purchase a specified number of shares of common stock.

The price at which holders of warrants can purchase a specified number of shares of common stock is normally referred to as the **exercise (or option) price.** This price is normally set at 10 to 20 percent above the market price of the firm's stock at the time of issuance. Until the market price of the stock exceeds the exercise price, holders of warrants would not be advised to exercise them, since they could purchase the stock more cheaply in the marketplace.

LIFE OF A WARRANT

Warrants normally have a life of no more than 10 years, although some have infinite lives. While, unlike convertible securities, warrants cannot be called, their limited life stimulates holders to exercise them when the exercise price is below the market price of the firm's stock.

WARRANT TRADING

A warrant is usually *detachable,* which means that the bondholder may sell the warrant without selling the security to which it is attached. Many detachable warrants are listed and actively traded on organized securities exchanges and on the over-the-counter exchange. The majority of actively traded warrants are listed on the American Stock Exchange. Warrants, as will be demonstrated in a later section, often provide investors with better opportunities for gain (with increased risk) than the underlying common stock.

COMPARISON OF WARRANTS AND RIGHTS

The similarity between a warrant and a right should be clear. Both result in new equity capital, although the warrant provides for *deferred* equity financing. The life of a right is typically not more than a few months; a warrant is generally exercisable for a period of years. Rights are issued at a subscription price below the prevailing market price of the stock; warrants are generally issued at an exercise price 10 to 20 percent above the prevailing market price.

COMPARISON OF WARRANTS AND CONVERTIBLES

The exercise of a warrant shifts the firm's capital structure to a less highly levered position because new common stock is issued without any change in debt. If a convertible bond were converted, the reduction in leverage would be even more pronounced, since common stock would be issued in exchange for a reduction in debt. In addition, the exercise of a warrant provides an influx of new capital; with convertibles the new capital is raised when the securities are originally issued rather than when converted. The influx of new equity capital resulting from the exercise of a warrant does not occur until the firm has achieved a certain degree of success that is reflected in an increased price for its stock. In this instance the firm conveniently obtains needed funds.

The implied price of an attached warrant

implied price of a warrant
The price effectively paid for each warrant attached to a bond.

When attached to a bond, the **implied price of a warrant**—the price that is effectively paid for each warrant attached to a bond—can be found by first using Equation 14.1:

Implied price of *all* warrants =
price of bond with warrants attached − straight bond value (14.1)

The straight bond value is found in a fashion similar to that used in valuing convertible bonds. Dividing the implied price of *all* warrants by the number of warrants attached to each bond results in the implied price of *each* warrant. This procedure can be demonstrated by using a simple example.

EXAMPLE

Martin Marine Products, a manufacturer of marine drive shafts and propellers, just issued a 10.5 percent coupon interest rate, $1,000 par, 20-year bond paying annual interest and having 20 warrants attached for the purchase of the firm's stock. The bonds were initially sold for their $1,000 par value. When issued, similar-risk straight bonds were selling to yield a 12 percent rate of return. The straight value of the bond would be the present value of its cash inflows discounted at the 12 percent yield on similar-risk straight bonds.

Years	Payments (1)	Present-value interest factor at 12 percent (2)	Present value[a] [(1) × (2)] (3)
1–20	$ 105[b]	7.469[c]	$784
20	1,000	.104[d]	104
		Straight bond value[e]	$888

[a]For convenience, these values have been rounded to the nearest $1.
[b]$1,000 at 10.5% = $105 interest per year.
[c]Present-value interest factor for an annuity, *PVIFA*, discounted at 12% for 20 years, from Table A-4.
[d]Present-value interest factor for $1, *PVIF*, discounted at 12% for year 20, from Table A-3.
[e]The value calculated by using a hand-held business/financial calculator and rounding to the nearest $1 is also $888.

Substituting the $1,000 price of the bond with warrants attached and the $888 straight value of the bond into Equation 14.1, we get an implied price of *all* warrants of $112:

Implied price of *all* warrants = $1,000 − $888 = $112

Dividing the implied price of *all* warrants by the number of warrants attached to each bond—20 in this case—we find the implied price of *each* warrant:

$$\text{Implied price of } each \text{ warrant} = \frac{\$112}{20} = \underline{\underline{\$5.60}}$$

Therefore by purchasing Martin Marine Products' bond with warrants attached for $1,000, one is effectively paying $5.60 for each warrant. ■

The implied price of each warrant is meaningful only when compared to the specific features of the warrant—the number of shares that can be purchased and the specified exercise price. Analysis of these features in light of the prevailing common stock price can be performed to estimate the true *market value* of each warrant. Clearly, if the implied price is above the estimated market value, the price of the bond with warrants attached may be too high, and if the implied price is below the estimated market value, the bond may be quite attractive. Firms must therefore price their bonds with warrants attached in a way that causes the implied price of its warrants to fall slightly below their estimated market value to "sweeten" the bond. Such an approach allows the firm to more easily sell the bonds at a lower coupon interest rate than would apply to a straight debt, thereby reducing its debt service costs.

The value of warrants

warrant premium
The difference between the actual market value and theoretical value of a warrant.

Like a convertible security, a warrant has both a market and a theoretical value. The difference between these values, or the **warrant premium,** depends largely on investor expectations and the ability of investors to get more leverage from the warrants than from the underlying stock.

THEORETICAL VALUE OF A WARRANT

The *theoretical value* of a stock-purchase warrant is the amount for which one would expect the warrant to sell in the marketplace. Equation 14.2 gives the theoretical value of a warrant:

$$TVW = (P_0 - E) \times N \tag{14.2}$$

where

TVW = theoretical value of a warrant
P_0 = current market price of a share of common stock
E = exercise price of the warrant
N = number of shares of common stock obtainable with one warrant

The use of Equation 14.2 can be illustrated by the following example.

EXAMPLE

Dustin Electronics, a major producer of transistors, has outstanding warrants that are exercisable at $40 per share and entitle holders to purchase three shares of common stock. The warrants were initially attached to a bond issue to sweeten the bond. The common stock of the firm is currently selling for $45 per share. Substituting P_0 =

\$45, $E = \$40$, and $N = 3$ into Equation 14.2 yields a theoretical warrant value of \$15 [(\$45 − \$40) × 3]. Therefore Dustin's warrants should sell for \$15 in the marketplace. ■

MARKET VALUE OF A WARRANT

The market value of a stock-purchase warrant is generally above the theoretical value of the warrant. Only when the theoretical value of the warrant is very high or the warrant is near its expiration date are the market and theoretical values close. The general relationship between the theoretical and market values of Dustin Electronics' warrants is presented graphically in Figure 14.2. The market value of warrants generally exceeds the theoretical value by the greatest amount when the stock's market price is close to the warrant exercise price per share. In addition, the amount of time until expiration also affects the market value of the warrant. Generally speaking, the closer the warrant is to its expiration date, the more likely that its market value will equal its theoretical value.

WARRANT PREMIUM

The *warrant premium,* or amount by which the market value of Dustin Electronics' warrants exceeds the theoretical value of these warrants, is also shown in Figure 14.2. This premium results from a combination of positive investor expectations and the ability of the investor with a fixed sum to invest to obtain much larger potential returns (and risk) by trading in warrants rather than the underlying stock. An example will clarify the effect of expected stock price movements and investor leverage opportunities on warrant market values.

FIGURE 14.2
The values and warrant premium for Dustin Electronics' stock-purchase warrants

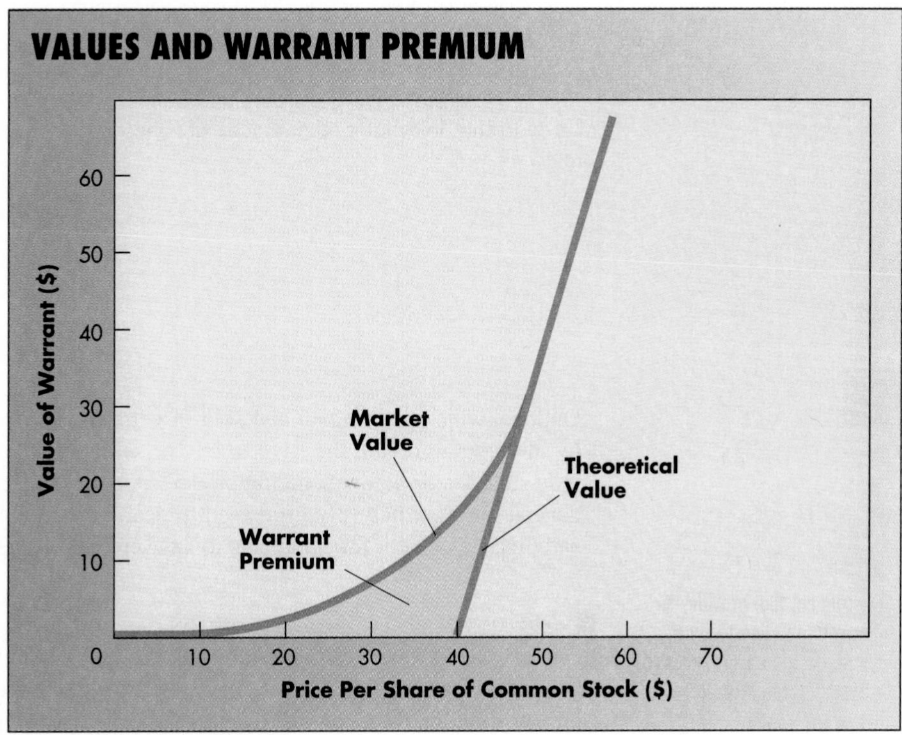

EXAMPLE

Stan Buyer has $2,430, which he is interested in investing in Dustin Electronics. The firm's stock is currently selling for $45 per share, and its warrants are selling for $18 per warrant. Each warrant entitles the holder to purchase three shares of Dustin's common stock at $40 per share. Since the stock is selling for $45 per share, the theoretical warrant value, calculated in the preceding example by using Equation 14.2, is $15 [($45 − $40) × 3].

The warrant premium is believed to result from positive investor expectations and leverage opportunities. Stan Buyer could spend his $2,430 in either of two ways. Ignoring brokerage fees, he could purchase 54 shares of common stock at $45 per share or 135 warrants at $18 per warrant. If Mr. Buyer purchases the stock, its price rises to $48, and he then sells the stock, he will gain $162 ($3 per share × 54 shares). If instead of purchasing the stock he purchases the 135 warrants and the stock price increases by $3 per share, Mr. Buyer will make approximately $1,215. Since the price of a share of stock rises by $3, the price of each warrant can be expected to rise by $9, since each warrant can be used to purchase three shares of common stock. A gain of $9 per warrant on 135 warrants means a total gain of $1,215 on the warrants. ■

The greater leverage associated with trading warrants should be clear from the preceding example. Of course, since leverage works both ways, it results in greater risk. If the market price fell by $3, the loss on the stock would be $162, whereas the loss on the warrants would be close to $1,215. Clearly, the use of warrants by investors is more risky.

CONCEPTS IN REVIEW

14-12 What are *stock-purchase warrants?* What are the similarities and key differences between the effects of warrants and those of convertibles on the firm's capital structure and its ability to raise new capital?

14-13 What is the *implied price of a warrant?* How is it estimated? To be effective, how should it relate to the estimated *market value* of a warrant?

14-14 What is the general relationship between the theoretical and market values of a warrant? In what circumstances are these values quite close? What is a *warrant premium?*

Options

LG 6

Options, which are created and sold in certain options markets, can be purchased by investors to obtain the right to buy or sell a specific number of shares of common stock on or before some future date at a stated price. Why do you think the financial manager has very little need to deal with options in his or her fund-raising activities? Devote a few moments to answering this question before reading on.

option
An instrument that provides its holder with an opportunity to purchase or sell a specified asset at a stated price on or before a set *expiration date.*

In the most general sense, an **option** can be viewed as an instrument that provides its holder with an opportunity to purchase or sell a specified asset at a stated price on or before a set *expiration date.* Today the interest in options centers on options on common stock. The development of organized options exchanges has created markets in which to trade these options, which themselves are securities. Three basic forms of options are rights, warrants, and calls and puts. Rights were discussed in Chapter 13, and warrants were described in the preceding section.

Calls and puts

call option
An option to *purchase* a specified number of shares of a stock (typically 100) on or before some future date at a stated price.

striking price
The price at which the holder of a call option can buy (or the holder of a put option can sell) a specified amount of stock at any time before the option's expiration date.

put option
An option to *sell* a given number of shares of a stock (typically 100) on or before a specified future date at a stated striking price.

The two most common types of options are calls and puts. A **call option** is an option to *purchase* a specified number of shares of a stock (typically 100) on or before some future date at a stated price. Call options usually have initial lives of one to nine months, occasionally one year. The **striking price** is the price at which the holder of the option can buy the stock at any time before the option's expiration date; it is generally set at or near the prevailing market price of the stock at the time the option is issued. For example, if a firm's stock is currently selling for $50 per share, a call option on the stock initiated today would likely have a striking price set at $50 per share. To purchase a call option, a specified price of normally a few hundred dollars must be paid.

A **put option** is an option to *sell* a given number of shares of a stock (typically 100) on or before a specified future date at a stated striking price. Like the call option, the striking price of the put is close to the market price of the underlying stock at the time of issuance. The lives and costs of puts are similar to those of calls.

How the options markets work

There are two ways of making options transactions. The first involves making a transaction through one of 20 or so call and put options dealers with the help of a stockbroker. The other, more popular mechanism is the organized options exchanges. The dominant exchange is the *Chicago Board Options Exchange (CBOE),* which was established in 1973. Other exchanges on which options are traded include the American Stock Exchange, the New York Stock Exchange, and several regional stock exchanges. Each exchange provides an organized marketplace in which purchases and sales of both call and put options can be made in an orderly fashion. The options traded on the options exchanges are standardized and thus are considered registered securities. Each option is for 100 shares of the underlying stock. The price at which options transactions can be made is determined by the forces of supply and demand.

Logic of options trading

The most common motive for purchasing call options is the expectation that the market price of the underlying stock will rise by more than enough to cover the cost of the option and thereby allow the purchaser of the call to profit.

EXAMPLE

Assume that Cindy Peters pays $250 for a three-month *call option* on Wing Enterprises, a maker of aircraft components, at a striking price of $50. This means that by paying $250, Cindy is guaranteed that she can purchase 100 shares of Wing at $50 per share at any time during the next three months. The stock price must climb $2.50 per share ($250 ÷ 100 shares) to $52.50 per share to cover the cost of the option (ignoring any brokerage fees or dividends). If the stock price were to rise to $60 per share during the period, Cindy's net profit would be $750 [(100 shares × $60/share) − (100 shares × $50/share) − $250]. Since this return would be earned on a $250 investment, it illustrates the high potential return on investment that options offer. Of course, had the stock price not risen above $50 per share, Cindy would have lost the $250, since there would have been no reason to exercise the option. Had the stock price risen to between $50 and $52.50 per share, Cindy probably would have exercised the option to reduce her loss to an amount less than $250. ■

Put options are purchased in the expectation that the share price of a given security will decline over the life of the option. Purchasers of puts commonly own the shares and wish to protect a gain they have realized since their initial purchase. By buying a put, they lock in the gain because it enables them to sell their shares at a known price during the life of the option. Investors gain from put options when the price of the underlying stock declines by more than the per-share cost of the option. The logic underlying the purchase of a put is exactly the opposite of that underlying the use of call options.

EXAMPLE

Assume that Don Kelly pays $325 for a six-month *put option* on Dante United, a baked goods manufacturer, at a striking price of $40. Don purchased the put option in expectation that the stock price would drop due to the introduction of a new product line by Dante's chief competitor. By paying $325, Don is assured that he can sell 100 shares of Dante at $40 per share at any time during the next six months. The stock price must drop by $3.25 per share ($325 ÷ 100 shares) to $36.75 per share to cover the cost of the option (ignoring any brokerage fees or dividends). If the stock price were to drop to $30 per share during the period, Don's net profit would be $675 [(100 shares × $40/share) − (100 shares × $30/share) − $325]. Since the return would be earned on a $325 investment, it again illustrates the high potential return on investment that options offer. Of course, had the stock price risen above $40 per share, Don would have lost the $325, since there would have been no reason to exercise the option. Had the stock price fallen to between $36.75 and $40.00 per share, Don probably would have exercised the option in order to reduce his loss to an amount less than $325. ■

Role of call and put options in fund raising

Although call and put options are extremely popular investment vehicles, they play *no* direct role in the fund-raising activities of the financial manager. These options are issued by investors, not businesses. *They are not a source of financing to the firm.* Corporate pension managers, whose job it is to invest and manage corporate pension funds, may use call and put options as part of their investment activities to earn a return or to protect or lock in returns already earned on securities. The presence of options trading in the firm's stock could—by increasing trading activity—stabilize the firm's share price in the marketplace, but the financial manager has no direct control over this. Buyers of options have neither any say in the firm's management nor any voting rights; only stockholders are given these privileges. Despite the popularity of call and put options as an investment vehicle, the financial manager has very little need to deal with them, especially as part of fund-raising activities.

Using options to protect against foreign currency exposures

Since 1983 the Philadelphia Stock Exchange (PHLX) has offered exchange-traded options contracts on the Canadian dollar, the Japanese yen, and several important European currencies. Currency options proved to be an immediate hit and today are used by a wide range of traders—from the largest multinational companies to small exporters and importers, as well as by individual investors and speculators. Unlike futures and forward contracts, options offer the key benefit of effectively protecting against the risk of adverse price movements while simultaneously preserving the possibility of profiting if prices move in your favor. The key drawback to using options to protect against foreign currency exposures is its high cost relative to using more traditional futures or forward contracts. The use of currency options is best demonstrated by an example.

EXAMPLE

Assume that a U.S. exporter just booked a sale denominated in Swiss francs with payment due upon delivery in three months. The company could protect against the risk of the dollar depreciating by purchasing a Swiss franc put option. This would give the company the right to sell Swiss francs at a fixed price (say, \$.65/Sf). This option would become very valuable if the Swiss franc were to depreciate from today's \$.66/Sf to, say, \$.60/Sf before expiration of the contract. On the other hand, if the Swiss franc were to appreciate from \$.66/Sf to, say, \$.72/Sf, the U.S. exporter would allow the put option to expire unexercised and would instead convert the Swiss francs received in payment on the sales contract into dollars on the open market at the new, higher dollar price. The exporter would be protected from adverse price risk but would still be able to profit from favorable price movements. ■

CONCEPTS IN REVIEW

14-15 What is an *option?* Define *calls* and *puts.* What role, if any, do call and put options play in the fund-raising activities of the financial manager?

14-16 How can the firm use currency options to protect its international business transactions against the risk of adverse movements in foreign exchange rates? Describe the key benefit and drawback of using currency options rather than the more traditional futures and forward contracts.

Summary

LG 1 Understand the basic rights of preferred stockholders, the features of preferred stock, special types of preferred stock, and the advantages and disadvantages of preferred stock financing. Preferred stockholders are given preference over common stockholders with respect to the distribution of earnings and assets and, as a result, do not normally receive voting privileges. Preferred stock issues may have certain restrictive covenants, cumulative dividends, participation in earnings, a call feature, and a conversion feature. Special types of preferred stock include adjustable-rate (or floating-rate) preferred stock (ARPS) and payment-in-kind (PIK) preferred stock. While most preferred stock is similar to debt in that it has stated fixed annual cash dividends, these special types do not. The basic advantages for preferred stock financing include its ability to increase the firm's leverage, the flexibility of the obligation, and its use in corporate restructuring. Disadvantages include the seniority of its claim over the common stockholders, its relatively high cost compared to debt financing, and the general difficulty of selling it.

LG 2 Review the basic types of leases, leasing arrangements, the lease contract, the lease-versus-purchase decision, the effects of leasing on future financing, and the advantages and disadvantages of leasing. A lease, like long-term debt, allows the firm to make contractual, tax-deductible payments to obtain the use of fixed assets. Operating leases are generally five or fewer years in term, cancelable, and renewable and provide for maintenance by the lessor. Financial leases are longer term, noncancelable, and not renewable and require the lessee to maintain the asset. FASB Standard No. 13 provides specific guidelines for defining a financial (or capital) lease. A lessor can obtain assets to be leased through a direct lease, a sale-leaseback arrangement, or a leveraged lease. The lease contract normally includes the term (duration) of the lease, provisions for its cancelation, lease payment amounts and dates, maintenance and associated costs and provisions, renewal options, purchase options, and other provisions specified in the lease-negotiation process. The lease-versus-purchase-decision can be evaluated by calculating the after-tax cash outflows associated with the leasing and purchasing alternatives. The more desirable alternative is the one that has the lower present value of after-tax cash outflows. FASB Standard No. 13 requires firms to show financial (or capital) leases as assets and corresponding liabilities on their balance sheets; operating leases must be shown in footnotes to the financial statements. A number of commonly cited advantages and disadvantages should be considered in making lease-versus-purchase decisions.

LG 3 Describe the basic types of convertible securities and their general features—including the conversion ratio, conversion period, conversion (or stock) value, and effects on earnings—and the use of convertible financing to raise long-term funds. Corporate bonds and preferred stocks may both be convertible into common stock. The conversion ratio indicates the number of shares for which a convertible can be exchanged and determines the conversion price. A conversion privilege is almost always available anytime during the life of the security. The conversion (or stock) value is the value of the convertible measured in terms of the market price of the common stock into which it can be converted. The presence of convertibles and other contingent securities (warrants and stock options) often requires the firm to report earnings (EPS) on both a primary basis and a fully diluted basis. Convertibles are used to obtain deferred common stock financing, to "sweeten" bond issues, to minimize restrictive covenants, and to raise cheap funds temporarily. The call feature is sometimes used to encourage or "force" conversion; occasionally, an overhanging issue results.

LG 4 Demonstrate the procedures for determining the straight bond value, conversion (or stock) value, and market value of a convertible bond. The straight bond value of a convertible is the price at which it would sell in the market without the conversion feature. It typically represents the minimum value at which a convertible bond will trade. The conversion (or stock) value of the convertible is found by multiplying the conversion ratio by the current market price of the underlying common stock. The market price of a convertible generally exceeds both its straight and conversion values, thus resulting in a market premium. The premium, which is largest when the straight and conversion values are nearly equal, is attributed to the attractive gains potential from the stock and the risk protection provided by the straight value of the convertible.

LG 5 Explain the basic characteristics of stock-purchase warrants, the implied price of an attached warrant, and the values of warrants—theoretical, market, and market premium. Stock-purchase warrants, like rights, provide their holders with the privilege of purchasing a certain number of shares of common stock at the specified exercise price. Warrants are often attached to debt issues as "sweeteners," generally have limited lives, are detachable, and may be listed and traded on securities exchanges. Warrants are similar to stock rights, except that the life of a warrant is generally longer than that of a right, and the exercise price of a warrant is initially set above the underlying stock's current market price. Warrants are similar to convertibles, but exercising them has a less pronounced effect on the firm's leverage and brings in new funds. The implied price of an attached warrant can be found by dividing the difference between the bond price with warrants attached and the straight bond value by the number of warrants attached to each bond. The market value of a warrant usually exceeds its theoretical value, creating a warrant premium. The premium results from positive investor expectations and the ability of investors to get more leverage from trading warrants than from trading the underlying stock.

LG 6 Define options and discuss the basics of calls and puts, options markets, options trading, and the role of call and put options in managerial finance. An option provides its holder with an opportunity to purchase or sell a specified asset at a stated price on or before a set expiration date. Rights, warrants, and calls and puts are all options. Calls are options to purchase common stock, and puts are options to sell common stock. Options exchanges, such as the Chicago Board Options Exchange (CBOE), provide organized marketplaces in which purchases and sales of both call and put options can be made in an orderly fashion. The options traded on the exchanges are standardized, and the price at which they trade is determined by the forces of supply and demand. Call and put options do not play a direct role in the fund-raising activities of the financial manager. On the other hand, currency options can be used, in lieu of futures and forward contracts, to protect the firm's international transactions against the risk of adverse movements in foreign exchange rates.

Self-test problems (Solutions in Appendix E)

ST 14-1 LG 2 Lease versus purchase The Hot Bagel Shop wishes to evaluate two plans, leasing and borrowing to purchase, for financing an oven. The firm is in the 40 percent tax bracket.

Lease The shop can lease the oven under a five-year lease requiring annual end-of-year payments of $5,000. All maintenance costs will be paid by the lessor, while insurance and other costs will be borne by the lessee. The lessee will exercise its option to purchase the asset for $4,000 at termination of the lease.

Purchase The oven costs $20,000 and will have a five-year life. It will be depreciated under MACRS using a five-year recovery period. (See Table 3.6 on page 83 for the applicable depreciation percentages.) The total purchase price will be financed by a five-year, 15 percent loan requiring equal annual end-of-year payments of $5,967. The firm will pay $1,000 per year for a service contract that covers all maintenance costs; insurance and other costs will be borne by the firm. The firm plans to keep the equipment and use it beyond its five-year recovery period.

a. For the leasing plan, calculate the following:
  (1) The after-tax cash outflows each year.
  (2) The present value of the cash outflows, using a *9 percent discount rate.*

b. For the purchasing plan, calculate the following:
  (1) The annual interest expense deductible for tax purposes for each of the five years.
  (2) The after-tax cash outflows resulting from the purchase for each of the five years.
  (3) The present value of the cash outflows, using a *9 percent discount rate.*

c. Compare the present value of the cash-outflow streams from each plan, and determine which would be preferable. Explain your answer.

ST 14-2 LG 4 Finding convertible bond values Mountain Mining Company has an outstanding issue of convertible bonds with a $1,000 par value. These bonds are convertible into 40 shares of common stock. They have an 11 percent annual coupon interest rate and a 25-year maturity. The interest rate on a straight bond of similar risk is currently 13 percent.

a. Calculate the straight bond value of the bond.

b. Calculate the conversion (or stock) values of the bond when the market price of the common stock is $20, $25, $28, $35, and $50 per share.

c. For each of the stock prices given in **b** at what price would you expect the bond to sell? Why?

d. What is the least you would expect the bond to sell for, regardless of the common stock price behavior?

Problems

14-1 LG 1 Preferred dividends Slater Lamp Manufacturing has an outstanding issue of preferred stock with an $80 par value and an 11 percent annual dividend.

a. What is the annual dollar dividend? If it is paid quarterly, how much will be paid each quarter?

b. If the preferred stock is *noncumulative* and the board of directors has passed the preferred dividend for the last three years, how much must be paid to preferred stockholders before dividends are paid to common stockholders?

c. If the preferred stock is *cumulative* and the board of directors has passed the preferred dividend for the last three years, how much must be paid to preferred stockholders before dividends are paid to common stockholders?

14-2 LG 1 **Preferred dividends** In each case in the table, how many dollars of preferred dividends per share must be paid to preferred stockholders before common stock dividends are paid?

Case	Type	Par value	Dividend per share per period	Periods of dividends passed
A	Cumulative	$ 80	$5	2
B	Noncumulative	110	8%	3
C	Noncumulative	100	$11	1
D	Cumulative	60	8.5%	4
E	Cumulative	90	9%	0

14-3 LG 1 **Participating preferred stock** Union Shipping Company has outstanding an issue of 3,000 shares of participating preferred stock that has a $100 par value and an 8 percent annual dividend. The preferred stockholders participate fully (on an equal per-share basis) with common stockholders in annual dividends of more than $9 per share for common stock. The firm has 5,000 shares of common stock outstanding.

a. If the firm pays preferred stockholders their dividends and then declares an additional $100,000 in dividends, what is the total dividend per share for preferred and common stock?

b. If the firm pays preferred stockholders their dividends and then declares an additional $40,000 in dividends, what is the total dividend per share for each type of stockholder?

c. If the firm's preferred stock is *cumulative* and the past two years' dividends have been passed, what dividends will be received by each type of stockholder if the firm declares a *total* dividend of $30,000?

d. Rework **c** assuming that the total dividend payment is $20,000.

e. Rework **a** and **b** assuming that the preferred stock is nonparticipating.

14-4 LG 2 **Lease cash flows** Given the following lease payments and terms, determine the yearly after-tax cash outflows for each firm, assuming that lease payments are made at the end of each year and that the firm is in the 40 percent tax bracket. Assume that no purchase option exists.

Firm	Annual lease payment	Term of lease
A	$100,000	4 years
B	80,000	14 years
C	150,000	8 years
D	60,000	25 years
E	20,000	10 years

14-5 LG 2 **Loan interest** For each of the following loan amounts, interest rates, annual payments, and loan terms, calculate the annual interest paid each year over the term of the loan, assuming that the payments are made at the end of each year.

Loan	Amount	Interest rate	Annual payment	Term
A	$14,000	10%	$ 4,416	4 years
B	17,500	12	10,355	2 years
C	2,400	13	1,017	3 years
D	49,000	14	14,273	5 years
E	26,500	16	7,191	6 years

14-6 LG 2 **Loan payments and interest** Schuyler Company wishes to purchase an asset costing $117,000. The full amount needed to finance the asset can be borrowed at 14 percent interest. The terms of the loan require equal end-of-year payments for the next six years. Determine the total annual loan payment, and break it into the amount of interest and the amount of principal paid for each year. (*Hint:* Use techniques presented in Chapter 5 to find the loan payment.)

14-7 LG 2 **Lease versus purchase** JLB Corporation is attempting to determine whether to lease or purchase research equipment. The firm is in the 40 percent tax bracket, and its after-tax cost of debt is currently 8 percent. The terms of the lease and the purchase are as follows:

Lease Annual end-of-year lease payments of $25,200 are required over the three-year life of the lease. All maintenance costs will be paid by the lessor; insurance and other costs will be borne by the lessee. The lessee will exercise its option to purchase the asset for $5,000 at termination of the lease.

Purchase The research equipment, costing $60,000, can be financed entirely with a 14 percent loan requiring annual end-of-year payments of $25,844 for three years. The firm in this case will depreciate the truck under MACRS using a three-year recovery period. (See Table 3.6 on page 83 for the applicable depreciation percentages.) The firm will pay $1,800 per year for a service contract that covers all maintenance costs; insurance and other costs will be borne by the firm. The firm plans to keep the equipment and use it beyond its three-year recovery period.

a. Calculate the after-tax cash outflows associated with each alternative.
b. Calculate the present value of each cash outflow stream using the after-tax cost of debt.
c. Which alternative, lease or purchase, would you recommend? Why?

14-8 LG 2 **Lease versus purchase** Northwest Lumber Company needs to expand its facilities. To do so, the firm must acquire a machine costing $80,000. The machine can be leased or purchased. The firm is in the 40 percent tax bracket, and its after-tax cost of debt is 9 percent. The terms of the lease and purchase plans are as follows:

Lease The leasing arrangement requires end-of-year payments of $19,800 over five years. All maintenance costs will be paid by the lessor; insurance and other costs will be borne by the lessee. The lessee will exercise its option to purchase the asset for $24,000 at termination of the lease.

Purchase If the firm purchases the machine, its cost of $80,000 will be financed with a five-year, 14 percent loan requiring equal end-of-year payments of $23,302. The machine will be depreciated under MACRS using a five-year recovery period. (See Table 3.6 on page 83 for the applicable depreciation percentages.) The firm will pay $2,000 per year for a service contract that covers all maintenance costs; insurance and other costs will be borne by the firm. The firm plans to keep the equipment and use it beyond its five-year recovery period.

a. Determine the after-tax cash outflows of Northwest Lumber under each alternative.
b. Find the present value of the after-tax cash outflows using the after-tax cost of debt.
c. Which alternative, lease or purchase, would you recommend? Why?

14-9 LG 2 **Capitalized lease values** Given the following lease payments, terms remaining until the leases expire, and discount rates, calculate the capitalized value of each lease, assuming that lease payments are made annually at the end of each year.

Lease	Lease payment	Remaining term	Discount rate
A	$ 40,000	12 years	10%
B	120,000	8 years	12
C	9,000	18 years	14
D	16,000	3 years	9
E	47,000	20 years	11

14-10 LG 3 **Conversion price** Calculate the conversion price for each of the following convertible bonds:

a. A $1,000-par-value bond that is convertible into 20 shares of common stock.
b. A $500-par-value bond that is convertible into 25 shares of common stock.
c. A $1,000-par-value bond that is convertible into 50 shares of common stock.

14-11 LG 3 **Conversion ratio** What is the conversion ratio for each of the following bonds?

a. A $1,000-par-value bond that is convertible into common stock at $43.75 per share.
b. A $1,000-par-value bond that is convertible into common stock at $25 per share.
c. A $600-par-value bond that is convertible into common stock at $30 per share.

14-12 LG 3 **Conversion (or stock) value** What is the conversion (or stock) value of each of the following convertible bonds?

a. A $1,000-par-value bond that is convertible into 25 shares of common stock. The common stock is currently selling at $50 per share.
b. A $1,000-par-value bond that is convertible into 12.5 shares of common stock. The common stock is currently selling for $42 per share.
c. A $1,000-par-value bond that is convertible into 100 shares of common stock. The common stock is currently selling for $10.50 per share.

14-13 LG 3 **Conversion (or stock) value** Find the conversion (or stock) value for each of the convertible bonds described in the following table.

Convertible	Conversion ratio	Current market price of stock
A	25	$42.25
B	16	50.00
C	20	44.00
D	5	19.50

14-14 LG 4 **Straight bond values** Calculate the straight bond value for each of the following bonds:

Bond	Par value	Coupon interest rate (paid annually)	Interest rate on equal-risk straight bond	Years to maturity
A	$1,000	10%	14%	20
B	800	12	15	14
C	1,000	13	16	30
D	1,000	14	17	25

14-15 LG 4 **Determining values—Convertible bond** Eastern Clock Company has an outstanding issue of convertible bonds with a $1,000 par value. These bonds are convertible into 50 shares of common stock. They have a 10 percent annual coupon interest rate and a 20-year maturity. The interest rate on a straight bond of similar risk is currently 12 percent.

a. Calculate the straight bond value of the bond.
b. Calculate the conversion (or stock) values of the bond when the market price of the common stock is $15, $20, $23, $30, and $45 per share.
c. For each of the stock prices given in **b**, at what price would you expect the bond to sell? Why?
d. What is the least you would expect the bond to sell for, regardless of the common stock price behavior?

14-16 LG 4 Determining values—Convertible bond Craig's Cake Company has an outstanding issue of 15-year convertible bonds with a $1,000 par value. These bonds are convertible into 80 shares of common stock. They have a 13 percent annual coupon interest rate, whereas the interest rate on straight bonds of similar risk is 16 percent.

a. Calculate the straight bond value of this bond.

b. Calculate the conversion (or stock) values of the bond when the market price is $9, $12, $13, $15, and $20 per share of common stock.

c. For each of the common stock prices given in **b**, at which price would you expect the bond to sell? Why?

d. Graph the straight value and conversion value of the bond for each common stock price given. Plot the per-share common stock prices on the x-axis and the bond values on the y-axis. Use this graph to indicate the minimum market value of the bond associated with each common stock price.

14-17 LG 5 Implied prices of attached warrants Calculate the implied price of *each* warrant for each of the following bonds.

Bond	Price of bond with warrants attached	Par value	Coupon interest rate (paid annually)	Interest rate on equal-risk straight bond	Years to maturity	Number of warrants attached to bond
A	$1,000	$1,000	12%	13%	15	10
B	1,100	1,000	9.5	12	10	30
C	500	500	10	11	20	5
D	1,000	1,000	11	12	20	20

14-18 LG 5 Evaluation of the implied price of an attached warrant Dinoo Mathur wishes to determine whether the $1,000 price asked for Stanco Manufacturing's bond is fair in light of the theoretical value of the attached warrants. The $1,000 par, 30-year, 11.5 percent coupon interest rate bond pays annual interest and has 10 warrants attached for purchase of common stock. The theoretical value of each warrant is $12.50. The interest rate on an equal-risk straight bond is currently 13 percent.

a. Find the straight value of Stanco Manufacturing's bond.

b. Calculate the implied price of *all* warrants attached to Stanco's bond.

c. Calculate the implied price of *each* warrant attached to Stanco's bond.

d. Compare the implied price for each warrant calculated in **c** to its theoretical value. On the basis of this comparison, what recommendation would you give Dinoo with respect to the fairness of Stanco's bond price? Explain.

14-19 LG 5 Warrant values Kent Hotels has warrants that allow the purchase of three shares of its outstanding common stock at $50 per share. The common stock price per share and the market value of the warrant associated with that stock price are summarized in the following table.

Common stock price per share	Market value of warrant
$42	$ 2
46	8
48	9
54	18
58	28
62	38
66	48

a. For each of the common stock prices given, calculate the theoretical warrant value.
b. Graph the theoretical and market values of the warrant on a set of per-share common stock price *(x-axis)*–warrant value *(y-axis)* axes.
c. If the warrant value is $12 when the market price of common stock is $50, does this contradict or support the graph you have constructed? Explain.
d. Specify the area of *warrant premium.* Why does this premium exist?
e. If the expiration date of the warrants is quite close, would you expect your graph to look different? Explain.

14-20 LG 5 **Common stock versus warrant investment** Susan Michaels is evaluating the Burton Tool Company's common stock and warrants to choose the better investment. The firm's stock is currently selling for $50 per share; its warrants to purchase three shares of common stock at $45 per share are selling for $20. Ignoring transactions costs, Ms. Michaels has $8,000 to invest. She is quite optimistic with respect to Burton because she has certain "inside information" about the firm's prospects with respect to a large government contract.
a. How many shares of stock and how many warrants can Ms. Michaels purchase?
b. Suppose Ms. Michaels purchased the stock, held it one year, then sold it for $60 per share. Ignoring brokerage fees and taxes, what total gain would she realize?
c. Suppose Ms. Michaels purchased warrants and held them for one year and the market price of the stock increased to $60 per share. Ignoring brokerage fees and taxes, what would be her total gain if the market value of warrants increased to $45 and she sold out?
d. What benefit, if any, would the warrants provide? Are there any differences in the risk of these two alternative investments? Explain.

14-21 LG 5 **Common stock versus warrant investment** Tom Baldwin can invest $6,300 in the common stock or the warrants of Lexington Life Insurance. The common stock is currently selling for $30 per share. Its warrants, which provide for the purchase of two shares of common stock at $28 per share, are currently selling for $7. The stock is expected to rise to a market price of $32 within the next year, so the expected theoretical value of a warrant over the next year is $8. The expiration date of the warrant is one year from the present.
a. If Mr. Baldwin purchases the stock, holds it for one year, and then sells it for $32, what is his total gain? (Ignore brokerage fees and taxes.)
b. If Mr. Baldwin purchases the warrants and converts them to common stock in one year, what is his total gain if the market price of common shares is actually $32? (Ignore brokerage fees and taxes.)
c. Repeat **a** and **b** assuming that the market price of the stock in one year is (1) $30 and (2) $28.
d. Discuss the two alternatives and the tradeoffs associated with them.

14-22 LG 6 **Options profits and losses** For each of the following *100-share options,* use the underlying stock price at expiration and other information to determine the amount of profit or loss an investor would have had, ignoring brokerage fees.

Option	Type of option	Cost of option	Striking price per share	Underlying stock price per share at expiration
A	Call	$200	$50	$55
B	Call	350	42	45
C	Put	500	60	50
D	Put	300	35	40
E	Call	450	28	26

14-23 LG 6 Call option Carol Krebs is considering buying 100 shares of Sooner Products, Inc., at $62 per share. Because she has read that the firm will likely soon receive certain large orders from abroad, she expects the price of Sooner to increase to $70 per share. As an alternative, Carol is considering purchase of a call option for 100 shares of Sooner at a striking price of $60. The 90-day option will cost $600. Ignore any brokerage fees or dividends.

a. What will Carol's profit be on the stock transaction if its price does rise to $70 and she sells?
b. How much will Carol earn on the option transaction if the underlying stock price rises to $70?
c. How high must the stock price rise for Carol to break even on the option transaction?
d. Compare, contrast, and discuss the relative profit and risk from the stock and the option transactions.

14-24 LG 6 Put option Ed Martin, the pension fund manager for Stark Corporation, is considering purchase of a put option in anticipation of a price decline in the stock of Carlisle, Inc. The option to sell 100 shares of Carlisle, Inc., at any time during the next 90 days at a striking price of $45 can be purchased for $380. The stock of Carlisle is currently selling for $46 per share.

a. Ignoring any brokerage fees or dividends, what profit or loss will Ed make if he buys the option, and the lowest price of Carlisle, Inc., stock during the 90 days is $46, $44, $40, and $35?
b. What effect would the fact that the price of Carlisle's stock slowly rose from its initial $46 level to $55 at the end of 90 days have on Ed's purchase?
c. In light of your findings, discuss the potential risks and returns from using put options to attempt to profit from an anticipated decline in share price.

Chapter 14 Case Financing L. Rashid Company's chemical-waste-disposal system

L. Rashid Company, a rapidly growing chemical processor, needs to raise $3 million in external funds to finance the acquisition of a new chemical-waste-disposal system. After carefully analyzing alternative financing sources, Denise McMahon, the firm's vice-president of finance, reduced the financing possibilities to three alternatives: (1) debt, (2) debt with warrants, and (3) a financial lease. The key terms of each of these financing alternatives are given below.

Debt The firm can borrow the full $3 million from First Shreveport Bank. The bank will charge 12 percent annual interest and require annual end-of-year payments of $1,249,050 over the next three years. The disposal system will be depreciated under MACRS using a three year recovery period. (See Table 3.6 on page 83 for the applicable depreciation percentages.) The firm will pay $45,000 at the end of each year for a service contract that covers all maintenance costs; insurance and other costs will be borne by the firm. The firm plans to keep the equipment and use it beyond its three-year recovery period.

Debt with Warrants The firm can borrow the full $3 million from Southern National Bank. The bank will charge 10 percent annual interest and will, in addition, require a grant of 50,000 warrants, each allowing the purchase of two shares of the firm's stock for $30 per share any time during the next 10 years. The stock is currently selling for $28 per share, and the warrants are estimated to have a market value of $1 each. The price (market value) of the debt with the warrants attached is estimated to equal the $3 million initial loan principal. The annual end-of-year payments on this loan will be $1,206,345 over the next three years. Depreciation, maintenance, and insurance will have the same costs and treatments under this alternative as those described above for the straight debt financing alternative.

Financial Lease The waste-disposal system can be leased from First International Capital. The lease will require annual end-of-year payments of $1,200,000 over the next three years. All maintenance costs will be paid by the lessor; insurance and other costs will be borne by the lessee.

The lessee will exercise its option to purchase the system for $220,000 at termination of the lease at the end of three years.

Denise decided to first determine which of the debt financing alternatives—debt or debt with warrants—would least burden the firm's cash flows over the next three years. In this regard, she felt that very few, if any, warrants would be exercised during this period. Once the best debt financing alternative was found, Denise planned to use lease-versus-purchase analysis to evaluate it in light of the lease alternative. The firm is in the 40 percent bracket, and its after-tax cost of debt would be 7 percent under the debt alternative and 6 percent under the debt with warrants alternative.

Required

a. Under the debt with warrants alternative, find:
  (1) Straight debt value.
  (2) Implied price of *all* warrants.
  (3) Implied price of *each* warrant.
  (4) Theoretical value of a warrant.

b. On the basis of your findings in **a**, do you think the price of the debt with warrants is too high or too low? Explain.

c. Assuming that the firm can raise the needed funds under the specified terms, which debt financing alternative—debt or debt with warrants—would you recommend in view of your findings above? Explain.

d. For the purchase alternative, financed as recommended in **c**, calculate the following:
  (1) The annual interest expense deductible for tax purposes for each of the next three years.
  (2) The after-tax cash outflows resulting from the purchase for each of the next three years.
  (3) The present value of the cash outflows using the appropriate discount rate.

e. For the lease alternative, calculate the following:
  (1) The after-tax cash outflows for each of the next three years.
  (2) The present value of the cash outflows using the appropriate discount rate applied in **d(3)**.

f. Compare the present values of the cash outflow streams for the purchase [in **d(3)**] and lease [in **e(2)**] alternatives, and determine which would be preferable. Explain and discuss your recommendation.

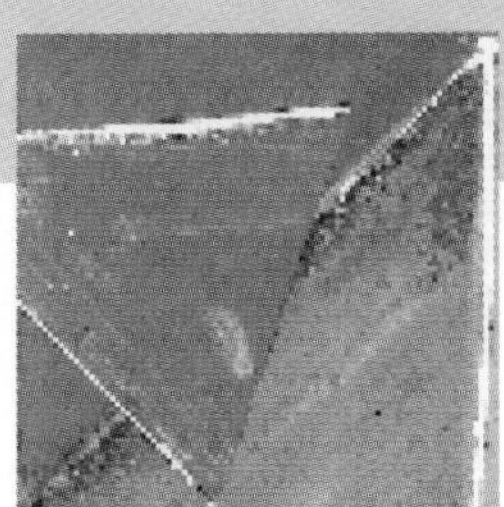

INTEGRATIVE CASE V
LONESTAR ENTERPRISES

Lonestar Enterprises, located in Dallas, Texas, began as a small radio station and in 1979 used a sizable loan to purchase a much larger company that is involved in the exterminating business. Net earnings have risen continuously through 1994, 12 years since Lonestar Enterprises first went public. Currently, the firm's equity base is quite small in comparison to the amount of debt financing on its books. The company is also doing well in its media, wallcovering, and burglary and fire protection systems businesses. Most important, the exterminating business—benefiting from wider markets, new customers, and higher fees—is performing magnificently. In the fiscal year ended June 30, 1994, gross income at Lonestar Enterprises rose 17 percent, while profits were held down somewhat by start-up costs in several new businesses.

The biggest factor in anticipating future gains is The Exterminator, Inc., a large termite and pest control organization, which was acquired in September 1984. Sales have grown over the first decade from $37 million to $108 million, accounting for 65 percent of Lonestar's revenues and 64 percent of its profits in fiscal 1994.

The Exterminator is expanding its operations and expects eventually to have a national network capable of handling the needs of any client. If The Exterminator achieves the same degree of market penetration on a national basis as it has achieved in Louisiana and Florida, it will be a $500 million a year business.

The second largest contributor to Lonestar Enterprises' profits is the media division. Lonestar began as a small radio station, which provided its basis for expansion into other fields such as television stations and cable television.

Lonestar currently owns three television stations in Texas, all of which have provided substantial revenues in the past few years. It is also the leading dealer in cable television in the southwestern United States. The cable television market is specialized, and Lonestar's experience and reputation have secured the company's position as a frontrunner in this field.

Another source of revenue is the Textura subsidiary, currently the nation's largest distributor of wallcovering. Textura is 75 years old and operates in 34 states and in Mexico. Wallcovering demand for redecorating is not subject to the uncertainties of the building cycle and provides the stability of diversification.

Lonestar Enterprises also sells burglary and fire protection systems for houses and commercial establishments through its newest division. The firm's electronics background in the media division helped to foster the growth of the burglary and fire protection division. This field is growing rapidly—the number of major markets served has expanded from 14 in December 1993 to 25 by September 1994, with nine more to be added in 1995. This activity is expected to account for over 12 percent of total revenues within a few years, greatly enhancing the firm's profitability.

Capital outlays have approximated $11 million in each of the past two fiscal years, but higher expansion levels are likely in the near future and are expected to require an additional $23 million of financing.

A few years ago, Lonestar's long-term debt equaled 85 percent of total capital, but debt has since been reduced to 70 percent of total capital. The debt carries an average interest rate of 11.7 percent before taxes. The debt reduction was partially financed through issuance of $7.7 million of 10 percent (annual dividend) preferred stock. On June 30, 1994, current assets were $55 million, current liabilities totaled $21 million, and net working capital was $34 million. Earnings before interest and taxes (EBIT) for the 1994 fiscal year amounted to $20 million. Because of the start-up costs of the expansion, the firm expects its EBIT to remain at the $20 million level for the next few years. The firm is in the 40 percent tax bracket.

Currently, the directors must decide upon a method of financing the $23 million expansion. The directors are primarily interested in an equity financing plan, since funds could be obtained without incurring added mandatory interest payments that would result in greater risk. Additional equity would allow Lonestar Enterprises to avoid restrictive covenants that are often tied to debt financing and would provide a more flexible foundation from which debt could be issued when interest rates fall. The decision, however, could result in lowering earnings per share (EPS) as well as diluting the current stockholders' control of the company. Jonathan Marks, the chief financial officer, has developed a number of capital structure alternatives (shown in Table 1 on page 605) and has presented them to the executive committee. He expects additional debt to have a before-tax cost of 11.7 percent, and additional preferred stock will pay a 10 percent annual dividend. The committee must now weigh the advantages, costs, and risks of each plan.

Required

a. Discuss the level of financial leverage associated with each plan.

b. Discuss the overall advantages of equity financing for this firm at this time.

c. Discuss the advantages and disadvantages of selling preferred stock.

d. (1) Discuss the advantages and disadvantages of selling common stock (be sure to discuss EPS effects).
(2) Explain how the firm's dividend policy might affect its ability to sell new common stock.

e. (1) Marks is also considering a rights offering to raise equity funds. With rights the price of the common stock is $50 per share, the subscription price per share is $43.50, and nine rights are required to purchase a share of stock. Determine the theoretical value of a right.
(2) Discuss the advantages and disadvantages of the proposed rights offering versus the public sale of new common stock.

f. (1) Calculate the (a) debt ratio, (b) times interest earned ratio, and (c) fixed-payment coverage ratio (assuming no principal repayments) for the current as well as each alternative capital structure.
(2) Use your finding in (1) to compare and contrast the financial risk of each alternative capital structure.

g. Recommend how Lonestar should finance its $23 million need. Justify your recommendation in light of the alternatives.

TABLE 1

CAPITAL STRUCTURE ALTERNATIVES

Capital structures	Amount (millions)	Percent of total capital
Current Structure		
Long-term debt	$ 53.9	70.0%
Preferred stock	7.7	10.0
Common stock equity (906,000 shares)	15.4	20.0
Total capital	$ 77.0	100.0%
Structure A		
Long-term debt	$ 70.0	70.0%
Preferred stock	10.0	10.0
Common stock equity (998,000 shares)	20.0	20.0
Total capital	$100.0	100.0%
Structure B		
Long-term debt	$ 53.9	53.9%
Preferred stock	7.7	7.7
Common stock equity (1,366,000 shares)	38.4	38.4
Total capital	$100.0	100.0%
Structure C		
Long-term debt	$ 53.9	53.9%
Preferred stock	30.7	30.7
Common stock equity (906,000 shares)	15.4	15.4
Total capital	$100.0	100.0%
Structure D		
Long-term debt	$ 53.9	53.9%
Preferred stock	23.0	23.0
Common stock equity (1,060,000 shares)	23.1	23.1
Total capital	$100.0	100.0%

part VI

Short-term financial decisions

CHAPTERS IN THIS PART

chapter 15

Financial planning

LEARNING GOALS

 Understand the financial planning process, including the role of and interrelationship between long-term (strategic) financial plans and short-term (operating) plans.

 Discuss the cash planning process, the role of sales forecasts, and the procedures for preparing the cash budget.

 Describe the cash budget evaluation process, procedures for coping with uncertainty, and the issue of cash flow within the month.

 Prepare a pro forma income statement using both the percent-of-sales method and a breakdown of costs and expenses into their fixed and variable components.

 Explain the procedures used to develop a pro forma balance sheet using the judgmental approach and the role and use of the plug figure—external funds required—in this process.

 Describe the weaknesses of the simplified approaches to pro forma preparation and the common uses of pro forma financial statements.

Financial planning is an essential part of any company's financial strategy. Planning statements such as cash budgets and pro forma statements provide a road map to guide the company toward its objectives. And although accrual-based statements are a good starting place, the company's survival depends on cash. Cash planning is the absolute backbone of the company. Without it, you don't know when you have enough cash to support operations or when you need bank financing. Companies that continually have cash shortages and need last-minute loans may discover that it's very hard to find a bank that will lend.

Financial planning for the Charlotte Hornets is not that different from planning in any other business except that we are extremely seasonal. Most of our cash inflow occurs from spring to fall, from season ticket renewals and general ticket sales, with heavy expenditures from fall to spring. The Hornets have very high season ticket sales—about 90 percent!—creating a predictable annual pattern of cash surplus followed by negative cash flow.

Our basic planning statements include the cash budget, cash flow projections, and pro forma income statement and balance sheet. The cash budget covers the next 12 months and is updated each month. The cash flow projections cover the following

Cash planning is the absolute backbone of the company.

three years; they are revised quarterly. We use cash rather than accrual statements to plan because our cash swings are so significant, and we prepare budgets in the spring and early summer from plans submitted by each department. We use zero-based budgeting to ensure that each prior expense is still needed in the coming year. We take a pragmatic approach and use actual expenditures and needs rather than historical percentages.

Like any industry, we have to factor both external and internal uncertainties into our planning process. External factors include the general economic situation, inflation rates, current and expected interest rates, tax laws, and cost increases. For example, in 1993 the tax deductibility of business entertainment expenses changed. This could significantly affect our cash flow because about 70 percent of our season ticket holders are businesses.

Some aspects of financial planning are relatively easy. Revenue and receipts from ticket sales are generally predictable. More difficult are the amount of advertising sales and the timing of ad receipts. With player salaries we consider all existing player contracts, those we expect to renegotiate, the player draft, the going rate for draft picks, and the National Basketball Association players' salary cap. To help management negotiate salaries more effectively, I use present-value calculations to analyze various payment plans. For example, some players get paid once a year, and others get paid twice a month. Ideally, we want a fairly steady payment stream, but we can't always control that.

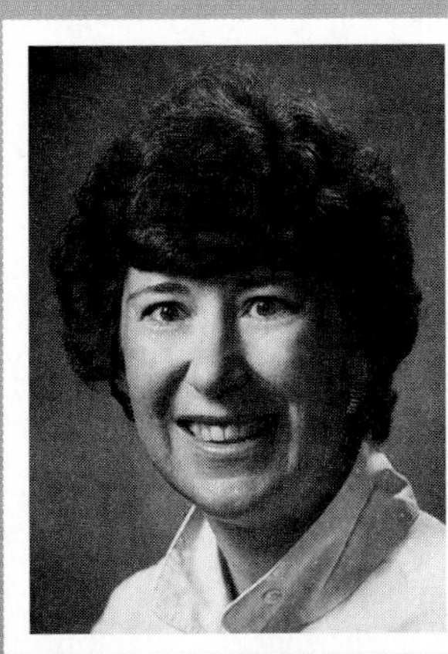

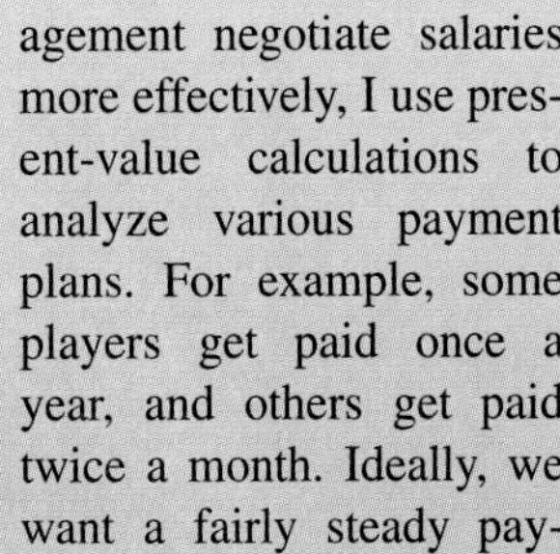

Then I develop one rather conservative scenario—I call it the "worst likely" case—and include a few notes on possible significant improvements on it, such as the financial impact of reaching the playoffs. I monitor budgets very closely, comparing budgeted to actual results every month. Overall, our planning process has worked well; our actual numbers are very close to budget.

Good financial planning requires common sense. First, you have to develop a broad base of business experience; then you look at how your company will be affected by external and internal forces; you can't view finance as an isolated area. It's not enough to put together a technically correct budget—if you can't evaluate the validity of the input, the numbers may be meaningless.

Shoon Ledyard, a Certified Public Accountant, became Controller of the Charlotte Hornets in 1989 after five years in public accounting. Ms. Ledyard received a B.A. in Mathematics from St. Andrews Presbyterian College and a B.S. in Accounting from the University of North Carolina at Charlotte.

The financial planning process

Firms use financial plans to guide their actions toward achievement of immediate and long-term goals. Why do lenders—present and prospective—frequently require submission of these plans by the firm? Before reading on, spend a few moments answering this question.

FINANCIAL PLANNING IS AN IMPORTANT ASPECT OF THE FIRM'S OPERATION AND LIVELIhood, since it provides road maps for guiding, coordinating, and controlling the firm's actions to achieve its objectives. Two key aspects of the financial planning process are *cash planning* and *profit planning.* Cash planning involves the preparation of the firm's cash budget; profit planning is usually done by means of pro forma financial statements. These statements not only are useful for internal financial planning but also are routinely required by present and prospective lenders.

financial planning process
Planning that begins with long-term (strategic) financial plans that in turn guide the formulation of short-term (operating) plans and budgets.

The **financial planning process** begins with long-term, or strategic, financial plans that in turn guide the formulation of short-term, or operating, plans and budgets. Generally, the short-term plans and budgets implement the firm's long-term strategic objectives. The major emphasis in this chapter is on short-term financial plans and budgets; the following three chapters in this part focus on the financial decisions involved in implementation of the firm's short-term financial plans. Here we begin with a few comments on long-term financial plans.

Long-term (strategic) financial plans

long-term (strategic) financial plans
Planned long-term financial actions and the anticipated financial impact of those actions.

Long-term (strategic) financial plans are planned long-term financial actions and the anticipated financial impact of those actions. Such plans tend to cover periods ranging from 2 to 10 years. The use of five-year strategic plans, which are periodically revised as significant new information becomes available, is common. Generally, firms that are subject to high degrees of operating uncertainty, relatively short production cycles, or both tend to use shorter planning horizons. Long-term financial plans are part of an integrated strategic plan that, along with production, marketing, and other plans, use a common set of assumptions and objectives to guide the firm toward achievement of its strategic goals. They consider proposed fixed-asset outlays, research and development activities, marketing and product development actions, capital structure, and major sources of financing. Also included would be termination of existing projects, product lines, or lines of business; repayment or retirement of outstanding debts; and any planned acquisitions. Such plans tend to be supported by a series of annual budgets and profit plans.

Short-term (operating) financial plans

short-term (operating) financial plans
Planned short-term financial actions and the anticipated financial impact of those actions.

Short-term (operating) financial plans are planned short-term financial actions and the anticipated financial impact of those actions. These plans most often cover a one- to two-year period. Key inputs include the sales forecast and various forms of operating and financial data. Key outputs include a number of operating budgets, the cash budget, and pro forma financial statements. The short-term financial planning process, from the initial sales forecast through the development of the cash budget and pro forma income statement and balance sheet, is presented in the flow diagram in Figure 15.1.

From the sales forecast are developed production plans that take into account lead (preparation) times and include estimates of the required types and quantities of raw materials. Using the production plans, the firm can estimate direct labor requirements, factory overhead outlays, and operating expenses. Once these estimates have been made, the firm's pro forma income statement and cash budget can be prepared. With the basic inputs—pro forma income statement, cash budget, fixed-asset outlay plan, long-term financing plan, and current-period balance sheet—the pro forma balance sheet can finally be developed. Throughout the remainder of this chapter we will concentrate on the key outputs of the short-term financial planning process: the cash budget, the pro forma income statement, and the pro forma balance sheet. Although they are not specifically discussed in this chapter, it is important to recognize that electronic spreadsheets (see Appendix C) such as Lotus 1–2–3, Excel, and QuattroPro, are widely used to streamline the process of preparing and evaluating these short-term financial planning statements.

FIGURE 15.1
The short-term (operating) financial planning process

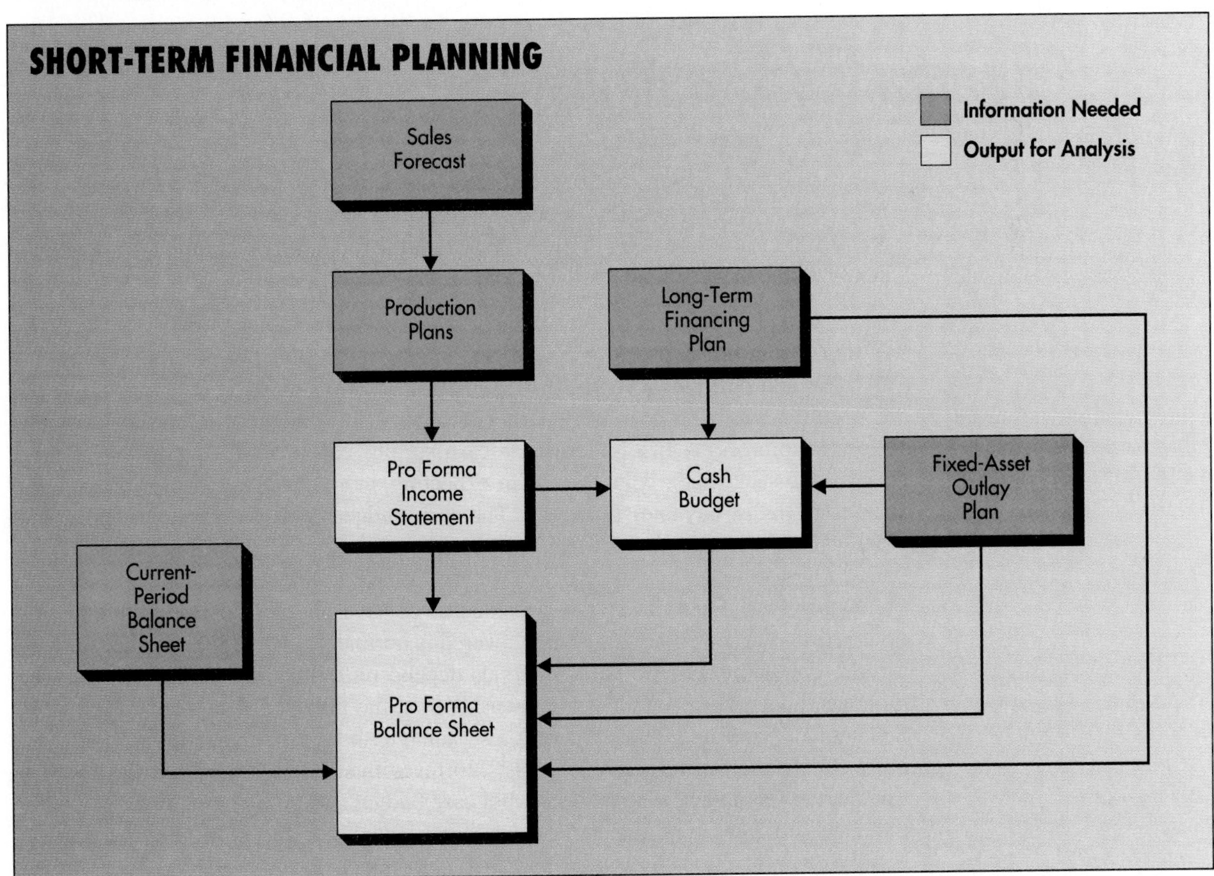

CONCEPT IN PRACTICE

Financial Planners Hope for the Best but Prepare for the Worst

What would you do if your business was bombed? Just dial Comdisco Disaster Recovery Services, Inc., a firm dedicated to helping managers find backup office locations, telephone and computer support, and even trauma counseling for shocked employees when disaster strikes. In early 1993, when a terrorist bomb blast disabled New York's World Trade Center for several months, Comdisco helped Fiduciary Trust Company—whose offices, computers, and corporate records were inside the disabled tower—open for business the very next day after the bombing. Even when catastrophe seems unlikely, effective disaster planning is a critical component of financial planning because a business that loses access to its corporate and human resources won't survive for long.

CONCEPTS IN REVIEW

15-1 What is the *financial planning process?* Define, compare, and contrast *long-term (strategic) financial plans* and *short-term (operating) financial plans.*

15-2 Which three statements result as part of the short-term (operating) financial planning process? Describe the flow of information from the sales forecast through the preparation of these statements.

Cash planning: Cash budgets

The cash budget allows the firm to forecast its short-term cash requirements, typically over a year divided into monthly intervals. Why is such a forecast important, even for the firm that's certain that it will have an annual cash surplus? Take a few moments to answer this question before reading on.

cash budget (cash forecast)
A statement of the firm's planned inflows and outflows of cash that is used to estimate its short-term cash requirements.

THE **CASH BUDGET,** OR **CASH FORECAST,** IS A STATEMENT OF THE FIRM'S PLANNED INflows and outflows of cash. It is used by the firm to estimate its short-term cash requirements. The firm gives particular attention to planning for surplus cash and for cash shortages. A firm expecting a cash surplus can plan short-term investments (marketable securities), whereas a firm expecting shortages in cash must arrange for short-term (notes payable) financing. The cash budget gives the financial manager a clear view of the timing of the firm's expected cash inflows and outflows over a given period.

Typically, the cash budget is designed to cover a one-year period, although any time period is acceptable. The period covered is normally divided into smaller time intervals. The number and type of intervals depend on the nature of the business. The more seasonal and uncertain a firm's cash flows, the greater the number of intervals. Since many firms are confronted with a seasonal cash flow pattern, the cash budget is quite often presented on a monthly basis. Firms with stable patterns of cash flow may use quarterly or annual time intervals. If a cash budget is developed for a period greater than one year, fewer time intervals may be warranted due to the difficulty and uncertainty of forecasting sales and other related cash items.

The sales forecast

sales forecast

The prediction of the firm's sales over a given period, based on external and/or internal data, and used as the key input to the short-term financial planning process.

The key input to the short-term financial planning process and therefore any cash budget is the firm's **sales forecast.** This is the prediction of the firm's sales over a given period and is ordinarily furnished to the financial manager by the marketing department. On the basis of this forecast, the financial manager estimates the monthly cash flows that will result from projected sales receipts and from production-related, inventory-related, and sales-related outlays. The manager also determines the level of fixed assets required and the amount of financing, if any, needed to support the forecast level of production and sales. In practice, obtaining good data is the most difficult aspect of forecasting; most forecasting techniques are relatively straightforward and easily automated.[1] The sales forecast may be based on an analysis of external or internal data or on a combination of the two.

CONCEPT IN PRACTICE

Baseball, Hot Dogs, Apple Pie, and . . . Cash Planning

On May 8, 1993, Major League Baseball announced a new six-year deal with two TV networks, ABC and NBC, to telecast baseball games for which each party would pay $14 million toward broadcasting and then share advertising profits from TV commercial revenues. Under the league's existing contract with CBS, the network pays a flat fee to the league for broadcast rights. If the new profit-sharing plan flies, then the league stands to gain only $158 million in 1994 from advertising sales, $107 million less than in the previous year. Owners of major league baseball teams are miffed by the lower returns because national broadcast and cable rights account for about 25 percent of baseball's total revenues. With many teams strapped for cash, 1994 is shaping up to be a lousy year to ask for a raise.

EXTERNAL FORECASTS

external forecast

A sales forecast based on the relationships observed between the firm's sales and certain key external economic indicators.

An **external forecast** is based on the relationships that can be observed between the firm's sales and certain key external economic indicators such as the gross domestic product (GDP), new housing starts, and disposable personal income. Forecasts containing these indicators are readily available. The rationale for this approach is that since the firm's sales are often closely related to some aspect of overall national economic activity, a forecast of economic activity should provide insight into future sales.

INTERNAL FORECASTS

internal forecast

A sales forecast based on a build-up, or consensus, of forecasts through the firm's own sales channels.

Internal forecasts are based on a build-up, or consensus, of sales forecasts through the firm's own sales channels. Typically, the firm's salespeople in the field are asked to estimate the number of units of each type of product that they expect to sell in the coming year. These forecasts are collected and totaled by the sales manager, who may adjust the figures using his or her own knowledge of specific markets or of the salesperson's forecasting ability. Finally, adjustments may be made for additional internal factors, such as production capabilities.

[1] A discussion of the calculation of the various forecasting techniques, such as regression, moving averages, and exponential smoothing, is not included in this text. For a description of the technical side of forecasting, refer to a basic statistics, econometrics, or management science text.

COMBINED FORECASTS

Firms generally use a combination of external and internal forecast data to make the final sales forecast. The internal data provide insight into sales expectations, and the external data provide a means of adjusting these expectations to take into account general economic factors. The nature of the firm's product also often affects the mix and types of forecasting methods used.

Preparing the cash budget

The general format of the cash budget is presented in Table 15.1. We will discuss each of its components individually.

CASH RECEIPTS

cash receipts
All items from which the firm receives cash inflows during a given financial period.

Cash receipts includes all items from which cash inflows result in any given financial period. The most common components of cash receipts are cash sales, collections of accounts receivable, and other cash receipts.

EXAMPLE

Coulson Industries, a defense contractor, is developing a cash budget for October, November, and December. Coulson's sales in August and September were $100,000 and $200,000, respectively. Sales of $400,000, $300,000, and $200,000 have been forecast for October, November, and December, respectively. Historically, 20 percent of the firm's sales have been for cash, 50 percent have generated accounts receivable collected after one month, and the remaining 30 percent have generated accounts receivable collected after two months. Bad-debt expenses (uncollectible accounts) have been negligible.[2] In December, the firm will receive a $30,000 dividend from stock in a subsidiary. The schedule of expected cash receipts for the company is presented in Table 15.2. It contains the following items.

TABLE 15.1

THE GENERAL FORMAT OF THE CASH BUDGET

	Jan.	Feb.	...	Nov.	Dec.
Cash receipts					
Less: Cash disbursements	____	____	...	____	____
Net cash flow					
Add: Beginning cash	____	↗____	↗...	↗____	↗____
Ending cash					
Less: Minimum cash balance	____	____	...	____	____
Required total financing			...		
Excess cash balance			...		

[2]Normally, it would be expected that the collection percentages would total slightly less than 100 percent to reflect the fact that some of the accounts receivable would be uncollectible. In this example the sum of the collection percentages is 100 percent (20% + 50% + 30%), which reflects the fact that all sales are assumed to be collected, since bad debts are said to be negligible.

TABLE 15.2

A SCHEDULE OF PROJECTED CASH RECEIPTS FOR COULSON INDUSTRIES ($000)

Forecast sales	Aug. $100	Sept. $200	Oct. $400	Nov. $300	Dec. $200
Cash sales (.20)	$ 20	$ 40	$ 80	$ 60	$ 40
Collections of A/R:					
Lagged one month (.50)		50	100	200	150
Lagged two months (.30)			30	60	120
Other cash receipts					30
Total cash receipts			$210	$320	$340

Forecast sales This initial entry is *merely informational.* It is provided as an aid in calculating other sales-related items.

Cash sales The cash sales shown for each month represent 20 percent of the total sales forecast for that month.

Collections of A/R These entries represent the collection of accounts receivable (A/R) resulting from sales in earlier months.

Lagged one month These figures represent sales made in the preceding month that generated accounts receivable collected in the current month. Since 50 percent of the current month's sales are collected one month later, the collections of accounts receivable with a one-month lag shown for September, October, November, and December represent 50 percent of the sales in August, September, October, and November, respectively.

Lagged two months These figures represent sales made two months earlier that generated accounts receivable collected in the current month. Since 30 percent of sales are collected two months later, the collections with a two-month lag shown for October, November, and December represent 30 percent of the sales in August, September, and October, respectively.

Other cash receipts These are cash receipts that are expected to result from sources other than sales. Items such as interest received, dividends received, proceeds from the sale of equipment, stock and bond sale proceeds, and lease receipts may show up here. For Coulson Industries the only other cash receipt is the $30,000 dividend due in December.

Total cash receipts This figure represents the total of all the cash receipt items listed for each month in the cash receipt schedule. In the case of Coulson Industries, we are concerned only with October, November, and December; the total cash receipts for these months are shown in Table 15.2. ■

CASH DISBURSEMENTS

cash disbursements
All cash outlays by the firm during a given financial period.

Cash disbursements include all outlays of cash in the period covered. The most common cash disbursements are

Cash purchases
Payments of accounts payable
Rent (and lease) payments
Wages and salaries
Tax payments
Fixed-asset outlays
Interest payments
Cash dividend payments
Principal payments (loans)
Repurchases or retirements of stock

It is important to recognize that *depreciation and other noncash charges are NOT included in the cash budget* because they merely represent a scheduled write-off of an earlier cash outflow. The impact of depreciation, as was noted in Chapter 3, is reflected in the level of cash outflow represented by the tax payments.

EXAMPLE

Coulson Industries has gathered the following data needed for the preparation of a cash disbursements schedule for the months of October, November, and December.

Purchases The firm's purchases represent 70 percent of sales. Ten percent of this amount is paid in cash, 70 percent is paid in the month immediately following the month of purchase, and the remaining 20 percent is paid two months following the month of purchase.[3]

Rent payments Rent of $5,000 will be paid each month.

Wages and salaries The firm's wages and salaries can be estimated by adding 10 percent of its monthly sales to the $8,000 fixed-cost figure.

Tax payments Taxes of $25,000 must be paid in December.

Fixed-asset outlays New machinery costing $130,000 will be purchased and paid for in November.

Interest payments An interest payment of $10,000 is due in December.

Cash dividend payments Cash dividends of $20,000 will be paid in October.

Principal payments (loans) A $20,000 principal payment is also due in December.

Repurchases or retirements of stock No repurchase or retirement of stock is expected during the October–December period.

---

[3]Unlike the collection percentages for sales, the total of the payment percentages should equal 100 percent, since it is expected that the firm will pay off all of its accounts payable. In line with this expectation, the percentages for Coulson Industries total 100 percent (10% + 70% + 20%).

TABLE 15.3

A SCHEDULE OF PROJECTED CASH DISBURSEMENTS FOR COULSON INDUSTRIES ($000)

Purchases (.70 × sales)	Aug. $70	Sept. $140	Oct. $280	Nov. $210	Dec. $140
Cash purchases (.10)	$ 7	$ 14	$ 28	$ 21	$ 14
Payments of A/P:					
Lagged one month (.70)		49	98	196	147
Lagged two months (.20)			14	28	56
Rent payments			5	5	5
Wages and salaries			48	38	28
Tax payments					25
Fixed-asset outlays				130	
Interest payments					10
Cash dividend payments			20		
Principal payments					20
Total cash disbursements			$213	$418	$305

The firm's cash disbursements schedule, based on the data above, is presented in Table 15.3. Some items in Table 15.3 are explained in greater detail below.

Purchases This entry is *merely informational.* The figures represent 70 percent of the forecast sales for each month. They have been included to facilitate the calculation of the cash purchases and related payments.

Cash purchases The cash purchases for each month represent 10 percent of the month's purchases.

Payments of A/P These entries represent the payment of accounts payable (A/P) resulting from purchases in earlier months.

Lagged one month These figures represent purchases made in the preceding month that are paid for in the current month. Since 70 percent of the firm's purchases are paid for one month later, the payments lagged one month shown for September, October, November, and December represent 70 percent of the August, September, October, and November purchases, respectively.

Lagged two months These figures represent purchases made two months earlier that are paid for in the current month. Since 20 percent of the firm's purchases are paid for two months later, the payments lagged two months for October, November, and December represent 20 percent of the August, September, and October purchases, respectively.

Wages and salaries These values were obtained by adding $8,000 to 10 percent of the *sales* in each month. The $8,000 represents the salary component; the rest represents wages.

The remaining items on the cash disbursements schedule are self-explanatory. ■

net cash flow

The mathematical difference between the firm's cash receipts and its cash disbursements in each period.

ending cash

The sum of the firm's beginning cash and its net cash flow for the period.

required total financing

Amount of funds needed by the firm if the ending cash for the period is less than the desired minimum cash balance; typically represented by notes payable.

excess cash balance

The (excess) amount available for investment by the firm if the period's ending cash is greater than the desired minimum cash balance; assumed to be invested in marketable securities.

NET CASH FLOW, ENDING CASH, FINANCING, AND EXCESS CASH

A firm's **net cash flow** is found by subtracting the cash disbursements from cash receipts in each period. By adding beginning cash to the firm's net cash flow, the **ending cash** for each period can be found. Finally, subtracting the desired minimum cash balance from ending cash yields the **required total financing** or the **excess cash balance.** If the ending cash is less than the minimum cash balance, *financing* is required. Such financing is typically viewed as short-term and therefore represented by notes payable. If the ending cash is greater than the minimum cash balance, *excess cash* exists. Any excess cash is assumed to be invested in a liquid, short-term, interest-paying vehicle and therefore is included in marketable securities.

EXAMPLE

Table 15.4 presents Coulson Industries' cash budget, based on the cash receipt and cash disbursement data already developed for the firm. Coulson's end-of-September cash balance was $50,000, and the company wishes to maintain as a reserve for unexpected needs a minimum cash balance of $25,000.

For Coulson Industries to maintain its required $25,000 ending cash balance, it will need to have borrowed $76,000 in November and $41,000 in December. In the month of October the firm will have an excess cash balance of $22,000, which can be held in an interest-earning marketable security. The required total financing figures in the cash budget refer to *how much will have to be owed at the end of the month;* they do *not* represent the monthly changes in borrowing.

The monthly changes in borrowing as well as excess cash can be found by further analyzing the cash budget in Table 15.4. It can be seen that in October the $50,000 beginning cash, which becomes $47,000 after the $3,000 net cash outflow is deducted, results in a $22,000 excess cash balance once the $25,000 minimum cash is deducted. In November the $76,000 of required total financing resulted from the $98,000 net cash outflow less the $22,000 of excess cash from October. The $41,000 of required total financing in December resulted from reducing November's $76,000 of required total financing by the $35,000 of net cash inflow during December. Summarizing, the financial activities for each month would be as follows:

October: Invest $22,000 of excess cash.

November: Liquidate $22,000 of excess cash and borrow $76,000.

December: Repay $35,000 of amount borrowed. ■

Evaluating the cash budget

The cash budget provides the firm with figures indicating the expected ending cash balance, which can be analyzed to determine whether a cash shortage or surplus is expected to result in each of the months covered by the forecast. Coulson Industries can expect a surplus of $22,000 in October, a deficit of $76,000 in November, and a deficit of $41,000 in December. Each of these figures is based on the internally imposed requirement of a $25,000 minimum cash balance and represents the total balance at the end of the month.

The excess cash balance in October can be invested in marketable securities. The deficits in November and December will have to be financed, typically, by short-term borrowing (notes payable). Since it may be necessary for the firm to borrow up to

TABLE 15.4

A CASH BUDGET FOR COULSON INDUSTRIES ($000)

	Oct.	Nov.	Dec.
Total cash receipts[a]	$210	$320	$340
Less: Total cash disbursements[b]	213	418	305
Net cash flow	$ (3)	$ (98)	$ 35
Add: Beginning cash	50	47	(51)
Ending cash	$ 47	$ (51)	$ (16)
Less: Minimum cash balance	25	25	25
Required total financing (notes payable)[c]	—	$ 76	$ 41
Excess cash balance (marketable securities)[d]	$ 22	—	—

[a]From Table 15.2.

[b]From Table 15.3.

[c]Values are placed in this line when the ending cash is less than the desired minimum cash balance, since in this instance financing is required. These amounts are typically financed short-term and therefore are represented by notes payable.

[d]Values are placed in this line when the ending cash is greater than the desired minimum cash balance, since in this instance an excess cash balance exists. These amounts are typically assumed to be invested short-term and therefore are represented by marketable securities.

$76,000 for the three-month period evaluated, the financial manager should be sure that a line of credit is established or some other arrangement made to ensure the availability of these funds. The manager will usually request or arrange to borrow more than the maximum financing indicated in the cash budget. This is necessary because of the uncertainty of the ending cash values, which are based on the sales forecast and other forecast values.

Coping with uncertainty in the cash budget

Aside from care in preparation of sales forecasts and other estimates included in the cash budget, there are two ways of coping with the uncertainty of the cash budget.[4] One is to prepare several cash budgets—one based on a pessimistic forecast, one based on the most likely forecast, and a third based on an optimistic forecast. An evaluation of these cash flows allows the financial manager to determine the amount of financing that is necessary to cover the most adverse situation. The use of several cash budgets, each based on differing assumptions, should also give the financial manager a sense of the riskiness of alternatives so that he or she can make more intelligent short-term financial decisions. The sensitivity or "what if" analysis approach is often used to analyze cash flows under a variety of possible circumstances. Computers and electronic spreadsheets (see Appendix C) are commonly used to greatly simplify the process of performing sensitivity analysis.

[4]The term *uncertainty* is used here to refer to the variability of the cash flow outcomes that may actually occur. A thorough discussion of risk and uncertainty is presented in Chapter 6.

EXAMPLE

Table 15.5 presents the summary results of Coulson Industries' cash budget prepared for each month of concern using a pessimistic, most likely, and optimistic estimate of cash receipts and cash disbursements. The most likely estimate is based on the expected outcomes presented earlier in Tables 15.2 through 15.4; the pessimistic and optimistic outcomes are based on the worst and best possible outcomes, respectively. During the month of October, Coulson will need a maximum of $15,000 of financing, while at best it will have a $62,000 excess cash balance available for short-term investment. During November its financing requirement will be between $0 and $185,000. It could experience an excess cash balance of $5,000 during November. The December projections reflect maximum borrowing of $190,000 with a possible excess cash balance of $107,000. By considering the extreme values reflected in the pessimistic and optimistic outcomes, Coulson Industries should be better able to plan cash requirements. For the three-month period, the peak borrowing requirement under the worst circumstances would be $190,000, which happens to be considerably greater than the most likely estimate of $76,000 for this period. ■

A second and much more sophisticated way of coping with uncertainty in the cash budget is *computer simulation.*[5] By simulating the occurrence of sales and other uncertain events, the firm can develop a probability distribution of its ending cash flows for each month. The financial decision maker can then use the probability distribution to determine the amount of financing necessary to provide a desired degree of protection against a cash shortage.

TABLE 15.5

A SENSITIVITY ANALYSIS OF COULSON INDUSTRIES' CASH BUDGET ($000)

	October			November			December		
	Pessimistic	Most likely	Optimistic	Pessimistic	Most likely	Optimistic	Pessimistic	Most likely	Optimistic
Total cash receipts	$160	$210	$285	$ 210	$320	$ 410	$ 275	$340	$422
Less: Total cash disbursements	200	213	248	380	418	467	280	305	320
Net cash flow	$(40)	$ (3)	$ 37	$ (170)	$ (98)	$ (57)	$ (5)	$ 35	$102
Add: Beginning cash	50	50	50	10	47	87	(160)	(51)	30
Ending cash	$ 10	$ 47	$ 87	$ (160)	$ (51)	$ 30	$(165)	$(16)	$132
Less: Minimum cash balance	25	25	25	25	25	25	25	25	25
Required total financing	$ 15	—	—	$ 185	$ 76	—	$ 190	$ 41	—
Excess cash balance	—	$ 22	$ 62	—	—	$ 5	—	—	$107

[5] A more detailed discussion of the use of simulation is included as part of the discussion of capital budgeting under risk in Chapter 9.

Cash flow within the month

Since the cash budget shows cash flows only on a total monthly basis, the information provided by the cash budget is not necessarily adequate for ensuring solvency. A firm must look more closely at its pattern of daily cash receipts and cash disbursements to ensure that adequate cash is available for meeting bills as they come due. The following example illustrates the importance of monitoring daily cash flows.

EXAMPLE

Coulson Industries found its actual pattern of cash receipts and cash disbursements during the month of October to be as shown in Table 15.6. Although the firm begins the month with $50,000 of cash and ends the month with $47,000 in cash, its cash balance is negative at various times within the month. Table 15.6 shows negative cash balances during the periods October 2–11 and October 17–22. The largest deficit, $72,000, occurs on October 4.

Although the cash budget presented in Table 15.4 indicates that Coulson Industries will not require any financing during the month of October, since a $22,000 excess cash balance is expected, a look at the firm's daily cash flows during October shows that it will need additional financing to make payments as they come due. At the maximum, $72,000 is required to meet daily cash flow requirements. ■

The example makes it quite clear that the synchronization of cash flows in the cash budget at month-end does not ensure that the firm will be able to meet daily cash requirements. Since a firm's cash flows are generally quite variable when viewed on a daily basis, effective cash planning requires a look beyond the cash budget. Although Coulson Industries' cash budget (Table 15.4) suggests that it does not need to borrow

TABLE 15.6

DAILY CASH FLOWS DURING OCTOBER FOR COULSON INDUSTRIES ($000)

Date	Amount received	Amount disbursed	Cash balance[a]
10/1	Beginning balance		$50
10/2		$100	− 50
10/4		22	− 72
10/5	$ 65	15	− 22
10/11	74		52
10/12	10	12	50
10/16		40	10
10/17	3	21	− 8
10/22	35		27
10/26	20	1	46
10/29	3		49
10/31		2	47
Total	$210	$213	

[a]These figures represent ending cash balances without any financing.

during October, the firm needs a maximum of $72,000 in additional funds, due to the nonsynchronized daily cash flows. The financial manager must therefore plan and monitor cash flow more frequently than on a monthly basis. The greater the variability of cash flows from day to day, the greater the attention required.

CONCEPTS IN REVIEW

15-3 What is the purpose of the *cash budget?* The key input to the cash budget is the sales forecast. What is the difference between *external* and *internal* forecast data?

15-4 Briefly describe the basic format of the cash budget, beginning with forecast sales and ending with required total financing or excess cash balance.

15-5 How can the two bottom lines of the cash budget be used to determine the firm's short-term borrowing and investment requirements?

15-6 What is the cause of uncertainty in the cash budget? What two techniques can be used to cope with this uncertainty?

15-7 What actions or analysis beyond preparation of the cash budget should the financial manager undertake to ensure that cash is available when needed? Why?

Profit planning: Pro forma statement fundamentals

Profit planning typically involves preparation of a pro forma—projected—income statement and balance sheet. What key inputs would you need to prepare pro forma statements for the coming year? Take a few minutes to answer this question before reading on.

pro forma statements Projected, or forecast, financial statements—income statements and balance sheets.

THE PROFIT-PLANNING PROCESS CENTERS ON THE PREPARATION OF **PRO FORMA STATEments**, which are projected, or forecast, financial statements—income statements and balance sheets. The preparation of these statements requires a careful blending of a number of procedures to account for the revenues, costs, expenses, assets, liabilities, and equity resulting from the firm's anticipated level of operations. The basic steps in this process were shown in the flow diagram presented in Figure 15.1. The financial manager frequently uses one of a number of simplified approaches to estimate the pro forma statements. The most popular approaches are based on the belief that the financial relationships reflected in the firm's historical (past) financial statements will not change in the coming period. The commonly used approaches are presented in subsequent discussions.

Two inputs are required for preparing pro forma statements using the simplified approaches: (1) financial statements for the preceding year and (2) the sales forecast for the coming year. A variety of assumptions must also be made in using simplified approaches. The company that we will use to illustrate the simplified approaches to pro forma preparation is Vectra Manufacturing, which manufactures and sells one product. It has two basic models—model X and model Y. Although each model is produced by the same process, each requires different amounts of raw material and labor.

CONCEPT IN PRACTICE

Is Corporate Reengineering Just a Fancy Phrase for Profit Planning?

Management courses may have introduced you to the quality movement, wherein businesses strive to improve processes for providing goods and services that consistently exceed customer expectations. Corporate reengineering is quite similar, if not synonymous. Developed by MIT computer scientist Michael Hammer and CSC/Index, Inc., reengineering involves focusing business processes on results and customers, not on traditional stovepipe functions like production, finance, marketing, and sales. Such redesigning encourages employees to concentrate externally on customers rather than internally on corporate hierarchy.

But does it work? Reengineered firms like Hallmark Cards, Taco Bell, and Bell Atlantic all answer *yes.* While the transition can be traumatic, companies that successfully implement reengineering plans make significant gains in financial performance measured by costs and profits. It boils down to doing more with less—less time, less money, and fewer people.

Past year's financial statements

The income statement for the firm's 1994 operations is given in Table 15.7. It indicates that Vectra had sales of $100,000, total cost of goods sold of $80,000, net profits before taxes of $9,000, and net profits after taxes of $7,650. The firm paid $4,000 in cash dividends, leaving $3,650 to be transferred to retained earnings. The firm's balance sheet at the end of 1994 is given in Table 15.8.

TABLE 15.7

AN INCOME STATEMENT FOR VECTRA MANUFACTURING FOR THE YEAR ENDED DECEMBER 31, 1994

Sales revenue		
Model X (1,000 units at $20/unit)	$20,000	
Model Y (2,000 units at $40/unit)	80,000	
Total sales		$100,000
Less: Cost of goods sold		
Labor	$28,500	
Material A	8,000	
Material B	5,500	
Overhead	38,000	
Total cost of goods sold		80,000
Gross profits		$ 20,000
Less: Operating expenses		10,000
Operating profits		$ 10,000
Less: Interest expense		1,000
Net profits before taxes		$ 9,000
Less: Taxes (.15 × $9,000)		1,350
Net profits after taxes		$ 7,650
Less: Common stock dividends		4,000
To retained earnings		$ 3,650

TABLE 15.8

A BALANCE SHEET FOR VECTRA MANUFACTURING (DECEMBER 31, 1994)

Assets		Liabilities and equities	
Cash	$ 6,000	Accounts payable	$ 7,000
Marketable securities	4,000	Taxes payable	300
Accounts receivable	13,000	Notes payable	8,300
Inventories	16,000	Other current liabilities	3,400
Total current assets	$39,000	Total current liabilities	$19,000
		Long-term debts	$18,000
Net fixed assets	$51,000	Stockholders' equity	
Total assets	$90,000	Common stock	$30,000
		Retained earnings	$23,000
		Total liabilities and stockholders' equity	$90,000

Sales forecast

Like the cash budget, the key input for the development of pro forma statements is the sales forecast. The sales forecast by model for the coming year, 1995, for Vectra Manufacturing is given in Table 15.9. This forecast is based on both external and internal data. The unit sales prices of the products reflect an increase from $20 to $25 for model X and from $40 to $50 for model Y. These increases are required to cover the firm's anticipated increases in the cost of labor, material, overhead, and operating expenses.

CONCEPT IN PRACTICE

Even a New Crystal Ball Won't Help Aldus's Forecasts

When creating pro forma financial statements, managers often assume that history repeats itself to some extent. However, as Aldus Corporation knows, such assumptions can be risky in this technologically progressive and competitive world. For four straight years this Seattle-based manufacturer of desktop publishing software

TABLE 15.9

1995 SALES FORECAST FOR VECTRA MANUFACTURING

Unit sales	
Model X	1,500
Model Y	1,950
Dollar sales	
Model X ($25/unit)	$ 37,500
Model Y ($50/unit)	97,500
Total	$135,000

appeared on *Business Week*'s list of hot growth companies, with an annual sales growth of 150 percent. In 1991, Aldus's earnings were up 26 percent over 1990. Then Aldus's fortune changed as competition increased in the desktop publishing industry. The firm not only botched a product introduction but incurred heavy sales and operating costs, so by the end of 1992, sales had increased only 4 percent, profits had crashed 70 percent, and stock prices fell from $60 a share in 1991 to around $15 by spring of 1993.

CONCEPT IN REVIEW

15-8 What is the purpose of *pro forma financial statements?* Which of the pro forma statements must be developed first? Why?

Preparing the pro forma income statement

The percent-of-sales method for preparing the pro forma income statement assumes that the relationships between various costs (or expenses) and sales in the coming year will be identical to those in the immediately preceding year. Why does use of this method typically understate the firm's profits when sales are increasing? Spend a few moments answering this question before reading ahead.

percent-of-sales method
A method for developing the pro forma income statement that expresses the cost of goods sold, operating expenses, and interest expense as a percentage of projected sales.

A SIMPLE METHOD FOR DEVELOPING A PRO FORMA INCOME STATEMENT IS TO USE THE **percent-of-sales method.** It forecasts sales and then expresses the cost of goods sold, operating expenses, and interest expense as a percentage of projected sales. The percentages used are likely to be the percentage of sales for these items in the immediately preceding year. For Vectra Manufacturing, these percentages are as follows:

$$\frac{\text{Cost of goods sold}}{\text{Sales}} = \frac{\$80{,}000}{\$100{,}000} = 80.0\%$$

$$\frac{\text{Operating expenses}}{\text{Sales}} = \frac{\$10{,}000}{\$100{,}000} = 10.0\%$$

$$\frac{\text{Interest expense}}{\text{Sales}} = \frac{\$1{,}000}{\$100{,}000} = 1.0\%$$

The dollar values used are taken from the 1994 income statement (Table 15.7).

Applying these percentages to the firm's forecast sales of $135,000, developed in Table 15.9, and assuming that the firm will pay $4,000 in common stock dividends in 1995, results in the pro forma income statement in Table 15.10 on page 626. The expected contribution to retained earnings is $6,327, which represents a considerable increase over $3,650 in the preceding year (Table 15.7).

Considering types of costs and expenses

The technique that is used to prepare the pro forma income statement in Table 15.10 assumes that all the firm's costs (or expenses) are *variable.* This means that the

TABLE 15.10

A PRO FORMA INCOME STATEMENT, USING THE PERCENT-OF-SALES METHOD, FOR VECTRA MANUFACTURING FOR THE YEAR ENDED DECEMBER 31, 1995

Sales revenue	$135,000
Less: Cost of goods sold (.80)	108,000
Gross profits	$ 27,000
Less: Operating expenses (.10)	13,500
Operating profits	$ 13,500
Less: Interest expense (.01)	1,350
Net profits before taxes	$ 12,150
Less: Taxes (.15 × $12,150)	1,823
Net profits after taxes	$ 10,327
Less: Common stock dividends	4,000
To retained earnings	$ 6,327

use of the historical (1994) ratios of cost of goods sold, operating expenses, and interest expense to sales assumes that for a given percentage increase in sales, the same percentage increase in each of these cost (or expense) components will result. For example, as Vectra's sales increased by 35 percent (from $100,000 in 1994 to $135,000 projected for 1995), its cost of goods sold also increased by 35 percent (from $80,000 in 1994 to $108,000 projected for 1995). On the basis of this assumption, the firm's net profits before taxes also increased by 35 percent (from $9,000 in 1994 to $12,150 projected for 1995).

In the approach just illustrated, the broader implication is that since the firm has no fixed costs, it will not receive the benefits often resulting from them.[6] Therefore the use of past cost and expense ratios generally tends to understate profits when sales are increasing and overstate profits when sales are decreasing. Clearly, if the firm has fixed operating and financial costs, when sales increase these costs do not change, thereby resulting in increased profits; when sales decline, these costs, by remaining unchanged, tend to lower profits. The best way to adjust for the presence of fixed costs when using a simplified approach for pro forma income statement preparation is to break the firm's historical costs and expenses into *fixed* and *variable components* and make the forecast using this relationship.[7]

[6]The potential returns as well as risks resulting from use of fixed (operating and financial) costs to create "leverage" are discussed in Chapter 11. The key point to recognize here is that when the firm's revenue is *increasing,* fixed costs can magnify returns.

[7]The application of *regression analysis*—a statistically based technique for measuring the relationship between variables—to past cost data as they relate to past sales could be used to develop equations that recognize the fixed and variable nature of each cost. Such equations could be employed in preparing the pro forma income statement from the sales forecast. The use of the regression approach in pro forma income statement preparation is widespread, and many computer software packages for use in pro forma preparation rely on this technique. Expanded discussions of the application of this technique can be found in most second-level managerial finance texts.

EXAMPLE

Vectra Manufacturing's last-year (1994) and pro forma (1995) income statements, which are broken into fixed- and variable-cost components, are given below.

Vectra Manufacturing's income statements

	Last year (1994)	Pro forma (1995)
Sales revenue	$100,000	$135,000
Less: Cost of goods sold		
Fixed cost	40,000	40,000
Variable cost (.40 × sales)	40,000	54,000
Gross profits	$ 20,000	$ 41,000
Less: Operating expenses		
Fixed expense	5,000	5,000
Variable expense (.05 × sales)	5,000	6,750
Operating profits	$ 10,000	$ 29,250
Less: Interest expense (all fixed)	1,000	1,000
Net profits before taxes	$ 9,000	$ 28,250
Less: Taxes (.15 × net profits before taxes)	1,350	4,238
Net profits after taxes	$ 7,650	$ 24,012

By breaking Vectra's costs and expenses into fixed and variable components, its pro forma profit is expected to provide a more accurate projection. Had the firm treated all costs as variable, its pro forma (1995) net profits before taxes would equal 9 percent of sales, just as was the case in 1994 ($9,000 net profits before taxes ÷ $100,000 sales). As shown in Table 15.10, by assuming that *all* costs are variable the net profits before taxes would have been $12,150 (.09 × $135,000 projected sales) instead of the $28,250 of net profits before taxes obtained above by using the firm's fixed-cost–variable-cost breakdown. ■

The preceding example should make it clear that a strict application of the percent-of-sales method is a naive approach that assumes that all costs (or expenses) are variable—there are *no* fixed costs. Because nearly all firms have fixed costs, ignoring them in the pro forma income statement preparation process typically results in misstatement of the firm's forecast profit. Therefore, in using a simplified approach to pro forma income statement preparation, it is advisable to consider first breaking down costs and expenses into fixed and variable components. For convenience, the pro forma income statement prepared for Vectra Manufacturing in Table 15.10 was based on the assumption that all costs were variable—which is *not* likely to be the case. Therefore Vectra's projected profits were understated when the percent-of-sales method was used.

CONCEPTS IN REVIEW

15-9 Briefly describe the pro forma income statement preparation process using the *percent-of-sales method.* What are the strengths and weaknesses of this simplified approach?

15-10 Comment on the following statement: "Because nearly all firms have fixed costs, ignoring them in the pro forma income statement preparation process typically results in misstatement of the firm's forecast profit." How can such a "misstatement" be avoided?

Preparing the pro forma balance sheet

The judgmental approach to pro forma balance sheet preparation involves estimating some account values and calculating others, thereby requiring a "plug" figure to bring the statement into balance. If a plug figure must be added to the right side of the firm's pro forma balance sheet, what does it indicate about the firm's financing requirements? Before reading further, spend a few moments answering this question.

judgmental approach
A method for developing the pro forma balance sheet in which the values of certain balance sheet accounts are estimated while others are calculated, using the firm's external financing as a balancing, or "plug," figure.

A NUMBER OF SIMPLIFIED APPROACHES ARE AVAILABLE FOR PREPARING THE PRO FORMA balance sheet. Probably the best and most popular is the judgmental approach.[8] Under the **judgmental approach** for developing the pro forma balance sheet, the values of certain balance sheet accounts are estimated, while others are calculated. When this approach is applied, the firm's external financing is used as a balancing, or "plug," figure. To apply the judgmental approach to prepare Vectra Manufacturing's 1995 pro forma balance sheet, a number of assumptions must be made:

1. A minimum cash balance of $6,000 is desired.
2. Marketable securities are assumed to remain unchanged from their current level of $4,000.
3. Accounts receivable will on average represent 45 days of sales. Since Vectra's annual sales are projected to be $135,000, accounts receivable should average $16,875 (⅛ × $135,000). (Forty-five days expressed fractionally is one-eighth of a year: 45/360 = ⅛.)
4. The ending inventory should remain at a level of about $16,000, of which 25 percent (approximately $4,000) should be raw materials, while the remaining 75 percent (approximately $12,000) should consist of finished goods.
5. A new machine costing $20,000 will be purchased. Total depreciation for the year will be $8,000. Adding the $20,000 acquisition to the existing net fixed assets of $51,000 and subtracting the depreciation of $8,000 will yield net fixed assets of $63,000.
6. Purchases are expected to represent approximately 30 percent of annual sales, which in this case would be approximately $40,500 (.30 × $135,000). The firm estimates that it can take 72 days on average to satisfy its accounts payable. Thus accounts payable should equal one-fifth (72 days ÷ 360 days) of the firm's purchases, or $8,100 (⅕ × $40,500).
7. Taxes payable are expected to equal one-fourth of the current year's tax liability, which would equal about $455 (one-fourth of the tax liability of $1,823 shown in the pro forma income statement presented in Table 15.10).
8. Notes payable are assumed to remain unchanged from their current level of $8,300.
9. No change in other current liabilities is expected. They will remain at the level of the previous year: $3,400.

[8]The judgmental approach represents an improved version of the often discussed *percent-of-sales approach* to pro forma balance sheet preparation. Because the judgmental approach requires only slightly more information and should yield better estimates than the somewhat naive percent-of-sales approach, it is presented here.

10. The firm's long-term debts and its common stock are expected to remain unchanged at $18,000 and $30,000, respectively, since no issues, retirements, or repurchases of bonds or stocks are planned.

11. Retained earnings will increase from the beginning level of $23,000 (from the balance sheet dated December 31, 1994, in Table 15.8) to $29,327. The increase of $6,327 represents the amount of retained earnings calculated in the year-end 1995 pro forma income statement in Table 15.10.

external funds required ("plug" figure)
Under the judgmental approach for developing a pro forma balance sheet, the amount of external financing needed to bring the statement into balance.

A 1995 pro forma balance sheet for Vectra Manufacturing based on these assumptions is presented in Table 15.11. A **"plug" figure**—called the **external funds required**—of $8,293 is needed to bring the statement into balance. This means that the firm will have to obtain about $8,293 of additional external financing to support the increased sales level of $135,000 for 1995.

A *positive* value for "external funds required," like that shown in Table 15.11 for Vectra Manufacturing, means that to support the firms forecast level of operation, it must raise funds externally using debt and/or equity financing. Once the form of financing is determined, the pro forma balance sheet is modified to replace "external funds required" with the planned increases in the debt and/or equity accounts. When the value for external funds required is *negative*, it indicates that the firm's forecast financing is in excess of its needs. In this case, funds would be available for use in repaying debt, repurchasing stock, or increasing dividends. Once the specific actions are determined, the external funds required are replaced in the pro forma balance sheet with the planned reductions in the debt and/or equity accounts. While the focus here is on the use of the judgmental approach to prepare the pro forma balance sheet, it is important to recognize that analysts frequently use this approach specifically to estimate the firms financing requirements.

TABLE 15.11

A PRO FORMA BALANCE SHEET, USING THE JUDGMENTAL APPROACH, FOR VECTRA MANUFACTURING (DECEMBER 31, 1995)

Assets			Liabilities and equities	
Cash		$ 6,000	Accounts payable	$ 8,100
Marketable securities		4,000	Taxes payable	455
Accounts receivable		16,875	Notes payable	8,300
Inventories			Other current liabilities	3,400
Raw materials	$ 4,000		Total current liabilities	$ 20,255
Finished goods	12,000		Long-term debts	$ 18,000
Total inventory		16,000	Stockholders' equity	
Total current assets		$ 42,875	Common stock	$ 30,000
Net fixed assets		$ 63,000	Retained earnings	$ 29,327
Total assets		$105,875	Total	$ 97,582
			External funds required[a]	$ 8,293
			Total liabilities and stockholders' equity	$105,875

[a]The amount of external funds needed to force the firm's balance sheet to balance. Due to the nature of the judgmental approach to preparing the pro forma balance sheet, the balance sheet is not expected to balance without some type of adjustment.

CONCEPTS IN REVIEW

15-11 Describe the *judgmental approach* for simplified preparation of the pro forma balance sheet. Contrast this with the more detailed approach shown in Figure 15.1.

15-12 What is the significance of the balancing ("plug") figure, *external funds required,* used with the judgmental approach for preparing the pro forma balance sheet? Differentiate between the interpretation and strategy associated with positive and negative values for *external funds required.*

Evaluation of pro forma statements

The percent-of-sales method and judgmental approach to pro forma preparation are popular because of their relative simplicity. What assumptions underlying these procedures account for their basic weaknesses? Spend a few moments answering this question before reading on.

IT IS DIFFICULT TO FORECAST THE MANY VARIABLES INVOLVED IN PRO FORMA STATEMENT preparation. As a result, analysts—including investors, lenders, and managers—frequently use the techniques presented here to make rough estimates of pro forma financial statements. Although the growing availability and acceptance of personal computers and electronic spreadsheets are streamlining the financial planning process, simplified approaches to pro forma preparation are expected to remain popular. An understanding of the basic weaknesses of these simplified approaches is therefore important. Equally important is the ability to effectively use pro forma statements to make financial decisions.

Weaknesses of simplified approaches

The basic weaknesses of the simplified pro forma approaches shown in the chapter lie in two assumptions: (1) that the firm's past financial condition is an accurate indicator of its future and (2) that certain variables, such as cash, accounts receivable, and inventories, can be forced to take on certain "desired" values. These assumptions cannot be justified solely on the basis of their ability to simplify the calculations involved. Good financial analysts do not generally assume that simplification of the forecasting model and assumptions enhances insight into what's going to happen. Because the quality of pro forma statements depends on the quality of the forecasting model and its assumptions, practicing analysts tend to spend time attempting to seek out the best models and assumptions for use in preparing these statements.

Other simplified approaches exist. Most are based on the assumption that certain relationships among revenues, costs, expenses, assets, liabilities, and equity will prevail in the future. For example, in preparing the pro forma balance sheet, all assets, liabilities, *and* equity are often increased by the percentage increase expected in sales. The financial analyst must know the techniques that have been used in preparing pro forma statements to judge the quality of the estimated values and thus the degree of confidence he or she can have in them.

Using pro forma statements

In addition to estimating the amount, if any, of external financing that is required to support a given level of sales, pro forma statements also provide a basis for analyzing in advance the level of profitability and overall financial performance of the firm in the coming year. Using pro forma statements, the financial manager, as well as lenders, can analyze the firm's sources and uses of cash as well as various aspects of performance, such as liquidity, activity, debt, and profitability. Sources and uses can be evaluated by preparing a pro forma statement of cash flows. Various ratios can be calculated from the pro forma income statement and balance sheet to evaluate performance.

After analyzing the pro forma statements, the financial manager can take steps to adjust planned operations to achieve short-term financial goals. For example, if profits on the pro forma income statement are too low, a variety of pricing or cost-cutting actions, or both, might be initiated. If the projected level of accounts receivable shown on the pro forma balance sheet is too high, changes in credit or collection policy may avoid this outcome. Pro forma statements are therefore of key importance in solidifying the firm's financial plans for the coming year.

CONCEPTS IN REVIEW

15-13 What are the two key weaknesses of the simplified approaches to pro forma statement preparation? How do practicing financial analysts deal with these weaknesses?

15-14 How may the financial manager wish to evaluate pro forma statements? What is his or her objective in evaluating these statements?

Summary

LG 1 Understand the financial planning process, including the role of and interrelationship between long-term (strategic) financial plans and short-term (operating) plans. The two key aspects of the financial planning process are cash planning and profit planning. Cash planning involves preparation of the cash budget or cash forecast. Profit planning relies on preparation of the pro forma income statement and balance sheet. Long-term (strategic) financial plans act as a guide for preparing short-term (operating) financial plans. Long-term plans tend to cover periods ranging from 2 to 10 years and are updated periodically. Short-term plans most often cover a one- to two-year period.

LG 2 Discuss the cash planning process, the role of sales forecasts, and the procedures for preparing the cash budget. The cash planning process uses the cash budget, which is based on a sales forecast, to estimate short-term cash surpluses and shortages. The sales forecast may be based on an analysis of external or internal data or on a combination of the two. The cash budget is typically prepared for a one-year period divided into months. It nets cash receipts and disbursements for each period to calculate net cash flow. Ending cash is estimated by adding beginning cash to the net cash flow. By subtracting the desired minimum cash balance from the ending cash, the financial manager can determine required total financing (typically represented by notes payable) or the excess cash balance (typically included in marketable securities).

LG 3 Describe the cash budget evaluation process, procedures for coping with uncertainty, and the issue of cash flow within the month. The cash budget allows the financial manager to plan investment of forecast cash surpluses in marketable securities and to arrange for adequate borrowing, typically through a line of credit to ensure the availability of funds to meet forecast investment cash shortages. Typically, to allow for uncertainty, borrowing in excess of the forecast maximum cash shortage is arranged. To cope with uncertainty in the cash budget, sensitivity analysis (which involves preparation of several cash budgets) or computer simulation can be used. A firm must also look beyond the cash budget and consider its pattern of daily cash receipts and cash disbursements to ensure that adequate cash is available to meet bills as they come due.

LG 4 Prepare a pro forma income statement using both the percent-of-sales method and a breakdown of costs and expenses into their fixed and variable components. A pro forma income statement can be developed by calculating past percentage relationships between certain cost and expense items and the firm's sales and then applying these percentages to forecasts. Because this approach implies that all costs (or expenses) are variable, it tends to understate profits when sales are increasing and overstate profits when sales are decreasing. This problem can be avoided by breaking down costs and expenses into fixed and variable components and using them to prepare the statement. In this case the fixed components will remain unchanged from the most recent year, and the variable costs and expenses will be forecast on a percent-of-sales basis.

LG 5 Explain the procedures used to develop a pro forma balance sheet using the judgmental approach and the role and use of the plug figure—external funds required—in this process. Under the judgmental approach for developing a pro forma balance sheet, the values of certain balance sheet accounts are estimated while others are calculated, frequently on the basis of their relationship to sales. When this approach is applied, the firm's external financing is used as a balancing, or "plug," figure. A positive value for "external funds required" means that to support the firm's forecast level of operations, it must raise funds externally; a negative value indicates that funds will be available for use in repaying debt, repurchasing stock, or increasing dividends.

LG 6 Describe the weaknesses of the simplified approaches to pro forma preparation and the common uses of pro forma financial statements. The use of simplified approaches for pro forma statement preparation, although quite popular, can be criticized for assuming that the firm's past condition is an accurate predictor of the future and for assuming that certain variables can be forced to take on desired values. Good financial analysts do not generally assume that simplification of the forecasting model and assumptions enhances insight into what's going to happen. Pro forma statements are commonly used by financial managers and lenders to analyze in advance the firm's level of profitability and overall financial performance. On the basis of their analysis, financial managers adjust planned operations to achieve short-term financial goals.

Self-test problems (Solutions in Appendix E)

ST 15-1 LG 2,5 Cash budget and pro forma balance sheet inputs Jane McDonald, a financial analyst for Carroll Company, has prepared the following sales and cash disbursement estimates for the period February–June of the current year.

Month	Sales	Cash disbursements
February	$500	$400
March	600	300
April	400	600
May	200	500
June	200	200

Ms. McDonald notes that historically, 30 percent of sales have been for cash. Of *credit sales,* 70 percent are collected one month after the sale, and the remaining 30 percent are collected two months after the sale. The firm wishes to maintain a minimum ending balance in its cash account of $25. Balances above this amount would be invested in short-term government securities (marketable securities), whereas any deficits would be financed through short-term bank borrowing (notes payable). The beginning cash balance at April 1 is $115.

a. Prepare a cash budget for April, May, and June.

b. How much financing, if any, at a maximum would Carroll Company need to meet its obligations during this three-month period?

c. If a pro forma balance sheet dated at the end of June were prepared from the information presented, give the size of each of the following: cash, notes payable, marketable securities, and accounts receivable.

ST 15-2 LG 4,6 Pro forma income statement Euro Designs, Inc., expects sales during 1995 to rise from the 1994 level of $3.5 million to $3.9 million. Due to a scheduled large loan payment, the interest expense in 1995 is expected to drop to $325,000. The firm plans to increase its cash dividend payments during 1995 to $320,000. The company's year-end 1994 income statement is given below.

Income Statement Euro Designs, Inc. for the Year Ended December 31, 1994	
Sales revenue	$3,500,000
Less: Cost of goods sold	1,925,000
Gross profits	$1,575,000
Less: Operating expenses	420,000
Operating profits	$1,155,000
Less: Interest expense	400,000
Net profits before taxes	$ 755,000
Less: Taxes (rate = 40%)	302,000
Net profits after taxes	$ 453,000
Less: Cash dividends	250,000
To retained earnings	$ 203,000

a. Use the percent-of-sales method to prepare a 1995 pro forma income statement for Euro Designs, Inc.
b. Explain why the statement may underestimate the company's actual 1995 pro forma income.

Problems

15-1 LG 2 Cash receipts A firm has actual sales of $65,000 in April and $60,000 in May. It expects sales of $70,000 in June and $100,000 in July and in August. Assuming that sales are the only source of cash inflows and that half of these are for cash and the remainder are collected evenly over the following two months, what are the firm's expected cash receipts for June, July, and August?

15-2 LG 2 Cash budget—Basic Grenoble Enterprises had sales of $50,000 in March and $60,000 in April. Forecast sales for May, June, and July are $70,000, $80,000, and $100,000, respectively. The firm has a cash balance of $5,000 on May 1 and wishes to maintain a minimum cash balance of $5,000. Given the following data, prepare and interpret a cash budget for the months of May, June, and July.

(1) Twenty percent of the firm's sales are for cash, 60 percent are collected in the next month, and the remaining 20 percent are collected in the second month following sale.
(2) The firm receives other income of $2,000 per month.
(3) The firm's actual or expected purchases, all made for cash, are $50,000, $70,000, and $80,000 for the months of May through July, respectively.
(4) Rent is $3,000 per month.
(5) Wages and salaries are 10 percent of the previous month's sales.
(6) Cash dividends of $3,000 will be paid in June.
(7) Payment of principal and interest of $4,000 is due in June.
(8) A cash purchase of equipment costing $6,000 is scheduled in July.
(9) Taxes of $6,000 are due in June.

15-3 LG 2 Cash budget—Advanced The actual sales and purchases for Xenocore, Inc., for September and October 1994, along with its forecast sales and purchases for the period November 1994 through April 1995, follow.

Year	Month	Sales	Purchases
1994	September	$210,000	$120,000
1994	October	250,000	150,000
1994	November	170,000	140,000
1994	December	160,000	100,000
1995	January	140,000	80,000
1995	February	180,000	110,000
1995	March	200,000	100,000
1995	April	250,000	90,000

The firm makes 20 percent of all sales for cash and collects on 40 percent of its sales in each of the two months following the sale. Other cash inflows are expected to be $12,000 in September and April, $15,000 in January and March, and $27,000 in February. The firm pays cash for 10 percent of its purchases. It pays for 50 percent of its purchases in the following month and for 40 percent of its purchases two months later.

Wages and salaries amount to 20 percent of the preceding month's sales. Rent of $20,000 per month must be paid. Interest payments of $10,000 are due in January and April. A principal payment of $30,000 is also due in April. The firm expects to pay cash dividends of $20,000 in January and April. Taxes of $80,000 are due in April. The firm also intends to make a $25,000 cash purchase of fixed assets in December.

a. Assuming that the firm has a cash balance of $22,000 at the beginning of November, determine the end-of-month cash balances for each month, November through April.

b. Assuming that the firm wishes to maintain a $15,000 minimum cash balance, determine the required total financing or excess cash balance for each month, November through April.

c. If the firm were requesting a line of credit to cover needed financing for the period November to April, how large would this line have to be? Explain your answer.

15-4 LG 2 Cash flow concepts The following represent financial transactions that Johnsfield & Co. will be undertaking in the next planning period. For each transaction, check the statement or statements that will be affected immediately.

	Statement		
Transaction	Cash budget	Pro forma income statement	Pro forma balance sheet
Cash sale			
Credit sale			
Accounts receivable are collected			
Asset with five-year life is purchased			
Depreciation is taken			
Amortization of goodwill is taken			
Sale of common stock			
Retirement of outstanding bonds			
Fire insurance premium is paid for the next three years			

15-5 LG 3 Multiple cash budgets—Sensitivity analysis Brownstein, Inc., expects sales of $100,000 during each of the next three months. It will make monthly purchases of $60,000 during this time. Wages and salaries are $10,000 per month plus 5 percent of sales. Brownstein expects to make a tax payment of $20,000 in the next month and a $15,000 purchase of fixed assets in the second month and to receive $8,000 in cash from the sale of an asset in the third month. All sales and purchases are for cash. Beginning cash and the minimum cash balance are assumed to be zero.

a. Construct a cash budget for the next three months.

b. Brownstein is unsure of the sales levels, but all other figures are certain. If the most pessimistic sales figure is $80,000 per month and the most optimistic is $120,000 per month, what are the monthly minimum and maximum ending cash balances that the firm can expect for each of the one-month periods?

c. Briefly discuss how the financial manager can use the data in **a** and **b** to plan for his or her financing needs.

15-6 LG 4 Pro forma income statement The marketing department of Metroline Manufacturing estimates that its sales in 1995 will be $1.5 million. Interest expense is expected to remain unchanged at $35,000, and the firm plans to pay $70,000 in cash dividends during 1995. Metroline Manufacturing's income statement for the year ended December 31, 1994, is given below, followed by a breakdown of the firm's cost of goods sold and operating expenses into its fixed- and variable-cost components.

Income statement
Metroline Manufacturing
for the year ended December 31, 1994

Sales revenue	$1,400,000
Less: Cost of goods sold	910,000
Gross profits	$ 490,000
Less: Operating expenses	120,000
Operating profits	$ 370,000
Less: Interest expense	35,000
Net profits before taxes	$ 335,000
Less: Taxes (rate = 40%)	134,000
Net profits after taxes	$ 201,000
Less: Cash dividends	66,000
To retained earnings	$ 135,000

Fixed- and variable-cost breakdown
Metroline Manufacturing
for the year ended December 31, 1994

Cost of goods sold	
Fixed cost	$210,000
Variable cost	700,000
Total cost	$910,000
Operating expenses	
Fixed expenses	$ 36,000
Variable expenses	84,000
Total expenses	$120,000

a. Use the *percent-of-sales method* to prepare a pro forma income statement for the year ended December 31, 1995.

b. Used the *fixed- and variable-cost data* to develop a pro forma income statement for the year ended December 31, 1995.

c. Compare and contrast the statements developed in **a** and **b**. Which statement will likely provide the better estimates of 1995 income? Explain why.

15-7 LG 5 Pro forma balance sheet—Basic Leonard Industries wishes to prepare a pro forma balance sheet for December 31, 1995. The firm expects 1995 sales to total $3,000,000. The following information has been gathered.

(1) A minimum cash balance of $50,000 is desired.
(2) Marketable securities are expected to remain unchanged.
(3) Accounts receivable represent 10 percent of sales.
(4) Inventories represent 12 percent of sales.
(5) A new machine costing $90,000 will be acquired during 1995. Total depreciation for the year will be $32,000.
(6) Accounts payable represent 14 percent of sales.
(7) Accruals, other current liabilities, long-term debt, and common stock are expected to remain unchanged.
(8) The firm's net profit margin is 4 percent, and it expects to pay out $70,000 in cash dividends during 1995.
(9) The December 31, 1994, balance sheet is given below.

Balance sheet
Leonard Industries
December 31, 1994

Assets		Liabilities and equities	
Cash	$ 45,000	Accounts payable	$ 395,000
Marketable securities	15,000	Accruals	60,000
Accounts receivable	255,000	Other current liabilities	30,000
Inventories	340,000	Total current liabilities	$ 485,000
Total current assets	$ 655,000	Long-term debt	$ 350,000
Net fixed assets	$ 600,000	Common stock	$ 200,000
Total assets	$1,255,000	Retained earnings	$ 220,000
		Total liabilities and stockholders'equity	$1,255,000

a. Use the *judgmental approach* to prepare a pro forma balance sheet dated December 31, 1995, for Leonard Industries.

b. How much, if any, additional financing will Leonard Industries require in 1995? Discuss.

c. Could Leonard Industries adjust its planned 1995 dividend to avoid the situation described in **b**? Explain how.

15-8 LG 5 Pro forma balance sheet Peabody & Peabody has 1994 sales of $10 million. It wishes to analyze expected performance and financing needs for 1996—two years ahead. Given the following information, answer questions **a** and **b**.

(1) The percent of sales for items that vary directly with sales are as follows:
Accounts receivable, 12 percent
Inventory, 18 percent
Accounts payable, 14 percent
Net profit margin, 3 percent

(2) Marketable securities and other current liabilities are expected to remain unchanged.
(3) A minimum cash balance of $480,000 is desired.
(4) A new machine costing $650,000 will be acquired in 1995, and equipment costing $850,000 will be purchased in 1996. Total depreciation in 1995 is forecast as $290,000, and in 1996 $390,000 of depreciation will be taken.
(5) Accruals are expected to rise to $500,000 by the end of 1996.
(6) No sale or retirement of long-term debt is expected.
(7) No sale or repurchase of common stock is expected.
(8) The dividend payout of 50 percent of net profits is expected to continue.
(9) Sales are expected to be $11 million in 1995 and $12 million in 1996.
(10) The December 31, 1994, balance sheet appears below.

Balance sheet
Peabody & Peabody
December 31, 1994
($000)

Assets		Liabilities and equities	
Cash	$ 400	Accounts payable	$1,400
Marketable securities	200	Accruals	400
Accounts receivable	1,200	Other current liabilities	80
Inventories	1,800	Total current liabilities	$1,880
Total current assets	$3,600	Long-term debt	$2,000
Net fixed assets	$4,000	Common equity	$3,720
Total assets	$7,600	Total liabilities and stockholders' equity	$7,600

a. Prepare a pro forma balance sheet dated December 31, 1996.
b. Discuss the financing changes suggested by the statement prepared in **a**.

15-9 LG 4,5,6 Integrative—Pro forma statements Red Queen Restaurants wishes to prepare financial plans. Use the financial statements and the other information provided below and on page 638 to prepare the financial plans.

Income statement
Red Queen Restaurants
for the year ended December 31, 1994

Sales revenue	$800,000
Less: Cost of goods sold	600,000
Gross profits	$200,000
Less: Operating expenses	100,000
Net profits before taxes	$100,000
Less: Taxes (rate = 40%)	40,000
Net profits after taxes	$ 60,000
Less: Cash dividends	20,000
To retained earnings	$ 40,000

Balance sheet
Red Queen Restaurants
December 31, 1994

Assets		Liabilities and equities	
Cash	$ 32,000	Accounts payable	$100,000
Marketable securities	18,000	Taxes payable	20,000
Accounts receivable	150,000	Other current liabilities	5,000
Inventories	100,000	Total current liabilities	$125,000
Total current assets	$300,000	Long-term debt	$200,000
Net fixed assets	$350,000	Common stock	$150,000
Total assets	$650,000	Retained earnings	$175,000
		Total liabilities and stockholders' equity	$650,000

The following financial data are also available:

(1) The firm has estimated that its sales for 1995 will be $900,000.
(2) The firm expects to pay $35,000 in cash dividends in 1995.
(3) The firm wishes to maintain a minimum cash balance of $30,000.
(4) Accounts receivable represent approximately 18 percent of annual sales.
(5) The firm's ending inventory will change directly with changes in sales in 1995.
(6) A new machine costing $42,000 will be purchased in 1995. Total depreciation for 1995 will be $17,000.
(7) Accounts payable will change directly in response to changes in sales in 1995.
(8) Taxes payable will equal one-fourth of the tax liability on the pro forma income statement.
(9) Marketable securities, other current liabilities, long-term debt, and common stock will remain unchanged.

a. Prepare a pro forma income statement for the year ended December 31, 1995, using the *percent-of-sales method.*
b. Prepare a pro forma balance sheet dated December 31, 1995, using the *judgmental approach.*
c. Analyze these statements, and discuss the resulting external funds required.

Chapter 15 Case Preparing Martin Manufacturing's 1995 pro forma financial statements

To improve its competitive position, Martin Manufacturing is planning to implement a major plant-modernization program. Included will be construction of a state-of-the-art manufacturing facility that will cost $400 million in 1995 and is expected to lower the variable cost per ton of steel. Terri Spiro, an experienced budget analyst, has been charged with preparing a forecast of the firm's 1995 financial position assuming construction of the proposed new facility. She plans to use the 1994 financial statements presented on page 147, along with the key projected financial data summarized in the table at the top of page 639.

Key projected financial data (1995) Martin Manufacturing Company ($000)	
Data item	**Value**
Sales revenue	$6,500,000
Minimum cash balance	$25,000
Inventory turnover (times)	7.0
Average collection period	50 days
Fixed-asset purchases	$400,000
Dividend payments	$20,000
Depreciation expense	$185,000
Interest expense	$97,000
Accounts payable increase	20%
Accruals and long-term debt	Unchanged
Preferred and common stock, notes payable	Unchanged

Required

a. Use the historic and projected financial data provided to prepare a pro forma income statement for the year ended December 31, 1995. (*Hint:* Use the *percent-of-sales method* to estimate all values *except* for depreciation expense and interest expense, which have been estimated by management and included in the table above.)

b. Use the projected financial data above along with relevant data from the pro forma income statement prepared in **a** to prepare the pro forma balance sheet at December 31, 1995. (*Hint:* Use the *judgmental approach.*)

c. Will Martin Manufacturing Company need to raise *external funds* to finance construction of the proposed facility? Explain.

chapter 16

Net working capital and short-term financing

LEARNING GOALS

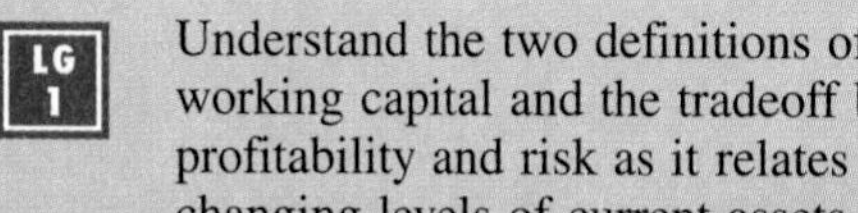

LG 1 Understand the two definitions of net working capital and the tradeoff between profitability and risk as it relates to changing levels of current assets and current liabilities.

LG 2 Discuss, in terms of profitability and risk, the aggressive financing strategy and the conservative financing strategy for meeting the firm's total—permanent and seasonal—funds requirement.

LG 3 Review the key features and characteristics of the two major sources of spontaneous short-term financing—accounts payable and accruals.

LG 4 Analyze credit terms offered by suppliers to determine, when the alternative is to borrow funds, whether to take or give up cash discounts and whether to stretch accounts payable.

LG 5 Describe the interest rates, basic types, and key features of unsecured bank sources of short-term loans, the use of commercial paper in short-term financing, and the role of international loans.

LG 6 Explain the characteristics of secured short-term loans and the use of accounts receivable (pledging and factoring) and inventory (floating lien, trust receipt, and warehouse receipt) as short-term loan collateral.

Working capital refers to the current assets that sustain day-to-day business operations. *Net working capital,* the difference between current assets and current liabilities, is a convenient measure of a company's liquidity and also reflects the company's ability to manage its vendor and customer relationships. Inefficient management of working capital will dramatically affect a company's cash flow. Failure to manage accounts payable could result in paying vendors too soon, draining the company's cash account.

Working capital requirements and management strategies vary by type of company and industry. The mix of current assets and current liabilities and the current-to-total-asset ratio also depend on the type of company. A computer services company's needs are different from those of a computer manufacturer. And a large multidivisional company—for example, one with both heavy manufacturing and distribution operations—must manage each unit's working capital requirements separately. A manufacturing operation has a larger fixed-to-total-assets ratio and tends to focus on long-term cash needs; distribution operations have a larger percentage in working capital–related accounts and focus on managing receivables, inventory, and accounts payable; a service company has few fixed assets and focuses primarily on accounts receivable.

The relationship between current assets and current liabilities plays a major role in establishing working capital management policies. A firm may set a target level for the current ratio (current assets divided by current liabilities) such as 2.5. Industry standards (for liquidity ratios and credit terms) and creditor requirements also affect these decisions. Companies with short-term bank loans may be required by loan agreement covenants to maintain a minimum level of net working capital or current ratio.

Inefficient management . . . will dramatically affect a company's cash flow.

Two very important considerations in managing working capital needs are economic cycles and the seasonality of a company's particular business. Changes in economic conditions affect sales volume, which in turn affects receivables and inventory levels. Companies with seasonal products may experience major accounts receivable and inventory build-ups because the product may be manufactured year-round but produce revenue only at a certain time of the year. These cycles present a challenge for financial managers, who must provide the necessary resources for company operations and arrange for short-term financing to cover working capital shortfalls.

A company's working capital strategy is also governed by the interest-rate environment and personal preference. Some companies use the conservative approach, financing both permanent and seasonal needs with medium- and long-term funds. Others are more aggressive and use long-term funds to finance permanent needs and less expensive short-term funds for seasonal needs, particularly when spreads between short- and long-term rates are favorable. Obviously, close monitoring of interest rates is critical to developing the best strategy for a company. Many companies hedge interest rate exposure through the use of derivative instruments.

The type of short-term financing that a company uses depends largely on its size and financial strength. Large, rated companies generally have access to commercial paper, bankers acceptances, money market types of bank debt, and other forms of unsecured debt. Smaller companies usually finance their working capital needs with short-term loans from local banks, and they sometimes have to secure the loan with accounts receivable or inventory.

Richard Moorman received a B.S. in marketing from Xavier University, Cincinnati, and has been involved in treasury management for 20 years. During his 13 years with Mead Corporation he held various international and domestic financial management positions, including Manager, Corporate Finance. A Certified Cash Manager who is active in the Treasury Management Association, he is currently Senior Vice President, Treasury Services Group, Bank One, Columbus.

Net working capital fundamentals

Generally, the higher a firm's net working capital (current assets minus current liabilities), the lower its profitability and the lower its risk of being unable to pay its bills as they come due; and the lower its net working capital, the higher its profitability and its risk of being unable to pay its bills as they come due. Why do you think profitability and risk respond in this fashion to changes in net working capital? Before reading further, spend a few minutes answering this question.

THE FIRM'S BALANCE SHEET PROVIDES INFORMATION ABOUT THE FIRM'S STRUCTURE—that is, the structure of its investments on the one hand and the structure of its financing sources on the other. In the most general sense, the overriding goal against which the alternative structures of assets and liabilities and equity are assessed is owner wealth maximization. The structures chosen should consistently lead to the maximization of the value of the owners' investment in the firm.

Important components of the firm's structure include the level of investment in current assets and the extent of current liability financing. In U.S. manufacturing firms, current assets currently account for about 40 percent of total assets; current liabilities represent about 26 percent of total financing. Therefore it should not be surprising to learn that **short-term financial management**—managing current assets and current liabilities—is one of the financial manager's most important and time-consuming activities. A study[1] of Fortune 1000 firms found that 60 percent of financial management time is spent on short-term financial management activities and 40 percent is spent on long-term financial management activities. The 60 percent represents 35 percent of financial management time spent managing current assets and 25 percent managing current liabilities. In other words, more than one-third of financial management time is spent managing current assets, and about one-fourth of financial management time is spent managing current liabilities.

short-term financial management
Management of current assets and current liabilities.

The goal of short-term financial management is to manage each of the firm's current assets (cash, marketable securities, accounts receivable, and inventory) and current liabilities (accounts payable, notes payable, and accruals) to achieve a balance between profitability and risk that contributes positively to the firm's value. Too much investment in current assets reduces profitability, whereas too little investment increases the risk of not being able to pay debts as they come due. Both situations generally lead to lower firm value. This chapter does not discuss the optimal level of current assets and current liabilities that a firm should have. This issue is as yet unresolved in the financial literature. Here attention is first given to the basic relationship between current assets and current liabilities, and then the key features of the major sources of short-term (current liability) financing are described. (Table 16.7, appearing at the end of this chapter, summarizes the key features of the common sources of short-term financing.) Subsequent chapters consider the management of current assets.

[1]Lawrence J. Gitman and Charles E. Maxwell, "Financial Activities of Major U.S. Firms: Survey and Analysis of Fortune's 1000," *Financial Management*, Winter 1985, pp. 57–65.

Net working capital

working capital
Current assets, which represent the portion of investment that circulates from one form to another in the ordinary conduct of business.

operating cycle
The recurring transition of a firm's working capital from cash to inventories to receivables and back to cash.

net working capital
The difference between the firm's current assets and its current liabilities, or, alternatively, the portion of current assets financed with long-term funds; can be *positive* or *negative.*

The current assets, commonly called **working capital,** represent the portion of investment that circulates from one form to another in the ordinary conduct of business. This idea embraces the recurring transition from cash to inventories to receivables and back to cash that forms the **operating cycle** of the firm. As cash substitutes, *marketable securities* are considered part of working capital. Similarly, *prepaid expenses* are included as working capital because they represent services owed to the company that are used in carrying out its activities, thereby eliminating the need for later cash outlays.

Current liabilities represent the firm's short-term financing, since they include all debts of the firm that come due (must be paid) in one year or less. These debts usually include amounts owed to suppliers (accounts payable), banks (notes payable), and employees and governments (accruals), among others.

As was noted in Chapter 4, **net working capital** is commonly defined as the difference between the firm's current assets and its current liabilities. When the current assets exceed the current liabilities, the firm has *positive net working capital.* In this most common case, net working capital is the portion of the firm's current assets financed with *long-term funds*—the sum of long-term debt and stockholders' equity—that are in excess of financing requirements of the firm's fixed assets. Since current liabilities represent the firm's sources of short-term funds, as long as current assets exceed current liabilities, the amount of the excess must be financed with long-term funds.

When current assets are less than current liabilities, the firm has *negative net working capital.* In this less common case, net working capital is the portion of the firm's fixed assets financed with current liabilities. This conclusion follows from the balance sheet equation: assets equal liabilities plus equity.

In general, the greater the margin by which a firm's current assets cover its short-term obligations (current liabilities), the better able it will be to pay its bills as they come due. This relationship results from the fact that the conversion of current assets from inventory to receivables to cash provides the source of cash used to pay the current liabilities, which represent a use of cash. The cash outlays for current liabilities are relatively predictable. When an obligation is incurred, the firm generally learns when the corresponding bill will be due. For instance, when merchandise is purchased on credit, the terms extended by the seller require payment by a known point in time. What is difficult to predict are the cash inflows—that is, the conversion of the current assets to more liquid forms. The more predictable its cash inflows, the less net working capital a firm needs. Because most firms are unable to match cash inflows to outflows with certainty, current assets that more than cover outflows for current liabilities are usually necessary. Stated differently, some portion of current assets is usually financed with long-term funds.

EXAMPLE

Nicholson Company, a packager of pork sausage, has the current position given in Table 16.1. All $600 of the firm's accounts payable, plus $200 of its notes payable and $100 of accruals, are due at the end of the current period. The $900 in outflows is certain; how the firm will cover these outflows is not certain. The firm can be sure that $700 will be available, since it has $500 in cash and $200 in marketable securities, which can easily be converted into cash. The remaining $200 must come from the collection

TABLE 16.1

THE CURRENT POSITION OF NICHOLSON COMPANY

Current assets		Current liabilities	
Cash	$ 500	Accounts payable	$ 600
Marketable securities	200	Notes payable	800
Accounts receivable	800	Accruals	200
Inventories	1,200	Total	$1,600
Total	$2,700		

of accounts receivable, the sale of inventory for cash, or both.[2] However, the firm cannot be sure when either the collection of an account receivable or a cash sale will occur. Generally, the more accounts receivable and inventories that are on hand, the greater the probability that some of these items will be converted into cash.[3] Thus a certain level of net working capital is often recommended to ensure the firm's ability to pay bills. Nicholson Company has $1,100 of net working capital (current assets minus current liabilities, or $2,700 − $1,600), which will most likely be sufficient to cover its bills. Its current ratio of 1.69 (current assets divided by current liabilities, or $2,700 ÷ $1,600) should provide sufficient liquidity as long as its accounts receivable and inventories remain relatively active. ■

The tradeoff between profitability and risk

Total investment in a firm consists of current assets (working capital) and fixed assets, and the firm's profitability and risk are affected by the ratio of current assets to fixed assets. A firm's level of fixed assets is determined by its scale and capital intensiveness of production. The level of current assets is closely tied to the firm's level of production. Thus, if production is increased, the need for current assets is increased, and if production is decreased, the need for current assets is decreased.

profitability
The relationship between revenues and costs generated by using the firm's assets—both current and fixed—in productive activities.

Profitability, in this context, is the relationship between revenues and costs generated by using the firm's assets—both current and fixed—in productive activities. A firm's profits can be increased by (1) increasing revenues or (2) decreasing costs. The most profitable firms are usually those with the largest market share for their products.

risk
The probability that a firm will be unable to pay its bills as they come due.

Risk, as was noted in Chapter 10, has two meanings. *Business risk* is the risk of being unable to cover operating costs. *Financial risk* is the risk of being unable to make the scheduled fixed payments associated with debt, leases, and preferred stock financing as they come due. For purposes of this chapter, **risk** will be defined as the proba-

[2]A sale of inventory for credit would show up as a new account receivable, which could not be easily converted into cash. Only a *cash sale* will guarantee the firm that its bill-paying ability during the period of the sale has been enhanced.

[3]It should be recognized that levels of accounts receivable or inventory can be too high, reflecting certain management inefficiencies. Acceptable levels for any firm can be calculated. The efficient management of accounts receivable and inventory is discussed in Chapter 18.

bility that a firm will be unable to pay its bills as they come due. A firm that cannot pay its bills as they come due is said to be **technically insolvent.**

technically insolvent
Describes a firm that is unable to pay its bills as they come due.

It is generally assumed that the greater the firm's net working capital, the lower its risk. In other words, the more net working capital, the more liquid the firm and therefore the lower its risk of becoming technically insolvent. However, such an assumption *may be* wrong. As was mentioned earlier, positive net working capital means that long-term funds are used to finance some part of the current assets. Long-term funds are usually more expensive than short-term funds and generally impose greater restrictions on the firm.

CHANGES IN CURRENT ASSETS

The effects of changing the level of the firm's current assets on its profitability-risk tradeoff can be demonstrated by using the ratio of current assets to total assets. This ratio indicates the *percentage of total assets* that is current. Assuming that the level of total assets remains unchanged,[4] the effects on both profitability and risk of an increase or decrease in this ratio are summarized in the upper portion of Table 16.2. When the ratio increases, profitability decreases because current assets are less profitable than fixed assets. Fixed assets are more profitable because they add more value to the product than that provided by current assets. Without the fixed assets, the firm could not produce the product.

The risk effect, however, decreases as the ratio of current assets to total assets increases. The increase in current assets increases net working capital, thereby reducing the risk of technical insolvency. In addition, as you go down the asset side of the balance sheet, the risk associated with the assets increases. Investment in cash and marketable securities is less risky than investment in accounts receivable, inventories, and fixed assets. Accounts receivable investment is less risky than investment in inventories and fixed assets. Investment in inventories is less risky than investment in fixed assets. The nearer an asset is to cash, the less risky it is. It is generally easier to turn receivables into the more liquid asset cash than it is to turn inventory into cash. As another example, fixed assets are long-term investments, and newer, more efficient, machines and facilities can quickly make the firm's fixed assets relatively inefficient or

TABLE 16.2

EFFECTS OF CHANGING RATIOS ON PROFITS AND RISK

Ratio	Change in ratio	Effect on profit	Effect on risk
$\frac{\text{Current assets}}{\text{Total assets}}$	**Increase**	Decrease	Decrease
	Decrease	Increase	Increase
$\frac{\text{Current liabilities}}{\text{Total assets}}$	**Increase**	Increase	Increase
	Decrease	Decrease	Decrease

[4]The level of total assets is assumed to be *constant* in this and the following discussion to isolate the effect of changing asset and financing mixes on the firm's profitability and risk.

obsolete. The opposite effects on profits and risk result from a decrease in the ratio of current assets to total assets.

CHANGES IN CURRENT LIABILITIES

The effects of changing the level of the firm's current liabilities on its profitability–risk tradeoff can be demonstrated by using the ratio of current liabilities to total assets. This ratio indicates the percentage of total assets that has been financed with current liabilities. Assuming that total assets remain unchanged, the effects on both profitability and risk of an increase or decrease in the ratio are summarized in the lower portion of Table 16.2. When the ratio increases, profitability increases because the firm uses more of the less expensive current-liability financing and less long-term financing. Current liabilities are less expensive because only notes payable, which represent about 20 percent of the typical manufacturer's current liabilities, have a cost. The other current liabilities are basically debts on which the firm pays no charge or interest. The risk of technical insolvency also increases because the increase in current liabilities in turn decreases net working capital. The opposite effects on profit and risk result from a decrease in the ratio of current liabilities to total assets.

CONCEPTS IN REVIEW

16-1 Why is *short-term financial management* one of the most important and time-consuming activities of the financial manager? What are the two most common definitions of *net working capital?*

16-2 What relationship would you expect there to be between the predictability of a firm's cash inflows and its required level of net working capital? How are net working capital, liquidity, and the risk of technical insolvency related?

16-3 Why is an increase in the ratio of current to total assets expected to decrease both profits and risk as measured by net working capital? How can changes in the ratio of current liabilities to total assets affect profitability and risk?

Net working capital strategies

Aggressive firms finance seasonal needs with current liabilities and permanent needs with long-term funds. Conservative firms meet both seasonal and permanent needs with long-term funds. In light of the fact that long-term financing is more expensive than current liability financing, why is the aggressive approach more profitable and more risky than the conservative one? Take a few moments to answer this question before reading on.

ONE OF THE MOST IMPORTANT DECISIONS THAT MUST BE MADE WITH RESPECT TO CURrent assets and liabilities is how current liabilities will be used to finance current assets. The amount of current liabilities that is available is limited by the dollar amount of purchases in the case of accounts payable, by the dollar amount of accrued liabilities in the case of accruals, and by the amount of seasonal borrowing considered acceptable by lenders in the case of notes payable and commercial paper. Lenders make short-term loans to allow a firm to finance seasonal build-ups of accounts receivable or inventory. *They generally do not lend short-term money for long-term uses.*[5]

There are two basic strategies—the aggressive strategy and the conservative strategy—for determining an appropriate mix of short-term (current liability) and long-term financing. Before discussing the cost and risk considerations of each of these strategies, it is helpful to consider the permanent and seasonal components of the firm's financing need. In these discussions the alternative definition that defines *net working capital* as *the portion of current assets financed with long-term funds* is applied.

CONCEPT IN PRACTICE

Rizzo's Receivables and Payables Priorities

Rizzo Associates, an environmental-engineering company based in Natick, Massachusetts, has a four-part approach to handling net working capital. One, to provide supervision from the top, the CEO schedules weekly half-hour sessions with the controller, collections manager, and accounts payable clerk. Two, Rizzo has individuals who are specifically assigned to accounts receivable and accounts payable. Three, Rizzo prioritizes receivables in terms of size and historical payment history. It also prioritizes payments, giving top priority to those firms on which it relies, though never paying until the bill is due. Four, to identify problems, Rizzo sends out letters 10 days before 30-day invoices are actually due, innocently asking whether the billing information is correct. On the liabilities side, each payable is analyzed by the payables specialist upon receipt. Rizzo's aggressive net working capital policy has minimized financing required from other sources.

permanent need
Financing requirements for the firm's fixed assets plus the permanent portion of the firm's current assets; these requirements remain unchanged over the year.

seasonal need
Financing requirements for temporary current assets, which vary over the year.

The firm's financing need

The firm's financing requirements can be separated into a permanent and a seasonal need. The **permanent need,** which consists of fixed assets plus the permanent portion of the firm's current assets, remains unchanged over the year. The **seasonal need,** which is attributable to the existence of certain temporary current assets, varies over the year. The relationship between current and fixed assets and permanent and seasonal funds requirements can be illustrated graphically with the aid of a simple example.

EXAMPLE

Nicholson Company's estimate of current, fixed, and total asset requirements on a monthly basis for the coming year is given in columns 1, 2, and 3 of Table 16.3. Note that the relatively stable level of total assets over the year reflects, for convenience, an absence of growth by the firm. Columns 4 and 5 present a breakdown of the total requirement into its permanent and seasonal components. The permanent component (column 4) is the lowest level of total assets during the period; the seasonal portion is the difference between the total funds requirement (i.e., total assets) for each month and the permanent funds requirement.

[5]The rationale for, techniques of, and parties to short-term business loans are discussed in detail later in this chapter. The primary sources of short-term loans to businesses—commercial banks—make these loans *only for seasonal or self-liquidating purposes* such as temporary build-ups of accounts receivable or inventory.

TABLE 16.3

ESTIMATED FUNDS REQUIREMENTS FOR NICHOLSON COMPANY

Month	Current assets (1)	Fixed assets (2)	Total assets[a] [(1) + (2)] (3)	Permanent funds requirement[b] (4)	Seasonal funds requirement [(3) − (4)] (5)
January	$4,000	$13,000	$17,000	$13,800	$3,200
February	3,000	13,000	16,000	13,800	2,200
March	2,000	13,000	15,000	13,800	1,200
April	1,000	13,000	14,000	13,800	200
May	800	13,000	13,800	13,800	0
June	1,500	13,000	14,500	13,800	700
July	3,000	13,000	16,000	13,800	2,200
August	3,700	13,000	16,700	13,800	2,900
September	4,000	13,000	17,000	13,800	3,200
October	5,000	13,000	18,000	13,800	4,200
November	3,000	13,000	16,000	13,800	2,200
December	2,000	13,000	15,000	13,800	1,200
Monthly average[c]				$13,800	$1,950

[a]This figure represents the firm's total funds requirement.

[b]This figure represents the minimum total asset requirement.

[c]Found by summing the monthly amounts for 12 months and dividing the resulting totals by 12.

By comparing the firm's fixed assets (column 2) to its permanent funds requirement (column 4), we see that the permanent funds requirement exceeds the firm's level of fixed assets. This result occurs because *a portion of the firm's current assets is permanent,* since they are apparently always being replaced. The size of the permanent component of current assets is $800 for Nicholson Company. This value represents the base level of current assets that remains on the firm's books throughout the entire year. This value can also be found by subtracting the level of fixed assets from the permanent funds requirement ($13,800 − $13,000 = $800). The relationships presented in Table 16.3 are depicted graphically in Figure 16.1. ■

aggressive financing strategy
Strategy by which the firm finances its seasonal needs, and possibly some of its permanent needs, with short-term funds and the balance of its permanent needs with long-term funds.

An aggressive financing strategy

An **aggressive financing strategy** results in the firm financing at least is seasonal needs, and possibly some of its permanent needs, with short-term funds. The balance is financed with long-term funds. This strategy can be illustrated graphically.

EXAMPLE

Nicholson Company's estimate of its total funds requirements (i.e., total assets) on a monthly basis for the coming year is given in column 3 of Table 16.3. Columns 4 and 5 divide this requirement into permanent and seasonal components.

An aggressive strategy may finance the permanent portion of the firm's funds requirement ($13,800) with long-term funds and finance the seasonal portion (ranging from $0 in May to $4,200 in October) with short-term funds. Much of the short-term financing may be in the form of *trade credit* (i.e., accounts payable). The application

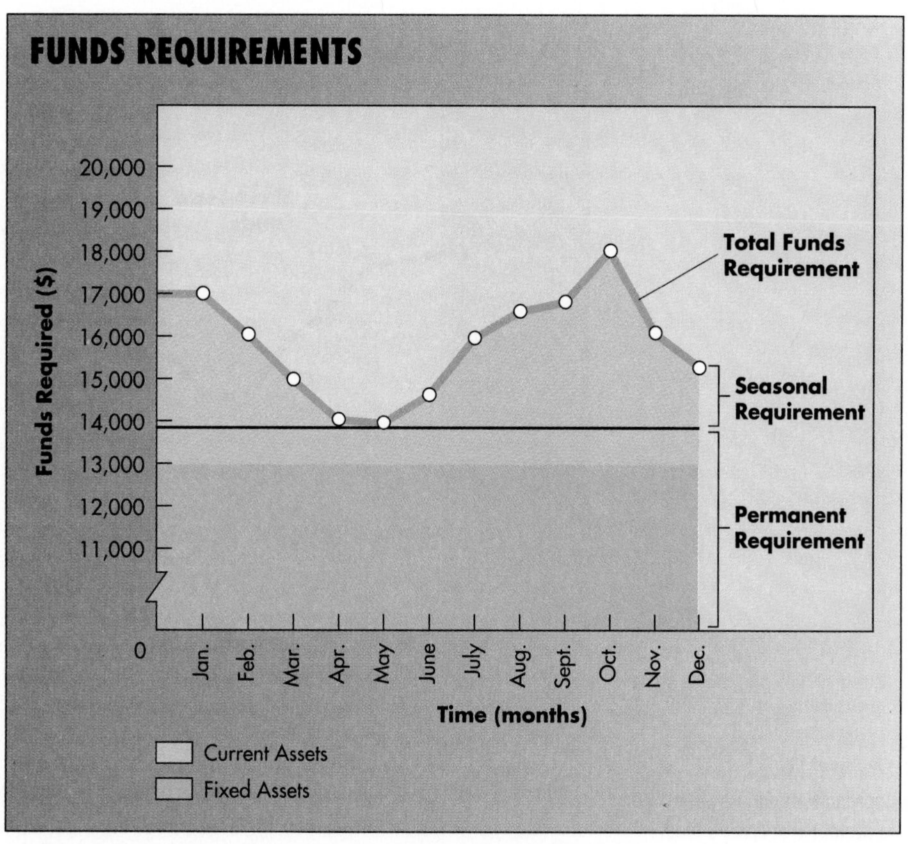

FIGURE 16.1
Nicholson Company's estimated funds requirements

of this financing strategy to the firm's total funds requirement is illustrated graphically in Figure 16.2 on page 650. ■

COST CONSIDERATIONS

Under the aggressive strategy, Nicholson's average short-term borrowing (seasonal funds requirement) is $1,950, and average long-term borrowing (permanent funds requirement) is $13,800 (see columns 4 and 5 of Table 16.3). If the annual cost of short-term funds needed by Nicholson is 3 percent and the annual cost of long-term financing is 11 percent, the total cost of the financing strategy is estimated as follows:

Cost of short-term financing	= 3% × $ 1,950 =	$ 58.50
Cost of long-term financing	= 11% × 13,800 =	1,518.00
Total cost		$1,576.50

The total annual cost of $1,576.50 will become more meaningful when compared to the cost of the conservative financing strategy. The relatively low cost of short-term financing results from using a high amount of free trade credit (a topic discussed later in the chapter).

RISK CONSIDERATIONS

The aggressive strategy operates with minimum net working capital, since only the permanent portion of the firm's current assets is being financed with long-term funds. For

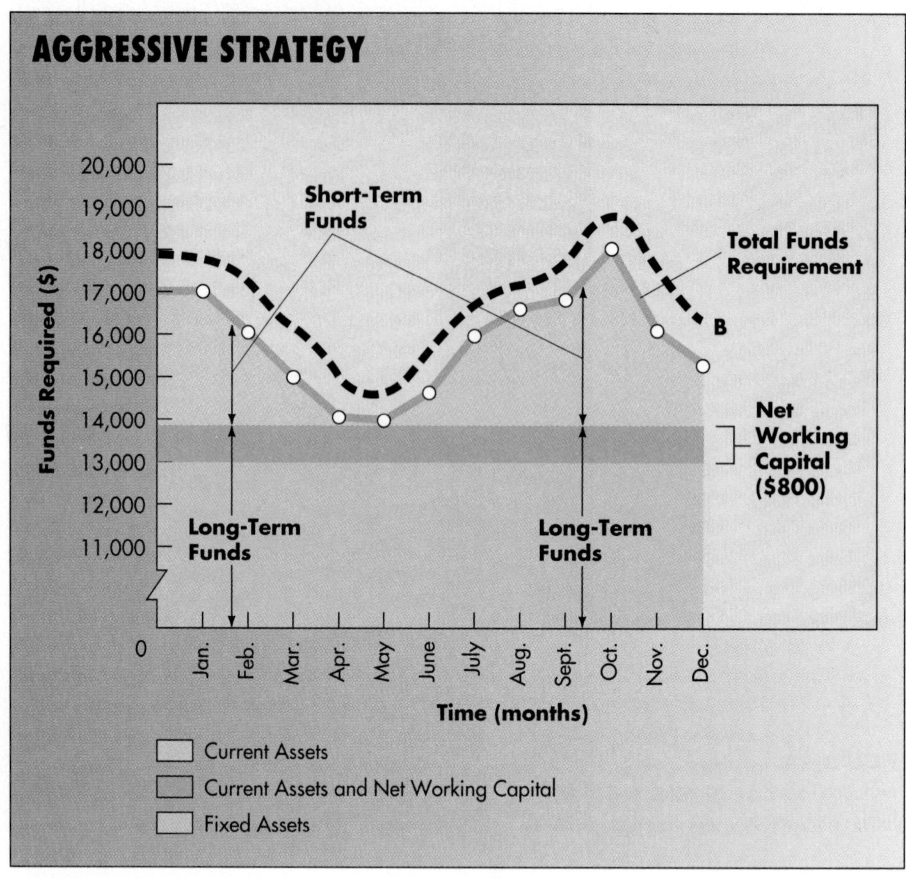

FIGURE 16.2
Applying the aggressive strategy to Nicholson Company's funds requirements

Nicholson Company, as noted in Figure 16.2, the level of net working capital is $800, which is the amount of permanent current assets ($13,800 permanent funds requirement − $13,000 fixed assets = $800).

The aggressive financing strategy is risky not only from the standpoint of low net working capital but also because the firm must draw as heavily as possible on its short-term sources of funds to meet seasonal fluctuations in its requirements. If its total requirement turns out to be, say, the level represented by the dashed curve B in Figure 16.2, the firm may find it difficult to obtain longer-term funds quickly enough to satisfy short-term needs. This aspect of risk associated with the aggressive strategy results from the fact that a firm has only a limited amount of short-term borrowing capacity. If it draws too heavily on this capacity, unexpected needs for funds may become difficult to satisfy.

conservative financing strategy
Strategy by which the firm finances all projected funds requirements with long-term funds and uses short-term financing only for emergencies or unexpected outflows.

A conservative financing strategy

The most **conservative financing strategy** should be to finance all projected funds requirements with long-term funds and use short-term financing in the event of an emergency or an unexpected outflow of funds. It is difficult to imagine how this strategy could actually be implemented, since the use of short-term financing tools, such as accounts payable and accruals, is virtually unavoidable. In illustrating this strategy, the spontaneous short-term financing provided by payables and accruals will be ignored.

EXAMPLE

Figure 16.3 shows graphically the application of the conservative strategy to the total funds requirement for Nicholson Company given in Table 16.3. Long-term financing of $18,000, which equals the firm's peak need (during October), is used under this strategy. Therefore all the funds required over the one-year period, including the entire $18,000 forecast for October, are financed with long-term funds. ■

COST CONSIDERATIONS

In the preceding example the annual cost of long-term funds was 11 percent per year. Since the average long-term financing balance under the conservative financing strategy is $18,000, the total cost of this strategy is $1,980 (11% × $18,000). Comparing this figure to the total cost of $1,576.50 using the aggressive strategy indicates the greater expense of the conservative strategy. The reason for this higher expense is apparent if we examine Figure 16.3. The area above the total funds requirement curve and below the long-term funds, or borrowing, line represents the level of funds that are not actually needed but for which the firm is paying interest. In spite of the fact that the financial manager will invest these excess available funds in some type of mar-

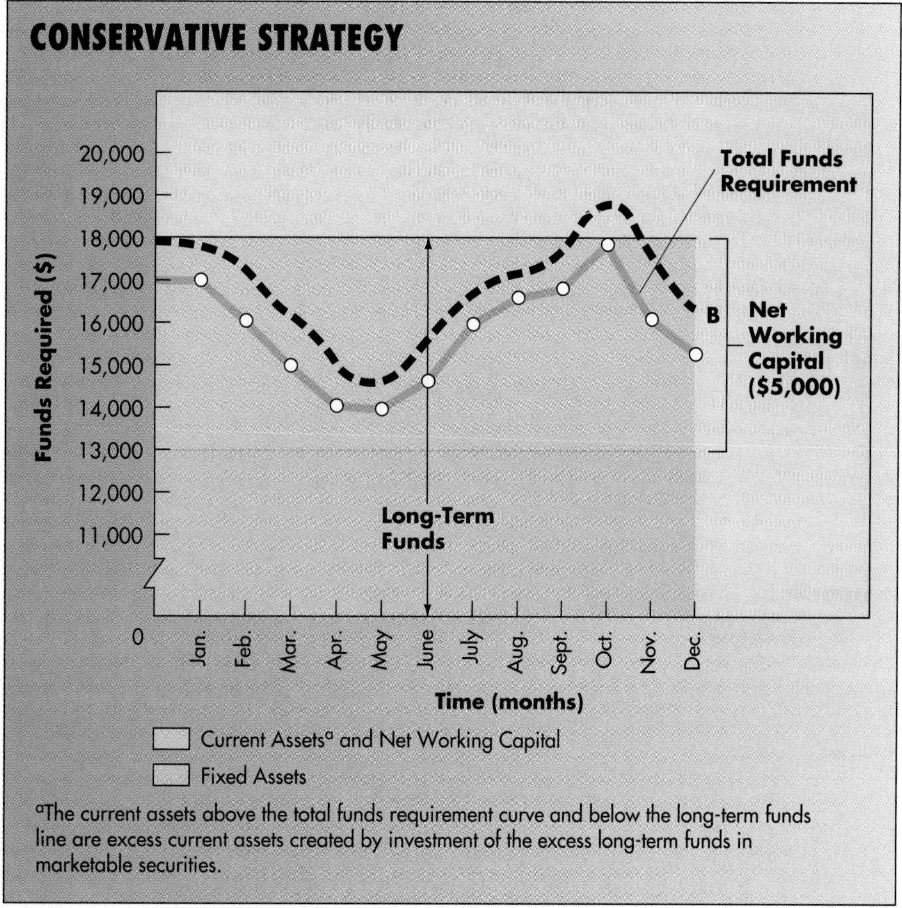

FIGURE 16.3
Applying the conservative strategy to Nicholson Company's funds requirements

ketable security so as partially to offset their borrowing cost, it is highly unlikely that the firm can earn a return on such funds in excess of their interest cost.

RISK CONSIDERATIONS

The $5,000 of net working capital ($18,000 long-term financing − $13,000 fixed assets) associated with the conservative strategy should mean a very low level of risk for the firm.[6] The firm's risk should also be lowered by the fact that the strategy does not require the firm to use any of its limited short-term borrowing capacity. In other words, if total required financing actually turns out to be the level represented by the dashed line B in Figure 16.3, sufficient short-term borrowing capacity should be available to cover the unexpected needs and avoid technical insolvency.

Conservative versus aggressive strategy

Unlike the aggressive strategy, the conservative strategy requires the firm to pay interest on unneeded funds. The lower cost of the aggressive strategy therefore makes it more profitable than the conservative strategy. However, the aggressive strategy involves much more risk. For most firms a tradeoff between the extremes represented by these two strategies should result in an acceptable financing strategy.

CONCEPT IN REVIEW

16-4 Describe both the *aggressive strategy* and the *conservative strategy* for meeting a firm's funds requirements. Compare and contrast the effects of each of these strategies on the firm's profitability and risk.

Spontaneous sources of short-term financing

Accounts payable, a major source of unsecured short-term financing, often allow the firm to take a cash discount and pay a reduced amount if payment is made by an earlier date than otherwise required. How would you go about deciding whether to take a cash discount that has been offered to your firm? Spend a short time answering this question before reading further.

spontaneous financing
Financing that arises from the normal operations of the firm, the two major short-term sources of which are accounts payable and accruals.

SPONTANEOUS FINANCING ARISES FROM THE NORMAL OPERATIONS OF THE FIRM. THE two major spontaneous sources of short-term financing are accounts payable and accruals. As the firm's sales increase, accounts payable increase in response to the increased purchases required to produce at higher levels. Also in response to increasing sales, the firm's accruals increase as wages and taxes rise due to greater labor re-

[6]The level of net working capital is constant throughout the year, since the firm has $5,000 in current assets that will be fully financed with long-term funds. Because the portion of the $5,000 in excess of the scheduled level of current assets is assumed to be held as marketable securities, the firm's current asset balance will increase to this level.

quirements and the increased taxes on the firm's increased earnings. There is normally no explicit cost attached to either of these current liabilities, although they do have certain implicit costs. In addition, both are forms of **unsecured short-term financing**—short-term financing obtained without pledging specific assets as collateral. The firm should take advantage of these often "interest-free" sources of unsecured short-term financing whenever possible.

unsecured short-term financing
Short-term financing obtained without pledging specific assets as collateral.

Accounts payable

Accounts payable are the major source of unsecured short-term financing for business firms. They result from transactions in which merchandise is purchased but no formal note is signed to show the purchaser's liability to the seller. The purchaser, by accepting merchandise, in effect agrees to pay the supplier the amount required in accordance with the terms of sale. The credit terms extended in such transactions are normally stated on the supplier's invoice. The discussion of accounts payable here is presented from the viewpoint of the purchaser rather than the supplier of "trade credit."[7]

CREDIT TERMS

The supplier's credit terms state the credit period, the size of the cash discount offered (if any), the cash discount period, and the date the credit period begins. Each of these aspects of a firm's credit terms is concisely stated in such expressions as "2/10 net 30 EOM." These expressions are a kind of shorthand containing the key information about the length of the credit period (30 days), the cash discount (2 percent), the cash discount period (10 days), and the time the credit period begins, which is the end of each month (EOM).

credit period
The number of days until full payment of an account payable is required.

CREDIT PERIOD The **credit period** of an account payable is the number of days until payment in full is required. Regardless of whether a cash discount is offered, the credit period associated with any transaction must always be indicated. Credit periods usually range from zero to 120 days, although in certain instances longer times are provided. Most credit terms refer to the credit period as the "net period." The word *net* indicates that the full amount of the purchase must be paid within the number of days indicated from the beginning of the credit period. For example, "net 30 days" indicates that the firm must make *full payment* within 30 days of the beginning of the credit period.

cash discount
A percentage deduction from the purchase price if the buyer pays within a specified time that is shorter than the credit period.

CASH DISCOUNT A **cash discount,** if offered as part of the firm's credit terms, is a percentage deduction from the purchase price if the buyer pays within a specified time that is shorter than the credit period. Cash discounts normally range from between 1 and 5 percent. A 2 percent cash discount indicates that the purchaser of $100 of merchandise need pay only $98 if payment is made within the specified shorter interval. Techniques for analyzing the benefits of taking a cash discount or paying at the end of the full credit period are discussed later.

cash discount period
The number of days after the beginning of the credit period during which the cash discount is available.

CASH DISCOUNT PERIOD The **cash discount period** is the number of days after the beginning of the credit period during which the cash discount is available. Typically, the cash discount period is between 5 and 20 days. Often, large customers

[7]An account payable of a purchaser is an account receivable on the supplier's books. Chapter 18 highlights the key strategies and considerations involved in extending credit to customers.

of smaller firms use their position as key customers as a form of leverage, enabling them to take cash discounts far beyond the end of the cash discount period. This strategy, although ethically questionable, is not uncommon.

date of invoice
Indicates that the beginning of the credit period is the date on the invoice for the purchase.

end of month (EOM)
Indicates that the credit period for all purchases made within a given month begins on the first day of the month immediately following.

BEGINNING OF THE CREDIT PERIOD The beginning of the credit period is stated as part of the supplier's credit terms. One of the most common designations for the beginning of the credit period is the **date of invoice.**[8] Both the cash discount period and the net period are then measured from the invoice date. **End of month (EOM)** indicates that the credit period for all purchases made within a given month begins on the first day of the month immediately following. These terms simplify record keeping on the part of the firm extending credit. The following example may help to clarify the differences between credit period beginnings.

EXAMPLE

Simpson Corporation, a producer of computer graphics software, made two purchases from a certain supplier offering credit terms of 2/10 net 30. One purchase was made on September 10, and the other on September 20. The payment dates for each purchase, based on date of invoice and end of month (EOM) credit period beginnings, are given in Table 16.4. The payment dates if the firm takes the cash discount and if it pays the net amount are shown. From the point of view of the recipient of trade credit, a credit period beginning at the end of the month is preferable in both cases, since purchases can be paid for without penalty at a later date than otherwise would have been possible. ■

To maintain their competitive position, firms within an industry generally offer the same terms. In many cases, stated credit terms are not the terms that are actually given to a customer. Special arrangements, or "deals," are made to provide certain customers with more favorable terms. The prospective purchaser is wise to look closely at the credit terms of suppliers when making a purchase decision. In many instances, concessions may be available.

ANALYZING CREDIT TERMS

The credit terms that a firm is offered by its suppliers allow it to delay payments for its purchases. Since the supplier's cost of having its money tied up in merchandise after it is sold is probably reflected in the purchase price, the purchaser is already indi-

TABLE 16.4

PAYMENT DATES FOR THE SIMPSON CORPORATION GIVEN VARIOUS ASSUMPTIONS

	September 10 purchase		September 20 purchase	
Beginning of credit period	Discount taken	Net amount paid	Discount taken	Net amount paid
Date of invoice	Sept. 20	Oct. 10	Sept. 30	Oct. 20
End of month (EOM)	Oct. 10	Oct. 30	Oct. 10	Oct. 30

[8]Occasionally, firms receive invoices before receiving the actual merchandise purchased. In these situations the beginning of the credit period is not tied to the invoice date, which could be 30 days prior to the receipt of goods.

rectly paying for this benefit. The purchaser should therefore carefully analyze credit terms to determine the best trade credit strategy.

TAKING THE CASH DISCOUNT If a firm is extended credit terms that include a cash discount, it has two options. Its first option is to *take the cash discount.* If a firm intends to take a cash discount, it should pay on the last day of the discount period. There is no cost associated with taking a cash discount.

EXAMPLE

Lawrence Industries, operator of a small chain of video stores, purchased $1,000 worth of merchandise on February 27 from a supplier extending terms of 2/10 net 30 EOM. If the firm takes the cash discount, it will have to pay $980 [$1,000 − (.02 × $1,000)] on March 10, thereby saving $20. ■

GIVING UP THE CASH DISCOUNT The second option open to the firm is to *give up the cash discount* and pay on the final day of the credit period. Although there is no direct cost associated with giving up a cash discount, there is an implicit cost. The **cost of giving up a cash discount** is the implied rate of interest paid to delay payment of an account payable for an additional number of days. In other words, the amount of the discount that is given up is the interest being paid by the firm to keep its money by delaying payment for a number of days. This cost can be illustrated by a simple example. The example assumes that if the firm takes a cash discount, payment will be made on the final day of the cash discount period, and if the cash discount is given up, payment will be made on the final day of the credit period.

cost of giving up a cash discount
The implied rate of interest paid to delay payment of an account payable for an additional number of days.

EXAMPLE

As in the preceding example, Lawrence Industries has been extended credit terms of 2/10 net 30 EOM on $1,000 worth of merchandise. If it takes the cash discount on its February 27 purchase, payment will be required on March 10. If the cash discount is given up, payment can be made on March 30. To keep its money for an extra 20 days (from March 10 to March 30), the firm must give up an opportunity to pay $980 for its $1,000 purchase. In other words, it will cost the firm $20 to delay payment for 20 days. Figure 16.4 shows the payment options that are open to the company.

To calculate the cost of giving up the cash discount, the *true purchase price* must be viewed as the discounted cost of the merchandise. For Lawrence Industries this discounted cost would be $980. To delay paying the $980 for an extra 20 days, the firm must pay $20 ($1,000 − $980). The annual percentage cost of giving up the cash discount can be calculated, by using Equation 16.1:[9]

$$\text{Cost of giving up cash discount} = \frac{CD}{100\% - CD} \times \frac{360}{N} \tag{16.1}$$

where

CD = the stated cash discount in percentage terms
N = the number of days payment can be delayed by giving up the cash discount

[9]Equation 16.1 and the related discussions are based on the assumption that there is only one discount period. In the event that multiple discount periods are offered, calculation of the cost of giving up the discount must be made for each alternative.

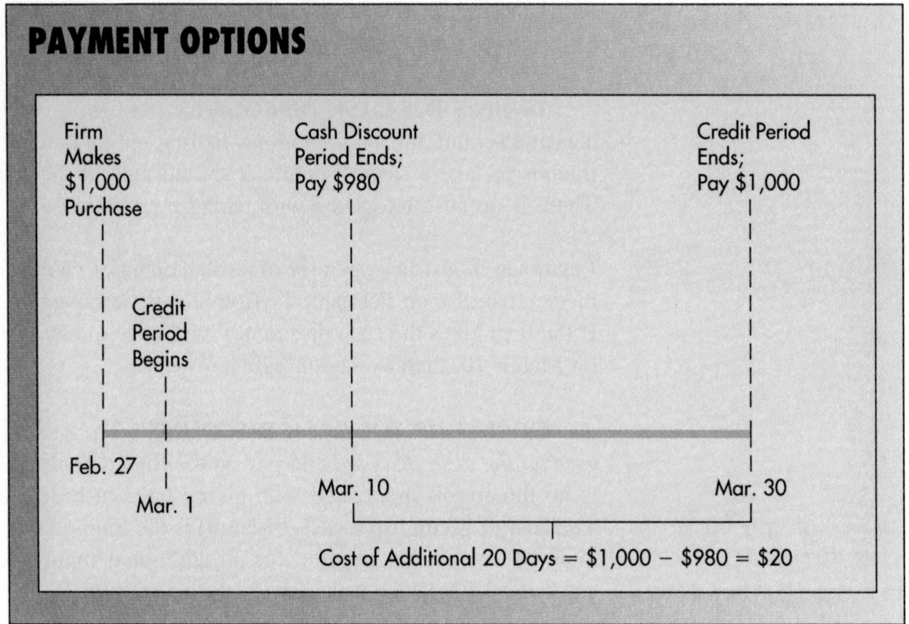

FIGURE 16.4
Payment options for Lawrence Industries

Substituting the values for *CD* (2%) and *N* (20 days) into Equation 16.1 results in an annualized cost of giving up the cash discount of 36.73 percent [(2% ÷ 98%) × (360 ÷ 20)]. A 360-day year is assumed.[10]

A simple way to *approximate* the cost of giving up a cash discount is to use the stated cash discount percentage, *CD,* in place of the first term of Equation 16.1:

$$\text{Approximate cost of giving up cash discount} = CD \times \frac{360}{N} \tag{16.2}$$

The smaller the cash discount, the closer the approximation to the actual cost of giving up the cash discount. Using this approximation, the cost of giving up the cash discount for Lawrence Industries is 36 percent [2% × (360 ÷ 20)]. ■

USING THE COST OF GIVING UP A CASH DISCOUNT IN DECISION MAKING The financial manager must determine whether it is advisable to take a cash discount. It is important to recognize that taking cash discounts may represent an important source of additional profitability for firms that are currently routinely giving them up.

[10]This example assumes that Lawrence Industries gives up only one discount during the year, which costs it 2.04 percent for 20 days (i.e., 2% ÷98%) or 36.73 percent when annualized. However, if Lawrence Industries *continually* gives up the 2 percent cash discounts, the effect of compounding will cause the annualized cost to rise to 43.84 percent:

$$\text{Annualized cost when discounts are continually given up} = \left[1 + \frac{CD}{100\% - CD}\right]^{360/N} - 1 \tag{16.1a}$$

$$= \left[1 + \frac{2\%}{100\% - 2\%}\right]^{360/20} - 1 = \underline{\underline{43.84\%}}$$

EXAMPLE

Mason Products, a large building supply company, has four possible suppliers, each offering different credit terms. Except for the differences in credit terms, their products and services are identical. Table 16.5 presents the credit terms offered by suppliers A, B, C, and D, respectively, and the cost of giving up the cash discounts in each transaction. The approximation method of calculating the cost of giving up a cash discount (Equation 16.2) has been used to simplify the analysis. The cost of giving up the cash discount from supplier A is 36 percent; from supplier B, 8 percent; from supplier C, 21.6 percent; and from supplier D, 28.8 percent.

If the firm needs short-term funds, which are currently available from its bank at an interest rate of 13 percent, and if each of the suppliers (A, B, C, and D) is viewed *separately,* which (if any) of the suppliers' cash discounts will the firm give up? To answer this question, each supplier's terms must be evaluated as they would be if it were the firm's sole supplier. In dealing with supplier A, the firm will take the cash discount, since the cost of giving it up is 36 percent. The firm will then borrow the funds it requires from its bank at 13 percent interest. In dealing with supplier B, the firm will do better to give up the cash discount, since the cost of this action is less than the cost of borrowing money from the bank (8 percent as opposed to 13 percent). In dealing with either supplier C or supplier D, the firm should take the cash discount, since in both cases the cost of giving up the discount is greater than the 13 percent cost of borrowing from the bank. ■

The example shows that the cost of giving up a cash discount is relevant in evaluating a single supplier's credit terms in light of certain *bank borrowing costs.* In comparing various suppliers' credit terms, the cost of giving up the cash discount may not be the most important factor in the decision process. Other factors relative to payment strategies may also need to be considered. It is important to note that some firms, particularly small firms and poorly managed firms, routinely give up *all* discounts because either they lack alternative sources of unsecured short-term financing or they fail to recognize the high implicit costs of their actions.

EFFECTS OF STRETCHING ACCOUNTS PAYABLE

stretching accounts payable
Paying bills as late as possible without damaging one's credit rating.

A strategy that is often employed by a firm is **stretching accounts payable**—that is, paying bills as late as possible without damaging its credit rating. Such a strategy can reduce the cost of giving up a cash discount. Although this strategy is financially attractive, it raises an important ethical issue: It may cause the firm to violate the agree-

TABLE 16.5

CASH DISCOUNTS AND ASSOCIATED COSTS FOR MASON PRODUCTS

Supplier	Credit terms	Approximate cost of giving up cash discount
A	2/10 net 30 EOM	36.0%
B	1/10 net 55 EOM	8.0
C	3/20 net 70 EOM	21.6
D	4/10 net 60 EOM	28.8

ment into which it entered with its supplier when it purchased merchandise. Clearly, a supplier would not look kindly on a customer who regularly and purposely postponed paying for purchases.

EXAMPLE

Lawrence Industries was extended credit terms of 2/10 net 30 EOM. The cost of giving up the cash discount, assuming payment on the last day of the credit period, was found to be approximately 36 percent [2% × (360 ÷ 20)]. If the firm were able to stretch its account payable to 70 days without damaging its credit rating, the cost of giving up the cash discount would be only 12 percent [2% × (360 ÷ 60)]. Stretching accounts payable reduces the implicit cost of giving up a cash discount. ■

CONCEPT IN PRACTICE

Double-Checking Accounts Payable Saved Fields & Associates $900

Fields & Associates is a California-based consulting firm that double-checks the accounts payable ledgers of 300 companies, including 20 FORTUNE 500 firms. The most frequent cause of overpayment is the inability of customer computers to recognize slight variations in bookkeeping entries. For instance, the software creates separate listings if a supplier's name pops up as L.A. Gear on one bill and LA Gear on another. Although suppliers reimburse customers for overpayments upon request, suppliers effectively have an interest-free loan in the interim. Fields estimates that $3.5 billion will be spent in duplicate payments during 1993 and admits that it recently made six duplicate payments for a total of $900. In every case, Fields had to ask for its money back. In a consulting role, Fields urges clients to pay only original bills.

Accruals

accruals
Liabilities for services received for which payment has yet to be made.

The second spontaneous source of short-term financing for a business is accruals. **Accruals** are liabilities for services received for which payment has yet to be made. The most common items accrued by a firm are wages and taxes. Since taxes are payments to the government, their accrual cannot be manipulated by the firm. However, the accrual of wages can be manipulated to some extent. This is accomplished by delaying payment of wages, thereby receiving an interest-free loan from employees who are paid sometime after they have performed the work. The pay period for employees who earn an hourly rate is often governed by union regulations or by state or federal law. However, in other cases the frequency of payment is at the discretion of the company's management.

EXAMPLE

The Tenney Company, a large janitorial service company, currently pays its employees at the end of each work week. The weekly payroll totals $400,000. If the firm were to extend the pay period so as to pay its employees one week later throughout an entire year, the employees would in effect be loaning the firm $400,000 for a year. If the firm could earn 10 percent annually on invested funds, such a strategy would be worth $40,000 per year (.10 × $400,000). By delaying payment of accruals in this way, the firm could save this amount of money. ■

CONCEPTS IN REVIEW

16-5 What are the two key sources of spontaneous short-term financing for a firm? Why are these sources considered spontaneous, and how are they related to the firm's sales? Do they normally have a stated cost?

16-6 Is there a cost associated with taking a cash discount? Is there any cost associated with giving up a cash discount? How is the decision to take a cash discount affected by the firm's cost of borrowing short-term funds?

Unsecured sources of short-term loans

Firms frequently establish lines of credit, which specify the amount of unsecured short-term borrowing that a bank will make available to them over a given period of time. Why is such an arrangement attractive from the viewpoint of both the borrowing firm and the lending bank? Before reading on, take a few moments to answer this question.

BUSINESSES OBTAIN UNSECURED SHORT-TERM LOANS FROM TWO MAJOR SOURCES—banks and commercial paper. Unlike the spontaneous sources of *unsecured short-term financing,* these sources are negotiated and result from deliberate actions taken by the financial manager. Bank loans are more popular because they are available to firms of all sizes; commercial paper tends to be available only to large firms. In addition, international loans can be used to finance international transactions.

Bank loans

short-term self-liquidating loan
An unsecured short-term loan in which the use to which the borrowed money is put provides the mechanism through which the loan is repaid.

Banks are a major source of unsecured short-term loans to businesses. The major type of loan made by banks to businesses is the **short-term self-liquidating loan.** Self-liquidating loans are intended merely to carry the firm through seasonal peaks in financing needs that are attributable primarily to build-ups of accounts receivable and inventory. It is expected that as receivables and inventories are converted into cash, the funds needed to retire these loans will automatically be generated. In other words, the use to which the borrowed money is put provides the mechanism through which the loan is repaid (hence the term *self-liquidating*). Banks lend unsecured short-term funds in three basic ways: through single-payment notes, lines of credit, and revolving credit agreements. Before we look at these types of loans, it is necessary to lay some groundwork about loan interest rates.

LOAN INTEREST RATES

The interest rate on a bank loan is typically based upon the *prime rate of interest* and can be a fixed or a floating rate. It should be evaluated by using the effective interest rate, which is calculated differently depending upon whether interest is paid when the loan matures or in advance. Each of these aspects of loan interest rates is evaluated below.

prime rate of interest (prime rate)
The lowest rate of interest charged by the nation's leading banks on business loans to their most important and reliable business borrowers.

PRIME RATE OF INTEREST The **prime rate of interest (prime rate)** is the lowest rate of interest charged by the nation's leading banks on business loans to their most important and reliable business borrowers.[11] The prime rate fluctuates with changing supply-and-demand relationships for short-term funds.[12] Banks generally determine the rate to be charged on loans to various borrowers by adding some type of premium to the prime rate to adjust it for the borrower's "riskiness." The premium may amount to 4 percent or more, although most unsecured short-term notes carry premiums of less than 2 percent. In general, commercial banks do not make short-term unsecured loans to businesses that are believed to be questionable risks.

fixed-rate loan
A loan whose rate of interest is determined at a set increment above the prime rate and remains unvarying at that fixed rate until maturity.

floating-rate loan
A loan whose rate of interest is established at an increment above the prime rate and is allowed to "float," or vary, above prime *as the prime rate varies* until maturity.

FIXED- AND FLOATING-RATE LOANS Loans can have either fixed or floating interest rates. On a **fixed-rate loan** the rate of interest is determined at a set increment above the prime rate on the date of the loan and remains unvarying at that fixed rate until maturity. On a **floating-rate loan** the increment above the prime rate is initially established, and the rate of interest is allowed to "float," or vary, above prime *as the prime rate varies* until maturity. Generally, the increment above the prime rate on a floating-rate loan will be *lower* than on a fixed-rate loan of equivalent risk because the lender bears less risk with a floating-rate loan. The highly volatile nature of the prime rate in recent years, coupled with the widespread use of computers by banks to monitor and calculate loan interest, has been responsible for the *current dominance of floating-rate loans.*

METHOD OF COMPUTING INTEREST Once the rate of interest has been established, the method of computing interest is determined. Interest can be paid either when a loan matures or in advance. If interest is paid at maturity, the *effective interest rate*—the actual rate of interest paid—for an assumed one-year period[13] is equal to

$$\frac{\text{Interest}}{\text{Amount borrowed}} \tag{16.3}$$

Most bank loans to businesses require the interest payment at maturity. When interest is paid in advance, it is deducted from the loan so that the borrower actually receives less money than is requested. These loans, on which interest is paid in advance, are of-

[11]Some, generally very large, firms can borrow from their banks at an interest rate slightly below the prime rate. This typically occurs when the borrowing firm either maintains high deposit balances at the bank over time or agrees to pay an upfront fee to "buy down" the interest rate. Below-prime-rate-loans are clearly the exception rather than the rule.

[12]From 1975 through the third quarter of 1978 the prime rate was generally below 9 percent. From the end of 1978 until June of 1985 the prime rate remained above 9.5 percent. In late December 1980 the prime rate reached a record high 21.5 percent. The prime rate slowly dropped from 9.5 percent in June 1985 to 7.5 percent in late August 1986, and in March 1987 it began a slow rise to 9.0 percent by November of 1987. It remained around 9.0 percent until the middle of 1988 when it began to rise, peaking at 11.5 percent in 1989. The prime rate then declined to and remained at about 10.0 percent through the end of 1990. By the middle of 1991 it had declined to 8.5 percent from which it further declined, reaching 6.0 percent in mid-1992. The prime rate remained at 6.0 percent through the middle of 1993. At that time the general expectation was a reasonably stable prime rate.

[13]Effective interest rates for loans with maturities of less than one year can be found by using the technique presented in Chapter 5 for finding effective interest rates when interest is compounded more frequently than annually. See Equation 5.10.

discount loans
Loans on which interest is paid in advance by deducting it from the amount borrowed.

ten called **discount loans**. The *effective interest rate for a discount loan* assuming a one-year period is calculated as

$$\frac{\text{Interest}}{\text{Amount borrowed} - \text{interest}} \tag{16.4}$$

Paying interest in advance therefore raises the effective interest rate above the stated interest rate. Let us look at an example.

EXAMPLE

The Wooster Company, a manufacturer of athletic apparel, wants to borrow \$10,000 at a stated rate of 10 percent interest for one year. If the interest on the loan is paid at maturity, the firm will pay \$1,000 (.10 × \$10,000) for the use of the \$10,000 for the year. Substituting into Equation 16.3, the effective interest rate will therefore be

$$\frac{\$1{,}000}{\$10{,}000} = 10.0 \text{ percent}$$

If the money is borrowed at the same *stated* rate but interest is paid in advance, the firm will still pay \$1,000 in interest, but it will receive only \$9,000 (\$10,000 − \$1,000). Thus the effective interest rate in this case is

$$\frac{\$1{,}000}{\$10{,}000 - \$1{,}000} = \frac{\$1{,}000}{\$9{,}000} = 11.1 \text{ percent}$$

Paying interest in advance thus makes the effective interest rate (11.1 percent) greater than the stated interest rate (10.0 percent). ■

SINGLE-PAYMENT NOTES

single-payment note
A short-term, one-time loan payable as a single amount at its maturity.

A **single-payment note** can be obtained from a commercial bank by a creditworthy business borrower. This type of loan is usually a "one-shot" deal made when a borrower needs additional funds for a short period but does not believe that this need will continue. The resulting instrument is a *note,* which must be signed by the borrower. The note states the terms of the loan, which include the length of the loan (the maturity date) and the interest rate charged. This type of short-term note generally has a maturity of 30 days to 9 months or more. The interest charged on the note is generally tied in some fashion to the prime rate of interest. A note may have either a fixed or floating rate. Let us look at an example.

EXAMPLE

Gordon Manufacturing, a producer of rotary mower blades, recently borrowed \$100,000 from each of two banks—bank A and bank B. The loans were incurred on the same day, when the prime rate of interest was 9 percent. Each loan involved a 90-day note with interest to be paid at the end of 90 days. The interest rate was set at 1½ percent above the prime rate on bank A's fixed-rate note. This means that over the 90-day period, the rate of interest will remain at 10½ percent (9% prime rate + 1½% increment) regardless of fluctuations in the prime rate. The total interest cost on this loan is \$2,625 [\$100,000 × (10½% × 90/360)]. The effective cost of this loan is 2.625 percent (\$2,625/\$100,000) for 90 days. Assuming that the loan is rolled over each 90 days throughout the year under the same terms and circumstances, its effective *annual* interest rate can be found by using Equation 5.10. Since the loan costs 2.625 percent for 90 days, it is necessary to compound (1 + 0.02625) for four periods in the year (i.e., 360/90) and then subtract 1:

$$\text{Effective annual interest rate} = (1 + 0.02625)^4 - 1$$
$$= 1.1092 - 1 = 0.1092 = \underline{\underline{10.92\%}}$$

The resulting effective annual rate of interest on Gordon's fixed-rate, 90-day note is 10.92 percent.

The interest rate was set at 1 percent above the prime rate on bank B's floating-rate note. This means that the rate charged over the 90 days will vary directly *with* the prime rate. Initially, the rate will be 10 percent (9% + 1%), but when the prime rate changes, so will the rate of interest on the note. For instance, if after 30 days the prime rate rises to 9.5 percent and after another 30 days it drops to 9.25 percent, the firm would be paying 0.833 percent for the first 30 days (10% × 30/360), 0.875 percent for the next 30 days (10.5% × 30/360), and 0.854 percent for the last 30 days (10.25% × 30/360). Its total interest cost would be $2,562 [$100,000 × (0.833% + 0.875% + 0.854%)] resulting in an effective cost of 2.562 percent ($2,562/$100,000) for 90 days. Again assuming that the loan is rolled over each 90 days throughout the year under the same terms and circumstances, its effective annual interest rate is 10.65 percent:

$$\text{Effective annual interest rate} = (1 + 0.02562)^4 - 1$$
$$= 1.1065 - 1 = 0.1065 = \underline{\underline{10.65\%}}$$

Clearly, in this case the floating-rate loan would have been less expensive (10.65 percent) than the fixed-rate loan (10.92 percent) due to its generally lower interest rates over the 90-day term of the note. ■

LINES OF CREDIT

line of credit
An agreement between a commercial bank and a business specifying the amount of unsecured short-term borrowing the bank will make available to the firm over a given period of time.

A **line of credit** is an agreement between a commercial bank and a business specifying the amount of unsecured short-term borrowing the bank will make available to the firm over a given period of time. It is similar to the agreement under which issuers of bank credit cards, such as MasterCard, Visa, and Discover, extend preapproved credit to cardholders. A line of credit agreement is typically made for a period of one year and often places certain constraints on the borrower. A line of credit agreement is *not a guaranteed loan* but indicates that if the bank has sufficient funds available, it will allow the borrower to owe it up to a certain amount of money. The amount of a line of credit is *the maximum amount the firm can owe the bank* at any point in time.

In applying for a line of credit, the borrower may be required to submit such documents as its cash budget, its pro forma income statement, its pro forma balance sheet, and its recent financial statements. If the bank finds the customer acceptable, the line of credit will be extended. The major attraction of a line of credit from the bank's point of view is that it eliminates the need to examine the creditworthiness of a customer each time it borrows money.

INTEREST RATES The interest rate on a line of credit is normally stated as a floating rate—the *prime rate plus a percent.* If the prime rate changes, the interest rate charged on new *as well as outstanding* borrowing will automatically change. The amount a borrower is charged in excess of the prime rate depends on its creditworthiness. The more creditworthy the borrower, the lower the interest increment above prime, and vice versa.

operating change restrictions
Contractual restrictions that a bank may impose on a firm as part of a line of credit agreement.

OPERATING CHANGE RESTRICTIONS In a line of credit agreement, a bank may impose **operating change restrictions,** which give it the contractual right to revoke the line if any major changes occur in the firm's financial condition or operations. The firm is usually required to submit for review periodically (quarterly or semiannually) up-to-date and, preferably, audited financial statements. In addition, the bank typically needs to be informed of shifts in key managerial personnel or in the firm's operations before changes take place. Such changes may affect the future success and debt-paying ability of the firm and thus could alter its credit status. If the bank does not agree with the proposed changes and the firm makes them anyway, the bank has the right to revoke the line of credit agreement.

compensating balance
A required checking account balance equal to a certain percentage of the borrower's short-term unsecured bank loan.

COMPENSATING BALANCES To ensure that the borrower will be a good customer, many short-term unsecured bank loans—single-payment notes and lines of credit—often require the borrower to maintain a **compensating balance** in a demand deposit account (checking account) equal to a certain percentage of the amount borrowed.[14] Compensating balances of 10 to 20 percent are frequently required. A compensating balance not only forces the borrower to be a good customer of the bank but may also raise the interest cost to the borrower, thereby increasing the bank's earnings. An example will illustrate.

EXAMPLE

Estrada Graphics, a graphic design firm, has borrowed $1 million under a line of credit agreement. It must pay a stated interest rate of 10 percent and maintain a compensating balance equal to 20 percent of the amount borrowed, or $200,000, in its checking account. Thus it actually receives the use of only $800,000. To use the $800,000 for a year, the firm pays interest of $100,000 (.10 × $1,000,000). The effective interest rate on the funds is therefore 12.5 percent ($100,000 ÷ $800,000), 2.5 percent more than the stated rate of 10 percent.

If the firm normally maintains a balance of $200,000 or more in its checking account, the effective interest rate will equal the stated interest rate of 10 percent because none of the $1 million borrowed is needed to satisfy the compensating balance requirement. If the firm normally maintains a $100,000 balance in its checking account, only an additional $100,000 will have to be tied up, leaving it with $900,000 ($1,000,000 − $100,000) of usable funds. The effective interest rate in this case would be 11.1 percent ($100,000 ÷ $900,000). Thus a compensating balance raises the cost of borrowing *only* if it is larger than the firm's normal cash balance. ■

annual cleanup
The requirement that for a certain number of days during the year, borrowers under a line of credit carry a zero loan balance (i.e., owe the bank nothing).

ANNUAL CLEANUPS To ensure that money lent under a line of credit agreement is actually being used to finance seasonal needs, many banks require an **annual cleanup.** This means that the borrower must have a loan balance of zero—that is, owe the bank nothing—for a certain number of days during the year. Forcing the borrower to carry a zero loan balance for a certain period of time ensures that short-term loans do not turn into long-term loans.

[14]Sometimes the compensating balance will be stated as a percentage of the amount of the line of credit rather than the amount borrowed. In other cases the compensating balance will be linked to both the amount borrowed and the amount of the line of credit.

All the characteristics of a line of credit agreement are negotiable to some extent. Today, banks bid competitively to attract large, well-known firms. A prospective borrower should attempt to negotiate a line of credit with the most favorable interest rate, for an optimal amount of funds, and with a minimum of restrictions. Borrowers today frequently pay fees to lenders in lieu of maintaining deposit balances as compensation for loans and other services provided by the lender. The lender will attempt to get a good return with maximum safety. These negotiations should produce a line of credit that is suitable to both borrower and lender.

revolving credit agreement
A line of credit *guaranteed* to the borrower by the bank for a stated time period and regardless of the scarcity of money.

REVOLVING CREDIT AGREEMENTS

A **revolving credit agreement** is nothing more than a *guaranteed line of credit.* It is guaranteed in the sense that the commercial bank making the arrangement assures the borrower that a specified amount of funds will be made available regardless of the scarcity of money. The interest rate and other requirements for a revolving credit agreement are similar to those for a line of credit. It is not uncommon for a revolving credit agreement to be for a period greater than one year.[15] Since the bank guarantees the availability of funds to the borrower, a **commitment fee** is normally charged on a revolving credit agreement.[16] This fee often applies to the average unused balance of the borrower's credit line. It is normally about .5 percent of the *average unused portion* of the funds. An example will clarify the nature of the commitment fees.

commitment fee
The fee that is normally charged on a revolving credit agreement, often based on the average unused balance of the borrower's credit line.

EXAMPLE

The REH Company, a major real estate developer, has a $2 million revolving credit agreement with its bank. Its average borrowing under the agreement for the past year was $1.5 million. The bank charges a commitment fee of .5 percent. Since the average unused portion of the committed funds was $500,000 ($2 million − $1.5 million), the commitment fee for the year was $2,500 (.005 × $500,000). Of course, REH also had to pay interest on the actual $1.5 million borrowed under the agreement. Assuming that $160,000 interest was paid on the $1.5 million borrowed, the effective cost of the agreement is 10.83 percent [($160,000 + $2,500)/$1,500,000]. Although more expensive than a line of credit, a revolving credit agreement can be less risky from the borrower's viewpoint, since the availability of funds is guaranteed by the bank. ■

Commercial paper

commercial paper
A form of financing consisting of short-term, unsecured promissory notes issued by firms with a high credit standing.

Commercial paper is a form of financing that consists of short-term, unsecured promissory notes issued by firms with a high credit standing. Generally, only quite large firms of unquestionable financial soundness and reputation are able to issue commercial paper. Most commercial paper has maturities ranging from 3 to 270 days. Although there is no set denomination, it is generally issued in multiples of $100,000 or more. A large portion of the commercial paper today is issued by finance companies;

[15]Many authors classify the revolving credit agreement as a form of *intermediate-term financing,* defined as having a maturity of one to seven years. In this text, the intermediate-term financing classification is not used; only short-term and long-term classifications are made. Since many revolving credit agreements are for more than one year, they can be classified as a form of long-term financing; however, they are discussed here because of their similarity to line of credit agreements.

[16]Some banks not only require payment of the commitment fee but also require the borrower to maintain, in addition to the compensating balance against actual borrowings, a compensating balance of 10 percent or so against the unused portion of the commitment.

manufacturing firms account for a smaller portion of this type of financing. As will be noted in Chapter 17, businesses often purchase commercial paper, which they hold as marketable securities, to provide an interest-earning reserve of liquidity.

INTEREST ON COMMERCIAL PAPER

The interest paid by the issuer of commercial paper is determined by the size of the discount and the length of time to maturity. Commercial paper is sold at a discount from its *par,* or *face, value,* and the actual interest earned by the purchaser is determined by certain calculations. These can be illustrated by the following example.

EXAMPLE

Bertram Corporation, a large shipbuilder, has just issued \$1 million worth of commercial paper that has a 90-day maturity and sells for \$980,000. At the end of 90 days the purchaser of this paper will receive \$1 million for its \$980,000 investment. The interest paid on the financing is therefore \$20,000 on a principal of \$980,000. This is equivalent to an annual interest rate for the Bertram Corporation commercial paper of 8.2 percent [(\$20,000 ÷ \$980,000) × (360 days ÷ 90 days)]. ■

An interesting characteristic of commercial paper is that it *normally* has a yield of 1 to 3 percent below the prime bank loan rate. In other words, firms are able to raise funds through the sale of commercial paper more cheaply than by borrowing from a commercial bank. The reason is that many suppliers of short-term funds do not have the option of making low-risk business loans at the prime rate.[17] They can invest only in marketable securities such as Treasury bills and commercial paper. The yields on these marketable securities on September 22, 1993, when the prime rate of interest was 6.0 percent, were about 2.9 percent for three-month Treasury bills and about 3.2 percent for three-month commercial paper.

Although the stated interest cost of borrowing through the sale of commercial paper is normally lower than the prime bank loan rate, the *overall cost* of commercial paper may not be cheaper than a bank loan. Additional costs include the fees paid by most issuers to obtain the bank line of credit used to back the paper, fees paid to obtain third-party ratings used to make the paper more salable, and flotation costs. In addition, it is important for the firm to maintain a good working relationship with its bank. Therefore even if it is slightly more expensive to borrow from a commercial bank, it may at times be advisable to do so to establish the necessary rapport with a particular institution. This strategy ensures that when money is tight, funds can be obtained promptly and at a reasonable interest rate.

SALE OF COMMERCIAL PAPER

Commercial paper is *directly placed with investors* by the issuer or is *sold by commercial paper dealers.* For performing the marketing function, the commercial paper dealer is paid a fee. Regardless of the method of sale, most commercial paper is pur-

[17]Commercial banks are legally prohibited from lending an amount greater than 15 percent (plus an additional 10 percent for loans secured by readily marketable collateral) of their unimpaired capital and surplus to any one borrower. This restriction is intended to protect depositors by forcing the commercial bank to spread its risk across a number of borrowers. In addition, smaller commercial banks do not have many opportunities to lend to large, high-quality business borrowers.

chased from a firm by other businesses, banks, life insurance companies, pension funds, and money market mutual funds.

CONCEPT IN PRACTICE

When NeXT to Broke, Ask Ross

After seven years of losses, NeXT Computer, Inc. earned its first-ever operating profit in the fourth quarter of 1992. Many lenders were attracted by their faith in Steven Jobs's ability to recreate the success he had experienced after co-founding Apple Computer. Canon, IBM, and Ross Perot provided lines of credit totaling $200 million. However, financing the development of object-oriented programming greatly limited the amount of funds available for operating units. NeXT's disgruntled marketing vice-president complained that his "fourth-quarter budget was too small to buy one advertisement in *Business Week*."

International loans

In some ways, arranging short-term financing for international trade is no different from financing purely domestic operations. In both cases, producers must finance the production and storage of goods for sale and then continue to finance accounts receivable before collecting any cash payments from sales. In other ways, however, the short-term financing of international sales and purchases is fundamentally different from strictly domestic trade.

INTERNATIONAL TRANSACTIONS

The important difference between international and domestic transactions is that payments are often made or received in a foreign currency. Not only does this require a U.S. company to pay the costs of doing business in the foreign exchange market; it also exposes the company to exchange rate risk if there is a delay between the date that a foreign-currency invoice is created and the date it is paid. A U.S.-based company that exports goods and has accounts receivable denominated in a foreign currency faces the risk that the U.S. dollar will appreciate in value relative to the foreign currency. The risk to a U.S. importer with foreign-currency-denominated accounts payable is that the dollar will depreciate. Although exchange rate risk can often be protected against by using currency forward, futures, or options markets, doing so is costly and possible only for relatively few foreign currencies.

Other distinguishing features of international trade include the large size and longer maturity date of typical transactions. Therefore companies that are involved in international trade generally have to finance larger dollar amounts for longer time periods than companies who operate domestically. Furthermore, because foreign companies are rarely well known in the United States, some financial institutions are reluctant to lend to U.S. exporters or importers, particularly smaller firms.

letter of credit

A letter written by a company's bank to the company's foreign supplier, stating that the bank will guarantee payment of an invoiced amount if all the underlying agreements are met.

FINANCING INTERNATIONAL TRADE

Many U.S. banks offer financing for international trade, and several specialized techniques have evolved. Perhaps the most important financing vehicle is the **letter of credit**, a letter written by a company's bank to the company's foreign supplier, stating that the bank will guarantee payment of an invoiced amount if all the underlying agreements are met. The bank receives a fee for issuing a letter of credit. The letter of credit essentially substitutes a well-known bank's reputation and creditworthiness for that of its commercial customer, increasing the likelihood that foreign suppliers will sell to a U.S. importer. Likewise, a U.S. exporter is more willing to sell goods to a foreign buyer if the transaction is covered by a letter of credit issued by a well-known bank in the buyer's home country.

Firms that do business in foreign countries on an ongoing basis often finance their operations, at least in part, in the local market. A company that has an assembly plant in Mexico, for example, might choose to finance its purchases of Mexican goods and services with peso funds borrowed from a Mexican bank. This not only minimizes exchange rate risk but also improves the company's business ties to the host community. Multinational companies, however, sometimes finance their international transactions through dollar-denominated loans from international banks. The depth and liquidity of *Eurocurrency loan markets* allows creditworthy borrowers to obtain financing on very attractive terms.

TRANSACTIONS BETWEEN SUBSIDIARIES

Much international trade involves transactions between corporate subsidiaries. A U.S. company might, for example, manufacture one part in an Asian plant and another part in the United States, assemble the product in Brazil, and sell it in Europe. The shipment of goods back and forth between subsidiaries creates accounts receivable and accounts payable, but the parent company has considerable discretion about how and when payments will be made. In particular, the parent can minimize foreign exchange fees and other transaction costs by "netting" what affiliates owe each other and paying only the net amount due rather than having both subsidiaries pay each other the gross amounts due.

CONCEPTS IN REVIEW

16-7 What is the *prime rate of interest,* and how is it relevant to the cost of short-term bank borrowing? What is a *floating-rate loan?* How does the *effective interest rate* differ between a loan requiring interest payments *at maturity* and another similar loan requiring interest *in advance?*

16-8 What are the basic terms and characteristics of a *single-payment note?* How is the *effective annual interest rate* on such a note found when it is assumed to be rolled over throughout the year under the same terms and circumstances?

16-9 What is a *line of credit?* Describe each of the following features that are often included in these agreements.

a. Operating change restrictions

b. Compensating balance

c. Annual cleanup

16-10 What is meant by *a revolving credit agreement?* How does this arrangement differ from the line of credit agreement? What is a *commitment fee?*

16-11 How is commercial paper used to raise short-term funds? Who can issue commercial paper? Who buys commercial paper? How is it sold?

16-12 What is the important difference between international and domestic transactions? How is a *letter of credit* used in financing international trade transactions? What is "netting," and how is it used in transactions between subsidiaries?

Secured sources of short-term loans

Secured short-term loans have specific assets—typically accounts receivable or inventory—pledged as collateral. Why do you think that in spite of the collateral, these loans have a higher cost to the borrower than do unsecured short-term loans? Spend a short time answering this question before reading ahead.

secured short-term financing
Short-term financing (loans) obtained by pledging specific assets as collateral.

security agreement
The agreement between the borrower and the lender that specifies the collateral held against a secured loan.

ONCE A FIRM HAS EXHAUSTED ITS UNSECURED SOURCES OF SHORT-TERM FINANCING, it may be able to obtain additional short-term loans on a secured basis. **Secured short-term financing** has specific assets pledged as collateral. The *collateral* commonly takes the form of an asset, such as accounts receivable or inventory. The lender obtains a security interest in the collateral through the execution of a contract (security agreement) with the borrower. The **security agreement** specifies the collateral held against the loan. In addition, the terms of the loan against which the security is held are attached to, or form part of, the security agreement. They specify the conditions required for the security interest to be removed, along with the interest rate on the loan, repayment dates, and other loan provisions. A copy of the security agreement is filed in a public office within the state—typically a county or state court. Filing provides subsequent lenders with information about which assets of a prospective borrower are unavailable for use as collateral. The filing requirement protects the lender by legally establishing the lender's security interest.

Characteristics of secured short-term loans

Although many people believe that holding collateral as security reduces the risk of the loan, lenders do not usually view loans in this way. Lenders recognize that by having an interest in collateral they can reduce losses if the borrower defaults, but *as far as changing the risk of default, the presence of collateral has no impact.* A lender requires collateral to ensure recovery of some portion of the loan in the event of default. What the lender wants above all, however, is to be repaid as scheduled. In general, lenders prefer to make less risky loans at lower rates of interest than to be in a position in which they are forced to liquidate collateral.

COLLATERAL AND TERMS

A number of factors relative to the characteristics that are desirable in collateral and the basic terms of secured short-term loans need to be examined.

COLLATERAL Lenders of secured short-term funds prefer collateral that has a life, or duration, that is closely matched to the term of the loan. This assures the lender that the collateral can be used to satisfy the loan in the event of a default. Current assets—accounts receivable and inventories—are the most desirable short-term loan collateral, since they normally convert into cash much sooner than do fixed assets. Thus the short-term lender of secured funds generally accepts only liquid current assets as collateral.

percentage advance
The percent of the book value of the collateral that constitutes the principal of a secured loan.

TERMS Typically, the lender determines the desirable **percentage advance** to make against the collateral. This percentage advance constitutes the principal of the secured loan and is normally between 30 and 100 percent of the book value of the collateral. It varies not only according to the type and liquidity of collateral but also according to the type of security interest being taken.

The interest rate that is charged on secured short-term loans is typically *higher* than the rate on unsecured short-term loans. Commercial banks and other institutions do not normally consider secured loans less risky than unsecured loans and therefore require higher interest rates on them. In addition, negotiating and administering secured loans is more troublesome for the lender than negotiating and administering unsecured loans. The lender therefore normally requires added compensation in the form of a service charge, a higher interest rate, or both. *The higher cost of secured as opposed to unsecured borrowing is attributable to the greater risk of default and to the increased administration costs involved.* (Remember that firms typically borrow on a secured basis only after exhausting less costly unsecured sources of short-term funds.)

INSTITUTIONS EXTENDING SECURED SHORT-TERM LOANS

commercial finance companies
Lending institutions that make *only* secured loans—both short-term and long-term—to businesses.

The primary sources of secured short-term loans to businesses are commercial banks and commercial finance companies. Both institutions deal in short-term loans secured primarily by accounts receivable and inventory. The operations of commercial banks have already been described. **Commercial finance companies** are lending institutions that make *only* secured loans—both short-term and long-term—to businesses. Unlike banks, finance companies are not permitted to hold deposits.

Only when its unsecured and secured short-term borrowing power from the commercial bank is exhausted will a borrower turn to the commercial finance company for additional secured borrowing. Because the finance company generally ends up with higher-risk borrowers, its interest charges on secured short-term loans are usually higher than those of commercial banks. The leading U.S. commercial finance companies include Associates Capital Company, The CIT Group, and GE Capital Services.

The use of accounts receivable as collateral

Two commonly used means of obtaining short-term financing with accounts receivable are pledging accounts receivable and factoring accounts receivable. Actually, only a pledge of accounts receivable creates a secured short-term loan; factoring really entails the *sale* of accounts receivable at a discount. Although factoring is not actually a form of secured short-term borrowing, it does involve the use of accounts receivable to obtain needed short-term funds.

PLEDGING ACCOUNTS RECEIVABLE

pledge of accounts receivable
The use of a firm's accounts receivable as security, or collateral, to obtain a short-term loan.

A **pledge of accounts receivable** is often used to secure a short-term loan. Because accounts receivable are normally quite liquid, they are an attractive form of short-term collateral. Both commercial banks and commercial finance companies extend loans against pledges of accounts receivable.

THE PLEDGING PROCESS When a firm approaches a prospective lender to request a loan against accounts receivable, the lender will first evaluate the firm's accounts receivable to determine their desirability as collateral. The lender will make a list of the acceptable accounts, along with the billing dates and amounts. If the borrowing firm requests a loan for a fixed amount, the lender will need to select only enough accounts to secure the funds requested. In some instances the borrower may want the maximum loan available. In this situation the lender will evaluate all the accounts to select the maximum amount of acceptable collateral. Let us look at an example.

EXAMPLE

The Second National Bank of Bryn Mawr is analyzing the accounts receivable ledger of the Crowe Company, an educational publisher, to find acceptable collateral for a pledge of accounts receivable. Each of Crowe's accounts receivable, along with its age and average payment period, is given in Table 16.6. Since Crowe extends credit terms of 2/10 net 30 EOM, the bank eliminates from further consideration all accounts that are currently overdue (those whose age is greater than 30 days). This immediately eliminates the accounts of customers C, E, and I.

The second step in the bank's evaluation process is to analyze the historical payment patterns of the customers. After calculating the average payment period for each customer (given in the last column of Table 16.6), the Second National Bank decides to eliminate customer B, whose account, although not currently overdue, normally requires 60 days to collect. Having eliminated the accounts of customers B, C, E, and I, the bank is left with $45,000 of acceptable accounts from customers A, D, F, G, and H (who owe $10,000, $4,000, $6,000, $14,000, and $11,000, respectively). The Crowe Company therefore has $45,000 of acceptable accounts receivable collateral. Each account that is used as collateral will be marked in the Crowe Company's ledger, and a list of the billing dates and amounts will be kept by the bank. ■

After selecting the acceptable accounts, the lender will normally adjust the dollar value of these accounts for expected returns on sales and other allowances. If a customer whose account has been pledged returns merchandise or receives some type of allowance, such as a cash discount for early payment, the amount of the collateral is automatically reduced. For protection from such occurrences, the lender will normally reduce the value of the acceptable collateral by a fixed percentage.

TABLE 16.6

THE CROWE COMPANY'S ACCOUNTS RECEIVABLE

Customer	Account receivable	Age[a]	Average payment period
A	$10,000	20 days	35 days
B	8,000	5	60
C	15,000	50	45
D	4,000	14	30
E	3,000	70	60
F	6,000	10	20
G	14,000	3	10
H	11,000	23	10
I	3,000	45	45

[a]Number of days since the beginning of the credit period.

EXAMPLE

The $45,000 of acceptable accounts receivable selected by the Second National Bank of Bryn Mawr from the Crowe Company's books must be adjusted for returns and allowances. The bank decides, after evaluating the company's accounts, that a 5 percent adjustment is appropriate. After this adjustment the Crowe Company has acceptable collateral of $42,750 [$45,000 × (1 − .05)]. ■

Once the lender has determined the acceptable accounts and made adjustments for returns on sales and other allowances, the percentage to be advanced against the collateral must be determined on the basis of the lender's overall evaluation of the quality of the acceptable receivables and the expected cost of their liquidation. This percentage represents the principal of the loan and typically ranges between 50 and 90 percent of the face value of acceptable accounts receivable. To protect its interest in the collateral, the lender will file a **lien,** which is a publicly disclosed legal claim on the collateral.

lien
A publicly disclosed legal claim on collateral.

EXAMPLE

After a reexamination of the Crowe Company's acceptable accounts receivable *and* general operations, the Second National Bank of Bryn Mawr decides to advance 85 percent of the value of the adjusted acceptable collateral. This means that the bank will lend the company about $36,338 ($42,750 × .85). ■

NOTIFICATION Pledges of accounts receivable are normally made on a **nonnotification basis.** This means that a customer whose account has been pledged as collateral is not notified of this action. Under the nonnotification arrangement, the borrower still collects the pledged account receivable, and the lender trusts that the borrower will remit these payments as they are received. If a pledge of accounts receivable is made on a **notification basis,** the customer is notified to remit payment directly to the lender.

nonnotification basis
The basis on which a borrower, having pledged an account receivable, continues to collect the account payments without notifying the account customer.

notification basis
The basis on which an account customer whose account has been pledged (or factored) is notified to remit payments directly to the lender (or factor) rather than to the borrower.

PLEDGING COST The stated cost of a pledge of accounts receivable is normally 2 to 5 percent above the prime rate of interest offered by banks. In addition to the stated interest rate, a service charge of up to 3 percent may be levied. Although the interest payment is expected to compensate the lender for making the loan, the service charge is needed to cover the administrative costs incurred by the lender. Clearly, pledges of accounts receivable are typically a high-cost source of short-term financing.

FACTORING ACCOUNTS RECEIVABLE

Factoring accounts receivable involves their outright sale at a discount to a factor or other financial institution. A **factor** is a financial institution that purchases accounts receivable from businesses. There are 15 to 20 firms currently operating in the United States that deal solely in factoring accounts receivable. Some commercial banks and commercial finance companies also factor accounts receivable. Although not actually the same as obtaining a short-term loan, factoring accounts receivable is similar to borrowing with accounts receivable as collateral. Factoring constitutes approximately one-third of the total financing secured by accounts receivable (including factoring) and inventory in the United States currently.

factoring accounts receivable
The outright sale of accounts receivable at a discount to a *factor* or other financial institution to obtain funds.

factor
A financial institution that specializes in purchasing accounts receivable from businesses.

FACTORING AGREEMENT A factoring agreement normally states the exact conditions, charges, and procedures for the purchase of an account. The factor, like a lender against a pledge of accounts receivable, chooses accounts for purchase, selecting only those that appear to be acceptable credit risks. Where factoring is to be on a continuing basis, the factor will actually make the firm's credit decisions, since this will guarantee the acceptability of accounts.[18] Factoring is normally done on a *notification basis,* and the factor receives payment of the account directly from the customer. In addition, most sales of accounts receivable to a factor are made on a **nonrecourse basis.** This means that the factor agrees to accept all credit risks. Thus if a purchased account turns out to be uncollectible, the factor must absorb the loss.

nonrecourse basis
The basis on which accounts receivable are sold to a factor with the understanding that the factor accepts all credit risks on the purchased accounts.

Typically, the factor is not required to pay the firm until the account is collected or until the last day of the credit period, whichever occurs first. The factor sets up an account similar to a bank deposit account for each customer. As payment is received or as due dates arrive, the factor deposits money into the seller's account, from which the seller is free to make withdrawals as needed. An example will illustrate.

EXAMPLE

The Ross Company, a manufacturer of aluminum baseball bats, has sold five accounts to a factor. All the accounts were due September 30. Each account, its amount, and its status on September 30 are given below.

Account	Amount	Status
A	$10,000	Collected Sept. 20
B	4,000	Collected Sept. 28
C	50,000	Collected Sept. 29
D	8,000	Uncollected
E	12,000	Collected Sept. 20

As of September 30, the factor has received payment from suppliers, A, B, C, and E. It therefore has already taken its fee, or discount, on each account and remitted the balance to Ross Company. On September 30, the factor has to remit the $8,000 due on account D, less the factoring fee on this account, even though it has not yet been collected. If account D is uncollectible, the factor will have to absorb the loss. ■

In many cases, if the firm leaves the money in the account, a *surplus* will exist on which the factor will pay interest. In other instances, the factor may make *advances* to the firm against uncollected accounts that are not yet due. These advances represent a negative balance in the firm's account, on which interest is charged.

FACTORING COST Factoring costs include commissions, interest levied on advances, and interest earned on surpluses. The factor deposits in the firm's account the book value of the collected or due accounts purchased by the factor, less the commissions. The commissions are typically stated as a 1 to 3 percent discount from the book value of factored accounts receivable. The *interest levied on advances* is generally

[18]The use of credit cards such as MasterCard, Visa, and Discover by consumers has some similarity to factoring, since the vendor accepting the card is reimbursed at a discount for purchases made by using the card. The difference between factoring and credit cards is that cards are nothing more than a line of credit extended by the issuer, which charges the vendors a fee for accepting the cards. In factoring, the factor does not analyze credit until after the sale has been made; in many cases (except when factoring is done on a continuous basis) the initial credit decision is the responsibility of the vendor, not the factor who purchases the account.

2 to 4 percent above the prime rate. It is levied on the actual amount advanced. The interest paid on surpluses or positive account balances left with a factor is generally around .5 percent per month.

EXAMPLE

The Graber Company, a producer of children's rainwear, has recently factored a number of accounts. The factor holds an 8 percent reserve, charges on and deducts from the book value of factored accounts a 2 percent factoring commission, and charges 1 percent per month interest (12 percent per year) on advances. Graber wishes to obtain an advance on a factored account having a book value of $1,000 and due in 30 days. The proceeds to the company are calculated as follows:

Book value of account	$1,000
Less: Reserve (8% × $1,000)	80
Less: Factoring commission (2% × $1,000)	20
Funds available for advance	$ 900
Less: Interest on advance (1% × $900)	9
Proceeds from advance	$ 891

The firm receives $891 now and expects eventually to receive the $80 reserve. The exact method that is used to calculate the amount of the advance will vary, depending on the terms of the factoring agreement. Since the Graber Company must pay the interest in advance, the effective *annual interest cost* of this transaction is not 12 percent but 12.12 percent [($9 ÷ $891) × 12].[19] Of course, if one includes both the factoring commission of $20 and the interest of $9, the *annual factoring cost* for the transaction would be approximately 39 percent [($29 ÷ $891) × 12]. ■

Although its costs may seem high, factoring has certain advantages that make it quite attractive to many firms. One is the ability it gives the firm to *turn accounts receivable immediately into cash* without having to worry about repayment. Another advantage of factoring is that it ensures a *known pattern of cash flows.* In addition, if factoring is undertaken on a continuous basis, the firm *can eliminate its credit and collection departments.*

CONCEPT IN PRACTICE

Gordon Brothers Gets Cash to Retailers

Bankers often avoid making loans to retailers because of the retailer's erratic borrowing needs and fears that they will have to sell off a borrower's inventory to recover capital. When facing cash shortages created by the absence of bank financing, retailers often turn to Gordon Brothers. This Boston-based financier offers special financing options to retailers. Three of the most popular services offered by the privately owned, 300-employee company are given below.

- **Inventory value guarantees** Gordon promises banks that it will buy specific inventory at a given price.

[19]Note that because this is deemed to be a single transaction, its cost is annualized without the necessity of compounding. It would be necessary to compound when finding the effective annual cost only when the transaction is assumed to be repeated on a continuous basis throughout the year under the same terms and circumstances.

- **Merchant credit support** Gordon buys inventory for cash-strapped clients, turns the inventory over to the client at full price, and takes any available trade discount.
- **Working capital loans** Gordon will extend short-term loans to retailers in the \$1-million-to-\$5-million range. Due to the absence of bank financing in this range and Gordon's guarantee that it will not cut back on the financing offered, Gordon has been able to charge four points above the prime rate on these loans.

The use of inventory as collateral

Inventory is generally second to accounts receivable in desirability as short-term loan collateral. Inventory is attractive as collateral because it normally has a market value that is greater than its book value, which is used to establish its value as collateral. A lender securing a loan with inventory will probably be able to sell it for at least book value if the borrower defaults on its obligations.

The most important characteristic of inventory being evaluated as loan collateral is *marketability,* which must be considered in light of its physical properties. A warehouse of *perishable* items, such as fresh peaches, may be quite marketable, but if the cost of storing and selling the peaches is high, they may not be desirable collateral. *Specialized items* such as moon-roving vehicles are not desirable collateral either, since finding a buyer for them could be difficult. In evaluating inventory as possible loan collateral, the lender looks for items with very stable market prices that have ready markets and that lack undesirable physical properties.

FLOATING INVENTORY LIENS

floating inventory lien
A lender's claim on the borrower's general inventory as collateral for a secured loan.

A lender may be willing to secure a loan under a **floating inventory lien,** which is a claim on inventory in general. This arrangement is most attractive when the firm has a stable level of inventory that consists of a diversified group of relatively inexpensive merchandise. Inventories of items such as auto tires, screws and bolts, and shoes are candidates for floating-lien loans. Since it is difficult for a lender to verify the presence of the inventory, the lender will generally advance less than 50 percent of the book value of the average inventory. The interest charge on a floating lien is 3 to 5 percent above the prime rate. Commercial banks often require floating liens as extra security on what would otherwise be an unsecured loan. A floating-lien inventory loan may also be available from commercial finance companies.

EXAMPLE

Prescott Toy Company, a manufacturer of inexpensive plastic children's toys, needs a loan of \$125,000 for 60 days. The company's primary bank has told management that a loan secured under a floating inventory lien is possible. The annual interest rate would be about 14 percent, which is 5 percent above the prime rate. Funds would be advanced up to 40 percent of the average book value of the secured inventory. This means that the company would have to put up \$312,500 in book value of inventory as collateral—the loan required divided by the loan advance ratio (\$125,000 ÷ .40). The cost of this loan is \$2,917 (\$125,000 × 14% × 2/12). This is equivalent to an effective rate of 2.33 percent for two months (\$2,917/\$125,000) or the stated 14 percent rate annually [2.33% × (12 ÷ 2)] assuming that this is a single transaction.[20] ■

[20]See footnote 19 on page 673.

TRUST RECEIPT INVENTORY LOANS

trust receipt inventory loan
An agreement under which the lender advances 80 to 100 percent of the cost of the borrower's relatively expensive inventory items in exchange for the borrower's promise to immediately repay the loan, with accrued interest, upon the sale of each item.

A **trust receipt inventory loan** can often be made against relatively expensive automotive, consumer-durable, and industrial equipment that can be identified by serial number. Under this agreement the borrower keeps the inventory and the lender may advance 80 to 100 percent of its cost. The lender files a *lien* on all the items financed. The borrower is free to sell the merchandise but is *trusted* to remit the amount lent against each item along with accrued interest to the lender immediately after the sale. The lender then releases the lien on the appropriate item. The lender makes periodic checks of the borrower's inventory to make sure that the required amount of collateral remains in the hands of the borrower. The interest charge to the borrower is normally 2 percent or more above the prime rate.

Trust receipt loans are often made by manufacturers' wholly owned financing subsidiaries, known as *captive finance companies,* to their customers.[21] *Floor planning* of automobile or equipment retailers is done under this arrangement. For example, General Motors Acceptance Corporation (GMAC), the financing subsidiary of General Motors, grants these types of loans to its dealers. Trust receipt loans are also available through commercial banks and commercial finance companies.

WAREHOUSE RECEIPT LOANS

warehouse receipt loan
An arrangement in which the lender receives control of the pledged inventory collateral, which is warehoused by a designated agent on the lender's behalf.

A **warehouse receipt loan** is an arrangement whereby the lender, who may be a commercial bank or commercial finance company, receives control of the pledged inventory collateral, which is stored, or warehoused, by a designated agent on the lender's behalf. After selecting acceptable collateral, the lender hires a warehousing company to act as its agent and take possession of the inventory. Two types of warehousing arrangements are possible: terminal warehouses and field warehouses. A *terminal warehouse* is a central warehouse that is used to store the merchandise of various customers. The lender normally uses such a warehouse when the inventory is easily transported and can be delivered to the warehouse relatively inexpensively. Under a *field warehouse* arrangement the lender hires a field warehousing company to set up a warehouse on the borrower's premises or to lease part of the borrower's warehouse as a repository for the pledged collateral. Regardless of whether a terminal or field warehouse is established, the warehousing company places a guard over the inventory. Only upon written approval of the lender can any portion of the secured inventory be released.

The actual lending agreement specifically states the requirements for the release of inventory. As in the case of other secured loans, the lender accepts only collateral that is believed to be readily marketable and advances only a portion—generally 75 to 90 percent—of the collateral's value. The specific costs of warehouse receipt loans are generally higher than those of any other secured lending arrangements due to the need to hire and pay a third party (the warehousing company) to guard and supervise the collateral. The basic interest charged on warehouse receipt loans is higher than that charged on unsecured loans, generally ranging from 3 to 5 percent above the prime rate. In addition to the interest charge, the borrower must absorb the costs of warehousing by paying the warehouse fee, which is generally between 1 and 3 percent of the amount of the loan. The borrower is normally also required to pay the insurance costs on the warehoused merchandise.

---

[21]Captive finance companies are especially popular in industries that manufacture consumer durable goods because they provide the manufacturer with a useful sales tool as well as other potential advantages.

EXAMPLE

GIT Industries, a manufacturer of adhesive products, needs to borrow $80,000 for one month to support a seasonal expansion of inventory. The financial manager has approached a commercial finance company about borrowing under a field warehouse receipt arrangement. The terms of the loan are prime plus 3 percent interest per annum, which makes the stated interest rate about 12 percent. Management thinks the prime rate will remain stable during the period of the loan. The finance company will loan 80 percent of the book value of inventory put up as collateral. The loan would require a warehousing charge of $500 per month plus 1 percent of the value of the inventory warehoused.

To be able to borrow $80,000, GIT Industries must provide collateral of $100,000—the amount needed ($80,000) divided by the loan ratio (0.80). The cost of the field warehouse receipt loan for one month is determined as follows:

Field warehouse charge	$ 500
1% of collateralized inventory charge	1,000
Loan interest (12%/12 × $80,000)	800
Total cost	$2,300

The effective interest rate on this loan is 2.875 percent ($2,300 ÷ $80,000) for one month. The effective annual cost of the loan is 34.5 percent (2.875% × 12) assuming that this is a single transaction.[22] ■

CONCEPTS IN REVIEW

16-13 In general, what kind of interest rates and fees are levied on secured short-term loans? Why are these rates generally *higher* than the rates on unsecured short-term loans?

16-14 Compare, contrast, and describe the basic features of the following forms of short-term financing. Be sure to mention the institutions offering each of them.

a. Pledging accounts receivable
b. Factoring accounts receivable

16-15 Describe the basic features and compare each of the following methods of using *inventory* as short-term loan collateral.

a. Floating lien
b. Trust receipt loan
c. Warehouse receipt loan

Summary

LG 1 Understand the two definitions of net working capital and the tradeoff between profitability and risk as it relates to changing levels of current assets and current liabilities. Net working capital is defined as the difference between current assets and current liabilities or, alternatively, as the portion of a firm's current assets financed with long-term funds. Profitability is the relationship between revenues and costs. Risk, in the context of short-term financial decisions, is the probability that a firm will become technically insolvent—unable to pay its bills as they come due. Assuming a constant level of total assets, the higher a firm's ratio of current assets to total assets, the less profitable the firm, and the less risky it is. The converse is also true. With constant total assets, the higher a firm's ratio of current liabilities to total assets, the more profitable and more risky the firm is. The converse of this statement is also true.

LG 2 Discuss, in terms of profitability and risk, the aggressive financing strategy and the conservative financing strategy for meeting the firm's total—permanent and seasonal—funds requirement. The aggressive strategy for deter-

[22]See footnote 19 on page 673.

mining the appropriate financing mix is a high-profit, high-risk financing strategy under which the firm finances at least its seasonal needs, and possibly some of its permanent needs, with short-term funds and the majority of its permanent needs with long-term funds. The conservative strategy is a low-profit, low-risk financing strategy under which all funds requirements—both permanent and seasonal—are financed with long-term funds. Short-term funds are saved for emergencies or unexpected outflows.

LG **3 Review the key features and characteristics of the two major sources of spontaneous short-term financing—accounts payable and accruals.** Spontaneous sources of short-term financing include accounts payable, which are the primary source of short-term funds, and accruals. Accounts payable result from credit purchases of merchandise, and accruals result primarily from wage and tax obligations. The key features of these forms of financing are summarized in part I of Table 16.7.

LG **4 Analyze credit terms offered by suppliers to determine, when the alternative is to borrow funds, whether to take or give up cash discounts and whether to stretch accounts payable.** Credit terms may differ with respect to the credit period, cash discount, cash discount period, and beginning of the credit period. The cost of giving up cash discounts is a factor in deciding whether to take or give up a cash discount. Cash discounts should be given up only when a firm in need of short-term funds must pay an interest rate on borrowing that is greater than the cost of giving up the cash discount. Stretching accounts payable can lower the cost of giving up a cash discount, thereby increasing the attractiveness of giving up the discount.

LG **5 Describe the interest rates, basic types, and key features of unsecured bank sources of short-term loans, the use of commercial paper in short-term financing, and the role of international loans.** Banks are the major source of unsecured short-term loans to businesses. The interest rate on these loans is tied to the prime rate of interest by a risk premium and may be fixed or may float. It should be evaluated by using the effective interest rate. This rate is calculated differently depending upon whether interest is paid when the loan matures or in advance. Bank loans may take the form of a single-payment note, a line of credit, or a revolving credit agreement. Commercial paper, IOUs issued by firms with a high credit standing, is directly placed with investors by the issuer or is sold by commercial paper dealers. The key features of the various types of bank loans as well as commercial paper are summarized in part II of Table 16.7. International sales and purchases expose firms to exchange rate risk; involve larger size and longer maturity dates on typical transactions; can be financed using a letter of credit, by borrowing in the local market, or through dollar-denominated loans obtained from international banks; and on transactions between subsidiaries "netting" can be used to minimize foreign exchange fees and other transactions costs.

LG **6 Explain the characteristics of secured short-term loans and the use of accounts receivable (pledging and factoring) and inventory (floating lien, trust receipt, and warehouse receipt) as short-term loan collateral.** Secured short-term loans are those for which the lender requires collateral—typically, current assets such as accounts receivable or inventory. Only a certain percentage of the book value of acceptable collateral is advanced by the lender. These loans are more expensive than unsecured loans; the presence of collateral does not lower the risk of default, and increased administrative costs result. Both commercial banks and commercial finance companies make secured short-term loans. Both pledging, which involves the use of accounts receivable as loan collateral, and factoring, which involves the outright sale of accounts receivable at a discount, involve the use of accounts receivable to obtain needed short-term funds. Inventory can be used as short-term loan collateral under a floating lien, a trust receipt arrangement, or a warehouse receipt loan. The key features of the popular forms of these loans are summarized in part III of Table 16.7.

Self-test problems (Solutions in Appendix E)

ST 16-1 LG 2 **Aggressive versus conservative financing strategy** Santo Gas has forecast its total funds requirements for the coming year as follows:

Month	Amount	Month	Amount
January	$7,400,000	July	$5,800,000
February	5,500,000	August	5,400,000
March	5,000,000	September	5,000,000
April	5,300,000	October	5,300,000
May	6,200,000	November	6,000,000
June	6,000,000	December	6,800,000

TABLE 16.7

SUMMARY OF KEY FEATURES OF COMMON SOURCES OF SHORT-TERM FINANCING

Type of short-term financing	Source	Cost or conditions	Characteristics
I. Spontaneous sources of short-term financing			
Accounts payable	Suppliers of merchandise	No stated cost except when a cash discount is offered for early payment.	Credit extended on open account for 0 to 120 days. The largest source of short-term financing.
Accruals	Employees and government	Free.	Result from the fact that wages (employees) and taxes (government) are paid at discrete points in time after the service has been rendered. Hard to manipulate this source of financing.
II. Unsecured sources of short-term loans			
Bank sources			
(1) Single-payment notes	Commercial banks	Prime plus 0% to 4% risk premium—fixed or floating rate.	A single-payment loan used to meet a funds shortage expected to last only a short period of time.
(2) Lines of credit	Commercial banks	Prime plus 0% to 4% risk premium—fixed or floating rate. Often must maintain 10% to 20% compensating balance and clean up the line.	A prearranged borrowing limit under which funds, if available, will be lent to allow the borrower to meet seasonal needs.
(3) Revolving credit agreements	Commercial banks	Prime plus 0% to 4% risk premium—fixed or floating rate. Often must maintain 10% to 20% compensating balance and pay a commitment fee of approximately .5% of the average unused balance.	A line of credit agreement under which the availability of funds is guaranteed. Often for a period greater than one year.
Commercial paper	Other businesses, banks, life insurance companies, pension funds, and money market mutual funds	Generally 1% to 3% below the prime rate of interest.	An unsecured short-term promissory note issued by the most financially sound firms. May be placed directly or sold through commercial paper dealers.

III. Secured sources of short-term loans			
Accounts receivable collateral			
(1) Pledging	Commercial banks and commercial finance companies	2% to 5% above prime plus up to 3% in fees. Advance 50% to 90% of collateral value.	Selected accounts receivable are used as collateral. The borrower is trusted to remit to the lender upon collection of pledged accounts. Done on a nonnotification basis.
(2) Factoring	Factors, commercial banks, and commercial finance companies	1% to 3% discount from face value of factored accounts. Interest levied on advances of 2% to 4% above prime. Interest earned on surplus balances left with factor of about .5% per month.	Selected accounts are sold—generally without recourse—at a discount. All credit risks go with the accounts. Factor will loan (make advances) against uncollected accounts that are not yet due. Factor will also pay interest on surplus balances. Typically done on a notification basis.
Inventory collateral			
(1) Floating liens	Commercial banks and commercial finance companies	3% to 5% above prime. Advance less than 50% of collateral value.	A loan against inventory in general. Made when firm has stable inventory of a variety of inexpensive items.
(2) Trust receipts	Manufacturers' captive financing subsidiaries, commercial banks, and commercial finance companies	2% or more above prime. Advance 80% to 100% of cost of collateral.	Loan against relatively expensive automotive, consumer-durable, and industrial equipment that can be identified by serial number. Collateral remains in possession of borrower, who is trusted to remit proceeds to lender upon its sale.
(3) Warehouse receipts	Commercial banks and commercial finance companies	3% to 5% above prime plus a 1% to 3% warehouse fee. Advance 75% to 90% of collateral value.	Inventory used as collateral is placed under control of the lender by putting it in a terminal warehouse or through a field warehouse. A third party—a warehousing company—guards the inventory for the lender. Inventory is released only upon written approval of the lender.

a. Divide the firm's monthly funds requirement into a *permanent* and a *seasonal* component, and find the monthly average for each of these components.

b. Describe the amount of long-term and short-term financing that is used to meet the total funds requirement under (1) an *aggressive strategy* and (2) a *conservative strategy.* Assume that under the aggressive strategy, long-term funds finance permanent needs and short-term funds are used to finance seasonal needs.

c. Assuming short-term funds cost 10 percent annually and long-term funds cost 16 percent annually, use the averages in **a** to calculate the total cost of each of the strategies described in **b**.

d. Discuss the profitability-risk tradeoffs associated with the aggressive strategy and the conservative strategy.

ST 16-2 LG 3 Cash discount decisions The credit terms for each of three suppliers are as follows:

Supplier	Credit terms
X	1/10 net 55 EOM
Y	2/10 net 30 EOM
Z	2/20 net 60 EOM

a. Determine the *approximate* cost of giving up the cash discount from each supplier.

b. Assuming that the firm needs short-term financing, recommend whether it would be better to give up the cash discount or take the discount and borrow from a bank at 15 percent annual interest. Evaluate each supplier separately using your findings in **a**.

c. What impact, if any, would the fact that the firm could stretch its accounts payable (net period only) by 20 days from supplier Z have on your answer in **b** relative to this supplier?

Problems

16-1 LG 2 Permanent versus seasonal funds requirements Manchester Industries' current, fixed, and total assets for each month of the coming year are summarized in the table below:

Month	Current assets (1)	Fixed assets (2)	Total assets [(1) + (2)] (3)
January	$15,000	$30,000	$45,000
February	22,000	30,000	52,000
March	30,000	30,000	60,000
April	18,000	30,000	48,000
May	10,000	30,000	40,000
June	6,000	30,000	36,000
July	9,000	30,000	39,000
August	9,000	30,000	39,000
September	15,000	30,000	45,000
October	20,000	30,000	50,000
November	22,000	30,000	52,000
December	20,000	30,000	50,000

a. Divide the firm's monthly total funds requirement (total assets) into a permanent and a seasonal component.

b. Find the monthly average (1) permanent and (2) seasonal funds requirements using your findings in **a**.

16-2 LG 2 **Annual loan cost** What are the average loan balance and the annual loan cost, given an annual interest rate on loans of 15 percent, for a firm with total monthly borrowings as follows?

Month	Amount	Month	Amount
January	$12,000	July	$6,000
February	13,000	August	5,000
March	9,000	September	6,000
April	8,000	October	5,000
May	9,000	November	7,000
June	7,000	December	9,000

16-3 LG 2 **Aggressive versus conservative financing strategy** Dynabase Tool has forecast its total funds requirements for the coming year as follows:

Month	Amount	Month	Amount
January	$2,000,000	July	$12,000,000
February	2,000,000	August	14,000,000
March	2,000,000	September	9,000,000
April	4,000,000	October	5,000,000
May	6,000,000	November	4,000,000
June	9,000,000	December	3,000,000

a. Divide the firm's monthly funds requirement into (1) a *permanent* and (2) a *seasonal* component, and find the monthly average for each of these components.

b. Describe the amount of long-term and short-term financing used to meet the total funds requirement under (1) an *aggressive strategy* and (2) a *conservative strategy.* Assume that under the aggressive strategy, long-term funds finance permanent needs and short-term funds are used to finance seasonal needs.

c. Assuming that short-term funds cost 12 percent annually and the cost of long-term funds is 17 percent annually, use the averages found in **a** to calculate the total cost of each of the strategies described in **b**.

d. Discuss the profitability–risk tradeoffs associated with the aggressive strategy and the conservative strategy.

16-4 LG 2 **Aggressive versus conservative financing strategy** Marbell International has forecast its seasonal financing needs for the next year as follows. Assuming that the firm's permanent funds requirement is $4 million, calculate the total annual financing costs using the aggressive strategy and the conservative strategy, respectively. Recommend one of the strategies under each of the following conditions:

a. Short-term funds cost 9 percent annually, and long-term funds cost 15 percent annually.
b. Short-term funds cost 10 percent annually, and long-term funds cost 13 percent annually.
c. Both short-term and long-term funds cost 11 percent annually.

Month	Seasonal requirement	Month	Seasonal requirement
January	$ 0	July	$700,000
February	300,000	August	400,000
March	500,000	September	0
April	900,000	October	200,000
May	1,200,000	November	700,000
June	1,000,000	December	300,000

16-5 LG 4 **Payment dates** Determine when a firm must make payment for purchases made and invoices dated on November 25 under each of the following credit terms.

a. net 30
b. net 30 EOM
c. net 45 date of invoice
d. net 60 EOM

16-6 LG 4 **Cost of giving up cash discounts** Determine the cost of giving up cash discounts under each of the following terms of sale.

a. 2/10 net 30
b. 1/10 net 30
c. 2/10 net 45
d. 3/10 net 45
e. 1/10 net 60
f. 3/10 net 30
g. 4/10 net 180

16-7 LG 4 **Cash discount versus loan** Erica Stone works in an accounts payable department. She has attempted to convince her boss to take the discount on the 3/10 net 45 credit terms most suppliers offer, but her boss argues that giving up the 3 percent discount is less costly than a short-term loan at 14 percent. Prove that either Erica or her boss is incorrect.

16-8 LG 4 **Cash discount decisions** Prairie Manufacturing has four possible suppliers, each offering different credit terms. Except for the differences in credit terms, their products and services are virtually identical. The credit terms offered by each supplier are as follows:

Supplier	Credit terms
J	1/10 net 30 EOM
K	2/20 net 80 EOM
L	1/20 net 60 EOM
M	3/10 net 55 EOM

a. Calculate the *approximate* cost of giving up the cash discount from each supplier.
b. If the firm needs short-term funds, which are currently available from its commercial bank at 16 percent, and if each of the suppliers is viewed *separately,* which, if any, of the suppliers' cash discounts should the firm give up? Explain why.
c. What impact, if any, would the fact that the firm could stretch its accounts payable (net period only) by 30 days from supplier M have on your answer in **b** relative to this supplier?

16-9 LG 4 Changing payment cycle Upon accepting the position of chief executive officer and chairman of Reeves Machinery, Frank Cheney changed the firm's weekly payday from Monday afternoon to the following Friday afternoon. The firm's weekly payroll was $10 million, and the cost of short-term funds was 13 percent. If the effect of this change was to delay check clearing by one week, what *annual* savings, if any, were realized?

16-10 LG 5 Cost of bank loan Data Back-Up Systems has obtained a $10,000, 90-day bank loan at an annual interest rate of 15 percent, payable at maturity. (*Note:* Assume a 360-day year.)
a. How much interest (in dollars) will the firm pay on the 90-day loan?
b. Find the effective cost of the loan for the 90 days.
c. Annualize your finding in **b** to find the effective annual interest rate for this loan, assuming that it is rolled over each 90 days throughout the year under the same terms and circumstances.

16-11 LG 5 Effective interest rate A financial institution made a $10,000, one-year discount loan at 10 percent interest, requiring a compensating balance equal to 20 percent of the face value of the loan. Determine the effective annual interest rate associated with this loan.

16-12 LG 5 Compensating balances and effective interest rates Lincoln Industries has a line of credit at Bank Two that requires it to pay 11 percent interest on its borrowing and maintain a compensating balance equal to 15 percent of the amount borrowed. The firm has borrowed $800,000 during the year under the agreement. Calculate the effective annual interest rate on the firm's borrowing in each of the following circumstances:
a. The firm normally maintains no deposit balances at Bank Two.
b. The firm normally maintains $70,000 in deposit balances at Bank Two.
c. The firm normally maintains $150,000 in deposit balances at Bank Two.
d. Compare, contrast, and discuss your findings in **a**, **b**, and **c**.

16-13 LG 5 Integrative—Comparison of loan terms Cumberland Furniture wishes to establish a prearranged borrowing agreement with its local commercial bank. The bank's terms for a line of credit are 3.30 percent over the prime rate, and the borrowing must be reduced to zero for a 30-day period. For an equivalent revolving credit agreement, the rate is 2.80 percent over prime with a commitment fee of .50 percent on the average unused balance. With both loans, the required compensating balance is equal to 20 percent of the amount borrowed. The prime rate is currently 8 percent. Both agreements have $4 million borrowing limits. The firm expects on average to borrow $2 million during the year no matter which loan agreement it decides to use.
a. What is the effective annual interest rate under the line of credit?
b. What is the effective annual interest rate under the revolving credit agreement? (*Hint:* Compute the ratio of the dollars that the firm will pay in interest and commitment fees to the dollars that the firm will effectively have use of.)
c. If the firm does expect to borrow an average of half the amount available, which arrangement would you recommend for the borrower? Explain why.

16-14 LG 5 Cost of commercial paper Commercial paper is usually sold at a discount. Fan Corporation has just sold an issue of 90-day commercial paper with a face value of $1 million. The firm has received $978,000.
a. What effective *annual* interest rate will the firm pay for financing with commercial paper?
b. If a brokerage fee of $9,612 was paid from the initial proceeds to an investment banker for selling the issue, what effective annual interest rate will the firm pay?

16-15 LG 6 **Accounts receivable as collateral** Kansas City Castings (KCC) is attempting to obtain the maximum loan possible using accounts receivable as collateral. The firm extends net 30-day credit. The amounts that are owed KCC by its 12 credit customers, the average age of each account, and customer's average payment period are as follows:

a. If the bank will accept all accounts that can be collected in 45 days or less as long as the customer has a history of paying within 45 days, which accounts will be acceptable? What is the total dollar amount of accounts receivable collateral? (*Note:* Accounts receivable that have an average age greater than the customer's average payment period are also excluded.)

b. In addition to the conditions in **a**, the bank recognizes that 5 percent of credit sales will be lost to returns and allowances. Also, the bank will lend only 80 percent of the acceptable collateral (after adjusting for returns and allowances). What level of funds would be made available through this lending source?

Customer	Account receivable	Average age of account	Average payment period of customer
A	$37,000	40 days	30 days
B	42,000	25	50
C	15,000	40	60
D	8,000	30	35
E	50,000	31	40
F	12,000	28	30
G	24,000	30	70
H	46,000	29	40
I	3,000	30	65
J	22,000	25	35
K	62,000	35	40
L	80,000	60	70

16-16 LG 6 **Accounts receivable as collateral** Springer Products wishes to borrow $80,000 from a local bank using its accounts receivable to secure the loan. The bank's policy is to accept as collateral any accounts that are normally paid within 30 days of the end of the credit period as long as the average age of the account is not greater than the customer's average payment period. Springer's accounts receivable, their average ages, and the average payment period for each customer are given in the following table. The company extends terms of net 30 days.

Customer	Account receivable	Average age of account	Average payment period of customer
A	$20,000	10 days	40 days
B	6,000	40	35
C	22,000	62	50
D	11,000	68	65
E	2,000	14	30
F	12,000	38	50
G	27,000	55	60
H	19,000	20	35

a. Calculate the dollar amount of acceptable accounts receivable collateral held by Springer Products.

b. The bank reduces collateral by 10 percent for returns and allowances. What is the level of acceptable collateral under this condition?

c. The bank will advance 75 percent against the firm's acceptable collateral (after adjusting for returns and allowances). What amount can Springer borrow against these accounts?

16-17 LG 6 Factoring Blair Finance factors the accounts of the Holder Company. All eight factored accounts are listed, with the amount factored, the date due, and the status as of May 30. Indicate the amounts Blair should have remitted to Holder as of May 30 and the dates of those remittances. Assume that the factor's commission of 2 percent is deducted as part of determining the amount of the remittance.

Account	Amount	Date due	Status on May 30
A	$200,000	May 30	Collected May 15
B	90,000	May 30	Uncollected
C	110,000	May 30	Uncollected
D	85,000	June 15	Collected May 30
E	120,000	May 30	Collected May 27
F	180,000	June 15	Collected May 30
G	90,000	May 15	Uncollected
H	30,000	June 30	Collected May 30

16-18 LG 6 Cost of factoring advance—Single amount Duff Industries wishes to receive an *advance* from its factor on an account of $100,000 due in 30 days. The factor holds a 10 percent factor's reserve, charges on and deducts from the book value of factored accounts a 2 percent factoring commission, and charges 16 percent annual interest (paid in advance) on advances.

a. Calculate the maximum dollar amount of interest to be paid.

b. What amount will the firm actually receive?

c. What is the effective annual interest cost of this transaction?

d. What is the annual factoring cost (in percent) for this transaction?

16-19 LG 6 Cost of factoring—Multiple accounts The Rohio Oil Company factors all its accounts. The factor charges on and deducts from the book value of factored accounts a 1 percent factoring commission, holds a 15 percent reserve, and charges 10 percent interest (paid in advance) on advances. Rohio wishes to receive an advance against the following accounts as of September 1:

Account	Amount	Date due
A	$ 60,000	September 30
B	100,000	September 30
C	120,000	September 30
D	75,000	September 30
E	40,000	September 30

a. Calculate the actual amount the firm can borrow.

b. Calculate the maximum dollar amount of interest that must be paid.

c. What is the effective annual interest cost of this advance?

d. What is the annual factoring cost (in percent) for this transaction? Can this rate be compared to a straight loan of the same amount? Why or why not?

e. Why might the actual interest and factoring costs be less than the amounts calculated in **b** and **d**?

16-20 LG 6 **Pledging versus factoring** American Manufacturing is considering obtaining funding through advances against receivables. Total credit sales are $12 million, terms are net 30 days, and payment is made on the average in 30 days. City State Bank will advance funds under a pledging arrangement for 15 percent annual interest. On the average, 80 percent of credit sales will be accepted as collateral. Friendly Finance offers factoring on a nonrecourse basis for a 2.5 percent factoring commission charged on and deducted from the book value of factored accounts, charges 1 percent per month on advances, and requires a 20 percent factor's reserve. Under this plan, the firm would factor all accounts and close its credit and collection department, saving $300,000 per year.

a. What are the effective annual interest rate and the average amount of funds made available under pledging and under factoring?

b. What other effects must be considered in choosing either of these plans?

c. Which plan do you recommend and why?

16-21 LG 6 **Inventory financing** Raymond Manufacturing faces a liquidity crisis—it needs a loan of $100,000 for 30 days. Having no source of additional unsecured borrowing, the firm must find a secured short-term lender. The firm's accounts receivable are quite low, but its inventory is considered liquid and reasonably good collateral. The book value of the inventory is $300,000, of which $120,000 is finished goods.

(1) City-Wide Bank will make a $100,000 trust receipt loan against the finished goods inventory. The annual interest rate on the loan is 12 percent on the outstanding loan balance plus a .25 percent administration fee levied against the $100,000 initial loan amount. Because it will be liquidated as inventory is sold, the average amount owed over the month is expected to be $75,000.

(2) Sun State Bank is willing to lend $100,000 against a floating lien on the book value of inventory for the 30-day period at an annual interest rate of 13 percent.

(3) Citizens' Bank and Trust will loan $100,000 against a warehouse receipt on the finished goods inventory and charge 15 percent annual interest on the outstanding loan balance. A .5 percent warehousing fee will be levied against the average amount borrowed. Because the loan will be liquidated as inventory is sold, the average loan balance is expected to be $60,000.

a. Calculate the dollar cost of each of the proposed plans for obtaining an initial loan amount of $100,000.

b. Which plan do you recommend? Why?

c. If the firm had made a purchase of $100,000 for which it had been given terms of 2/10 net 30, would it increase the firm's profitability to give up the discount and not borrow as recommended in **b**? Why or why not?

Chapter 16 Case Selecting Kanton Company's financing strategy and unsecured short-term borrowing arrangement

Morton Mercado, the CFO of Kanton Company, carefully developed the following estimates of the firm's total funds requirements for the coming year.

Month	Total Funds	Month	Total Funds
January	$1,000,000	July	$6,000,000
February	1,000,000	August	5,000,000
March	2,000,000	September	5,000,000
April	3,000,000	October	4,000,000
May	5,000,000	November	2,000,000
June	7,000,000	December	1,000,000

In addition, Morton expects short-term financing costs of about 10 percent and long-term financing costs of about 14 percent during that period. He developed the three possible financing strategies described below.

Strategy 1—Aggressive: Finance seasonal needs with short-term funds and permanent needs with long-term funds.

Strategy 2—Conservative: Finance an amount equal to the peak need with long-term funds and use short-term funds only in an emergency.

Strategy 3—Tradeoff: Finance $3,000,000 with long-term funds and finance the remaining funds requirements with short-term funds.

To ensure that, along with spontaneous financing from accounts payable and accruals, adequate short-term financing will be available, Morton plans to establish an unsecured short-term borrowing arrangement with its local bank, Third National. The bank has offered either a line of credit or a revolving credit agreement. Third National's terms for a line of credit are an interest rate of 2.50 percent above the prime rate, and the borrowing must be reduced to zero for a 30-day period during the year. On an equivalent revolving credit agreement, the interest rate would be 3.00 percent above prime with a commitment fee of .50 percent on the average unused balance. Under both loans, a compensating balance equal to 20 percent of the amount borrowed would be required. The prime rate is currently 7 percent. Both the line of credit and the revolving credit agreement would have borrowing limits of $1,000,000. For purposes of his analysis, Morton estimates that Kanton will borrow $600,000 on the average during the year, regardless of the financing strategy and loan arrangement it chooses.

Required

a. Divide Kanton's monthly funds requirements into (1) a *permanent* component and (2) a *seasonal* component, and find the monthly average for each.

b. For each of the three possible financing strategies, determine (1) the amount of long-term and short-term financing required and (2) the total annual cost of each strategy.

c. Assuming that the firm expects its current assets to total $4 million throughout the year, determine the average amount of net working capital under each financing strategy. (*Hint:* Current liabilities equal average short-term financing.)

d. Discuss the profitability–risk tradeoff associated with each financing strategy. Which strategy would you recommend to Morton Mercado for Kanton Company? Why?

e. Find the effective annual interest rate under:

(1) The line of credit agreement.

(2) The revolving credit agreement. (*Hint:* Compare the ratio of the dollars that the firm will pay in interest and commitment fees to the dollars that the firm will effectively have use of.)

f. If the firm does expect to borrow an average of $600,000, which borrowing arrangement would you recommend to Kanton? Explain why.

chapter 17

Cash and marketable securities

LEARNING GOALS

 Discuss the motives for holding cash and marketable securities and the two models—Baumol model and the Miller-Orr model—that can be used to determine the appropriate transactional cash balances.

 Use the firm's operating and cash conversion cycles to define and demonstrate the three basic strategies for managing its cash to minimize its financing needs.

 Explain *float,* including its three basic components, and the firm's major objective with respect to the levels of collection float and disbursement float.

 Review popular techniques for speeding up collections and slowing down disbursements, the role of strong banking relationships in cash management, and international cash management.

 Understand the basic characteristics of marketable securities *and* the key government issues—Treasury bills, Treasury notes, and federal agency issues.

 Describe the key features of the popular nongovernment marketable securities—negotiable certificates of deposit, commercial paper, banker's acceptances, Eurodollar deposits, money market mutual funds, and repurchase agreements.

Good cash management affects a company's profitability by shortening the collection time line and reducing transaction costs to process collections and disbursements. Although cash management is part of the Treasury Department, it involves working closely with other departments, particularly the accounting and systems groups. Treasury's cash collection and disbursement systems are also used by accounting to record and reconcile transactions. Other departments use this information to develop policies for payment terms, inventory levels, budgeting methods, and security.

The McDonald's System collects over \$22 billion in cash worldwide each year. McDonald's Corporation has two main sources of cash inflows: sales from company-owned restaurants (about 20 percent of the nearly 13,400 restaurants worldwide), and monthly franchisee payments for rent and service fees. For day-to-day operations our goal is to keep daily cash levels as close to zero as possible. We accomplish this with a controlled disbursement system that tells us early in the day how much we need to cover our debit payments. When daily cash receipts do not cover cash disbursements, we issue commercial paper and repay it when we have a cash surplus. Our large daily cash collections provide the liquidity that we need to operate with very low cash balances.

Another company, such as a manufacturer with large accounts receivable, probably could not operate this way.

Because we have restaurants around the world, international cash management presents many challenges for McDonald's. Banks in some other countries aren't as technologically advanced as U.S. banks, and cash management practices abroad differ considerably. There are foreign exchange risks; you might collect in one currency, then have to pay bills in another. It's hard to get money out of some countries. These situations call for new types of creativity. In Russia we try to use the rubles generated by our Moscow restaurants within the country. We built an office building in Moscow with rubles. Our restaurant is on the ground floor, and we rent the other floors, receiving payment in dollars, which can be more easily repatriated.

Our large daily cash collections provide the liquidity that we need to operate with very low cash balances.

Cash management practices are affected by the business environment. In recent years there have been many bank consolidations and mergers. As a result, we hope to consolidate our banking relationships—we currently use 500 different banks for our 1,400 company-owned restaurants in the U.S.—and reduce our banking costs. In the current low-interest-rate environment, transaction costs are more of an issue than float. To reduce these costs, we've automated a substantial portion of our banking activities. For example, we automatically verify daily deposits using data received directly from our banks. We're also developing systems to bring some banking services in-house. As a result, we have more control, especially on the collections side. In the future electronic data interchange and electronic payments will be increasingly important.

The field of cash management offers many interesting job opportunities, including corporate positions and sales, product development, and management positions at commercial banks. In addition to finance, cash managers also need good accounting and information technology skills, with good general knowledge of their business and strong interpersonal skills. To effectively coordinate the needs of all departments affecting the cash flow time line, they must understand how sales are generated, what triggers cash needs, and how to manage liquidity levels. All these factors are critical to establishing effective cash management policies for the company.

Before joining McDonald's Corporation in December 1987, Karen Leets was an Audit Manager at Coopers & Lybrand, where she worked for eight years. She received both a B.S. in Accounting and an M.B.A. from Indiana State University and is a CPA and a Certified Cash Manager.

Cash and marketable security balances

Cash and marketable securities are held by firms to reduce the risk of technical insolvency by providing a pool of liquid resources for use in making planned as well as unexpected outlays. What basic economic tradeoffs do you think the firm must consider when deciding how to split its liquidity between cash and marketable securities? Take a few moments to answer this question before reading further.

cash
The ready currency to which all liquid assets can be reduced.

marketable securities
Short-term, interest-earning, money-market instruments used by the firm to obtain a return on temporarily idle funds.

CASH AND MARKETABLE SECURITIES ARE THE MOST LIQUID OF THE FIRM'S ASSETS. **CASH** is the ready currency to which all liquid assets can be reduced. **Marketable securities** are short-term, interest-earning, money market instruments that are used by the firm to obtain a return on temporarily idle funds. Together, cash and marketable securities act as a pool of funds that can be used to pay bills as they come due and to meet any unexpected outlays. Because the rate of interest applied by banks to checking accounts is relatively low, firms tend to use excess bank balances to purchase marketable securities. The firm must therefore determine the appropriate balances for both cash and marketable securities to reduce the risk of technical insolvency to an acceptable level. The desired balances are determined by carefully considering the motives for holding them. The higher these balances are, the lower the risk of technical insolvency, and the lower they are, the higher the risk of technical insolvency.

Motives for holding cash and near-cash balances

near-cash
Marketable securities, which are viewed the same as cash because of their high liquidity.

There are three motives for holding cash and **near-cash** (marketable securities) balances. Each motive is based on two underlying questions: (1) What is the appropriate degree of liquidity to maintain? and (2) What is the appropriate distribution of liquidity between cash and marketable securities?

transactions motive
A motive for holding cash or near-cash—to make planned payments for items such as materials and wages.

TRANSACTIONS MOTIVE

A firm maintains cash balances to satisfy the **transactions motive,** which is to make planned payments for items such as materials and wages. If cash inflows and cash outflows are closely matched, transaction cash balances can be smaller. While firms *must* achieve this motive, they typically *try to* achieve the following two motives as well.

safety motive
A motive for holding cash or near-cash—to protect the firm against being unable to satisfy unexpected demands for cash.

SAFETY MOTIVE

Balances held to satisfy the **safety motive** are invested in highly liquid marketable securities that can be immediately transferred from securities to cash. Such securities protect the firm against being unable to satisfy unexpected demands for cash.

speculative motive
A motive for holding cash or near-cash—to put unneeded funds to work or to be able to quickly take advantage of unexpected opportunities that may arise.

SPECULATIVE MOTIVE

At times, firms invest in marketable securities in excess of needs to satisfy the safety motive, as well as in long-term instruments. A firm may do so because it currently has no other use for certain funds or because it wants to be able to quickly take advantage of unexpected opportunities that may arise. These funds satisfy the **speculative motive,** which is the least common of the three motives.

Estimating cash balances

Management's goal should be to *maintain levels of transactional cash balances and marketable securities investments that contribute to improving the value of the firm.* If levels of cash or marketable securities are too high, the profitability of the firm will be lower than if more optimal balances were maintained. This concept was examined in the preceding chapter in the profitability–risk tradeoff discussion. Firms can use either *subjective approaches* or *quantitative models* to determine appropriate transactional cash balances. A subjective approach might be to maintain transactional balance equal to 10 percent of the following month's forecast sales. If the forecast amount of sales for the following month is $500,000, the firm would maintain a $50,000 (i.e., .10 × $500,000) transactional cash balance. Two quantitative models that management can use to determine the appropriate transactional cash balances are the Baumol model and the Miller-Orr model.

BAUMOL MODEL

Baumol model
A model that provides for cost-efficient transactional cash balances; assumes that the demand for cash can be predicted with certainty and determines the *economic conversion quantity (ECQ).*

economic conversion quantity (ECQ)
The cost-minimizing quantity in which to convert marketable securities to cash.

The **Baumol model**[1] is a simple approach that provides for cost-efficient transactional cash balances by determining the optimal cash conversion quantity. It treats cash as an inventory item whose *future demand for settling transactions can be predicted with certainty.* In other words, cash inflows and cash outflows are assumed to be known with certainty. A portfolio of marketable securities acts as a reservoir for replenishing transactional cash balances. The firm manages this cash inventory on the basis of the cost of converting marketable securities into cash (the conversion cost) and the cost of holding cash rather than marketable securities (opportunity cost). The **economic conversion quantity (ECQ),** the cost-minimizing quantity in which to convert marketable securities to cash, is

$$\text{ECQ} = \sqrt{\frac{2 \times \text{conversion cost} \times \text{demand for cash}}{\text{opportunity cost (in decimal form)}}} \qquad (17.1)$$

CONVERSION COST *Conversion cost* includes the fixed cost of placing and receiving an order for cash in the amount ECQ. It includes the cost of communicating the necessity to transfer funds to the cash account, associated paperwork costs, and the cost of any follow-up action. The conversion cost is stated as dollars per conversion.

OPPORTUNITY COST *Opportunity cost* is the interest earnings per dollar given up during a specified time period as a result of holding funds in a non-interest-earning cash account rather than having them invested in interest-earning marketable securities.

CONCEPT IN PRACTICE

Community Credit Union: Higher, Friendly Returns on Excess Cash

Although credit unions have been around since 1909, their popularity was limited until 1986, when their deposits became insured by the "full faith and credit of

[1]William J. Baumol, "The Transactions Demand for Cash: An Inventory Theoretic Approach," *Quarterly Journal of Economics,* November 1952, pp. 545–556.

the United States Government." Credit unions are a cooperative business, owned by members, with eligibility for membership dependent upon a common bond, which is specified in its charter. Most credit unions require employment by a specific business. Others base membership upon residence in a given locale. Although numerous, with 13,000 credit unions nationwide compared with almost 12,000 FDIC-insured banks, only about 10 percent make business loans.

One such operation is Community Credit Union, located in La Crosse, Wisconsin. Like credit unions nationwide, low loss experience and low marketing costs have resulted in higher interest on savings and lower charges on loans. Member services include money market accounts and interest-earning checking accounts.

TOTAL COST The *total cost* of cash is the sum of the total conversion and total opportunity costs. Total conversion cost equals the cost per conversion times the number of conversions per period. The *number of conversions* per period can be found by dividing the period's cash demand by the economic conversion quantity (ECQ). The total dollar opportunity cost equals the opportunity cost (in decimal form) times the average cash balance. The *average cash balance* is found by dividing ECQ by 2. The total cost equation is

$$\text{Total cost} = (\text{cost per conversion} \times \text{number of conversions}) + [\text{opportunity cost (in decimal form)} \times \text{average cash balance}] \quad (17.2)$$

The objective of the Baumol model is to determine the economic conversion quantity (ECQ) of cash that minimizes total cost: conversion cost + opportunity cost. Cash transfers that are larger or smaller than ECQ result in higher total cost.

Graphically, the Baumol model can be depicted as a sawtooth pattern of cash holdings as shown in Figure 17.1. The initial ECQ-dollar cash balance calculated by the equation decreases steadily to zero as the firm spends the cash. When the cash account reaches a zero balance, additional ECQ dollars are transferred from marketable securities to cash. The model can be demonstrated by using a simple example.

EXAMPLE

The management of JanCo, a small distributor of sporting goods, anticipates $1,500,000 in cash outlays (demand) during the coming year. A recent study indicates that it costs

FIGURE 17.1
Baumol model

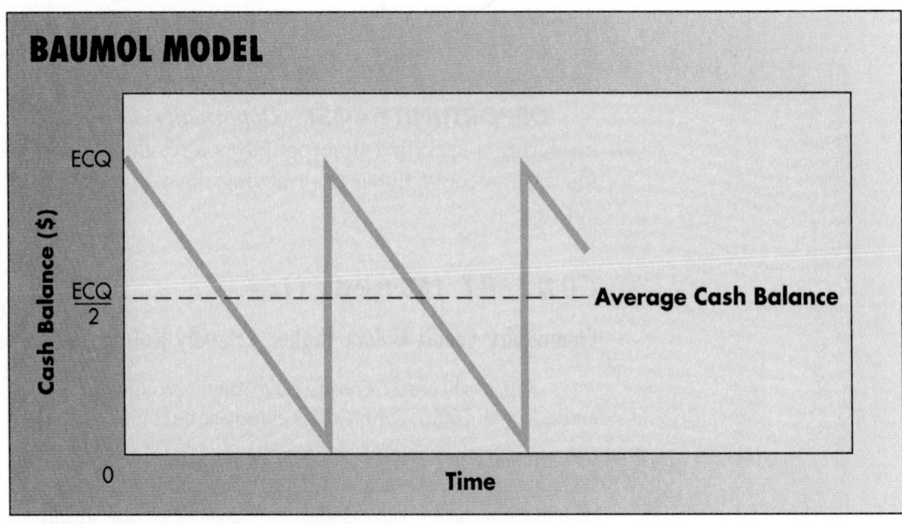

$30 to convert marketable securities to cash. The marketable securities portfolio currently earns an 8 percent annual rate of return. Substituting into Equation 17.1 results in the economic conversion quantity (ECQ) of cash:

$$\text{ECQ} = \sqrt{\frac{2 \times \$30 \times \$1{,}500{,}000}{.08}} = \underline{\underline{\$33{,}541}}$$

Since $33,541 is received each time the cash account is replenished, there will be 45 conversions during the year to replenish the account—$1,500,000/$33,541 = 44.7. The average cash balance is $16,770.50 ($33,541/2). The total cost of managing the cash is found by substituting the appropriate values into Equation 17.2:

$$\text{Total cost} = (\$30 \times 45) + (.08 \times \$16{,}770.50) = \underline{\underline{\$2{,}692}}$$ ■

MILLER-ORR MODEL

Miller-Orr model
A model that provides for cost-efficient transactional cash balances; assumes uncertain cash flows and determines an upper limit and return point for cash balances.

When much *uncertainty* surrounds future cash flows—the firm cannot accurately predict cash inflows and cash outflows—the Miller-Orr model,[2] although more difficult to apply, is generally considered more realistic and appropriate than the Baumol model. The **Miller-Orr model** provides for cost-efficient transactional cash balances by determining an *upper limit* (i.e., maximum amount) and a *return point* for them. The return point represents the level at which the cash balance is set, either when cash is converted to marketable securities or vice versa. Cash balances are allowed to fluctuate between the upper limit and a zero balance.

RETURN POINT The value for the return point depends on (1) conversion costs, (2) the daily opportunity cost of funds, and (3) the variance of daily net cash flows. The variance is estimated by using daily net cash flows (inflows minus outflows for the day). The equation for determining the return point is

$$\text{Return point} = \sqrt[3]{\frac{3 \times \text{conversion cost} \times \text{variance of daily net cash flows}}{4 \times \text{daily opportunity cost (in decimal form)}}} \quad (17.3)$$

where $\sqrt[3]{\ }$ means to take the cube root of the solution under the $\sqrt{\ }$ sign.

UPPER LIMIT The *upper limit for the cash balance* is three times the return point.

CASH BALANCE REACHES THE UPPER LIMIT When the cash balance reaches the upper limit, an amount equal to the *upper limit minus the return point* is converted to marketable securities:

$$\text{Cash converted to marketable securities} = \text{upper limit} - \text{return point} \quad (17.4)$$

CASH BALANCE FALLS TO ZERO When the cash balance falls to zero, the amount converted from marketable securities to cash is the amount represented by the *return point:*

[2]Merton H. Miller and Daniel Orr, "A Model of the Demand for Money by Firms," *Quarterly Journal of Economics,* August 1966, pp. 413–435.

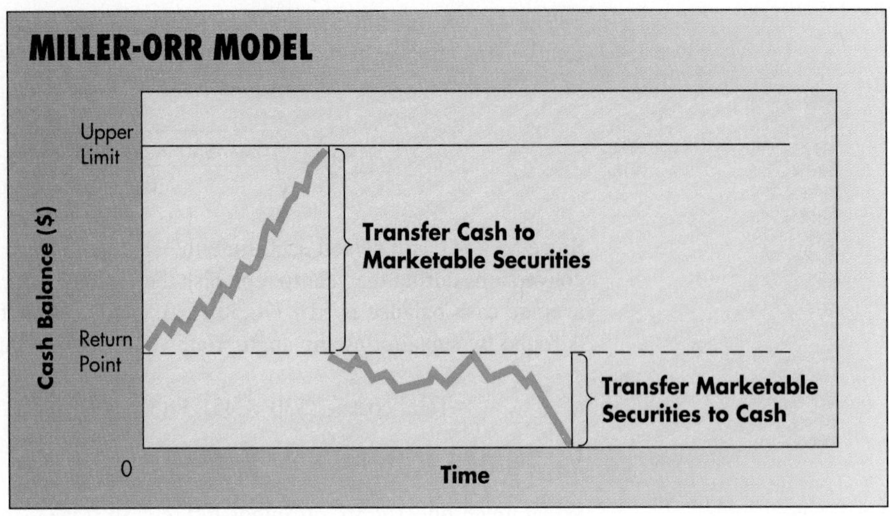

FIGURE 17.2
Miller-Orr model

$$\text{Marketable securities converted to cash} = \text{return point} - \text{zero balance} \quad (17.5)$$

Figure 17.2 depicts this model. An example will help to demonstrate its application.

EXAMPLE

Continuing with the prior example, it costs JanCo $30 to convert marketable securities to cash, or vice versa; the firm's marketable securities portfolio earns an 8 percent annual return, which is 0.0222 percent daily (8%/360 days). The variance of JanCo's daily net cash flows is estimated to be $27,000. Substituting into Equation 17.3 yields the return point:

$$\text{Return point} = \sqrt[3]{\frac{3 \times \$30 \times \$27{,}000}{4 \times 0.000222}} = \underline{\underline{\$1{,}399}}$$

The upper limit is 3 × return point:

$$\text{Upper limit} = 3 \times \$1{,}399 = \underline{\underline{\$4{,}197}}$$

The firm's cash balance will be allowed to vary between $0 and $4,197. When the upper limit is reached, $2,798 ($4,197 − $1,399) is converted (see Equation 17.4) from cash to marketable securities that will earn interest. When the cash balance falls to zero, $1,399 ($1,399 − $0) is converted (see Equation 17.5) from marketable securities to cash. ■

The level of marketable securities investment

In addition to earning a positive return on temporarily idle funds, the marketable securities portfolio serves as a safety stock of cash that can be used to satisfy unexpected demands for funds. The level of the safety stock is the difference between management's desired liquidity level and the level of transactional cash balances determined by either the Baumol or the Miller-Orr models. For example, if management wishes to maintain $25,000 of liquid funds and a transactional cash balance of $18,000 is desired, a $7,000 ($25,000 − $18,000) safety stock of cash would be held as marketable securities. The firm may use a line of credit (as was discussed in Chapter 16) instead of a portfolio of marketable securities, or a combination of line of credit reserves and marketable securities, as safety stocks.

CONCEPTS IN REVIEW

17-1 List and describe the three motives for holding cash and near-cash (marketable securities). Which are the most common motives?

17-2 What is management's goal with respect to the management of cash and marketable securities?

17-3 What purpose do the *Baumol* and *Miller-Orr models* serve? Briefly describe their similarities and differences.

The efficient management of cash

A firm's cash conversion cycle represents the amount of time that elapses between its payment for production inputs and the time when payment is received from the sale of the finished product containing these inputs. What basic strategies would you pursue when managing inventory, accounts receivable, and accounts payable to shorten the cash conversion cycle? Before reading on, spend a few moments answering this question.

CASH BALANCES AND SAFETY STOCKS OF CASH ARE SIGNIFICANTLY INFLUENCED BY THE firm's production and sales techniques and by its procedures for collecting sales receipts and paying for purchases. These influences can be better understood through analysis of the firm's operating and cash conversion cycles.[3] By efficiently managing these cycles, the financial manager can maintain a low level of cash investment and thereby contribute toward maximization of share value.

The operating cycle

operating cycle (OC)
The amount of time that elapses from the point at which the firm begins to build inventory to the point at which cash is collected from sale of the resulting finished product.

The **operating cycle (OC)** of a firm is defined as the amount of time that elapses from the point at which the firm inputs material and labor into the production process (i.e., begins to build inventory) to the point at which cash is collected from the sale of the finished product that contains these production inputs. The cycle is made up of two

[3]The conceptual model that is used in this part to demonstrate basic cash management strategies was developed by Lawrence J. Gitman in "Estimating Corporate Liquidity Requirements: A Simplified Approach," *The Financial Review,* 1974, pp. 79–88, and refined and operationalized by Lawrence J. Gitman and Kanwal S. Sachdeva in "A Framework for Estimating and Analyzing the Required Working Capital Investment," *Review of Business and Economic Research,* Spring 1982, pp. 35–44.

components: the average age of inventory and the average collection period of sales. The firm's operating cycle (OC) is simply the sum of the *average age of inventory (AAI)* and the *average collection period (ACP):*

$$OC = AAI + ACP \tag{17.6}$$

The concept of the operating cycle can be illustrated by using a simple example.

EXAMPLE

MAX Company, a producer of paper dinnerware, sells all its merchandise on credit. The credit terms require customers to pay within 60 days of a sale. The firm's calculations reveal that, on average, it takes 85 days to manufacture, warehouse, and ultimately sell a finished good. In other words, the firm's average age of inventory (AAI) is 85 days. Calculation of the average collection period (ACP) indicates that it is taking the firm, on average, 70 days to collect its accounts receivable. Substituting AAI = 85 days and ACP = 70 days into Equation 17.6, we find MAX's operating cycle to be 155 days (85 days + 70 days). It is graphically depicted above the time line in Figure 17.3. ■

The cash conversion cycle

A company can usually purchase many of its production inputs (i.e., raw materials and labor) on credit. The time it takes the firm to pay for these inputs is called the *average payment period (APP).* These production inputs therefore generate sources

FIGURE 17.3
MAX Company's operating and cash conversion cycles

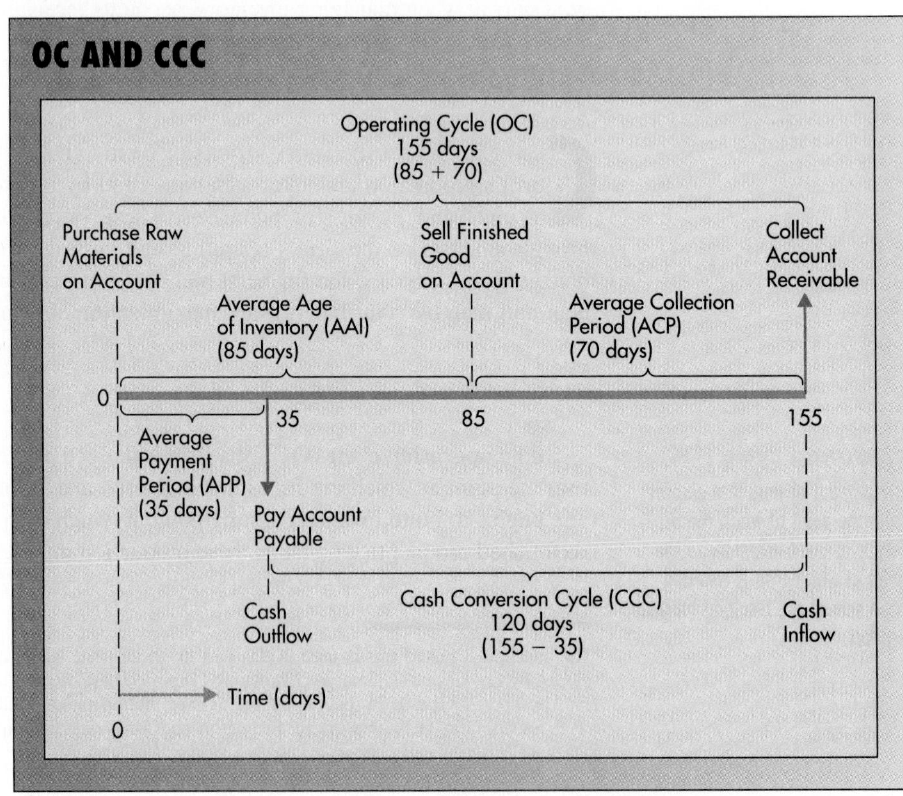

cash conversion cycle (CCC)
Represents the amount of time the firm's cash is tied up between payment for production inputs and receipt of payment from the sale of the resulting finished product; calculated as the number of days in the firm's operating cycle minus the average payment period for inputs to production.

of spontaneous short-term financing. As was noted in Chapter 16, spontaneous financing represents free financing as long as the firm takes any cash discounts offered. The ability to purchase production inputs on credit allows the firm to partially (or maybe even totally) offset the length of time resources are tied up in the operating cycle. The total number of days in the operating cycle less the average payment period for inputs to production represents the **cash conversion cycle (CCC):**

$$\text{CCC} = \text{OC} - \text{APP} = \text{AAI} + \text{ACP} - \text{APP} \tag{17.7}$$

A continuation of the MAX Company example illustrates this concept.

EXAMPLE

The credit terms extended the firm for raw material purchases currently require payment within 40 days of a purchase, and employees are paid every 15 days. The firm's calculated weighted average payment period for raw materials and labor is 35 days, which represents the average payment period (APP). Substituting MAX Company's 155-day operating cycle (OC), found in the preceding example, and its 35-day average payment period (APP) into Equation 17.7 results in its cash conversion cycle (CCC):

$$\begin{aligned} \text{CCC} &= \text{OC} - \text{APP} \\ &= 155 - 35 = 120 \text{ days} \end{aligned}$$

MAX Company's cash conversion cycle is graphically depicted below the time line in Figure 17.3. There are 120 days between the cash *outflow* to pay the accounts payable (on day 35) and the cash *inflow* from the collection of the account receivable (on day 155). During this period—the cash conversion cycle—the firm's money is tied up. ■

Managing the cash conversion cycle

A *positive* cash conversion cycle, as in the case of MAX Company in the above example, means that the firm must use nonspontaneous (i.e., negotiated) forms of financing, such as unsecured short-term loans or secured sources of financing, to support the cash conversion cycle. This should be obvious from the above discussion, since the cash conversion cycle is the difference between the number of days resources are tied up in the operating cycle and the average number of days the firm can use spontaneous financing before payment is made.

Ideally, a firm would like to have a *negative* cash conversion cycle. A negative CCC means the average payment period (APP) exceeds the operating cycle (OC) (see Equation 17.7). Manufacturing firms usually will not have negative cash conversion cycles unless they extend their average payment periods an unreasonable length of time, a topic that will be further discussed later. Nonmanufacturing firms are more likely to have negative cash conversion cycles because they generally carry smaller, faster-moving inventories and often sell their products for cash. As a result, these firms have shorter operating cycles. These shorter operating cycles may be exceeded in length by the firm's average payment periods, thereby resulting in negative cash conversion cycles. When a firm's cash conversion cycle is negative, the firm should benefit by being able to use spontaneous financing to help support aspects of the business other than just the operating cycle.

In the more common case in which the cash conversion cycle is positive, the firm needs to pursue strategies to minimize it without causing harm to the company in the form of lost sales or the inability to purchase on credit. The basic strategies that should be employed by the firm to manage the cash conversion cycle are as follows:

1. Turn over inventory as quickly as possible, avoiding stockouts (depletions of stock) that might result in a loss of sales.
2. Collect accounts receivable as quickly as possible without losing future sales because of high-pressure collection techniques. Cash discounts, if they are economically justifiable, may be used to accomplish this objective.
3. Pay accounts payable as late as possible without damaging the firm's credit rating, but take advantage of any favorable cash discounts.[4]

The effects of implementing each of these strategies are described in the following paragraphs using the MAX Company data. The costs of implementing each proposed strategy are ignored; in practice these costs would be measured against the calculated savings to make the appropriate strategic decision.

EFFICIENT INVENTORY-PRODUCTION MANAGEMENT

One strategy available to MAX is to increase inventory turnover. To do so, the firm can increase raw materials turnover, shorten the production cycle, or increase finished goods turnover. Regardless of which of these approaches is used, the result will be a reduction in the amount of negotiated financing required—that is, the cash conversion cycle will be shortened.

EXAMPLE

If MAX Company manages to increase inventory turnover by reducing the average age of inventory from the current level of 85 days to 70 days—a reduction of 15 days—the effect on the firm can be estimated as follows. Suppose MAX currently spends $12 million annually on operating cycle investments. The daily expenditure is $33,333 (i.e., $12 million ÷ 360 days). Since the cash conversion cycle is reduced 15 days, $500,000 (i.e., $33,333 × 15) of financing can be repaid. If MAX pays 10 percent for its negotiated financing, the firm will reduce financing costs and thereby increase profit by $50,000 (.10 × $500,000) as a result of managing inventory more efficiently. ■

ACCELERATING THE COLLECTION OF ACCOUNTS RECEIVABLE

Another means of reducing the cash conversion cycle (and the negotiated financing need) is to speed up, or accelerate, the collection of accounts receivable. Accounts receivable, like inventory, tie up dollars that could otherwise be used to reduce financing or be invested in earning assets. Let us consider the following example.

EXAMPLE

If MAX Company, by changing its credit terms, is able to reduce the average collection period from the current level of 70 days to 50 days, it will reduce its cash conversion cycle by 20 days (70 days − 50 days) to 100 days (CCC = 120 days − 20 days = 100 days). Again, assume that $12 million is spent annually—$33,333 daily—to support the operating cycle. By improving the management of accounts receivable

[4]A discussion of the variables to consider in determining whether to take cash discounts appears in Chapter 16. A cash discount is often an enticement to pay accounts payable early to effectively reduce the purchase price of goods. Strategies for the use of accruals as a free source of short-term financing are also discussed in Chapter 16.

by 20 days, the firm will require \$666,666 (i.e., \$33,333 × 20) less in negotiated financing. With an interest rate of 10 percent, the firm is able to reduce financing costs and thereby increase profits by \$66,666 (.10 × \$666,666). ■

STRETCHING ACCOUNTS PAYABLE

A third strategy is to *stretch accounts payable*—that is, as noted in Chapter 16, a firm pays its bills as late as possible without damaging its credit rating. Although this approach is financially attractive, it raises an important ethical issue: Clearly, a supplier would not look favorably on a customer that purposely postponed payment.[5]

EXAMPLE

If MAX Company can stretch the payment period from the current average of 35 days to an average of 45 days, its cash conversion cycle will be reduced to 110 days (CCC = 85 days + 70 days − 45 days = 110 days). Once more, if operating cycle expenditures total \$12 million annually, stretching accounts payable (i.e., spontaneous financing) 10 additional days will reduce the firm's negotiated financing need by \$333,333 [(\$12 million ÷ 360) × 10 days]. With an interest rate of 10 percent, the firm can reduce its financing costs and thereby increase profits by \$33,333 (.10 × \$333,333). ■

Combining cash management strategies

Firms typically do not attempt to implement just one cash management strategy; they attempt to use them all to reduce their reliance on negotiated financing. Of course, when implementing these policies, firms should take care to avoid having a large number of inventory stockouts, to avoid losing sales because of the use of high-pressure collection techniques, and not to damage the firm's credit rating by overstretching accounts payable. Using a combination of these strategies would have the following effects on MAX Company.

EXAMPLE

If MAX simultaneously decreased the average age of inventory by 15 days, sped the collection of accounts receivable by 20 days, and increased the average payment period by 10 days, its cash conversion cycle would be reduced to 75 days, as shown here.

Initial cash conversion cycle		120 days
Reduction due to:		
1. Decreased inventory age		
85 days to 70 days =	15 days	
2. Decreased collection period		
70 days to 50 days =	20 days	
3. Increased payment period		
35 days to 45 days =	10 days	
Less: Total reduction in cash conversion cycle		45 days
New cash conversion cycle		75 days

[5]The resolution of this ethical issue is not further addressed in this text. Suffice it to say that although the use of various techniques to slow down payments is widespread due to its financial appeal, it may not be justifiable on purely ethical grounds.

The 45-day reduction in MAX Company's cash conversion cycle means that it can reduce its reliance on interest-bearing financing (i.e., negotiated financing). If annual expenditures for operations are $12 million, then interest-bearing financing can be reduced by $1.5 million [($12 million + 360 days) × 45 days]. If the company pays 10 percent interest on its financing, then it can save $150,000 (i.e., .10 × $1,500,000) through improved management of the cash conversion cycle. ■

CONCEPTS IN REVIEW

17-4 What is the firm's *operating cycle*? What is the *cash conversion cycle*? Compare and contrast them. What is the firm's objective with respect to each of them?

17-5 What are the *key strategies* with respect to inventory, accounts receivable, and accounts payable for the firm that wants to manage its cash conversion cycle efficiently?

17-6 If a firm reduces the average age of its inventory, what effect might this action have on the cash conversion cycle? On the firm's total sales? Is there a tradeoff between average inventory and sales? Give reasons for your answer.

Cash management techniques

To minimize the firm's negotiated financing requirements, financial managers attempt to speed collections and slow disbursements. Can you think of any techniques or strategies that the financial manager might employ to speed collections or slow disbursements? Before reading ahead, spend a few moments answering this question.

FINANCIAL MANAGERS HAVE AT THEIR DISPOSAL A VARIETY OF CASH MANAGEMENT TECHniques that can provide additional savings. These techniques are aimed at minimizing the firm's negotiated financing requirements by taking advantage of certain imperfections in the collection and payment systems. Assuming that the firm has done all that it can to stimulate customers to pay promptly and to select vendors offering the most attractive and flexible credit terms, certain techniques can further speed collections and slow disbursements. These procedures take advantage of the "float" existing in the collection and payment systems.

CONCEPT IN PRACTICE

GE Capital Services: Making Money with Money

The scope of GE Capital Services is a far cry from its Depression-era origin, when General Electric used excess cash to finance refrigerator purchases. As GE Capital Services grew, it has held to the manufacturing mind-set of General Electric, viewing money as a raw material to be transformed into a service that can be marked up and sold for a profit. Today, GE Capital Services extends financing worldwide. It provided a $100 million loan for the recapitalization of the Six Flags amusement park chain and a performance loan to Toronto's Skydome. It has issued 65 million credit cards to customers of many retailers, including R.H. Macy and Montgomery Ward. Beyond retailers, GE Capital Services provides financing in the leasing of cars, planes, and shipping containers. As a result of the strong performance of its cash management division, profits at GE Capital Services offset cutbacks in jet engine and home appliance sales at General Electric.

Float

float
Funds dispatched by a payer that are not yet in a form that can be spent by the payee.

In the broadest sense, **float** refers to funds that have been dispatched by a payer (the firm or individual *making* payment) but are not yet in a form that can be spent by the payee (the firm or individual *receiving* payment). Float also exists when a payee has received funds in a spendable form but these funds have not been withdrawn from the account of the payer. Delays in the collection-payment system resulting from the transportation and processing of checks are responsible for float. With electronic payment systems as well as deliberate action by the Federal Reserve System, it seems clear that in the foreseeable future, float will virtually disappear. Until that time, however, financial managers must continue to understand and take advantage of float.

TYPES OF FLOAT

collection float
The delay between the time when a payer or customer deducts a payment from its checking account ledger and the time when the payee or vendor actually receives the funds in a spendable form.

disbursement float
The lapse between the time when a firm deducts a payment from its checking account ledger (disburses it) and the time when funds are actually withdrawn from its account.

Currently, business firms and individuals can experience both collection and disbursement float as part of the process of making financial transactions. **Collection float** results from the delay between the time when a payer or customer deducts a payment from its checking account ledger and the time when the payee or vendor actually receives these funds in a spendable form. Thus collection float is experienced by the payee and is a delay in the receipt of funds. **Disbursement float** results from the lapse between the time when a firm deducts a payment from its checking account ledger (disburses it) and the time when funds are actually withdrawn from its account. Disbursement float is experienced by the payer and is a delay in the actual withdrawal of funds.

COMPONENTS OF FLOAT

mail float
The delay between the time when a payer mails a payment and the time when the payee receives it.

processing float
The delay between the receipt of a check by the payee and its deposit in the firm's account.

clearing float
The delay between the deposit of a check by the payee and the actual availability of the funds.

Both collection float and disbursement float have the same three basic components:

1. **Mail float:** The delay between the time when a payer places payment in the mail and the time when it is received by the payee.
2. **Processing float:** The delay between the receipt of a check by the payee and the deposit of it in the firm's account.
3. **Clearing float:** The delay between the deposit of a check by the payee and the actual availability of the funds. This component of float is attributable to the time required for a check to clear the banking system.[6] It is important to note that the use of new electronic methods to process checks within the banking system continues to reduce clearing float.

Figure 17.4 illustrates the key components of float resulting from the issuance and mailing of a check by the payer company to the payee company on day zero. The entire process required a total of nine days: three days' mail float, two days' processing float, and four days' clearing float. To the payer company, the delay is disbursement float; to the payee company, the delay is collection float.

[6]Currently, on checks cleared through the Federal Reserve banking system, clearing time of less than two days is guaranteed to the collecting bank, but, of course, this does not assure the depositor (payee) that the bank will make the money available within two days. With the passage of the *Expedited Funds Availability Act of 1987,* banks are required to make funds available to payees within two business days of deposit on local (same Federal Reserve processing region) checks and within five business days on out-of-town checks.

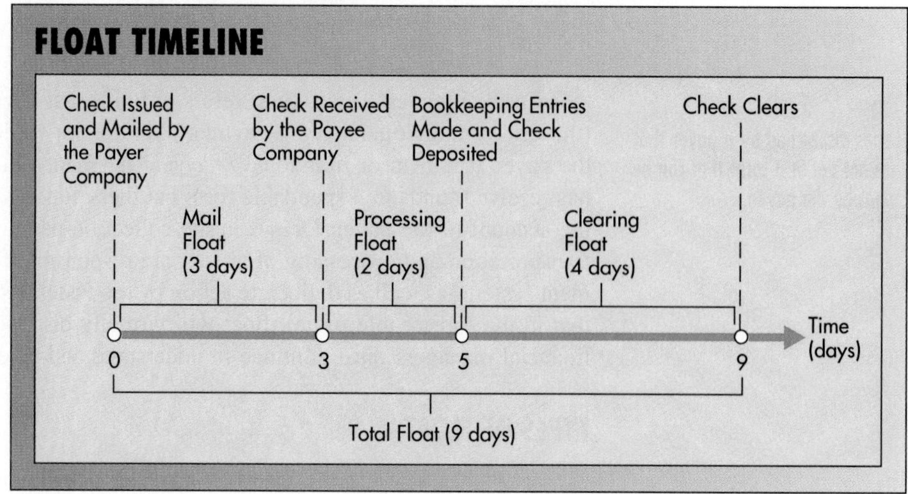

FIGURE 17.4
Float resulting from a check issued and mailed by the payer company to the payee company

Speeding up collections

The firm's objective is not only to stimulate customers to pay their accounts as promptly as possible but also to convert their payments into a spendable form as quickly as possible—in other words, to *minimize collection float.* A variety of techniques aimed at *speeding up collections,* and thereby reducing collection float, are available.

CONCENTRATION BANKING

Firms with numerous sales outlets throughout the country often designate certain offices as collection centers for given geographic areas. Customers in these areas remit their payments to these sales offices, which in turn deposit the receipts in local banks. At certain times, or on a when-needed basis, funds are transferred by wire from these regional banks to a concentration, or disbursing, bank, from which bill payments are dispatched.[7]

concentration banking
A collection procedure in which payments are made to regionally dispersed collection centers, then deposited in local banks for quick clearing. Reduces collection float by shortening mail and clearing float.

Concentration banking is used to reduce collection float by shortening the mail and clearing float components. Mail float is reduced because regionally dispersed collection centers bring the collection point closer to the point from which the check is sent. Clearing float should also be reduced, since the payee's regional bank is likely to be in the same Federal Reserve district or the same city as the bank on which the check is drawn; it may even be the same bank. A reduction in clearing float will, of course, make funds available to the firm more quickly.

EXAMPLE

Suppose Erich, Inc., a hair products manufacturer, could go to concentration banking and reduce its collection period by 3 days. If the company normally carried $10 million in receivables and that level represented 30 days of sales, cutting 3 days from the collection process would result in a $1 million decline in receivables [(3 ÷ 30) ×

[7]Most large firms disburse funds, or pay bills, only from certain banks. Normally, separate payroll and general expense accounts are maintained.

$10,000,000]. Given a 10 percent opportunity cost, the gross annual benefits (profits) of concentration banking would amount to $100,000 (.10 × $1,000,000). Clearly, assuming no change in risk, as long as total annual costs—*incremental* administrative costs and bank service fees and the opportunity cost of holding specified minimum bank balances—are less than the expected annual benefits of $100,000, Erich, Inc.'s proposed program of concentration banking should be implemented. ■

LOCKBOXES

lockbox system
A collection procedure in which payers send their payments to a nearby post office box that is emptied by the firm's bank several times daily; the bank deposits the payment checks in the firm's account. Reduces collection float by shortening processing float as well as mail and clearing float.

Another method that is used to reduce collection float is the **lockbox system,** which differs from concentration banking in several important ways. Instead of mailing payment to a collection center, the payer sends it to a post office box that is emptied by the firm's bank one or more times each business day. The bank opens the payment envelopes, deposits the checks in the firm's account, and sends a deposit slip (or, under certain arrangements, a computer file) indicating the payments received, along with any enclosures, to the collecting firm. Lockboxes normally are geographically dispersed, and the funds, when collected, are wired from each lockbox bank to the firm's disbursing bank.

The lockbox system is superior to concentration banking because it reduces processing float as well as mail and clearing float. The receipts are immediately deposited in the firm's account by the bank so that processing occurs after, rather than before, funds are deposited in the firm's account. This allows the firm to use the funds almost immediately for disbursing payments. Additional reductions in mail float may also result, since payments do not have to be delivered but are picked up by the bank at the post office.

EXAMPLE

Dennison Group, a manufacturer of disposable razors, has annual credit sales of $6 million, which are billed at a constant rate each day. It takes about four days to receive customers' payments at corporate headquarters. It takes another day for the credit department to process receipts and deposit them in the bank. A cash management consultant has told Dennison that a lockbox system would shorten the mail float from 4 days to 1½ days and completely eliminate the processing float. The lockbox system would cost the firm $8,000 per year. Dennison currently earns 12 percent on investments of comparable risk. The lockbox system would free $58,333 of cash [($6 million ÷ 360 days) × (4 days mail float + 1 day processing float − 1½ days mail float)] that is currently tied up in mail and processing float. The gross annual benefit would be $7,000 (.12 × $58,333). Since the $7,000 gross annual benefit is less than the $8,000 annual cost, Dennison should *not* use the lockbox. ■

DIRECT SENDS

direct send
A collection procedure in which the payee presents payment checks directly to the banks on which they are drawn, thus reducing clearing float.

To reduce clearing float, firms that have received large checks drawn on distant banks or a large number of checks drawn on banks in a given city may arrange to present these checks directly for payment to the bank on which they are drawn. Such a procedure is called a **direct send.** Rather than depositing these checks in its collection account, the firm arranges to present the checks to the bank on which they are drawn and receive immediate payment. The firm can use Express Mail or private express services to get the checks into a bank in the same city or to a sales office where an employee can take the checks to the bank and present them for payment. In most cases the funds will be transferred via wire into the firm's disbursement account.

Deciding whether to use direct sends is relatively straightforward. If the benefits from the reduced clearing time are greater than the cost, the checks should be sent directly for payment rather than cleared through normal banking channels.

EXAMPLE

If a firm with an opportunity to earn 10 percent on its idle balances can, through a direct send, make available $1.2 million three days earlier than would otherwise be the case, the benefit of this direct send would be $1,000 [.10 × (3 days ÷ 360 days) × $1,200,000]. If the cost of achieving this three-day reduction in float is less than $1,000, the direct send would be recommended. ■

OTHER TECHNIQUES

preauthorized check (PAC)
A check written by the payee against a customer's checking account for a previously agreed-upon amount. Because of prior legal authorization, the check does not require the customer's signature.

depository transfer check (DTC)
An unsigned check drawn on one of the firm's bank accounts and deposited into its account at a concentration or major disbursement bank, thereby speeding up the transfer of funds.

wire transfers
Telegraphic communications that, via bookkeeping entries, remove funds from the payer's bank and deposit them into the payee's bank, thereby reducing collection float.

ACH (automated clearinghouse) debits
Preauthorized electronic withdrawals from the payer's account that are then transferred to the payee's account via a settlement among banks by the automated clearinghouse. They clear in one day, thereby reducing mail, processing, and clearing float.

A number of other techniques can be used to reduce collection float. One method that is commonly used by firms that collect a fixed amount from customers on a regular basis, such as insurance companies, is the preauthorized check. A **preauthorized check (PAC)** is a check written against a customer's checking account for a previously agreed-upon amount by the firm to which it is payable. Because the check has been legally authorized by the customer, it does not require the customer's signature. The payee merely issues and then deposits the PAC in its account. The check then clears through the banking system just as if it were written by the customer and received and deposited by the firm.

A method that is used by firms with multiple collection points to speed up the transfer of funds is the depository transfer check. A **depository transfer check (DTC)** is an unsigned check drawn on one of the firm's bank accounts and deposited into its account at another bank—typically a concentration or major disbursing bank. Once the DTC has cleared the bank on which it is drawn, the actual transfer of funds is completed. Most firms currently transmit deposit information via telephone rather than by mail to their concentration banks, which then prepare and deposit DTCs into the firm's accounts.

Firms also frequently use wire transfers to reduce collection float by quickly transferring funds from one bank account to another. **Wire transfers** are telegraphic communications that, via bookkeeping entries, remove funds from the payer's bank and deposit them into the payee's bank. Wire transfers can eliminate mail and clearing float and may provide processing float reductions as well. They are sometimes used instead of DTCs to move funds into key disbursing accounts, although a wire transfer is more expensive than a DTC.

Another popular method of accelerating cash inflows involves the use of **ACH (automated clearinghouse) debits.** These are preauthorized electronic withdrawals from the payer's account. A computerized clearing facility (called an automated clearinghouse, or ACH) makes a paperless transfer of funds between the payer and payee banks. An ACH settles accounts among participating banks. Individual depositor accounts are settled by respective bank balance adjustments. ACH transfers clear in one day, in most cases reducing mail, processing, and clearing float.

Slowing down disbursements

The firm's objective relative to accounts payable is not only to pay its accounts as late as possible but also to slow down the availability of funds to suppliers and employees once the payment has been dispatched—in other words, to *maximize disbursement float.* A variety of techniques aimed at *slowing down disbursements,* and thereby increasing disbursement float, are available.

CONTROLLED DISBURSING

controlled disbursing
The strategic use of mailing points and bank accounts to lengthen mail float and clearing float, respectively.

Controlled disbursing involves the strategic use of mailing points and bank accounts to lengthen mail float and clearing float, respectively. When the date of postmark is considered the effective date of payment by the supplier, the firm may be able to lengthen the mail time associated with disbursements.[8] It can place payments in the mail at locations from which it is known that they will take a considerable amount of time to reach the supplier. Typically, small towns that are not close to major highways and cities provide excellent opportunities to increase mail float. Of course, the benefits of using selected mailing points may not justify the costs of this strategy, particularly in light of the fact that the U.S. Postal Service gives rate reductions on mail that is presorted by ZIP Code and sent from designated major post offices.

The widespread availability of computers and data on check clearing times allows firms to develop disbursement schemes that maximize clearing float on their payments. These methods involve assigning payments going to vendors in certain geographic areas to be drawn on specific banks from which maximum clearing float will result.

Data on clearing time among banks located in various cities can be developed by the firm itself, it can be obtained from a major bank's cash management service department, or it can be purchased from a firm that sells such information to banks and other firms. Firms that are attempting to assign checks to be drawn on banks providing maximum float to the vendor city will typically run a computer program each payment cycle. The program will draw on the clearing-time database and assign the checks to be drawn on the bank account that provides maximum clearing float to each vendor. The number of potential bank accounts considered will depend on the economics of the system. Once the computer has assigned payments to banks, the computer will print the checks on blank check forms, and the checks can then be sorted and mailed from remote points, as was mentioned earlier. Although such controlled disbursement systems are used today, their cost must be justified by the additional earnings achieved by the firm on the disbursement float created.

PLAYING THE FLOAT

playing the float
A method of consciously anticipating the resulting float, or delay, associated with the payment process and using it to keep funds in an interest-earning form for as long as possible.

Playing the float is a method of consciously anticipating the resulting float, or delay, associated with the payment process. Firms often play the float by writing checks against funds that are not currently in their checking accounts. They can do this because they know that a delay will occur between the receipt and the deposit of checks by suppliers and the actual withdrawal of funds from their checking accounts. It is likely that the firm's bank account will not be drawn down by the amount of the payments for a few additional days. Although the ineffective use of this practice could result in problems associated with "bounced checks," many firms use float to stretch out their accounts payable.[9]

---

[8]A supplier's credit terms as well as any penalties associated with late payment are typically stated in the invoice that accompanies the shipment of merchandise. Of course, depending on the supplier, the terms of the invoice may or may not be enforced. Knowledge of the strictness of suppliers' credit terms is often useful for developing the firm's accounts payable strategies.

[9]Issuing checks against nonexistent funds can be prosecuted only if the check is drawn on insufficient funds. The fact that a check bounces is viewed as prima facie—but not irrefutable—evidence of fraud. The burden of proof that the act causing insufficient funds was not willful is placed on the issuer. If such proof cannot be given, the issuer will be convicted of fraud. Prosecution rarely results, since the issuer usually obtains sufficient funds to satisfy the obligation prior to the filing of any criminal charges.

Firms play the float in a variety of ways—all of which are aimed at keeping funds in an interest-earning form for as long as possible. For example, one way of playing the float is to deposit a certain proportion of a payroll or payment into the firm's checking account on several successive days *following* the actual issuance of a group of checks. This technique is commonly referred to as **staggered funding.** If the firm can determine from historic data that only 25 percent of its payroll checks are cashed on the day immediately following the issuance of the checks, then only 25 percent of the value of the payroll needs to be in its checking account one day later. The amount of checks cashed on each of several succeeding days can also be estimated until the entire payroll is accounted for. Normally, however, to protect itself against any irregularities, a firm will place slightly more money in its account than is needed to cover the expected withdrawals.

staggered funding
A way to play the float by depositing a certain proportion of a payroll or payment into the firm's checking account on several successive days *following* the actual issuance of checks.

Another way of playing the float is to use payable-through drafts, rather than checks, to pay large sums of money like the payroll. A **payable-through draft** is similar to a check in that it is drawn on the payer's checking account and is payable to a given payee. Unlike a check, however, it is not payable on demand; approval of the draft by the payer is required before the bank pays the draft. The advantage of these drafts to the payer is that money does not have to be placed on deposit until the draft clears the bank; instead, the firm can invest it in short-term money market vehicles. As the drafts are cleared for payment by the payer, the investments can be liquidated and the funds used to cover the drafts. Banks may charge a modest fee for processing the drafts, but this technique enables the firm to keep its money more fully invested for a longer period of time.

payable-through draft
A draft drawn on the payer's checking account, payable to a given payee but not payable on demand; approval of the draft by the payer is required before the bank pays the draft.

EXAMPLE

Assume that by using payable-through drafts in place of checks to meet its payroll, Mardon Manufacturing, a producer of chain-link fencing, can increase its disbursement float by five days. If its monthly payroll is $12 million, this increase in float will translate into profits of $200,000 per year given an opportunity cost of 10 percent. That is the amount of profit that the firm would realize by keeping $12 million invested at 10 percent (per year) for five additional days each month for an entire year [.10 × (5 days ÷ 360 days) × $12,000,000 × (12 months/year) = $200,000]. ■

But note that many vendors will not accept payable-through drafts as payment for the goods or services provided, and in some states the use of these drafts is prohibited by law.

OVERDRAFT SYSTEMS, ZERO-BALANCE ACCOUNTS, AND ACH CREDITS

Firms that aggressively manage cash disbursements will often arrange for some type of overdraft system or a zero-balance account. In an **overdraft system,** if the firm's checking account balance is insufficient to cover all checks presented against the account, the bank will automatically lend the firm enough money to cover the amount of the overdraft. The bank, of course, will charge the firm interest on the funds lent and will limit the amount of overdraft coverage. Such an arrangement is important for a business that actively plays the float.

overdraft system
Automatic coverage by the bank of all checks presented against the firm's account, regardless of the account balance.

Firms can also establish **zero-balance accounts**—checking accounts in which zero balances are maintained. Under this arrangement, each day the bank will notify the firm of the total amount of checks presented against the account. The firm then transfers only that amount—typically from a master account or through liquidation of a portion of its marketable securities—into the account. Once the corresponding checks have

zero-balance account
A checking account in which a zero balance is maintained and the firm is required to deposit funds to cover checks drawn on the account only as they are presented for payment.

been paid, the account balance reverts to zero. The bank, of course, must be compensated for this service.

ACH (automated clearinghouse) credits

Deposits of payroll directly into the payees' (employees') accounts. Sacrifices disbursement float but may generate goodwill for the employer.

ACH (automated clearinghouse) credits are frequently used by corporations for making direct bank deposits of payroll into the payees' (employees') accounts. Disbursement float is sacrificed with this technique because ACH transactions immediately draw down the company's payroll account on payday, whereas in check-based payroll systems, not all employees cash their checks on payday, thus allowing the firm to use *staggered funding* as discussed earlier. The benefit of ACH credits is that employees enjoy convenience, which may generate enough goodwill to justify the firm's loss of float.

The role of strong banking relationships

Establishing and maintaining strong banking relations are among the most important elements in an effective cash management system. Banks have become keenly aware of the profitability of corporate accounts and in recent years have developed a number of innovative services and packages designed to attract various types of businesses. No longer are banks simply a place to establish checking accounts and secure loans; instead, they have become the source of a wide variety of cash management services. For example, banks are selling sophisticated information-processing packages to commercial clients. These packages deal with everything from basic accounting and budgeting to complex multinational disbursement and centralized cash control. All are designed to help financial managers maximize day-to-day cash availability and facilitate short-term investing.

Today, most bank services are offered to corporations on a direct-fee basis, but some of the depository functions are still paid for with deposit balances rather than direct charges. Banks prefer the *compensating balance* approach—giving credit against bank service charges for amounts maintained in the customer's checking account—because it fosters deposit growth and provides a foundation for the future growth of bank earnings. Of course, bank services should be used only when the benefits derived from them are greater than their costs.

EXAMPLE

Clear, Inc., an optical lens manufacturer, has been offered a cash management service that should eliminate "excess" cash on deposit and reduce certain administrative and clerical costs. The service, which costs $50,000 per year, involves the collection, movement, and reporting of corporate cash. The purported benefits are these: (1) The firm should be able to reduce the negotiated financing required to support operations by some $600,000 (as a result of tighter control over the cash flow), and (2) administrative and clerical costs should drop by about $1,000 per month (since the bank will be taking on administrative and clerical duties as part of the service). Using a 10 percent opportunity cost, the benefits and costs would be as follows:

Benefits (annual)	
Savings from reduced financing (.10 × $600,000)	$60,000
Reduced administrative and clerical costs ($1,000 × 12)	12,000
Total annual benefits	$72,000
Less: Costs (annual)	
Bank service charge	50,000
Net annual benefits	$22,000

From a benefit–cost perspective the proposal looks promising. The major risk, of course, is that the purported benefits will fall far short of the mark. Management, however, can get at least an idea of such risk. A simple calculation, for example, may be used to estimate the minimum reduction in financing or opportunity cost required to generate a sufficient level of total benefits. On the other hand, some positive risk reductions may result from adoption of the bank's program, such as less exposure to volatile interest rates, and these should obviously also be considered. ■

International cash management

Although the motivations for holding cash balances and the basic concepts underlying optimal cash management are the same worldwide, there are dramatic differences in practical cash management techniques for international versus strictly domestic business transactions. In fact, the differences between U.S. and international banking and payment systems are so great that only an elementary comparison is made here. More detailed information about payments and cash management systems abroad can be found in textbooks on international finance or short-term financial (working capital) management.

DIFFERENCES IN BANKING SYSTEMS

Giro system
System through which retail transactions are handled in association with a foreign country's national postal system.

value dating
A procedure used by non-U.S. banks to delay, often for days or even weeks, the availability of funds deposited with them.

Banking systems outside the United States differ fundamentally from the U.S. model in several key aspects. First, foreign banks are generally far less restricted either geographically or in the services they are allowed to offer. Second, retail transactions are typically routed through a **Giro system** that is usually operated by, or in association with, the national postal system. Because of this direct payment system, checks are used much less frequently than in the United States. Third, banks in other countries are allowed to pay interest on corporate demand deposits, and they also routinely provide overdraft protection. To recoup the cost of these services, however, non-U.S. banks generally charge more and higher fees for services and also engage in the practice of **value dating.** This involves delaying, often for days or even weeks, the availability of funds deposited with the bank. This lag between the date funds are deposited and when they are usable obviously complicates cash management procedures, and if a transaction involves collecting on a foreign-currency-denominated check drawn on a bank outside of the host country, the delay in availability of good funds can be very long indeed.

CASH MANAGEMENT PRACTICES

intracompany netting technique
A technique used by multinational firms to minimize their cash requirements by transferring across national boundaries only the net amount of payments owed between them. Sometimes bookkeeping entries are substituted for international payments.

The cash management practices of multinational corporations are made more complicated by the need to both maintain local currency deposit balances in banks in every country in which the firm operates and to retain centralized control over cash balances and cash flows that, in total, can be quite large. The largest multinational corporations have honed their treasury operations to such an extent that they can balance these conflicting objectives efficiently and even profitably. To do so, they rely on the cash collection, disbursement, and foreign-exchange trading expertise of large international banks, all of which operate very sophisticated computerized treasury services.

Multinational firms can also minimize their cash requirements by using an **intracompany netting technique.** For example, when two subsidiaries in different countries trade with each other—thereby generating payment obligations to each other—

only the net amount of payment owed will be transferred across national boundaries. In fact, it may be possible to handle many of these transactions strictly internally (on the books of the parent company) without having to resort to the international payment system at all.

When it becomes necessary to make large international cash payments, these are almost invariably handled by one of the wire transfer services operated by international banking consortia. The most important of these networks is the **Clearing House Interbank Payment System,** called **CHIPS.** It has been estimated that over $600 billion worth of payments are settled *every day* using wire transfer and settlement services. While the bulk of these transactions result from foreign exchange trading, many are also due to settlement of international payment obligations.

Clearing House Interbank Payment System (CHIPS)
The most important wire transfer service; operated by international banking consortia.

Multinational companies with excess funds to invest benefit from having access to a wide variety of government and corporate investment vehicles. Companies naturally have access to all of the marketable securities offered to U.S. investors (described in the following section). Multinational companies can also invest funds in foreign government securities, or they can invest directly in the *Eurocurrency market* either in dollars or in other convertible currencies. This financial flexibility often provides multinational corporations with a key competitive advantage, particularly if they need to transfer funds into or out of countries experiencing political or financial difficulties.

CONCEPT IN PRACTICE

High-Tech Cash Management Offered Through Columbus Bank & Trust

Heightened competition prompted Columbus Bank & Trust to upgrade the way in which it handles customers' cash management needs. The Columbus, Georgia, subsidiary of Synovus felt that it would lose market share if it didn't offer automated cash management. Using Columbus Bank's new computer network, corporate treasurers can invest idle funds overnight or longer by requesting that they be put into certificates of deposit, commercial paper, money market mutual funds, or repurchase agreements. By 7:00 A.M. the following day, users can access funds, transmit funds, and reconcile accounts. Additional on-line services include stop-payment orders, concentration banking, and electronic mail. The cost to the user is $225 per month. As a result of these new services, Columbus Bank & Trust has been able to cut the size of its cash management department (which handles service requests) from seven to four employees.

CONCEPTS IN REVIEW

17-7 Define *float,* and describe its three basic components. Compare and contrast collection and disbursement float, and state the financial manager's goal with respect to each of these types of float.

17-8 Briefly describe the key features of each of the following techniques for speeding up collections.

a. Concentration banking
b. Lockboxes
c. Direct sends
d. Preauthorized checks (PACs)
e. Depository transfer checks (DTCs)
f. Wire transfers
g. ACH (automated clearinghouse) debits

17-9 Briefly describe the key features of each of the following techniques for slowing down disbursements.

a. Controlled disbursing
b. Playing the float
c. Overdraft systems
d. Zero-balance accounts
e. ACH (automated clearinghouse) credits

17-10 Describe the role of strong banking relationships in the cash management process. How should available bank services be evaluated?

17-11 Describe the key differences between banking systems outside of the United States and the U.S. model. What is *value dating,* and how does it affect international cash management?

17-12 What is an *intracompany netting technique,* and what is its purpose? What is *CHIPS* and what role does it play in the international payment system?

Marketable securities

Marketable securities are highly liquid, short-term, interest-earning government and nongovernment money market instruments. Can you name and briefly describe a few of the marketable securities that are commonly held by firms? Spend a short time answering this question before reading on.

MARKETABLE SECURITIES ARE SHORT-TERM, INTEREST-EARNING, MONEY MARKET INstruments that can easily be converted into cash.[10] Marketable securities are classified as part of the firm's liquid assets. The securities that are most commonly held as part of the firm's marketable securities portfolio are divided into two groups: (1) government issues and (2) nongovernment issues. Before describing the popular government and nongovernment marketable securities, we discuss the basic characteristics of marketable securities. Table 17.1 summarizes the key features and recent (September 22, 1993) yields for the marketable securities described in the sections that follow.

Characteristics of marketable securities

The basic characteristics of marketable securities affect the degree of their salability. To be truly marketable, a security must have two basic characteristics: (1) a ready market and (2) safety of principal (no likelihood of loss in value).

A READY MARKET

The market for a security should have both breadth and depth to minimize the amount of time required to convert it into cash. The **breadth of a market** is determined by the

breadth of a market
A characteristic of a ready market, determined by the number of participants (buyers) in the market.

[10]As was explained in Chapter 2, the *money market* results from a financial relationship between the suppliers and demanders of short-term funds, that is, marketable securities.

TABLE 17.1

FEATURES AND RECENT YIELDS ON POPULAR MARKETABLE SECURITIES[a]

Security	Issuer	Description	Initial maturity	Risk and return	Yield on September 22, 1993[b]
Government Issues					
Treasury Bills	U.S. Treasury	Issued weekly at auction; sold at a discount; strong secondary market	91 and 182 days, occasionally 1 year	Lowest, virtually risk free	2.93%
Treasury notes	U.S. Treasury	Stated interest rate; interest paid semiannually; strong secondary market	1 to 10 years	Low, but slightly higher than U.S. Treasury bills	2.96
Federal agency issues	Agencies of federal government	Not an obligation of U.S. Treasury; strong secondary market	9 months to 30 years	Slightly higher than U.S. Treasury issues	3.01[c]
Nongovernment Issues					
Negotiable certificates of deposit (CDs)	Commercial banks	Represent specific cash deposits in commercial banks; amounts and maturities tailored to investor needs; large denominations; good secondary market	1 month to 3 years	Higher than U.S. Treasury issues and comparable to commercial paper	3.13
Commercial paper	Corporation with a high credit standing	Unsecured note of issuer; large denominations	3 to 270 days	Higher than U.S. Treasury issues and comparable to negotiable CDs	3.20
Banker's acceptances	Banks	Results from a bank guarantee of a business transaction; sold at discount from maturity value	30 to 180 days	Slightly lower than negotiable CDs and commercial paper but higher than U.S. Treasury issues	3.06
Eurodollar deposits	Foreign banks	Deposits of currency not native to the country in which the bank is located; large denominations; active secondary market	1 day to 3 years	Highest, due to less regulation of depository banks and some foreign exchange risk	3.25
Money market mutual funds	Professional portfolio management companies	Professionally managed portfolios of marketable securities; provide instant liquidity	None—depends on wishes of investor	Vary, but generally higher than U.S. Treasury issues and comparable to negotiable CDs and commercial paper	2.91[d]
Repurchase agreements	Bank or security dealer	Bank or security dealer sells specific securities to firm and agrees to repurchase them at a specific price and time	Customized to purchaser's needs	Generally slightly below that associated with the outright purchase of the security	—

[a]The prime rate of interest at this time was 6.00%.

[b]Yields obtained for three-month maturities of each security.

[c]A Federal Home Loan Bank (FHLB) issue maturing in January 1994 is used here in the absence of any average-yield data.

[d]The Value Line Money Market Fund with an average maturity of 61 days is used here in the absence of any average-yield data.

Source: The Wall Street Journal, September 23, 1993, pp. C19, C20, C27.

number of participants (buyers). A broad market is one that has many participants. The **depth of a market** is determined by its ability to absorb the purchase or sale of a large dollar amount of a particular security. It is therefore possible to have a broad market that has no depth. Thus 100,000 participants each willing to purchase one share of a security is less desirable than 1,000 participants each willing to purchase 2,000 shares. Although both breadth and depth are desirable for a security to be salable, it is much more important for a market to have depth.

depth of a market
A characteristic of a ready market, determined by its ability to absorb the purchase or sale of a large dollar amount of a particular security.

SAFETY OF PRINCIPAL (NO LIKELIHOOD OF LOSS IN VALUE)

There should be little or no loss in the value of a marketable security over time. Consider a security that was recently purchased for $1,000. If it can be sold quickly for $500, does that make it marketable? No. According to the definition of marketability, the security not only must be salable quickly, but also must be salable for close to the $1,000 that was initially invested. This aspect of marketability is referred to as **safety of principal.** Only securities that can be easily converted into cash without experiencing any appreciable reduction in principal are candidates for short-term investment.

safety of principal
The ease of salability of a security for close to its initial value.

Government issues

The short-term obligations issued by the federal government and available as marketable security investments are Treasury bills, Treasury notes, and federal agency issues. These securities have relatively low yields due to their low risk and the fact that the interest income on all Treasury issues and most federal agency issues, although taxable at the federal level, is exempt from state and local taxes.

TREASURY BILLS

Treasury bills are obligations of the U.S. Treasury that are issued weekly on an auction basis. The most common maturities are 91 and 182 days, although bills with one-year maturities are occasionally sold. Treasury bills are sold by competitive bidding. Because they are issued in bearer form, there is a strong *secondary (resale) market.* The bills are sold at a discount from their face value, the face value being received at maturity. The smallest denomination of a Treasury bill currently available is $10,000. Since Treasury bills are issues of the United States government, they are considered to be virtually risk-free. For this reason, and because of the strong secondary market for them, Treasury bills are one of the most popular marketable securities. The yields on Treasury bills are generally lower than those on any other marketable securities due to their virtually risk-free nature and favorable tax status.

Treasury bills
U.S. Treasury obligations issued weekly on an auction basis, having varying maturities, generally under a year, and virtually no risk.

TREASURY NOTES

Treasury notes have initial maturities of between one and ten years; due to the existence of a strong secondary market, they are quite attractive marketable security investments. They are generally issued in minimum denominations of either $1,000 or $5,000, carry a coupon interest rate, and pay interest semiannually. A firm that purchases a Treasury note that has less than one year left to maturity is in the same position as if it had purchased a marketable security with an initial maturity of less than one year. Because of their virtually risk-free nature and favorable tax status, Treasury notes generally have a low yield relative to other securities with similar maturities.

Treasury notes
U.S. Treasury obligations with initial maturities of between one and ten years, paying interest at a stated rate semiannually, and having virtually no risk.

FEDERAL AGENCY ISSUES

federal agency issues
Low-risk securities issued by government agencies but not guaranteed by the U.S. Treasury, having generally short maturities, and offering slightly higher yields than comparable U.S. Treasury issues.

Certain agencies of the federal government issue their own debt. These **federal agency issues** are not part of the public debt, are not a legal obligation of the U.S. Treasury, and are not guaranteed by the U.S. Treasury. Regardless of their lack of direct government backing, the issues of government agencies are readily accepted as low-risk securities, since most purchasers feel that they are implicitly guaranteed by the federal government. Agency issues generally have minimum denominations of $1,000 or more and are issued either with a stated interest rate or at a discount. Agencies commonly issuing short-term instruments include the Farm Credit Banks (FCB), the Federal Home Loan Banks (FHLB), and the Federal National Mortgage Association (FNMA). Of course, instead of agency issues with short initial maturities, other longer-term agency issues with less than one year to maturity could be purchased. Most agency issues offer slightly higher yields than U.S. Treasury issues having similar maturities. Agency issues have a strong secondary market, which is most easily reached through government securities dealers.

Nongovernment issues

A number of additional marketable securities are issued by banks or businesses. These nongovernment issues typically have slightly higher yields than government issues with similar maturities due to the slightly higher risks associated with them and the fact that their interest income is taxable at all levels—federal, state, and local. The principal nongovernment marketable securities are negotiable certificates of deposit, commercial paper, banker's acceptances, Eurodollar deposits, money market mutual funds, and repurchase agreements.

NEGOTIABLE CERTIFICATES OF DEPOSIT (CDS)

negotiable certificates of deposit (CDs)
Negotiable instruments representing specific cash deposits in commercial banks, having varying maturities and yields based on size, maturity, and prevailing money market conditions. Yields are generally above those on U.S. Treasury issues and comparable to those on commercial paper with similar maturities.

Negotiable certificates of deposit (CDs) are negotiable instruments representing the deposit of a certain number of dollars in a commercial bank. The amounts and maturities are normally tailored to the investor's needs. Average maturities of 30 days are quite common. A good secondary market for CDs exists. Normally, the smallest denomination for a negotiable CD is $100,000. The yields on CDs are initially set on the basis of size, maturity, and prevailing money market conditions. They are typically above those on U.S. Treasury issues and comparable to the yields on commercial paper with similar maturities.

COMMERCIAL PAPER

commercial paper
A short-term, unsecured promissory note issued by a corporation that has a very high credit standing, having a yield above that paid on U.S. Treasury issues and comparable to that available on negotiable CDs with similar maturities.

Commercial paper is a short-term, unsecured promissory note issued by a corporation that has a very high credit standing.[11] These notes are issued, generally in multiples of $100,000, by all types of firms and have initial maturities of anywhere from 3 to 270 days.[12] They can be sold directly by the issuer or through dealers. The yield on

[11]The role of commercial paper from the point of view of the issuer is included in the discussion of the various sources of short-term financing available to business in Chapter 16.

[12]The maximum maturity is 270 days because the Securities and Exchange Commission (SEC) requires formal registration of corporate issues having maturities greater than 270 days.

commercial paper typically is above that paid on U.S. Treasury issues and comparable to that available on negotiable CDs with similar maturities.

BANKER'S ACCEPTANCES

banker's acceptances
Short-term, low-risk marketable securities arising from bank guarantees of business transactions; are sold by banks at a discount from their maturity value and provide yields slightly below those on negotiable CDs and commercial paper, but higher than those on U.S. Treasury issues.

Banker's acceptances arise from a short-term credit arrangement used by businesses to finance transactions, especially those involving firms in foreign countries or firms with unknown credit capacities. The purchaser, to ensure payment to the seller, requests its bank to issue a *letter of credit* on its behalf, authorizing the seller to draw a *time draft*—an order to pay a specified amount at a specified time—on the bank in payment for the goods. Once the goods are shipped, the seller presents a time draft along with proof of shipment to its bank. The seller's bank then forwards the draft with appropriate shipping documents to the buyer's bank for acceptance and receives payment for the transaction. The buyer's bank may either hold the acceptance to maturity or sell it at a discount in the money market. If sold, the size of the discount from the acceptance's maturity value and the amount of time until the acceptance is paid determine the purchaser's yield.

As a result of its sale, the banker's acceptance becomes a marketable security that can be traded in the marketplace. The initial maturities of banker's acceptances are typically between 30 and 180 days, 90 days being most common. A banker's acceptance is a low-risk security because at least two, and sometimes three, parties may be liable for its payment at maturity. The yields on banker's acceptances are generally slightly below those on negotiable CDs and commercial paper, but higher than those on U.S. Treasury issues.

CONCEPT IN PRACTICE

Investing Cash in a Lending Circle Allows Magna to Bypass the Bank

In 1993, Magna Publications reported that a new financial union was being organized to allow small firms like itself to pool cash for a rainy day. The Madison, Wisconsin–based group is known as a neighborhood lending circle, which consists of five small business owners pooling their extra cash to make small, short-term loans to each other. Advantages include (1) cutting out the bank middleman and thereby reducing costs, (2) providing small amounts of money, which some banks avoid, and (3) focusing on circle members' character, not their assets. After the receivable is collected, the cash is made available to another circle member. Of course, circle members earn interest on the surplus cash that they invest in the pool.

EURODOLLAR DEPOSITS

Eurodollar deposits
Deposits of currency not native to the country in which the bank is located; negotiable, usually pay interest at maturity, and are typically denominated in units of $1 million. Provide yields above nearly all other marketable securities with similar maturities.

Eurodollar deposits are deposits of currency that are not native to the country in which the bank is located. London is the center of the Eurodollar market. Other important centers are Paris, Frankfurt, Zurich, Nassau (Bahamas), Singapore, and Hong Kong. Nearly 75 percent of these deposits are in the form of U.S. dollars. The deposits are negotiable, usually pay interest at maturity, and are typically denominated in units of $1 million. Maturities range from overnight to several years, most of the money being in the 1-week to 6-month maturity range. Eurodollar deposits tend to provide yields above nearly all other marketable securities, government or nongovernment, with similar maturities. These higher yields are attributable to (1) the fact that the depository banks are generally less closely regulated than U.S. banks and are therefore more risky and (2) some foreign exchange risk may be present. An active secondary market allows Eurodollar deposits to be used to meet all three motives for holding cash and near-cash balances.

MONEY MARKET MUTUAL FUNDS

money market mutual funds
Professionally managed portfolios of various popular marketable securities, having instant liquidity, competitive yields, and low transactions costs.

Money market mutual funds, often called *money funds,* are professionally managed portfolios of marketable securities such as those described earlier. Shares or interests in these funds can be easily acquired—often without paying any brokerage commissions. A minimum initial investment of as low as $500, but generally $1,000 or more, is required. Money funds provide instant liquidity in much the same fashion as a checking or savings account. In exchange for investing in these funds, investors earn returns that are comparable to or higher than—especially during periods of high interest rates—those obtainable from negotiable CDs and commercial paper. Due to the high liquidity, competitive yields, and often low transactions costs, these funds have achieved significant growth in size and popularity in recent years.

REPURCHASE AGREEMENTS

repurchase agreement
An agreement whereby a bank or securities dealer sells a firm specific securities and agrees to repurchase them at a specific price and time.

A **repurchase agreement** is not a specific security. It is an arrangement whereby a bank or securities dealer sells specific marketable securities to a firm and agrees to repurchase them at a specific price at a specified point in time. In exchange for the tailor-made maturity date provided by this arrangement, the bank or securities dealer provides the purchaser with a return slightly below that obtainable through outright purchase of similar marketable securities. The benefit to the purchaser is the guaranteed repurchase, and the tailor-made maturity date ensures that the purchaser will have cash at a specified point in time. The actual securities involved may be government or nongovernment issues. Repurchase agreements are ideal for marketable securities investments made to satisfy the transactions motive.

CONCEPTS IN REVIEW

17-13 What two characteristics are deemed essential for a security to be marketable? Which aspect of a market for a security is more important—breadth or depth? Why?

17-14 Discuss the two reasons why government issues of marketable securities have generally lower yields than do nongovernment issues with similar maturities.

17-15 For each of the following government-based marketable securities, give a brief description emphasizing issuer, initial maturity, liquidity, risk, and return.

- **a.** Treasury bill
- **b.** Treasury note
- **c.** Federal agency issue

17-16 Describe the basic features—including issuer, initial maturity, liquidity, risk, and return—of each of the following nongovernment marketable securities.

- **a.** Negotiable certificate of deposit (CD)
- **b.** Commercial paper
- **c.** Banker's acceptance
- **d.** Eurodollar deposit

17-17 Briefly describe the basic features of the following marketable securities, and explain how they both involve other marketable securities.

- **a.** Money market mutual fund
- **b.** Repurchase agreement

Summary

LG 1 **Discuss the motives for holding cash and marketable securities and the two models—the Baumol model and the Miller-Orr model—that can be used to determine the appropriate transactional cash balances.** The three motives for holding cash and near-cash (marketable securities) balances are (1) the transactions motive, (2) the safety motive, and (3) the speculative motive. Cash is held to satisfy transactional needs, whereas investment in marketable securities provides a safety stock of liquid resources and, possibly, the ability to profit from unexpected events that may arise. Estimating the cost-efficient transactional cash balances is difficult. However, the Baumol model and the Miller-Orr model can help management with this task. The Baumol model assumes that the future demand for cash—the firm's cash inflows and cash outflows—is known with certainty, whereas the Miller-Orr model incorporates the more realistic assumption of uncertain cash flows.

LG 2 **Use the firm's operating and cash conversion cycles to define and demonstrate the three basic strategies for managing its cash to minimize its financing needs.** The efficient management of cash is affected by the firm's operating and cash conversion cycles. Ideally, management wants to minimize the length of these cycles without jeopardizing profitability. Three basic strategies for achieving this objective are (1) turning over inventory as quickly as possible, (2) collecting accounts receivable as quickly as possible, and (3) paying accounts payable as late as possible without damaging the firm's credit rating. Employment of these strategies should reduce the firm's cash conversion cycle and negotiated financing need, thereby improving its profitability.

LG 3 **Explain *float*, including its three basic components, and the firm's major objective with respect to the levels of collection float and disbursement float.** Float refers to funds that have been collected by a payer (the firm or individual *making* payment) but are not yet in a form that can be spent by the payee (the firm or individual *receiving* payment). Both collection and disbursement float have the same three basic components: (1) mail float, (2) processing float, and (3) clearing float. The firm's major objective with respect to float is to minimize collection float and maximize disbursement float within reasonable limits.

LG 4 **Review popular techniques for speeding up collections and slowing down disbursements, the role of strong banking relationships in cash management, and international cash management.** Popular techniques for speeding up collections include concentration banking, lockboxes, direct sends, preauthorized checks (PACs), depository transfer checks (DTCs), wire transfers, and ACH (automated clearinghouse) debits. Techniques for slowing down disbursements include controlled disbursing, playing the float, overdraft systems, zero-balance accounts, and ACH (automated clearinghouse) credits. Establishing and maintaining strong banking relationships are crucial for effective cash management. Dramatic differences between foreign and domestic banking systems exist and result in more complex cash management practices for international firms than for purely domestic firms.

LG 5 **Understand the basic characteristics of marketable securities *and* the key government issues—Treasury bills, Treasury notes, and federal agency issues.** Marketable securities allow the firm to earn a return on temporarily idle funds. For a security to be considered marketable, it must have a ready market that has both breadth and depth. Furthermore, the risk associated with the safety of the principal must be quite low. The key features and recent yields for each of the three key government issues are summarized in the upper portion of Table 17.1. These securities have relatively low yields due to their low risk and the fact that interest income on all Treasury issues and most federal agency issues, although taxable at the federal level, is exempt from state and local taxes.

LG 6 **Describe the key features of the popular nongovernment marketable securities—negotiable certificates of deposit, commercial paper, banker's acceptances, Eurodollar deposits, money market mutual funds, and repurchase agreements.** The key features and recent yields for each of the principal nongovernment marketable securities are summarized in the lower portion of Table 17.1. These securities have slightly higher yields than government issues with similar maturities due to the slightly higher risks associated with them and the fact that their interest income is taxable at all levels—federal, state, and local.

Self-test problems (Solutions in Appendix E)

ST 17-1 LG 2 **Cash conversion cycle** The Hurkin Manufacturing Company pays accounts payable on the tenth day after purchase. The average collection period is 30 days, and the average age of inventory is 40 days. The firm currently spends about $18 million on operating cycle investments. The firm is considering a plan that would stretch its accounts payable by 20 days. If the firm pays 12 percent per year for its financing, what annual savings can it realize by this plan? Assume no discount for early payment of trade credit and a 360-day year.

ST 17-2 LG 4 Lockbox decision A firm that has an annual opportunity cost of 9 percent is contemplating installation of a lockbox system at an annual cost of $90,000. The system is expected to reduce mailing time by 2½ days and reduce check clearing time by 1½ days. If the firm collects $300,000 per day, would you recommend the system? Explain.

Problems

17-1 LG 1 Baumol model Namtig Industries forecasts cash outlays of $1.8 million for its next fiscal year. To minimize investment in the cash account, management intends to apply the Baumol model. A financial analyst for the company has estimated the conversion cost of converting marketable securities to cash to be $45 per conversion transaction and the annual opportunity cost of holding cash instead of marketable securities to be 8 percent.

a. Calculate the optimal amount of cash to transfer from marketable securities to cash (i.e., the economic conversion quantity, ECQ). What will be the average cash balance?
b. How many transactions will be required for the year?
c. Calculate the total cost resulting from use of the ECQ calculated in **a**.
d. If management makes 12 equal conversions (i.e., one per month), what will be (1) the total conversion cost, (2) the total opportunity cost, and (3) the total cost? Contrast and discuss this value in light of your finding in **c**.

17-2 LG 1 Miller-Orr model STIC Corporation uses the Miller-Orr model to manage its cash account. Recently, someone asked how sensitive is the solution for the return point and upper limit to changes in the conversion cost, the variance of daily net cash flows, and the *daily* opportunity cost rate. The values that are currently being used are a $50 conversion cost, a $2 million daily net cash flow variance, and a 10 percent *annual* opportunity cost.

a. Calculate the return point and upper limit using the current values.
b. Simultaneously increase each of the three variable values used in **a** by 50 percent and recalculate the return point and upper limit.
c. Discuss the sensitivity of the model to changes in the values of the input variables.

17-3 LG 1 Miller-Orr model The financial manager of YARL Corporation recently learned that application of the Miller-Orr cash-balance model has resulted in significant savings to another company in the industry. Anxious to see whether it could provide savings to YARL, she studied YARL's cash system and found:

(1) Currently, about $100,000 is maintained in a non-interest-earning cash account.
(2) Conversion costs to transfer marketable securities to cash, or vice versa, average $30 per conversion.
(3) The variance of daily net cash flows is $1.5 million.
(4) Marketable securities can earn 9 percent *annually*, assuming a 360-day year.

The financial manager has asked you to do the following:

a. Calculate the return point and upper limit using the Miller-Orr model.
b. Determine how much additional profit YARL can earn by using the Miller-Orr model instead of maintaining its current cash balance. The average cash balance for the Miller-Orr model is: Return point × 4/3.
c. Recommend whether YARL should rely on the Miller-Orr model or continue to use its current system of maintaining a large cash balance if YARL's variance of daily net cash flows rises to $3 million.

17-4 LG 2 Cash conversion cycle American Products is concerned about managing cash efficiently. On the average, inventories have an average age of 90 days, and accounts receivable are collected in 60 days. Accounts payable are paid approximately 30 days after they arise. The firm spends $30 million on operating cycle investments each year, at a constant rate. Assuming a 360-day year:

a. Calculate the firm's operating cycle.
b. Calculate the firm's cash conversion cycle.
c. Calculate the amount of negotiated financing required to support the firm's cash conversion cycle.
d. Discuss how management might be able to reduce the cash conversion cycle.

17-5 LG 2 **Cash conversion cycle** Harris & Company has an inventory turnover of 12, an average collection period of 45 days, and an average payment period of 40 days. The firm spends $1 million on operating cycle investments each year. Assuming a 360-day year:
a. Calculate the firm's operating cycle.
b. Calculate the firm's cash conversion cycle.
c. Calculate the amount of negotiated financing required to support the firm's cash conversion cycle.
d. If the firm's operating cycle were lengthened, without any change in its average payment period (APP), how would this affect its cash conversion cycle and negotiated financing need?

17-6 LG 2 **Comparison of cash conversion cycles** A firm turns its inventory, on average, every 105 days. Its accounts receivable are collected, on the average, after 75 days, and accounts payable are paid an average of 60 days after they arise. Assuming a 360-day year, what changes will occur in the cash conversion cycle under each of the following circumstances?
a. The average age of inventory changes to 90 days.
b. The average collection period changes to 60 days.
c. The average payment period changes to 105 days.
d. The circumstances in **a, b,** and **c** occur simultaneously.

17-7 LG 2 **Changes in cash conversion cycles** A firm is considering several plans that affect its current accounts. Given the five plans and their probable results in the following table, which one would you favor? Explain.

	Change		
Plan	**Average age of inventory**	**Average collection period**	**Average payment period**
A	+30 days	+20 days	+5 days
B	+20 days	−10 days	+15 days
C	−10 days	0 days	−5 days
D	−15 days	+15 days	+10 days
E	+5 days	−10 days	+15 days

17-8 LG 2 **Changing cash conversion cycle** Camp Manufacturing turns its inventory eight times each year, has an average payment period of 35 days, and has an average collection period of 60 days. The firm's total annual outlays for operating cycle investments are $3.5 million. Assuming a 360-day year:
a. Calculate the firm's operating and cash conversion cycles.
b. Calculate the firm's daily cash operating expenditure. How much negotiated financing is required to support its cash conversion cycle?
c. Assuming the firm pays 14 percent for its financing, by how much would it increase its annual profits by *favorably* changing its current cash conversion cycle by 20 days?

17-9 LG 2 **Multiple changes in cash conversion cycle** Garrett Industries turns its inventory six times each year; it has an average collection period of 45 days and an average payment period of 30 days. The firm's annual operating cycle investment is $3 million. Assuming a 360-day year:

a. Calculate the firm's cash conversion cycle, its daily cash operating expenditure, and the amount of negotiated financing required to support its cash conversion cycle.

b. Find the firm's cash conversion cycle and negotiated financing requirement if it makes the following changes simultaneously.

(1) Shortens the average age of inventory by five days.

(2) Speeds the collection of accounts receivable by an average of 10 days.

(3) Extends the average payment period by 10 days.

c. If the firm pays 13 percent for its negotiated financing, by how much, if anything, could it increase its annual profit as a result of the changes in **b**?

d. If the annual cost of achieving the profit in **c** is $35,000, what action would you recommend to the firm? Why?

17-10 LG 3 **Float** Simon Corporation has daily cash receipts of $65,000. A recent analysis of its collections indicated that customers' payments were in the mail an average of 2½ days. Once received, the payments are processed in 1½ days. After payments are deposited, it takes an average of three days for these receipts to clear the banking system.

a. How much collection float (in days) does the firm currently have?

b. If the firm's opportunity cost is 11 percent, would it be economically advisable for the firm to pay an annual fee of $16,500 to reduce collection float by three days? Explain why or why not.

17-11 LG 4 **Concentration banking** Mead Enterprises sells to a national market and bills all credit customers from the New York City office. Using a continuous billing system, the firm has collections of $1.2 million per day. Under consideration is a concentration banking system that would require customers to mail payments to the nearest regional office to be deposited in local banks.

Mead estimates that the collection period for accounts will be shortened an average of 2½ days under this system. The firm also estimates that *annual* service charges and administrative costs of $300,000 will result from the proposed system. The firm can earn 14 percent on equal-risk investments.

a. How much cash will be made available for other uses if the firm accepts the proposed concentration banking system?

b. What savings will the firm realize on the 2½-day reduction in the collection period?

c. Would you recommend the change? Explain your answer.

17-12 LG 4 **Concentration banking—Range of outcomes** Pet-Care Company markets its products through widely dispersed distributors in the United States. It currently takes between six and nine days for cash-receipt checks to become available to the firm once they are mailed. Through use of a concentration banking system, the firm estimates that the collection float can be reduced to between two and four days. Daily cash receipts currently average $10,000. The firm's minimum opportunity cost is 5.5 percent.

a. Use the data given to determine the minimum and maximum annual savings from implementing the proposed system.

b. If the annual cost of the concentration banking system is $7,500, what recommendation would you make?

c. What impact, if any, would the fact that the firm's opportunity cost is 12 percent have on your analysis? Explain.

17-13 LG 4 **Lockbox system** Eagle Industries feels that a lockbox system can shorten its accounts receivable collection period by three days. Credit sales are $3,240,000 per year, billed on a continuous basis. The firm has other equally risky investments with a return of 15 percent. The cost of the lockbox system is $9,000 per year.

a. What amount of cash will be made available for other uses under the lockbox system?

b. What net benefit (cost) will the firm receive if it adopts the lockbox system? Should it adopt the proposed lockbox system?

17-14 LG 4 Direct send—Single Ocean Research of San Diego, California, just received a check in the amount of $800,000 from a customer in Bangor, Maine. If the firm processes the check in the normal manner, the funds will become available in six days. To speed up this process, the firm could send an employee to the bank in Bangor on which the check is drawn to present it for payment. Such action will cause the funds to become available after two days. If the cost of the direct send is $650 and the firm can earn 11 percent on these funds, what recommendation would you make? Explain.

17-15 LG 4 Direct sends—Multiple Delta Company just received four sizable checks drawn on various distant banks throughout the United States. The data on these checks are summarized in the following table. The firm, which has a 12 percent opportunity cost, can lease a small business jet with pilot to fly the checks to the cities of the banks on which they are drawn and present them for immediate payment. This task can be accomplished in a single day—thereby reducing to one day the funds availability from each of the four checks. The total cost of leasing the jet with pilot and other incidental expenditures is $4,500. Analyze the proposed action and make a recommendation.

Check	Amount	Number of days until funds are available
1	$ 600,000	7 days
2	2,000,000	5
3	1,300,000	4
4	400,000	6

17-16 LG 4 Controlled disbursing A large Texas firm has annual cash disbursements of $360 million made continuously over the year. Although annual service and administrative costs would increase by $100,000, the firm is considering writing all disbursement checks on a small bank in Oregon. The firm estimates that this will allow an additional 1½ days of cash usage. If the firm earns a return on other equally risky investments of 12 percent, should it change to the distant bank? Why or why not?

17-17 LG 4 Playing the float Clay Travel, Inc., routinely funds its checking account to cover all checks when written. A thorough analysis of its checking account discloses that the firm could maintain an average account balance that is 25 percent below the current level and adequately cover all checks presented. The average account balance is currently $900,000. If the firm can earn 10 percent on short-term investments, what, if any, annual savings would result from maintaining the lower average account balance?

17-18 LG 4 Payroll account management Cord Products has a weekly payroll of $250,000. The payroll checks are issued on Friday afternoon each week. In examining the check-cashing behavior of its employees, it has found the following pattern:

Number of business days[a] since issue of check	Percentage of checks cleared
1	20%
2	40
3	30
4	10

[a]Excludes Saturday and Sunday.

Given the information on page 720, what recommendation would you make to the firm with respect to managing its payroll account? Explain.

17-19 LG 4 **Zero-balance account** Union Company is considering establishment of a zero-balance account. The firm currently maintains an average balance of $420,000 in its disbursement account. As compensation to the bank for maintaining the zero-balance account, the firm will have to pay a monthly fee of $1,000 and maintain a $300,000 non-interest-earning deposit in the bank. The firm currently has no other deposits in the bank. Evaluate the proposed zero-balance account, and make a recommendation to the firm assuming that it has a 12 percent opportunity cost.

Chapter 17 Case Assessing Roche Publishing Company's cash management efficiency

Lisa Pinto, vice president of finance at Roche Publishing Company, a rapidly growing publisher of college texts, is concerned about the firm's high level of short-term negotiated financing. She feels that the firm can improve the management of its cash and, as a result, reduce its heavy reliance on negotiated financing. In this regard, she charged Arlene Bessenoff, the treasurer, with assessing the firm's cash management efficiency. Arlene decided to begin her investigation by studying the firm's operating and cash conversion cycles.

Arlene found that Roche's average payment period was 25 days. She consulted industry data, which showed that the average payment period for the industry was 40 days. Investigation of three similar publishing companies revealed that their average payment period was also 40 days.

Next, Arlene studied the production cycle and inventory policies. The average age of inventory was 120 days. She determined that the industry standard as reported in a survey done by *Publishing World*, the trade association journal, was 85 days.

Further analysis showed Arlene that the firm's average collection period was 60 days. The trade association and three similar publishing companies averages were found to be 42 days—30 percent lower than Roche's.

Roche Publishing Company was spending an estimated $14,400,000 per year on its operating cycle investments. Arlene considered this expenditure level to be the minimum that she could expect the firm to disburse during the coming year. Her concern was whether the firm's cash management was as efficient as it could be. She estimated that the firm could achieve the industry standards in managing its payables, inventory, and receivables by incurring an annual cost of $120,000. Arlene knew that the company paid 12 percent for its negotiated financing. For this reason she was concerned about the financing cost resulting from any inefficiencies in the management of Roche's cash conversion cycle.

Required

a. Assuming a constant rate for purchases, production, and sales throughout the year, what are Roche's existing operating cycle (OC), cash conversion cycle (CCC), and negotiated financing need?

b. If Roche can optimize operations according to industry standards, what would its operating cycle (OC), cash conversion cycle (CCC), and negotiated financing need be under these more efficient conditions?

c. In terms of negotiated financing requirements, what is the annual cost of Roche Publishing Company's operational inefficiency?

d. Should the firm incur the $120,000 annual cost to achieve the industry level of operational efficiency? Explain why or why not.

chapter 18

Accounts receivable and inventory

LEARNING GOALS

Discuss the key aspects of credit selection, including the five Cs of credit, obtaining credit information, analyzing credit information, credit scoring, and managing international credit.

Understand how to isolate and measure the key variables and use them to evaluate quantitatively the effects of either relaxing or tightening a firm's credit standards.

Review the three basic components of a firm's credit terms, the effects of changes in each of them on key variables and profits, and the procedure for evaluating the quantitative effects of proposed cash discount changes.

Explain the key features of collection policy, including aging accounts receivable, the basic tradeoffs, and the types of collection techniques.

Understand the types of inventory, differing viewpoints about inventory level, inventory as an investment, the relationship between inventory and accounts receivable, and international inventory management.

Describe the common techniques for managing inventory, including the ABC system, the basic economic order quantity (EOQ) model, the reorder point, the materials requirement planning (MRP) system, and the just-in-time (JIT) system.

A wholesale distributor like Hydro-Scape Products—we sell irrigation products—doesn't have many fixed assets. Accounts receivable and inventory account for 80 to 85 percent of our total assets. The faster we can convert these assets to cash, the better. We sell to over 15,000 customers and stock about 19,000 products. Obviously, good receivables and inventory management is critical to our financial success.

About 75 percent of our sales are credit sales, creating an interesting financing situation. In effect, we become the "Bank of Hydro-Scape." Many of our customers are small local landscapers that don't qualify for bank credit lines; typically, they aren't paid until they finish a job. Unless we provide financing by extending credit terms, our customers won't buy from us. Our basic credit terms are set by the industry; we have to offer them to be competitive. However, we offer better terms to some customers to induce quick payment. In fact, we have 21 different discount classifications.

With so many credit customers the "Five C's" of credit—character, capacity, capital, collateral, and conditions—are key factors in analyzing creditworthiness and determining a customer's credit limit. Character is very important in a people-oriented business like ours. It's simple: We sell products and we expect to be paid; we don't want the product back. Practically speaking, collateral doesn't matter if the customer decides not to pay us. To assess the "Five C's," we check credit reporting agencies such as Dun & Bradstreet and bank and industry references, looking at not only the primary source of repayment, but also the secondary and even tertiary sources.

> **"Five C's" of credit—character, capacity, capital, collateral, and conditions.**

The sales staff works closely with the credit department and must follow through on sales until collection. Our salespeople must also take responsibility for cash generation. Merit increases and bonuses are tied into company performance, which depends on *quality* sales—collected dollars. This minimizes any potential conflict between the sales and marketing effort and financial management.

We carefully monitor accounts receivable and take prompt action once an account becomes 30 days past due. The longer an account goes uncollected, the lower the probability of receiving payment. On the whole, our collection policies work well, and our allowance for doubtful accounts is between 3 and 5 percent. It has actually decreased, despite difficult times for our construction and real estate customers.

Hydro-Scape's profits are directly related to its ability to take cash discounts. Our suppliers offer incentives to pay them more quickly. To take those discounts, we must sell inventory and convert accounts receivable to cash quickly. This means having the right products in the right quantities. Inventory—in our case, finished goods only—represents 40 percent of assets, so we manage it closely. We also have to know what products sell during each season. In addition, certain manufacturers offer special incentives, such as lower prices and extended credit terms, to buy off-season. By spreading our purchases over a longer time period, we save money.

We don't finance inventory but use bank lines to finance accounts receivable, so we can take cash discounts. A good banking relationship is a very important part of managing accounts receivable. We understand our cash cycle and that of our customers and can explain to our bankers just how much we need and why. It never fails to surprise me how many multimillion-dollar companies don't understand their cash cycle or calculate the value of taking cash discounts. Unless they do, they will lose money.

During his 11 years as a retail and corporate banker at First Interstate and Security Pacific (now Bank of America), Kevin Hall served as Hydro-Scape's loan officer before becoming its Controller in 1988. He received a B.A. from San Diego State University and an M.B.A. from Chapman College, where he also taught finance.

Credit selection

A firm's credit selection activity focuses on determining whether to extend credit to a customer and how much credit to extend. What information would you need, and from what sources would you obtain it, to assess the creditworthiness of a business customer? Before reading on, spend a few moments answering this question.

ACCOUNTS RECEIVABLE REPRESENT THE EXTENSION OF CREDIT BY THE FIRM TO ITS CUStomers. For the average manufacturer they account for about 37 percent of *current assets* and about 16 percent of *total assets.* The extension of credit to customers by most manufacturers is a cost of doing business. By keeping its money tied up in accounts receivable, the firm loses the time value of the money and runs the risk of nonpayment by its customers. In return for incurring these costs, the firm can be competitive, attract and retain customers, and improve and maintain sales and profits.

credit policy
The determination of credit selection, credit standards, and credit terms.

Generally, the firm's financial manager directly controls accounts receivable through involvement in the establishment and management of (1) **credit policy,** which includes determining credit selection, credit standards, and credit terms, and (2) *collection policy.* The firm's approach to managing each of these aspects of accounts receivable is heavily influenced by competitive conditions—typically, greater leniency enhances competition, and less leniency hinders competition. Here we discuss credit selection; in the following sections we look at credit standards, credit terms, and collection policy.

credit selection
The decision whether to extend credit to a customer and how much credit to extend.

A firm's **credit selection** activity involves deciding whether to extend credit to a customer and how much credit to extend. Appropriate *sources of credit information* and *methods of credit analysis* must be developed. Each of these aspects of credit policy is important to the successful management of accounts receivable. First we look at the five C's of credit, which are the traditional focus of credit investigation.

The five C's of credit

five C's of credit
The five key dimensions—character, capacity, capital, collateral, and conditions—used by a firm's credit analysts in their analysis of an applicant's creditworthiness.

A firm's credit analysts often use the **five C's of credit** to focus their analysis on the key dimensions of an applicant's creditworthiness. Each of these five dimensions—character, capacity, capital, collateral, and conditions—is briefly described in the following list.

1. *Character:* The applicant's record of meeting past obligations—financial, contractual, and moral. Past payment history as well as any pending or resolved legal judgments against the applicant would be used to evaluate its character.
2. *Capacity:* The applicant's ability to repay the requested credit. Financial statement analysis (see Chapter 4) with particular emphasis on liquidity and debt ratios is typically used to assess the applicant's capacity.
3. *Capital:* The financial strength of the applicant as reflected by its ownership position. Analysis of the applicant's debt relative to equity and its profitability ratios are frequently used to assess its capital.
4. *Collateral:* The amount of assets the applicant has available for use in securing the credit. The larger the amount of available assets, the greater the chance that a firm will recover its funds if the applicant defaults. A review of the applicant's

balance sheet, asset value appraisals, and any legal claims filed against the applicant's assets can be used to evaluate its collateral.

5. *Conditions:* The current economic and business climate as well as any unique circumstances affecting either party to the credit transaction. For example, if the firm has excess inventory of the item the applicant wishes to purchase on credit, the firm may be willing to sell on more favorable terms or to less creditworthy applicants. Analysis of general economic and business conditions, as well as special circumstances that may affect the applicant or firm, is performed to assess conditions.

The credit analyst typically gives primary attention to the first two C's—character and capacity—since they represent the most basic requirements for extending credit to an applicant. Consideration of the last three C's—capital, collateral, and conditions—is important in structuring the credit arrangement and making the final credit decision, which is affected by the credit analyst's experience and judgment.

Obtaining credit information

When a business is approached by a customer desiring credit terms, the credit department typically begins the evaluation process by requiring the applicant to fill out various forms that request financial and credit information and references. Working from the application, the firm obtains additional information from other sources. If the firm has previously extended credit to the applicant, it will have its own information on the applicant's payment history. The major external sources of credit information are as follows:

FINANCIAL STATEMENTS

By requiring the credit applicant to provide financial statements for the past few years, the firm can analyze the applicant firm's liquidity, activity, debt, and profitability positions.

DUN & BRADSTREET

Dun & Bradstreet (D&B)
The largest mercantile credit-reporting agency in the United States.

Dun & Bradstreet (D&B) is the largest mercantile credit-reporting agency in the United States. It provides subscribers with a copy of its *Reference Book,* which contains credit ratings and keyed estimates of overall financial strength for virtually millions of U.S. and international companies. The key to the D&B ratings is shown in Figure 18.1. For example, a firm rated 2A3 would have estimated financial strength (net worth) in the range of $750,000 to $999,999 and would have a *fair* credit appraisal. D&B subscribers can also purchase detailed reports on specific companies and electronic access to D&B's database of business information through its *Electronic Access Systems.*

CREDIT INTERCHANGE BUREAUS

Firms can obtain credit information through the National Credit Interchange System, a national network of local credit bureaus that exchange information on a reciprocal basis. The reports obtained through these exchanges contain factual data rather than analyses. A fee is usually levied for each inquiry.

KEY TO RATINGS

Key to Ratings

Estimated Financial Strength			Composite Credit Appraisal			
			High	Good	Fair	Limited
5A	$50,000,000	and over	1	2	3	4
4A	$10,000,000 to	49,999,999	1	2	3	4
3A	1,000,000 to	9,999,999	1	2	3	4
2A	750,000 to	999,999	1	2	3	4
1A	500,000 to	749,999	1	2	3	4
BA	300,000 to	499,999	1	2	3	4
BB	200,000 to	299,999	1	2	3	4
CB	125,000 to	199,999	1	2	3	4
CC	75,000 to	124,999	1	2	3	4
DC	50,000 to	74,999	1	2	3	4
DD	35,000 to	49,999	1	2	3	4
EE	20,000 to	34,999	1	2	3	4
FF	10,000 to	19,999	1	2	3	4
GG	5,000 to	9,999	1	2	3	4
HH	Up to	4,999	1	2	3	4

DUN & BRADSTREET
Information Services
DB a company of The Dun & Bradstreet Corporation

FIGURE 18.1
The key to Dun & Bradstreet's ratings

DIRECT CREDIT INFORMATION EXCHANGES

Another means of obtaining credit information is through local, regional, or national credit associations. Often, an industry association maintains certain credit information that is available to members. Another method is to contact other suppliers that sell to the applicant and ask what its payment patterns are like.

BANK CHECKING

It may be possible for the firm's bank to obtain credit information from the applicant's bank. However, the type of information obtained will most likely be vague unless the applicant assists the firm in obtaining it. Typically, an estimate of the firm's cash balance is provided. For instance, it may be found that a firm maintains a "high five-figure" balance.

Analyzing credit information

credit analysis
The evaluation of credit applicants.

line of credit
The maximum amount a credit customer can owe the lending firm at any one time.

Firms typically establish set procedures for use in **credit analysis**—the evaluation of credit applicants. Often the firm not only must determine the creditworthiness of a customer but also must estimate the maximum amount of credit the customer is capable of supporting. Once this is done, the firm can establish a **line of credit,** the maximum amount the customer can owe the firm at any point in time. This type of line of credit extended by a firm to its customer is similar to a line of credit extended by a bank to a short-term borrower as described in Chapter 16. Lines of credit are established to eliminate the necessity of checking a major customer's credit each time a large purchase is made. We now consider procedures for analyzing credit information, the economic considerations involved in such analyses, and the small business problem.

PROCEDURES

A credit applicant's financial statements and accounts payable ledger can be used to calculate its "average payment period." This value can be compared to the credit terms currently extended to the firm. For customers requesting large amounts of credit or lines of credit, a thorough ratio analysis of the firm's liquidity, activity, debt, and profitability should be performed by using the relevant financial statements. A time-series comparison (discussed in Chapter 4) of similar ratios for various years should uncover any developing trends. The *Dun & Bradstreet Reference Book* can be used for estimating the maximum line of credit to extend. Dun & Bradstreet suggests no more than 10 percent of a customer's "estimated financial strength" (see Figure 18.1).

One of the key inputs to the final credit decision is the credit analyst's *subjective judgment* of a firm's creditworthiness. Experience provides a "feel" for the nonquantifiable aspects of the quality of a firm's operations. The analyst will add his or her knowledge of the character of the applicant's management, references from other suppliers, and the firm's historic payment patterns to any quantitative figures developed to determine creditworthiness. The analyst will then make the final decision as to whether to extend credit to the applicant and possibly what amount of credit to extend. Often these decisions are made not by one individual but by a credit review committee.

ECONOMIC CONSIDERATIONS

Regardless of whether the firm's credit department is evaluating the creditworthiness of a customer desiring credit for a specific transaction or that of a regular customer to establish a line of credit, the basic procedures are the same. The only difference is the depth of the analysis. A firm would be unwise to spend $100 to investigate the creditworthiness of a customer making a one-time $40 purchase, but $100 for a credit investigation may be a good investment in the case of a customer that is expected to make credit purchases of $60,000 annually. Clearly, the firm's credit selection procedures must be established on a sound economic basis that considers the benefits and costs of obtaining and analyzing credit information.

CONCEPT IN PRACTICE

SPS Facilitates and Enhances Credit Card Sales

Have you ever wondered what happens when a merchant slips a customer's credit card through a reader at the checkout counter? The information goes via SPS Transaction Services' telecommunications network to the card issuer, which authorizes or rejects the credit request. Beyond the high-tech wizardry, SPS also manages private-label credit card programs for Radio Shack, Goodyear, and other companies. The Riverwoods, Illinois, firm offers card design, card production, and billing services. As a special service, SPS promotes the business' product line. Beyond calling past-due Radio Shack accounts, SPS will distribute information on current sales promotions. According to SPS, which spun off from Sears in March 1992, the service provides goodwill and revenues at no incremental cost.

THE SMALL BUSINESS PROBLEM

Management of accounts receivable is one of the biggest financial problems facing small businesses. These firms typically lack the appropriate personnel and processes needed to make informed credit decisions. In addition, they are eager to increase sales volumes through the extension of credit, sometimes at the expense of bad debts. Frequently, for small firms, their credit customers are other local businesses managed by personal friends, which makes it particularly difficult to deny them credit. However, the credit decision must be made on the basis of sound financial and business principles. Clearly, it is better to have a potential credit customer get upset than for excessive uncollectible receivables to bankrupt the firm.

Credit scoring

credit scoring
A procedure resulting in a score reflecting an applicant's overall credit strength, derived as a weighted average of scores on key financial and credit characteristics.

Consumer credit decisions, because they involve a large group of similar applicants, each representing a small part of the firm's total business, can be handled by using impersonal, computer-based credit decision techniques. One popular technique is **credit scoring**—a procedure resulting in a score reflecting an applicant's overall credit strength, derived as a weighted average of the scores obtained on a variety of key financial and credit characteristics. Credit scoring is often used by large credit card operations such as oil companies and department stores. This technique can best be illustrated by an example.

EXAMPLE

Haller's Stores, a major regional department store chain, uses a credit scoring model to make its consumer credit decisions. Each credit applicant fills out and submits a credit application to the company. The application is reviewed and scored by one of the company's credit analysts, and then the relevant information is entered into the computer. The rest of the process, including making the credit decision, generating a letter of acceptance or rejection to the applicant, and dispatching the preparation and mailing of a credit card, is automated.

Table 18.1 demonstrates the calculation of Barb Buyer's credit score. The firm's predetermined credit standards are summarized in Table 18.2. The cutoff credit scores were developed to accept the group of credit applicants that will result in a positive contribution to the firm's share value. In evaluating Barb Buyer's credit score of 80.25 in light of the firm's credit standards, Haller's would decide to *extend standard credit terms* to her (80.25 > 75). ■

TABLE 18.1

CREDIT SCORING OF BARB BUYER BY HALLER'S STORES

Financial and credit characteristics	Score (0 to 100) (1)	Predetermined weight (2)	Weighted score [(1) × (2)] (3)
Credit references	80	.15	12.00
Home ownership	100	.15	15.00
Income range	70	.25	17.50
Payment history	75	.25	18.75
Years at address	90	.10	9.00
Years on job	80	.10	8.00
	Total	1.00	Credit score 80.25

Key: Column 1: Scores assigned by analyst or computer using company guidelines on the basis of data presented in credit application. Scores range from 0 (lowest) to 100 (highest). Column 2: Weights based on the company's analysis of the relative importance of each financial and credit characteristic in predicting whether or not a customer will pay an account. The sum of these weights must be 1.00.

TABLE 18.2

CREDIT STANDARDS FOR HALLER'S STORES

Credit score	Action
Greater than 75	Extend standard credit terms.
65 to 75	Extend limited credit; if account is properly maintained, convert to standard credit terms after one year.
Less than 65	Reject application.

The attractiveness of credit scoring should be clear from the above example. Unfortunately, most manufacturers sell to a diversified group of different-sized businesses, not to individuals. The statistical characteristics necessary for applying credit scoring to decisions regarding *mercantile credit*—credit extended by business firms to other business firms—rarely exist. In the following discussion we concentrate on the basic concepts of mercantile credit decisions, which cannot easily be expressed in quantifiable terms.

Managing international credit

Whereas credit management is difficult enough for managers of purely domestic companies, these tasks become much more complex for companies that operate internationally. This is partly because (as we have seen before) international operations typically expose a firm to *exchange rate risk*. It is also due to the dangers and delays involved in shipping goods long distances and having to cross at least two international borders.

Exports of finished goods are usually denominated in the currency of the importer's local market; most commodities, on the other hand, are denominated in dollars. Therefore, a U.S. company that sells a product in, for example, France would have to price that product in French francs and extend credit to a French wholesaler in the local currency (francs). Were the franc to depreciate against the dollar before the U.S. exporter collected on its account receivable, the U.S. company would experience an exchange rate loss because the francs collected would be worth fewer dollars than expected at the time the sale was made. Of course, the dollar could just as easily depreciate against the franc, yielding an exchange rate gain to the U.S. exporter, but most companies fear the loss more than they welcome the gain.

For a major currency like the French franc, the exporter can protect against this risk by using the currency futures, forward, or options markets, but it is costly to do so, particularly for relatively small amounts. If the exporter is selling to a customer in a developing country—where 40 percent of U.S. exports are now sold—there will probably be no effective instrument available for protecting against exchange rate risk at any price. This risk may be further magnified because credit standards (and acceptable collection techniques) may be much lower in developing countries than in the United States. While it may seem tempting to just "not bother" with exporting, U.S. companies no longer have the luxury of conceding foreign markets to international rivals. These export sales, if carefully monitored and, where possible, effectively protected against exchange rate risk, often prove to be very profitable. Beginning and/or infrequent exporters may choose to rely on *factors* (see Chapter 16) to manage their international export (credit) sales. While expensive, these firms typically have much better credit evaluation capabilities regarding foreign customers, and they are better able to bear credit risk than are most small exporters.

CONCEPTS IN REVIEW

18-1 What do the *accounts receivable* of a firm typically represent? What is meant by a firm's *credit policy?*

18-2 What does the *credit selection* activity include? Briefly list, define, and discuss the role of the *five C's of credit* in this process.

18-3 Summarize the basic sources of credit information. What procedures are commonly used to analyze credit information?

18-4 How do economic considerations affect the depth of credit analysis performed by a firm on a potential credit customer? Explain why the management of accounts receivable is one of the biggest financial problems facing small firms.

18-5 Describe *credit scoring,* and explain why this technique is typically applied to consumer credit decisions rather than to mercantile credit decisions.

18-6 Describe why the risks involved in international credit management are more complex than those associated with purely domestic credit sales.

Changing credit standards

A firm's credit standards reflect the minimum level of creditworthiness for which it would extend credit to a customer. What effect do you think raising a firm's credit standards would have on its sales, level of accounts receivable investment, and bad debts as a percentage of sales? Take a few moments to consider this question before reading on.

credit standards
The minimum requirements for extending credit to a customer.

THE FIRM'S **CREDIT STANDARDS** ARE THE MINIMUM REQUIREMENTS FOR EXTENDING credit to a customer. Our concern here is with the nonrestrictiveness or restrictiveness of a firm's overall policy. Understanding the key variables that must be considered when a firm is contemplating relaxing or tightening its credit standards will give a general idea of the kinds of decisions involved.

Key variables

The major variables that should be considered in evaluating proposed changes in credit standards are (1) sales volume, (2) the investment in accounts receivable, and (3) bad debt expenses.[1] Let us examine each in more detail.

SALES VOLUME

Changing credit standards can be expected to change the volume of sales. If credit standards are relaxed, sales are expected to increase; if credit standards are tightened, sales

[1]A relaxation of credit standards would be expected to add to the *clerical costs* as a result of the need for a larger credit department, whereas a tightening of credit standards might save clerical costs. Because these costs are assumed to be included in the variable cost per unit, they are not explicitly isolated in the analyses presented in this chapter.

are expected to decrease. Generally, increases in sales affect profits positively, whereas decreases in sales affect profits negatively.

INVESTMENT IN ACCOUNTS RECEIVABLE

Carrying, or maintaining, accounts receivable involves a cost to the firm. This cost is attributable to the forgone earnings opportunities resulting from the necessity to tie up funds in accounts receivable. Therefore the higher the firm's investment in accounts receivable, the greater the carrying cost, and the lower the firm's investment in accounts receivable, the lower the carrying cost. If the firm relaxes its credit standards, the volume of accounts receivable increases, and so does the firm's carrying cost (investment). This change results from increased sales and longer collection periods due to slower payment on average by credit customers.[2] The opposite occurs if credit standards are tightened. Thus a relaxation of credit standards is expected to affect profits negatively because of higher carrying costs, whereas tightening credit standards would affect profits positively as a result of lower carrying costs.

BAD DEBT EXPENSES

The probability, or risk, of acquiring a bad debt increases as credit standards are relaxed. The increase in bad debts associated with relaxation of credit standards raises bad debt expenses and affects profits negatively. The opposite effects on bad debt expenses and profits result from a tightening of credit standards.

The basic changes and effects on profits expected to result from the *relaxation* of credit standards are tabulated as follows:

Variable	Direction of change	Effect on profits
Sales volume	Increase	Positive
Investment in accounts receivable	Increase	Negative
Bad debt expenses	Increase	Negative

If credit standards were tightened, the opposite effects would be expected.

Determining values of key variables

The way in which the key credit standard variables are determined can be illustrated by the following example.[3]

[2]Because of the forward-looking nature of accounts receivable analysis, certain items such as sales, collections, and bad debts resulting from changes in the management of accounts receivable must be estimated. The need to estimate these future values may introduce a great deal of uncertainty into the decision process. Some of the techniques discussed in Chapter 9, such as sensitivity and scenario analysis and simulation, can be applied to these estimates to adjust them for uncertainty.

[3]Because various credit policy decisions tend to commit the firm to long-run behaviors, a number of authors have suggested that credit policy decisions should be made by using a present-value framework. See Yong H. Kim and Joseph C. Atkins, "Evaluating Investments in Accounts Receivable: A Maximizing Framework," *Journal of Finance* 33 (May 1978), pp. 402–412. Although their suggestions are valid, a more recent article by Kanwal S. Sachdeva and Lawrence J. Gitman, "Accounts Receivable Decisions in a Capital Budgeting Framework," *Financial Management* 10 (Winter 1981), pp. 45–49, has shown that single-period decision rules similar to those applied throughout this chapter will provide correct accept-reject decisions without the computational rigor of the present-value approach.

EXAMPLE

Dodd Tool, a manufacturer of lathe tools, is currently selling a product for $10 per unit. Sales (all on credit) for last year were 60,000 units. The variable cost per unit is $6. The firm's total fixed costs are $120,000.

The firm is currently contemplating a *relaxation of credit standards* that is expected to result in a 5 percent increase in unit sales to 63,000 units, an increase in the average collection period from its current level of 30 days to 45 days, and an increase in bad debt expenses from the current level of 1 percent of sales to 2 percent. The firm's required return on equal-risk investments, which is the opportunity cost of tying up funds in accounts receivable, is 15 percent.

To determine whether to implement the proposed relaxation of credit standards, Dodd Tool must calculate the effect on the firm's additional profit contribution from sales, the cost of the marginal investment in accounts receivable, and the cost of marginal bad debts.

Additional Profit Contribution from Sales The additional profit contribution from sales expected to result from the relaxation of credit standards can be calculated easily. Because fixed costs are "sunk" and thereby unaffected by a change in the sales level, the only cost relevant to a change in sales would be out-of-pocket or variable costs. Sales are expected to increase by 5 percent, or 3,000 units. The profit contribution per unit will equal the difference between the sale price per unit ($10) and the variable cost per unit ($6). The profit contribution per unit will therefore be $4. Thus the total additional profit contribution from sales will be $12,000 (3,000 units × $4 per unit).

Cost of the Marginal Investment in Accounts Receivable The cost of the marginal investment in accounts receivable can be calculated by finding the difference between the cost of carrying receivables before and after the introduction of the relaxed credit standards. Because our concern is only with the out-of-pocket costs rather than the fixed costs (which are sunk and unaffected by this decision), *the relevant cost in this analysis is the variable cost.* The average investment in accounts receivable can be calculated by using the following formula:

$$\text{Average investment in accounts receivable} = \frac{\text{total variable cost of annual sales}}{\text{turnover of accounts receivable}} \quad (18.1)$$

where

$$\text{Turnover of accounts receivable}^4 = \frac{360}{\text{average collection period}}$$

The total variable cost of annual sales under the proposed and present plans can be found as noted below.

Total variable cost of annual sales:

Under proposed plan: ($6 × 63,000 units) = $378,000
Under present plan: ($6 × 60,000 units) = $360,000

[4]The turnover of accounts receivable can also be calculated by *dividing annual sales by accounts receivable.* For the purposes of this chapter, only the formula transforming the average collection period to a turnover of accounts receivable is emphasized.

The calculation of the total variable cost for both plans involves the straightforward use of the variable cost per unit of $6. The total variable cost under the proposed plan is $378,000, and under the present plan it is $360,000. Therefore implementation of the proposed plan will cause the total variable cost of annual sales to increase from $360,000 to $378,000.

The turnover of accounts receivable refers to the number of times each year the firm's accounts receivable are actually turned into cash. In each case it is found by dividing the average collection period into 360—the number of days in a year.

Turnover of accounts receivable:

$$\text{Under proposed plan: } \frac{360}{45} = 8$$

$$\text{Under present plan: } \frac{360}{30} = 12$$

With implementation of the proposed plan, the accounts receivable turnover would slow from 12 to 8 times per year.

By substituting the cost and turnover data just calculated into Equation 18.1 for each case, the following average investments in accounts receivable result:

Average investment in accounts receivable:

$$\text{Under proposed plan: } \frac{\$378{,}000}{8} = \$47{,}250$$

$$\text{Under present plan: } \frac{\$360{,}000}{12} = \$30{,}000$$

The marginal investment in accounts receivable as well as its cost are calculated as follows:

Cost of marginal investment in accounts receivable:

Average investment under proposed plan	$47,250
− Average investment under present plan	30,000
Marginal investment in accounts receivable	$17,250
× Required return on investment	.15
Cost of marginal investment in A/R[5]	$ 2,588

The cost of investing an additional $17,250 in accounts receivable was found by multiplying this marginal investment by 15 percent (the firm's required return on investment). The resulting value of $2,588 is considered a cost because it represents the maximum amount that could have been earned on the $17,250 had it been placed in the best equal-risk investment alternative available.

Cost of Marginal Bad Debts The cost of marginal bad debts is found by taking the difference between the level of bad debts before and after the relaxation of credit standards, as shown at the top of page 734.

[5]Throughout the text, *A/R* will frequently be used interchangeably with *accounts receivable.*

Cost of marginal bad debts:

Under proposed plan: (.02 × \$10/unit × 63,000 units)	=	\$12,600
Under present plan: (.01 × \$10/unit × 60,000 units)	=	6,000
Cost of marginal bad debts		\$ 6,600

Note that the bad debt costs are calculated by using the sale price per unit (\$10) to back out not just the true loss of variable (or out-of-pocket) cost (\$6) that results when a customer fails to pay its account, but also the profit contribution per unit—in this case \$4 (\$10 sales price − \$6 variable cost)—that is included in the "additional profit contribution from sales." Thus the resulting cost of marginal bad debts is \$6,600. ■

Making the credit standard decision

To decide whether the firm should relax its credit standards, the additional profit contribution from sales must be compared to the sum of the cost of the marginal investment in accounts receivable and the cost of marginal bad debts. If the additional profit contribution is greater than marginal costs, credit standards should be relaxed; otherwise, present standards should remain unchanged. Let us look at an example.

EXAMPLE

The results and key calculations relative to Dodd Tool's decision to relax its credit standards are summarized in Table 18.3. Since the additional profit contribution from the increased sales would be \$12,000, which exceeds the sum of the cost of the marginal investment in accounts receivable and the cost of marginal bad debts, the firm *should* relax its credits standards as proposed. The net addition to total profits resulting from such an action will be \$2,812 per year. ■

TABLE 18.3

THE EFFECTS ON DODD TOOL OF A RELAXATION OF CREDIT STANDARDS

Additional profit contribution from sales [3,000 units × (\$10 − \$6)]		\$12,000
Cost of marginal investment in A/R[a]		
Average investment under proposed plan:		
$\frac{(\$6 \times 63{,}000)}{8} = \frac{\$378{,}000}{8}$	\$47,250	
Average investment under present plan:		
$\frac{(\$6 \times 60{,}000)}{12} = \frac{\$360{,}000}{12}$	30,000	
Marginal investment in A/R	\$17,250	
Cost of marginal investment in A/R (.15 × \$17,250)		(\$2,588)
Cost of marginal bad debts		
Bad debts under proposed plan (.02 × \$10 × 63,000)	\$12,600	
Bad debts under present plan (.01 × \$10 × 60,000)	6,000	
Cost of marginal bad debts		(\$6,600)
Net profit from implementation of proposed plan		\$2,812

[a]The denominators 8 and 12 in the calculation of the average investment in accounts receivable under the proposed and present plans are the accounts receivable turnovers for each of these plans (360/45 = 8 and 360/30 = 12).

The technique described here for making a credit standard decision is commonly used for evaluating other types of changes in the management of accounts receivable as well. If the firm in the preceding example had been contemplating tightening its credit standards, the cost would have been a reduction in the profit contribution from sales, and the return would have been from reductions in the cost of the marginal investment in accounts receivable and in bad debts. Another application of this analytical technique is demonstrated later in the chapter.

CONCEPT IN PRACTICE

Tightening Credit Standards at Household International

Among the companies tracked by the investment advisory department of LBS Capital Management, Household International, a large provider of consumer financial services, stood out in early 1993. Paine Webber analysts also viewed Household as an attractive investment. Both firms agreed that Household International's earnings would be 50 percent higher in 1993 and rise another 20 percent in 1994. The reason for the enthusiasm and run-up in share price from $44 to $64 was Household International's tightening of credit standards. Despite the continuing recession, Household's delinquent loans had dropped to 4.5 percent of total loans, the lowest for the industry. This performance was considered to be evidence that Household was serious about tightening its credit standards.

CONCEPT IN REVIEW

18-7 What key variables should be considered in evaluating possible changes in a firm's *credit standards?* What are the basic tradeoffs in a *tightening* of credit standards?

Changing credit terms

A firm's credit terms specify the repayment requirements that it places on all of its credit customers. What impact do you think the firm's introduction of a cash discount for early payment would have on its sales, level of accounts receivable investment, bad debts as a percentage of sales, and average profit per unit? Spend a short time answering this question before reading further.

credit terms
Specify the repayment terms required of a firm's credit customers.

A FIRM'S **CREDIT TERMS** SPECIFY THE REPAYMENT TERMS REQUIRED OF ALL ITS CREDIT customers.[6] Typically, a type of shorthand is used. For example, credit terms may be stated as *2/10 net 30,* which means that the purchaser receives a 2 percent cash discount if the bill is paid within 10 days after the beginning of the credit period; if the customer does not take the cash discount, the full amount must be paid within 30 days after the beginning of the credit period. Credit terms cover three things: (1) the cash discount, if any (in this case 2 percent); (2) the cash discount period (in this

[6]An in-depth discussion of credit terms as viewed by the *customer*—that is, *accounts payable*—is presented in Chapter 16. In this chapter our concern is with *accounts receivable*—credit terms from the point of view of the *seller*.

case 10 days); and (3) the credit period (in this case 30 days). Changes in any aspect of the firm's credit terms may have an effect on its overall profitability. The positive and negative factors associated with such changes and quantitative procedures for evaluating them are presented in this section.

Cash discount

When a firm initiates or *increases* a cash discount, the changes and effects on profits shown in the following table can be expected.

Variable	Direction of change	Effect on profits
Sales volume	Increase	Positive
Investment in accounts receivable due to nondiscount takers paying earlier	Decrease	Positive
Investment in accounts receivable due to new customers	Increase	Negative
Bad debt expenses	Decrease	Positive
Profit per unit	Decrease	Negative

The sales volume should increase because if a firm is willing to pay by day 10, the unit price decreases. The net effect on the accounts receivable investment is difficult to determine because the nondiscount takers paying earlier will reduce the accounts receivable investment, while the new customer accounts will increase this investment. The bad debt expenses should decline, since, as customers on the average will pay earlier, the probability of their not paying at all will decrease.[7] Both the decrease in the receivables investment and the decrease in bad debt expenses should result in increased profits. The negative aspect of an increased cash discount is a decreased profit per unit as more customers take the discount and pay the reduced price.

Decreasing or eliminating a cash discount would have opposite effects. The quantitative effects of changes in cash discounts can be evaluated by a method similar to that used earlier to evaluate changes in credit standards.

EXAMPLE

Assume that Dodd Tool is considering initiating a cash discount of 2 percent for payment prior to day 10 after a purchase. The firm's current average collection period is 30 days [turnover = (360/30) = 12], credit sales of 60,000 units are made, and the variable cost per unit is $6. The firm expects that if the cash discount is initiated, 60 percent of its sales will be on discount, and sales will increase by 5 percent to 63,000 units. The average collection period is expected to drop to 15 days [turnover = (360/15) = 24]. Bad debt expenses are expected to drop from the current level of 1 percent of sales to .5 percent of sales. The firm's required return on equal-risk investments remains at 15 percent.

[7]This contention is based on the fact that the longer a person has to pay, the less likely it is that the person will pay. The more time that elapses, the more opportunities there are for a customer to become technically insolvent or fail. Therefore the probability of a bad debt is expected to increase directly with increases in the credit period.

The analysis of this decision is presented in Table 18.4. The calculations are similar to those presented for Dodd's credit standard decision in Table 18.3[8] except for the final entry, "Cost of cash discount." This cost of \$7,560 reflects the fact that *profits will be reduced* as a result of a 2 percent cash discount being taken on 60 percent of the new level of sales. Dodd Tool can increase profit by \$9,428 by initiating the proposed cash discount. Such an action therefore seems advisable. This type of analysis can also be applied to decisions concerning the elimination or reduction of cash discounts. ■

Cash discount period

The net effect of changes in the cash discount period is quite difficult to analyze because of the nature of the forces involved. For example, if the cash discount period were *increased,* the changes noted in the table at the top of page 738 could be expected.

TABLE 18.4

THE EFFECTS ON DODD TOOL OF INITIATING A CASH DISCOUNT

Additional profit contribution from sales [3,000 units × (\$10 − \$6)]		\$12,000
Cost of marginal investment in A/R		
Average investment under proposed plan:		
$\frac{(\$6 \times 63{,}000)}{24} = \frac{\$378{,}000}{24}$	\$15,750	
Average investment under present plan:		
$\frac{(\$6 \times 60{,}000)}{12} = \frac{\$360{,}000}{12}$	30,000	
Marginal investment in A/R	(\$14,250)	
Cost of marginal investment in A/R (.15 × \$14,250)		\$2,138[a]
Cost of marginal bad debts		
Bad debts under proposed plan (.005 × \$10 × 63,000)	\$ 3,150	
Bad debts under present plan (.01 × \$10 × 60,000)	6,000	
Cost of marginal bad debts		\$2,850[a]
Cost of cash discount[b] (.02 × .60 × \$10 × 63,000)		(\$7,560)
Net profit from implementation of proposed plan		\$9,428

[a]This value is positive, since it represents a savings rather than a cost.

[b]This calculation reflects the fact that a 2 percent cash discount will be taken on 60 percent of the new level of sales—63,000 units at \$10 each.

[8]The calculation of the average investment in accounts receivable presented for both the present and proposed plans is not entirely correct. Whenever a change in credit terms or some other aspect of accounts receivable is expected to change the payment pattern of existing customers, formal analysis should recognize that the firm's pattern of receipt of both cost *and* profit from these customers is being altered. Therefore the average investment in receivables for existing customers whose payment patterns have been altered should be measured at the sale price, not at cost. For an excellent discussion of this point, see Edward A. Dyl, "Another Look at the Investment in Accounts Receivable," *Financial Management* 6 (Winter 1977), pp. 67–70. To convey the key concepts throughout the remainder of this chapter without confusing the reader, the average accounts receivable investment is calculated at cost regardless of whether or not existing customers' payment patterns are altered by the proposed action.

Variable	Direction of change	Effect on profits
Sales volume	Increase	Positive
Investment in accounts receivable due to nondiscount takers paying earlier	Decrease	Positive
Investment in accounts receivable due to discount takers still getting cash discount but paying later	Increase	Negative
Investment in accounts receivable due to new customers	Increase	Negative
Bad debt expenses	Decrease	Positive
Profit per unit	Decrease	Negative

The problems in determining the exact results of changes in the cash discount period are directly attributable to the three forces affecting the firm's *investment in accounts receivable.* If the firm were to shorten the cash discount period, the effects would be the opposite of those described above.

Credit period

Changes in the credit period also affect the firm's profitability. The following effects on profits can be expected from an *increase* in the length of the credit period:

Variable	Direction of change	Effect on profits
Sales volume	Increase	Positive
Investment in accounts receivable	Increase	Negative
Bad debt expenses	Increase	Negative

Increasing the length of the credit period should increase sales, but both the investment in accounts receivable and bad debt expenses are likely to increase as well. Thus the net effect on profits of the sales increase is positive, while the increases in accounts receivable investment and bad debt expenses will negatively affect profits. A decrease in the length of the credit period is likely to have the opposite effect. The credit period decision is analyzed in the same ways as the credit standard decision illustrated in Table 18.3.

CONCEPTS IN REVIEW

18-8 Discuss what is meant by *credit terms.* What are the three components of credit terms? How do credit terms affect the firm's accounts receivable?

18-9 What are the expected effects of a *decrease* in the firm's cash discount on sales volume, investment in accounts receivable, bad debt expenses, and per-unit profits, respectively?

18-10 What are the expected effects of a *decrease* in the firm's credit period? What is likely to happen to sales volume, investment in accounts receivable, and bad debt expenses, respectively?

Collection policy

Collection policy includes the procedures used to collect accounts receivable once they are due. How would you go about collecting from those customers whose accounts have become overdue? Devote a few moments to answering this question before reading on.

collection policy
The procedures for collecting a firm's accounts receivable when they are due.

THE FIRM'S **COLLECTION POLICY** IS THE SET OF PROCEDURES FOR COLLECTING ACcounts receivable when they are due. The effectiveness of this policy can be partly evaluated by looking at the level of bad debt expenses. This level depends not only on collection policy but also on the policy on which the extension of credit is based. If one assumes that the level of bad debts attributable to *credit policy* is relatively constant, increasing collection expenditures can be expected to reduce bad debts. This relationship is depicted in Figure 18.2. As the figure indicates, beyond point A, additional collection expenditures will not reduce bad debt losses sufficiently to justify the outlay of funds. Popular approaches used to evaluate credit and collection policies include the *average collection period ratio* (presented in Chapter 4) and *aging accounts receivable.*

aging
A technique used to evaluate credit and/or collection policies that indicates the proportion of the accounts receivable balance that has been outstanding for a specified period of time.

Aging accounts receivable

Aging is a technique that indicates the proportion of the accounts receivable balance that has been outstanding for a specified period of time. By highlighting irregu-

FIGURE 18.2
Collection expenditures and bad debt losses

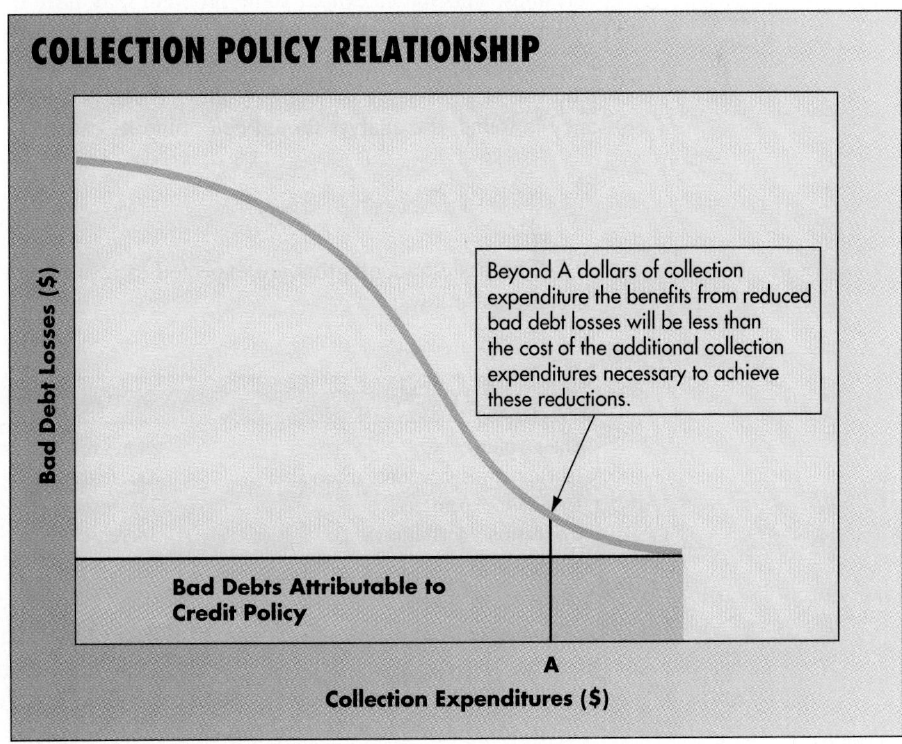

larities it allows the analyst to pinpoint the cause of credit and/or collection problems. Aging requires that the firm's accounts receivable be broken down into groups based on the time of origin. This breakdown is typically made on a month-by-month basis, going back three or four months. Let us look at an example.

EXAMPLE

Assume that Dodd Tool extends 30-day EOM credit terms to its customers. The firm's December 31, 1994, balance sheet shows $200,000 of accounts receivable. An evaluation of the $200,000 of accounts receivable results in the following breakdown:

Days	Current	0–30	31–60	61–90	Over 90	
Month	December	November	October	September	August	Total
Accounts receivable	$60,000	$40,000	$66,000	$26,000	$8,000	$200,000
Percentage of total	30	20	33	13	4	100

Since it is assumed that Dodd Tool gives its customers 30 days after the end of the month in which the sale is made to pay off their accounts, any December receivables that are still on the firm's books are considered current. November receivables are between zero and 30 days overdue, October receivables still unpaid are 31 to 60 days overdue, and so on.

The table shows that 30 percent of the firm's receivables are current, 20 percent are one month late, 33 percent are two months late, 13 percent are three months late, and 4 percent are more than three months late. While payment seems generally slow, a noticeable irregularity in these data is the high percentage represented by October receivables. This indicates that some problem may have occurred in October. Investigation may find that the problem can be attributed to the hiring of a new credit manager, the acceptance of a new account that has made a large credit purchase it has not yet paid for, or ineffective collection policy. When accounts are aged and such a discrepancy is found, the analyst should determine its cause. ■

Basic tradeoffs

The basic tradeoffs that are expected to result from an *increase* in collection efforts are as follows:

Variable	Direction of change	Effect on profits
Sales volume	None or decrease	None or negative
Investment in accounts receivable	Decrease	Positive
Bad debt expenses	Decrease	Positive
Collection expenditures	Increase	Negative

Increased collection efforts should reduce the investment in accounts receivable and bad debt expenses, increasing profits. The cost of this strategy may include lost sales in addition to increased collection expenditures if the level of collection effort is too intense. In other words, if the firm pushes its customers too hard to pay their accounts, they may be angered and may take their business elsewhere. The firm should therefore be careful not to be overly aggressive. The basic collection policy tradeoffs can be evaluated quantitatively in a manner similar to that used to evaluate the tradeoffs for credit standards and cash discounts.

Types of collection techniques

A number of collection techniques are employed. As an account becomes more and more overdue, the collection effort becomes more personal and more strict. The basic techniques are presented in the order typically followed in the collection process.

LETTERS

After an account receivable becomes overdue a certain number of days, the firm normally sends a polite letter reminding the customer of its obligation. If the account is not paid within a certain period of time after the letter has been sent, a second, more demanding letter is sent. This letter may be followed by yet another letter if necessary. Collection letters are the first step in the collection process for overdue accounts.

TELEPHONE CALLS

If letters prove unsuccessful, a telephone call may be made to the customer to personally request immediate payment. Such a call is typically directed to the customer's accounts payable department, where the responding employee acts on instructions of his or her boss. If the customer has a reasonable excuse, arrangements may be made to extend the payment period. A call from the seller's attorney may be used if all other discussions seem to fail.

PERSONAL VISITS

This technique is much more common at the consumer credit level, but it may be effectively employed by industrial suppliers. Sending a local salesperson or a collection person to confront the customer can be a very effective collection procedure. Payment may be made on the spot.

USING COLLECTION AGENCIES

A firm can turn uncollectible accounts over to a collection agency or an attorney for collection. The fees for this service are typically quite high; the firm may receive less than 50 cents on the dollar from accounts collected in this way.

LEGAL ACTION

Legal action is the most stringent step in the collection process. It is an alternative to the use of a collection agency. Not only is direct legal action expensive, but it may force the debtor into bankruptcy, thereby reducing the possibility of future business without guaranteeing the ultimate receipt of the overdue amount.

Computerization of accounts receivable management

The use of computers in the billing and collection of accounts is widespread. A computer is used to bill credit customers at the appropriate time following a purchase. As payments are received, a record of them is keyed into the computer. A computer can be programmed to monitor accounts receivable after a customer has been billed. Periodic checks are automatically made at certain points in time after billing to see whether the accounts have been paid. If payment has not been received at certain predetermined points, collection letters are sent. After a prescribed number of these letters have been sent without any receipt of payment, a special notice will be generated, probably as part of a report to the credit manager. At this point the collection efforts become more directly personal. Actions such as telephone calls, personal visits, and use of a collection agency will then be taken. Legal action is also a possibility.

Currently, computers are being used not only to monitor accounts but also to aid in the credit decision process. Data on each customer's payment patterns are maintained and can be called forth to evaluate requests for renewed or additional credit. A computer can also be used to monitor the effectiveness of the collection department by generating data on the status of outstanding accounts. Although the computer cannot carry out the entire accounts receivable management function, it will continue to reduce the amount of paperwork required.

CONCEPTS IN REVIEW

18-11 What is meant by a firm's *collection policy?* Explain how *aging accounts receivable* can be used to evaluate the effectiveness of both the credit policy and the collection policy.

18-12 Describe the basic tradeoffs involved in collection policy decisions, and describe the popular types of collection techniques.

Inventory management

Although inventory generally represents a sizable investment by the firm, its management is typically the responsibility of manufacturing personnel. What general viewpoint do you think the financial manager takes with respect to the level of inventory, and how does it compare to the views of the marketing manager, the manufacturing manager, and the purchasing manager? Before reading further, take a few moments to answer this question.

INVENTORY, OR GOODS ON HAND, IS A NECESSARY CURRENT ASSET THAT PERMITS THE PRODUCTION-sale process to operate with a minimum of disturbance. Like accounts receivable, inventory represents a significant monetary investment on the part of most firms. For the average manufacturer it accounts for about 42 percent of *current assets* and about 18 percent of *total assets.* Chapter 17 illustrated the importance of turning over inventory quickly to reduce financing costs. The financial manager generally acts as a "watchdog" and advisor in matters concerning inventory; he or she does not have direct control over inventory but does provide input into the inventory management process.

Inventory fundamentals

Two aspects of inventory require some elaboration. One is the *types of inventory;* the other concerns differing viewpoints as to the *appropriate level of inventory.*

TYPES OF INVENTORY

raw materials inventory
Items purchased by the firm for use in the manufacture of a finished product.

work-in-process inventory
All items that are currently in production.

finished goods inventory
Items that have been produced but not yet sold.

The three basic types of inventory are raw materials, work in process, and finished goods. **Raw materials inventory** consists of items purchased by the firm—usually basic materials such as screws, plastic, raw steel, or rivets—for use in the manufacture of a finished product. If a firm manufactures complex products with numerous parts, its raw materials inventory may consist of manufactured items that have been purchased from another company or from another division of the same firm. **Work-in-process inventory** consists of all items that are currently in production. These are normally partially finished goods at some intermediate stage of completion. **Finished goods inventory** consists of items that have been produced but not yet sold.

DIFFERING VIEWPOINTS ABOUT INVENTORY LEVEL

Differing viewpoints concerning appropriate inventory levels commonly exist among the finance, marketing, manufacturing, and purchasing managers of a company. Each sector views inventory levels in light of its own objectives. The *financial manager's* general disposition toward inventory levels is to keep them low. The financial manager must police the inventories, making sure that the firm's money is not being unwisely invested in excess resources. The *marketing manager,* on the other hand, would like to have large inventories of each of the firm's finished products. This would ensure that all orders could be filled quickly, eliminating the need for backorders due to stockouts.

The *manufacturing manager's* major responsibility is to make sure that the production plan is correctly implemented and that it results in the desired amount of finished goods of acceptable quality at a low cost. In fulfilling this role the manufacturing manager would keep raw materials inventories high to avoid production delays and would favor high finished goods inventories by making large production runs for the sake of lower unit production costs. The *purchasing manager* is concerned solely with the raw materials inventories. He or she is responsible for seeing that whatever raw materials are required by production are available in the correct quantities at the desired times and at a favorable price. Without proper control, the purchasing manager may purchase larger quantities of resources than are actually needed to get quantity discounts or in anticipation of rising prices or a shortage of certain materials.

CONCEPT IN PRACTICE

Blue-Light Specials on Bread Create Inventory Headaches at Kmart

Kmart, the nation's second largest discount retailer, is planning to open 450 Super Kmarts. These locations would consist of both a supermarket and a discount store. Although the expansion is necessary to counter Wal-Mart's combination of discount stores and Sam's grocery stores, inventory management presents a problem.

The typical discount store turns over inventory about four times a year. Meanwhile, the typical grocery store turns over inventory about 25 times per year. It takes a nimbler distribution system to keep perishables stocked and fresh. Analysts are worried that Kmart may have to utilize blue-light specials to sell bread.

Inventory as an investment

Inventory is an investment in the sense that it requires that the firm tie up its money, thereby forgoing certain other earnings opportunities. In general, the higher a firm's average inventories, the larger the dollar investment and cost required, and the lower its average inventories, the smaller the dollar investment and cost required. In evaluating planned changes in inventory levels, the financial manager should consider such changes from a benefit-versus-cost standpoint.

EXAMPLE

Ultimate Manufacturing is contemplating making larger production runs to reduce the high setup costs associated with the production of its only product, industrial hoists. The total *annual* reduction in setup costs that can be obtained has been estimated to be $20,000. As a result of the larger production runs, the average inventory investment is expected to increase from $200,000 to $300,000. If the firm can earn 25 percent per year on equal-risk investments, the *annual* cost of the additional $100,000 ($300,000 − $200,000) inventory investment will be $25,000 (.25 × $100,000). Comparing the annual $25,000 cost of the system with the annual savings of $20,000 shows that the proposal should be rejected, since it results in a net annual *loss* of $5,000. ■

The relationship between inventory and accounts receivable

The level and management of inventory and accounts receivable are closely related.[9] Generally, in the case of manufacturing firms, when an item is sold, it moves from inventory to accounts receivable and ultimately to cash. Because of the close relationship between inventory and accounts receivable, management of them should not be viewed independently. For example, the decision to extend credit to a customer can result in an increased level of sales, which can be supported only by higher levels of inventory and accounts receivable. The credit terms extended will also affect the investment in inventory and receivables, since longer credit terms may allow a firm to move items from inventory to accounts receivable. Generally, there is an advantage to such a strategy, since the cost of carrying an item in inventory is greater than the cost of carrying an account receivable. This is true because the cost of carrying inventory includes, in addition to the required return on the invested funds, the costs of storing, insuring, and otherwise maintaining the physical inventory. This relationship can be shown, using a simple example.

EXAMPLE

Mills Industries, a producer of PVC pipe, estimates that the annual cost of carrying $1 of merchandise in inventory for a one-year period is 25 cents, whereas the annual cost

[9]While this chapter emphasizes primarily the financial considerations involved in accounts receivable and inventory decisions, other nonfinancial considerations may significantly influence a firm's decisions in these areas.

of carrying $1 of receivables is 15 cents. The firm currently maintains average inventories of $300,000 and an average *investment* in accounts receivable of $200,000. The firm believes that by altering its credit terms, it can cause its customers to purchase in larger quantities on the average, thereby reducing its average inventories to $150,000 and increasing the average investment in accounts receivable to $350,000. The altered credit terms are not expected to generate new business but will result only in a shift in purchasing and payment patterns. The costs of the present and proposed inventory–accounts receivable systems are calculated in Table 18.5.

Table 18.5 shows that by shifting $150,000 of inventory to accounts receivable, Mills Industries is able to lower the cost of carrying inventory and accounts receivable from $105,000 to $90,000—a $15,000 ($105,000 − $90,000) addition to profits. This profit is achieved without changing the level of average inventory and accounts receivable investment from its $500,000 total. Rather, the profit is attributed to a shift in the mix of these current assets so that a larger portion of them is held in the form of accounts receivable, which is less costly to hold than inventory. ■

The inventory–accounts receivable relationship is affected by decisions made in all areas of the firm—finance, marketing, manufacturing, and purchasing. The financial manager should consider the interactions between inventory and accounts receivable when developing strategies and making decisions related to the production-sale process. This interaction is especially important in making credit decisions, since the required as well as actual levels of inventory will be directly affected.

International inventory management

International inventory management is typically much more complicated for exporters in general, and for multinational companies in particular, than for purely domestic companies. The production and manufacturing economies of scale that would seem to come from selling products globally may prove elusive if products must be tailored for individual local markets, as very frequently happens, or if actual production of goods takes place in factories around the world. When raw materials, intermediate goods, or finished products have to be transported long distances—particularly by ocean shipping—there will inevitably be more delays, confusion, damage, theft, and other difficulties to overcome than occurs in a one-country operation. The international

TABLE 18.5

ANALYSIS OF INVENTORY–ACCOUNTS RECEIVABLE SYSTEMS FOR MILLS INDUSTRIES

		Present		Proposed	
Variable	Cost/return (1)	Average investment (2)	Cost [(1) × (2)] (3)	Average investment (4)	Cost [(1) × (4)] (5)
Average inventory	25%	$300,000	$ 75,000	$150,000	$37,500
Average receivables	15	200,000	30,000	350,000	52,500
Totals		$500,000	$105,000	$500,000	$90,000

inventory manager therefore puts a premium on flexibility, and he or she is usually less concerned about ordering the economically optimal quantity of inventory than about making sure that sufficient quantities of materials are delivered where they are needed, when they are needed, and in a condition to be used as planned.

CONCEPTS IN REVIEW

18-13 What is the financial manager's role with respect to the management of inventory? What are likely to be the viewpoints of each of the following managers about the levels of the various types of inventory?

a. Finance
b. Marketing
c. Manufacturing
d. Purchasing

18-14 Explain the relationship between inventory and accounts receivable. Assuming that the total investment in inventory and accounts receivable remains constant, what impact would lengthening the credit terms have on the firm's profits? Why?

18-15 What factors make managing inventory more difficult for exporters and multinational companies?

Techniques for managing inventory

The economic order quantity (EOQ) model is a frequently cited technique that is used to find the optimal inventory order quantity, which is the one that minimizes the total cost—order cost plus carrying cost—of inventory. Why would the financial manager be concerned with this and other inventory management techniques in spite of the fact that he or she is not directly involved in their use? Spend a few moments answering this question before reading on.

TECHNIQUES THAT ARE COMMONLY USED IN MANAGING INVENTORY ARE (1) THE ABC system, (2) the basic economic order quantity (EOQ) model, (3) the reorder point, (4) the materials requirement planning (MRP) system, and (5) the just-in-time (JIT) system. Although these techniques are not strictly financial, it is helpful for the financial manager to understand them.

The ABC system

ABC system
Inventory management technique that divides inventory into three categories of descending importance based on the dollar investment in each.

A firm using the **ABC system** divides its inventory into three groups, A, B, and C. The *A group* includes those items that require the largest dollar investment. In the typical distribution of inventory items this group consists of the 20 percent of inventory items that account for 80 percent of the firm's dollar investment. The *B group* consists of the items accounting for the next largest investment. The *C group* typically consists of a large number of items accounting for a relatively small dollar investment. Dividing its inventory into A, B, and C items allows the firm to determine the level and types of inventory control procedures needed. Control of the A items should be most intensive because of the high dollar investment involved; the use of *perpetual in-*

ventory record keeping that allows daily monitoring of these inventory levels is appropriate. B items are frequently controlled through *periodic checking*—possibly weekly—of their levels. C items could be controlled by using unsophisticated procedures such as a **red-line method,** in which a reorder is placed when enough inventory has been removed from a bin containing the inventory item to expose a red line that has been drawn around the inside of the bin. The economic order quantity (EOQ) model, discussed next, is appropriate for use in monitoring A and B items.

red-line method
Unsophisticated inventory management technique in which a reorder is placed when sufficient use of inventory items from a bin exposes a red line drawn inside the bin.

The basic economic order quantity (EOQ) model

One of the most commonly cited sophisticated tools for determining the optimal order quantity for an item of inventory is the **economic order quantity (EOQ) model.** It takes into account various operating and financial costs and determines the order quantity that minimizes total inventory cost.[10]

economic order quantity (EOQ) model
An inventory management technique for determining an item's optimal order quantity, which is the one that minimizes the total of its order and carrying costs.

BASIC COSTS

Excluding the actual cost of the merchandise, the costs associated with inventory can be divided into three broad groups: order costs, carrying costs, and total cost. Each has certain key components and characteristics.

order costs
The fixed clerical costs of placing and receiving an inventory order.

ORDER COSTS **Order costs** include the fixed clerical costs of placing and receiving an order—the cost of writing a purchase order, of processing the resulting paperwork, and of receiving an order and checking it against the invoice. Order costs are normally stated as dollars per order.

carrying costs
The variable costs per unit of holding an item in inventory for a specified time period.

CARRYING COSTS **Carrying costs** are the variable costs per unit of holding an item in inventory for a specified time period. These costs are typically stated as dollars per unit per period. Carrying costs include storage costs, insurance costs, the cost of deterioration and obsolescence, and most important, the opportunity, or financial, cost of tying up funds in inventory. A commonly cited rule of thumb suggests that the cost of carrying an item in inventory for one year is between 20 and 30 percent of the cost (value) of the item.

total cost
The sum of the order costs and carrying costs of inventory.

TOTAL COST The **total cost** of inventory is defined as the sum of the order and carrying costs. Total cost is important in the EOQ model, since the model's objective is to determine the order quantity that minimizes it.

A GRAPHIC APPROACH

The stated objective of the EOQ model is to find the order quantity that minimizes the firm's total inventory cost. The economic order quantity can be found graphically by plotting order quantities on the x, or horizontal, axis and costs on the y, or vertical,

[10]The EOQ methodology is also applied to situations in which the firm wishes to minimize a total cost with fixed and variable components. It is commonly used to determine optimal production quantities when there is a fixed setup cost and a variable operating cost. The EOQ methodology, referred to as the *Baumol model,* is applied in Chapter 17 to determine the economic conversion quantity (ECQ) for converting marketable securities to cash and vice versa.

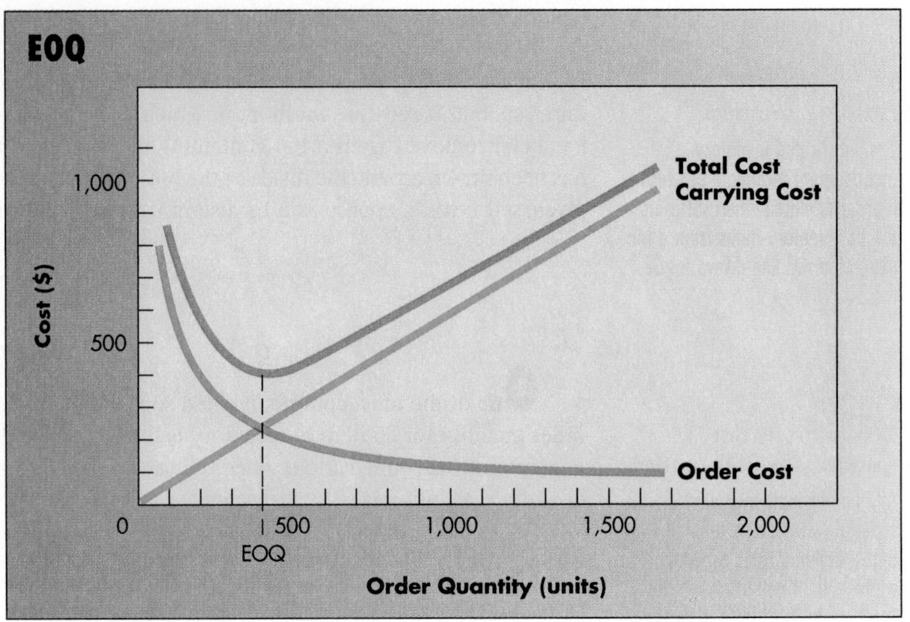

FIGURE 18.3
A graphic presentation of an EOQ

axis. Figure 18.3 shows the general behavior of these costs. The total cost line represents the sum of the order costs and carrying costs for each order quantity. The minimum total cost occurs at the point labeled EOQ, where the order cost line and the carrying cost line intersect.

A MATHEMATICAL APPROACH

A formula can be developed for determining the firm's EOQ for a given inventory item. By letting

S = usage in units per period
O = order cost per order
C = carrying cost per unit per period
Q = order quantity in units

we can develop the firm's total cost equation. The first step in deriving the total cost equation is to develop an expression for the order cost function and the carrying cost function. The order cost can be expressed as the product of the cost per order and the number of orders. Since the number of orders equals the usage during the period divided by the order quantity (S/Q), the order cost can be expressed as follows:

$$\text{Order cost} = O \times S/Q \tag{18.2}$$

The carrying cost is defined as the cost of carrying a unit per period multiplied by the firm's average inventory. The average inventory is defined as the order quantity divided by 2 ($Q/2$), since inventory is assumed to be depleted at a constant rate. Thus the carrying cost can be expressed as follows:

$$\text{Carrying cost} = C \times Q/2 \tag{18.3}$$

Analyzing Equations 18.2 and 18.3 shows that as the order quantity, Q, increases, the order cost will decrease while the carrying cost increases proportionately.

The total cost equation is obtained by combining the order cost and carrying cost expressions in Equations 18.2 and 18.3, as follows:

$$\text{Total cost} = (O \times S/Q) + (C \times Q/2) \tag{18.4}$$

Since the EOQ is defined as the order quantity that minimizes the total cost function, Equation 18.4 must be solved for the EOQ.[11] The following formula results:

$$\text{EOQ} = \sqrt{\frac{2 \times S \times O}{C}} \tag{18.5}$$

EXAMPLE

Assume that RSP, Inc., a manufacturer of electronic test equipment, uses 1,600 units of an item annually. Its order cost is \$50 per order, and carrying cost is \$1 per unit per year. Substituting $S = 1{,}600$, $O = \$50$, and $C = \$1$ into Equation 18.5 yields an EOQ of 400 units:

$$\text{EOQ} = \sqrt{\frac{2 \times 1{,}600 \times \$50}{\$1}} = \sqrt{160{,}000} = \underline{\underline{400 \text{ units}}}$$

If the firm orders in quantities of 400 units, it will minimize its total inventory cost. This solution is depicted in Figure 18.3. ■

Although even the simple EOQ model has weaknesses, it certainly provides decision makers with better grounds for a decision than subjective observations. Despite the fact that the financial manager is normally not directly associated with the use of the EOQ model, he or she must be aware of its utility. The financial manager must also provide certain financial inputs, specifically with respect to inventory carrying costs, to enable the firm to use the EOQ model.

The reorder point

Once the firm has calculated its economic order quantity, it must determine when to place orders. A reorder point is required that considers the lead time needed to place

[11]The solution can be found by either (1) taking the first derivative of Equation 18.4 with respect to Q, setting it equal to zero, and solving for Q, the EOQ, or (2) setting the order cost equal to the carrying cost and solving for Q, the EOQ, as demonstrated below.

(1) Multiply both sides by Q $\qquad O \times \frac{S}{Q} = C \times \frac{Q}{2}$

(2) Multiply both sides by 2 $\qquad O \times S = C \times \frac{Q^2}{2}$

(3) Divide both sides by C $\qquad 2 \times O \times S = C \times Q^2$

(4) Take the square root of both sides $\qquad \frac{2 \times O \times S}{C} = Q^2$

$$\sqrt{\frac{2 \times S \times O}{C}} = Q = \text{EOQ}$$

reorder point
The point at which to reorder inventory, expressed equationally as: lead time in days × daily usage.

and receive orders. Assuming a constant usage rate for inventory, the **reorder point** can be determined by the following equation:

$$\text{Reorder point} = \text{lead time in days} \times \text{daily usage} \tag{18.6}$$

For example, if a firm knows that it requires 10 days to place and receive an order, and if it uses five units of inventory daily, the reorder point would be 50 units (10 days × 5 units per day). Thus as soon as the firm's inventory level reaches 50 units, an order will be placed for an amount equal to the economic order quantity. If the estimates of lead time and daily usage are correct, the order will be received exactly when the inventory level reaches zero. Because of the difficulty in precisely predicting lead times and daily usage rates, many firms typically maintain **safety stocks**, which are extra inventories that can be drawn down when actual outcomes are greater than expected.

safety stocks
Extra inventories that can be drawn down when actual lead times and/or usage rates are greater than expected.

CONCEPT IN PRACTICE

Designs Inc. Puts Inventory Management in Levi's Hands

Designs Inc., a retail clothing chain, has an unorthodox technique designed to reduce inventory cost. The technique is based on Designs' selection of Levi Strauss & Company as its sole supplier. Designs' cash registers are connected to an automated inventory service called LeviLink that automatically replenishes stores. Since Levi Strauss ships directly to Designs' 111 stores, Designs does not need a warehouse or distribution center. Designs' inventory management technique has effectively made the firm a distribution center of Levi Strauss and dependent upon the demand for Levi Strauss apparel. In the process, Designs was able to eliminate its purchasing department, which at competing retail chains pays the salaries of those employees who select and order inventory.

Materials requirement planning (MRP) system

materials requirement planning (MRP) system
Inventory management system that uses EOQ concepts and a computer to compare production needs to available inventory balances and determine when orders should be placed for various items on a product's *bill of materials.*

Many companies use a **materials requirement planning (MRP) system** to determine what to order, when to order, and what priorities to assign to ordering materials. MRP uses EOQ concepts to determine how much to order. It simulates, using a computer, each product's bill of materials structure, inventory status, and process of manufacturing. The *bill of materials* structure simply refers to every part or material that goes into making the finished product. For a given production plan, the computer simulates needed materials requirements by comparing production needs to available inventory balances. On the basis of the time it takes for a product that is in process to move through the various production stages and the lead time required to get materials, the MRP system determines when orders should be placed for the various items on the bill of materials. The advantage of the MRP system is that it forces the firm to more thoughtfully consider its inventory needs and plan accordingly. The objective is to lower the firm's inventory investment without impairing production. If the firm's opportunity cost of capital for investments of equal risk is 25 percent, every dollar of investment released from inventory increases before-tax profits by $.25.

Just-in-time (JIT) system

just-in-time (JIT) system
Inventory management system that minimizes inventory investment by having material inputs arrive at exactly the time they are needed for production.

The **just-in-time (JIT) system** is used to minimize inventory investment. The philosophy is that materials should arrive at exactly the time they are needed for production. Ideally, the firm would have only work-in-process inventory. Since its objective is to minimize inventory investment, a JIT system uses no, or very little, safety stocks. Extensive coordination must exist between the firm, its suppliers, and shipping companies to ensure that material inputs arrive on time. Failure of materials to arrive on time results in a shutdown of the production line until the materials arrive. Likewise, a JIT system requires high-quality parts from suppliers. When quality problems arise, production must be stopped until the problems are resolved.

The goal of the JIT system is manufacturing efficiency. It uses inventory as a tool for attaining efficiency by emphasizing quality in terms of both the materials used and their timely delivery. When JIT is working properly it forces process inefficiencies to surface and be resolved. A JIT system requires cooperation among all parties involved in the process—suppliers, shipping companies, and the firm's employees. Employees must encourage competitive excellence, continuous improvements, and 100 percent quality items. If employees are not committed to these goals, the JIT system will likely be unsuccessful.

CONCEPTS IN REVIEW

18-16 Briefly describe each of the following techniques for managing inventory.
- **a.** ABC system
- **b.** Reorder point
- **c.** Materials requirement planning (MRP) system
- **d.** Just-in-time (JIT) system

18-17 What is the *EOQ model?* To which group of inventory items is it most applicable? What costs does it consider? What financial cost is involved?

Summary

LG 1 Discuss the key aspects of credit selection, including the five C's of credit, obtaining credit information, analyzing credit information, credit scoring, and managing international credit. Credit selection includes deciding whether to extend credit to a customer and how much credit to extend. The five C's of credit—character, capacity, capital, collateral, and conditions—are often used to guide credit investigation. Credit information can be obtained from a variety of external sources and can be analyzed in a number of ways. An analyst's subjective judgment is an important input to the final decision. At the consumer level, impersonal credit decision techniques, such as credit scoring, are often used. Credit management is much more difficult for companies that operate internationally than for purely domestic companies due to the presence of exchange rate risk and difficulties in shipping long distances across international borders and assessing and bearing the credit risks of foreign customers.

LG 2 Understand how to isolate and measure the key variables and use them to evaluate quantitatively the effects of either relaxing or tightening a firm's credit standards. At the mercantile level, credit standards—the minimum criteria for extension of credit to a customer—must be set by considering the tradeoffs between the key variables, which are the profit contribution from sales, the cost of investment in accounts receivable, and the cost of bad debts. Generally, when credit standards are relaxed, the profit contribution from sales increases, as do the costs of investment in accounts receivable and bad debts. If the increased profit contribution exceeds the increased costs, the credit standards should be relaxed. A tightening of credit standards would result in decreases in each of the key variables; if the cost reductions exceed the reduced profit contribution, credit standards should be tightened.

LG 3 Review the three basic components of a firm's credit terms, the effects of changes in each of them on key vari-

ables and profits, and the procedure for evaluating the quantitative effects of proposed cash discount changes. Credit terms have three components: (1) the cash discount, (2) the cash discount period, and (3) the credit period. Changes in each of these variables affect the firm's sales, investment in accounts receivable, bad debt expenses, and profit per unit. Quantitatively, a proposed increase (or initiation) of a cash discount is evaluated by comparing the profit increases attributable to the added sales, the reduction in accounts receivable investment, and the reduction in bad debts to the cost of the cash discount. If the profit increases exceed the cost, the discount increase should be undertaken. The proposed decrease (or elimination) of a cash discount would be analyzed similarly, except that the profit and cost factors would be reversed.

LG 4 Explain the key factors of collection policy, including aging accounts receivable, the basic tradeoffs, and the types of collection techniques. Collection policy determines the type and degree of effort exercised to collect overdue accounts. In addition to looking at the average collection period ratio, firms often age accounts receivable to evaluate the effectiveness of the firm's credit and collection policies. The procedures that are used to evaluate changes in collection policy are similar to those used to evaluate credit standards and credit terms. Generally, increased collection expenditures will have little effect on sales volume and will reduce the investment in accounts receivable and bad debt expenses. The basic collection techniques include letters, telephone calls, personal visits, the use of collection agencies, and, as a last resort, legal action.

LG 5 Understand the types of inventory, differing viewpoints about inventory level, inventory as an investment, the relationship between inventory and accounts receivable, and international inventory management. The respective viewpoints held by marketing, manufacturing, and purchasing managers regarding the appropriate levels of various types of inventory (raw materials, work in process, and finished goods) tend to conflict with that of the financial manager. The financial manager views inventory as an investment that consumes dollars and should be maintained at a low level. Because it is more expensive to carry an item in inventory than to carry an account receivable, the financial manager must consider the relationship between inventory and accounts receivable when making decisions related to the production-sale process. Because international inventory management is more complex than the purely domestic situation, international inventory managers place greater emphasis on making sure that sufficient quantities of materials are delivered where they are needed, when they are needed, and in the right condition than on ordering the economically optimal quantities.

LG 6 Describe the common techniques for managing inventory, including the ABC system, the basic economic order quantity (EOQ) model, the reorder point, the materials requirement planning (MRP) system, and the just-in-time (JIT) system. The ABC system determines which inventories require the most attention according to dollar investment. One of the most common techniques for determining optimal order quantities is the economic order quantity (EOQ) model. Once the optimal order quantity has been determined, the firm can set the reorder point, the level of inventory at which an order will be placed. Materials requirement planning (MRP) is a system that can be used to determine when orders should be placed for various items on a firm's bill of materials. Just-in-time (JIT) systems are used to minimize inventory investment by having materials arrive at exactly the time they are needed for production.

Self-test problems (Solutions in Appendix E)

ST 18-1 LG 2 Easing collection efforts The Regency Rug Repair Company is attempting to evaluate whether it should ease collection efforts. The firm repairs 72,000 rugs per year at an average price of $32 each. Bad debt expenses are 1 percent of sales, and collection expenditures are $60,000. The average collection period is 40 days, and the variable cost per unit is $28. By easing the collection efforts, Regency expects to save $40,000 per year in collection expense. Bad debts will increase to 2 percent of sales, and the average collection period will increase to 58 days. Sales will increase by 1,000 repairs per year. If the firm has a required rate of return on equal-risk investments of 24 percent, what recommendation would you give the firm? Use your analysis to justify your answer.

ST 18-2 LG 6 EOQ analysis The Thompson Paint Company uses 60,000 gallons of pigment per year. The cost of ordering pigment is $200 per order, and the cost of carrying the pigment in inventory is $1 per gallon per year. The firm uses pigment at a constant rate every day throughout the year.

a. Calculate the EOQ.
b. Calculate the total cost of the plan suggested by the EOQ.
c. Determine the total number of orders suggested by this plan.
d. Assuming that it takes 20 days to receive an order once it has been placed, determine the reorder point in terms of gallons of pigment. (*Note:* Use a 360-day year.)

Problems

18-1 LG 1 Credit scoring Clemens Department Store uses credit scoring to evaluate retail credit applications. The financial and credit characteristics considered and weights indicating their relative importance in the credit decision are given in the following table. The firm's credit standards are to accept all applicants with credit scores of 80 or more, to extend limited credit on a probationary basis to applicants with scores of greater than 70 and less than 80, and to reject all applicants with scores below 70.

Financial and credit characteristics	Predetermined weight
Credit references	.25
Education	.15
Home ownership	.10
Income range	.10
Payment history	.30
Years on job	.10

The firm currently needs to process three applications that were recently received and scored by one of its credit analysts. The scores for each of the applicants on each of the financial and credit characteristics are summarized in the following table:

	Applicant		
Financial and credit characteristics	A	B Score (0 to 100)	C
Credit references	60	90	80
Education	70	70	80
Home ownership	100	90	60
Income range	75	80	80
Payment history	60	85	70
Years on job	50	60	90

a. Use the data presented to find the credit score for each of the applicants.
b. Recommend the appropriate action for each of the three applicants.

18-2 LG 2 Accounts receivable and costs Randolph Company currently has an average collection period of 45 days and annual credit sales of \$1 million. Assume a 360-day year.
a. What is the firm's average accounts receivable balance?
b. If the variable cost of each product is 60 percent of sales, what is the average *investment* in accounts receivable?
c. If the equal-risk opportunity cost of the investment in accounts receivable is 12 percent, what is the total opportunity cost of the investment in accounts receivable?

18-3 LG 2 Accounts receivable changes without bad debts Tara's Textiles currently has credit sales of \$360 million per year and an average collection period of 60 days. Assume that the price of Tara's products is \$60 per unit and the variable costs are \$55 per unit. The firm is considering an account receivable change that will result in a 20 percent increase in sales and an equal 20 percent increase in the average collection period. No change in bad debts is expected. The firm's equal-risk opportunity cost on its investment in accounts receivable is 14 percent.

a. Calculate the additional profit contribution from new sales that the firm will realize if it makes the proposed change.

b. What marginal investment in accounts receivable will result?

c. Calculate the cost of the marginal investment in accounts receivable.

d. Should the firm implement the proposed change? What other information would be helpful in your analysis?

18-4 LG 2 Accounts receivable changes and bad debts A firm is evaluating an account receivable change that would increase bad debts from 2 percent to 4 percent of sales. Sales are currently 50,000 units, the selling price is $20 per unit, and the variable cost per unit is $15. As a result of the proposed change, sales are forecast to increase to 60,000 units.

a. What are bad debts in dollars currently and under the proposed change?

b. Calculate the cost of the marginal bad debts to the firm.

c. Ignoring the additional profit contribution from increased sales, if the proposed change saves $3,500 and causes no change in the average investment in accounts receivable, would you recommend it? Explain.

d. Considering *all* changes in costs and benefits, would you recommend the proposed change? Explain.

e. Compare and discuss your answers in **c** and **d**.

18-5 LG 2 Tightening credit standards—Sales and bad debt effects only Michael's Menswear feels that its credit costs are too high. By tightening its credit standards, bad debts will fall from 5 percent of sales to 2 percent. However, sales will fall from $100,000 to $90,000 per year. The variable cost per unit is 50 percent of the sale price, and the average investment in receivables is expected to remain unchanged.

a. What cost will the firm face in a reduced contribution to profits from sales?

b. Should the firm tighten its credit standards? Explain your answer.

18-6 LG 2 Relaxation of credit standards Lewis Enterprises is considering relaxing its credit standards to increase its currently sagging sales. As a result of the proposed relaxation, sales are expected to increase by 10 percent from 10,000 to 11,000 units during the coming year, the average collection period is expected to increase from 45 to 60 days, and bad debts are expected to increase from 1 percent to 3 percent of sales. The sale price per unit is $40, and the variable cost per unit is $31. If the firm's required return on equal-risk investments is 25 percent, evaluate the proposed relaxation, and make a recommendation to the firm.

18-7 LG 3 Initiating a cash discount Gardner Company currently makes all sales on credit and offers no cash discount. The firm is considering a 2 percent cash discount for payment within 15 days. The firm's current average collection period is 60 days, sales are 40,000 units, selling price is $45 per unit, and variable cost per unit is $36. The firm expects that the change in credit terms will result in an increase in sales to 42,000 units, that 70 percent of the sales will take the discount, and that the average collection period will fall to 30 days. If the firm's required rate of return on equal-risk investments is 25 percent, should the proposed discount be offered?

18-8 LG 3 Shortening the credit period A firm is contemplating *shortening* its credit period from 40 to 30 days and believes that as a result of this change, its average collection period will decline from 45 to 36 days. Bad debt expenses are expected to decrease from 1.5 percent to 1 percent of sales. The firm is currently selling 12,000 units but believes that as a result of the proposed change, sales will decline to 10,000 units. The sale price per unit is $56, and its variable cost per unit is $45.

The firm has a required return on equal-risk investments of 25 percent. Evaluate this decision, and make a recommendation to the firm.

18-9 LG 3 Lengthening the credit period Parker Tool is considering lengthening its credit period from 30 to 60 days. All customers will continue to pay on the net date. The firm currently bills $450,000 for sales and has $345,000 in variable costs. The change in credit terms is expected to increase sales to $510,000. Bad debt expense will increase from 1 percent to 1.5 percent of sales. The firm has a required rate of return on equal-risk investments of 20 percent.

a. What additional profit contribution from sales will be realized from the proposed change?
b. What is the cost of the marginal investment in accounts receivable?
c. What is the cost of the marginal bad debts?
d. Do you recommend this change in credit terms? Why or why not?

18-10 LG 4 Aging accounts receivable Burnham Services' accounts receivable totaled $874,000 on August 31, 1994. A breakdown of these outstanding accounts on the basis of the month in which the credit sale was initially made is given below. The firm extends 30-day EOM credit terms to its credit customers.

Month of credit sale	Accounts receivable
August 1994	$320,000
July 1994	250,000
June 1994	81,000
May 1994	195,000
April 1994 or before	28,000
Total (August 31, 1994)	$874,000

a. Prepare an aging schedule for Burnham Services' August 31, 1994, accounts receivable balance.
b. Using your findings in **a**, evaluate the firm's credit and collection activities.
c. What are some probable causes of the situation discussed in **b**?

18-11 LG 5 Inventory investment Paterson Products is considering leasing a computerized inventory control system to reduce its average inventories. The annual cost of the system is $46,000. It is expected that with the system the firm's average inventory will decline by 50 percent from its current level of $980,000. The level of stockouts is expected to be unaffected by this system. The firm can earn 20 percent per year on equal-risk investments.

a. How much of a reduction in average inventory will result from the proposed installation of the computerized inventory control system?
b. How much, if any, annual savings will the firm realize on the reduced level of average inventory?
c. Should the firm lease the computerized inventory control system? Explain why or why not.

18-12 LG 5 Inventory versus accounts receivable costs Hamilton Supply estimates the annual cost of carrying a dollar of inventory is $.27, while the annual carrying cost of an equal investment in accounts receivable is $.17. The firm's current balance sheet reflects its average inventory of $400,000 and average investment in accounts receivable of $100,000. If the firm can convince its customers to purchase in large quantities, the average level of inventory can be reduced by $200,000, and the average investment in receivables can be increased by the same amount. Assuming no change in annual sales, what addition to profits will be generated from this shift? Explain your answer.

18-13 LG 6 Inventory—The ABC system Newton, Inc., has 16 different items in its inventory. The average number of units held in inventory and the average unit cost for each item are listed below. The firm wishes to introduce the ABC system of inventory management. Suggest a breakdown of the items into classifications of A, B, and C. Justify your selection, and point out items that could be considered borderline cases.

Item	Average number of units in inventory	Average cost per unit
1	1,800	$ 0.54
2	1,000	8.20
3	100	6.00
4	250	1.20
5	8	94.50
6	400	3.00
7	80	45.00
8	1,600	1.45
9	600	0.95
10	3,000	0.18
11	900	15.00
12	65	1.35
13	2,200	4.75
14	1,800	1.30
15	60	18.00
16	200	17.50

18-14 LG 6 Graphic EOQ analysis Knoll Manufacturing uses 10,000 units of raw material per year on a continuous basis. Placing and processing an order for additional inventory cost $200 per order. The firm estimates the cost of carrying one unit in inventory at $.25 per year.

a. What are the annual order costs, carrying costs, and total costs of inventory if the firm orders in quantities of 1,000, 2,000, 3,000, 4,000, 5,000, 6,000, and 7,000 units?

b. Graph the order cost, carrying cost, and total cost (y-axis) relative to order quantity (x-axis). Label the EOQ.

c. On the basis of your graph, in what quantity would you order? Is this consistent with the EOQ equation? Explain why or why not.

18-15 LG 6 EOQ analysis Tiger Corporation purchases 1,200,000 units per year of one component. The fixed cost per order is $25. The annual carrying cost of the item is 27 percent of its $2 cost.

a. Determine the EOQ under the following conditions: (1) no changes, (2) order cost of zero, (3) carrying cost of zero.

b. What do your answers illustrate about the EOQ model? Explain.

18-16 LG 6 Reorder point Beeman Gas and Electric (BG&E) is required to carry a minimum of 20 days' average coal usage, which is 100 tons of coal. It takes 10 days between order and delivery. At what level of coal would BG&E reorder?

18-17 LG 6 EOQ, reorder point, and safety stock A firm uses 800 units of a product per year on a continuous basis. The product has a fixed cost of $50 per order, and its carrying cost is $2 per unit per year. It takes five days to receive a shipment after an order is placed, and the firm wishes to hold in inventory 10 days' usage as a safety stock.

a. Calculate the EOQ.

b. Determine the average level of inventory. (*Note:* Use a 360-day year to calculate daily usage.)

c. Determine the reorder point.

d. Which of the following variables change if the firm does not hold the safety stock: (1) order cost, (2) carrying cost, (3) reorder point, (4) total inventory cost, (5) average level of inventory, (6) number of orders per year, (7) economic order quantity? Explain.

Chapter 18 Case Evaluating Global Textiles' proposed change in credit terms

Ken Steinbacher, a financial analyst for Global Textiles, has been asked to investigate a proposed change in the firm's credit terms. The company's founder and president believes that by increasing the credit period from 30 to 65 days, two important benefits will result: (1) sales will increase as a result of attracting *new customers,* and (2) some *existing customers* will purchase merchandise sooner to ensure its availability, given the unpredictable timing of the selling seasons. Annual sales are estimated to increase from the current level of $4,000,000 to $4,800,000. Eighty percent of this increase is expected to be attributable to new customers, and the other 20 percent is expected to result from existing customers. Because some existing customers will be making their purchases earlier than in the past, their actions will merely result in a shifting of inventory to accounts receivable. Ken estimated that the decline in inventory investment attributable to the actions of existing customers would just equal the additional accounts receivable investment associated with their actions.

Ken's investigation indicates that with the extended credit period, the firm's average collection period will increase from 45 to 90 days. In addition, bad debts will increase from 1 percent to 2½ percent of sales. The firm's variable costs are expected to continue to amount to 80 percent of each $1 of sales. Global currently requires a 16 percent rate of return on equal-risk accounts receivable investments and its cost of carrying $1 of inventory for one year is 26 cents.

Required

a. Find the additional annual profit contribution expected from the increased credit period.

b. Determine the increase in Global's average investment in accounts receivable and the resulting annual cost attributable to the proposed increase in the credit period.

c. Calculate the annual savings resulting from the reduced inventory investment attributable to the existing customers' earlier purchases.

d. Calculate the annual cost expected to result from the increase in bad debt expenses attributable to the proposed lengthening of the credit period.

e. Use your findings in **a** through **d** to advise Ken on whether or not the proposed increase in the credit period can be financially justified. Explain your recommendation.

f. What impact, if any, would ignoring the effect of the proposed increase in the credit period on the level of inventory investment found in **c** have on your recommendation in **e**? Explain.

INTEGRATIVE CASE VI

CASA DE DISEÑO

In January 1995, Teresa Leal was named treasurer of Casa de Diseño. She decided that she could best orient herself by systematically examining each area of the company's financial operations. She began by studying the firm's short-term financial activities.

Casa de Diseño is located in southern California and specializes in a furniture line called "Ligne Moderna." Of high quality and contemporary design, the furniture appeals to the customer who wants something unique for his or her home or apartment. Most Ligne Moderna furniture is built by special order, since a wide variety of upholstery, accent trimming, and colors is available. The product line is distributed through exclusive dealership arrangements with well-established retail stores. Casa de Diseño's manufacturing process virtually eliminates the use of wood. Plastic and metal provide the basic framework, and wood is used only for decorative purposes.

Casa de Diseño entered the plastic furniture market in late 1989. The company markets its plastic furniture products as indoor-outdoor items under the brand name "Futuro." Futuro plastic furniture emphasizes comfort, durability, and practicality and is distributed through wholesalers. The Futuro line has been very successful, accounting for nearly 40 percent of the firm's sales and profits in 1994. Casa de Diseño anticipates some additions to the Futuro line and also some limited change of direction in its promotion in an effort to expand the applications of the plastic furniture.

Ms. Leal has decided to study the firm's cash management practices. To determine the effects of these practices, she must first determine the current operating and cash conversion cycles. In her investigations she found that Casa de Diseño purchases all of its raw materials and production supplies on open account. The company is operating at production levels that preclude volume discounts. Most suppliers do not offer cash discounts, and Casa de Diseño usually receives credit terms of net 30. An analysis of Casa de Diseño's accounts payable showed that its average payment period is 30 days. Leal consulted industry data and found that the industry average payment period was 39 days. Investigation of six California furniture manufacturers revealed that their average payment period was also 39 days.

Next, Leal studied the production cycle and inventory policies. Casa de Diseño tries not to hold any more inventory in either raw materials or finished goods than necessary. The average inventory age was 110 days. Leal determined that the industry standard as reported in a survey done by *Furniture Age,* the trade association journal, was 83 days.

Casa de Diseño sells to all of its customers on a net 60 basis, in line with the industry trend to grant such credit terms on specialty furniture. Leal discovered, by aging the accounts receivable, that the average collection period for the firm was 75 days. Investigation of the trade association's and California manufacturers' averages showed that the same collection period existed where net 60 credit terms were given. Where cash discounts were offered, the collection period was significantly shortened. Leal believed that if Casa de Diseño were to offer credit terms of 3/10 net 60, the average collection period could be reduced by 40 percent.

Casa de Diseño was spending an estimated $26,500,000 per year on operating cycle investments. Leal considered this expenditure level to be the minimum she could expect the firm to disburse during 1995. Her concern was whether the firm's cash management was as efficient as it could be. She knew that the company paid 15 percent for its negotiated financing. For this reason she was concerned about the financing cost resulting from any inefficiencies in the management of Casa de Diseño's cash conversion cycle.

Required

a. Assuming a constant rate for purchases, production, and sales throughout the year, what are Casa de Diseño's existing operating cycle (OC), cash conversion cycle (CCC), and negotiated financing needs?

b. If Leal can optimize Casa de Diseño's operations according to industry standards, what would Casa de Diseño's operating cycle (OC), cash conversion cycle (CCC), and negotiated financing need be under these more efficient conditions?

c. In terms of negotiated financing requirements, what is the cost of Casa de Diseño's operational inefficiency?

d. (1) If in addition to achieving industry standards for payables and inventory, the firm can reduce the average collection period by offering 3/10 net 60 credit terms, what additional savings in negotiated financing costs would result from the shortened cash conversion cycle, assuming that the level of sales remains constant?

(2) If the firm's sales (all on credit) are $40,000,000 and 45 percent of the customers are expected to take the cash discount, how much will the firm's annual revenues be reduced by as a result of the discount?

(3) If the firm's variable cost of the $40,000,000 in sales is 80 percent, determine the reduction in the average investment in accounts receivable and the annual savings resulting from this reduced investment assuming that sales remain constant. (Assume a 360-day year.)

(4) If the firm's bad debt expenses decline from 2 percent of sales to 1.5 percent of sales, what annual savings would result, assuming that sales remain constant?

(5) Use your findings in (2) through (4) to assess whether offering the cash discount can be justified financially. Explain why or why not.

e. On the basis of your analysis in **a** through **d**, what recommendations would you offer Teresa Leal?

part VII

Special managerial finance topics

CHAPTERS IN THIS PART

chapter 19

Mergers, LBOs, divestitures, and failure

LEARNING GOALS

 Understand merger fundamentals, including basic terminology, motives for merging, and types of mergers.

 Describe the objectives and procedures used in leveraged buyouts (LBOs) and divestitures.

 Demonstrate the procedures used to analyze mergers, including valuing the target company and the effect of stock swap transactions on earnings per share.

 Discuss the merger negotiation process, the role of holding companies, and international mergers.

 Understand the types and major causes of business failure and the use of voluntary settlements to sustain or liquidate the failed firm.

 Explain bankruptcy legislation and the procedures involved in reorganizing or liquidating a bankrupt firm.

At Hershey Foods, a major diversified food company producing chocolate, confectionery, and pasta products, our mission includes becoming a leader in each product line. A portion of our growth has come from acquisitions, so we actively seek companies that increase market share and offer new but related products or special technology. Our objective is to significantly improve operating margins through our market knowledge and economies of scale—and, in the process, add shareholder value. Each acquisition must stand on its own economic merit. As Director of Corporate Financial Planning and Analysis, I assist management in developing the value on which we base our offer for the target company. Consequently, I analyze a potential acquisition, using such techniques as ratio analysis, discounted cash flow, valuation, and development of financial plans.

I work closely with divisional personnel on assumptions and valuation, asking them, "How would you run this business more efficiently if we owned it?" For example, in 1986 I assisted the Hershey Chocolate USA management team in valuing the Dietrich Corporation. The team decided to focus Dietrich's business on four—rather than 750—products. Our marketing department estimated sales and our engineers provided estimated production costs, and I valued the acquisition on the basis of these assumptions.

Good assumptions are obviously key in this type of capital-budgeting decision. The divisions are pretty careful about their assumptions—they have to live up to those performance expectations! In most cases our business knowledge makes product cost and operating expenses fairly easy to determine. The revenue stream is the hardest to predict. Good historical information and brand knowledge provide patterns for our forecasts, and we always include sensitivity analysis using growth and margin as the two key variables.

Successful acquisition and divestiture analysis requires good qualitative and quantitative skills plus sound business judgment.

We value acquisitions using the discounted cash flow method with the company-wide cost of capital as the discount rate because we are interested in only one industry: branded food processors. The bidding process usually has two or three rounds, starting with a nonbinding offer. In our preliminary analysis we don't have much financial data, so we adjust the hurdle (discount) rate for risk and add a percent or two to our cost of capital. If we proceed to the next round, our management visits the company, meets its officers, and gets more operating and financial information. Then my department does a more complete analysis. By the time we have our binding offer, we can usually reduce our risk assessment (because we have more data) and use our cost of capital in the valuation calculation.

We do a very thorough job of valuation analysis, so we've been quite successful overall. We have exceeded our acquisition plans in terms of growth and margin in virtually all our acquisitions. We continually refine our business strategy and may decide to sell an existing business unit. My group uses similar techniques to value divestitures. We sold Friendly restaurants to an experienced restaurant company at a profit when management decided that restaurants didn't fit our corporate objectives.

Successful acquisition and divestiture analysis requires good qualitative and quantitative skills plus sound business judgment. It's a particularly challenging part of my job, one that I really enjoy because it is a stimulating application of financial theory with immediate practical results. This area of finance is fast-paced, has a long-term implications for the company's future, and provides interesting career opportunities.

Samuel C. Weaver joined Hershey Foods in 1978 as a Senior Financial Analyst, continuing to work for the company part-time while pursuing an M.B.A. and a Ph.D. in Economics and Finance from Lehigh University (where he earned a B.S. in Accounting). After receiving his Ph.D. in 1984, he became Manager of Corporate Financial Analysis and was promoted to Director of this department in 1990.

Merger fundamentals

Mergers are a form of external expansion that should be undertaken only when they are expected to enhance share value. What do you think are some of the specific motives that actually cause firms to pursue mergers? Spend a few moments answering this question before reading on.

FIRMS SOMETIMES USE MERGERS TO EXPAND EXTERNALLY BY ACQUIRING CONTROL OF another firm. While the overriding objective for a merger should be to improve and, hopefully, maximize the firm's share value, a number of more immediate motivations such as diversification, tax considerations, and increasing owner liquidity frequently exist. Sometimes mergers are pursued to acquire needed assets rather than the going concern. Although the "merger mania" of the 1980s has cooled somewhat, brisk merger activity continues to take place today. Here we discuss merger fundamentals—terminology, motives, and types. In the following sections we'll briefly describe the related topics of leveraged buyouts and divestitures and review the procedures used to analyze and negotiate mergers.

Basic terminology

The high level of merger activity occurring over the last 10 to 15 years has resulted in the coining of numerous new terms to describe various actions, strategies, participants, and techniques. In the broadest sense, activities involving expansion or contraction of a firm's operations or changes in its asset or financial (ownership) structure are called **corporate restructuring.** The topics addressed in this chapter—mergers, LBOs, and divestitures—are some of the most common forms of corporate restructuring; there are many others, which are beyond the scope of this text.[1] Below we define some basic merger terminology; other terms are introduced and defined as needed in subsequent discussions.

corporate restructuring
The activities involving expansion or contraction of a firm's operations or changes in its asset or financial (ownership) structure.

MERGERS, CONSOLIDATIONS, AND HOLDING COMPANIES

A **merger** occurs when two or more firms are combined and the resulting firm maintains the identity of one of the firms. Usually, the assets and liabilities of the smaller firm are merged into those of the larger firm. **Consolidation**, on the other hand, involves the combination of two or more firms to form a completely new corporation. The new corporation normally absorbs the assets and liabilities of the companies from which it is formed. Because of the similarity of mergers and consolidations, the term *merger* is used throughout this chapter to refer to both. A **holding company** is a corporation that has voting control of one or more other corporations. Having control in large, widely held companies generally requires ownership of between 10 and 20 percent of the outstanding stock. The companies controlled by a holding company are nor-

merger
The combination of two or more firms, in which the resulting firm maintains the identity of one of the firms, usually the larger one.

consolidation
The combination of two or more firms to form a completely new corporation.

holding company
A corporation that has voting control of one or more other corporations.

[1]For comprehensive coverage of the many aspects of corporate restructuring, see J. Fred Weston, Kwang S. Chung, and Susan E. Hoag, *Mergers, Restructuring, and Corporate Control* (Englewood Cliffs, NJ: Prentice Hall, 1990).

subsidiaries
The companies controlled by a holding company.

mally referred to as its **subsidiaries.** Control of a subsidiary is typically obtained by purchasing (generally for cash) a sufficient number of shares of its stock.

ACQUIRING VERSUS TARGET COMPANIES

acquiring company
The firm in a merger transaction that attempts to acquire another firm.

target company
The firm in a merger transaction that the acquiring company is pursuing.

The firm in a merger transaction that attempts to acquire another firm is commonly called the **acquiring company.** The firm that the acquiring company is pursuing is referred to as the **target company.** Generally, the acquiring company identifies, evaluates, and negotiates with the management and/or shareholders of the target company. Occasionally, the management of a target company initiates its acquisition by seeking to be acquired.

FRIENDLY VERSUS HOSTILE TAKEOVERS

friendly merger
A merger transaction endorsed by the target firm's management, approved by its stockholders, and easily consummated.

hostile merger
A merger transaction not supported by the target firm's management, forcing the acquiring company to try to gain control of the firm by buying shares in the marketplace.

Mergers can occur on either a friendly or a hostile basis. Typically, after isolating the target company, the acquirer initiates discussions with its management. If the target management is receptive to the acquirer's proposal, it may endorse the merger and recommend shareholder approval. If the stockholders approve the merger, the transaction is typically consummated either through a cash purchase of shares by the acquirer or through an exchange of the acquirer's stock, bonds, or some combination for the target firm's shares. This type of negotiated transaction is known as a **friendly merger.** If, on the other hand, the takeover target's management does not support the proposed takeover for any of a number of possible reasons, such as too low an offering price, a desire to maintain the firm's autonomy, or a "poor fit," it can fight the acquirer's actions. In this case the acquirer can attempt to gain control of the firm by buying sufficient shares of the target firm in the marketplace. This is typically accomplished by using *tender offers,* which, as was noted in Chapter 13, are formal offers to purchase a given number of shares at a specified price. This type of unfriendly transaction is commonly referred to as a **hostile merger.** Clearly, hostile mergers are more difficult to consummate because the target firm's management acts to deter rather than facilitate the acquisition. Regardless, hostile takeovers are sometimes successful.

STRATEGIC VERSUS FINANCIAL MERGERS

strategic merger
A merger transaction undertaken to achieve economies of scale.

financial merger
A merger transaction undertaken with the goal of restructuring the acquired company to improve its cash flow and unlock its hidden value.

Mergers are undertaken for either strategic or financial reasons. **Strategic mergers** involve merging firms to achieve various economies of scale by eliminating redundant functions, increasing market share, improving raw material sourcing and finished product distribution, and so on. In these mergers the operations of the acquiring and target firms are somehow combined to achieve economies and thereby cause the performance of the merged firm to exceed that of the premerged firms. The mergers of Bristol Meyers and Squibb (both drug firms), The *New York Times* and the *Boston Globe* (both publishers), Sara Lee (food) and Champion Products (apparel), and AT&T (telecommunications) and NCR (computers) are examples of strategic mergers. An interesting variation of the strategic merger involves the purchase of specific product lines (rather than the whole company) for strategic reasons. Examples include Colgate-Palmolive (consumer products) buying the Softsoap Liquid line from Minnetonka Labs and Shaw Industries' (textiles) purchase of the carpet division of Armstrong World Industries.

Financial mergers, on the other hand, are based on the acquisition of companies that can be restructured to improve their cash flow. These mergers involve the acquisition of the target firm by an acquirer, which may be another company or a group of investors—often the firm's existing management. The objective of the acquirer is to drastically cut costs and sell off certain unproductive or noncompatible assets to increase the firm's cash flows. The increased cash flows are used to service the sizable debt that is typically incurred to finance these transactions. Financial mergers are not based on the firm's ability to achieve economies of scale, but rather on the acquirer's belief that through restructuring, the firm's hidden value can be unlocked. The ready availability of *junk bond* financing throughout the 1980s fueled the financial merger mania during that period. Examples of financial mergers include the takeover of RJR Nabisco by Kohlberg Kravis Roberts (KKR), Campeau Corporation's (real estate) acquisition of Allied Stores and Federated Department Stores, and Merv Griffin's acquisition of Resorts International (hotels/casinos) from Donald Trump. With the collapse of the junk bond market in the early 1990s, financial mergers have fallen on relatively hard times. The heavy debt burdens involved in many of the glamour financial mergers of the 1980s caused many of them to subsequently file for bankruptcy. As a result, the strategic merger, which does not rely as heavily on debt, tends to dominate today.

Motives for merging

Firms merge to fulfill certain objectives. The overriding goal for merging is the maximization of the owners' wealth as reflected in the acquirer's share price. Specific motives, which include growth or diversification, synergy, fund raising, increased managerial skill or technology, tax considerations, increased ownership liquidity, and defense against takeover, should be pursued when they are believed to be consistent with owner wealth maximization.

GROWTH OR DIVERSIFICATION

Companies that desire rapid growth in *size* or *market share* or diversification in *the range of their products* may find that a merger can be used to fulfill this objective. Instead of going through the time-consuming process of internal growth or diversification, the firm may achieve the same objective in a short period of time by merging with an existing firm. In addition, such a strategy is often less costly than the alternative of developing the necessary production capability and capacity. If a firm that wants to expand operations in existing or new product areas can find a suitable going concern, it may avoid many of the risks associated with the design, manufacture, and sale of additional or new products. Moreover, when a firm expands or extends its product line by acquiring another firm, it also removes a potential competitor.[2]

SYNERGY

The *synergy* of mergers is the economies of scale resulting from the merged firms' lower overhead. Synergy is said to be present when a whole is greater than the sum of the parts ("1 plus 1 equals 3"). The economies of scale that generally result from a merger lower the combined overhead, thereby increasing earnings to a level greater than the sum of the earnings of each of the independent firms. Synergy is most obvious when firms merge with other firms in the same line of business, since many re-

[2]Certain legal constraints on growth exist—especially when the elimination of competition is expected. The various antitrust laws, which are closely enforced by the Federal Trade Commission (FTC) and the Justice Department, prohibit business combinations that eliminate competition, especially when the resulting enterprise would be a monopoly.

dundant functions and employees can thereby be eliminated. Staff functions, such as purchasing and sales, are probably most greatly affected by this type of combination.

FUND RAISING

Often, firms combine to enhance their fund-raising ability. A firm may be unable to obtain funds for its own internal expansion but able to obtain funds for external business combinations. Quite often, one firm may combine with another that has high liquid assets and low levels of liabilities. The acquisition of this type of "cash-rich" company immediately increases the firm's borrowing power by decreasing its financial leverage. This should allow funds to be raised externally at lower cost.

INCREASED MANAGERIAL SKILL OR TECHNOLOGY

Occasionally, a firm will have good potential that it finds itself unable to develop fully because of deficiencies in certain areas of management or an absence of needed product or production technology. If the firm cannot hire the management or develop the technology it needs, it might combine with a compatible firm that has the needed managerial personnel or technical expertise. Of course, any merger, regardless of the specific motive for it, should contribute to the maximization of owners' wealth.

TAX CONSIDERATIONS

tax loss carryforward
In a merger, the tax loss of one of the firms that can be applied against a limited amount of future income of the merged firm either over 15 years or until the total tax loss has been fully recovered, whichever is shorter.

Quite often, tax considerations are a key motive for merging. In such a case the tax benefit generally stems from the fact that one of the firms has a **tax loss carryforward.** This means that the company's tax loss can be applied against a limited amount of future income of the merged firm either over 15 years or until the total tax loss has been fully recovered, whichever is shorter.[3] Two situations could actually exist. A company with a tax loss could acquire a profitable company to utilize the tax loss. In this case the acquiring firm would boost the combination's after-tax earnings by reducing the taxable income of the acquired firm. A tax loss may also be useful when a profitable firm acquires a firm that has such a loss. In either situation, however, the merger must be justified not only on the basis of the tax benefits but also on grounds consistent with the goal of owner wealth maximization. Moreover, the tax benefits described can be used only in mergers—not in the formation of holding companies—since only in the case of mergers are operating results reported on a consolidated basis. An example will clarify the use of the tax loss carryforward.

EXAMPLE

The Bergen Company, a wheel bearing manufacturer, has a total of $450,000 in tax loss carryforwards resulting from operating tax losses of $150,000 a year in each of the past three years. To use these losses and to diversify its operations, the Hudson Company, a molder of plastics, has acquired Bergen through a merger. Hudson expects to have *earnings before taxes* of $300,000 per year. We assume that these earnings are realized, that they fall within the annual limit that is legally allowed for application of the tax loss carryforward resulting from the merger (see footnote 3), that the Bergen

[3]The *Tax Reform Act of 1986,* to deter firms from combining solely to take advantage of tax loss carryforwards, initiated an annual limit on the amount of taxable income against which such losses can be applied. The annual limit is determined by formula and is tied to the value of the loss corporation before the combination. While not fully eliminating this motive for combination, the act makes it more difficult for firms to justify combinations solely on the basis of tax loss carryforwards.

TABLE 19.1

TOTAL TAXES AND AFTER-TAX EARNINGS FOR HUDSON COMPANY WITHOUT AND WITH MERGER

Total taxes and after-tax earnings without merger				
	Year			Total for
	1	2	3	3 years
(1) Earnings before taxes	$300,000	$300,000	$300,000	$900,000
(2) Taxes [.40 × (1)]	120,000	120,000	120,000	360,000
(3) Earnings after taxes [(1) − (2)]	$180,000	$180,000	$180,000	$540,000
Total taxes and after-tax earnings with merger				
(4) Earnings before losses	$300,000	$300,000	$300,000	$900,000
(5) Tax loss carryforward	300,000	150,000	0	450,000
(6) Earnings before taxes [(4) − (5)]	$ 0	$150,000	$300,000	$450,000
(7) Taxes [.40 × (6)]	0	60,000	120,000	180,000
(8) Earnings after taxes [(4) − (7)]	$300,000	$240,000	$180,000	$720,000

portion of the merged firm just breaks even, and that Hudson is in the 40 percent tax bracket. The total taxes paid by the two firms and their after-tax earnings without and with the merger are calculated as shown in Table 19.1.

With the merger the total tax payments are less—$180,000 (total of line 7) versus $360,000 (total of line 2). With the merger the total after-tax earnings are more—$720,000 (total of line 8) versus $540,000 (total of line 3). The merged firm is able to deduct the tax loss either for 15 years subsequently or until the total tax loss has been fully recovered, whichever period is shorter. In this example the shorter is at the end of year 2. ■

INCREASED OWNERSHIP LIQUIDITY

The merger of two small firms or a small and a larger firm may provide the owners of the small firm(s) with greater liquidity. This is due to the higher marketability associated with the shares of larger firms. Instead of holding shares in a small firm that has a very "thin" market, the owners will receive shares that are traded in a broader market and can thus be liquidated more readily. Not only does the ability to convert shares into cash quickly have appeal, but owning shares for which market price quotations are readily available provides owners with a better sense of the value of their holdings. Especially in the case of small, closely held firms, the improved liquidity of ownership obtainable through merger with an acceptable firm may have considerable appeal.

DEFENSE AGAINST TAKEOVER

Occasionally, when a firm becomes the target of an unfriendly takeover, it will as a defense acquire another company. Such a strategy typically works like this: The original target firm takes on additional debt to finance its defensive acquisition; because of the debt load, the target firm becomes too large and too highly levered financially to be of any further interest to its suitor. To be effective, a defensive takeover must create greater value for shareholders than they would have realized had the firm been merged with its suitor. An example of such a defense was the 1988 incurrence of about $2.5 billion in debt a year after Harcourt Brace Jovanovich's (HBJ's) (publishing, insurance, theme parks) acquisition of Holt, Rinehart and Winston (publishing) from CBS, Inc. to ward off its suitor, Robert Maxwell (British takeover specialist, now deceased). To service the huge debt incurred in this transaction, HBJ subsequently sold its Sea World theme parks to Anheuser-Busch Co. (alcoholic beverages) but subsequently defaulted on many of its debts. After much negotiation, HBJ (now called Harcourt Brace, HB) was acquired by General Cinema in 1991. In retrospect it appears that HBJ's defense may have been its downfall. Clearly, the use of a merger with a large amount of debt financing as a takeover defense, while effectively deterring the takeover, can result in subsequent financial difficulty and possibly failure.

Types of mergers

horizontal merger
A merger of two firms *in the same line of business.*

vertical merger
A merger in which a firm acquires *a supplier or a customer.*

congeneric merger
A merger in which one firm acquires another firm that is *in the same general industry* but neither in the same line of business nor a supplier or customer.

conglomerate merger
A merger combining firms in *unrelated businesses.*

The four types of mergers are the (1) horizontal merger, (2) vertical merger, (3) congeneric merger, and (4) conglomerate merger. A **horizontal merger** results when two firms *in the same line of business* are merged. An example would be the merger of two machine-tool manufacturers. This form of merger results in the expansion of a firm's operations in a given product line and at the same time eliminates a competitor. A **vertical merger** occurs when a firm acquires *a supplier or a customer.* For example, the merger of a machine-tool manufacturer with its supplier of castings would be a vertical merger. The economic benefit of this type of merger stems from the firm's increased control over the acquisition of raw materials or the distribution of finished goods.

A **congeneric merger** is achieved by acquiring a firm that is *in the same general industry* but neither in the same line of business nor a supplier or customer. An example is the merger of a machine-tool manufacturer with the manufacturer of industrial conveyor systems. The benefit of this type of merger is the resulting ability to use the same sales and distribution channels to reach customers of both businesses. A **conglomerate merger** involves the combination of firms in *unrelated businesses.* The merger of a machine-tool manufacturer with a chain of fast-food restaurants would be an example of this kind of merger. The key benefit of the conglomerate merger is its ability to *reduce risk* by merging firms with different seasonal or cyclical patterns of sales and earnings.[4]

CONCEPTS IN REVIEW

19-1 Define and differentiate each of the following sets of terms.
- **a.** Mergers, consolidations, and holding companies
- **b.** Acquiring versus target company
- **c.** Friendly versus hostile mergers
- **d.** Strategic versus financial mergers

[4]A discussion of the key concepts underlying the portfolio approach to the diversification of risk was presented in Chapter 6. In the theoretical literature some questions exist relating to whether diversification by the firm is a proper motive consistent with shareholder wealth maximization. Many scholars argue that by buying shares in different firms, investors can obtain the same benefits as they would realize from owning stock in the merged firm. It appears that other benefits need to be available to justify mergers.

19-2 Briefly describe each of the following motives for merging.
- **a.** Growth or diversification
- **b.** Synergy
- **c.** Fund raising
- **d.** Increased managerial skill or technology
- **e.** Tax considerations
- **f.** Increased ownership liquidity
- **g.** Defense against takeover

19-3 Briefly describe each of the following types of mergers.
- **a.** Horizontal merger
- **b.** Vertical merger
- **c.** Congeneric merger
- **d.** Conglomerate merger

LBOs and divestitures

During the 1980s many firms were involved in leveraged buyouts (LBOs), which involve the use of a large amount of debt to finance the acquisition of other firms. What basic attributes do you think an attractive LBO candidate should possess? Before reading further, take a few minutes to answer this question.

BEFORE ADDRESSING THE MECHANICS OF MERGER ANALYSIS AND NEGOTIATION, IT IS IMportant to understand two topics that are closely related to mergers—LBOs and divestitures. An LBO is a method of structuring a financial merger, whereas divestitures involve the sale of a firm's assets.

Leveraged buyouts (LBOs)

leveraged buyout (LBO)
An acquisition technique involving the use of a large amount of debt to purchase a firm; an example of a *financial merger.*

A popular technique that was widely used during the 1980s to make acquisitions is the **leveraged buyout (LBO),** which involves the use of a large amount of debt to purchase a firm. LBOs are a clear-cut example of a *financial merger* undertaken to create a high-debt private corporation with improved cash flow and value. Typically in an LBO, 90 percent or more of the purchase price is financed with debt. A large part of the borrowing is secured by the acquired firm's assets, and the lenders, because of the high risk, take a portion of the firm's equity. *Junk bonds* have been routinely used to raise the large amounts of debt needed to finance LBO transactions. Of course, the purchasers in an LBO expect to use the improved cash flow to service the large amount of junk bond and other debt incurred in the buyout. The acquirers in LBOs are other firms or groups of investors that frequently include key members of the firm's existing management.

An attractive candidate for acquisition through leveraged buyout should possess three basic attributes:

1. It must have a good position in its industry with a solid profit history and reasonable expectations of growth.
2. The firm should have a relatively low level of debt and a high level of "bankable" assets that can be used as loan collateral.

3. It must have stable and predictable cash flows that are adequate to meet interest and principal payments on the debt and provide adequate working capital.

Of course, a willingness on the part of existing ownership and management to sell the company on a leveraged basis is also needed.

The leveraged buyout of Gibson Greeting Cards by a group of investors and managers headed by William Simon, former Secretary of the Treasury, is the classic example of a highly successful LBO. In the early 1980s, Simon's group, Wesray, purchased Gibson from RCA for $81 million. The group put up $1 million and borrowed the remaining $80 million, using the firm's assets as collateral. Within three years after Gibson had been acquired, Wesray had publicly sold 50 percent of the company for $87 million. Wesray still owned 50 percent of Gibson and had earned $87 million on a $1 million investment. While success of this magnitude is indeed not typical, it does point out the potential rewards from the use of LBOs to finance acquisitions. Another successful LBO was the management buyout of Topps Co. (baseball cards, Bazooka bubble gum), which was subsequently taken public, resulting in sizable profits for the buyout group.

Many LBOs did not live up to original expectations. The largest ever was the $24.5 billion buyout of RJR Nabisco by KKR, mentioned earlier. RJR was later taken public and the company is still struggling with the very heavy debt burden from the LBO. Campeau Corporation's buyouts of Allied Stores and Federated Department Stores resulted in its later filing for bankruptcy protection, from which reorganized companies have recently emerged. In recent years, other highly publicized LBOs have defaulted on the high yield debt incurred to finance the buyout. While the LBO remains a viable financing technique under the right circumstances, its use in the future will be greatly diminished from the frenzied pace of the 1980s. Whereas the LBOs of the 1980s were used, often indiscriminately, for hostile takeovers, today LBOs are most often used to finance management buyouts.

CONCEPT IN PRACTICE

Wall Street Grounds Gulfstream Aerospace's Approach to Flying Again

In 1983, when it went public, Gulfstream Aerospace had a reputation for making high-quality business jets. Chrysler acquired Gulfstream two years later but put it on the auction block in 1989. A year later, Forstmann Little, a New York LBO firm, bought Gulfstream for $850 million. From 1988 to 1992, delivery of new jets nosedived from 50 to 25. To ease the debt burden arising from the LBO, Forstmann Little attempted to sell shares in Gulfstream. However, investment bankers couldn't find enough investors to purchase shares at a minimum total value of $100 million. In early 1993, investors in Forstmann Little were experiencing a bumpy ride as Gulfstream prepared for another initial public offering.

Divestitures

operating unit
A part of a business, such as a plant, division, product line, or subsidiary, that contributes to the actual operations of the firm.

divestiture
The selling of some of a firm's assets for various strategic motives.

It is important to recognize that companies often achieve external expansion by acquiring an **operating unit**—plant, division, product line, subsidiary, etc.—of another company. In such a case the seller generally believes that the value of the firm will be enhanced by converting the unit into cash or some other more productive asset. The selling of some of a firm's assets is called **divestiture.** Unlike business failure, the motive for divestiture is often positive: to generate cash for expansion of other product lines, to get rid of a poorly performing operation, to streamline the corporation, or to restructure the corporation's business consistent with its strategic goals.

There is a variety of methods by which firms divest themselves of operating units. One involves the *sale of a product line to another firm.* Examples include Dow Jones & Co.'s (newspaper publishing) sale of Richard D. Irwin (publishing) to Times Mirror (newspapers) to concentrate on its business publishing and Clorox Company's (soap and cleaning products) sale of its Lucite/Olympic Paint business to focus entirely on its supermarket-distributed products. These outright sales can be accomplished on a cash or stock swap basis using the procedures described later in this chapter. A second method that has become quite popular in recent years involves the *sale of the unit to existing management.* This sale is often achieved through the use of a *leveraged buyout (LBO),* examples of which were given in the preceding section. Sometimes divestiture is achieved through a **spin-off**, which results in an operating unit becoming an independent company. A spin-off is accomplished by issuing shares in the operating unit being divested on a pro rata basis to the parent company's shareholders. Such an action allows the unit to be separated from the corporation and to trade as a separate entity. An example was the decision by The Quaker Oats Company to spin off Fisher-Price Toys to focus entirely on its supermarket-distributed brand-name products. Like outright sale, this approach achieves the divestiture objective, although it does not bring additional cash or stock to the parent company. The final and least popular approach to divestiture involves *liquidation of the operating unit's individual assets.*

spin-off
A form of divestiture in which an operating unit becomes an independent company by issuing shares in it on a pro rata basis to the parent company's shareholders.

Regardless of the method used to divest a firm of an unwanted operating unit, the goal typically is to create a more lean and focused operation that will enhance the efficiency as well as the profitability of the enterprise and create maximum value for shareholders. Recent divestitures seem to suggest that many operating units are worth much more to others than to the firm itself. Comparisons of postdivestiture and predivestiture market values have shown that the "breakup value" of many firms is significantly greater than their combined value. As a result of market valuations, divestiture often creates value in excess of the cash or stock received in the transaction. Unlike LBOs, the use of divestitures in corporate restructuring is expected to remain popular.

CONCEPT IN PRACTICE

Attempting a Spin-Off to Remedy Humana's Ills

In the 1970s, Humana was transformed from a leading nursing home chain into a 77-unit hospital chain. In the 1980s the company developed a health maintenance organization (HMO) to help fill Humana's beds. In 1993 the firm planned to separate into two units: a spin-off of the hospitals, to be known as Galen Health Care, and a health-insurance company, which would retain the Humana name. The realization that there was a clear contradiction in the vertically integrated firm motivated the split. Health plans attempt to cut usage and cost, while hospitals attempt to increase admissions and revenues. In splitting, the firm hopes to expand both businesses: the insurance operation was expected to benefit from anticipated health-care cost management, while the hospital chain was expected to attract patients insured by firms other than Humana.

CONCEPTS IN REVIEW

19-4 What is a *leveraged buyout (LBO)?* What are the three key attributes of an attractive candidate for acquisition using an LBO?

19-5 What is a *divestiture?* What is an *operating unit?* What are four common methods used by firms to divest themselves of operating units?

Analyzing and negotiating mergers

Whether a firm is planning to acquire a target firm for cash or through a stock swap, it must first determine the target firm's value. How would you go about estimating the value of a target firm that you are interested in acquiring as a going concern? Before reading ahead, spend a short time answering this question.

THIS PORTION OF THE CHAPTER DESCRIBES THE PROCEDURES THAT ARE USED TO ANAlyze and negotiate mergers. Initially, we will consider valuing the target company and using stock swap transactions to acquire companies. Next, we will look at the merger negotiation process. Then, we will review the major advantages and disadvantages of holding companies. Finally, we will briefly discuss international mergers.

Valuing the target company

Once the acquiring company isolates a target company that it wishes to acquire, it must estimate the target's value. The value would then be used, along with a proposed financing scheme, to negotiate the transaction—on a friendly or hostile basis. The value of the target would be estimated by using the valuation techniques presented in Chapter 7 and applied to long-term investment decisions in Chapters 8 and 9. Similar capital budgeting techniques would be applied whether the target firm is being acquired for its assets or as a going concern.

ACQUISITIONS OF ASSETS

Occasionally, a firm is acquired not for its income-earning potential but as a collection of assets (generally fixed assets) that the acquiring company needs. The price paid for this type of acquisition depends largely on which assets are being acquired; consideration must also be given to the value of any tax losses. To determine whether the purchase of assets is financially justified, the acquirer must estimate both the costs and benefits of the target assets. This is a capital budgeting problem (see Chapters 8 and 9), since an initial cash outlay is made to acquire assets and, as a result, future cash inflows are expected.

EXAMPLE

Clark Company, a major manufacturer of electrical transformers, is interested in acquiring certain fixed assets of Noble Company, an industrial electronics company. Noble, which has tax loss carryforwards from losses over the past five years, is interested in selling out, but it wishes to sell out entirely, not just get rid of certain fixed assets. A condensed balance sheet for Noble Company appears at the top of page 774.

Clark Company needs only machines B and C and the land and buildings. However, it has made some inquiries and has arranged to sell the accounts receivable, inventories, and machine A for \$23,000. Since there is also \$2,000 in cash, Clark will get \$25,000 for the excess assets. Noble wants \$200,000 for the entire company, which means that Clark will have to pay the firm's creditors \$80,000 and its owners \$20,000. The actual outlay required of Clark after liquidating the unneeded assets will be \$75,000 [(\$80,000 + \$20,000) − \$25,000]. In other words, to obtain the use of the desired assets (machines B and C and the land and buildings) and the benefits of Noble's tax losses, Clark must pay \$75,000. The *after-tax cash inflows* that are expected to result from the new assets and applicable tax losses are \$14,000 per year for the next five

Balance sheet Noble Company			
Assets		**Liabilities and stockholders' equity**	
Cash	$ 2,000	Total liabilities	$ 80,000
Marketable securities	0	Stockholders' equity	120,000
Accounts receivable	8,000	Total liabilities and	
Inventories	10,000	stockholders' equity	$200,000
Machine A	10,000		
Machine B	30,000		
Machine C	25,000		
Land and buildings	115,000		
Total assets	$200,000		

years and $12,000 per year for the following five years. The desirability of this asset acquisition can be determined by calculating the net present value of this outlay using the Clark Company's 11 percent cost of capital, as shown in Table 19.2. *Since the net present value of $3,072 is greater than zero, Clark's value should be increased by acquiring Noble Company's assets.* ■

ACQUISITIONS OF GOING CONCERNS

Acquisitions of target companies that are going concerns are best analyzed by using capital budgeting techniques similar to those described for asset acquisitions. The basic difficulty in applying the capital budgeting approach to the acquisition of a going concern is the *estimation of cash flows* and certain *risk considerations.* The methods of estimating expected cash flows from an acquisition are similar to those used in estimating

TABLE 19.2

NET PRESENT VALUE OF NOBLE COMPANY'S ASSETS

Year(s)	Cash inflow (1)	Present value factor at 11% (2)	Present value [(1) × (2)] (3)
1–5	$14,000	3.696[a]	$51,744
6	12,000	.535[b]	6,420
7	12,000	.482[b]	5,784
8	12,000	.434[b]	5,208
9	12,000	.391[b]	4,692
10	12,000	.352[b]	4,224
	Present value of inflows		$78,072
	Less: Cash outlay required		75,000
	Net present value[c]		$ 3,072

[a]The present-value interest factor for an annuity, *PVIFA*, with a five-year life discounted at 11 percent obtained from Table A-4.

[b]The present-value interest factor, *PVIF,* for $1 discounted at 11 percent for the corresponding year obtained from Table A-3.

[c]By using a hand-held business/financial calculator the net present value is $3,063.

capital budgeting cash flows. Typically, *pro forma income statements* reflecting the postmerger revenues and costs attributable to the target company are prepared (see Chapter 15). They are then adjusted to reflect the expected cash flows over the relevant time period. Whenever a firm considers acquiring a target company that has different risk behaviors, it should adjust the cost of capital appropriately before applying the appropriate capital budgeting techniques (see Chapter 9). An example will clarify this procedure.

EXAMPLE

The Square Company, a major media company, is contemplating the acquisition of the Circle Company, a small independent film producer that can be purchased for $60,000. Square currently has a high degree of financial leverage, which is reflected in its 13 percent cost of capital. Because of the low financial leverage of the Circle Company, Square estimates that its overall cost of capital will drop to 10 percent after the acquisition. Since the effect of the less risky capital structure resulting from the acquisition of Circle Company cannot be reflected in the expected cash flows, the postmerger cost of capital (10 percent) must be used to evaluate the cash flows that are expected from the acquisition. The postmerger cash flows attributable to the target company are forecast over a 30-year time horizon. These estimated cash flows (all inflows) are $5,000 for years 1 through 10, $13,000 for years 11 through 18, and $4,000 for years 19 through 30. The net present value (i.e., value) of the target company, Circle Company, is calculated in Table 19.3.

Since the net present value of the target company of $2,357 is greater than zero, the merger is acceptable. It is interesting to note that, had the effect of the changed capital structure on the cost of capital not been considered, the acquisition would have been found unacceptable, since the net present value *at a 13 percent cost of capital* is − $11,864, which is less than zero. (The value calculated by using a hand-held business/financial calculator is − $11,868.) ■

TABLE 19.3

NET PRESENT VALUE OF THE CIRCLE COMPANY ACQUISITION

Year(s)	Cash inflow (1)	Present value factor at 10%[a] (2)	Present value [(1) × (2)] (3)
1–10	$ 5,000	6.145	$30,725
11–18	13,000	(8.201 − 6.145)[b]	26,728
19–30	4,000	(9.427 − 8.201)[b]	4,904
	Present value of inflows		$62,357
	Less: Cash purchase price		60,000
	Net present value[c]		$ 2,357

[a]Present-value interest factors for annuities, *PVIFA*, obtained from Table A-4.

[b]These factors are found by using a shortcut technique that can be applied to annuities for periods of years beginning at some point in the future. By finding the appropriate interest factor for the present value of an annuity given for the last year of the annuity and subtracting the present-value interest factor of an annuity for the year immediately preceding the beginning of the annuity, the appropriate interest factor for the present value of an annuity beginning sometime in the future can be obtained. You can check this shortcut by using the long approach and comparing the results.

[c]The net present value calculated by using a hand-held business/financial calculator is $2,364.

Stock swap transactions

Once the value of the target company is determined, the acquirer must develop a proposed financing package. The simplest, but probably least common, case would be a pure cash purchase. Beyond this extreme case there are virtually an infinite number of financing packages that use various combinations of cash, debt, preferred stock, and common stock. Here we look at the other extreme—**stock swap transactions** in which the acquisition is paid for using an exchange of common stock. The acquiring firm exchanges its shares for shares of the target company according to a predetermined ratio. The *ratio of exchange* of shares is determined in the merger negotiations. This ratio affects the various financial yardsticks that are used by existing and prospective shareholders to value the merged firm's shares. With the demise of LBOs, the use of stock swaps to finance mergers has grown in popularity during the past few years.

stock swap transaction
An acquisition method in which the acquiring firm exchanges its shares for shares of the target company according to a predetermined ratio.

RATIO OF EXCHANGE

When one firm swaps its stock for the shares of another firm, the firms must determine the number of shares of the acquiring firm to be exchanged for each share of the target firm. The first requirement, of course, is that the acquiring company have sufficient shares available to complete the transaction. Often, a firm's repurchase of shares (which was discussed in Chapter 13) is necessary to obtain sufficient shares for such a transaction. The acquiring firm generally offers more for each share of the target company than the current market price of its publicly traded shares. The actual **ratio of exchange** is merely the ratio of the amount *paid* per share of the target company to the per-share market price of the acquiring firm. It is calculated in this manner because the acquiring firm pays the target firm in stock, which has a value equal to its market price. An example will clarify the calculation.

ratio of exchange
The ratio of the amount *paid* per share of the target company to the per-share market price of the acquiring firm.

EXAMPLE

The Grand Company, a leather products concern, whose stock is currently selling for \$80 per share, is interested in acquiring the Small Company, a producer of belts. To prepare for the acquisition, Grand has been repurchasing its own shares over the past three years. Small's stock is currently selling for \$75 per share, but in the merger negotiations, Grand has found it necessary to offer Small \$110 per share. Since Grand does not have sufficient financial resources to purchase the firm for cash and it does not wish to raise these funds, Small has agreed to accept Grand's stock in exchange for its shares. As stated, Grand's stock currently sells for \$80 per share, and it must pay \$110 per share for Small's stock. Therefore the ratio of exchange is 1.375 (\$110 ÷ \$80). This means that the Grand Company must exchange 1.375 shares of its stock for each share of Small's stock. ■

EFFECT ON EARNINGS PER SHARE

Ordinarily, the resulting earnings per share differ from the premerger earnings per share for both the acquiring firm and the target firm. They depend largely on the ratio of exchange and the premerger earnings per share of each firm. It is best to view the initial and long-run effects of the ratio of exchange on earnings per share (EPS) separately.

INITIAL EFFECT When the ratio of exchange is equal to 1 and both the acquiring firm and the target firm have the *same* premerger earnings per share, the merged firm's earnings per share will initially remain constant. In this rare instance, both the acquiring and target firms would also have equal price/earnings (P/E) ratios. In actuality the earnings per share of the merged firm are generally above the premerger earnings per share of one firm and below the premerger earnings per share of the other, af-

TABLE 19.4

GRAND COMPANY AND SMALL COMPANY FINANCIAL DATA

Item	Grand Company	Small Company
(1) Earnings available for common stock	\$500,000	\$100,000
(2) Number of shares of common stock outstanding	125,000	20,000
(3) Earnings per share [(1) ÷ (2)]	\$4	\$5
(4) Market price per share	\$80	\$75
(5) Price/earnings (P/E) ratio [(4) ÷ (3)]	20	15

ter the necessary adjustment has been made for the ratio of exchange. These differences can be illustrated by a simple example.

EXAMPLE

The Grand Company is contemplating acquiring the Small Company by swapping 1.375 shares of its stock for each share of Small's stock. The current financial data related to the earnings and market price for each of these companies are given in Table 19.4. Although Small's stock currently has a market price of \$75 per share, Grand has offered it \$110 per share. As was seen in the preceding example, this results in a ratio of exchange of 1.375.

To complete the merger and retire the 20,000 shares of Small Company stock outstanding, Grand will have to issue and (or) use treasury stock totaling 27,500 shares (1.375 × 20,000 shares). Once the merger is completed, Grand will have 152,500 shares of common stock (125,000 + 27,500) outstanding. If the earnings of each of the firms remain constant, the merged company will be expected to have earnings available for the common stockholders of \$600,000 (\$500,000 + \$100,000). The earnings per share of the merged company should therefore equal approximately \$3.93 per share (\$600,000 ÷ 152,500 shares).

It would appear at first that the Small Company's shareholders have sustained a decrease in per-share earnings from \$5 to \$3.93, but since each share of the Small Company's original stock is equivalent to 1.375 shares of the merged company, the equivalent earnings per share are actually \$5.40 (\$3.93 × 1.375). In other words, as a result of the merger, the Grand Company's original shareholders experience a decrease in earnings per share from \$4 to \$3.93 to the benefit of the Small Company's shareholders, whose earnings per share increase from \$5 to \$5.40. These results are summarized in Table 19.5. ■

TABLE 19.5

SUMMARY OF THE EFFECTS ON EARNINGS PER SHARE OF A MERGER BETWEEN GRAND COMPANY AND SMALL COMPANY AT \$110 PER SHARE

Stockholders	Earnings per share: Before merger	Earnings per share: After merger
Grand Company	\$4.00	\$3.93[a]
Small Company	5.00	5.40[b]

[a] $\frac{\$500,000 + \$100,000}{125,000 + (1.375 \times 20,000)} = \$3.93$

[b] \$3.93 × 1.375 = \$5.40

TABLE 19.6

EFFECT OF PRICE/EARNINGS (P/E) RATIOS ON EARNINGS PER SHARE (EPS)

	Effect on EPS	
Relationship between P/E paid and P/E of acquiring company	Acquiring company	Target company
P/E paid > P/E of acquiring company	Decrease	Increase
P/E paid = P/E of acquiring company	Constant	Constant
P/E paid < P/E of acquiring company	Increase	Decrease

The postmerger earnings per share for owners of the acquiring and target companies can be explained by comparing the price/earnings (P/E) ratio paid by the acquiring company with its initial P/E ratio. This relationship is summarized in Table 19.6. By paying more than its current value per dollar of earnings to acquire each dollar of earnings (P/E paid > P/E of acquiring company), the acquiring firm transfers the claim on a portion of its premerger earnings to the owners of the target firm. Therefore on a postmerger basis the target firm's EPS increases, and the acquiring firm's EPS decreases. Note that this outcome is *almost always* the case, since the acquirer typically pays a 50 percent, on average, premium above the target firm's market price, thereby resulting in the P/E paid being much above its own P/E. Examples include Bristol-Myers paying 26 times Squibb's EPS when its own P/E was 16 and Procter & Gamble paying 27 times Noxell's EPS when its own P/E was only 17. If the acquiring company were to pay less than its current value per dollar of earnings to acquire each dollar of earnings (P/E paid < P/E of acquiring company), the opposite effects would result. The P/E ratios associated with the Grand-Small merger can be used to explain the effect of the merger on earnings per share.

EXAMPLE

Grand Company's P/E ratio is 20, while the P/E ratio paid for Small Company's earnings was 22 ($110 ÷ $5). Since the P/E paid for Small Company was greater than the P/E for Grand Company (22 versus 20), the effect of the merger was to decrease the EPS for original holders of shares in Grand Company (from $4.00 to $3.93) and to increase the effective EPS of original holders of shares in Small Company (from $5.00 to $5.40). ■

LONG-RUN EFFECT The long-run effect of a merger on the earnings per share of the merged company depends largely on whether the earnings of the merged firm grow. Often, although a decrease in the per-share earnings of the stock held by the original owners of the acquiring firm is expected initially, the long-run effects of the merger on earnings per share are quite favorable. Since business firms generally expect growth in earnings, the key factor enabling the acquiring company, which initially experiences a decrease in EPS, to experience higher future EPS than it would have without the merger is the fact that the earnings attributable to the target company's assets grow at a faster rate than those resulting from the acquiring company's premerger assets. An example will clarify this point.

EXAMPLE

In 1994, Grand Company acquired Small Company by swapping 1.375 shares of its common stock for each share of Small Company. Other key financial data and the effects of this exchange ratio were discussed in the preceding examples. The total earnings of Grand Company were expected to grow at an annual rate of 3 percent without the merger; Small Company's earnings were expected to grow at a 7 percent annual rate without the merger. The same growth rates are expected to apply to the component earnings streams with the merger.[5] The table in Figure 19.1, on page 780, shows the future effects on EPS for Grand Company without and with the proposed Small Company merger, based on these growth rates.

The table indicates that the earnings per share without the merger will be greater than the EPS with the merger for the years 1994 through 1996. After 1996, however, the EPS will be higher than they would have been without the merger as a result of the faster earnings growth rate of Small Company (7 percent versus 3 percent). Although a few years are required for this difference in the growth rate of earnings to pay off, it can be seen that in the future, Grand Company will receive an earnings benefit as a result of merging with Small Company at a 1.375 ratio of exchange. The relationships in the table are shown in the graph in Figure 19.1. The long-run earnings advantage of the merger is clearly depicted by this graph.[6] ■

EFFECT ON MARKET PRICE PER SHARE

ratio of exchange in market price
The ratio of the market price per share of the acquiring firm *paid* to each dollar of market price per share of the target firm.

The market price per share does not necessarily remain constant after the acquisition of one firm by another. Adjustments occur in the marketplace in response to changes in expected earnings, the dilution of ownership, changes in risk, and certain other operating and financial changes. Using the ratio of exchange, a **ratio of exchange in market price** can be calculated. It indicates the market price per share of the acquiring firm *paid* for each dollar of market price per share of the target firm. This ratio, the *MPR*, is defined by Equation 19.1:

$$MPR = \frac{MP_{\text{acquiring}} \times RE}{MP_{\text{target}}} \tag{19.1}$$

where

MPR = market price ratio of exchange
$MP_{\text{acquiring}}$ = market price per share of the acquiring firm
MP_{target} = market price per share of the target firm
RE = ratio of exchange

The following example can be used to illustrate the calculation of this ratio.

EXAMPLE

In the Grand-Small example the market price of the Grand Company's stock was \$80, and that of the Small Company's was \$75. The ratio of exchange was 1.375. Substituting these values into Equation 19.1 yields a ratio of exchange in market price of 1.47 [(\$80 × 1.375) ÷ \$75]. This means that \$1.47 of the market price of Grand Company is given in exchange for every \$1.00 of the market price of Small Company. ■

---

[5]Frequently, because of synergy, the combined earnings stream is greater than the sum of the individual earnings streams. This possibility is ignored here.

[6]To discover properly whether the merger is beneficial, the earnings estimates under each alternative would have to be made over a long period of time, say, 50 years, and then converted to cash flows and discounted at the appropriate rate. The alternative with the higher present value would be preferred. In the interest of simplicity, only the basic intuitive view of the long-run effect is presented here.

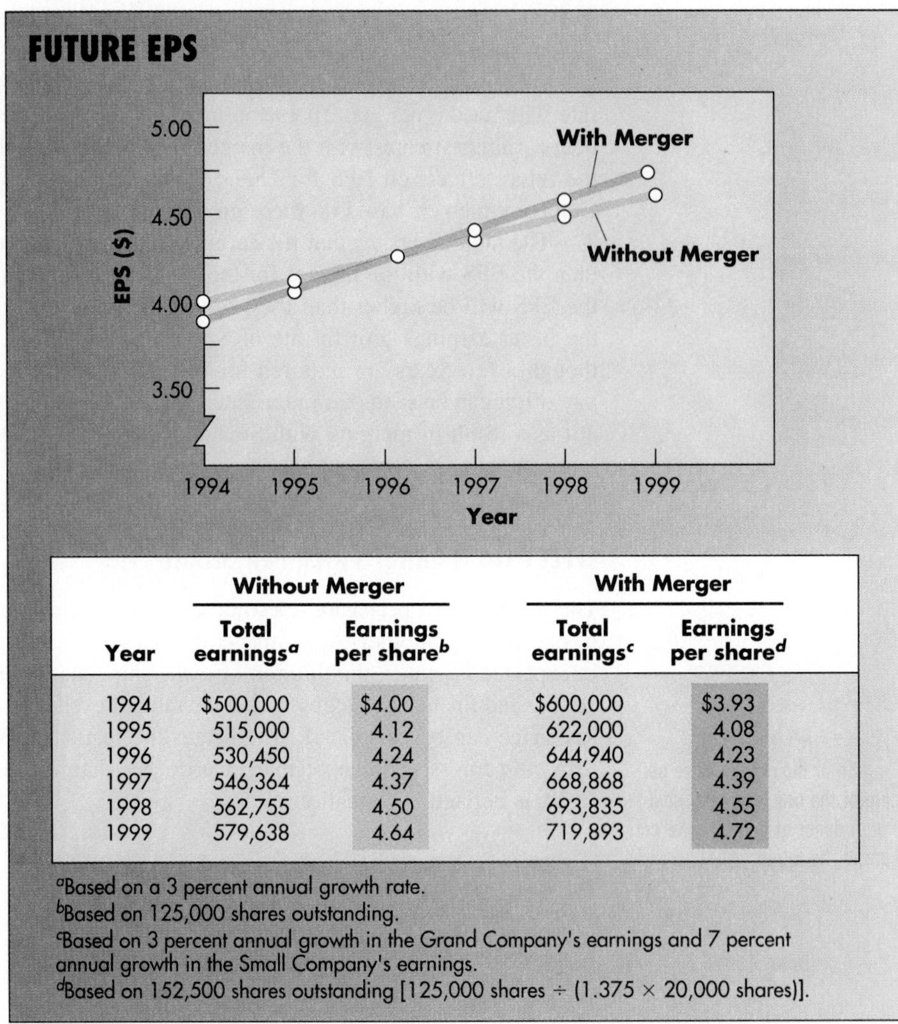

	Without Merger		With Merger	
Year	Total earnings[a]	Earnings per share[b]	Total earnings[c]	Earnings per share[d]
1994	$500,000	$4.00	$600,000	$3.93
1995	515,000	4.12	622,000	4.08
1996	530,450	4.24	644,940	4.23
1997	546,364	4.37	668,868	4.39
1998	562,755	4.50	693,835	4.55
1999	579,638	4.64	719,893	4.72

[a]Based on a 3 percent annual growth rate.
[b]Based on 125,000 shares outstanding.
[c]Based on 3 percent annual growth in the Grand Company's earnings and 7 percent annual growth in the Small Company's earnings.
[d]Based on 152,500 shares outstanding [125,000 shares ÷ (1.375 × 20,000 shares)].

FIGURE 19.1
Future EPS without and with the Grand-Small merger

The ratio of exchange in market price is normally greater than 1, which indicates that to acquire a firm, the acquirer must pay a premium above its market price. Even so, the original owners of the acquiring firm may still gain because the merged firm's stock may sell at a price/earnings ratio above the individual premerger ratios. This results from the improved risk and return relationship perceived by shareholders and other investors.

EXAMPLE

The financial data developed earlier for the Grand-Small merger can be used to explain the market price effects of a merger. If the earnings of the merged company remain at the premerger levels, and if the stock of the merged company sells at an assumed multiple of 21 times earnings, the values in Table 19.7 can be expected. In spite of the fact that Grand Company's earnings per share decline from $4.00 to $3.93 (see Table 19.5), the market price of its shares will increase from $80.00 (see Table 19.4) to $82.53 as a result of the merger. ■

Although the kind of behavior exhibited in this example is not unusual, the financial manager must recognize that only with proper management of the merged en-

TABLE 19.7

POSTMERGER MARKET PRICE OF GRAND COMPANY USING A P/E RATIO OF 21

Item	Merged company
(1) Earnings available for common stock	$600,000
(2) Number of shares of common stock outstanding	152,500
(3) Earnings per share [(1) ÷ (2)]	$3.93
(4) Price/earnings (P/E) ratio	21
(5) Expected market price per share [(3) × (4)]	$82.53

terprise can its market value be improved. If the merged firm cannot achieve sufficiently high earnings in view of its risk, there is no guarantee that its market price will reach the forecast value. Nevertheless, a policy of acquiring firms with low P/Es can produce favorable results for the owners of the acquiring firm. Acquisitions are especially attractive when the acquiring firm's stock price is high, since fewer shares must be exchanged to acquire a given firm.

The merger negotiation process

investment bankers
Financial intermediates hired by acquirers in mergers to find suitable target companies and assist in negotiations.

Mergers are often handled by **investment bankers**—financial intermediaries hired by acquirers to find suitable target companies and assist in negotiations. A firm seeking a potential acquisition can hire an investment banker to find firms meeting its requirements. Once a target company is selected, the investment banker negotiates with its management or investment banker. Frequently, when management wishes to sell the firm or a division of the firm, it will hire an investment banker to seek out potential buyers.

In the event that attempts to negotiate with the management of the target company break down, the acquiring firm, often with the aid of its investment banker, can make a direct appeal to shareholders by using *tender offers* (as explained below). The investment banker is typically compensated with a fixed fee, a commission tied to the transaction price, or with a combination of fees and commissions. Frequently, particularly in LBOs, the investment banker will take an equity position in the target company.

Many observers attribute the frenzied merger activity of the 1980s largely to the aggressive actions of investment bankers who initiated most of the many transactions that took place. The huge fees extracted by investment bankers, as well as attorneys, from their clients in these transactions in effect fueled the market. Today, with the collapse of the junk bond market and the related demise of LBOs and other forms of purely financial mergers, the investment banking community—especially the segment of investment bankers involved in mergers and acquisitions—is smaller and less active than during the 1980s. Although the merger business is not expected to disappear, investment banking revenues from this activity are not expected to experience significant growth in the future.

MANAGEMENT NEGOTIATIONS

To initiate the negotiation process, the acquiring firm must make an offer either in cash or based on a stock swap with a specified ratio of exchange. The target company must then review the offer and, in light of alternative offers, accept or reject the terms presented. A desirable merger candidate usually receives more than a single offer. Normally, certain nonfinancial issues relating to the disposition and compensation of the existing management, product-line policies, financing policies, and the independence of the target firm must be resolved. The key factor, of course, is the per-share price offered in cash or reflected in the ratio of exchange. Although the negotiations are generally based on the expectation of a merger, sometimes negotiations will break down.

TENDER OFFERS

two-tier offer
A tender offer in which the terms offered are more attractive to those who tender shares early.

takeover defenses
Strategies for fighting hostile takeovers.

When management negotiations for an acquisition break down, tender offers may then be used to negotiate a "hostile merger" directly with the firm's stockholders. As was noted in Chapter 13, a *tender offer* is a formal offer to purchase a given number of shares of a firm's stock at a specified price. The offer is made to all the stockholders at a premium above the market price. Occasionally, the acquirer will make a **two-tier offer** in which the terms offered are more attractive to those who tender shares early. For example, the acquirer offers to pay $25 per share for the first 60 percent of the outstanding shares tendered and only $23 per share for the remaining shares. The stockholders are advised of a tender offer through announcements in financial newspapers or through direct communications from the offering firm. Sometimes a tender offer is made to add pressure to existing merger negotiations. In other cases the tender offer may be made without warning as an attempt at an abrupt corporate takeover.

FIGHTING HOSTILE TAKEOVERS

white knight
A takeover defense in which the target firm finds an acquirer more to its liking than the initial hostile acquirer and prompts the two to compete to take over the firm.

poison pill
A takeover defense in which a firm issues securities that give their holders certain rights that become effective when a takeover is attempted; these rights make the target firm less desirable to a hostile acquirer.

greenmail
A takeover defense under which a target firm repurchases through private negotiation a large block of stock at a premium from one or more shareholders to end a hostile takeover attempt by those shareholders.

leveraged recapitalization
A takeover defense in which the target firm pays a large debt-financed cash dividend, increasing the firm's financial leverage and deterring the takeover attempt.

If the management of a target firm does not favor a merger or considers the price offered in a proposed merger too low, it is likely to take defensive actions to ward off the hostile tender offer. Such actions are generally developed with the assistance of investment bankers and lawyers who, for generally sizable fees, help the firm to develop and employ effective **takeover defenses.** Numerous strategies for fighting hostile takeovers were developed during the 1980s. There are obvious strategies such as informing stockholders of the alleged damaging effects of a takeover, acquiring another company (discussed earlier in the chapter), or attempting to sue the acquiring firm on antitrust or other grounds. In addition, many other defenses (some with colorful names) exist—white knight, poison pills, greenmail, leveraged recapitalization, golden parachutes, and shark repellents. We now take a brief look at each of these strategies.

The **white knight** strategy involves the target firm finding a more suitable acquirer (the "white knight") and prompting it to compete with the initial hostile acquirer to take over the firm. The basic premise of this strategy is that if being taken over is nearly certain, the target firm ought to attempt to be taken over by the firm that is deemed most acceptable to its management. **Poison pills** typically involve the creation of securities that give their holders certain rights that become effective when a takeover is attempted. The "pill" allows the shareholders to receive special voting rights or securities that, once issued, cause the firm to be much less desirable to the hostile acquirer. **Greenmail** is a strategy by which the firm repurchases through private negotiation a large block of stock at a premium from one or more shareholders to end a hostile takeover attempt by those shareholders. Clearly, greenmail is a form of corporate blackmail by the holders of a large block of shares.

Another hostile takeover defense involves the use of a **leveraged recapitalization,** which is a strategy involving the payment of a large debt-financed cash dividend. This strategy significantly increases the firm's financial leverage, thereby deterring the takeover attempt. In addition, as a further deterrent the recapitalization is often structured to increase the equity and control of the existing management. **Golden parachutes** are provisions in the employment contracts of key executives that provide them with sizable compensation if the firm is taken over. Golden parachutes deter hostile takeovers to the extent that the cash outflows required by these contracts are large enough to make the takeover unattractive to the acquirer. Another defense is use of **shark repellents,** which are antitakeover amendments to the corporate charter that constrain the firm's ability to transfer managerial control of the firm as a result of a merger. Although this defense could entrench existing management, many firms have had these amendments ratified by shareholders.

golden parachutes
Provisions in the employment contracts of key executives that provide them with sizable compensation if the firm is taken over; deters hostile takeovers to the extent that the cash outflows required are large enough to make the takeover unattractive.

shark repellents
Antitakeover amendments to a corporate charter that constrain the firm's ability to transfer managerial control of the firm as a result of a merger.

Because takeover defenses tend to insulate management from shareholders, the potential for litigation is great when these strategies are employed. Lawsuits are sometimes filed against management by dissident shareholders. In addition, federal and state governments frequently intervene when a proposed takeover is deemed to be in violation of federal or state law. A number of states have legislation on their books limiting or restricting hostile takeovers of companies domiciled within their boundaries. While new takeover defenses will surely be developed in the future, so too will new legislation be passed to regulate merger activity to protect the interests not only of stockholders but also of employees, customers, suppliers, creditors, and other "stakeholders" in target firms.

Holding companies

As defined earlier, a *holding company* is a corporation that has voting control of one or more other corporations. The holding company may need to own only a small percentage of the outstanding shares to have this voting control. In the case of companies with a relatively small number of shareholders, as much as 30 to 40 percent of the stock may be required. In the case of firms with a widely dispersed ownership, 10 to 20 percent of the shares may be sufficient to gain voting control. A holding company that wants to obtain voting control of a firm may use direct market purchases or tender offers to acquire needed shares. Although there are relatively few holding companies and they are far less important than mergers, it is helpful to understand their key advantages and disadvantages.

ADVANTAGES OF HOLDING COMPANIES

The primary advantage of the holding company arrangement is the *leverage effect* that permits the firm to control a large amount of assets with a relatively small dollar investment. In other words, the owners of a holding company can *control* significantly larger amounts of assets than they could *acquire* through mergers. The following example illustrates the leverage effect.

EXAMPLE

Carr Company, a holding company, currently holds voting control of two subsidiaries—company X and company Y. The balance sheets for Carr Company and its two subsidiaries are presented in Table 19.8. It owns approximately 17 percent ($10 ÷ $60) of company X and 20 percent ($14 ÷ $70) of company Y. It is assumed that these holdings are sufficient for voting control.

The owners of Carr Company's $12 worth of equity have control over $260 worth of assets (company X's $100 worth and company Y's $160 worth). Thus the owners' equity represents only about 4.6 percent ($12 ÷ $260) of the total assets controlled.

TABLE 19.8

BALANCE SHEETS FOR CARR COMPANY AND ITS SUBSIDIARIES

Assets		Liabilities and stockholders' equity	
Carr Company			
Common stock holdings		Long-term debt	$ 6
Company X	$10	Preferred stock	6
Company Y	14	Common stock equity	12
Total	$24	Total	$24
Company X			
Current assets	$ 30	Current liabilities	$ 15
Fixed assets	70	Long-term debt	25
Total	$100	Common stock equity	60
		Total	$100
Company Y			
Current assets	$ 20	Current liabilities	$ 10
Fixed assets	140	Long-term debt	60
Total	$160	Preferred stock	20
		Common stock equity	70
		Total	$160

From the discussions of ratio analysis, leverage, and capital structure in Chapters 4 and 11 you should recognize that this is quite a high degree of leverage. If an individual stockholder or even another holding company owns $3 of Carr Company's stock, which is assumed to be sufficient for its control, it will in actuality control the whole $260 of assets. The investment itself in this case would represent only 1.15 percent ($3 ÷ $260) of the assets controlled. ■

pyramiding
An arrangement among holding companies wherein one holding company controls other holding companies, thereby causing an even greater magnification of earnings and losses.

The high leverage obtained through a holding company arrangement greatly magnifies earnings and losses for the holding company. Quite often, a **pyramiding** of holding companies occurs when one holding company controls other holding companies, thereby causing an even greater magnification of earnings and losses. The greater the leverage, the greater the risk involved. The risk-return tradeoff is a key consideration in the holding company decision.

Another commonly cited advantage of the holding company arrangement is the *risk protection* resulting from the fact that the failure of one of the companies (such as Y in the preceding example) does not result in the failure of the entire holding company. Since each subsidiary is a separate corporation, the failure of one company should cost the holding company, at maximum, no more than its investment in that subsidiary. Other advantages include the following: (1) certain state *tax benefits* may be realized by each subsidiary in its state of incorporation; (2) *lawsuits or legal actions* against a subsidiary will not threaten the remaining companies; and (3) it is *generally easy to gain control* of a firm, since stockholder or management approval is not generally necessary.

DISADVANTAGES OF HOLDING COMPANIES

A major disadvantage of the holding company arrangement is the *increased risk* resulting from the leverage effect. When general economic conditions are unfavorable, a loss by one subsidiary may be magnified. For example, if subsidiary company X in Table 19.8 experiences a loss, its inability to pay dividends to Carr Company could result in Carr Company's inability to meet its scheduled payments.

Another disadvantage is *double taxation.* Before paying dividends a subsidiary must pay federal and state taxes on its earnings. Although a 70 percent tax exclusion is allowed on dividends received by one corporation from another, the remaining 30 percent received is taxable. (In the event that the holding company owns between 20 and 80 percent of the stock in a subsidiary, the exclusion is 80 percent, and if it owns more than 80 percent of the stock in the subsidiary, 100 percent of the dividends are excluded.) If a subsidiary were part of a merged company, double taxation would *not* exist.

The fact that holding companies are *difficult to analyze* is another disadvantage. Security analysts and investors typically have difficulty understanding holding companies because of their complexity. As a result these firms tend to sell at low multiples, of earnings (P/Es). This means that the shareholder value of holding companies may suffer.

A final disadvantage of holding companies is the generally *high cost of administration* resulting from maintaining each subsidiary company as a separate entity. A merger, on the other hand, would likely result in certain administrative economies of scale. The need for coordination and communication between the holding company and its subsidiaries may further elevate these costs.

CONCEPT IN PRACTICE

As the Toronto Blue Jays Win the World Series, Its Owners Strike Out

At its peak, the Bronfman brothers' holding company controlled firms representing more than 10 percent of the value of the Toronto Stock Exchange, touching nearly every sector of Canada's economy. Starting with $25 million left by their uncle, Samuel Bronfman, who built the Seagram Co. liquor fortune, Edward and Peter Bronfman injected these funds and subsequent earnings into holding companies. Next, the Bronfmans offered public shareholders the chance to match their investment. The combined funds were then funneled into a second firm, in which investors were again given the chance to match the Bronfmans' investment. However, the Bronfmans' success relied upon the operating companies on the bottom earning enough to pay the required rate of return to higher-level holding companies. When earnings fell, operating companies slashed dividends, cutting income to senior holding companies. Suddenly, the Bronfmans became dependent on external financing to meet interest charges and capital expenditures. In 1993 the Bronfmans obtained external funds by restructuring the financing of its real estate division and selling John Labatt Brewing and baseball's Toronto Blue Jays.

International mergers

Perhaps in no other area does U.S. financial practice differ more fundamentally from practices in other countries than in the field of mergers. Outside of the United States (and, to a lesser degree, Great Britain), hostile takeovers are virtually nonexistent, and in some countries (such as Japan), takeovers of any kind are uncommon. The corporate control model that applies to large U.S. and British companies, with its emphasis on shareholder value and reliance on public capital markets for financing, is generally inapplicable in continental Europe—where companies are generally smaller and other stakeholders such as employees, bankers, and governments are accorded greater consideration than in the United States and United Kingdom. The model is a poor fit for Japan and other Asian nations, where large and very stable industrial groupings, called *Keiretsu,* dominate the corporate scene.

CHANGES IN WESTERN EUROPE

Today, there are signs that Western Europe is moving more toward a U.S.-style corporate control and financing model. Since the final plan for European economic integration was unveiled in 1988, the number, size, and importance of crossborder European mergers have exploded. Nationally focused companies want to achieve economies of scale in manufacturing, encourage international product development strategies, and develop distribution networks across the continent. They are also driven by the need to compete with U.S. companies, which have been operating on a continentwide basis in Europe for decades.

These larger European-based companies will probably prove to be even more formidable competitors once national barriers are fully removed in the mid-1990s. While the vast majority of these cross-border mergers (and joint ventures, which have also increased recently) are friendly in nature, a few have been actively resisted by target firm managements. It seems clear that as European companies come to rely more on public capital markets for financing, and as the market for common stock becomes more truly European in character—rather than French or British or German—these will inevitably evolve into active markets for corporate control as well.

FOREIGN TAKEOVERS OF U.S. COMPANIES

Both European and Japanese companies have been active as acquirers of U.S. companies in recent years. In fact, during the 1980s, foreign takeovers of U.S. companies for the first time exceeded in number and dollar volume the acquisitions by U.S. firms of companies in Europe, Canada, and the Pacific Rim excluding Japan. Foreign companies have purchased U.S. firms for two major reasons: access to the world's single largest, richest, and least regulated market and to acquire world-class technology at a bargain price. Because the dollar has depreciated against most major currencies since 1987, the effective price of purchasing U.S. assets has declined. British companies have historically been the most active acquirers of U.S. firms. For example, Grand Metropolitan acquired Pillsbury Corp. in 1989. In the late 1980s, Japanese corporations surged to prominence with a series of very large acquisitions, including two in the entertainment industry: Sony's purchase of Columbia Pictures and Matsushita's acquisition of MCA. More recently, German firms have become especially active acquirers of U.S. companies as the cost of producing export goods in Germany has become prohibitively expensive. (German workers now have the world's highest wages and shortest workweek.) It seems inevitable that in the years ahead, foreign companies will continue to acquire U.S. firms even as U.S. companies continue to seek attractive acquisitions or joint-venture partners abroad.

CONCEPTS IN REVIEW

19-6 Describe the procedures that are typically used by an acquirer to value a target company, whether it is being acquired for its assets or as a going concern.

19-7 What is the *ratio of exchange?* Is it based on the current market prices of the shares of the acquiring and target firms? Why may a long-run view of the merged firm's earnings per share change a merger decision?

19-8 What role do *investment bankers* often play in the merger negotiation process? What is a *tender offer?* When and how is it used?

19-9 Briefly describe each of the following *takeover defenses* against a hostile merger.

- **a.** White knight
- **b.** Poison pill
- **c.** Greenmail
- **d.** Leveraged recapitalization
- **e.** Golden parachutes
- **f.** Shark repellents

19-10 What are the key advantages and disadvantages cited for the holding company arrangement? What is *pyramiding,* and what are its consequences?

19-11 Discuss the differences in merger practices between U.S. companies and companies in other countries. What changes are occurring in international merger activity, particularly in Western Europe and Japan?

Business failure fundamentals

Businesses fail by having negative or low returns, being unable to pay liabilities as they come due, or having more liabilities than assets, for a variety of reasons. What do you think are some of the major causes of business failure? Take a few moments to answer this question before reading further.

A BUSINESS FAILURE IS AN UNFORTUNATE CIRCUMSTANCE. ALTHOUGH THE MAJORITY OF firms that fail do so within the first year or two of life, other firms grow, mature, and fail much later. The failure of a business can be viewed in a number of ways and can result from one or more causes.

Types of business failure

A firm may fail because its *returns are negative or low.* A firm that consistently reports operating losses will probably experience a decline in market value. If the firm fails to earn a return that is greater than its cost of capital, it can be viewed as having failed. Negative or low returns, unless remedied, are likely to result eventually in one of the following more serious types of failure.

technical insolvency
Business failure that occurs when a firm is unable to pay its liabilities as they come due.

bankruptcy
Business failure that occurs when a firm's liabilities exceed the fair market value of its assets.

A second type of failure, **technical insolvency,** occurs when a firm is unable to pay its liabilities as they come due. When a firm is technically insolvent, its assets are still greater than its liabilities, but it is confronted with a *liquidity crisis.* If some of its assets can be converted into cash within a reasonable period, the company may be able to escape complete failure. If not, the result is the third and most serious type of failure, **bankruptcy.** Bankruptcy occurs when a firm's liabilities exceed the fair market value of its assets. A bankrupt firm has a *negative* stockholders' equity.[7] This means that the claims of creditors cannot be satisfied unless the firm's assets can be liquidated for more than their book value. Although bankruptcy is an obvious form of failure, *the courts treat technical insolvency and bankruptcy in the same way.* They are both considered to indicate the financial failure of the firm.

Major causes of business failure

The primary cause of business failure is *mismanagement,* which accounts for more than 50 percent of all cases. Numerous specific managerial faults can cause the firm to fail. Overexpansion, poor financial actions, an ineffective sales force, and high production costs can all singly or in combination cause the ultimate failure of the firm. Since all major corporate decisions are eventually measured in terms of dollars, the financial manager may play a key role in avoiding or causing a business failure. It is his or her duty to monitor the firm's financial pulse.

Economic activity—especially economic downturns—can contribute to the failure of a firm.[8] If the economy goes into a recession, sales may decrease abruptly, leaving the firm with high fixed costs and insufficient revenues to cover them. In addition, rapid rises in interest rates just prior to a recession can further contribute to cash flow problems and make it more difficult for the firm to obtain and maintain needed financing. If the recession is prolonged, the likelihood of survival decreases even further. Recently, a number of major business failures such as those of Olympia and York (real estate), America West Airlines, and Southmark Corporation (convenience stores) have resulted from overexpansion and a recessionary economy.

A final cause of business failure is *corporate maturity.* Firms, like individuals, do not have infinite lives. Like a product, a firm goes through the stages of birth, growth, maturity, and eventual decline. The firm's management should attempt to prolong the growth stage through research, the development of new products, and mergers. Once the firm has matured and has begun to decline, it should seek to be acquired by another firm or liquidate before it fails. Effective management planning should help the firm to postpone decline and ultimate failure.

Voluntary Settlements

voluntary settlement
An arrangement between a technically insolvent or bankrupt firm and its creditors enabling it to bypass many of the costs involved in legal bankruptcy proceedings.

When a firm becomes technically insolvent or bankrupt, it may arrange with its creditors a **voluntary settlement,** which enables it to bypass many of the costs involved in legal bankruptcy proceedings. The settlement is normally initiated by the debtor firm, since such an arrangement may enable it to continue to exist or to be liq-

[7] Since on a balance sheet the firm's assets equal the sum of its liabilities and stockholders' equity, the only way a firm that has more liabilities than assets can balance its balance sheet is to have a *negative* stockholders' equity.

[8] The success of some firms runs countercyclical to economic activity, and other firms are unaffected by economic activity. For example, the sale of sewing machines is likely to increase during a recession, since people are more willing to make their own clothes and less willing to pay for the labor of others. The sale of boats and other luxury items may decline during a recession, while sales of staple items such as electricity are likely to be unaffected. In terms of beta—the measure of nondiversifiable risk developed in Chapter 6—a negative-beta stock would be associated with a firm whose behavior is generally countercyclical to economic activity.

uidated in a manner that gives the owners the greatest chance of recovering part of their investment. The debtor, possibly with the aid of a key creditor, arranges a meeting between itself and all its creditors. At the meeting, a committee of creditors is selected to investigate and analyze the debtor's situation and recommend a plan of action. The recommendations of the committee are discussed with both the debtor and the creditors, and a plan for sustaining or liquidating the firm is drawn up.

VOLUNTARY SETTLEMENT TO SUSTAIN THE FIRM

extension
An arrangement whereby the firm's creditors receive payment in full, although not immediately.

composition
A pro rata cash settlement of creditor claims by the debtor firm; a uniform percentage of each dollar owed is paid.

creditor control
An arrangement in which the creditor committee replaces the firm's operating management and operates the firm until all claims have been settled.

Normally, the rationale for sustaining a firm is that it is reasonable to believe that the firm's recovery is feasible. By sustaining the firm the creditor can continue to receive business from it. A number of strategies are commonly used. An **extension** is an arrangement whereby the firm's creditors receive payment in full, although not immediately. Normally, when creditors grant an extension, they agree to require cash payments for purchases until all past debts have been paid. A second arrangement, called **composition,** is a pro rata cash settlement of creditor claims. Instead of receiving full payment of their claims, as in the case of an extension, creditors receive only a partial payment. A uniform percentage of each dollar owed is paid in satisfaction of each creditor's claim. A third arrangement is **creditor control.** In this case the creditor committee may decide that the only circumstance in which maintaining the firm is feasible is if the operating management is replaced. The committee may then take control of the firm and operate it until all claims have been settled. Sometimes, a plan involving some combination of extension, composition, and creditor control will result. An example of this would be a settlement whereby the debtor agrees to pay a total of 75 cents on the dollar in three annual installments of 25 cents on the dollar, while the creditors agree to sell additional merchandise to the firm on 30-day terms if the existing management is replaced by new management that is acceptable to them.

VOLUNTARY SETTLEMENT RESULTING IN LIQUIDATION

After the situation of the firm has been investigated by the creditor committee, recommendations have been made, and talks among the creditors and the debtor have been held, the only acceptable course of action may be liquidation of the firm. Liquidation can be carried out in two ways—privately or through the legal procedures provided by bankruptcy law. If the debtor firm is willing to accept liquidation, legal procedures may not be required. Generally, the avoidance of litigation enables the creditors to obtain *quicker* and *higher* settlements. However, all the creditors must agree to a private liquidation for it to be feasible.

assignment
A voluntary liquidation procedure by which a firm's creditors pass the power to liquidate the firm's assets to an adjustment bureau, a trade association, or a third party, which is designated the *assignee.*

The objective of the voluntary liquidation process is to recover as much per dollar owed as possible. Under voluntary liquidation, common stockholders, who are the firm's true owners, cannot receive any funds until the claims of all other parties have been satisfied. A common procedure is to have a meeting of the creditors at which they make an **assignment** by passing the power to liquidate the firm's assets to an adjustment bureau, a trade association, or a third party, which is designated the *assignee.* The assignee's job is to liquidate the assets, obtaining the best price possible. The assignee is sometimes referred to as the *trustee,* since it is entrusted with the title to the company's assets and the responsibility to liquidate them efficiently. Once the trustee has liquidated the assets, it distributes the recovered funds to the creditors and owners (if any funds remain for the owners). The final action in a private liquidation is for the creditors to sign a release attesting to the satisfactory settlement of their claims.

CONCEPTS IN REVIEW

19-12 What are the three types of business failure? What is the difference between *technical insolvency* and *bankruptcy*? What are the major causes of business failure?

19-13 Define an *extension* and a *composition,* and explain how they might be combined to form a voluntary settlement plan to sustain the firm. How is a voluntary settlement resulting in liquidation handled?

Reorganization and liquidation in bankruptcy

When a firm that fails is liquidated under the prevailing bankruptcy law, a specified priority of claims must be maintained in distributing funds. Of all parties that a firm might owe, in what basic order of priority do you think their claims must be satisfied? Devote a few moments to answering this question before reading ahead.

If a voluntary settlement for a failed firm cannot be agreed upon, the firm can be forced into bankruptcy by its creditors. As a result of bankruptcy proceedings, the firm may be either reorganized or liquidated.

Bankruptcy legislation

Bankruptcy Reform Act of 1978
The current governing bankruptcy legislation in the United States.

Chapter 7
The portion of the *Bankruptcy Reform Act of 1978* that details the procedures to be followed in liquidating a failed firm.

Chapter 11
The portion of the *Bankruptcy Reform Act of 1978* that outlines the procedures for reorganizing a failed (or failing) firm, whether its petition is filed voluntarily or involuntarily.

As was already stated, *bankruptcy* in the legal sense occurs when the firm cannot pay its bills or when its liabilities exceed the fair market value of its assets. In either of these situations a firm may be declared legally bankrupt. However, creditors generally attempt to avoid forcing a firm into bankruptcy if it appears to have opportunities for future success.

The governing bankruptcy legislation in the United States today is the **Bankruptcy Reform Act of 1978,** which significantly modified earlier bankruptcy legislation. This law contains eight odd-numbered (1 through 15) and one even-numbered (12) chapters. A number of these chapters would apply in the instance of failure; the two key ones are Chapters 7 and 11. **Chapter 7** of the Bankruptcy Reform Act of 1978 details the procedures to be followed in liquidating a failed firm. This chapter typically comes into play once it has been determined that a fair, equitable, and feasible basis for the reorganization of a failed firm does not exist (although a firm may of its own accord choose not to reorganize and may instead go directly into liquidation). **Chapter 11** outlines the procedures for reorganizing a failed (or failing) firm, whether its petition is filed voluntarily or involuntarily. If a workable plan for reorganization cannot be developed, the firm will be liquidated under Chapter 7.

Reorganization in bankruptcy

voluntary reorganization
A petition filed by a failed firm on its own behalf for reorganizing its structure and paying its creditors.

There are two basic types of reorganization petitions—voluntary and involuntary. Any firm that is not a municipal or financial institution can file a petition for **volun-**

involuntary reorganization
A petition initiated by an outside party, usually a creditor, for the reorganization and payment of creditors of a failed firm.

tary reorganization on its own behalf.[9] **Involuntary reorganization** is initiated by an outside party, usually a creditor. An involuntary petition against a firm can be filed if one of three conditions is met:

1. The firm has past-due debts of $5,000 or more.
2. Three or more creditors can prove that they have aggregate unpaid claims of $5,000 against the firm. If the firm has fewer than 12 creditors, any creditor that is owed more than $5,000 can file the petition.
3. The firm is *insolvent,* which means (a) that it is not paying its debts as they come due, (b) that within the immediately preceding 120 days a custodian (a third party) was appointed or took possession of the debtor's property, or (c) that the fair market value of the firm's assets is less than the stated value of its liabilities.

CONCEPT IN PRACTICE

R-TEK and 96,000 Other Firms

R-Tek Corporation, a record and video marketer, has the distinction of being the worst-performing stock in 1992. The company lost millions of dollars when a German subsidiary went into receivership and its share price fell from $7.75 to pennies per share. R-Tek was not alone. According to Dun & Bradstreet Information Services, business failures in 1992 were more common than ever. Approximately 96,000 businesses closed their doors, 9 percent more than in 1991 and 50 percent more than in 1990. The dollar value of unpaid liabilities associated with these failures amounted to $105 billion. The one bright spot was that the number of bankruptcies leaving liabilities greater than $1 million dropped.

PROCEDURES

The procedures for initiation and execution of corporate reorganizations entail five separate steps: filing, appointment, development and approval of a reorganization plan, acceptance of the plan, and payment of expenses.

FILING A reorganization petition under Chapter 11 must be filed in a federal bankruptcy court. In the case of an involuntary petition, if it is challenged by the debtor, a hearing must be held to determine whether the firm is insolvent. If it is, the court enters an "Order for Relief" that formally initiates the process.

debtor in possession (DIP)
The term assigned to a firm that files a reorganization petition under Chapter 11 and then develops, if feasible, a reorganization plan.

APPOINTMENT Upon the filing of a reorganization petition, the filing firm becomes the **debtor in possession (DIP)** of the assets. If creditors object to the filing firm being the debtor in possession, they can ask the judge to appoint a trustee.

REORGANIZATION PLAN After reviewing its situation the debtor in possession submits a plan of reorganization to the court. The plan and a disclosure statement summarizing the plan are filed. A hearing is held to determine whether the plan is *fair,*

[9]Firms sometimes file a voluntary petition to obtain temporary legal protection from creditors or from prolonged litigation. Once they have straightened out their financial or legal affairs—prior to further reorganization or liquidation actions—they will have the petition dismissed. Although such actions are not the intent of the bankruptcy law, difficulty in enforcing the law has allowed this abuse to occur.

equitable, and *feasible* and whether the disclosure statement contains adequate information. The court's approval or disapproval is based on its evaluation of the plan in light of these standards. A plan is considered *fair and equitable* if it *maintains the priorities* of the contractual claims of the creditors, preferred stockholders, and common stockholders. The court must also find the reorganization plan *feasible,* meaning that it must be *workable.* The reorganized corporation must have sufficient working capital, sufficient funds to cover fixed charges, sufficient credit prospects, and sufficient ability to retire or refund debts as proposed by the plan.

ACCEPTANCE OF THE REORGANIZATION PLAN Once approved, the plan, along with the disclosure statement, is given to the firm's creditors and shareholders for their acceptance. Under the Bankruptcy Reform Act, creditors and owners are separated into groups with similar types of claims. In the case of creditor groups, approval by holders of at least two-thirds of the dollar amount of claims as well as a numerical majority of creditors in the group is required. In the case of ownership groups (preferred and common stockholders), two-thirds of the shares in each group must approve the reorganization plan for it to be accepted. Once accepted and confirmed by the court, the plan is put into effect as soon as possible.

PAYMENT OF EXPENSES After the reorganization plan has been approved or disapproved, all parties to the proceedings whose services were beneficial or contributed to the approval or disapproval of the plan file a statement of expenses. If the court finds these claims acceptable, the debtor must pay these expenses within a reasonable period of time.

ROLE OF THE DEBTOR IN POSSESSION (DIP)

Since reorganization activities are largely in the hands of the debtor in possession (DIP), it is useful to understand the DIP's responsibilities. The DIP's first responsibility is the valuation of the firm to determine whether reorganization is appropriate. To do this, the DIP must estimate both the *liquidation value* of the business and its value as a *going concern.* If the DIP finds that its value as a going concern is less than its liquidation value, it will recommend liquidation. If the opposite is found to be true, the DIP will recommend reorganization. If the reorganization of the firm is recommended by the DIP, a plan of reorganization must be drawn up. The key portion of the reorganization plan generally concerns the firm's capital structure. Since most firms' financial difficulties result from high fixed charges, the company's capital structure is generally *recapitalized,* or altered, to reduce these charges. Under **recapitalization,** debts are generally exchanged for equity, or the maturities of existing debts are extended. The DIP, in recapitalizing the firm, places a great deal of emphasis on building a mix of debt and equity that will allow the firm to meet its debts and provide a reasonable level of earnings for its owners.

recapitalization
The reorganization procedure under which a failed firm's debts are generally exchanged for equity or the maturities of existing debts are extended.

Once the optimal capital structure has been determined, the DIP must establish a plan for exchanging outstanding obligations for new securities. The guiding principle is to *observe priorities.* Senior claims (those with higher legal priority) must be satisfied before junior claims (those with lower legal priority). To comply with this principle, senior suppliers of capital must receive a claim on new capital equal to their previous claims. The common stockholders are the last to receive any new securities. (It is not unusual for them to receive nothing.) Security holders do not necessarily have to receive the same type of security they held before; often they receive a combination of securities. Once the debtor in possession has determined the new capital structure and distribution of capital, it will submit the reorganization plan and disclosure statement to the court as described.

Liquidation in bankruptcy

The liquidation of a bankrupt firm usually occurs once the courts have determined that reorganization is not feasible. A petition for reorganization must normally be filed by the managers or creditors of the bankrupt firm. If no petition is filed, if a petition is filed and denied, or if the reorganization plan is denied, the firm must be liquidated. Three important aspects of liquidation in bankruptcy are the procedures, the priority of claims, and the final accounting.

PROCEDURES

When a firm is adjudged bankrupt, the judge may appoint a *trustee* to perform the many routine duties required in administering the bankruptcy. The trustee takes charge of the property of the bankrupt firm and protects the interest of its creditors. Once the firm has been adjudged bankrupt, a meeting of creditors must be held between 20 and 40 days thereafter. At this meeting, the creditors are made aware of the prospects for the liquidation. The meeting is presided over by the bankruptcy court clerk. The trustee is then given the responsibility to liquidate the firm, keep records, examine creditors' claims, disburse money, furnish information as required, and make final reports on the liquidation. In essence the trustee is responsible for the liquidation of the firm. Occasionally, the court will call subsequent creditor meetings, but only a final meeting for closing the bankruptcy is required.

PRIORITY OF CLAIMS

It is the trustee's responsibility to liquidate all the firm's assets and to distribute the proceeds to the holders of *provable claims*. The courts have established certain procedures for determining the provability of claims. The priority of claims, which is specified in Chapter 7 of the Bankruptcy Reform Act, must be maintained by the trustee in distributing the funds from liquidation. It is important to recognize that any **secured creditors** have specific assets pledged as collateral and, in liquidation, receive proceeds from the sale of those assets. If these proceeds are inadequate to meet their claim, the secured creditors become **unsecured, or general, creditors** for the unrecovered amount, since specific collateral no longer exists. These and all other unsecured creditors will divide up, on a pro rata basis, any funds remaining after all prior claims have been satisfied. If the proceeds from the sale of secured assets are in excess of the claims against them, the excess funds become available to meet claims of unsecured creditors. The complete order of priority of claims is as follows:

secured creditors
Creditors who have specific assets pledged as collateral and in liquidation of the failed firm receive proceeds from the sale of those assets.

unsecured, or general, creditors
Creditors who have a general claim against all the firm's assets other than those specifically pledged as collateral.

1. The expenses of administering the bankruptcy proceedings.
2. Any unpaid interim expenses incurred in the ordinary course of business between filing the bankruptcy petition and the entry of an Order for Relief in an involuntary proceeding. (This step is *not* applicable in a voluntary bankruptcy.)
3. Wages of not more than $2,000 per worker that have been earned by workers in the 90-day period immediately preceding the commencement of bankruptcy proceedings.

4. Unpaid employee benefit plan contributions that were to be paid in the 180-day period preceding the filing of bankruptcy or the termination of business, whichever occurred first. For any employee, the sum of this claim plus eligible unpaid wages (item 3) cannot exceed $2,000.
5. Claims of farmers or fishermen in a grain-storage or fish-storage facility, not to exceed $2,000 for each producer.
6. Unsecured customer deposits, not to exceed $900 each, resulting from purchasing or leasing a good or service from the failed firm.
7. Taxes legally due and owed by the bankrupt firm to the federal government, state government, or any other governmental subdivision.
8. Claims of secured creditors, who receive the proceeds from the sale of collateral held, regardless of the priorities above. If the proceeds from the liquidation of the collateral are insufficient to satisfy the secured creditors' claims, the secured creditors become unsecured creditors for the unpaid amount.
9. Claims of unsecured creditors. The claims of unsecured, or general, creditors and unsatisfied portions of secured creditors' claims (item 8) are all treated equally.
10. Preferred stockholders, who receive an amount up to the par, or stated, value of their preferred stock.
11. Common stockholders, who receive any remaining funds, which are distributed on an equal per-share basis. If different classes of common stock are outstanding (see Chapter 13), priorities may exist.

In spite of the priorities listed in items 1 through 7, secured creditors have first claim on proceeds from the sale of their collateral. The claims of unsecured creditors, including the unpaid claims of secured creditors, are satisfied next and, finally, the claims of preferred and common stockholders. The application of these priorities by the trustee in bankruptcy liquidation proceedings can be illustrated by a simple example.

EXAMPLE

Cambridge Company, a manufacturer of portable computers, has the balance sheet presented in Table 19.9. The trustee, as was her obligation, has liquidated the firm's assets, obtaining the highest amounts she could get. She managed to obtain $2.3 million for the firm's current assets and $2 million for the firm's fixed assets. The total proceeds from the liquidation were therefore $4.3 million. It should be clear that the firm is legally bankrupt, since its liabilities of $5.6 million dollars exceed the $4.3 million fair market value of its assets.

The next step is to distribute the proceeds to the various creditors. The only liability that is not shown on the balance sheet is $800,000 in expenses for administering the bankruptcy proceedings and satisfying unpaid bills incurred between the time of filing the bankruptcy petition and the entry of an Order for Relief. The distribution of the $4.3 million among the firm's creditors is shown in Table 19.10. The table shows that once all prior claims on the proceeds from liquidation have been satisfied, the unsecured creditors get the remaining funds. The pro rata distribution of the $700,000 among the unsecured creditors is given in Table 19.11, on page 796. The disposition of funds in the Cambridge Company liquidation should be clear from Tables 19.10 and 19.11. Since the claims of the unsecured creditors have not been fully satisfied, the preferred and common stockholders receive nothing. ■

FINAL ACCOUNTING

After the trustee has liquidated all the bankrupt firm's assets and distributed the proceeds to satisfy all provable claims in the appropriate order of priority, he or she makes

TABLE 19.9

BALANCE SHEET FOR CAMBRIDGE COMPANY

Assets		Liabilities and stockholders' equity	
Cash	$ 10,000	Accounts payable	$ 200,000
Marketable securities	5,000	Notes payable—bank	1,000,000
Accounts receivable	1,090,000	Accrued wages[a]	320,000
Inventories	3,100,000	Unpaid employee benefits[b]	80,000
Prepaid expenses	5,000	Unsecured customer deposits[c]	100,000
Total current assets	$4,210,000	Taxes payable	300,000
Land	$2,000,000	Total current liabilities	$2,000,000
Net plant	1,810,000	First mortgage[d]	$1,800,000
Net equipment	80,000	Second mortgage[d]	1,000,000
Total fixed assets	$3,890,000	Unsecured bonds	800,000
Total	$8,100,000	Total long-term debt	$3,600,000
		Preferred stock (5,000 shares)	$ 400,000
		Common stock (10,000 shares)	500,000
		Paid-in capital in excess of par	1,500,000
		Retained earnings	100,000
		Total stockholders' equity	$2,500,000
		Total	$8,100,000

[a]Represents wages of $800 per employee earned within 90 days of filing bankruptcy for 400 of the firm's employees.

[b]These unpaid employee benefits were due in the 180-day period preceding the firm's bankruptcy filing, which occurred simultaneously with the termination of its business.

[c]Unsecured customer deposits not exceeding $900 each.

[d]The first and second mortgages are on the firm's total fixed assets.

a final accounting to the bankruptcy court and creditors. Once the court approves the final accounting, the liquidation is complete.

TABLE 19.10

DISTRIBUTION OF THE LIQUIDATION PROCEEDS OF CAMBRIDGE COMPANY

Proceeds from liquidation	$4,300,000
−Expenses of administering bankruptcy and paying interim bills	$ 800,000
−Wages owed workers	320,000
−Unpaid employee benefits	80,000
−Unsecured customer deposits	100,000
−Taxes owed governments	300,000
Funds available for creditors	$2,700,000
−First mortgage, paid from the $2 million proceeds from the sale of fixed assets	$1,800,000
−Second mortgage, partially paid from the remaining $200,000 of fixed assets proceeds	200,000
Funds available for unsecured creditors	$ 700,000

TABLE 19.11

PRO RATA DISTRIBUTION OF FUNDS AMONG UNSECURED CREDITORS OF CAMBRIDGE COMPANY

Unsecured creditors' claims	Amount	Settlement at 25%[a]
Unpaid balance of second mortgage	$ 800,000[b]	$200,000
Accounts payable	200,000	50,000
Notes payable—bank	1,000,000	250,000
Unsecured bonds	800,000	200,000
Totals	$2,800,000	$700,000

[a]The 25 percent rate is calculated by dividing the $700,000 available for unsecured creditors by the $2.8 million owed unsecured creditors. Each is entitled to a pro rata share.

[b]This figure represents the difference between the $1 million second mortgage and the $200,000 payment on the second mortgage from the proceeds from the sale of the collateral remaining after satisfying the first mortgage.

CONCEPTS IN REVIEW

19-14 What is the concern of Chapter 11 of the Bankruptcy Reform Act of 1978? How is the *debtor in possession (DIP)* involved in (1) the valuation of the firm, (2) the recapitalization of the firm, and (3) the exchange of obligations using the priority rule?

19-15 What is the concern of Chapter 7 of the Bankruptcy Reform Act of 1978? Under which conditions is a firm liquidated in bankruptcy? Describe the procedures (including the role of the *trustee*) involved in liquidating the bankrupt firm.

19-16 In which order would the following claims be settled in distributing the proceeds from liquidating a bankrupt firm?

- **a.** Claims of preferred stockholders
- **b.** Claims of secured creditors
- **c.** Expenses of administering the bankruptcy
- **d.** Claims of common stockholders
- **e.** Claims of unsecured, or general, creditors
- **f.** Taxes legally due
- **g.** Unsecured deposits of customers
- **h.** Certain eligible wages
- **i.** Unpaid employee benefit plan contributions
- **j.** Unpaid interim expenses incurred between the time of filing and the entry of an Order for Relief
- **k.** Claims of farmers or fishermen in a grain-storage or fish-storage facility

Summary

LG **1 Understand merger fundamentals, including basic terminology, motives for merging, and types of mergers.** Mergers, including consolidations, result from the combining of firms. Typically, the acquiring company pursues and attempts to merge with the target company, on either a friendly or a hostile basis. Mergers are undertaken either for strategic reasons to achieve economies of scale or for financial reasons to restructure the firm to improve its cash flow. Although the overriding goal of merging is maximization of owners' wealth (share price), other specific merger motives include growth or diversification, synergy, fund raising, increased managerial skill or technology, tax considerations, increased ownership liquidity, and defense against takeover. The four basic types of mergers are horizontal—the merger of two firms in the same line of business, vertical—acquisition of a supplier or customer, congeneric—acquisition of a firm in the same general industry but neither in the same business nor a supplier or customer, and conglomerate—merger between unrelated businesses.

LG 2 **Describe the objectives and procedures used in leveraged buyouts (LBOs) and divestitures.** A popular technique for structuring financial mergers during the 1980s was the leveraged buyout (LBO), a financial merger involving the use of a large amount of debt to purchase a firm. While still used today, LBOs are fewer in number and generally used for management buyouts. Divestiture involves the sale of a firm's assets, typically an operating unit, to another firm or existing management, the spin-off of assets into an independent company, or the liquidation of assets. Motives for divestiture include cash generation and corporate restructuring consistent with strategic goals. The result is typically a more focused and efficient company.

LG 3 **Demonstrate the procedures used to analyze mergers, including valuing the target company and the effect of stock swap transactions on earnings per share.** The value of a target company can be estimated by using valuation techniques. Capital budgeting techniques are applied to the relevant cash flows whether the target firm is being acquired for its assets or as a going concern. All proposed mergers with positive net present values would be considered acceptable. In a stock swap transaction in which an exchange of common stock is used to pay for the acquisition, a ratio of exchange must be established. This ratio measures the amount paid per share of the target company relative to the per-share market price of the acquiring firm. The resulting relationship between the price/earnings (P/E) ratio paid by the acquiring firm and its initial P/E affects the merged firm's earnings per share (EPS) and market price. If the P/E paid is greater than the P/E of the acquiring company, the EPS of the acquiring company decreases and the EPS of the target company increases; if the P/E paid is less than the P/E of the acquiring firm, the converse is the case.

LG 4 **Discuss the merger negotiation process, the role of holding companies, and international mergers.** Investment bankers are commonly hired by the acquirer to find a suitable target company and assist in negotiations. A merger can be negotiated with the target firm's management or, in the case of a hostile merger, directly with the firm's shareholders by using tender offers. When the management of the target firm does not favor the merger, it can employ any of a number of takeover defenses, which include a white knight, poison pills, greenmail, leveraged recapitalization, golden parachutes, and shark repellents. A holding company can be created by one firm gaining control of other companies, often by owning as little as 10 to 20 percent of their stock. The chief advantages of holding companies are the leverage effect, risk protection, tax benefits, protection against lawsuits, and the fact that it is generally easy to gain control of a subsidiary. Commonly cited disadvantages include increased risk due to the magnification of losses, double taxation, difficulty of analysis, and the high cost of administration. While U.S. merger practices differ greatly from practices in other countries, during recent years mergers of companies in western European countries have exploded as they move toward the U.S.-style corporate control and financing model, and both European and Japanese companies have become active acquirers of U.S. companies.

LG 5 **Understand the types and major causes of business failure and the use of voluntary settlements to sustain or liquidate the failed firm.** A firm may fail because it has negative or low returns, because it is technically insolvent, or because it is bankrupt. The major causes of business failure are mismanagement, downturns in economic activity, and corporate maturity. Voluntary settlements are initiated by the debtor and can result in sustaining the firm through an extension, a composition, creditor control of the firm, or a combination of these strategies. If creditors do not agree to a plan to sustain a firm, they may recommend voluntary liquidation, which bypasses many of the legal requirements and costs of bankruptcy proceedings.

LG 6 **Explain bankruptcy legislation and the procedures involved in reorganizing or liquidating a bankrupt firm.** A failed firm that cannot or does not want to arrange a voluntary settlement can voluntarily or involuntarily file in federal bankruptcy court for reorganization under Chapter 11 or liquidation under Chapter 7 of the Bankruptcy Reform Act of 1978. Under Chapter 11 the judge will appoint the debtor in possession, who with court supervision develops, if feasible, a reorganization plan. A firm that cannot be reorganized under Chapter 11 of the bankruptcy law or does not petition for reorganization is liquidated under Chapter 7. The responsibility for liquidation is placed in the hands of a court-appointed trustee, whose duties include the liquidation of assets, the distribution of the proceeds, and making a final accounting. Liquidation procedures follow a priority of claims for distribution of the proceeds from the sale of assets.

Self-test problems (Solutions in Appendix E)

ST 19-1 LG 3 **Cash acquisition decision** Luxe Foods is contemplating acquisition of Valley Canning Company for a cash price of $180,000. Luxe currently has high financial leverage and therefore has a cost of capital of 14 percent. As a result of acquiring Valley Canning, which is financed entirely with equity, the firm expects its financial leverage to be reduced and its cost of capital therefore to drop to 11 percent. The acquisition of Valley Canning is expected to increase Luxe's cash inflows by $20,000 per year for the first 3 years and by $30,000 per year for the following 12 years.

a. Determine whether the proposed cash acquisition is desirable. Explain your answer.

b. If the firm's financial leverage would actually remain unchanged as a result of the proposed acquisition, would this alter your recommendation? Support your answer with numerical data.

ST 19-2 LG 3 **Expected EPS—Merger decision** At the end of 1994, Lake Industries had 80,000 shares of common stock outstanding and had earnings available for common of $160,000. The Butler Company, at the end of 1994, had 10,000 shares of common stock outstanding and had earned $20,000 for common shareholders. Lake's earnings are expected to grow at an annual rate of 5 percent, while Butler's growth rate in earnings should be 10 percent per year.

a. Calculate earnings per share (EPS) for Lake Industries for each of the next five years, assuming that there is no merger.

b. Calculate the next five years' earnings per share (EPS) for Lake if it acquires Butler at a ratio of exchange of 1.1.

c. Compare your findings in **a** and **b**, and explain why the merger looks attractive when viewed over the long run.

ST 19-3 LG 6 **Liquidation and priority of claims** The Leto Company recently failed and was left with the balance sheet shown below. The trustee liquidated the firm's assets, obtaining net proceeds of $2.2 mil-

Balance sheet of Leto Company

Assets		Liabilities and stockholders' equity	
Cash	$ 80,000	Accounts payable	$ 400,000
Marketable securities	10,000	Notes payable—bank	800,000
Accounts receivable	1,090,000	Accrued wages[a]	500,000
Inventories	2,300,000	Unpaid employee benefits[b]	100,000
Prepaid expenses	20,000	Unsecured customer deposits[c]	50,000
		Taxes payable	250,000
Total current assets	$3,500,000	Total current liabilities	$2,100,000
Land	$1,000,000	First mortgage[d]	$2,000,000
Net plant	2,000,000	Second mortgage[d]	800,000
Net equipment	1,500,000	Unsecured bonds	500,000
Total fixed assets	$4,500,000	Total long-term debt	$3,300,000
Total	$8,000,000	Preferred stock (10,000 shares)	$300,000
		Common stock (5,000 shares)	300,000
		Paid-in capital in excess of par	1,500,000
		Retained earnings	500,000
		Total stockholders' equity	$2,600,000
		Total	$8,000,000

[a]Represents wages of $250 per employee earned within 90 days of filing bankruptcy for 2,000 of the firm's employees.

[b]These unpaid employee benefits were due in the 180-day period preceding the firm's bankruptcy filing, which occurred simultaneously with the termination of its business.

[c]Unsecured customer deposits not exceeding $900 each.

[d]The first and second mortgages are on the firm's total fixed assets.

lion from the current assets and $2.5 million from the fixed assets. In the process of liquidating the assets, the trustee incurred expenses totaling $400,000. Because of the speed with which the Order for Relief was entered, no interim expenses were incurred.

a. Prepare a table indicating the amount, if any, to be distributed to each claimant except unsecured creditors. Indicate the amount to be paid, if any, to the group of unsecured creditors.

b. After all claims other than those of unsecured creditors have been satisfied, how much, if any, is still owed to the second-mortgage holders? Why?

c. Prepare a table showing how the remaining funds, if any, would be distributed to the firm's unsecured creditors.

Problems

19-1 LG 1,3 Tax effects of acquisition The Connors Shoe Company is contemplating the acquisition of Salinas Boots, a firm that has shown large operating tax losses over the past few years. As a result of the acquisition, Connors believes that the total pretax profits of the merger will not change from their present level for 15 years. The tax loss carryforward of Salinas is $800,000, while Connors projects annual earnings before taxes to be $280,000 per year for each of the next 15 years. These earnings are assumed to fall within the annual limit legally allowed for application of the tax loss carryforward resulting from the proposed merger (see footnote 3 on page 767). The firm is in the 40 percent tax bracket.

a. If Connors does not make the acquisition, what are the company's tax liability and earnings after taxes each year over the next 15 years?

b. If the acquisition is made, what are the company's tax liability and earnings after taxes each year over the next 15 years?

c. If Salinas can be acquired for $350,000 in cash, should Connors make the acquisition, based on tax considerations? (Ignore present value.)

19-2 LG 1,3 Tax effects of acquisition Trapani Tool Company is evaluating the acquisition of Sussman Casting. Sussman has a tax loss carryforward of $1.8 million. Trapani can purchase Sussman for $2.1 million. It can sell the assets for $1.6 million—their book value. Trapani expects earnings before taxes in the five years after the merger to be as follows:

Year	Earnings before taxes
1	$150,000
2	400,000
3	450,000
4	600,000
5	600,000

The expected earnings given above are assumed to fall within the annual limit that is legally allowed for application of the tax loss carryforward resulting from the proposed merger (see footnote 3 on page 767). Trapani is in the 40 percent tax bracket.

a. Calculate the firm's tax payments and earnings after taxes for each of the next five years *without* the merger.

b. Calculate the firm's tax payments and earnings after taxes for each of the next five years *with* the merger.

c. What are the total benefits associated with the tax losses from the merger? (Ignore present value.)

d. Discuss whether you would recommend the proposed merger. Support your decision with figures.

19-3 LG 1,3 Tax benefits and price Hahn Textiles has a tax loss carryforward of $800,000. Two firms are interested in acquiring Hahn for the tax loss advantage. Reilly Investment Group has expected earnings before taxes of $200,000 per year for each of the next seven years and a cost of capital of 15 percent. Webster Industries has expected earnings before taxes for the next seven years as indicated:

Webster Industries	
Year	**Earnings before taxes**
1	$ 80,000
2	120,000
3	200,000
4	300,000
5	400,000
6	400,000
7	500,000

Both Reilly's and Webster's expected earnings are assumed to fall within the annual limit legally allowed for application of the tax loss carryforward resulting from the proposed merger (see footnote 3 on page 767). Webster has a cost of capital of 15 percent. Both firms are subject to 40 percent tax rates on ordinary income.

a. What is the tax advantage of the merger each year for Reilly?
b. What is the tax advantage of the merger each year for Webster?
c. What is the maximum cash price each interested firm would be willing to pay for Hahn Textiles? (*Hint:* Calculate the present value of the tax advantages.)
d. Use your answers in **a** through **c** to explain why a target company can have different values to different potential acquiring firms.

19-4 LG 3 Asset acquisition decision Zarin Printing Company is considering the acquisition of Freiman Press at a cash price of $60,000. Freiman Press has liabilities of $90,000. Freiman has a large press that Zarin needs; the remaining assets would be sold to net $65,000. As a result of acquiring the press, Zarin would experience an increase in cash inflow of $20,000 per year over the next 10 years. The firm has a 14 percent cost of capital.

a. What is the effective or net cost of the large press?
b. If this is the only way Zarin can obtain the large press, should the firm go ahead with the merger? Explain your answer.
c. If the firm could purchase a press that would provide slightly better quality and $26,000 annual cash inflow for 10 years for a price of $120,000, which alternative would you recommend? Explain your answer.

19-5 LG 3 Cash acquisition decision Benson Oil is being considered for acquisition by Dodd Oil. The combination, Dodd believes, would increase its cash inflows by $25,000 for each of the next five years and $50,000 for each of the following five years. Benson has high financial leverage, and Dodd can expect its cost of capital to increase from 12 to 15 percent if the merger is undertaken. The cash price of Benson is $125,000.

a. Would you recommend the merger?
b. Would you recommend the merger if Dodd could use the $125,000 to purchase equipment returning cash inflows of $40,000 per year for each of the next 10 years?
c. If the cost of capital does not change with the merger, would your decision in **b** be different? Explain.

19-6 LG 3 Ratio of exchange and EPS Marla's Cafe is attempting to acquire the Victory Club. Certain financial data on these corporations are summarized as follows:

Item	Marla's Cafe	Victory Club
Earnings available for common stock	$20,000	$8,000
Number of shares of common stock outstanding	20,000	4,000
Market price per share	$12	$24

Marla's Cafe has sufficient authorized but unissued shares to carry out the proposed merger.

a. If the ratio of exchange is 1.8, what will be the earnings per share (EPS) based on the original shares of each firm?

b. If the ratio of exchange is 2.0, what will be the earnings per share (EPS) based on the original shares of each firm?

c. If the ratio of exchange is 2.2, what will be the earnings per share (EPS) based on the original shares of each firm?

d. Discuss the principle illustrated by your answers to **a** through **c**.

19-7 LG 3 **EPS and merger terms** Cleveland Corporation is interested in acquiring the Lewis Tool Company by swapping $4/10$ shares of its stock for each share of Lewis stock. Certain financial data on these companies are given.

Item	Cleveland Corporation	Lewis Tool
Earnings available for common stock	$200,000	$50,000
Number of shares of common stock outstanding	50,000	20,000
Earnings per share (EPS)	$4.00	$2.50
Market price per share	$50.00	$15.00
Price/earnings (P/E) ratio	12.5	6

Cleveland has sufficient authorized but unissued shares to carry out the proposed merger.

a. How many new shares of stock will Cleveland have to issue to make the proposed merger?

b. If the earnings for each firm remain unchanged, what will the postmerger earnings per share be?

c. How much, effectively, has been earned on behalf of each of the original shares of Lewis stock?

d. How much, effectively, has been earned on behalf of each of the original shares of Cleveland Corporation's stock?

19-8 LG 3 **Ratio of exchange** Calculate the ratio of exchange (1) of shares and (2) in market price for each of the following cases. What does each ratio signify? Explain.

	Current market price per share		
Case	Acquiring company	Target company	Price per share offered
A	$50	$25	$ 30.00
B	80	80	100.00
C	40	60	70.00
D	50	10	12.50
E	25	20	25.00

19-9 LG 3 Expected EPS—Merger decision Graham & Sons wishes to evaluate a proposed merger into the RCN Group. Graham had 1994 earnings of $200,000, has 100,000 shares of common stock outstanding, and expects earnings to grow at an annual rate of 7 percent. RCN had 1994 earnings of $800,000, has 200,000 shares of common stock outstanding, and expects its earnings to grow at 3 percent per year.

a. Calculate the expected earnings per share (EPS) for Graham & Sons for each of the next five years without the merger.

b. What would Graham's stockholders earn in each of the next five years on each of their Graham shares swapped for RCN shares at a ratio of (1) 0.6 and (2) 0.8 shares of RCN for one share of Graham?

c. Graph the premerger and postmerger EPS figures developed in **a** and **b** on a set of year (x-axis)–EPS (y-axis) axes.

d. If you were the financial manager for Graham & Sons, which would you recommend from **b**, (1) or (2)? Explain your answer.

19-10 LG 3 EPS and postmerger price Data for the Henry Company and Mayer Services are given. Henry Company is considering merging with Mayer by swapping 1.25 shares of its stock for each share of Mayer stock. Henry Company expects to sell at the same price/earnings (P/E) multiple after the merger as before merging.

Item	Henry Company	Mayer Services
Earnings available for common stock	$225,000	$50,000
Number of shares of common stock outstanding	90,000	15,000
Market price per share	$45	$50

a. Calculate the ratio of exchange in market price.

b. Calculate the earnings per share (EPS) and price/earnings (P/E) ratio for each company.

c. Calculate the price/earnings (P/E) ratio used to purchase Mayer Services.

d. Calculate the postmerger earnings per share (EPS) for the Henry Company.

e. Calculate the expected market price per share of the merged firm. Discuss this result in light of your findings in **a**.

19-11 LG 4 Holding company Scully Corporation holds stock in company A and company B. Simplified balance sheets for the companies are presented at the top of page 803. Scully has voting control over both company A and company B.

a. What percentage of the total assets controlled by Scully Corporation does its common stock equity represent?

b. If another company owns 15 percent of the common stock of Scully Corporation and, by virtue of this fact, has voting control, what percentage of the total assets controlled does the outside company's equity represent?

c. How does a holding company effectively provide a great deal of control for a small dollar investment?

d. Answer **a** and **b** in light of the following additional facts.

(1) Company A's fixed assets consist of $20,000 of common stock in company C. This provides voting control.

(2) Company C, which has total assets of $400,000, has voting control of company D, which has $50,000 of total assets.

(3) Company B's fixed assets consist of $60,000 of stock in both company E and company F. In both cases this gives it voting control. Companies E and F have total assets of $300,000 and $400,000, respectively.

Assets		Liabilities and stockholders' equity	
Scully Corporation			
Common stock holdings		Long-term debt	$ 40,000
Company A	$ 40,000	Preferred stock	25,000
Company B	60,000	Common stock equity	35,000
Total	$100,000	Total	$100,000
Company A			
Current assets	$100,000	Current liabilities	$100,000
Fixed assets	400,000	Long-term debt	200,000
Total	$500,000	Common stock equity	200,000
		Total	$500,000
Company B			
Current assets	$180,000	Current liabilities	$100,000
Fixed assets	720,000	Long-term debt	500,000
Total	$900,000	Common stock equity	300,000
		Total	$900,000

19-12 LG 5 Voluntary settlements Classify each of the following voluntary settlements as an extension, a composition, or a combination of the two.

a. Paying all creditors 30 cents on the dollar in exchange for complete discharge of the debt.
b. Paying all creditors in full in three periodic installments.
c. Paying a group of creditors with claims of $10,000 in full over two years and immediately paying the remaining creditors 75 cents on the dollar.

19-13 LG 5 Voluntary settlements For a firm with outstanding debt of $125,000, classify each of the following voluntary settlements as an extension, a composition, or a combination of the two.

a. Paying a group of creditors in full in four periodic installments and paying the remaining creditors in full immediately.
b. Paying a group of creditors 90 cents on the dollar immediately and paying the remaining creditors 80 cents on the dollar in two periodic installments.
c. Paying all creditors 15 cents on the dollar.
d. Paying all creditors in full in 180 days.

19-14 LG 5 Voluntary settlements—Payments Jacobi Supply Company recently ran into certain financial difficulties that have resulted in the initiation of voluntary settlement procedures. The firm currently has $150,000 in outstanding debts and approximately $75,000 in liquidable short-term assets. Indicate, for each plan below, whether the plan is an extension, a composition, or a combination of the two. Also indicate the cash payments and timing of the payments required of the firm under each plan.

a. Each creditor will be paid 50 cents on the dollar immediately, and the debts will be considered fully satisfied.
b. Each creditor will be paid 80 cents on the dollar in two quarterly installments of 50 cents and 30 cents. The first installment is to be paid in 90 days.
c. Each creditor will be paid the full amount of its claims in three installments of 50 cents, 25 cents, and 25 cents on the dollar. The installments will be made in 60-day intervals, beginning in 60 days.
d. A group of creditors with claims of $50,000 will be immediately paid in full; the rest will be paid 85 cents on the dollar, payable in 90 days.

19-15 LG 6 Unsecured creditors A firm has $450,000 in funds to distribute to its unsecured creditors. Three possible sets of unsecured creditor claims are presented. Calculate the settlement, if any, to be received by each creditor in each case.

Unsecured creditors' claims	Case I	Case II	Case III
Unpaid balance of second mortgage	$300,000	$200,000	$ 500,000
Accounts payable	200,000	100,000	300,000
Notes payable—bank	300,000	100,000	500,000
Unsecured bonds	100,000	200,000	500,000
Total	$900,000	$600,000	$1,800,000

19-16 LG 6 Liquidation and priority of claims Keck Business Forms recently failed and was liquidated by a court-appointed trustee who charged $200,000 for her services. Between the time of filing of the bankruptcy petition and the entry of an Order for Relief, a total of $100,000 in unpaid bills was incurred and remain unpaid. The preliquidation balance sheet follows.

Assets		Liabilities and stockholders' equity	
Cash	$ 40,000	Accounts payable	$ 200,000
Marketable securities	30,000	Notes payable—bank	300,000
Accounts receivable	620,000	Accrued wages[a]	50,000
Inventories	1,200,000	Unsecured customer deposits[b]	30,000
Prepaid expenses	10,000	Taxes payable	20,000
Total current assets	$1,900,000	Total current liabilities	$ 600,000
		First mortgage[c]	$ 700,000
Land	$ 300,000	Second mortgage[c]	400,000
Net plant	400,000	Unsecured bonds	300,000
Net equipment	400,000	Total long-term debt	$1,400,000
Total fixed assets	$1,100,000	Preferred stock (15,000 shares)	$ 200,000
Total	$3,000,000	Common stock (10,000 shares)	200,000
		Paid-in capital in excess of par	500,000
		Retained earnings	100,000
		Total stockholders' equity	$1,000,000
		Total	$3,000,000

[a]Represents wages of $500 per employee earned within 90 days of filing bankruptcy for 100 of the firm's employees.

[b]Unsecured customer deposits not exceeding $900 each.

[c]The first and second mortgages are on the firm's total fixed assets.

a. Assume that the trustee liquidates the assets for $2.5 million—$1.3 million from current assets and $1.2 million from fixed assets.

(1) Prepare a table indicating the amount to be distributed to each claimant. Indicate whether the claimant is an unsecured creditor.
(2) Before satisfying unsecured creditor claims, how much is owed to first-mortgage holders and second-mortgage holders?
(3) Do the firm's owners receive any funds? If so, in what amounts?

b. Assume the trustee liquidates the assets for $1.8 million—$1.2 million from current assets and $600,000 from fixed assets; rework your answers in **a**.

c. Compare, contrast, and discuss your findings in **a** and **b**.

Chapter 19 Case Deciding whether to acquire or liquidate Procras Corporation

Sharon Scotia, CFO of Rome Industries, must decide what to do about Procras Corporation, a major customer that is bankrupt. Rome Industries is a large plastic-injection-molding firm that produces plastic products to customer order. Procras Corporation is a major customer of Rome Industries that designs and markets a variety of plastic toys. As a result of mismanagement and inventory problems, Procras has become bankrupt. Among its unsecured debts are total past due accounts of $1.9 million owed to Rome Industries.

Recognizing that it is probably cannot recover the full $1.9 million that Procras Corporation owes it, the management of Rome Industries has isolated two mutually exclusive alternative actions: (1) Acquire Procras through an exchange of stock or (2) let Procras be liquidated and recover Rome Industries' proportionate claim against any funds available for unsecured creditors. Rome's management feels that acquisition of Procras would have appeal in that it would allow Rome to vertically integrate and expand its business from strictly industrial manufacturing to include product development and marketing. Of course, the firm wants to select the alternative that will create the most value for its shareholders. Charged with making a recommendation as to whether Rome should acquire Procras Corporation or allow it to be liquidated, Ms. Scotia gathered the following data.

Acquire Procras Corporation Negotiations with Procras management have resulted in a planned ratio of exchange of .60 Rome Industries' shares for each share of Procras Corporation common stock. The following table reflects current data for Rome Industries and Rome's expectations of the data values for Procras Corporation with proper management in place.

Item	Rome Industries	Procras Corporation
Earnings available for common stock	$640,000	$180,000
Number of shares of common stock outstanding	400,000	60,000
Market price per share	$32	$30

Rome Industries estimates that after the proposed acquisition of Procras Corporation its price/earnings (P/E) ratio will be 18.5.

Liquidation of Procras Corporation Procras Corporation was denied its petition for reorganization, and the court-appointed trustee was expected to charge $150,000 for his services in liquidating the firm. In addition, $100,000 in unpaid bills were expected to be incurred between the time of filing the bankruptcy petition and the entry of an Order for Relief. The firm's preliquidation balance sheet is given below.

Assets		Liabilities and stockholders' equity	
Cash	$ 20,000	Accounts payable	$2,700,000
Marketable securities	1,000	Notes payable—bank	1,300,000
Accounts receivable	1,800,000	Accrued wages[a]	120,000
Inventories	3,000,000	Unsecured customer deposits[b]	60,000
Prepaid expenses	14,000	Taxes payable	70,000
Total current assets	$4,835,000	Total current liabilities	$4,250,000
Land	$ 415,000	First mortgage[c]	$ 300,000
Net plant	200,000	Second mortgage[c]	200,000
Net equipment	350,000	Unsecured bonds	400,000
Total fixed assets	$ 965,000	Total long-term debt	$ 900,000
Total	$5,800,000	Common stock (60,000 shares)	$ 120,000
		Paid-in capital in excess of par	480,000
		Retained earnings	50,000
		Total stockholders' equity	$ 650,000
		Total	$5,800,000

[a]Represents wages of $600 per employee earned within 90 days of filing bankruptcy for 200 of the firm's employees.

[b]Unsecured customer deposits not exceeding $900 each.

[c]The first and second mortgages are on the firm's total fixed assets.

The trustee expects to liquidate the assets for $3.2 million—$2.5 million from current assets and $.7 million from fixed assets.

Required

a. Calculate (1) the ratio of exchange in market price and (2) the earnings per share (EPS) and price/earnings (P/E) ratio for each company based on the data given in the acquisition alternative table on page 805.

b. Find the postmerger earnings per share (EPS) for Rome Industries assuming that it acquires Procras Corporation under the terms given above.

c. Use the estimated postmerger price/earnings (P/E) ratio and your finding in **b** to find the postmerger share price.

d. Use your finding in **c** to determine how much, if any, the *total market value* of Rome Industries will change as a result of acquiring Procras Corporation.

e. Determine how much each claimant will receive if Procras Corporation is liquidated under the terms given.

f. How much, if any, will Rome Industries recover of its $1.9 million balance due from Procras Corporation as a result of liquidation of Procras?

g. Compare your findings in **d** and **f**, and make a recommendation for Rome Industries with regard to its best action—acquisition of Procras or its liquidation.

h. Which alternative would the shareholders of Procras Corporation prefer? Why?

chapter 20

International managerial finance

LEARNING GOALS

LG 1 Understand the major factors influencing the financial operations of multinational companies (MNCs).

LG 2 Describe the key differences between purely domestic and international financial statements—particularly consolidation, translation of individual accounts, and international profits.

LG 3 Discuss the two risks—exchange rate and political—requiring special consideration by the multinational company, and explain how MNCs manage them.

LG 4 Describe foreign investment cash flows and decisions, the factors that influence an MNC's capital structure, and the international debt and equity instruments that are available to MNCs.

LG 5 Demonstrate use of the Eurocurrency market in short-term borrowing and investing (lending) and the basics of cash, credit and inventory management in international operations.

LG 6 Discuss the growth of and special factors relating to international mergers and joint ventures.

Today's speed of communications and ease of traveling have made most of the world a global marketplace. The same consumer products are available in Europe, Latin America, and Asia as in the United States. Debt and equity financing have become global in concept and execution. To survive in the 21st century, managers must understand how business is conducted internationally.

The Gillette Company became multinational within seven years of incorporating in the United States in 1901, establishing manufacturing operations in Europe and Canada. Expansion overseas was due to the immediate success of our product—Gillette invented the safety razor—and patent laws in some countries that protected the product only if it was manufactured locally. Over time we acquired other consumer product lines such as toiletries, pens and stationery products, toothbrushes, and personal appliances. Today, Gillette manufactures in 57 locations in 28 countries and markets in over 200 countries. Our international business has grown twice as fast as our U.S. business in the past five years because the United States is a mature market for most of our products. Currently, non-U.S. operations account for 69 percent of sales, 72 percent of operating profits, and 67 percent of assets.

Operating internationally means dealing with heavy political and financial risks. Political risk could involve expropriation of company-owned assets, which we experienced in Cuba and Iran, price freezes or controls, or closing the borders for products or funds flow. Financial risk is primarily exchange-related, such as sudden large currency devaluations. When these occur, as happened in 1993 in Spain and Italy, price increases cannot, in the short term, compensate for revenue loss. We use currency hedging to reduce financial risk and protect earnings against exchange rate fluctuations.

Financial management becomes extremely complex for a multinational company.

Financial management becomes extremely complex for a multinational company. Preparing financial statements involves translating the accounting conventions used in various countries into U.S. accounting principles. Unfortunately, as yet there are no universal accounting standards. Accounting for foreign exchange becomes quite challenging and complicated, especially in consolidating cash flows.

We are active participants in the international capital markets. Our equity financing originates in the United States, although our stock is also listed on various foreign exchanges. Long-term borrowing, on the other hand, is both U.S.- and foreign-sourced for three reasons. First, interest rates are sometimes lower overseas. Second, our tax position may be better if we borrow abroad. Third, we have a large number of foreign assets. Long-term borrowing in the same place where we have those assets reduces our economic exposure and protects those assets because it is a natural form of hedging.

Although Gillette was one of the first multinational corporations, today most companies operate in the global marketplace. Many foreign corporations now own real estate and corporations in the United States. Working for one of those companies requires understanding its corporate culture, how it operates, and the parent company's social customs, all of which may be quite different from ours. With the growth of international business it is important to gain a breadth of experience and add to your knowledge of what exists in this country.

Anthony Lucas received Bachelor's and M.B.A. degrees from McGill University and then worked for Deloitte Touche in Montreal, during which time he became a Canadian Chartered Accountant. He joined Gillette Canada in 1962 as Assistant to the Controller, became Canadian Controller in 1966, and moved to Gillette's corporate headquarters in Boston in 1968. He held various financial positions, principally in the international area, before becoming Corporate Controller in 1980 and Vice President and Controller in 1983.

The multinational company and its environment

Multinational companies have assets and operations in foreign markets and generate a portion of their total revenue and profits from those operations. As a result, they pay taxes to more than one country and make financial transactions in other countries. How do you think these factors create additional challenges for the financial manager of a multinational company? Before reading on, spend a few moments answering this question.

multinational companies (MNCs)
Firms that have international assets and operations in foreign markets and draw part of their total revenue and profits from such markets.

IN RECENT YEARS, AS WORLD MARKETS HAVE BECOME SIGNIFICANTLY MORE INTERDEPENDENT, international finance has become an increasingly important element in the management of **multinational companies (MNCs).** These firms, being based in the United States, Western Europe, Japan, and many other countries, have international assets and operations in foreign markets and draw part of their total revenue and profits from such markets. The principles of managerial finance presented in this text are applicable to the management of MNCs. However, certain factors unique to the international setting tend to complicate the financial management of multinational companies. A simple comparison between a domestic U.S. firm (firm A) and a U.S.-based MNC (firm B), as illustrated in Table 20.1, can give an indication of the influence of some of the international factors on MNCs' operations.

TABLE 20.1

INTERNATIONAL FACTORS AND THEIR INFLUENCE ON MNCs' OPERATIONS

Factor	Firm A (Domestic)	Firm B (MNC)
Foreign ownership	All assets owned by domestic entities	Portions of equity of foreign investments owned by foreign partners, thus affecting foreign decision making and profits
Multinational capital markets	All debt and equity structures based on the domestic capital market	Opportunities and challenges arise from the existence of different capital markets where debt and equity can be issued
Multinational accounting	All consolidation of financial statements based on one currency	The existence of different currencies and of specific translation rules influences the consolidation of financial statements into one currency
Foreign exchange risks	All operations in one currency	Fluctuations in foreign exchange markets can affect foreign revenues and profits as well as the overall value of the firm

In the present international environment, multinationals face a variety of laws and restrictions when operating in different nation-states. The legal and economic complexities existing in this environment are significantly different from those a domestic firm would face. Here we take a brief look at the newly emerging trading blocs in North America and Western Europe, legal forms of business, taxation of MNCs, and financial markets. Subsequent sections discuss the international aspects of financial statements, risk, long-term investment and financing decisions, short-term financial decisions, and mergers and joint ventures.

Emerging trading blocs: NAFTA and the European Open Market

During the early 1990s, two important trading blocs emerged, centered in North America and Western Europe. Chile, Mexico, and several other Latin American countries began to adopt market-oriented economic policies in the late 1980s, forging very close financial and economic ties to the United States. In 1988, Canada and the United States negotiated essentially unrestricted trade between the countries, and this free trade zone was extended to include Mexico in late 1992 when the **North American Free Trade Agreement (NAFTA)** was signed by the presidents of the United States and Mexico and the Prime Minister of Canada. Eventually, the agreement will probably include Chile and other countries. Although NAFTA has yet to be ratified by the U.S. Senate, the trade pact simply mirrors underlying economic reality. Canada is already the United States' largest trading partner, and Mexico is the third largest (after Japan) and fastest growing U.S. export market.

North American Free Trade Agreement (NAFTA)
The treaty establishing free trade and open markets between Canada, Mexico, and the United States.

The European Economic Community (EC or, as also referred to, EEC) has been in existence since 1959. It has a current membership of 12 nations. With a total population estimated at more than 350 million and an overall gross national income paralleling that of the United States, the EC is a significant global economic force. Now, because of a series of major economic, monetary, financial, and legal provisions set forth by the member countries during the 1980s, the countries of Western Europe opened a new era of free trade within the community when tariff barriers fell at the end of 1992. This transformation is commonly called the **European Open Market.** Although the EC has managed to reach agreements on most of these provisions, debates continue on certain other aspects (some key), including those related to automobile production and imports, monetary union, taxes, and workers' rights.

European Open Market
The transformation of the European Economic Community (EC) into a *single* market at year-end 1992.

It is generally believed that the EC can expect to enjoy enhanced economic growth rates for much of the 1990s and perhaps beyond. The new community will offer both challenges and opportunities to a variety of players, including multinational firms. MNCs, especially those based in the United States, will face heightened levels of competition when operating inside the EC. As more of the existing restrictions and regulations are eliminated, for instance, U.S. multinationals will have to face other MNCs. Some, such as the larger and perhaps more efficient firms resulting from mergers, will come from within the community. Others, including the giants from Japan, could challenge the U.S. MNCs in a manner similar to that already done in the U.S. market.

U.S. companies can benefit from a single European market, but only if they are prepared. They must offer the correct mix of products to a collection of varied consumers and be ready to take advantage of a variety of currencies (including the EC's own, the *European Currency Unit, ECU*) as well as financial markets and instruments (such as the emerging Euro-equities). They must staff their operations with the appropriate combination of local and foreign personnel and, when necessary, enter into joint ventures and strategic alliances.

Legal forms of business

In many countries outside the United States, operating a foreign business as a subsidiary or affiliate can take two forms, both similar to the U.S. corporation. In German-speaking nations the two forms are the *Aktiengesellschaft* (A.G.) or the *Gesellschaft mit beschrankter Haftung* (GmbH). In many other countries the similar forms are a *Société Anonyme* (S.A.) or a *Société à Responsibilité Limitée* (S.A.R.L.). The A.G. or the S.A. is the most common form, but the GmbH or the S.A.R.L. enjoys much greater freedom and requires fewer formalities for formation and operation.

Although establishing a business in a form such as the S.A. can involve most of the provisions that govern a U.S.-based corporation, to operate in many foreign countries, especially in most of the less-developed nations, it is often essential to enter into joint-venture business agreements with private investors or with government-based agencies of the host country. A **joint venture** is a partnership under which the participants have contractually agreed to contribute specified amounts of money and expertise in exchange for stated proportions of ownership and profit. The governments of numerous countries, such as Brazil, Colombia, Mexico, and Venezuela in Latin America as well as Indonesia, Malaysia, the Philippines, and Thailand in East Asia, have in recent years instituted new laws and regulations governing MNCs. The basic rule introduced by most of these nations requires that the majority ownership (i.e., at least 51 percent of the total equity) of MNCs' joint-venture projects be held by domestically based investors. In other regions of the world, MNCs, especially those based in the United States and Japan, will face new challenges and opportunities, particularly in terms of ownership requirements, and mergers. Two regions providing these challenges and opportunities in the near future are Western Europe as it approaches a truly open trading system and Eastern Europe as it attempts to adopt more market-based economic principles.

joint venture
A partnership under which the participants have contractually agreed to contribute specified amounts of money and expertise in exchange for stated proportions of ownership and profit.

The existence of joint-venture laws and restrictions has certain implications for the operation of foreign-based subsidiaries. First of all, majority foreign ownership may result in a substantial degree of management and control by host-country participants; this in turn can influence day-to-day operations to the detriment of the managerial policies and procedures that are normally pursued by MNCs. Next, foreign ownership may result in disagreements among the partners as to the exact distribution of profits and the portion to be allocated for reinvestment. Moreover, operating in foreign countries, especially on a joint-venture basis, can entail problems regarding the actual remission of profits. In the past, the governments of Argentina, Brazil, Nigeria, and Thailand, among others, have imposed ceilings not only on the repatriation (return) of capital by MNCs but also on profit remittances by these firms back to the parent companies. These governments usually cite the shortage of foreign exchange as the motivating factor. Finally, from a "positive" point of view, it can be argued that to operate in many of the less-developed countries, it would be beneficial for MNCs to enter into joint-venture agreements, given the potential risks stemming from political instability in the host countries. This issue will be addressed in detail in subsequent discussions.

CONCEPT IN PRACTICE

U.S. Regulation May Be Foreign, But That's No Defense at Daiwa, Nomura, and Yamaichi

While the difficulties encountered by U.S. firms expanding abroad are widely reported, less attention is paid to the cultural differences faced by foreign firms who do business in the United States. For example, U.S. securities firms diligently ensure that their employees are properly licensed. In contrast, brokers do not have to be licensed in Japan. As a result, Daiwa, Nomura, and Yamaichi, three of the four largest Japanese brokerage firms, have routinely violated U.S. licensing rules and other requirements. In 1991 the Securities and Exchange Commission (SEC) found that 20 of the 50 Daiwa traders who are regularly rotated to the United States did not have sales licenses. In 1992 the SEC accused these firms of reimbursing customers for trading losses, a practice that is not acceptable under U.S. regulations. In 1993 the SEC reported that Yamaichi's head of institutional sales, research, and mergers and acquisitions had not passed a supervisory exam. Because U.S. regulations permit customers to hold firms liable for losses on transactions executed by unregistered representatives, the cost of overlooking U.S. regulations could be high.

Taxes

Multinational companies, unlike domestic firms, have financial obligations—as well as opportunities—in foreign countries. One of their basic responsibilities is international taxation—a complex issue because national governments follow a variety of tax policies. In general, from the point of view of a U.S.-based MNC, several factors must be taken into account.

TAX RATES AND TAXABLE INCOME

First, the *level* of foreign taxes needs to be examined. Among the major industrial countries, corporate tax rates do not vary too widely. For many less industrialized nations, relatively moderate rates are maintained, partly as an incentive for attracting foreign capital inflows. Certain countries, meanwhile, including the Bahamas, Switzerland, Liechtenstein, the Cayman Islands, and Bermuda, are known for their "low" tax levels. These nations typically have no withholding taxes on *intra-MNC dividends.*

Next, there is a question as to the definition of *taxable income.* Some countries tax profits as received on a cash basis, whereas others tax profits earned on an accrual basis. Differences can also exist in treatments of noncash charges, such as depreciation, amortization, and depletion. Finally, the existence of tax agreements between the United States and other governments can influence not only the total tax bill of the parent MNC, but also its international operations and financial activities. Effective January 1, 1988, for example, the U.S. Treasury terminated a 1948 tax treaty with the Netherlands Antilles, affecting about $32 billion of debt issued by U.S.-based MNCs. Under this treaty, debt issued in the Netherlands Antilles had been exempt from a 30 percent withholding tax imposed by the United States.

TAX RULES

Different parent or home countries apply varying tax rates and rules to the global earnings of their own multinationals. Moreover, tax rules are subject to frequent modifications. In the United States, for instance, the Tax Reform Act of 1986 resulted in certain changes affecting the taxation of U.S.-based MNCs. Special provisions apply to tax deferrals by MNCs on foreign income; operations set up in U.S. possesssions, such as the U.S. Virgin Islands, Guam, and American Samoa; capital gains from the sale of stock in a foreign corporation; and withholding taxes. Furthermore, MNCs (both U.S. and foreign) can be subject to national as well as local taxes. As an example, a number of individual state governments in the United States have in recent years introduced new measures—in the form of special **unitary tax laws**—that tax the multinationals on a percentage of their *total* worldwide income rather than, as is generally accepted elsewhere, on their earnings arising within the jurisdiction of each respective government. (As a part of their response to unitary tax laws, the multinationals have already pressured a number of state governments into abolishing the laws. In addition, some MNCs have relocated their investments away from those states that continue to apply such laws.) For updated details on various countries' tax laws, consult relevant publications by international accounting firms.

unitary tax laws
Laws in some U.S. states that tax multinationals (both American and foreign) on a percentage of their *total* worldwide income rather than the usual taxation of the MNCs' earnings arising within their jurisdiction.

As a general practice, the U.S. government claims jurisdiction over *all* the income of an MNC, wherever earned. (Special rules apply to foreign corporations conducting business in the United States.) However, it may be possible for a multinational company to take foreign income taxes as a direct credit against its U.S. tax liabilities. The following simple example illustrates one way of accomplishing this objective.

EXAMPLE

American Enterprises, a U.S.-based MNC that manufactures heavy machinery, has a foreign subsidiary that earns $100,000 before local taxes. All of the after-tax funds are available to the parent in the form of dividends. The applicable taxes consist of a 35 percent foreign income tax rate, a foreign dividend withholding tax rate of 10 percent, and a U.S. tax rate of 34 percent.

Subsidiary income before local taxes	$100,000
Foreign income tax at 35%	− 35,000
Dividend available to be declared	$ 65,000
Foreign dividend withholding tax at 10%	− 6,500
MNC's receipt of dividends	$ 58,500

Using the so-called *grossing up procedure,* the MNC will add the full before-tax subsidiary income to its total taxable income. Next, the U.S. tax liability on the grossed-up income is calculated. Finally, the related taxes paid in the foreign country are applied as a credit against the additional U.S. tax liability.

Additional MNC income		$100,000
U.S. tax liability at 34%	$34,000	
Total foreign taxes paid to be used as a credit ($35,000 + $6,500)	− 41,500	− 41,500
U.S. taxes due		0
Net funds available to the parent MNC		$ 58,500

Since the U.S. tax liability is less than the total taxes paid to the foreign government, *no additional U.S. taxes are due* on the income from the foreign subsidiary. In our example, if tax credits had not been allowed, then "double taxation" by the two authorities, as shown, would have resulted in a substantial drop in the overall net funds available to the parent MNC.

Subsidiary income before local taxes	$100,000
Foreign income tax at 35%	− 35,000
Dividend available to be declared	$ 65,000
Foreign dividend withholding tax at 10%	− 6,500
MNC's receipt of dividends	$ 58,500
U.S. tax liability at 34%	− 19,890
Net funds available to the parent MNC	$ 38,610

■

The preceding example clearly demonstrates that the existence of bilateral tax treaties and the subsequent application of tax credits can significantly enhance the overall net funds available to MNCs from their worldwide earnings. Consequently, in an increasingly complex and competitive international financial environment, international taxation is one of the variables that multinational corporations should fully utilize to their advantage.

Financial markets

Euromarket
The international financial market that provides for borrowing and lending currencies outside their country of origin.

During the last two decades the **Euromarket**—which provides for borrowing and lending currencies outside their country of origin—has grown quite rapidly. The Euromarket provides multinational companies with an "external" opportunity to borrow or lend funds with the additional feature of less government regulation.

GROWTH OF THE EUROMARKET

Several reasons can be offered to explain why the Euromarket has grown so large. First, beginning in the early 1960s, the Russians wanted to maintain their dollar earnings outside the legal jurisdiction of the United States, mainly because of the Cold War. Second, the consistently large U.S. balance of payments deficits helped to "scatter" dollars around the world. Third, the existence of specific regulations and controls on dollar deposits in the United States, including interest rate ceilings imposed by the government, helped to send such deposits to places outside the United States.

These and other factors have combined and contributed to the creation of an "external" capital market whose size cannot be accurately determined, mainly because of its lack of regulation and control. Several sources that periodically estimate its size are the Bank for International Settlements (BIS), Morgan Guaranty Trust, the World Bank, and the Organization for Economic Cooperation and Development (OECD). The latest available estimates put the overall size of the market at over $4.0 trillion *net* international lending.

offshore centers
Certain cities or states (including London, Singapore, Bahrain, Nassau, Hong Kong, and Luxembourg) that have achieved prominence as major centers for Euromarket business.

One aspect of the Euromarket is the so-called **offshore centers.** Certain cities or states around the world—including London, Singapore, Bahrain, Nassau, Hong Kong, and Luxembourg—have achieved prominence and are considered major offshore centers for Euromarket business. The availability of communication and transportation facilities, along with the importance of language, costs, time zones, taxes, and local banking regulations, are among the main reasons for the prominence of these centers.

Another important point to note is that in recent years a variety of new financial instruments have appeared in the international financial markets. One is interest rate and currency swaps (with a total outstanding balance of approximately $4.5 trillion in mid-1993, over half of which is in nondollar currencies). Another is various combinations of forward and options contracts on different currencies. A third is new types of bonds and notes—along with an international version of U.S. commercial paper—with flexible characteristics in terms of currency, maturity, and interest rate. More details will be provided in subsequent discussions.

MAJOR PARTICIPANTS

The Euromarket is still dominated by the U.S. dollar. However, activities in other major currencies, including the Deutsche mark, Swiss franc, Japanese yen, British pound sterling, French franc, and European Currency Unit (ECU), have in recent years grown much faster than those denominated in the U.S. currency. Similarly, while U.S. banks and other financial institutions continue to play a significant role in the global markets, financial giants from Japan and Europe have become major participants in Euromarkets. At the end of 1992, for example, eight of the top ten largest banks in the world as measured in terms of total assets were based in Japan.

Following the oil price increases by the Organization of Petroleum Exporting Countries (OPEC) in 1973–1974 and 1979–1980, massive amounts of dollars were placed in various Euromarket financial centers. International banks, in turn, as part of the so-called *redistribution* of "oil money," began lending to different groups of borrowers. At the end of 1992, for example, a group of Latin American countries had total borrowings outstanding of about $357 billion. Although developing countries have become a major borrowing group in recent years, the industrialized nations continue to borrow actively in international markets. Included in the latter group's borrowings are the funds obtained by multinational companies. The multinationals use the Euromarket to raise additional funds as well as to invest excess cash. Both Eurocurrency and Eurobond markets are extensively used by MNCs. Further details on MNCs' Euromarket activities are presented later.

CONCEPTS IN REVIEW

20-1 What are *NAFTA* and the *European Open Market?* What challenges and opportunities will they offer to MNCs, especially those based in the United States?

20-2 What is a *joint venture?* Why is it often essential to use this arrangement? What effect do joint-venture laws and restrictions have on the operation of foreign-based subsidiaries?

20-3 From the point of view of a U.S.-based MNC, what key tax factors need to be considered? What are *unitary tax laws?*

20-4 Discuss the major reasons for the growth of the Euromarket. What is an *offshore center?* Name the major participants in the Euromarket.

Financial statements

Specific requirements of the government and the accounting profession exist with respect to preparing the financial statements of U.S. multinational corporations. What do you think are the key issues with respect to consolidation, translation of international items for inclusion on domestic statements, and determination of the MNC's profits? Spend a short time responding to this question before reading ahead.

SEVERAL FEATURES DISTINGUISH DOMESTICALLY ORIENTED FINANCIAL STATEMENTS AND internationally based reports. Among these are the issues of consolidation, translation of individual accounts within the financial statements, and overall reporting of international profits.

Consolidation

At the present time, the rules in the United States require the consolidation of financial statements of subsidiaries according to the percentage of ownership by the parent of the subsidiary. Table 20.2 illustrates this point. As indicated, the regulations range from requiring a one-line income-item reporting of dividends to a pro rata inclusion of profits and losses to a full disclosure in the balance sheet and income statement. (When ownership is less than 50 percent, since the balance sheet and thus the subsidiary's financing do not get reported, it is possible for the parent MNC to have off-balance-sheet financing.)

FASB No. 52
Statement issued by the FASB requiring U.S. multinationals first to convert the financial statement accounts of foreign subsidiaries into their *functional currency* and then to translate the accounts into the parent firm's currency using the *all-current-rate method.*

Translation of individual accounts

Unlike domestic items in financial statements, international items require translation back into U.S. dollars. Since December 1982, all financial statements of U.S. multinationals have to conform to Statement No. 52 issued by the Financial Accounting Standards Board (FASB). The basic rules of FASB No. 52 are given in Figure 20.1.

functional currency
The currency of the economic environment in which a business entity primarily generates and expends cash and in which its accounts are maintained.

Under **FASB No. 52,** the *current rate method* is implemented in a two-step process. First, each entity's balance sheet and income statement are *measured* in terms of their functional currency by using generally accepted accounting principles (GAAP). That is, foreign currency elements are translated by each subsidiary into the **functional currency**—the currency of the economic environment in which an entity primarily generates and expends cash and in which its accounts are maintained before financial statements are submitted to the parent for consolidation.

all-current-rate method
The method by which the *functional currency*–denominated financial statements of an MNC's subsidiary are translated into the parent company's currency.

Through the second step, as shown in Figure 20.1, by using the **all-current-rate method** (which requires the translation of all balance sheet items at the closing rate

TABLE 20.2

UNITED STATES RULES FOR CONSOLIDATION OF FINANCIAL STATEMENTS

Percentage of beneficial ownership by parent in subsidiary	Consolidation for financial reporting purposes
0–19%	Dividends as received
20–49%	Pro rata inclusions of profits and losses
50–100%	Full consolidation[a]

[a]Consolidation may be avoided in the case of some majority-owned foreign operations if the parent can convince its auditors that it does not have control of the subsidiaries or if there are substantial restrictions on the repatriation of cash.

Source: Rita M. Rodriguez and E. Eugene Carter, *International Financial Management,* 3rd ed. (Englewood Cliffs, NJ: Prentice-Hall, 1984), p. 492.

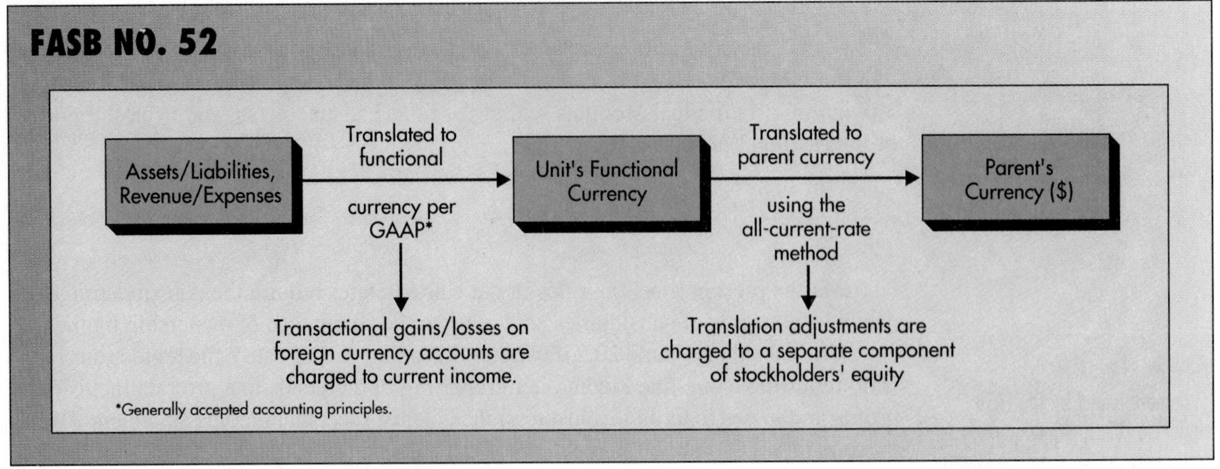

FIGURE 20.1
Details of FASB No.52

Source: John B. Giannotti, "FAS 52 Gives Treasurers the Scope FAS 8 Denied Them," *Euromoney,* April 1982, pp. 141–151.

and all income statement items at average rates), the functional currency–denominated financial statements are translated into the parent's currency.

Each of these steps can result in certain gains or losses. The first step can lead to transaction (cash) gains or losses, which, whether realized or not, are charged directly to net income. The completion of the second step can result in translation (accounting) adjustments, which are excluded from current income. Instead, they are disclosed and charged to a separate component of stockholders' equity.

International profits

Before January 1976 the practice for most U.S. multinationals was to utilize a special account called the *reserve account* to show "smooth" international profits. Excess international profits due to favorable exchange fluctuations were deposited in this account. Withdrawals were made during periods of high losses stemming from unfavorable exchange movements. The overall result was to display a smooth pattern in an MNC's international profits.

Between 1976 and 1982, however, the existence of *FASB No. 8* required that both transaction gains or losses and translation adjustments be included in net income, with the separate disclosure of only the aggregate foreign exchange gain or loss. This requirement caused highly visible swings in the reported net earnings of U.S. multinationals. Under FASB No. 52, only certain transactional gains or losses are reflected in the income statement. Overall, assuming a positive income flow for a subsidiary, the income statement risk will be positive and will be similarly enhanced or reduced by an appreciation or depreciation of the functional currency.

CONCEPT IN REVIEW

20-5 State the rules for consolidation of foreign subsidiaries. Under *FASB No. 52,* what are the translation rules for financial statement accounts?

Risk

LG 3

Two risks requiring special consideration by the multinational firm are concerned with exchange rates and political factors relating to the policies and actions of host governments. How can changes in each of these areas adversely affect the MNC's success? Take a short time to answer this question before reading further.

THE CONCEPT OF RISK CLEARLY APPLIES TO INTERNATIONAL INVESTMENTS AS WELL AS purely domestic ones. However, MNCs must take into account additional factors including both exchange rate and political risks.

Exchange rate risks

Since multinational companies operate in many different foreign markets, portions of these firms' revenues and costs are based on foreign currencies. To understand the **exchange rate risk** caused by varying exchange rates between two currencies, we examine both the relationships that exist among various currencies and the impact of currency fluctuations.

exchange rate risk The risk caused by varying exchange rates between two currencies.

RELATIONSHIPS AMONG CURRENCIES

Since the mid-1970s, the major currencies of the world have had a *floating*—as opposed to *fixed*—relationship with respect to the U.S. dollar and to one another. Among the currencies regarded as being major (or "hard") are the British pound sterling (£), the Swiss franc (Sf), the Deutsche mark (DM), the French franc (Ff), the Japanese yen (¥), the Canadian dollar (C$), and, of course, the U.S. dollar (US$). The value of two currencies with respect to each other, or their **foreign exchange rate,** is expressed as follows:

foreign exchange rate The value of two currencies with respect to each other.

US$ 1.00 = Sf 1.42
Sf 1.00 = US$ .704

The usual exchange rate quotation in international markets is given as Sf 1.42/US$, where the unit of account is the Swiss franc and the unit of currency being priced is one U.S. dollar.

For the major currencies the existence of a **floating relationship** means that the value of any two currencies with respect to each other is allowed to fluctuate on a daily basis. On the other hand, many of the nonmajor currencies of the world try to maintain a **fixed (or semi-fixed) relationship** with respect to one of the major currencies, a combination (basket) of major currencies, or some type of international foreign exchange standard.

floating relationship The fluctuating relationship of the values of two currencies with respect to each another.

fixed (or semi-fixed) relationship The constant (or relatively constant) relationship of a currency to one of the major currencies, a combination (basket) of major currencies, or some type of international foreign exchange standard.

On any given day the relationship between any two of the major currencies will contain two sets of figures, one reflecting the **spot exchange rate** (the rate on that day) and the other indicating the **forward exchange rate** (the rate at some specified future date). The foreign exchange rates given in Figure 20.2 can be used to illustrate these concepts. For instance, the figure shows that on Wednesday, June 2, 1993, the spot rate for the Swiss franc was Sf 1.4242/US$, while the forward (future) rate was Sf

spot exchange rate The rate of exchange between two currencies on any given day.

forward exchange rate The rate of exchange between two currencies at some specified future date.

CURRENCY TRADING

EXCHANGE RATES

Wednesday, June 2, 1993

The New York foreign exchange selling rates below apply to trading among banks in amounts of $1 million and more, as quoted at 3 p.m. Eastern time by Bankers Trust Co., Telerate and other sources. Retail transactions provide fewer units of foreign currency per dollar.

	U.S. $ equiv.		Currency per U.S. $	
Country	**Wed.**	**Tues.**	**Wed.**	**Tues.**
Argentina (Peso)	1.01	1.01	.99	.99
Australia (Dollar)	.6782	.6788	1.4745	1.4732
Austria (Schilling)	.08887	.08940	11.25	11.19
Bahrain (Dinar)	2.6522	2.6522	.3771	.3771
Belgium (Franc)	.03044	.03060	32.85	32.68
Brazil (Cruzeiro)	.0000244	.0000247	40972.02	40447.00
Britain (Pound)	1.5405	1.5485	.6491	.6458
30-Day Forward	1.5368	1.5448	.6507	.6473
90-Day Forward	1.5302	1.5388	.6535	.6499
180-Day Forward	1.5223	1.5304	.6569	.6534
Canada (Dollar)	.7867	.7862	1.2712	1.2719
30-Day Forward	.7857	.7852	1.2728	1.2735
90-Day Forward	.7837	.7833	1.2760	1.2767
180-Day Forward	.7797	.7793	1.2825	1.2832
Czech. Rep. (Koruna)				
Commercial rate	.0358809	.0358809	27.8700	27.8700
Chile (Peso)	.002544	.002544	393.12	393.11
China (Renminbi)	.174856	.174856	5.7190	5.7190
Colombia (Peso)	.001514	.001501	660.54	666.40
Denmark (Krone)	.1632	.1641	6.1258	6.0953
Ecuador (Sucre)				
Floating rate	.000535	.000535	1870.03	1870.03
Finland (Markka)	.18375	.18498	5.4422	5.4061
France (Franc)	.18563	.18613	5.3870	5.3725
30-Day Forward	.18484	.18530	5.4101	5.3967
90-Day Forward	.18352	.18404	5.4491	5.4335
180-Day Forward	.18192	.18238	5.4970	5.4830
Germany (Mark)	.6254	.6287	1.5990	1.5905
30-Day Forward	.6228	.6260	1.6057	1.5975
90-Day Forward	.6183	.6217	1.6173	1.6084
180-Day Forward	.6133	.6166	1.6306	1.6217
Greece (Drachma)	.004609	.004624	216.95	216.25
Hong Kong (Dollar)	.12947	.12947	7.7237	7.7235
Hungary (Forint)	.0115500	.0116050	86.5800	86.1700
India (Rupee)	.03211	.03211	31.14	31.14
Indonesia (Rupiah)	.0004811	.0004811	2078.53	2078.53
Ire!and (Punt)	1.5243	1.5319	.6560	.6528
Israel (Shekel)	.3763	.3681	2.6575	2.7170
Italy (Lira)	.0006842	.0006804	1461.50	1469.64
Japan (Yen)	.009320	.009337	107.30	107.10
30-Day Forward	.009319	.009337	107.30	107.10
90-Day Forward	.009320	.009337	107.30	107.10
180-Day Forward	.009326	.009344	107.23	107.02
Jordan (Dinar)	1.4984	1.4984	.6674	.6674
Kuwait (Dinar)	3.3267	3.3267	.3006	.3006
Lebanon (Pound)	.000577	.000577	1733.00	1733.00
Malaysia (Ringgit)	.3914	.3915	2.5550	2.5542
Malta (Lira)	2.7248	2.7248	.3670	.3670
Mexico (Peso)				
Floating rate	.3197953	.3197953	3.1270	3.1270
Netherland (Guilder)	.5574	.5604	1.7939	1.7845
New Zealand (Dollar)	.5425	.5407	1.8433	1.8495
Norway (Krone)	.1474	.1480	6.7862	6.7584
Pakistan (Rupee)	.0373	.0373	26.81	26.81
Peru (New Sol)	.5219	.5233	1.92	1.91
Philippines (Peso)	.03752	.03752	26.65	26.65
Poland (Zloty	.00006202	.00006196	16125.13	16140.00
Portugal (Escudo)	.006508	.006522	153.66	153.32
Saudi Arabia (Rival)	.26702	.26702	3.7450	3.7450
Singapore (Dollar)	.62X8	.6243	1.6005	1.6018
Slovak Rep. (Koruna)	.0358809	.0358809	27.87000	27.8700
South Africa (Rand)				
Commercial rate	.3141	.3144	3.1838	3.1811
Financial rate	.2162	.2165	4.6250	4.6200
South Korea (Won)	.0012449	.0012466	803.30	802.20
Spain (Peseta)	.007984	.007964	125.25	125.57
Sweden (Krona)	.1388	.1391	7.2059	7.1914
Switzerland (Franc)	.7021	.7030	1.4242	1.4225
30-Day Forward	.7009	.7017	1.4268	1.4252
90-Day Forward	.6987	.6996	1.4312	1.4294
180-Day Forward	.6965	.6973	1.4358	1.4342
Taiwan (Dollar)	.038685	.038256	25.85	26.14
Thailand (Baht)	.03981	.03981	25.12	25.12
Turkey (Lira)	.0001004	.0001004	9956.00	9956.00
United Arab (Dirham)	.2723	.2723	3.6725	3.6725
Uruguary (New Peso)				
Financial	.251256	.251256	3.98	3.98
Venezuela (Bolivar)				
Floating rate	.01155	.01162	86.58	86.07
SDR	1.42658	1.43064	.70098	.6899

ECU	1.21940	1.22460		

Special Drawing Rights (SDR) are based on exchange rates for the U.S., German, British, French and Japanese currencies. Source: International Monetary Fund.

European Currency Unit (ECU) is based on a basket of community currencies.

FIGURE 20.2
Spot and forward exchange rate quotations
Source: The Wall Street Journal, June 3, 1993, p. C14.

1.4268/US$ for 30-day delivery. In other words, on June 2, 1993, one could take a contract on Swiss francs for 30 days hence at an exchange rate of Sf 1.4268/US$. *Forward delivery rates* are also available for 90-day and 180-day contracts. For all such contracts, the agreements and signatures are completed on, say, June 2, 1993, whereas the actual exchange of dollars and Swiss francs between buyers and sellers will take place on the future date, say, 30 days later.

Figure 20.2 can also be used to illustrate the differences between floating and fixed currencies. All the major currencies previously mentioned have spot and forward rates with respect to the U.S. dollar. Moreover, a comparison of the exchange rates prevailing on Wednesday, June 2, 1993, *versus* those on Tuesday, June 1, 1993, indicates that the floating major currencies (or other currencies that also float in relation to the U.S. dollar, such as the Austrian schilling and the Belgian franc) experienced changes in rates. Other currencies, however, such as the United Arab dirham, do not exhibit relatively large fluctuations on a daily basis with respect to either the U.S. dollar or the currency to which they are pegged (i.e., they have very limited movements with respect to either the U.S. dollar or other currencies).

A final point to note is the concept of changes in the value of a currency with respect to the U.S. dollar or another currency. For the floating currencies, changes in the value of foreign exchange rates are called *appreciation* or *depreciation.* For example, referring to Figure 20.2, it can be seen that the value of the French franc has depreciated from Ff 5.3725/US$ on Tuesday to Ff 5.3870/US$ on Wednesday. In other words, it takes more francs to buy one dollar. For the fixed currencies, changes in values are called official *revaluation* or *devaluation,* but these terms have the same meanings as *appreciation* and *depreciation,* respectively.

IMPACT OF CURRENCY FLUCTUATIONS

Multinational companies face foreign exchange risks under both floating and fixed arrangements. The case of floating currencies can be used to illustrate these risks. Returning to the U.S. dollar–Swiss franc relationship, we note that the forces of international supply and demand as well as internal and external economic and political elements help to shape both the spot and forward rates between these two currencies. Since the MNC cannot control much (or most) of these "outside" elements, the company faces potential changes in exchange rates in the form of appreciation or depreciation. These changes can in turn affect the MNC's revenues, costs, and profits as measured in U.S. dollars. For currencies that are fixed in relation to each other, the risks come from the same set of elements indicated above. Again, these official changes, like the ones brought about by the market in the case of floating currencies, can affect the MNC's operations and its dollar-based financial position.

The risks stemming from changes in exchange rates can be illustrated by examining the balance sheet and income statement of MNC, Inc. We will focus on its subsidiary in Switzerland.

EXAMPLE

MNC, Inc., a multinational manufacturer of dental drills, has a subsidiary in Switzerland that at the end of 1994 had the financial statements shown in Table 20.3. The figures for the balance sheet and income statement are given in the local currency, Swiss franc (Sf). Using the foreign exchange rate of Sf 1.50/US$ for December 31, 1994, MNC has translated the statements into U.S. dollars. For simplicity it is assumed that all the local figures are expected to remain the same during 1995. As a result, as of January 1, 1995, the subsidiary expects to show the same Swiss franc figures on 12/31/95 as on 12/31/94. However, because of the change in the value of the Swiss franc relative to the dollar, from Sf 1.50/US$ to Sf 1.30/US$, the translated dollar values of the items on the balance sheet, along with the dollar profit value on 12/31/95, are higher than those of the previous year, the changes being due only to fluctuations in foreign exchange. ■

There are additional complexities attached to each individual account in the financial statements. For instance, it is important whether a subsidiary's debt is all in the local currency, in U.S. dollars, or in several currencies. Moreover, it is important which currency (or currencies) the revenues and costs are denominated in. The risks shown so far relate to what is called the **accounting exposure.** In other words, foreign exchange fluctuations affect individual accounts in the financial statements. A different, and perhaps more important, risk element concerns **economic exposure,** which is the potential impact of exchange rate fluctuations on the firm's value. Given that all future revenues and thus net profits can be subject to exchange rate changes, it is obvious that the *present value* of the net profits derived from foreign operations will have, as a part of its total diversifiable risk, an element reflecting appreciation (revaluation) or depreciation (devaluation) of various currencies with respect to the U.S. dollar.

accounting exposure
The risk resulting from the effects of changes in foreign exchange rates on the translated value of a firm's financial statement accounts denominated in a given foreign currency.

economic exposure
The risk resulting from the effects of changes in foreign exchange rates on the firm's value.

What can the management of MNCs do about these risks? The actions will depend on the attitude of the management toward risk. This attitude, in turn, translates

TABLE 20.3

FINANCIAL STATEMENTS FOR MNC, INC.'S, SWISS SUBSIDIARY

Translation of Balance Sheet	12/31/94		12/31/95
Assets	**Sf**	**US$**	**US$**
Cash	8.00	5.33	6.15
Inventory	60.00	40.00	46.15
Plant and equipment (net)	32.00	21.33	24.61
Total	100.00	66.66	76.91
Liabilities and stockholders' equity			
Debt	48.00	32.00	36.92
Paid-in capital	40.00	26.66	30.76
Retained earnings	12.00	8.00	9.23
Total	100.00	66.66	76.91
Translation of Income Statement			
Sales	600.00	400.00	461.53
Cost of goods sold	550.00	366.66	423.07
Operating profits	50.00	33.34	38.46

Note: This example is simplified to show how the balance sheet and income statement are subject to exchange rate fluctuations. For the applicable rules on the translation of foreign accounts, review the discussion of international financial statements presented earlier.

into how aggressively management wants to hedge (i.e. protect against) the company's undesirable positions and exposures. The money markets, the forward (futures) markets, and the foreign currency options markets can be used—either individually or in conjunction with one another—to hedge foreign exchange exposures. Further details on certain hedging strategies are described later.

political risk
The potential discontinuity or seizure of an MNC's operations in a host country due to the host's implementation of specific rules and regulations (such as nationalization, expropriation, or confiscation).

Political risks

Another important risk facing MNCs is political risk. **Political risk** refers to the implementation by a host government of specific rules and regulations that can result in the discontinuity or seizure of the operations of a foreign company in that country. Political risk is usually manifested in the form of nationalization, expropriation, or confiscation. In general, the assets and operations of a foreign firm are taken over by the host government, usually without proper (or any) compensation.

macro political risk
The subjection of *all* foreign firms to political risk (takeover) by a host country because of political change, revolution, or the adoption of new policies.

micro political risk
The subjection of an individual firm, a specific industry, or companies from a particular foreign country to political risk (takeover) by the host country.

Political risk has two basic paths: *macro* and *micro.* **Macro political risk** means that because of political change, revolution, or the adoption of new policies by a host government, *all* foreign firms in the country will be subjected to political risk. In other words, no individual country or firm is treated differently; all assets and operations of foreign firms are taken over wholesale. An example of macro political risk is China in 1949 or Cuba in 1959–1960. **Micro political risk,** on the other hand, refers to the case in which an individual firm, a specific industry, or companies from a particular foreign country will be subjected to takeover. Examples include the nationalization by a majority of the oil-exporting countries of the assets of the international oil companies in their territories.

CONCEPT IN PRACTICE

Shifting Sands and Risks for General Motors and Citibank in Saudi Arabia

Following Desert Storm, the Saudi Arabian economy swelled, providing profits to U.S. firms that were hurting elsewhere. General Motors sold the Saudis $600 million worth of Chevrolet Caprices and Cadillacs. Yet a short distance from the capital's opulent, Westernized neighborhoods are poor sections that display religious fare that often attacks the United States. While Citibank's Saudi-American Bank earned $300 million in 1992, religious gangs roamed the streets and assaulted people wearing "inappropriate" attire. Anxiety mounted with reports that pro-American King Fahd was in poor health. Despite a competent governmental apparatus, including the state-owned Saudi Arabia Oil Company, concerns abounded that a decline in oil revenues would lead to a fundamentalist takeover and nationalization of U.S. facilities.

Although political risk can take place in any country—even in the United States—the political instability of the Third World generally makes the positions of multinational companies most vulnerable there. At the same time, some of the countries in this group have the most promising markets for the goods and services being offered by MNCs. The main question, therefore, is how to engage in operations and foreign investment in such countries and yet avoid or minimize the potential political risk.

Table 20.4 shows some of the approaches that MNCs may be able to adopt to cope with political risk. The negative approaches are generally used by firms in extractive

TABLE 20.4

APPROACHES FOR COPING WITH POLITICAL RISKS

Positive approaches		Negative approaches
Prior negotiation of controls and operating contracts Prior agreement for sale Joint venture with government or local private sector	Direct	License or patent restrictions under international agreements Control of external raw materials
Use of locals in management Joint venture with local banks Equity participation by middle class Local sourcing Local retail outlets	Indirect	Control of transportation to (external) markets Control of downstream processing Control of external markets
External approaches to minimize loss		
International insurance or investment guarantees Thinly capitalized firms: Local financing External financing secured only by the local operation		

Source: Rita M. Rodriguez and E. Eugene Carter, *International Financial Management,* 3rd ed. (Englewood Cliffs, NJ: Prentice-Hall, 1984), p. 512.

industries. The external approaches are also of limited use. The best policies MNCs can follow are the positive approaches, which have both economic and political aspects.

In recent years, MNCs have been relying on a variety of complex forecasting techniques whereby "international experts," using available historical data, predict the chances for political instability in a host country and the potential effects on MNC operations. Events in Iraq and Yugoslavia, among others, however, point to the limited use of such techniques and tend to reinforce the usefulness of the positive approaches.

national entry control systems
Comprehensive rules, regulations, and incentives aimed at regulating inflows of *foreign direct investments* involving MNCs and at the same time extracting more benefits from their presence.

A final point relates to the introduction by most "host" governments in the last two decades of comprehensive sets of rules, regulations, and incentives. Known as **national entry control systems,** they are aimed at regulating inflows of *foreign direct investments* involving MNCs. They are designed to extract more benefits from MNCs' presence by regulating such flows in terms of a variety of factors—local ownership, level of exportation, use of local inputs, number of local managers, internal geographic location, level of local borrowing, and the respective percentages of profits to be remitted and of capital to be repatriated back to parent firms. Host countries expect that as MNCs comply with these regulations, the potential for acts of political risk will decline, thus benefiting MNCs as well.

CONCEPTS IN REVIEW

20-6 Define *spot* and *forward exchange rates.* Define and compare *accounting exposures* and *economic exposures* to exchange rate fluctuations.

20-7 Discuss *macro* and *micro political risk.* Describe some techniques for dealing with political risk.

Long-term investment and financing decisions

Multinational firms make long-term investments by transferring money and other assets from their home country to a host country and obtain long-term financing by issuing debt and equity in the international capital markets. Why do you think political risk plays a much more important role in these activities than in short-term, foreign investment and financing activities? Devote a few moments to answering this question before reading more.

IMPORTANT LONG-TERM ASPECTS OF INTERNATIONAL MANAGER/FINANCE INCLUDE FOREIGN direct investment, investment cash flows and decisions, capital structure, long-term debt, and equity capital. Here we briefly consider the international demensions of each of these topics.

Foreign direct investment

foreign direct investment (FDI)
The transfer, by a multinational firm, of capital, managerial, and technical assets from its home country to a host country.

Foreign direct investment (FDI) is the transfer by a multinational firm of capital, managerial, and technical assets from its home country to a host country. The equity participation on the part of an MNC can be 100 percent (resulting in a wholly owned foreign subsidiary) or less (leading to a joint-venture project with foreign participants). In contrast to short-term, foreign portfolio investments undertaken by individuals and companies (e.g., internationally diversified mutual funds), FDI involves equity participation, managerial control, and day-to-day operational activities on the part of MNCs. Therefore FDI projects will be subjected not only to business, financial, inflation, and foreign exchange risks (as would foreign portfolio investments) but also to the additional element of political risk.

For a number of decades, U.S.-based MNCs had dominated the international scene in terms of both the *flow* and *stock* of FDI. The total FDI stock of U.S.-based MNCs, for instance, increased from $7.7 billion in 1929 to over $450.2 billion at the end of 1991. Since the 1970s, though, their global presence is being challenged by MNCs based in Western Europe, Japan, and other developed and developing nations. In fact, even the "home" market of U.S. multinationals is being challenged by foreign firms. For instance, in 1960, FDI into the United States amounted to only 11.5 percent of U.S. investment overseas. By the end of 1991, the *book value* of FDI into the United States, at US$407.6 billion, was almost as large as the comparable figure of US$450.2 billion, for U.S. FDI abroad. However, the *market value* of U.S. FDI, at US$802 billion, still exceeded that of FDI into the United States at US$654 billion, by a substantial margin at year-end 1991.

Investment cash flows and decisions

Measuring the amount invested in a foreign project, its resulting cash flows, and the associated risk is difficult. The returns and NPVs of such investments can significantly vary from the subsidiary's and parent's points of view. Therefore several factors that are unique to the international setting need to be examined in making long-term investment decisions.

First, elements relating to a parent company's *investment* in a subsidiary and the concept of taxes must be considered. For example, in the case of manufacturing investments, questions may arise as to the value of the equipment a parent may contribute to the subsidiary. Is the value based on the market conditions in the parent country or the local host economy? In general, the market value in the host country is the relevant "price."

The existence of different taxes–as was pointed out earlier—can complicate measurement of the *cash flows* to be received by the parent because different definitions of taxable income can arise. There are still other complications when it comes to measuring the actual cash flows. From a parent firm's viewpoint the cash flows are those that are repatriated from the subsidiary. In some countries, however, such cash flows may be totally or partially blocked. Obviously, depending on the life of the project in the host country, the returns and net present values (NPVs) associated with such projects can vary significantly from the subsidiary's and the parent's point of view. For instance, for a project of only five years' duration, if all yearly cash flows are blocked by the host government, the subsidiary may show a "normal" or even superior return and NPV, although the parent may show no return at all. On the other hand, for a project of longer life, even if cash flows are blocked for the first few years, the remaining years' cash flows can contribute toward the parent's returns and NPV.

Finally, there is the issue of *risk* attached to international cash flows. The three basic types of risk categories are (1) business and financial risks, (2) inflation and exchange rate risks, and (3) political risks. The first category relates to the type of industry the subsidiary is in as well as its financial structure (more details on financial risks are presented later). As for the other two categories, we have already discussed both the risks of having investments, profits, and assets/liabilities in different currencies and the potential impacts of political risks and how MNCs can combat them.

The important point to note here is that the presence of such risks will influence the discount rate (or the cost of capital) to be used in evaluating international cash flows. The basic rule, however, is that the *local cost of equity capital* (applicable to the local business and financial environments within which a subsidiary operates) is the starting discount rate to which risks stemming from exchange rate and political factors can be added and from which benefits reflecting the parent's lower capital costs may be subtracted.

Capital structure

Both theory and empirical evidence indicate that the capital structures of multinational companies differ from those of purely domestic firms. Furthermore, differences are also observed among the capital structures of MNCs domiciled in various countries. Several factors tend to influence the capital structures of MNCs. Each will be briefly discussed here.

INTERNATIONAL CAPITAL MARKETS

MNCs, unlike smaller-size domestic firms, have access to the Euromarket (discussed earlier) and the variety of financial instruments available there (to be described later). Because of their access to the international bond and equity markets, MNCs may have lower costs of various sources of long-term financing, thus resulting in differences between the capital structures of these firms and those of purely domestic companies. Similarly, MNCs based in different countries and regions, such as those domiciled in the United States, Western Europe, and Japan, may have access to different currencies and markets, resulting in variances in capital structures for these multinationals.

INTERNATIONAL DIVERSIFICATION

It is well-established that MNCs, in contrast to domestic firms, can achieve further risk reduction in their cash flows by diversifying internationally. International diversification, in turn, may lead to varying degrees of debt versus equity. Empirically, mixed evidence exists on debt ratios. Some studies have found MNCs' debt proportions to be higher than those of domestic firms. Other studies have concluded the opposite, citing imperfections in certain foreign markets, political risk factors, and complexities in the international financial environment that cause higher agency costs of debt for MNCs.

COUNTRY FACTORS

A number of studies have concluded that certain factors unique to each host country, including legal, tax, political, social, and financial aspects, as well as the overall relationship between the public and private sectors can cause differences in capital structures. Owing to these factors, differences have been found not only among MNCs based in various countries but among the foreign affiliates of an MNC as well. However, since no one capital structure is ideal for all MNCs, each multinational has to consider a set of global and domestic factors in deciding on the appropriate capital structure for both the overall corporation and its affiliates.

CONCEPT IN PRACTICE

Toyota Puts Research and Development in the Driver's Seat

A 1993 survey conducted by the Massachusetts Institute of Technology found that Japanese firms are less likely to cut research and development staffs than are their counterparts in North America and Europe. Only 4 percent of the Japanese firms surveyed anticipated cutting their research and development staffs, while 32 percent of North American firms and 54 percent of European firms planned staff cuts. When faced with the need to trim expenses, Japanese firms, such as Toyota, reduce travel, equipment, and external consulting expenditures.

Japanese firms were also found to be more likely to focus on core research, while North American and European firms concentrated on applied research. The survey also ranked Japan's machinery and electronics industries first and second in overall research performance. While North American firms focus on current cash flows, Japanese firms concentrate on market share and long-term profitability.

Long-term debt

As was noted earlier, multinational companies, in conducting their global operations, have access to a variety of international financial instruments. International bonds are among the most widely used, so we will begin by focusing on them. Next, we discuss the role of international financial institutions in underwriting such instruments. Finally, we consider the use of various techniques (such as swaps) by MNCs to change the structure of their long-term debt.

INTERNATIONAL BONDS

international bond
A bond that is initially sold outside the country of the borrower and often distributed in several countries.

foreign bond
An international bond that is sold primarily in the country of the currency of the issue.

Eurobond
An international bond that is sold primarily in countries other than the country of the currency in which the issue is denominated.

In general, an **international bond** is one that is initially sold outside the country of the borrower and often distributed in several countries. When a bond is sold primarily in the country of the currency of the issue, it is called a **foreign bond.** For example, an MNC based in West Germany might float a bond issue in the French capital market underwritten by a French syndicate and denominated in French francs. When an international bond is sold primarily in countries other than the country of the currency in which the issue is denominated, it is called a **Eurobond.** Thus an MNC based in the United States might float a Eurobond in several European capital markets, underwritten by an international syndicate and denominated in U.S. dollars.

The U.S. dollar continues to dominate the Eurobond issues, with the Japanese yen gaining popularity. The importance of the U.S. currency in all aspects of international transactions, and thus its importance to MNCs, can explain this continued dominance. In the foreign bond category the Swiss franc continues to be the major choice. Low interest rates, the general stability of the currency, and the overall efficiency of the Swiss capital markets are among the primary reasons for the ongoing popularity of the Swiss franc. However, Eurobonds are much more widely used than foreign bonds. These instruments are heavily used, especially in relation to Eurocurrency loans in recent years, by major market participants, including U.S. corporations. These so-called equity-linked Eurobonds (i.e., convertible to equity), especially those offered by a number of U.S. firms, have found strong demand among Euromarket participants. It is expected that more of these innovative types of instruments will emerge on the international scene in the coming years.

A final point concerns the levels of interest rates in international markets. In the case of foreign bonds, interest rates are usually directly correlated with the domestic rates prevailing in the respective countries. For Eurobonds several interest rates may be influential. For instance, for a Eurodollar bond, the interest rate will reflect several different rates, most notably the U.S. long-term rate, the Eurodollar rate, and long-term rates in other countries.

THE ROLE OF INTERNATIONAL FINANCIAL INSTITUTIONS

For *foreign bonds* the underwriting institutions are those that handle bond issues in the respective countries in which such bonds are issued. For *Eurobonds* a number of financial institutions in the United States, Western Europe and Japan, form international underwriting syndicates. The underwriting costs for Eurobonds are comparable to those for bond flotation in the U.S. domestic market. Although U.S. institutions used to dominate the Eurobond scene, recent economic and financial strengths exhibited by some Western European (especially German) and Japanese financial firms have led to a change in that dominance. Since 1986 a number of European and Japanese firms have held the top positions in terms of acting as lead underwriters of Eurobond issues. However, U.S. investment banks continue to dominate most other international security issuance markets—such as international equity, medium-term note, syndicated loan, and commercial paper markets—and U.S. corporations accounted for almost three-quarters of the $1.12 trillion in worldwide securities issues in 1992.

To raise funds through international bond issues, many MNCs establish their own financial subsidiaries. Many U.S.-based MNCs, for example, have created subsidiaries in the United States and Western Europe, especially in Luxembourg. Such subsidiaries can be used to raise large amounts of funds in "one move," the funds being redistributed wherever MNCs need them. (Special tax rules applicable to such subsidiaries also make them desirable to MNCs.)

CHANGING THE STRUCTURE OF DEBT

As will be noted in a subsequent discussion, MNCs can use *hedging strategies* to change the structure/characteristics of their long-term assets and liabilities. For instance, multinationals can utilize *interest rate swaps* to obtain a desired stream of interest payments (e.g., fixed-rate) in exchange for another (e.g., floating-rate), and *currency swaps* to exchange an asset/liability denominated in one currency (e.g., U.S. dollar) for another (e.g., Swiss franc). The use of these tools allows MNCs to gain access to a broader set of markets, currencies, and maturities, thus leading to both cost savings and a means of restructuring the existing assets/liabilities. Such use has experienced significant growth during the last few years, and this trend is expected to continue.

Equity capital

Here we look at how multinational companies can raise equity capital abroad. First, they can sell their shares in international capital markets. Second, they can use joint ventures, which are sometimes required by the host country. We also consider the role of equity (versus debt) in the MNCs' foreign direct investment in international joint ventures.

EQUITY ISSUES AND MARKETS

One means of raising equity funds for MNCs is to have the parent's stock distributed internationally and owned by stockholders of different nationalities. In the 1980s the world's equity markets became more "internationalized" (i.e., becoming more standardized and thus closer in character to the Eurobond market discussed earlier). In other words, while distinct *national* stock markets (such as New York, London, and Tokyo) continue to exist and grow, an *international* stock market has also emerged on the global financial scene.

Euro-equity market
The capital market around the world that deals in international equity issues; London has become the center of Euro-equity activity.

In recent years the terms **Euro-equity market** and "Euro-equities" have become widely known. While a number of capital markets—including New York, Tokyo, Frankfurt, Zurich, and Paris—play major roles by being hosts to international equity issues, London has become *the* center of Euro-equity activity. For the year 1992, for instance, the *new issue* volume was close to $23 billion and included 360 offerings. As in most recent years, a large part of this issue volume represented government sales of state-owned firms to private investors, referred to as *share-issue privatizations.*

As the time for the full financial integration of the EC approaches, some European stock exchanges continue to compete with each other. Others have called for more cooperation in forming a single market capable of competing with New York and Tokyo. From the multinationals' perspective the most desirable outcome would be to have uniform international rules and regulations with respect to all the major national stock exchanges. Such uniformity would allow MNCs to have unrestricted access to an international equity market paralleling that of the international currency and bond markets.

JOINT VENTURES

The basic aspects of foreign ownership of international operations were discussed earlier. Worth emphasizing here is that certain laws and regulations enacted during the 1960s and 1970s by a number of host countries require MNCs to maintain less than 50 percent ownership in their subsidiaries in most of those countries. For a U.S.-based MNC, for example, establishing foreign subsidiaries in the form of joint ventures means that a certain portion of the firm's total international equity stock is (indirectly) held by foreign owners.

Some of the advantages and disadvantages of joint ventures have previously been highlighted. In establishing a foreign subsidiary an MNC may wish to have as little equity and as much debt as possible, the debt coming from local sources in the host country or the MNC itself. Each of these actions can be supported. The host country may allow *more local debt* for a subsidiary; this is a good protective measure in terms of lessening the potential impacts of political risk. In other words, since local sources are involved in the capital structure of a subsidiary, there may be fewer threats from local authorities in the event of changes in government or the enactment of new regulations on foreign business.

In support of the other action—having *more MNC-based debt* in a subsidiary's capital structure—it is true that many host governments are less restrictive, in terms of taxation and actual repatriation, toward intra-MNC interest payments than toward intra-MNC dividend remittances. The parent firm may therefore be in a better position if it has more MNC-based debt than equity in the capital structure of its subsidiaries.

CONCEPTS IN REVIEW

20-8 Indicate how net present value (NPV) can differ if measured from the parent MNC's point of view or from that of the foreign subsidiary when cash flows may be blocked by local authorities.

20-9 Briefly discuss some of the international factors that cause the capital structures of MNCs to differ from those of purely domestic firms.

20-10 Describe the difference between *foreign bonds* and *Eurobonds*. Explain how each is sold, and discuss the determinant(s) of their interest rates.

20-11 What are the long-run advantages of having more *local* debt and less MNC-based equity in the capital structure of a foreign subsidiary?

Short-term financial decisions

The Eurocurrency market offers nondomestic short-term borrowing and investing (lending) opportunities to the multinational firm. How do you think the financial manager chooses the best borrowing and investing opportunities in the Eurocurrency market? Before reading ahead, spend a short time answering this question.

IN INTERNATIONAL OPERATIONS THE USUAL DOMESTIC SOURCES OF SHORT-TERM FINANCING, along with other sources, are available to MNCs. Included are accounts payable as well as accruals, bank and nonbank sources in each subsidiary's local environment, and the Euromarket discussed earlier. Our emphasis here is on the "foreign" sources.

For a subsidiary of a multinational company its local economic market is a basic source of both short- and long-term financing. Moreover, the subsidiary's borrowing and lending status, relative to a local firm in the same economy, can be superior, since the subsidiary can rely on the potential backing and guarantee of its parent MNC. One drawback, however, is that most local markets and local currencies are regulated by local authorities. Thus a subsidiary may ultimately choose to turn to the Euromarket and take advantage of borrowing and investing in an unregulated financial forum.

Eurocurrency markets
The portion of the Euromarket that provides short-term foreign-currency financing to subsidiaries of MNCs.

nominal interest rate
In the international context, the stated interest rate charged on financing when only the MNC parent's currency is involved.

effective interest rate
In the international context, the rate equal to the nominal rate plus (or minus) any forecast appreciation (or depreciation) of a foreign currency relative to the currency of the MNC parent.

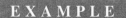

The Euromarket offers nondomestic financing opportunities for both the short term (Eurocurrency) and the long term (Eurobonds). (Eurobonds were discussed earlier.) In the case of short-term financing, the forces of supply and demand are among the main factors determining exchange rates in **Eurocurrency markets.** Each currency's normal interest rate is influenced by economic policies pursued by the respective "home" government. In other words, the interest rates offered in the Euromarket on, for example, the U.S. dollar are greatly affected by the prime rate inside the United States, and the dollar's exchange rates with other major currencies are influenced by the supply and demand forces acting in such markets (and in response to interest rates).

Unlike borrowing in the domestic markets, where only one currency and a **nominal interest rate** is involved, financing activities in the Euromarket can involve several currencies and both nominal and effective interest rates. **Effective interest rates** are equal to nominal rates plus (or minus) any forecast appreciation (or depreciation) of a foreign currency relative to the currency of the MNC parent—say, the U.S. dollar. An example will illustrate the issues involved.

EXAMPLE

A multinational plastics company, International Molding, has subsidiaries in Switzerland (local currency, Swiss franc, Sf) and Belgium (local currency, Belgian franc, Bf). Based on each subsidiary's forecast operations, the short-term financial needs (in equivalent U.S. dollars) are as follows:

Switzerland: $80 million excess cash to be invested (lent)
Belgium: $60 million funds to be raised (borrowed)

On the basis of all the available information, the parent firm has provided each subsidiary with the figures, given below, regarding exchange rates and interest rates. (The figures for the effective rates shown are derived by adding the forecast percentage changes to the nominal rates.)

Item	Currency		
	US$	Sf	Bf
Spot exchange rates		Sf 1.42/US$	Bf 32.85/US$
Forecast % change		+1.0%	−2.5%
Interest rates			
Nominal			
Euromarket	4.6%	6.2%	8.5%
Domestic	4.0	5.5	9.0
Effective			
Euromarket	4.6%	7.2%	6.0%
Domestic	4.0	6.5	6.5

From the point of view of a multinational the effective rates of interest, which take into account each currency's forecast percentage change (appreciation or depreciation) relative to the U.S. dollar, are the main items to be considered for investment and borrowing decisions. (It is assumed here that because of local regulations, a subsidiary is *not* permitted to use the domestic market of *any other* subsidiary.) The relevant question is, where should funds be invested and borrowed?

For investment purposes the highest available rate of interest is the effective rate for the Swiss franc in the Euromarket. Therefore the Swiss subsidiary should invest the $80 million in Swiss francs in the Euromarket. In the case of raising funds the cheapest source *open* to the Belgian subsidiary is the 4.6 percent in the US$ Euromarket. The subsidiary should therefore raise the $60 million in U.S. dollars. These two transactions will result in the most revenues and least costs, respectively. ■

Several points should be made with respect to the preceding example. First of all, this is a simplified case of the actual workings of the Eurocurrency markets. The example ignores taxes, intersubsidiary investing and borrowing, and periods longer or shorter than a year. Nevertheless, it shows how the existence of many currencies can provide both challenges and opportunities for MNCs. Next, the focus has been solely on accounting values; of greater importance would be the impact of these actions on market value. Finally, it is important to note the following details about the figures presented. The forecast percentage change (appreciation or depreciation) data are regarded as those normally supplied by the MNC's international financial managers. The management may have a *range of forecasts,* from the most likely to the least likely. In addition, the company's management is likely to take a specific position in terms of its response to any remaining foreign exchange exposures. If any action is to be taken, certain amounts of one or more currencies will be borrowed and then invested in other currencies in the hope of realizing potential gains to offset potential losses associated with the exposures.

Cash management

In its international cash management a multinational firm can respond to foreign exchange risks by protecting (hedging) its undesirable cash and marketable securities exposures or by certain adjustments in its operations. While the former approach is more applicable in responding to *accounting exposures,* the latter is better suited against *economic exposures.* Each of these two approaches is examined here.

HEDGING STRATEGIES

hedging strategies
Techniques used to offset or protect against risk; in the international context these include borrowing or lending in different currencies, undertaking contracts in the forward, futures, and/or options markets, and also swapping assets/liabilities with other parties.

Hedging strategies are techniques used to offset or protect against risk. In international cash management these strategies include actions such as borrowing or lending in different currencies, undertaking contracts in the forward, futures, and/or options markets, and also swapping assets/liabilities with other parties. Table 20.5 provides a brief summary of some of the major hedging tools available to MNCs.

ADJUSTMENTS IN OPERATIONS

In responding to exchange rate fluctuations, MNCs can give some protection to international cash flows through appropriate adjustments in assets and liabilities. Two routes are available to a multinational company. The first centers on the operating relationships that a subsidiary of an MNC maintains with *other* firms—*third parties.* Depending on management's expectation of a local currency's position, adjustments in operations would involve the reduction of liabilities if the currency is appreciating or the reduction of financial assets if it is depreciating. For example, if a U.S.-based MNC with a subsidiary in Mexico expects the Mexican currency to *appreciate* in value relative to the U.S. dollar, local customers' accounts receivable would be *increased* and accounts payable would be reduced if at all possible. Because the dollar is the currency in which the MNC parent will have to prepare consolidated financial statements, the net result in this case would be to favorably increase the Mexican subsidiary's resources in local currency. If the Mexican currency were, instead, expected to *depreciate,* the local customers' accounts receivable would be *reduced* and accounts payable would be increased, thereby reducing the Mexican subsidiary's resources in the local currency.

The second route focuses on the operating relationship a subsidiary has with its parent or with other subsidiaries within the same MNC. In dealing with exchange rate risks, a subsidiary can rely on *intra-MNC accounts.* Specifically, undesirable foreign exchange exposures can be corrected to the extent that the subsidiary can take the following steps:

1. In appreciation-prone countries, intra-MNC accounts receivable are collected as soon as possible, and payment of intra-MNC accounts payable is delayed as long as possible.
2. In devaluation-prone countries, intra-MNC accounts receivable are collected as late as possible, and intra-MNC accounts payable are paid as soon as possible.

Again using the example of a Mexican subsidiary, the net result of step 1 or step 2 would be the potential increase or decrease of that subsidiary's resources in the Mexican currency, depending on whether that currency is appreciating or depreciating relative to the parent MNC's main currency, the U.S. dollar.

From a *global* point of view and as far as an MNC's consolidated intracompany accounts are concerned, the manipulation of such accounts by one subsidiary can pro-

TABLE 20.5

EXCHANGE RATE RISK HEDGING TOOLS

Tool	Description	Impact on risk
Borrowing or lending	Borrowing or lending in different currencies to take advantage of interest rate differentials and foreign exchange appreciation/depreciation; can be either on a certainty basis with "up-front" costs or speculative.	Can be used to offset exposures in existing assets/liabilities and in expected revenues/expenses.
Forward contract	"Tailor-made" contracts representing an *obligation* to buy/sell, with the amount, rate, and maturity agreed upon between the two parties; has little up-front cost.	Can eliminate downside risk but locks out any upside potential.
Futures contract	Standardized contracts offered on organized exchanges; same basic tool as a forward contract, but less flexible because of standardization; more flexibility because of secondary market access; has some up-front cost/fee.	Can also eliminate downside risk, plus position can be nullified, creating possible upside potential.
Options	Tailor-made or standardized contracts providing the *right* to buy or to sell an amount of the currency, at a particular price, during a specified time period; has up-front cost (premium).	Can eliminate downside risk and retain unlimited upside potential.
Interest rate swap	Allows the trading of one interest rate stream (e.g., on a fixed-rate U.S. dollar instrument) for another (e.g., on a floating-rate U.S. dollar instrument); fee to be paid to the intermediary.	Permits firms to change the interest rate structure of their assets/liabilities and achieves cost savings due to broader market access.
Currency swap	Two parties exchange principal amounts of two different currencies initially; they pay each other's interest payments, then reverse principal amounts at a pre-agreed exchange rate at maturity; more complex than interest rate swaps.	All the features of interest rate swaps, plus it allows firms to change the currency structure of their assets/liabilities.
Hybrids	A variety of combinations of some of the above tools; may be quite costly and/or speculative.	Can create, with the right combination, a perfect hedge against certain foreign exchange exposures.

Note: The participants in the above activities include MNCs, financial institutions, and brokers. The organized exchanges include Amsterdam, Chicago, London, New York, Philadelphia, and Zurich, among others. It should be emphasized that while most of these tools can be utilized for short-term exposure management, some, such as swaps, are more appropriate for long-term hedging strategies.

duce the opposite results for another subsidiary or the parent firm. For example, if an MNC's subsidiaries in Brazil and Mexico are dealing with each other, the Brazilian subsidiary's manipulations of intra-MNC accounts, along the lines just discussed, in anticipation of an appreciation of that country's currency relative to that of Mexico can mean exchange gains for the Brazilian subsidiary but losses for the Mexican one. The exact degree and direction of the actual manipulations, however, may depend on the tax status of each country. The MNC obviously would want to have the exchange losses in the country with the higher tax rate. Finally, changes in intra-MNC accounts can also be subject to restrictions and regulations put forward by the respective host countries of various subsidiaries.

Credit and inventory management

Multinational firms based in different countries compete for the same global export markets. Therefore it is essential that they offer attractive credit terms to potential customers. Increasingly, however, the maturity and saturation of developed markets is forcing MNCs to maintain and increase revenues by exporting and selling a higher percentage of their output to developing countries. Given the risks associated with the latter group of buyers, as partly evidenced by their lack of a major (hard) currency, the MNC must use a variety of tools to protect such revenues. In addition to the use of hedging and various asset and liability adjustments (described earlier), MNCs should seek the backing of their respective governments in both identifying target markets and extending credit. Multinationals based in a number of Western European nations and those based in Japan currently benefit from extensive involvement of government agencies that provide them with the needed service and financial support suggested here. For U.S.-based MNCs the international positions of government agencies such as the Export-Import Bank currently do not provide a comparable level of support.

In terms of inventory management, MNCs must consider a number of factors related to both economics and politics. In the former category, in addition to maintaining the appropriate level of inventory in various locations around the world, a multinational firm is compelled to deal with exchange rate fluctuations, tariffs, nontariff barriers, integration schemes such as the EC, and other rules and regulations. Politically, inventories could be subjected to wars, expropriations, blockages, and other forms of government intervention.

CONCEPTS IN REVIEW

20-12 What is the *Eurocurrency market?* What are the main factors determining exchange rates in that market? Define and differentiate between the *nominal interest rate* and *effective interest rate* in this market.

20-13 Discuss the steps to be followed in adjusting a subsidiary's accounts relative to *third parties* when that subsidiary's local currency is expected to appreciate in value in relation to the currency of the parent MNC.

20-14 Outline the changes to be undertaken in *intra-MNC accounts* if a subsidiary's currency is expected to depreciate in value relative to the currency of the parent MNC.

Mergers and joint ventures

International mergers and joint ventures are formed for reasons similar to those motivating purely domestic mergers. Why do you think that over the past few years many developing nations have become more flexible in their dealings with MNCs wishing to form joint ventures in their countries? Spend a short time answering this question before reading on.

THE MOTIVES FOR DOMESTIC MERGERS—GROWTH OR DIVERSIFICATION, SYNERGY, FUND raising, increased managerial skill or technology, tax considerations, increased ownership liquidity, and defense against takeover—are all applicable to MNCs' international mergers and joint ventures. Several points, nevertheless, need attention.

First, international mergers and joint ventures, especially those involving European firms acquiring assets in the United States, increased significantly beginning in the 1980s. MNCs based in Western Europe, Japan, and North America have made substantial contributions to this increase. Moreover, a fast-growing group of MNCs has emerged in the past two decades, based in the so-called newly industrializing countries (which include, among others, Brazil, Argentina, Mexico, Hong Kong, Singapore, South Korea, Taiwan, India, and Pakistan). This growth has added further to the number and value of international mergers.

Foreign direct investments (i.e., *new* investments and/or *mergers,* on the basis of either wholly owned or joint ventures) in the United States have gained popularity in the past few years. Most of the foreign direct investors in the United States come from seven countries: Britain, Canada, France, the Netherlands, Japan, Switzerland, and Germany. The heaviest investments are concentrated in manufacturing, followed by the petroleum and trade/service sectors. Another interesting trend is the current rise in the number of joint ventures between companies based in Japan and firms domiciled elsewhere in the industrialized world, especially U.S.-based MNCs. While Japanese authorities continue their discussions and debates with other governments regarding Japan's international trade surpluses as well as perceived trade barriers, mergers and joint ventures continue to take place. In the eyes of some U.S. corporate executives, such business ventures are viewed as a "ticket into the Japanese market" as well as a way to curb a potentially tough competitor.

CONCEPT IN PRACTICE

General Magic: Making Science Fiction Real

Once, hand-held communications devices that used wireless phone networks to keep people in touch were science fiction; the devices and the wireless networks didn't speak the same language. Today, people can share messages, faxes, and hand-drawn sketches anytime, anywhere, thanks to General Magic, a joint venture of Apple Computer, AT&T, Japan's Matsushita Electric and Sony, and others. Along with money, each partner contributed knowledge from its area of specialization. Apple provided input on software. AT&T contributed expertise on wired and wireless communications. Matsushita developed a pen-based communicator with AT&T. Sony contributed insight into miniaturization. The last partner that General Magic needs to create a new industry is Microsoft, which controls PC programming standards.

Developing countries, too, have been attracting foreign direct investments in both horizontal and vertical industries. Meanwhile, during the last two decades a number of these nations have adopted specific policies and regulations aimed at controlling the inflows of foreign investments, a major provision being the 49 percent ownership limitation applied to MNCs. Of course, international competition among differently based MNCs has been of benefit to some developing countries in their attempts to extract concessions from the multinationals. However, an increasing number of such nations have shown greater flexibility in their recent dealings with MNCs as the latter group has become more reluctant to form joint ventures under the stated conditions. Furthermore, given the present, as well as the expected, international economic and trade status, it is likely that as more Third World countries recognize the need for foreign capital and technology, they will show even greater flexibility in their agreements with MNCs.

A final point to note relates to the existence of international *holding companies.* Places such as Liechtenstein and Panama have long been considered favorable spots for forming holding companies because of their conducive legal, corporate, and tax environments. International holding companies control many business entities in the form of subsidiaries, branches, joint ventures, and other agreements. For international legal (especially tax-related) reasons, as well as anonymity, such holding companies have become increasingly popular in recent years.

CONCEPT IN REVIEW

20-15 What are some of the major reasons for the rapid expansion in international business mergers and joint ventures of firms?

Summary

LG **1** **Understand the major factors influencing the financial operations of multinational companies (MNCs).** The emergence of new trading blocs, especially in North America and Western Europe, will result in new challenges and opportunities for MNCs. Setting up operations in foreign countries can entail special problems due to, among other things, the legal form of business organization chosen, the degree of ownership allowed by the host country, and possible restrictions and regulations on the return of capital and profits. Taxation of multinational companies is a complex issue because of the existence of varying tax rates, differing definitions of taxable income, measurement differences, and tax treaties. For U.S. MNCs it may be possible to take foreign taxes as a direct credit against U.S. tax liabilities. The existence and expansion of dollars held outside the United States have contributed in recent years to the development of a major international financial market, the Euromarket. The large international banks, developing and industrialized nations, and multinational companies participate as borrowers and lenders in this market.

LG **2** **Describe the key differences between purely domestic and international financial statements—particularly consolidation, translation of individual accounts, and international profits.** Certain regulations that apply to international operations tend to complicate the preparation of foreign-based financial statements. Rulings in the United States require the consolidation of financial statements of subsidiaries according to the percentage of ownership by the parent in the subsidiary. Individual accounts of subsidiaries must be translated back into U.S. dollars by using the procedures outlined in FASB No. 52. This standard also requires that only certain transactional gains or losses from international operations be included in the U.S. parent's income statement.

LG **3** **Discuss the two risks—exchange rate and political—requiring special consideration by the multinational company, and explain how MNCs manage them.** Operating in international markets involves certain factors that can influence the risk and return characteristics of an MNC. Economic exposure from exchange rate risk results from the existence of different currencies and the potential impact they can have on the value of foreign operations. The money markets, the forward (futures) markets, and the foreign currency options markets can be used to hedge (i.e., protect against) foreign exchange exposure. Political risks stem mainly from political instability in a number of countries and from the associated implications for the assets and operations of MNCs with subsidiaries located in such countries. MNCs can employ negative, external, and positive approaches to cope with political risk.

LG **4** **Describe foreign direct investment, investment cash flows and decisions, the factors that influence an MNC's capital structure, and the international debt and equity instruments that are available to MNCs.** Foreign direct investment (FDI) involves an MNC's transfer of capital, managerial, and technical assets from its home country to the host country. The investment cash flows of FDIs are subject to a variety of factors, including local taxes in host countries, host-country regulations that may block the return (repatriation) of MNCs' cash flow, the usual business and financial risks, risks stemming from inflation and different currency and political actions by host governments, and the application of a local cost of capital. The capital structures of MNCs differ from those of purely domestic firms because of the MNCs' access to the Euromarket and the variety of financial instruments it offers, the ability to reduce risk in their cash flows through international diversification, and the impact of legal, tax, political, social, and financial factors unique to each host country. International capital markets provide MNCs with an opportunity to raise long-term debt through the issuance of international bonds in various currencies. Foreign bonds are sold primarily in the country of the currency of issue; Eurobonds are sold primarily in countries other than the country of the currency in which the issue is denominated. MNCs can raise equity through the sale of their shares in the international capital markets or through joint ventures. In establishing foreign subsidiaries it may be more advantageous to issue debt (either local or MNC-based) than MNC-owned equity.

LG **5 Demonstrate use of the Eurocurrency market in short-term borrowing and investing (lending) and the basics of cash, credit, and inventory management in international operations.** Eurocurrency markets allow multinationals to take advantage of unregulated financial markets to invest (lend) and raise (borrow) short-term funds in a variety of currencies and to protect themselves against foreign exchange risk exposures. The effective rates of interest, which take into account each currency's forecast percentage change relative to the MNC parent's currency, are the main items considered by an MNC in making investment and borrowing decisions. The MNC invests in the currency with the highest effective rate and borrows in the currency with the lowest effective rate. MNCs must offer competitive credit terms and maintain adequate inventories to provide timely delivery to foreign buyers. Obtaining the backing of foreign governments is helpful to the MNC in effectively managing credit and inventory.

LG **6 Discuss the growth of and special factors relating to international mergers and joint ventures.** International mergers and joint ventures, including international holding companies, increased significantly in the last decade. Special factors affecting these mergers relate to various regulations imposed on MNCs by host countries and economic and trade conditions.

Self-test problem (Solution in Appendix E)

ST 20-1 LG 1 **Tax credits** A U.S.-based MNC has a foreign subsidiary that earns $150,000 before local taxes, with all the after-tax funds to be available to the parent in the form of dividends. The applicable taxes consist of a 32 percent foreign income tax rate, a foreign dividend withholding tax rate of 8 percent, and a U.S. tax rate of 34 percent. Calculate the net funds available to the parent MNC if:

a. Foreign taxes can be applied as a credit against the MNC's U.S. tax liability.

b. No tax credits are allowed.

Problems

20-1 LG 1 **Tax credits** A U.S.-based MNC has a foreign subsidiary that earns $250,000 before local taxes, with all the after-tax funds to be available to the parent in the form of dividends. The applicable taxes consist of a 33 percent foreign income tax rate, a foreign dividend withholding tax rate of 9 percent, and a U.S. tax rate of 34 percent. Calculate the net funds available to the parent MNC if:

a. Foreign taxes can be applied as a credit against the MNC's U.S. tax liability.

b. No tax credits are allowed.

20-2 LG 2 Translation of financial statements A U.S.-based MNC has a subsidiary in France. The balance sheet and income statement of the subsidiary are given below. On 12/31/94 the exchange rate is Ff 5.50/US$. Assume that the local (French franc, Ff) figures for the statements remain the same on 12/31/95. Calculate the U.S. dollar–translated figures for the two ending time periods, assuming that between 12/31/94 and 12/31/95 the French currency has appreciated against the U.S. dollar by 6 percent.

Translation of Balance Sheet			
	12/31/94		12/31/95
Assets	Ff	US$	US$
Cash	40.00		
Inventory	300.00		
Plant and equipment (net)	160.00	____	____
Total	500.00	____	____
Liabilities and stockholders' equity			
Debt	240.00		
Paid-in capital	200.00		
Retained earnings	60.00	____	____
Total	500.00	____	____
Translation of Income Statement			
Sales	3,000.00		
Cost of goods sold	2,750.00	____	____
Operating profits	250.00	____	____

20-3 LG 5 Euromarket investment and fund raising A U.S.-based multinational company has two subsidiaries, one in Germany (local currency, Deutsche mark, DM) and one in Switzerland (local currency, Swiss franc, Sf). Forecasts of business operations indicate the following short-term financing position for each subsidiary (in equivalent U.S. dollars):

Germany: $80 million excess cash to be invested (lent)
Switzerland: $60 million funds to be raised (borrowed)

The management gathered the following data:

	Currency		
Item	US$	DM	Sf
Spot exchange rates		DM 1.62/US$	Sf 1.42/US$
Forecast % change		+1.5%	+1.0%
Interest rates			
Nominal			
Euromarket	5.0%	6.5%	6.2%
Domestic	4.5	6.1	5.7
Effective			
Euromarket			
Domestic			

Determine the effective rates of interest for all three currencies in both the Euromarket and the domestic market; then indicate where the funds should be invested and raised. (*Note:* Assume that because of local regulations, a subsidiary is *not* permitted to use the domestic market of *any other* subsidiary.)

Chapter 20 Case Assessing a direct investment in Chile by U.S. Computer Corporation

David Smith is Chief Financial Officer for U.S. Computer Corporation (USCC), a successful and rapidly growing manufacturer of personal computers. He has been asked to evaluate an investment project calling for USCC to build a factory in Chile to assemble the company's most popular computer for sale in the Chilean market. David knows that Chile has been a real business success story in recent years—having achieved economic growth rates of over 9 percent per year during the early 1990s, even as it made the transition from military dictatorship to democracy—and USCC is eager to invest in this developing economy if an attractive opportunity arises. David's job is to use the information below to see whether this particular proposal meets the company's investment standards.

On the basis of the current Chilean peso (Ps)-to-dollar exchange rate of Ps 400/US$, David calculates that the factory would cost Ps 4,000,000,000 ($10,000,000) to build and would generate sales of Ps 8,000,000,000 ($20,000,000) per year for the first several years. An additional $1,000,000 in dollar-denominated working capital and Ps 400,000,000 in peso-denominated working capital would be required as part of the initial investment. The working capital needs can be financed in one of two ways. Either the entire amount can be borrowed in dollars in the Euromarket at 5% annual interest and half the proceeds converted to pesos, or the dollar portion can be borrowed in the Euromarket and the peso portion can be borrowed locally at 12% annual interest.

Initially, the factory would import key components from the United States and assemble the computers in Chile using local labor. Smith estimates that half the company's costs will be dollar-denominated components, and half will be local currency (peso) costs, but all USCC's revenues will be in pesos. As long as the peso/$ exchange rate is stable, the company's operating cash flow is expected to equal 20 percent of sales. If, however, the peso were to depreciate relative to the dollar, the company's peso cost of acquiring dollar-denominated components would increase, and its profit margin would shrink because the peso sale prices of its computers would not change.

If USCC made this investment, they would set up a subsidiary in Chile and structure the factory investment so that the subsidiary's capital structure was 60 percent debt and 40 percent equity. Therefore to finance the Ps 4,000,000,000 factory cost, USCC must obtain Ps 2,400,000,000 ($6,000,000) in debt and Ps 1,600,000,000 ($4,000,000) in equity. The debt can be obtained either by issuing $6,000,000 of dollar-denominated bonds in the Eurobond market at a 6% annual rate and then converting the proceeds into pesos or by borrowing the Ps 2,400,000 in the Chilean market at a 14% annual interest rate. If borrowing is done in dollars, however, the parent company must also service and repay the debt in dollars, even though all project revenues will be in pesos.

The parent company also has two ways to obtain the required equity financing. First, USCC can contribute $4,000,000 to the subsidiary from either retained earnings or newly issued stock. This equity financing would then be converted to pesos. Alternatively, the subsidiary could sell Ps 1,600,000,000 of stock to Chilean investors by listing shares on the Santiago Stock Exchange. USCC has a 12% required return on equity on its dollar-denominated investments, while Chilean investors have an annual required return on equity of 20% per year.

Required

a. Compute the weighted average cost of capital for this project, assuming that all financing (including the peso working capital requirement) is in dollars.

b. Assuming that the peso/$ exchange rate remains unchanged, compute the present value of the first five years of the project's cash flows, using the weighted average cost of capital computed in **a**. (*Note:* Round your answer in **a** to the nearest 1 percent prior to making this calculation.) What happens to the present value if the dollar appreciates against the peso?

c. Identify the exchange rate risks involved in this project. Given that no forward, futures, or options markets exist for the Chilean peso, how might USCC minimize the exchange rate risk of this project by changes in production, sourcing, and sales? (*Hint:* Exchange rate risk can be minimized either by decreasing dollar-denominated costs or by increasing dollar-denominated revenue or both.)

d. What are the risks involved in financing this project as much as possible with local funds (pesos)? Which financing strategy—dollar versus peso—would minimize the project's exchange rate risk? Would your answer change if Chile began to experience political instability? What would happen to the attractiveness of the project if Chile joined NAFTA?

INTEGRATIVE CASE VII
ORGANIC SOLUTIONS

Organic Solutions (OS), one of the nation's largest plant wholesalers in the Southeastern United States, was poised for expansion. Through strong profitability, a conservative dividend policy, and some recent realized gains in real estate, OS had a strong cash position and was searching for a target company to acquire. The executive members on the acquisition search committee had agreed that they preferred to find a firm in a similar line of business rather than one that would provide broad diversification. This would be their first acquisition, and they preferred to stay in a familiar line of business. Jennifer Morgan, director of marketing, had identified through exhaustive market research the targeted lines of business.

Ms. Morgan had determined that the servicing of plants in large commercial offices, hotels, zoos, and theme parks would complement the existing wholesale distribution business. Frequently, OS was requested by its large clients to bid on a service contract. However, Organic Solutions was neither staffed nor equipped to enter this market. Ms. Morgan was familiar with the major plant service companies in the Southeast and had suggested Green Thumbs, Inc. (GTI) as an acquisition target because of its significant market share and excellent reputation.

GTI had successfully commercialized a market that had been dominated by small local contractors and in-house landscaping departments. By first winning a contract from one of the largest theme parks in the United States, GTI's growth in sales had compounded remarkably over its eight-year history.

GTI had also been selected because of its large portfolio of long-term service contracts with several major Fortune 500 companies. These contracted clients would provide a captive customer base for the wholesale distribution of OS's plant products.

At the National Horticultural meeting in Los Angeles this past March, Ms. Morgan and OS's chief financial officer, Jack Levine, had approached the owner of GTI (a closely held corporation) to determine whether a merger offer would be welcomed. GTI's majority owner and president, Herb Merrell, had reacted favorably and subsequently provided financial data including GTI's earnings record and current balance sheet. These figures are presented in Tables 1 and 2 at the top of page 842.

Jack Levine had estimated that the incremental cash flow after taxes from the acquisition would be $18,750,000 for years 1 and 2, $20,500,000 for year 3, $21,750,000 for year 4, $24,000,000 for year 5, and $25,000,000 for years 6 through 30. He also estimated that the company should earn a rate of return of at least 16 percent on an investment of this type. Additional financial data for 1994 are available in Table 3 (on page 842) to analyze the acquisition potential of GTI.

TABLE 1

GREEN THUMBS, INC., EARNING RECORD

Year	EPS	Year	EPS
1987	\$2.20	1991	\$2.85
1988	2.35	1992	3.00
1989	2.45	1993	3.10
1990	2.60	1994	3.30

TABLE 2

GREEN THUMBS, INC., BALANCE SHEET (DECEMBER 31, 1994)

Assets		Liabilities and equity	
Cash	\$ 2,500,000	Current liabilities	\$ 5,250,000
Accounts receivable	1,500,000	Mortgage payable	3,125,000
Inventories	7,625,000	Common stock	15,625,000
Land	7,475,000	Retained earnings	9,000,000
Fixed assets (net)	13,900,000	Total liabilities	
Total assets	\$33,000,000	and equity	\$33,000,000

TABLE 3

OS AND GTI FINANCIAL DATA (DECEMBER 31, 1994)

Item	OS	GTI
Earnings available for common stock	\$35,000,000	\$15,246,000
Number of shares of common stock outstanding	10,000,000	4,620,000
Market price per share	\$50	\$30[a]

[a]Estimated by Organic Solutions.

Required

a. What is the maximum price Organic Solutions should offer GTI for a cash acquisition? (*Note:* Assume that the relevant time horizon for analysis is 30 years.)

b. (1) What is the ratio of exchange in a stock swap acquisition if OS pays \$30 per share for GTI? Explain why.

(2) What effect will this swap of stock have on the EPS of the original shareholders of (a) Organic Solutions and (b) Green Thumbs, Inc.? Explain why.

(3) If the earnings attributed to GTI's assets grow at a much slower rate than those attributed to OS's premerger assets, what effect might this have on the EPS of the merged firm over the long run?

c. What other merger proposals could OS make to GTI's owners?

d. What impact would the fact that GTI is actually a foreign-based company have on the foregoing analysis? Describe the added regulations, costs, benefits, and risks that are likely to be associated with such an international merger.

APPENDIXES

appendix A

Financial tables

TABLE A-1 Future-Value Interest Factors for One Dollar Compounded at *k* Percent for *n* Periods:

$$FVIF_{k,n} = (1 + k)^n$$

TABLE A-2 Future-Value Interest Factors for a One-Dollar Annuity Compounded at *k* Percent for *n* Periods:

$$FVIFA_{k,n} = \sum_{t=1}^{n} (1 + k)^{t-1}$$

TABLE A-3 Present-Value Interest Factors for One Dollar Discounted at *k* Percent for *n* Periods:

$$PVIF_{k,n} = \frac{1}{(1 + k)^n}$$

TABLE A-4 Present-Value Interest Factors for a One-Dollar Annuity Discounted at *k* Percent for *n* Periods:

$$PVIFA_{k,n} = \sum_{t=1}^{n} \frac{1}{(1 + k)^t}$$

TABLE A-1 Future-Value Interest Factors for One Dollar Compounded at k Percent for n Periods: $FVIF_{k,n} = (1 + k)^n$

Period	1%	2%	3%	4%	5%	6%	7%	8%	9%	10%	11%	12%	13%	14%	15%	16%	17%	18%	19%	20%
1	1.010	1.020	1.030	1.040	1.050	1.060	1.070	1.080	1.090	1.100	1.110	1.120	1.130	1.140	1.150	1.160	1.170	1.180	1.190	1.200
2	1.020	1.040	1.061	1.082	1.102	1.124	1.145	1.166	1.188	1.210	1.232	1.254	1.277	1.300	1.322	1.346	1.369	1.392	1.416	1.440
3	1.030	1.061	1.093	1.125	1.158	1.191	1.225	1.260	1.295	1.331	1.368	1.405	1.443	1.482	1.521	1.561	1.602	1.643	1.685	1.728
4	1.041	1.082	1.126	1.170	1.216	1.262	1.311	1.360	1.412	1.464	1.518	1.574	1.630	1.689	1.749	1.811	1.874	1.939	2.005	2.074
5	1.051	1.104	1.159	1.217	1.276	1.338	1.403	1.469	1.539	1.611	1.685	1.762	1.842	1.925	2.011	2.100	2.192	2.288	2.386	2.488
6	1.062	1.126	1.194	1.265	1.340	1.419	1.501	1.587	1.677	1.772	1.870	1.974	2.082	2.195	2.313	2.436	2.565	2.700	2.840	2.986
7	1.072	1.149	1.230	1.316	1.407	1.504	1.606	1.714	1.828	1.949	2.076	2.211	2.353	2.502	2.660	2.826	3.001	3.185	3.379	3.583
8	1.083	1.172	1.267	1.369	1.477	1.594	1.718	1.851	1.993	2.144	2.305	2.476	2.658	2.853	3.059	3.278	3.511	3.759	4.021	4.300
9	1.094	1.195	1.305	1.423	1.551	1.689	1.838	1.999	2.172	2.358	2.558	2.773	3.004	3.252	3.518	3.803	4.108	4.435	4.785	5.160
10	1.105	1.219	1.344	1.480	1.629	1.791	1.967	2.159	2.367	2.594	2.839	3.106	3.395	3.707	4.046	4.411	4.807	5.234	5.695	6.192
11	1.116	1.243	1.384	1.539	1.710	1.898	2.105	2.332	2.580	2.853	3.152	3.479	3.836	4.226	4.652	5.117	5.624	6.176	6.777	7.430
12	1.127	1.268	1.426	1.601	1.796	2.012	2.252	2.518	2.813	3.138	3.498	3.896	4.334	4.818	5.350	5.936	6.580	7.288	8.064	8.916
13	1.138	1.294	1.469	1.665	1.886	2.133	2.410	2.720	3.066	3.452	3.883	4.363	4.898	5.492	6.153	6.886	7.699	8.599	9.596	10.699
14	1.149	1.319	1.513	1.732	1.980	2.261	2.579	2.937	3.342	3.797	4.310	4.887	5.535	6.261	7.076	7.987	9.007	10.147	11.420	12.839
15	1.161	1.346	1.558	1.801	2.079	2.397	2.759	3.172	3.642	4.177	4.785	5.474	6.254	7.138	8.137	9.265	10.539	11.974	13.589	15.407
16	1.173	1.373	1.605	1.873	2.183	2.540	2.952	3.426	3.970	4.595	5.311	6.130	7.067	8.137	9.358	10.748	12.330	14.129	16.171	18.488
17	1.184	1.400	1.653	1.948	2.292	2.693	3.159	3.700	4.328	5.054	5.895	6.866	7.986	9.276	10.761	12.468	14.426	16.672	19.244	22.186
18	1.196	1.428	1.702	2.026	2.407	2.854	3.380	3.996	4.717	5.560	6.543	7.690	9.024	10.575	12.375	14.462	16.879	19.673	22.900	26.623
19	1.208	1.457	1.753	2.107	2.527	3.026	3.616	4.316	5.142	6.116	7.263	8.613	10.197	12.055	14.232	16.776	19.748	23.214	27.251	31.948
20	1.220	1.486	1.806	2.191	2.653	3.207	3.870	4.661	5.604	6.727	8.062	9.646	11.523	13.743	16.366	19.461	23.105	27.393	32.429	38.337
21	1.232	1.516	1.860	2.279	2.786	3.399	4.140	5.034	6.109	7.400	8.949	10.804	13.021	15.667	18.821	22.574	27.033	32.323	38.591	46.005
22	1.245	1.546	1.916	2.370	2.925	3.603	4.430	5.436	6.658	8.140	9.933	12.100	14.713	17.861	21.644	26.186	31.629	38.141	45.923	55.205
23	1.257	1.577	1.974	2.465	3.071	3.820	4.740	5.871	7.258	8.954	11.026	13.552	16.626	20.361	24.891	30.376	37.005	45.007	54.648	66.247
24	1.270	1.608	2.033	2.563	3.225	4.049	5.072	6.341	7.911	9.850	12.239	15.178	18.788	23.212	28.625	35.236	43.296	53.108	65.031	79.496
25	1.282	1.641	2.094	2.666	3.386	4.292	5.427	6.848	8.623	10.834	13.585	17.000	21.230	26.461	32.918	40.874	50.656	62.667	77.387	95.395
30	1.348	1.811	2.427	3.243	4.322	5.743	7.612	10.062	13.267	17.449	22.892	29.960	39.115	50.949	66.210	85.849	111.061	143.367	184.672	237.373
35	1.417	2.000	2.814	3.946	5.516	7.686	10.676	14.785	20.413	28.102	38.574	52.799	72.066	98.097	133.172	180.311	243.495	327.988	440.691	590.657
40	1.489	2.208	3.262	4.801	7.040	10.285	14.974	21.724	31.408	45.258	64.999	93.049	132.776	188.876	267.856	378.715	533.846	750.353	1051.642	1469.740
45	1.565	2.438	3.781	5.841	8.985	13.764	21.002	31.920	48.325	72.888	109.527	163.985	244.629	363.662	538.752	795.429	1170.425	1716.619	2509.583	3657.176
50	1.645	2.691	4.384	7.106	11.467	18.419	29.456	46.900	74.354	117.386	184.559	288.996	450.711	700.197	1083.619	1670.669	2566.080	3927.189	5988.730	9100.191

Using the calculator to compute the future value of a single amount

Before you begin, make sure to clear the memory, ensure that you are in the correct mode, and set the number of decimal places that you want (usually two for dollar-related accuracy).

SAMPLE PROBLEM

You place $800 in a savings account at 6 percent compounded annually. What is your account balance at the end of five years?

Hewlett-Packard HP 12C, 17 BII, and 19 BII[a]

Inputs: [800] [5] [6]

Functions: [CHS] [PV] [n] [i] [FV]

Outputs: [*1070.58*]

[a]For the 17 BII and 19 BII you would use the [+/−] key instead of the [CHS] key, the [N] key instead of the [n] key, and the [I% YR] key instead of the [i] key.

TABLE A-1 (Continued)

Period	21%	22%	23%	24%	25%	26%	27%	28%	29%	30%	31%	32%	33%	34%	35%	40%	45%	50%
1	1.210	1.220	1.230	1.240	1.250	1.260	1.270	1.280	1.290	1.300	1.310	1.320	1.330	1.340	1.350	1.400	1.450	1.500
2	1.464	1.488	1.513	1.538	1.562	1.588	1.613	1.638	1.664	1.690	1.716	1.742	1.769	1.796	1.822	1.960	2.102	2.250
3	1.772	1.816	1.861	1.907	1.953	2.000	2.048	2.097	2.147	2.197	2.248	2.300	2.353	2.406	2.460	2.744	3.049	3.375
4	2.144	2.215	2.289	2.364	2.441	2.520	2.601	2.684	2.769	2.856	2.945	3.036	3.129	3.224	3.321	3.842	4.421	5.063
5	2.594	2.703	2.815	2.932	3.052	3.176	3.304	3.436	3.572	3.713	3.858	4.007	4.162	4.320	4.484	5.378	6.410	7.594
6	3.138	3.297	3.463	3.635	3.815	4.001	4.196	4.398	4.608	4.827	5.054	5.290	5.535	5.789	6.053	7.530	9.294	11.391
7	3.797	4.023	4.259	4.508	4.768	5.042	5.329	5.629	5.945	6.275	6.621	6.983	7.361	7.758	8.172	10.541	13.476	17.086
8	4.595	4.908	5.239	5.589	5.960	6.353	6.767	7.206	7.669	8.157	8.673	9.217	9.791	10.395	11.032	14.758	19.541	25.629
9	5.560	5.987	6.444	6.931	7.451	8.004	8.595	9.223	9.893	10.604	11.362	12.166	13.022	13.930	14.894	20.661	28.334	38.443
10	6.727	7.305	7.926	8.594	9.313	10.086	10.915	11.806	12.761	13.786	14.884	16.060	17.319	18.666	20.106	28.925	41.085	57.665
11	8.140	8.912	9.749	10.657	11.642	12.708	13.862	15.112	16.462	17.921	19.498	21.199	23.034	25.012	27.144	40.495	59.573	86.498
12	9.850	10.872	11.991	13.215	14.552	16.012	17.605	19.343	21.236	23.298	25.542	27.982	30.635	33.516	36.644	56.694	86.380	129.746
13	11.918	13.264	14.749	16.386	18.190	20.175	22.359	24.759	27.395	30.287	33.460	36.937	40.745	44.912	49.469	79.371	125.251	194.620
14	14.421	16.182	18.141	20.319	22.737	25.420	28.395	31.691	35.339	39.373	43.832	48.756	54.190	60.181	66.784	111.119	181.614	291.929
15	17.449	19.742	22.314	25.195	28.422	32.030	36.062	40.565	45.587	51.185	57.420	64.358	72.073	80.643	90.158	155.567	263.341	437.894
16	21.113	24.085	27.446	31.242	35.527	40.357	45.799	51.923	58.808	66.541	75.220	84.953	95.857	108.061	121.713	217.793	381.844	656.841
17	25.547	29.384	33.758	38.740	44.409	50.850	58.165	66.461	75.862	86.503	98.539	112.138	127.490	144.802	164.312	304.911	553.674	985.261
18	30.912	35.848	41.523	48.038	55.511	64.071	73.869	85.070	97.862	112.454	129.086	148.022	169.561	194.035	221.822	426.875	802.826	1477.892
19	37.404	43.735	51.073	59.567	69.389	80.730	93.813	108.890	126.242	146.190	169.102	195.389	225.517	260.006	299.459	597.625	1164.098	2216.838
20	45.258	53.357	62.820	73.863	86.736	101.720	119.143	139.379	162.852	190.047	221.523	257.913	299.937	348.408	404.270	836.674	1687.942	3325.257
21	54.762	65.095	77.268	91.591	108.420	128.167	151.312	178.405	210.079	247.061	290.196	340.446	398.916	466.867	545.764	1171.343	2447.515	4987.883
22	66.262	79.416	95.040	113.572	135.525	161.490	192.165	228.358	271.002	321.178	380.156	449.388	530.558	625.601	736.781	1639.878	3548.896	7481.824
23	80.178	96.887	116.899	140.829	169.407	203.477	244.050	292.298	349.592	417.531	498.004	593.192	705.642	838.305	994.653	2295.829	5145.898	11222.738
24	97.015	118.203	143.786	174.628	211.758	256.381	309.943	374.141	450.974	542.791	652.385	783.013	938.504	1123.328	1342.781	3214.158	7461.547	16834.109
25	117.388	144.207	176.857	216.539	264.698	323.040	393.628	478.901	581.756	705.627	854.623	1033.577	1248.210	1505.258	1812.754	4499.816	10819.242	25251.164
30	304.471	389.748	497.904	634.810	807.793	1025.904	1300.477	1645.488	2078.208	2619.936	3297.081	4142.008	5194.516	6503.285	8128.426	24201.043	69348.375	191751.000
35	789.716	1053.370	1401.749	1861.020	2465.189	3258.053	4296.547	5653.840	7423.988	9727.598	12719.918	16598.906	21617.363	28096.695	36448.051	130158.687	*	*
40	2048.309	2846.941	3946.340	5455.797	7523.156	10346.879	14195.051	19426.418	26520.723	36117.754	49072.621	66519.313	89962.188	121388.437	163433.875	700022.688	*	*
45	5312.758	7694.418	11110.121	15994.316	22958.844	32859.457	46897.973	66748.500	94739.937	134102.187	*	*	*	*	*	*	*	*
50	13779.844	20795.680	31278.301	46889.207	70064.812	104354.562	154942.687	229345.875	338440.000	497910.125	*	*	*	*	*	*	*	*

*Not shown due to space limitations.

Texas Instruments BA-35, BAII, BAII Plus[b]

Inputs:	800		5	6		
Functions:	+/–	PV	N	%i	CPT	FV
Outputs:						1070.58

[b]For the Texas Instrument BAII you would use the 2nd key instead of the CPT key; for the Texas Instruments BAII Plus you would use the I/Y key instead of the %i key. When using the Texas Instruments BAII Plus, make sure that your calculator is set to *1 payment per year* I/Y *key* to work with annual compounding.

TABLE A-2 Future-Value Interest Factors for a One-Dollar Annuity Compounded at k Percent for n Periods: $FVIFA_{k,n} = \sum_{t=1}^{n} (1 + k)^{t-1}$

Period	1%	2%	3%	4%	5%	6%	7%	8%	9%	10%	11%	12%	13%	14%	15%	16%	17%	18%	19%	20%
1	1.000	1.000	1.000	1.000	1.000	1.000	1.000	1.000	1.000	1.000	1.000	1.000	1.000	1.000	1.000	1.000	1.000	1.000	1.000	1.000
2	2.010	2.020	2.030	2.040	2.050	2.060	2.070	2.080	2.090	2.100	2.110	2.120	2.130	2.140	2.150	2.160	2.170	2.180	2.190	2.200
3	3.030	3.060	3.091	3.122	3.152	3.184	3.215	3.246	3.278	3.310	3.342	3.374	3.407	3.440	3.472	3.506	3.539	3.572	3.606	3.640
4	4.060	4.122	4.184	4.246	4.310	4.375	4.440	4.506	4.573	4.641	4.710	4.779	4.850	4.921	4.993	5.066	5.141	5.215	5.291	5.368
5	5.101	5.204	5.309	5.416	5.526	5.637	5.751	5.867	5.985	6.105	6.228	6.353	6.480	6.610	6.742	6.877	7.014	7.154	7.297	7.442
6	6.152	6.308	6.468	6.633	6.802	6.975	7.153	7.336	7.523	7.716	7.913	8.115	8.323	8.535	8.754	8.977	9.207	9.442	9.683	9.930
7	7.214	7.434	7.662	7.898	8.142	8.394	8.654	8.923	9.200	9.487	9.783	10.089	10.405	10.730	11.067	11.414	11.772	12.141	12.523	12.916
8	8.286	8.583	8.892	9.214	9.549	9.897	10.260	10.637	11.028	11.436	11.859	12.300	12.757	13.233	13.727	14.240	14.773	15.327	15.902	16.499
9	9.368	9.755	10.159	10.583	11.027	11.491	11.978	12.488	13.021	13.579	14.164	14.776	15.416	16.085	16.786	17.518	18.285	19.086	19.923	20.799
10	10.462	10.950	11.464	12.006	12.578	13.181	13.816	14.487	15.193	15.937	16.722	17.549	18.420	19.337	20.304	21.321	22.393	23.521	24.709	25.959
11	11.567	12.169	12.808	13.486	14.207	14.972	15.784	16.645	17.560	18.531	19.561	20.655	21.814	23.044	24.349	25.733	27.200	28.755	30.403	32.150
12	12.682	13.412	14.192	15.026	15.917	16.870	17.888	18.977	20.141	21.384	22.713	24.133	25.650	27.271	29.001	30.850	32.824	34.931	37.180	39.580
13	13.809	14.680	15.618	16.627	17.713	18.882	20.141	21.495	22.953	24.523	26.211	28.029	29.984	32.088	34.352	36.786	39.404	42.218	45.244	48.496
14	14.947	15.974	17.086	18.292	19.598	21.015	22.550	24.215	26.019	27.975	30.095	32.392	34.882	37.581	40.504	43.672	47.102	50.818	54.841	59.196
15	16.097	17.293	18.599	20.023	21.578	23.276	25.129	27.152	29.361	31.772	34.405	37.280	40.417	43.842	47.580	51.659	56.109	60.965	66.260	72.035
16	17.258	18.639	20.157	21.824	23.657	25.672	27.888	30.324	33.003	35.949	39.190	42.753	46.671	50.980	55.717	60.925	66.648	72.938	79.850	87.442
17	18.430	20.012	21.761	23.697	25.840	28.213	30.840	33.750	36.973	40.544	44.500	48.883	53.738	59.117	65.075	71.673	78.978	87.067	96.021	105.930
18	19.614	21.412	23.414	25.645	28.132	30.905	33.999	37.450	41.301	45.599	50.396	55.749	61.724	68.393	75.836	84.140	93.404	103.739	115.265	128.116
19	20.811	22.840	25.117	27.671	30.539	33.760	37.379	41.446	46.018	51.158	56.939	63.439	70.748	78.968	88.211	98.603	110.283	123.412	138.165	154.739
20	22.019	24.297	26.870	29.778	33.066	36.785	40.995	45.762	51.159	57.274	64.202	72.052	80.946	91.024	102.443	115.379	130.031	146.626	165.417	186.687
21	23.239	25.783	28.676	31.969	35.719	39.992	44.865	50.422	56.764	64.002	72.264	81.698	92.468	104.767	118.809	134.840	153.136	174.019	197.846	225.024
22	24.471	27.299	30.536	34.248	38.505	43.392	49.005	55.456	62.872	71.402	81.213	92.502	105.489	120.434	137.630	157.414	180.169	206.342	236.436	271.028
23	25.716	28.845	32.452	36.618	41.430	46.995	53.435	60.893	69.531	79.542	91.147	104.602	120.203	138.295	159.274	183.600	211.798	244.483	282.359	326.234
24	26.973	30.421	34.426	39.082	44.501	50.815	58.176	66.764	76.789	88.496	102.173	118.154	136.829	158.656	184.166	213.976	248.803	289.490	337.007	392.480
25	28.243	32.030	36.459	41.645	47.726	54.864	63.248	73.105	84.699	98.346	114.412	133.333	155.616	181.867	212.790	249.212	292.099	342.598	402.038	471.976
30	34.784	40.567	47.575	56.084	66.438	79.057	94.459	113.282	136.305	164.491	199.018	241.330	293.192	356.778	434.738	530.306	647.423	790.932	966.698	1181.865
35	41.659	49.994	60.461	73.651	90.318	111.432	138.234	172.314	215.705	271.018	341.583	431.658	546.663	693.552	881.152	1120.699	1426.448	1816.607	2314.173	2948.294
40	48.885	60.401	75.400	95.024	120.797	154.758	199.630	259.052	337.872	442.580	581.812	767.080	1013.667	1341.979	1779.048	2360.724	3134.412	4163.094	5529.711	7343.715
45	56.479	71.891	92.718	121.027	159.695	212.737	285.741	386.497	525.840	718.881	986.613	1358.208	1874.086	2590.464	3585.031	4965.191	6879.008	9531.258	13203.105	18280.914
50	64.461	84.577	112.794	152.664	209.341	290.325	406.516	573.756	815.051	1163.865	1668.723	2399.975	3459.344	4994.301	7217.488	10435.449	15088.805	21812.273	31514.492	45496.094

Using the calculator to compute future value of an annuity

Before you begin, make sure to clear the memory, ensure that you are in the correct mode, and set the number of decimal places that you want (usually two for dollar-related accuracy).

SAMPLE PROBLEM

You want to know what the future value will be at the end of five years if you place five end-of-year deposits of $1,000 in an account paying 7 percent annually. What is your account balance at the end of five years?

Hewlett-Packard HP 12C, 17 BII, and 19 BII[a]

Inputs: 1000 | 5 | 7

Functions: CHS | PMT | n | i | FV

Outputs: *5750.74*

[a]For the 17 BII and 19 BII you would use the +/− key instead of the CHS key, the N key instead of the n key, and the I% YR key instead of the i key.

ABLE A-2 (Continued)

Period	21%	22%	23%	24%	25%	26%	27%	28%	29%	30%	31%	32%	33%	34%	35%	40%	45%	50%
1	1.000	1.000	1.000	1.000	1.000	1.000	1.000	1.000	1.000	1.000	1.000	1.000	1.000	1.000	1.000	1.000	1.000	1.000
2	2.210	2.220	2.230	2.240	2.250	2.260	2.270	2.280	2.290	2.300	2.310	2.320	2.330	2.340	2.350	2.400	2.450	2.500
3	3.674	3.708	3.743	3.778	3.813	3.848	3.883	3.918	3.954	3.990	4.026	4.062	4.099	4.136	4.172	4.360	4.552	4.750
4	5.446	5.524	5.604	5.684	5.766	5.848	5.931	6.016	6.101	6.187	6.274	6.362	6.452	6.542	6.633	7.104	7.601	8.125
5	7.589	7.740	7.893	8.048	8.207	8.368	8.533	8.700	8.870	9.043	9.219	9.398	9.581	9.766	9.954	10.946	12.022	13.188
6	10.183	10.442	10.708	10.980	11.259	11.544	11.837	12.136	12.442	12.756	13.077	13.406	13.742	14.086	14.438	16.324	18.431	20.781
7	13.321	13.740	14.171	14.615	15.073	15.546	16.032	16.534	17.051	17.583	18.131	18.696	19.277	19.876	20.492	23.853	27.725	32.172
8	17.119	17.762	18.430	19.123	19.842	20.588	21.361	22.163	22.995	23.858	24.752	25.678	26.638	27.633	28.664	34.395	41.202	49.258
9	21.714	22.670	23.669	24.712	25.802	26.940	28.129	29.369	30.664	32.015	33.425	34.895	36.429	38.028	39.696	49.152	60.743	74.887
10	27.274	28.657	30.113	31.643	33.253	34.945	36.723	38.592	40.556	42.619	44.786	47.062	49.451	51.958	54.590	69.813	89.077	113.330
11	34.001	35.962	38.039	40.238	42.566	45.030	47.639	50.398	53.318	56.405	59.670	63.121	66.769	70.624	74.696	98.739	130.161	170.995
12	42.141	44.873	47.787	50.895	54.208	57.738	61.501	65.510	69.780	74.326	79.167	84.320	89.803	95.636	101.840	139.234	189.734	257.493
13	51.991	55.745	59.778	64.109	68.760	73.750	79.106	84.853	91.016	97.624	104.709	112.302	120.438	129.152	138.484	195.928	276.114	387.239
14	63.909	69.009	74.528	80.496	86.949	93.925	101.465	109.611	118.411	127.912	138.169	149.239	161.183	174.063	187.953	275.299	401.365	581.858
15	78.330	85.191	92.669	100.815	109.687	119.346	129.860	141.302	153.750	167.285	182.001	197.996	215.373	234.245	254.737	386.418	582.980	873.788
16	95.779	104.933	114.983	126.010	138.109	151.375	165.922	181.867	199.337	218.470	239.421	262.354	287.446	314.888	344.895	541.985	846.321	1311.681
17	116.892	129.019	142.428	157.252	173.636	191.733	211.721	233.790	258.145	285.011	314.642	347.307	383.303	422.949	466.608	759.778	1228.165	1968.522
18	142.439	158.403	176.187	195.993	218.045	242.583	269.885	300.250	334.006	371.514	413.180	459.445	510.792	567.751	630.920	1064.689	1781.838	2953.783
19	173.351	194.251	217.710	244.031	273.556	306.654	343.754	385.321	431.868	483.968	542.266	607.467	680.354	761.786	852.741	1491.563	2584.665	4431.672
20	210.755	237.986	268.783	303.598	342.945	387.384	437.568	494.210	558.110	630.157	711.368	802.856	905.870	1021.792	1152.200	2089.188	3748.763	6648.508
21	256.013	291.343	331.603	377.461	429.681	489.104	556.710	633.589	720.962	820.204	932.891	1060.769	1205.807	1370.201	1556.470	2925.862	5436.703	9973.762
22	310.775	356.438	408.871	469.052	538.101	617.270	708.022	811.993	931.040	1067.265	1223.087	1401.215	1604.724	1837.068	2102.234	4097.203	7884.215	14961.645
23	377.038	435.854	503.911	582.624	673.626	778.760	900.187	1040.351	1202.042	1388.443	1603.243	1850.603	2135.282	2462.669	2839.014	5737.078	11433.109	22443.469
24	457.215	532.741	620.810	723.453	843.032	982.237	1144.237	1332.649	1551.634	1805.975	2101.247	2443.795	2840.924	3300.974	3833.667	8032.906	16579.008	33666.207
25	554.230	650.944	764.596	898.082	1054.791	1238.617	1454.180	1706.790	2002.608	2348.765	2753.631	3226.808	3779.428	4424.301	5176.445	11247.062	24040.555	50500.316
30	1445.111	1767.044	2160.459	2640.881	3227.172	3941.953	4812.891	5873.172	7162.785	8729.805	10632.543	12940.672	15737.945	19124.434	23221.258	60500.207	154105.313	383500.000
35	3755.814	4783.520	6090.227	7750.094	9856.746	12527.160	15909.480	20188.742	25596.512	32422.090	41028.887	51868.563	65504.199	82634.625	104134.500	325394.688	*	*
40	9749.141	12936.141	17153.691	22728.367	30088.621	39791.957	52570.707	69376.562	91447.375	120389.375	*	*	*	*	*	*	*	*
45	25294.223	34970.230	48300.660	66638.937	91831.312	126378.937	173692.875	238384.312	326686.375	447005.062	*	*	*	*	*	*	*	*

ot shown due to space limitations.

Texas Instruments BA-35, BAII, BAII Plus[b]

Inputs:	1000		5	7		
Functions:	+/−	PMT	N	%i	CPT	FV
Outputs:						5750.74

[b]For the Texas Instrument BAII you would use the 2nd key instead of the CPT key; for the Texas Instruments BAII Plus you would use the I/Y key instead of the %i key. When using the Texas Instruments BAII Plus, make sure that your calculator is set to *1 payment per year* I/Y *key* to work with annual compounding.

TABLE A-3 Present-Value Interest Factors for One Dollar Discounted at *k* Percent for *n* Periods: $PVIF_{k,n} = \frac{1}{(1+k)^n}$

Period	1%	2%	3%	4%	5%	6%	7%	8%	9%	10%	11%	12%	13%	14%	15%	16%	17%	18%	19%	20%
1	.990	.980	.971	.962	.952	.943	.935	.926	.917	.909	.901	.893	.885	.877	.870	.862	.855	.847	.840	.833
2	.980	.961	.943	.925	.907	.890	.873	.857	.842	.826	.812	.797	.783	.769	.756	.743	.731	.718	.706	.694
3	.971	.942	.915	.889	.864	.840	.816	.794	.772	.751	.731	.712	.693	.675	.658	.641	.624	.609	.593	.579
4	.961	.924	.888	.855	.823	.792	.763	.735	.708	.683	.659	.636	.613	.592	.572	.552	.534	.516	.499	.482
5	.951	.906	.863	.822	.784	.747	.713	.681	.650	.621	.593	.567	.543	.519	.497	.476	.456	.437	.419	.402
6	.942	.888	.837	.790	.746	.705	.666	.630	.596	.564	.535	.507	.480	.456	.432	.410	.390	.370	.352	.335
7	.933	.871	.813	.760	.711	.665	.623	.583	.547	.513	.482	.452	.425	.400	.376	.354	.333	.314	.296	.279
8	.923	.853	.789	.731	.677	.627	.582	.540	.502	.467	.434	.404	.376	.351	.327	.305	.285	.266	.249	.233
9	.914	.837	.766	.703	.645	.592	.544	.500	.460	.424	.391	.361	.333	.308	.284	.263	.243	.225	.209	.194
10	.905	.820	.744	.676	.614	.558	.508	.463	.422	.386	.352	.322	.295	.270	.247	.227	.208	.191	.176	.162
11	.896	.804	.722	.650	.585	.527	.475	.429	.388	.350	.317	.287	.261	.237	.215	.195	.178	.162	.148	.135
12	.887	.789	.701	.625	.557	.497	.444	.397	.356	.319	.286	.257	.231	.208	.187	.168	.152	.137	.124	.112
13	.879	.773	.681	.601	.530	.469	.415	.368	.326	.290	.258	.229	.204	.182	.163	.145	.130	.116	.104	.093
14	.870	.758	.661	.577	.505	.442	.388	.340	.299	.263	.232	.205	.181	.160	.141	.125	.111	.099	.088	.078
15	.861	.743	.642	.555	.481	.417	.362	.315	.275	.239	.209	.183	.160	.140	.123	.108	.095	.084	.074	.065
16	.853	.728	.623	.534	.458	.394	.339	.292	.252	.218	.188	.163	.141	.123	.107	.093	.081	.071	.062	.054
17	.844	.714	.605	.513	.436	.371	.317	.270	.231	.198	.170	.146	.125	.108	.093	.080	.069	.060	.052	.045
18	.836	.700	.587	.494	.416	.350	.296	.250	.212	.180	.153	.130	.111	.095	.081	.069	.059	.051	.044	.038
19	.828	.686	.570	.475	.396	.331	.277	.232	.194	.164	.138	.116	.098	.083	.070	.060	.051	.043	.037	.031
20	.820	.673	.554	.456	.377	.312	.258	.215	.178	.149	.124	.104	.087	.073	.061	.051	.043	.037	.031	.026
21	.811	.660	.538	.439	.359	.294	.242	.199	.164	.135	.112	.093	.077	.064	.053	.044	.037	.031	.026	.022
22	.803	.647	.522	.422	.342	.278	.226	.184	.150	.123	.101	.083	.068	.056	.046	.038	.032	.026	.022	.018
23	.795	.634	.507	.406	.326	.262	.211	.170	.138	.112	.091	.074	.060	.049	.040	.033	.027	.022	.018	.015
24	.788	.622	.492	.390	.310	.247	.197	.158	.126	.102	.082	.066	.053	.043	.035	.028	.023	.019	.015	.013
25	.780	.610	.478	.375	.295	.233	.184	.146	.116	.092	.074	.059	.047	.038	.030	.024	.020	.016	.013	.010
30	.742	.552	.412	.308	.231	.174	.131	.099	.075	.057	.044	.033	.026	.020	.015	.012	.009	.007	.005	.004
35	.706	.500	.355	.253	.181	.130	.094	.068	.049	.036	.026	.019	.014	.010	.008	.006	.004	.003	.002	.002
40	.672	.453	.307	.208	.142	.097	.067	.046	.032	.022	.015	.011	.008	.005	.004	.003	.002	.001	.001	.001
45	.639	.410	.264	.171	.111	.073	.048	.031	.021	.014	.009	.006	.004	.003	.002	.001	.001	.001	*	*
50	.608	.372	.228	.141	.087	.054	.034	.021	.013	.009	.005	.003	.002	.001	.001	.001	*	*	*	*

**PVIF* is zero to three decimal places.

Using the calculator to compute the present value of a single amount

Before you begin, make sure to clear the memory, ensure that you are in the correct mode, and set the number of decimal places that you want (usually two for dollar-related accuracy).

SAMPLE PROBLEM

Calculate the present value of $1,700 to be received in eight years, assuming an 8 percent opportunity cost.

Hewlett-Packard HP 12C, 17 BII, and 19 BII[a]

Inputs: 1700 8 8

Functions: CHS FV n i PV

Outputs: 918.46

TABLE A-3 (Continued)

Period	21%	22%	23%	24%	25%	26%	27%	28%	29%	30%	31%	32%	33%	34%	35%	40%	45%	50%
1	.826	.820	.813	.806	.800	.794	.787	.781	.775	.769	.763	.758	.752	.746	.741	.714	.690	.667
2	.683	.672	.661	.650	.640	.630	.620	.610	.601	.592	.583	.574	.565	.557	.549	.510	.476	.444
3	.564	.551	.537	.524	.512	.500	.488	.477	.466	.455	.445	.435	.425	.416	.406	.364	.328	.296
4	.467	.451	.437	.423	.410	.397	.384	.373	.361	.350	.340	.329	.320	.310	.301	.260	.226	.198
5	.386	.370	.355	.341	.328	.315	.303	.291	.280	.269	.259	.250	.240	.231	.223	.186	.156	.132
6	.319	.303	.289	.275	.262	.250	.238	.227	.217	.207	.198	.189	.181	.173	.165	.133	.108	.088
7	.263	.249	.235	.222	.210	.198	.188	.178	.168	.159	.151	.143	.136	.129	.122	.095	.074	.059
8	.218	.204	.191	.179	.168	.157	.148	.139	.130	.123	.115	.108	.102	.096	.091	.068	.051	.039
9	.180	.167	.155	.144	.134	.125	.116	.108	.101	.094	.088	.082	.077	.072	.067	.048	.035	.026
10	.149	.137	.126	.116	.107	.099	.092	.085	.078	.073	.067	.062	.058	.054	.050	.035	.024	.017
11	.123	.112	.103	.094	.086	.079	.072	.066	.061	.056	.051	.047	.043	.040	.037	.025	.017	.012
12	.102	.092	.083	.076	.069	.062	.057	.052	.047	.043	.039	.036	.033	.030	.027	.018	.012	.008
13	.084	.075	.068	.061	.055	.050	.045	.040	.037	.033	.030	.027	.025	.022	.020	.013	.008	.005
14	.069	.062	.055	.049	.044	.039	.035	.032	.028	.025	.023	.021	.018	.017	.015	.009	.006	.003
15	.057	.051	.045	.040	.035	.031	.028	.025	.022	.020	.017	.016	.014	.012	.011	.006	.004	.002
16	.047	.042	.036	.032	.028	.025	.022	.019	.017	.015	.013	.012	.010	.009	.008	.005	.003	.002
17	.039	.034	.030	.026	.023	.020	.017	.015	.013	.012	.010	.009	.008	.007	.006	.003	.002	.001
18	.032	.028	.024	.021	.018	.016	.014	.012	.010	.009	.008	.007	.006	.005	.005	.002	.001	.001
19	.027	.023	.020	.017	.014	.012	.011	.009	.008	.007	.006	.005	.004	.004	.003	.002	.001	*
20	.022	.019	.016	.014	.012	.010	.008	.007	.006	.005	.005	.004	.003	.003	.002	.001	.001	*
21	.018	.015	.013	.011	.009	.008	.007	.006	.005	.004	.003	.003	.003	.002	.002	.001	*	*
22	.015	.013	.011	.009	.007	.006	.005	.004	.004	.003	.003	.002	.002	.002	.001	.001	*	*
23	.012	.010	.009	.007	.006	.005	.004	.003	.003	.002	.002	.002	.001	.001	.001	*	*	*
24	.010	.008	.007	.006	.005	.004	.003	.003	.002	.002	.002	.001	.001	.001	.001	*	*	*
25	.009	.007	.006	.005	.004	.003	.003	.002	.002	.001	.001	.001.	.001	.001	.001	*	*	*
30	.003	.003	.002	.002	.001	.001	.001	.001	*	*	*	*	*	*	*	*	*	*
35	.001	.001	.001	.001	*	*	*	*	*	*	*	*	*	*	*	*	*	*
40	*	*	*	*	*	*	*	*	*	*	*	*	*	*	*	*	*	*
45	*	*	*	*	*	*	*	*	*	*	*	*	*	*	*	*	*	*
50	*	*	*	*	*	*	*	*	*	*	*	*	*	*	*	*	*	*

*$PVIF$ is zero to three decimal places.

Texas Instruments BA-35, BAII, BAII Plus[b]

Inputs:	1700		8	8		
Functions:	+/−	FV	N	%i	CPT	PV
Outputs:						918.46

[a]For the 17 BII and 19 BII you would use the +/− key instead of the CHS key, the N key instead of the n key, and the I% YR key instead of the i key.

[b]For the Texas Instrument BAII you would use the 2nd key instead of the CPT key; for the Texas Instruments BAII Plus you would use the I/Y key instead of the %i key. When using the Texas Instruments BAII Plus, make sure that your calculator is set to *1 payment per year* I/Y *key* to work with annual compounding.

TABLE A-4 Present-Value Interest Factors for a One-Dollar Annuity Discounted at *k* Percent for *n* Periods: $PVIFA_{k,n} = \sum_{t=1}^{n} \frac{1}{(1+k)^t}$

Period	1%	2%	3%	4%	5%	6%	7%	8%	9%	10%	11%	12%	13%	14%	15%	16%	17%	18%	19%	20%
1	.990	.980	.971	.962	.952	.943	.935	.926	.917	.909	.901	.893	.885	.877	.870	.862	.855	.847	.840	.833
2	1.970	1.942	1.913	1.886	1.859	1.833	1.808	1.783	1.759	1.736	1.713	1.690	1.668	1.647	1.626	1.605	1.585	1.566	1.547	1.528
3	2.941	2.884	2.829	2.775	2.723	2.673	2.624	2.577	2.531	2.487	2.444	2.402	2.361	2.322	2.283	2.246	2.210	2.174	2.140	2.106
4	3.902	3.808	3.717	3.630	3.546	3.465	3.387	3.312	3.240	3.170	3.102	3.037	2.974	2.914	2.855	2.798	2.743	2.690	2.639	2.589
5	4.853	4.713	4.580	4.452	4.329	4.212	4.100	3.993	3.890	3.791	3.696	3.605	3.517	3.433	3.352	3.274	3.199	3.127	3.058	2.991
6	5.795	5.601	5.417	5.242	5.076	4.917	4.767	4.623	4.486	4.355	4.231	4.111	3.998	3.889	3.784	3.685	3.589	3.498	3.410	3.326
7	6.728	6.472	6.230	6.002	5.786	5.582	5.389	5.206	5.033	4.868	4.712	4.564	4.423	4.288	4.160	4.039	3.922	3.812	3.706	3.605
8	7.652	7.326	7.020	6.733	6.463	6.210	5.971	5.747	5.535	5.335	5.146	4.968	4.799	4.639	4.487	4.344	4.207	4.078	3.954	3.837
9	8.566	8.162	7.786	7.435	7.108	6.802	6.515	6.247	5.995	5.759	5.537	5.328	5.132	4.946	4.772	4.607	4.451	4.303	4.163	4.031
10	9.471	8.983	8.530	8.111	7.722	7.360	7.024	6.710	6.418	6.145	5.889	5.650	5.426	5.216	5.019	4.833	4.659	4.494	4.339	4.192
11	10.368	9.787	9.253	8.760	8.306	7.887	7.499	7.139	6.805	6.495	6.207	5.938	5.687	5.453	5.234	5.029	4.836	4.656	4.486	4.327
12	11.255	10.575	9.954	9.385	8.863	8.384	7.943	7.536	7.161	6.814	6.492	6.194	5.918	5.660	5.421	5.197	4.988	4.793	4.611	4.439
13	12.134	11.348	10.635	9.986	9.394	8.853	8.358	7.904	7.487	7.013	6.750	6.424	6.122	5.842	5.583	5.342	5.118	4.910	4.715	4.533
14	13.004	12.106	11.296	10.563	9.899	9.295	8.745	8.244	7.786	7.367	6.982	6.628	6.302	6.002	5.724	5.468	5.229	5.008	4.802	4.611
15	13.865	12.849	11.938	11.118	10.380	9.712	9.108	8.560	8.061	7.606	7.191	6.811	6.462	6.142	5.847	5.575	5.324	5.092	4.876	4.675
16	14.718	13.578	12.561	11.652	10.838	10.106	9.447	8.851	8.313	7.824	7.379	6.974	6.604	6.265	5.954	5.668	5.405	5.162	4.938	4.730
17	15.562	14.292	13.166	12.166	11.274	10.477	9.763	9.122	8.544	8.022	7.549	7.120	6.729	6.373	6.047	5.749	5.475	5.222	4.990	4.775
18	16.398	14.992	13.754	12.659	11.690	10.828	10.059	9.372	8.756	8.201	7.702	7.250	6.840	6.467	6.128	5.818	5.534	5.273	5.033	4.812
19	17.226	15.679	14.324	13.134	12.085	11.158	10.336	9.604	8.950	8.365	7.839	7.366	6.938	6.550	6.198	5.877	5.584	5.316	5.070	4.843
20	18.046	16.352	14.878	13.590	12.462	11.470	10.594	9.818	9.129	8.514	7.963	7.469	7.025	6.623	6.259	5.929	5.628	5.353	5.101	4.870
21	18.857	17.011	15.415	14.029	12.821	11.764	10.836	10.017	9.292	8.649	8.075	7.562	7.102	6.687	6.312	5.973	5.665	5.384	5.127	4.891
22	19.661	17.658	15.937	14.451	13.163	12.042	11.061	10.201	9.442	8.772	8.176	7.645	7.170	6.743	6.359	6.011	5.696	5.410	5.149	4.909
23	20.456	18.292	16.444	14.857	13.489	12.303	11.272	10.371	9.580	8.883	8.266	7.718	7.230	6.792	6.399	6.044	5.723	5.432	5.167	4.925
24	21.244	18.914	16.936	15.247	13.799	12.550	11.469	10.529	9.707	8.985	8.348	7.784	7.283	6.835	6.434	6.073	5.746	5.451	5.182	4.937
25	22.023	19.524	17.413	15.622	14.094	12.783	11.654	10.675	9.823	9.077	8.422	7.843	7.330	6.873	6.464	6.097	5.766	5.467	5.195	4.948
30	25.808	22.396	19.601	17.292	15.373	13.765	12.409	11.258	10.274	9.427	8.694	8.055	7.496	7.003	6.566	6.177	5.829	5.517	5.235	4.979
35	29.409	24.999	21.487	18.665	16.374	14.498	12.948	11.655	10.567	9.644	8.855	8.176	7.586	7.070	6.617	6.215	5.858	5.539	5.251	4.992
40	32.835	27.356	23.115	19.793	17.159	15.046	13.332	11.925	10.757	9.779	8.951	8.244	7.634	7.105	6.642	6.233	5.871	5.548	5.258	4.997
45	36.095	29.490	24.519	20.720	17.774	15.456	13.606	12.108	10.881	9.863	9.008	8.283	7.661	7.123	6.654	6.242	5.877	5.552	5.261	4.999
50	39.196	31.424	25.730	21.482	18.256	15.762	13.801	12.233	10.962	9.915	9.042	8.304	7.675	7.133	6.661	6.246	5.880	5.554	5.262	4.999

Using the calculator to compute the present value of an annuity

Before you begin, make sure to clear the memory, ensure that you are in the correct mode, and set the number of decimal places that you want (usually two for dollar-related accuracy).

SAMPLE PROBLEM

You want to know what the present value will be of an annuity of $700 per year at the end of each year for five years, given a required return of 8 percent.

Hewlett-Packard HP 12C, 17 BII, and 19 BII[a]

Inputs: [700] [5] [8]

Functions: [CHS] [PMT] [n] [i] [PV]

Outputs: [2794.90]

[a]For the 17 BII and 19 BII you would use the [+/−] key instead of the [CHS] key, the [N] key instead of the [n] key, and the [I% YR] key instead of the [i] key.

TABLE A-4 (Continued)

Period	21%	22%	23%	24%	25%	26%	27%	28%	29%	30%	31%	32%	33%	34%	35%	40%	45%	50%
1	.826	.820	.813	.806	.800	.794	.787	.781	.775	.769	.763	.758	.752	.746	.741	.714	.690	.667
2	1.509	1.492	1.474	1.457	1.440	1.424	1.407	1.392	1.376	1.361	1.346	1.331	1.317	1.303	1.289	1.224	1.165	1.111
3	2.074	2.042	2.011	1.981	1.952	1.923	1.896	1.868	1.842	1.816	1.791	1.766	1.742	1.719	1.696	1.589	1.493	1.407
4	2.540	2.494	2.448	2.404	2.362	2.320	2.280	2.241	2.203	2.166	2.130	2.096	2.062	2.029	1.997	1.849	1.720	1.605
5	2.926	2.864	2.803	2.745	2.689	2.635	2.583	2.532	2.483	2.436	2.390	2.345	2.302	2.260	2.220	2.035	1.876	1.737
6	3.245	3.167	3.092	3.020	2.951	2.885	2.821	2.759	2.700	2.643	2.588	2.534	2.483	2.433	2.385	2.168	1.983	1.824
7	3.508	3.416	3.327	3.242	3.161	3.083	3.009	2.937	2.868	2.802	2.739	2.677	2.619	2.562	2.508	2.263	2.057	1.883
8	3.726	3.619	3.518	3.421	3.329	3.241	3.156	3.076	2.999	2.925	2.854	2.786	2.721	2.658	2.598	2.331	2.109	1.922
9	3.905	3.786	3.673	3.566	3.463	3.366	3.273	3.184	3.100	3.019	2.942	2.868	2.798	2.730	2.665	2.379	2.144	1.948
10	4.054	3.923	3.799	3.682	3.570	3.465	3.364	3.269	3.178	3.092	3.009	2.930	2.855	2.784	2.715	2.414	2.168	1.965
11	4.177	4.035	3.902	3.776	3.656	3.544	3.437	3.335	3.239	3.147	3.060	2.978	2.899	2.824	2.752	2.438	2.185	1.977
12	4.278	4.127	3.985	3.851	3.725	3.606	3.493	3.387	3.286	3.190	3.100	3.013	2.931	2.853	2.779	2.456	2.196	1.985
13	4.362	4.203	4.053	3.912	3.780	3.656	3.538	3.427	3.322	3.223	3.129	3.040	2.956	2.876	2.799	2.469	2.204	1.990
14	4.432	4.265	4.108	3.962	3.824	3.695	3.573	3.459	3.351	3.249	3.152	3.061	2.974	2.892	2.814	2.478	2.210	1.993
15	4.489	4.315	4.153	4.001	3.859	3.726	3.601	3.483	3.373	3.268	3.170	3.076	2.988	2.905	2.825	2.484	2.214	1.995
16	4.536	4.357	4.189	4.033	3.887	3.751	3.623	3.503	3.390	3.283	3.183	3.088	2.999	2.914	2.834	2.489	2.216	1.997
17	4.576	4.391	4.219	4.059	3.910	3.771	3.640	3.518	3.403	3.295	3.193	3.097	3.007	2.921	2.840	2.492	2.218	1.998
18	4.608	4.419	4.243	4.080	3.928	3.786	3.654	3.529	3.413	3.304	3.201	3.104	3.012	2.926	2.844	2.494	2.219	1.999
19	4.635	4.442	4.263	4.097	3.942	3.799	3.664	3.539	3.421	3.311	3.207	3.109	3.017	2.930	2.848	2.496	2.220	1.999
20	4.657	4.460	4.279	4.110	3.954	3.808	3.673	3.546	3.427	3.316	3.211	3.113	3.020	2.933	2.850	2.497	2.221	1.999
21	4.675	4.476	4.292	4.121	3.963	3.816	3.679	3.551	3.432	3.320	3.215	3.116	3.023	2.935	2.852	2.498	2.221	2.000
22	4.690	4.488	4.302	4.130	3.970	3.822	3.684	3.556	3.436	3.323	3.217	3.118	3.025	2.936	2.853	2.498	2.222	2.000
23	4.703	4.499	4.311	4.137	3.976	3.827	3.689	3.559	3.438	3.325	3.219	3.120	3.026	2.938	2.854	2.499	2.222	2.000
24	4.713	4.507	4.318	4.143	3.981	3.831	3.692	3.562	3.441	3.327	3.221	3.121	3.027	2.939	2.855	2.499	2.222	2.000
25	4.721	4.514	4.323	4.147	3.985	3.834	3.694	3.564	3.442	3.329	3.222	3.122	3.028	2.939	2.856	2.499	2.222	2.000
30	4.746	4.534	4.339	4.160	3.995	3.842	3.701	3.569	3.447	3.332	3.225	3.124	3.030	2.941	2.857	2.500	2.222	2.000
35	4.756	4.541	4.345	4.164	3.998	3.845	3.703	3.571	3.448	3.333	3.226	3.125	3.030	2.941	2.857	2.500	2.222	2.000
40	4.760	4.544	4.347	4.166	3.999	3.846	3.703	3.571	3.448	3.333	3.226	3.125	3.030	2.941	2.857	2.500	2.222	2.000
45	4.761	4.545	4.347	4.166	4.000	3.846	3.704	3.571	3.448	3.333	3.226	3.125	3.030	2.941	2.857	2.500	2.222	2.000
50	4.762	4.545	4.348	4.167	4.000	3.846	3.704	3.571	3.448	3.333	3.226	3.125	3.030	2.941	2.857	2.500	2.222	2.000

Texas Instruments BA-35, BAII, BAII Plus[b]

Inputs:	700		5	8		
Functions:	+/−	PMT	N	%i	CPT	FV
Outputs:						2794.90

[b]For the Texas Instrument BAII you would use the 2nd key instead of the CPT key; for the Texas Instruments BAII Plus you would use the I/Y key instead of the %i key. When using the Texas Instruments BAII Plus, make sure that your calculator is set to *1 payment per year* I/Y *key* to work with annual compounding.

appendix B

Instructions for using the *PMF Disk*

The *PMF Disk* contains three different sets of routines: the *PMF Tutor, PMF Problem-Solver,* and the *PMF Lotus Templates.* These programs are designed for use on IBM PC/XT/AT and compatible microcomputers. All programs are extremely user friendly.

The *Tutor, Problem-Solver,* and *Lotus Templates* routines are arranged in the same order as the text discussions. For convenience, text page references are shown on the screen for each associated computational routine in the *Problem-Solver* and the *Tutor.* As noted in the text Preface as well as in Chapter 1, applicability of the software throughout the text and study guide is keyed to related text discussions, end-of-chapter problems, and end-of-part cases by a computer icon for the *Tutor,* by a diskette icon for the *Problem-Solver,* and by a spreadsheet icon for the *Lotus Templates.* Thus you can integrate the procedures on the disk with the corresponding text discussions.

What is the *PMF Tutor?*

The *PMF Tutor* is a collection of managerial finance problem types constructed by random number generation. It is based on the *Finance Tutor* by Hansen, Bush, and Flowers, also published by HarperCollins. Its purpose is to give you an essentially unlimited number of problems to work so that you can practice until you are satisfied that you understand a concept. In using the *Tutor* the following sequence should produce the best results:

1. **Work the problem first yourself.** It is tempting to save time by letting the computer solve the problem for you and then studying the computer's answer. You won't learn much that way. Even if you make mistakes when you try the problem on your own, you will learn from those mistakes.
2. **Enter your answer.** The computer will check your answer against the correct answer.
3. If you do not get the same answer as the computer, **check your work step-by-step** against the correct solution displayed on the computer screen. Doing so will help you to pinpoint your mistakes. Practice each type of problem until you have genuinely mastered it. Don't have false pride about your mastery. When you take the course exams, you won't be able to fake your knowledge level. So don't stop until *you* know that you have mastered the idea.

The *Tutor* uses randomizing procedures to choose the specific numbers, so it is unlikely that you will ever see a combination of numbers twice. This gives you an effectively unlimited number of practice problems. The only limit is your willingness to practice.

What is the *PMF Problem-Solver?*

The *PMF Problem-Solver* is a collection of financial computation routines. The purpose of the *PMF Problem-Solver* is to aid the student's learning and understanding of managerial finance by providing a fast and easy method for performing the often time-consuming mathematical computations required. It is not the intent of the *PMF Problem-Solver* to eliminate the need for learning the various concepts, but to assist in solving the problems once the appropriate formulas have been studied. The *PMF Problem-Solver* differs from the *Tutor* in that it solves for the answer, given the input data supplied by the user, whereas the *Tutor* supplies the input data and looks to the student to perform the calculations. The *Tutor* should be used to practice application of basic concepts; the *PMF Problem-Solver* should be used to save computational time once the concepts are understood.

What are the *PMF Lotus Templates?*

The *PMF Lotus Templates* are a collection of preprogrammed Lotus worksheets. The templates enable students to enter data and solve problems using perhaps the most popular and widely accepted practical software application. The template files correspond to selected end-of-chapter problems, and the template file names are based on the chapter number and the problem number. For selected problems there are additional templates that are not tied to the problems in the text. These templates can be used to provide students with additional opportunities for solving financial problems on their own.

Hardware requirements

To use the *PMF Disk,* the following equipment is needed:

- An IBM PC or true compatible with MS-DOS® operating system Version 2.1
- 640 Kb of RAM
- At least one floppy or fixed (hard) disk drive
- Monochrome, Hercules®, CGA, EGA, or VGA card and monitor

Checking the master diskette

The *PMF Disk* comes on a diskette labeled "PMF Master Diskette." Some pointers in handling diskettes:

- *Never* put your fingers on the recording window. Always hold the diskette at the label end or by the hub (hole in the center).
- *Never* allow the diskette near a magnetic object or intense heat.
- *Never* apply pressure to the diskette with a ballpoint pen, pencil, or other sharp object. If you want to write something on the label of the diskette, use a soft-tip pen of some kind.
- *Never* bend the diskette.

The PMF Master Diskette comes with the following files on it:

```
PMFTUTOR.EXE...................The PMF Tutor program

PMFSOLVE.EXE...................The PMF Problem-Solver program
```

The PMF Master Diskette also comes with a directory that contains the Lotus 123 templates:

```
PMFSPR <DIR> ..................The Directory that contains the
                               PMF Lotus templates
```

You should verify through a directory listing that all of these files are on your master diskette. To display a directory listing, place the diskette in diskette drive A (shown in Figure B.1) and type the command:

DIR A:

You should see the following directory listing on your screen:

```
                Volume in drive A has no label
                       Directory of A:\
PMFTUTOR        EXE        xxxxxx        dd-dd-dd        tt:ttt
PMFSOLVE        EXE        xxxxxx        dd-dd-dd        tt:ttt
PMFSPR          <DIR>      xxxxxx        dd-dd-dd        tt:ttt
COLOR           BAT        xxxxxx        dd-dd-dd        tt:ttt
             2 File(s)               XXXXXX bytes free
```

where xxxxxx represents numbers, dd-dd-dd dates, and tt:ttt clock times. Since these will vary with the particular release of the *PMF Disk,* no specific values are given here. If you see these same eight files on your listing, your diskette should be all right. If you do not see this same directory, your diskette is probably defective and should be returned to the publisher as soon as possible. You can access the Lotus templates by accessing the Template Directory (TYPE CD\PMFSPR and press enter) and repeat the "DIR A:" command. A listing of the *PMF Templates* is illustrated in Figure B.2.

Getting started

COPYING THE *PMF DISK* TO A HARD DISK

If a hard disk is available and you wish to run the *PMF Disk* from it, execute the following sequence of steps to place the *PMF Disk* on the hard disk of your computer.

1. Make certain you are in the root directory by typing the command:

CD\ ↵

(The symbol ↵ means press the **ENTER** or **RETURN** key.)

FIGURE B.1

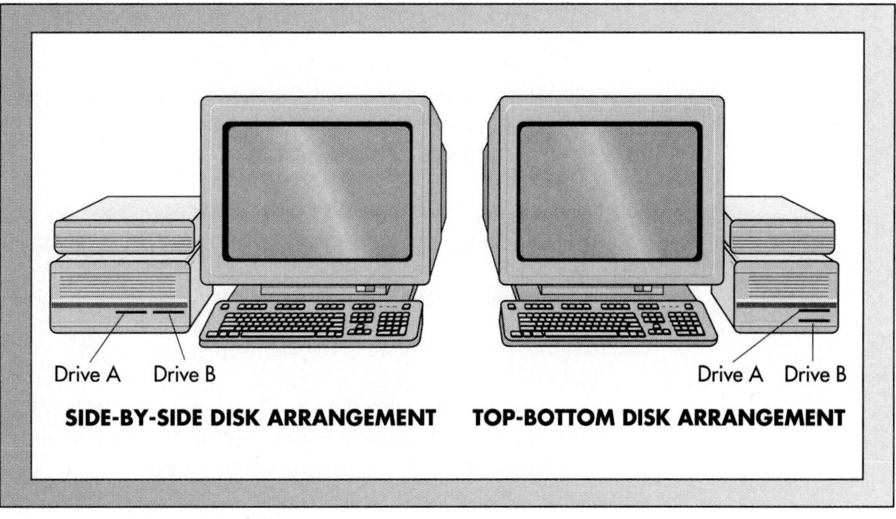

```
Volume in drive A has no label
Volume Serial Number is 3145-07C8
Directory of A:\PMFSPR

[.]           [..]          CH10-6.FMT    CH10-6.WK1    CH10-7.FMT
CH10-7.WK1    CH11-12.FMT   CH11-2.WK1    CH12-1.FMT    CH12-1.WK1
CH13-17.FMT   CH13-17.WK1   CH14-7.FMT    CH14-7.WK1    CH15-2.FMT
CH15-2.WK1    CH16-10.FMT   CH16-10.WK1   CH17-4.FMT    CH17-4.WK1
CH18-11.FMT   CH18-11.WK1   CH18-2.FMT    CH18-2.WK1    CH18-5.FMT
CH18-5.WK1    CH19-1.FMT    CH19-1.WK1    CH19-4.FMT    CH19-4.WK1
CH19-7.FMT    CH19-7.WK1    CH2-1.FMT     CH2-1.WK1     CH2-11.FMT
CH2-11.WK1    CH2-12.FMT    CH2-12.WK1    CH20-1.FMT    CH20-1.WK1
CH3-14.FMT    CH3-14.WK1    CH3-5.FMT     CH3-5.WK1     CH3-ST1.FMT
CH3-ST1.WK1   CH4-4.FMT     CH4-4.WK1     CH5-ST1.FMT   CH5-ST1.WK1
CH5-ST2.FMT   CH5-ST2.WK1   CH5-ST3.FMT   CH5-ST3.WK1   CH5-ST4.FMT
CH5-ST4.WK1   CH6-22.FMT    CH6-22.WK1    CH6-7.FMT     CH6-7.WK1
CH6-ST1.FMT   CH2-ST1.WK1   CH6-ST2.FMT   CH6-ST2.WK1   CH7-11.FMT
CH7-11.WK1    CH7-13.FMT    CH7-13.WK1    CH7-14.FMT    CH7-14.WK1
CH7-ST1.FMT   CH7-ST1.WK1   CH7-ST2.FMT   CH7-ST2.WK1   CH8-12.FMT
CH8-12.WK1    CH9-10.FMT    CH9-10.WK1    CH9-3.FMT     CH9-3.WK1
        80 file(s)       227765 bytes
                         186368 bytes free

A:\PMFSPR>
```

FIGURE B.2

2. Create a subdirectory by typing the following command:

MD\PMFSOFT↵

3. Go to the new subdirectory by typing the following command:

CD\PMFSOFT↵

4. Place the PMF Master Diskette in the floppy disk drive A, and type the following command:

COPY A:.**↵

5. When the copy operation is completed, store the Master Diskette in a safe place, and begin using the *PMF Disk* from your hard disk. Now see the section entitled "Running the *PMF Disk* (Hard Disk)" on page B-6.

COPYING THE *PMF DISK* TO A FLOPPY DISKETTE

To execute the *PMF Disk* from a floppy diskette, you need to create a diskette with a copy of the MS-DOS operating system (version 2.1 or later). To do this, place a MS-DOS master diskette (which your instructor may need to supply) in drive A and a blank diskette in drive B. Press the CRTL and ALT keys simultaneously and, without releasing these keys, press the DEL key. This will cause the computer to "reboot" to the MS-DOS operating system on your MS-DOS master diskette. Depending on what machine you have, you may be asked to enter the date and time; you may simply press the ENTER or RETURN key, or you may enter the actual date and time.

1. When you see the A > (called the "A prompt") characters on the screen, you should type:

FORMAT B: /S↵

(It is important that there be a space between *FORMAT* and *B:* and a space between *B:* and */S*.) This will cause the blank diskette in drive B to be prepared to receive the *PMF Disk*. You will first see a message on the screen:

```
Insert new diskette for drive B:
and strike ENTER when ready:
```

When you have placed the blank diskette in the B drive and closed the drive door, press the **ENTER** key (on most keyboards this key has the ↵ symbol on it).

2. The computer will next display a message that looks like the following:

```
Head: x Cylinder: xx
```

This is describing the progress of the format operation and will be updated by the computer. You should do nothing but watch at this stage.

3. When the format operation is complete, the computer will display another message:

```
Format complete
System transferred
 362496 bytes total disk space
   xxxxx bytes used by the system
 xxxxxx bytes available on disk
```

where xxxxx and xxxxxx are numbers that will vary depending on the version of MS-DOS that you use. However, they will always add up to 362496. You may occasionally see a slightly different form of the message:

```
362496 bytes total disk space
  xxxxx bytes used by the system
  xxxxx bytes in bad sectors
xxxxxx bytes available on disk
```

If you get this second form of the message, do not use the diskette. Use another diskette and repeat, starting at Step 1. This message means that the diskette is partially damaged and probably will not have enough space for all of the *PMF Disk* files.

4. The format operation will end with the message:

```
Format another (Y/N)?
```

You should press the N key and then press **ENTER.** This will return you to the prompt (A>). Now remove the MS-DOS master diskette from the A drive, and put the Gitman Master Diskette in the A drive. Next, type in the following command:

*COPY *.* B:*

(It is important that there be a space between *COPY* and *.* and a space between *.* and *B:*.) The message

```
copying files
```

will appear on the screen, and the names of the files on the PMF Master Diskette will appear on the screen as they are copied. When this is finished, you will see the A prompt (A>) again on the screen.

5. Remove the PMF Master Diskette from drive A, and store it in a safe place. Remove the diskette from drive B, and label it "PMF Diskette Working Copy." Remember to use a soft-tip pen to do this, never a pencil or hard-tip pen. This is the copy that you should use when you run the *PMF Disk*. Now see the section entitled "Running the *PMF Disk* (Floppy Diskette)" below.

RUNNING THE *PMF DISK* (HARD DISK)

To run the *PMF Disk* from a hard disk drive, type the command

CD\PMFSOFT↵

where the symbol ↵ means press the ENTER or RETURN key. You are now in the subdirectory for the *PMF Disk*. To start the program, type the following command:

PMFSOFT↵

Now skip to the section entitled "Running the *PMF Disk* (Combined)" below.

RUNNING THE *PMF DISK* (FLOPPY DISKETTE)

To run the *PMF Disk* from a floppy disk drive, place the PMF Diskette Working Copy in the floppy disk drive A. Now simultaneously press CTRL, ALT and DEL keys. When you are asked to enter the date and the time, you may simply press the ENTER or RETURN key (↵), or you may enter the actual date and time. To run the *PMFTUTOR* type PMFTUTOR and ENTER (↵). To run the *PMFSOLVER,* type PMFSOLVE and press ENTER (↵).

If you select the *PMF Tutor* option, go to the section "Running the *PMF Tutor*" below for further instruction. If you select *PMF Problem-Solver,* go to the section "Running the *PMF Problem-Solver*" (page B-12) for further instruction. If you select *PMF Lotus Templates,* go to the section "Running the PMF Lotus Templates" (page B-13) for further instructions.

Running the *PMF Tutor*

If you select the *PMF Tutor* option, the screen shown in Figure B.3 will appear. The screen has what appear to be a group of "buttons" on it. You can either move the mouse cursor to the option that you want to select and press the left mouse button or, using the left and right arrow keys, move the black highlight bar to the "button" for the option that you want and then press the ENTER key.

FIGURE B.3

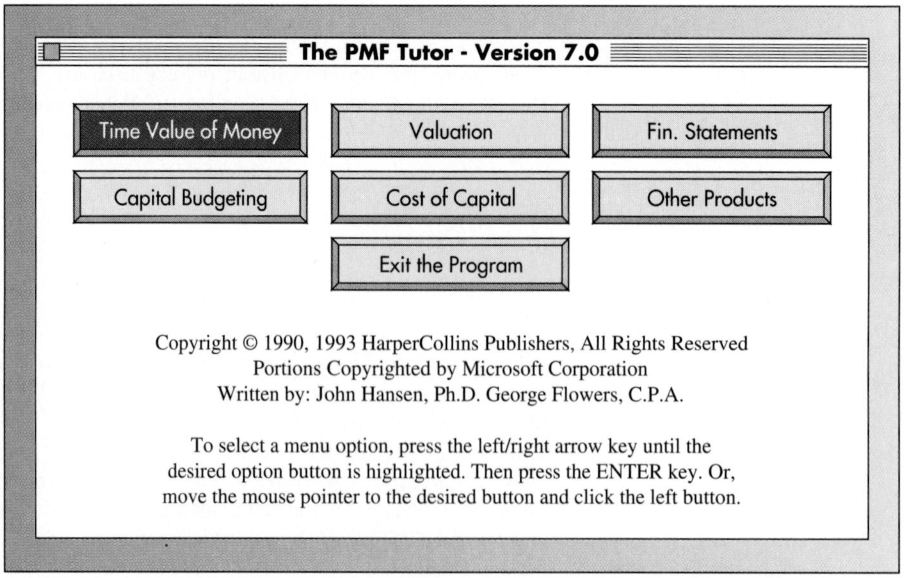

The PMF Tutor - Version 7.0

Time Value of Money	Valuation	Fin. Statements
Capital Budgeting	Cost of Capital	Other Products
	Exit the Program	

Copyright © 1990, 1993 HarperCollins Publishers, All Rights Reserved
Portions Copyrighted by Microsoft Corporation
Written by: John Hansen, Ph.D. George Flowers, C.P.A.

To select a menu option, press the left/right arrow key until the desired option button is highlighted. Then press the ENTER key. Or, move the mouse pointer to the desired button and click the left button.

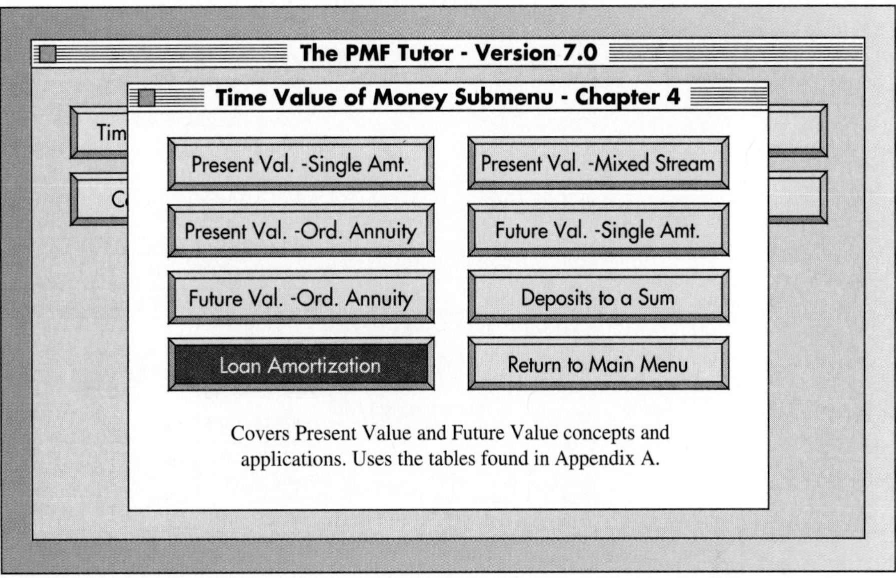

FIGURE B.4

If you select the TIME VALUE OF MONEY option, you will get the submenu screen shown in Figure B.4. As in the main menu screen, move the mouse cursor to the option that you want, or use the left and right arrow keys to move the highlight bar to the option that you want. To select this option, press the left mouse key or press the ENTER key on the keyboard.

If you select the LOAN AMORTIZATION option, you will get a screen like the one shown in Figure B.5. There are five "buttons" at the bottom of the screen. Initially, the black highlight is on the "Answer" button. These buttons have the following meanings:

ANSWER: Allows you to enter an answer and obtain a detailed solution

REPEAT: Gives you a new problem with a different set of numbers

QUIT: Returns you to the previous menu

FIGURE B.5

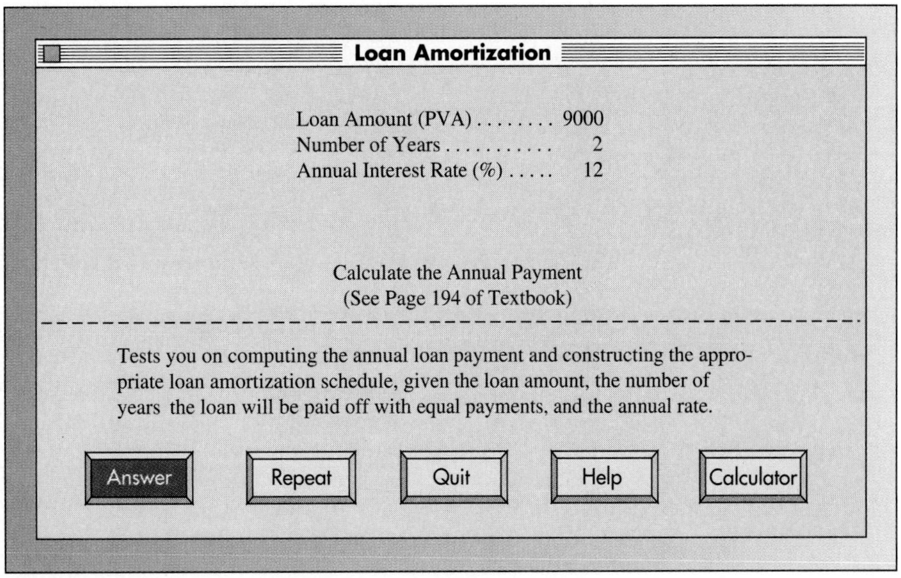

Loan Amortization

Loan Amount (PVA) 9000
Number of Years 2
Annual Interest Rate (%) 12

Calculate the Annual Payment
(See Page 194 of Textbook)

Tests you on computing the annual loan payment and constructing the appropriate loan amortization schedule, given the loan amount, the number of years the loan will be paid off with equal payments, and the annual rate.

Answer | Repeat | Quit | Help | Calculator

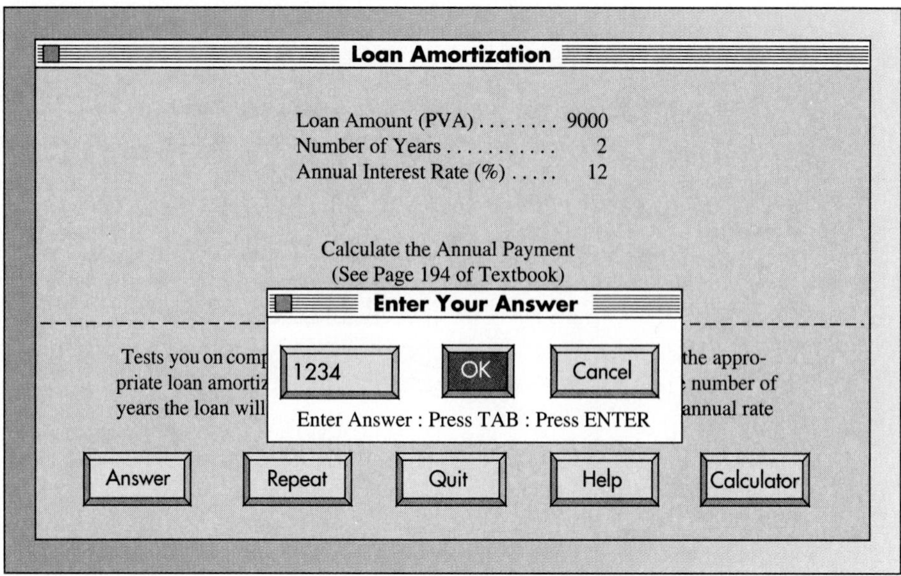

FIGURE B.6

HELP: Gives you directions on working the problem

CALCULATOR: Brings the "pop-up" calculator to the screen (see the next section)

Before you look at the solution, you should try to work the problem yourself. When you select the "Answer" option (using either the mouse or the keyboard), a screen like the one in Figure B.6 appears. Type in your answer, and press the TAB key to highlight the "OK" button. If for some reason you do not wish to continue with this problem, press the TAB key a second time to highlight the "Cancel" button. Press ENTER.

If you select "OK," you will see a screen like the one illustrated in Figure B.7. This shows your answer along with the correct answer using a calculator and the correct answer using the three-place tables. You have three options at this point:

FIGURE B.7

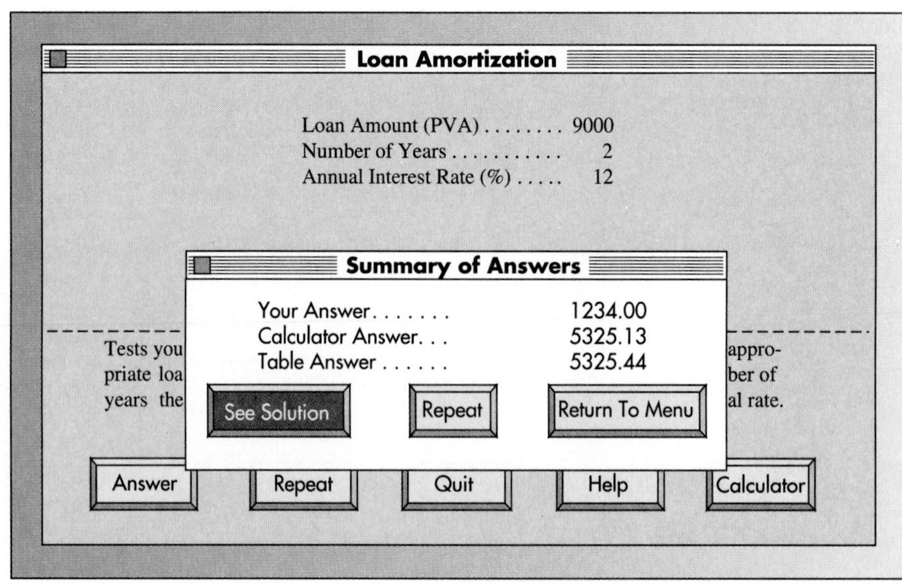

SEE SOLUTION: Shows a detailed solution for this problem

REPEAT: Performs another problem of the same type

RETURN TO MENU: Puts you back in the previous menu

If you select "See Solution," you will next see a screen like the one in Figure B.8. Again you have three options:

CONTINUE: Shows the remainder of the detailed solution

REPEAT: Discontinue looking at the solution and see another problem of the same type

RETURN TO MENU: Puts you back in the previous menu

If you select "Continue," you will see a screen like the one illustrated in Figure B.9. Again you have three options:

REPEAT: Runs another problem of the same type

GO BACK: Puts you back in the previous solution screen (Figure B.8)

RETURN TO MENU: Puts you back in the previous menu screen

Using the pop-up calculator

Any time you select the "calculator" option while running the *PMF Tutor,* the picture of a calculator will appear on the screen in the lower left-hand corner, as shown in Figure B.10. As in the rest of the program, pressing the CTRL and F4 keys will take you out of the pop-up calculator.

There are ten command keys associated with the calculator: **=, +, −, *, /, %, C, P, S,** and **R.** The effect of these command keys is summarized in Table B.1. For the four letter command keys, it does not matter whether you enter an uppercase or a lowercase letter (for example, R or r). You can either press the keys on the keyboard or move the mouse cursor to the calculator key on the screen and press the left mouse key.

FIGURE B.8

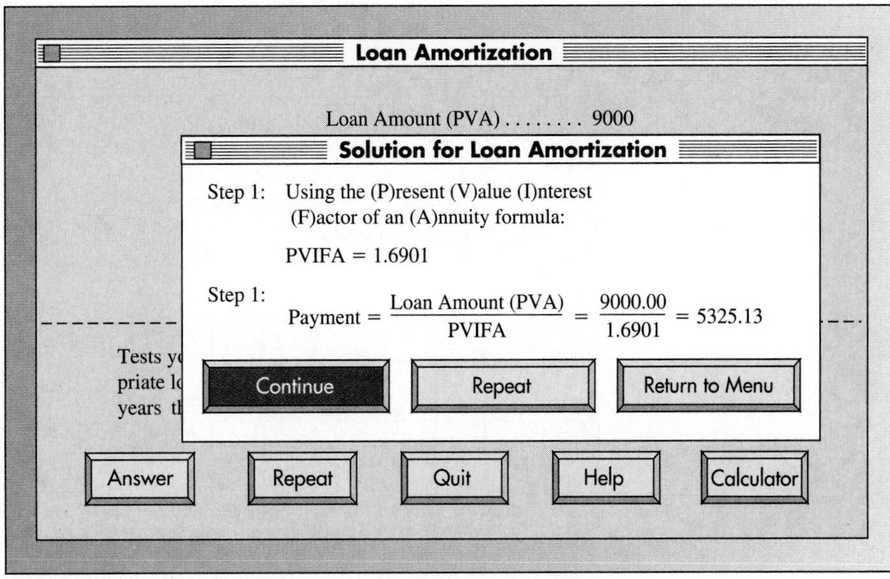

Loan Amortization

Loan Amount (PVA) 9000

Loan Amortization Schedule

Principal 9000.00 Rate 12% 2-Year Repayment Period

End of Year	Loan Payment	Beginning of Year Principal	Payments: Interest	Payments: Principal	End of Year Principal
1	5325.13	9000.00	1080.00	4245.13	4754.87
2	5325.13	4754.87	570.58	4754.54	.33

Tes
pria
yea

Answ | Repeat | Go Back | Return to Menu

FIGURE **B.9**

USING THE COMMAND KEYS

Four-function arithmetic is performed on the pop-up calculator just as it would be on a hand-held calculator. For example, to add 23.7 to 46.2, the following sequence of steps would be executed:

Step 1 Select the calculator option to display the pop-up calculator on the screen.
Step 2 Enter the number 23.7. (It does not matter whether you use the number on the typewriter part of the keyboard or on the numeric keypad or use the mouse to select the keys on the screen.)
Step 3 Press the + key.
Step 4 Enter the second number, 46.2.

FIGURE **B.10**

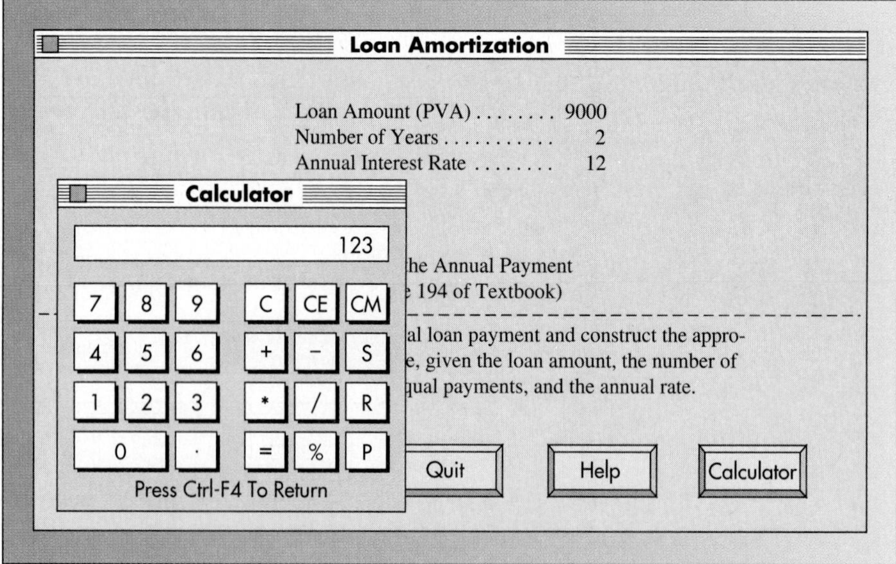

TABLE B.1

SUMMARY OF CALCULATOR COMMAND KEYS

Command key	Effect/operation
=	Causes the calculator to perform the current calculation
+	Addition
–	Subtraction
*	Multiplication
/	Division
%	Compute percentage
C	Clears the display of the calculator
P	Power function raises the previous number to the power of the next number
S	Saves the current display into the calculator memory
R	Recalls the current content of the memory to the display

Step 5 Press the = key to display the resulting answer. You should see the number 69.9 appear on the output display.

Similar sequences can be used on the pop-up calculator for subtraction, multiplication, and division.

POWER FUNCTION To raise a number to a power, the P key must be used. To raise 1.09 to the seventh power, for example, the following sequence would be executed:

Step 1 Select the calculator option to display the pop-up calculator on the screen.
Step 2 Enter the number 1.09.
Step 3 Press the P key.
Step 4 Enter the power 7.
Step 5 Press the = key to display the resulting answer. You should see the number 1.82803912081669 appear on the output display.

CLEAR DISPLAY FUNCTION Just like hand-held calculators, the pop-up calculator allows you to clear the output display. To do this, simply press the backspace key at any time, and the calculator will reset. You can also use the mouse cursor to press the C on the screen calculator.

SAVE-TO-MEMORY AND RECALL-TO-DISPLAY FUNCTIONS Sometimes, there is a need to save the result of a calculation while another calculation is being performed. Hand-held calculators offer this capability, and so does the pop-up calculator. To save a result that is still on the output display, press the S key. When you need to recall the saved result, just press the R key.

To illustrate the use of this feature, let's say that we want to compute the present value interest factor for a dollar to be received five years from today where the opportunity cost of money is 8 percent per year. The present value interest factor is computed by:

$$\frac{1}{(1.08)^5} = .681 \text{ (rounded to three decimal places)}$$

To perform this calculation on the pop-up calculator, you should perform the following steps:

Step 1 Select the calculator option to display the pop-up calculator on the screen.
Step 2 Enter the number 1.08.
Step 3 Press the P key.
Step 4 Enter the power 5.
Step 5 Press the = key to display the resulting answer. You should see the number 1.469328 appear on the output display.
Step 6 Press the s key.
Step 7 Enter the number 1 (the numerator).
Step 8 Press the / key.
Step 9 Press the R key. At this point you are dividing 1 by the first result.
Step 10 Press the = key to display the resulting answer. You should see the number 0.68058 appear on the output display.

CHAINING OPERATIONS

The rules for chaining operations on the pop-up calculator are about the same as they are on many hand-held calculators. The key to successful chaining of operations is to remember to press the = key for the previous operation before beginning a new operation. For example, to multiply 23.7 by 46.2 and then divide by 15.3, you should first enter 23.7, then press the * key, then enter 46.2, then press the = key, then press the / key, then enter the number 15.3, and finally press the = key again to get the result of 71.5647.

Running the *PMF Problem-Solver*

If you select the *Problem-Solver* at the Master Menu, you will see the Main Menu screen shown in Figure B.11. This menu controls the *PMF Problem-Solver* and is used as the starting point for all of the financial routines. The left side of the screen will have the menu items, and the right side will display a brief explanation of the currently highlighted item.

By pressing the ENTER or RETURN key (↵), the highlighted routine or its submenu is brought up. If there are no subchoices, the routine will begin; otherwise, a new menu will be displayed, offering the subchoices that are available for that routine.

FIGURE B.11

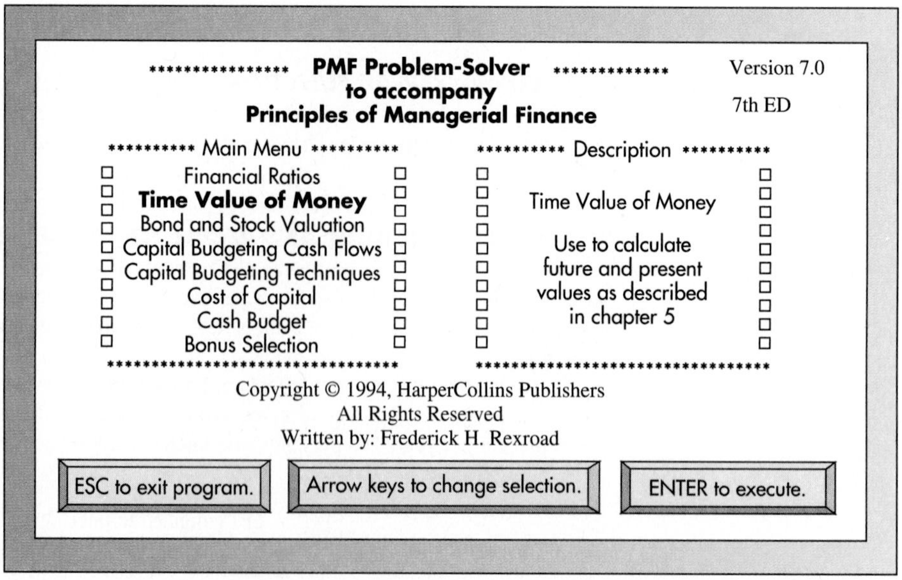

PMF Problem-Solver
to accompany
Principles of Managerial Finance

Version 7.0
7th ED

Main Menu

Financial Ratios
Time Value of Money
Bond and Stock Valuation
Capital Budgeting Cash Flows
Capital Budgeting Techniques
Cost of Capital
Cash Budget
Bonus Selection

Description

Time Value of Money

Use to calculate future and present values as described in chapter 5

Copyright © 1994, HarperCollins Publishers
All Rights Reserved
Written by: Frederick H. Rexroad

ESC to exit program. | Arrow keys to change selection. | ENTER to execute.

For example, if you select "Time Value of Money" (by pressing the down arrow once and then pressing the ENTER key), a third window opens on the screen showing that you have two further options: "Single Payment/Annuity" and "Mixed Stream." To make a selection, you again move the highlight bar to the line for the option that you want (using the cursor movement arrows ↑ and ↓ as before), and press the ENTER (↵) key. If you select the "Single Payment Annuity" option, you will next see a screen that gives you four further options: You can solve for (1) the interest, (2) the number of time periods required, (3) the future value, or (4) the present value. On this screen, you must use the ← and → keys to move between options. You should notice that as you press one of those keys, the highlighting around INTEREST shifts to another of the four words. Move the highlighting to the type of calculation you want to do, and press the ENTER key as before. **Once you have reached this point,** you can return to a prior menu without entering data by pressing the ESC key (as you can to move backwards through the menus).

Once you have answered all the questions, an answer will be displayed. After the answer has been shown, you can either select another option or return to an earlier menu by pressing the ESC key until you get back to the master menu. Please note that the *PMF Problem-Solver* will yield exact answers which may differ from answers derived through the use of financial tables which are rounded. Also, your own rounding during multiple steps may cause differences. DON'T PANIC if your pennies do not match the *PMF Problem-Solver*.

Running the *PMF Lotus Templates*

The *PMF Lotus Templates* are designed to be used with the LOTUS 1-2-3 spreadsheet program. To use the templates, you must have a copy of LOTUS 1-2-3, Version 2.2 or higher, installed in your computer and a copy of the *PMF Disk*. See Figure B.12 for an explanation of the Lotus 1-2-3 screen layout.

The template files correspond to selected end-of-chapter problems. The name of each file incorporates the chapter number and the problem number. For example, Problem 6 from Chapter

FIGURE B.12

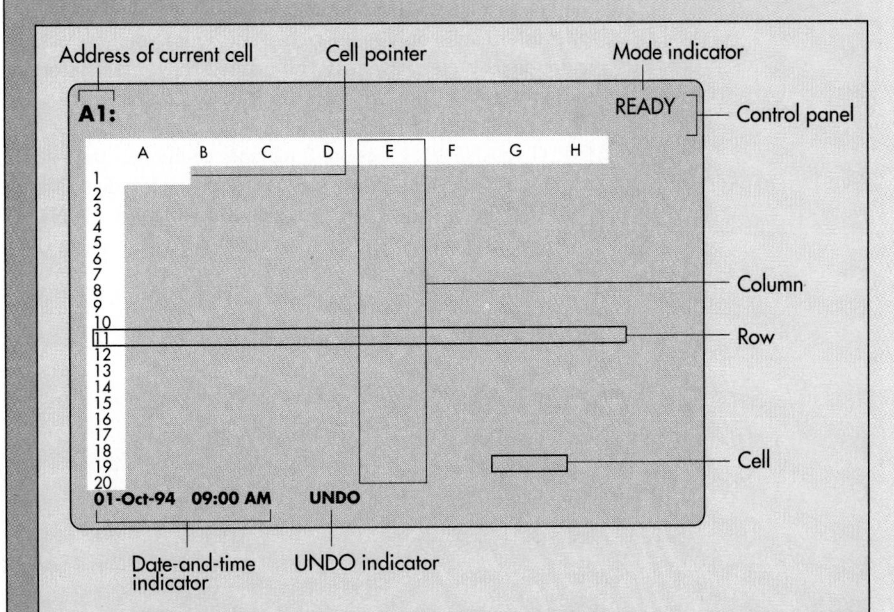

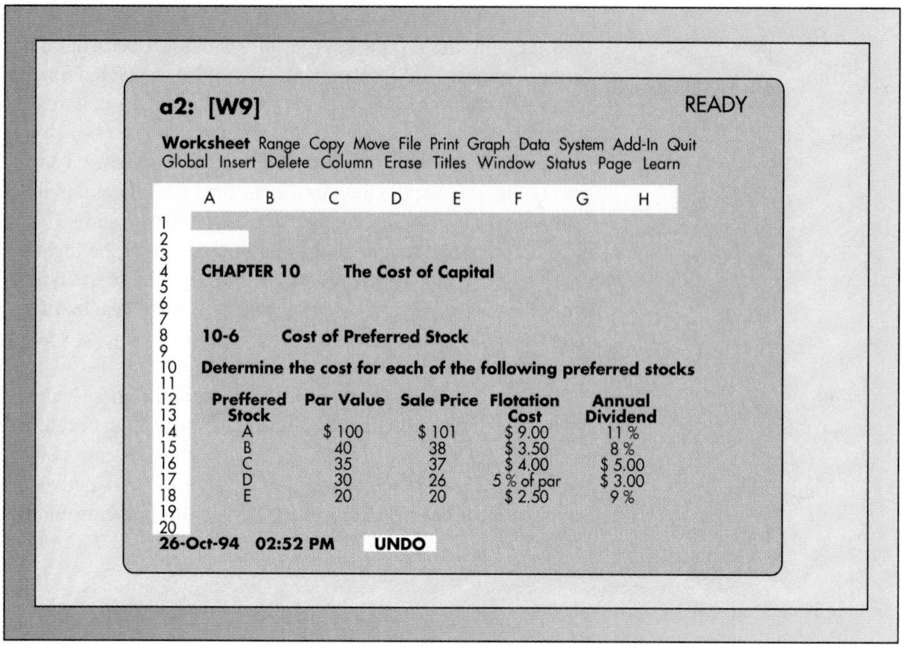

a2: [W9] READY

Worksheet Range Copy Move File Print Graph Data System Add-In Quit
Global Insert Delete Column Erase Titles Window Status Page Learn

CHAPTER 10 The Cost of Capital

10-6 Cost of Preferred Stock

Determine the cost for each of the following preferred stocks

Preffered Stock	Par Value	Sale Price	Flotation Cost	Annual Dividend
A	$ 100	$ 101	$ 9.00	11 %
B	40	38	$ 3.50	8 %
C	35	37	$ 4.00	$ 5.00
D	30	26	5 % of par	$ 3.00
E	20	20	$ 2.50	9 %

26-Oct-94 02:52 PM UNDO

FIGURE B.13

10 is called "CH10-6.WK1." To load a file from the Lotus main menu, choose FILE-RETRIEVE-Name of File "A:CH10-6.WK1." You will then see the screen shown in Figure B.13.

Each problem included in the *PMF Lotus Templates* fits on the width of the screen. To scroll up or down, use the **PgUp** and **PgDn** keys. The first part of each file describes the problem. For example, the description for Problem 6 from Chapter 10 would be: DETERMINE THE COST FOR EACH OF THE FOLLOWING PREFERRED STOCKS.

If you use the **PgDn** key, you will get to the INPUT & ANSWER section. In this section you enter the required information in the shaded areas. The template is protected so that you can enter information only in the right place. Once you have entered data, the template will automatically display the answer. If you entered the correct information, you will see "OK." If your input is incorrect, you will see TRY AGAIN! or ERROR.

Some problems include a section called ON YOUR OWN. This section appears below the INPUT & ANSWER section. It includes additional templates that are not tied to the problems in the text. You can use these templates to solve additional financial problems on your own.

To print any portion of the spreadsheet, choose PRINT-PRINTER-RANGE from the Lotus main menu, and specify the range as A1..E65. Then select GO to begin printing.

appendix C

Using computers and spreadsheets in managerial finance

Harnessing massive amounts of information is the challenge of every manager today. Fortunately, many tools are available for gathering, storing, analyzing, and processing mounds of data. Here we will briefly discuss the two key components of a computer system—hardware and software—and some of the key features of electronic spreadsheets—an extremely popular type of software that is widely used by financial managers.

Hardware

Hardware refers to the physical components of a computer system. The basic components of a personal computer are a microprocessor (the "brain"), an input device (keyboard and/or mouse), a video display terminal, an output device (printer), and one or more storage devices (disk, tape, or CD-ROM drives). Critical to the decision of which type of computer is appropriate for the application software is the amount of memory available. Most general management applications programs (word processor, database management, and spreadsheets) require at least 1 MB of memory. Systems based on the 80286, 80386, and 80486 processors and the Macintosh series are able to run the most popular management applications software available.

Software

Software consists of the programs that instruct the computer about the functions it is to perform. Without adequate software the computer is useless. With the increased ownership of personal computers (PCs) has come a growing proliferation of software programs that cater to the financial manager. Moreover, PCs have become more "user friendly" (the user can communicate more easily with the computer and thus utilize it more fully), enabling managers to design programs to meet their objectives. The three basic tools of information management for use on the personal computer are word processing, database management, and spreadsheet software. In addition, integrated software packages are available.

WORD PROCESSING SOFTWARE

Word processing software is rapidly making the conventional typewriter obsolete. It allows text to be keyed into a computer and saved. While viewing the document on the display terminal, the user may easily edit, delete, or add more text. A variety of formats, type styles, and other features are available in most word processing programs to ease document preparation. (For a listing of popular word processing software, see Table C.1.)

DATABASE MANAGEMENT SOFTWARE

Database management software stores information in discrete "parcels." These parcels may then be sorted in a variety of ways. Needed information can be easily extracted from the database by user-specified criteria. The parcel may contain only a single piece of data or hundreds of pieces of data. For example, some common applications of a database management program are storage of customer data (name, address, and city), inventory records, personnel data, and accounts receivable information. (For a listing of popular database management software, see Table C.1.)

SPREADSHEET SOFTWARE

Spreadsheet software facilitates extensive calculations based on models developed by the user. A spreadsheet appears on the screen divided into cells of rows and columns. Spreadsheet rows are generally numbered 1, 2, 3, etc., and columns are lettered A, B, C, etc. Some programs have as many as 16,000 rows and columns available. The user may enter text or numeric data or program a formula into each cell. Most programs also allow data to be shown graphically. (For a listing of popular spreadsheet software, see Table C.1.)

INTEGRATED SOFTWARE

Integrated software combines more than one function into a single program. For example, an integrated software package might include a word processor, database, graphics, and spreadsheet. With this type of software the same information can be used in the different modules of the program. Integrated software packages have become quite popular and can be an economical alternative to purchasing separate programs. However, the individual modules generally have fewer features than single-purpose programs, so it is important to review the package carefully to see what compromises were made when the component programs were combined. (For a listing of popular integrated software, see Table C.1.)

Electronic spreadsheets

A strength of electronic spreadsheets is the ability to customize formulas to make automatic calculations using the desired model. Since the automatic calculation feature takes the drudgery out of the financial analysis of large amounts of data, the analyst may spend more time asking "what if." The data or the formulas may be easily changed, often by a mere keystroke, to simulate various business conditions. (Table C.2 illustrates a spreadsheet with data and formulas.)

ADDITIONAL FEATURES

The most powerful spreadsheet software has several additional features beyond the basic calculating power: linking worksheets, using predefined functions, auditing of design logic, and the

TABLE C.1

POPULAR WORD PROCESSING, DATABASE MANAGEMENT, SPREADSHEET, AND INTEGRATED SOFTWARE PACKAGES*

Title	Hardware family	Company
	Word Processing	
Microsoft Word	Available for both IBM PC compatibles and Macintosh	Microsoft Corp. One Microsoft Way Redmond, WA 98073
WordPerfect	Available for both IBM PC compatibles and Macintosh	WordPerfect Corp. 1555 N. Technology Way Oren, UT 84057
MacWrite II	Macintosh	Claris Corporation 440 Clyde Ave. Mountain View, CA 94043
	Database Management	
dBase IV	IBM PC compatibles	Ashton-Tate 20101 Hamilton Ave. Torrance, CA 90502
FileMaker II	Macintosh	Claris Corporation 440 Clyde Ave. Mountain View, CA 94043
Paradox	IBM PC compatibles	Borland International 4585 Scotts Valley Drive Scotts Valley, CA 95066
Access	IBM PC compatibles	Microsoft Corp. One Microsoft Way Redmond, WA 98073
	Spreadsheet	
Lotus 1-2-3	Available for both IBM PC compatibles and Macintosh	Lotus Development Corp. 55 Cambridge Parkway Cambridge, MA 92142
Excel	Available for both IBM PC compatibles and Macintosh	Microsoft Corp. One Microsoft Way Redmond, WA 98073
Quattro Pro	IBM PC compatibles	Borland International 4585 Scotts Valley Drive Scotts Valley, CA 95066
SuperCalc5	IBM PC compatibles	Computer Associates International Inc. Micro Products Division 1240 McKay Drive San Jose, CA 95131
Wingz	Macintosh	Informix Software 16011 College Blvd. Lenexa, KS 66219
	Integrated	
Microsoft Works	Available for both IBM PC compatibles and Macintosh	Microsoft Corp. One Microsoft Way Redmond, WA 98073
First Choice	IBM PC compatibles	Software Publishing Corp. 1901 Landings Drive Mountain View, CA 94039

*It is important to check the specific system requirements (such as amount of memory) of a software package to make sure that the program is compatible with your hardware.

TABLE C.2

ILLUSTRATION OF A SPREADSHEET WITH DATA AND FORMULAS

A	B C D E	F
	INPUT SECTION	
7	Sun Valley Prune Company	
8	Income Statement	
9	For the Year Ended December 31	
10		1994
11	SALES	$4,300,000
12	COST OF GOODS SOLD	
13	FIXED	$300,000
14	VARIABLE	$2,250,000
15	GROSS PROFIT	$1,750,000
16	GENERAL AND ADMIN EXPENSES	
17	FIXED	$100,000
18	VARIABLE	$333,000
19	EARNINGS BEFORE INT AND TAX	$1,317,000
20	INTEREST EXPENSE (ALL FIXED)	$150,000
21	EARNINGS BEFORE TAXES	$1,167,000
22	TAXES (40%)	$466,800
23	NET INCOME	$700,200
24	RESULTS SECTION	
25	Sun Valley Prune Company	
26	Pro Forma Income Statement	
27	Percent-of-Sales Method	
28	For the Year Ended December 31	
29		1995
30	SALES	$4,750,000
31	COST OF GOODS SOLD	FORMULA A
32	GROSS PROFIT	FORMULA B
33	GENERAL AND ADMIN EXPENSES	FORMULA C
34	EARNINGS BEFORE INT AND TAX	FORMULA D
35	INTEREST EXPENSE (ALL FIXED)	FORMULA E
36	EARNINGS BEFORE TAXES	FORMULA F
37	TAXES (40%)	FORMULA G
38	NET INCOME	FORMULA H

FORMULA A:	+(F13+F14)/F11*F30	FORMULA B:	+F30-F31
FORMULA C:	+(F17+F18)/F11*F30	FORMULA D:	+F32-F33
FORMULA E:	+F20/F11*F30	FORMULA F:	+F34-F35
FORMULA G:	+F36*0.4	FORMULA H:	+F36-F37

ability to use macros. These features are necessary for the serious "number cruncher" or "power user." *Worksheet linking* allows the user to maintain multiple spreadsheets to support a final spreadsheet. For example, in developing a pro forma income statement, multiple supporting spreadsheets like sales, cost of goods sold, and general and administrative expense forecasts, among others, may be linked to produce the final summary pro forma spreadsheet. A *predefined function* is one that need not be programmed by the user. Some programs have predefined functions like depreciation calculation using the sum-of-the-years'-digits method or net present value and internal rate of return calculations. The *auditing feature* is a simple check of the programmer's logic to ensure the model's feasibility. It does not, however, make the program design foolproof. *Macros* allow the user to program a sequence of operations to be used to manipulate data. For complicated manipulation, using a macro to record a frequently used sequence of operations reduces tedious duplication of effort.

SPREADSHEET APPLICATIONS

For the financial manager the electronic spreadsheet can be customized to fit a range of financial tasks, from a simple return on investment calculation to a sophisticated merger analysis. The most common applications are forecasting models for preparation of cash budgets and pro forma income statements and balance sheets.

PRO FORMA BALANCE SHEET ILLUSTRATION In the case of the pro forma balance sheet, the final spreadsheet may be supported by multiple spreadsheets that calculate various asset and liability values. For instance, the depreciation schedule for the existing fixed assets plus the projected purchases and sales of fixed assets might support the calculation of the net fixed asset account. Likewise, a supporting spreadsheet for the amortization of debt might take into account all existing loans, lines of credit, and their payment terms and interest rates and project the pro forma balance with no new borrowings. All other asset and liability account spreadsheets may then be linked to the final spreadsheet, which has user-defined mathematical relationships common to balance sheets. The user may impose any type of restriction, such as a minimum cash balance or a desired current ratio.

OTHER APPLICATIONS A wide variety of financial analysis applications are available to the user who is willing to spend the time to develop the model. Accounts receivable and inventory management can be achieved through the use of database software (for large amounts of data stored) and spreadsheets to analyze the data stored in the database. Capital-budgeting analysis is made easier by many of the spreadsheet programs having predefined functions such as net present value and the internal rate of return formulas. The WMCC and IOS analysis and breakeven analysis may be brought to life through the graphic abilities of an integrated spreadsheet program that translates the numerical data into a chart or graph. Other financial applications include cost of capital, lease-versus-purchase decisions, economic order quantity for inventory, and merger analysis, among many others.

SPREADSHEET DESIGN

Designing a spreadsheet is as basic as the preparation of blueprints before building a house. Spreadsheets may contain four basic sections: the assumptions, the input data, the calculations, and the results summary. The *assumptions* are often grouped together at the top of the spreadsheet and are used as references to drive the calculations section. If the user decides that an assumption is not reasonable, it may be changed and the entire spreadsheet immediately recalculated. Stating the assumptions up front also aids the reader of the report. The *input data* section is the area where the data are to be manipulated and stored. For large sets of data, multiple spreadsheets are recommended. The data may then be imported from various other worksheets for manipulation. The *calculation* section sets forth the mathematical relationships among the data. The *results summary* section ends the spreadsheet and capsulizes the results. A spreadsheet that is divided into the four sections may more clearly communicate the what, how, and why of the report to its reader and allows for easy verification. Planning the layout of a spreadsheet is essential to its success.

SPREADSHEET ERRORS

The ease with which a spreadsheet may be programmed and calculations performed may disguise the fact that errors are easy to make. Two independent Silicon Valley consulting firms, Input and Palo Alto Research, estimated that approximately one out of three business spreadsheets has some kind of error! The error to which these consulting firms refer is not a bug in the computer program; it is a programmer error—an illogical command or misplaced data. It is essential to test the program with simplified data and to verify the expected results with a hand-held calculator on the first pass. The results are only as good as the program.

Conclusion

Financial management applications for the computer are plentiful, but first, many decisions need to be made. The selection of hardware and software is one that must be investigated thoroughly to determine whether the capabilities of each meet the manager's needs. Actually using a computer at a dealer location and requesting "demo" disks to "test drive" the software are recommended. Talk with other professionals about the products that they use and keep current on new products through computer periodicals. Once the hardware and software selection is made and the program has been mastered, the manager will be one step closer to conquering the massive amount of information that complicates most business decisions.

appendix D

Key equations and disk routines

Topic	Equation	Page	PMF Tutor	PMF Problem-Solver	PMF Lotus Templates
PART I/THE GOAL AND ENVIRONMENT OF MANAGERIAL FINANCE					
Chapter 2 The Operating Environment of the Firm					
Real rate of interest					■
Nominal rate of interest					
Nominal rate of interest					
Risk-free rate of interest					
Risk-free rate of interest					
Interest vs. dividend income					■
Interest vs. dividend expense					■
Chapter 3 Financial Statements, Depreciation, and Cash Flow					
Calculation of EPS and Retained Earnings					■
Cash flow from operations	3.1	80			
Depreciation and cash flow					■
Finding dividends paid	3.2	88			■
Chapter 4 The Analysis of Financial Statements					
Net working capital				■	
Current ratio			■	■	
Quick ratio			■	■	
Inventory turnover			■	■	
Average collection period			■	■	
Average payment period				■	
Fixed asset turnover			■	■	
Total asset turnover			■	■	
Debt ratio			■	■	■
Debt-equity ratio			■	■	■
Times interest earned			■	■	■
Fixed-payment coverage ratio				■	■
Gross profit margin			■	■	

Topic	Equation	Page	PMF Tutor	PMF Problem-Solver	PMF Lotus Templates
Operating profit margin			■	■	
Net profit margin			■	■	
Return on total assets (ROA)			■	■	
Return on equity (ROE)			■	■	
Earnings per share (EPS)			■	■	
Price/Earnings (P/E) ratio			■	■	
DuPont formula			■		
Modified DuPont formula			■		
Financial leverage multiplier (FLM)			■		

PART II/BASIC FINANCIAL CONCEPTS

Chapter 5 The Time Value of Money

Topic	Equation	Page	PMF Tutor	PMF Problem-Solver	PMF Lotus Templates
Future value tables				■	
Future value at the end of period n	5.4	163	■	■	■
Future-value interest factor	5.5	164			
Future value at the end of period n	5.6	165			
Compounding more frequently than annually	5.7	168		■	
Future-value interest factor for continuous compounding	5.9	170			
Effective interest rate	5.10	171		■	
Future-value interest factor for an annuity	5.14	176			
Future value (annuity)	5.15	176	■	■	■
Future value of an annuity due	5.16	178		■	
Present value of a future amount	5.19	181	■	■	■
Present-value interest factor	5.21	182	■	■	
Present-value interest factor	5.22	182			
Present-value interest factor for an annuity	5.26	188			
Present value (annuity)	5.27	188	■	■	
Present value—mixed streams			■	■	
Present-value interest factor for a perpetuity discounted at rate k	5.28	191			
Deposits to accumulate a future sum			■	■	■
Loan amortization			■	■	
Growth rates			■	■	

Chapter 6 Risk and Return

Topic	Equation	Page	PMF Tutor	PMF Problem-Solver	PMF Lotus Templates
Rate of return earned on any asset over period t	6.1	215			
Expected value of a return	6.2	220			
Expected value of a return when all outcomes are known and their related probabilities are assumed to be equal	6.2a	220			
Standard deviation of returns	6.3	220			
Standard deviation of returns when all outcomes are known and their related probabilities are assumed to be equal	6.3a	220			
Coefficient of variation	6.4	222			■
Portfolio return	6.5	225			■

Topic	Equation	Page	PMF Tutor	PMF Problem-Solver	PMF Lotus Templates
Total risk	6.6	234			
Beta of a portfolio	6.7	236			
Capital Asset Pricing Model (CAPM)	6.8	238			■
Security Market Line (SML)					■

Chapter 7 Valuation

Topic	Equation	Page	PMF Tutor	PMF Problem-Solver	PMF Lotus Templates
Value of any asset at time zero	7.1	262			
Value of any asset at time zero ($PVIF_{k,n}$) notation	7.2	262			
Basic bond value	7.3	264			■
Basic bond value	7.3a	264			
Yield to maturity (YTM)			■	■	■
Approximate yield	7.4	270			
Bond valuation, semiannual interest				■	■
Bond valuation, quarterly interest					■
Zero growth model	7.8	277			■
Constant growth model	7.10	278		■	
Variable growth model	7.11	280			

PART III/LONG-TERM INVESTMENT DECISIONS

Chapter 8 Capital Budgeting and Cash Flow Principles

Topic	Equation	Page	PMF Tutor	PMF Problem-Solver	PMF Lotus Templates
Initial investment			■	■	
Incremental operating cash flows			■	■	■
Terminal cash flow			■	■	
Relevant cash flow			■	■	
Book value	8.1	315			

Chapter 9 Capital Budgeting Techniques: Certainty, Risk, and Some Refinements

Topic	Equation	Page	PMF Tutor	PMF Problem-Solver	PMF Lotus Templates
Payback period			■	■	
Payback comparisons			■	■	
Net present value (NPV)	9.1	345	■	■	■
Internal rate of return (IRR)	9.2	346	■	■	■
Breakeven cash inflow	9.3	358			
NPV when certainty equivalents are used for risk adjustments	9.5	364			
RADR	9.6	366			
Total risk	9.7	366			
Capital asset pricing model (CAPM)	9.8	366	■		
Annualized net present value (ANPV)	9.10	375			

PART IV/COST OF CAPITAL, LEVERAGE, AND CAPITAL STRUCTURE

Chapter 10 The Cost of Capital

Topic	Equation	Page	PMF Tutor	PMF Problem-Solver	PMF Lotus Templates
Approximate before-tax cost of debt	10.2	407	■	■	
After-tax cost of debt	10.3	408	■	■	
Cost of preferred stock	10.4	409	■	■	■
Constant growth valuation (Gordon) model	10.5	410	■	■	
Cost of common stock equity	10.6	410	■	■	■

Topic	Equation	Page	PMF Tutor	PMF Problem-Solver	PMF Lotus Templates
Capital asset pricing model (CAPM)	10.7	412	✓	✓	✓
Cost of retained earnings	10.8	413	✓	✓	
Cost of new issue of common stock	10.9	414	✓	✓	
Weighted average cost of capital (WACC)	10.10	415	✓	✓	
Breaking point	10.11	419			
Weighted marginal cost of capital (WMCC)				✓	

Chapter 11 Leverage and Capital Structure

Topic	Equation	Page	PMF Tutor	PMF Problem-Solver	PMF Lotus Templates
Breakeven comparisons					✓
Earnings before interest and taxes (EBIT)	11.1	440			
Simplified EBIT	11.2	440			
Operating breakeven point	11.3	440		✓	
Degree of operating leverage (DOL)	11.4	444			
Direct formula for DOL	11.5	445			
Degree of financial leverage (DFL)	11.6	448			
Direct formula for DFL	11.7	448			
Degree of total leverage (DTL)	11.8	449			
Direct formula for DTL	11.9	449			
Relationship between the degrees of operating, financial, and total leverage	11.10	450			
Value of the firm	11.11	463			
Per-share value of the firm	11.12	470			

PART V/LONG-TERM FINANCING DECISIONS

Chapter 12 Long-Term Debt and Investment Banking

Topic	Equation	Page	PMF Tutor	PMF Problem-Solver	PMF Lotus Templates
Bond discounts or premiums					✓

Chapter 13 Common Stock and Dividend Policy

Topic	Equation	Page	PMF Tutor	PMF Problem-Solver	PMF Lotus Templates
Number of shares to elect a certain number of directors	13.1	527			
Theoretical value of a right when stock is selling with rights	13.2	531			
Market value of stock trading ex rights	13.3	532			
Theoretical value of a right when stock is trading ex rights	13.4	532			
Stock dividend–investor					✓

Chapter 14 Preferred Stock, Leasing, Convertibles, Warrants, and Options

Topic	Equation	Page	PMF Tutor	PMF Problem-Solver	PMF Lotus Templates
Lease versus purchase				✓	✓
Implied price of a warrant	14.1	587			
Theoretical value of a warrant	14.2	588			

PART VI/SHORT-TERM FINANCIAL DECISIONS

Chapter 15 Financial Planning

Topic	Equation	Page	PMF Tutor	PMF Problem-Solver	PMF Lotus Templates
Cash budget—Basic				✓	✓
Cash budget—Advanced				✓	

Topic	Equation	Page	PMF Tutor	PMF Problem-Solver	PMF Lotus Templates
Chapter 16 Net Working Capital and Short-Term financing					
Cost of giving up cash discount	16.1	655			
Approximate cost of giving up cash discount	16.2	656			
Effective interest rate	16.3	660			■
Effective interest rate for a discount loan	16.4	661			
Chapter 17 Cash and Marketable Securities					
Operating cycle	17.6	696			
Cash conversion cycle	17.7	697			■
Chapter 18 Accounts Receivable and Inventory					
Average investment in accounts receivable	18.1	732			
Economic order quantity	18.5	749			
Accounts receivable and costs					■
Tightening credit standards					■
Inventory investment					■
PART VII/SPECIAL MANAGERIAL FINANCE TOPICS					
Chapter 19 Mergers, LBOs, Divestitures, and Failure					
Tax effects of acquisition					■
Asset acquisition decision					■
EPS and merger terms					■
Market price ratio of exchange	19.1	779			
Chapter 20 International Managerial Finance					
Tax credits					■

appendix E

Solutions to self-test problems

Chapter 2

ST 2-1 **a.** Capital gains = \$180,000 sale price − \$150,000 original purchase price = \$30,000

b. Total taxable income = \$280,000 operating earnings + \$30,000 capital gain = \$310,000

c. Firm's tax liability:

Using Table 2.3:

$$\begin{aligned}\text{Total taxes due} &= \$22{,}250 + [.39 \times (\$310{,}000 - \$100{,}000)]\\ &= \$22{,}250 + (.39 \times \$210{,}000) = \$22{,}250 + \$81{,}900\\ &= \underline{\underline{\$104{,}150}}\end{aligned}$$

d. $\text{Average tax rate} = \dfrac{\$104{,}150}{\$310{,}000} = \underline{\underline{33.6\%}}$

Marginal tax rate = $\underline{\underline{39\%}}$

Chapter 3

ST 3-1 **a.** Depreciation Schedule

Year	Cost* (1)	Percentages (from Table 3.6) (2)	Depreciation [(1) × (2)] (3)
1	\$150,000	20%	\$ 30,000
2	150,000	32	48,000
3	150,000	19	28,500
4	150,000	12	18,000
5	150,000	12	18,000
6	150,000	5	7,500
	Totals	100%	\$150,000

*\$140,000 asset cost + \$10,000 installation cost.

b. Cash flow schedule

Year	EBDT (1)	Deprec. (2)	Net profits before taxes [(1) − (2)] (3)	Taxes [.4 × (3)] (4)	Net profits after taxes [(3) − (4)] (5)	Operating cash flows [(2) + (5)] (6)
1	$160,000	$30,000	$130,000	$52,000	$78,000	$108,000
2	160,000	48,000	112,000	44,800	67,200	115,200
3	160,000	28,500	131,500	52,600	78,900	107,400
4	160,000	18,000	142,000	56,800	85,200	103,200
5	160,000	18,000	142,000	56,800	85,200	103,200
6	160,000	7,500	152,500	61,000	91,500	99,000

c. The purchase of the asset allows the firm to deduct depreciation—a noncash charge—for tax purposes. This results in lower taxable income and therefore lower tax payments. As a result the firm's operating cash flows (in column 6 of the table above) exceed its net profits after taxes (in column 5 of the table).

Chapter 4

ST 4-1

Ratio	Too high	Too low
Current ratio = current assets/current liabilities	May indicate that the firm is holding excessive cash, accounts receivable, or inventory.	May indicate poor ability to satisfy short-term obligations.
Inventory turnover = CGS/inventory	May indicate lower level of inventory, which may cause stockouts and lost sales.	May indicate poor inventory management, excessive inventory, or obsolete inventory.
Times interest earned = earnings before interest and taxes/interest		May indicate poor ability to pay contractual interest payments.
Gross profit margin = gross profits/sales	Indicates the low cost of merchandise sold relative to the sales price; may indicate noncompetitive pricing and potential lost sales.	Indicates the high cost of the merchandise sold relative to the sales price; may indicate either a low sales price or a high cost of goods sold.
Return on total assets = net profits after taxes/total assets		Indicates ineffective management in generating profits with the available assets.

ST 4-2

Balance sheet
O'Keefe Industries
December 31, 1994

Cash	$ 30,000	Accounts payable	$ 120,000
Marketable securities	25,000	Notes payable	160,000[e]
Accounts receivable	200,000[a]	Accruals	20,000
Inventories	225,000[b]	Total current liabilities	$ 300,000[d]
Total current assets	$ 480,000		
Net fixed assets	$1,020,000[c]	Long-term debt	$ 600,000[f]
Total assets	$1,500,000	Stockholders' equity	$ 600,000
		Total liabilities and stockholders' equity	$1,500,000

[a]Average collection period (ACP) = 40 days
ACP = accounts receivable/average sales per day
40 = accounts receivable/($1,800,000/360)
40 = accounts receivable/$5,000
$200,000 = accounts receivable

[b]Inventory turnover = 6.0
Inventory turnover = cost of goods sold/inventory
6.0 = [sales × (1 − gross profit margin)]/inventory
6.0 = [$1,800,000 × (1 − .25)]/inventory
$225,000 = inventory

[c]Total asset turnover = 1.20
Total asset turnover = sales/total assets
1.20 = $1,800,000/total assets
$1,500,000 = total assets
Total assets = current assets + net fixed assets
$1,500,000 = $480,000 + net fixed assets
$1,020,000 = net fixed assets

[d]Current ratio = 1.60
Current ratio = current assets/current liabilities
1.60 = $480,000/current liabilities
$300,000 = current liabilities

[e]Notes payable = total current liabilities − accounts payable − accruals
= $300,000 − $120,000 − $20,000
= $160,000

[f]Debt ratio = .60
Debt ratio = total liabilities/total assets
.60 = total liabilities/$1,500,000
$900,000 = total liabilities
Total liabilities = current liabilities + long-term debt
$900,000 = $300,000 + long-term debt
$600,000 = long-term debt

Chapter 5

ST 5-1 a. *Bank A*

$$FV_3 = \$10,000 \times FVIF_{4\%/3\text{yrs}} = \$10,000 \times 1.125 = \underline{\underline{\$11,250}}$$

(Calculator solution = $11,248.64)

Bank B

$$FV_3 = \$10,000 \times FVIF_{4\%/2,2 \times 3\text{yrs}} = \$10,000 \times FVIF_{2\%,6\text{yrs}}$$
$$= \$10,000 \times 1.126 = \underline{\underline{\$11,260}}$$

(Calculator solution = $11,261.62)

Bank C

$$FV_3 = \$10{,}000 \times FVIF_{4\%/4,4 \times 3\text{yrs}} = \$10{,}000 \times FVIF_{1\%,12\text{yrs}}$$
$$= \$10{,}000 \times 1.127 = \underline{\underline{\$11{,}270}}$$
$$(\text{Calculator solution} = \$11{,}268.25)$$

b. Bank A: $k_{eff.} = (1 + 4\%/1)^1 - 1 = (1 + 0.4)^1 - 1 = 1.04 - 1 = .04 = \underline{\underline{4\%}}$

Bank B: $k_{eff.} = (1 + 4\%/2)^2 - 1 = (1 + .02)^2 - 1 = 1.0404 - 1 = .0404 = \underline{\underline{4.04\%}}$

Bank C: $k_{eff.} = (1 + 4\%/4)^4 - 1 = (1 + .01)^4 - 1 = 1.0406 - 1 = .0406 = \underline{\underline{4.06\%}}$

c. Ms. Martin should deal with Bank C: The quarterly compounding of interest at the given 4 percent rate results in the highest future value as a result of the corresponding highest effective interest rate.

d. *Bank D*

$$FV_3 = \$10{,}000 \times FVIF_{4\%,3\text{yrs}} \text{ (continuous compounding)}$$
$$= \$10{,}000 \times e^{.04 \times 3} = \$10{,}000 \times e^{.12}$$
$$= \$10{,}000 \times 1.127497$$
$$= \underline{\underline{\$11{,}274.97}}$$

This alternative is better than Bank C, since it results in a higher future value because of the use of continuous compounding, which with otherwise identical cash flows always results in the higher future value of any compounding period.

ST 5-2 a. On a purely subjective basis, annuity X looks more attractive than annuity Y. The fact that annuity Y's cash flows occur at the end of the year (an ordinary annuity) while annuity X's cash flows occur at the beginning of the year (an annuity due) favors annuity X, since its beginning-of-year cash flows will have more time to compound than the end-of-year cash flows of annuity Y. On the other hand, it would seem that the extra $1,000 per year in cash flow from annuity Y ($10,000 for annuity Y and $9,000 for annuity X) would outweigh the benefit of annuity X's longer compounding period. As noted below, only after making necessary computations can the more attractive annuity be determined.

b. *Annuity X (annuity due)*

$$FVA_6 = \$9{,}000 \times FVIFA_{15\%,6\text{yrs}} \times (1 + .15)$$
$$= \$9{,}000 \times 8.754 \times 1.15 = \underline{\underline{\$90{,}603.90}}$$
$$(\text{Calculator solution} = \$90{,}601.19)$$

Annuity Y (ordinary annuity)

$$FVA_6 = \$10{,}000 \times FVIFA_{15\%,6\text{yrs}}$$
$$= \$10{,}000 \times 8.754 = \underline{\underline{\$87{,}540.00}}$$
$$(\text{Calculator solution} = \$87{,}537.38)$$

c. Annuity X is more attractive, since its future value at the end of year 6, FVA_6, of $90,603.90 is greater than annuity Y's end-of-year-6 future value, FVA_6, of $87,540.00. Clearly, the subjective assessment in **a** was incorrect. The benefit of receiving annuity X's cash flows at the beginning of the year more than offset the fact that its cash flows are $1,000 less than those of annuity Y, which has end-of-year cash flows. The high interest rate of 15 percent added to the attractiveness of annuity X (the annuity due), since each of its cash flows earns at this rate for an extra year, thereby enhancing its future value.

ST 5-3 *Alternative A*

Cash flow stream:

$$PVA_5 = \$700 \times PVIFA_{9\%,5\text{yrs}}$$
$$= \$700 \times 3.890 = \underline{\underline{\$2,723}}$$

(Calculator solution = \$2,722.76)

Lump sum: $\underline{\underline{\$2,825}}$

Alternative B

Cash flow stream:

Year (n)	Cash flow (1)	$FVIF_{9\%,n}$ (2)	Present value [(1) × (2)] (3)
1	\$1,100	.917	\$1,088.70
2	900	.842	757.80
3	700	.772	540.40
4	500	.708	354.00
5	300	.650	195.00
	Present value		\$2,855.90

(Calculator solution = \$2,856.41)

Lump-sum: $\underline{\underline{\$2,800}}$

Conclusion: Alternative B in the form of a cash flow stream is preferred since its present value of \$2,855.90 is greater than the other three values.

ST 5-4 $FVA_5 = \$8,000$; $FVIFA_{7\%,5\text{yrs}} = 5.751$; $PMT = ?$

$FVA_n = PMT \times (FVIFA_{k,n})$ [Equation 5.15 or 5.29]

$\$8,000 = PMT \times 5.751$

$PMT = \$8,000/5.751 = \underline{\underline{\$1,391.06}}$

(Calculator solution = \$1,391.13)

Judi should deposit \$1,391.06 at the end of each of the five years in order to meet her goal of accumulating \$8,000 at the end of the fifth year.

Chapter 6

ST 6-1 a. Expected return, $\bar{k} = \dfrac{\Sigma\text{Returns}}{3}$ *(Equation 6.2a in footnote 8)*

$$\bar{k}_A = \frac{12\% + 14\% + 16\%}{3} = \frac{42\%}{3} = \underline{\underline{14\%}}$$

$$\bar{k}_B = \frac{16\% + 14\% + 12\%}{3} = \frac{42\%}{3} = \underline{\underline{14\%}}$$

$$\bar{k}_C = \frac{12\% + 14\% + 16\%}{3} = \frac{42\%}{3} = \underline{\underline{14\%}}$$

b. Standard deviation, $\sigma_k = \sqrt{\frac{\sum_{i=1}^{3}(k_i - \bar{k})^2}{n-1}}$ *(Equation 6.3a in footnote 9)*

$$\sigma_{k_A} = \sqrt{\frac{(12\% - 14\%)^2 + (14\% - 14\%)^2 + (16\% - 14\%)^2}{3-1}}$$

$$= \sqrt{\frac{4\% + 0\% + 4\%}{2}} = \sqrt{\frac{8\%}{2}} = \underline{\underline{2\%}}$$

$$\sigma_{k_B} = \sqrt{\frac{(16\% - 14\%)^2 + (14\% - 14\%)^2 + (12\% - 14\%)^2}{3-1}}$$

$$= \sqrt{\frac{4\% + 0\% + 4\%}{2}} = \sqrt{\frac{8\%}{2}} = \underline{\underline{2\%}}$$

$$\sigma_{k_C} = \sqrt{\frac{(12\% - 14\%)^2 + (14\% - 14\%)^2 + (16\% - 14\%)^2}{3-1}}$$

$$= \sqrt{\frac{4\% + 0\% + 4\%}{2}} = \sqrt{\frac{8\%}{2}} = \underline{\underline{2\%}}$$

c.

	Annual expected returns	
Year	**Portfolio AB**	**Portfolio AC**
1995	(.50 × 12%) + (.50 × 16%) = 14%	(.50 × 12%) + (.50 × 12%) = 12%
1996	(.50 × 14%) + (.50 × 14%) = 14%	(.50 × 14%) + (.50 × 14%) = 14%
1997	(.50 × 16%) + (.50 × 12%) = 14%	(.50 × 16%) + (.50 × 16%) = 16%

Over the three-year period:

$$\bar{k}_{AB} = \frac{14\% + 14\% + 14\%}{3} = \frac{42\%}{3} = \underline{\underline{14\%}}$$

$$\bar{k}_{AC} = \frac{12\% + 14\% + 16\%}{3} = \frac{42\%}{3} = \underline{\underline{14\%}}$$

d. AB is perfectly negatively correlated.
AC is perfectly positively correlated.

e. Standard deviation portfolios

$$\sigma_{k_{AB}} = \sqrt{\frac{(14\% - 14\%)^2 + (14\% - 14\%)^2 + (14\% - 14\%)^2}{3-1}}$$

$$= \sqrt{\frac{0\% + 0\% + 0\%}{2}} = \sqrt{\frac{0\%}{2}} = \underline{\underline{0\%}}$$

$$\sigma_{k_{AC}} = \sqrt{\frac{(12\% - 14\%)^2 + (14\% - 14\%)^2 + (16\% - 14\%)^2}{3-1}}$$

$$= \sqrt{\frac{4\% + 0\% + 4\%}{2}} = \sqrt{\frac{8\%}{2}} = \underline{\underline{2\%}}$$

f. Portfolio AB is preferred, since it provides the same return (14%) as AC but with less risk $[(\sigma_{k_{AB}} = 0\%) < (\sigma_{k_{AC}} = 2\%)]$.

ST 6-2 a. When the market return increases by 10 percent, the project's required return would be expected to increase by 15 percent ($1.50 \times 10\%$). When the market return decreases by 10 percent, the project's required return would be expected to decrease by 15 percent $[1.50 \times (-10\%)]$.

b.
$$k_j = R_F + [b_j \times (k_m - R_F)]$$
$$= 7\% + [1.50 \times (10\% - 7\%)]$$
$$= 7\% + 4.5\% = \underline{\underline{11.5\%}}$$

c. No, the project should be rejected, since its expected return of 11 percent is less than the 11.5 percent return required from the project.

d.
$$k_j = 7\% + [1.50 \times (9\% - 7\%)]$$
$$= 7\% + 3\% = \underline{\underline{10\%}}$$

The project would now be acceptable, since its expected return of 11 percent is now in excess of the required return, which has declined to 10 percent as a result of investors in the marketplace becoming less risk-averse.

Chapter 7

ST 7-1 a. $B_0 = I \times (PVIFA_{k_d,n}) + M \times (PVIF_{k_d,n})$

$I = .08 \times \$1{,}000 = \$80$

$M = \$1{,}000$

$n = 12$ yrs.

(1) $k_d = 7\%$

$$B_0 = \$80 \times (PVIFA_{7\%,12\text{yrs}}) + \$1{,}000 \times (PVIF_{7\%,12\text{yrs}})$$
$$= (\$80 \times 7.943) + (\$1{,}000 \times .444)$$
$$= \$635.44 + \$444.00 = \underline{\underline{\$1{,}079.44}}$$

(Calculator solution = \$1,079.43)

(2) $k_d = 8\%$

$$B_0 = \$80 \times (PVIFA_{8\%,12\text{yrs}}) + \$1{,}000 \times (PVIF_{8\%,12\text{yrs}})$$
$$= (\$80 \times 7.536) + (\$1{,}000 \times .397)$$
$$= \$602.88 + \$397.00 = \underline{\underline{\$999.88}}$$

(Calculator solution = \$1,000)

(3) $k_d = 10\%$

$$B_0 = \$80 \times (PVIFA_{10\%,12\text{yrs}}) + \$1{,}000 \times (PVIF_{10\%,12\text{yrs}})$$
$$= (\$80 \times 6.814) + (\$1{,}000 \times .319)$$
$$= \$545.12 + \$319.00 = \underline{\underline{\$864.12}}$$

(Calculator solution = \$863.73)

b. (1) $k_d = 7\%$, $B_0 = \$1{,}079.44$; sells at a *premium*
(2) $k_d = 8\%$, $B_0 = \$999.88 \approx \$1{,}000.00$; sells at its *par value*
(3) $k_d = 10\%$, $B_0 = \$864.12$; sells at a *discount*

c.
$$B_0 = \frac{I}{2} \times (PVIFA_{k_d/2,2n}) + M \times (PVIF_{k_d/2,2n})$$
$$= \frac{\$80}{2} \times (PVIFA_{10\%/2,2\times 12\text{periods}}) + \$1{,}000 \times (PVIF_{10\%/2,2\times 12\text{periods}})$$

$= \$40 \times (PVIFA_{5\%,24\text{periods}}) + \$1{,}000 \times (PVIF_{5\%,24\text{periods}})$

$= (\$40 \times 13.799) + (\$1{,}000 \times .310)$

$= \$551.96 + \$310.00 = \underline{\underline{\$861.96}}$

(Calculator solution = \$862.01)

ST 7-2 a. $B_0 = \$1{,}150$

$I = .11 \times \$1{,}000 = \$110$

$M = \$1{,}000$

$n = 18$ yrs.

$\$1{,}150 = \$110 \times (PVIFA_{k_d,18\text{ yrs}}) + \$1{,}000 \times (PVIF_{k_d,18\text{ yrs}})$

Since if $k_d = 11\%$, $B_0 = \$1{,}000 = M$, try $k_d = 10\%$.

$B_0 = \$110 \times (PVIFA_{10\%,18\text{yrs}}) + \$1{,}000 \times (PVIF_{10\%,18\text{yrs}})$

$= (\$110 \times 8.201) + (\$1{,}000 \times .180)$

$= \$902.11 + \$180.00 = \$1{,}082.11$

Since \$1,082.11 < \$1,150, try $k_d = 9\%$.

$B_0 = \$110 \times (PVIFA_{9\%,18\text{yrs}}) + \$1{,}000 \times (PVIF_{9\%,18\text{yrs}})$

$= (\$110 \times 8.756) + (\$1{,}000 \times .212)$

$= \$963.16 + \$212.00 = \$1{,}175.16$

Since the \$1,175.16 value at 9 percent is higher than \$1,150, and the \$1,082.11 value at 10 percent rate is lower than \$1,150, the bond's yield to maturity must be between 9 and 10 percent. Since the \$1,175.16 value is closer to \$1,150, to the nearest whole percent the YTM is 9 percent. (Using interpolation, the more precise YTM value is 9.27 percent.)

(Calculator solution = 9.26%)

b. Substituting into the *approximate yield formula:*

$$\text{Approximate yield} = \frac{I + \dfrac{M - B_0}{n}}{\dfrac{M + B_0}{2}}$$

$$= \frac{\$110 + \dfrac{\$1{,}000 - \$1{,}150}{18}}{\dfrac{\$1{,}000 + \$1{,}150}{2}} = \frac{\$110 - \$8.33}{\$1{,}075}$$

$$= \frac{\$101.67}{\$1{,}075} = \underline{\underline{9.46\%}}$$

c. The approximate yield of 9.46 percent is a reasonably good estimate of the actual yield (found by using interpolation) of 9.27 percent. Comparing the 9.46 percent approximation to the 9.00 percent estimate to the nearest 1 percent, the use of the approximate yield formula seems appealing, since its estimate is about as accurate (using the 9.27 percent value as the actual) as the use of the precise method rounded to the nearest whole percent.

d. The calculated YTM of 9+ percent is below the bond's 11 percent coupon interest rate, since the bond's market value of \$1,150 is above its \$1,000 par value. Whenever a bond's market value is above its par value (it sells at a *premium*), its YTM will be below its coupon interest rate; when a bond sells at *par,* the YTM will equal its coupon interest rate; and when the bond sells for less than par (at a *discount*), its YTM will be greater than its coupon interest rate.

ST 7-3 $D_0 = \$1.80/\text{share}$
$k_s = 12\%$

a. *Zero growth*

$$P_0 = \frac{D_1}{k_s} = \frac{D_1 = D_0 = \$1.80}{.12} = \underline{\underline{\$15/\text{share}}}$$

b. *Constant growth, $g = 5\%$*

$$D_1 = D_0 \times (1 + g) = \$1.80 \times (1 + .05) = \$1.89/\text{share}$$

$$P_0 = \frac{D_1}{k_s - g} = \frac{\$1.89}{.12 - .05} = \frac{\$1.89}{.07} = \underline{\underline{\$27/\text{share}}}$$

c. *Variable growth, $N = 3$, $g_1 = 5\%$* for years 1 to 3 and $g_2 = 4\%$ for years 4 to ∞.

$$D_1 = D_0 \times (1 + g_1)^1 = \$1.80 \times (1 + .05)^1 = \$1.89/\text{share}$$
$$D_2 = D_0 \times (1 + g_1)^2 = \$1.80 \times (1 + .05)^2 = \$1.98/\text{share}$$
$$D_3 = D_0 \times (1 + g_1)^3 = \$1.80 \times (1 + .05)^3 = \$2.08/\text{share}$$
$$D_4 = D_3 \times (1 + g_2) = \$2.08 \times (1 + .04) = \$2.16/\text{share}$$

$$P_0 = \sum_{t=1}^{N} \frac{D_0 \times (1 + g_1)^t}{(1 + k_s)^t} + \left(\frac{1}{(1 + k_s)^N} \times \frac{D_{N+1}}{k_s - g_2}\right)$$

$$\sum_{t=1}^{N} \frac{D_0 \times (1 + g_1)^t}{(1 + k_s)^t} = \frac{\$1.89}{(1 + .12)^1} + \frac{\$1.98}{(1 + .12)^2} + \frac{\$2.08}{(1 + .12)^3}$$
$$= [\$1.89 \times (PVIF_{12\%,1\text{yr}})] + [\$1.98 \times (PVIF_{12\%,2\text{yrs}})] + [\$2.08 \times (PVIF_{12\%,3\text{yrs}})]$$
$$= (\$1.89 \times .893) + (\$1.98 \times .797) + (\$2.08 \times .712)$$
$$= \$1.69 + \$1.58 + \$1.48 = \$4.75$$

$$\left(\frac{1}{(1 + k_s)^N} \times \frac{D_{N+1}}{(k_s - g_2)}\right) = \frac{1}{(1 + .12)^3} \times \frac{D_4 = \$2.16}{.12 - .04}$$
$$= (PVIF_{12\%,3\text{yrs}}) \times \frac{\$2.16}{.08}$$
$$= .712 \times \$27.00 = \$19.22$$

$$P_0 = \sum_{t=1}^{N} \frac{D_0 \times (1 + g_1)^t}{(1 + k_s)^t} + \left(\frac{1}{(1 + k_s)^N} \times \frac{D_{N+1}}{k_s - g_2}\right) = \$4.75 + \$19.22$$
$$= \underline{\underline{\$23.97/\text{share}}}$$

Chapter 8

ST 8-1 **a.** Book value = installed cost − accumulated depreciation

Installed cost = $50,000

Accumulated depreciation = $50,000 × (.20 + .32 + .19 + .12)
= $50,000 × .83 = $41,500

Book value = $50,000 − $41,500 = $\underline{\underline{\$8,500}}$

b. Taxes on sale of old equipment:

Capital gain = sale price − initial purchase price
= $55,000 − $50,000 = $5,000

Recaptured depreciation = initial purchase price − book value
= $50,000 − $8,500 = $41,500

Taxes = (.40 × $5,000) + (.40 × $41,500)
= $2,000 + $16,600 = $18,600

c. Initial investment:

Installed cost of new equipment		
Cost of new equipment	$75,000	
+ Installation costs	5,000	
Total installed cost—new		$80,000
− After-tax proceeds from sale of old equipment		
Proceeds from sale of old equipment	$55,000	
− Taxes on sale of old equipment	18,600	
Total after-tax proceeds—old		36,400
+ Change in net working capital		15,000
Initial investment		$58,600

ST 8-2 a. Initial investment:

Installed cost of new machine		
Cost of new machine	$140,000	
+ Installation costs	10,000	
Total installed cost—new (depreciable value)		$150,000
− After-tax proceeds from sale of old machine		
Proceeds from sale of old machine	$ 42,000	
− Taxes on sale of old machine[1]	9,120	
Total after-tax proceeds—old		32,880
+ Change in net working capital[2]		20,000
Initial investment		$137,120

[1]Book value of old machine = $40,000 − [(.20 + .32) × $40,000]
= $40,000 − (.52 × $40,000)
= $40,000 − $20,800 = $19,200

Capital gain = $42,000 − $40,000 = $2,000

Recaptured depreciation = $40,000 − $19,200 = $20,800

Taxes = (.40 × $2,000) + (.40 × $20,800) = $800 + $8,320 = $9,120

[2]Change in net working capital = +$10,000 + $25,000 − $15,000
= $35,000 − $15,000 = $20,000

b. Incremental operating cash inflows:

CALCULATION OF DEPRECIATION EXPENSE FOR NEW MACHINE

Year	Cost (1)	Applicable MACRS depreciation percentages (from Table 3.6) (2)	Depreciation [(1) × (2)] (3)
With new machine			
1	$150,000	33%	$ 49,500
2	150,000	45	67,500
3	150,000	15	22,500
4	150,000	7	10,500
Totals		100%	$150,000

CALCULATION OF DEPRECIATION EXPENSE FOR OLD MACHINE

Year	Cost (1)	Applicable MACRS depreciation percentages (from Table 3.6) (2)	Depreciation [(1) × (2)] (3)
With old machine			
1	$40,000	19% (year 3 depreciation)	$ 7,600
2	40,000	12 (year 4 depreciation)	4,800
3	40,000	12 (year 5 depreciation)	4,800
4	40,000	5 (year 6 depreciation)	2,000
		Total	$ 19,200[a]

[a]The total of $19,200 represents the book value of the old machine at the end of the second year, which was calculated in part **a**.

CALCULATION OF OPERATING CASH INFLOWS

Year	Profits before depreciation and taxes (1)	Depreciation[a] (2)	Net profits before taxes [(1) − (2)] (3)	Taxes [.40 × (3)] (4)	Net profits after taxes [(3) − (4)] (5)	Operating cash inflows [(2) + (5)] (6)
New machine						
1	$120,000	$49,500	$ 70,500	$28,200	$42,300	$ 91,800
2	130,000	67,500	62,500	25,000	37,500	105,000
3	130,000	22,500	107,500	43,000	64,500	87,000
4	0	10,500	− 10,500	− 4,200	− 6,300	4,200
Old machine						
1	$ 70,000	$ 7,600	$ 62,400	$24,960	$37,440	$ 45,040
2	70,000	4,800	65,200	26,080	39,120	43,920
3	70,000	4,800	65,200	26,080	39,120	43,920
4	0	2,000	− 2,000	− 800	− 1,200	800

[a]From column 3 of the preceding table.

CALCULATION OF INCREMENTAL OPERATING CASH INFLOWS

	Operating cash inflows		
Year	New machines[a] (1)	Old machine[a] (2)	Incremental (relevant) [(1) − (2)] (3)
1	$ 91,800	$45,040	$46,760
2	105,000	43,920	61,080
3	87,000	43,920	43,080
4	4,200	800	3,400

[a]From column 6 of the preceding table.

c. Terminal cash flow (end of year 3):

After-tax proceeds from sale of new machine		
Proceeds from sale of new machine	$35,000	
− Taxes on sale of new machine[1]	9,800	
Total after-tax proceeds		$25,200
− After-tax proceeds from sale of old machine		
Proceeds from sale of old machine	$ 0	
− Taxes on sale of old machine[2]	− 800	
Total after-tax proceeds—old		800
+ Change in net working capital		20,000
Terminal cash flow		$44,400

[1]Book value of new machine at end of year 3

= $150,000 − [(.33 + .45 + .33 + .15) × $150,000] = $150,000 − (.93 × $150,000)

= $150,000 − $139,500 = $10,500

Tax on sale = .40 × ($35,000 sale price − $10,500 book value)

= .40 × $24,500 = $9,800

[2]Book value of old machine at end of year 3

= $40,000 − [(.20 + .32 + .19 + .12 + .12) × $40,000] = $40,000 − (.95 × $40,000)

= $40,000 − $38,000 = $2,000

Tax on sale = .40 × ($0 sale price − $2,000 book value)

= .40 × (− $2,000) = −$800 (i.e., $800 tax saving)

d.

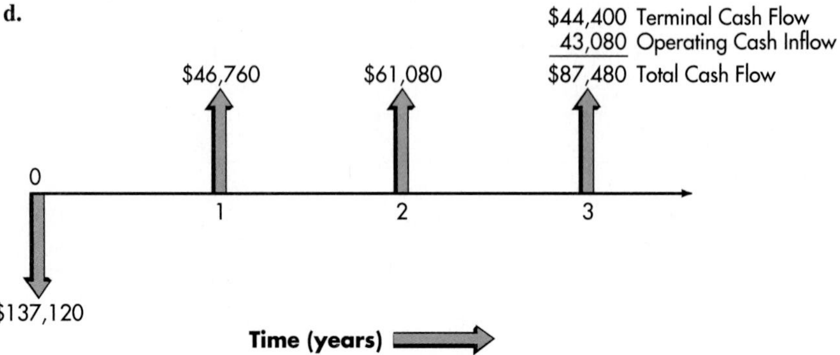

Note: The year 4 incremental operating cash inflow of $3,400 is not directly included; it is instead reflected in the book values used to calculate the taxes on sale of the machines at the end of year 3 and is therefore part of the terminal cash flow.

Chapter 9

ST 9-1 a. Payback period:

Project M: $\frac{\$28,500}{\$10,000} = \underline{\underline{2.85 \text{ years}}}$

Project N:

Year (t)	Cash inflows (CF_t)	Cumulative cash inflows
1	$11,000	$11,000
2	10,000	21,000 ←
3	9,000	30,000
4	8,000	38,000

$$2 + \frac{\$27{,}000 - \$21{,}000}{\$9{,}000} \text{ years}$$

$$2 + \frac{\$6{,}000}{\$9{,}000} \text{ years} = \underline{\underline{2.67 \text{ years}}}$$

b. Net present value (NPV):

Project M: NPV $= (\$10{,}000 \times PVIFA_{14\%,4\text{yrs}}) - \$28{,}500$

$= (\$10{,}000 \times 2.914) - \$28{,}500$

$= \$29{,}140 - \$28{,}500 = \underline{\underline{\$640}}$

(Calculator solution = $637.12)

Project N:

Year (t)	CF_t (1)	$PVIF_{14\%,t}$ (2)	Present value at 14% [(1) × (2)] (3)
1	$11,000	.877	$ 9,647
2	10,000	.769	7,690
3	9,000	.675	6,075
4	8,000	.592	4,736
	Present value of cash inflows		$28,148
	− Initial investment		$27,000
	Net present value (NPV)		$ 1,148

(Calculator solution = $1,155.18)

c. Internal rate of return (IRR):

Project M: $\frac{\$28{,}500}{\$10{,}000} = 2.850$

$PVIFA_{\text{IRR},4\text{yrs}} = 2.850$

From Table A-4:

$PVIFA_{15\%,4\text{yrs}} = 2.855$

$PVIFA_{16\%,4\text{yrs}} = 2.798$

IRR = $\underline{\underline{15\%}}$ (2.850 is closest to 2.855)

(Calculator solution = 15.09%)

Project N: Average annuity $= \frac{\$11{,}000 + \$10{,}000 + \$9{,}000 + \$8{,}000}{4}$

$= \frac{\$38{,}000}{4} = \$9{,}500$

$$PVIFA_{k,4yrs} = \frac{\$27,000}{\$9,500} = 2.842$$

$$k \approx 15\%$$

Try 16%, since there are more cash inflows in early years.

Year (t)	CF_t (1)	$PVIF_{16\%,t}$ (2)	Present value at 16% [(1) × (2)] (3)	$PVIF_{17\%,t}$ (4)	Present value at 17% [(1) × (4)] (5)
1	$11,000	.862	$ 9,482	.855	$ 9,405
2	10,000	.743	7,430	.731	7,310
3	9,000	.641	5,769	.624	5,616
4	8,000	.552	4,416	.534	4,272
	Present value of cash inflows		$27,097		$26,603
	− Initial investment		27,000		27,000
	NPV		$ 97		−$ 397

IRR = 16% (rounding to nearest whole percent)

(Calculator solution = 16.19%)

d.

	Project	
	M	N
Payback period	2.85 years	2.67 years*
NPV	$640	$1,148*
IRR	15%	16%*

*Preferred project.

Project N is recommended, since it has the shorter payback period and the higher NPV, which is greater than zero, and the larger IRR, which is greater than the 14 percent cost of capital

e. Net present value profiles:

Data

Discount rate	NPV	
	Project M	Project N
0%	$11,500[a]	$11,000[b]
14	640	1,148
15	0	—
16	—	0

[a]($10,000 + $10,000 + $10,000 + $10,000) − $28,500 = $40,000 − $28,500 = $11,500

[b]($11,000 + $10,000 + $9,000 + $8,000) − $27,000 = $38,000 − $27,000 = $11,000

From the NPV profile below it can be seen that if the firm has a cost of capital below approximately 6 percent (exact value is 5.75 percent), conflicting rankings of the projects would exist using the NPV and IRR decision techniques. Since the firm's cost of capital is 14 percent, it can be seen in part **d** that no conflict exists.

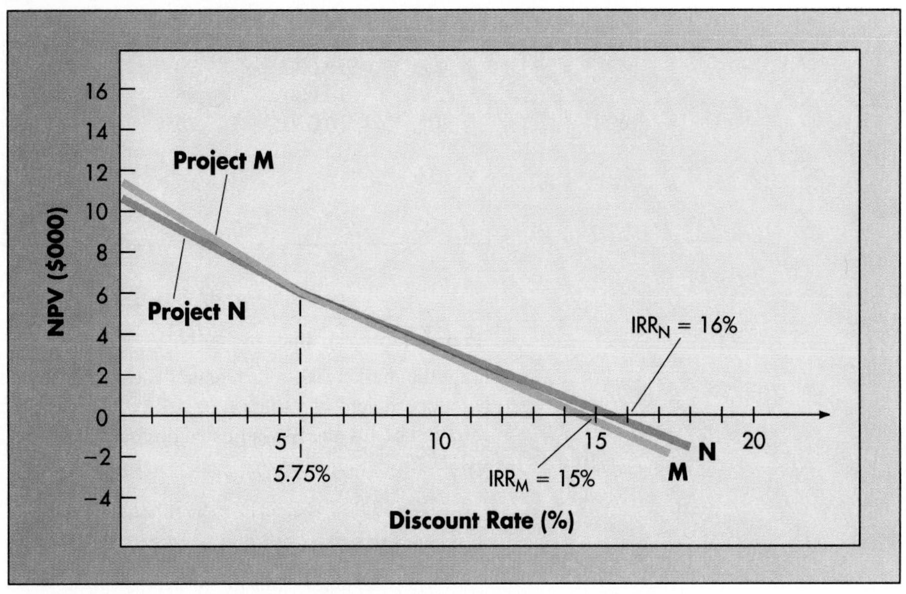

ST 9-2 a. $NPV_A = (\$7{,}000 \times PVIFA_{10\%,3yrs}) - \$15{,}000$

$= (\$7{,}000 \times 2{,}487) - \$15{,}000$

$= \$17{,}409 - \$15{,}000 = \underline{\underline{\$2{,}409}}$

(Calculator solution = $2,407.96)

$NPV_B = (\$10{,}000 \times PVIFA_{10\%,3yrs}) - \$20{,}000$

$= (\$10{,}000 \times 2.487) - \$20{,}000$

$= \$24{,}870 - \$20{,}000 = \underline{\underline{\$4{,}870^*}}$

(Calculator solution = $4,868.52)

*Preferred project, since higher NPV.

b. Project A:

Year (t)	CF_t (1)	Certainty equivalent factors (α_t) (2)	Certain CF_t [(1) × (2)] (3)	$PVIF_{7\%,t}$ (4)	Present value at 7% [(3) × (4)] (5)
1	$7,000	.95	$6,650	.935	$ 6,218
2	7,000	.90	6,300	.873	5,500
3	7,000	.90	6,300	.816	5,141
			Present value of cash inflows		$16,859
			− Initial investment		15,000
			NPV		$1,859*

(Calculator solution = $1,860.29)

Project B:

Year (t)	CF_t (1)	Certainty equivalent factors (α_t) (2)	Certain CF_t [(1) × (2)] (3)	$PVIF_{7\%,t}$ (4)	Present value at 7% [(3) × (4)] (5)
1	$10,000	.90	$9,000	.935	$ 8,415
2	10,000	.85	8,500	.873	7,421
3	10,000	.70	7,000	.816	5,712
			Present value of cash inflows		$21,548
			− Initial investment		20,000
			NPV		$1,548

(Calculator solution = $1,549.53)

*Preferred project, since higher NPV.

c. From the market risk-return data, the risk-adjusted discount rate for project A, which has a coefficient of variation of 0.4, is *9 percent;* for project B, with a coefficient of variation of 1.8, the risk-adjusted discount rate is *16 percent.*

$$NPV_A = (\$7{,}000 \times PVIFA_{9\%,3yrs}) - \$15{,}000$$
$$= (\$7{,}000 \times 2.531) - \$15{,}000$$
$$= \$17{,}717 - \$15{,}000 = \$2{,}717^*$$
(Calculator solution = $2,719.06)

$$NPV_B = (\$10{,}000 \times PVIFA_{16\%,3yrs}) - \$20{,}000$$
$$= (\$10000 \times 2.246) - \$20{,}000$$
$$= \$22{,}460 - \$20{,}000 = \$2{,}460$$
(Calculator solution = $2,458.90)

*Preferred project, since higher NPV.

d. When the differences in risk were ignored in **a**, project B is preferred over project A; but when the higher risk of project B is incorporated in the analysis using either certainty equivalents (**b**) or risk-adjusted discount rates (**c**), *project A is preferred over project B.* Clearly, project A should be implemented.

Chapter 10

ST 10-1 a. Cost of debt, k_i (using approximation formula)

$$k_d = \frac{1 + \frac{\$1{,}000 - N_d}{n}}{\frac{N_d + \$1{,}000}{2}}$$

$$I = .10 \times \$1{,}000 = \$100$$
$$N_d = \$1{,}000 - \$30 \text{ discount} - \$20 \text{ flotation cost} = \$950$$
$$n = 10 \text{ years}$$

$$k_d = \frac{\$100 + \frac{\$1{,}000 - \$950}{10}}{\frac{\$950 + \$1{,}000}{2}} = \frac{\$100 + \$5}{\$975} = 10.8\%$$

(Calculator solution = 10.8%)

$$k_i = k_d \times (1 - T)$$
$$T = .40$$
$$k_i = 10.8\% \times (1 - .40) = \underline{\underline{6.5\%}}$$

Cost of preferred stock, k_p

$$k_p = \frac{D_p}{N_p}$$

$$D_p = .11 \times \$100 = \$11$$
$$N_p = \$100 - \$4 \text{ flotation cost} = \$96$$

$$k_p = \frac{\$11}{\$96} = \underline{\underline{11.5\%}}$$

Cost of retained earnings, k_r

$$k_r = k_s = \frac{D_1}{P_0} + g$$

$$= \frac{\$6}{\$80} + 6.0\% = 7.5\% + 6.0\% = \underline{\underline{13.5\%}}$$

Cost of new common stock, k_n

$$k_n = \frac{D_1}{N_n} + g$$

$$D_1 = \$6$$
$$N_n = \$80 - \$4 \text{ underpricing} - \$4 \text{ flotation cost} = \$72$$
$$g = 6.0\%$$

$$k_n = \frac{\$6}{\$72} + 6.0\% = 8.3\% + 6.0\% = \underline{\underline{14.3\%}}$$

b. (1) Breaking point, BP

$$BP_{\text{common equity}} = \frac{AF_{\text{common equity}}}{w_{\text{common equity}}}$$

$$AF_{\text{common equity}} = \$225{,}000$$
$$w_{\text{common equity}} = 45\%$$

$$BP_{\text{common equity}} = \frac{\$225{,}000}{.45} = \underline{\underline{\$500{,}000}}$$

(2) WACC for total new financing < \$500,000

Source of capital	Weight (1)	Cost (2)	Weighted cost [(1) × (2)] (3)
Long-term debt	.40	6.5%	2.6%
Preferred stock	.15	11.5	1.7
Common stock equity	.45	13.5	6.1
Totals	1.00		10.4%
Weighted average cost of capital = 10.4%			

(3) WACC for total new financing > $500,000

Source of capital	Weight (1)	Cost (2)	Weighted cost [(1) × (2)] (3)
Long-term debt	.40	6.5%	2.6%
Preferred stock	.15	11.5	1.7
Common stock equity	.45	14.3	6.4
Totals	1.00		10.7%
Weighted average cost of capital = 10.7%			

c. IOS data for graph

Investment opportunity	Internal rate of return (IRR)	Initial investment	Cumulative investment
D	16.5%	$200,000	$ 200,000
C	12.9	150,000	350,000
E	11.8	450,000	800,000
A	11.2	100,000	900,000
G	10.5	300,000	1,200,000
F	10.1	600,000	1,800,000
B	9.7	500,000	2,300,000

d. Projects D, C, E, and A should be accepted because their respective IRRs exceed the WMCC. They will require $900,000 of total new financing.

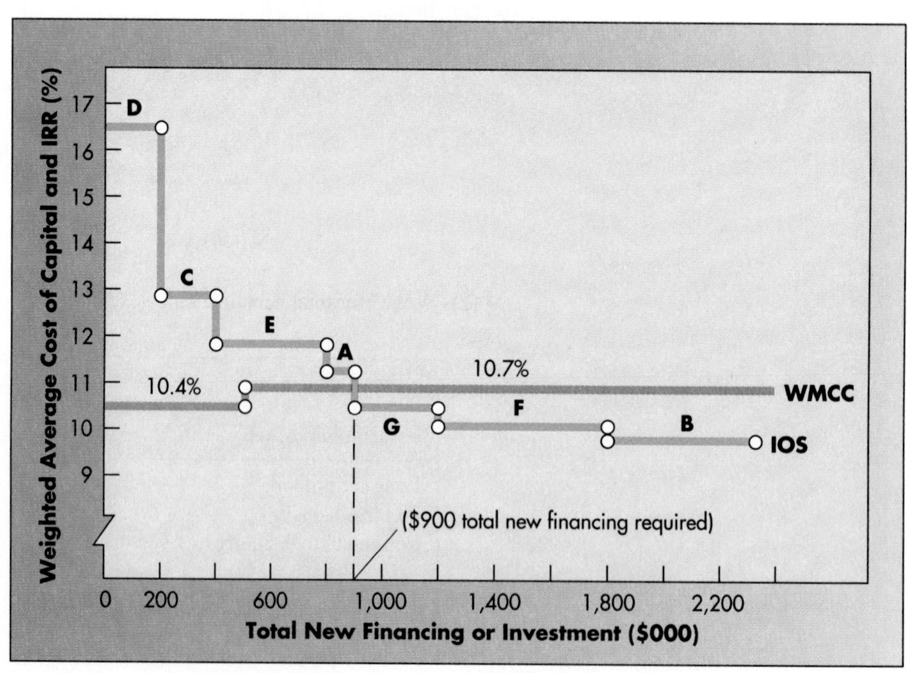

Chapter 11

ST 11-1 a. $Q = \frac{FC}{P - VC}$

$$= \frac{\$250{,}000}{\$7.50 - \$3.00} = \frac{\$250{,}000}{\$4.50} = \underline{\underline{55{,}556 \text{ units}}}$$

b.

		+20%	
Sales (in units)	100,000		120,000
Sales revenue (units × \$7.50/unit)	\$750,000		\$900,000
Less: Variable operating costs (units × \$3.00/unit)	300,000		360,000
Less: Fixed operating costs	250,000		250,000
Earnings before interest and taxes (EBIT)	\$200,000		\$290,000
Less: Interest	80,000	+45%	80,000
Net profits before taxes	\$120,000		\$210,000
Less: Taxes (T = .40)	48,000		84,000
Net profits after taxes	\$ 72,000		\$126,000
Less: Preferred dividends (8,000 shares × \$5.00/share)	40,000		40,000
Earnings available for common	\$ 32,000		\$ 86,000
Earnings per share (EPS)	\$32,000/20,000 = \$1.60/share		\$86,000/20,000 = \$4.30/share
		+169%	

c. $\text{DOL} = \frac{\text{\% change in EBIT}}{\text{\% change in sales}} = \frac{+45\%}{+20\%} = \underline{\underline{2.25}}$

d. $\text{DFL} = \frac{\text{\% change in EPS}}{\text{\% change in EBIT}} = \frac{+169\%}{+45\%} = \underline{\underline{3.76}}$

e. $\text{DTL} = \text{DOL} \times \text{DFL}$

$= 2.25 \times 3.76 = \underline{\underline{8.46}}$

Using the other DTL formula:

$$\text{DTL} = \frac{\text{\% change in EPS}}{\text{\% change in sales}}$$

$$8.46 = \frac{\text{\% change in EPS}}{+50\%}$$

% change in EPS = 8.46 × .50 = 4.23 = $\underline{\underline{+423\%}}$

ST 11-2

Data summary for alternative plans		
Source of capital	**Plan A (bond)**	**Plan B (stock)**
Long-term debt	\$60,000 at 12% annual interest	\$50,000 at 12% annual interest
Annual interest =	.12 × \$60,000 = \$7,200	.12 × \$50,000 = \$6,000
Common stock	10,000 shares	11,000 shares

a.

	Plan A (bond)		Plan B (stock)	
EBIT*	$30,000	$40,000	$30,000	$40,000
Less: Interest	7,200	7,200	6,000	6,000
Net profits before taxes	$22,800	$32,800	$24,000	$34,000
Less: Taxes (T = .40)	9,120	13,120	9,600	13,600
Net profits after taxes	$13,680	$19,680	$14,400	$20,400
EPS (10,000 shares)	$1.37	$1.97		
(11,000 shares)			$1.31	$1.85

*Values were arbitrarily selected; other values could have been utilized.

Coordinates		
	EBIT	
	$30,000	$40,000
Financing plan	Earnings per share (EPS)	
A (Bond)	$1.37	$1.97
B (Stock)	1.31	1.85

b.

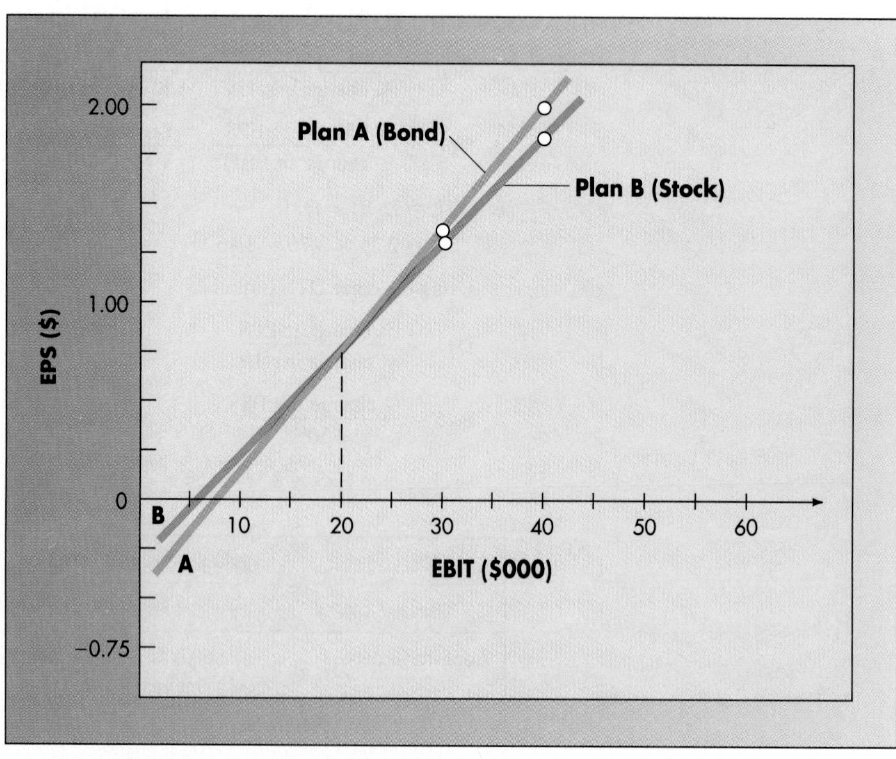

c. The bond plan (Plan A) becomes superior to the stock plan (Plan B) at *around $20,000* of EBIT as represented by the dashed vertical line in the figure in **b** above. (*Note:* The actual point is $19,200, which was determined algebraically by using the technique described in footnote 21.)

ST 11-3 a.

Capital structure debt ratio (%)	Expected EPS ($) (1)	Required return, k_s (2)	Estimated share value ($) [(1) ÷ (2)] (3)
0%	$3.12	.13	$24.00
10	3.90	.15	26.00
20	4.80	.16	30.00
30	5.44	.17	32.00
40	5.51	.19	29.00
50	5.00	.20	25.00
60	4.40	.22	20.00

b. Using the table in **a** above:

(1) Maximization of EPS: *40 percent debt ratio,* EPS = $5.51/share (see column 1).

(2) Maximization of share value: *30 percent debt ratio,* share value = $32.00 (see column 3).

c. Recommend *30 percent debt ratio,* since it results in the maximum share value and is therefore consistent with the firm's goal of owner wealth maximization.

Chapter 12

ST 12-1 a. Tabular Calculation of the Initial Investment for Torbert Manufacturing's Bond-Refunding Decision

a. Call premium		
Before tax [($1,130 − $1,000) × 20,000 bonds]	$2,600,000	
Less: Taxes (.40 × $2,600,000)	1,040,000	
After-tax cost of call premium		$1,560,000
b. Flotation cost of new bond		400,000
c. Overlapping interest		
Before tax (.13 × 3/12[a] × $20,000,000)	$ 650,000	
Less: Taxes (.40 × $650,000)	260,000	
After-tax cost of overlapping interest		390,000
d. Tax savings from unamortized discount on old bond [20/30[b] × (20,000 bonds × $12/bond discount) × .40]		(64,000)
e. Tax savings from unamortized flotation cost of old bond (20/30[b] × $150,000 × .40)		(40,000)
Initial investment		$2,246,000

[a]3 months overlapping interest ÷ 12 months per year

[b]20 years to maturity ÷ 30 year initial maturity

b. Tabular Calculation of the Annual Cash Flow Savings for Torbert Manufacturing's Bond-Refunding Decision

Old bond			
a. Interest cost			
Before tax (.13 × $20,000,000)	$2,600,000		
Less: Taxes (.40 × $2,600,000)	$1,040,000		
After-tax interest cost		$1,560,000	
b. Tax savings from amortization of discount [($240,000[a] ÷ 30) × .40]		(3,200)	
c. Tax savings from amortization of flotation cost [($150,000 ÷ 30) × .40]		(2,000)	
(1) Annual after-tax debt payment			$1,554,800
New bond			
d. Interest cost			
Before tax (.11 × $20,000,000)	$2,200,000		
Less: Taxes (.40 × $2,200,000)	880,000		
After-tax interest cost		$1,320,000	
e. Tax savings from amortization of flotation cost [($400,000 ÷ 20) × .40]		(8,000)	
(2) Annual after-tax debt payment			1,312,000
Annual cash flow savings [(1) − (2)]			$ 242,800

[a]20,000 bonds × $12 per-bond discount

c. Tabular Calculation of the Net Present Value of Torbert Manufacturing's Bond-Refunding Decision

Present value of annual cash flow savings (from **b**)	
$242,800 × $PVIFA_{7\%,20yrs}$	
$242,800 × 10.594 =	$2,572,223
Less: Initial investment (from **a**)	2,246,000
Net present value (NPV) of refunding[a]	$ 326,223

Decision: The proposed refunding is *recommended* because the NPV of refunding of $326,223 is greater than $0.

[a]By using a hand-held business/financial calculator, the present value of cash flow savings would be $2,572,227, which would have resulted in a NPV of refunding of $326,227.

Chapter 13

ST 13-1 a. Number of new shares $= \dfrac{\$1{,}000{,}000 \text{ to be raised}}{\$25 \text{ subscription price}} = \underline{\underline{40{,}000 \text{ shares}}}$

b. Number of shares per right $= \dfrac{40{,}000 \text{ new shares}}{500{,}000 \text{ shares outstanding}} = \underline{\underline{.08 \text{ shares}}}$

c. Candy Lopez's additional shares = .08 shares/right × 5,000 rights (1 right/share)

= $\underline{\underline{400 \text{ shares}}}$

d. *Variables:*

$M_w = \$27$ market value of stock with rights

$S = \$25$ subscription price

$N = \dfrac{1}{.08} = 12.5$ rights needed to purchase one share of stock.

Theoretical value of right with rights, R_w:

$$R_w = \frac{M_w - S}{N + 1} = \frac{\$27 - \$25}{12.5 + 1} = \frac{\$2}{13.5} = \underline{\underline{\$0.148}}$$

Theoretical value of right ex rights, R_e:

$M_e = M_w - R_w = \$27 - \$0.148 = \$26.852$ market value of stock trading ex rights

$$R_e = \frac{M_e - S}{N} = \frac{\$26.852 - \$25}{12.5} = \frac{\$1.852}{12.5} = \underline{\underline{\$0.148}}$$

e. Candy should receive at least the theoretical value of $0.148 per right—a total of $740 for her 5,000 rights ($0.148 × 5,000 = $740). If investors expect the price of Bulah Gas to rise during the period the rights are exercisable, the market value of the rights would be above their theoretical value.

ST 13-2 a. Earnings per share (EPS) $= \dfrac{\$2{,}000{,}000 \text{ earnings available}}{500{,}000 \text{ shares of common outstanding}}$

$= \underline{\underline{\$4.00/\text{share}}}$

Price/earnings (P/E) ratio $= \dfrac{\$60 \text{ market price}}{\$4.00 \text{ EPS}} = \underline{\underline{15}}$

b. Proposed dividends = 500,000 shares × $2 per share = $1,000,000

Shares that can be repurchased $= \dfrac{\$1{,}000{,}000}{\$62} = \underline{\underline{16{,}129 \text{ shares}}}$

c. *After proposed repurchase:*
Shares outstanding = 500,000 − 16,129 = 483,871

$\text{EPS} = \dfrac{\$2{,}000{,}000}{483{,}871} = \underline{\underline{\$4.13/\text{share}}}$

d. Market price = $4.13/share × 15 = $\underline{\underline{\$61.95/\text{share}}}$

e. The earnings per share (EPS) are higher after the repurchase, since there are fewer shares of stock outstanding (483,871 shares versus 500,000 shares) to divide up the firm's $2,000,000 of available earnings.

f. In both cases the stockholders would receive $2 per share—a $2 cash dividend in the dividend case or an approximately $2 increase in share price ($60.00 per share to $61.95 per share) in the repurchase case. (*Note:* The $.05 per share ($2.00 − $1.95) difference is due to rounding).

Chapter 14

ST 14-1 a. (1) and (2) In tabular form—after-tax cash outflows in column 3 and present value of the cash outflows in column 5.

End of year	Lease payment (1)	Tax adjustment [(1 − .40) = .60] (2)	After-tax cash outflows [(1) × (2)] (3)	Present-value factors[a] (4)	Present-value of outflows [(3) × (4)] (5)
1	$5,000	.60	$3,000	.917	$ 2,751
2	5,000	.60	3,000	.842	2,526
3	5,000	.60	3,000	.772	2,316
4	5,000	.60	3,000	.708	2,124
5	5,000	.60	7,000[b]	.650	4,550
			Present value of cash outflows		$14,267

[a]From Table A-3, *PVIF*, for 9 percent and the corresponding year.

[b]After-tax lease payment outflow of $3,000 plus the $4,000 cost of exercising the purchase option.

(Calculator solution = $14,269)

b. (1) In tabular form—annual interest expense in column 3.

End of year	Loan payments (1)	Beginning-of-year principal (2)	Payments: Interest [.15 × (2)] (3)	Payments: Principal [(1) − (3)] (4)	End-of-year principal [(2) − (4)] (5)
1	$5,967	$20,000	$3,000	$2,967	$17,033
2	5,967	17,033	2,555	3,412	13,621
3	5,967	13,621	2,043	3,924	9,697
4	5,967	9,697	1,455	4,512	5,185
5	5,967	5,185	778	5,189	—[a]

[a]The values in this table have been rounded to the nearest dollar, which results in a slight difference ($4) between the beginning-of-year 5 principal (in column 2) and the year 5 principal payment (column 4).

(2) In tabular form—after-tax cash outflows in column 9.

End of year	Loan payments (1)	Maintenance costs (2)	Cost of oven (3)	Depreciation percentages[a] (4)	Depreciation [(3) × (4)] (5)	Interest[b] (6)	Total deductions [(2) + (5) + (6)] (7)	Tax shields [.40 × (7)] (8)	After-tax cash outflows [(1) + (2) − (8)] (9)
1	$5,967	$1,000	$20,000	.20	$4,000	$3,000	$8,000	$3,200	$3,767
2	5,967	1,000	20,000	.32	6,400	2,555	9,955	3,982	2,985
3	5,967	1,000	20,000	.19	3,800	2,043	6,843	2,737	4,230
4	5,967	1,000	20,000	.12	2,400	1,455	4,855	1,942	5,025
5	5,967	1,000	20,000	.12	2,400	778	4,178	1,671	5,296

[a]From Table 3.6 on page 83.

[b]From column 3 of table in **b**(1).

(3) In tabular form—present value of the cash outflows in column 3.

End of year	After-tax cash outflows[a] (1)	Present-value factors[b] (2)	Present-value of outflows [(1) × (2)] (3)
1	$3,767	.917	$ 3,454
2	2,985	.842	2,513
3	4,230	.772	3,266
4	5,025	.708	3,558
5	5,296	.650	3,442
		Present value of cash outflows	$16,233

[a]From column 9 of table in **b**(2).

[b]From Table A-3, *PVIF,* for 9 percent and the corresponding year.

(Calculator solution = $16,237)

c. Because the present value of the lease outflows of $14,267 is well below the present value of the purchase outflows of $16,233, *the lease is preferred.* Leasing rather than purchasing the oven should result in an incremental savings of $1,966 ($16,233 purchase cost = $14,267 lease cost).

ST 14-2 a. In tabular form:

Year(s)	Payments (1)	Present-value interest factor at 13 percent (2)	Present value [(1) × (2)] (3)
1–25	$ 110[a]	7.330[b]	$806.30
25	1,000	.047[c]	47.00
		Straight bond value	$853.30

[a]$1,000 at 11% = $110 interest per year.

[b]Present-value interest factor for an annuity, *PVIFA,* discounted at 13 percent for 25 years, from Table A-4.

[c]Present-value interest factor for $1, *PVIF,* discounted at 13 percent for year 25, from Table A-3.

(Calculator solution = $853.40)

b. In tabular form:

Market price of stock (1)	Conversion ratio (2)	Conversion value [(1) × (2)] (3)
$20	40	$ 800
25 (conversion price)	40	1,000 (par value)
28	40	1,120
35	40	1,400
50	40	2,000

c. The bond would be expected to sell at the higher of the conversion value or straight value. In no case would it be expected to sell for less than the straight value of $853.30. Therefore at a price of $20 the bond would sell for its straight value of $853.30, and at prices of $25, $28, $35, and $50 the bond would be expected to sell at the associated conversion values (calculated in **b**) of $1,000, $1,120, $1,400, and $2,000, respectively.

d. The straight bond value of $853.30.

Chapter 15

ST 15-1 a.

Cash Budget Carroll Company April–June						Accounts receivable at end of June	
	February	March	April	May	June	July	August
Forecast sales	$500	$600	$400	$ 200	$200		
Cash sales (.30)	$150	$180	$120	$ 60	$ 60		
Collections of A/R							
Lag 1 mo. [(.7 × .7) = .49]		245	294	196	98	$ 98	
Lag 2 mo. [(.3 × .7) = .21]			105	126	84	42	$42
						$140 + $42 = $182	
Total cash receipts			$519	$ 382	$242		
Less: Total cash disbursements			600	500	200		
Net cash flow			$ (81)	$(118)	$ 42		
Add: Beginning cash			115	34	(84)		
Ending cash			$ 34	$ (84)	$ (42)		
Less: Minimum cash balance			25	25	25		
Required total financing (notes payable)			—	$ 109	$ 67		
Excess cash balance (marketable securities)			$ 9	—	—		

b. Carroll Company would need a maximum of $109 in financing over the three-month period.

c.

Account	Amount	Source of amount
Cash	$ 25	Minimum cash—June
Notes payable	67	Required total financing—June
Marketable securities	0	Excess cash balance—June
Accounts receivable	182	Calculation at right of cash budget statement

ST 15-2 a.

Pro forma income statement
Euro Designs, Inc.
for the year ended December 31, 1995

Sales revenue (given)	$3,900,000
Less: Cost of goods sold (.55)	2,145,000
Gross profits	$1,755,000
Less: Operating expenses (.12)	468,000
Operating profits	$1,287,000
Less: Interest expense (given)	325,000
Net profits before taxes	$ 962,000
Less: Taxes (.40 × $962,000)	384,800
Net profits after taxes	$ 577,200
Less: Cash dividends (given)	320,000
To retained earnings	$ 257,200

b. The percent-of-sales method may underestimate actual 1995 pro forma income by assuming that all costs are variable. If the firm has fixed costs, which by definition would not increase with increasing sales, the 1995 pro forma income would likely be underestimated.

Chapter 16

ST 16-1 a.

Month	Total funds requirement (1)	Permanent funds requirement[a] (2)	Seasonal funds requirement [(1) − (2)] (3)
January	$7,400,000	$5,000,000	$2,400,000
February	5,500,000	5,000,000	500,000
March	5,000,000	5,000,000	0
April	5,300,000	5,000,000	300,000
May	6,200,000	5,000,000	1,200,000
June	6,000,000	5,000,000	1,000,000
July	5,800,000	5,000,000	800,000
August	5,400,000	5,000,000	400,000
September	5,000,000	5,000,000	0
October	5,300,000	5,000,000	300,000
November	6,000,000	5,000,000	1,000,000
December	6,800,000	5,000,000	1,800,000
Monthly average[b]		$5,000,000	$ 808,333

[a]Represents the lowest level of total funds required over the 12-month period.

[b]Found by summing the monthly amounts for 12 months and dividing the resulting totals by 12. For the permanent funds requirement, $60,000,000/12 = $5,000,000, and for the seasonal funds requirement, $9,700,000/12 = $808,333.

b. (1) *Aggressive strategy*—Applying this strategy would result in a perfect matching of long-term financing with the permanent funds requirement and short-term financing with the seasonal funds requirement. Therefore $5,000,000 of long-term financing and average monthly short-term financing of $808,333 would be used.

(2) *Conservative strategy*—Applying this strategy would result in enough long-term financing to meet all projected funds requirements; short-term financing would be used only to meet emergency or unexpected financial needs. In this case, $7,400,000 of long-term financing would be used to meet the peak funds requirement (during January), and no short-term financing would be used.

c. (1) *Aggressive strategy*

$$\text{Total cost} = (\$5{,}000{,}000 \times .16) + (\$808{,}333 \times .10)$$
$$= \$800{,}000 + \$80{,}833 = \underline{\underline{\$880{,}833}}$$

(2) *Conservative strategy*

$$\text{Total cost} = (\$7{,}400{,}000 \times .16) + (\$0 \times .10)$$
$$= \$1{,}184{,}000 + \$0 = \underline{\underline{\$1{,}184{,}000}}$$

d. The *aggressive strategy is more profitable,* since, as was noted in **c**, its total cost is $880,833 compared to the total cost of $1,184,000 under the conservative strategy. This difference results because the aggressive strategy uses as much of the less expensive short-term (current liability) financing as possible, whereas the conservative strategy finances all needs with the more expensive long-term financing. Also, under the aggressive strategy, interest is paid only on necessary financing; under the conservative strategy, interest is paid on unneeded funds. (For example, under the conservative strategy, interest is paid on $7,400,000 in July while only $5,800,000 of financing is needed.)

The *aggressive strategy, on the other hand, is more risky,* since it relies heavily on the *limited* short-term financing, while the conservative strategy reserves short-term borrowing for emergency or unexpected financial needs. In addition, the aggressive strategy results in lower net working capital than the conservative strategy, thereby resulting in lower liquidity and a higher risk of technical insolvency.

ST 16-2 a.

Supplier	Approximate cost of giving up cash discount
X	1% × [360/(55 − 10)] = 1% × 360/45 = 1% × 8 = 8%
Y	2% × [360/(30 − 10)] = 2% × 360/20 = 2% × 18 = 36%
Z	2% × [360/(60 − 20)] = 2% × 360/40 = 2% × 9 = 18%

b.

Supplier	Recommendation
X	8% cost of giving up discount < 15% interest cost from bank; therefore, *give up discount.*
Y	36% cost of giving up discount > 15% interest cost from bank; therefore, *take discount and borrow from bank.*
Z	18% cost of giving up discount > 15% interest cost from bank; therefore, *take discount and borrow from bank.*

c. Stretching accounts payable for supplier Z would change the cost of giving up the cash discount to:

$$2\% \times [360/[(60 + 20) - 20]] = 2\% \times 360/60 = 2\% \times 6 = \underline{\underline{12\%}}$$

In this case, in light of the 15 percent interest cost from the bank, the recommended strategy in **b** would be to *give up the discount,* since the 12 percent cost of giving up the discount would be less than the 15 percent bank interest cost.

Chapter 17

ST 17-1

Basic data		
Time component	**Current**	**Proposed**
Average payment period (APP)	10 days	30 days
Average collection period (ACP)	30 days	30 days
Average age of inventory (AAI)	40 days	40 days

Cash conversion cycle (CCC) = AAI + ACP − APP

$$CCC_{current} = 40 \text{ days} + 30 \text{ days} - 10 \text{ days} = 60 \text{ days}$$

$$CCC_{proposed} = 40 \text{ days} + 30 \text{ days} - 30 \text{ days} = \underline{40 \text{ days}}$$

Reduction in CCC $\underline{\underline{20 \text{ days}}}$

Annual operating cycle investment = $18,000,000

Daily expenditure = $18,000,000 ÷ 360 = $50,000

Reduction in financing = $50,000 × 20 days = $1,000,000

Annual profit increase = .12 × $1,000,000 = $\underline{\underline{\$120,000}}$

ST 17-2 Time reduction

Mailing time	2½ days
Clearing time	1½ days
Total time reduction	4 days

Float reduction

$$4 \text{ days} \times \$300{,}000/\text{day} = \underline{\underline{\$1{,}200{,}000}}$$

Gross annual benefit of float reduction

$$.09 \times \$1{,}200{,}000 = \underline{\underline{\$108{,}000}}$$

Since the annual earnings from the float reduction of $108,000 exceed the annual cost of $90,000, *the proposed lockbox should be implemented.* It will result in a net annual savings of $18,000 ($108,000 earnings − $90,000 cost).

Chapter 18

ST 18-1 Tabular Calculation of the Effects of Easing Collection Efforts on Regency Rug Repair Company

Additional profit contribution from sales		
[1,000 rugs × ($32 avg. sale price − $28 var. cost)]		$ 4,000
Cost of marginal investment in accounts receivable		
Average investment under proposed plan:		
$\frac{(\$28 \times 73{,}000 \text{ rugs})}{360/58} = \frac{\$2{,}044{,}000}{6.21}$	$329,147	
Average investment under present plan:		
$\frac{(\$28 \times 72{,}000 \text{ rugs})}{360/40} = \frac{\$2{,}016{,}000}{9}$	224,000	
Marginal investment in A/R	$105,147	
Cost of marginal investment in A/R (.24 × $105,147)		($25,235)
Cost of marginal bad debts		
Bad debts under proposed plan (.02 × $32 × 73,000 rugs)	$ 46,720	
Bad debts under present plan (.01 × $32 × 72,000 rugs)	23,040	
Cost of marginal bad debts		($23,680)
Annual savings in collection expense		$40,000
Net loss from implementation of proposed plan		($ 4,915)

Recommendation: Since a net loss of $4,915 is expected to result from easing collection efforts, *the proposed plan should not be implemented.*

ST 18-2 **a.** *Data:*

S = 60,000 gallons

O = $200 per order

C = $1 per gallon per year

Calculation:

$$\text{EOQ} = \sqrt{\frac{2 \times S \times O}{C}} = \sqrt{\frac{2 \times 60{,}000 \times \$200}{\$1}} = \sqrt{24{,}000{,}000} = \underline{\underline{4{,}899 \text{ gallons}}}$$

b. Total cost = $(O \times S/Q) + (C \times Q/2)$

Q = EOQ = 4,899 gallons

Total Cost = [$200 × (60,000/4,899)] + [$1 × (4,899/2)]

= ($200 × 12.25) + ($1 × 2,449.5)

= $2,450 + $2,449.5 = $\underline{\underline{\$4{,}899.50}}$

c. Number of orders = S/Q

= 60,000/4,899 = $\underline{\underline{12.25 \text{ orders}}}$

d. *Data:*

Lead time = 20 days
Daily usage = 60,000 gallons/360 days
= 166.67 gallons/day

Calculation:

Reorder point = lead time in days × daily usage
= 20 days × 166.67 gallons/day
= 3,333.4 gallons

Chapter 19

ST 19-1 a. Net present value at 11%

Year(s)	Cash inflow (1)	Present value factor at 11%[a] (2)	Present value [(1) × (2)] (3)
1–3	$20,000	2.444	$ 48,880
4–15	30,000	(7.191 − 2.444)	142,410
		Present value of inflows	$191,290
		Less: Cash purchase price	180,000
		Net present value (NPV)	$ 11,290

[a]Present-value interest factors for annuities, *PVIFA,* from Table A-4.

(Calculator solution = $11,289)
Since the NPV of $11,290 is greater than zero, *Luxe Foods should acquire Valley Canning.*

b. In this case the 14 percent cost of capital must be used.
Net present value at 14%.

Year(s)	Cash inflow (1)	Present value factor at 14%[a] (2)	Present value [(1) × (2)] (3)
1–3	$20,000	2.322	$ 46,440
4–15	30,000	(6.142 − 2.322)	114,600
		Present value of inflows	$161,040
		Less: Cash purchase price	180,000
		Net present value (NPV)	($ 18,960)

[a]Present-value interest factors for annuities, *PVIFA,* from Table A-4.

[Calculator solution = ($18,951)]
At the higher cost of capital the *acquisition of Valley by Luxe cannot be justified.*

ST 19-2 a. Lake Industries' EPS without merger

Year	Earnings available for common: Initial value (1)	Future value factor at 5%[a] (2)	End-of-year value [(1) × (2)] (3)	Number of shares outstanding (4)	EPS [(3) ÷ (4)] (5)
1994	$160,000	1.000	$160,000	80,000	$2.00
1995	160,000	1.050	168,000	80,000	2.10
1996	160,000	1.102	176,320	80,000	2.20
1997	160,000	1.158	185,280	80,000	2.32
1998	160,000	1.216	194,560	80,000	2.43
1999	160,000	1.276	204,160	80,000	2.55

[a]Future-value interest factors, *FVIF,* from Table A-1.

b. Number of postmerger shares outstanding for Lake Industries

$$\text{Number of new shares issued} = \text{Initial number of Butler Company shares} \times \text{Ratio of exchange}$$

= 10,000 × 1.1 = 11,000 shares

Plus: Lake's premerger shares 80,000

Lake's postmerger shares 91,000 shares

Year	Butler Company: Initial value (1)	Butler Company: Future value factor at 10%[a] (2)	Butler Company: End-of-year value [(1) × (2)] (3)	Lake Industries Without merger: End-of-year value[b] (4)	Lake Industries With merger: End-of-year value [(3) + (4)] (5)	Number of shares outstanding[c] (6)	EPS [(5) ÷ (6)] (7)
1994	$20,000	1.000	$20,000	$160,000	$180,000	91,000	$1.98
1995	20,000	1.100	22,000	168,000	190,000	91,000	2.09
1996	20,000	1.210	24,200	176,320	200,520	91,000	2.20
1997	20,000	1.331	26,620	185,280	211,900	91,000	2.33
1998	20,000	1.464	29,280	194,560	223,840	91,000	2.46
1999	20,000	1.611	32,220	204,160	236,380	91,000	2.60

(Columns 1–5: Earnings available for common)

[a]Future-value interest factors, *FVIF,* from Table A-1.

[b]From column 3 of table in part **a**.

[c]Calculated at beginning of this part.

c. Comparing the EPS without the proposed merger calculated in **a** (see column 5 of table in **a**) with the EPS with the proposed merger calculated in **b** (see column 7 of table **b** above), we can see that after 1996 the EPS *with* the merger rises above the EPS without the merger. Clearly, over the long run the EPS with the merger will exceed those without the merger. This outcome is attributed to the higher rate of growth associated with Butler's earnings (10% versus 5% for Lake).

ST 19-3 a.

Proceeds from liquidation	$4,700,000
—Trustee's expenses	$400,000
—Wages owed workers	500,000
—Unpaid employee benefits	100,000
—Unsecured customer deposits	50,000
—Taxes owed governments	250,000
Funds available for creditors	$3,400,000
—First mortgage, paid from the $2.5 million proceeds from the sale of fixed assets	$2,000,000
—Second mortgage, partially paid from the remaining $500,000 of fixed assets proceeds	500,000
Funds available for unsecured creditors	$ 900,000

b. The second-mortgage holders are *still owed $300,000,* since they have recovered from the sale of the fixed assets $500,000 of the $800,000 owed them.

c.

Unsecured creditors' claims	Amount	Settlement at 45%[a]
Unpaid balance of second mortgage	$ 300,000[b]	$135,000
Accounts payable	400,000	180,000
Notes payable—bank	800,000	360,000
Unsecured bonds	500,000	225,000
Totals	$2,000,000	$900,000

[a]The 45 percent rate is calculated by dividing the $900,000 available for unsecured creditors by the $2,000,000 owed unsecured creditors. Each is entitled to a pro rata share.

[b]Value calculated in part **b**.

Chapter 20

ST 20-1 MNC's receipt of dividends can be calculated as follows:

Subsidiary income before local taxes	$150,000
Foreign income tax at 32%	− 48,000
Dividend available to be declared	$102,000
Foreign dividend withholding tax at 8%	− 8,160
MNC's receipt of dividends	$ 93,840

a. If tax credits are allowed, then the so-called "grossing up" procedure will be applicable:

Additional MNC income		$150,000
U.S. tax liability at 34%	$51,000	
Total foreign taxes paid to be used as a credit ($48,000 + $8,160)	− 56,160	− 56,160
U.S. taxes due		0
Net funds available to the MNC		$ 93,840

b. If no tax credits are permitted, then:

MNC's receipt of dividends	$93,840
U.S. tax liability at 34%	− 31,905
Net funds available to the parent MNC	$61,935

appendix F

Answers to selected end-of-chapter problems

The following list of answers to selected problems and portions of problems is included to provide "check figures" for use in preparing detailed solutions to end-of-chapter problems requiring calculations. For problems that are relatively straightforward the key answer is given; for more complex problems, answers to a number of parts of the problem are included. Detailed calculations are not shown—only the final and, in some cases, intermediate answers, which should help to confirm whether the correct solution is being developed. Answers to problems involving present and future value were solved by using the appropriate tables; calculator solutions are not given. For problems containing a variety of cases for which similar calculations are required, the answers for only one or two cases have been included. The only verbal answers included are simple yes-or-no or "choice of best alternative" responses; answers to problems requiring detailed explanations or discussions are not given.

The problems and portions of problems for which answers have been included were selected randomly; therefore there is no discernible pattern to the choice of problem answers given. The answers given are based on what are believed to be the most obvious and reasonable assumptions related to the given problem; in some cases, other reasonable assumptions could result in equally correct answers.

1-1 a. Ms. Harper has unlimited liability; $60,000.
c. Ms. Harper has limited liability.
2-1 b. 4%
2-4 a. B: 3%
E: 3.1%
2-6 a. C: 11%
E: 14%
c. C: 13%
E: 15%
2-8 a. $19,700
2-10 a. Tax on $90,000 = $18,850
2-13 a. X: $250
Y: $5,000
3-4 b. $27,050
3-5 a. $1.16
3-8 a. EPS = $1.9375
b. Total assets: $926,000
3-11 $80,000
3-16 a. Total sources: $2,900
3-17 a. Total sources: $70,800
4-2 a. Average age of inventory: 97.6 days
4-6 a. 1993 Johnson ROE = 22.13%
Industry ROE = 16.92%
4-8 a.

	Actual 1994
Current ratio:	1.04
Average collection period:	56 days
Debt-equity:	40%
Net profit margin:	4.1%
Return on equity:	11.3%

5-4 A: $530.60
D: $78,450
5-6 a. (1) Annual: $8,810
Semiannual: $8,955
Quarterly: $9,030
5-13 A: $3,862.50
B: $138,450.00
C: $6,956.80
5-18 a. PV of stream A = $109,890
5-19 c. PV of stream C = $52,410
5-21 E: $85,297.50
5-22 a. $43,691.48
5-27 Future value of retirement home in 20 years = $272,595
Annual deposit = $4,759.49
5-28 b. Deposit = $3,764.82
5-30 b.

Year	Interest	Principal
2	$1,489.61	$4,970.34

5-33 $PVIFA_{k,10} = 5.303$
$13\% < k < 14\%$
6-1 a. X: 12.5%
Y: 12.36%
6-2 A: 25%
6-4 a. A: 8%
B: 20%
6-5 a. R: 10%
S: 20%
b. R: 25%
S: 25.5%
6-8 a. (4) Project 257 CV: .368
Project 432 CV: .354
6-9 a. F: 4%
b. F: 13.38%
c. F: 3.345
6-11 b. Portfolio return: 15.5%
c. Standard deviation: 1.638%
6-16 a. 18% increase
b. 9.6% decrease
c. No change
6-20 A: 8.9%
D: 15%
6-21 b. 10%
7-2 C: $16,660
E: $14,112
7-4 a. $1,156.88
7-5 A: $1,149,66
D: $450.80
7-9 a. 12.69%
b. 12.58%
7-11 $841.15
7-15 a. $68.82
b. $7.87
7-17 a. $37.75
b. $60.40
7-18 $81.18
7-19 a. $34.12
b. $20.21
c. $187.87
7-24 2.67
7-25 a. 14.8%
b. $29.55
8-1 a. Current expenditure
d. Current expenditure
f. Capital expenditure
8-5 A: $275,500
B: $26,800
8-7 a. Total tax: $49,600
d. Total tax: ($6,400)
8-9 Initial investment: $22,680
8-10 a. Initial investment: $18,240
c. Initial investment: $23,100
8-12 c. Cash inflow, Year 3: $584,000
8-14 b. Incremental cash flow, Year 3: $1,960
8-16 Terminal cash flow: $76,640
8-20 a. Initial investment, Asset B: $51,488

b. Incremental cash flow, Year 2, Hoist A: $8,808
c. Terminal cash flow, Hoist B: $18,600

9-2 **a.** Machine 1: 4 years, 8 months
Machine 2: 5 years, 3 months

9-4 **a.** (1) $2,675
(2) Accept

9-6 **a.** NPV = ($320); reject

9-8 **a.** Project A: 3.08 years; Project C: 2.38 years
b. Project C: NPV = $5,451

9-9 Project A: 17%
Project D: 21%

9-12 **a.** NPV = $1,222
b. IRR = 12%
c. Accept

9-14 **a.** Project A
NPV = $15,245
b. Project B
IRR = 18%

9-17 **a.** Initial Investment: $1,480,000
b.

Year	Cash flow
1	$656,000
2	761,600
3	647,200
4	585,600
5	585,600
6	44,000

c. 2.1 years
d. NPV = $959,289
IRR = 35%

9-20 **a.** Range A: $1,600
Range B: $200

9-23 **a.** NPV = $22,320
b. NPV = ($5,596)

9-25 **a.** Project E: NPV = $2,130
Project F: NPV = $1,678
Project G: NPV = $1,144
c. Project E: NPV = $834
Project F: NPV = $1,678
Project G: NPV = $2,138

9-29 **b.** X: $920.04
Y: $1,079.54
Z: $772.80

9-31 **b.** Projects C, F, and G

10-2 **b.** 12.4%

10-3 **a.** $980
c. 12.31%
d. Before-tax: 12.26%; after-tax: 7.36%

10-4 A: 5.66%
E: 7.10%

10-8 **c.** 15.91%
d. 16.54%

10-11 **a.** Weighted cost: 8.344%
b. Weighted cost: 10.854%

10-14 **a.** $k_i = 5.2\%$; $k_p = 8.4\%$; $k_n = 15.0\%$; $k_r = 13.8\%$
b. (1) $200,000
(2) 10.1%
(3) 10.7%

10-15 **b.** $500,000 and $800,000
c. WACC, over $800,000: 16.2%

11-4 **a.** 21.000 CDs
d. $10,500

11-7 **a.** Q = 8,000 units
e. DOL = 5.00

11-9 **a.** EPS = $0.375

11-11 **a.** DFL = 1.5

11-12 **a.** (1) 175,000 units
d. DTL = 2.40

11-14

Debt ratio	Debt	Equity
40%	$400,000	$600,000

11-20 **a.** EBIT: $60,000; $240,000; $420,000
d. At 15% debt ratio, EPS = $0.85, $4.02, $7.20
e. (1) At 15% debt ratio, expected EPS = $4.03
g. $0 < EBIT < $100,000; choose 0%
$100,000 < EBIT < $198,000; choose 30%
$198,000 < EBIT < ∞; choose 60%
h. At 15% debt ratio, share price = $38.38
i. Maximize EPS at 60% debt ratio
Maximize share value at 30% debt ratio

12-1 Bond A: **a.** Discount; **b.** $400,000; **c.** $16,000; **d.** $320,000; **e.** $128,000

12-3 **b.** Bond B: $20,000

12-4 **a.** Bond A: $40,000
b. Bond A: $16,000

12-5 **a.** $80,000
b. $8,000
f. $1,016,216

12-6 **a.** $1,294,000
b. $178,933
c. Net present value of refunding: $237,666; bond refunding should be initiated.

12-8 $3.60 per share spread

13-1 **a.**

Common stock (10,000 shares @ $1 par)	$ 10,000
Paid in capital in excess of par	120,000
Common stock equity	$130,000

13-3 **a.** Majority: A, B, C, D, E: (.54 × 1,000 = 540)
b. Majority can elect 3, and minority can elect 2.

13-6 Case E: (1) With rights: $1.11
(2) Ex rights: $1.11

13-8 **a.** 24,000 shares
b. 12.5 rights
c. 3,840 shares
d. (1) R_w = $0.296

(2) $M_e = \$28.704$
$R_e = \$0.296$

13-11 **a.** $4.75/share
b. $0.40/share
d. A decrease in retained earnings and hence stockholder's equity by $80,000.

13-14 **a.** 1992 = $0.60
b. 1992 = $0.50
c. 1992 = $0.62
d. 1992 = $0.62

13-15 **a.** Retained earnings = $85,000
b. (1) Retained earnings = $70,000
(2) Retained earnings = $40,000

13-17 **a.** EPS = $2
b. 1%
c. 1%; stock dividends do not have a real value.

14-3 **a.** Preferred dividends = $14.88/share
Common dividends = $15.88/share
c. Preferred dividends = $10.00/share
Common dividends = $0.00/share

14-7 **b.** Lease: PV = $42,934
Purchase: PV = $43,773

14-9

Lease	Capitalized value
A	$272,560
B	$596,160
E	$374,261

14-12 **a.** $1,250
b. $525
c. $1,050

14-16 **a.** $832.75
b. At $9: $720
c. At $9: $832.75

14-17 Bond A: $6.46 per warrant

14-20 **a.** 160 shares, 400 warrants
b. 20%
c. 125%

14-23 **a.** $800 profit
b. $400
c. $6/share

15-3

	Feb.	Mar. (in $000)	Apr.
a. Ending cash	$37	$67	($22)
b. Required total financing			$37
Excess cash balance	$22	$52	

c. Line of credit should be at least $37,000 to cover borrowing needs for the month of April.

15-6 **a.** Net profit after taxes: $216,600
b. Net profit after taxes: $227,400

15-8 **a.** Accounts receivable $1,400,000
Net fixed assets $4,820,000
Total current liabilities $2,260,000
External funds required $ 775,000
Total assets $9,100,000

15-9 **a.** Net profits after taxes $67,500
b.

	Judgmental
Total assets	$697,500
External funds required	$ 11,250

16-1 **b.** (1) $36,000
(2) $10,333

16-2 Annual loan cost: $1,200

16-5 **c.** January 9

16-7 Effective interest rate = 31.81%

16-9 $1,300,000

16-14 **a.** 9.0%
b. 13.06%

16-17 Total $886,900

16-18 **a.** Interest: $1,173

17-1 **a.** ECQ = $45,000

17-2 **a.** Return point = $6,463

17-4 **a.** OC = 150 days
b. CCC = 120 days
c. $10,000,000

17-5 **b.** CCC = 35 days
c. $97,222

17-7 Plan E

17-10 **a.** 7 days
b. $21,450

17-12 **a.** Maximum savings = $3,850
Minimum savings = $1,100

17-17 $22,500 annual savings

18-1 **a.** Credit score applicant B: 81.5

18-2 **b.** $75,000
c. $9,000

18-4 **a.** Present plan: $20,000
Proposed plan: $48,000

18-6 The credit standards should not be relaxed, since the proposed plan results in a loss.

18-7 Net profit of the proposal $20,040

18-9 **a.** $14,000 additional profit contribution
b. $36,432 marginal investment in accounts receivable

18-11 **b.** $52,000 net savings

18-14 **c.** 4,000 units

18-17 **a.** 200 units
b. 123 units
c. 33 units

19-1 **a.** Total tax liability = $1,680,000
b. Tax liability: Year 1 = $0
Year 2 = $0
Year 3 = $16,000
Year 4–15 = $112,000/year

19-3 **a.** Total tax advantage = $320,000; Years 1–4 = $80,000/year
b. Total tax advantage = $320,000

c. Reilly Investment Group: $228,400
Webster Industries $205,288

19-5 **a.** Yes, the NPV = $42,150
b. Yes, the NPV = $101,000

19-6 **a.** EPS merged firm = $1.029
b. EPS Marla's = $1.00
c. EPS Victory = $2.139

19-8 Ratio of exchange: (1) of shares; (2) market price
A: 0.60; 1.20
D: 0.25; 1.25
E: 1.00; 1.25

19-10 **a.** 1.125
b. Henry Co.: EPS = $2.50, P/E = 18
c. 16.89

19-15 Case II:

Unpaid balance of 2nd mortgage	$150,000
Accounts payable	$ 75,000
Notes payable	$ 75,000
Unsecured bonds	$150,000

19-16 **b.** (1)

1st mortgage	$61,539
2nd mortgage	$246,154
Unsecured bonds	$184,615

20-1 **a.** Net funds available $152,425

20-3 Effective rate, Euromarket:
US$ 5.0%
DM 8.0%
Sf 7.2%

INDEX

Page numbers in italics indicate figures; page numbers followed by n indicate footnotes; page numbers followed by t indicate tables. Marginal terms are boldface.

THE PMF DISK

The *PMF Disk* (enclosed opposite) contains three different sets of routines: the *PMF Tutor,* the *PMF Problem-Solver* and the *PMF Lotus Templates.* The disk is designed for use on IBM PC/XT/AT and compatible microcomputers. All programs are extremely user friendly. Many software products make this claim; you'll see for yourself that the *PMF Disk* really lives up to it.

The *PMF Tutor* is a collection of managerial finance problem types constructed by random number generation. Its purpose is to provide an essentially unlimited number of problems to work, so that users can practice until they are satisfied that they understand a concept. The *PMF Problem-Solver* is a collection of financial computation routines. Its purpose is to provide a fast and easy method for performing the often time-consuming mathematical computations required. The *PMF Lotus Templates* are a collection of pre-programmed Lotus worksheets. The templates enable students to enter data and solve problems using perhaps the most popular and widely accepted software application. The *Tutor* should be used to reinforce application of basic concepts; the *Problem-Solver* should be used to save computational time once the concepts are understood. The *Lotus Templates* should be used to provide students with opportunities to use spreadsheets to solve selected problems.

The *Tutor, Problem-Solver,* and *Templates* routines are arranged on the software in the same order as the text discussions, with page reference shown on the screen. Text and problems that utilize the disk are keyed to the text and study guide by a computer icon, ▪, for the *Tutor,* by a diskette icon, ▫, for the *Problem-Solver,* and by a spreadsheet icon, ▪, for the *Templates.*

Complete and clear instructions for using the *PMF Disk* are included in Appendix B of the book.